Frank Maloney Judge (ret)
Tx Cd Crim. Apps

HANDBOOK

of

MASSACHUSETTS

EVIDENCE

HANDBOOK

of

MASSACHUSETTS

EVIDENCE

Seventh Edition

PAUL J. LIACOS
Chief Justice
Supreme Judicial Court
of Massachusetts

Seventh Edition prepared by

MARK S. BRODIN
Professor of Law
Boston College Law School

and

MICHAEL AVERY
Professor of Law
Suffolk University Law School

Aspen Law & Business
A Division of Aspen Publishers, Inc.
Gaithersburg   New York

This publication is designed to provide accurate and authoritative information in regard to the subject matter covered. It is sold with the understanding that the publisher is not engaged in rendering legal, accounting, or other professional services. If legal advice or other professional assistance is required, the services of a competent professional person should be sought.

Permissions
Aspen Law & Business
1185 Avenue of the Americas
New York, NY 10036

Printed in the United States of America

1 2 3 4 5 6 7 8 9 0

Library of Congress Cataloging-in-Publication Data

Liacos, Paul J.
 Handbook of Massachusetts evidence / Paul J. Liacos. — 7th ed. / prepared by Michael Avery and Mark S. Brodin.
 p. cm.
 Includes index.
 ISBN 0-7355-0532-2 (hardback)
 1. Evidence (Law) — Massachusetts. I. Avery, Michael, 1944- II. Brodin, Mark S., 1947- III. Title.

KFM2940.Z9 L4 1999
347.774'06 — dc21

99-052436

About Aspen Law & Business

Aspen Law & Business — comprising the former Prentice Hall Law & Business, Little, Brown and Company's Professional Division, and Wiley Law Publications — is a leading publisher of authoritative treatises, practice manuals, services, and journals for attorneys, financial and tax advisors, corporate and bank directors, and other business professionals. Our mission is to provide practical solution-based how-to information keyed to the latest legislative, judicial, and regulatory developments.

We offer publications in the areas of banking and finance; bankruptcy; business and commercial law; construction law; corporate law; pensions, benefits, and labor; insurance law; securities; taxation; intellectual property; government and administrative law; real estate law; matrimonial and family law; environmental and health law; international law; legal practice and litigation; and criminal law.

Other Aspen Law & Business products treating litigation and evidence issues include

Civil Discovery and Depositions
The Deposition Handbook
Discovery Practice
Drunk Driving Defense
Inside Litigation
Jury Selection
Mauet's Trial Notebook
Motion Practice
Witness Preparation

Handbook of Connecticut Evidence
Handbook of Illinois Evidence
New York Evidence Handbook
Wigmore on Evidence
The New Wigmore

ASPEN LAW & BUSINESS
A Division of Aspen Publishers, Inc.
A Wolters Kluwer Company
www.aspenpublishers.com

SUBSCRIPTION NOTICE

This Aspen Law & Business product is updated on a periodic basis with supplements to reflect important changes in the subject matter. If you purchased this product directly from Aspen Law & Business, we have already recorded your subscription for the update service.

If, however, you purchased this product from a bookstore and wish to receive future updates and revised or related volumes billed separately with a 30-day examination review, please contact our Customer Service Department at 1-800-234-1660 or send your name, company name (if applicable), address, and the title of the product to:

ASPEN LAW & BUSINESS
A Division of Aspen Publishers, Inc.
7201 McKinney Circle
Frederick, MD 21704

This edition is dedicated to Paul J. Liacos, who committed his dazzling intellect and boundless energy to the pursuit of equal and impartial justice for all inhabitants of the Commonwealth. We are forever thankful for the privilege of working with him on one of his many contributions to the law.

M. S. B.
M. A.

Summary of Contents

Table of Contents

CHAPTER

3

MACHINERY of the TRIAL   43

Table of Contents

CHAPTER

4

RELEVANCE and CIRCUMSTANTIAL PROOF

107

CHAPTER

5

BURDEN of PROOF, PRESUMPTIONS, and INFERENCES   193

CHAPTER

6

WITNESSES   255

CHAPTER

7

OPINION and EXPERT EVIDENCE   367

CHAPTER

8

HEARSAY   461

CHAPTER

9

CONFESSIONS and INCRIMINATING STATEMENTS   575

CHAPTER

10

EYEWITNESS IDENTIFICATION EVIDENCE

657

CHAPTER

11

REAL and DEMONSTRATIVE EVIDENCE   703

CHAPTER
12
DOCUMENTARY EVIDENCE and RELATED MATTERS 733

Preface to the
Seventh Edition

When we assumed the daunting task of revising and updating the *Handbook of Massachusetts Evidence* seven years ago, we took for granted that we would always have the wisdom and insight of Paul Liacos to guide us. Now, as do countless others, we suffer his untimely departure from our midst. We have nonetheless endeavored to continue the *Handbook's* great tradition of providing the reader with a one-volume illumination of the Commonwealth's uncodified law of evidence.

The reader will note some reorganization in this edition. Most notably, we have substantially expanded the treatment of expert testimony and scientific proof in Chapter Seven, providing an assessment of the impact of the United States Supreme Court's groundbreaking decisions in *Daubert v. Merrell Dow Pharmaceuticals, Inc.,* and *Kumho Tire Co., Ltd. v. Carmichael.* A more functional table of contents divides topics into the physical, biological, behavioral, and forensic sciences to enhance the reader's access to the case law relevant to particular categories of proof.

A new Chapter Fourteen combines all materials concerning evidence in administrative proceedings, and Chapters Five and Nine have been reorganized somewhat to reflect the new importance of certain topics.

Throughout the edition, we have discarded many older citations in order to restore the volume to a portable size. Readers desiring access to this history would be advised to keep their Sixth Editions close at hand.

Finally, we gratefully acknowledge those many law students who have assisted us with this project over the years since the last edition: Gabriel N. Devitto, Christine R. Dutt, Jennifer A. Leahy, Robert J. Malionek, Jeremy L. Pearlman, Amy B. Spagnole, Jennifer Tumminelli, and Robert Zaffrann.

Michael Avery
Mark S. Brodin

November 1999

Preface to the
Sixth Edition

The opportunity to participate in a revision of the *Handbook of Massachusetts Evidence* is both a great honor and a formidable challenge. The task of preparing a new edition of a volume that has for many years been authored by Paul J. Liacos, the Chief Justice of the Supreme Judicial Court, is, to say the least, somewhat anxiety-provoking.

Given the great respect which the *Handbook* has enjoyed among the trial bar and the bench, we have sought to retain as much of the original manuscript as possible. Developments in the law over the eight years since the last supplement, however, have required a number of significant changes. Where substantial redrafting of the text or the incorporation of new material was necessary, we have sought to remain true to the style and spirit of previous editions.

In addition to thorough updating of case citations and selected reorganization of topics to reflect recent approaches to evidence rules and practice, we have added two new chapters and expanded others. Chapter 4, *Relevance and Circumstantial Proof,* one of the new chapters, includes extensive treatment of direct and circumstantial proof, statistical and probabilistic evidence, character evidence, prejudice versus probative value, and the policy rules of exclusion. Chapter 9, *Confessions,* which is also new, approaches the question of the admissibility of a defendant's statement from both common-law and constitutional perspectives. Much of the chapter is organized around an analysis of the substantive protections afforded by the Fourth, Fifth, and Sixth Amendments to the United States Constitution. The substantial body of recent case law in this area is also examined.

Chapter 8, *Hearsay,* has been modernized and reorganized, collecting in one place material that previously appeared in various sections of the Fifth Edition. Chapter 7, *Opinion and Expert Testimony,* has been expanded to include the latest developments in this critical area, particularly with respect to scientific evidence.

Unfortunately, given the wealth of new material, it has not been possible to maintain a chapter on search and seizure in the *Handbook.* Constitutional developments on the federal level in the last eight years have rendered the law in this area so complex that space simply does not allow an adequate treatment of these issues in the present volume. Fortunately, there are several highly regarded treatises specifically devoted to the law of search and seizure. We have retained, however, analysis of constitutional principles with regard to the admissibility of confessions in the chapter devoted to that topic. In addition, constitutional law is discussed at some length in the chapters on identification evidence and privilege.

We have included all citations we believe are significant in cases decided through the end of calendar year 1992. Several cases from 1993 have been cited as well, although no systematic effort to analyze 1993 cases was undertaken, given the constraints of manuscript and publication deadlines. We will provide the reader with annual supplements, in order to keep the text as current as possible.

Preface to the Sixth Edition

We are grateful to the law students, many of whom are now lawyers, who assisted us in locating and analyzing the recent citations that have been added to the *Handbook*. We wish to take this opportunity to express formally our gratitude to Julie Cardonick, Susan Finegan, Simeon Goldstein, Richard Hayber, Christopher Jernigan, Mark LaBollita, Marianne LeBlanc, Lynn Muster, Nadine Nasser, G. Thomas Pauling, David Sgan, David Wiseman, and Stephen Zamansky. In addition, we both wish to express our gratitude and respect for the work of Susan Moore, whose secretarial and organizational skills were invaluable in the preparation of the manuscript.

We would like to acknowledge the significant part played by Thomas W. Lincoln, Sandy Doherty, and Jay Boggis of Little, Brown and Company, in bringing this project to completion.

Without the leadership of Chief Justice Liacos, of course, continued revision of the *Handbook* would not be possible. We are particularly grateful to the Chief Justice for allowing us substantial flexibility and freedom in the preparation of the manuscript, while setting the overall direction and philosophy of the project.

Finally, we wish to thank our wives, Garland Waller and Andrea Brodin, and our children, Katherine, David, and Samantha Avery and Rachel and Laura Brodin, for their patience and understanding during a period in which the preparation of this text created a substantial distraction from our family lives.

Mark S. Brodin
Michael Avery

September 1993

Historical Note to the
Sixth Edition

The concept of *Handbook of Massachusetts Evidence* originated with W. Barton Leach, the late Story Professor of Law at Harvard University, who prepared the editions of 1940, 1948, and 1956. Professor Leach asked me to undertake the work that resulted in the Fourth and Fifth Editions in 1967 and 1981. His compilation and organization of the materials in the first three editions and his guidance in preparing the Fourth Edition made this handbook what has been called (by others) "the Bible" on evidence in the Commonwealth of Massachusetts. With the help of my former law clerk, Dean Richlin, Esquire, of Boston, I prepared the Fifth Edition (1981) and the 1985 Supplement.

Responding to requests from members of the bench and bar, my publishers asked me to prepare an updated Sixth Edition, but, after assuming the office of Chief Justice of the Supreme judicial Court of Massachusetts in 1989, I found it impossible to accede to this proper request. Happily, however, two distinguished authorities on litigation and evidence agreed to act as editors: Professor Mark S. Brodin of Boston College School of Law and Mr. Michael Avery, a trial lawyer in Boston. They are the ones who have done the painstaking work of updating and integrating the previous edition and supplement. My role has been to give counsel, to make suggestions I felt would be helpful, and to review the draft manuscript they prepared. I am delighted with their outstanding work.

They have remained true to the original concept of the book that has made it so useful to students of evidence. As stated in the Preface to the Fifth Edition in 1981, the purposes of this edition remain:

(1) to serve as an aid to members of the bench and bar for quick reference in trial of cases,

(2) to help prepare for Massachusetts bar examinations, and

(3) to serve as a text in Evidence courses.

The Sixth Edition should also prove useful in pretrial discovery and preparation. The *Handbook* again sets out to provide, in brief compass, a reasoned analytical statement of the Massachusetts law of evidence, with the text of significant statutes and rules and with citations to leading cases. The Handbook also treats federal decisions, particularly those of constitutional dimension, that have significance in administering the rules of evidence.

It is always difficult to write succinctly and clearly in such a dynamic area of the law; as always, changes had to be made to reflect developments in case law, constitutional precepts, statutory enactments, and relevant rules of court. The Editors have managed this task very well. I hope that readers of the Sixth Edition will continue to find this work not only useful but illuminating, for the rules of evidence are most important in establishing truth at trial, that justice may be given to all.

I conclude by acknowledging the support of Maureen, my beloved wife of forty years, and of our children, James,

Historical Note to the Sixth Edition

Diana, Mark, and Gregory. Their patience and love for me and each other has made this effort, and all others, possible.

Paul J. Liacos
Chief Justice

September 1993

HANDBOOK
of
MASSACHUSETTS
EVIDENCE

CHAPTER

1

INTRODUCTION — THE SOURCES and APPLICABILITY of MASSACHUSETTS EVIDENCE LAW

§1.1 Sources
§1.2 Applicability

§1.1 Sources

Massachusetts evidence law derives from various sources, including common law, statutes, procedural rules, and the federal and state constitutions. Unlike the federal system and that of many states, Massachusetts evidence law remains uncodified. An effort to adopt a code in the form of the Proposed Massachusetts Rules of Evidence was rejected by the Supreme Judicial Court on December 30, 1982. In its announcement, the court explained:

> The Justices recognize that if the Proposed Rules were to be adopted, (1) there would have to be careful coordination with the legislature to repeal, revise, or modify many statutes which deal with the admissibility and effect of evidence; (2)

many of the Proposed Rules involve departures from the principles set forth in the Federal Rules of Evidence; (3) some of the Proposed Rules are subject to significant and arguably valid criticisms.

A majority of the Justices conclude that promulgation of rules of evidence would tend to restrict the development of common law principles pertaining to the admissibility of evidence. The valid objective of uniformity of practice in federal and State courts would not necessarily be advanced because the Proposed Rules, in their present form, depart significantly from the Federal Rules of Evidence. Additionally, in the view of some of the justices, the Federal Rules of Evidence have not led to uniform practice in the various Federal courts and are, in some instances, less well adapted to the needs of modern trial practice than current Massachusetts law. Accordingly, a majority of the Justices have concluded that it would not be advisable to adopt the Proposed Massachusetts Rules of Evidence at the present time. The Proposed Rules have substantial value as a comparative standard in the continued and historic role of the courts in developing principles of law relating to evidence. Parties are invited to cite the Proposed Rules, wherever appropriate, in briefs and memoranda submitted.

Consistent with its announcement, the Supreme Judicial Court has continued to make reference to the Proposed Rules in its decisions and has, on a case-by-case basis, adopted some in Massachusetts practice. See, e.g., *Com. v. Daye*, 393 Mass 55, 65-75, 469 NE2d 483, 490-496 (1984), discussed in §6.7.2.g, and *Flood v. Southland Corp.*, 416 Mass 62, 616 NE2d 1068 (1993), discussed in §8.21.2. In large part as a result of the Proposed Rules and developments surrounding them, evidence law in the Commonwealth has in recent years been in a heightened state of evolution. See generally Healy, Ten Years After: A Reconsideration of the Codification of Evidence Law in Massachusetts, 15 Western New England L Rev 1 (1993).

§1.2 Applicability

Massachusetts evidence law is generally applicable to all proceedings, civil and criminal, in the courts of the Commonwealth. Proposed Mass R Evid 1101, which reflects currect practice, provides that the rules of evidence (except with respect to privileges) do not apply in the following situations:

(1) Preliminary questions of fact. The determination of questions of fact preliminary to admissibility of evidence when the issue is to be determined by the court . . .

(2) Grand jury. Proceedings before grand juries.

(3) Miscellaneous proceedings. Proceedings for small claims; sentencing, or granting or revoking probation; issuance of warrants for arrest, criminal summonses, and search warrants; and proceedings with respect to release on bail or otherwise.

(4) Contempt proceedings. Contempt proceedings in which the court may act summarily.

Thus, hearsay may be admitted in the above proceedings. For grand jury proceedings, see Mass R Crim P 4(c); *Com. v. Pina*, 406 Mass 540, 549, 549 NE2d 106, 112 (1990); *Com. v. Dilone*, 385 Mass 281, 284, 431 NE2d 576, 578 (1982) (hearsay alone may support indictment); *Com. v. St. Pierre*, 377 Mass 650, 654-657, 387 NE2d 1135, 1139-1140 (1979) (fact that indictments based entirely on hearsay did not require their dismissal where no showing that integrity of grand jury proceedings was impaired; but sound policy dictates preference for direct testimony); *Com. v. Fort*, 33 Mass App 181, 182-184, 597 NE2d 1056, 1058 (1992) (hearsay account by police of what witnesses said immediately after shooting incident). See also *Com. v. Fleury*, 417 Mass 810, 816-817, 632 NE2d 1230, 1233-1234 (1994) (integrity of grand jury not impaired by introduction of videotape of interview of victim). Compare *Com. v. Salman*, 387 Mass 160, 439 NE2d 245 (1982) (judge acted properly in dismissing indictments where defendant made substantial showing that false hearsay testimony was knowingly presented to grand jury).

For hearings on pretrial detention on ground of dangerousness (GL 276, §58A), see *Mendonza v. Com.*, 423 Mass 771, 785-786, 673 NE2d 22, 31-32 (1996) (upholding constitutionality of pretrial detention statute). For probation revocation hearings, see *Com. v. Durling*, 407 Mass 108, 118, 551 NE2d 1193, 1199 (1990) (hearsay must bear substantial indicia of reliability and trustworthiness when it is only evidence of alleged violation). Compare *Com. v. Delaney*, 36 Mass App 930, 629 NE2d 1007 (1994) (hearsay testimony of defendant's ex-wife improperly admitted at probation revocation hearing where declarant was available to be called and statement did not bear indicia of reliability).

Additionally, the rules of evidence do not apply strictly in the following proceedings:

- Prison disciplinary hearings. See *Murphy v. Superintendent, Massachusetts Correctional Institution*, 396 Mass 830, 489 NE2d 661 (1986) (hearsay may be admitted).
- Domestic abuse prevention order proceedings (GL 209A). See *Frizado v. Frizado*, 420 Mass 592, 597-598, 651 NE2d 1206, 1211 (1995) (provided there is fairness in what evidence is admitted and relied on).
- Court inquiries such as disbarment proceedings. Board of Bar Overseers Rule 3.39 (admissibility of evidence governed by GL 30A, State Administrative Procedure Act). See also *Matter of Tobin*, 417 Mass 92, 102, 628 NE2d 1273, 1279 (1994); *Matter of Jordan*, 332 Mass 520, 521-522, 125 NE2d 925 (1955). But compare GL 211C, §7(3) (at hearing before Commission on Judicial Conduct, "all testimony

shall be under oath" and "the rules of evidence applicable to civil proceedings shall apply"). See also *Matter of King*, 409 Mass 590, 600, 568 NE2d 588, 593-594 (1991); *Matter of Troy*, 364 Mass 15, 24-25, 306 NE2d 203 (1973).

- Juvenile transfer hearings. See *Com. v. Spencer*, 45 Mass App 33, 36-37, 695 NE2d 677, 680 (1998) (& citations) (hearsay admissible; test for admissibility is fundamental fairness).

Hearsay is not admissible at either the adjudicatory or dispositional phase of a care and protection proceeding. See *Custody of Two Minors*, 19 Mass App 552, 476 NE2d 235 (1985) (& citations).

Evidence in proceedings seeking equitable relief is taken in the same manner as actions seeking legal remedies, except that more liberal use of affidavits is permitted. GL 233, §67.

The rules of evidence at a probable cause hearing (GL 276, §38) should in general be the same rules that are applicable at the criminal trial. *Myers v. Com.*, 363 Mass 843, 854, 298 NE2d 819 (1973).

The rules of evidence applicable at hearings on workers' compensation claims are the rules applied at court proceedings. See 452 CMR 1.11(5).

Evidence in administrative proceedings is discussed in Chapter 14.

CHAPTER
2
JUDICIAL ADMISSIONS, JUDICIAL NOTICE, and BINDING TESTIMONY

§2.1   Introduction

This chapter discusses two classes of matter that are material to the outcome of a trial but with respect to which no evidence need be presented: (1) propositions of fact that the opponent has conclusively admitted are true (judicial admissions); and (2) propositions of law and of fact that are unquestionably true and are either well-known or easily confirmed (judicial notice). This chapter also discusses the subject of binding testimony.

A.   JUDICIAL ADMISSIONS[1]

§2.2   Effect of Judicial Admissions

Some acts and statements of a party or his attorney, including failures to act, are such as to conclusively determine an issue. Such acts always occur in connection with the court proceedings themselves. They are called judicial admissions. They are unlike evidentiary admissions in that because they conclusively determine an issue they relieve the other party of the necessity of presenting evidence on it. Moreover, they usually deprive the parties of the right to present evidence on the admitted point, although the trial court in its discretion may permit evidence to be introduced. *Dorr v. Tremont National Bank,* 128 Mass 349, 360

---

§2.1   [1] For a discussion of the admissibility of statements by a party opponent ("admissions") generally, see §8.8.

8

(1880); *Com. v. Costello,* 120 Mass 358, 364, 369 (1876); Mass R Civ P 36(b); Wigmore §§2588-2591 (Chad rev 1981).

§2.3   Admissions under the Massachusetts Rules of Civil Procedure

§2.3.1   Rule 36

Mass R Civ P 36 provides, in part:

> (a) *Request for admission.* A party may serve upon any other party a written request for admission, for purposes of the pending action, only, of the truth of any matters within the scope of Rule 26(b) set forth in the request that relate to statements or opinions of fact or of the application of law to fact, including the genuineness of any documents described in the request. Copies of documents shall be served with the request unless they have been or are otherwise furnished or made available for inspection and copying. The request may, without leave of court, be served upon the plaintiff after commencement of the action and upon any other party with or after service of the summons and complaint upon that party.
>
> Each matter of which an admission is requested shall be separately set forth. . . .

Rule 36, by incorporating the relevancy standard of Mass R Civ P 26(b), permits requests for admission of any matter that is relevant to the subject matter involved in the pending action. Pursuant to Rule 36, a party has 30 days to respond to a request for an admission, as compared with the ten days permitted under the statute. A request under Rule 36 need not be served by registered mail. Under the rule, a party may not give lack of information or of knowledge as a reason for failing to admit or deny unless he states that he has made a reasonable inquiry and that the information known or readily obtainable by him is not sufficient to enable him to admit or deny.

The rule allows the requesting party to move to determine the sufficiency of the answer or objection. If the court determines that the objection is not justified, it can order that an answer be made; if it determines that an answer is deficient, it can order that the matter be admitted. Sanctions for noncompliance are prescribed in Mass R Civ P 37(c).

The rule provides that any matter admitted is "conclusively established" for the purpose of the pending action. The admission binds the party making it, as well as the one requesting it. See subsection (b) of the rule. This subsection also authorizes the court, under certain prescribed conditions, to permit withdrawal or amendment of the admission. Subsection (b) further provides: "Any admission made by a party under this rule is for the purpose of the pending action only and is not an admission by him for any other purpose nor may it be used against him in any other proceeding."

Rule 36 governs district, municipal, superior courts, and the Housing Court, suits of a civil nature in the Land Court, and proceedings seeking equitable relief in the Probate and Family Court.

Facts established by use of Rule 36 may be the basis, in whole or in part, of summary judgment proceedings under Mass R Civ P 56.

A Request for Admissions of Fact should not be confused with interrogatories. Unlike admissions made by a party by answering, or not answering a request, admissions contained in answers to interrogatories are not binding upon the admitting party. At most, the answers of a party to interrogatories may be read by the other party into evidence at trial. See GL 231, §89; Mass R Civ P 33(b).

§2.3.2   Rule 16

Mass R Civ P 16 provides for a pretrial proceeding at which the parties may make admissions of fact and stipulate to the authenticity of documents, which will avoid unnecessary proof. The court enters an order which recites the action taken at the conference including, among other matters, any agreements made by the parties, and which limits the issues for trial to those not disposed of by admissions or agreements of counsel. The order when entered controls the subsequent course of the action, unless modified at the trial to prevent manifest injustice. Agreements and stipulations by the parties are binding, unless they are later vacated for good cause shown. See *Slade v. Slade,* 43 Mass App 376, 682 NE2d 1385 (1997) and cases cited therein; *Norton v. Vaughan,* 13 Mass App 1075, 435 NE2d 634 (1982) (plaintiff bound by counsel's admission that there was no evidence of medical malpractice, case dismissed).

See Mass R Crim P 11 for pretrial procedures in criminal cases in district and superior courts.

§2.3.3   *Rules 8(b) and 9(a)*

Mass R Civ P 8(b) provides, in part: "The signature to an instrument set forth in any pleading shall be taken as admitted unless a party specifically denies its genuineness." The rule is consistent with GL 106, §3-307 (Uniform Commercial Code), which requires a specific denial of genuineness.

Mass R Civ P 8(b) also provides, in part: "An allegation in any pleading that a place is a public way shall be taken as admitted unless a party specifically denies such allegation."

As to matters pertaining to fiduciary capacity or corporate existence, Mass R Civ P 9(a) provides:

> It is not necessary to aver the capacity of a party to sue or be sued or the authority of a party to sue or be sued in a representative capacity or the legal existence of an organized association of persons that is made a party. When a party desires to raise an issue as to the legal existence of any party

or the capacity of any party to sue or be sued or the authority of a party to sue or be sued in a representative capacity, he shall do so by specific negative averment, which shall include such supporting particulars as are peculiarly within the pleader's knowledge.

A party is not required to allege that it is an executor, administrator, guardian, trustee, assignee, conservator, receiver, or corporation. Under Rule 9(a), the matter will be raised only by an opposing party who, by "specific negative averment," wishes to raise the issue. It would also appear that a judicial admission will come about when the issue is not so raised.

§2.4   Statutory Admissions

§2.4.1   Demand for Admission of Fact or Execution of Paper

GL 231, §69, provides for admissions in district court actions not governed by the District-Municipal Courts Rules of Civil Procedure. Admissions made in response to a notice to admit are, unless the court otherwise directs, conclusive on the admitting party, not merely an item of evidence the admitting party is free to contradict. *Gishen v. Dura Corp.*, 362 Mass 177, 285 NE2d 117 (1972); *Snowden v. Cheltenham*, 337 Mass 295, 149 NE2d 606 (1958). Cf. Mass R Civ P 36 (discussed supra at §2.3.1). Strict compliance with the terms of §69 is required to avoid a binding admission thereunder. *Plante v. Louro*, 345 Mass 456, 463, 187 NE2d 866, 871 (1963) (affidavit of counsel rather than party was not compliance with the statute). The *Plante* case contains extensive discussion as to the nature of the statute and the power of a trial judge to relieve a party of binding admissions improvidently made due to lack of diligence of his counsel. Strict compliance with the procedures set forth in the statute is required of the demanding party in order to obtain the benefits of §69. *Deutsch v. Ormsby*, 354 Mass 485, 238 NE2d 339 (1968); *McElaney v. Hubby*, 3 Mass App 717, 323 NE2d 770 (1975).

Facts admitted under §69 do not preclude a finding of other facts by a judge. *Manoogian v. Manoogian*, 1 Mass App 825, 296 NE2d 516 (1973). For other cases discussing GL 231, §69, see *Loew v. Minasian*, 361 Mass 390, 280 NE2d 688 (1972); *Merchants National Bank v. New York Life Ins. Co.*, 346 Mass 745, 196 NE2d 201 (1964); *Town Bank & Trust Co. v. Sheraton Investment Corp.*, 2 Mass App 852, 312 NE2d 592 (1974).

Although there is no case authority on the point, it has been argued that §69 precludes evidence not only from the party admitting the fact but also from the party demanding it; that a denial duly made will preclude the party so denying the fact from taking a contradictory position at the trial; and that an express admission withdrawn by authority of the court, while no longer binding, may nonetheless be offered in evidence as an evidentiary admission. See 5 Ann Survey Mass L §22.2 (1958).

§2.4.2   Pleadings as Admissions

GL 231, §87, provides: "In any civil action pleadings shall not be evidence on the trial, but the allegations therein shall bind the party making them." Matters admitted in the pleadings are not open to dispute. *Willett v. Webster*, 337 Mass 98, 101, 105, 148 NE2d 267, 270, 272 (1958) (order for judgment given on the pleadings); *Provincetown Chamber of Commerce, Inc. v. Grace*, 14 Mass App 903, 436 NE2d 177 (1982); *General Electric Co. v. Brady Electrical Co.*, 2 Mass App 522, 317 NE2d 91 (1974).

The word "pleadings" under §87 includes matter filed in response to a motion for a more definite statement under Mass R Civ P 12(e); documents or articles attached to the pleadings and incorporated by reference, *H. P. Hood & Sons v. Whiting Milk Co.*, 345 Mass 287, 186 NE2d 904

(1963); Mass R Civ P 10(c); but not formal allegations as to unliquidated damages made by the attorney without special instructions from his client, *Maney v. Maney*, 340 Mass 350, 164 NE2d 146 (1960). Pleadings amended or withdrawn are not binding and may not be used as evidence in the same case. *Harrington v. MTA*, 345 Mass 371, 187 NE2d 818 (1963); *McCray v. Weinberg*, 4 Mass App 13, 340 NE2d 518 (1976); *Mastandrea v. Baressi*, 2 Mass App 54, 308 NE2d 573 (1974).

However, such pleadings from another case may come in as evidence if otherwise competent. Pleadings from another case are admissible against the party who made them, see §8.8.3, including from a case that has been discontinued. *Clarke v. Taylor*, 269 Mass 335, 168 NE 806 (1929). Pleadings from another case introduced as statements by a party opponent are not judicial admissions and thus do not conclusively determine an issue. *Hibernia Savings Bank v. Bomba*, 35 Mass App 378, 620 NE2d 787 (1993).

In *Com. v. Zuluaga*, 43 Mass App Ct 629, 686 NE2d 463 (1997), the court questioned whether the Commonwealth's statements made in opposition to a motion to suppress were judicial admissions. The court ruled that, in any event, it was not error for the trial court to relieve the Commonwealth of the consequences of having made them.

While a party may be bound by allegations of fact he makes or admits, *Zaleski v. Zaleski*, 330 Mass 132, 111 NE2d 451 (1953), admissions as to allegations of law or jurisdictional facts are not binding, although admissions of allegations of mixed fact and law may conclude the issue. *Wasserman v. Tonelli*, 343 Mass 253, 178 NE2d 477 (1961).

The prior practice under GL 231, §§87 and 90 (limited to the district courts by amendment in 1973 and repealed in 1975), was not changed by the enactment of the Massachusetts Rules of Civil Procedure (Mass R Civ P 8(e)). *Linthicum v. Archambault*, 379 Mass 381, 398 NE2d 482 (1979). The cases construing these statutes held that parties could plead on separate issues without being bound thereby on other issues and that such pleas could not be used as evidence with regard to other issues. One may plead inconsistent or alternative defenses without fear of making binding judicial admissions. *Linthicum v. Archambault,* supra, and cases cited therein. An admission by one party does not bind a co-party, even if the co-party is his insurer. *Kneeland v. Bernardi,* 317 Mass 517, 520, 58 NE2d 823, 824 (1945).

Although pleadings are binding on the party making them, *Adiletto v. Brockton Cut Sole Corp.,* 322 Mass 110, 75 NE2d 926 (1947); *Ciarletta v. Commissioner of Corporations & Taxation,* 3 Mass App 737, 326 NE2d 353 (1975), and findings to the contrary cannot be made, *DeNunzio v. City Manager of Cambridge,* 341 Mass 420, 169 NE2d 877 (1960), the court may allow the party to amend where the contrary fact is established. *Wasserman v. Tonelli,* supra; *Carson v. Brady,* 329 Mass 36, 40-41, 106 NE2d 1, 3-4 (1952).

Mass R Civ P 15 provides a liberal opportunity for a party to amend pleadings. Rule 15(a) allows amendment as a matter of right before a responsive pleading is served. Rules 15(b) through (d) deal with amendments to conform pleadings to the evidence and provide for supplemental pleadings. While amendments other than those specified in Rule 15(a) require leave of court or written consent, the rule states that leave to amend "shall be freely given when justice so requires." See, e.g., *Sullivan v. Iantosca,* 409 Mass 796, 569 NE2d 822 (1991), and cases cited therein. Unexcused delay and prejudice to the opposing party may, however, justify the denial of a motion to amend. See, e.g., *Mathis v. Massachusetts Electric Co.,* 409 Mass 256, 565 NE2d 1180 (1991), and cases cited therein.

§2.5 Common-Law Admissions

The attorney for a party may make a judicial admission binding upon his client. *Lucia v. Water & Sewer Commissioners of Medford,* 332 Mass 468, 125 NE2d 776 (1955); *Lewis v.*

Sumner, 54 Mass (13 Metc) 269 (1847). Such admissions may be made (a) by stipulations during the trial or before it; (b) by the opening statement of counsel at the trial; (c) by remarks or statements made by counsel during the trial; or (d) by conduct of counsel during the trial.

Otherwise controvertible facts may be agreed to and eliminated as issues by stipulation. *Mirashefski v. White City Apartments, Inc.,* 343 Mass 774, 178 NE2d 30 (1961). A fact may be admitted prior to the trial under the authority of a court rule such as Mass R Civ P 16 or Mass R Crim P 11.[1] Ordinarily, stipulations made prior to the trial or other than in open court must be in writing in order to be valid and binding. Neither the rules nor the statutes apply to agreements made in open court and acted on by the court. *Savage v. Blanchard,* 148 Mass 348, 19 NE 396 (1889) (dealing with an earlier version of GL 231, §72).

Stipulations may have binding effect in subsequent parts of the same proceeding. *Household Fuel Corp. v. Hamacher,* 331 Mass 653, 121 NE2d 846 (1954); Wigmore §2593 (Chad rev 1981). Compare *Com. v. Arsenault,* 361 Mass 287, 298, 280 NE2d 129, 136 (1972), distinguishing stipulations from a retrial on a different theory of the case.

Either the trial court or the appellate court has power, in its discretion, to relieve a party from a stipulation improvidently made or one not conducive to justice. See *Pastene Wine & Spirits Co. v. Alcoholic Beverages Control Comm'n,* 401 Mass 612, 615, 518 NE2d 841, 843 (1988) (party claiming to have been misled by opposing counsel not relieved from stipulation where material information was readily discoverable); *Com. v. Walker,* 392 Mass 152, 466 NE2d 71 (1984) (stipulation that result of polygraph test would be admissible will not be enforced even if all parties

---

§2.5 [1]GL 231, §§71 and 72, govern civil proceedings that are not "governed by the Massachusetts Rules of Civil Procedure or by the District-Municipal Courts Rules of Civil Procedure." These statutes provide for pretrial orders and written agreements of counsel in a manner similar to Mass R Civ P 16 and Mass R Crim P 11.

have agreed in writing to admissibility); *Pereira v. New England LNG Co.*, 364 Mass 109, 114, 301 NE2d 441, 445 (1973); *Gore v. Daniel O'Connell's Sons, Inc.*, 17 Mass App 645, 649, 461 NE2d 256, 260 (1984) (Appeals Court vacated stipulation as "improvident and not conducive to justice"). The courts may discharge a stipulation where fuller development of the facts is desired by the court. *Francesconi v. Planning Board of Wakefield*, 345 Mass 390, 187 NE2d 807 (1963). In interpreting a stipulation that is unclear, a court should attempt to effectuate the parties' manifested intentions. *Granby Heights Ass'n, Inc. v. Dean*, 38 Mass App 266, 647 NE2d 75 (1995).

Stipulations as to facts are to be distinguished from stipulations as to law. *Forbes v. Commissioner*, 82 F2d 204, 207-208 (1st Cir 1936). Stipulations as to questions of law are of no effect. *Swift & Co. v. Hocking Valley Railway*, 243 US 281, 289, 37 S Ct 287, 290, 61 L Ed 722, 725-726 (1917); *Kolda v. National Ben Franklin Fire Ins. Co.*, 290 Mass 182, 195 NE 331 (1935); cf. *Marotta v. Board of Appeals*, 336 Mass 199, 143 NE2d 270 (1957). However, parties are bound by a stipulation that an item of evidence is admissible unless the court vacates it as improvident or not conducive to justice. *Com. v. Sanchez*, 405 Mass 369, 377, 540 NE2d 1316, 1322 (1989).

An agreed statement of facts may be entered into by the parties and may serve as the basis of determination of their rights and obligations under, for example, the provisions of Mass R Civ P 56 (motions for summary judgment). Thus, an "agreed statement of facts" or a "case stated" involves an agreement as to all material ultimate facts upon which the rights of the parties depend; a stipulation as to facts involves an agreement as to certain facts with the remaining facts to be found from evidence submitted.

Distinguishable from a "case stated" and a stipulation of facts is a stipulation or agreement as to testimony or evidence. In the latter case, there is an agreement not as to the facts but as to the evidence of them. This leaves to the trier of fact the determination of those facts based on the agreed evidence and to the appellate court only the question of whether the evidence as stated warrants the finding of the trier of fact. *Benmosche v. Board of Reg. in Medicine*, 412 Mass 82, 588 NE2d 621 (1992); *Cambridge v. Somerville*, 329 Mass 658, 110 NE2d 99 (1953); *Frati v. Jannini*, 226 Mass 430, 115 NE 746 (1917).

Opening statements by counsel that fail to indicate that the party will establish a cause of action or defense have been construed as binding judicial admissions. *Cohen v. Suburban Sidney-Hill, Inc.*, 343 Mass 217, 178 NE2d 19 (1961) (judge properly granted directed verdict for defendant after hearing plaintiff's opening statement); *Gynan v. Jeep Corp.*, 13 Mass App 504, 434 NE2d 688 (1982) (same); cf. *Com. v. Sandler*, 368 Mass 729, 335 NE2d 903 (1975); *Mallard v. Waldman*, 340 Mass 288, 163 NE2d 658 (1960) (trial judge may refuse to grant a motion for a directed verdict). Mass R Civ P 50, which explicitly provides for a motion for a directed verdict following the close of the opponent's evidence, does not by its terms preclude a motion for directed verdict at the close of an opening.

Remarks, statements, or admissions by counsel during the course of the trial will also be binding judicial admissions. *Brocklesby v. Newton*, 294 Mass 41, 42-43, 200 NE 351, 352 (1936). But it must appear with reasonable certainty that such an admission was made. *Marotta v. Board of Appeals*, 336 Mass 199, 201, 143 NE2d 270, 272 (1957). So, too, conduct by counsel during the course of the trial may constitute an admission. *Drinkwater v. D. Guschov Co.*, 347 Mass 136, 140, 196 NE2d 863, 865 (1964); *Owens v. Dinkins*, 345 Mass 106, 185 NE2d 645 (1962) (acquiescence by silence of counsel); *Dalton v. Post Publishing Co.*, 328 Mass 595, 105 NE2d 385 (1952)(choice of one theory of defense held waiver as to another); *Forte v. Muzi Motors, Inc.*, 5 Mass App 700, 369 NE2d 1030 (1977) (same). Cf. *Bouley v. Reisman*, 38 Mass App 118, 129, 645 NE2d 708, 715 (1995) (questions asked during cross-examination by party's attorney did not constitute a judicial admission).

An admission made by a party while testifying at the trial is distinguishable from the judicial admissions discussed above. A testimonial admission is not binding on the party making the admission in the sense that further evidence on the matter is irrelevant. Such an admission may be "binding" in a different sense—in the sense that the jury is not free to disbelieve it if it is uncontradicted by other evidence (see §2.11).

§2.5.1 Judicial Estoppel

The Supreme Judicial Court has not yet thoroughly developed how it will treat the doctrine of judicial estoppel. The court has, however, indicated that it would apply the doctrine of judicial estoppel to preclude a party from asserting a position in one proceeding that is contrary to a position that the party previously asserted successfully in another proceeding. See *East Cambridge Savings Bank v. Wheeler*, 422 Mass 621, 664 NE2d 446 (1996); *Fay v. Federal National Mortgage Ass'n*, 419 Mass 782, 647 NE2d 422 (1995); *Tinkham v. Jenny Craig, Inc.*, 45 Mass App 567, 574, 699 NE2d 1255, 1259 (1998) (plaintiffs who sought remand to state court from federal court based on representation that claims were not greater than monetary threshold for diversity actions could not demand greater damages in state court). In *Wheeler*, the court held that settlement of the former action would not be defined as representing success for the purpose of invoking the doctrine of judicial estoppel. Cf. *Paixao v. Paixao*, 429 Mass 307, 708 NE2d 91 (1999) (judicial estoppel applies to oral separation agreements, but parties must acknowledge their assent to agreement in open court); *Blanchette v. School Committee of Westwood*, 427 Mass 176, 692 NE2d 21 (1998) (no inconsistency in party's position); *Labonte v. Hutchins & Wheeler*, 424 Mass 813, 820, 678 NE2d 853 (1997) (plaintiff was not estopped from pursuing handicap discrimination claim because of application for disability benefits without reasonable accommodation, but could perform it with reasonable accommodations).

Other decisions of the court have recognized the principle that "[a] party who has successfully maintained a certain position at a trial cannot in a subsequent trial between the same parties be permitted to assume a position relative to the same subject that is directly contrary to that taken at the first trial." *Gordon v. Lewitsky,* 333 Mass 379, 381, 131 NE2d 174 (1955) and see cases cited therein. Cf. *Spilios v. Cohen,* 38 Mass App 338, 340 n.2, 647 NE2d 1218, 1220 n.2 (1995) (collecting recent decisions supporting proposition that a party's affidavit, submitted to avoid summary judgment, may be disregarded where it directly contradicts that party's earlier statements made under oath, by deposition or otherwise).

B. JUDICIAL NOTICE [1]

§2.6   Meaning and Purpose of Judicial Notice

The purpose of a trial is to settle disputes according to law. To do this rationally, the court must have two general kinds of information: (1) information as to the law relevant according to the facts; and (2) information as to the facts relevant according to the law. The relevant law may range from well-known local statutes to remote foreign law and obscure municipal ordinances. The relevant facts may

---

§2.6 [1]For a general treatment of judicial notice, see Mueller & Kirkpatrick, Evidence §§2.1-2.13 (2d ed 1999). Regarding the counterpart of judicial notice before administrative tribunals, see Davis, Official Notice, 62 Harv L Rev 537 (1949). See also GL 30A, §11(5). With reference to judicial notice in the federal courts, see Fed R Evid 201; Fed R Civ P 44.1, Fed R Crim P 26.1.

range from specific facts directly bearing on the case to propositions of generalized knowledge useful only to put the particular facts in a meaningful context. Experience of the courts has been that much of this information is most efficiently obtained by way of evidence adduced at the trial. Some information, on the other hand, the court either already has or prefers to get in some way other than from evidence. For example, with respect to laws, the court would require evidence to prove that a bylaw of the town of Arlington prohibits speed in excess of 20 m.p.h. in the business district; it would already know that GL 90, §17, provides that speeds in excess of 20 m.p.h. while driving in an established school zone are prima facie unreasonably fast; it would look at the statute book of Pennsylvania to discover what is the speed limit in that state.

As for particular facts, the court would require evidence to prove that it rained in Boston on June 20, 1979; it would already know that Pearl Harbor was bombed on December 7, 1941; it would look at a calendar to discover that December 18, 1948, was a Saturday. As for propositions of generalized knowledge, the court would require evidence as to the distance an automobile will travel after the brakes are applied at a particular speed; it would already know that cancer tends to shorten life; it might refer to a standard scientific treatise or to reports of a prior case to learn that a child with type O blood cannot be the progeny of a man with type AB blood.

When the information is permitted to influence the outcome of the case without its having been introduced in evidence—that is, when the information is already a part of the court's knowledge or when the court gets the information from an almanac, statute book, court report, or other material not in evidence—the matter is said to have been judicially noticed. Matters are judicially noticed only when they are indisputably true. *Dimino v. Secretary of the Commonwealth*, 427 Mass 704, 707, 695 NE2d 659, 662 (1998). Such matters are generally categorized as either being matters that the judge knows because of his judicial function, matters of common knowledge within the community, or subjects of generalized knowledge that are readily ascertainable from authoritative sources.

Another method of classifying matters that might be the subject of judicial notice is to designate such matters as: (1) legislative; (2) adjudicative; (3) political; or (4) as being of law. This classification was suggested by Professor Davis in 1942. See Davis, An Approach to Problems of Evidence in the Administrative Process, 55 Harv L Rev 364, 404-407 (1942). Drafters of rules of evidence and of procedure have tended to accept this approach. Thus, Fed R Evid 201 deals only with "adjudicative" facts (i.e., facts of common knowledge in the jurisdiction or facts of generalized knowledge that are readily ascertainable). Matters of foreign law are treated in the rules of procedure (e.g., Fed R Civ P 44.1 and Fed R Crim P 26.1). Proposed Mass R Evid 201 takes the same approach, as do Mass R Civ P 44.1 and Mass R Crim P 39(b). Cf. GL 233, §70. It is doubtful, however, that the adoption of this method of classification materially alters prior practice.

§2.7   Judicial Notice under the Proposed Massachusetts Rules of Evidence and the Federal Rules of Evidence

Proposed Mass R Evid 201 provides:

> (a) *Scope of rule.* This rule governs only judicial notice of adjudicative facts.
> (b) *Kinds of facts.* A judicially noticed fact must be one not subject to reasonable dispute in that it is either
> (1) generally known within the territorial jurisdiction of the trial court or

(2) capable of accurate and ready determination by resort to resources whose accuracy cannot reasonably be questioned.

(c) *When discretionary.* A court may take judicial notice, whether requested or not.

(d) *When mandatory.* A court shall take judicial notice if requested by a party and supplied with the necessary information.

(e) *Opportunity to be heard.* A party is entitled upon timely request to an opportunity to be heard as to the propriety of taking judicial notice and the tenor of the matter noticed. In the absence of prior notification, the request may be made after judicial notice has been taken.

(f) *Time of taking notice.* Judicial notice may be taken at any stage of the proceeding.

(g) *Instructing jury.* In a civil action or proceeding, the court shall instruct the jury to accept as conclusive any fact judicially noticed. In a criminal case, the court shall instruct the jury that it may, but is not required to, accept as conclusive any fact judicially noticed.

Proposed Mass R Evid 201 is identical with Fed R Evid 201. It is the only rule of evidence dealing with the subject of judicial notice. Excluded from its scope are "facts" classified as political, legislative, or of law. Hence, the rule provides for judicial notice of those facts in issue that are indisputable and well-known but necessary to the resolution of the dispute between the parties. Matters that are material to the interpretation, determination, nature, and application of the law, whether it be constitutional, statutory, or judicial in nature, are not included; nor are matters necessary to judicial reasoning properly designated "adjudicative." The practice and power of the courts to consider matters legislative, political, or legal in nature as part of the process of dispute resolution and the determination of valid principles of law is unaffected by the limited scope of Rule 201. Procedural aspects of determination of law are covered in part by the procedure rules cited above.

§2.8   Matters Subject to Judicial Notice

§2.8.1   Law

a.   Domestic Law

General or public law of the Commonwealth is judicially noticed without request. *DiMaggio v. Mystic Building Wrecking Co.*, 340 Mass 686, 689, 166 NE2d 213, 216 (1960); *Burnham v. Webster*, 5 Mass (5 Tyng) 266, 269 (1809). See also, *Chopelas v. City Clerk of Malden*, 1 Mass App 241, 295 NE2d 395 (1973) (city charter and amendments thereto will be judicially noticed when charter found in statute). But whether a public statute has been accepted in a particular locality will not be judicially noticed. *City of Worcester v. Hoffman*, 345 Mass 647, 189 NE2d 226 (1963) (court refused to judicially notice whether statute was accepted by city); *Nayor v. Rent Board of Brookline*, 334 Mass 132, 135, 134 NE2d 419, 421 (1956) (same with regard to acceptance by town); *Bouchard v. City of Haverhill*, 342 Mass 1, 171 NE2d 848 (1961) (particular form of charter adopted by city would not be judicially noticed). Compare *American Mutual Liability Ins. Co. v. Com.*, 379 Mass 398, 403 n.11, 398 NE2d 491, 495 n.11 (1980) (court took judicial notice of unsuccessful legislative attempts to amend statute to require local approval of state agency decision); *Pereira v. New England LNG Co.*, 364 Mass 109, 301 NE2d 441 (1973) (same).

It should be noticed that under GL 233, §74, legislative acts of incorporation are "public acts" and therefore subject to judicial notice without request. *Salisbury Water Supply Co. v. Town of Salisbury*, 341 Mass 42, 167 NE2d 320 (1960) (statute incorporating public water supply company and subsequent amendments thereto); *Grant v. Aldermen of Northampton*, 316 Mass 432, 435, 55 NE2d 705, 706 (1944) (city charter); *Mariani v. Trustees of Tufts College*, 1 Mass App 869, 306 NE2d 833 (1974) (charter of Tufts College); *Baizen v. Board of Public Works of Everett*, 1 Mass App 602, 304

NE2d 586 (1973) (statute authorizing establishment and operation of water system and city charter).

Similarly, county and town limits are prescribed by public statutes. Thus, it is noticed that Suffolk is a Massachusetts county, *Com. v. Desmond*, 103 Mass 445, 447 (1869); that the town of Springfield is in Hampshire County, *Com. v. Springfield*, 7 Mass 9, 11 (1810); and that Milton is very close to Boston, *Brush Hill Development, Inc. v. Com.*, 338 Mass 359, 366, 155 NE2d 170, 175 (1959). The identity of government officers of any considerable importance (including the medical examiner of a county, clerk of the state senate, and federal deputy controller of the currency) is judicially noticed. *Gahn v. Leary*, 318 Mass 425, 426, 61 NE2d 844, 846 (1945). Compare *Com. v. Ficksman*, 340 Mass 744, 166 NE2d 726 (1960) (whether investigators employed by state Alcoholic Beverages Control Commission were public officers of the Commonwealth could not be determined without evidence).

Matters pertaining to the organization, structure, and jurisdiction of the courts of the Commonwealth are judicially noticed. *Cohen v. Assessors of Boston*, 344 Mass 268, 182 NE2d 138 (1962) (rules of Appellate Tax Board judicially noticed); *Com. v. Desmond*, supra. Judicial notice extends to the identity of judicial officers, *Assessors of Lawrence v. Arlington Mills*, 320 Mass 272, 69 NE2d 2 (1946); *Broitman v. Silver*, 278 Mass 510, 180 NE 311 (1932); and to their duties and function, *Martin v. Wyzanski*, 191 F Supp 931 (D Mass 1961).

Records and files of the court as to the case in issue, including proceedings ancillary thereto, will be judicially noticed. *Adoption of Simone*, 427 Mass 34, 691 NE2d 538 (1998) (in proceeding to dispense with biological parents' consent to adoption, permissible to judicially notice earlier findings in care and protection proceeding, although such findings could not be given dispositive effect in later proceeding); *In re Andrews*, 368 Mass 468, 476, 334 NE2d 15, 20 (1975); *Dwight v. Dwight*, 371 Mass 424, 357 NE2d 772 (1972); *Miller v. Norton*, 353 Mass 395, 232 NE2d 351

(1967); *In re Welansky*, 319 Mass 205, 65 NE2d 202 (1946). Cf. *Board of Assessors v. Ogden Suffolk Downs*, 398 Mass 604, 605, 499 NE2d 1200, 1201 (1986) (Board of Assessors may notice its previous determination of value of subject premises).

As to such related proceedings, a court may also take judicial notice of the records of other courts. *Nantucket Conservation Foundation v. Russell*, 2 Mass App 868, 316 NE2d 625 (1974); *Flynn v. Brassard*, 1 Mass App 678, 306 NE2d 446 (1974) (Appeals Court, in both cases, took judicial notice of the records of the Supreme Judicial Court); *Brookline v. Goldstein*, 388 Mass 443, 447 n.5, 447 NE2d 641, 644 n.5 (1983) (court examined certified copies of pleadings in related cases to discover nature of the claims asserted).

Court records of other proceedings in the same or another court need not be judicially noticed. *Grenda v. Kitchen*, 270 Mass 559, 170 NE 619 (1930); *Great Northern Indemnity v. Hartford Acc.*, 40 Mass App 686, 666 NE2d 1320, 1323 (1996) (impermissible to take judicial notice of facts purportedly established in a separate case between different parties) (Text cited). A judge may not take judicial notice of the undisclosed basis of his decree in an earlier case. *Morrison v. Krauss*, 353 Mass 761, 233 NE2d 301 (1968); *Ferriter v. Borthwick*, 346 Mass 391, 193 NE2d 335 (1963). Nor may a judge reviewing an administrative agency's decision go beyond the administrative record to judicially notice the defense of collateral estoppel, where such defense was neither pleaded nor proved. *Methuen Retirement Board v. Contributory Retirement Appeal Board*, 384 Mass 797, 424 NE2d 242 (1981).

Private acts of the legislature are not judicially noticed. *Brodsky v. Fine*, 263 Mass 51, 160 NE 335 (1928); *Burnham v. Webster*, supra. Nor are municipal ordinances or town by-laws properly the subject of judicial notice. *Warren v. Board of Appeals of Amherst*, 383 Mass 1, 8, 416 NE2d 1382, 1386 (1981); *Trustees of Stigmatine Fathers, Inc. v. Secretary of Administration & Finance*, 369 Mass 562, 568, 341 NE2d 662,

666 (1976); *Boulter Brothers Construction Co., Inc. v. Zoning Board of Appeals of Norfolk,* 45 Mass App 283, 697 NE2d 997 (1998) (zoning bylaws are not judicial noticed); *Rose v. Board of Selectmen of Falmouth,* 36 Mass App 34, 627 NE2d 478 (1994); *Shwachman v. Khoroshansky,* 15 Mass App 1002, 448 NE2d 409 (1983) (trial judge not required to take judicial notice of Boston rent control ordinance); *Perini Corp. v. Building Inspector of North Andover,* 7 Mass App 72, 78, 385 NE2d 1035, 1038 (1979). Cf. *Camara v. Board of Appeals of Tewksbury,* 40 Mass App 209, 662 NE2d 719 (1996) (although judge could not take judicial notice of municipal bylaw not in evidence, court could rely on findings in earlier Supreme Judicial Court opinion based on evidence introduced in that case). Regulations of executive departments are not judicially noticed. *York v. Sullivan,* 369 Mass 157, 160, 338 NE2d 341, 344 (1975) (regulations of the state attorney general); *Building Comm'r of Boston v. Santilli,* 358 Mass 816, 266 NE2d 634 (1971) (zoning code of the city of Boston); *Com. v. Berney,* 353 Mass 571, 233 NE2d 739 (1968) (traffic rules and regulations promulgated by traffic commission of town). A ruling by an officer of the executive department is not judicially noticed. *White v. Universal Underwriters Ins. Co.,* 347 Mass 367, 373, 197 NE2d 868, 872 (1964).

Generally, it had been stated that a court would not take judicial notice of the rules and regulations of administrative bodies. *Baxter v. Com.,* 359 Mass 175, 177, 268 NE2d 670, 671 (1971); *Kearney v. Board of Registration in Pharmacy,* 4 Mass App 25, 340 NE2d 515 (1976). However, judicial notice of administrative regulations has been taken in recent cases where the regulations were readily accessible in a state publication. See, e.g., *Ferreira v. Arrow Mutual Liability Ins. Co.,* 15 Mass App 633, 447 NE2d 1258 (1983); *Bagge's Case,* 5 Mass App 839, 363 NE2d 1321 (1977); *Sullivan v. Labor Relations Comm'n,* 5 Mass App 532, 364 NE2d 1099 (1977). Cf. *Paananen v. Rhodes,* 1 Mass App 12, 294 NE2d 434 (1972) (court declined to take judicial notice of administrative regulations where defendant had not had an opportunity to litigate the applicability of the regulation).

The question of administrative regulations appears to have been resolved, in large part, by legislative enactment. St 1976, c459, rewrote GL 30A, §6, to provide for the publication by the Secretary of State of a "Massachusetts Register" and designated its contents to include, inter alia, certain executive orders and regulations filed under GL 30A, §5. It is also provided by §6 that the contents of the Massachusetts Register "shall be judicially noticed." But see *Shafnacker v. Raymond James & Associates, Inc.*, 425 Mass 724, 683 NE2d 662 (1997) (not error to decline to judicially notice regulations of National Association of Securities Dealers); *Saxon Coffee Shop, Inc. v. Boston Licensing Board*, 380 Mass 919, 407 NE2d 311 (1980) (regulations not published in the Massachusetts Register will not be judicially noticed and must be made part of the appellate record).

GL 233, §75, simplifies proof of private acts, regulations, municipal ordinances and the like, but it does not dispense with such proof. (See §12.3.4)

b.   Law of Other Jurisdictions

In the absence of statute, the law of other jurisdictions, except well-known admiralty law, is not judicially noticed. *Hellenic Lines Ltd. v. Rhoditis*, 412 F2d 919, 922 (5th Cir 1969), *aff'd*, 398 US 306, 90 S Ct 1731 (1970).

GL 233, §70, provides: "The courts shall take judicial notice of the law of the United States or of any state, territory or dependency thereof or of a foreign country whenever the same shall be material." Section 70 applies to criminal as well as civil proceedings. *Com. v. White*, 358 Mass 488, 265 NE2d 473 (1970). The word "law" in GL 233, §70, includes "decisions," *Lenn v. Riche*, 331 Mass 104, 117 NE2d 129 (1954), but does not include judgments of foreign courts. GL 233, §69, and the applicable rules provide the manner in which records and judicial proceedings (including judgments) of the courts of another state or of the United States are admissible in evidence. (See §12.3.4)

In addition to GL 233, §70, Mass R Civ P 44.1 and Mass R Crim P 39 deal with proof of the law of foreign countries and the laws of the United States and its states and territories. Mass R Civ P 44.1 provides:

> A party who intends to raise an issue concerning the law of the United States or of any state, territory or dependency thereof or of a foreign country shall give notice in his pleadings or other reasonable written notice. The court, in determining such law, may consider any relevant material or source, including testimony, whether or not submitted by a party or admissible under Rule 43. The court's determination shall be treated as a ruling on a question of law.

Rule 44.1 does not materially alter pre-rule practice under GL 233, §70. Under both the statute and the rule, a court is not required to take judicial notice of foreign law unless it is brought to its attention. The statute does not make it the duty of the trial court to make an independent inquiry regarding foreign law, and it is unlikely that Rule 44.1 changed this. Rule 44.1 permits the court to consider "any relevant material or source." The rule is in accord with practice under the statute. The last sentence of Rule 44.1 makes it clear that the trial court's determination of foreign law is a question of law and therefore is reversible if the appellate court is in disagreement.

Mass R Crim P 39, which is applicable in district and superior courts, provides:

> (a) *Records of Courts of Other States or of the United States.* The records and judicial proceedings of a court of another state or of the United States shall be competent evidence in this Commonwealth if authenticated by the attestation of the clerk or other officer who has charge of the records of such court under its seal.
> (b) *Notice of Foreign Law.* The court shall upon request take judicial notice of the law of the United States or of any

state, territory, or dependency thereof or of a foreign country whenever it shall be material.

Subsection (a) of Rule 39 follows GL 233, §69. A complete record is not required under §69 as long as the essential facts are set forth on the portion produced. *Com. v. Rondoni*, 333 Mass 384, 131 NE2d 187 (1955). It can be assumed that this is so under Rule 39(a). Rule 39(b) is taken, with no material difference, from GL 233, §70. The rule provides that a court shall notice, upon request, material foreign law. This does not limit a court's authority under §70 to notice foreign law on its own initiative.

Federal courts judicially notice the laws of every state of the United States. *The President Wilson*, 30 F2d 466 (D Mass 1929).

Fed R Civ P 44.1 governs the procedure for establishing the law of a foreign country before a federal court. This rule does not employ the term "judicial notice," but makes the determination of foreign law a question of law for the court. The rule provides:

> A party who intends to raise an issue concerning the law of a foreign country shall give notice in his pleadings or other reasonable written notice. The court, in determining foreign law, may consider any relevant material or source, including testimony, whether or not submitted by a party or admissible under the Federal Rules of Evidence. The court's determination shall be treated as a ruling on a question of law.

The procedure in federal criminal trials is essentially the same. Fed R Crim P 26.1. Under these rules of procedure, the federal courts have wide discretion in the materials to which they may resort to determine the content of foreign law. *Pancotto v. Sociedade de Safaris de Mocambique, S.A.R.L.*, 422 F Supp 405 (ND Ill 1976).

Federal Law.   Taking judicial notice of federal law in Massachusetts courts raises special problems. Public acts of

Congress and presidential proclamations and reports to Congress are noticed. *Stankus v. New York Life Ins. Co.*, 312 Mass 366, 369, 44 NE2d 687, 689 (1942). However, even though §70 provides that the courts shall take judicial notice of the "law" of the United States and 44 USC §1507 provides that the contents of the Federal Register shall be judicially noticed, it is not clear that a Massachusetts court must notice regulations of federal offices and boards. It is clear that a Massachusetts court need not notice a federal regulation if the regulation is not brought to its attention. *Mastrullo v. Ryan*, 328 Mass 621, 105 NE2d 469 (1952). The appellate court may or may not take judicial notice of such a regulation where the attention of the trial court has not been called to it. *Gilbert v. Merrimack Development Corp.*, 333 Mass 758, 759, 133 NE2d 491, 492 (1956) (notice refused); *Ralston v. Comm'r of Agriculture*, 334 Mass 51, 133 NE2d 589 (1956) (notice taken). It is also clear that a federal court sitting in Massachusetts may notice a federal regulation without having had the regulation called to the attention of the trial court. *Green v. United States*, 176 F2d 541 (1st Cir 1949) (notice by district court); *Batista v. Nicolls*, 213 F2d 20 (1st Cir 1954) (notice by circuit court). The problems associated with notice of federal regulations in Massachusetts courts, as in the case of foreign state law, discussed below, may not be problems of judicial notice but rather of invited error. The language of the *Mastrullo* case implies that judicial notice is to be taken of a federal regulation if it is brought to the attention of the trial court.

Foreign Law in General. Under GL 233, §70, the correct procedure for the party desiring to establish the law of some other jurisdiction is: (1) to call the attention of the trial court to the statutes and decisions upon which he relies; (2) to have it appear in the record on appeal that this was done; and then (3) to refer again to those statutes and decisions in the brief on appeal. *Tsacoyeanes v. Canadian Pacific Railway Co.*, 339 Mass 726, 162 NE2d 23 (1959); *Bradbury v. Central Vermont Railway*, 299 Mass 230, 234, 12 NE2d 732, 734 (1938). One method of placing the authorities relied upon in the record is to place references to them in the requests for instructions or rulings. The following rules have been adopted in the handling of foreign law under the statute:

(1) The foreign law will be noticed if it is brought to the attention of the trial court. *Goodale v. Morrison*, 343 Mass 607, 180 NE2d 67 (1962) (failure of trial judge to charge jury on applicable New Hampshire law after proper request and citation held error). See also *Cameron v. Gunstock Acres, Inc.*, 370 Mass 378, 348 NE2d 791 (1976).

(2) The statute does not make it the duty of the trial court to make independent inquiry as to foreign law. *Murphy v. Brilliant Co.*, 323 Mass 526, 529, 83 NE2d 166, 168 (1948); *Knych v. Trustees of New York, N.H. & H.R.R. Co.*, 320 Mass 339, 340, 69 NE2d 575, 576 (1946). However, the court is not precluded from doing so if it so chooses. In *Petition of Mazurowski*, 331 Mass 33, 116 NE2d 854 (1954), the court held that it was proper for the probate judge and the Supreme Judicial Court to seek information from the State, Justice, and Treasury Departments relating to foreign exchange laws and regulations, even though such information was not directly available to the courts or litigants. Where the trial court takes judicial notice of foreign law, the appellate court will do so also, and it may consider other authorities not brought to the attention of the trial court. *Dicker v. Klein*, 360 Mass 735, 277 NE2d 514 (1972). However, the appellate court is not required to go beyond the authorities considered by the trial court. *Dadmun v. Dadmun*, 279 Mass 217, 220, 181 NE 264, 265 (1932).

(3) The law of a foreign common-law jurisdiction is presumed to be the same as the common (not statutory) law of Massachusetts to the extent that the foreign law is not brought to the attention of the court. *Commercial Credit Corp. v. Stan Cross Buick, Inc.*, 343 Mass 622, 180 NE2d 88 (1962); *Stern v. Lieberman*, 307 Mass 77, 78, 29 NE2d 839, 841 (1940); *Swift v. Swift*, 8 Mass App 875, 391 NE2d 930 (1979). The presumption does not apply to the law of a

foreign non-common-law jurisdiction. *Aslanian v. Dostumian*, 174 Mass 328, 330-332, 54 NE 845, 846 (1899).

(4) Where the law of the foreign state is not shown by the record to have been brought to the attention of the trial court, it may or may not—depending on the interests of "justice"—be considered when called to the attention of the appellate court. Compare *De Gategno v. De Gategno*, 336 Mass 426, 146 NE2d 497 (1957) (notice of Nevada statute taken); *Madeiros v. Perry*, 332 Mass 158, 124 NE2d 240 (1955) (Rhode Island common-law decision noticed); *Hiller v. American Tel. & Tel. Co.*, 324 Mass 24, 84 NE2d 548 (1949) (appellate court noticed that New York had adopted Uniform Stock Transfer Act), with *Donahue v. Dal, Inc.*, 314 Mass 460, 463, 50 NE2d 207, 209 (1943) (refused to consider New York law under which contract sued upon allegedly would be void).

(5) As to foreign law in a foreign language, it is not sufficient to call the court's attention to authorities without providing authentic translations. See *Rodrigues v. Rodrigues*, 286 Mass 77, 83, 190 NE 20, 22 (1934). Expert testimony as to the status of such law has been received. *Vergnani v. Guidetti*, 308 Mass 450, 454, 32 NE2d 272, 275 (1941); compare *Eastern Offices, Inc. v. P. F. O'Keefe Advertising Agency*, 289 Mass 23, 26, 193 NE 837, 838 (1935).

§2.8.2 Fact

Dates, the chief facts of history, and a broad and indefinite group of indisputable and either generally known or easily ascertainable facts are judicially noticed. There is a plethora of such cases. See the following examples:

History. *Nickols v. Commissioners of Middlesex County*, 341 Mass 13, 22, 166 NE2d 911, 918 (1960) (the reputation of Walden Pond that grew out of Thoreau's book *Walden*); *DeSautels, Petitioner*, 1 Mass App 787, 307 NE2d 576 (1974) (notice of the conquest of Lithuania in 1940 by Soviet

Russia and of the fact that the United States did not recognize the forced incorporation of Lithuania into the Soviet Union).

Government. *Michaud v. Sheriff of Essex County*, 390 Mass 523, 535, 458 NE2d 702, 709 (1983) (prison facilities of the Commonwealth are filled beyond capacity); *Com. v. Harris*, 383 Mass 655, 421 NE2d 447 (1981) (threats of violent acts directed at courthouses give rise to urgent need for protective measures); *Karchmar v. Worcester*, 364 Mass 124, 301 NE2d 570 (1973) (many collective bargaining agreements governing public employees are for a short period of time); *Sheridan v. Gardner*, 347 Mass 8, 196 NE2d 303 (1964) (legislation frequently is proposed by governor and other executive officers); *Allston Finance Co., Inc. v. Hanover Ins. Co.*, 18 Mass App 96, 463 NE2d 562 (1984) (1977 policy year was one of unusual regulatory turbulence).

Geography. *Crowe v. Ward*, 363 Mass 85, 292 NE2d 716 (1973) (distance between weather station and locus of accident); *Chin Kee v. Com.*, 354 Mass 156, 164, 235 NE2d 787, 793 (1968) (save for a few family-owned business operations there were few persons of Oriental heritage in Middlesex County in 1932); *May v. Boston & M.R.R.*, 340 Mass 609, 165 NE2d 910 (1960) (Porter Square in North Cambridge is thickly settled with industrial plants and businesses); *Opinion of the Justices*, 333 Mass 773, 780, 128 NE2d 557, 562 (1955) (historic nature and character of Nantucket); *Com. v. King*, 150 Mass 221, 22 NE 905 (1889) (location of a river).

Traffic and Transportation. *Berger v. MBTA*, 355 Mass 695, 246 NE2d 665 (1969) (occasional jolts and jerks are a normal incident to riding streetcars); *Medford v. Marnucci Brothers & Co.*, 344 Mass 50, 57, 181 NE2d 584, 588 (1962) (Commonwealth must often act through others to construct roads and bridges of a modern highway system); *Wilmington v. Department of Public Utilities*, 340 Mass 432, 438, 165 NE2d 99, 103 (1960) (matters of public transportation are of great importance to persons living in the communities surrounding Boston); *Green v. Wilmington*, 339 Mass 142, 158 NE2d 143 (1959) (many streets in suburbs and rural communities have no sidewalks); *American Oil Co. v. Alexanderian*, 338 Mass 112, 154 NE2d 127 (1958) (a way eight feet in width is required for passage of motor vehicles); *Mann v. Parkway Motor Sales*, 324 Mass 151, 85 NE2d 210 (1949) (existence of parkways in metropolitan Boston).

Science. *Com. v. Wilborne*, 382 Mass 241, 250, 415 NE2d 192, 199 (1981) (dosage and effect of Demerol as set forth in Physician's Desk Reference book); *Richards v. McKeown*, 9 Mass App 838, 399 NE2d 877 (1980) (reliability of standard mortality tables); *Com. v. Whynaught*, 377 Mass 14, 384 NE2d 1212 (1979) (radar speed meter is an accurate and reliable means of measuring velocity); *Com. v. LePage*, 352 Mass 403, 226 NE2d 200 (1967) (capacity of trained dogs to follow a human's trail); *Com. v. D'Avella*, 339 Mass 642, 162 NE2d 19 (1959) (conclusive reliability of properly administered blood tests showing nonpaternity); *Vincent v. Nicholas E. Tsiknas Co.*, 337 Mass 726, 151 NE2d 263 (1958) (propensity of glass to break under pressure); *Brookline v. Barnes*, 327 Mass 201, 97 NE2d 651 (1951) (recent emphasis on preventive medicine); *Deerfoot Farms, Inc. v. New York, N.H. & H.R. Co.*, 327 Mass 51, 96 NE2d 872 (1951) (wind tends to communicate fire from one property to another); *Silke v. Silke*, 325 Mass 487, 91 NE2d 200 (1950) (normal period of human gestation is approximately 280 days).

It should be noted that questions involving scientific or technological facts are constantly moving from the realm of the unknown or debatable to the realm of the accepted and established, but in some instances the reverse occurs. What facts of generalized knowledge are judicially noticeable thus depends on the state of knowledge more than it does on questions of stare decisis or precedent. Wigmore §2580 (Chad rev 1981). The appropriateness of judicial notice of scientific facts frequently arises in making the determination of whether evidence of scientific tests or procedures is admissible. See §§7.8, 7.9.4, 7.9.5.

General Knowledge. *In re McInerney*, 389 Mass 528, 536, 451 NE2d 401, 406 (1983) (fact that attorney continued to list himself as an attorney in telephone directory after suspension from practice); *Com. v. Stowell*, 389 Mass 171, 175, 449 NE2d 357, 360 (1983) (adultery frequently has a destructive impact on a marital relationship and is a factor in many divorces); *Smith v. Ariens Co.*, 375 Mass 620, 377 NE2d 954 (1978) (reliance of public on trademarks and trade names as proof of identity of manufacturer of product); *Sorensen v. Sorensen*, 369 Mass 350, 339 NE2d 907 (1975) (widespread existence of automobile liability insurance); *Benavides v. Stop & Shop, Inc.*, 346 Mass 154, 190 NE2d 894 (1963) (bland, pure, neutral soap sometimes causes slight, temporary burning sensation when introduced into the eye); *Mudge v. Stop & Shop, Inc.*, 339 Mass 763, 162 NE2d 670 (1959) (grocery carts and stock trucks are frequently used in aisles of supermarkets); *Samuel v. White Fuel Corp.*, 332 Mass 264, 124 NE2d 270 (1955) (fuel oil is customarily pumped into basement tank through hose to opening on outside of building); *Shaw v. Boston American League Baseball Co.*, 325 Mass 419, 90 NE2d 840 (1947) (spectators at baseball games are subjected to possibility of being hit by ball); *Katz v. Gow*, 321 Mass 666, 75 NE2d 438 (1947) (golf ball hit by unskilled person does not always fly straight toward intended mark).

The courts found that judicial notice of the proposed facts was not appropriate in the following cases:

Stasiukevich v. Nicolls, 168 F2d 474 (1st Cir 1948) (the Communist Party advocates the violent overthrow of United States government); *Com. v. Hartman*, 404 Mass 306, 313 n.9, 534 NE2d 1170 n.9 (1990) (symptoms of insulin shock); *Mendel Kern, Inc. v. Workshop, Inc.*, 400 Mass 277, 282, 508 NE2d 853, 856 (1987) (location of redevelopment project where location was not subject of general knowledge); *Weinberg v. MBTA*, 348 Mass 669, 205 NE2d 5 (1965) (whether fracture of ankle can give rise to varicose veins and shortness of breath); *Faulkner v. J. H. Corcoran & Co.*, 342 Mass 94, 172 NE2d 94 (1961) (that a terrazzo floor becomes dangerously slippery when wet); *Jensen v. McEldowney*, 341 Mass 485, 170 NE2d 472 (1960) (Registry of Motor Vehicles table showing distance car will travel at given speeds after brakes are applied); *Foss v. Mutual Life Ins. Co.*, 247 Mass 10, 15, 141 NE 498, 499 (1923) (that angina pectoris tends to shorten life); *Com. v. Kirk*, 39 Mass App 225, 654 NE2d 938 (1995) (not proper to take judicial notice of earlier 209A order to establish identity of victim's assailant; judicial notice cannot be taken of material factual issues that can only be decided by fact finder on competent evidence); *Com. v. Gonzales*, 33 Mass App 728, 604 NE2d 1317 (1992) (whether a particular school was an elementary, vocational, or secondary school not subject to judicial notice); *Rice v. James Hanrahan & Sons*, 20 Mass App 701, 707, 482 NE2d 833, 838 (1985) (judicial notice of administrative regulations not appropriate to prove insulation governed by them was hazardous).

Judicial notice is limited to subjects of general knowledge and is not extended to personal observations of the judge or juror. *Nantucket v. Beinecke*, 379 Mass 345, 398 NE2d 458 (1979); *Com. v. Byfield*, 32 Mass App 912, 585 NE2d 746 (1992) (peculiar experience and knowledge of magistrate may not support issuance of search warrant); *DeSautels, Petitioner*, 1 Mass App 787, 307 NE2d 576 (1974). Cf., *Com. v. Howard*, 42 Mass App 322, 326, 677 NE2d 233, 236 (1997) (error for sentencing judge to attempt to send a message to residents of town based on his perception of the extent of child abuse in the area). This rule does not preclude the finder of fact from considering the evidence in the light of general human knowledge and experience. *Com. v. Kingsbury*, 378 Mass 751, 393 NE2d 391 (1979); *Crowe v. Ward*, 363 Mass 85, 292 NE2d 716 (1973); *Richmond v. Richmond*, 340 Mass 367, 164 NE2d 155 (1960); *Com. v. Peckham*, 68 Mass (2 Gray) 514 (1854). Compare *Casey's Case*, 348 Mass 572, 204 NE2d 710 (1965), with *Lovely's Case*, 336 Mass 512, 146 NE2d 488 (1957), as to the extent that lay members of an administrative body can rely on such knowledge with regard to medical questions.

§2.9   Conclusiveness of Judicial Notice

Historically, judicial notice was conclusive. The court might hear argument of counsel and consider submissions by the parties before taking notice of a fact, but once the court had resolved to take judicial notice it would not receive evidence offered to contradict a matter judicially noticed. *Com. v. Marzynski*, 149 Mass 68, 72, 21 NE 228, 229 (1889) (refusal to hear evidence that cigars were drugs or medicine). Cf. *Stasiukevich v. Nicolls*, 168 F2d 474 (1st Cir 1948) (authenticity of report of legislative committee noticed; evidence admissible to dispute truth of assertions in report).[1]

Fed R Evid 201 is in accord with Massachusetts law on the conclusiveness of judicial notice, except as to criminal cases. As to criminal matters, Fed R Evid 201(g) provides that the jury is to be instructed "that it may, but is not required to, accept as conclusive any fact judicially noticed." Proposed Mass R Evid 201(g) contains the same language. In a criminal trial, the judge must expressly submit all factual issues to the jury, including matters of which the court has taken judicial notice. *Com. v. Kingsbury*, 378 Mass 751, 755, 393 NE2d 391, 393-394 (1979); *Com. v. Finegan*, 45 Mass App 921, 699 NE2d 1228 (1998) (judge may not implicitly take judicial notice of an element of the crime). Proof of an essential element of a crime may not be supplied by judicial notice taken at the appellate level, and where the trial court has failed to take judicial notice of an essential element of a crime, even though it could have done so, the defendant is entitled to a required finding of not guilty. *Com. v. Green*, 408 Mass 48, 50, 556 NE2d 387, 389 (1990); *Com. v. Kingsbury*, supra. See also *Com. v. Barrett*, 1 Mass App 332, 296 NE2d 712 (1973) (appellate court

---

§2.9   [1]Wigmore's earlier dictum to the contrary, §2567 (3d ed 1940), is not followed by Massachusetts or federal courts. Cf. Wigmore §2567(a) (Chad rev 1981) where the revisor's note takes a position consonant with that of the Massachusetts cases.

will not take judicial notice that defendant was represented by counsel in prior criminal proceeding).

§2.10   Miscellaneous Statutes

There are a number of special statutory provisions relating to judicial notice: GL 21, §24(8) (seal of supervisors of conservation districts); GL 25, §1 (seal of Department of Telecommunications and Energy); GL 58A, §1 (seal of Appellate Tax Board); GL 111, §13 (signature and office of analyst of narcotic drugs, poisons, etc.); GL 138, §36 (signature and office of alcoholic beverage analyst); and GL 271, §27 (general methods and character of lotteries). See also GL 30A, §6 (added by St 1976, c459) (providing that the contents of the Massachusetts Register shall be judicially noticed); GL 30A, §11(5) (administrative agencies may, in addition to judicial notice, "take notice of general, technical or scientific facts within their specialized knowledge"); and GL 277, §33 (matters that may be judicially noticed need not be alleged in criminal indictments).

C.   BINDING TESTIMONY

§2.11   Definition and Application of Doctrine

Generally speaking, it is the jury's function to pass on the credibility of testimony. *Com. v. Fitzgerald*, 376 Mass 402, 412, 381 NE2d 123, 131 (1978); *Kane v. Learned*, 17 Mass 190 (1875). There are, however, certain limitations to this prerogative. A party may be "bound" by his own testimony. He is bound not in the judicial admission sense that his testimony renders other evidence on the point immaterial, but rather in the sense that his testimony may be disbelieved only to his disadvantage. A party is bound by his testimony if

(1) the testimony was given in the pending trial, *291 Washington Street v. School Street Liquors*, 331 Mass 150, 117 NE2d 809 (1954); *Brown v. MTA*, 345 Mass 636, 189 NE2d 214 (1963) (party's testimony at auditor's hearing admissible at trial but not binding); and

(2) where (a) there is no evidence more favorable to him than his own testimony, *Jacquot v. William Filene's Sons Co.*, 337 Mass 312, 316, 149 NE2d 635, 639 (1958); *Gaynor v. Laverdure*, 362 Mass 828, 841, 291 NE2d 617, 625 (1973) (but where the party gives evidence leading to inconsistent conclusions, the jury may decide which version it will accept as true); *McClean v. University Club*, 327 Mass 68, 73, 97 NE2d 174, 178-179 (1951); *Gow v. Buckminster Hotel, Inc.*, 336 Mass 606, 608, 146 NE2d 924, 926 (1958); or (b) there has been an election by a witness between conflicting statements and any evidence more favorable to the party has been repudiated, *Harlow v. Chin*, 405 Mass 697, 706 n.11, 545 NE2d 602, 608 n.11 (1989); *Siira v. Shields*, 360 Mass 874, 277 NE2d 825 (1972) (see §6.6.3); *Ravosa v. Zais*, 40 Mass App 47, 661 NE2d 111 (1996); or (c) the testimony concerns the witness-party's subjective emotions, feelings, motives, intentions or knowledge, whether or not there is more favorable evidence from other witnesses, *Carey v. Lynn Ladder and Scaffolding Co., Inc.*, 427 Mass 1003, 691 NE2d 223 (1998) (plaintiff bound by his testimony as to his knowledge of ladder's instability); *Davidonis v. Levielle*, 356 Mass 716, 248 NE2d 645 (1969); *Hultberg v. Truex*, 344 Mass 414, 182 NE2d 483 (1962); *Fraser v. Fraser*, 334 Mass 4, 133 NE2d 236 (1956); *Motta v. Mello*, 338 Mass 170, 154 NE2d 364 (1958). Cf. *Charles Dowd Box Co. v. Fireman's Fund Ins. Co.*, 351 Mass 113, 121, 218 NE2d 64, 69 (1966) (knowledge of objective or physical facts not included within this doctrine); *Reynolds v. Sullivan*, 330 Mass 549, 116 NE2d 128 (1953). See generally Wigmore §2594(a) (Chad rev 1981) and Spalding, When Is a Party Bound by His Testimony?, 12 Boston Bar Bull 37 (1941).

Subject to similar limitations, a party who introduces in evidence his opponent's answers to interrogatories is in the same sense bound by them. *Tanguay v. Wood Conversion Co.*, 347 Mass 530, 533, 199 NE2d 181, 183 (1964) (introducing party bound by opponent's uncontradicted answers); *Hoban v. Trustees of New York, N.H. & H.R.R. Co.*, 326 Mass 566, 569-570, 95 NE2d 651, 654 (1950) (introducing party not bound by opponent's contradicted answers); *Gannon v. Summerfield Co.*, 323 Mass 25, 80 NE2d 51 (1948) (answers introduced by answering party; interrogating party not bound).

Testimonial admissions relating to questions of law, and not of fact, are not binding within the meaning of these rules. *Adams v. Adams*, 338 Mass 776, 780, 157 NE2d 405, 408 (1959). See also *Wasserman v. Tonelli*, 343 Mass 253, 178 NE2d 477 (1961). Compare *Shamrock Liquors, Inc. v. Alcoholic Beverages Control Comm'n*, 7 Mass App 333, 387 NE2d 204 (1979).

The jury is not required to believe the uncontradicted testimony of a witness unless it comes within the special rules described above. *Manias v. Director of Division of Employment Security*, 388 Mass 201, 205 n.7, 445 NE2d 1068, 1070 n.7 (1983) (Text cited); *Lenn v. Riche*, 331 Mass 104, 111, 117 NE2d 129, 133 (1954). Cf. *Shipp v. Boston & M.R.R. Co.*, 283 Mass 266, 186 NE 653 (1933) (court invoked federal rule in Federal Employees Liability Act case that testimony of witness cannot be disregarded when not open to doubt from any reasonable point of view). Specifically, a party is not bound by the testimony of a witness called by him, even if the testimony is uncontradicted. *Com. v. Britt*, 358 Mass 767, 770, 267 NE2d 223, 225 (1971); *Salvato v. DiSilva Transportation Co.*, 329 Mass 305, 108 NE2d 51 (1952) (witness is not a party); *Gordon v. Bedard*, 265 Mass 408, 164 NE 374 (1929) (witness is party opponent).

The jury may believe part and disbelieve part of a witness's testimony, provided it does not distort an integral portion of the witness's statements. *Donovan v. DiPaolo*, 4 Mass App 576, 355 NE2d 484 (1976). See also *Com. v. Cinelli*, 389 Mass 197, 204, 449 NE2d 1207, 1211 (1983); *Com. v. Hill*, 387 Mass 619, 624, 442 NE2d 24, 28 (1982);

Com. v. Fitzgerald, 376 Mass 402, 411, 381 NE2d 123, 131 (1978); *Lydon v. Boston Elevated Railway Co.*, 309 Mass 205, 34 NE2d 642 (1941).

A. PRESENTING EVIDENCE

§3.1 Order of Presentations and Examination of Witnesses; Role of the Trial Judge

The party having the burden of proof is required to put in its entire affirmative case first. Thereafter, the opposing party rebuts and puts in its entire affirmative case. The party that presented first may then introduce evidence to rebut new matters. A wide discretion is allowed the trial judge on the order of evidence. See *Com. v. Rancourt*, 399 Mass 269, 277, 503 NE2d 960, 965 (1987); *Boyd v. Lawrence Redevelopment Authority*, 348 Mass 83, 84, 202 NE2d 297, 298 (1964) (trial judge may admit evidence de bene out of order); *Horowitz v. Bokron*, 337 Mass 739, 742, 151 NE2d 480, 483 (1958) (judge had discretion to permit medical witnesses to testify on damages before evidence of liability was offered); Proposed Mass R Evid 611(a).[1] See also *Finance Commission of Boston v. McGrath*, 343 Mass 754, 768,

---

§3.1 [1] Rule 611(a) provides:

The court shall exercise reasonable control over the mode and order of interrogating witnesses and presenting evidence on direct and cross-examination so as to (1) make the interrogation and presentation effective for the ascertainment of the truth, (2) avoid needless consumption of time, and (3) protect witnesses from harassment or undue embarrassment. The court has discretion to admit evidence conditionally upon the representation that its relevancy will be established by evidence subsequently offered.

180 NE2d 808, 817 (1962) (administrative body has discretion to determine order of testimony).

It has been said that rebuttal is a matter of right where the proponent seeks to refute evidence of new facts presented by the opposing party. *Com. v. Wood*, 302 Mass 265, 267, 19 NE2d 320, 322 (1939). There is no right to rebut evidence that was not unanticipated, or to present rebuttal evidence that merely supports the proponent's affirmative case. See *Drake v. Goodman*, 386 Mass 88, 92, 434 NE2d 1211, 1214 (1982); *Urban Investment & Development Co. v. Turner Construction Co.*, 35 Mass App 100, 103-104, 616 NE2d 829, 832 (1993); *Teller v. Schepens*, 25 Mass App 346, 351, 518 NE2d 868, 881 (1988). Although courts are generally strict in forbidding affirmative evidence in rebuttal, the judge is accorded wide discretion to allow it. See *Mason v. General Motors Corp.*, 397 Mass 183, 193, 490 NE2d 437, 443 (1986); *Drake v. Goodman*, supra, 386 Mass at 92-94, 43 NE2d at 1213-1215 (extensive discussion of issue); *Chadbourn v. Franklin*, 71 Mass (5 Gray) 312 (1855); *Teller v. Schepens*, supra, 25 Mass App at 350, 518 NE2d at 870; *Com. v. Guidry*, 22 Mass App 907, 909, 491 NE2d 281, 283 (1986).

The usual procedure for interrogation of a witness is that the party producing him conducts direct examination about all matters as to which he is to testify. The witness is then cross-examined by the opponent on the matters as to which he has testified and, under Massachusetts practice, on any other matters relevant to the case.[2] See §3.2, infra. There may then be a redirect examination by the proponent and a re-cross-examination by the opponent; occasionally there are several redirect and re-cross-examinations. See §3.4, infra. The same witness may be called later as the opposing party's witness, in which case the original

---

[2]Mass R Civ P 43(g) provides: "Unless otherwise permitted by the court, the examination and cross-examination of any witness shall be conducted by one attorney only for each party. The attorney shall stand while so examining or cross-examining unless the court otherwise permits." See also Mass Superior Court Rule 69 (same; applicable in criminal cases).

proponent conducts cross-examination. The court in its discretion may permit a witness to be recalled by either side; but the judge is not required to allow a party to recall a witness. *Com. v. Bradley*, 35 Mass App 525, 531, 622 NE2d 1386, 1390 (1993) (& citations).

While the trial judge has wide discretion to impose reasonable limits on the length of witness examination, the judge may not impose arbitrary time limits on the taking of testimony in a manner that prevents the parties from presenting their entire case. See *Chandler v. FMC Corp.*, 35 Mass App 332, 619 NE2d 626 (1993). Compare *Guardianship of Brandon*, 424 Mass 482, 492-494, 677 NE2d 114, 122-123 (1997) (parties stipulated to time limits).

Mass R Civ P 43(a) provides in perinent part: "In all trials the testimony of witnesses shall be taken orally in open court, unless otherwise provided by these rules.[3] In general, evidence in a jury trial can be given only in the presence of the judge, whose duty it is to be present and to be the directing mind over whatever goes on. . . . It is a part of the right of trial by jury as established by the law of this Commonwealth that each party is entitled to the assistance and protection of the judge throughout the trial." *Com. v. Bergstrom*, 402 Mass 534, 551, 524 NE2d 366 (1988) (citation omitted). See also *Barrett v. Leary*, 34 Mass App 659, 614 NE2d 1035 (1993) (trial judge's presence in courtroom required while videotape deposition of medical experts was played for jury). But compare *McSweeney v. Build Safe Corp.*, 417 Mass 610, 632 NE2d 1185 (1994) (reversal not required where counsel failed to object to judge absenting himself

---

[3]Evidence offered as a basis for a motion may, in the discretion of the court, be received by way of affidavit. Mass R Civ P 43(e); Mass Superior Court Rule 9, 9A. See also Fed R Civ P 43(e); Fed R Crim P 47. Affidavits may be an essential part of certain types of preliminary proceedings. See, e.g., Mass R Civ P 56 and Fed R Civ P 56 (summary judgment); Mass R Civ P 12(c) and Fed R Civ P 12(c) (motion for judgment on the pleadings); Mass R Crim P 13 and Fed R Crim P 47 (pretrial motions); Mass Superior Court Rule 61 (motion to suppress).

during videotaped testimony and there was no showing of prejudice arising from absence).

It has been observed that a judge is "not a mere functionary to preserve order and lend ceremonial dignity to the proceedings but rather the directing and controlling mind at the trial." *Adoption of Seth*, 29 Mass App 343, 350, 560 NE2d 708, 712 (1990) (citations and internal quotes omitted). In this regard a judge has "the right, and perhaps the duty . . . to intervene occasionally in the examination of witnesses" to develop the most trustworthy testimony. *Com. v. Festa*, 369 Mass 419, 422, 341 NE2d 276, 279 (1976). "A trial judge is empowered to question witnesses in order to clarify an issue, to prevent perjury, or to develop trustworthy testimony." *Com. v. Paradise*, 405 Mass 141, 157, 539 NE2d, 1006, 1016-1017 (1989). The judge may participate in the questioning of a witness "so long as the examination is not partisan in nature, biased, or a display of belief in the defendant's guilt." *Com. v. Festa*, supra, 369 Mass at 422, 341 NE2d at 279. See also *Com. v. Marangiello*, 410 Mass 452, 457-462, 573 NE2d 500, 503-506 (1991) (judge's questioning of the victim, who because of a handicap was testifying through interpreters, not inappropriate where he properly determined there was need for clarification and his involvement was not overbearing); *Nancy P. v. D'Amato*, 401 Mass 516, 525, 517 NE2d 824, 829 (1988) (judge entitled to question witness not called as an expert as to her opinions); *Com. v. Fiore*, 364 Mass 819, 826-827, 308 NE2d 902, 907 (1974) (no error where judge questioned witness about discrepancy between proferred testimony and earlier testimony); *Com. v. DeJesus*, 44 Mass App 349, 353, 691 NE2d 234, 238 (1998) (trial judge's brief take-over of cross-examination of prosecution witness, to ask seven simple questions clarifying description of robbery location, not prejudicial to defendant) (& citations); *Com. v. Meadows*, 33 Mass App 534, 539-540, 602 NE2d 583, 586-587 (1992) (trial judge did not give robbery victim's testimony judicial imprimatur of credibility or undercut cross-examination when he intervened by questioning witness to clarify testimony); *Com. v. Jiminez*, 22 Mass App 286, 291-293, 493 NE2d 501, 505-506 (& citations). Compare *Com. v. Ragonesi*, 22 Mass App 320, 493 NE2d 527 (1986) (& citations) (reversal of convictions required because of judge's extensive and excessive questioning of complainant at pretrial hearing) and *Com. v. Hassey*, 40 Mass App 806, 668 NE2d 357 (1996) (judge's examination of defense witness went beyond clarification and was partisan).

"So far as possible, a judge should not dress down counsel before the jury, but when examination of witnesses veers off the point, it is not unreasonable for a trial judge to rein in counsel." *Com. v. Meadows*, supra, 33 Mass App at 536-537, 602 NE2d at 585 (citations omitted). Compare *Com. v. Keniston*, 423 Mass 304, 310, 667 NE2d 1127, 1132-1133 (1996) (no unfair prejudice where judge reprimanded defense counsel for theatrics) with *Com. v. Sylvester*, 388 Mass 749, 751-752, 448 NE2d 1106, 1107-1108 (1983) (judge's remarks disparaging defense counsel's skill, some with personal overtones, deprived defendant of a fair trial) and *Kuczynski v. Alfano*, 402 Mass 1001, 520 NE2d 150 (1988) (judge's repeated and combative interruptions of counsel and his sharp comments and questions to plaintiff's witnesses were not consistent with judge's role as impartial magistrate).

For a discussion of the judge's role regarding a pro se litigant, see *Com. v. Jackson*, 419 Mass 716, 721-722, 647 NE2d 401, 405 (1995). On the question of judicial bias, see *City of Boston v. U.S. Gypsum Co.*, 37 Mass App 253, 256-259, 638 NE2d 1387, 1389-1391 (1994).

For a discussion of the propriety of permitting the questioning of witnesses by jurors, see *Com. v. Urena*, 417 Mass 692, 632 NE2d 1200 (1994).

The trial judge has discretion to permit a criminal defendant to make an unsworn statement in lieu of testifying under oath. See *Com. v. Gallagher*, 408 Mass 510, 518, 562 NE2d 80, 85-86 (1990) (& citations) (but defendant has no right to make statement).

Although apparently rarely exercised, Massachusetts law permits the judge to comment on the evidence, provided of course that it is done in a fair and impartial manner and does not invade the jury's sole function to assess the credibility of witnesses and find the facts. See GL c231, 81 ("The courts [in civil actions] shall not charge juries with respect to matters of fact, but they may state the testimony and the law."); *Com. v. Perez*, 390 Mass 308, 319, 455 NE2d 632, 638 (1983) (judge may state the evidence and discuss possible inferences to be drawn therefrom, but may not directly or indirectly express an opinion as to the credibility of particular witnesses); *Com. v. McColl*, 375 Mass 316, 321-322, 376 NE2d 562, 565-566 (1978) (& citations) (judge may properly engage in analysis of evidence). Compare *Com. v. Kane*, 19 Mass App 129, 138, 472 NE2d 1343, 1349-1350 (1984) (& citations) (judge improperly conveyed his own view of evidence); *Com. v. Borges*, 2 Mass App 869, 316 NE2d 627 (1974) (judge's comment during instructions, "You don't go around paying somebody else's doctor's bills if you didn't cause the reason for it," amounted to instruction as to inference which jury should draw from victim's testimony and had effect of throwing judge's opinion onto scales decisively against defendant).

§3.2 Scope and Extent of Cross-Examination

"Parties to litigation are entitled as a matter of right to the reasonable cross-examination of witnesses against them for the purpose of attempting to impeach or discredit their testimony. The scope of cross-examination, including to what extent the accuracy, veracity, and credibility of a witness may be tested, rests largely in the sound discretion of the judge, not subject to revision unless prejudice is shown to a party by reason of too narrow restriction or too great breadth of inquiry." *Com. v. Gagnon*, 408 Mass 185, 192, 557 NE2d 728, 733-734 (1990) (citations and internal quotations omitted). See also *Roche v. MBTA*, 400 Mass 217,

222-223, 508 NE2d 614, 617 (1987) (judge's quashing of subpoena issued to plaintiff's expert whose videotaped deposition was admitted at trial improperly restricted defendants' right of cross-examination); *Com. v. Maltais*, 387 Mass 79, 90, 438 NE2d 847, 859 (1982). This rule applies to the criminal defendant who chooses to testify in his own behalf: he thereby renders himself subject to cross-examination on all facts relevant to the crime. *Com. v. Judge*, 420 Mass 433, 445, 650 NE2d 1242, 1250 (1995). But compare *Com. v. McClendon*, 39 Mass App 122, 128-130, 653 NE2d 1138, 1142-1143 (1995) (even though defendant opened himself up to cross-examination by taking stand, prosecution not entitled to impeach his credibility by way of prior bad acts).

Massachusetts practice defines a broad scope of cross-examination, as summarized in Proposed Mass R Evid 611(b): "A witness may be cross-examined on any matter relevant to any issue in the case, including credibility. In the interests of justice, the judge may limit cross-examination with respect to matters not testified to on direct examination." See *O'Connell v. Dow*, 182 Mass 541, 546, 66 NE 788, 789 (1903); *Com. v. Bibby*, 35 Mass App 938, 940, 624 NE2d 624, 627 (1993) (citing Text). See also Mass R Civ P 43(b). But see *Nuger v. Robinson*, 32 Mass App 959, 591 NE2d 1116 (1992) (trial court's ruling in contract action limiting scope of plaintiff's cross-examination of defendant to specific subjects raised on direct examination was reversible error). This approach contrasts with the more restrictive scope of cross-examination in the federal courts. See Fed R Evid 611(b): "Cross-examination should be limited to the subject matter of the direct examination and matters affecting the credibility of the witness. The court may, in the exercise of disrection, permit inquiry into additional matters as if on direct examination."[1]

---

§3.2 [1] In explaining the preference for the broader scope, Chief Justice Lemuel Shaw wrote:

Thus, when a proponent produces a witness, the opposing counsel may cross-examine the witness as to all relevant aspects of the case, whether or not a particular aspect was elicited during direct examination. *Nuger v. Robinson,* supra, 32 Mass App at 960, 591 NE2d at 1116-1117. Consequently, a party may put in its own affirmative case on cross-examination of the opposing party's witness, regardless of whether the matters were raised on direct.

GL 233, §22 and Mass R Civ P 43(b) permit a party to call the adverse party (or an officer, director, or managing agent of an institutional party) as a witness and interrogate that witness by leading questions. In such case, the witness may be "cross-examined" by his own counsel only upon the subject matter of his examination-in-chief. Mass R Civ P 43(b). See also *Phillips v. Vorenberg,* 259 Mass 46, 73, 156 NE 61, 65 (1927). The court may permit the use of leading questions when the adverse witness is "cross-examined." See *Westland Housing Corp. v. Scott,* 312 Mass 375, 383, 44 NE2d 959, 964 (1942). See §3.5, infra.

Both Proposed Mass R Evid 611(c) and Fed R Evid 611(c) broaden the concept of adverse party in this context to include "a witness identified with an adverse party." This approach is consistent with the view of the Supreme Judicial Court, which has upheld cross-examination of a witness called by a proponent to whom the witness is "essentially,

---

[W]here a witness is called to a particular fact, he is a witness to all purposes, and may be fully cross-examined to the whole case. . . . It is most desireable that rules of general practice, of so much importance and of such frequent recurrence, should be as few, simple and practical as possible, and that distinctions should not be multiplied without good cause. It would be often difficult, in a long and complicated examination, to decide whether a question applies wholly to new matter, or to matter already examined to in chief. . . . [I]t would not be useful to engraft upon [practice] a distinction not in general necessary to attain the purposes of justice, in the investigation of the truth of facts, that it would be often difficult of application, and that all the practical good expected from it may be as effectually attained by the exercise of the discretionary power of the court. . . .

Moody v. Rowell, 34 Mass (17 Pick) 490, 499-500 (1836).

although not technically, an adverse party." *Virta v. Mackey*, 343 Mass 286, 291, 178 NE2d 571, 574 (1961).

The judge has wide discretion to exclude cross-examination in the following circumstances:

(1)   in collateral or remote areas. See, e.g., *Com. v. Franklin*, 366 Mass 284, 288, 318 NE2d 469, 473 (1974); *Com. v. Fidler*, 23 Mass App 506, 516-517, 503 NE2d 1302, 1309 (1987); *Com. v. Shaheen*, 15 Mass App 302, 308, 445 NE2d 619, 623-624.

(2)   where the proposed inquiry is repetitious or cumulative. See, e.g., *Com. v. Jackson*, 419 Mass 716, 722, 726-727, 647 NE2d 401, 405, 407-408 (1995); *Com. v. Carroll*, 360 Mass 580, 589, 276 NE2d 705, 711 (1971); *Com. v. Meadows*, 33 Mass App 534, 540, 602 NE2d 583, 587 (1992).

(3)   to limit general or indefinite cross-examination, particularly in non-jury trials. See, e.g., *Nancy P. v. D'Amato*, 401 Mass 516, 524, 517 NE2d 824, 829 (1988).

It is improper for the cross-examiner to ask a question that implies the truth of a proposition he knows to be false; the cross-examiner should have a basis in fact for asking any such question and must be prepared to disclose that reason to the judge. See *Com. v. Mahoney*, 400 Mass 524, 531-532, 510 NE2d 759, 763-764 (1987) (& cases cited); *Com. v. Fitzgerald*, 376 Mass 402, 411 n.8, 414, 381 NE2d 123, 131 n.8, 133 (1978) (& citations). "The attempt to communicate impressions by innuendo through questions which are answered in the negative, . . . when the questioner has no evidence to support the innuendo, is an improper tactic which has often been condemned by the courts." *Com. v. Syrafos*, 38 Mass App 211, 219, 646 NE2d 429, 434 (1995) (citation omitted). See also §3.6.

For a discussion of the appropriate limits of cross-examination directed at discrediting a witness, see *Com. v. Rooney*, 365 Mass 484, 495-496, 313 NE2d 105, 112-113

(1974) ("The judge presiding over the trial of a case has the power to keep the examination of witnesses within the limits of common decency and fairness, and he has the duty to exercise that power promptly and firmly when it becomes necessary to do so."). See also *Com. v. Blake*, 409 Mass 146, 156-162, 564 NE2d 1006, 1012-1016 (1991). For an extensive discussion of impeachment approaches on cross-examination, see §§6.6 through 6.12.

§3.3   Cross-Examination in Criminal Cases—Right of Confrontation

The extent of cross-examination assumes a constitutional dimension in criminal cases, where the defendant is guaranteed the right to confront the Commonwealth's witnesses by both the Sixth Amendment to the United States Constitution[1] and art. 12 of the Massachusetts Declaration of Rights.[2] See *Com. v. Miles*, 420 Mass 67, 71, 648 NE2d 719, 723 (1995); *Com. v. Fuller*, 399 Mass 678, 684, 506 NE2d 852, 856 (1987); *Com. v. Johnson*, 365 Mass 534, 543, 313 NE2d 571, 579-580 (1974). "[T]he decisions of [the United States Supreme Court] and other courts throughout the years have constantly emphasized the necessity for cross-examination as a protection for defendants in criminal cases. . . There are few subjects, perhaps, upon which [the Supreme] Court and other courts have been more nearly unanimous than in their expressions of belief that the right of confrontation and cross-examination is an essential and fundamental requirement for the kind of fair trial which is this country's constitutional goal." *Com. v. Tanso*, 411 Mass 640, 650, 583 NE2d 1247, 1253-1254 (citation omitted).

---

§3.3   [1] "In all criminal prosecutions, the accused shall enjoy the right . . . to be confronted with the witnesses against him."

[2] "[E]very subject shall have a right . . . to meet the witnesses against him face to face."

Nonetheless, the right of confrontation is not absolute. *Com. v. Buckley*, 410 Mass 209, 221, 571 NE2d 609, 616 (1991). A trial judge may of course curtail cross-examination if the questions are not relevant or the relevance is attenuated. See, e.g., *Com. v. Souza*, 39 Mass App 103, 108, 653 NE2d 1127, 1131 (1995). Questions as to how far cross-examination may go are committed to the trial judge's discretion, and the burden of showing an abuse of that discretion and resulting prejudice is on the defendant, with the reviewing court considering the cross-examination in its entirety. *Com. v. Fordham*, 417 Mass 10, 19-20, 627 NE2d 901, 906 (1994) (but while defendant bears burden of showing both abuse of discretion and prejudice, defendant ought not be required to prove what opposing witness's testimony would have been had cross-examination been permitted); *Com. v. O'Connor*, 407 Mass 663, 672, 555 NE2d 865, 870-871 (1990); *Com. v. Fuller*, supra, 399 Mass, at 684-685, 506 NE2d at 856.

Determining whether a defendant's constitutional right of cross-examination has been violated requires weighing "the materiality of the witness's direct testimony and the degree of the restriction on cross-examination." *Com. v. DeJesus*, 44 Mass App 349, 352, 691 NE2d 234, 237 (1998) (citation omitted). Compare *Com. v. Reynolds*, 429 Mass 388, 390-392, 708 NE2d 658, 661-662 (1999) (reversible error to prevent defense counsel from cross-examining police officer concerning failure to pursue leads concerning other possible suspects), *Com. v. Miles*, supra, 420 Mass at 71-75, 648 NE2d at 723-724 (error to exclude cross-examination of police officer concerning other suspect), *Com. v. Franklin*, supra, 366 Mass at 288-291, 318 NE2d at 472-474 (error to exclude cross-examination about the victims' mistaken identification of other assailant), and *Com. v. Rescia*, 44 Mass App 909, 688 NE2d 1026 (1998) (remand required where defendant not permitted to cross-examine victim at restitution hearing regarding specifics of property taken in purse) with *Com. v. Sands*, 424 Mass 184, 189 n.7, 675 NE2d 370, 373 n.7 (1997) (no violation of art.

12 where defendant chose to avoid extensive questioning of trooper as matter of trial strategy), *Com. v. Barbosa*, 399 Mass 841, 845, 507 NE2d 694, 696 (1987) (rejecting defendant's contention that his right to confront the witness against him was denied because of limited language skills of the deaf-mute victim and inability of the interpreter to interpret critical questions on cross-examination), *Com. v. Doherty*, 394 Mass 341, 349-350, 476 NE2d 169, 175-176 (1985) (trial judge was within his discretion to limit cross-examination concerning promises and inducements to prosecution witness, as well as specific facts of charges pending against witness), *Com. v. McGrath*, 364 Mass 243, 250-252, 303 NE2d 108, 113-114 (1973) (no violation of defendant's right of confrontation where judge excluded question on cross-examination as to present address of witness), *Com. v. Montez*, 45 Mass App 802, 810, 702 NE2d 40, 46-47 (1998) (no error in refusing to allow defendant to cross-examine victim by showing her altered photo array), *Com. v. Lloyd*, 45 Mass App 931, 702 NE2d 395 (1998) (judge properly refused to permit defendant to cross-examine victim about her alleged use of Prozac at time of incident), and *Com. v. Munafo*, 45 Mass App 597, 603-604, 700 NE2d 556, 560-561 (1998) (no error in refusing to permit defendant to cross-examine concerning victim's leaving her children with defendant after prior assault). See also *Com. v. Conefrey*, 410 Mass 1, 8-14, 570 NE2d 1384, 1388-1391 (1991) (discussing the right to cross-examine in context of defendant representing himself); *Com. v. Massey*, 402 Mass 453, 523 NE2d 781 (1988) (discussing right to cross-examine during voir dire of witness to determine competency to testify).

"Where there is no opportunity to cross-examine a witness, because, for example, he is uncooperative, fails to appear, or invokes his privilege against self-incrimination, the striking of any direct testimony by that witness may be constitutionally required." *Com. v. Santiago*, 30 Mass App 207, 221, 567 NE2d 943, 951-952 (1991) (& citations). See, e.g., *Com. v. Kirouac*, 405 Mass 557, 560-564, 542 NE2d 270

(1989); *Com. v. Funches,* 379 Mass 283, 397 NE2d 1097 (1979) (& citations) (trial judge erred in refusing to strike direct testimony of prosecution's chief witness who asserted privilege against self-incrimination on cross-examination); *Com. v. Johnson,* supra, 365 Mass at 539-548, 313 NE2d at 576-581 (defendant's right to confrontation violated where judge, concerned with safety of the prosecution witness, refused to order him to answer questions on cross-examination). But compare *Com. v. Amirault,* 404 Mass 221, 234-235, 535 NE2d 193, 202-203 (1989) (child witness's lapse of memory was not comparable to a refusal to answer questions); *Com. v. Santiago,* supra, 30 Mass App at 221-222 (exclusion of police officer's testimony regarding defendant's inculpatory statements not required even though he could not remember, and made no notes of, any exculpatory statements).

The right of "face to face" confrontation protected by art. 12 of the Massachusetts Declaration of Rights precludes witnesses from testifying outside the physical presence of the defendant and the jury. See *Com. v. Bergstrom,* 402 Mass 534, 524 NE2d 366 (1988) (holding that GL 278, §16D, which permits child witnesses in sexual assault cases to testify by closed-circuit television transmission, violates art. 12). Compare *Maryland v. Craig,* 497 US 836, 110 S Ct 3157, 111 L Ed 2d 666 (1990) (upholding against Sixth Amendment challenge statutory procedure allowing use of one-way closed-circuit television to present testimony of child abuse victim). Art. 12 is not violated, however, where the child's testimony is taken on videotape in the presence of the defendant, and upon a showing of a compelling need to do so. See *Com. v. Tufts,* 405 Mass 610, 542 NE2d 586 (1989); *Com. v. Dockham,* 405 Mass 618, 622-625, 542 NE2d 591, 594-595 (1989); *Com. v. Amirault,* 404 Mass 221, 240-243, 535 NE2d 193, 205-207 (1989). Art. 12 forbids a special courtroom seating arrangement that impedes the defendant's view of the faces of minor complainants as they testify. See *Com. v. Amirault,* 424 Mass 618, 632, 677 NE2d 652, 662 (1997); *Com. v. Souza,* 44 Mass App 238, 689 NE2d

1359 (1998); *Com. v. Spear*, 43 Mass App 583, 686 NE2d 1037 (1997) (special seating arrangement allowing nine-year-old complainant to testify facing jury box and not defendant violated confrontation rights, even if defendant could see complainant's profile). Compare *Com. v. Sanchez*, 423 Mass 591, 596-598, 670 NE2d 377, 380-381 (1996) (no violation of confrontation right where judge seated child witness at table in front of jury box while defendant sat 20 feet away at counsel table); *Com. v. Johnson*, 417 Mass 498, 631 NE2d 1002 (1994). See also *Coy v. Iowa*, 487 US 1012, 108 S Ct 2798 (1988) (Sixth Amendment violated when child witnesses were shielded from defendant by a screen).

Because a GL 209A proceeding alleging domestic abuse is civil, not criminal, it has been held that the constitutional right to confront witnesses does not apply. A defendant against whom a domestic abuse prevention order is sought has a general right to cross-examine witnesses against him, but the judge in appropriate circumstances may limit and even deny cross-examination for good cause. *Frizado v. Frizado*, 420 Mass 592, 596-598, 651 NE2d 1206, 1210-1211 (1995); *Silvia v. Duarte*, 421 Mass 1007, 657 NE2d 1262 (1995) (failure to allow defendant to cross-examine domestic abuse complainant not abuse of discretion given defendant's established history of violence directed at complainant). Similarly, there is no constitutional right to confront witnesses in a divorce matter. *White v. White*, 40 Mass App 132, 133, 662 NE2d 230, 232 (1996) (but judge lacked authority to take 22-year-old daughter's testimony outside presence of parties and attorneys to resolve conflicting testimony about father's alleged sexual misconduct).

The right to cross-examine extends to witnesses only, and not to persons present in the courtroom as "demonstrative evidence" but who do not testify. See *Com. v. Roderick*, 411 Mass 817, 820, 586 NE2d 967, 969 (1992).

For further discussion of the right to cross-examine to show bias, see §6.9. For discussion of the confrontation issue in regard to a non-testifying codefendant (*Bruton v. United States*), see §8.8.7, infra.

§3.4   Redirect and Re-Cross-Examination

The primary purpose of redirect examination is to give the witness who has been cross-examined an opportunity to explain, correct, or modify evidence elicited from him on cross-examination. *Com. v. Olszewski*, 416 Mass 707, 718, 625 NE2d 529, 536 (1993); *Com. v. Allen*, 395 Mass 448, 459, 480 NE2d 630, 638 (1985). Thus, a subject opened during cross-examination may be explored on redirect. *Com. v. Marrero*, 427 Mass 65, 68-69, 691 NE2d 918, 921-922 (1998); *Com. v. Johnson*, 412 Mass 318, 325, 588 NE2d 684, 688 (1992); *Com. v. Otsuki*, 411 Mass 218, 236, 581 NE2d 999, 1009-1010 (1991); *Com. v. Smith*, 403 Mass 489, 498-499, 531 NE2d 556, 561-562 (1988) (& citations).

The scope of redirect examination is within the discretion of the trial judge, and a party who claims an abuse of discretion assumes a heavy burden. *Com. v. Gordon*, 407 Mass 340, 352, 553 NE2d 915, 921-922 (1990); *Com. v. Maltais*, 387 Mass 79, 92, 438 NE2d 847, 854 (1982). Redirect examination to explain testimony adduced on cross-examination is, however, treated as a matter of right. See *Com. v. Helfant*, 398 Mass 214, 222, 496 NE2d 433, 439-440 (1986) (defendant had right to explain why he lied to police); *Com. v. Mandeville*, 386 Mass 393, 400, 436 NE2d 912, 917-918 (1982) (defendant had right to explain damaging testimony elicited on cross-examination); *Com. v. Fatalo*, 345 Mass 85, 185 NE2d 754 (1962) (defendant had right to explain testimony developed on cross-examination that had impeached his alibi); *Com. v. Smith*, 329 Mass 477, 109 NE2d 120 (1952) (refusal of judge to permit alibi witness to explain apparently contradictory statements made during direct and cross-examination prejudicial error). Compare *Martel v. MBTA*, 403 Mass 1, 7, 525 NE2d 662, 665 (1988) (since no erroneous impression was created on cross-examination, judge did not err in excluding clarifying evidence on redirect); *Footit v. Monsees*, 26 Mass App 173, 182, 525 NE2d 423, 429 (1988) (judge properly limited efforts to rehabilitate witness on redirect that went to collateral matters).

Although the scope of inquiry on redirect is generally limited to those matters raised on cross-examination, the judge has discretion to allow redirect concerning matters not touched on in cross-examination. *Com. v. Allen*, supra, 395 Mass at 459, 480 NE2d at 638; *Com. v. Nawn*, 394 Mass 1, 5, 474 NE2d 545, 549 (1985).

Where parts of a prior statement are testified to on cross-examination, detailed examination of the entire statement is permitted on redirect. *Com. v. Hoffer*, supra, 375 Mass at 376, 377 NE2d at 690. See also §3.12, infra.

For a discussion of the rehabilitation of a witness on redirect, see §§6.15 and 6.16.

A defendant has no right to re-cross-examination unless the examination addresses a new matter brought out for the first time on redirect examination. Otherwise, re-cross-examination is allowed within the sound discretion of the trial judge, and is generally limited to new matters raised on redirect. *Com. v. O'Brien*, 419 Mass 470, 476, 645 NE2d 1170, 1174 (1995); *Com. v. Riley*, 17 Mass App 950, 952, 457 NE2d 660, 662-663 (1983) (citing Text) (same ground had been well-plowed by the direct, cross-, and redirect examination).

§3.5 Leading Questions

Leading questions are questions that suggest to the witness the answer desired by the examiner, and for that reason are generally objectionable on direct examination of one's own witness. Proposed Mass R Evid 611(c), which is substantially identical to Fed R Evid 611(c), provides:

Leading questions should not be used on the direct examination of a witness except as may be necessary to develop his testimony. Ordinarily leading questions should be permitted on cross-examination. When a party calls a hostile witness, an adverse party, *or a witness identified with an adverse party,* interrogation may be by leading questions (emphasis supplied).

The rule is consistent with present Massachusetts practice, except for the italicized phrase, which the Advisory Committee pointed out is broader than Mass R Civ P 43(b) and GL 233, §22, both of which confine the use of leading questions in this context to the adverse party or an officer, director, or managing agent of the adverse party.

Leading questions are permissible on direct examination in the following circumstances:

- When examining a hostile witness, including the adverse party, as noted in §3.2, supra. See also *Com. v. LaFrance,* 361 Mass 53, 57, 278 NE2d 394, 397 (1972); *Com. v. Greene,* 9 Mass App 688, 693, 404 NE2d 110, 113 (1980). Massachusetts practice also permits the use of leading questions when the adverse witness is then "cross-examined" by his own counsel. See *Westland Housing Corp. v. Scott,* 312 Mass 375, 383, 44 NE2d 959, 964 (1942).
- If necessary to refresh the failing or confused memory of a friendly witness. *Com. v. Fiore,* 364 Mass 819, 825-826, 308 NE2d 902, 907-908 (1974); *DiMarzo v. S. & P. Realty Corp.,* 364 Mass 510, 512, 306 NE2d 432, 433-434 (1974). See also §6.19.
- To elicit testimony from a witness of limited understanding due to age, mental disability, difficulty with the English language, or other similar reason. *Com. v. Carrion,* 370 Mass 408, 411, 348 NE2d 754, 756 (1976) (child witness); *Com. v. Aronson,* 330 Mass 453, 460, 115 NE2d 362, 367 (1953) (witness under emotional stress); *Guiffre v. Carapezza,* 298 Mass 458, 11 NE2d 433 (1937) (witness unable to

read list); *Gray v. Kelley*, 190 Mass 184, 187, 76 NE 724, 726 (1906) (elderly witness); *Com. v. Baran*, 21 Mass App 989, 991, 490 NE2d 479, 480-481 (1986) (child witness); *Com. v. Clark*, 3 Mass App 481, 487, 334 NE2d 68, 72 (1975) (non-English-speaking witness).

- In bringing out preliminary matters such as name, age, business, place of residence, and so on. See *Moody v. Rowell*, 34 Mass (17 Pick) 490, 498 (1836).

The allowance of leading questions is almost wholly a matter within the court's discretion. *Com. v. Mitchell*, 367 Mass 419, 326 NE2d 6 (1975); *DiMarzo v. S. & P. Realty Corp.*, supra, 364 Mass 512 ("We are aware of no decision in this Commonwealth in which exceptions have been sustained because of the allowance of leading questions." citation omitted); *Dorfman v. TDA Industries, Inc.*, 16 Mass App 714, 719, 455 NE2d 457, 460 (1983) (remedy for abusive use of leading questions is committed to the broad discretion of trial judge). The judge may instruct the jury that facts suggested in leading questions which are answered in the negative are not evidence. See *Com. v. Judge*, 420 Mass 433, 452 n.12, 650 NE2d 1242, 1254 n.12 (1995) (& citation).

Although the use of leading questions in presenting evidence to a grand jury has been challenged on occasion, there appears to be no federal or state reported decisions in which an indictment was dismissed solely because the prosecutor used leading questions. See *Com. v. Martinez*, 420 Mass 622, 625-626, 651 NE2d 380, 382-383 (1995) (& citations).

§3.6 Questions Improper as to Form

By way of example, the following are objectionable:

- Questions that are argumentative—i.e., that assume as true a material fact not in evidence. See

Cleary v. St. George, 335 Mass 245, 250, 139 NE2d
180, 183-184 (1957); *Reardon v. Boston Elevated
Railway,* 311 Mass 228, 231, 40 NE2d 865, 866-867
(1942); *Com. v. McHugh,* 17 Mass App 1015, 1016,
460 NE2d 613, 614 (1984).

- Questions that communicate impressions by innuendo when the questioner has no evidence to support the innuendo. See *Com. v. Fordham,* 417 Mass
  10, 20-21, 627 NE2d 901, 906-907 (1994); *Com. v.
  Syrafos,* 38 Mass App 211, 219, 646 NE2d 429, 434
  (1995).

- Questions that are repetitious. See *LaCroix v. Zoning Board of Appeals of Methuen,* 344 Mass 489, 183
  NE2d 99 (1962); *Com. v. Roukous,* 2 Mass App 378,
  382-383, 313 NE2d 143, 147 (1974).

- Questions that are overbroad and confusing. See
  Com. v. Blake, 409 Mass 146, 159, 564 NE2d 1006,
  1014 (1991).

- Questions that are too vague or indefinite to likely
  be understood by the witness or jury. See *Com. v.
  Tarver,* 369 Mass 302, 313, 345 NE2d 671, 680
  (1975); *Footit v. Monsees,* 26 Mass App 173, 183, 525
  NE2d 423, 430 (1988).

- Questions that ask a witness to comment on the
  credibility of other witnesses. See §6.5 and §7.3, infra.

§3.7 Closing Argument

In closing argument counsel may argue to the jury the
evidence and reasonable inferences that might be drawn
from that evidence. *Com. v. Murchison,* 418 Mass 58, 59, 634
NE2d 561, 562 (1994) (noting that in general the standards
are the same for prosecutor and defense counsel); *Com. v.
Dinkins,* 415 Mass 715, 725, 615 NE2d 570, 575 (1993) (the
inferences suggested by prosecutor need only be reasonable, not necessary or inescapable); *Com. v. Viriyahiranpai-*

boon, 412 Mass 224, 231, 588 NE2d 643, 649 (1992); *Com. v. Blake,* 409 Mass 146, 161, 564 NE2d 1006, 1015-1016 (1991); *Com. v. Paradise,* 405 Mass 141, 152, 539 NE2d 1006, 1013-1014 (1989). Counsel may "attempt to assist the jury in their task of analyzing, evaluating, and applying evidence," including "suggestions by counsel as to what conclusions the jury should draw from the evidence." *Com. v. Grimshaw,* 412 Mass 505, 510, 590 NE2d 681, 684-685 (1992) (citation omitted). Counsel may "fit all the pieces of evidence together so that they form a comprehensive and comprehensible picture for the jury." *Com. v. Corriveau,* 396 Mass 319, 336, 486 NE2d 29, 41 (1985) (citation omitted).

"[E]nthusiastic rhetoric, strong advocacy, and excusable hyperbole are not grounds for reversal. The jury is presumed to have a certain measure of sophistication in sorting out excessive claims on both sides." *Com. v. Wilson,* 427 Mass 336, 350, 693 NE2d 158, 171 (1998) (citations and internal quotes omitted). See also *Com. v. Lawrence,* 404 Mass 378, 391-392, 536 NE2d 571, 579-580 (1989) ("The rules governing prosecutors' closing arguments are clear in principle. We have never criticized a prosecutor for arguing forcefully for a conviction based on the evidence and on inferences that may reasonably be drawn from the evidence." (citations omitted)). If in accord with reasonable inferences from the evidence, counsel may present an argument by dramatizing it in imaginary dialogue or with a hypothetical account. *Com. v. Good,* 409 Mass 612, 625-626, 568 NE2d 1127, 1135-1136 (1991) (& citations). See also *Com. v. Nol,* 39 Mass App 901, 652 NE2d 898 (1995) (demonstration in which prosecutor showed that handkerchief held over face would not preclude identification of defendant was proper illustration of testimony). But compare *Com. v. Masello,* 428 Mass 446, 452, 702 NE2d 1153, 1157 (1998) (prosecutor's argument about what defendant had been thinking prior to shooting not based on any testimony, nor permissible "enthusiastic rhetoric"); *Com. v. Andrews,* 427 Mass 434, 443-444, 694 NE2d 329, 336 (1998) (no evidence supported prosecutor's characterizations of shooting); *Com. v. Hubbard*, 45 Mass App 277, 697 NE2d 551 (1998) (reversal required where prosecutor, without support in admissible evidence, referred in opening and closing to prior assault incident involving defendant).

Counsel may properly comment on the trial tactics of the opponent, including pointing out conflicts in the opponent's version of events. *Com. v. Jackson*, 428 Mass 455, 463-464, 702 NE2d 1158, 1164 (1998) (references to defense counsel's use of "smoke screen and mirrors" permissible); *Com. v. Evans*, 415 Mass 422, 428-429, 614 NE2d 653, 658 (1993); *Com. v. Grimshaw*, supra, 412 Mass at 507, 590 NE2d at 683; *Com. v. Cohen*, 412 Mass 375, 384, 589 NE2d 289, 296 (1992). Further, counsel have been permitted to engage in otherwise improper argument to counteract improper argument by their opponent. See, e.g., *Com. v. Mello*, 420 Mass 375, 380-381, 649 NE2d 1106, 1111 (1995) (& citations); *Com. v. Amirault*, 404 Mass 221, 236-237, 535 NE2d 193, 203 (1989) ("Defense counsel clearly invited the prosecutor's comments with remarks in his own closing argument.")

"Within the bounds of the evidence and the fair inferences from the evidence, great latitude should be permitted to counsel in argument," and the judge should not invade the province of the jury to decide what inferences to draw from certain evidence. *Com. v. Gilmore*, 399 Mass 741, 745, 506 NE2d 883, 886 (1987) (citations omitted) (judge improperly interrupted defense counsel's argument). See also *Com. v. Murchison*, supra, 418 Mass at 60, 634 NE2d at 562 (trial court's special curative instruction, following defense counsel's argument that testifying police officers were lying, prejudiced defendant).

Counsel may not, however, go beyond the scope of the evidence or refer to matters that have been excluded. See *Com. v. Grimshaw*, supra, 412 Mass at 508-509, 590 NE2d at 683-684; *Harlow v. Chin*, 405 Mass 697, 704-705 n.6, 545 NE2d 602, 607 n.6 (1989); *Com. v. Amirault*, 404 Mass 221, 238-240, 535 NE2d 193, 204-205 (1989). Counsel may not misstate the evidence, *Com. v. Fitzgerald*, 376 Mass 402, 416-

417, 381 NE2d 123, 134 (1978), or misstate principles of law,[1] nor may their summations infringe or denigrate constitutional rights. *Com. v. Thomas,* 401 Mass 109, 113, 514 NE2d 1309, 1312 (1987) (citation omitted); *Com. v. Smith,* 387 Mass 900, 903, 444 NE2d 374, 377-378 (1983).

Appeals to racial, religious, or ethnic prejudices are especially improper. See *Com. v. Phoenix,* 409 Mass 408, 424-425, 567 NE2d 193, 202-203 (1991); *Com. v. Mahdi,* 388 Mass 679, 691-693, 448 NE2d 704, 712-713 (1983); *Com. v. Lara,* 39 Mass App 546, 658 NE2d 692 (1995); *Com. v. Kines,* 37 Mass App 540, 640 NE2d 1117 (1994). It has been observed that "even a totally benign reference to group membership may awaken or even exacerbate latent biases among some jurors. For this reason, prosecutors would be well advised to steer . . . clear of making such characterizations in future cases to avoid the possibility of needless retrials." *Com. v. Berrio,* 43 Mass App 836, 842, 687 NE2d 644 (1997); *Com. v. West,* 44 Mass App 150, 152, 688 NE2d 1378, 1380 (1998). But compare *Com. v. Dixon,* 425 Mass 223, 230-231, 680 NE2d 84, 89-90 (1997) (no error although prosecutor's extensive reference to defendant and witnesses as "these people" coming from "a whole different planet" with a "whole different moral code" arguably had racial overtones).

The prosecution may not appeal to the jury to convict on the basis of emotion or sympathy for the victim or suggest that the jury put themselves in the victim's position. See *Com. v. Kent,* 427 Mass 754, 759-762, 696 NE2d 511, 515-517 (1998) (repeated statement that victim was nine years old and shot on birthday); *Com. v. Hamilton,* 426 Mass 67, 75, 686 NE2d 975, 981 (1997) (remarks concerning

---

§3.7 [1] The court must inform counsel of its proposed action upon requests for jury instructions prior to closing argument. Mass R Civ P 51(b); Mass R Crim P 24(b). Trial court judges have been instructed that charging conferences should be held on the record, and trial counsel have been advised where necessary to remind the judge of this requirement. See *Com. v. Adams,* 34 Mass App 516, 517 n.3, 613 NE2d 118, 120 n.3 (1993).

victim's right to live amounted to improper appeal for sympathy); *Com. v. Santiago,* 425 Mass 491, 494-495, 681 NE2d 1205, 1209-1210 (1997) (prosecutor may humanize victim, but reversal required where prosecutor impermissibly appealed to jury's sympathy for victim by repeatedly referring to her age, pregnancy, and fact she was shot on day before her 18th birthday); *Com. v. Cowels,* 425 Mass 279, 287, 680 NE2d 924, 929 (1997) (prosecutor's repeated mention of defendants' statements that victim was a "fucking dirty pig," and "I wish I could bottle up [the victim's] screams" were improper effort to stimulate sympathy); *Com. v. Barros,* 425 Mass 572, 682 NE2d 849 (1997) (victim's "right to live" argument was impermissible effort to sway jury); *Com. v. Sanchez,* 405 Mass 369, 375-376, 377, 540 NE2d 1316, 1320-1321 (1989) (improper for prosecutor to urge jury to convict defendant in order to end the victim's nightmares, or to ask jury to put themselves in victim's position); *Com. v. Worcester,* 44 Mass App 258, 263-264, 690 NE2d 451, 455 (1998) (reversal required where prosecutor called upon sympathy of jury by arguing victim's right to live, pain victim and family suffered, and that defendant determined victim's life was of no value); *Com. v. Drumgold,* 423 Mass 230, 251-253, 668 NE2d 300, 315-316 (1996) (improper for prosecutor to characterize murder case as dispute between innocent young victim and defendant); *Com. v. Depradine,* 42 Mass App 401, 409, 677 NE2d 262, 268 (1997) (prosecutor's remarks concerning what victim had gone through crossed the line of permissibility); *Com. v. Lorette,* 37 Mass App 736, 742-743, 643 NE2d 67, 70-71 (1994) (prosecutor's appeal to jury to respond to victim's family's nightmares required reversal); *Com. v. Bibby,* 35 Mass App 938, 941, 624 NE2d 624, 627 (1993) (prosecutor crossed line of propriety when she asked jury to "remember the specter of the victim"); *Com. v. McLeod,* 30 Mass App 543, 571 NE2d 29 (1991) (prosecutor's argument that it was "tragedy" that victim had to take witness stand and jury had opportunity to rectify tragedy was improper).

Compare *Com. v. Pearce*, 427 Mass 642, 644-645, 695 NE2d 1059, 1062 (1998) (prosecutor did not go beyond tolerable hyperbole); *Com. v. Wilson*, 427 Mass 336, 351, 693 NE2d 158, 172 (1998) (prosecutor's references to gruesomeness of crime and suffering of victims not improper because relevant to issue of extreme atrocity and cruelty); *Com. v. Lyons*, 426 Mass 466, 688 NE2d 1350 (1998) (prosecutor's depiction of brutal murder not improper appeal to jury's sympathy); *Com. v. Judge*, 420 Mass 433, 451-452, 650 NE2d 1242, 1253 (1995) (single reference to victim's terror not so inflammatory to require new trial); *Com. v. Marquetty*, 416 Mass 445, 449-452, 622 NE2d 632, 636-637 (1993) (prosecutor's references to murder victim's desire to live and his own personal desire to keep his children safe were innocuous in context); *Com. v. Woods*, 414 Mass 343, 357-358, 607 NE2d 1024, 1033-1034 (1993) (prosecutor's statement that vehicular homicide defendant was more "fortunate" than passengers who died in accident evoked emotional reaction but did not require mistrial); *Com. v. Pontes*, 402 Mass 311, 317-318, 522 NE2d 931 (1988) (rhetorical question in prosecutor's closing that suggested jurors place themselves in rape victim's father's position did not constitute reversible error where question appeared to be attempt to explain father's conduct); *Com. v. DeCicco*, 44 Mass App 111, 121, 688 NE2d 1010, 1017 (1998) ("right of victim to live" argument not improper where prosecutor did not exploit manner of death). See also *Com. v. Matthews*, 45 Mass App 444, 446-447, 699 NE2d 347, 349-350 (1998) (judge's comments that jurors put themselves in place of victim was balanced by suggestion they place themselves in position of defendant).

For a discussion of the related issue of generating sympathy for the victim by the presence, behavior, or demeanor of others in the courtroom, see *Com. v. Harris*, 409 Mass 461, 469-471, 567 NE2d 899, 905 (1991) (victim advocate); *Com. v. Woods*, supra, 414 Mass at 358 (victim's parents).

It is improper for the prosecutor to suggest that the jury would have to answer to the victim for their verdict, or that they are "the conscience of the community." See *Com. v. Payne*, 426 Mass 692, 696, 690 NE2d 443, 447 (1998) (closing arguments referring to jury's duty to convict are disfavored); *Com. v. Andrade*, 422 Mass 236, 661 NE2d 1308 (1996) (suggestion that evidence in murder trial "cried out for justice"); *Com. v. Walker*, 421 Mass 90, 103-104, 653 NE2d 1080, 1087-1088 (1995) (suggestion that jury had duty to vindicate victim's faith in the system); *Com. v. Smith*, 413 Mass 275, 282 n.6, 596 NE2d 346, 350 n.6 (1992) (as conscience of community, jury had duty to convict); *Com. v. Worcester*, supra, 44 Mass App at 264, 690 NE2d at 456 (improper to ask jury to do something about the killing); *Com. v. Coyne*, 44 Mass App 1, 686 NE2d 1321 (1997) (suggesting jurors should convict to play their part in war on drugs); *Com. v. Matthews*, 31 Mass App 564, 572-573, 581 NE2d 1304, 1310-1311 (1992) (& citations).

The "conscience of the community" argument has been upheld where the issue is whether the defendant committed murder by extreme atrocity or cruelty. See, e.g., *Com. v. Fitzmeyer*, 414 Mass 540, 547, 609 NE2d 81, 85 (1993); *Com. v. Lawrence*, 404 Mass 378, 393, 536 NE2d 571 (1989). See also *Com. v. Perez*, 44 Mass App 911, 689 NE2d 843 (1998) ("Do justice" argument was artless, but did not improperly call upon jurors to be avenging angels); *Com. v. Wojcik*, 43 Mass App 595, 686 NE2d 452 (1997) (remarks did not constitute exhortation to jurors to vindicate society).

The prosecutor may not inflame the jury with references to the potential consequences of a verdict of not guilty, or make the jury aware of sentencing consequences. *Com. v. Thomas*, supra, 401 Mass at 117, 514 NE2d at 1314 (& citations); *Com. v. Smith*, supra, 387 Mass at 910-911, 444 NE2d at 381-382 (improper for prosecutor to argue person like defendant should not be let loose on society). Compare *Com. v. Westerman*, 414 Mass 688, 701, 611 NE2d 215, 224 (1993) (prosecutor's statements regarding effect of defendant's actions on the community were not unfairly prejudicial in light of evidence of his involvement with organized crime).

It is impermissible for counsel to inject his or her own credibility or personal beliefs into his or her closing argument. *Com. v. Chavis*, 415 Mass 703, 712-714, 616 NE2d 423, 429 (1993); *Com. v. Thomas*, supra, 401 Mass at 114-116, 514 NE2d at 1313 (& citations); *Rolanti v. Boston Edison Corp.*, 33 Mass App 516, 528-529, 603 NE2d 211, 220-221 (1992). "To permit counsel to express his personal belief in the testimony (even if not phrased so as to suggest knowledge of additional evidence not known to the jury), would afford him a privilege not even accorded to witnesses under oath and subject to cross-examination. Worse, it creates the false issue of the reliability and credibility of counsel. This is peculiarly unfortunate if one of them has the advantage of official backing." *Com. v. Thomas*, supra, 401 Mass at 115-116, 514 NE2d at 1313-1314 (citations omitted). See also *Com. v. Santiago*, 425 Mass 491, 498, 681 NE2d 1205, 1212 (1997) (prosecutor's statement "I suggest to you I overwhelmingly proved who fired that fatal shot" was improper subjective assessment of evidence); *Com. v. Fitzgerald*, supra, 376 Mass at 421-422, 381 NE2d at 137 (prosecutor may not convey impression that he possesses independent knowledge of defendant's guilt). But compare *Com. v. Johnson*, 412 Mass 318, 326, 588 NE2d 684, 689 (1992) (although prosecutor's restating of witness's prior statements to him came "perilously close to injecting his own personal knowledge and integrity into his closing argument," no error because witness had agreed she had made the statements); *Com. v. Grimshaw*, supra, 412 Mass at 508, 590 NE2d at 683 (prosecutor may express his view of the strength of the evidence); *Com. v. Cohen*, supra, 412 Mass at 386, 589 NE2d at 297 (prosecutor's use of term "obvious" in arguing defendant's guilt did not interject his own belief); *Com. v. Smith*, supra, 387 Mass at 906-907, 444 NE2d at 380 (prosecutor may express his view of the strength of the evidence, and may comment on defendant's demeanor);

Com. v. LaFontaine, 32 Mass App 529, 537, 591 NE2d 1103, 1107-1108 (1992) (prosecutor's use of "I submit" was rhetorical device and not assertion of personal belief); *Com. v. Jones*, 42 Mass 378, 384, 677 NE2d 683, 688 (1997) (prosecutor's use of phrase "I think" regrettable, but not in context an assertion of personal knowledge or opinion).

The prosecutor may not comment (either positively or negatively) from personal knowledge on the credibility of a witness. See *Com. v. Pearce*, supra, 427 Mass at 644-645, 695 NE2d at 1062; *Com. v. Wilson*, 427 Mass 336, 351-352, 693 NE2d 158, 172 (1998); *Com. v. Richardson*, 425 Mass 765, 767, 682 NE2d 1354, 1356 (1997); *Com. v. Raymond*, 424 Mass 382, 391-392, 676 NE2d 824, 831 (1997) (discouraging use by prosecutors of ambiguous statements which jury could interpret as vouching for credibility of witness); *Com. v. Kosilek*, 423 Mass 449, 459, 668 NE2d 808, 816 (1996); *Com. v. Olszewski*, 416 Mass 707, 726, 625 NE2d 529, 541 (1993); *Com. v. Chavis*, supra, 415 Mass at 713; *Com. v. Meuse*, 38 Mass App 772, 653 NE2d 186 (1995) (prosecutor's references to credibility of witness testifying pursuant to plea agreement suggested government had verified testimony and thus required reversal; see §6.9); *Com. v. Nicholson*, 20 Mass App 9, 17-18, 477 NE2d 1038, 1044-1045 (1985) (& citations) (prosecutor description of victim, "[I]n my years of experience, [she] is one of the most truthful, sincere, candid witnesses that I have seen in any courtroom," improper). Compare *Com. v. Drumgold*, 423 Mass 230, 250-251, 668 NE2d 300, 314-315 (1996) (in context prosecutor's remarks did not amount to impermissible vouching); *Com. v. Marangiello*, 410 Mass 452, 573 NE2d 500 (1991) (prosecutor did not impermissibly vouch for credibility of witness); *Com. v. Berrio*, 43 Mass App 836, 838-840, 687 NE2d 644, 646-647 (1997) (while prosecutor's use of first-person voice was unfortunate, no impermissible vouching); *Com. v. Zuluaga*, 43 Mass App 629, 647-648, 686 NE2d 463, 476-477 (1997) (if prosecutor's description of defendants' version of events as "unbelievable" constituted insertion of his own opinion as to credibility of defense witnesses, curative instruction mitigated harm); *Com. v. Traylor*, 43 Mass App 239, 246, 681 NE2d 1249, 1253-1254 (1997) (no impermissible vouching where prosecutor merely characterized victims as honest witnesses); *Com. v. Mayne*, 38 Mass App 282, 286, 647 NE2d 89, 92 (1995).

Otherwise, the credibility of witnesses is a proper subject of comment. *Com. v. Murchison*, supra, 418 Mass at 60, 634 NE2d at 563; *Com. v. Smiledge*, 419 Mass 156, 160, 643 NE2d 41, 44 (1994); *Com. v. Lapointe*, 402 Mass 321, 331, 522 NE2d 937, 942-943 (1988). A prosecutor may permissibly argue that defense witnesses, including the defendant, are not credible. *Com. v. Donovan*, 422 Mass 349, 357, 662 NE2d 692, 698-699 (1996); *Com. v. Cohen*, supra, 412 Mass at 388, 589 NE2d at 298 (proper for prosecutor to suggest that defendant contrived his story); *Com. v. Yesilciman*, 406 Mass 736, 746, 550 NE2d 378, 384 (1990); *Com. v. Thomas*, 44 Mass App 521, 525, 692 NE2d 97, 101 (1997) (although prosecutor's harping on word "lie" was excessive regarding defendant's testimony, it was not improper); *Com. v. Padgett*, 44 Mass App 359, 369, 691 NE2d 239 (1998); *Com. v. Johnson*, 41 Mass App 81, 89-90, 669 NE2d 212, 217 (1996) (not improper for prosecutor to urge jury not to let defendant "talk his way out of" the charges); *Com. v. Azar*, 32 Mass App 290, 306-307, 588 NE2d 1352, 1363 (1992) (prosecutor's comments contrasting defendant's response to his family with subsequent testimony were permissible attacks on his credibility). Compare *Com. v. Waite*, 422 Mass 792, 800-801, 665 NE2d 982, 989 (1996) (clear error for prosecutor to make bald assertion that defendant, who never took the stand, was "a liar"); *Com. v. Smith*, 40 Mass App 770, 775-776, 667 NE2d 1160, 1163 (1996) (sloganeering manner in which prosecutor admonished jury not to be "conned by the cons," referring to defense witnesses, should have been avoided). Similarly, the defense counsel, with a basis in the record and expressed as a conclusion and not as a personal opinion, may properly argue that a police officer witness was lying. *Com. v. Murchison*, supra, 418 Mass at 60, 634 NE2d at 563.

A prosecutor may argue in support of the credibility of the Commonwealth's witnesses based on their demeanor, motive, and the consistency of their stories. *Com. v. Payne,* 426 Mass 692, 695-696, 690 NE2d 443, 447 (1998) (prosecutor could ask jury to consider witnesses' fearful demeanor in assessing credibility); *Com. v. Dixon,* 425 Mass 223, 232-234, 680 NE2d 84, 90-91 (1997) (no improper vouching where prosecutor mentioned that witness would be subjecting himself to prosecution for perjury if he lied on stand). *Com. v. Chavis,* supra, 415 Mass at 713-714 (prosecutor could respond to attack on credibility of government witness by arguing, based on the evidence, that witness told truth); *Com. v. Gordon,* 41 Mass App 459, 466-467, 671 NE2d 972, 977 (1996) (vouching in response to defense attack); *Com. v. Gurney,* 413 Mass 97, 104, 595 NE2d 320, 324-325 (1992) (prosecutor suggested that jury ought to believe Commonwealth's witnesses because their testimony was reasonable and they had no reason to target defendant with false accusations); *Com. v. Sanchez,* supra, 405 Mass at 377, 540 NE2d at 1322 (& citations). See also *Com. v. Valentin,* 420 Mass 263, 274, 649 NE2d 1079, 1085 (1995) (prosecutor's suggestion that jurors put themselves in shoes of murder eyewitnesses, though poorly phrased, not reversible error; remarks intended to explain inconsistencies in testimony).

For an extensive discussion of the limits of prosecutorial argument, see *Com. v. Kozec,* 399 Mass 514, 516-521, 505 NE2d 519, 520-523 (1987). For additional cases reversing convictions because of improper argument, see *Com. v. Kelly,* 417 Mass 266, 629 NE2d 999 (1994) (argument that arresting officers' credibility could not be challenged, and that the officers would not have risked their pensions by giving false testimony); *Com. v. Rosa,* 412 Mass 147, 587 NE2d 767 (1992) (improper use of hearsay testimony that had been admitted solely for impeachment); *Com. v. Person,* 400 Mass 136, 139-143, 508 NE2d 88, 90-92 (1987) (arguments that because defendant had sat silently through his trial he was able to tailor a cover story, and that jury should infer consciousness of guilt from defendant's decision to consult with attorney after the shooting); *Com. v. Clary*, 388 Mass 583, 589-594, 447 NE2d 1217, 1221-1223 (1983) (cumulative effect of prosecutor's improper closing argument in which he referred to matters not in evidence, misstated evidence, and hypothesized an unproved lesbian relationship between defendant and a female companion as the motive for attack); *Com. v. Hoppin*, 387 Mass 25, 28-32, 438 NE2d 820, 823-824 (1982) (prosecutor displayed piece of rawhide not in evidence and which fit victim's description of the thong with which she had been bound); *Com. v. Smith*, supra, 387 Mass at 906-912, 444 NE2d at 379-383 (prosecutor commented on defendant's failure to testify, made inflammatory appeals to jury's sympathy, and remarked on consequences of their decision); *Com. v. Jones*, 45 Mass App 254, 697 NE2d 140 (1998) (prosecutor's comments that defendant had had pre-trial access to Commonwealth's evidence and had remained silent prior to testifying to fabricate version of events); *Com. v. West*, 44 Mass App 150, 688 NE2d 1378 (1998) (prosecutor asserted personal opinion that certain evidence was hearsay and should not have been admitted, distorted defendant's theory of defense, made unsupported assertions that defendant had placed witnesses in fear, and made irrelevant reference to race of defense witness).

Compare *Com. v. Dixon*, 425 Mass 223, 680 NE2d 84 (1997) (misstatements and reference to evidence admitted for limited purpose did not require reversal); *Com. v. Wilson*, 427 Mass 336, 353, 693 NE2d 158, 173 (1998) (misstatements regarding evidence not prejudicial); *Com. v. Simmons*, 419 Mass 426, 646 NE2d 97 (1995) (improper references to defendant's service in Army "where he knew how to kill" did not require reversal); *Com. v. Cook*, 419 Mass 192, 644 NE2d 203 (1994) (statement that jury should "not be intimidated by phrase 'unreasonable doubt'" not improper comment when viewed in connection with other statements and judge's instructions); *Com. v. Benson*, 419 Mass 114, 642 NE2d 1035 (1994) (reference to nursery rhyme about spider luring victim fly, and excessive attack on credibility of defense expert, not prejudicial); *Com. v. Fructman*, 418 Mass 8, 633 NE2d 369 (1994) (misstatements and improper appeal to sympathy remedied by judge's instructions); *Com. v. Olszewski*, 416 Mass 707, 725-727, 625 NE2d 529, 541-542 (1993) (improprieties in prosecutor's argument, including reference to evidence that had been excluded and to defendant's lack of remorse, promptly remedied by judge's instructions); *Com. v. Cohen*, supra, 412 Mass at 388, 589 NE2d at 298 (although it is "hard to imagine a more potentially prejudicial analogy for the role of the jury and the status of the accused than that of a 'hunter' and a 'hunted' prey," no substantial likelihood of a miscarriage of justice); *Com. v. Thomas*, 44 Mass App 521, 525, 692 NE2d 97, 101 (1997) (reference to defendant's prior convictions was "blow below the belt," but not reversible error); *Com. v. Vermette*, 43 Mass App 789, 802, 686 NE2d 1071, 1079 (1997) (prosecutor should not have made reference to defense counsel's frequent objections, but in its context as a retaliatory reply error was harmless); *Com. v. Carter*, 38 Mass App 952, 649 NE2d 782 (1995) (no reversal required even though prosecutor improperly suggested defendant had intimidated witness without hint of evidence in record to support suggestion); *Com. v. Davis*, 38 Mass App 932, 636 NE2d 1093 (1995) (remark that "the only thing it takes for evil to triumph is for a few good men and good women to do nothing" did not, standing alone, require reversal); *Com. v. Elberry*, 38 Mass App 912, 645 NE2d 41 (1995) (statement that defendant was only witness with opportunity to hear all evidence and accordingly tailor his testimony was improper, but judge adequately corrected matter); *Com. v. Costello*, 36 Mass App 689, 635 NE2d 255 (1994) (comments attacking character of defendant and remark that, for jury to believe defendant's version, all prosecution witnesses had to have conspired against him were improper but did not require reversal); *Com. v. Deveau*, 34 Mass App 9, 606 NE2d 921 (1993) (unfortunate use of phrase "people like Mr. Deveau" in child molestation case did not create substantial risk of miscarriage of justice; distasteful reference to defendant's "abiding interest in children" was nonetheless permissible commentary on the evidence; insinuation that victims had suffered further sexual trauma through defense counsel's lawful cross-examination was crude impropriety, but not reversible error); *Com. v. Azar*, supra, 32 Mass App at 307-308, 588 NE2d at 1363-1364 (misstatement that defendant had been silent when questioned by police could not have harmed defendant). See also *Com. v. Vazquez*, 419 Mass 350, 644 NE2d 978 (1995) (statement that victim's body was best evidence of defendant's intent and jury should "take with [them] the body of [the victim] and go into [the] jury room and deliberate" not improper); *Com. v. Rogers*, 43 Mass App 782, 785, 686 NE2d 486, 490 (1997) (while rhetorical questions potentially shifting burden of proof to defendant and reflecting unfavorably on defense counsel should be avoided, no impropriety here).

A prosecutor may not comment on the defendant's failure to testify. See §13.14.8.

In order to ascertain whether improper statements during argument require reversal, the court will view the particular statements in the context of the entire argument, the judge's instructions, and the evidence at trial. *Com. v. Wallace*, 417 Mass 126, 131, 627 NE2d 935, 939 (1994); *Com. v. Marquetty*, 416 Mass 445, 450, 622 NE2d 632, 636 (1993). "[T]he prejudicial impact of the prosecutor's charge should be assessed by looking at the combined effect of all his errors." *Com. v. Borodine*, 371 Mass 1, 11, 353 NE2d 649, 656 (1976). See also *Com. v. Griffith*, 45 Mass App 784, 785, 702 NE2d 17, 18 (1998) (multiple instances of misconduct, when aggregated, deprived defendant of fair trial).

The courts attribute a "certain sophistication to the jury as aided by the cautionary remarks of the judge. The jury [can] be expected to take [closing] arguments with a grain of salt." *Com. v. Wallace*, supra, 417 Mass at 134 (citations omitted). See also *Com. v. Masello*, supra, 428 Mass at 452-

453, 702 NE2d at 1157; *Com. v. Bibby*, supra, 35 Mass App at 941 ("Kept in perspective, the prosecutor's remark was not of a sort which would inflame the passion of a jury with normal ignition temperatures. We may assume a certain amount of common sense capacity by jurors to filter out overstatement. . . .").

Thus, "the consequences of prosecutorial error depend on a number of factors, such as: Did the defendant reasonably object to the argument? Was the prosecutor's error limited to 'collateral issues' or did it go to the heart of the case? What did the judge tell the jury, generally or specifically, that may have mitigated the prosecutor's mistake, and generally did the error in the circumstances possibly make a difference in the jury's conclusions?" *Com. v. Kelly*, 417 Mass 266, 271, 629 NE2d 999, 1002 (1994) (citations omitted).

"Extraevidentiary remarks in closing arguments are normally neutralized by a timely curative instruction and a general reminder that arguments of counsel are not evidence." *Com. v. Giguere*, 420 Mass 226, 234, 648 NE2d 1279, 1284 (1995) (& citations). See, e.g., *Com. v. Gordon*, 422 Mass 816, 832, 666 NE2d 122, 133 (1996); *Com. v. Depradine*, 42 Mass App 401, 409, 677 NE2d 262, 268 (1997). But compare *Com. v. Griffith*, supra, 45 Mass App at 789, 702 NE2d at 20 (multiple instances of prosecutorial misconduct suffusing entire trial not cured by general reminder).

Reversals have not been required where the inappropriate remarks of opposing counsel neutralize each other. See *Com. v. Mello*, 420 Mass 375, 380-381, 649 NE2d 1106, 1111 (1995); *Com. v. Cohen*, supra, 412 Mass at 388, 589 NE2d at 298 (& citations). While a prosecutor may not "fight fire with fire," an improper argument from the defense may undermine the claim that the prosecutor's improper argument requires reversal. See *Com. v. Pearce*, supra, 427 Mass at 646, 695 NE2d at 1063.

Objection at the conclusion of the opponent's closing argument is sufficient to preserve appellate rights. *Com. v. Person*, supra, 400 Mass at 139, 508 NE2d at 90 (& citations); *Com. v. Kelly*, supra, 417 Mass at 270-271. But see *Com. v. Richardson*, 38 Mass App 384, 392, 648 NE2d 445, 450 (1995) (objection not preserved where defense counsel, told by judge to defer objections until conclusion of charge, failed to make any further objection).

A failure to object to the prosecutor's closing argument will limit appellate review to the question of whether there is a substantial likelihood of a miscarriage of justice. *Com. v. Marquetty*, supra, 416 Mass at 450, 622 NE2d at 636. See §3.8.1, infra. Moreover, the absence of any objection is important because it indicates that trial counsel "did not consider the tone, manner, and substance of the prosecutor's statement when it was made to be harmful." *Com. v. Talbot*, 35 Mass App 766, 779, 625 NE2d 1374, 1382 (1994), (citations and internal quotes omitted). See also *Com. v. Myer*, 38 Mass App 140, 145-146, 646 NE2d 155, 158 (1995).

When a specific objection is made and rejected by the judge without curative instructions, error in closing argument must be treated as prejudicial, and requiring a new trial, unless the appellate court can conclude with confidence that the error was not likely to influence the jury's verdict. *Com. v. Loguidice*, 420 Mass 453, 455-456, 650 NE2d 1254, 1256 (1995).

The criminal defendant's right to present closing argument has been held integral to the fundamental right to the assistance of counsel in both jury and jury-waived trials. See *Herring v. New York*, 422 US 853 (1975); *Com. v. Martelli*, 38 Mass App 669, 651 NE2d 414 (1995); *Com. v. Miranda*, 22 Mass App 10, 490 NE2d 1195 (1986).

Reasonable time limits may be imposed on counsel during closing argument as long as adequate time is allowed to address the pertinent aspects of the case. See *Com. v. Johnson*, 42 Mass App 948, 951, 679 NE2d 261, 263-264 (1997) (& citations).

The fact that an expert witness was retained and paid by an opposing party is a proper subject for argument, but use of the term "hired gun" is disfavored. *Com. v. Grimshaw*, supra, 412 Mass at 511, 590 NE2d at 685 (& citation); *Com.*

v. Benson, 419 Mass 114, 119-120, 642 NE2d 1035, 1038-1039 (1994). See also *Com. v. Cruz*, 424 Mass 207, 212, 675 NE2d 764, 767-768 (1997) (improper for prosecutor to refer to defense psychologist witness as "charlatan").

Counsel should not encourage the jury to conduct experiments or obtain outside information. See *Com. v. Beauchamp*, 424 Mass 682, 691, 677 NE2d 1135, 1140 (1997).

In civil cases, there have been only rare instances in which a new trial was granted because of an overreaching closing argument. See *Rolanti v. Boston Edison Corp.*, 33 Mass App 516, 529-530, 603 NE2d 211, 220-221, (1992) (& cases collected). See also *Harlow v. Chin*, 405 Mass 697, 704, 545 NE2d 602, 606-607 (1989) (plaintiff's counsel's references to large verdicts in other cases and to salaries of professional athletes improper, but reversal not required).

B.   EXCLUDING EVIDENCE

§3.8   Objection/Motion to Strike/Offer of Proof

§3.8.1   *Necessity for Objection or Motion to Strike*

Failure to object to offered evidence operates to waive objections to its admissibility. *Com. v. Haley*, 363 Mass 513, 517, 296 NE2d 207, 210 (1973) (& citations). See also Mass R Civ P 46; Mass R Crim P 22. The evidence, even though it would have been excluded upon objection, retains its full probative force. *Nancy P. v. D'Amato*, 401 Mass 516, 524-525, 517 NE2d 824, 829 (1988); *Com. v. Keevan*, 400 Mass 557, 562, 511 NE2d 534, 538 (1987) (hearsay); *Com. v. Luce*, 399 Mass 479, 482, 505 NE2d 178, 180 (1987) (prior inconsistent statement); *Abraham v. Woburn*, 383 Mass 724, 726 n.1, 421 NE2d 1206, 1209 n.1 (1981); *Pataskas v. Judeikis*, 327 Mass 258, 260, 98 NE2d 265, 266 (1951) (opinion evidence); *MacDonald's Case*, 277 Mass 418, 422, 178 NE 647, 649 (1931) (private conversation between husband and wife). But see *Com. v. Reynolds*, 338 Mass 130, 135-136, 154 NE2d 130, 134 (1958) (reserving question "whether circumstances could ever exist in which the requirements of due process of law and substantial justice would make it necessary to consider the extent to which highly prejudicial but palpably incompetent evidence improvidently admitted without objection or proper limitation should be used as the basis of a conviction").

"The purpose of requiring an objection is to afford the trial judge an opportunity to act promptly to remove from the jury's consideration evidence which has no place in the trial." *Abraham v. Woburn*, supra, 383 Mass at 726 n.1, 421 NE2d at 1209 n.1.

A motion to strike is the proper means of eliminating an answer that is objectionable either on substantive grounds—e.g., that it is hearsay—or on the ground that it is non-responsive.[1] See, e.g., *Com. v. Pickles*, 364 Mass 395, 399, 305 NE2d 107, 109-110 (1973) (& citations); *Com. v. Bishop*, 5 Mass App 738, 370 NE2d 452 (1977). If the answer challenged is admissible, although not strictly responsive, the allowance of a motion to strike is discretionary. *Com. v. Silvia*, 343 Mass 130, 137, 177 NE2d 571, 576 (1961).

Absent plain error, a timely objection or motion to strike is necessary to preserve an issue for appeal. See Proposed Mass R Evid 103(a)(1);[2] *Nancy P. v. D'Amato*, 401

---

§3.8 [1]Indications in the case law suggest that under Massachusetts practice, either examining or opposing counsel may move to strike a non-responsive answer. See, e.g., *Burke v. Kellough*, 235 Mass 405, 408, 126 NE 787, 788 (1920).

[2] (a) Effect of erroneous rulings. Error may not be predicated upon a ruling which admits or excludes evidence unless a substantial right of the party is affected, and

(1) Objection. In case the ruling is one admitting evidence, a timely objection or motion to strike appears of record, stating the specific ground of objection, if the specific ground was not apparent from the context; or

(2) Offer of proof. In case the ruling is one excluding evidence, the substance of the evidence was made known to the court by offer or was apparent from the context within which questions were asked.

Mass 516, 524, 517 NE2d 824, 829 (1988); *Com. v. Comtois*, 399 Mass 668, 674, 506 NE2d 503, 507 (1987). "This rule of procedure stems from the neccesity of placing an affirmative obligation on trial counsel to inform both the trial court and subsequent courts of review of alleged error in the admission of evidence at the earliest possible time and in the most direct manner. Furthermore, since it is not uncommon for a lawyer to forego the exercise of such a right as part of the trial tactics or strategy being employed for his client, this court cannot be put in a position of giving defense counsel the benefit of hindsight and in effect allowing the opportunity to compensate for erroneous, but conscious strategic decisions." *Com. v. Harris*, 371 Mass 462, 471, 358 NE2d 982, 987-988 (1976) (citations and internal quotations omitted). "A lawyer cannot try a case on one theory and then, having lost on that theory, argue before an appellate court about alleged issues which might have been, but were not, raised at the trial. That is true whether or not the trial lawyer and the appellate lawyer are the same person, and whether or not they are in any way associated. The appeal must be based on what took place at the trial, not on anything which is presented for the first time before an appellate court." *Com. v. Olson*, 24 Mass App 539, 544, 510 NE2d 787, 790 (1987). See also *Vassallo v. Baxter Healthcare Corp.*, 428 Mass 1, 11, 696 NE2d 909, 917 (1998) ("established principle" that in civil cases issues not properly raised in trial court will not be considered on appeal); *Adoption of Astrid*, 45 Mass App 538, 542,

---

(b) Record of offer and ruling. The court may add any other of further statement which shows the character of the evidence, the form in which it was offered, the objection made, and the ruling thereon. It may direct the making of an offer in question and answer form.

(c) Hearing of jury. In jury cases, proceedings shall be conducted, to the extent practicable, so as ro prevent inadmissible evidence from being suggested to the jury by any means, such as statements or offers of proof or asking questions in the hearing of the jury.

(d) Plain error. Nothing in this rule precludes taking notice of plain errors affecting substantial rights although they were not brought to the attention of the court.

PMRE 103.

700 NE2d 275, 278 (1998); *Com. v. Huertas*, 34 Mass App 939, 940-941, 613 NE2d 113, 115 (1993).

The filing of a motion in limine to prevent the introduction of evidence does not, by itself, preserve appellate rights. *Com. v. Whelton*, 428 Mass 24, 25-26, 696 NE2d 540, 543-544 (1998); *Com v. Keniston*, 423 Mass 304, 308, 667 NE2d 1127, 1131-1132 (1996); *Com. v. Shea*, 401 Mass 731, 740, 519 NE2d 1283, 1288-1289 (1988); *Com. v. Chase*, 26 Mass App 578, 582-583, 530 NE2d 185, 188-189 (1988).

An objection is generally necessary to preserve an issue regarding the giving or failure to give an instruction to the jury. See Mass R Civ P 51(b) and Mass R Crim P 24(b); *Harlow v. Chin*, 405 Mass 697, 703 n.5, 545 NE2d 602, 703 n.5 (1989); *Com. v. Barbosa*, 399 Mass 841, 844, 507 NE2d 694, 696 (1987) (in absence of objection, review limited to determining whether instructions created substantial risk of miscarriage of justice). The objection must be made before the jury retires. See *Jarry v. Corsaro*, 40 Mass App 601, 609, 666 NE2d 1012, 1017 (1996). Compare *Com. v. Biancardi*, 421 Mass 251, 253-254, 656 NE2d 1234, 1235-1236 (1995) (request for instruction, judge's rejection of request, and giving of instruction inconsistent with request sufficient to preserve appellate rights) and *Com. v. Grenier*, 415 Mass 680, 686 n.8, 615 NE2d 922, 925 n.8 (1993) (defendant saved appellate rights where he submitted written request for instruction that judge denied at charging conference stating defendant's exception was saved) with *Com. v. Torres*, 420 Mass 479, 651 NE2d 360 (1995) (party must bring alleged error in instructions to judge's attention in specific terms to give judge opportunity to rectify). Counsel are advised to renew any earlier objection with specificity following the charge. See *Fein v. Kahan*, 36 Mass App 967, 968 n.4, 635 NE2d 1, 2 n.4 (1994) (citation omitted).

Notwithstanding the general requirement for a timely objection, Proposed Mass R Evid 103(d) permits an appellate court to take notice of "plain errors affecting substantial rights although they were not brought to the attention of the [trial] court." The case law recognizes that in criminal matters, error may be entertained by an appellate court in the absence of an objection if it constitutes a "substantial risk of a miscarriage of justice." See, e.g., *Com. v. Hamilton*, 411 Mass 313, 323, 582 NE2d 929, 935 (1991); *Com. v. Sullivan*, 410 Mass 521, 524, 574 NE2d 966, 969 (1991) (admission of plea agreement); *Com. v. Pares-Ramirez*, 400 Mass 604, 610, 511 NE2d 344, 348 (1987) (jury instructions); *Com. v. Keevan*, supra, 400 Mass at 562, 564, 511 NE2d at 538, 539 (admission of hearsay; jury instructions); *Com. v. Comtois*, supra, 399 Mass at 674, 506 NE2d at 507 (admission of testimony as to victim's statements). See also GL 278, §33E (mandatory review by Supreme Judicial Court of first degree murder convictions).[3] Such power is "rarely used," exercised only when a "decisive matter has not been raised at trial." *Com. v. Young*, 35 Mass App 427, 442, 621 NE2d 1180, 1189 (1993) (citations omitted). For cases reversing convictions on this standard, see *Com. v. Thomas*, 401 Mass 109, 118-119, 514 NE2d 1309, 1315 (1987) (jury instructions); *Com. v. Cobb*, 397 Mass 105, 109, 489 NE2d 1246, 1247-1248 (1986) (missing witness instruction); *Com. v. Harris*, supra, 371 Mass at 471, 358 NE2d at 988 (admission of confession).

The so-called clairvoyance exception permits an appellate court to entertain an error of constitutional dimension where the principle was not sufficiently developed at the time of the trial to afford a meaningful opportunity to raise it. See *Com. v. Hinckley*, 422 Mass 261, 264-267, 661 NE2d 1317, 1319-1321 (1996); *Com. v. D'Agostino*, 421 Mass 281, 284-286, 657 NE2d 217, 219-220 (1995); *In re Redgate*, 417 Mass 799, 801-802, 633 NE2d 380, 382 (1994); *DeJoinville v. Com.*, 381 Mass 246, 248, 408 NE2d 1353, 1354 (1980); *Com. v. Pagan*, 35 Mass App 788, 793, 625 NE2d 579, 582 (1994). For an extensive discussion of this and the other recognized exceptions to the rule requiring objec-

---

[3] Massachusetts case law apparently does not follow the "plain error" doctrine in civil cases. See Reporter's Notes to Mass R Civ P 46.

tion at trial to preserve appellate review, see *Com. v. Miranda,* 22 Mass App 10, 14-19, 490 NE2d 1195, 1198-1201 (1986). For other "exceptional circumstances," see *White v. White,* 40 Mass App 132, 133, 662 NE2d 230, 232 (1996) and *Atlas Tack Corp. v. DiMasi,* 37 Mass App 66, 70-71, 637 NE2d 230, 233 (1994). For a discussion of the issue with regard to review of denials of motions for new trial, see *Com. v. Hallet,* 427 Mass 552, 694 NE2d 845 (1998) and *Com. v. Curtis,* 417 Mass 619, 632 NE2d 821 (1994).

In appropriate circumstances, the judge may exclude or limit evidence on her own, even in the absence of an objection. See *Com. v. Haley,* 363 Mass 513, 516-519, 296 NE2d 207, 210-211 (1973). See also *Com. v. Smith,* 387 Mass 900, 911 & n.7, 444 NE2d 374, 382 & n.7 (1983) (where prejudicial excesses in prosecutor's closing are clear, "preferable practice is for the judge to intervene then and there on his own motion." (citations omitted)).

The rules pertaining to objections at trial to the admissibility of a deposition transcript are found in Mass R Civ P 32(b) and Mass R Crim P 35(f). See also Fed R Civ P 32(b) and Fed R Crim P 15(f).

The requirement (long a part of Massachusetts practice) for a formal "exception" to a ruling, in addition to an objection, has been abandoned. See Mass R Civ P 46; Mass R Crim P 22.

§3.8.2   Timeliness

The objection to evidence must be made as soon as the error is apparent. *Com. v. Baptiste,* 372 Mass 700, 706, 363 NE2d 1303, 1307 (1977). Thus, an objection to a question that calls for inadmissible testimony or is improper in form must usually be made before the answer is given. *Com. v. Baptiste,* supra; *Com. v. Miskel,* 364 Mass 783, 792-793, 308 NE2d 547, 553 (1974) (objection to earlier question does not carry over to later one); *Com. v. Silvia,* 343 Mass 130, 135-136, 177 NE2d 571, 576 (1961) (objection based upon motion to strike answer that is responsive to a question to which no objection was made is of no avail); *Com. v. Hinckley,* 1 Mass App 195, 199, 294 NE2d 562, 565 (1973) (objection to "line of questioning" after questioning was concluded not timely). Objection to an item of real evidence must usually be made before the item is admitted in evidence. *Com. v. Silvia,* supra, 343 Mass at 136, 177 NE2d at 575. With regard to objections to argument, counsel need not immediately interrupt opposing counsel on each occasion when he believes the argument is improper; it is usually sufficient if the matter is called to the attention of the judge at the end of the argument. *Com. v. Cancel,* 394 Mass 567, 574, 476 NE2d 610, 616 (1985) (& citations).

If grounds for the objection are not apparent until after the evidence is admitted or because the answer came too quickly for the objection to be made, such fact should be called to the attention of the court and a motion to strike the evidence should immediately be made; "[t]he judge then would be in a position to determine at once whether justice required some relief and to grant it if it required." *Buckley v. Frankel,* 262 Mass 13, 15, 159 NE 459, 460 (1928). See also *Com. v. Cancel,* supra, 394 Mass at 571, 476 NE2d at 614 (once it became clear that testimony concerning defendant's out-of-court statement was hearsay, it was incumbent upon counsel to renew objection or move to strike); *Com. v. Wood,* 17 Mass App 304, 307, 457 NE2d 1131, 1133 (1983) (failure of defendant to make motion to strike after it became apparent that adequate factual basis for expert testimony was lacking constituted waiver of the objection); *Com. v. Prince,* 4 Mass App 799, 344 NE2d 202 (1976) (objection based on hearsay waived by the failure to make a motion to strike the testimony after it became apparent that witness's knowledge was "second-hand."). Mass R Civ P 46 and Mass R Crim P 22 provide that "if a party has no opportunity to object to a ruling or order at the time it is made, the absence of an objection does not thereafter prejudice him."

A motion to strike erroneously admitted evidence must be made prior to the close of the evidence. See *Jarry v. Corsaro*, 40 Mass App 601, 609, 666 NE2d 1012, 1017 (1996).

Where evidence is admitted conditionally, it is incumbent upon the objecting party to move to strike it if the condition has not been satisfied. See §3.11, infra.

§3.8.3   Form of the Objection/Specificity

When objecting, counsel should state the specific ground of the objection unless it is apparent from the context. See Proposed Mass R Evid 103(a)(1) (§3.8 n.2); Mass R Civ P 46; Mass R Crim P 22 and Superior Court Rule 8 (objecting party "may" state the precise grounds of his objection). Specificity serves to call the attention of the judge and the opposing party to the particular problem asserted at a time when it can still be corrected, thus avoiding the necessity of a new trial. See *Harlow v. Chin*, 405 Mass 697, 706, 545 NE2d 602, 608 (1989); *Com. v. Keevan*, 400 Mass 557, 563-564, 511 NE2d 534, 538-539 (1987). Compare *Com. v. De La Cruz*, 405 Mass 269, 271, 540 NE2d 168, 169-170 (1989) and *Com. v. Susi*, 394 Mass 784, 788 n.3, 477 NE2d 995, 998 n.3 (1985) (defendants' requests, although not precisely on point, made judge aware of juror selection issue); *Com. v. Cancel*, 394 Mass 567, 573, 476 NE2d 610, 615 (1985) (ground for exclusion should have been obvious to judge and opposing counsel); *Fein v. Kahan*, 36 Mass App 967, 968, 635 NE2d 1, 2 (1994) (request for instruction, although imperfect, sufficient to alert judge); *Com. v. Gee*, 36 Mass App 154, 158-159, 628 NE2d 1296 (1994) (although not model of clarity, defense counsel's objection to unsanitized mug shot adequate to alert judge to potential errors). The adequacy of an objection must be assessed in the context of the trial as a whole. See *Com. v. Koney*, 421 Mass 295, 298-300, 657 NE2d 210, 213-214 (1995) (defendant's objection, although not specifically mentioning art. 12, nonetheless sufficient).

A general objection must be overruled if the evidence is admissible for any purpose. *Com. v. Errington*, 390 Mass 875, 882, 460 NE2d 598, 601-602 (1984). "Where evidence is excluded upon a general objection, the ruling will be upheld on appeal by the proponent if any ground existed for exclusion. It will be assumed that the ruling was based upon the right ground." *Palm v. Kulesza*, 333 Mass 461, 463, 131 NE2d 472, 473 (1956). See also *G.E.B. v. S.R.W.*, 422 Mass 158, 168, 661 NE2d 646, 654 (1996).

If the objection is too broad, including unobjectionable matter within its scope, the overruling of the objection is not error. *Bruyer v. P. S. Thorsen Co.*, 327 Mass 684, 686-687, 100 NE2d 684, 686 (1951). Similarly, a motion to strike that is directed to both admissible as well as inadmissible evidence may properly be denied. *Griffin v. General Motors Corp.*, 380 Mass 362, 365, 403 NE2d 402, 404-405 (1980); *Com. v. Sandler*, 368 Mass 729, 738-739, 335 NE2d 903, 909-910 (1975) (motion to strike "entire testimony" of witness properly denied); *Afienko v. Harvard Club of Boston*, 365 Mass 320, 335, 312 NE2d 196, 207 (1974) (motion to strike entire answer properly denied where part of answer was responsive); *Adoption of Sean*, 36 Mass App 261, 264, 630 NE2d 604, 606 (1994).

A party who has made an objection at trial specifically stating the grounds therefor is not entitled to urge different grounds upon appeal of the court's overruling of the objection. *Com. v. Tyree*, 387 Mass 191, 213, 439 NE2d 263, 276 (1982). Thus, the overruling of an incorrect specific objection is not error even if a correct ground for exclusion appears to exist. *Holbrook v. Jackson*, 61 Mass 7 (Cush) 136, 154-155 (1851).

The general rule is that no error will be found when an incorrect specific objection is sustained, if some other proper ground for exclusion exists, since a retrial would probably only result in the exclusion of the evidence on the correct ground. *Com. v. Mandeville,* 386 Mass 393, 397-398, 436 NE2d 912, 916 (1982).

The proponent of evidence objected to is obliged "to bring to the judge's attention with sufficient clarity the grounds upon which the admission of the evidence was sought, so that, upon its exclusion, the points of law actually presented for the judge's consideration would be apparent and provide a basis for correction of the ruling if there was error." *H. H. Hawkins & Sons v. Robie,* 338 Mass 61, 66, 153 NE2d 768, 770 (1958). If the proponent urges its admissibility on an incorrect ground at trial, he cannot press on appeal that it should have been admitted on a different ground, even if it appears that the evidence was admissible on the other ground. *Com. v. White,* 353 Mass 409, 420-421, 232 NE2d 335, 343 (Mass 1967).

§3.8.4   *Offer of Proof*

Where evidence is excluded the proponent must, in order to preserve the issue for appeal, make an offer of proof stating the substance of the evidence—for example, what the witness would have answered to an excluded question. See Proposed Mass R Evid 103(a)(2) (§3.8 n.2); Mass R Civ P 43(c) (examining counsel "may" make offer). See also *Mazzaro v. Paull,* 372 Mass 645, 652-653, 363 NE2d 509, 514 (1977); *Palmer v. Palmer,* 27 Mass App 141, 149, 535 NE2d 611, 616 (1989). "The offer of proof requirement serves several purposes. An offer of proof may assist the trial judge in making the correct ruling. And the presence of an offer of proof in a record on appeal enables an appellate court to determine whether an error was made and, if so, how harmful it was to the [proponent]." *Com. v. Chase,* 26 Mass App 578, 581-582, 530 NE2d 185, 188 (1998) (& citations; citing text). See also *Com. v. Blake,* 409 Mass 146, 159, 564 NE2d 1006, 1014-1015 (1991).

Ordinarily, no formal offer of proof is required when the evidence is excluded on cross-examination, since an offer must point to evidence "actually available, and the cross-examiner will often be unable to state what the answer would have been if the question had been allowed." *Com. v. Barnett*, 371 Mass 87, 95, 354 NE2d 879, 884-885 (1976). In cases where the purpose or significance of the question is obscure or the prejudice to the cross-examiner is not clear, an offer may be required. See *Com. v. Ahearn*, 370 Mass 283, 286, 346 NE2d 907, 909 (1976); *Breault v. Ford Motor Co.*, 364 Mass 352, 357-358, 305 NE2d 824, 828 (1973). The cross-examiner should certainly be permitted to make an offer of proof if he wishes to do so to show the pertinency of the question excluded where it is not otherwise apparent. *Com. v. Barnett*, supra, 371 Mass at 95, 354 NE2d at 884-885.

No offer of proof has been required on direct examination where the trial judge has in effect treated the witness as not qualified to testify at all on a particular issue or has otherwise excluded all evidence on that issue. *First National Bank of Mount Dora v. Shawmut Bank of Boston, N.A.*, 378 Mass 137, 141, 389 NE2d 1002, 1005 (1979); *Ratner v. Canadian Universal Ins. Co.*, 359 Mass 375, 385, 269 NE2d 227, 232 (1971) (but it is "better practice" to make offer); *Ford v. Worcester*, 339 Mass 657, 659, 162 NE2d 264, 266 (1959); *Charles River Mortgage Co., Inc. v. Baptist Home of Massachusetts*, 36 Mass App 277, 280, 630 NE2d 304, 306 (1994).

Where the general nature and purpose of the expected testimony are sufficiently known to enable the judge to make an informed decision, an offer of proof may not be necessary. See *Urban Investment & Development Co. v. Turner Construction Co.*, 35 Mass App 100, 102, 616 NE2d 829, 832 (1993) (& citations). See also *Com. v. Caldron*, 383 Mass 86, 89 n.2, 417 NE2d 958 (1981) (offer of proof may be dispensed with where there is no doubt what testimony would be given).

The offer of proof must of course be responsive to the question excluded. *Com. v. Hubbard*, 371 Mass 160, 174, 355 NE2d 469, 478 (1976).

§3.9 The Ruling

§3.9.1 Preliminary Questions of Fact

It frequently happens that a ruling on evidence requires the determination of a preliminary question of fact —e.g., the "good faith" of a declaration under GL 233, §65 or §78 (see §8.5), or the unavailability of the original document under the best evidence rule. See §12.7.1. Although questions of fact are ordinarily for the jury, it is the province of the judge to determine these preliminary questions, and she may hear evidence on them in the absence of the jury. See Proposed Mass R Evid 104(a),(c);[1] *Fauci v. Mulready*, 337 Mass 532, 540, 150 NE2d 286, 291 (1958).

The rules of evidence are not binding on the judge in the determination of such preliminary questions, except those rules concerning privileges and except on preliminary questions concerning the existence of a conspiracy or arising in hearings on motions to suppress. Proposed Mass R Evid 104(a). Compare Fed R Evid 104(a) (only exception is for rules concerning privileges). The determination of the trial judge on preliminary questions concerning admissibility of evidence is conclusive upon appeal as long as there is evidence to support it. *Fauci v. Mulready*, supra, 337 Mass at 540, 150 NE2d at 291; *Torre v. Harris-Seybold Co.*, 9 Mass App 660, 672-673, 404 NE2d 96, 106 (1980).

---

§3.9 [1](a) Questions of admissibility generally. Preliminary questions concerning the qualification or competency of a person to be a witness, the existence of a privilege, or the admissibility of evidence shall be determined by the court, subject to the provisions of subdivisions (b) and (f). In making its determination it is not bound by the rules of evidence except those with respect to privilege, the existence of a conspiracy, and on questions arising in hearings on motions to suppress evidence.

(c) Hearing of jury. Hearings on the admissibility of confessions shall in all cases be conducted out of the hearing of the jury. Hearings on other preliminary matters shall be so conducted, when the interests of justice require or, when an accused is a witness, if he so requests.

PMRE 104

With respect to certain preliminary facts in criminal cases, it is the practice for the judge, after finding the facts and admitting the evidence over objection, to nonetheless instruct the jurors to disregard the evidence if they do not believe that the preliminary facts exist. Where the voluntariness of a confession is in issue, for example, the accused is entitled under the so-called "humane practice" to both a voir dire examination in the absence of the jury, and in the event the judge admits the confession, to an instruction that the jury disregard the confession if upon their reconsideration of the issue they conclude that it was involuntary. Proposed Mass R Evid 104(f).[2] See generally §9.1.

Other situations in which the determination of a preliminary question is shared between the judge and the jury include:

- the question of whether the requirements for a dying declaration have been established. See *Com. v. Key*, 381 Mass 19, 22, 407 NE2d 327, 330-331 (1980); *Com. v. Polian*, 288 Mass 494, 497-498, 193 NE 68, 69-70 (1934); Proposed Mass R Evid 104(f).
- the question of whether in a criminal case the foundational requirements for admission of a document as a business record have been met. See GL 233, §78.
- the question of whether a document is in the handwriting of a particular person. See *Com. v. Tucker*, 189 Mass 457, 471, 76 NE 127, 133-134 (1905).

---

[2] "In a criminal case tried to a jury, if the court admits evidence of a confession, or a statement under Rule 804(b)(2) [dying declaration], it shall submit for determination by the jury the respective questions of the voluntariness of the confession and the belief that death was imminent." PMRE 104(f).

While the "reasonable doubt" standard of proof applies to the admission of a confession (see §9.1), a "preponderance of the evidence" is sufficient to warrant admission in these other situations. *Com. v. Polian*, supra, 288 Mass at 498-499, 193 NE2d at 70 (explicitly rejecting the "reasonable doubt" standard); *Com. v. Key*, supra, 381 Mass at 25. The jury, of course, has no role to play unless the judge has made an affirmative finding that the evidence is admissible. See *Com. v. Reagan*, 175 Mass 335, 56 NE 577 (1900) (judge erred in permitting witness to testify and leaving question of competency to the jury after he determined as a preliminary matter that she was not competent).

In the absence of an express finding of preliminary facts, the appellate court will make the following inferences:

(1) If the evidence is admitted, it will be inferred from the admission that the necessary preliminary findings were made and that there was evidence to support them, unless the record shows that no such finding was or could have been made. See *Com. v. Bjorkman*, 364 Mass 297, 302, 303 NE2d 715, 718 (1973) ("It was not necessary for the trial judge explicitly to state his conclusion as to relevancy as a preliminary finding, since that conclusion was implicit in his ruling that the evidence was admissible."); *Greenberg v. Weisman*, 345 Mass 700, 703, 189 NE2d 531, 534 (1963) ("The admission of the [business] records imports the necessary findings."); *Mitchell v. Hastings & Koch Enterprises, Inc.*, 38 Mass App 271, 275, 647 NE2d 78, 81 (1995) (failure to articulate preliminary findings for admission of declaration of deceased person). Compare *Middlesex Supply, Inc. v. Martin & Sons, Inc.*, 354 Mass 373, 237 NE2d 692 (1968) (rule permitting inference of foundational facts does not apply where facts concerning admission are not in dispute and declaration itself shows that it is not within statute). See also *Ricciutti v. Sylvania Electric Products Inc.*, 343 Mass 347, 351, 178 NE2d 857, 860 (1961) (admission of document implies finding of prerequisite facts, but latter may be

reviewed and error found where necessary findings could not be made); *Old Colony Trust Co. v. Shaw*, 348 Mass 212, 216, 202 NE2d 785, 789 (1964) (same).

A preliminary finding by the judge that a confession of a criminal defendant was voluntary beyond a reasonable doubt must, however, appear from the record with "unmistakable clarity." See §9.1.

(2) If the evidence is excluded, it will be presumed that the trial judge did not find the necessary preliminary facts to exist. *Day Trust Co. v. Malden Savings Bank*, 328 Mass 576, 580, 105 NE2d 363, 365 (1952). See also *H. E. Fletcher Co. v. Com.*, 350 Mass 316, 321, 214 NE2d 721, 724-725 (1966) and *H. H. Hawkins & Sons v. Robie*, 338 Mass 61, 66, 153 NE2d 768, 770 (1958) (judge not required to state grounds for excluding testimony).

§3.9.2   *Correction of Erroneous Ruling*

It sometimes happens that the court, having admitted evidence, becomes convinced that it should have been excluded. Ordinarily this can be corrected by an instruction to the jury to disregard the evidence. See, e.g., *Com. v. Gordon*, 356 Mass 598, 604, 254 NE2d 901, 904 (1970) ("While we recognize that there are certain circumstances under which error is not alleviated by instructions to the jury, we shall not assume that jurors will slight strong and precise instructions of the trial judge to disregard the matters which have been withdrawn from their consideration." (citations omitted)). See also *Com. v. Amirault*, 404 Mass 221, 231-232, 535 NE2d 193, 200-201 (1989) (& cases cited); *Bouley v. Reisman*, 38 Mass App 118, 128, 645 NE2d 708, 714 (1995). The practice, however, is disfavored because it is "always desirable that the person who determines the facts, whether he be judge or juror, should hear only what the law says he may hear" and it is "hard to be sure of one's self after the evidence is introduced, even if one tries to disregard it." *Holcombe v. Hopkins*, 314 Mass 113, 118, 49 NE2d 722, 724 (1943).

There are cases, of course, in which the evidence is so damaging that nothing but a new trial will remedy the error. See, e.g., *Bruton v. United States*, 391 US 123, 88 S Ct 1620, 20 L Ed 2d 476 (1968) (admission of codefendant's confession implicating defendant); *Com. v. Perkins*, 39 Mass App 577, 584, 658 N.E.2d 975, 980 (1995). See also *Com. v. Adamides*, 37 Mass App 339, 341-344, 639 N.E.2d 1092, 1094-1095 (1994) (cases collected). For such cases involving improper closing arguments, see *Com. v. Hoppin*, 387 Mass 25, 31, 438 NE2d 820, 823-824 (1982) and *Com. v. Clary*, 388 Mass 583, 589-594, 447 NE2d 1217, 1221-1223 (1983). Compare *Com. v. Charles*, 397 Mass 1, 12, 489 NE2d 679, 687 (1986) ("It is well within the discretion of the trial judge to deny a mistrial and rely on appropriate curative instructions to erase error even in a case of intentional mistatement.").

C.   GENERAL CONSIDERATIONS CONCERNING ADMISSIBILITY[1]

§3.10   Limited Admissibility/Limiting Instructions

Certain evidence may be admissible only on one issue, or for one purpose, or (in a multiparty trial) against one party. Thus, for example, a prior statement of a witness may be admissible to impeach his credibility, but not to prove the truth of the matters asserted. It has long been recognized that "evidence admissible for one purpose, if offered for that purpose in good faith, is not made inadmissible by the fact that it could not be used for another with regard to

---

§3.10   [1]The threshold requirement of relevance is discussed in Chap. 4.

which it has a tendency to influence the mind." *Whipple v. Rich*, 180 Mass 477, 479, 63 NE 5, 6 (1902).

A party desiring to restrict the scope of the evidence must, at the time the evidence is offered or admitted, specifically call the attention of the judge to any limitations by moving to have the jury so instructed. See Proposed Mass R Evid 105;[2] *Com. v. Errington*, 390 Mass 875, 882, 460 NE2d 598, 603-604 (1984) (where evidence was admissible for one purpose, admission over a general objection was not error; and since no request was made for a limiting instruction, judge's failure to give one was not error); *Com. v. Pinnick*, 354 Mass 13, 16-17, 234 NE2d 756, 758 (1968) (general objection to the evidence is insufficient to raise issue of limited admissibility at trial or preserve it for appeal). The judge may refuse to limit the scope of the evidence where the objecting party fails to request limiting instructions until a later point in the trial. *Solomon v. Dabrowski*, 295 Mass 358, 360, 3 NE2d 744, 745 (1936). See also *Com. v. De La Cruz*, 405 Mass 269, 275-276, 540 NE2d 168, 172-173 (1989) (failure of counsel to object to adequacy of limiting instruction deprived judge of opportunity to correct error and thus appellate review is limited to whether there was substantial risk of miscarriage of justice).

If the nature of the evidence is such that a jury could not reasonably be expected to adhere to a limiting instruction, exclusion of the evidence may be required to protect the rights of the objecting party. See, e.g., *Bruton v. United States*, 391 US 123, 88 S Ct 1620, 20 L Ed 2d 476 (1968) (limiting charge could not effectively protect defendant where codefendant's confession was admitted), discussed in §8.8.7.

---

[2] "When evidence which is admissible as to one party or for one purpose but not admissible as to another party or for another purpose is admitted, the court, upon request, shall restrict the evidence to its proper scope and instruct the jury accordingly." PMRE 105.

§3.11 Conditional Admissibility

It is within the discretion of the trial court to admit evidence de bene, on the representation of counsel to produce other evidence upon which the admissibility of the original offer depends. See Proposed Mass R Evid 104(b)[1] and 611(a).[2] See, e.g., *Boyd v. Lawrence Redevelopment Authority*, 348 Mass 83, 202 NE2d 297 (1964) (evidence about sales of four parcels admitted before evidence of comparability). If the promised evidence is not produced, the evidence provisionally admitted may be stricken; but it is the obligation of opposing counsel to move to strike, and if counsel fails to make such a motion, no error is committed by the failure of the court to strike it out. *Muldoon v. West End Chevrolet, Inc.*, 338 Mass 91, 98, 153 NE2d 887, 893 (1958); *Foreign Car Center, Inc. v. Salem Suede, Inc.*, 40 Mass App 15, 23, 660 NE2d 687, 694 (1996); *Com. v. Navarro*, 39 Mass App 161, 166, 654 NE2d 71, 75 (1995). But see *Roddy v. Fleishman Distilling Sales Corp.*, 360 Mass 623, 625-626, 277 NE2d 284, 287 (1971) (failure to make motion to strike did not foreclose defendant from challenging de bene evidence on appeal because of subsequent evidentiary developments).

A court may exclude evidence with the proviso that it may be reoffered after other evidence establishing its relevancy has been adduced. Proposed Mass R Evid 104(b). If the other evidence is admitted, it is the proponent's obligation to offer the original evidence again. See *Thalin v. Friden Calculating Machine Co., Inc.*, 338 Mass 67, 69, 153 NE2d 658, 660 (1958).

---

§3.11 [1]"When the relevancy of evidence depends upon the fulfillment of a condition of fact, the court shall admit it upon, or subject to, the introduction of evidence sufficient to support a finding that the condition has been fulfilled." PMRE 104(b).

[2]In pertinent part the rule provides: "The court has discretion to admit evidence conditionally upon the representation that its relevancy will be established by evidence subsequently offered." PMRE 611(a).

§3.12   Rule of Verbal Completeness

Whenever a portion of an oral or written statement of a person is introduced into evidence, the opponent may require that the remainder of the statement, insofar as it relates to the same subjects, be admitted as well. The rule of completeness permits the opponent to put before the trier of fact the context of the fragmentary statement admitted, as well as any contradictions, modifications, or explanations made at the same time (but which would not otherwise be admissible). It does not render automatically admissible portions of the statement that do not explain or qualify the portion admitted, or that relate to other subject matters. The doctrine permits an opposing party to add what has been omitted to give a full picture; it does does not open the gate for admission of everything in a document or statement. See generally *McAllister v. Boston Housing Authority*, 429 Mass 300, 302-303, 708 NE2d 95, 97-98 (1999) (& citations).

For an extensive discussion of the rule of completeness including cases and authorities, see *Com. v. Watson*, 377 Mass 814, 824-833, 388 NE2d 680, 686-691 (1979) (quoting Treatise). For cases applying the doctrine, see *Com. v. Carmona*, 428 Mass 268, 271-272, 700 NE2d 823, 827 (1998) (once defendant presented portion of teletype showing he had turned himself in he opened door for admission of portion explaining why he had done so); *Com. v. Robles*, 423 Mass 62, 69, 666 NE2d 497, 502 (1996) (not error to exclude codefendant's admission that he was the shooter since defendant objected to the admission of other portions of the statement which would clarify its meaning); *Com. v. Hamilton*, 411 Mass 313, 321-322, 582 NE2d 929, 934-935 (1991) (when defendant introduced portions of his tape-recorded interrogation, that rendered entire recording admissible); *Com. v. Owens*, 402 Mass 639, 641 n.2, 524 NE2d 387, 388 n.2 (1988) (where one party puts part of conversation in evidence, other party is entitled to put in evidence balance of what was said); *Com. v. Slonka*, 42 Mass

App 760, 771-772, 680 NE2d 103, 110-111 (1997) (rule requires that if entry of one page of victim's medical record is admitted by prosecution, another page offered by defendant should be admitted notwithstanding privileged status); *Kobayashi v. Orion Ventures, Inc.*, 42 Mass App 492, 497-498, 678 NE2d 180, 185 (1997) (excluded parts of memo should have been admitted to give full picture); *Com. v. Thatch*, 39 Mass App 904, 653 NE2d 1121 (1995) (once defense counsel introduced portion of rape victim's statement to police officer, prosecutor was entitled to put into evidence complete version); *Com. v. Graves*, 35 Mass App 76, 87-88, 616 NE2d 817, 824 (1993) (rape victim, who had been referred to a portion of her written statement given to police, was properly allowed to read entire statement).

Compare *Com. v. Eason*, 427 Mass 595, 597-598, 694 NE2d 1264, 1266 (1998) (fact that declarant made two statements in course of same conversation did not make second admissible, where it did not concern same subject as first statement which was admitted); *Com. v. Hanlon*, 44 Mass App 810, 823, 694 NE2d 358, 368-369 (1998) (rule did not require admission of entire transcript of defendant's testimony at first trial where state trooper read portions at second trial); *Com. v. Henry*, 37 Mass App 429, 432, 640 NE2d 503, 506 (1994) (doctrine did not require admission of rape defendant's statement that he was "not guilty of anything" to explain statement that he fled from police because he was afraid; exculpatory statement went beyond explanation of why defendant was afraid); *Com. v. Hearn*, 31 Mass App 707, 710, 583 NE2d 279, 281-282 (1991) (doctrine did not require admission of portions of defendant's statement that did not relate to portion admitted); *Com. v. Crowe*, 21 Mass App 456, 478-479, 488 NE2d 780, 794 (1986) (where portions of defendant's statement were admitted against him, rule of verbal completeness did not require the admission of other portions offered by defendant because they did furnish an explanation or qualification of the admitted portions). See also *Com. v. Santiago*, 30 Mass

App 207, 221, 567 NE2d 943, 952 (1991) (doctrine is one of inclusion, not exclusion, and thus does not require exclusion of testimony concerning defendant's statements on the grounds that the witness was unable to recall entire conversation).

In order to give the jury the full picture at the outset, the better practice is to require an objection from the opposing party and contemporaneous introduction of the complete statements when the original is offered. *McAllister v. Boston Housing Authority*, supra, 429 Mass at 303, 708 NE2d at 98.

Proposed Mass R Evid 106[1] limits application of the verbal completeness doctrine to written or recorded statements, although the Advisory Committee's Note adds that "[t]he availability of oral statements is left to the discretion of the court." The rule requires contemporaneous admission of the completing statements, whereas the case law doctrine discussed above envisions subsequent admission by the opposing party.

For a discussion of the common-law origins and application of the completeness doctrine, see Dale A. Nance, A Theory of Verbal Completeness, 80 Iowa L Rev 825 (1995).

§3.13 Curative Admissibility

§3.13.1 Inadmissible Evidence to Offset Inadmissible Evidence

Where A introduces, without objection by B, evidence that is inadmissible and immaterial, it is within the discretion of the trial court to permit B to introduce evidence

---

§3.12 [1]"When a writing or recorded statement or part thereof is introduced by a party, an adverse party may require him at that time to introduce any other part or any other writing or recorded statement which ought in fairness to be considered contemporaneously with it." PMRE 106

that contradicts A's evidence; but it is generally not error to refuse to permit B to introduce evidence otherwise inadmissible. "A party cannot gain an absolute right to introduce evidence of facts not otherwise admissible, by permitting his opponent to introduce evidence of part of them, or evidence of similar facts. A trial judge cannot be compelled to listen to the trial of immaterial issues which in his judgment would prolong the trial, confuse the jury, and make likely an unjust result. The settled rule is that the introduction or exclusion of immaterial evidence to meet immaterial evidence is within the discretion of the court." *Goodyear Park Co. v. Holyoke*, 298 Mass 510, 511-512, 11 NE2d 439, 441 (1937) (internal quotations and citation omitted). Compare *Com. v. Schnackenberg*, 356 Mass 65, 70, 248 NE2d 273, 277 (1969) ("it does not follow that because the Commonwealth introduced hearsay statements, to which there was no objection, the defence then may similarly introduce such testimony over proper objections") with *Com. v. Cataldo*, 326 Mass 373, 377, 94 NE2d 761, 763 (1950) (defendant could not object to cross-examination by Commonwealth concerning otherwise inadmissible hearsay evidence that defense counsel raised on direct examination).

Where the evidence admitted without objection is incompetent but otherwise material and relevant, it may be rebutted by the opponent as a matter of right under the doctrine of curative admissibility. Thus, a judge who erroneously, but without objection, admitted hearsay evidence of a face-to-face accusation of defendant by the victim committed reversible error in refusing to allow defendant to introduce otherwise inadmissible evidence that he had denied the accusations at the time. See *Com. v. Ruffen*, 399 Mass 811, 813-814, 507 NE2d 684, 686-687 (1987). See also *Com. v. Wakelin*, 230 Mass 567, 576, 120 NE 209, 213 (1918) (evidence of third-party's confession, generally inadmissible but admitted without objection, could be rebutted by Commonwealth as of right); *Burke v. Memorial Hospital*, 29 Mass App 948, 950, 558 NE2d 1146, 1149-1150 (1990) (performance evaluations of patient's work by supervisor admissible to rebut supervisor's memo, portions of which were improperly admitted).

The doctrine of curative admissibility allows a party harmed by incompetent evidence to rebut it only where:

- the original evidence being rebutted was improperly admitted. See *Vassallo v. Baxter Healthcare Corp.*, 428 Mass 1, 17, 696 NE2d 909, 920 (1998); *Com. v. Henry*, 37 Mass App 429, 433 n.3, 640 NE2d 503, 507 n.3 (1994); and
- the evidence created significant prejudice. *Judge Rotenberg Educational Center, Inc. v. Commissioner of Department of Mental Retardation*, 424 Mass 430, 462, 677 NE2d 127, 148-149 (1997) (& citation).

On a related matter, there has been "modest recognition" in the Commonwealth of the notion that a party should be permitted some latitude to "fight fire with fire," —i.e., to rebut improper argument with improper argument. *Com. v. Amirault*, 404 Mass 221, 237-238, 535 NE2d 193, 203 (1989) (& citations). See, e.g., *Com. v. Mello*, 420 Mass 375, 380-381, 649 NE2d 1106, 1111 (1995); *Com. v. Smith*, 342 Mass 180, 186, 172 NE2d 597, 601-602 (1961). Compare *Com. v. Smith*, 387 Mass 900, 908, 444 NE2d 374, 380-381 (1983) (concept is limited to correcting error by opponent).

§3.13.2   Documents Called For and Examined by a Party at Trial

Under Massachusetts practice, where one party at trial calls for a document from the other party and in response to the call receives it and examines it, the document may be put in evidence by the party who produced it, even if it would have been otherwise inadmissible. *Leonard v. Taylor,* 315 Mass 580, 53 NE2d 705 (1944); *Clark v. Fletcher,* 83 Mass (1 All) 53, 57 (1861). The rule was originally premised on the notion that a party should not be able to require his adversary to produce a document at trial and, after examining it, "insist on excluding it from the case altogether." *Clark v. Fletcher,* supra. The more pressing concern seems to be with "the disastrous effect upon a jury in a perfectly good case or defense of a bold and dramatic demand by opposing counsel for the production of a document at some critical moment of the trial. It may be impossible to refuse without creating an impression of evasion and concealment, and even if the demand is acceded to it may be practically impossible to prevent the same impression without showing the document itself to the jury." *Leonard v. Taylor,* supra, 315 Mass at 582-583, 53 NE2d at 706.

Application of the rule is not dependent upon the giving of a notice to produce the document prior to the trial. *Leonard v. Taylor,* supra, 315 Mass at 581, 53 NE2d at 706. There must, however, be a demand at trial for the document in order to trigger the *Leonard* rule. See *Com. v. Kenneally,* 10 Mass App 162, 179, 406 NE2d 714, 725 (1980).

The rule making documents called for and examined at trial admissible at the option of the producing party does not apply to documents used by a witness to refresh his recollection *while* testifying (see §6.20, infra). *Nussenbaum v. Chambers & Chambers, Inc.,* 322 Mass 419, 424, 77 NE2d 780, 783-784 (1948). It does apply to documents used for that purpose by the witness *before* trial. *Leonard v. Taylor,* supra, 315 Mass at 583, 53 NE2d at 707. The logic of this distinction has been questioned. See *Com. v. Marsh,* 354 Mass 713, 721-722, 242 NE2d 545, 551 (1968) ("It is an artificial distinction to allow inspection of notes on the stand to refresh recollection [without rendering the notes admissible] and to decline it where the witness inspects his notes just before being called to the stand."). Nonetheless, Proposed Mass. R Evid. 612 carries forward the distinction.[1]

The rule is of limited applicability in criminal cases. It has been held inapplicable where the defendant demands to inspect prior statements of a prosecution witness in the possession of the Commonwealth. See *Com. v. Ellison*, 376 Mass 1, 22-23, 379 NE2d 560, 571 (1978). Similarly, neither defense counsel's request to see the notes referred to by a prosecution witness to refresh his recollection at trial nor counsel's use of them in cross-examination make the notes admissible at the option of the Commonwealth. *Com. v. Beaulieu*, 333 Mass 640, 648-650, 133 NE2d 226, 231-232 (1955). The court has also suggested that the judge should have discretion to permit inspection of a prosecution witness's notes without a formal demand, and that where the request is on a voir dire, there are substantial reasons for exercising discretion in favor of the inspection. *Com. v. Marsh*, supra, 354 Mass at 721, 242 NE2d at 551. Application of the rule has also been questioned in the case where a defense attorney requests and obtains a police report at trial. See *Com. v. Kenneally, supra,* 10 Mass App at 179, 406 NE2d at 725.

The *Leonard* rule does not apply unless the document produced is found by the judge to be the one demanded by the opponent. See *O'Connell v. Kennedy*, 328 Mass 90, 95-96, 101 NE2d 892, 895-896 (1951).

The wisdom of the rule making admissible a document called for and examined at trial was raised by the *Leonard*

---

§3.13 [1]The Advisory Committee writes that PMRE 612(b), providing that the judge has discretion to order production of a document used by a witness before testifying, "does not change the practice under Leonard v. Taylor, which held that a demand for a writing used prior to trial made such writing admissible at the option of the party producing it, though it would have otherwise been incompetent. Leonard v. Taylor, supra, is considered to be disciplinary in nature in order to discourage the 'bravado' demand, and does not impair appropriate discovery." Advisory Committee Note to R.612 (citations omitted).

court itself, see 315 Mass at 582, 53 NE2d at 706; and the current status of the rule has been questioned by the Supreme Judicial Court. See *Com. v. Ellison,* supra, 376 Mass at 22, 379 NE2d at 570. Moreover, because the rule is designed to avoid prejudicial impact on the jury, there is serious question as to whether it should apply at all in jury-waived cases.

D. JUROR SELECTION

§3.14 Individual Juror Voir Dire for Bias or Prejudice

A trial judge is required to question prospective jurors individually when it appears that their impartiality may be affected by extraneous influences, including "community attitudes, possible exposure to potentially prejudicial material or possible preconceived opinions toward the credibility of certain classes of persons." GL 234, §28. See also Mass R Crim P 20(b); Mass R Civ P 47(a). Individual voir dire has been mandated in the following categories of cases:

- Interracial rape or other sexual offense, with respect to racial prejudice. See *Com. v. Sanders,* 383 Mass 637, 640-641, 421 NE2d 436, 438 (1981); *Com. v. Hobbs,* 383 Mass 863, 873, 434 NE2d 633, 641 (1982) (interracial sexual abuse); *Com. v. Hooper,* 42 Mass App 730, 679 NE2d 602 (1997) (any case involving interracial sex and violence). But compare *Com. v. De La Cruz,* 405 Mass 269, 540 NE2d 168 (1989) (Hispanic defendant and white sexual assualt victim not interracial).
- Interracial murder. *Com. v. Young,* 401 Mass 390, 398, 517 NE2d 130, 135 (1987). But the requirement has not been extended to cases where defendant and victim are of different ethnic back-

grounds. See *Com. v. Hunter*, 427 Mass 651, 656, 695 NE2d 653, 654 (1998).

- Child sexual abuse, with respect to each prospective juror's own experience with such abuse. *Com. v. Flebotte*, 417 Mass 348, 353-356, 630 NE2d2 265, 268-270 (1994). See also *Com. v. Holloway*, 44 Mass App 469, 691 NE2d 985 (1998) (reversible error to refuse rape defendant's request to interview jurors individually as to whether they or a member of their families had been victims of sexual assault). But see *Com. v. Sanchez*, 423 Mass 591, 594-595, 670 NE2d 377, 379-380 (1996) (*Flebotte* not retroactive).

- Cases involving the insanity defense, with respect to any opinion that would prevent the juror from returning a verdict of not guilty by reason of insanity. *Com. v. Seguin*, 421 Mass 243, 249, 656 NE2d 1229, 1233 (1995).

In addition, in cases where the victim is a homosexual or bisexual, the subject of juror attitudes towards those groups "requires careful attention." *Com. v. Plunkett*, 422 Mass 634, 641, 664 NE2d 833, 838 (1996) (but refusing to mandate individual voir dire).

For an extensive discussion of challenge for cause, see generally *Com. v. Long*, 419 Mass 798, 647 NE2d 1162 (1995) (& citations); *Com. v. Auguste*, 414 Mass 51, 605 NE2d 819 (1992) (& citations) (discussing obligation of judge to adequately question venirepersons who expressed concerns about impartiality). For a discussion of GL 234, §28 in a civil case, see *Blank v. Hubbuch*, 36 Mass App 955, 633 NE2d 439 (1994).

For discussion of the process of removal of a juror for cause after final submission of the case, see *Com. v. Caldwell*, 45 Mass App 42, 694 NE2d 1309 (1998) (& citations); *Com. v. Federici*, 427 Mass 740, 746-747, 696 NE2d 111, 116 (1998) (& citations).

§3.15 Discriminatory Use of Peremptory Challenges

Peremptory challenges, which by definition require no statement of reason, cannot be used to exclude prospective jurors solely by virtue of their membership in, or affiliation with, particular defined groupings in the community. *Com. v. Long,* 419 Mass 798, 806, 647 NE2d 1162, 1167-1168 (1995) (citing *Com. v. Soares,* 377 Mass 461, 486, 387 NE2d 499, 515 (1979) (art. 12 of Massachusetts Declaration of Rights); *Com. v. LeClair,* 429 Mass 313, 319, 708 NE2d 107, 112 (1999) (gender). See also *Batson v. Kentucky,* 476 US 79, 106 S Ct 1712, 90 L Ed 2d 69 (1986) (equal protection clause of federal constitution). The party raising the issue must demonstrate a prima facie showing of impropriety, generally by showing that: (1) a pattern of conduct has developed whereby prospective jurors who have been challenged peremptorily are members of a discrete group;[1] and (2) there is a likelihood that they are being excluded from the jury solely on the basis of their group membership. If the judge determines that a sufficient showing has been made, the burden shifts to the allegedly offending party to provide a group-neutral reason for challenging the prospective juror. *Com. v. LeClair,* supra, 429 Mass at 319-320, 708 NE2d at 112-113; *Com. v. Long,* supra, 419 Mass at 806, 647 NE2d at 1168 (& citations). The party challenging the use of the peremptory strikes must then be given the chance to rebut the proffered explanation as a pretext. *Com. v. LeClair,* supra, 429 Mass at 323, 708 NE2d at 114; *Com. v. Futch,* 38 Mass App 174, 178, 647 NE2d 59, 62

---

§3.15 [1]A prima facie case can be established based even on a single peremptory challenge. See, e.g., *Com. v. Curtiss,* 424 Mass 78, 79, 676 NE2d 431, 432 (1997) (disallowed white defendant's challenge to only black potential juror); *Com. v. Fryar,* 414 Mass 732, 737, 610 NE2d 903, 907 (1993) (& citations) (prosecutor's use of peremptory challenge against only eligible black venireperson). But compare *Com. v. Roche,* 44 Mass App 372, 378, 691 NE2d 946, 951 (1998) (challenge to single prospective juror within class does not, by itself, constitute prima facie showing of impropriety in all circumstances).

(1995). See generally *Com. v. Burnett*, 418 Mass 769, 642 NE2d 294 (1994).

§4.1 Relevance

§4.1.1 Defined

Proposed Mass R Evid 401 defines "relevant evidence" as "evidence having any tendency to make the existence of any fact that is of consequence to the determination of the action more or less probable than it would be without the evidence." This is in accord with Massachusetts case law, which defines as relevant that evidence which has a "rational tendency to prove an issue in the case." *Com. v. Fayerweather*, 406 Mass 78, 83, 546 NE2d 345, 350 (1989); *Com. v. LaCorte*, 373 Mass. 700, 702, 369 NE2d 1006, 1008 (1977).

The concept of relevancy thus has two components: (1) the evidence must have some tendency to prove or disprove a particular fact; and (2) that particular fact must be material to an issue in the case. The first concept, that of inherent probative worth, is as much practical as legal. To determine the probative value of a fact (B) offered to establish another fact (A), it must be shown that from the viewpoint of logic, experience or common sense, proof of B tends to prove A.

It has generally been held with regard to the second requirement that evidence may be admitted even if the issue is conceded or there is an offer to stipulate. See *Com.*

v. Roderick, 411 Mass 817, 819-820, 586 NE2d 967, 968-969 (1992) (fact that evidence is relevant to issue that opponent concedes does not render it inadmissible, but such concession is factor to be weighed in assessing propriety of discretionary exclusion on grounds of potential prejudicial impact, discussed in §4.3, infra); *Com. v. Nadworny,* 396 Mass 342, 367, 486 NE2d 675, 690 (1985); *Com. v. Nassar,* 351 Mass 37, 46-47, 218 NE2d 72, 78 (1966); *Com. v. Worcester,* 44 Mass App 258, 262, 690 NE2d 451, 454 (1998) (defendant prepared to stipulate to identity of deceased). But compare *Old Chief v. United States,* 519 U.S. 172 (1997) (in prosecution for violation of 18 U.S.C. §922(g), defendant's offer to stipulate to prior felony element of firearm possession charge precludes introduction of full record).

It is often stated that any evidence that "throws light" on an issue is properly admitted. *Adoption of Carla,* 416 Mass 510, 513, 623 NE2d 1118, 1120 (1993); *Com. v. Woods,* 414 Mass 343, 355, 607 NE2d 1024, 1033 (1993). Alternatively, the test of admissibility has been described as follows: The evidence "must render the desired inference more probable than it would be without the evidence." *Com. v. Fayerweather,* supra, 406 Mass at 83, 546 NE2d at 350; *Com. v. Mandeville,* 386 Mass 393, 398, 436 NE2d 912, 917 (1982). See also FRE 401.

§4.1.2   Relevancy and Admissibility

Generally speaking, evidence that is relevant is admissible unless barred by some statute, rule, or policy of exclusion; evidence that is not relevant is not admissible. *Green v. Richmond,* 369 Mass 47, 59, 337 NE2d 691, 699 (1975); *Poirier v. Plymouth,* 374 Mass 206, 210, 372 NE2d 212, 218 (1978); *Com. v. Vitello,* 376 Mass 426, 438-439, 381 NE2d 582, 590 (1978); Proposed Mass R Evid 402.[1] The trial judge

---

§4.1   [1]"All relevant evidence is admissible, except as limited by constitutional requirements, or as otherwise provided by statute or by

is accorded substantial discretion in deciding whether evidence is relevant. See *In re Wyatt*, 428 Mass 347, 355, 701 NE2d 337, 343 (1998) (& citations). But see *Com. v. Santiago*, 425 Mass 491, 497 n.4, 681 NE2d 1205, 1211 n.4 (1997) (where victim's sister was permitted to testify in substantial detail about victim's life, it was "abundantly clear" she offered no evidence relevant to the crime charged).[2] Once admitted, the weight to be accorded the evidence is a question for the jury. *Com. v. Weichell*, 390 Mass 62, 74, 453 NE2d 1038, 1045 (1983); *Poirier v. Plymouth*, supra, 374 Mass at 215, 372 NE2d at 218.

To be admissible, it is not necessary that the evidence in question bear directly on the issue or be conclusive of it. *Com. v. Ashley*, 427 Mass 620, 624-625, 694 NE2d 862, 867 (1998) (no requirement that evidence of motive be conclusive). It is sufficient if it tends to establish the issue or constitutes a link in the chain of proof. *Com. v. Gordon*, 407 Mass 340, 351, 553 NE2d 915, 921 (1990); *Liarikos v. Mello*, 418 Mass 669, 672, 639 NE2d 716, 718 (1994); *Com. v. Cross*, 33 Mass App 761, 763, 605 NE2d 298, 301 (1992). "Evidence must go in piecemeal, and evidence having a tendency to prove a proposition is not inadmissible simply because it does not wholly prove the proposition. It is

---

these rules, or by other rules applicable in the courts of this Commonwealth. Evidence which is not relevant is not admissible." PMRE 402.

[2] An error by the trial judge in excluding relevant evidence must be shown to have been "prejudicial" in order to constitute grounds for a new trial. See *DeJesus v. Vogel*, 404 Mass 44, 47-49, 533 NE2d 1318, 1321-1322 (1989). The proponent must make a plausible showing that the trier of fact might have reached a different result if the evidence had been admitted. "[T]he erroneous exclusion of relevant evidence is reversible error unless, on the record, the appellate court can say with substantial confidence that the error would not have made a material difference." *Foreign Car Center, Inc. v. Salem Suede, Inc.*, 40 Mass App 15, 17, 660 NE2d 687, 691 (1996) (citation omitted).

enough if in connection with other evidence it helps a little." *Com. v. Tucker,* 189 Mass 457, 467, 76 NE 127, 130 (1905). Evidence that bloodstains were found inside defendant's automobile and on his clothes was, for example, held admissible even though it could not be scientifically determined that the blood came from the murder victim: "The evidence was relevant to the issue whether the defendant was the perpetrator. Other evidence introduced at trial made it clear that whoever committed the crime would have gotten blood on himself or on his clothing. Therefore, evidence that there was blood in the defendant's car and on an item of his clothing was a link in the chain of proof of his identity as the perpetrator of the crime." *Com. v. Yesilciman,* 406 Mass 736, 744, 550 NE2d 378, 383 (1990). See also *Com. v. Voisine,* 414 Mass 772, 781-782, 610 NE2d 926, 931 (1993).

Similarly, evidence that two knives were found in the vicinity of the defendant at the time of his arrest two months after the stabbing was held properly admitted to show that he possessed instruments that could have been used in the commission of the crime, despite the lack of any demonstrable connection between the knives and the murder weapon. *Com. v. Marangiello,* 410 Mass 452, 456-457, 573 NE2d 500, 503-504 (1991). See also *Com. v. James,* 424 Mass 770, 779-780, 678 NE2d 1170, 1177-1178 (1997); *Com. v. Marquetty,* 416 Mass 445, 447-448, 622 NE2d 632, 635 (1993); *Com. v. Hamilton,* 411 Mass 313, 322, 582 NE2d 929, 934-935 (1991). Compare *Com. v. Chasson,* 383 Mass 183, 186-187, 423 NE2d 306, 308-309 (1981) (knives found near murder scene several weeks after stabbings too remote to be admissible).

It is not a basis for excluding relevant evidence that it is "self-serving." *Com. v. Caldron,* 383 Mass 86, 90, 417 NE2d 958 (1981) (error to exclude testimony by defendant as to his intent at time of alleged crime).

The issue of admissibility must, of course, be distinguished from the question of the sufficiency of the evidence. See, e.g., *Com. v. Morris*, 422 Mass 254, 662 NE2d 683 (1996) (fact that defendant's fingerprint was found on mask left at crime scene was admissible, but evidence was insufficient to warrant finding beyond reasonable doubt that print was placed on mask during crime).

For cases illustrative of the breadth of the relevancy concept, see *Com. v. Barnoski*, 418 Mass 523, 538, 638 NE2d 9, 17 (1994) (testimony that defendant repeatedly rubbed hand through his hair admissible to show why gunshot residue test might have been negative); *Com. v. Gordon*, supra, 407 Mass at 351, 553 NE2d at 921 (evidence of prior confrontation between victim and defendant was relevant to issue of victim's reasonable fear of defendant); *Com. v. Fayerweather*, 406 Mass 78, 83, 546 NE2d 345, 350 (1989) ("Evidence that the complainant claimed to hear the voice of the defendant telling her to do things could have made it more likely, in the jury's view, that the complainant did not perceive the event accurately. The evidence could have been helpful for the jury to determine whether the complainant was telling the truth or whether she imagined the entire incident. The evidence, then, met the threshold test of relevancy. . . ."); *Com. v. Borodine*, 371 Mass 1, 7-9, 353 NE2d 649, 653 (1976) (evidence that homicide victim had abandoned plans to marry defendant and planned to terminate their relationship was relevant to motive, even in absence of direct evidence that this was communicated to defendant); *Sydney Binder, Inc. v. Jewelers Mutual Ins. Co.*, 28 Mass App 459, 461-463, 552 NE2d 568, 569-570 (1990) (evidence that principal officer of corporate plaintiff was in financial straits admissible as tending to establish motive for burglary of his own store); *Com. v. Phong Thu Ly*, 19 Mass App 901, 471 NE2d 383 (1984) (rubber dishwashing gloves found on defendant held probative of intent to conceal fingerprints, which was probative of defendant's actual robbery attempt).

§4.1.3 Limits on Relevancy—"Remote" or "Speculative" Evidence

Where the links in the chain are too attenuated, evidence will be excluded as "remote" or "speculative."[3] In *Com. v. Burke*, 339 Mass 521, 533-534, 159 NE2d 856, 864 (1959), for example, evidence showing that the defendant and a woman had occupied an apartment together for a short time seven months before his wife's death was held, in the absence of any proof that the relationship continued to a later period, too remote on the issue of hostility towards the victim or motive to kill her. See also *Com. v. Gilbert*, 423 Mass 863, 870-871, 673 NE2d 46, 51 (1996) (evidence that victim turned down long-term job offered to show she was contemplating suicide too attenuated); *Com. v. Kirkpatrick*, 423 Mass 436, 447-448, 668 NE2d 790, 797 (1996) (in absence of medical testimony explaining records, jury could only have speculated on importance of presence of sexually transmitted disease in defendant and absence of it in alleged victim of sexual assault); *Com. v. Woods*, 414 Mass 343, 355, 607 NE2d 1024, 1032-1033 (1993) (chain of inference from evidence that front seat passenger possessed marijuana at time of accident to conclusion that he, not vehicular homicide defendant, was driving too tenuous and approached impermissible speculation); *Maillet v. ATF-Davidson Co.*, 407 Mass 185, 186-189, 552 NE2d 95, 96-98 (1990) (evidence that beer was available on premises of industrial accident and that plaintiff was seen handling a beer can irrelevant to prove that plaintiff had consumed a beer prior to the accident); *Com. v. Palmariello*, 392 Mass 126, 137, 466 NE2d 805, 812 (1984) (evidence that victim threatened defendant in 1979 too

---

[3] The Supreme Judicial Court has observed: "Our older cases sustaining the exclusion of evidence on the ground that it was 'too remote' may fairly be read as saying that, in the circumstances, the evidence was not relevant." *DeJesus v. Vogel,* supra, 404 Mass at 47 n.3, 533 NE2d at 1320 n.3.

remote to be relevant to the circumstances of murder in 1981); *Com. v. LeCain,* 19 Mass App 1034, 1035-1036, 477 NE2d 205, 207 (1985) (evidence that mother of one-year-old murder victim had been upset immediately after birth of child and had failed to bond with her too remote from subsequent crime); *Com. v. Jacobson,* 19 Mass App 666, 678-679, 477 NE2d 158, 166 (1985) (evidence that on two occasions more than six weeks before arson fire a security company had investigated burglar alarms and discovered fresh footprints and unlocked door too remote to be probative of possibility that someone other than defendant had set the fire); *Com. v. Glen,* 12 Mass App 317, 321-322, 423 NE2d 1048, 1051 (1981) (testimony of rape defendant's brother that victim had on one occasion tried to get defendant to go home with her properly excluded as there was no indication when that had occurred).

Compare *DeJesus v. Vogel,* 404 Mass 44, 46-47, 533 NE2d 1318, 1320-1321 (1989) (evidence that porch railing was loose two months before accident and no repairs were made during intervening period relevant and not remote); *Com. v. Machado,* 339 Mass 713, 715, 162 NE2d 71, 73 (1959) (testimony that defendant was in bed with victim six months after alleged occurrence of carnal knowledge of the girl not too remote to show an inclination to commit the earlier crime); *Com. v. Taylor,* 426 Mass 189, 687 NE2d 631 (1997) (notebook and tape-recorded conversation disclosing discordant relationship between defendant and murder victim's parents relevant to possible motive, even though they predated trial by three years); *Com. v. Lora,* 43 Mass App 136, 141-142, 681 NE2d 876, 880-881 (1997) (defendant's medical records relevant to necessity defense, even though they dated back six years before his arrest); *Com. v. Rockett,* 41 Mass App 5, 667 NE2d 1168 (1996) (evidence that unidentified voice called out defendant's first name as perpetrator fled scene admissible because inference that it referred to defendant was plausible); *Cocco v. Deluxe Systems, Inc.,* 25 Mass App 151, 155, 516 NE2d 1171, 1173 (1987) ("notwithstanding the gap in the evidence of direct observations, the jury was justified in drawing an inference that the starter switch delivered with the shredder was the same type of unguarded starter switch which was on the shredder five years later at the time of the accident and about which the expert testified").

§4.2   Direct and Circumstantial Evidence

Probative evidence takes two forms. Direct proof is evidence that actually asserts or demonstrates the fact proposition for which it is offered, and which, "if believed by the trier of fact, will prove the particular fact in question without reliance upon inference or presumption." *Rolanti v. Boston Edison Corp.*, 33 Mass App 516, 521, 603 NE2d 211, 216 (1992) (citations omitted). Circumstantial proof, on the other hand, requires the trier of fact to make inferences to reach the fact proposition. See generally *Abraham v. Woburn*, 383 Mass 724, 730, 421 NE2d 1206, 1210 (1981). It is not necessary that the inference proposed to be drawn from the circumstantial evidence be the *only* one possible. Rather, it is sufficient if the inference is a reasonable one. *Com. v. Marquetty*, 416 Mass 445, 452, 622 NE2d 632, 638 (1993); *Com. v. Cohen*, 412 Mass 375, 378, 589 NE2d 289, 292-293 (1992); *Com. v. Talbot*, 35 Mass App 766, 772, 625 NE2d 1374, 1378 (1994). Nor is it required that every inference be premised on an independently proven fact; in certain circumstances a jury is permitted to make an inference based on an inference, as long as it is not speculative. *Com. v. Doste*, 425 Mass 372, 375-376, 681 NE2d 282, 284 (1997) (& citations).

The scope of circumstantial evidence is as broad as human experience and, although "indirect," can carry persuasive value equal to or even greater than that of direct proof. See *Abraham v. Woburn*, supra, 383 Mass at 729, 421 NE2d at 1210 (1981) (citing Text).

It is well-settled that circumstantial evidence may be sufficient to establish guilt beyond a reasonable doubt in a criminal case. See *Com. v. Cohen*, supra, 412 Mass at 380, 589 NE2d at 293-294; *Com. v. Kater*, 409 Mass 433, 444, 567 NE2d 885, 891-892 (1991) (*Kater III*); *Com. v. Anderson*, 396 Mass 306, 311, 486 NE2d 19, 22-23 (1985); *Com. v. Nadworny*, 396 Mass 342, 354, 486 NE2d 675, 690 (1985).

Where, however, the evidence tends equally to support inconsistent conclusions as to the defendant's guilt, the evidence is insufficient to support a conviction. See *Com. v. Lombard*, 419 Mass 585, 589, 646 NE2d 400, 404 (1995); *Com. v. Salemme*, 395 Mass 594, 601, 481 NE2d 471, 476 (1985). Compare *Com. v. Smith*, 368 Mass 126, 330 NE2d 197 (1975) and *Com. v. Doyle*, 12 Mass App 786, 429 NE2d 346 (evidence sufficient to support conclusion that defendant had been operator of vehicle involved in accident) with *Corson v. Com.*, 428 Mass 193, 699 NE2d 814 (1998) (evidence insufficient to permit inference that defendant had requisite criminal intent) and *Com. v. Mullen*, 3 Mass App 25, 322 NE2d 195 (1975) (evidence insufficient to permit inference that defendant had been driving vehicle).[1]

In order to convict on circumstantial evidence, it is not necessary to show that no person other than the defendant could have committed the crime. *Cramer v. Com.*, 419 Mass 106, 111-112, 642 NE2d 1039, 1043-1044 (1994); *Com. v. Keaton*, supra, 36 Mass App at 86 (& citations). The question of guilt must not, however, be left to conjecture or surmise. *Com. v. Anderson*, supra, 396 Mass at 312, 486 NE2d at 22-23 (citation omitted); *Berry v. Com.*, 393 Mass 793, 795-796, 473 NE2d 1115, 1117 (1985); *Com. v. Keaton*, 36 Mass App 81, 85, 628 NE2d 1286, 1288 (1994).

For cases discussing jury instructions on circumstantial proof, see *Com. v. Gil*, 393 Mass 204, 221-222, 471 NE2d 30

---

§4.2 [1] The standard of sufficiency in criminal cases is discussed in *Jackson v. Virginia*, 443 US 307, 99 S Ct 2781, 61 L Ed 2d 560 (1979) and *Berry v. Com.*, 393 Mass 793, 473 NE2d 1115 (1985) (& citations).

(1984) ("footprints in the snow" anology); *Com. v. Rosa*, 422 Mass 1, 26-29, 661 NE2d 56, 61-63 (1996) (& cases cited) (warning against numeric or quantifiable examples to explain circumstantial proof); *Com. v. Brooks*, 422 Mass 574, 578-579, 664 NE2d 801, 806 (1996) (same).

§4.2.1   *Consciousness of Guilt/Consciousness of Liability Evidence*

Illustrative of the nature of circumstantial proof is "consciousness of guilt" evidence frequently encountered in criminal cases. Evidence of flight, escape, or concealment is admissible under appropriate circumstances as probative of the defendant's guilty state of mind. See *Com. v. Lavalley*, 410 Mass 641, 649, 574 NE2d 1000, 1005 (1991); *Com. v. Roberts*, 407 Mass 731, 735-736, 555 NE2d 588 (1990); *Com. v. Epsom*, 399 Mass 254, 258-259, 503 NE2d 954, 957-958 (1987). "While proof of mere consciousness of guilt alone may be insufficient to convict of the crime, evidence of such a state of mind when coupled with other probable inferences, may be sufficient to amass the quantum of proof necessary to prove guilt." *Com. v. Porter*, 384 Mass 647, 653, 429 NE2d 14, 15 (1981) (citation omitted). Standing alone, evidence of consciousness of guilt is insufficient to warrant submission of the case to a jury. *Com. v. Fancy*, 349 Mass 196, 201, 207 NE2d 276, 280 (1965); *Com. v. Butler*, 7 Mass App 918, 389 NE2d 431 (1979). Such evidence may tip the scale where the other evidence is conflicting. *Com. v. Best*, 381 Mass 472, 483, 411 NE2d 442, 449 (1980). See also *Com. v. Paniaqua*, 413 Mass 796, 803 n.7, 604 NE2d 1278, 1283 n.7 (1992).

"There are two assumptions that underlie the inference of guilt that may be drawn from evidence of flight, concealment, or similar acts. The first assumption is that a person who flees or hides after a criminal act has been committed does so because he feels guilt concerning the act. The second is that one who feels guilt concerning an act has committed that act." *Com. v. Toney,* 385 Mass 575, 585-586, 433 NE2d 425, 432 (1982). Both assumptions have been the subject of some judicial criticism. Id., 385 Mass at 585, 433 NE2d at 432.

Consciousness of guilt evidence may be admitted even though the defendant presents plausible alternative explanations for the conduct that are consistent with innocence of the crime charged. In *Com. v. Booker,* 386 Mass 466, 469-471, 436 NE2d 160, 163-164 (1982), for example, evidence that the defendant attempted to hide from the police was held properly admitted despite the fact that there was an outstanding default warrant for him on an unrelated crime that he had knowledge of at the time police arrived. "That there may have been other reasons for the flight presents a question for the jury in considering the probability that the defendant fled because of a consciousness of guilt of the crime charged in the indictments for which he was on trial." Id., 386 Mass at 470-471, 436 NE2d at 163. See also *Com. v. Sheriff,* 425 Mass 186, 199-200, 680 NE2d 75, 83 (1997) (evidence of defendant's attempt at suicide admissible despite argument that paranoid schizophrenics are ten times more likely to kill themselves); *Com. v. Burke,* 414 Mass 252, 260-261, 607 NE2d 991, 997 (1993) (evidence of defendant's flight from police properly submitted to jury despite defendant's contention it resulted from house-break just committed, and not murder charged; also rejecting federal authority excluding consciousness of guilt evidence where defendant stands trial for an offense that occurred before the offense that allegedly prompted defendant to flee); *Com. v. Toney,* supra, 385 Mass at 584-585, 433 NE2d at 431 ("it was for the jury to determine which explanation for defendant's absence from home and work after the murder was most credible"); *Com. v. Goldoff,* 24 Mass App 458, 465-466, 510 NE2d 277, 281-282 (1987).

Evidence tending to show consciousness of guilt is not rendered inadmissible simply because it may reveal to the jury that the defendant has committed another offense.

Com. v. Burke, supra, 414 Mass at 260 (& citation); *Com. v. Jackson,* 419 Mass 716, 731, 647 NE2d 401, 410 (1995); *Com. v. Fernandes,* 427 Mass 90, 94, 692 NE2d 3, 6 (1998).

It has been held that the defendant has an unqualified right to negate the inference of consciousness of guilt by explaining to the jury why he took the action in question. *Com. v. Chase,* 26 Mass App 578, 580-581, 530 NE2d 185, 187-188 (1988) (& citations); *Com. v. Garuti,* 23 Mass App 561, 566-569, 504 NE2d 357, 360-362 (1987).

For other examples of consciousness of guilt evidence, see *Com. v. Miles,* 420 Mass 67, 75-76, 648 NE2d 719, 726 (1995) (threats to key prosecution witness); *Com. v. Jackson,* supra, 419 Mass at 730-731, 647 NE2d at 409 (giving false name to police officer); *Cramer v. Com.,* 419 Mass 106, 111, 642 NE2d 1039, 1043 (1994) (conflicting explanations about how child was burned); *Com. v. Cruz,* 416 Mass 27, 29, 616 NE2d 804, 805 (1993) (false statements to police); *Com. v. Paniaqua,* supra, 413 Mass at 803 (running from police, discarding bag, giving false name, and changing appearance by time of trial); *Com. v. Scanlon,* 412 Mass 664, 676-677, 592 NE2d 1279, 1286-1287 (1992) (possible threat or intimidation of prosecution witnesses by defendant); *Com. v. Otsuki,* 411 Mass 218, 237, 581 NE2d 999, 1010 (1991) (flight and hiding in Mexico); *Com. v. Hamilton,* 411 Mass 313, 326, 582 NE2d 929, 937 (1991) (false name to police); *Com. v. Lavalley,* supra, 410 Mass at 647-650, 574 NE2d at 1004-1006 (false statement concerning incident with victim); *Com. v. Merola,* 405 Mass 529, 546-547, 542 NE2d 249, 259-260 (1989) (false statements to police and denial of having seen bruises on victim's body); *Com. v. Paradise,* 405 Mass 141, 157, 539 NE2d 1006, 1016-1017 (1989) (hiding clothing, change of appearance); *Com. v. Tyree,* 387 Mass 191, 439 NE2d 263 (1982) (defendant authored anonymous statement that exculpated him in attempt to mislead police); *Com. v. Basch,* 386 Mass 620, 624-625, 437 NE2d 200, 203 (1982) (defendant faked break-in to divert suspicion from himself); *Com. v. Blaikie,*

375 Mass 601, 378 NE2d 1361 (1978) (concealment of body, misleading and false statements to police, and flight); *Com. v. Montecalvo*, 367 Mass 46, 323 NE2d 888 (1975) (inordinate interest in case, particularly in whether victim's clothing had been found); *Com. v. Bray*, 19 Mass App 751, 759, 477 NE2d 596, 601-602 (1985) (defendant and other youths met together days after crime and agreed upon statement to make to police).

But compare *Com. v. Barnoski*, 418 Mass 523, 537-538, 638 NE2d 9, 17 (1994) (testimony that defendant repeatedly rubbed his hand through his hair admissible only if it is shown he knew this might affect gunshot residue test); *Com. v. Brown*, 414 Mass 123, 126-127, 605 NE2d 837, 839 (1993) (judge erred in instructing jury concerning flight as evidence of consciousness of guilt where defendant's peculiar behavior at crime scene was not "flight" in the common sense of the term); *Com. v. Hightower*, 400 Mass 267, 269, 508 NE2d 850, 852 (1987) (where there was no evidence to show that defendant's failure to appear for trial was motivated by choice to avoid trial on the charges, reversible error to admit evidence of the default and instruct the jury as to consciousness of guilt).

An escape or attempted escape need not be contemporaneous with the crime or arrest to be probative of consciousness of guilt. See *Com. v. Lam*, 420 Mass 615, 617-618, 650 NE2d 796, 798 (1995) (evidence of attempted escape shortly before defendant's trial was scheduled to begin admissible even though several years after offense).

Acts of a joint venturer amounting to evidence of consciousness of guilt may be attributed to another joint venturer if the acts occurred during the course of the joint venture and in the furtherance of it. *Com. v. Mahoney*, 405 Mass 326, 330-331, 540 NE2d 179, 182 (1989) (& citations). But compare *Com. v. Pringle*, 22 Mass App 746, 751-752, 498 NE2d 131, 134-135 (1986) (error to instruct jury that companion's use of false name could be considered evidence of defendant's own consciousness of guilt where defendant gave his correct name).

While consciousness of guilt evidence is admissible on the question of whether a homicide was committed, it cannot be used to prove that a homicide was murder rather than manslaughter. See *Com. v. Niland,* 45 Mass App 526, 529, 699 NE2d 1236, 1239 (1998) (& citations).

Because a suspect has the right to remain silent and is under no obligation to say anything to police (see §9.7, infra), it is improper for the Commonwealth to invite the jury to infer consciousness of guilt from a defendant's failure to deny his guilt during interrogation. See *Com. v. Haas,* 373 Mass 545, 558-562, 369 NE2d 692, 702-703 (1977); *Com. v. Harris,* 371 Mass 462, 358 NE2d 982 (1976) (defendant's "hanging his head" and "biting his lips" in response to police interrogation could not be viewed as evidence of consciousness of guilt in light of defendant's right to remain silent while in custody.) See also *Com. v. Martinez,* 34 Mass App 131, 608 NE2d 740 (1993) (reversal required where prosecutor suggested in cross-examination of rape defendant that inference of guilt could be drawn from defendant's pretrial failure to voluntarily offer to furnish physical evidence to district attorney's office). But compare *Com. v. Lavalley,* supra, 410 Mass at 649, 574 NE2d at 1005-1006 (prosecutor did not refer to defendant's failure to deny the crime, but only his failure to mention in his first statement to police that victim and had made sexual advances).

When consciousness of guilt evidence is admitted, the jury should be instructed that they are not to convict on the basis of that evidence alone; they may, but need not, consider the evidence as one factor tending to prove the guilt of the defendant. *Com. v. Toney,* 385 Mass 575, 585-586, 433 NE2d 425, 432 (1982) (required cautionary instruction set out). In the absence of a request, however, the judge is not required to instruct the jury *sua sponte* on their evaluation of such evidence. See *Com. v. Brousseau,* 421 Mass 647, 652, 659 NE2d 724, 727 (1996); *Com. v. Simmons,* 419 Mass 426, 434-436, 646 NE2d 97, 102-103 (1995). *Com. v. Simmons* appears to call into question the propriety of a judge giving a *Toney* instruction over the objection of defense counsel, as had been permitted by *Com. v. Cruz*, 416 Mass 27, 616 NE2d 804 (1993) and *Com. v. De Los Santos*, 37 Mass App 526, 640 NE2d 1124 (1994). But see *Com. v. Robles*, 423 Mass 62, 70-72, 666 NE2d 497, 503-504 (1996) (no error in judge instructing jury on consciousness of guilt over defendant's repeated objection).

For cases reversing convictions based on the failure to give proper instructions, see *Com. v. Matos*, 394 Mass 563, 476 NE2d 608 (1985); *Com. v. Estrada*, 25 Mass App 907, 908, 514 NE2d 1099, 1100 (1987); *Com. v. Rivera*, 23 Mass App 605, 608-610, 504 NE2d 371, 372-374 (1987). Compare *Com. v. Avellar*, 416 Mass 409, 421, 622 NE2d 625, 631-632 (1993) (failure to instruct unlikely to have affected verdict); *Com. v. Lavalley*, supra, 410 Mass at 650-652, 574 NE2d at 1006-1007 (no reversal required where judge omitted supplemental instruction in his written instructions but included it in oral charge); *Com. v. Mercado*, 24 Mass App 391, 400, 509 NE2d 300, 306 (1987) (no reversal required because failure to give supplemental instruction had negligible effect on verdict). See also *Com. v. Nadworny*, 396 Mass 342, 371 n.14, 486 NE2d 675, 692 n.14 (1985) (while instruction was "not a model of clarity regarding the fact that a defendant may not be convicted on consciousness of guilt evidence alone, it contained the substance of what we required in *Toney*"); *Com. v. Colantonio*, 31 Mass App 299, 310-311, 577 NE2d 314, 321-322 (1991) (same); *Com. v. Henry*, 37 Mass App 429, 434-439, 640 NE2d 503, 507-509 (1994) (trial court not required to give *Toney* instructions verbatim); *Com. v. Pagan*, 35 Mass App 788, 793-794, 625 NE2d 579, 582 (1994) (in absence of argument that defendant's conflicting statements demonstrated consciousness of guilt, no instruction required).

It is preferable for the judge to explicitly limit the consciousness of guilt instruction to only those defendants whose conduct is in question. See *Com. v. Gordon*, 422 Mass 816, 852-853, 666 NE2d 122, 144 (1996).

A judge is not required to draw the jury's attention to the defendant's own innocent explanation for the act alleged to imply consciousness of guilt; "consciousness of innocence is a matter more appropriately left to the defendant's closing argument." *Com. v. Knap*, 412 Mass 712, 716-717, 592 NE2d 747, 749-750 (1992). See also *Com. v. Sowell*, 22 Mass App 959, 961, 494 NE2d 1359, 1362-1363 (1986). Nor is a judge required to instruct on defendant's evidence of consciousness of innocence (such as nonflight). *Com. v. Lam*, supra, 420 Mass at 619-620, 650 NE2d at 799.

"Consciousness of liability" may be shown in civil cases by evidence of the following:

- leaving the scene of an accident without identifying oneself, *Olofson v. Kilgallon*, 362 Mass 803, 806, 291 NE2d 600, 602-603 (1973); but see *Kelliher v. General Transportation Services*, 29 F3d 750, 754 (1st Cir 1995) (there must be evidence that defendant knew he had been involved in an accident before leaving scene in order to entitle plaintiff to instruction);
- evasive conduct and false statements to police, *Parsons v. Ryan*, 340 Mass 245, 248, 163 NE2d 293, 295 (1960);
- giving a false name, *Rich v. Finley*, 325 Mass 99, 105, 89 NE2d 213, 216 (1949);
- testimony by a litigant that the jury could have found to be intentionally false and inconsistent with statements made out of court, *Sheehan v. Goriansky*, 317 Mass 10, 16-17, 56 NE2d 883, 886 (1944);
- conveying one's property away immediately before action was begun, *Credit Service Corp. v. Barker*, 308 Mass 476, 481, 33 NE2d 293, 295 (1941); compare *Matteo v. Livingston*, 40 Mass App 658, 663-664, 666 NE2d 1309, 1313 (1996) (defendant's conveyance of property five years after accident and two years after lawsuit was filed was temporally too remote);

- suborning a witness to testify falsely, bribing a juror, or suppressing evidence, *Bennett v. Susser*, 191 Mass 329, 331, 77 NE 884, 885 (1906) (& citations).

Such evidence will not, however, warrant submitting a case to the jury where there is no other evidence of liability. *Miles v. Caples*, 362 Mass 107, 114, 284 NE2d 231, 236 (1972); *Parsons v. Ryan*, supra, 340 Mass at 249, 163 NE2d at 296; *Credit Service Corp. v. Barker*, supra, 308 Mass at 481, 33 NE2d at 295.

§4.2.2　Statistical and Probabilistic Evidence

Although it has been said that "the admission of evidence of statistical probability is disfavored in this Commonwealth," *Com. v. Beausoleil*, 397 Mass 206, 217 n.15, 490 NE2d 788, 795 n.15 (1986) (& citations) (HLA tests in paternity actions), such evidence may be admitted where the probabilities upon which the evidence depends are based on established empirical data rather than on speculation, and where the evidence is more probative than prejudicial. See, e.g., *Com. v. Gomes*, 403 Mass 258, 273-275, 526 NE2d 1270, 1279-1280 (1988) (genetic markers in bloodstain). See also §7.8.3.

§4.2.3　Negative Evidence

Testimony that something did *not* happen may be of probative value. Such negative testimony, however, is usually less reliable than positive testimony. A witness's failure to recall perceiving an event, for example, can often be explained by many hypotheses other than that the event did not occur—e.g., the witness may not have been in a position to perceive the event or may not have been paying attention. As the Supreme Judicial Court explained in *Schwartz v. Feinberg*, 306 Mass 331, 334-335, 28 NE2d 249,

250-251 (1940), such evidence is admissible on a proper foundation:

> There was no direct evidence to show . . . the condition or appearance of the stairway in question on any exact date. At best, the evidence relative to conditions or appearances goes no further than that the witnesses did not notice or see any [protruding] nail. . . . The probative value of testimony of witnesses as to sensory reactions depends upon the attendant circumstances. If it appears that there was no particular reason why their senses should, or should not, react, such testimony is merely negative and of no value as evidence. But, if the circumstances are such, and the witnesses are in a position where such reactions would have been likely to occur, then their failure to hear a signal that should have been given, or to see an object, is evidence from which it is permissible to draw the inference that the signal was not given or that the object was not there to be seen (citations omitted).

For similar examples of negative evidence, see *Nickerson v. Boston & M.R.R.*, 342 Mass 306, 173 NE2d 248 (1961), and *Slattery v. New York, N.H. & H.R.R. Co.*, 203 Mass 453, 457-458, 89 NE 622, 623-624 (1909) (no warning bell rung); *Byrne v. Dunn*, 296 Mass 184, 5 NE2d 10 (1936) (no warning horn blown); *Sodekson v. Lynch*, 314 Mass 161, 49 NE2d 901 (1943) (no will executed).

Evidence of the absence of a record may be admitted to establish that a particular event or transaction did not occur. See, e.g., *Cohen v. Boston Edison Co.*, 322 Mass 239, 76 NE2d 766 (1948) (no bank ledger card belonging to plaintiff); *Com. v. Scanlan*, 9 Mass App 173, 181-182, 400 NE2d 1265, 1271 (1980) (citing Text) (witness may testify that he has examined records and did not find particular entry); *Johnson v. Wilmington Sales, Inc.*, 5 Mass App 858, 364 NE2d 1291 (1977) (lack of entry in cash journal admissible to show absence of cash payment). Compare *Bouley v. Reisman*, 38 Mass App 118, 123, 645 NE2d 708, 712 (1995) (evidence that there was no notation of telephone call from defendant doctor did not necessarily warrant jury's drawing inference that doctor did not make call).

For cases admitting evidence of lack of complaints, see §8.2.7, infra.

It is well established that disbelief of testimony does not of itself warrant a finding that the contrary fact is true. See *Com. v. Michaud*, 389 Mass 491, 498, 451 NE2d 396, 400 (1983); *Com. v. Eramo*, 377 Mass 912, 387 NE2d 558 (1979); *Com. v. Marino*, 343 Mass 725, 728, 180 NE2d 662, 664 (1962); *Fraser v. Fraser*, 336 Mass 597, 147 NE2d 165 (1958); *Hopping v. Whirlaway, Inc.*, 37 Mass App 121, 126, 637 NE2d 866, 869 (1994); *Atkinson v. Rosenthal*, 33 Mass App 219, 224, 598 NE2d 666, 669-670 (1992); *Kunkel v. Alger*, 10 Mass App 76, 86, 406 NE2d 402, 408-409 (1980).

§4.3   Discretion to Exclude Relevant Evidence

Even if determined to be relevant, evidence may nonetheless be excluded within the sound discretion of the trial judge because its probative value is outweighed by the risk of confusion, surprise, undue consumption of time, or unfair prejudice to the opposing party. See *Com. v. Lewin (No. 2)*, 407 Mass 629, 631, 555 NE2d 557, 558-559 (1990); *Com. v. Mandeville*, 386 Mass 393, 398-399, 436 NE2d 912, 918 (1982); *Green v. Richmond*, 369 Mass 47, 59-60, 337 NE2d 691, 699 (1975); Proposed Mass R Evid 403.[1] "[T]rial judges must take care to avoid exposing the jury unnecessarily to inflammatory material that might inflame the jurors' emotions and possibly deprive the defendant of an impartial jury." *Com. v. Berry*, 420 Mass 95, 109, 648 NE2d 732, 741 (1995). In balancing probative value against risk

---

§4.3   [1]"Although relevant, evidence may be excluded if its probative value is substantially outweighed by the danger of unfair prejudice, confusion of the issues, or misleading the jury, or considerations of undue delay, waste of time, or needless presentation of cumulative evidence." PMRE 403.

of prejudice, the fact that the evidence goes to a central issue in the case weighs in favor of admission. See *Com. v. Medeiros*, 395 Mass 336, 352, 479 NE2d 1371, 1381 (1985); *Com. v. Lamoureux*, 348 Mass 390, 204 NE2d 115 (1965).

By way of example, prejudice was sufficiently demonstrated in *Com. v. LaSota*, 29 Mass App 15, 557 NE2d 34 (1990), where defendant's conviction for rape and abuse of his daughter was reversed because a pamphlet found among his papers had been admitted into evidence. Underlined passages spoke favorably about incest. In holding that the admission constituted palpable error, the court observed:

> Even if we were to ascribe some probative value to the pamphlet, its prejudicial potential and probable impact were considerable. The ideas expressed in the pamphlet were likely to offend the jury. The prosecutor's use of the pamphlet, and particularly her numerous references to it as "that Penthouse publication," sought to make the most of probable juror revulsion so as to depict the defendant as a lewd man and to lead the jury to believe that a man of his character would be likely to commit the crimes charged.

29 Mass App at 26-27, 557 NE2d at 40-42 (citations and internal quotes omitted). Similarly in *Com. v. Lewin (No. 2)*, supra, 407 Mass at 631-632, 555 NE2d at 558-559, the court affirmed an order excluding from evidence the homicide defendant's statement (made while detained in a holding cell) that he would be agreeable to pleading guilty to manslaughter. Noting that the statement was of probative value but nonetheless might be weighed heavily by the jury as an admission of guilt, the court concluded: "The judge could draw on his knowledge and particular experiences with the case in balancing the factors of probative value and prejudicial effect and in deciding whether exclusion of the evidence was necessary in the interests of a fair trial." 407 Mass at 632, 555 NE2d at 559. See also *Com. v. Demars*, 38 Mass App 596, 650 NE2d 368 (1995) (prejudicial impact

of testimony suggesting defendant had previously engaged in sexual misconduct far outweighed its relevance); *Com. v. Fallon*, 38 Mass App 366, 648 NE2d 767 (1995) (defendant unfairly prejudiced by reference to his incarceration for civil contempt for discovery violations in victim's civil suit); *Com. v. Benitez*, 37 Mass App 722, 643 NE2d 468 (1994) (defendant unfairly prejudiced by evidence of 900 packets of heroin seized from supplier's apartment).

Whether the probative value of evidence is outweighed by its prejudicial effect is, like the question of relevance itself, within the sound discretion of the trial judge, whose determination will be upheld on appeal unless there is palpable error. *Com. v. Woods*, 414 Mass 343, 355, 607 NE2d 1024, 1033 (1993); *Com. v. Roderick*, 411 Mass 817, 819, 586 NE2d 967, 968-969 (1992). In reviewing such determinations, the effectiveness of limiting instructions in minimizing the risk of prejudice will be considered. In *Com. v. Dunn*, 407 Mass 798, 807, 556 NE2d 30, 35-36 (1990), for example, the defendant argued that the trial judge erred in admitting evidence that the murder victim, his wife, was pregnant at the time of her death and carrying a 22-week-old fetus. Given other evidence indicating that the defendant believed someone other than himself was the father, the evidence was held to be highly relevant in proving motive. Observing that "the chance of prejudice was minimized by a specific limiting instruction cautioning the jury to consider the testimony only on the issue of the defendant's state of mind at the time of the crime," the court concluded that the probative value outweighed the potential prejudicial effect. 407 Mass at 807, 556 NE2d at 807-808. See also *Com. v. Harvey*, 397 Mass 351, 358-359, 491 NE2d 607, 612 (1986) (judge's instruction to jury that it consider videotape evidence of witness solely on question of his sobriety, and not consider his allegations against defendant, sufficient to alleviate potential prejudice); *Com. v. Cruz*, 373 Mass 676, 692, 369 NE2d 996, 1006 (1977); *Com. v. Azar*, 32 Mass App 290, 300, 588 NE2d 1352, 1359-1360 (1992) (limiting instructions on prior injury evidence). Cf. *Com. v. Ashley*, 427 Mass 620, 625-626 n.5, 694 NE2d 862, 867 n.5 (1998) (judge limited use of photographs of defendant's girlfriend's car to aiding witnesses to identify car seen at shooting). For a discussion of the different standard for measuring prejudicial harm in bench trials, see *Com. v. Darby*, 37 Mass App 650, 655-656, 642 NE2d 303, 306 (1994).

On the admissibility of evidence concerning the effect of the crime on the victim, see *Com. v. Sanchez*, 405 Mass 369, 540 NE2d 1316 (1989) (evidence that child rape victim frequently awoke at night trembling and screaming tended to show he did not fabricate his story and was not unduly prejudicial); *Com. v. Gill*, 37 Mass App 457, 640 NE2d 798 (1994) (medical testimony concerning victim's extensive brain injuries relevant to establish that assault was intentional and to demonstrate reason for victim's lack of memory of incident). On the admissibility of evidence concerning the effect of the crime on the victim's family, compare *Com. v. Santiago*, 425 Mass 491, 497, 681 NE2d 1205, 1211 (1997) (testimony of victim's sister evoking sympathy improperly admitted) and *Com. v. Lorette*, 37 Mass App 746, 643 NE2d 67 (1994) (defendant unfairly prejudiced by testimony of rape victim's father that "this whole thing has ruined my life") with *Com. v. Murphy*, 426 Mass 395, 402, 688 NE2d 966, 972 (1998) (evidence that victim's two-year-old son was in room and possibly witnessed death of victim relevant in prosecution for murder by extreme atrocity or cruelty).

Another frequently recurring question balancing probative value and prejudicial harm is the admissibility of photographs of the victim. This matter is discussed at length in §11.6.

In sum, the legal concept of relevancy is made up of a blend of: (1) inherent probative value; (2) materiality; and (3) the discretionary application of safeguards against prejudicial unfairness, confusion, surprise, and undue consumption of time. Against this backdrop, several special rules operate to exclude certain categories of circumstantial evidence that repeatedly appear in the courts and in which probative value is generally outweighed by the risk of undue prejudice. Attention will now be turned to these categorical rules.

§4.4　Character Evidence

§4.4.1　General Inadmissibility of Character Evidence to Prove Conduct

As a general rule, evidence of a person's character is not admissible to prove that he acted in conformity with that character on a particular occasion. See *Com. v. Doherty*, 23 Mass App 633, 636-637, 504 NE2d 681, 683-684 (1987) (& citations); Proposed Mass R Evid 404(a).[1] Thus, for example, the plaintiff is not permitted to offer evidence that the defendant is a "careless person" or "accident prone" in order to establish an increased probability that he drove negligently at the time of the accident. See *Com. v. Mandell*, 29 Mass App 504, 507, 562 NE2d 111, 113 (1990). The prosecution is similarly barred from offering evidence that the accused is a "violent person" in order to demonstrate that he has a propensity to commit the crime charged (although, as we shall see at §4.4.2, such evidence may be offered once the defendant "opens the door" by offering favorable character evidence). *Com. v. Kozec*, 399 Mass 514, 525, 505 NE2d 519, 525-526 (1987).

Moreover, it generally is not permissible for purposes of proving that A did a particular act to show that he did a similar act at a prior or subsequent time. *Maillet v. ATF-Davidson Co.*, 407 Mass 185, 188, 552 NE2d 95, 97 (1990); *Della Jacova v. Widett*, 355 Mass 266, 274-275, 244 NE2d 580,

---

§4.4　[1] "Evidence of a person's character or a trait of his character is not admissible for the purpose of proving that he acted in conformity therewith on a particular occasion. . . ." PMRE 404(a).

586 (1969). See also Proposed Mass R Evid 404(b).[2] Thus, it may not be shown that the defendant had been negligent on a prior occasion in order to create an inference that he was negligent at the time of the litigated event. See *Com. v. Mandell,* 29 Mass App 504, 507, 562 NE2d 111, 113 (1990) (affirming trial judge's exclusion of testimony that defendant had previously caused minor accidents). Nor may it be shown that a criminal defendant has committed a crime on a prior occasion to raise an inference of guilt on the charges in issue. *Com. v. Bassett,* 21 Mass App 713, 717, 490 NE2d 459, 461 (1986). "This rule stems from the belief that such evidence forces the defendant to answer accusations not set forth in the indictment, confuses his defense, diverts the attention of the jury, and may create undue prejudice against him." *Com. v. Clifford,* 374 Mass 293, 298, 372 NE2d 1267, 1271 (1978).

The exclusion of character evidence, in both its general trait and specific act form, is referred to as the "propensity doctrine" because the purpose of such circumstantial evidence is to establish a propensity to act in a particular manner. It should be noted that this category of evidence is not disfavored strictly on relevance grounds, because in fact it may in certain contexts make it somewhat more likely that the subject acted in conformity with an established trait or pattern of conduct on the occasion in question. Rather, the rule of exclusion is premised on the high risk that such evidence will have a prejudicial impact on the jury and will result in a decision motivated by something other than the particular facts of the incident before the court.

Despite the general exclusion, character evidence is admissible in several contexts. First, a limited exception has

---

[2] "Evidence of other crimes, wrongs, or acts is not admissible to prove the character of a person in order to show that he acted in conformity therewith. It may, however, be admissible for other purposes, such as proof of motive, opportunity, intent, preparation, plan, knowledge, identity, or absence of mistake or accident." PMRE 404(b).

long been recognized for the character of the criminal defendant and the victim. See §§4.4.2 and 4.4.3. Second, character evidence is admissible in certain civil actions where the character of a party is directly in issue, such as defamation cases. See §4.4.5. Third, evidence of specific crimes, wrongs, or acts is admissible where it has relevance beyond mere propensity logic, as discussed in §4.4.6. Finally, evidence of poor character for truthfulness and veracity may be used to impeach the testimony of a witness at trial. See §6.10.

§4.4.2   *Character of the Criminal Defendant*

The prosecution may not offer evidence of the defendant's bad character as part of its case in chief. *Com. v. O'Brien*, 119 Mass 342 (1876); Proposed Mass R Evid 404(a). This prohibition includes evidence from which bad character may be inferred. Thus, for example, the fact that the defendant possessed weapons (not directly connected to the crime charged) has generally been excluded because of the unfavorable impact it might have on the jury. See *Com. v. Toro*, 395 Mass 354, 480 NE2d 19 (1985) (& cases cited). But compare *Com. v. Otsuki*, 411 Mass 218, 235-237, 581 NE2d 999, 1009-1010 (1991) (no error in admission of evidence that defendant was seen with handgun months before murder, because relevant to his possession of means to commit it); *Com. v. Sims*, 41 Mass App 902, 667 NE2d 1165 (1996) (no error in admitting evidence that defendant possessed handgun after shooting, where he testified he "never had a gun"). See also *Com. v. Morse*, 42 Mass App 936, 939, 678 NE2d 175, 178-179 (1997).

For other examples of "bad character" evidence, compare *Com. v. Harris*, 409 Mass 461, 469, 567 NE2d 899, 905 (1991) (testimony that witness warned victim that defendant might be carrying a knife, objected to as the "functional equivalent" of improper character evidence, should not be admitted on retrial), *Com. v. Kozec*, 399 Mass

514, 524, 525, 505 NE2d 519, 524-526 (1987) (admission of testimony that defendant was jello wrestler prejudicial error because it presented defendant in demeaning light), and *Com. v. Wolcott*, 28 Mass App 200, 210-211, 548 NE2d 1271, 1277 (1990) (testimony of police officer that defendant was member of street gang irrelevant and prejudicial) with *Com. v. Adams*, 416 Mass 55, 60, 617 NE2d 594, 597 (1993) (no error in admission of videotape of murder defendant smiling into camera just after arrest, over objection that it was introduced as improper character evidence to suggest lack of remorse, because relevant to claim that defendant had been beaten by police), *Com. v. Otsuki*, supra, 411 Mass at 237, 581 NE2d at 1010 (evidence that defendant was fugitive properly admitted as relevant to defendant's motive to flee when police arrived), and *Com. v. Drew*, 397 Mass 65, 78-79, 489 NE2d 1233, 1234 (1986) (evidence of defendant's participation in Satanic cult rituals at which murder victim was present admissible to show relationship between victim and defendant). It has been recognized that aliases can be suggestive of bad character and prior criminality and thus present a risk of unfair prejudice. See *Com. v. Carter*, 423 Mass 505, 515, 669 NE2d 203, 208 (1996). But compare *Com. v. Manning*, 44 Mass App 695, 705, 693 NE2d 704, 712 (1998) (testimony that defendant had used aliases properly admitted as relevant to issue of identity of shooter).

For a discussion of the unique issues raised by evidence that the defendant has AIDS or has tested positive for HIV, see *Com. v. Martin*, 424 Mass 301, 304-306, 676 NE2d 451, 453-455 (1997) (rape victim's testimony that she was informed by defendant that he had tested positive for HIV relevant on issue of consent).

It is "well settled that the prosecution may not introduce evidence that a defendant previously has misbehaved, indictably or not, for the purposes of showing his bad character, or propensity to commit the crime charged." *Com. v. Helfant*, 398 Mass 214, 224, 496 NE2d 433, 440-441 (1986). See also *Com. v. Otsuki*, supra, 411 Mass at 236, 581

NE2d at 1009-1010; *Com. v. Trapp*, 396 Mass 202, 206, 485 NE2d 162, 165-166 (1985); *Com. v. Nassar*, 351 Mass 37, 44-46, 218 NE2d 72, 78-79 (1966) (error to admit testimony of police officers as to conversation at time of murder defendant's arrest in which officer referred to defendant's involvement in the "same thing" many years before); *Com. v. Welcome*, 348 Mass 68, 70-71, 201 NE2d 827, 828-829 (1964) (error to admit testimony, in prosecution for indecent assault on minor female, that defendant admitted having been "involved in something like this before" with other little girls); *Com. v. McClendon*, 39 Mass App 122, 126-128, 653 NE2d 1138, 1141-1142 (1995) (error to admit evidence regarding murder defendant's bad temper when drinking and alleged prior attempt to strangulate stepmother). Compare *Com. v. Vanetzian*, 350 Mass 491, 494-495, 215 NE2d 658, 661 (1966) and *Com. v. Lacey*, 2 Mass App 889, 318 NE2d 843 (1974) (vague reference to prior misconduct of defendant harmless); *Com. v. Evans*, 415 Mass 422, 424-426, 614 NE2d 653, 656 (1993) (no error allowing Commonwealth to rehabilitate witness on redirect even though testimony permitted inference that defendant had prior criminal record); *Com. v. Grammo*, 8 Mass App 447, 395 NE2d 476 (1979) (judge's explicit instructions erased potential for error).

Evidence of other crimes, wrongs or acts may, however, be admissible if relevant for non-propensity purposes. See generally §4.4.6, infra.

Identification evidence such as "mug shot" photographs which might reveal to the jury that the defendant had been previously arrested or convicted must either be excluded or purged of any characteristics from which a prior record may be inferred. See *Com. v. Blaney*, 387 Mass 628, 634-640, 442 NE2d 389, 394-396 (1982) (& cases cited); *Com. v. Nassar*, supra, 351 Mass at 42-43, 218 NE2d at 77. But compare *Com. v. Picher*, 46 Mass App 409, 415-416, 706 NE2d 710, 715 (1999) (where defense claims misidentification and alibi, Commonwealth may admit mug shots to explain how defendant became suspect). *Blaney* includes an extensive discussion of the procedures to be followed to sanitize such evidence, including the testimony of witnesses who have previously viewed mug shots. See also *Com. v. Valentin*, 420 Mass 263, 270-272, 649 NE2d 1079, 1083-1084 (1995); *Com. v. Perez*, 405 Mass 339, 344, 540 NE2d 681, 684 (1989). For further discussion, see §10.1, infra.

According to long-standing practice, the accused may introduce evidence of his own good character to show that he is not the type of person to commit the crime charged. *Com. v. Belton*, 352 Mass 263, 265, 225 NE2d 53, 56-57 (1967); *Com. v. Beal*, 314 Mass 210, 230, 50 NE2d 14, 25 (1943); Proposed Mass R Evid 404(a)(1).[3] Reputation is the only permissible form of character evidence that may be offered for this purpose. See §4.4.4. When such evidence is offered by the accused and there is a proper foundation, it has been held that there is no discretion to exclude it. See *Com. v. Schmukler*, 22 Mass App 432, 437-438, 494 NE2d 48, 52 (1986).

Defendant's evidence is, however, limited to character traits that are relevant to the crime charged, such as peacefulness for assault crimes and honesty for crimes of fraud. Evidence of a character trait not pertinent to the crime charged is not admissible. See *Com. v. DeVico*, 207 Mass 251, 253, 93 NE 570 (1911) (evidence offered by defendant charged with assault that he was of an excitable disposition would have no tendency to show that he acted in self defense).

The Commonwealth has the right to cross-examine the defendant's character witnesses on matters that are inconsistent with the character trait to which the witness has testified, including reports of misconduct or criminal activity. *Michelson v. United States*, 335 US 469 (1948); *Com. v. Piedra*, 20 Mass App 155, 160-161, 478 NE2d 1284,

---

[3] "Evidence of a pertinent trait of his character offered by an accused, or by the prosecution to rebut the same is admissible." PMRE 404(a)(1).

1288-1289 (1985) (& cases cited). "The credibility of the [reputation] witness is tested in the following manner—if the witness states that he has not heard of the report of prior misconduct, his professed knowledge of the defendant's reputation in the community may be doubted by the jury or, if he states that he has heard of the report but still testifies that the defendant's reputation is good in the community, the jury may consider whether the witness is fabricating or whether the community standards in regard to character are too low." *Com. v. Montanino*, 27 Mass App 130, 136, 535 NE2d 617, 621 (1989). See also *Com. v. Brown*, 411 Mass 115, 118, 579 NE2d 153, 155 (1991) (witness who testifies to defendant's reputation for truthfulness may be cross-examined as to allegedly false statements defendant made as to his military record). Proposed Mass R Evid 405(a) is in accord with the case law.[4] Thus, in the absence of a showing of bad faith, a prosecutor may ask a witness called to testify to the defendant's good character whether she has heard that the defendant had committed certain criminal acts. The defendant is entitled to a limiting instruction to protect against undue prejudice. *Com. v. Piedra*, supra, 20 Mass App at 161, 478 NE2d at 1286-1287.

Once the accused has "opened the door" by offering evidence of good character, the prosecution may present in rebuttal evidence of defendant's bad character through its own reputation witnesses. *Com. v. Maddocks*, 207 Mass 152, 157, 93 NE 253, 254 (1910); Proposed Mass R Evid 404(a)(1).

When character evidence is admitted, its weight is left to the jury; and if a reasonable doubt of guilt is generated from such evidence in the mind of the jury, it is its duty to acquit. *Com. v. Leonard*, 140 Mass 473, 479-481, 4 NE 96, 101 (1886). Under Massachusetts law, however, the defendant has no right to a specific instruction that favorable character evidence itself may create a reasonable doubt; it is

---

[4]"On cross examination [of a character witness], inquiry is allowable into relevant specific instances of conduct." PMRE 405(a).

sufficient if the judge adequately charges the jury on the burden of proof and how to evaluate the evidence generally. See *Com. v. Dilone*, 385 Mass 281, 288-289, 431 NE2d 576, 581 (1982); *Com. v. Simmons*, 383 Mass 40, 42-44, 417 NE2d 430, 431-432 (1981). The federal circuit courts are split on whether the defendant is entitled to the "standing alone" instruction, and the Supreme Court has not resolved the conflict. See *Spangler v. United States*, 487 US 1224, 108 S Ct 2884, 101 L Ed 2d 918 (1988) (& citations) (White, J, dissenting from denial of certiorari).

§4.4.3   Character of the Victim in a Criminal Case

a.   Self-Defense

In criminal cases, the character of the alleged victim may be relevant to the issue of the defendant's guilt, and an exception to the general rule against propensity evidence is recognized in certain situations. Thus, the defendant in a prosecution for homicide or assault and battery may offer evidence of the victim's character for violence when the defendant asserts a claim of self-defense, but under the Massachusetts rule he may do so only if he shows that the violent character of the victim was known to him prior to the incident in question.[5] *Com. v. Edmonds*, 365 Mass 496, 499-504, 313 NE2d 429, 432-433 (1974); *Com. v. Connolly*, 356 Mass 617, 625-626, 255 NE2d 191, 197-198 (1970). See also *Com. v. Papadinis*, 23 Mass App 570, 503 NE2d 1334 (1987) (error to exclude evidence offered by murder defendant of what he had heard and read about police officer victim, because relevant to explain his fear of victim); *Com. v. Kamishlian*, 21 Mass App 931, 933, 486

---

[5] Compare Fed R Evid 404(a)(2), which does not impose a requirement of knowledge on the part of the defendant, and thus permits evidence respecting the victim to be used for a propensity purpose — i.e., to suggest that the "victim" had been violent in the past and may have been the aggressor on the occasion in question.

NE2d 743, 746 (1985) (no error in excluding evidence that assault victim was known by nickname "Weapon," because even if equivalent to showing reputation for violence, there was no evidence that defendant knew of victim's nickname); *Com. v. Fortini,* 44 Mass App 562, 566-568, 692 NE2d 110, 113-114 (1998) (no prejudice to defendant in excluding evidence of victim's involvement in violent episode shortly before defendant shot him, where defendant did not know of episode at time). The knowledge requirement results from the fact that "the victim's reputation for violence is relevant solely on the issue of reasonable apprehension, and, accordingly, admissible only if the defendant has knowledge of the reputation." Advisory Committee Note, Proposed Mass R Evid 404. See also *Com. v. Dilone,* 385 Mass 281, 431 NE2d 576 (1982).

Evidence of the victim's violent character is admissible in reputation form, but not as the private opinion of a witness. *Com. v. Connolly,* supra, 356 Mass 617, 313 NE2d 429. It is not necessary for the defendant himself to take the stand to offer such testimony; other witnesses may testify to the victim's reputation and to the defendant's knowledge of that reputation. *Com. v. Edmonds,* supra, 365 Mass at 502, 313 NE2d at 433. It is necessary that a proper foundation be shown as to defendant's knowledge. *Com. v. Gibson,* 368 Mass 518, 525-527, 333 NE2d 400, 406 (1975).

In 1986, the Supreme Judicial Court adopted a new rule permitting introduction of evidence of a victim's specific acts of violence toward third persons, and known to the homicide defendant, to prove that at the time of the killing the defendant reasonably believed he was in imminent danger.[6] *Com. v. Fontes,* 396 Mass 733, 488 NE2d 760 (1986). See also *Com. v. Pidge,* 400 Mass 350, 509 NE2d 281

---

[6] Evidence of the victim's threats of violence against the defendant, even if unknown to him, has long been held admissible as tending to show that the victim was attempting to carry out the threat. *Com. v. Rubin,* 318 Mass 587, 588-589, 63 NE2d 344, 345 (1945); *Com. v. Young,* 35 Mass App 427, 442-443, 621 NE2d 1180, 1189 (1993).

(1987) (evidence that defendant was told on night of killing of previous assaults committed by victim admissible on claim of self-defense). The incidents must be close in time to the killing and not remote, a matter for the discretion of the trial judge. *Com. v. Fontes*, supra, 396 Mass at 736, 488 NE2d at 762-763; *Com. v. Phachansiri*, 38 Mass App 100, 105-106, 645 NE2d 60, 63-64 (1995) (evidence of victim's violent acts nine years before homicide too remote). Recognizing the potential risks of admitting such evidence—i.e., the intrusion of collateral points and the propensity inference created by the negative information about the victim—the *Fontes* court nonetheless concluded that a "jury assessing the reasonableness of the defendant's reaction to the events leading to the homicide should in fairness have that information." 396 Mass at 737, 488 NE2d at 763. Compare *Com. v. Kosilek*, 423 Mass 449, 458-459, 668 NE2d 808, 815 (1996) (no error in excluding evidence that victim had used physical force to discipline her son); *Com. v. Doherty*, 23 Mass 633, 636-637, 504 NE2d 681, 683-684 (1987) (no error in excluding evidence of victim's aggressive behavior toward third parties where defendant had already been permitted to inquire concerning victim's reputation for violence and acts of violent behavior directed against, or committed in presence of, defendant); *Com. v. Zitano*, 23 Mass App 403, 405-406, 502 NE2d 952, 954-955 (1987) (no error where record revealed defense counsel made no offer at trial to prove specific incidents of violence).

When admitted, there is no requirement that a judge specifically instruct the jury as to the relevance of the defendant's knowledge of the victim's character for violence. *Com. v. Simmons*, 383 Mass 40, 42-43, 417 NE2d 430, 432 (1981). The trial judge would, however, be "well advised to point out to the jury the limited purpose for which the evidence has been admitted"—i.e., it is to be considered solely on the question of the defendant's reasonable apprehension of danger, and not to show that the victim was more likely to have been the aggressor. *Com. v. Fontes,* supra, 396 Mass at 736 n.1, 488 NE2d at 763 n.1.

Once the defense has opened the door on the issue of the victim's violent character, the prosecution can rebut with evidence of the victim's reputation for peacefulness. *Com. v. Lapointe,* 402 Mass 321, 325, 522 NE2d 937, 939-940 (1988). Such evidence may not, however, be admitted unless and until the defense presents some evidence of the victim's violent character. An opening statement by the defense attorney is not evidence and thus does not constitute opening the door on the issue of the victim's character. *Com. v. Lapointe,* supra, 402 Mass at 325, 522 NE2d at 939-940.

Evidence of specific violent acts directed at the defendant by the victim, and not too remote in time, are relevant to the defense of self-defense. See *Com. v. Rodriquez,* 418 Mass 1, 633 NE2d 1039 (1994) (exclusion of evidence of prior abuse required new trial). See also GL 233, §23F, added by St 1996, c450, §248[7] (making admissible evidence that defendant suffered abuse as well as expert testimony concerning patterns of abusive relationships).

---

[7]   In the trial of criminal cases charging the use of force against another where the issue of defense of self or another, defense of duress or coercion, or accidental harm is asserted, a defendant shall be permitted to introduce either or both of the following in establishing the reasonableness of the defendant's apprehension that death or serious bodily injury was imminent, the reasonableness of the defendant's belief that he had availed himself of all available means to avoid physical combat or the reasonableness of a defendant's perception of the amount of force necessary to deal with the perceived threat:

    (a) evidence that the defendant is or has been the victim of acts of physical, sexual or psychological harm or abuse;

    (b) evidence by expert testimony regarding the common pattern in abusive relationships; the nature and effects of physical, sexual or psychological abuse and typical responses thereto, including how those effects relate to the perception of the imminent nature of the threat of death or serious bodily harm; the relevant facts and circumstances which form the basis for such opinion; and evidence whether the defendant displayed characteristics common to victims of abuse.

    Nothing in this section shall be interpreted to preclude the introduction of evidence or expert testimony as described in clause (a) or (b) in any civil or criminal action where such evidence or expert testimony is otherwise now admissible.

b.   "Rape Shield" Statute

A second situation where the character of the victim may be relevant to the defendant's guilt is in rape cases. In a prosecution for rape, assault with intent to rape, or indecent assault, the defense often is that the complaining witness gave her consent to the sexual act. In this instance, the Massachusetts rule until 1977 was that the defendant could offer evidence of the unchaste character of the victim. *Com. v. Gouveia*, 371 Mass 566, 569, 358 NE2d 1001, 1003-1004 (1976).

This matter is now governed by GL 233, §21B (added by St 1977, c110). Aimed at eliminating a common defense strategy of placing the complaining witness "on trial," resulting in the further humiliation of the victim and the discouragement of other victims from coming forward, see *Com. v. Joyce*, 382 Mass 222, 415 NE2d 181 (1981), the "rape shield" law provides:

> Evidence of the reputation of a victim's sexual conduct shall not be admissible in any investigation or proceeding before a grand jury or any court of the Commonwealth for a violation of sections thirteen B, thirteen F, thirteen H, twenty-two, twenty-two A, twenty-three, twenty-four and twenty-four B of chapter two hundred and sixty-five or section five of chapter two hundred and seventy-two [indecent assault and battery on child under fourteen; indecent assault and battery on mentally retarded person; indecent assault and battery on person fourteen or older; rape; rape of a child; assault with intent to commit rape; assault of a child with intent to commit rape]. Evidence of specific instances of a victim's sexual conduct in such an investigation or proceeding shall not be admissible except evidence of the victim's sexual conduct with the defendant or evidence of recent conduct of the victim alleged to be the cause of any physical feature, characteristic, or condition of the victim; provided, however, that such evidence shall be admissible only after an in camera hearing on a written motion for admission of same and an offer of proof. If, after said hearing, the court finds that the weight and relevancy of said

evidence is sufficient to outweigh its prejudicial effect to the victim, the evidence shall be admitted; otherwise not. If the proceeding is a trial with jury, said hearing shall be held in the absence of the jury. The finding of the court shall be in writing and filed but shall not be made available to the jury.[8]

Evidence of the victim's reputation for promiscuity as well as specific acts of sexual conduct is excluded because such evidence "tends to put the witness on trial, it can be highly prejudicial to the prosecution, it tends to encourage litigation of collateral matters, and it has little probative value on the issue of consent." *Com. v. Simcock*, 31 Mass App 184, 197-198, 575 NE2d 1137, 1144-1145 (1991) (internal quotation omitted). For a general discussion of GL 233, §21B, see Burnim, Massachusetts Rape Shield Law—An Overstep in the Right Direction, 64 Mass L Rev 61 (1979); *Com. v. Thevenin*, 33 Mass App 588, 591, 603 NE2d 222, 225 (1992) (apart from rape shield statute, defendant would have right to introduce evidence concerning his state of mind tending to disprove criminal act, such as evidence of victim's past sexual conduct); *Com. v. Edgerly*, 13 Mass App 562, 565-569, 435 NE2d 641, 644-645 (1982). See also *Com. v. McGregor*, 39 Mass App 919, 655 NE2d 1278 (1995) (evidence that male rape victim had previously engaged in homosexual activities and that defendant, based on what he had been told concerning victim's sexuality, had good faith belief that victim consented to intercourse not admissible).

The statutory exceptions authorize admission of evidence of specific acts of sexual conduct by the victim in two contexts: (1) where the prior acts were with the defendant; or (2) where the acts are offered to explain the victim's physical condition subsequent to the alleged crime, such as the presence of semen or bruises in the vaginal area.[9] Prior

---

[8] Fed R Evid 412 is comparable to GL 233, §21B, in excluding evidence of the victim's character but permitting the introduction of evidence of specific acts of sexual conduct in specified situations.

[9] Case law and constitutional exceptions are discussed below.

acts of intercourse of the victim with the defendant may be relevant to the issue of consent, particularly if there is a pattern of recent consensual activity. See, e.g, *Com. v. Grieco*, 386 Mass 484, 436 NE2d 167 (1982). Compare *Com. v. Fionda*, 33 Mass App 316, 321-322, 599 NE2d 635, 638-639 (1992) (primary issue pertaining to relevance of prior activities with defendant is consent; provocative conversation and kissing on prior occasion not probative of consent to intercourse on later occasion). Prior acts with another person may be relevant to establishing an alternative cause for the victim's physical condition. See, e.g., *Com. v. Fitzgerald*, 402 Mass 517, 524 NE2d 72 (1988), and *Com. v. Fitzgerald*, 412 Mass 516, 590 NE2d 1151 (1992) (citing Text) (presence of sperm, where defendant had had vasectomy); *Com. v. Cardoza*, 29 Mass App 645, 647-648, 563 NE2d 1384, 1386-1387 (1990) (evidence of presence on victim of foreign pubic hair not belonging to defendant improperly excluded where offered not to show complainant's sexual behavior but on issue of identification). Compare *Com. v. Martin*, 424 Mass 301, 312-313, 676 NE2d 451, 458-459 (1997) (testimony that victim was with another man on night of rape properly excluded where no particularity as to time-frame or identity of man).

Lack of virginity is not generally deemed a "condition" under the exception in GL 233, §21B, which would justify the admission of prior sexual conduct by way of explanation. *Com. v. Elder*, 389 Mass 743, 452 NE2d 1104, 1111 (1983). "Normally, lack of virginity cannot be linked to the time of the rape, nor can the identity of the sexual partner be determined from this physical characteristic. Evidence of lack of virginity is unlike evidence of the presence of sperm, bruises in the vaginal area, and other data which are more relevant to the proof of rape. Since lack of virginity has such a tenuous connection to most rape cases, it ordinarily should not be admitted." Id.

Specific act evidence is admissible under the exceptions in GL 233, §21B, only after a written motion for admission, an offer of proof, and an in camera hearing in which the judge determines (and makes a finding in writing) that the prejudicial effect to the victim is outweighed by the probative value of the evidence. See *Com. v. Grieco,* supra, 386 Mass at 488-489, 436 NE2d at 170-171. Failure to comply with these requirements is "no trifling procedural omission; the sharply limited exception to the rape shield statute is not to be made available on the basis of surprise and snap reaction by a trial judge." *Com. v. Gauthier,* 32 Mass App 130, 133, 586 NE2d 34 (1992).

When a defendant seeks to admit evidence under one of the statutory exceptions, he must have a demonstrable good faith basis for asking any question even remotely connected with complainant's sexual conduct, *Com. v. Mosby,* 11 Mass App 1, 413 NE2d 754 (1980); and he must make a preliminary showing that the theory under which he proceeds is based on more than mere hope or speculation. *Com. v. Chretien,* 383 Mass. 123, 138, 417 NE2d 1203, 1210 (1981) (judge properly refused to permit defendant to question victim in front of jury regarding her sexual activities with other men, for purpose of explaining the presence of semen, when victim categorically denied out of presence of jury that she had had any contacts with other men for one week prior to event); *Com. v. Hynes,* 40 Mass App 927, 929, 664 NE2d 864, 867 (1996) (no evidence to support defendant's contention that victim confused incidents of abuse by third party); *Com. v. Whitman,* 29 Mass App 972, 561 NE2d 525 (1990).

Even for matters covered by GL 233, §21B, the statute is not always interpreted strictly. Where the proponent of evidence of prior sexual conduct is not seeking to use it for a purpose forbidden by the statute—i.e., to attack the victim's credibility by depicting her as promiscuous—the inquiry may be viewed as outside the scope of the statute. See *Com. v. Thevenin,* supra, 33 Mass App at 592, 603 NE2d at 225-226 (& citations); *Com. v. Baxter,* 36 Mass App 45, 51, 627 NE2d 487, 491 (1994) (statute did not require exclusion of evidence that complainant had previously been raped, offered to show that resulting psychiatric problems and similarities to present incident rendered her unable to distinguish between the two situations). But compare *Com. v. Syrafos*, 38 Mass App 211, 217-219, 646 NE2d 429, 433 (1994).

Thus, evidence of specific instances of a complainant's sexual conduct has been held admissible where it is relevant to show the complainant's bias.[10] In *Com. v. Joyce*, 382 Mass 222, 415 NE2d 181 (1981), defendant unsuccessfully sought to introduce evidence that the rape complainant had been charged with prostitution on two prior occasions; his purpose was to show that her allegation may have been motivated by a desire to avoid further prosecution. Emphasizing that it was not departing from the policy of the statute in viewing evidence of prostitution or lack of chastity as inadmissible, the court held: "Where, however, such facts are relevant to a showing of bias or motive to lie, the general evidentiary rule of exclusion must give way to the constitutionally based right of effective cross-examination." 382 Mass at 231, 415 NE2d at 187. But compare *Com. v. Houston*, 46 Mass App 378, 379-381, 706 NE2d 308, 310 (1999) (where no showing that evidence was relevant to bias or motive to lie, victim's prior conviction for prostitution-related offenses was properly excluded). See also *Com. v. Stockhammer*, 409 Mass 867, 873-880, 570 NE2d 992, 996-1001 (1991) (trial judge erred in preventing defense counsel from pursuing on cross-examination questions designed to demonstrate that rape complainant was motivated to lie because she did not want her parents to learn that she was sexually active with boyfriend); *Com. v. McGregor*, supra, 39 Mass App 919, 655 NE2d 1278 (exclusion of previous statements made by victim of homosexual prison rape that could have shown motive to lie created substantial risk of miscarriage of justice); *Com. v. Shaw*, 29 Mass App 39, 43, 556 NE2d 1058, 1060 (1990) (discussing line of cases admitting evidence of victim's sexual relation-

---

[10] For a general discussion of bias, see generally §6.9.

ship with third party to demonstrate motive to fabricate rape accusation against defendant).

Compare *Com. v. Pearce*, 427 Mass 642, 647-648, 695 NE2d 1059, 1063-1064 (1998) (relevance of evidence that victim had been previously molested and raped, offered to demonstrate bias, outweighed by prejudicial effect to victim); *Com. v. Frey*, 390 Mass 245, 250-252, 454 NE2d 478, 481-482 (1983) (evidence of statutory rape complainant's prior sexual conduct not admissible where only marginally probative of bias); *Com. v. Elder*, 389 Mass 743, 749-751, 452 NE2d 1104, 1109-1110 (1983) (evidence of complainant's prior sexual conduct inadmissible where defendant was able to elicit evidence of hostility and bias without the proffered evidence); *Com. v. Gagnon*, 45 Mass App 584, 587-589, 699 NE2d 1260, 1263-1264 (1998) (same); *Com. v. Herrick*, 39 Mass App 291, 294-295, 655 NE2d 637, 639-640 (1995) (by merely offering at voir dire that victim was romantically involved with third party, defendant failed to make plausible showing of motive to lie); *Com. v. Pyne*, 35 Mass App 36, 38, 616 NE2d 470, 471 (1993) ("When other evidence of bias is available, evidence of a complainant's prior sexual history should not be admitted."); *Com. v. Heath*, 24 Mass App 437, 441-445, 509 NE2d 1212, 1214-1217 (1987) (no prejudice in exclusion of questions on cross-examination of rape victim concerning her relationship to her boyfriend where other evidence of possible motive to fabricate had been admitted).

In prosecutions for rape or indecent assault on a child, prior sexual abuse of the victim may be admissible (with proper instructions to the jury) to show knowledge about sexual acts and terminology apart from any experience with the defendant. *Com. v. Ruffen*, 399 Mass 811, 814-816, 507 NE2d 684, 686-688 (1987); *Com. v. Rathburn*, 26 Mass App 699, 706-708, 532 NE2d 691, 695-697 (1988). But compare *Com. v. Pyne*, supra, 35 Mass App at 37-38 (no abuse of discretion in excluding evidence of prior sexual experiences of alleged statutory rape victim to show alternative source of knowledge of sexual matters where victim's testimony did not display knowledge extraordinary to teenage boy). The defendant must have a good faith basis for the inquiry, upon which showing the judge should permit voir dire to determine whether the child has been a victim of prior sexual abuse that is factually similar to the abuse in the case on trial. See *Com. v. Walker*, 426 Mass 301, 306, 687 NE2d 1246, 1250 (1997) (& citations) (insufficient foundation to require voir dire); *Com. v. Scheffer*, 43 Mass App 398, 683 NE2d 1043 (1997).

Evidence of prior false allegations of rape is not a matter covered by GL 233, §21B, and may be admissible to impeach a complainant. See *Com. v. Bohannon*, 376 Mass 90, 378 NE2d 987 (1978) (*Bohannon I*) (trial judge erred in excluding evidence of prior false accusations of rape made by complainant where her credibility as to consent was the critical issue in the case, her testimony was inconsistent and confused, and defendant made offer of proof indicating an independent factual basis for concluding the prior allegations were false). Such allegations may be admitted only if there is evidence of falsity. See *Com. v. Scanlon*, 412 Mass 664, 675-676, 592 NE2d 1279, 1285-1286 (1992) ("No evidence was proffered which would create a basis to conclude that any prior accusation was made falsely. A mere hope of recantation is not a justification for a fishing expedition under the guise of the *Bohannon* rule."); *Com. v. Vieira*, 401 Mass 828, 838-839, 519 NE2d 1320, 1326-1327 (1988); *Com. v. McDonough*, 400 Mass 639, 650, 511 NE2d 551, 558 (1987); *Com. v. Sherry*, 386 Mass 682, 691-693, 437 NE2d 224, 230-231 (1982). See also *Com. v. Pyne*, supra, 35 Mass App at 38-41 (trial court abused discretion by denying defense counsel's request for brief continuance or leave to conduct voir dire to determine whether alleged statutory rape victim had falsely accused another woman of sexual abuse).

The false allegations cannot be shown by incompetent hearsay evidence. *Com. v. Bohannon*, 385 Mass 733, 749-752, 434 NE2d 163, 172-174 (1982) (*Bohannon II*). Rather, there must be a basis in independent third-party records for concluding that the prior accusations were made and were false. *Com. v. Fruchtman*, 418 Mass 8, 17-18, 633 NE2d 369, 374 (1994); *Com. v. Hrycenko*, 417 Mass 309, 319, 630 NE2d 258, 264 (1994).

Evidence that the victim failed to pursue the prior accusation is not evidence that it was falsely made. Id. Nor is the circumstance that authorities did not pursue the case sufficient basis for inferring falsity. *Com. v. Wise*, 39 Mass App 922, 655 NE2d 643 (1995).

The *Bohannon* exception has been held to apply even though the false allegations were made *after* the complaint against defendant. See *Com. v. Nichols*, 37 Mass App 332, 639 NE2d 1088 (1994).

The court has characterized *Bohannon I* as a narrow exception applicable in "special circumstances." *Com. v. Sperrazza*, 379 Mass 166, 169, 396 NE2d 449, 451 (1979). See also *Com. v. Haynes*, 45 Mass App 192, 199-201, 696 NE2d 555, 560-561 (1998) (prior accusation was not of "crying wolf" type and was not part of pattern; complainant's testimony was neither inconsistent nor confused); *Com. v. LaVelle*, 33 Mass App 36, 39, 596 NE2d 364, 366-367 (1992) (exception not applicable to informer's false accusation of threats); *Com. v. Rathburn*, supra, 26 Mass App 699, 532 NE2d 691.

The Commonwealth is under no obligation to seek information on behalf of the defendant concerning previously reported sexual assaults. See *Com. v. Beal*, 429 Mass 530, 533 n.2, 709 NE2d 413, 416 n.2 (1999).

In certain instances, exclusion of evidence falling squarely within the prohibitions of GL 233, §21B has been found to conflict impermissibly with the defendant's constitutional right to present a full defense. See *Com. v. Thevenin*, supra, 33 Mass App at 592-594, 603 NE2d at 225-227 (& citations) (evidence that defendant had been told by friend that he had had intercourse with victim and developed pubic lice as result highly relevant to defense; but rejecting "an open-ended exception for state-of-mind evidence concerning a defendant's fear of contacting a disease"). See also *Com. v. Baxter*, supra, 36 Mass App at 52, 627 NE2d at 491 (& citations).[11]

Although GL 233, §21B, does not by its terms apply to criminal proceedings for incest (GL 272, §17), evidence relating to the complainant's prior sexual activity and pregnancy has been held excludable under common-law principles. *Com. v. Domaingue*, 397 Mass 693, 696-700, 493 NE2d 841, 844-845 (1986). "At common law, evidence of the prior sexual conduct of the victim with persons other than the defendant is inadmissible for the purpose of impeaching the victim's credibility. Prior unrelated instances of sexual conduct also are inadmissible for the purpose of proving consent to intercourse with the defendant. These evidentiary principles have been applied not only to charges of rape, but also to charges of assault and battery, sodomy, and unnatural and lascivious acts. They reflect a judicial determination that prior sexual acts are simply not relevant to the victim's trustworthiness, or to consent to sexual activity on a particular occasion." 397 Mass at 698-699, 493 NE2d at 845 (citations omitted).

Finally, it should be noted that GL 233, §21B does not come into play if the evidence offered fails to meet the threshold standard of relevance. Evidence that the victim was taking birth control pills, for example, was properly excluded as irrelevant without regard to the applicability of the rape shield statute. *Com. v. Chretien*, supra, 383 Mass at 136, 417 NE2d at 1211.

§4.4.4   *Form of Character Evidence/Reputation*

Where character evidence is admissible, it generally must be offered in the form of reputation evidence.[12] Thus,

---

[11] FRE 412, the federal rape shield statute, explicitly excepts "evidence the exclusion of which would violate the constitutional rights of the defendant." FRE 412(b)(1)(C).

[12] Specific act evidence may be admissible to prove motive, intent, plan, knowledge, identity, etc. See §4.4.6.

the only permissible form of character evidence that may be offered by the criminal defendant, or the prosecution in rebuttal (see §4.4.2) is reputation evidence. *Com. v. Roberts*, 378 Mass 116, 129, 389 NE2d 989, 997 (1979). The witness must testify as to the composite opinion of the defendant held by those likely to have observed a representative sample of his conduct. See generally *Michelson v. United States*, 335 US 469, 477-478 (1948). Evidence in the form of either private opinions or specific acts is not admissible. *Com. v. Roberts*, supra, 378 Mass at 129, 389 NE2d at 997 ("Personal opinions and isolated acts are not evidence of general reputation"); *Com. v. Belton*, 352 Mass 263, 269, 225 NE2d 53, 57 (1967) (recognizing, however, that the "distinction between general reputation and individual opinions often is difficult to determine").

As explained in *Miller v. Curtis*, 158 Mass 127, 131, 32 NE 1039, 1040 (1893), the principal reason for the rule precluding proof of character by evidence of specific acts is

> that a multiplicity of issues would be raised if special acts, covering perhaps a lifetime, could be shown. It might be necessary to go into the circumstances attending each act before it could be determined what its nature was, and what effect should be given to it. It would be impossible for the opposing party to be prepared to meet evidence upon matters in regard to which he had no notice, and great injustice might be done by hearing biased and false testimony to which no answer could be made.

The case law rejection of character evidence in opinion form contrasts with Proposed Mass R Evid 405(a) and Fed R Evid 405(a): "In all cases in which evidence of character or a trait of character of a person is admissible, proof may be made by testimony as to reputation *or by testimony in the form of an opinion* (emphasis added)."

Prior to 1947, the only reputation evidence deemed admissible was testimony as to the subject's reputation in the community in which he resided. *F. W. Stock & Sons v.*

Dellapenna, 217 Mass 503, 105 NE2d 378 (1914). However, GL 233, §21A now provides:

> Evidence of the reputation of a person in a group with the members of which he has habitually associated in his work or business shall be admissible to the same extent and subject to the same limitations as is evidence of such reputation in a community in which he has resided.

Cf. *United States v. Mandel,* 591 F2d 1347, 1370 (4th Cir 1979) ("the realities of our modern, mobile, impersonal society should also recognize that a witness may have a reputation for truth and veracity in the community in which he works and may have impressed on others in that community his character for truthfulness or untruthfulness"). On the reputation of a business, see GL 108A, §35(2)(b); *Warner v. Modano,* 340 Mass 439, 444, 164 NE2d 904, 907 (1960) (business reputation of a partnership is its standing in the business community).

A trial judge may exclude reputation evidence if a proper foundation is lacking for the testimony. See, e.g., *Com. v. Gomes,* 11 Mass App 933, 416 NE2d 551 (1981) (character witness who had known subject for two years and spoken of her with five other persons who knew her did not have a sufficient basis to offer reputation evidence).

A character witness may be cross-examined as to the witness's knowledge of a specific instance of conduct inconsistent with the reputation vouched for. See §4.4.2.

For a discussion of the use of reputation evidence to impeach a witness, see §6.10.1.

§4.4.5   Character Evidence in Civil Cases

As noted in §4.4.1, evidence of the character of either party to a civil action is generally inadmissible. "The fact that a person's habits or character are such that he would be apt to do an act is not competent evidence that he did the act." *Cucchiara v. Settino,* 328 Mass 116, 117-118, 102

NE2d 430 (1951). See also *Brennan v. Bongiorno*, 304 Mass 476, 477, 23 NE2d 1007 (1939) (evidence that defendant's employee, alleged to have committed assault, had reputation as prize fighter improperly admitted); *Whitney v. Lynch*, 222 Mass 112, 109 NE 826 (1915) (in action for deceit, evidence of reputation of defendant for honesty and fair dealing inadmissible).

The general rule against admission of character evidence applies even if the civil action is one for which a criminal prosecution might have been brought, or where the offense set up in justification involves a crime. *Stearns v. Long*, 215 Mass 152, 155, 102 NE 326, 327 (1926); *Geary v. Stevenson*, 169 Mass 23, 31, 47 NE 508, 509 (1897) (in tort action for assault and battery and false imprisonment, plaintiff's offer of evidence of good reputation properly excluded). Compare *Davidson v. Massachusetts Casualty Ins. Co.*, 325 Mass 115, 122, 89 NE2d 201, 205 (1949) (evidence of plaintiff's good character would not have been admissible to rebut defense that he made misrepresentations in application for insurance) with *Crumpton v. Confederation Life Ins. Co.*, 672 F.2d 1248 (5th Cir. 1982) (where civil case raises issue akin to criminal case, such as insurer's defense that insured died as result of commission of crime, character evidence admissible under FRE 404(a)).

Character evidence has been held admissible where the character of a party is more directly in issue, as in actions of malicious prosecution and libel or slander. *Geary v. Stevenson*, supra; *Clark v. Eastern Massachusetts Street Railway Co.*, 254 Mass 441, 442-443, 150 NE 184, 185 (1926) ("The ordinary rule, that the reputation of a party in a civil action is inadmissible, does not apply in actions for malicious prosecution of a criminal charge, if it is known to the person responsible for the complaint."). Evidence of the plaintiff's good reputation, if known to the defendant, is deemed relevant in proving absence of probable cause because "the same facts, which would raise a strong suspicion in the mind of a cautious and reasonable man, against a person of notoriously bad character for honesty and integrity, would make a slighter impression if they tended to throw a charge of guilty upon a man of good reputation." *Lewis v. Goldman*, 241 Mass 577, 578, 136 NE 67, 67-68 (1922) (citation omitted).

In actions for defamation, evidence of the plaintiff's good character is admissible on the issue of damages. It may also be admissible on the liability issue where the defamation involves an allegation of the commission of a crime by the plaintiff. See *Stearns v. Long*, supra, 215 Mass at 155-156, 102 NE at 327; *Howland v. George F. Blake Manufacturing Co.*, 156 Mass 543, 568-570, 31 NE 656, 657 (1892). The defendant may offer evidence of the plaintiff's poor reputation in those respects assailed by the alleged slander in mitigation of damages. *Clark v. Brown*, 116 Mass 504 (1875). The defendant may show that "the plaintiff's general reputation for integrity and moral worth was so bad that any damage done by the slander uttered by the defendant would be but nominal." *Hastings v. Stetson*, 130 Mass 76, 78 (1881).

Certain statutes explicitly provide for the admission of character evidence in civil proceedings. GL 139, §9, for example, provides that "[f]or the purpose of proving the existence of [a] nuisance the general reputation of a place shall be admissible in evidence." Thus, the general reputation of a lounge as a place where acts of prostitution occur is admissible on the issue of whether a nuisance exists. See *Com. v. United Food Corp.*, 374 Mass 765, 767-770, 374 NE2d 1331, 1336 (1978).

For the unique questions of admissibility of character evidence in proceedings under the "sexually dangerous person" statute, GL 123A, see *Com. v. Bladsa*, 362 Mass 539, 288 NE2d 813 (1972) and *In re Wyatt*, 428 Mass 347, 701 NE2d 337 (1998).

§4.4.6   *Specific Act Evidence for Non-Propensity Purposes*

Although inadmissible to prove conduct in conformity with a particular character trait (see §4.4.1), evidence of specific acts may be admissible for another purpose.[13] Where evidence of other crimes, wrongs, or acts is relevant in establishing motive, opportunity, intent, preparation, plan, knowledge, identity, absence of mistake or accident, or a particular way of doing an act or a particular skill, the evidence may be admitted if its probative value is not substantially outweighed by any prejudice. *Com. v. Fordham,* 417 Mass 10, 22, 627 NE2d 901, 908 (1994); *Com. v. Martino,* 412 Mass 267, 280, 588 NE2d 651, 659 (1992); *Com. v. Otsuki,* 411 Mass 218, 236, 581 NE2d 999, 1009-1010 (1991); *Com. v. Helfant,* 398 Mass 214, 224, 496 NE2d 433, 440-441 (1986); *Com v. Chalifoux,* 362 Mass 811, 815-816, 291 NE2d 635, 638 (1973); Proposed Mass R Evid 404(b).[14] Admission is justified on the theory that the evidence relates not to a general disposition to commit the crime, but rather tends to prove other facts relevant to the ultimate issues in the case. *Com. v. Trapp,* 396 Mass 202, 206, 485 NE2d 162, 165 (1985). If, for example, a prior crime functions as an identifying feature because it is so unusual and distinctive as to be like a signature, evidence of it may be admitted to connect the defendant to the crime charged. *Com. v. Jackson,* 428 Mass 455, 459-460, 702 NE2d 1158, 1162 (1998); *Com. v. Cordle,* 404 Mass 733, 537 NE2d 130 (1989).

It has been observed that the Supreme Judicial Court "may have been more willing recently than in prior years to allow evidence of bad acts to be admitted to prove an element of a crime." See *Com. v. Brusgulis,* 406 Mass 501,

---

[13] A sentencing judge may of course properly consider information concerning uncharged misconduct. See *Com. v. Goodwin,* 414 Mass 88, 605 NE2d 827 (1993) (& citations).

[14] See §4.4.1, note 2, supra.

505, 548 NE2d 1234, 1237 (1990). Given the risk of undue prejudice, caution must nonetheless be exercised in the admission of such evidence.

To be admissible, evidence of uncharged conduct must usually be related in time, place, and/or form to the charges being tried. There must be, in other words, a sufficient nexus to render the conduct relevant and probative. *Com. v. Barrett*, 418 Mass 788, 794, 641 NE2d 1302, 1307 (1994). Compare *Com. v. Burke*, 339 Mass 521, 533-534, 159 NE2d 856, 864 (1959) (evidence of murder defendant's relationship to another woman improperly admitted because too remote in time to be probative of motive to kill wife), *Com. v. Yetz*, 37 Mass App 970, 643 NE2d 1062 (1995) (evidence of defendant's sexual abuse of another child improperly admitted where it occurred two years before alleged abuse of complainant, and type of conduct was dissimilar), and *Com. v. Johnson*, 35 Mass App 211, 617 NE2d 1040 (1993) (testimony about alleged sexual touching occurring 40 months after alleged sexual offense improperly admitted) with *Com. v. Jackson*, 417 Mass 830, 841-842, 633 NE2d 1031, 1037-1038 (1994) (two years between incidents, although near limit, not too great considering distinctiveness of incidents), *Com. v. Hanlon*, 44 Mass App 810, 819-820, 694 NE2d 358, 366-367 (1998) (evidence of abuse of altar boys over decade admissible despite fact that last incident occurred nine years after last charged act), *Com. v. Scullin*, 44 Mass App 9, 15-16, 687 NE2d 1258, 1263 (1997) (gap of two and one-half years did not prevent admission of prior assault, given the two incidents were nearly identical), and *Com. v. Calcagno*, 31 Mass App 25, 27-28, 574 NE2d 420, 422 (1991) (evidence of defendant's abuse of victim going back eight years probative to put single instance charged into comprehensible context).

"There is no bright-line test for determining temporal remoteness of evidence of prior misconduct. Where the prior misconduct is merely one instance in a continuing course of related events, the allowable time period is greater. Where the logical relationship between the charged and the uncharged offenses is more attenuated, a time span of fifteen minutes may be too much." *Com. v. Helfant*, supra, 398 Mass at 228 n.13, 496 NE2d at 443 n.13 (& cases cited).

Specific act evidence relevant for non-propensity purposes is not rendered inadmissible merely because it tends to prove the commission of other crimes. *Com. v. Jackson*, 384 Mass 572, 577, 428 NE2d 289, 292 (1981); *Com. v. Titus*, 32 Mass App 216, 225, 587 NE2d 800, 805-806 (1992). Nor is the fact that the "bad acts" occurred after the event that is the subject of the pending charges in itself a bar to admission. *Com. v. Myer*, 38 Mass App 140, 143 n.2, 646 NE2d 155, 157 n.2 (1995). As with any other evidence, there is no requirement that the prior bad acts be proved beyond a reasonable doubt. *Com. v. Azar*, 32 Mass App 290, 309, 588 NE2d 1352, 1364 (1992).

If the probative value of the specific acts evidence is substantially outweighed by the danger of uncorrectable prejudice, the evidence should be excluded. *Com v. Chalifoux*, supra, 362 Mass at 816, 291 NE2d at 638-639. See, e.g., *Com. v. Montanino*, 409 Mass 500, 505-507, 567 NE2d 1212, 1215-1216 (1991) (reversible error for judge to admit testimony from complainant that he came forward four years after sexual abuse incident because he had found out "that it was still going on;" reference to other sexual misconduct not relevant and highly prejudicial). This determination is for the trial judge and will be overturned on appeal only upon a showing of abuse of discretion. *Com. v. Fordham*, supra, 417 Mass at 22-23; *Com. v. Robertson*, 408 Mass 747, 750, 563 NE2d 223, 225 (1990); *Com. v. King*, 387 Mass 464, 472, 441 NE2d 248, 254 (1982); *Com. v. Young*, 382 Mass 448, 462-463, 416 NE2d 944, 953 (1981). Because of the substantial risk of prejudice, "other crimes" evidence should be admitted only where it has substantial probative value. *Com. v. Burke*, supra, 339 Mass at 533-534, 159 NE2d at 864.

Prompt cautionary instructions to the jury are critical to protecting a defendant against prejudice where such evidence is admitted. The instructions should "offset any improper prejudicial effect of evidence that might be thought to show the defendant's bad character or propensity for violent acts" and should "focus the jury's attention on the proper application of the evidence." *Com. v. McGeoghean*, 412 Mass 839, 842, 593 NE2d 229, 231 (1992). See, e.g., *Com. v. De La Cruz*, 405 Mass 269, 274-276, 540 NE2d 168, 171-173 (1989); *Com. v. Sawyer*, 389 Mass 686, 696-699, 452 NE2d 1094, 1100-1101 (1983). See also *Com. v. Kent K.*, 427 Mass 754, 756-757, 696 NE2d 511, 514-515 (1998) (curative instruction adequately instructed jury to ignore testimony concerning mug shot of defendant). The judge should carefully instruct the jury as to the limited admissibility of "other crimes" evidence, as well as the need to connect up the other event with the defendant before the jury can consider it at all. See, e.g., *Com. v. Collins*, 26 Mass App 1021, 1022-1023, 533 NE2d 214, 215-216 (1989). But compare *Com. v. Leonardi*, 413 Mass 757, 764, 604 NE2d 23, 28 (1992) (no requirement that judge give limiting instruction unless so requested by defendant); *Com. v. Myer*, 38 Mass App 140, 145 n.3, 646 NE2d 155, 158 n.3 (1995) (where limiting instruction not requested, bad acts evidence competent for all purposes).

Where evidence of prior bad acts is offered, it must of course be in the form of otherwise admissible evidence. See *Com. v. Hubbard*, 45 Mass App 277, 697 NE2d 551 (1998) (prosecutor's references to prior assault incident required reversal because based on hearsay). Before the evidence can be admitted, the Commonwealth must satisfy the judge that the jury could reasonably conclude that the act occurred and that the defendant was the actor. *Com. v. Leonard*, 428 Mass 782, 785-786, 705 NE2d 247, 250 (1999) (& citations). The Commonwealth need only show these facts by a preponderance of the evidence. Id.

By way of example, evidence of other acts, crimes, or wrongs was held admissible because relevant to a non-propensity purpose in the following cases:

Intent: *Com. v. Fallon*, 423 Mass 92, 668 NE2d 296 (1996) (evidence of defendant's incarceration for civil contempt for refusal to disclose location of victim's money relevant on issue of fraudulent intent); *Com. v. McGeoghean*, supra, 412 Mass at 841, 593 NE2d at 231 (evidence that defendant had inflicted cigarette burns on daughter's chest six weeks prior to daughter's death relevant to defendant's intent and malice); *Com. v. Rancourt*, 399 Mass 269, 275-276, 503 NE2d 960, 964-965 (1987) (evidence that defendant attempted forcibly to enter car in which two women were riding shortly before he entered rape victim's car relevant to issues of intent, motive, and consent); *Com. v. Helfant*, 398 Mass 214, 496 NE2d 433 (1986) (at trial of indictment for rape and drugging a person for unlawful sexual inter-course, evidence that defendant doctor had the year before sexually assaulted two women after injecting them with valium probative of defendant's illegal intent); *Com. v. Harvey*, 397 Mass 803, 809-810, 494 NE2d 382, 386-387 (1986) (at murder trial in which defendant claimed shooting was accidental, testimony regarding prior shooting incident relevant to establish defendant's intent and to rebut defense of accident); *Com. v. Jordan (No.1)*, 397 Mass 489, 491-492, 492 NE2d 349, 350-351 (1986) (at trial of indictments for armed assault with intent to murder and related offenses, evidence that defendant beat and mis-treated victim on prior occasions within the months before crime probative of defendant's mental state and intent to murder victim); *Com. v. Shraiar*, 397 Mass 16, 26, 489 NE2d 689, 696 (1986) (evidence of subsequent uncharged larce-nies admissible to rebut larceny defendant's defense that he intended to repay monies taken); *Com. v. Walker*, 370 Mass 548, 568-569, 350 NE2d 678, 692-693 (1976) (testi-mony that witness and defendant had stolen a car prior to robbery charged properly admitted because probative on issue of criminal intent); *Morris's Case*, 354 Mass 420, 238

NE2d 35 (1968) (evidence that employer of claimant employed other minors probative of intent to hire minors and knowledge of minor status).

Knowledge: *Com. v. Stewart*, 411 Mass 345, 354, 582 NE2d 514, 520 (1991) (evidence that codefendant shot cat prior to shooting of victim relevant to defendant's knowledge that codefendant was armed); *Com. v. Cordle*, 404 Mass 733, 744, 537 NE2d 130, 137 (1989) (evidence of defendant's prior break-in into murder victim's home relevant to show knowledge of how to break into home); *Com. v. Imbruglia*, 377 Mass 682, 693-696, 387 NE2d 559, 567-568 (1979) (evidence of defendant's fencing activities within same time period of alleged crime probative of defendant's knowledge that bonds in question had been stolen); *Com. v. Robinson*, 43 Mass App 257, 260, 682 NE2d 903, 906 (1997) (association with drug dealer relevant to show defendant's knowledge). Compare *Com. v. Sapoznik*, 28 Mass App 236, 239-245, 549 NE2d 116, 118-123 (1990) (evidence of defendant's prior arrest on drug-related charge only minimally relevant to issue of knowledge and highly prejudicial).

Motive/State of Mind: *Com. v. Cormier*, 427 Mass 446, 449-450, 693 NE2d 1015, 1018 (1998) (evidence of defendant's prior attacks on and threats to wife admissible to establish possible motive and intent in her murder); *Com. v. Gunter*, 427 Mass 259, 262-263, 692 NE2d 515, 519-520 (1997) (evidence of prior history of drug dealing admissible to prove motive to murder individual who allegedly stole drugs); *Com. v. Wilson*, 427 Mass 336, 349, 693 NE2d 158, 170 (1998) (evidence of prior domestic incident relevant to motive for killings); *Com. v. Arce*, 426 Mass 601, 690 NE2d 806 (1998) (evidence of hostile relationship between murder victim and defendant admissible to show motive); *Com. v. Magraw*, 426 Mass 589, 690 NE2d 400 (1998) (evidence of incident in which defendant placed rifle on bed of murder victim admissible to show discord between the two); *Com. v. Rivera*, 424 Mass 266, 273, 675 NE2d 791, 797 (1997) (evidence regarding drug organization admissible to prove defendant's motive to kill victim); *Com. v. Diaz*, 422 Mass 269, 273, 661 NE2d 1326, 1329 (1996) (evidence that murder defendant discussed possibility of killing competitor of drug operation tended to show motive for killings); *Com. v. Fordham*, 417 Mass 10, 22-23, 627 NE2d 901, 907-908 (1994) (evidence of defendant's prior assault on murder victim probative of his attitude toward her and reason to kill her); *Com. v. Phinney*, 416 Mass 364, 375, 622 NE2d 617, 624 (1993) (evidence of defendant's prior activities photographing and ogling woman relevant to motive); *Com. v. Sneed*, 413 Mass 387, 396-397, 597 NE2d 1346, 1351 (1992) (evidence of defendant's violent striking of victim shortly before death admissible to show defendant's state of mind or motive, and to negate accident as cause of victim's injuries); *Com. v. Robertson*, supra, 408 Mass at 749-752, 563 NE2d at 224-226 (evidence that defendant was pimp for victims in murder case and that he had previously beaten them probative of defendant's reason to kill them); *McEvoy Travel Bureau, Inc. v. Norton Co.*, 408 Mass 704, 714-715, 563 NE2d 188, 194-195 (1990) (evidence of defendant's possible illegal dealings with another company relevant to show motive for rejection of plaintiff's arrangement); *Com. v. Libran*, 405 Mass 634, 640-641, 543 NE2d 5, 9 (1989) (evidence of fight between defendant and another person night before murder relevant to defendant's sanity and issue of premeditation); *Com. v. Drew*, 397 Mass 65, 79-80, 489 NE2d 1233, 1243 (1986) (evidence of defendant's involvement in earlier murder admissible to show motive because victim had been eyewitness to prior crime); *Com. v. Gil*, 393 Mass 204, 215-217, 471 NE2d 30 (1984) (restraining orders issued against defendant seven months before murder of wife admissible to show motive); *Com. v. Hoffer*, 375 Mass 369, 372, 377 NE2d 685, 688 (1978) (evidence that defendant did not have a driver's license probative of motive for armed robbery of victim's wallet and license); *Com. v. Cokonougher*, 35 Mass App 502, 622 NE2d 1365 (1993) (evidence that defendant had talked about having abortion when pregnant with infant son victim admissible to show state of mind). See also *Com. v. LeFave*, 407 Mass 927, 935-938, 556 NE2d 83, 89-91 (1990) (at trial of indictments for sexual abuse of children, testimony of expert on child pornography concerning general practices of pornographers relevant to possible motive of defendants). Compare *Com. v. Valcourt*, 333 Mass 706, 717-718, 133 NE2d 217, 225 (1956) (evidence that arson defendant had not paid any federal or state income taxes for two years preceding fire too prejudicial and not probative of weak financial condition as motive for crime).

Plan, Common Scheme, or Course of Conduct: *Com. v. Feijoo*, 419 Mass 486, 494-495, 646 NE2d 118, 124-125 (1995) (karate instructor's use of relationship to students as modus operandi to induce submission to homosexual activity); *Com. v. Daggett*, 416 Mass 347, 349-352, 622 NE2d 272, 274 (1993) (evidence that defendant had been previously arrested for soliciting a prostitute at time when his log records indicated he was working at plant admissible in prosecution for murder of another prostitute when records again indicated defendant was at work, to show plan or scheme and opportunity to commit crime); *Com. v. Scott*, 408 Mass 811, 817-820, 564 NE2d 370, 375-377 (1990) (evidence of defendant's harassment of three women days before alleged murder probative of plan, motive, and intent to procure a sexual encounter at the time of murder); *Com. v. King*, 387 Mass 464, 469-473, 441 NE2d 248, 251-253 (1982) (at trial of indictment charging unlawful intercourse with child under 16, evidence that defendant had had similar sexual relations with sibling of victim probative of pattern of conduct) (citing Text); *Com. v. Baldassini*, 357 Mass 670, 677-679, 260 NE2d 150, 155 (1970) (evidence of prior illegal betting acts of defendant charged with gambling offenses probative of general scheme to violate gaming laws); *Com. v. Campbell*, 371 Mass 40, 353 NE2d 740 (1976) (evidence of other burglaries committed by defendant properly admitted because probative of common scheme to use specialized knowledge as police officer to engage in burglarious enterprises); *Newton Centre Trust Co. v. Stuart*, 208 Mass 221, 225-226, 94 NE 454, 456 (1911) (evidence of other stock transactions admissible to show scheme to conceal transactions); *Com. v. Maimoni*, 41 Mass App 321, 326-328, 670 NE2d 189, 192-193 (1996) (evidence of sexual advances made in week preceding victim's death upon two women invited to sail in defendant's boat admissible to show plan or pattern of conduct); *Com. v. Wotan*, 37 Mass App 727, 731-732, 643 NE2d 62, 65 (1995) (evidence of prior phone calls admissible to show pattern); *Com. v. Odell*, 34 Mass App 100, 102-105, 607 NE2d 423, 425-426 (1993) (in trial on charges defendant administered drugs to teenage girls with intent to facilitate unlawful sexual intercourse, defendant's post-indictment note to nephew seeking his aid in bringing teenage girls over and finding out what drugs or drink they liked admissible to prove common scheme or pattern of operations); *Com. v. Brown*, 34 Mass App 222, 228, 609 NE2d 100, 104 (1993) (earlier drug transaction admissible in prosecution for trafficking as probative of method and pattern of operation, even though the identity of person who handled transaction behind door not established); *Com. v. Lanning*, 32 Mass App 279, 282-284, 589 NE2d 318, 321-322 (1992) (other acts of sexual misconduct properly admitted to show common scheme and pattern of behavior); *Com. v. Fleury-Ehrhart*, 20 Mass App 429, 430-432, 480 NE2d 661, 663 (1985) (at trial on indictment charging indecent assault and battery upon a patient, evidence that defendant doctor committed similar misconduct against two other female patients probative of common scheme, pattern of conduct, and absence of accident or mistake).

Identity/Modus Operandi: *Com v. Leonard*, 428 Mass 782, 787-788, 705 NE2d 250, 251 (1999) (prior and current fires had meaningfully distinctive similarities); *Com. v. Jackson*, 428 Mass 455, 459-460, 702 NE2d 1158, 1162 (1998) (prior crime to which defendant had already pled guilty involving kicking in door in close proximity and time to crime charged had sufficiently similar modus operandi to identify defendant); *Com. v. Jackson,* 417 Mass 830, 633 NE2d 1031 (1994) (prior incident involving "hog-tied" victim admissible in murder trial alleging similar means); *Com. v. Zagranski,* 408 Mass 278, 281, 558 NE2d 933, 935-936 (1990) (proposed scheme to purchase parcel of land and kill owner properly admitted because it tended to identity defendant as person who killed victim); *Com. v. Lacy,* 371 Mass 363, 358 NE2d 419 (1976) (evidence of defendant's visits to apartment of other woman probative of identity of perpetrator because method of gaining entry was same); *Com. v. Montez,* 45 Mass App 802, 808-810, 702 NE2d 40, 45-46 (1998) (evidence of two uncharged burglaries admissible on question of identity of assailant); *Com. v. Madyun,* 17 Mass App 965, 458 NE2d 745 (1983) (testimony of two victims of subsequent rapes probative of central issue of identity in rape trial because of "striking similarities" in crimes). Compare *Com. v. Brusgulis,* 406 Mass 501, 507, 548 NE2d 1234, 1238 (1990) (evidence of other sexual assaults by defendant not sufficiently distinctive or unique to be relevant to identity of perpetrator: "The fact is that the circumstances of each incident were characteristic of numerous assaults on women walking or jogging in unpopulated portions of public parks or in similar areas. If we were to uphold the admission of the evidence of prior bad acts in this case, we would be endorsing a rule that evidence of prior assaults by a person is admissible in the trial of every future assault charge against that person, provided that there is a general, although less than unique or distinct, similarity between the incidents. Such a rule would be unfair to defendants and inconsistent with our well-established law on the use of evidence of prior bad acts to prove identity"); *Com. v. McClendon,* 39 Mass App 122, 129-130, 653 NE2d 1138, 1143 (1995) (evidence that defendant became violent when drunk and attempted to strangle someone was not distinguishing pattern of conduct to constitute signature or absence of accident).

Other Purposes: *Com. v. Moure,* 428 Mass 313, 318-320, 701 NE2d 319, 323-324 (1998) (prior bad acts of gang members to establish motivation of prosecution witness to testify); *Com. v. Marrero,* 427 Mass 65, 67-69, 691 NE2d 918, 920-921 (1998) (context for the killing); *Com. v. Richardson,* 423 Mass 180, 187, 677 NE2d 257, 263 (1996) (evidence that victim's friend told her she was also raped by defendant admissible to explain delay in reporting); *Com. v. Robles,* 423 Mass 62, 68-69, 666 NE2d 497, 501-502 (1996) (evidence of defendant's drug activities connected him to homicide victim); *Com. v. Brousseau,* 421 Mass 647, 650-651, 659 NE2d 724, 726-727 (1996) (evidence of defendant's prior use of murder weapon relevant to show control over weapon); *Com. v. Austin,* 421 Mass 357, 364-365, 657 NE2d 458, 462-463 (1995) (videotape depicting another bank robbery for limited purpose of assisting jury in assessing reliability of identification evidence); *Com. v. Elam,* 412 Mass 583, 585-586, 591 NE2d 186, 188-189 (1992) (evidence that weapon carried by codefendant had been fired into house in unrelated incident relevant to rebut defendants' evidence that others were responsible for crimes charged); *Com. v. Gordon,* 407 Mass 340, 351, 553 NE2d 915, 921 (1990) (evidence of prior confrontation between defendant and victim wife relevant to proving her fear of husband in prosecution for violation of protective order); *Com. v. Connor,* 392 Mass 838, 852, 467 NE2d 1340, 1350 (1984) (evidence of defendant's prior incarceration intertwined with the circumstances of the crimes charged); *Com. v. Errington,* 390 Mass 875, 882, 460 NE2d 598, 603 (1984) (evidence that defendant had committed similar sex offenses with another child admissible to explain witness's fear of going to police); *Com. v. Caine,* 366 Mass 366, 318 NE2d 901 (1974) (evidence that defendant stole gun probative to show that he possessed means to commit crime); *Com. v. Green,* 302 Mass 547, 551-553, 20 NE2d 417, 420-421 (1939) (admission of defendant's letter written in jail narrating other crimes and a plan of escape probative of consciousness of guilt); *Lally v. Volkswagen Aktiengesell-*

schaft, 45 Mass App 317, 334-335, 698 NE2d 28, 41-42 (1998) (evidence of prior substance abuse relevant to issue of whether accident caused plaintiff's deteriorating condition); *McLaughlin v. Vinios*, 39 Mass App 5, 8, 653 NE2d 189, 191 (1995) (evidence of prior crime near locus admissible to prove owner failed to take reasonable steps to protect patrons from injury); *Com. v. Titus*, 32 Mass App 216, 225, 587 NE2d 800, 805 (1992) (evidence of kidnapping of victim admissible to show rape defendant's guilty state of mind); *Com. v. Azar*, 32 Mass App 290, 298-300, 588 NE2d 1352, 1359 (1992) (evidence of injuries inflicted upon victim admissible to show someone in custodial relation bore her ill will); *Com. v. Englehart*, 27 Mass App 1201, 543 NE2d 1154 (1989) (photographs of defendant taken by surveillance camera at another bank one month before robbery in question admissible to rebut alibi testimony).

It has been held that "when a defendant is charged with any form of illicit sexual intercourse, evidence of the commission of similar crimes by the same parties though committed in another place, if not too remote in time, is competent to prove an inclination to commit the [acts] charged in the indictment . . . and is relevant to show the probable existence of the same passion or emotion at the time in issue." *Com. v. Barrett*, 418 Mass 788, 794, 641 NE2d 1302, 1307 (1994); *Com. v. Hanlon*, 44 Mass App 810, 817-819, 694 NE2d 358, 365-366 (1998) (evidence of sexual assualts of four other altar boys by defendant priest, establishing pattern of conduct); *Com. v. Kelleher*, 42 Mass App 911, 675 NE2d 802 (1997).[15] Evidence of similar misconduct may also be used to show the relationship between the defendant and the victim. *Com. v. Holloway*, 44 Mass App

---

[15] FRE 413, 414, and 415 render admissible in federal criminal and civil cases charging sexual assault or child molestation evidence of the defendant's commission of another offense or offenses of sexual assault or child molestation.

469, 474-477, 691 NE2d 985, 989-990 (1998); *Com. v. Sos-nowski,* 43 Mass App 367, 682 NE2d 944 (1997).

Where an entrapment defense is raised, evidence of past similar crimes may be offered by the Commonwealth to prove that defendant was predisposed to commit the crime. See *Com. v. Vargas,* 417 Mass 792, 632 NE2d 1223 (1994) (& cases cited); *Com. v. Penta,* 32 Mass App 36, 47-49, 586 NE2d 996, 1002-1003 (1992).

Specific act evidence was held inadmissible in the following cases: *Com. v. Triplett,* 398 Mass 561, 562-564, 500 NE2d 262, 263-264 (1986) (evidence that murder defendant had assaulted his mother, lost his job because he could not control his temper, and received a dishonorable discharge from the Army; the evidence portrayed defendant as a violent and dangerous person and was not relevant to any issue other than propensity to act violently); *Com. v. Trapp,* 396 Mass 202, 205-210, 485 NE2d 162, 166 (1985) (at murder trial in which defense was insanity, evidence that defendant had made threats against persons other than the victim four years before and that defendant had been subject to disciplinary action while in jail awaiting trial); *Com. v. Brown,* 389 Mass 382, 450 NE2d 172 (1983) (references in defendant's confession to unrelated robberies could not be justified by either need to give complete picture of confession or by common scheme relevance); *Com. v. Banuchi,* 335 Mass 649, 654, 141 NE2d 835, 838 (1957) (evidence that arson defendant possessed large knife and intended to use it to assault divorced wife); *Com. v. Almeida,* 42 Mass App 607, 679 NE2d 561 (1997) (evidence that rape defendant had previously impregnated complainant and procured an abortion for her); *Com. v. Cokonougher,* 32 Mass App 54, 58-60, 585 NE2d 345, 348-349 (1992) (evidence concerning defendant's treatment of her other children in trial on charge of manslaughter of infant son, where other conduct occurred seven months prior to victim's death and constituted negligence, which did not support Commonwealth's theory of intentional smothering of son); *Com. v. Salone,* 26 Mass App 926, 525 NE2d 430

(1988) (evidence of specific acts demonstrating that assault defendant had bad temper); *Com. v. Key*, 21 Mass App 293, 295-298, 486 NE2d 1139, 1142-1143 (1985) (evidence that photograph of rape defendant which victim identified was taken after he was arrested for unrelated indecent assault committed days later in same location as rape); *Com. v. Yelle*, 19 Mass App 465, 468-472, 475 NE2d 427, 430-431 (1985) (testimony that rape defendant had offered ride to another young girl 20 minutes before picking up complainant); *Com. v. Hogan*, 12 Mass App 646, 650-654 428 NE2d 314, 316-318 (1981) (evidence that defendant was suspect in murder of witness in another case); *Com. v. Fillippini*, 2 Mass App 179, 185-187, 310 NE2d 147, 150-151 (1974) (evidence that armed robbery defendant had been previously convicted, on testimony of same witness, of similar crime perpetrated jointly with present codefendant).

Where the defendant takes the stand and opens the subject on direct examination, questions relating to other crimes and bad acts (otherwise inadmissible) may be permissible within the proper scope of cross-examination. *Com. v. Key*, 381 Mass 19, 28-29, 407 NE2d 327, 334 (1980). But compare *Com. v. McClendon*, supra, 39 Mass App at 129-130, 653 NE2d at 1143 (1995) (subjects not sufficiently opened up on direct); *Com. v. Hogan*, 12 Mass App 646, 649, 428 NE2d 314, 316 (1981) (same).

The defendant who testifies may be impeached by proof of a prior conviction. See generally §6.10.2. In this instance, the conviction bears solely on the credibility of the defendant and may not be used as evidence of guilt. Such use of prior convictions to impeach a witness must be distinguished from the substantive use of other crimes to prove such matters as knowledge, scheme or identity, as discussed above. First, use of prior convictions for impeachment is possible only if the defendant chooses to testify in his own behalf. In contrast, when admissible for substantive purposes "specific acts" evidence may be offered whether the defendant testifies or not. Second, when prior crimes are used for impeachment purposes, they may be proven only by the record of conviction. See §6.10.2. No such requirement exists for specific act evidence, which need only be shown by a preponderance of the evidence or by such evidence as warrants submission to the jury. *Com. v. Leonard,* supra, 428 Mass at 785-786, 705 NE2d at 250 (citing *Huddleston v. United States,* 485 US 681 (1988)). See also *Dowling v. United States,* 493 US 342, 110 S Ct 668 (1990) (evidence of prior crime admissible on issue of identity under Fed R Evid 404(b) even though defendant had been tried and acquitted of prior offense).

§4.4.7 *Specific Act Evidence Offered by Defendant*

Evidence of other similar crimes or acts may be introduced by the defendant as well as the prosecution. "It is well established that a defendant should be allowed to introduce evidence that another person recently committed a similar crime by similar methods, since such evidence tends to show that someone other than the accused committed the particular crime." *Com. v. Scott,* 408 Mass 811, 815-816, 564 NE2d 370, 374-375 (1990). See also *Com. v. Brusgulis,* 406 Mass 501, 506 n.7, 548 NE2d 1234, 1237 n.7 (1990); *Com. v. Signorine,* 404 Mass 400, 407-408, 535 NE2d 601, 605-606 (1989); *Com. v. Jewett,* 392 Mass 558, 562, 467 NE2d 155, 158 (1984).

The acts must be "so closely connected in point of time and method of operation as to cast doubt upon the identification of defendant as the person who committed the crime." *Com. v. Keizer,* 377 Mass 264, 267, 385 NE2d 1001, 1003 (1979). See, e.g., *Com. v. Rosa,* 422 Mass 18, 22-25, 661 NE2d 56, 59-61 (1996) (look-alike evidence properly excluded because insufficient similarities between crimes); *Com. v. Perito,* 417 Mass 674, 684-686, 632 NE2d 1190 (1994) (other robberies committed after defendant's arrest not significantly comparable to require admission; robbery committed before defendant's arrest properly excluded where defendant failed to show he was not the perpetrator of that crime); *Com. v. Hunter,* 426 Mass 715, 690 NE2d 815 (1998) (no error in excluding evidence that neighbor may have strangled victim, because prior incident too dissimilar); *Com. v. Clarke,* 44 Mass App 502, 508-509, 692 NE2d 85, 89-90 (1998) (crimes committed by other person not unique or unusual so as to compel inference that he alone was likely perpetrator); *Com. v. Sneed,* 413 Mass 387, 397, 597 NE2d 1346, 1351 (1992) (no abuse of discretion in excluding evidence of mother's disciplinary treatment of children, because level of violence not substantial enough to show she may have caused victim's injuries); *Com. v. Mayfield,* 398 Mass 615, 628, 500 NE2d 774, 782 (1986) (alleged assault incident between witness and third party not sufficiently similar to murder charged to implicate third party); *Com. v. Harris,* 395 Mass 296, 300-301, 479 NE2d 690, 693 (1985) (evidence offered by defendant of similar attack that occurred while he was in custody properly excluded because "the points of similarity are not particularly distinguishing or unique"); *Com. v. Brown,* 27 Mass App 72, 76, 534 NE2d 806, 808 (1989) (evidence of other crime properly excluded because the two crimes were "commonplace" and "there was nothing in them so striking or salient as to connect them to a single putative offender"). The judge has considerable discretion in determining whether the proferred evidence meets these conditions. *Com. v. Lawrence,* 404 Mass 378, 387, 536 NE2d 571, 577 (1989); *Com. v. Carver,* 33 Mass App 378, 381-383, 600 NE2d 588, 592-593 (1992).

"Moreover, there must be reasonable assurance that the defendant at bar did not commit the 'similar' offense, that it was in fact committed by someone else; thus the cases admitting evidence of similar crimes customarily establish that the particular defendant was in custody or in jail or in some predicament at the time." *Com. v. Brown,* supra, 27 Mass App at 76, 534 NE2d at 808-809. It has been held error to bar the defendant's evidence of prior misidentification of him by another victim of a similar crime based on the same police photograph used to identify defendant in the case on trial. *Com. v. Jewett,* supra, 392 Mass 558, 467 NE2d 165.

§4.4.8   Habit and Custom

While "character" encompasses a broad aggregate of attributes and qualities, "habit" refers to a specific and routine response to a particular set of circumstances. Because habitual conduct may be viewed as semiautomatic, it is thought to be more probative of how the actor conducted himself on the particular occasion in question. Evidence of the habit of a person and the routine practice of an organization is thus admissible in the federal courts to prove conduct in conformity with it. Fed R Evid 406. Proposed Mass R Evid 406 takes the same position, although with a caveat limiting the use of habit evidence in negligence trials and with a requirement not explicit in the federal rule that habit be proven by specific instances of conduct, not reputation or opinion evidence.[16]

---

[16] Rule 406 provides:

(a) Admissibility. Evidence of the habit of a person or of the routine practice of an organization, whether corroborated or not and regardless of the presence of eyewitnesses, is relevant to prove that the conduct of the person or organization on a particular occasion was in conformity with the habit or routine practice, but such evidence is not admissible for the purpose of proving that a person or organization did or did not conform on a particular occasion to the prescribed standard of care.

(b) Method of Proof. Habit or routine practice may be proved by specific instances of conduct sufficient in number to warrant a finding that the habit existed or that the practice was routine.

With regard to the caveat for negligence cases, the Advisory Committee Notes explain:

A majority of the Committee believes that habit evidence would have a disruptive effect on the trial of negligence cases and therefore favored the express prohibition in subdivision (a). Negligence, they urge, is a deviation from the norm and proof of a habit of care does not warrant the inference of conformity with the habit on the occasion giving rise to the lawsuit. The minority thinks that adoption of the rule without this exclusion would not significantly change Massachusetts law and that the exclusion reflects undue

Massachusetts case law, however, rejects the use of habit evidence to prove the conduct of an individual. "For the purpose of proving that one has or has not done a particular act, it is not competent to show that he has or has not been in the habit of doing similar acts." *Davidson v. Massachusetts Casualty Ins. Co.*, 325 Mass 115, 122, 89 NE2d 201, 205 (1949) (citation omitted). See, e.g, *Figueiredo v. Hamill*, 385 Mass 1003, 431 NE2d 231 (1982) (evidence that pedestrian accident victim habitually acted in reckless manner properly excluded); *Com. v. Hodge (No.2)*, 380 Mass 858, 862, 406 NE2d 1015, 1018 (1980) (evidence that defendant frequently used phrase "he'll leave in a hearse" in a joking, non-threatening manner properly excluded); *Brownhill v. Kivlin*, 317 Mass 168, 171, 57 NE2d 539, 540 (1944) (evidence that deceased had caused three prior fires by falling asleep with cigarette in mouth inadmissible); *Com. v. Mandell*, 29 Mass App 504, 507-508, 562 NE2d 111, 113 (1990) (evidence that victim was habitually accident-prone properly excluded). It should be noted that the evidence offered in these cases probably fell short of demonstrating "habit" when defined as "the regular practice of a person to meet a particular kind of situation with a specific type of conduct." Advisory Committee Notes, Proposed Mass R Evid 406.

Habit evidence has been held admissible where it related to the habits of intoxication of the defendant's watchman, which was relevant to establish that he was not a suitable person to be employed in that capacity and that the defendant "by reasonable diligence might have [so] discovered." See *Cox v. Vermont Central Railroad Co.*, 170

---

rigidity. In any event the judge has discretion to exclude habit evidence pursuant to Rule 403 if he finds its probative value to be substantially outweighed by the danger of unfair prejudice.

The Supreme Judicial Court has refused to revise the Committee's judgment. See *Figueiredo v. Hamill*, 385 Mass 1003, 1005, 431 NE2d 231, 232-233 (1982).

Mass 129, 139-140, 49 NE 97, 102 (1898). But see *Com. v. Shine*, 25 Mass App 613, 614-615, 521 NE2d 749, 750 (1988) (references to possibility that deceased accident victim had been an alcoholic properly excluded; possibility that the decedent had been an alcoholic had no relevance on the question whether he was in fact intoxicated at the time of the accident). Evidence of the decedent's "acts and habits of dealing tending to disprove or to show the improbability of making of" a disputed oral promise is admissible in an action on the promise. See GL 233, §66.

In recognition of the reality that with regard to large organizations such evidence is often the only practical means of proof, evidence of the custom or routine practice of a business or institution is generally admitted to prove that a particular act was performed. See *Com. v. Robles*, 423 Mass 62, 73-74, 666 NE2d 497, 504-505 (1996) (usual practice of court clerk relevant to inquiry on correctness of transcript); *Palinkas v. Bennett*, 416 Mass 273, 620 NE2d 775 (1993) (& cases cited) (pediatrician's routine practice followed when discharging premature infants could be found to be business habit admissible on issue of whether he gave instructions on proper care); *Prudential Trust Co. v. Hayes*, 247 Mass 311, 315, 142 NE 73, 74 (1924) (evidence that it was clerk's invariable practice to mail all letters forwarded to him competent to prove that particular letters were mailed; "in large banks and business houses, it must often be practically impossible to honestly obtain more definite evidence as to mailing than the delivery of letters to the mailing clerk, whose duty it is to deposit them in the post office in the usual course of his employment"). See also *Com. v. Carroll*, 360 Mass 580, 276 NE2d 705 (1971) (evidence that common police department practice in case of fugitives returned to state is to impound any money in their possession properly admitted); *Singer Sewing Machine Co. v. Assessors of Boston*, 341 Mass 513, 519, 170 NE2d 687, 691 (1960) (evidence of customary practice of mail clerk competent to prove that bills in dispute were mailed); *Irving v. Goodimate Co.*, 320 Mass 454, 460, 70 NE2d 414, 417 (1946) (other letters sent by defendant admissible to show manner in which defendant routinely signed letters as bearing on question of whether letters in dispute were actually those of defendant); *Com. v. Torrealba*, 316 Mass 24, 54 NE2d 939 (1944) (testimony from manager that it was custom of store to give a sales slip with each purchase properly admitted in shoplifting prosecution); *O'Connor v. Smithkline Bio-Science Laboratories, Inc.*, 36 Mass App 360, 631 NE2d 1018 (1994) (citing Text) (usual practice of lab technician); *Elias v. Suran*, 35 Mass App 7, 11-13, 616 NE2d 134, 136-137 (1993) (practice at hospital of administering morphine in particular doses to angiogram patients admissible to corroborate defendant's testimony as to dosage given plaintiff). But compare *Com. v. Levin*, 11 Mass App 482, 503, 417 NE2d 440, 451 (1981) (insufficient foundation to establish insurance broker's practice of signing names of customers to insurance applications).

The line between a personal habit and a business habit is often not a bright line, and a trial judge has broad discretion in making this determination. *Palinkas v. Bennett*, supra, 416 Mass at 277.

Evidence of the habits of animals is generally admissible. "It is a familiar fact that animals are more likely to act in a certain way at a particular time, if the action is in accordance with their established habit or usual conduct, than if it is not. There is a probability that an animal will act as he is accustomed to act under like circumstances. For this reason, when disputes have arisen in regard to the conduct of an animal, evidence of his habits in that particular has often been received." *Broderick v. Higginson*, 169 Mass 482, 485, 48 NE 269, 270 (1897) (proof that dog had habit of attacking passing teams competent to prove that he attacked team on particular occasion). See also *Palmer v. Coyle*, 187 Mass 136, 72 NE 844 (1905).

§4.4.9 Similar Circumstances Offered for Various Purposes

a. Similar Occurrences

The occurrence of an event or transaction similar to the one in issue is sometimes offered as circumstantial evidence. For example, to prove that a particular defect in the road caused the plaintiff's accident, the plaintiff may seek to offer evidence that similar accidents have occurred at the same location. Such offers of evidence are generally viewed with disfavor on the ground that they raise collateral issues that distract from the central questions in the case. (This type of evidence is sometimes referred to as *res inter alios acta*, or a thing done between others. See *Denton v. Park Hotel, Inc.*, 343 Mass 524, 527, 180 NE2d 70, 72 (1962)). As the Supreme Judicial Court has cautioned:

> The admissibility of evidence of injury to others at other times by reason of the same thing that caused the plaintiff's injury, for the purpose of showing that thing to be dangerous, has often come before this court. Such evidence is open to grave objections. Its persuasive force depends upon the similarity in the circumstances of different injuries, of which it is hard to be certain. Substantial identity in the alleged defective condition is only the first essential. The person who was injured at the time to which the offered evidence related may have been defective in eyesight, feeble, or careless. The fact that he was injured may have little or no bearing upon the danger to the normal traveller. Moreover, though the same defective condition may have been present at both times, the actual causes of the two injuries may have been different. Unless a comparison of the circumstances and causes of the two injuries is made, the injury to another is without significance. But if such comparison is undertaken, the minds of the jurors must be diverted from the injury on trial into a detailed and possibly protracted inquiry as to injuries received by others at various times. Those injuries have only a collateral and often minor bearing upon the case. As to them the opposing party will

often be ill prepared to present evidence. There is danger that a jury may disregard the real differences in the circumstances of the two incidents, and find upon mere superficial similarity that a dangerous condition existed. Similar considerations apply where evidence that other people, confronted at other times with the same alleged danger, suffered no injury, is offered to prove the want of a dangerous condition.

Robitaille v. Netoco Community Theatre, 305 Mass 265, 266-267, 25 NE2d 749, 750-751 (1940) (in action for personal injuries sustained in fall on stairway, evidence that other persons had fallen at same spot two weeks before not admissible to prove carpet was loose). See also *Kromhout v. Com.*, 398 Mass 687, 692-694, 500 NE2d 789, 792-794 (1986) (in action to recover for motorist's death allegedly caused by defect in highway, reversible error to admit plaintiff's evidence that 21 other accidents occurred at the intersection during past five years in absence of showing that circumstances were substantially similar); *Reil v. Lowell Gas Co.*, 353 Mass 120, 135-136, 228 NE2d 707, 719 (1967) (in action for personal injuries sustained in plant explosion, judge properly excluded evidence of other fires in plant and in another plant of same proprietor because it would be of little help in determining cause of explosion); *Sweeney v. Boston & M.R.R.*, 341 Mass 357, 169 NE2d 875 (1960) (in action for personal injuries sustained by passenger when train stopped suddenly, evidence concerning sudden jolts of train on return trip properly excluded because similarity of conditions not shown); *Guidara & Terenzio v. R. Guastavino Co.*, 286 Mass 502, 190 NE 716 (1934) (evidence that plaster material from same batch used in plaintiff's building worked perfectly in another building properly excluded: "Such evidence would require the jury to compare the buildings in many respects in order to determine whether the conditions were in all ways similar. . . . A multitude of collateral issues might be opened, with no assurance that the jury would be aided rather than misled."); *Read v. Mt. Tom Ski Area, Inc.*, 37 Mass App 901, 639 NE2d 391 (1994) (plaintiff not entitled to submit accident reports to show other rear-end collisions on slide); *Com. v. Levin*, 11 Mass App 482, 503, 417 NE2d 440, 451 (1981) (testimony of other customers that they authorized defendant insurance broker to sign their applications not admissible to prove that insured had authorized defendant to sign his application).

However, "where substantial identity in the circumstances appears, and the danger of unfairness, confusion or undue expenditure of time in the trial of collateral issues reasonably seems small to the trial judge, he has generally been left free to admit such evidence in his discretion." *Robitaille v. Netoco Community Theatre*, supra, 305 Mass at 266, 25 NE2d at 750 (& cases cited). Evidence of the similar behavior of machinery or animals has, for example, generally been held admissible. See *Edward Rose Co. v. Globe & Rutgers Fire Ins. Co.*, 262 Mass 469, 160 NE2d 306 (1928) (evidence of other cotton fires under substantially same conditions near time of fire admissible to prove cause was spark from milling machine); *Bemis v. Temple*, 162 Mass 342, 38 NE 970 (1894) (in nuisance action for injuries occasioned by plaintiff's horse becoming frightened at flag suspended across street, evidence that ordinarily safe and gentle horses had been frightened at flag on other occasions improperly excluded). Similarly, the noxious or harmless character of food and other substances may be shown by their effect upon other persons similarly exposed. *Brek's Case*, 335 Mass 144, 149, 138 NE2d 748, 751 (1948) (testimony of physician that all asbestosis patients he had ever treated had worked at insurer's plant admissible to refute evidence of absence of asbestos dust in plant); *Carter v. Yardley & Co.*, 319 Mass 92, 94, 64 NE2d 693, 694 (1946) (evidence that other users of defendant's perfume suffered skin irritation after applying product properly admitted to show causation); *Johnson v. Kanavos*, 296 Mass 373, 375, 6

NE2d 434, 436 (1937) ("When, under the same conditions, several persons who have eaten the same food become similarly ill an inference may be warranted that the food which all had eaten was unwholesome and was the cause of their illness.").

Conversely, the lack of similar occurrences has been held admissible to prove absence of a dangerous condition. See *Haskell v. Boat Clinton-Serafina, Inc.*, 412 F.2d 896 (1st Cir. 1969) (& citations) (evidence that no prior accident had occurred on ship's deck properly admitted to contradict plaintiff's testimony that there was large patch of slime there).

Evidence of a similar occurrence may also be admissible for the limited purpose of proving knowledge, notice, or state of mind. See, e.g., *Burnham v. Mark IV Homes, Inc.*, 387 Mass 575, 584-585, 441 NE2d 1027, 1033 (1982) (testimony that dealer informed sales manager of leakage problems in roofs of other units admissible to prove notice of defect); *Saldi v. Brighton Stock Yard Co.*, 344 Mass 89, 97-98, 181 NE2d 687, 692 (1962) (in action for personal injuries resulting when plaintiff was butted by defendant's cow, evidence of prior escapes of cows from defendant's yard admissible to show defendant's knowledge of the defective premises); *Denton v. Park Hotel, Inc.*, supra, 343 Mass at 527-528, 180 NE2d at 72 (evidence of prior falls on defendant's dance floor admissible to show defendant's knowledge of the dangerous condition). But see *Williams v. Winthrop*, 213 Mass 581, 584-585, 100 NE 1101, 1103 (1913) (evidence that wagons had been thrown up at particular point in road several times during week prior to accident not admissible to show notice because too many collateral issues); *Read v. Mt. Tom Ski Area, Inc.*, supra, 37 Mass App at 902, 639 NE2d at 393 (evidence of other accidents not admissible to prove knowledge of dangerous condition because no showing other accidents were substantially identical).

b.   Sale Price of Similar Land

Evidence of similar transactions has been held admissible in a variety of commercial law settings. See, e.g., *Steranko v. Inforex*, 8 Mass App 523, 530-531, 395 NE2d 1303, 1307 (1979) (evidence of other sales of similar stock admissible for purpose of showing what might have been a reasonable time in which stock in question could have been sold). Perhaps the most common is proof of the value of a parcel of land by evidence as to the sale price of other similar land. Such evidence must relate to similar property sold at a time not too remote from the time relevant in the disputed case and sold at a noncompulsory sale between a willing seller and a willing buyer. See *United-Carr, Inc. v. Cambridge Redevelopment Authority*, 362 Mass 597, 599-601, 289 NE2d 833, 834-835 (1972). Admissibility of evidence of comparable sales is within the broad discretion of the trial judge, and the judge's decision will be reversed only if manifestly erroneous. See *Anthony's Pier Four, Inc. v. HBC Associates*, 411 Mass 451, 479, 583 NE2d 806, 824 (1991); *Analogic Corp. v. Board of Assessors of Peabody*, 45 Mass App 605, 609-610, 700 NE2d 548, 552-553 (1998).

The sale price of land to a party possessing the power of eminent domain may be admissible if found to be voluntary. *Amory v. Com.*, 321 Mass 240, 256, 72 NE2d 549, 559 (1947). See also *Pankauski v. Greater Lawrence Sanitary District Com.*, 13 Mass App 929, 430 NE2d 1228 (1982) (even though evidence of sale price of comparable land may have been excluded as "under duress" because of pending eminent domain taking, not error to admit evidence in view of owner's failure to develop involuntary nature of sale). The court has given a narrow definition to the "compulsion" that requires exclusion of evidence of a comparable sale, and the burden is on the party opposing the evidence to show that the sale price should be disregarded because it was not the product of free bargaining. See *Westwood Group, Inc. v. Board of Assessors of Revere*, 391 Mass 1012, 462 NE2d 115 (1984); *Ramacorti v. Boston Rede-*

velopment Authority, 341 Mass 377, 170 NE2d 323 (1960) (plaintiff unsuccessfully sought to refute low sale price of land by offering evidence of "compelled" sale due to age of sellers); *Joseph DeVries & Sons, Inc. v. Com.*, 339 Mass 663, 665, 162 NE2d 269, 271 (1959) (fact that parcel was land-locked did not require finding of forced sale).

Zoning differences may properly preclude evidence of the sale price of otherwise similar land. See *Congregation of Mission of St. Vincent de Paul v. Com.*, 336 Mass 357, 145 NE2d 681 (1957) (at trial of petition for assessment of damages for taking of land half of which was located in business zone, no abuse of discretion in exclusion of evidence of sale price of nearby land located entirely in residential zone). There is, however, "no hard and fast rule that a difference in zones in and of itself renders such evidence inadmissible." See *Gregori v. City of Springfield*, 348 Mass 395, 397, 204 NE2d 113, 114 (1965). Nor would the absence of water rights necessarily bar evidence of otherwise comparable sales. *Valley Paper Co. v. Holyoke Housing Authority*, 346 Mass 561, 569, 194 NE2d 700, 705-706 (1963). The sale price of land whose value has been enhanced by a nearby taking for turnpike purposes is clearly inadmissible. *Alden v. Com.*, 351 Mass 83, 87, 217 NE2d 743, 746-747 (1966). Compare *Burchell v. Com.*, 350 Mass 488, 490, 215 NE2d 649, 651 (1966) and *Zambarano v. Massachusetts Turnpike Authority*, 350 Mass 485, 215 NE2d 652 (1966) (nothing in record to indicate enhancement in value because of taking).

For cases holding admissible evidence of sale prices of similar properties, see *Nonni v. Com.*, 356 Mass 264, 268-269, 249 NE2d 644, 646 (1969) (sale price of property five miles away and three years prior); *H. E. Fletcher Co. v. Com.*, 350 Mass 316, 324-326, 214 NE2d 721, 725-727 (1966) (sale price of several parcels of comparable land where sales not too remote in time to assist jury); *Boyd v. Lawrence Redevelopment Authority*, 348 Mass 83, 202 NE2d 297 (1964) (sale price of land similarly zoned and in same general area admissible despite minor differences between parcels);

179

Consolini v. Com., 346 Mass 501, 194 NE2d 407 (1963) (prices paid in sales, near the time of the taking, of two contiguous lots despite substantial difference in size from the property taken). Compare *Massachusetts-American Water Co. v. Grafton Water District*, 36 Mass App 944, 946, 631 NE2d 59, 61 (1994) (significant dissimilarities between sales); *Brush Hill Development, Inc. v. Com.*, 338 Mass 359, 366-367, 155 NE2d 170, 175 (1959) (comparable property four miles away); *Wright v. Com.*, 286 Mass 371, 190 NE2d 593 (1934) (differences in parcels and a question about the voluntary nature of the comparable sale). See also *North American Philips Lighting Corp. v. Board of Assessors of Lynn*, 392 Mass 296, 465 NE2d 782 (1984) (board did not err in assigning little weight to taxpayer's evidence of other sales where there were differences in size, location, and market conditions).

For discussion of expert testimony concerning the value of property, see §7.8.7.

c. Experimental Evidence[17]

If certain natural forces produce a particular effect on one occasion, it is likely that they will do so on another similar occasion. When such a cause-effect relationship is in issue in a case, the outcome of an experiment duplicating the alleged causes may be probative. The evidentiary problem in these cases usually relates to the similarity of the conditions between the experiment and the disputed event.

The general rule is that evidence of an experiment is admissible provided that the conditions are sufficiently similar to make the experiment of value in aiding the jury. This judgment rests in the discretion of the judge, who must determine whether the differences in conditions raise so many collateral issues that the jury will be confused or

---

[17] The use of experiments and demonstrations conducted in court is discussed in §11.12.

misled. Admission of such evidence requires that the trial judge weigh its probative value against the possibility that it will prejudice the jury. See *Griffin v. General Motors Corp.*, 380 Mass 362, 365-366, 403 NE2d 402, 405 (1980) (in negligence action by plaintiff burned when car burst into flames as she was lighting cigarette, judge did not abuse discretion by admitting evidence of test conducted on similar vehicle, but using ammonia rather than gasoline, to rebut defendant manufacturer's theory that it was not possible for fumes to enter passenger compartment from the engine area); *Lally v. Volkswagen Aktiengesellschaft*, 45 Mass App 317, 332-334, 698 NE2d 28, 40-41 (1998) (no abuse of discretion in admitting evidence of sled test performed by defendant which sought to recreate accident); *Calvanese v. W. W. Babcock Co.*, 10 Mass App 726, 729-731, 412 NE2d 895, 899-900 (1980). Compare *Fusco v. General Motors Corp.*, 11 F3d 259 (1st Cir 1993) (judge properly excluded videotaped simulation of car accident because circumstances of test were not substantially similar to those of accident).

The standard for admissibility does not require precise replication. *Ducharme v. Hyundai Motor America*, 45 Mass App 401, 408, 698 NE2d 412, 417 (1998) (crash tests). "Evidence of tests or experiments, which do not exactly replicate the conditions giving rise to the alleged injury, are admissible upon a showing of adequate test controls where there is a substantial similarity between experimental conditions and the conditions that gave rise to the litigation." *Welch v. Keene Corp.*, 31 Mass App 157, 166, 575 NE2d 766, 772 (1991) (& cases cited); *Lally v. Volkswagen Aktiengesellschaft*, supra, 45 Mass App at 333, 698 NE2d at 41 (standard is whether test is similar enough to allow jury to infer "something material"). Dissimilarities go to the weight of such evidence, not its admissibilty. *Ducharme v. Hyundai Motor America*, supra, 45 Mass App 401 at 408-409, 698 NE2d at 417. See, e.g., *Com. v. Ellis*, 373 Mass 1, 4-6, 364 NE2d 808, 811-812 (1977) (no error in admission of expert ballistics evidence even though some dissimilarities between experiment and actual shooting); *Sarkesian v. Cedric Chase Photographic Laboratories, Inc.*, 324 Mass 620, 621-622, 87 NE2d 745, 746 (1949) (on issue of whether roll of photographic film lost by defendant contained pictures, testimony that plaintiff had obtained satisfactory pictures using the same camera and film type sufficient to warrant finding that pictures had been recorded); *Guinan v. Famous Players-Lasky Corp.*, 267 Mass 501, 521-522, 167 NE 235, 245 (1929) (in action by street car passenger for personal injuries caused by explosion of scrap motion picture film, no error in admission of evidence of experiments subjecting pieces of film to various tests to determine explosive quality).

Compare *Com. v. Weichell*, 390 Mass 62, 78, 453 NE2d 1038, 1047 (1983) (evidence of photographic experiment offered by defendant on issue of witness's ability to perceive and identify a human figure at scene of murder properly excluded because conditions of experiment not sufficiently similar); *Com. v. Geagan*, 339 Mass 487, 511, 159 NE2d 870, 887 (1959) (at Brink's robbery trial judge properly excluded evidence of chauffeur called by defendants to testify that he drove route allegedly traveled by defendants and they could not have arrived in time to commit robbery, because no showing that traffic, weather, and light conditions sufficiently similar); *Fahey v. Osol*, 338 Mass 429, 433-434, 155 NE2d 454, 457 (1959) (evidence of expert's tensile strength tests on rope that broke causing collapse of staging upon which plaintiff stood should have been excluded because insufficient similarity between test and actual conditions); *Read v. Mt. Tom Ski Area, Inc.*, 37 Mass App 901, 903-904, 639 NE2d 391, 393-394 (1994) (judge properly excluded experimental evidence where expert testified he had no information about actual conditions at time of plaintiff's accident); *Sacks v. Roux Laboratories, Inc.*, 25 Mass App 672, 674-676, 521 NE2d 1050, 1051-1052 (1988) (judge acted within discretion in excluding results of product test conducted under control of manufacturer because test lacked probative value); *Terrio v. McDonough*, 16 Mass App 163, 173, 450 NE2d 190, 196 (1983) (judge did not abuse discretion by excluding from evidence videotape reenactment of plaintiff's fall down staircase because it did not sufficiently represent actual event).

Experimental evidence is useful and commonly offered to prove that an undisputed effect may have resulted from a cause other than the one alleged. See, e.g., *Lincoln v. Taunton Copper Manufacturing Co.*, 91 Mass 181, 191-192 (1864) (in action alleging injury to land caused by noxious substances from defendant's nearby copper mill, evidence from defendant's expert concerning results of experiment indicating that copper was found in grasses remote from mill properly admitted to rebut plaintiff's evidence that copper was found on his grass); *Calvanese v. W. W. Babcock Co.*, supra, 10 Mass App at 729-731, 412 NE2d at 901 (in action for personal injuries sustained when plaintiff fell from ladder manufactured by defendant, results of tests conducted by defendant's expert to show that ladder could not have failed under normal use described by plaintiff, but that substantially similar damage could be reproduced in an identical ladder by improper loading); *Szeliga v. General Motors Corp.*, 728 F2d 566 (1st Cir 1984) (films depicting experiment conducted by defendant's expert to demonstrate that impact of car, and not loss of lug nuts, was cause of wheel leaving axle).

Experimental evidence may also be used to prove that a particular feat is at least possible. See, e.g., *Griffin v. General Motors Corp.*, supra, 380 Mass at 365-366, 403 NE2d at 405; *Com. v. Makarewicz*, 333 Mass 575, 592-593, 132 NE2d 294, 303-304 (1956) (evidence of experiment conducted by police officer four months after crime to prove that person of defendant's size could climb through particular window at scene of murder).

§4.5 Subsequent Repairs

Although arguably probative, the fact that an alleged defect was repaired or other safety measures were taken after an accident is not admissible as proof of negligence or the existence of the defect. *Martel v. MBTA*, 403 Mass 1, 4, 525 NE2d 662, 664 (1988); Proposed Mass R Evid 407.[1] The predominant reason for this exclusionary rule derives from public policy unrelated to the fact-finding process, that a contrary rule would discourage owners from making repairs to dangerous property. *Martel v. MBTA*, supra (citation omitted). Thus, the following post-accident measures have been held inadmissible to prove liability: installation of a flashing light signal at a railroad crossing, *Ladd v. New York, N.H. & H.R.R.*, 335 Mass 117, 120, 138 NE2d 346, 347-348 (1956); precautions taken to avoid another collapse of a trench, *Shinners v. Proprietors of Locks & Canals on Merrimack River*, 154 Mass 168, 28 NE 10 (1891); repositioning barrier across sidewalk, *Manchester v. Attleboro*, 288 Mass 492, 193 NE 4 (1934); installation of iron bar to prevent wagon from sagging, *Albright v. Sherer*, 223 Mass 39, 42, 111 NE2d 711, 712 (1915); sweeping sidewalk, *Nelson v. Economy Grocery Stores Corp.*, 305 Mass 383, 389, 25 NE2d 986, 990 (1940); sanding street, *National Laundry Co. v. Newton*, 300 Mass 126, 127, 14 NE2d 108, 109 (1938); nailing down board, *Goodell v. Sviokcla*, 262 Mass 317, 159 NE 728 (1928); repairing steps, *Hubley v. Lilley*, 28 Mass App 468, 474, 552 NE2d 573, 576-577 (1990).

---

§4.5 [1] "When, after an event, measures are taken which, if taken previously, would have made the event less likely to occur, evidence of the subsequent measures is not admissible to prove negligence or culpable conduct in connection with the event. This rule does not require the exclusion of evidence of subsequent measures when offered for another purpose, such as proving ownership, control, or feasibility of precautionary measures, if controverted, or impeachment.

PMRE 407.

The exclusion has been extended to the results of a defendant's investigation into the causes of the accident. See *Martel v. MBTA*, supra. The Supreme Judicial Court reasoned:

> Although not itself a "repair" of a dangerous condition, the investigation is the prerequisite to any remedial safety measure. . . . The investigation is inextricably bound up with the subsequent remedial measures to which it may lead, and questions of admissibility of evidence as to each should be analyzed in conjunction and answered consistently. If, as a result of the investigation, the defendant had discharged the bus driver, or required him to undergo additional safety training, evidence of these steps would fall squarely within the rule excluding evidence of subsequent remedial measures. The investigation cannot sensibly be treated differently. To do so would discourage potential defendants from conducting such investigations, and so preclude safety improvements, and frustrate the salutary public policy underlying the rule.

403 Mass at 5, 525 NE2d at 664.

Evidence of a subsequent repair or measure is admissible, however, to prove disputed issues other than negligence such as:

Ownership or Control Over the Premises. See, e.g., *Finn v. Peters*, 340 Mass 622, 625, 165 NE2d 896, 898 (1960) (where oral tenancy was ambiguous as to retention of control by landlord over porch where plaintiff fell because of defective railing, evidence that landlord had subsequently repaired railing admissible); *Perkins v. Rice*, 187 Mass 28, 30, 72 NE 323, 324 (1904) ("When repairs are made on premises by those whom it is sought to charge with liability for their defective condition, evidence of this fact has been deemed competent whether they were made before or after the accident, as being inconsistent with a denial of ownership, although such evidence is not competent as an admission of liability for the accident itself."). But see *Dias v. Woodrow*, 342 Mass 218, 172 NE2d 705

(1961) (evidence that building owner had entranceway cleaned and step repaired after accident admissible on, but not sufficient in itself to establish, issue of control).

The Feasibility of Giving Adequate Warnings. See, e.g., *Schaeffer v. General Motors Corp.*, 372 Mass 171, 175-177, 360 NE2d 1062, 1066 (1977) (text from defendant's owners' manuals admissible to prove practical possibility of giving cautionary warnings regarding cars equipped with controlled differential); *Fiorentino v. A. E. Staley Manufacturing Co.*, 11 Mass App 428, 437-438, 416 NE2d 998, 1005 (1981) (evidence of pre-accident and post-accident changes in warnings admissible to prove feasibility of providing adequate warnings).

The Feasibility of Safety Improvements. See, e.g., *doCanto v. Ametek, Inc.*, 367 Mass 776, 779-782, 328 NE2d 873, 876-877 (1975) (evidence of safety features developed by manufacturer of ironing machinery after sale to plaintiff's employer, but before accident, admissible for limited purposes of showing feasibility of redesign of safety features, defendant's knowledge of defects, and duty to warn of safety deficiencies); *Coy v. Boston Elevated Railway*, 212 Mass 307, 309-310, 98 NE 1041 (1912) (evidence that following accident defendant put up fence to prevent passengers from crossing tracks admissible to show practical possibility of doing so); *Torre v. Harris-Seybold Co.*, 9 Mass App 660, 677, 404 NE2d 96, 108 (1980) (evidence concerning subsequent technological advances or safety improvements utilized by same manufacturer before or after accident admissible in discretion of judge on issues of feasibility and knowledge of risk).

Knowledge of the Danger at Time of Accident. See, e.g., *Reardon v. Country Club at Coonamessett, Inc.*, 353 Mass 702, 704-705, 234 NE2d 881, 883 (1968) (testimony of manager that protective screen was in place at time of accident together with rebuttal evidence that screen was not erected until after accident relevant to prove defendant's knowledge of danger that golfer could be hit with ball).

186

A general concession by the defendant that design improvements were practical does not defeat the admissibility of the evidence to establish feasibility of redesign. See *doCanto v. Ametek, Inc.*, supra, 367 Mass at 781, 328 NE2d at 876; *Schaeffer v. General Motors Corp.*, supra, 372 Mass at 176 n.3 (feasibility of safety warnings). Compare *Cameron v. Otto Bock Orthopedic Indus., Inc.*, 43 F3d 14 (1st Cir 1994) (plaintiff failed to satisfy "if controverted" condition of FRE 407 when manufacturer offered to stipulate to feasibility and did not deny that certain measures might have avoided accident).

Although there does not appear to be direct authority on point in Massachusetts law, the federal subsequent remedial measures exclusionary rule (FRE 407) has been held inapplicable to third-party repairs. See *United States Fidelity & Guaranty Co. v. Baker Material Handling Corp.*, 62 F3d 24 (1st Cir 1995) (& citations).

Failure to comply with safety regulations or a contractual standard may be relevant to the question of negligence. See §8.8.4.

§4.6   Compromise and Offers to Compromise/Offers to Plead Guilty

A party's offer to compromise a dispute is not admissible in evidence as an admission of the validity or invalidity of the claim. *Enga v. Sparks*, 315 Mass 120, 124, 51 NE2d 984, 987 (1943). "This rule is founded in policy, that there may be no discouragement to amicable adjustment of disputes, by a fear, that if not completed, the party amicably disposed may be injured." *Strauss v. Skurnik*, 227 Mass 173, 175, 116 NE 404 (1917). The exclusion applies to offers and actual compromises with third parties as well. See *Murray v. Foster*, 343 Mass 655, 659-669, 180 NE2d 311, 313-314 (1962); *Ricciutti v. Sylvania Electric Products, Inc.*, 343 Mass 347, 349, 178 NE2d 857, 859 (1961). See also *Anonik v. Ominsky*, 261 Mass 65, 158 NE 267 (1927) (statement to third party of willingness to buy peace from litigation by paying a certain amount of money treated as offer to compromise and thus inadmissible to prove liability).

"While it is well settled that offers of settlement are inadmissible to establish liability, whether a particular discussion is in fact a settlement offer may require the resolution of conflicting testimony and is a preliminary question for the trial judge." *Marchand v. Murray*, 27 Mass App 611, 615, 541 NE2d 371, 374 (1989) (conversation in question was offer to purchase, and not offer of settlement). A unilateral statement made by a person who injured a child in an automobile accident to the child's father that he would "fix it up, everything" was held to be an admission of liability, not an offer to compromise, and thus admissible. *Bernasconi v. Bassi*, 261 Mass 26, 28, 158 NE 341, 342 (1927). See also *Hurwitz v. Bocian*, 41 Mass App 365, 371-372, 670 NE2d 408, 413 (1996) (telephone message asking defendant to "come up with a number" to settle business differences with plaintiff admissible, since no indication that lawsuit was planned at time); *Cassidy v. Hollingsworth*, 324 Mass 424, 426, 86 NE2d 663, 664 (1949) (statement made after accident that "I guess I owe you a fender" admissible); *Dennison v. Swerdlove*, 250 Mass 507, 146 NE 27 (1925) (defendant's statement immediately after automobile accident that he would "adjust the damage to your car" not an offer to compromise but admissible as admission of fault). An expression of sympathy such as "I'm sorry" does not qualify as an admission of liability. *Denton v. Park Hotel, Inc.*, 343 Mass 524, 528, 180 NE2d 70, 73 (1962) (such statements have "no probative value as an admission of responsibility or liability" and "[c]ommon decency should not be penalized by treating such statements as admissions"); *Casper v. Lavoie*, 1 Mass App 809, 294 NE2d 466 (1973).

While both Proposed Mass R Evid 408[1] and Fed R Evid 408 provide that admissions of fact made in the course of the compromise negotiations are also inadmissible, Massachusetts case law is to the contrary. See *Puzo v. Puzo,* 342 Mass 775, 173 NE2d 268 (1961); *Calvin Hosmer, Stolte Co. v. Paramount Cone Co.,* 285 Mass 278, 281, 189 NE 192, 194 (1934); *Wagman v. Ziskind,* 234 Mass 509, 125 NE 633 (1920). Where, however, the parties "understood at [the time of the negotiations] that what was said at that time was said without prejudice to either party," admissions of fact will not be admissible at trial. *Garber v. Levine,* 250 Mass 485, 490, 146 NE 21, 22-23 (1925).

The Supreme Judicial Court has adapted the basic principle of Proposed Mass R Evid 408 to settlements between the plaintiff and a joint tortfeasor: unless evidence of the settlement is relevant for some purpose other than to prove liability, it is not admissible. Regarding the mitigation of damages based on the settlement, the judge shall instruct the jury to determine the damages substantially caused by the defendant, and then the judge (not the jury) will make the appropriate reduction in any amount awarded. See *Morea v. Cosco, Inc.,* 422 Mass 601, 664 NE2d 822 (1996) (abandoning the so-called "jury rule" for the "court rule").

An offer to pay medical expenses is inadmissible to prove liability for the underlying injury, again based on the public policy of encouraging such payments. See *Gallo v. Veliskakis,* 357 Mass 602, 606, 259 NE2d 568, 570 (1970)

---

§4.6   [1]Evidence of (1) furnishing or offering or promising to furnish, or (2) accepting or offering or attempting to compromise a claim which was disputed as to either validity or amount, is not admissible to prove liability for, invalidity of, or amount of the claim or any other claim. Evidence of conduct or statements made in compromise negotiations is likewise not admissible. This rule does not require exclusion when the evidence is offered for another purpose, such as proving bias or prejudice of a witness, negativing a contention of undue delay, or proving an effort to obstruct a criminal investigation or prosecution.

PMRE 408.

(statement by owner of automobile to parent of passenger injured while it was operated by nephew that owner was sorry about accident and would take care of medical bills not an admission of liability and lacking in probative value); Proposed Mass R Evid 409.[2]

Massachusetts practice bars the use in evidence in any criminal or civil proceeding of a withdrawn guilty plea or an offer to plead guilty. Mass R Crim P 12(f); Proposed Mass R Evid 410.[3] Except in a prosecution for perjury, the bar created by Rules 12(f) and 410 applies to any statement made in the course of the plea negotiations as long as it is relevant to the negotiations. But see *Com. v. Luce*, 34 Mass App 105, 111-112, 607 NE2d 427, 430-431 (1993) (judge found meetings between defendant and counsel and government officers did not constitute plea bargaining). See also §8.8.2.

§4.7   Liability Insurance

Evidence of insurance coverage or lack thereof is not admissible on the issue of negligence or liability. It may be

---

[2] "Evidence of furnishing or offering or promising to pay medical, hospital, or similar expenses occasioned by an injury is not admissible to prove liability for the injury." PMRE 409. Note that Rule 409, unlike Rule 408, does not bar specific admissions of liability made in conjunction with such offers.

[3] Both Mass R Crim P 12(f) and Proposed Mass R Evid 410 provide:

> [E]vidence of a plea of guilty, later withdrawn, or a plea of nolo contendere, or an offer to plead guilty or nolo contendere to the crime charged or any other crime, or statements made in connection with, and relevant to, any of the foregoing pleas or offers, is not admissible in any civil or criminal proceedings against the person who made the plea or offer. However, evidence of a statement made in connection with, and relevant to, a plea of guilty, later withdrawn, or a plea of nolo contendere, or an offer to plead guilty or nolo contendere to the crime charged or any other crime, is admissible in a criminal proceeding for perjury if the statement was made by the defendant under oath, on the record, and in the presence of counsel.

These provisions changed prior law in the Commonwealth. See *Morrissey v. Powell*, 304 Mass 268, 23 NE2d 411 (1939).

admissible for other purposes, such as showing ownership or control where those issues are genuinely in dispute. See *Goldstein v. Gontarz,* 364 Mass 800, 807-814, 309 NE2d 196, 202-205 (1974) (extensive discussion of principles and authorities); *Leavitt v. Glick Realty Corp.,* 362 Mass 370, 372, 285 NE2d 786, 787-788 (1972); Proposed Mass R Evid 411.[1]

"Exposing juries to [insurance coverage] information is condemned because it is not itself probative of any relevant proposition and is taken to lead to undeserved verdicts for plaintiffs and exaggerated awards which jurors will readily load on faceless insurance companies supposedly paid for taking the risk." *Goldstein v. Gontarz,* supra, 364 Mass at 808, 309 NE2d at 202.[2] The exclusion covers: (1) evidence offered by the plaintiff that the defendant is insured; (2) evidence offered by the defendant that the plaintiff has received third-party compensation for his injury; (3) evidence offered by the defendant that he is not protected by insurance (considered a "plea of poverty" that might influence the jury to give defendant "compassionate but strictly unmerited relief from personal liability"); and (4) evidence offered by the plaintiff that he has no resort to insurance or other coverage for his loss. *Goldstein v. Gontarz,* supra, 364 Mass at 808-810, 309 NE2d at 202-204.

Evidence of a policy of indemnity insurance is admissible on the disputed issue of control over the covered premises, because the jury could properly infer that "the defendants would not have deemed it prudent to secure indemnity insurance on [an area] not within their control, or for the careless management or defective condition of

---

§4.7   [1] "Evidence that a person was or was not insured against liability is not admissible upon the issue whether he acted negligently or otherwise wrongfully. This rule does not require the exclusion of evidence of insurance against liability when offered for another purpose, such as proof of agency, ownership, or control, or bias or prejudice of a witness." PMRE 411.

[2] But see *McDaniel v. Pickens,* 45 Mass App 63, 70, 695 NE2d 215, 219 (1998) (raising but not reaching issue of "whether jurors have attained to such a level of sophistication that they can take insurance and related things in stride when properly instructed").

which they could not be held responsible." *Perkins v. Rice*, 187 Mass 28, 30, 72 NE 323, 324 (1904). A blanket insurance policy covering more than one location is not, however, admissible to show control. See *Camerlin v. Marshall*, 411 Mass 394, 398, 582 NE2d 539, 542 (1991) (& cases cited).

Evidence of insurance coverage or lack thereof may also be admissible to establish the bias of a witness. See, e.g., *McDaniel v. Pickens*, 45 Mass App 63, 695 NE2d 215 (1998) (& citations) (bias of expert in medical malpractice case); *Com. v. Danis*, 38 Mass App 968, 650 NE2d 802 (1995) (showing that policy did not cover collision damage to prosecution witness' car relevant to her possible bias in trial of vehicular offenses).

Evidence of insurance coverage has been held inadmissible in intra-family tort actions even though jurors may wrongfully assume that one family member is seeking to deplete the assets of another family member and that institution of the lawsuit has disrupted family harmony. *Shore v. Shore*, 385 Mass 529, 432 NE2d 526 (1982).

Ordinarily evidence of collateral source payments (such as workers' compensation benefits) is excluded because jurors may be led to consider the plaintiff's claims unimportant or trivial or to refuse or reduce a verdict in the plaintiff's favor, believing that otherwise there would be unjust double recovery. In some limited circumstances, however, such evidence may be admissible as probative of a relevant proposition, such as the credibility of a witness. See *Goldstein v. Gontarz*, supra, 364 Mass at 809, 309 NE2d at 202; *Corsetti v. Stone Co.*, 396 Mass 1, 16-21, 483 NE2d 793, 801-804 (1985); *West v. Shawmut Design & Construction*, 39 Mass App 247, 655 NE2d 136 (1995) (& citations) (extensive discussion). See generally *Fitzgerald v. Expressway Sewerage Construction, Inc.*, 177 F3d 71 (1st Cir 1999).

§5.1   Burden of Proof Defined

"Burden of proof" has two distinct meanings. The burden of persuasion is the burden to convince the jury (or other fact finder) that a fact exists. The burden of production is the burden to produce sufficient evidence to "get to the jury" — i.e., evidence sufficient to convince the judge that a reasonable jury could find that the fact exists. See *City of Lawrence v. Commissioners of Public Works*, 318 Mass 520, 527-528, 62 NE2d 850, 854 (1945); *Epstein v. Boston Housing Authority*, 317 Mass 297, 302, 58 NE2d 135, 139 (1944); *Smith v. Hill*, 232 Mass 188, 190-191, 122 NE 310, 310-311 (1919). For a general treatment of burdens of proof, see Wigmore §§2485-2489 (Chad rev 1981).

The burden of persuasion instructs the fact finder concerning the "degree of confidence our society thinks [it] should have in the correctness of factual conclusions for a particular type of adjudication." *C.C. v. A.B.*, 406 Mass 679, 686-687, 550 NE2d 365, 370-371 (1990) (quoting *In re Winship*, 397 US 358, 370 (1970) (Harlan, J, concurring)). For an extensive discussion of the policy implications and constitutional requirements concerning the standard of proof, see *Santosky v. Kramer*, 455 US 745 (1982); *Care and Protection of Robert*, 408 Mass 52, 556 NE2d 993 (1990) (& citations);

Spence v. Gormley, 387 Mass 258, 274-277, 439 NE2d 741, 750-751 (1982). If, at the close of the evidence, the fact finder determines that a fact has not been proven to the required level of certainty, the fact finder must decide the issue against the burdened party.

As a general rule, the burden of persuasion does not shift between the parties during the course of the trial because it does not come into play until the fact finder deliberates on its decision. See *Wylie v. Marinofsky,* 201 Mass 583, 88 NE 448 (1909); *Powers v. Russell,* 30 Mass (13 Pick) 69, 76 (1832); Proposed Mass R Evid 301(b) and Fed R Evid 301 ("the burden of proof in the sense of the risk of nonpersuasion remains throughout the trial upon the party on whom it was originally cast."). Certain types of presumptions, however, may have the practical effect of shifting the burden of persuasion as to a particular fact. See §§5.5.3.a, infra.

The burden of production requires the party who bears it to come forward with some evidence that a fact exists. If the party does not satisfy this burden, the court will decide the issue against it without submitting the issue to the jury. Unlike the burden of persuasion, the burden of production as to an issue can, and often does, shift between the parties during the course of the trial. *Powers v. Russell,* supra, 30 Mass at 76.

Adequate proof in both civil and criminal cases may come from either direct or circumstantial evidence. *Abraham v. Woburn,* 383 Mass 724, 729, 421 NE2d 1206, 1210 (1981) (& citations). See generally §4.2.

§5.2   Burden of Production of Evidence

§5.2.1   Amount of Evidence Required

A party has sustained its burden of production when it has adduced evidence sufficient to form a reasonable basis for a verdict in that party's favor. Generally speaking, for the judge to submit an issue to the jury for final determination in a civil case, the evidence must be such that the jury could reasonably find either way as to the existence of the fact. *West v. Molders Foundry Co.*, 342 Mass 8, 171 NE2d 860 (1961). Where there is sufficient evidence to support a verdict either way, the case must be given to the jury even though it appears that "the preponderance of the evidence on one side is so great that [the judge] would set aside a verdict rendered against such preponderance." See *Hartmann v. Boston Herald-Traveler Corp.*, 323 Mass 56, 59-60, 80 NE2d 16, 18 (1948); *Lubianez v. Metropolitan Life Insurance Co.*, 323 Mass 16, 20, 79 NE2d 876, 878-879 (1948).

Whether the party with the burden of production of evidence has adduced enough evidence to warrant submission of the case to the jury may be tested by a motion for a directed verdict in a civil case, Mass R Civ P 50(a), and a motion for required finding of not guilty in criminal cases. Mass R Crim P 25. Mass R Crim P 25(a) authorizes the judge to enter a finding of not guilty on his own motion. Although Mass R Civ P 50(a) does not similarly authorize such action in a civil case, older precedent does. See *Field v. Hamm*, 254 Mass 268, 150 NE 3 (1926). Mass R Crim P 25(c) provides the Commonwealth with a right of appeal where the judge directs a verdict or sets aside a verdict of guilty.

Under present civil practice, a judge may grant a motion for directed verdict or defer ruling on the motion until after the jury renders a decision and then the judge may entertain a motion under Mass R Civ P 50(b) to enter a judgment notwithstanding the verdict (n.o.v.). Under Rule 50, the filing of a motion for directed verdict is a predicate for a motion for judgment n.o.v. *Davis v. DelRosso*, 371 Mass 768, 359 NE2d 313 (1977). The litigant is required to state the specific grounds in support of the motion for directed verdict. *Rhode Island Hospital Trust National Bank v. Varadian*, 419 Mass 841, 846-847, 647 NE2d 1174, 1177 (1995). The standard of appellate review is the same under both motions. *Turnpike Motors, Inc. v. Newbury Group, Inc.*, 413 Mass 119, 121, 596 NE2d 989, 991 (1992) (*Turnpike Motors II*) (whether "anywhere in the evidence, from whatever source derived, any combination of circumstances could be found from which a reasonable inference could be drawn in favor of" the party moved against); *Stapleton v. Macchi*, 401 Mass 725, 728, 519 NE2d 273, 275, (1988) (same); *Abraham v. Woburn*, 383 Mass 724, 727, 421 NE2d 1206, 1209-1210 (1981) (same); *Corbin v. Hudson*, 9 Mass App 900, 402 NE2d 1115 (1980) (standard of review requires appellate court to view evidence, including all reasonable inferences therefrom, in light most favorable to party moved against).

In close questions, it is preferable practice to allow the matter to go to the jury since the motion for judgment n.o.v. may be allowed later, if appropriate, and the benefit of a jury verdict may preclude the necessity of a new trial subsequent to appellate review. See *Brady v. Nestor*, 398 Mass 184, 187, 496 NE2d 148, 150 (1986); *Abraham v. Woburn*, supra, 383 Mass at 727 n.3, 421 NE2d at 1209 n.3; *Smith v. Ariens Co.*, 375 Mass 620, 627, 377 NE2d 954, 959 (1978).

On motions for a directed verdict or for judgment n.o.v. in a civil case, where the judge, considering the evidence in the light most favorable to the party against whom the motion is directed and, without weighing the credibility of the witnesses or otherwise considering the weight of the evidence, determines that the jury could reasonably find just *one* way, the motion must be allowed. *Bonin v. Chestnut Hill Towers Realty Corp.*, 392 Mass 58, 61, 466 NE2d 90, 92 (1984); *Adams v. Herbert*, 345 Mass 588, 188 NE2d 577 (1963); *O'Shaughnessy v. Besse*, 7 Mass App 727, 389 NE2d 1049 (1979). A court will not substitute its interpretation of facts for the jury's; as long as the jury's verdict would be (or is) supported by reasonable inferences, a motion for directed verdict (or judgment n.o.v.) should be denied. *Abraham v. Woburn*, supra, 383 Mass at 730, 421 NE2d at 1209. See, e.g., *Turnpike Motors II*, supra, 413 Mass at 121-126, 596 NE2d at 990-993 (judge incorrectly allowed plaintiff sellers' motion for judgment n.o.v. where defendant broker had introduced sufficient evidence to support finding of reasonable reliance).

If the evidence is so scant or ambiguous that the jury could reasonably find *either* way as to the existence of the fact, the judge should direct a finding against the party with the burden of persuasion. *Alholm v. Wareham*, 371 Mass 621, 358 NE2d 788 (1976) (no evidence); *Spano v. Wilson Tisdale Co.*, 361 Mass 209, 279 NE2d 725 (1972) (scant evidence); *LeBlanc v. Atlantic Building & Supply Co.*, 323 Mass 702, 84 NE2d 10 (1949) (ambiguous evidence); *Hillyer v. Dickinson*, 154 Mass 502, 28 NE 905 (1891) (scintilla of evidence in favor not enough). See also *Stapleton v. Macchi*, supra, 401 Mass at 728, 519 NE2d at 275 (party may not avoid directed verdict or entry of judgment n.o.v. against it if any essential element of its case rests upon mere scintilla of evidence); *Gram v. Liberty Mutual Insurance Co.*, 384 Mass 659, 429 NE2d 21 (1981) (no basis for reasonable inference); *Laurendeau v. Kewaunee Scientific Equipment Corp.*, 17 Mass App 113, 122-124, 456 NE2d 767, 772-773 (1983). This is so even though mathematically the chances somewhat favor the proposition to be proved. *Friese v. Boston Consolidated Gas Co.*, 324 Mass 623, 631, 88 NE2d 1, 5 (1949); *Smith v. Rapid Transit, Inc.*, 317 Mass 469, 58 NE2d 754 (1945).

Alternatively, a verdict may be set aside as being contrary to the weight of the evidence. Mass R Civ P 59; Mass R Crim P 25(b)(2). The judge, however:

> should not decide the case as if sitting without a jury; rather, the judge should only set aside the verdict if satisfied that the jury failed to exercise an honest and reasonable judgment in accordance with the controlling principles of law. Moreover, a judge should exercise this discretion only when the verdict is so greatly against the weight of the evidence as to induce in his mind the strong belief that it was not due to a careful consideration of the evidence, but that it was the product of bias, misapprehension or prejudice.

Turnpike Motors II, supra, 413 Mass at 127, 596 NE2d at 994 (citations and internal quotations omitted). For further discussion of the standard for setting aside a verdict, see *J. Edmund & Co. v. Rosen*, 412 Mass 572, 576, 591 NE2d 179, 181 (1992); *Oldham v. Nerolich*, 389 Mass 1005, 452 NE2d 225 (1983); *Brown v. MTA*, 345 Mass 636, 189 NE2d 214 (1963); *Lubianez v. Metropolitan Life Insurance Co.*, supra, 323 Mass at 20-21, 79 NE2d at 878-879; *Massachusetts General Hospital v. Brody*, 16 Mass App 993, 454 NE2d 1281 (1983).

While directed findings for opponents are common, they are rarely given in favor of the party having the burden of proof because such a ruling would mean that as a matter of law it had sustained its burden of persuasion as well as its burden of production of evidence. See *Workmen's Circle Education Center v. Board of Assessors of City of Springfield*, 314 Mass 616, 621, 51 NE2d 313, 317 (1943); *Giles v. Giles*, 204 Mass 383, 90 NE 595 (1910); *Spence v. Gillis*, 16 Mass App 905, 449 NE2d 391 (1983) (citing Text). Directed findings are given in such situations only where the facts are undisputed or undisputable, or shown by evidence by which the opponent is bound. *Goldstein v. Gontarz*, 364 Mass 800, 309 NE2d 196 (1974); *O'Neill v. Middlesex & Boston Railway*, 244 Mass 510, 138 NE 841 (1923); *Gaston v. Gordon*, 208 Mass 265, 94 NE 307 (1911). Compare *J. Edmund & Co. v. Rosen*, supra, 412 Mass at 575, 591 NE2d at 181 and *Lubianez v. Metropolitan Life Insurance Co.*, supra, 323 Mass at 19, 79 NE2d at 878 (verdict can rarely be directed in favor of party having burden of proof where evidence consists of oral testimony).

In criminal cases, a motion for a required finding of not guilty must be allowed if the evidence and the inferences permitted to be drawn therefrom cannot reasonably support a finding of guilt beyond a reasonable doubt on each element of the crime charged. *Com. v. Kappler*, 416 Mass 574, 578-579, 625 NE2d 513 (1993); *Com. v. Pratt*, 407 Mass 647, 651, 555 NE2d 559, 562 (1990); *Com. v. Sherry*, 386 Mass 682, 687, 437 NE2d 224, 227-228 (1982); *Com. v. DeStefano*, 16 Mass App 208, 214-215, 450 NE2d 637, 640 (1983). The question on review of a denial of such a motion is whether, after viewing the evidence in the light most favorable to the prosecution, any rational trier of fact could have found the essential elements of the crime beyond a reasonable doubt. *Jackson v. Virginia*, 443 US 307, 319, 99 S Ct 2781, 61 L Ed 2d 560 (1979); *Com. v. Pratt*, supra; *Com. v. Salim*, 399 Mass 227, 228, 503 NE2d 1267, 1268 (1987); *Com. v. Lowe*, 391 Mass 97, 107, 461 NE2d 192, 199 (1984); *Com. v. Dunphy*, 377 Mass 453, 455-456, 386 NE2d 1036, 1038 (1979).

In making a ruling of the kinds considered here, the judge must resolve all questions as to the weight of evidence and credibility of the witnesses against the party making the motion. *Gram v. Liberty Mutual Insurance Co.*, supra; *Com. v. Soares*, 377 Mass 461, 464, 387 NE2d 499, 503 (1979); *Adams v. Herbert*, 345 Mass 588, 188 NE2d 577 (1963). In connection with such rulings, the following points should also be kept in mind:

(1)   a number of facts are questions for the court and not the jury — e.g., preliminary questions of fact (see §3.9.1, supra);

(2)   the judge and jury may not be free to disbelieve certain testimony (see §2.11, supra);

(3)   mere disbelief of testimony does not constitute proof of the contrary proposition, and a case lacking adequate affirmative proof is insufficient to support a verdict in favor of the party with the burden of proof on the issue (see *Forrey v. Dedham Taxi, Inc.*, 19 Mass App 955, 473 NE2d 726 (1985) (& citations) and §4.2.3, supra);

(4)   in a criminal case, only the evidence introduced up to the time the Commonwealth rested its case and the defendant first filed a motion for directed verdict may be considered (see *Com. v. Dunnington*, 390 Mass 472, 475, 457 NE2d 1109, 1112 (1983); *Com. v. Bongarzone*, 390 Mass 326, 348, 455 NE2d 1183, 1196 (1983); *Com. v. Wilborne*, 382 Mass 241, 415 NE2d 192 (1981)).

§5.2.2   Allocation of Burden of Production

The party with the burden of persuasion has the burden of production at the outset of the trial. The burden shifts to the opponent, back to proponent, and so on, if and when the evidence becomes such that the jury could reasonably find only for the other party. The burden of production of evidence thus may be on one, on the other, or on neither party as the trial progresses. *Com. v. Taylor*, 383 Mass 272, 281-282 n.10, 418 NE2d 1226, 1232 n.10 (1981) (quoting *Powers v. Russell*, 30 Mass (13 Pick) 69, 76 (1832)). When the proponent has presented "prima facie evidence" on an issue, the burden of production shifts to the opponent; and if the opponent does not carry that burden, a finding against the opponent is required. See *Ford Motor Co. v. Barrett*, 403 Mass 240, 242-243, 526 NE2d 1284, 1286 (1988) (& citations) (citing Text) (arbitrator's findings constitute prima facie evidence in action under "Lemon Law"); *Pryor v. Holiday Inns, Inc.*, 401 Mass 506, 508-510, 517 NE2d 472, 474-475 (1988) (& citations) (prima facie showing of discrimination shifts to employer burden of coming forward with evidence of lawful reason for discharge). For a discussion of the shifting burdens in discrimination cases, see §5.3.1.d, infra. For a discussion of the various factors weighed in deciding which party has the burden of production on a particular issue, see *Eliot Discount Corp. v. Dame*, 19 Mass App 280, 284-285, 473 NE2d 711, 714-715 (1985) (& citations) (citing Text).

In a criminal case, the Commonwealth has both the burden of production and the burden of persuasion as to each element of the offense charged. See *Com. v. Burke*, 390 Mass 480, 483-484, 457 NE2d 622, 624-625 (1983). For a discussion of the burden of production on a criminal defendant seeking to raise an insanity defense, see *Com. v. Mills*, 400 Mass 626, 511 NE2d 572 (1987) (& citations).

§5.3   Burden of Persuasion in Civil Cases

§5.3.1   Allocation of Burden of Persuasion in Civil Cases

a.   General Principles

In civil cases, the burden of persuasion is on the plaintiff as to some issues and on defendant as to others. If a fact must be pleaded, the burden of persuasion is usually on the party who must plead that fact. See, e.g., *Freeman v. Travelers Insurance Co.*, 144 Mass 572, 12 NE 372 (1887) (burden on defendant to prove insured did not use due diligence to prevent accident); *Phipps v. Mahon*, 141 Mass 471, 5 NE 835 (1886) (burden on plaintiff to prove contract alleged by him); *Crownenshield v. Crownenshield*, 68 Mass (2 Gray) 524 (1854) (burden on party offering will for probate to prove requisite formalities).

It is variously stated that the burden of persuasion should properly fall on the party who:

(1)   initiated the suit;
(2)   would change the status quo;
(3)   asserts the affirmative proposition;
(4)   asserts the unlikely proposition;
(5)   has freer access to the evidence; or
(6)   by winning will cause socially undesirable results.

In accordance with these considerations, the burden of persuasion has been allocated to the plaintiff as to most classes of disputed facts. See, e.g., *Jernigan v. Giard*, 398 Mass 721, 500 NE2d 806 (1986) (burden on plaintiff in legal malpractice action to prove that judgment would have been collectible). For examples of allocation analysis, see *Cleary v. Cleary*, 427 Mass 286, 692 NE2d 955 (1998) (in general, party challenging will or other document on ground it was procured through fraud or undue influence bears burden of proving allegation; but burden shifts when fiduciary benefits from transaction with principal); *Cantres v. Director of the Division of Employment Security*, 396 Mass 226, 484 NE2d 1336 (1985) (citing Text); *Eliot Discount Corp. v. Dame*, 19 Mass App 280, 284-285, 473 NE2d 711, 715 (1985) (& citations) (citing Text).

b.   Actions Alleging Statutory Liability

In actions alleging statutory liability, the burden of persuasion is on the plaintiff as to all facts that by statute are necessary to create the liability. *Tileston v. Inhabitants of Brookline*, 134 Mass 438 (1883). Similarly, one who seeks relief under a statute has the burden of proving himself within its terms. *William Rodman & Sons v. State Tax Comm'n*, 373 Mass 606, 610-611, 368 NE2d 1382, 1384-1385 (1977); *Treasurer & Receiver General v. Cunniff*, 357 Mass 206, 257 NE2d 459 (1970). The party seeking to come within a statutory exception has the burden of persuasion on that matter. *In re Acushnet River & New Bedford Harbor*, 722 F Supp 893, 901 & n.21 (D Mass 1989); *Cantres v. Director of the Division of Employment Security*, supra, 396 Mass at 231, 484 NE2d at 1340; *Wheeler v. Director of Division of Employment Security*, 347 Mass 730, 200 NE2d 272 (1964).

The legislature may by statute designate the party with the burden of persuasion. See, e.g., GL 231, §85 (comparative negligence). The Uniform Commercial Code (GL 106) has various provisions pertaining to burdens of persuasion. See, e.g., §1-201(8) (definition of burden of persuasion); §1-208 (burden of establishing lack of good faith on party against whom power to accelerate was exercised); §2-607(4) (burden on buyer to establish breach after goods accepted); §3-115 (burden of establishing unauthorized completion of paper on party so asserting); §3-307 (burden of establishing genuineness of signature on party claiming under signature; burden of proving party is holder in due course is on party claiming those rights); §3-408 (burden as to want or failure of consideration); §4-202(2) (collecting bank has burden of establishing it took proper action within reasonable time when that time was longer than that expressly stipulated by §4-202); §4-403 (customer has burden of establishing fact and amount of loss from payment contrary to binding stop order). See also *Universal CIT Credit Corp. v. Ingel*, 347 Mass 119, 125, 196 NE2d 847, 851 (1964) (burden on defendants to rebut plaintiff's prima facie case of holder in due course).

c. Affirmative Defenses

The burden of persuasion is on the defendant as to affirmative defenses. An affirmative defense is one that, rather than meeting or negating the allegations of the proponent, sets up new and distinct propositions that avoid the effect of the proponent's allegations even if they are established. *Perley v. Perley*, 144 Mass 104, 10 NE 726 (1887); *Powers v. Russell*, 30 Mass (13 Pick) 69, 76 (1832). Examples of affirmative defenses include arbitration and award, comparative negligence, fraud, payment, and res judicata.

GL 231, §85, eliminated the defenses of contributory negligence and assumption of risk in negligence cases, substituting comparative negligence which may diminish the amount of recovery. The burden of alleging and proving comparative negligence is upon the party who seeks to establish such negligence.

Although illegality is an affirmative defense to be pleaded by the defendant, the court will not act to enforce an illegal contract contrary to public policy even though neither party raises the issue. See *Cadillac Automobile Co. of Boston v. Engeian*, 339 Mass 26, 29-30, 157 NE2d 657, 659-660 (1959); *O'Donnell v. Bane*, 385 Mass 114, 117, 431 NE2d 190, 192 (1982) (extensive review of authorities) (contingent fee agreement for attorney's representation in criminal matter).

For a sampling of cases illustrating the variety of affirmative defenses, see *Highlands Insurance Co. v. Aerovox, Inc.*, 424 Mass 226, 231, 676 NE2d 801, 805 (1997) (insured has burden of proving "sudden and accidental" release exception to pollution exclusion); *McGinnis v. Aetna Life & Casualty Co.*, 398 Mass 37, 494 NE2d 1322 (1986) (burden of proof on insurer to prove plaintiff intentionally procured loss); *Three Sons, Inc. v. Phoenix Insurance Co.*, 357 Mass 271, 257 NE2d 774 (1970) (laches); *Benoit v. Fisher*, 341 Mass 386, 169 NE2d 905 (1960) (cancellation of insurance coverage prior to accident); *Wellesley v. Brossi*, 340 Mass 456, 164 NE2d 883 (1960) (nonconforming use); *Corbett v. Derman Shoe Co.*, 338 Mass 405, 412-413, 155 NE2d 423, 428 (1959) (lessee has burden to qualify under separate and distinct covenant of exception in lease); *Lubianez v. Metropolitan Life Insurance Co.*, 323 Mass 16, 18-19, 79 NE2d 876-878 (1948) (exception in contract); *City of Lawrence v. Commissioners of Public Works*, 318 Mass 520, 527, 62 NE2d 850, 854 (1945) (that person was de facto officer at time license was issued); *Zani v. Garrison Hall, Inc.*, 300 Mass 128, 14 NE2d 118 (1938) (recoupment); *Merry v. Priest*, 276 Mass 592, 599, 177 NE 673, 674 (1931) (extent of right of way); *McCarthy v. Simon*, 247 Mass 514, 521, 142 NE 806, 807 (1924) (payment); *Smith v. Hill*, 232 Mass 188, 122 NE 310 (1919) (discharge in bankruptcy).

There are certain matters that must be affirmatively pleaded by way of defense, but that do not cast the burden of persuasion upon the defendant. See *Cluff v. Picardi*, 331 Mass 320, 321, 118 NE2d 753, 754 (1954) (Statute of Frauds); *Lariviere v. Lariviere*, 304 Mass 627, 628, 24 NE2d 659, 661 (1939) (Statute of Limitations, GL 260); *Breen v. Burns*, 280 Mass 222, 182 NE 294 (1932) (Statute of Limitations, GL 197, §9).

Mass R Civ P 8(b) (requiring specific denial as to genuineness of a signature to an instrument set forth in a pleading and as to an allegation that a place is a public way), Mass R Civ P 8(c) (requiring that enumerated defenses "and any other matter constituting an avoidance or affirmative defense" be set forth affirmatively in party's pleading), and Mass R Civ P 9(a) (requiring issue as to party's legal existence, capacity to sue or be sued, or representative capacity to be raised by specific negative averment) do not

205

purport to establish either a burden of persuasion or production of evidence, but instead deal only with pleading. See Reporters' Notes to Rule 8.

d. Discrimination Cases

In discrimination cases, although the plaintiff's establishment of a prima facie case shifts the burden of producing a lawful explanation for the adverse treatment to the defendants, the plaintiff bears the ultimate burden of proving intentional discrimination. *Lynn Teachers Union, Local 1037 v. Massachusetts Commission Against Discrimination,* 406 Mass 515, 526-527, 549 NE2d 97, 103-104 (1990); *Pryor v. Holiday Inns, Inc.,* 401 Mass 506, 508-510, 517 NE2d 472, 474-475 (1988); *Lewis v. Area II Homecare for Senior Citizens, Inc.,* 397 Mass 761, 765-766, 493 NE2d 867, 870 (1986); *Sarni Original Dry Cleaners, Inc. v. Cooke,* 388 Mass 611, 614-615, 447 NE2d 1228, 1233 (1983); *City of Salem v. Massachusetts Commission Against Discrimination,* 44 Mass App 627, 641-642, 693 NE2d 1026, 1037-1038 (1998). See generally *Texas Department of Community Affairs v. Burdine,* 450 US 248, 101 S Ct 1089, 67 L Ed 2d 207 (1981) (shifting burdens in federal Title VII action).

Although the elements of the plaintiff's initial burden may vary depending on the specific facts of the case, a prima facie case of discrimination is generally made out with evidence that: (1) the plaintiff is a member of a protected class; (2) the plaintiff was qualified for the position in question; (3) the plaintiff was not hired, terminated, or otherwise adversely treated; and (4) the employer sought to fill the position with individuals of similar qualifications to plaintiff's. See *Dartt v. Browning-Ferris Industries, Inc.,* 427 Mass 1, 691 NE2d 526 (1998) (handicap); *Blare v. Husky Injection Molding Systems Boston, Inc.,* 419 Mass 437, 441, 646 NE2d 111, 115 (1995) (age); *Beal v. Board of Selectmen of Hingham,* 419 Mass 535, 541, 646 NE2d 131, 136 (1995) (handicap and gender); *Tate v. Department of Mental Health*, 419 Mass 361-364, 645 NE2d 1163, 1165 (1995) (handicap and retaliation). The plaintiff does not have to prove each of the four elements to avoid a directed verdict; rather, the plaintiff must merely produce evidence that, if believed, would be sufficient to establish facts entitling the plaintiff to judgment. *Whalen v. NYNEX Information Resources Co.*, 419 Mass 792, 796, 647 NE2d 716, 719 (1995). It is not a requirement that the plaintiff show, as part of his prima facie case, that he was terminated *solely* because of discrimination. *Dartt v. Browning-Ferris Industries, Inc.*, supra, 427 Mass at 2, 691 NE2d at 528.

The burden of production then shifts to the defendant employer, who must rebut by articulating a legitimate, non-discriminatory reason(s) for its decision. This requires credible evidence that the reason or reasons were the real reasons. If the employer fails to meet its burden, the plaintiff is entitled to judgment. *Blare v. Husky Injection Molding Systems Boston, Inc.*, supra, 419 Mass 441-442, 646 NE2d at 115. If the defendant meets the burden, the proceedings enter a third stage where the plaintiff has the opportunity to prove that the stated reasons are pretextual. Proof of pretext entitles the plaintiff to judgment under Massachusetts law. *Blare v. Husky Injection Molding Sysytems Boston, Inc.*, supra, 419 Mass 441-442, 646 NE2d at 115. Compare *St. Mary's Honor Center v. Hicks*, 509 US 502, 113 S Ct 2742, 125 L Ed 2d 407 (1993) (in federal Title VII action, proof of pretext does not constitute proof of discrimination entitling plaintiff to judgment). See generally Brodin, The Demise of Circumstantial Proof in Employment Discrimination Litigation: *St. Mary's Honor Center v. Hicks*, Pretext and the "Personality" Excuse, 18 Berkeley Journal of Employment and Labor Law 183 (1997). For discussion of the analysis in cases involving mixed-motive decision-making, see *Brownlie v. Kanzaki Speciality Papers, Inc.*, 44 Mass App 408, 416-419, 691 NE2d 953, 960-961 (1998).

§5.3.2   Degree of Persuasion in Civil Cases

a.   Preponderance of the Evidence

Generally in civil cases the party who bears the burden of persuasion must persuade the fact finder that its contention is more probably true than false, referred to as proof "by a preponderance of the evidence." See *Lynch v. Merrell-National Laboratories,* 830 F2d 1190, 1197 (1st Cir 1987); *Goffredo v. Mercedes-Benz Truck Co.,* 402 Mass 97, 102-103, 520 NE2d 1315, 1318 (1988); *Corsetti v. The Stone Co.,* 396 Mass 1, 23-24, 483 NE2d 793, 805 (1985); *School Committee of Brookline v. Bureau of Special Education Appeals,* 389 Mass 705, 716, 452 NE2d 476, 482 (1983); *LaClair v. Silberline Manufacturing Co., Inc.,* 379 Mass 21, 32, 393 NE2d 867, 873-874 (1979) (jury must conclude it was more probable than not that event was caused by defendant's product); *Evangelio v. Metropolitan Bottling Co., Inc.,* 339 Mass 177, 180, 158 NE2d 342, 345 (1959). See also Uniform Commercial Code, GL 106, §1-201(8) ("'Burden of establishing a fact' means the burden of persuading the triers of fact that the existence of the fact is more probable than its non-existence."). Preponderance of the evidence is the standard applied to the plaintiff's case in a domestic abuse prevention proceeding pursuant to GL 209A. See *Frizado v. Frizado,* 420 Mass 592, 597, 651 NE2d 1206, 1210 (1995).

The jury must find for the opponent if it believes either that the burdened party's contention is more probably false than true, *or* is as probably false as true. See *Corsetti v. The Stone Co.,* supra, 396 Mass at 24, 483 NE2d at 805; *Sargent v. Massachusetts Accident Co.,* 307 Mass 246, 251, 29 NE2d 825, 827-828 (1940) (where evidence tends to equally support two inconsistent propositions, neither can be found to be true).

"After the evidence has been weighed, that proposition is proved by a preponderance of the evidence if it is made to appear more likely or probable in the sense that actual belief in its truth, derived from the evidence, exists in the mind or minds of the tribunal notwithstanding any doubts that may still linger there." *Sargent v. Massachusetts Accident Co.*, supra, 307 Mass at 250, 29 NE2d at 827. For cases dealing with the wording of the instructions in this regard, see also *Stepakoff v. Kantar*, 393 Mass 836, 842-843, 473 NE2d 1131, 1136 (1985); *Sullivan v. Hamacher*, 339 Mass 190, 158 NE2d 301 (1959); *Knox v. Lamoureaux*, 338 Mass 167, 154 NE2d 342 (1958); *Tucker v. Pearlstein*, 334 Mass 33, 133 NE2d 489 (1956); *Footit v. Monsees*, 26 Mass App 173, 178-180, 525 NE2d 423, 427-428 (1988); *Grassis v. Retik*, 25 Mass App 595, 601-602, 521 NE2d 411, 415 (1988); *Fire Commissioner of Boston v. Joseph*, 23 Mass App 76, 82, 498 NE2d 1368, 1372 (1986). Instructions using "firm and abiding conviction" language to explain the preponderance of the evidence standard are disfavored. See *Shafnacker v. Raymond James & Associates*, 425 Mass 724, 736-737, 683 NE2d 662, 670-671 (1997).

While the phrase "preponderance of the evidence" has frequently been defined in terms of probabilities, see, e.g., *Evangelio v. Metropolitan Bottling Co., Inc.*, supra, 339 Mass at 182, 158 NE2d at 346 ("balance of probabilities"), statistical preponderance is not sufficient. As noted in the oft-quoted case, it is "not enough that mathematically the chances somewhat favor a proposition to be proved; for example, the fact that colored automobiles made in the current year outnumber black ones would not warrant a finding that an undescribed automobile of the current year is colored and not black, nor would the fact that only a minority of men die of cancer warrant a finding that a particular man did not die of cancer." *Sargent v. Massachusetts Accident Co.*, supra, 307 Mass at 250, 29 NE2d at 827. See also *King's Case*, 352 Mass 488, 491-492, 225 NE2d 900, 902 (1967). The preponderance which determines the verdict must be a preponderance of credible testimony, not a "balance of probabilities." *Callahan v. Fleischman Co.*, supra, 262 Mass at 437, 160 NE at 250.

Where the private interests of the litigant are not "fundamental," there is no unusual risk of error, and the onus on the government that a higher standard of proof would entail is substantial, special degrees of proof (as described in the following sections) have not been required. See, e.g., *Spence v. Gormley*, 387 Mass 258, 274-277, 439 NE2d 741, 750-751 (1982) (in proceedings to evict public housing tenant on basis of violent acts of member of tenant's household, ordinary civil standard of proof by preponderance of evidence is sufficient); *Phipps v. Barbera*, 23 Mass App 1, 4-6, 498 NE2d 411, 413-414 (1986) (with regard to latent ambiguity in will, claimant is required to show only by preponderance of evidence that it was intended beneficiary).

It should be noted that the allocation of burdens of proof under the Massachusetts drug forfeiture statute, GL 94C, §47(d), have been upheld despite the fact that the Commonwealth need only prove the existence of probable cause to institute the action, shifting to the claimant the burden of proving the property is not forfeitable. See *Com. v. Brown*, 426 Mass 475, 688 NE2d 1356 (1998).

b.   Clear and Convincing Evidence

As to certain issues in civil cases where "particularly important individual interests or rights are at stake," see *Medical Malpractice Joint Underwriting Association of Massachusetts v. Commissioner of Insurance*, 395 Mass 43, 46, 478 NE2d 936, 939 (1985) (citation omitted), an intermediate standard of proof greater than "a preponderance" but less than "beyond a reasonable doubt" is required. This degree is called "clear and convincing" evidence. See generally *Stone v. Essex County Newspapers, Inc.*, 367 Mass 849, 871, 330 NE2d 161, 175 (1975). It is applicable in the following contexts:

- **Issue of malice in a public figure defamation case.** *New York Times Co. v. Sullivan*, 376 US 254, 84 S Ct 710, 11 L Ed 2d 686 (1964); *Tosti v. Ayik*, 394 Mass 482, 491, 476 NE2d 928, 935 (1985); *Callahan v. Westinghouse Broadcasting Co., Inc.*, 372 Mass 582,

363 NE2d 240 (1977); *Stone v. Essex County Newspapers, Inc.*, supra, 367 Mass at 870, 330 NE2d at 174. See also *Bose Corp. v. Consumers Union of the United States*, 466 US 485, 104 S Ct 1949, 80 L Ed 2d 502 (1984) (issue of malice in defamation action for product disparagement).

- **Action by putative father to establish paternity of child born out of wedlock to married woman.** *C.C. v. A.B.*, 406 Mass 679, 686-687, 550 NE2d 365, 370-371 (1990).

- **Claim for reformation of contract for mutual mistake.** *Kidder v. Greenman*, 283 Mass 601, 613-614, 187 NE 42, 47-48 (1933) (distinguishing reformation for mutual mistake, to which higher standard applies, from reformation for unauthorized completion of instrument, to which higher standard does not apply); *Covich v. Chambers*, 8 Mass App 740, 397 NE2d 1115 (1979).

- **Contents of a lost will.** *Coghlin v. White*, 273 Mass 53, 55, 172 NE 786 (1930) (& citations) (evidence must be "strong, positive and free from doubt"). But compare *Rubenstein v. Royal Insurance Company of America*, 44 Mass App 842, 846, 694 NE2d 381, 384 (1998) (only preponderance of evidence required to prove existence and contents of lost insurance policy).

- **Gift causa mortis.** *Foley v. Coan*, 272 Mass 207, 172 NE 74 (1930).

- **Irregularity of official proceedings.** *Newcomb v. Aldermen of Holyoke*, 271 Mass 565, 171 NE 826 (1930).

- **Transfer hearing under former GL 119, §61, to determine whether juvenile should be tried as adult.** *Com. v. Kelley*, 411 Mass 212, 213 n.2, 581 NE2d 472, 473 n.2 (1991). But see *Com. v. Berry*, 420 Mass 95, 100 n.3, 648 NE2d 732, 736 n.3 (1995) and *Com. v. Clifford C.*, 415 Mass 38, 42, 610 NE2d 967, 970 (1993), noting that the Legislature has lowered the Commonwealth's burden of proof to a preponderance of the evidence where the transfer case involves a charge of murder or other violent crime.

- **Pretrial detention on grounds of dangerousness pursuant to GL 276, §58A.** See *Mendonza v. Com.*, 423 Mass 771, 782-784, 673 NE2d 22, 30-31 (1996) (failure to require proof beyond reasonable doubt does not violate constitutional protections).

- **Termination of parental rights.** As a matter of federal constitutional law, termination of parental rights requires proof by "clear and convincing" evidence. *Santosky v. Kramer*, 455 US 745, 102 S Ct 1388, 71 L Ed 599 (1982). For Massachusetts cases adopting this standard, see *Adoption of Carla*, 416 Mass 510, 517-518, 623 NE2d 1118, 1122 (1993) (GL 210, §3); *Adoption of Carlos*, 413 Mass 339, 348, 596 NE2d 1383, 1388 (1992) (& citations); *Care and Protection of Martha*, 407 Mass 319, 327, 553 NE2d 902, 906-907 (1990) (& citations) (GL 119, §24); *Custody of a Minor (No. 2)*, 392 Mass 719, 467 NE2d 1286 (1984) (GL 119, §§21, 35). See also *Petitions of the Department of Social Services to Dispense with Consent to Adoption*, 389 Mass 793, 802-803, 452 NE2d 497, 503 (1983) (declaring invalid GL 210, §3(c), establishing presumption against parental rights for child in the care of the DSS or licensed child care agency for more than one year). But see *Opinion of the Justices*, 427 Mass 1201, 691 NE2d 911 (1998) (finding constitutional proposed burden-shifting bill that would provide that in custody dispute, if one parent proves by preponderance of evidence that other parent engaged in abuse of child, rebuttable presumption arises that it is not in child's best interest to be in custody of challenged parent).

In the parental rights area, careful factual inspection and specific, detailed findings by the trial court are mandated. *Adoption of Hugo*, 428 Mass 219, 224, 700 NE2d 516, 520 (1998); *Care and Protection of Three Minors*, 392 Mass 704,

467 NE2d 851 (1984). See, e.g., *Adoption of Stuart*, 39 Mass App 380, 656 NE2d 916 (1995) (reversing trial court's termination of parental rights); *Petition of the Department of Social Services to Dispense with Consent to Adoption*, 391 Mass 113, 461 NE2d 186 (1984) (judge's findings inadequate to sustain conclusion of unfitness of putative biological father); *Adoption of Inez*, 45 Mass App 171, 696 NE2d 164 (1998) (clear and convincing evidence did not support finding of unfitness). Subsidiary evidentiary findings, however, need only be proved by a fair preponderance of the evidence. *Adoption of Hugo*, supra; *In re Care and Protection of Rebecca*, 419 Mass 67, 81, 643 NE2d 26, 34 (1994).

Where the proceeding can deprive the parent of custody only temporarily, the lesser standard of "fair preponderance of the evidence" governs. See *Care and Protection of Manuel*, 428 Mass 527, 534, 703 NE2d 211, 216 (1998) and *Care and Protection of Robert*, 408 Mass 52, 556 NE2d 993 (1990) (72 hour hearings pursuant to GL 119, §§24 and 25).

Clear and convincing proof generally requires that the evidence must be sufficient to convey a "high degree of probability" that the proposition is true. *Tosti v. Ayik*, supra, 394 Mass at 493 n.9, 476 NE2d at 936 n.9. The proof must be "strong, positive and free from doubt;" it has also been described as "full, clear and decisive." *Callahan v. Westinghouse Broadcasting Co., Inc.*, supra, 372 Mass at 584, 363 NE2d at 241.

The Supreme Judicial Court has suggested the following form of jury instruction with regard to the clear and convincing evidence standard:

> The burden of persuasion, therefore, in those cases requiring a showing of clear and convincing proof is sustained if evidence induces in the mind of the trier a reasonable belief that the facts asserted are highly probably true, that the probability that they are true or exist is substantially greater than the probability that they are false or do not exist.

Callahan v. Westinghouse Broadcasting Co., Inc., supra, 372 Mass at 588, 363 NE2d at 244. The instruction should be preceded by an instruction that the jury should examine the evidence and weigh the probabilities with particular care. Id.

The Supreme Judicial Court has indicated a reluctance to extend the clear and convincing evidence standard beyond the instances set out above, suggesting that it too often serves as the "functional equivalent" for the reasonable doubt standard. See *Medical Malpractice Joint Underwriting Association of Massachusetts v. Commissioner of Insurance*, supra, 395 Mass at 47, 478 NE2d at 939 (& citations); *Department of Public Health v. Cumberland Cattle Co.*, 361 Mass 817, 282 NE2d 895 (1967).

On a petition brought by a guardian of a mentally incompetent person seeking an order to permit involuntary sterilization of the ward, the court has rejected both the "proof beyond a reasonable doubt" and the "clear and convincing evidence" standards. The preponderance of the evidence standard, augmented by the requirement of "utmost care" and "detailed written findings" by the judge, was found sufficient to protect the incompetent ward's rights. *In re Moe*, 385 Mass 555, 570-572, 432 NE2d 712, 723-724 (1982) (but suggesting that such petition brought by the Commonwealth might require a higher standard of proof). See also *In re Moe*, 31 Mass App 473, 479, 579 NE2d 682, 686-687 (1991) (judge erred in requiring "a higher standard of proof" on petition seeking authorization for abortion and sterilization of ward).

c.   Beyond a Reasonable Doubt

Certain types of proceedings designated "civil" involve fundamental interests that warrant a requirement of proof beyond a reasonable doubt:

- **Involuntary commitment to or retention in mental health facility.** *D. L. v. Commissioner of Social Services,*

412 Mass 558, 564 n.11, 591 NE2d 173, 176 n.11 (1992) (& citations). But compare *Addington v. Texas*, 441 US 418, 99 S Ct 1804, 60 L Ed 2d 323 (1979) (federal due process requires only "clear and convincing" proof); *Jones v. United States*, 463 US 354, 368, 103 S Ct 3043, 77 L Ed 2d 694 (1983) (preponderance of evidence standard satisfies due process for commitment of insanity acquittees).

- **Petition to retain custody of juvenile under GL 120, §17.** *Department of Youth Services v. A Juvenile*, 384 Mass 784, 791-793, 429 NE2d 709, 713-714 (1981).
- **Need for involuntary administration of antipsychotic drugs.** *In re Guardianship of Roe*, 383 Mass 415, 422-426, 421 NE2d 40, 45-47 (1981) (but rejecting requirement of proof beyond a reasonable doubt in regard to appointment of guardian under GL 201, §6).
- **Commitment or transfer to treatment center for sexually dangerous persons.** *In re Wyatt*, 428 Mass 347, 360, 701 NE2d 337, 346 (1998) (& citations). But compare *Doe v. Sex Offender Registry Board*, 428 Mass 90, 100-104, 697 NE2d 512, 518-520 (1998) (Board must show risk of reoffense by preponderance of evidence for purpose of classification under sex offender registration act).
- **Adjudication of delinquency.** See GL 119, §58.

Allegations in a civil proceeding as to acts that may be penal in nature nonetheless require no more proof than a preponderance of the evidence. See, e.g., *Com. v. Guilfoyle*, 402 Mass 130, 136, 521 NE2d 984, 987 (1988) (issuance of injunction for civil rights violations); *Vaspourakan Ltd. v. Alcoholic Beverages Control Commission*, 401 Mass 347, 352, 516 NE2d 1153, 1157 (1987) (& citations) (violation of criminal antidiscrimination statute); *Craven v. State Ethics Commission*, 390 Mass 191, 199-201, 454 NE2d 471, 476-477 (1983) (& citations) (civil action alleging conduct for which criminal sanctions could have been imposed); *In re Mayberry*, 295

Mass 155, 3 NE2d 248 (1936) (disbarment proceedings); *Grella v. Lewis Wharf Co.*, 211 Mass 54, 97 NE 745 (1912) (wrongful death action); *Kline v. Baker*, 106 Mass 61 (1870) (allegations of fraud).

d.   Administrative Procedure Act

See §14.2, infra.

§5.4   Burden of Persuasion in Criminal Cases

§5.4.1   Allocation of Burden of Persuasion in Criminal Cases

In criminal cases, the burden of persuasion as to all elements of the crime is on the Commonwealth. *Sandstrom v. Montana*, 442 US 510, 99 S Ct 2450, 61 L Ed 2d 39 (1979); *Mullaney v. Wilbur*, 421 US 684, 95 S Ct 1881, 44 L Ed 2d 508 (1975); *In re Winship*, 397 US 358, 90 S Ct 1068, 25 L Ed 2d 368 (1970); *Com. v. Amirault*, 404 Mass 221, 240, 535 NE2d 193, 205 (1989); *Com. v. Claudio*, 405 Mass 481, 541 NE2d 993 (1989); *Com. v. Pickles*, 393 Mass 775, 778, 473 NE2d 694, 696-697 (1985) (& citations). See also *Com. v. Burke*, 390 Mass 480, 483-484, 457 NE2d 622, 624-625 (1983) (Commonwealth has both burden of production and burden of persuasion as to each element of offense).

Thus, where the issue is raised,[1] the Commonwealth must prove the following beyond a reasonable doubt:

---

§5.4 [1]The question of whether a defendant has sufficiently "raised" an issue of insanity or other defense "relates not to the burden of persuasion but to the burden of producing evidence." *Com. v. Mills*, 400 Mass 626, 632, 511 NE2d 572, 576 (1987) (O'Connor, J, dissenting). See §5.2.1, supra. See also *Simopoulos v. Virginia*, 462 US 506, 103 S Ct 2532, 76 L Ed 2d 755 (1983) (defense of medical necessity must be disproved by state only where defendant's evidence raises issue).

- **The sanity of the defendant.** See *Com. v. Keita*, 429 Mass 843, 712 NE2d 65 (1999) (declining to change burden of proof on criminal responsibility from prosecution to defendant); *Com. v. Kappler*, 416 Mass 574, 586, 625 NE2d 513 (1993) (but Abrams, J, concurring, would place the burden of proving lack of criminal responsibility on the defendant); *Com. v. Mills*, 400 Mass 626, 630, 511 NE2d 572, 575 (1987); *United States v. Pasarell*, 727 F2d 13 (1st Cir 1984).

- **The absence of mental disease or defect or diminished capacity.** See *Com. v. Goudreau*, 422 Mass 731, 735-736, 666 NE2d 112, 115 (1996); *Com. v. Angelone*, 413 Mass 82, 84, 594 NE2d 866, 867 (1992).

- **The absence of self-defense or use of excessive force.** See *Com. v. Rodriguez*, 370 Mass 684, 352 NE2d 203 (1976); *Com. v. Haddock*, 46 Mass App 246, 248, 704 NE2d 537, 540 (1999); *Com. v. A Juvenile*, 17 Mass App 988, 459 NE2d 134 (1984). See also *Com. v. Baseler*, 419 Mass 500, 502-503, 645 NE2d 1179, 1181 (1995) (conviction reversed because jury instructions lowered state's burden of proof on self-defense); *Com. v. Koonce*, 418 Mass 367, 370-375, 636 NE2d 1305, 1307-1309 (1994) (patently erroneous instruction on excessive force did not shift burden to defendant).

- **The absence of accident.** See *Com. v. Lowe*, 391 Mass 97, 108-112, 461 NE2d 192, 199-200 (1984) (& citations).

- **The presence of malice or intent, or the absence of reasonable provocation or heat of passion.** See *Francis v. Franklin*, 471 US 307, 105 S Ct 1965, 85 L Ed 2d 344 (1985); *Sandstrom v. Montana*, supra; *Mullaney v. Wilbur*, supra; *Com. v. Acevedo*, 427 Mass 714, 695 NE2d 1065 (1998) (absence of provocation); *Com. v. Giguere*, 420 Mass 226, 230, 648 NE2d 1279, 1282 (1995) (use of phrase "reduce murder to manslaughter" did not shift burden of proof to defendant); *Com. v. Eagles*, 419 Mass 825, 834-837, 648 NE2d 410, 416-418 (1995); *Com. v. A Juvenile (No. 1)*, 396 Mass 108, 115, 483 NE2d 822, 826-827 (1985); *Com. v. McLeod*, 394 Mass 727, 738-740, 477 NE2d 972, 982 (1985); *Com. v. Zezima*, 387 Mass 748, 443 NE2d 1282 (1982); *DeJoinville v. Com.*, 381 Mass 246, 408 NE2d 1353 (1980). But compare *Com. v. Mandeville*, 386 Mass 393, 406-408, 436 NE2d 912, 921-922 (1982) (court would not consider argument that judge's instructions on malice improperly shifted burden of proof in absence of objection and where only seriously contested issue was identity).

- **Predisposition of defendant where entrapment defense is presented**. See *Com. v. Monteagudo*, 427 Mass 484, 487, 693 NE2d 1381, 1384 (1998).
- **In wilful non-support case, the defendant's financial ability to support the child.** See *Com. v. Teixera*, 396 Mass 746, 488 NE2d 775 (1986).
- **When age is an element of offense charged, the Commonwealth must prove that fact.** See *Com. v. Pittman*, 25 Mass App 25, 514 NE2d 857 (1987).

Where it is raised to negate the element of malice in a homicide case, the Commonwealth need not disprove defendant's intoxication beyond a reasonable doubt. *Com. v. Purcell*, 423 Mass 880, 882, 673 NE2d 53, 54 (1996).

Instructions concerning alibi which appear to shift the burden of proof to the defendant must be avoided. See *Com. v. Berth*, 385 Mass 784, 434 NE2d 192 (1982); *Com. v. Bowden*, 379 Mass 472, 399 NE2d 482 (1980); *Com. v. Williams*, 378 Mass 242, 390 NE2d 1114 (1979).

Instructions using "finding" language — "if you find that defendant acted in self-defense" — may erroneously lead the jury to believe the defendant has the burden of proof, and are thus disfavored. See *Com. v. Beauchamp*, 424 Mass 682, 689-8-690, 677 NE2d 1135, 1139 (1997) (& citations). Compare *Com. v. Shea*, 401 Mass 731, 742-743,

519 NE2d 1283, 1289-1290 (1988) (judge's use of "finding language" did not require reversal).

Presumptions that relieve the government of its burden of persuasion on each element of the offense are impermissible. See §5.5.6, infra.

§5.4.2   Degree Of Persuasion in Criminal Cases

a.   Proof Beyond a Reasonable Doubt

In criminal cases, proof of guilt beyond a reasonable doubt is required by the Due Process Clause of the Fourteenth Amendment to the United States Constitution. *In re Winship*, 397 US 358, 364, 90 S Ct 1068, 25 L Ed 2d 368 (1970) (1970). The requirement applies to every element of the offense charged and also extends to non-existence of facts or circumstances that would mitigate the degree of the defendant's culpability (as discussed in §5.4.1, supra). *Mullaney v. Wilbur*, 421 US 684 (1975); *Com. v. Teixera*, 396 Mass 746, 748, 488 NE2d 775, 777-778 (1986); *Com. v. Nieves*, 394 Mass 355, 359-360, 476 NE2d 179, 182 (1985).[2]

"The reasonable-doubt standard plays a vital role in the American scheme of criminal procedure. It is a prime instrument for reducing the risk of convictions resting on factual error. The standard provides concrete substance for the presumption of innocence — that bedrock axiomatic and elementary principle whose enforcement lies at the foundation of the administration of our criminal law." *In re Winship*, supra, 397 US at 363 (citation and internal quotations omitted). See also *Com. v. Blanchette*, 409 Mass 99, 105, 564 NE2d 992, 995-996 (1991).

---

[2]Although every necessary element of the crime must be proved beyond a reasonable doubt, it does not follow that every piece of evidence must be admissible beyond a reasonable doubt or that any inference drawn be proved beyond a reasonable doubt. *Com. v. Azar*, 32 Mass App 290, 309-310, 588 NE2d 1352, 1364-1365 (1992) (citation omitted).

b.   "Reasonable Doubt" Defined/Jury Instructions

The accepted definition of reasonable doubt in Massachusetts was set forth nearly a century and a half ago in *Com. v. Webster*, 59 Mass (5 Cush) 295, 320 (1850):

> [Reasonable doubt] is a term often used, probably pretty well understood, but not easily defined. It is not mere possible doubt; because everything relating to human affairs, and depending on moral evidence, is open to some possible or imaginary doubt. It is that state of the case, which, after the entire comparison and consideration of all the evidence, leaves the minds of jurors in that condition that they cannot say they feel an abiding conviction, to a moral certainty, of the truth of the charge.

See also *Com. v. Dinkins*, 415 Mass 715, 723-724, 615 NE2d 570, 575 (1993) ("a judge's explanation of reasonable doubt is usually best made in close reliance on the time-tested language of [*Webster*]"); *Com. v. Scanlon*, 412 Mass 664, 677-678, 592 NE2d 1279, 1287 (1992) (referring to "time tested and widely approved" language of *Com. v. Webster)*; *Com. v. A Juvenile (No. 2)*, 396 Mass 215, 217-219 & n.2, 485 NE2d 170, 172 n.2 (& citations) 173-174 (1985) (setting out Model Jury Instruction for Criminal Offenses Tried in the District Courts 2.051, which incorporates *Com. v. Webster)*; *Com. v. Rembiszewski*, 391 Mass 123, 130, 461 NE2d 201 (1984) (a fact is proved beyond a reasonable doubt "when it is proved to a moral certainty, when it is proved to a degree of certainty that satisfies the judgment and conscience of the jury as reasonable men and leaves in their minds as reasonable men a clear and settled conviction of guilt"); *Com. v. Costley*, 118 Mass 1, 24-25 (1875). The "moral certainty" required is to be distinguished from "absolute or mathematical certainty, the kind of certainty when you add two and two and get four." *Com. v. A Juvenile (No. 2)*, supra, 396 Mass at 218 n.2, 485 NE2d at 172 n.2.

Although the First Circuit Court of Appeals has repeatedly criticized the practice of defining reasonable doubt in terms of moral certainty, it has not found use of the phrase in a state trial to be constitutional error. See *Lanigan v. Maloney*, 853 F2d 40, 47 n.4 (1st Cir 1988) (& citations); *Smith v. Butler*, 696 F Supp 748, 753-759 (D Mass 1988) (& citations). Use of the phrase "proof to a degree of moral certainty" has, however, been found constitutionally deficient. *Lanigan v. Maloney*, supra, 853 F2d at 45-47. For a discussion of the different approaches to the definition of reasonable doubt between the state and federal courts in Massachusetts, see *Smith v. Butler*, supra, 696 F Supp at 753-766 (referring to "clear and unavoidable conflict" over use of the term "moral certainty" in defining reasonable doubt); *Com. v. Tavares*, 385 Mass 140, 147, 430 NE2d 1198, 1203 (1982); *Com. v. Garcia*, 379 Mass 422, 440 n.11, 399 NE2d 460, 472 n.11 (1980).

The United States Supreme Court, while criticizing the "moral certainty" language contained in the *Webster* charge, has nonetheless upheld its constitutionality when used in conjunction with language impressing on the jury the need to reach a state of near certitude of guilt. See *Victor v. Nebraska*, 511 US 1, 14-15, 114 S Ct 1239, 127 L Ed 2d 583 (1994). Compare *Cage v. Louisiana*, 498 US 39, 111 S Ct 328, 112 L Ed 2d 339 (1990) (invalidating charge requiring "moral certainty" where reasonable juror could have interpreted instructions to allow finding of guilt based on degree of proof below that constitutionally required).

The Supreme Judicial Court has adopted the approach of *Victor v. Nebraska*. In *Com. v. Gagliardi*, 418 Mass 562, 571, 638 NE2d 20, 25 (1994), the Court indicated that use of the term "moral certainty" in isolation and without further explanation might constitute reversible error; but when used in conjunction with an explanation of the high degree of certainty necessary to convict, the instruction is permissible. Compare *Com. v. Bonds*, 424 Mass 698, 677 NE2d 1131 (1997) (instructions that equate proof beyond reasonable doubt with moral certainty, and then compare that with certainty required to make important personal decisions, are unconstitutional), *Com. v. Pinckney*, 419 Mass 341, 644

NE2d 973 (1995) (conviction reversed where "moral certainty" language was not used in context that expressed proper degree of proof), and *Com. v. Viera*, 42 Mass App 916, 676 NE2d 66 (1997) (same) with *Com. v. Andrews*, 427 Mass 434, 444-445, 694 NE2d 329, 336-337 (1998) (judge used "moral certainty" in context of *Webster* charge), *Com. v. Smith*, 427 Mass 245, 251-254, 692 NE2d 65, 70-72 (1998) (remainder of instructions sufficient to inform jurors of high degree of certainty they must possess to convict), *Com. v. Watkins*, 425 Mass 830, 836-839, 683 NE2d 653, 658-659 (1997) (same), *Com. v. Gagnon*, 37 Mass App 626, 643 NE2d 1045 (1994) (instruction conveyed proper standard of proof despite use of phrase "moral certainty"), and *Com. v. Ewing*, 30 Mass App 285, 289-290, 567 NE2d 1262, 1265 (1991) (no error in judge's charge that "proof beyond a reasonable doubt is proof to a moral certainty" in light of rest of instructions).

Use of the so-called *Madeiros* charge language that "if an unreasonable doubt or a mere possibility of innocence were sufficient to prevent a conviction, practically every criminal would be set free to prey upon the community," see *Com. v. Madeiros*, 255 Mass 304, 151 NE 297 (1926), has been severely criticized. See *Com. v. Pinckney*, supra, 419 Mass at 347-349, 644 NE2d at 977-978. But see *Com. v. Smith*, supra, 427 Mass at 250-251, 692 NE2d at 69-70 (disfavored language balanced by emphasis on Commonwealth's substantial burden of proof and warning that guilty verdict could not be based on prejudice); *Com. v. Gagnon*, supra, 37 Mass App at 631-632, 643 NE2d at 1049 (use of disfavored language cured by *Webster* definition of reasonable doubt).

While there is no constitutional requirement to specifically charge the jury to presume the defendant innocent, the instructions on the Commonwealth's burden of proof must amply fulfill the protective purposes of such a charge. See *Com. v. Viera*, 42 Mass App 916, 917-918, 676 NE2d 66, 67 (1997) (& citations).

The reasonable doubt standard defies easy explication, and no precise formulation is mandated. *Com. v. Anderson*,

425 Mass 685, 689, 682 NE2d 859, 863 (1997) (conformity to *Webster* charge not required); *Com. v. James*, 424 Mass 770, 788, 678 NE2d 1170, 1182 (1997) (& citations). The following guidance may be discerned from the decisional law.

Because it detracts from the seriousness of the issue before them and trivializes the degree of certainty required, it is error to include in the instruction specific examples of personal decisions in the jurors' own lives and then state "proof beyond a reasonable doubt is the same kind of proof and degree of satisfaction or conviction which you wanted for yourself when you were considering one of those very important decisions." *Com. v. Rembiszewski*, supra, 391 Mass at 130-132, 461 NE2d at 206. See also *Com. v. Bonds*, 424 Mass 698, 677 NE2d 1131 (1997) (instructions that equate proof beyond reasonable doubt with moral certainty, and then compare that with certainty required to make important personal decisions, are unconstitutional); *Com. v. Murphy*, 415 Mass 161, 168, 612 NE2d 1137 (1993); *Com. v. Limone*, 410 Mass 364, 573 NE2d 1 (1991) (use of specific examples does not necessarily require reversal); *Com. v. Kelleher*, 395 Mass 821, 826-827, 482 NE2d 804, 807-808 (1985); *Com. v. Garcia*, supra, 379 Mass at 440-442, 399 NE2d at 471-472 (& citations); *Com. v. Payton*, 35 Mass App 586, 597, 623 NE2d 1127, 1134 (1993); *Com. v. Ferreira*, 373 Mass 116, 128-130, 364 NE2d 1264, 1272-1273 (1977). Cf. *Com. v. Doherty*, 394 Mass 341, 350-351, 476 NE2d 169, 176-177 (1985) (no error where judge used "ordinary incidents" language when charging jury on reasonable inference rather than reasonable doubt); *Com. v. Holmes*, 32 Mass App 906, 909, 584 NE2d 1150, 1154 (1992) (& citations) (rejecting argument that judge trivialized task of jury by using "chocolate cake" analogy).

Attempts to quantify proof beyond a reasonable doubt or to give numeric examples create a risk of lowering the burden of proof and should be avoided. See *Com. v. Rosa*, 422 Mass 18, 27-29, 661 NE2d 56, 62-63 (1996) (& cases cited).

Use of the phrase "doubt based upon a reason" should be avoided because of its potential to shift the burden of proof to the defendant; but the phrase "doubt based *on reason*" is permissible. See *Com. v. Anderson*, 425 Mass 685, 690, 682 NE2d 859, 863 (1997) (& citations). See also *Com. v. Slonka*, 42 Mass App 760, 762, 680 NE2d 103, 105-106 (1997) (use of phrase "fair doubt" could lower Commonwealth's burden of proof, and constituted reversible error); *Com. v. Burke*, 44 Mass App 76, 80-81, 687 NE2d 1279, 1283 (1997) (term "reservoir of doubt" should be avoided).

Instructions that incorporate negative definitions of reasonable doubt—what reasonable doubt is not—have been repeatedly upheld where the negative definitions are counterbalanced by instructions following *Com. v. Webster*. See *Com. v. Scanlon*, supra, 412 Mass at 677-678, 592 NE2d at 1287 (& citations). A judge may contrast reasonable doubt with absolute certainty, see *Com. v. Gonzalez*, 426 Mass 313, 318, 688 NE2d 455, 458 (1997), or the doubt that might exist in the mind of someone searching for doubt. See *Com. v. Watkins*, 425 Mass 830, 839, 683 NE2d 653, 659 (1997). But see *Com. v. Richardson*, 425 Mass 765, 768, 682 NE2d 1354, 1356 (1997) (contrasts with proof beyond shadow of doubt should be avoided). See also *Com. v. Crawford*, 417 Mass 358, 367-368, 629 NE2d 1332, 1337 (1994) (judge should not refer to civil preponderance of evidence standard by way of comparison).

For other cases dealing with the proper articulation of the reasonable doubt standard, see *Com. v. Grant*, 418 Mass 76, 84-85, 634 NE2d 565, 570-571 (1994) (judge's misstatement that jury must find defendant guilty unless his guilt has been proven beyond reasonable doubt could not have misled a reasonable juror); *Com. v. Cook*, 419 Mass 192, 203, 644 NE2d 203, 210 (1994) (prosecutor's statement that jury should "not be intimidated by phrase 'reasonable doubt'" not improper when viewed in context); *Com. v. Thomas*, 401 Mass 109, 112-114, 514 NE2d 1309, 1311-1312 (1987) (prosecutor's misstatements of reasonable doubt standard, which adversely implicated presumption of innocence, did not create substantial risk of miscarriage of justice); *Com. v. Atkins*, 386 Mass 593, 601-602, 436 NE2d 1203, 1208-1209 (1982) (no reversal required where prosecutor's misstatement of standard, referring to the heart as a source of decision-making, was corrected by proper *Webster* instructions).

The determination of whether the definition of reasonable doubt has been conveyed accurately to the jury requires consideration of the charge as a whole, and not an isolated portion that misstates the burden. See *Com. v. Limone*, supra, 410 Mass at 367, 573 NE2d at 3; *Com. v. Morse*, 402 Mass 735, 737, 525 NE2d 364, 365-366 (1988) (& citations); *Com. v. A Juvenile (No. 2)*, supra, 396 Mass at 218-220 & n.3, 485 NE2d at 172-174 & n.3 (1985) (& citations); *Com. v. LaFontaine*, 32 Mass App 529, 535-536, 591 NE2d 1103, 1107 (1992). See also *Smith v. Butler*, 696 F Supp 748, 754 n.9 (D Mass 1988) (& cases collected). In assessing the possible impact of an alleged error, the Massachusetts courts ask whether a reasonable juror *could have* used the instruction incorrectly; in contrast, the more strict federal standard requires reversal only where there is a "reasonable likelihood" that the jury used an inappropriate standard. See *Com. v. Rosa*, supra, 422 Mass at 27 n.10, 661 NE2d at 62 n.10 (& cases cited); *Com. v. Torres*, 420 Mass 479, 490-491 n.10, 651 NE2d 360, 367 n.10 (1995).

Failure to instruct the jury properly on reasonable doubt can never be deemed harmless error. See *Sullivan v. Louisiana*, 508 US 275, 280-281, 113 S Ct 2078, 124 L Ed 2d 182 (1993). See also *Com. v. Garcia*, supra, 379 Mass at 445-446, 389 NE2d at 474-475 (Liacos, J, dissenting).

It has been held that a trial judge's failure to give any instruction on the meaning of reasonable doubt is error. See *Com. v. Stellberger*, 25 Mass App 148, 149, 515 NE2d 1207, 1207-1208 (1987).

A judge may provide the jury with an accurate statement of the elements of the crimes charged, including the use of a blackboard, as long as the Commonwealth's burden of proof with regard to each element is made clear. See

Com. v. DiBenedetto, 427 Mass 414, 421-422, 693 NE2d 1007, 1013 (1998).

§5.5   Presumptions/Prima Facie Evidence

Generalization with respect to "presumptions" is difficult at best, mainly because the word is used to describe a number of quite different concepts.[1] Five such concepts are described and illustrated below:

- conclusive or irrebuttable presumptions
- presumptions as shorthand references
- prima facie evidence that shifts the burden of persuasion
- prima facie evidence that shifts the burden of production
- inferences (sometimes erroneously referred to as "presumptions of fact").

---

§5.5 [1]The confusion in terminology is evident when looking at cases dealing with the "presumption" that a plaintiff had normal skin. See *Payne v. R. H. White Co.,* 314 Mass 63, 49 NE2d 425 (1943) (may be an inference, a presumption, or the sum of the two — prima facie evidence — that plaintiff had normal skin); *Graham v. Jordan Marsh Co.,* 319 Mass 690, 67 NE2d 404 (1946) (jury could draw an inference that plaintiff's skin was normal); *Jacquot v. William Filene's Sons Co.,* 337 Mass 312, 149 NE2d 635 (1958) (there might be a presumption or permissible inference that plaintiff's skin was normal); and *Casagrande v. F. W. Woolworth Co.,* 340 Mass 552, 165 NE2d 109 (1960) (presumption, as distinguished from inference, that skin is normal). See also *Connolly v. John Hancock Mut. Life Ins. Co.,* 322 Mass 678, 79 NE2d 189 (1948) (whatever "presumption" there is that a person is in sound health, it could not itself satisfy plaintiff's burden of proving that he was in sound health at time policy was issued); *Goodman v. New York, N.H.& H. R.R.,* 295 Mass 330, 3 NE2d 777 (1936) ("presumption" that damage to goods happened while in possession of last of a series of common carriers).

The word "presumption" is sometimes used to describe nonevidentiary observations. See, e.g., *Moroni v. Brawders,* 317 Mass 48, 55-56, 57 NE2d 14, 18 (1944) ("presumption" that the conduct of a person is lawful, regular, proper, innocent, honest and in good faith, because most human conduct is of that sort).

Proposed Mass R Evid 301(a) proposes a single rule for all presumptions in civil cases. Taking the approach formerly espoused by the drafters of the Uniform Rules of Evidence and Professor Morgan, Proposed Mass R Evid 301(a) provides that "a presumption imposes on the party against whom it is directed the burden of proving that the non-existence of the presumed fact is more probable than its existence." Compare Fed R Evid 301 ("a presumption imposes on the party against whom it is directed the burden of going forward with evidence to rebut or meet the presumption, but does not shift to such party the burden of proof in the sense of the risk of nonpersuasion").[2] This rule does not apply to criminal cases (see Proposed Mass R Evid 302), nor does it apply to presumptions provided by statutes that prescribe a different effect. See, e.g., GL 106, §1-201 (31). The relationship of both the Proposed Massachusetts Rules of Evidence and the Federal Rules of Evidence to present Massachusetts practice will be discussed below.

For an excellent analysis of the concept of presumptions and a vigorous critique of Proposed Mass R Evid 301, see Hecht & Pinzler, *Rebutting Presumptions: Order Out of Chaos*, 58 BUL Rev 527 (1978).

§5.5.1   Conclusive or Irrebuttable Presumptions

"Conclusive" or "irrebutable" presumptions may be statutory or common-law in nature. In truth they are not presumptions at all, but rules of substantive law removing the issue from the area of evidence and proof. The following are illustrative:

---

[2] In federal diversity cases, "the effect of a presumption respecting a fact which is an element of a claim or defense as to which State law supplies the rule of decision is determined in accordance with State law." Fed R Evid 302.

- Conclusive presumption of dependency of spouses under worker's compensation law. GL 152, §32.
- Acts constituting constructive eviction make actual intention of landlord immaterial. *Westland Housing Corp. v. Scott*, 312 Mass 375, 381-383, 44 NE2d 959, 962-963 (1942); *Lowery v. Robinson*, 13 Mass App 982, 432 NE2d 543 (1982).
- Presumption of no consent by female under 16 in civil action for indecent assault. *Glover v. Callahan*, 299 Mass 55, 58, 12 NE2d 194, 196 (1937).
- Consent of child immaterial in prosecution for rape and abuse under GL 265, §23. *Com. v. Gallant*, 373 Mass 577, 369 NE2d 707 (1977).
- Presumption of incapacity of child under seven to commit crime. *Com. v. Mead*, 92 Mass (10 All) 398 (1865).

Compare *Com. v. Walter R.*, 414 Mass 714, 610 NE2d 323 (1993) (repudiating common-law presumption of incapacity of boy under 14 to commit rape); *Com. v. Burke*, 390 Mass 480, 484, 457 NE2d 622, 625 (1983) (declining to establish "age of consent" below which child is to be considered incapable of consent as a matter of law in prosecution for indecent assault and battery on child under GL 265, §13B; lack of consent must be proved); *Commissioner of Corporations & Taxation v. Bullard*, 313 Mass 72, 79, 46 NE2d 557, 561 (1943) (no general irrebuttable presumption applicable to all classes of cases that a woman is capable of bearing children throughout her life). See also *Nelson v. Hamlin*, 258 Mass 331, 340, 155 NE 18, 21 (1926) (parol evidence rule: unambiguous written agreement ordinarily conclusively presumed to express whole intent of parties).

§5.5.2   *Presumptions as Shorthand References*

Some "presumptions" serve merely as a reference to the allocation of the burden of persuasion to one party or the other from the outset of the case. By way of example, the "presumption of innocence" in criminal cases is not a presumption in the usual sense, but a "shorthand reference to the premises from which a criminal trial proceeds," with the burden of persuasion falling upon the government at all times. *Com. v. Drayton*, 386 Mass 39, 46, 434 NE2d 997, 1003 (1982); *Com. v. Blanchette*, 409 Mass 99, 105, 564 NE2d 992, 995-996 (1991). The "presumption" of validity of assessments is similarly a restatement that the taxpayer bears the burden to prove the property has been overvalued. *Analogic Corp. v. Board of Assessors of Peabody*, 45 Mass App 605, 607, 700 NE2d 548, 550 (1998). For other examples, see *Coyne v. John S. Tilley Co.*, 368 Mass 230, 331 NE2d 541 (1975) (presumption of due care created by comparative negligence statute, GL 231, §85); *Gynan v. Hayes*, 9 Mass App 721, 404 NE2d 122 (1980) (same); 20 ALR2d 235 (presumptions of survivorship created by Uniform Simultaneous Death Law, GL 190A); *St. Germaine v. Pendergast*, 416 Mass 698, 703, 626 NE2d 857, 860 (1993) (& citations) (presumption that a statute is constitutional; challenging party bears heavy burden).

§5.5.3   *Prima Facie Evidence*

"Prima facie evidence" is described as "evidence which, standing alone and unexplained, maintains the proposition and warrants the conclusion to support which it is introduced. If such evidence is not in any way met or controlled, and relates to the decisive issue in the case, a verdict or finding is required in accordance with its effect." *Thomes v. Meyer Store, Inc.*, 268 Mass 587, 588, 168 NE 178, 179 (1929); *Scheffler's Case*, 419 Mass 251, 258-259, 643 NE2d 1023, 1027 (1994) (citations omitted).

The Massachusetts decisions distinguish prima facie evidence from presumptions by emphasizing the different consequences that ensue with regard to the rebuttal of prima facie evidence. See generally *Cook v. Farm Service*

Stores, Inc., 301 Mass 564, 566-567, 17 NE2d 890, 893 (1938). Like presumptions, prima facie evidence retains its artificial legal force only until evidence appears that warrants a finding to the contrary. *McGovern v. Tinglof*, 344 Mass 114, 181 NE2d 573 (1962); *Malloy v. Coldwater Seafood Corp.*, 338 Mass 554, 564-565, 156 NE2d 61, 67 (1959). Unlike presumptions, however, the effect of prima facie evidence does not "disappear" upon being rebutted, but rather remains as evidence sufficient to get the case to the jury. *Tuttle v. McGeeney*, 344 Mass 200, 181 NE2d 655 (1962); *Ferreira v. Franco*, 273 Mass 272, 173 NE 529 (1930). And the jury may consider such evidence. *Com. v. Cox*, 327 Mass 609, 100 NE2d 14 (1951). See also *Anderson's Case*, 373 Mass 813, 370 NE2d 692 (1977) (same principles apply to administrative proceedings in workers' compensation cases). In sum, prima facie evidence is "evidence," remains evidence throughout the trial, and is entitled to be weighed like any other evidence upon any question of fact to which it is relevant. *Cook v. Farm Service Stores, Inc.*, supra, 301 Mass at 566, 17 NE2d at 892.

While it has been held that the jury should not hear of a presumption that has been rebutted, see *Potter v. John Bean Division of Food Machinery & Chemical Corp.*, 344 Mass 420, 425, 182 NE2d 834, 838 (1962), the judge must (when properly requested) charge the jury as to the effect of prima facie evidence in such event. *Newgent v. Colonial Contractors & Builders, Inc.*, 348 Mass 582, 204 NE2d 922 (1965).

Prima facie evidence by rule of law shifts either the burden of persuasion or the burden production to the opponent.

a.   Shifting Burden of Persuasion

The examples below reflect situations where a rule of law makes proof of fact A "prima facie evidence" of fact B in the sense that proof of fact A places on the opponent the burden of persuasion as to the nonexistence of fact B:

- In a motor vehicle accident case, proof of registration in the name of the defendant creates "prima facie evidence" that the vehicle was operated by and under the control of a person for whom the defendant was legally responsible, and lack of responsibility is an affirmative defense. GL 231, §85A; §85B. See *Mitchell v. Hastings & Koch Enterprises, Inc.*, 38 Mass App 271, 647 NE2d 78 (1995); *Cheek v. Econo-Car Rental System of Boston, Inc.*, 393 Mass 660, 662, 473 NE2d 659, 660 (1985); *Falden v. Crook*, 342 Mass 173, 172 NE2d 686 (1961) (limiting effect of statute); *Arrigo v. Lindquist*, 324 Mass 278, 85 NE2d 782 (1949) (construing statute); *Thomes v. Meyer Store, Inc.*, supra, 168 Mass at 589, 168 NE at 179 (construing statute). But see *Gallo v. Veliskakis*, 357 Mass 602, 259 NE2d 568 (1970) (statute does not make registration prima facie evidence that operator was empowered by owner to invite others to ride with him). Where there is evidence to contradict the prima facie evidence created by the statute, the agency issue is a question of fact for the jury — or in the case of a bench trial, the judge. *Cheek v. Econo-Car Rental System of Boston, Inc.*, supra, 393 Mass at 662, 473 NE2d at 661 (in view of evidence contradicting agency relationship, judge's ruling that finding of agency was compelled was erroneous; Nolan, Liacos, and Abrams, JJ, dissenting, concluding that the "judge's findings indicate that the force of the statutory prima facie evidence of agency had not been overcome" and that "the agency created by registration of the motor vehicle in the name of the defendant was [not] sufficiently rebutted."393 Mass at 665; 473 NE2d at 662); *Feltch v. General Rental Co.*, 383 Mass 603, 421 NE2d 67 (1981). Compare *Nugent v. Classic Car Corp.*, 379 Mass 913, 393 NE2d 934 (1979) (error to direct verdict on issue of control where GL 231, §85A, applies) with *Bergdoll v. Suprynowicz*, 359 Mass 173,

268 NE2d 362 (1971) (GL 231, §85A, does not preclude judge from ordering new trial on ground that verdict against owner-defendant was against weight of evidence on issue of control).

- Presumption that accident vehicle was operated with the consent of the owner. GL 231, §85C. See *Scaltreto v. Shea*, 352 Mass 62, 223 NE2d 525 (1967) (construing presumption); *Owens v. Dinkins*, 345 Mass 106, 108, 185 NE2d 645, 647 (1962) (failure of insurer to plead affirmative defense of absence of consent was waived by plaintiff where there was full trial on issue of consent without objection by him).

- Presumption that a vehicle was parked by its registered owner. GL 266, §120A.

- Where the plaintiff in a dog bite case is a child under seven, "it shall be presumed that such minor was not committing a trespass or other tort, or teasing, tormenting or abusing such dog, and the burden of proof thereof shall be upon the defendant in such action." GL 140, §155

- In a worker's compensation case where the employee is physically or mentally unable to testify, certain facts "shall be prima facie evidence that the employee was performing his regular duties on the day of the injury" and that the claim is compensable. GL 152, §7A. See *Anderson's Case*, 373 Mass 813, 370 NE2d 692 (1977); *Collin's Case*, 21 Mass App 557, 559, 488 NE2d 46, 48 (1986).

- The impartial physician's report is prima facie evidence of the medical issues in a worker's compensation case. GL 152, §11A(2). See *Scheffler's Case*, supra, 419 Mass at 259, 643 NE2d at 1028; *O'Brien's Case*, 424 Mass 16, 673 NE2d 567 (1996) (rejecting due process challenge to statute). See also *Tobin's Case*, 424 Mass 250, 255, 675 NE2d 781, 785 (1997) (rejecting due process challenge to presumption cutting off worker's compensation benefits at age 65, GL 152, §35E).

- Where not otherwise provided in a judgment of divorce or in an agreement between the parties, the recipient spouse's remarriage does not of itself automatically terminate alimony, but makes a prima facie case that requires the court to end alimony absent proof of some extraordinary circumstances, established by the recipient spouse, warranting continuation. *Keller v. O'Brien*, 420 Mass 820, 652 NE2d 589 (1995)
- Docket entries are prima facie evidence of the facts recorded therein. See *Com. v. Mattos*, 404 Mass 672, 677 (1989); *Com. v. Sigman*, 41 Mass App 574, 575 n. 2, 671 NE2d 1008, 1010 n.2 (1996).

The common-law presumption of legitimacy, see *Taylor v. Whittier*, 240 Mass 514, 138 NE 6 (1922), has been effectively eliminated by legislative and judicial action. See *C. C. v. A. B.*, 406 Mass 679, 688-691, 550 NE2d 365, 371-373 (1990). See also *P. B. C. v. D. H.*, 396 Mass 68, 483 NE2d 1094 (1985).

Some older Massachusetts decisions strongly assert that this class of prima facie evidence cannot exist because the burden of persuasion should never shift. See *Hanna v. Shaw*, 244 Mass 57, 60, 138 NE 247, 248 (1923). See also *Cook v. Farm Service Stores, Inc.*, 301 Mass 564, 569, 17 NE2d 890, 893 (1938) (shift of burden of persuasion called "heresy"). Nevertheless, it seems clear that such a shift is the practical effect of the presumptions mentioned above. As noted above, Proposed Mass R Evid 301(a) would generally treat presumptions in civil cases (except as otherwise provided in statutes) as shifting the burden of persuasion.

It should be noted that where the presumptions mentioned in this section are created by statute, the statutes usually contain more than a mere reference to "presumption" or "prima facie evidence," but rather go on to describe the response as an affirmative defense, see, e.g., *Hurley v. Flanagan*, 313 Mass 567, 575, 48 NE2d 621, 626 (1943) (GL 231, §85C), or require that a "showing" contrary to the presumption be "demonstrated." See *Yazbek v. Board of Appeal on Motor Vehicle Liability Policies*, 41 Mass App 915, 670 NE2d 200 (1996), discussed in the next section.

b. Shifting Burden of Production

This section considers those rules of law that make proof of fact A "prima facie evidence" of fact B in the sense that proof of fact A by proponent places upon opponent the burden of production of evidence as to the nonexistence of fact B. The additional effect of such a presumption, while it is still operative, is to assist proponent in carrying its burden of persuasion on that issue and, in the absence of countervailing evidence as to the presumed fact B, to require a finding of fact B as a matter of law. As the court explained in *Com. v. Pauley*, 368 Mass 286, 290-291, 331 NE2d 901, 904 (1975) (citing Text):

> According to the Massachusetts view, when, by statute or common law, one fact probative of another is denominated prima facie evidence of that second fact, proof of the first or basic fact requires a finding that the second, the inferred or presumed fact, is also true. The finding is mandatory. To avert this result, the opponent must assume the burden of production (the burden of persuasion remains with the proponent). It is only when the opponent has introduced sufficient evidence, which, cast against the natural inferential value of the basic fact, creates an issue of fact for the trier, that the opponent has satisfied his burden and the mandatory effect disappears. In a case tried by jury where the opponent does not assume his burden, the judge should charge that if the jury find the basic fact, they are required to find the inferred fact; if the basic fact is admitted or otherwise undisputed, the judge should charge that the jury must find the inferred fact, and if the inferred fact encom-

passes the substance of the case, the judge should direct a verdict.

See also *Epstein v. Boston Housing Authority*, 317 Mass 297, 302, 58 NE2d 135, 139 (1944). Compare *Dobija v. Hopey*, 353 Mass 600, 233 NE2d 920 (1968) (evidence insufficient to rebut presumption that testator knew contents of will) with *Duchesneau v. Jaskoviak*, 360 Mass 730, 277 NE2d 507 (1972) (evidence sufficient to rebut such presumption).

The definition of a presumption in the Uniform Commercial Code GL 106, §1-201(31), seems to come within this concept of prima facie evidence. Section 1-201(31) defines a presumption as follows: "'Presumption' or 'presumed' means that the trier of fact must find the existence of the fact presumed unless and until evidence is introduced which would support a finding of its non-existence." These are the classic "presumptions of law" recognized by Thayer and Wigmore, although the Massachusetts decisions take pains to emphasize that the concept is more properly described as "prima facie evidence." See, e.g., *Com. v. Crosscup*, 369 Mass 228, 339 NE2d 731 (1975); *Com. v. Norton*, 339 Mass 592, 161 NE2d 766 (1959); *Hobart-Farrell Plumbing & Heating Co. v. Klayman*, 302 Mass 508, 19 NE2d 805 (1939); *Com. v. Koney*, 421 Mass 295, 303-304, 657 NE2d 210, 215 (1995).

Illustrative of this type of presumption is that the mailing of a properly addressed postpaid letter is deemed "prima facie evidence" of delivery in due course of post. *Com. v. Crosscup*, supra. Consistent with the so-called bursting bubble theory of presumptions, the courts have explained: "As soon as evidence is introduced that warrants a finding that the letter failed to reach its destination, the artificial compelling force of the prima facie evidence disappears, and the evidence of nondelivery has to be weighed against the likelihood that the mail service was efficient in the particular instance, with no artificial weight on either side of the balance." *Hobart-Farrell Plumbing & Heating Co. v. Klayman*, supra, 302 Mass at 510, 19 NE2d at

805. See also *Bouley v. Reisman*, 38 Mass App 118, 125-126, 645 NE2d 708, 713 (1995) (refusing to apply presumption in face of evidence of nondelievery of radiologist's report).

In contrast, where the rule of law requires not merely the introduction of some contradictory evidence in order to overcome the presumption but rather that a "showing" contrary to the presumption be "demonstrated," the presumption will survive the mere production of some contrary evidence. See *Yazbek v. Board of Appeal on Motor Vehicle Liability Policies*, 41 Mass App 915, 670 NE2d 200 (1996) (regulation concerning insurance surcharges) and §5.5.3.a, supra.

Other examples of this type of prima facie evidence include:

- Bills of lading in due form issued by third party are prima facie evidence of its own authenticity and genuineness and the facts stated in the document by the third party. GL 106, §1-202. See also *Joseph Freedman Co. v. North Penn Transfer, Inc.*, 388 Mass 551, 555, 447 NE2d 657, 659 (1983) (bill of lading prima facie evidence that, as to all circumstances which were open to inspection and visible, goods were in good order).
- Birth, marriage, and death certificates are prima facie evidence of the facts therein recorded. GL 46, §19.
- A certificate signed and sworn to by a state police chemist is prima facie evidence of the percentage of alcohol in motorist's blood. GL 90, §24(1)(e).
- Certificate of certain state-employed chemists is prima facie evidence of the composition, quality, and the net weight of the narcotic or other drug analyzed. GL 111, §13; GL 22C, §39. But see *Com. v. Malcolm*, 35 Mass App 938, 624 NE2d 968 (1993) (& cases cited) (error for judge to instruct jury that certificate of analysis from DPH must be accepted by jury unless contrary evidence was introduced).

See also GL 22C, §41 (certificate by state police chemist prima facie evidence of presence of sperm cells or seminal fluid). For a discussion of these provisions, see *Com. v. Westerman*, 414 Mass 688, 699-700, 611 NE2d 215 (1993); *Com. v. Villella*, 39 Mass App 426, 430, 657 NE2d 237, 239-240 (1995) (prior misfeasance of state chemist could be introduced to rebut prima facie effect of certificate); *Smola v. Higgins*, 42 Mass App 724, 679 NE2d 593 (1997) (state laboratory lead detection report under GL 111, §195).

- The "presumption" of death from an unexplained absence for more than seven years has the effect of shifting to the party denying death the burden of production on this issue; it does not shift the ultimate burden of persuasion, which remains on the party alleging death. *Jacobs v. Town Clerk of Arlington*, 402 Mass 824, 827, 525 NE2d 658, 660 (1988) (& citations). See also *Stamper v. Stanwood*, 339 Mass 549, 159 NE2d 865 (1959).

- Corporate charter is prima facie evidence of charitable character and purpose. *Boxer v. Boston Symphony Orchestra, Inc.*, 342 Mass 537, 174 NE2d 363 (1961).

- An affidavit of the tax collector sending a tax bill or notice as to the time of sending shall be prima facie evidence that the same was sent at such time. GL 60, §3. See also *Singer Sewing Machine Co. v. Assessors of Boston*, 341 Mass 513, 519, 170 NE2d 687, 691 (1960) (prima facie effect of affidavit of mailing under GL 60, §3, and inference behind it destroyed by vague and unsatisfactory form of affidavit and misstated fact it contained); *Roda Realty Trust v. Board of Assessors of Belmont*, 385 Mass 493, 495, 432 NE2d 522, 524 (1983) (affidavit submitted under GL 60, §3, is prima facie evidence of date real estate notices were sent).

- Death certificate is prima facie evidence of time of death. GL 46, §19 (construed in *Com. v. Lykus*, 406 Mass 135, 143-144, 546 NE2d 159, 164-165 (1989)).
- Certificate by ballistics expert of Department of Public safety is prima facie evidence that item is a "firearm." GL 140, §12A (construed in *Com. v. Rhodes*, 389 Mass 641, 644 n.4, 451 NE2d 1151, 1153 n.4 (1983)).

See also GL 231, §102C ("The decision, and the amount of damages assessed, if any, by a district court shall be prima facie evidence upon such matters as are put in issue by the pleadings [in the superior court]."), construed in *Lubell v. First National Stores, Inc.*, 342 Mass 161, 172 NE2d 689 (1961), *Dwyer v. Piccicuto*, 25 Mass App 910, 515 NE2d 596 (1987), *Forrey v. Dedham Taxi, Inc.*, 19 Mass App 955, 473 NE2d 726 (1985), and *Garrity v. Valley View Nursing Home, Inc.*, 10 Mass App 822, 406 NE2d 423 (1980); GL 218, §23 ("A finding for the plaintiff [in small claims case] in the district court department shall be prima facie evidence for the plaintiff in the trial by jury of six. At such trial the plaintiff may, but need not, introduce evidence."), construed in *Todino v. Arbella Mutual Insurance Co.*, 415 Mass 298, 612 NE2d 1181 (1993); Mass R Civ P 53(i)(1) ("the master's findings upon all issues submitted to him are admissible as prima facie evidence of the matters found and may be read to the jury and, in the discretion of the court, may be submitted to the jury as an exhibit, subject, however, to the rulings of the court upon any objections properly preserved."), construed in *Delano Growers' Cooperative Winery v. Supreme Wine Co., Inc.*, 393 Mass 666, 671-672, 473 NE2d 1066, 1070 (1985).

§5.5.4 Inferences

Sometimes confused with the evidentiary devices discussed above is the concept of inference, which simply describes the situation where proof of fact A logically permits (but does not require) a finding that fact B exists because of the relationship of the two facts in light of common experience. The inference is a generalization based on the logical connection between facts, and does not carry any artificial evidentiary weight.[3] See, e.g., *Com. v. Pratt*, 407 Mass 647, 652-653, 555 NE2d 559, 562 (1990) (inference of possession of contraband from proximity to defendant's personal effects; inference of intent to distribute from possession of large quantity of contraband); *Lynn Teachers Union, Local 1037 v. Massachusetts Commission Against Discrimination*, 406 Mass 515, 526-527, 549 NE2d 97, 103-104 (1990) (discriminatory intent may be inferred from mere fact of differences in treatment); *Com. v. Lawrence*, 404 Mass 378, 392, 536 NE2d 571, 580 (1989) (fact that an empty condom package was found in pocket of jacket found next to nude body of victim supports inference that sexual activity occurred); *Com. v. Seven Thousand Two Hundred Forty-Six Dollars*, 404 Mass 763, 537 NE2d 144 (1989) (insufficient evidence to support inference that monies seized were proceeds of marijuana sales); *Com. v. Ridge*, 37 Mass App 943, 641 NE2d 1059 (1994) (inference of intent to distribute from large quantity of cocaine possessed); *Com. v. Watson*, 36 Mass App 252, 260, 629 NE2d 1341, 1346 (1994) (& citations) (inference of possession from defendant's possession of similar drugs in similar packages); *Com. v. Reilly*, 23 Mass App 53, 55, 498 NE2d 1366, 1368 (1986) (inference that defendant had "carried" pistol drawn from proximity of gun to other items in van defendant admittedly owned); *Com. v. Rarick*, 23 Mass App 912, 499 NE2d 1233 (1986) (inference that defendant was in possession of contraband drawn from proximity of contraband to personal effects of defendant in dwelling); *Com. v. Broderick*, 16

---

[3]But see *Rolanti v. Boston Edison Corp.*, 33 Mass App 516, 522, 603 NE2d 211, 216-217 (1992) ("An inference is an important means by which a party may satisfy his burden of persuasion sufficiently to transfer the burden of going forward to the other party, who may be in a better position to know certain facts essential to the case.")

Mass App 941, 943, 450 NE2d 1116, 1117 (1983) (inference of criminal intent from defendant's conduct); *Com. v. Diaz*, 15 Mass App 469, 471-472, 446 NE2d 415, 416 (1983) (inference of knowledge of presence of firearm); *Com. v. Porter*, 15 Mass App 331, 332-335, 445 NE2d 631, 632-634 (1983) (inference of guilty knowledge). Compare *Com. v. True*, 16 Mass App 709, 711-712, 455 NE2d 453, 454 (1983) (intent to defraud may not be inferred from mere nonperformance of a promise) with *Com. v. Wilson*, 16 Mass App 369, 451 NE2d 727 (1983) (citing Text) (construing GL 140, §12, to permit inference of intent to defraud from refusal to pay hotel bill upon demand).

References to "familiar rules," — e.g., a state of things once proved to exist may generally be found to continue — seem to fall within the category of inference. See, e.g., *Galdston v. McCarthy*, 302 Mass 36, 18 NE2d 331 (1938); *Com. v. Bono*, 7 Mass App 849, 384 NE2d 1260 (1978) (continued existence of a corporation); *Panesis v. Loyal Protective Life Insurance Co.*, 5 Mass App 66, 359 NE2d 319 (1977) (mental condition and total disability) (Text cited); *Conroy v. Fall River Herald News Co.*, 306 Mass 488, 28 NE2d 729 (1940) (inference that state of things once proved to exist existed earlier). See also *Com. v. Carson*, 349 Mass 430, 208 NE2d 792 (1965) (regularity of corporate proceedings is "presumed"); *Swartz v. Sher*, 344 Mass 636, 640, 184 NE2d 51, 54 (1962) (presumption that a person's conduct is lawful); *Newcomb v. Aldermen of Holyoke*, 271 Mass 565, 171 NE 826 (1930) (presumption of regularity of official proceedings); *Stamper v. Stanwood*, 339 Mass 549, 553, 159 NE2d 865, 868 (1959) (presumption of good faith). Compare *Flynn v. Coffee*, 94 Mass (12 Allen) 133 (1866) (presumption of death after unexplained absence of more than seven years); *Allen v. Mazurowski*, 317 Mass 218, 57 NE2d 544 (1944) (presumption of continuity of life); *Krantz v. John Hancock Mutual Life Insurance Co.*, 335 Mass 703, 141 NE2d 719 (1957); *Bohaker v. Travelers Insurance Co.*, 215 Mass 32, 36, 102 NE 342, 344 (1913) ("presumption against suicide").

For a discussion of inferences in the context of circumstantial proof and relevance, see §§4.1 and 4.2.

§5.5.5 Presumptions, Prima Facie Evidence, and Inferences Distinguished

For additional cases discussing the effect of, and contrasting, presumptions, prima facie evidence and inferences, see *DiLoreto v. Fireman's Fund Insurance Co.*, 383 Mass 243, 418 NE2d 612 (1981) (rebuttable administrative presumption of fault in excess of 50 percent where automobile whose doors are open is involved in collision); *Com. v. Pauley*, 368 Mass 286, 290-294, 331 NE2d 901, 904-908 (1975); *Scaltreto v. Shea*, 353 Mass 62, 223 NE2d 525 (1967); *Pahigian v. Manufacturer's Life Insurance Co.*, 349 Mass 78, 85, 206 NE2d 660, 666 (1965); *Universal C.I.T. Corp. v. Ingel*, 347 Mass 119, 125, 196 NE2d 847, 851 (1962); *Akers Motor Lines, Inc. v. State Tax Commission*, 344 Mass 359, 363, 182 NE2d 476, 478 (1962); *Boxer v. Boston Symphony Orchestra, Inc.*, 342 Mass 537, 174 NE2d 363 (1961); *Casagrande v. F. W. Woolworth Co.*, 340 Mass 552, 555-557, 165 NE2d 109, 112 (1960); *Duarte v. Kavanaugh*, 340 Mass 640, 165 NE2d 746 (1960); *Jacquot v. William Filene's Sons Co.*, 337 Mass 312, 149 NE2d 635 (1958); *Planning Board of Springfield v. Board of Appeals of Springfield*, 338 Mass 160, 163, 154 NE2d 349, 351 (1958); *Marotta v. Board of Appeals*, 336 Mass 199, 204, 143 NE2d 270, 274 (1957); *Perry v. Boston Elevated Railway*, 322 Mass 206, 76 NE2d 653 (1948); *Thomes v. Meyer Store, Inc.*, 268 Mass 587, 589, 168 NE 178, 179 (1929); *Redstone v. Board of Appeals of Chelmsford*, 11 Mass App 383, 416 NE2d 543 (1981).

In the case of conflict between presumptions or prima facie evidence, both lose their artificial compelling force and neither prevails as a matter of law over the other. The issue is then thrown open to be decided as a fact upon all the evidence. *Turner v. Williams*, 202 Mass 500, 505, 89 NE 110, 112 (1909) (conflicting presumptions); *Town of Lexing-*

ton v. Ryder, 296 Mass 566, 6 NE2d 828 (1937) (conflicting prima facie evidence); *Boyas v. Raymond*, 302 Mass 519, 20 NE2d 411 (1939) (conflict between two types of statutory prima facie evidence); *Krantz v. John Hancock Mutual Life Insurance Co.*, 335 Mass 703, 141 NE2d 719 (1957) (conflict between prima facie evidence of suicide and presumption against suicide). Proposed Mass R Evid 301(c) would alter Massachusetts practice by providing: "If two presumptions arise which are conflicting with each other, the court shall apply the presumption which is founded on the weightier considerations of policy and logic. If there is no such preponderance, both presumptions shall be disregarded."

§5.5.6   Presumptions in Criminal Cases

The use of presumptions raises special problems in criminal cases, where care must be taken to avoid giving the jury the impression that the burden of persuasion shifts to the defendant on any element of the crime. See generally *Francis v. Franklin*, 471 US 307 (1985); *Connecticut v. Johnson*, 460 US 73 (1983); *Sandstrom v. Montana*, 442 US 510 (1979); *Mullaney v. Wilbur*, 421 US 684 (1975); *Com. v. Lykus*, 406 Mass 135, 143, 546 NE2d 159, 165 (1989); *Com. v. Claudio*, 405 Mass 481, 541 NE2d 993 (1989); *Com. v. Johnson*, 405 Mass 488, 542 NE2d 248 (1989); *Com. v. Teixera*, 396 Mass 746, 488 NE2d 775 (1986); *Com. v. Nieves*, 394 Mass 355, 476 NE2d 179 (1985); *DeJoinville v. Com.*, 381 Mass 246, 408 NE2d 1353 (1980). Also, because of the long-established principle that a verdict may not be directed against a defendant in a criminal case, as well as the corollary proposition that the trier of fact cannot be compelled to find against the defendant as to any element of the crime, neither a presumption nor prima facie evidence, even if unrebutted, can have the effect it does in a civil case. See *Com. v. Pauley*, 368 Mass 286, 291, 331 NE2d 901, 904-905 (1975); *DeJoinville v. Com.*, supra.

Instructions to the jury in criminal cases must be phrased in permissive, not mandatory, terms. The use of the word "presumed" should be avoided. The essential fact-finding process must be left to the jury, which may perform that function by drawing reasonable inferences from the evidence provided that there is a rational connection between the underlying fact and the presumed fact and that the burden remains on the prosecution to establish every element of the crime beyond a reasonable doubt. *McInerney v. Berman*, 621 F2d 20 (1st Cir 1980); *Com. v. Lykus*, supra, 406 Mass at 143-144, 546 NE2d at 164-165; *Com. v. Pauley*, supra; *Com. v. Callahan*, 401 Mass 627, 633, 519 NE2d 245, 249-250 (1988) (*Callahan III*); *Com. v. Callahan*, 380 Mass 821, 406 NE2d 385 (1980) (*Callahan I*); *Com. v. Medina*, 380 Mass 565, 577-580, 404 NE2d 1228, 1236-1237 (1980); *Com. v. Campbell*, 375 Mass 308, 376 NE2d 872 (1978). See also *Connecticut v. Johnson*, supra; *Com. v. Doucette*, 391 Mass 443, 450-452, 462 NE2d 1084, 1092-1093 (1984); *Com. v. Palmer*, 386 Mass 35, 434 NE2d 983 (1982); *Com. v. Moreira*, 385 Mass 792, 434 NE2d 196 (1982) (error to charge jury under GL 90, §24(1)(e), that statutory presumption of intoxication binds jury);[4] *Com. v. McDuffee*, 379 Mass 353, 398 NE2d 463 (1979) (materiality in perjury case); *Com. v. Sibinich*, 33 Mass App 246, 598 NE2d 673 (1992) (instruction that "everybody is presumed to intend what he or she did in fact do" did not impermissibly shift burden of proof on issue of intent to armed robbery defendant).

On the elements of intent and malice, compare *Com. v. Sires*, 405 Mass 598, 542 NE2d 580 (1989) (instructions on intent referring to "the natural presumption of malice" impermissibly shifted burden of proof to defendant) and *Com. v. Repoza*, 400 Mass 516, 510 NE2d 755 (1987) (*Repoza II*) (instruction that intentional use of a deadly weapon created presumption of malice violated *Sandstrom v. Montana*, supra) with *Com. v. Blake*, 409 Mass 146, 149-154, 564

---

[4] Section 5 of St. 1994, c. 25, substituted "permissible inference" for "presumption" in GL 90, §24(1)(e).

NE2d 1006, 1009-1012 (1991) (instructions permitting jury to infer malice from deliberate or cruel act did not shift burden of proof), *Com. v. Pierce*, 419 Mass 28, 37-38, 642 NE2d 579, 585 (1994) (judge properly instructed jury that they might, but were not required to, draw inference of malice from use of deadly weapon), and *Com. v. Sime*, 35 Mass App 928, 623 NE2d 500 (1993) (same). See also *Com. v. Wallace*, 417 Mass 126, 132, 627 NE2d 935, 939 (1994) (prosecutor's statement during closing argument that human beings intend natural consequences of their acts did not, in context, require reversal); *Com. v. Doherty*, 411 Mass 95, 578 NE2d 411 (1991) (instruction regarding presumption of malice, while generally impermissible, was not error in case where there was no evidence justifying a finding of involuntary manslaughter or raising reasonable doubt whether killing was excused or justified); *Com. v. Matos*, 36 Mass App 958, 961, 634 NE2d 138, 141 (1994) (jury could properly infer malice from intentional shooting); *Com. v. Alves*, 35 Mass App 935, 937, 625 NE2d 559, 561 (1993) (no error in instruction that intentional killing without justification or excuse was unlawful killing with malice aforethought).

When instructing a jury in a criminal case on use of prima facie evidence, as with a certificate of analysis of drugs, the judge must convey that such evidence carries no particular presumption of validity. *Com. v. Berrio*, 43 Mass App 836, 837-838, 687 NE2d 644, 644-646 (1997).

Proposed Mass R Evid 302(c) takes cognizance of these principles in providing:

> Whenever the existence of a presumed fact against the accused is submitted to the jury, the court shall instruct the jury that it may regard the basic facts as sufficient evidence of the presumed fact but is not required to do so. In addition, if the presumed fact establishes guilt or is an element of the offense or negatives a defense, the court shall instruct the jury that its existence, on all the evidence, must be proved beyond a reasonable doubt.

Although earlier decisions[5] allowing a presumption of sanity to assist the prosecution in carrying its burden of proof have been questioned, the Supreme Judicial Court has rejected the argument that an instruction allowing a permissive inference of sanity based on the fact "that a great majority of men are sane" violates art. 12 of the Massachusetts Declaration of Rights. *Com. v. Kappler,* 416 Mass 574, 585-587, 625 NE2d 513 (1993) (O'Connor, J, dissenting, would invalidate the presumption once the issue of insanity is raised by sufficient evidence). See also *Com. v. Keita,* 429 Mass 843, 712 NE2d 65 (1999). The jury may be advised of the reasonable inference of sanity and may rely on it together with other evidence. *Com. v. Amaral,* 389 Mass 184, 190-193, 450 NE2d 142, 146-147 (1983); *Com. v. Brown,* 387 Mass 220, 439 NE2d 296 (1982); *Com. v. Robinson,* 14 Mass App 591, 594, 441 NE2d 553, 556 (1982) (jury may consider "presumption of sanity" as "shorthand expression for fact that the majority of people are sane"). Indeed, the court has never held that the presumption of sanity is alone insufficient to meet the Commonwealth's burden. See *Com. v. Keita,* supra, 419 Mass at 847, 712 NE2d at 69.

For a discussion of the role of an appellate court in assessing the impact of constitutionally erroneous burden-shifting language in jury instructions and the question of harmless error, see *Com. v. Doherty,* supra, 411 Mass at 102-105 (& citations); *Com. v. Repoza II,* supra, 400 Mass at 521-522, 510 NE2d at 758-759.

§5.6   Adverse Inferences

§5.6.1   In General

In certain situations a negative inference may be drawn from the failure of a party to produce evidence or take

---

[5] See, e.g., *Com. v. Kostka,* 370 Mass 516, 350 NE2d 444 (1976).

other action that might reasonably be expected of it. Thus, for example, the failure to conduct scientific tests, evidence of inadequacies of tests performed, or the existence of more reliable tests is relevant to rebut the Commonwealth's evidence. See *Com. v. Cordle*, 412 Mass 172, 176-178, 587 NE2d 1372, 1375-1376 (1992); *Com. v. Benoit*, 382 Mass 210, 221, 415 NE2d 818, 825 (1981); *Com. v. Bowden*, 379 Mass 472, 485-486, 399 NE2d 482, 491 (1980); *Com. v. Flanagan*, 20 Mass App 472, 475-476, 481 NE2d 205, 208-209 (1985); *Com. v. Phong Thu Ly*, 19 Mass App 901, 471 NE2d 383 (1984).[1] See also *Com. v. Reynolds*, 429 Mass 388, 390-392, 708 NE2d 658, 661-662 (1999) (failure to pursue leads concerning other suspects); *Com. v. Viriyahiranpaiboon*, 412 Mass 224, 231-232, 588 NE2d 643, 649 (1992) (prosecutor argued defense expert failed to perform certain tests). Compare *Com. v. Brown*, 411 Mass 115, 119, 579 NE2d 153, 155-156 (1991) (no error in refusal to instruct jury that adverse inference could be drawn from failure of police to conduct tests where there was nothing to show shirt in question was ever in police custody). The decision to give the so-called *Bowden* instruction allowing the jury to draw an inference from the failure to conduct tests is within the trial judge's discretion. See *Com. v. Rivera*, 424 Mass 266, 274, 675 NE2d 791, 797 (1997); *Com. v. Leitzsey*, 421 Mass 694, 702, 659 NE2d 1168, 1173 (1996); *Com. v. Cordle*, supra, 412 Mass at 177, 587 NE2d at 1375; *Com. v. Daye*, 411 Mass 719, 740-741, 587 NE2d 194, 206-207 (1992); *Com. v. Adams*, 34 Mass App 516, 519, 613 NE2d 118, 121 (1993) ("The failure to conduct certain tests or make certain investigations is a permissible ground on which to build a defense, and the judge may not remove that issue from the jury's considera-

---

§5.6 [1] "To prevent the jury from reaching unwarranted inferences concerning a failure to test, the prosecution should also be allowed to elicit on direct or redirect examination the reason for the omission of a test, such as that the test could not be performed . . . or would have had little probative value." *Com. v. Flanagan*, supra, 20 Mass App at 476 n.2, 481 NE2d at 208 n.2 (citations omitted).

tion. However, a judge need not give instructions on what inferences the jury may draw." (citations omitted).

Similarly, the jury may consider the lack of adequate medical records to justify drug prescriptions and draw an adverse inference from the absence of such records. *Com. v. Wood*, 17 Mass App 304, 457 NE2d 1131 (1983). Refusal of a plaintiff claiming personal injuries to permit a physical examination is proper cause for comment. *Stack v. New York, N. H. & H. R.R. Co.*, 177 Mass 155, 157, 58 NE 686, 686 (1900). See also Mass R Civ P 35. In an action to establish paternity, the "fact that any party refuses to submit to a genetic marker test shall be admissible and the court may draw an adverse inference from such refusal." GL 209C, §17, as amended in 1998.

§5.6.2   *Failure to Call Witnesses*

Perhaps the most common example of an adverse inference of this type involves the failure to call a witness who would normally be expected to be called. "Where a party has knowledge of a person who can be located and brought forward, who is friendly to, or at least not hostilely disposed toward, the party, and who can be expected to give testimony of distinct importance to the case, the party would naturally offer that person as a witness. If, then, without explanation, he does not do so, the jury may, if they think reasonable in the circumstances, infer that person, had he been called, would have given testimony unfavorable to the party. . . ." *Com. v. Figueroa*, 413 Mass 193, 199, 595 NE2d 779, 783 (1992) (quoting *Com. v. Schatvet*, 23 Mass App 130, 134, 499 NE2d 1208, 1210-1211 (1986)); *Com. v. Zagranski*, 408 Mass 278, 287, 558 NE2d 933, 939 (1990). See also *Com. v. Niziolek*, 380 Mass 513, 404 NE2d 643 (1980) (rejecting argument that inference erodes presumption of innocence).

Failure to call witnesses to support an alibi is a typical example. See, e.g., *Com. v. Thomas*, 429 Mass 146, 706 NE2d

669 (1999); *Com. v. MacKenzie*, 413 Mass 498, 515-516, 597 NE2d 1037, 1048 (1992); *Com. v. Lee*, 394 Mass 209, 219, 475 NE2d 363, 369-370 (1985); *Com. v. Luna*, 46 Mass App 90, 94-96, 703 NE2d 740, 743-744 (1998) (defendant properly cross-examined about his failure to search for alibi witnesses); *Com. v. Tavares*, 27 Mass App 637, 642-643, 541 NE2d 578, 581-582 (1989). But compare *Com. v. Johnson*, 46 Mass App 398, 407-408, 706 NE2d 716, 723-724 (1999) (no foundation for inference where defendant never mentioned being with anyone). See also *Graves v. R.M. Packer, Inc.*, 45 Mass App 760, 770, 702 NE2d 21, 28 (1998) (failure of defendant to call its president and controlling stockholder, person presumably most knowledgeable of facts in question and present during entire trial).

The courts have advised that "[b]ecause the inference, when it is made, can have a seriously adverse effect on the noncalling party — suggesting, as it does, that the party has willfully attempted to withhold or conceal significant evidence — it should be invited only in clear cases, and with caution." *Com. v. Figueroa*, supra, 413 Mass at 199, 595 NE2d at 783 (citation omitted). See also *Com. v. Lo*, 428 Mass 45, 50-51, 696 NE2d 935, 939-940 (1998); *Com. v. Zagranski*, supra ("This is a delicate area, requiring caution."); *Com. v. Groce*, 25 Mass App 327, 329-331, 517 NE2d 1297, 1298-1299 (1988) (judge failed to exercise caution in instructing jury that it could draw adverse inference from defendant's failure to call mother and girlfriend).

Whether an inference can be drawn from the failure to call witnesses necessarily depends upon the "posture of the particular case and the state of the evidence." *Com. v. Anderson*, 411 Mass 279, 282, 581 NE2d 1296, 1298 (1991) (citation omitted) (citing Text). "When it appears that the witness may be as favorable to one party as the other, no inference is warranted. Further, if the circumstances, considered by ordinary logic and experience, suggest a plausible reason for nonproduction of the witness, the jury should not be advised of the inference." 411 Mass at 282-283, 581 NE2d at 1298 (citations omitted). There is no basis for the inference when it appears that the testimony would be "unimportant — merely corroborative of, or merely cumulative upon, the testimony of one or more witnesses who have been called." *Com. v. Schatvet*, supra, 23 Mass App at 134, 499 NE2d at 1211. See also *Com. v. Richardson*, 429 Mass 182, 184, 706 NE2d 664, 666 (1999); *Com. v. Lo*, supra, 428 Mass at 51, 696 NE2d at 940 (missing witness's testimony would probably have been cumulative); *Com. v. Wilson*, 38 Mass App 680, 685-688, 651 NE2d 854, 857-858 (1995) (no error in warning jury not to draw adverse inference where missing informant and officers were not present during transaction in question).

A showing of availability is a foundational prerequisite for the inference. See *Com. v. Gagnon*, 408 Mass 185, 198 n.8, 557 NE2d 728, 737 n.8 (1990) (no inference permitted where missing witness has successfully invoked testimonial privilege); *Com. v. Cobb*, 397 Mass 105, 108, 489 NE2d 1246, 1247-1248 (1986) (substantial risk of miscarriage of justice where jury was permitted to draw adverse inference from defendant's failure to produce store employees where nothing to suggest that missing witnesses were available or within his control); *Com. v. Fredette*, 396 Mass 455, 465-466, 486 NE2d 1112, 1119-1120 (1986); *Com. v. United Food Corp.*, 374 Mass 765, 374 NE2d 1331 (1978); *Com. v. Franklin*, 366 Mass 284, 318 NE2d 469 (1974) (extensive discussion); *Grady v. Collins Transportation Co.*, 341 Mass 502, 170 NE2d 725 (1960) (extensive review of cases and principles, especially relating to availability); *Horowitz v. Bokron*, 337 Mass 739, 743-744, 151 NE2d 480, 483-484 (1958) (error to comment in absence of showing of availability of doctor witness); *Thornton v. First National Stores, Inc.*, 340 Mass 222, 226, 163 NE2d 264, 267 (1960) (mere showing that doctor practiced in nearby community not sufficient to show availability); *Com. v. Crawford*, 46 Mass App 423, 428-429, 706 NE2d 1141, 1145-1146 (1999) (where evidence was that missing witness was arrested at same time as defendant, and is silent as to outcome of arrest, inference and instruction improper because witness might still be in custody); *Com. v.*

Vasquez, 27 Mass App 655, 659, 542 NE2d 296, 298-299 (1989) (insufficient foundation for inference where no evidence of physical availability of missing witness).

Where a witness is equally available to both sides, no inference should be drawn against either side for failing to call the witness. *Com. v. Crawford*, 417 Mass 358, 366-367, 629 NE2d 1332, 1337 (1994); *Com. v. Figueroa*, supra, 413 Mass at 199, 595 NE2d at 783-784; *Com. v. Cobb*, supra, 397 Mass at 108, 489 NE2d at 1247-1248; *Berry v. Stone*, supra, 345 Mass at 756, 189 NE2d at 855. But compare *Com. v. Johnson*, 39 Mass App 410, 412, 656 NE2d 929, 931 (1995) (mere fact that witness appears equally available to both parties does not preclude missing witness instruction if it appears that defendant would be naturally expected to call friend).

Availability does not necessarily mean proof of actual whereabouts. Rather, it refers to the likelihood that the party against whom the inference is to be drawn would be able to procure the missing witness' physical presence in court. *Com. v. Happnie*, 3 Mass App 193, 197, 326 NE2d 25, 29 (1975). Comment may nonetheless be impermissible if the witness cannot easily be called or if the negative inference would otherwise be unfair. See *Com. v. Melendez*, 12 Mass App 980, 428 NE2d 824 (1981).

The most significant factors considered by courts in determining whether to give a "missing witness" instruction against a party have been summarized as follows: (1) the case against the party is strong, so that the party would naturally be expected to call favorable witnesses; (2) the purported evidence of the missing witnesses is not unimportant, collateral, or cumulative; (3) the party has superior knowledge of the identity and whereabouts of the witness; and (4) the party has not furnished a plausible reason, in the light of ordinary logic and experience, for nonproduction of the witness (stated otherwise, the evidence did not establish the missing witness' unavailability to the party). *Com. v. Graves*, 35 Mass App 76, 81-87, 616 NE2d 817, 821-824 (1993). See also *Com. v. Olszewski*, 416 Mass 707, 723-724, 625 NE2d 529, 540 (1993). A jury should ordinarily not be permitted to draw inferences from failure of defendant to call witnesses unless it appears to be within his power to do so and unless the evidence against him is so strong that, if innocent, he would be expected to call them. *Com. v. Fredette*, 396 Mass 455, 466, 486 NE2d 1112, 1119-1120 (1986) (& citations).

"A party need not call everyone who might have information on a given subject, on pain, if he omits any, of suffering a jury inference that he is wrongly withholding damaging evidence." *Com. v. Schatvet*, supra, 23 Mass App at 136, 499 NE2d at 1212. Compare *Bencosme v. Kokoras*, 400 Mass 40, 44, 507 NE2d 748, 751 (1987) (no indication that missing witness knew anything bearing on issues at trial, and thus not clear that defendants naturally would be expected to call her), *Com. v. Matthews*, 45 Mass App 444, 447-450, 699 NE2d 347, 349-352 (1998) (improper for prosecutor to argue inference where defendant claimed he did not have opportunity to produce witnesses and unlikely that they would have offered important and helpful testimony), *Com. v. Resendes*, 30 Mass App 430, 569 NE2d 413 (1991) (cross-examination, prosecutor's comment, and instruction on missing witness constituted reversible error where evidence strongly suggested that defendant and missing witness were unfriendly), *Com. v. LeBlanc*, 30 Mass App 1, 7-8, 565 NE2d 797, 801 (1991) (in view of facts that defendant's testimony inculpated missing witness in drug activity and person does not appear to have any personal knowledge of the transactions in question, caution is advised regarding missing witness inference upon retrial), *Com. v. Vasquez*, 27 Mass App 655, 659, 542 NE2d 296, 298-299 (1989) (insufficient foundation for inference where testimony from missing witness would not have been crucial to Commonwealth's case), and *Com. v. Fulgham*, 23 Mass App 422, 423-427, 502 NE2d 960, 961-963 (1987) (judge did not err in refusing to give missing witness instruction against Commonwealth for failure to call two witnesses to testify as to fresh complaint where their testimony would have been cumulative of police officer's testimony and where prosecutor provided satisfactory explanation for not calling them) with *Com. v. Olszewski,* 416 Mass 707, 724-725, 625 NE2d 529, 541 (1993) (where defendant offered no convincing reason why he failed to call father and sister to challenge confession, proper foundation for inference was laid), *Com. v. Bryer,* 398 Mass 9, 12-13, 494 NE2d 1335, 1337-1338 (1986) (fact that defendant's roommate could not have fully corroborated defendant's testimony did not bar prosecutorial comment since defendant would be expected to call him for even partial corroboration), *Com. v. Caldwell,* 36 Mass App 570, 581-582, 634 NE2d 124, 131 (1994) (partial corroboration), *Berry v. Stone,* 345 Mass 752, 756, 189 NE2d 852, 855 (1963) ("It is reasonable in the usual case to expect a plaintiff to call an available physician who first attended her after her injury."), and *Grassis v. Retik,* 25 Mass App 595, 600-601, 521 NE2d 411, 414 (1988) (same).

Failure to call a witness who would normally be expected to be called is a proper subject for comment in argument in both civil and criminal cases. Before commenting on the absence of a witness, the better practice is to notify the court and opposing counsel. See *Com. v. Fredette,* supra, 396 Mass at 466, 486 NE2d at 1120; *Com. v. Matthews,* supra, 45 Mass App at 448, 699 NE2d at 351; *Com. v. Calcagno,* 31 Mass App 25, 29, 574 NE2d 420, 423 (1991). The trial judge should rule that there is sufficient foundation for such inference in the record before comment is made. *Com. v. Vasquez,* supra, 27 Mass App at 658, 542 NE2d at 298 (citations omitted). But see *Com. v. Caldwell,* supra, 36 Mass App at 582, 634 NE2d at 131 (failure of prosecutor to obtain favorable ruling from judge before commenting on missing witness does not of itself ordinarily create basis for reversal; it merely creates risk that attorney will be interrupted by judge who may then give an unfavorable instruction to the jury).

The decision to give a missing witness instruction to the jury is within the discretion of the judge, and a party who seeks the instruction cannot require it of right. *Com. v. Figueroa,* supra, 413 Mass at 199, 595 NE2d at 784; *Com. v.*

Anderson, supra, 411 Mass at 283, 581 NE2d at 1298. See also *Rolanti v. Boston Edison Corp.*, 33 Mass App 516, 526-527, 603 NE2d 211, 219 (1992) (no error in judge's refusal to give missing witness instruction where he allowed defense counsel extensive questioning regarding doctor's assessment). It has been suggested, however, that once a judge authorizes counsel at the charge conference to make a "missing witness" comment to the jury, the judge must also give a missing witness instruction to the jury; otherwise, the effect is to undercut counsel's closing argument. *Com. v. Sena*, 29 Mass App 463, 468 n.7, 561 NE2d 528, 531 n.7 (1990). See also *Com. v. Pratt*, 407 Mass 647, 654-658, 555 NE2d 559, 565-566 (1990) (judge's instructions admonishing jury to refrain from speculation regarding credibility of informants not called by Commonwealth did not impermissibly frustrate defendant's missing witness inference argument).

There are suggestions in the cases that the judge should instruct that, with regard to a criminal defendant, the jury should not draw an inference from the defendant's failure to call a witness unless it is persuaded of the truth of the inference beyond a reasonable doubt. See *Com. v. Olszewski*, supra, 416 Mass at 724 n.18, 625 NE2d at 540 (& citation); *Com. v. Johnson*, supra, 39 Mass App at 412-413, 656 NE2d at 931. But compare *Com. v. Lawrence*, 404 Mass 378, 394, 536 NE2d 571, 581 (1989) (defendant not entitled to instruction that in order to draw inferences, Commonwealth must prove subsidiary facts beyond reasonable doubt); *Com. v. Ruggerio*, 32 Mass App 964, 966, 592 NE2d 753, 753 (1992) (no requirement that each inference from facts made must be proved beyond reasonable doubt).

A missing witness instruction need not identify the missing witness by name. See *Com. v. Johnson*, supra, 39 Mass App at 412-413, 656 NE2d at 931 (identity of witness clear from arguments).

The failure of a party to take the stand in his own behalf is a proper subject for comment in a civil case (see *McGinnis v. Aetna Life & Casualty Co.*, 398 Mass 37, 39, 494

NE2d 1322, 1323 (1986) (& citations)), but not in the case of a criminal defendant, who enjoys the privilege against self-incrimination. See §13.14.8. See also *Frizado v. Frizado,* 420 Mass 592, 596, 651 NE2d 1206, 1210 (1995) (adverse inference permissible in domestic abuse case even where criminal proceedings are pending against defendant); *Custody of Two Minors,* 396 Mass 610, 617, 487 NE2d 1358, 1363-1364 (1986) (privilege against self-incrimination applicable in criminal proceedings, which prevents drawing negative inference from a defendant's failure to testify, not applicable in child custody case); *Adoption of Nadia,* 42 Mass 304, 306-308, 676 NE2d 1165, 1167 (1997) (negative inference of unfitness permissible from father's failure to testify at hearing to dispense with need for consent to adoption).

The adverse inference drawn from the failure of a party to testify is not sufficient, by itself, to meet an opponent's burden of proof. *Frizado v. Frizado,* supra, 420 Mass at 596, 651 NE2d at 1210; *McGinnis v. Aetna Life & Casualty Co.,* supra; *Custody of Two Minors,* supra, 396 Mass at 616, 487 NE2d at 1363.

The same adverse inference may apply to the failure to produce evidence. See, e.g., *Com. v. Ramey,* 368 Mass 109, 111-112, 330 NE2d 193, 195 (1975) (failure to produce time cards in support of alibi); *Com. v. Matthews,* supra, 45 Mass App at 450, 699 NE2d at 352 (& citations) (proper to question defendant and comment upon his lack of documentation of employment).

A.   BASICS

§6.1   Attendance/Compulsory Process

In Massachusetts, subpoenas run throughout the Commonwealth and mandate attendance in court as long as
accompanied by one day's witness fees and travel fare to
and from court. GL 233, §§1-3; GL 262, §29. The form and
process for the issuance of a subpoena in civil proceedings
are set forth in Mass R Civ P 45, and for criminal matters in
Mass R Crim P 17.

A defendant in a state criminal proceeding is entitled
to compulsory process to obtain witnesses in his or her favor

under both the Sixth and Fourteenth Amendments to the United States Constitution and Article 12 of the Massachusetts Declaration of Rights. See *Washington v. Texas*, 388 US 14, 87 S Ct 1920, 18 L Ed 1019 (1967); *Blazo v. Superior Court*, 366 Mass 141, 315 NE2d 857 (1974) (indigent defendants entitled to compel attendance of witnesses at misdemeanor trials at public expense); *Com. v. Degrenier*, 40 Mass App 212, 214-215, 662 NE2d 1039, 1041-1042 (1996) (defendant had constitutional right to compel presence of inmate witness); *Com. v. Adderley*, 36 Mass App 918, 919-920, 629 NE2d 308, 310-311 (1994) (judge's refusal to issue bench warrant for defense witness deprived defendant of right to present defense).

A witness "necessary" to an adequate defense is one whose testimony is relevant, material, and not cumulative. *Com. v. Degrenier*, supra, 40 Mass App at 215, 662 NE2d at 1041. This right, however, is not absolute and may be lost by the failure to make timely disclosure of the intention to call the witness. See *Com. v. Durning*, 406 Mass 485, 494-498, 548 NE2d 1242, 1248-1250 (1990) (witness not listed on pretrial conference report); *Com. v. Chappee*, 397 Mass 508, 516-519, 492 NE2d 719, 724-726 (1986) (expert witnesses not disclosed to prosecution as required by pretrial agreement); *Com. v. Porcher*, 26 Mass App 517, 529 NE2d 1348 (1988) (alibi witness not disclosed as required by Mass R Crim P 14(b)). But compare *Com. v. Steinmeyer*, 43 Mass App 185, 681 NE2d 893 (1997) (trial court abused discretion in striking testimony of defense witness as sanction for defense counsel's failure to furnish prosecution with copy of witness's pretrial notes as required by pretrial conference agreement). Another limitation on a defendant's right to call a witness is the latter's invocation of the privilege against self-incrimination. See *Com. v. Drumgold*, 423 Mass 230, 247-249, 668 NE2d 300, 313-314 (1996) (& citations); §13.14, infra.

Defendants are entitled as of right to have access to witnesses who are in the custody of the Commonwealth, including the opportunity for an interview. See generally

Com. v. Rivera, 424 Mass 266, 271-272, 675 NE2d 791, 796 (1997); *Com. v. Penta*, 423 Mass 546, 669 NE2d 767 (1996). Witnesses may, however, refuse to grant an interview with defense counsel; if they chose to be interviewed, they have "the right to impose reasonable conditions on the conduct of the interview." GL 258B, §3(m). On the issue of the Commonwealth's duty to produce informers for testimony, see *Com. v. Penta*, supra.

The defendant's constitutional right to prepare a defense is abridged where a prospective defense witness decides not to testify because of the prosecutor's threats to prosecute him. See *Com. v. Turner*, 37 Mass App 385, 640 NE2d 488 (1994) (& citations). Compare *Com. v. Penta*, supra, 423 Mass at 548-550, 669 NE2d at 769-770 (prosecution did not improperly prevent informer from testifying by requesting perjury prosecution warning in open court).

GL 268, §13B, makes it a crime to intimidate, influence, or otherwise interfere with a witness. See generally *Com. v. Belle Isle*, 44 Mass App 226, 694 NE2d 5 (1998). See also *Com. v. Belete*, 37 Mass App 424, 640 NE2d 511 (1994) (court interpreter is not "witness" for purposes of GL 268, §13B); *Com. v. Auguste*, 418 Mass 643, 646-648, 639 NE2d 388, 390-391 (1994) (questions regarding witness's fear of testifying, whether or not caused by defendant, are allowable at judge's discretion).

Witness fees may be paid by the government on written ex parte application of an indigent criminal defendant. Mass R Crim P 17(b) and (c). A defendant indicted for a capital offense may have process issued at the expense of the Commonwealth without regard to proof of indigence. GL 277, §66. Fees and mileage need not be tendered when a subpoena is issued on behalf of the United States, the Commonwealth, a political subdivision or agency, or an officer of a political subdivision or agency. Mass R Civ P 45(c); Fed R Civ P 45(c). For a discussion of the recovery of witness fees (including expert witness fees) as taxable costs by a successful civil litigant, see *Waldman v. American Honda Motor Co.*, 413 Mass 320, 597 NE2d 404 (1992); *City of Boston v. United States Mineral Products Co.*, 37 Mass App 933, 641 NE2d 132 (1994).

In criminal cases, Massachusetts witnesses can be summoned into other states, and witnesses from other states can be summoned into Massachusetts, provided the other state in question has enacted reciprocal legislation and certain other conditions are met. GL 233, §§13A-B (Uniform Act to Secure the Attendance of Witnesses from Without a State in Criminal Proceedings); Mass R Crim P 17(d)(2). See generally *Matter of Rhode Island Grand Jury Subpoena*, 414 Mass 104, 605 NE2d 840 (1993) (& citations) (extensive discussion of issues of standing, privilege, and application of Uniform Act). Penalties, warrants, and contempt powers for failure of a witness to appear in accordance with a valid subpoena are found in both statutes and rules of court. See GL 233, §§5-11 (courts and nonjudicial tribunals); GL 3, §28A (General Court); Mass R Civ P 45(f), Fed R Civ P 45(f), and Fed R Crim P 17(g) (contempt); Mass R Crim P 17(e) (warrant). Regarding discovery within the Commonwealth for proceedings held in another jurisdiction, see GL 223A, §11 ("A court of this Commonwealth may order a person who is domiciled or is found within this Commonwealth to give his testimony or statement or to produce documents or other things for use in a proceeding in a tribunal outside this Commonwealth. . . ."), construed in *Matter of a Rhode Island Select Commission Subpoena*, 415 Mass 890, 616 NE2d 458 (1993).

§6.2   Sequestration

Sequestration of witnesses is designed to prevent perjury by keeping them out of the courtroom during each other's testimony. See *Com. v. Jackson*, 384 Mass 572, 582, 428 NE2d 289, 295 (1981) (citing Text). Unlike the federal practice where sequestration is mandatory upon the request of a party (see Fed R Evid 615), the sequestration of witnesses in the Massachusetts courts lies within the discretion of the trial judge. See *Com. v. Watkins*, 373 Mass 849, 370 NE2d 701 (1977); *Com. v. Vanderpool*, 367 Mass 743, 748, 328 NE2d 833, 837 (1975); *Com. v. Blackburn*, 354 Mass 200, 205, 237 NE2d 35, 38 (1968); *Zambarano v. Massachusetts Turnpike Authority*, 350 Mass 485, 215 NE2d 652 (1966); *Com. v. Bonner*, 33 Mass App 471, 473-474, 601 NE2d 32, 33-34 (1992) (citing Text) (judge acted within discretion in denying motion to sequester child victim's mother); *Com. v. Sevieri*, 21 Mass App 745, 757, 490 NE2d 481, 488-489 (1986) (discretion should be exercised based on reasons related to particular case rather than as matter of general practice); Proposed Mass R Evid 615;[1] Mass R Crim P 21.[2] The better practice in "capital cases" is to order sequestration. *Com. v. Vanderpool*, supra (but failure to order sequestration not abuse of discretion here); *Com. v. Watkins*, supra.

Similarly left to the discretion of the judge is the modification or revocation of sequestration orders. See *Com. v. Jackson*, supra, 384 Mass at 581-582, 428 NE2d at 295 (judge acted within discretion in allowing expert witness for prosecution to remain in courtroom to assist prosecution, and permitting police officer witness to resume testimony after hearing testimony of other witnesses, despite general sequestration order) and *Com. v. Parry*, 1 Mass App 730, 735-736, 306 NE2d 855, 859-860 (1974) (judge did not abuse his discretion by permitting witness to remain in courtroom and hear testimony of other witnesses after having initially ordered her to be sequestered), as well as the appropriate remedy for violation. See *Com. v. Pope*, 392 Mass 493, 506,

---

§6.2 [1]"At the request of a party the court may order witnesses excluded so that they cannot hear the testimony of other witnesses, and it may make the order on its own motion. This rule does not authorize exclusion of (1) a party who is a natural person, or (2) an officer or employee of a party which is not a natural person designated as its representative by its attorney, or (3) a person whose presence is shown by a party to be essential to the presentation of his cause." PMRE 615.

[2]"Upon his own motion or the motion of either party, the judge may, prior to or during the examination of a witness, order any witness or witnesses other than the defendant to be excluded from the courtroom."

467 NE2d 117, 126 (1984) (judge acted within discretion in deciding that counsel should be responsible for enforcing sequestration order); *Com. v. Gogan*, 389 Mass 255, 261-262, 449 NE2d 365, 369 (1983) (judge did not abuse discretion in denying motion for mistrial after police officer witnesses violated order not to discuss case with one another); *Com. v. Navarro*, 2 Mass App 214, 223, 310 NE2d 372, 378 (1974) (judge acted within discretion in refusing to declare mistrial because of violation of sequestration order).

Parties to the case and prospective witnesses whose presence is essential to the management and presentation of the party's case, such as the police officer in charge of the investigation, are exempt from exclusion. See *Com. v. Perez*, 405 Mass 339, 343, 540 NE2d 681, 683 (1989) (& cases cited); *Com. v. Therrien*, 359 Mass 500, 508, 269 NE2d 687, 693 (1971); *Com v. Washburn*, 5 Mass App 195, 197, 360 NE2d 908, 909 (1977); *Com. v. Clark*, 3 Mass App 481, 485-486, 334 NE2d 68, 72 (1975); Proposed Mass R Evid 615. As to the propriety of allowing a police officer witness to sit at the Commonwealth's table during trial, see *Com. v. Auguste*, 414 Mass 51, 59-60, 605 NE2d 819, 824 (1992) (& citations); *Com. v. Duffy*, 36 Mass App 937, 939, 629 NE2d 1347, 1349 (1994).

§6.3 Competency

"Any person of sufficient understanding, although a party, may testify in any proceeding, civil or criminal. . . ." GL 233, §20. Thus, the only requirement of competency to testify as a witness in the Massachusetts courts is sufficient mental capacity to: (1) observe, remember, and give expression to that which she has seen, heard, or evidenced; and (2) comprehend the difference between truth and falsehood. *Com. v. Brusgulis*, 398 Mass 325, 329, 496 NE2d 652, 655 (1986); *Com. v. Whitehead*, 379 Mass 640, 656, 400 NE2d 821,

833-834 (1980); Proposed Mass R Evid 601.[1] Under the modern trend, a judge may find a witness competent even though his reliability is, in the judge's eyes, "marginally sufficient." *Demoulas v. Demoulas,* 428 Mass 555, 564, 703 NE2d 1149, 1159 (1998) (challenge to competency of deponent's testimony). It is left to the trier of fact to "make any proper discount for the quality of [the witnesses'] understanding." Id. (citation omitted). See also *Com. v. Echavarria,* 428 Mass 593, 595-596, 703 NE2d 1137, 1139 (1998) (although witness was illiterate, recently arrived in the United States, and unable to speak English, he was "far from failing the not very stringent test of competence" applied).

Witnesses have been deemed competent to testify although they were:

- *young children* — see, e.g., *Com. v. Trowbridge,* 419 Mass 750, 754-755, 647 NE2d 413, 417 (1995) (eight-year-old); *Com. v. LeFave,* 407 Mass 927, 941-942, 556 NE2d 83, 92-93 (1990); *Com. v. Dockham,* 405 Mass 618, 542 NE2d 591 (1989) (four-year-old); *Malchanoff v. Truehart,* 354 Mass 118, 236 NE2d 89 (1968) (eight-year-old testifying to events that occurred when she was three); *Com. v. Welcome,* 348 Mass 68, 201 NE2d 827 (1964) (seven-year-old); *Com. v. Tatisos,* 238 Mass 322, 325, 130 NE 495, 497 (1921) (six-year-old); *Com. v. Lamontagne,* 42 Mass App 213, 675 NE2d 1169 (1997) (four-year-old testifying to events at age three); *Com. v. Gamache,* 35 Mass

---

§6.3 [1] Rule 601 provides:

(a) General rule of competency. Every person is competent to be a witness except as otherwise provided in these rules.

(b) Disqualification of witness; interpreters. A person is disqualified to be a witness if the court finds that the proposed witness (1) lacked the capacity to perceive, or (2) is incapable of remembering, or (3) is incapable of expressing himself concerning the matter so as to be understood by the judge and jury either directly or through interpretation by one who can understand him, or (4) is incapable of understanding the duty of a witness to tell the truth. An interpreter is subject to all the provisions of these rules relating to witnesses.

App 805, 806-809, 626 NE2d 616, 618-620 (1994) (five-year-old testifying to acts committed when she was 22 to 33 months old); *Com. v. Baran,* 21 Mass App 989, 991, 490 NE2d 479, 480-481 (1986). For a discussion of special arrangements for the taking of testimony from a child witness, see §6.4.

- *emotionally disturbed or learning disabled* —see, e.g., *Com. v. Sylvia,* 35 Mass App 310, 619 NE2d 360 (1993) (witness mentally competent to testify even though she had suffered nervous breakdown and was under hospital treatment); *Com. v. Jimenez,* 10 Mass App 441, 409 NE2d 204 (1980).
- *mentally ill or insane* —see, e.g., *Com. v. Zelenski,* 287 Mass 125, 129, 191 NE2d 355, 357 (1934); *Com. v. Piedra,* 20 Mass App 155, 159-160, 478 NE2d 1284, 1288 (1985).
- *of limited intelligence* —see, e.g., *Com. v. Whitehead,* supra.
- *alcoholic* —see, e.g., *Com. v. Sires,* 370 Mass 541, 546, 350 NE2d 460, 464 (1976).

Neither a child's inability to place events in a temporal framework, nor inconsistencies or lapses in the child's answers, renders the child incompetent to testify. See *Com. v. Trowbridge,* supra, 419 Mass at 755, 647 NE2d at 418; *Com. v. Gamache,* supra, 35 Mass App at 806-809, 626 NE2d at 618-620. Nor is it necessary that the child have a full understanding of the obligation of the oath; it is sufficient if she demonstates an understanding of the difference between truth and falsehood and an awareness of the duty to tell the truth. *Com. v. LeFave,* supra; *Com. v. Welcome,* supra; *Com. v. Healey,* 8 Mass App 938, 396 NE2d 1027 (1979). Compare *Com. v. Corbett,* 26 Mass App 773, 775-777, 533 NE2d 207, 209-210 (1989) (judge did not abuse discretion in ruling four-year-old witness incompetent to testify because her answers indicated confusion as to difference between truth and lie). There is no requirement that the child be able to explain the concept of punishment for the telling of a lie. *Com. v. Brusgulis,* supra, 398 Mass at 330, 496 NE2d at 655-656. Once deemed competent, the testimony of a child is not rendered inadmissible by the failure to formally administer the oath. *Com. v. McCaffrey*, 36 Mass App 583, 589-590, 633 NE2d 1062, 1066 (1994).

Unlike some jurisdictions, Massachusetts does not mandate a pretrial hearing to give the defendant an opportunity to show that a child's memory of events is the product of suggestive or coercive interview techniques. Such hearing is within the discretion of the judge. See *Com. v. Allen*, 40 Mass App 458, 462-463, 665 NE2d 105, 108-109 (1996).

The competency of a person to testify is a question "peculiarly for the trial judge, and his determination will be rarely faulted on appellate review." *Com. v. Whitehead*, supra, 379 Mass at 656, 400 NE2d at 833-834. Except in quite clear cases of incompetency, the tendency is to let the witness testify and have the triers make any proper discount for the quality of her "understanding." Id. "The established safeguards of the Anglo-American legal system leave the veracity of a witness to be tested by cross-examination, and the credibility of his testimony to be determined by a properly instructed jury." *Com. v. Colon*, 408 Mass 419, 443, 558 NE2d 974, 989 (1990) (quoting *Hoffa v. United States*, 385 US 293, 311, 87 S Ct 408, 418 (1966)). Thus, inconsistencies or lapses in testimony as well as the witness's inability to remember details of events all go to credibility and the weight of the evidence, not competence to testify. See, e.g., *Com. v. Lamontagne*, supra, 42 Mass App at 218, 675 NE2d at 1173; *Com. v. Capone*, 39 Mass App 606, 610 n.1, 659 NE2d 1196, 1199 n.1 (1996); *Com. v. Gamache*, supra, 35 Mass App at 806-807; *Com. v. Jimenez*, supra, 10 Mass App at 444, 409 NE2d at 205-206.

Ordinarily when an issue is raised as to competency, the trial judge should require a voir dire examination to determine the issue. "The judge is afforded wide discretion — indeed, is obliged — to tailor the competency inquiry to the particular circumstances and intellect of the witness." *Com. v. Brusgulis*, supra, 398 Mass at 329-330, 496 NE2d at 655. See also *Com. v. Doucette*, 22 Mass App 659, 496 NE2d 837 (1986) (judge did not abuse discretion in conducting voir dire on his own and refusing to allow defense counsel to ask questions); *Com. v. Rockwood*, 27 Mass App 1137, 538 NE2d 40 (1989) (trial judge is not required to administer oath to child witness who undergoes voir dire to determine competency).

Upon a proper showing, the judge may require an examination of the witness's mental condition by a qualified physician under the authority of GL 123, §19.[2] For a discussion of the statute and the limitations on the judge's power thereunder, see *Com. v. Gibbons*, 378 Mass 766, 393 NE2d 400 (1979). The decision whether to employ an expert is entirely within the judge's discretion. *Com. v. Trowbridge*, supra, 419 Mass at 755, 647 NE2d at 418. See also *Com. v. Santos*, 402 Mass 775, 787-788, 525 NE2d 388, 395-396 (1988) (judge erred in not ordering competency evaluation of witness with Down's syndrome); *Com. v. Gamache*, supra, 35 Mass App at 809 (judge did not improperly delegate to psychiatrist determination of competence). The judge is not empowered to order a psychiatric examination merely for purposes of assessing a witness's credibility. See *Com. v. Widrick*, 392 Mass 884, 467 NE2d 1353 (1984).

GL 233, §23E provides alternative procedures for determining the competency of a witness with mental retardation where the court finds that the usual procedures will likely cause severe psychological or emotional trauma. The statute also provides alternative methods of taking the testimony, including videotape, but in a criminal proceeding the defendant has the right to be present during the taking of the testimony, to have an unobstructed view of the witness, and to have the witness's view of the defendant be unobstructed. §23E(d).

Although competency is determined before a witness testifies, the judge may reconsider the decision (either sua

---

[2]"In order to determine the mental condition of any party or witness before any court of the Commonwealth, the presiding judge may, in his discretion, request the department [of Mental Health] to assign a qualified physician or psychologist, who, if assigned shall make such examinations as the judge may deem necessary."

sponte or on motion) if he entertains doubts about the correctness of the ruling. *Com. v. Brusgulis*, supra, 398 Mass at 331, 496 NE2d at 656. "While the judge must be careful not to invade the jury's province of deciding the witness's credibility, he may consider whether the witness's performance on the stand demonstrates a lack of awareness of the obligation to tell the truth or an inability to observe, remember, and recount." Id. But see *Com. v. Lamontagne*, supra, 42 Mass App at 218-219, 675 NE2d at 1173 (judge did not abuse discretion in refraining from sua sponte inquiry into child's competency).

Objections to the competency of a witness must generally be raised before the testimony is given. See *Com. v. Domanski*, 332 Mass 66, 73-74, 123 NE2d 368, 373 (1954); *Com. v. Sylvia*, supra, 35 Mass App at 312. But see *Com. v. Whitehead*, supra, 379 Mass at 655, 400 NE2d at 833 (objection to competency made by "novel" method of motion to strike).

On the question of jury instructions regarding witnesses of limited competency, see *Com. v. Figueroa*, 413 Mass 193, 196-198, 595 NE2d 779, 781-783 (1992) (judge not required to give defendant's requested instruction regarding mentally retarded victim); *Com. v. Perkins*, 39 Mass App 577, 580, 658 NE2d 975, 977-978 (1995) (judge not required to give special instruction on credibility and suggestibility of child witness).

Despite the general rule of competency, certain witnesses under certain circumstances are precluded by law from testifying as to certain matters. In other circumstances, witnesses are privileged not to reveal, or privileged to prevent others from revealing, certain matters. These disqualifications and privileges are discussed in Chapter 13.

§6.4   Special Arrangements for the Child Witness

GL 278, §16D provides for alternative procedures for the taking of testimony if the court finds by a preponderance of the evidence "that the child witness is likely to suffer psychological or emotional trauma as a result of testifying in open court, as a result of testifying in front of the defendant, or as a result of both. . . ." See generally *Com. v. Dockham*, 405 Mass 618, 622-625, 542 NE2d 591, 594-595 (1989) (& cases cited). A child can give videotaped testimony, but it must be taken in the defendant's presence. *Com. v. Tufts*, 405 Mass 610, 614-615, 542 NE2d 586, 589 (1989).

Although permitted by GL 278, §16D, testimony by closed circuit television outside the presence of the defendant has been held violative of the art. 12 right to confront one's accusers "face to face." See *Com. v. Bergstrom*, 402 Mass 534, 524 NE2d 366 (1988). Similarly, a special seating arrangement in the courtroom during the testimony of a minor witness that results in the defendant being unable to see the face of the witness, or that permits the witness to give testimony without facing the accused, violates art. 12. See *Com. v. Amirault*, 424 Mass 618, 631-632, 677 NE2d 652, 662 (1997); *Com. v. Johnson*, 417 Mass 498, 631 NE2d 1002 (1994).

GL 278, §16A, mandates closure of proceedings during the testimony of minor complainants of sexual offenses, but the decisional law dictates a case-by-case determination of the necessity of closure. See *Com. v. Martin*, 417 Mass 187, 191-196, 629 NE2d 297, 300-303 (1994) (& citations).

GL 233, §§81, 82, and 83 provide for the admission of out-of-court statements of children not available or competent to testify, relating to acts of sexual abuse. See §8.21.

§6.5 Personal Knowledge

Competency to testify is to be distinguished from the separate requirement that a witness have personal knowledge of the matters he is testifying about. See *Com. v. Whitehead*, 379 Mass 640, 657, 400 NE2d 821, 833 (1980); *Malchanoff v. Truehart*, 354 Mass 118, 121-122, 236 NE2d 89,

92-93 (1968); Proposed Mass R Evid 602.[1] Testimony must be based on first-hand observations derived from the witness's own senses. *Com. v. Whitehead,* supra. Thus, for example, a witness's testimony that she had an instinct or suspicion that the defendant had had sexual relations with the complainant cannot be admitted. *Com. v. Martin,* 417 Mass 187, 189-190, 629 NE2d 297, 299-300 (1994).

A preliminary question to the witness is sometimes required to establish personal knowledge. In the absence of a showing of personal knowledge concerning the matter inquired into, the judge may exclude the question. *Com. v. LaCorte,* 373 Mass 700, 706-707, 369 NE2d 1006, 1011 (1977). Lack of sufficient personal knowledge to testify about a matter may also be raised by a motion to strike. *Com. v. Whitehead,* supra; *Com. v. Boris,* 317 Mass 309, 318, 58 NE2d 8, 14 (1944).

When an extrajudicial statement is offered for its truth, the proponent of the statement may be required to establish that the declarant had personal knowledge of the information contained in the statement. See *Com. v. Crawford,* 417 Mass 358, 363, 629 NE2d 1332, 1334 (1994) (& citations).

B. IMPEACHMENT

§6.6 Introduction

The credibility of a witness is of course a question for the jury to decide — "they may accept or reject, in whole or in part, the testimony presented to them." *Com. v. Fitzgerald,*

---

§6.5 [1] "A witness may not testify to a matter unless evidence is introduced sufficient to support a finding that he has personal knowledge of the matter. Evidence to prove personal knowledge may, but need not, consist of the testimony of the witness himself. This rule is subject to the provisions of Rule 703, relating to opinion testimony by expert witnesses." PMRE 602.

376 Mass 402, 411, 381 NE2d 123, 131 (1978). See also *Com. v. Hoffer,* 375 Mass 369, 377, 377 NE2d 685, 691 (1978) (rejecting contention that key prosecution witness's testimony was so inherently contradictory and had been so fully impeached that it was incredible as a matter of law). A Massachusetts jury is not required to credit a witness's testimony merely because he tells a plausible story and is not impeached. See *Com. v. McInerney,* 373 Mass 136, 143-144, 365 NE2d 815, 820 (1977) (& cases cited).

A party may seek to discredit or impeach a witness in four basic ways:

(1)   contradict his testimony;
(2)   challenge his testimonial faculties;
(3)   show that he has a bias, prejudice, or motive to lie in the particular case;
(4)   show that he has a bad character for truthfulness and veracity.

Impeachment may be accomplished on cross-examination and, as to noncollateral matters (see §6.7.1), by the introduction of extrinsic evidence. As the Court put it long ago:

> [I]n cross-examination, an adverse party is usually allowed great latitude of inquiry, limited only by the sound discretion of the court, with a view to test the memory, the purity of principle, the skill, accuracy, and judgment of the witness; the consistency of his answers with each other, and with his present testimony; his life and habits, his feelings towards the parties respectively, and the like; to enable the jury to judge of the degree of confidence they may safely place in his testimony.

Hathaway v. Crocker, 48 Mass (7 Metc) 262, 266 (1843).

It is improper to ask one witness to comment (positively or negatively) on the credibility of another witness, or to ask whether another witness is lying. See *Com. v. Johnson,*

412 Mass 318, 327-328, 588 NE2d 684, 689-690 (1992) (& citations); *Com. v. Triplett,* 398 Mass 561, 567, 500 NE2d 262 (1986); *Com. v. DeMars,* 42 Mass App 788, 792, 682 NE2d 885, 887-888 (1997); *Com. v. Lorette,* 37 Mass App 736, 739-740, 643 NE2d 67, 69 (1994) (complainant's mother's testimony had improper effect of affirming credibility of complainant); *Com. v. Kines,* 37 Mass App 540, 542-543, 640 NE2d 1117, 1119 (1994); *Com. v. Powers,* 36 Mass App 65, 627 NE2d 953 (1994) (reversible error to admit testimony of four fresh complaint witnesses with regard to credibility of complainant); *Com. v. Krepon,* 32 Mass App 945, 948, 590 NE2d 1165, 1168 (1992); *Com. v. Carver,* 33 Mass App 378, 383, 600 NE2d 588, 592-593 (1992); *Com. v. Morris,* 20 Mass App 114, 119, 478 NE2d 750, 753-754 (1985) (improper for defendant to be asked on cross-examination: "There is no reason for [the alleged child victims] to lie, is there?"); *Com. v. Flanagan,* 20 Mass App 472, 477-478, 481 NE2d 205, 209 (1985); *Com. v. Long,* 17 Mass App 707, 708-709, 462 NE2d 330, 331 (1984). Compare *Com. v. Grenier,* 415 Mass 680, 690, 615 NE2d 922, 927 (1993) (police officer's testimony that he told defendant in course of questioning that he did not believe him, and that defendant then became noticeably nervous, not same as testimony of witness at trial who expresses opinion about credibility of another witness); *Com. v. Federico,* 40 Mass App 616, 619-621, 666 NE2d 1017, 1020-1021 (1996) (child victim's testimony that she told her mother "the truth" was colloquial use of term and not comment on witness's own credibility).

The main evil of this line of questioning is that it "implies to the jury that differences in the testimony of the witness and any other witness could only be the result of lying and not because of misrecollection, failure of recollection or other innocent reason." *Com. v. Ward,* 15 Mass App 400, 401-402, 446 NE2d 89, 91 (1983) (citation and internal quotes omitted). It is of course proper for counsel through questioning to point out inconsistencies between the witness's testimony and that of other witnesses. See *Com. v. Johnson,* supra, 412 Mass at 326, 558 NE2d at 689.

It is equally well-settled that an expert may not offer an opinion (directly or indirectly) on another witness's credibility. See §7.3.

Although a judge may summarize the evidence, discuss possible inferences to be drawn therefrom, and point out factors to be considered by the jury in weighing the credibility of witnesses, the judge may not (directly or indirectly) express an opinion as to the credibility of particular witnesses. See *Com. v. Keniston*, 423 Mass 304, 313, 667 NE2d 1127, 1134 (1996) (& citations); *Com. v. Perez*, 390 Mass 308, 319-321, 455 NE2d 632, 638-639 (1983) (& cases cited); *Com. v. Ortiz*, 39 Mass App 70, 653 NE2d 1119 (1995) (instructing jury that quality of police officer's report was not important impermissibly implied that omissions had no impeachment value). Compare *Com. v. Mello*, 420 Mass 375, 388-389, 649 NE2d 1106, 1115-1116 (1995) (although challenged instruction may have impermissibly warned jury not to accept defendant's testimony, in context of entire charge it did not create substantial likelihood of miscarriage of justice).

For an example of a general instruction to the jury on the credibility of witnesses, see *Com. v. Whitlock*, 39 Mass App 514, 521, 658 NE2d 182, 187 (1995) (judge not required to specifically instruct that police officer's testimony is not to be accorded any greater weight or credibility than other witness).

Polygraph (lie detector) evidence may not be used to impeach a witness in Massachusetts. See §7.8, note 1.

§6.7 By Contradiction

The testimony of W1 may be contradicted in three ways:

(1) by testimony of W2 as to the same subject matter;
(2) by evidence of a statement made by W1 prior to trial that is inconsistent with his testimony;
(3) by inconsistent testimony of W1 given at the trial.

§6.7.1   Contradiction by W2

The testimony of W1 may be challenged by calling W2 to contradict it. The right to present contradictory testimony is limited, however, to matters that are otherwise directly relevant to the issues in the lawsuit. Thus, while W1 may be cross-examined as to collateral facts that cast doubt on his credibility by suggesting that if he was wrong about one matter, "other portions of his testimony also might be inaccurate," *Com. v. Fleury-Ehrhart*, 20 Mass App 429, 434, 480 NE2d 661, 665 (1985), the opponent must take the answer as it is given and generally cannot resort to extrinsic proof (such as testimony of W2) to contradict these matters.[1] *Leone v. Doran*, 363 Mass 1, 15, 292 NE2d 19, 30; *Alexander v. Kaiser*, 149 Mass 321, 21 NE 376 (1889); *Hathaway v. Crocker*, 48 Mass (7 Metc) 262, 266 (1843). See, e.g., *Com. v. Sherry*, 386 Mass 682, 693, 437 NE2d 224, 231 (1982) ("The out-of-court statement of the [rape] victim was . . . offered only to impeach her credibility generally and not as to her description of the events in issue. Consequently, [evidence of the statement] was collateral to all issues in the case, save the victim's credibility. The victim's testimony on matters not relevant to contested issues in the case cannot, as of right, be contradicted by extrinsic evidence.") (citing Text); *Com. v. Chase*, 372 Mass 736, 746-748, 363 NE2d 1105, 1112-1113 (1977) (prior statement of one police officer to another concerning what prosecution witness told him); *Com. v. Zezima*, 365 Mass 238, 242 n.5, 310 NE2d 590, 593 n.5 (1974); *Com. v. Doherty*, 353 Mass 197, 213-214, 229

---

§6.7   [1]The common-law *Hitchcock* rule provided:

If the answer of a witness is [about] a matter which you would be allowed on your part to prove in evidence—if it have such connection with the issue, that you would be allowed to give it in evidence——then it is a matter on which you may contradict him [with extrinsic evidence].

Attorney-General v. Hitchcock, 1 Exch 91, 99 (Eng 1847). For more on the test for collateralness and the modern application of the doctrine, see *United States v. Pisari*, 636 F2d 855 (1st Cir 1981) (& citations).

NE2d 267, 277 (1967) (extrinsic evidence contradicting prosecution witness's denial that she had known victim); *Com. v. Connolly*, 308 Mass 481, 495, 33 NE2d 303, 311 (1941) (extrinsic proof contradicting prosecution witness's denial that defendant clerk had been compelled to reprove him in unrelated matter); *Klein v. Keresey*, 307 Mass 51, 29 NE2d 703 (1940) (applying collateral matter rule under GL 233, §23, where plaintiff sought to contradict defendant whom he had called to testify); *Com. v. Wheeler*, 42 Mass App 933, 678 NE2d 168 (1997) (defendant's lack of belligerence at police station, shown on videotape, collateral to issue of earlier assault); *Com. v. Doyle*, 5 Mass App 544, 550, 364 NE2d 1283, 1288 (1977) (whether arson defendant intended to divorce his wife was collateral; contradictory testimony thus properly excluded).

The limitation on contradiction by extrinsic proof is premised upon a desire to avoid a proliferation of tangential issues as well as unfair surprise to the opposing party. As the Supreme Judicial Court long ago recognized, "if a different rule were adopted . . . the trial of a cause would branch out into collateral issues without limit." *Hathaway v. Crocker*, 48 Mass (7 Metc) 262, 266 (1843). See also *Leone v. Doran*, supra, 363 Mass at 15, 292 NE2d at 30 (& citations).

Notwithstanding the general prohibition, a judge may permit impeachment by extrinsic evidence even on collateral points. See, e.g., *Com. v. Ferguson*, 425 Mass 349, 355-356, 680 NE2d 1166, 1170 (1997) (rebuttal testimony contradicting murder defendant on collateral issue of his treatment of female employees properly admitted because it cast doubt on his credibility); *Simon v. Solomon*, 385 Mass 91, 107, 431 NE2d 556, 567 (1982) (no error where exhibits admitted not likely to delay trial or confuse jury, and no unfair surprise to opponent); *Com. v. Chase*, supra, 372 Mass at 747, 363 NE2d at 1113.

When the matter is relevant to an issue in the lawsuit and not merely to the credibility of the witness, extrinsic proof can always be offered to contradict. See *Hathaway v. Crocker*, supra, 48 Mass at 266 (W1 could be contradicted on denial that he had told W2 that his son was partner in business because son's partnership was central issue in case).

§6.7.2   Contradiction by Prior Inconsistent Statement

a.   General Considerations

The testimony of W1 may be challenged by showing that he made a contradictory statement (either oral or written) at some time prior to trial. This may be done on cross-examination or, for noncollateral matters (see previous section), by extrinsic proof such as the testimony of W2 who heard the statement. "The rule of evidence is well settled that if a witness either upon his direct or cross-examination testifies to a fact which is relevant to the issue on trial the adverse party, for the purpose of impeaching his testimony, may show that the witness has made previous inconsistent or conflicting statements, either by eliciting such statements upon cross-examination of the witness himself, or proving them by other witnesses." *Robinson v. Old Colony Street Railway,* 189 Mass 594, 596, 76 NE 190, 191 (1905). See also *Com. v. Gil,* 393 Mass 204, 219, 471 NE2d 30, 41 (1984). The witness may be asked to explain inconsistencies between prior statements and trial testimony. See *Com. v. Dickinson,* 394 Mass 702, 706, 477 NE2d 381, 383-384 (1985).[2]

When the prior statement bears upon a central issue in the case it has been held that the judge has no discretion to

---

[2] It is to be noted that "simply because a witness alters some portion of his testimony at the time of trial is not sufficient reason to conclude that the new testimony was false, or that the [proponent] knew or had reason to know that it was false." *Com. v. McLeod,* 394 Mass 727, 743, 477 NE2d 972, 984; *Com. v. Sullivan,* 410 Mass 521, 532, 574 NE2d 966, 973 (1991).

exclude extrinsic evidence of it, even if it would otherwise be inadmissible. See *Schwartz v. Goldstein,* 400 Mass 152, 508 NE2d 97 (1987) (prior inconsistent statement of physican witness admissible for impeachment even though it constituted breach of confidentiality); *Com. v. Domaingue,* 397 Mass 693, 701-702, 493 NE2d 841, 847 (1986) (prior recorded statement obtained in violation of GL 272, §99); *Com. v. West,* 312 Mass 438, 440-441, 45 NE2d 260, 262 (1942) (statement may not be excluded even though it incidentally shows witness's conviction of crime).

For examples of the use of prior inconsistent statements see *Com. v. Basch,* 386 Mass 620, 623, 437 NE2d 200, 203-204 (1982) (prior report of coroner contradicting time of death testified to); *Com. v. A Juvenile,* 361 Mass 214, 217-218, 280 NE2d 144, 147 (1972); *Assessors of Pittsfield v. W. T. Grant Co.,* 329 Mass 359, 360, 108 NE2d 536, 537 (1952); *Com. v. Campbell,* 37 Mass App 960, 963, 643 NE2d 462, 464 (1994) (citing Text); *Com. v. Donnelly,* 33 Mass App 189, 196-198, 597 NE2d 1060, 1065-1066 (1992) (state trooper's diagrams of accident scene, which he had used to illustrate grand jury testimony, to impeach contradictory trial testimony); *Com. v. Cogswell,* 31 Mass App 691, 696-699, 583 NE2d 266, 269-271 (1991) (complaining witness's diary that contradicted testimony); *Com. v. Smith,* 26 Mass App 673, 679-680, 532 NE2d 57, 61-62 (1988) (victim's prior inconsistent statement to co-worker concerning name perpetrator was addressed by); *Com. v. Pimental,* 25 Mass App 971, 519 NE2d 795 (1988) (victim's prior inconsistent statement to police); *Com. v. Allen,* 22 Mass App 413, 417-423, 494 NE2d 55, 58-62 (1986) (transcript of telephone conversation between victim witness and emergency operator, offered to impeach testimony concerning identification of defendant). Compare *Com. v. Clarke,* 418 Mass 207, 211-213, 635 NE2d 1197, 1200-1201 (1994) (no error in excluding written prior statements made by prosecution witness where witness admitted making the statements, which had been prepared by defense counsel, and statements were read to jury); *Com. v. McGowan,* 400 Mass 385, 390-391, 510 NE2d 239, 243

(1987) (judge properly refused to permit proof of prior statement where it did not bear directly on any central issue); *Com. v. Fazzino,* 27 Mass App 485, 489, 539 NE2d 1060, 1063 (1989) (same); *Com. v. Campbell,* supra, 37 Mass App at 963, 643 NE2d at 465 (where testimony allegedly inconsistent with prior statement is stricken from record, prior statement should not have been admitted).

With the exception of certain statutory limitations discussed below (§§6.7.2.c and 6.7.2.d), evidence of prior inconsistent statements may be gathered from a wide variety of sources including:

- pretrial depositions and other discovery materials (see Mass R Civ P 26-37).
- prior statements and reports of a witness that are in the possession of the adverse party (see Mass R Crim P 23).
- transcripts of grand jury testimony (see Mass R Crim P 14(a)(1)(B)).
- transcripts of prior hearings or trials.
- accident and other reports (see *Genova v. Genova,* 28 Mass App 647, 554 NE2d 1221 (1990) (motorist's accident report filed under GL 90, §26 admissible as prior inconsistent statement); see also GL 175, §111F (requiring insurance companies to deliver to an injured party medical reports as to his examination by insurance doctors if said party furnishes, in exchange, copies of medical reports by his physicians).
- letters and documents.
- witnesses who heard the statement.

Any materials in the possession of the prosecution that are of an exculpatory nature must be disclosed to the defendant. Mass R Crim P 14(a)(1)(C). Prior inconsistent statements of a prosecution witness that constitute exculpatory evidence must be disclosed in a timely fashion. See

Com. v. Vieira, 401 Mass 828, 832, 519 NE2d 1320, 1322 (1988).

b.   Nature of Inconsistency

In order to be used to impeach W1, it is not necessary that the prior statement be a complete, categorical, or explicit contradiction of his trial testimony. *Com. v. Simmonds*, 386 Mass 234, 242, 434 NE2d 1270, 1276 (1982). It is sufficient if "taken as a whole, either by what it says or by what it omits to say, [it] affords some indication that the fact was different from the testimony." *Com. v. West*, supra, 312 Mass at 440, 45 NE2d at 262. Put another way, it is enough that the statement's "implications tend in a different direction" from the trial testimony. *Com. v. Pickles*, 364 Mass 395, 402, 305 NE2d 107, 111 (1973); *Com. v. Granito*, 326 Mass 494, 500, 95 NE2d 539, 543 (1950). See also *Com. v. Lopes*, 34 Mass App 179, 185-186, 608 NE2d 749, 753 (1993); *Com. v. Donnelly*, supra, 33 Mass App at 197, 597 NE2d at 1065 (citing Text); *Com. v. Tiexeira*, 29 Mass App 200, 202, 559 NE2d 408, 410 (1990). But see *Com. v. Hesketh*, 386 Mass 153, 160-161, 434 NE2d 1238, 1244 (1982) (judge has wide discretion to exclude prior statement where it is not plainly contradictory); *Com. v. Fazzino*, 27 Mass App 485, 489, 539 NE2d 1060, 1063 (1989) (same); *Com. v. Accetta*, 422 Mass 642, 644-645, 664 NE2d 830, 831-832 (1996) (witness' statement to grand jury that defendant used recoil from pistol to break it free of victim not inconsistent with trial testimony that victim held defendant's wrist).

The inconsistency may lie not only in the prior assertion, but in an omission to speak as well. "A prior statement may be inconsistent . . . if by what it omits to say the facts look different than those suggested by the in-court testimony of the witness." *Com. v. Kindell*, 44 Mass App 200, 204, 689 NE2d 845, 848 (1998) (& citations). A police officer's trial testimony may thus be impeached with the officer's report omitting important details that it would have been natural to include. See, e.g., *Com. v. Ortiz,* 39 Mass App 70, 71-72, 653 NE2d 1119, 1120 (1995). Similarly, a witness's prior failure to dispute the accuracy of a statement made to her was held to bear upon the credibility of her contradictory trial testimony. *Com. v. Goldenberg,* 338 Mass 377, 385, 155 NE2d 187, 192 (1959). In sum, "[d]eclarations or acts, or omissions to speak or to act when it would have been natural to do so if the fact were as testified to, may be shown by way of contradiction or impeachment of the testimony of a witness, when they fairly tend to control or qualify his testimony." *Foster v. Worthing,* 146 Mass 607, 608, 16 NE 572, 574 (1888). See §6.7.2.e, infra. For impeachment by silence in criminal cases, see §9.7.8, infra.

It has generally been held that for purposes of impeachment, there is no inconsistency between a present failure of memory on the witness stand and a past existence of memory. See *Com. v. Martin,* 417 Mass 187, 197, 629 NE2d 297, 303 (1994) (citing Text) (prior statement of witness not admissible where witness had no present memory of substance of prior statement); *Corsick v. Boston Elevated Railway Co.,* 218 Mass 144, 147, 105 NE 600, 601 (1914) (evidence of prior statement that he had made report that "the car was no good" not inconsistent with conductor's testimony that he did not remember whether he made report); *Com. v. Chin Kee,* 283 Mass 248, 260-262, 186 NE 253, 258-259 (1933). "Where a witness has no present memory as to the substance of the prior statement, its admissibility generally is precluded because opposing counsel would not have an opportunity for meaningful cross-examination of the witness at trial." *Com. v. Martin,* supra, 417 Mass at 197, 629 NE2d at 303. The rule is designed to avoid the admission of prior statements carrying dubious probative value but a high degree of risk that the jury would give affirmative testimonial value to the statement. See *Langan v. Pianowski,* 307 Mass 149, 151, 29 NE2d 700, 701 (1940).

A witness's failure to recall certain details of a prior interview with a trooper did not, however, preclude impeachment testimony from the trooper. See *Com. v. Gil,* 393 Mass 204, 219-220, 471 NE2d 30, 41 (1984). See also *Com. v. Granito,* supra, 326 Mass at 500, 95 NE2d at 543 ("It was open to the prosecution to show that at the time of his arrest, nine days after the robbery, the defendant's reply to [police] questions bearing on [his whereabouts at the time of the crime] was that he did not know. These replies were admissible to discredit the detailed alibi testified to at the trial. And the fact that the defendant testified in several instances that he did not remember being asked such questions or giving such answers did not deprive the Commonwealth of the right to put them in evidence."); *Com. v. Cappellano,* 17 Mass App 272, 278-279, 457 NE2d 1121, 1125 (1983) (witness's lack of memory of details of detective's interview in hospital did not preclude impeachment). Similarly a witness who admitted signing a statement could not escape impeachment through use of it merely by claiming he did not remember giving the statement. See *Langan v. Pianowski,* 307 Mass 149, 29 NE2d 700 (1940). See also *Com. v. Hartford,* 346 Mass 482, 486-487, 194 NE2d 401, 404 (1963) (illustrating the use of leading questions to refresh recollection concerning a prior conversation).

The court has left open the question "whether, when the circumstances at trial indicate that a witness is falsifying a lack of memory, a judge may admit the statement as 'inconsistent' with the claim of lack of memory." *Com. v. Daye,* 393 Mass 55, 73 n.17, 469 NE2d 483, 494 n.17 (1984).

A statement may be admitted as a prior inconsistent statement only if it can be clearly attributed to the witness. See, e.g., *Com. v. Fruchtman,* 418 Mass 8, 18, 633 NE2d 369, 374 (1994) (no error in excluding attempted impeachment where allegedly prior inconsistent statement in social worker's reports not shown to be based on communication by victim); *Wingate v. Emery Air Freight Corp.,* 385 Mass 402, 405, 432 NE2d 474, 478 (1982) (evidence did not warrant inference that injury report contained statements made by witness); *Com. v. Beauregard*, 25 Mass App 983, 521 NE2d 404 (1988) (notation in hospital record, "Cannot identify assailant," could not be sufficiently attributed to victim). See also *Pina v. McGill Development Corp.*, 388 Mass 159, 164, 445 NE2d 1059, 1062 (1983) (insurance forms containing prior statements not signed by plaintiff witness).

The fact that the prior inconsistent statement is in the form of an opinion does not necessarily preclude its use to impeach the witness. This is obviously true where the witness has expressed a contrary opinion on the stand. Thus, a physician called by the defendant who minimized the plaintiff's injuries in his testimony could be contradicted by a prior statement that the plaintiff was "the worst accident case he handled in the last ten years." *McGrath v. Fash*, 244 Mass 327, 139 NE 303 (1923). See also *Schwartz v. Goldstein*, 400 Mass 152, 508 NE2d 97 (1987) (physician witness's prior statement that "he felt there was no malpractice" and "the case should be thrown out."). But see *Loftus v. Fall River Laundry Co.*, 217 Mass 240, 243, 104 NE 575, 576 (1914) (evidence of what expert witness previously said he would have done under circumstances of accident properly excluded even though it contradicted his testimony as to propriety of plaintiff's actions).

Where a lay witness testifies as to specific facts, evidence of a prior inconsistent opinion may be used only if the facts testified to lead directly to a contrary conclusion. See, e.g., *Com. v. Grossman*, 261 Mass 68, 71-72, 158 NE 338, 339 (1927) (prior statement by character witness that "it looked bad for [defendant]"); *Whipple v. Rich*, 180 Mass 477, 63 NE 5 (1902) (prior statement that railway driver was "not to blame" for accident properly admitted to impeach witness's testimony). The prior inconsistent opinion is admissible for the limited purpose of impeachment even though the witness would not otherwise be permitted to state an opinion on the matter. *Hogan v. Roche*, 179 Mass 510, 61 NE 57 (1901) (statements and conduct of witness indicating opinion on sanity of testator admissible to impeach witness who testified to facts tending to show testator was of unsound mind); *Bonnemort v. Gill*, 165 Mass 493, 43 NE 299 (1896). See also *Com. v. Tiexeira*, supra, 29 Mass App at 202, 559 NE2d at 410 (prior statement of lay witness admissible even though it involved inference drawn from her observations).

c.   *Special Provisions for Impeachment in Criminal Cases*

Like any witness, a criminal defendant who takes the stand may be impeached by use of a prior inconsistent statement. Under federal constitutional standards this may be accomplished even if the statement was obtained in violation of the *Miranda* safeguards (and thus otherwise inadmissible), provided the statement is voluntary and trustworthy. *Harris v. New York*, 401 US 222, 91 S Ct 643, 28 L Ed 2d 1 (1971). Massachusetts law is in accord. See *Com. v. Harris*, 364 Mass 236, 238-241, 303 NE2d 115, 117-118 (1973); *Commonwealth v. Mahnke*, 368 Mass 662, 691-697, 335 NE2d 660, 678-681 (1975); see §9.7.7, infra.

In the context of the retrial of a criminal case, any admission the defendant made in the first trial, as well as any prior testimony that tends to contradict later testimony, is admissible in the second trial. See *Com. v. Cassidy*, 29 Mass App 651, 655 n.4, 564 NE2d 400, 402 n.4 (1990) (citing Text). Moreover, a defendant's testimony or affidavit in support of a motion to suppress evidence on Fourth Amendment grounds may be used as a prior inconsistent statement to impeach the defendant's later testimony at trial. See *Com. v. Rivera*, 425 Mass 633, 637-638, 682 NE2d 636, 640-641 (1997).

There are, however, several limitations that apply specially to criminal cases. GL 233, §23B,[3] provides that any

_____

[3] "In the trial of an indictment or complaint for any crime, no statement made by a defendant therein subjected to psychiatric examination pursuant to sections fifteen or sixteen of chapter one hundred and twenty-three for the purposes of such examination or treatment shall be admissible in evidence against him on any issue other

statement made by a criminal defendant pursuant to a psychiatric examination ordered by the court is inadmissible in evidence against him on any issue other than his mental condition. See generally *Blaisdell v. Com.*, 372 Mass 753, 364 NE2d 191 (1977). See also *Com. v. Martin*, 393 Mass 781, 473 NE2d 1099 (1985) (defendant's statements made during court-ordered psychiatric examination, which revealed his thought processes at time of shooting, were improperly admitted in violation of §23B); *Com. v. Callahan*, 386 Mass 784, 438 NE2d 45 (1982) (defendant's inculpatory statements in course of court-ordered psychiatric examination constituted strong evidence of premeditation and thus were improperly admitted in violation of §23B). The statute has been read to preclude the use of the defendant's statements for purposes of impeachment. *Blaisdell v. Com.*, supra, 372 Mass at 763, 364 NE2d at 197-198. See also Mass R Crim P 14(b)(2) (preventing disclosure to prosecutor of incriminating statements made by defendant during course of court-ordered psychological examination); GL 233, §20B (dealing with privileged communications between patient and psychotherapist, see §13.5.2, infra).

Any evidence given in a delinquency proceeding is rendered inadmissible against the child in any subsequent proceeding (except in a delinquency or sentencing proceeding involving the same person) by a broad confidentiality provision, GL 119, §60. See generally *Police Commissioner of Boston v. Municipal Court of the Dorchester District*, 374 Mass 640, 651-652, 374 NE2d 272, 288 (1978) (construing earlier version of statute). This has been held to preclude the use against a defendant at a criminal proceeding of prior testimony given by the defendant and other witnesses at a prior delinquency hearing. See *Com. v. Wallace*, 346 Mass 9, 15-16, 190 NE2d 224, 228 (1963); *Com. v. Franklin*, 366 Mass

---

than of his mental condition, nor shall it be admissible in evidence against him on that issue if such statement constitutes a confession of guilt of the crime charged."

284, 291, 318 NE2d 469, 474 (1974) (Commonwealth cannot confront defense witnesses with prior testimony at delinquency proceeding). GL 119, §60 does not appear to prevent the use of prior inconsistent testimony when offered by the juvenile to impeach prosecution witnesses in a subsequent proceeding. See *Com. v. A Juvenile*, 361 Mass 214, 217-218, 280 NE2d 144, 146 (1972) (but deciding case on different ground). For a discussion of the constitutional limits on GL 119, §60, when the information is relevant to a witness's bias, see §6.8.2.

For a discussion of the limits on impeachment of a defendant by his prior silence, see §9.7.8, infra.

d.   *Special Provisions for Impeachment in*
      Tort Actions and Worker's Compensation
      Proceedings

Two statutory limitations affect the impeachment use of prior statements in tort actions.

GL 233, §23A, renders inadmissible in an action for personal injuries any signed written or recorded statement of a party concerning the event unless a copy of the statement was promptly provided to the party upon request prior to trial. The purpose of the statute is to enable a party before trial to ascertain what he has written to an adversary, and "to disallow ambushes of injured persons by their adversaries, because statements are sometimes obtained before the injured person is represented . . . [a]nd it's not fair to permit a defendant at the trial to spring on the plaintiff such a statement." See *Mazzoleni v. Cotton*, 33 Mass App 147, 149-150, 597 NE2d 59, 60-61 (1992) (quoting Superior Court Judge J. Harold Flannery); *Spellman v. Metropolitan Transit Authority*, 328 Mass 446, 104 NE2d 493 (1952) (§23A applies to written statements given by injured person on his own accord as well as those solicited by defendant or insurer). The trial judge has some discretion to admit a statement notwithstanding the failure to strictly comply with the statute. See *Mazzoleni v. Cotton*, supra (statement not furnished upon plaintiff's demand nonetheless admissible where it was ultimately furnished long before trial and plaintiff could demonstrate no prejudice from delay). A similar statute applies to worker's compensation proceedings. See GL 152, §7B.

GL 271, §44, renders inadmissible in tort actions for personal injuries any settlement, general release, or statement in writing signed by a patient confined in a hospital or sanitarium that refers to any personal injuries for which the patient is confined if the statement was obtained within 15 days after the injuries were sustained. "The apparent purpose of the statute is to protect persons who might be weakened and vulnerable following injury and treatment and, therefore, unwittingly act against their best legal interests." *Fahey v. Rockwell Graphic Systems, Inc.*, 20 Mass App 642, 655, 482 NE2d 519, 528 (1985). The statute excepts by its terms statements given to police or Registry of Motor Vehicle inspectors acting in the performance of their duty as well as statements given to members of the patient's family or to his attorney, and it does not apply to worker's compensation proceedings under GL 152.

Several significant points distinguish GL 271, §44, from GL 233, §23A:

(1)   statements covered by §44 are barred even though no demand for a copy thereof was made;

(2)   §44 is not limited to statements of a "party" or one acting in his behalf (and thus arguably applies to a statement given by one passenger in an action brought by another passenger against the vehicle's operator); and

(3)   §44 applies only to written, and not tape-recorded, statements. See *Fahey v. Rockwell Graphic Systems, Inc.,* supra.

e. Impeachment by Silence or Failure to Come Forward

A prior contradictory statement of a witness may consist of silence in circumstances where denial would be called for. *Com. v. Nickerson*, 386 Mass 54, 57, 434 NE2d 992, 994 (1982). "It is generally appropriate to impeach a witness by showing that he was silent in circumstances in which he naturally would have been expected to deny some asserted fact or that, in the circumstances, the witness would be expected to disclose some fact and did not do so." Id. (citations omitted). Thus, a witness testifying for the taxpayer in an abatement action could be impeached with evidence that he never expressed disapproval of the assessors' valuation when he participated in an earlier discussion on the subject in which the proposed valuation plan was distributed. *Assessors of Pittsfield v. W. T. Grant Co.*, 329 Mass 359, 108 NE2d 536 (1952). See also *Com. v. Azar*, 32 Mass App 290, 303, 588 NE2d 1352 (1992) (defendant's failure to offer explanation of child's death to mother admissible to impeach defendant at trial).

It is for the court (and ultimately the jury) to determine whether the witness understood the statements made to him or in his presence, had the opportunity to reply to them, and conducted himself in such a manner that by his silence he must be deemed to have acquiesced in the statements. *Hill v. Crompton*, 119 Mass 376, 382 (1876).

If the witness is a party to the litigation the silence may be offered as an adoptive admission, in which case it is admissible as probative evidence and not merely for impeachment, and is thus admissible even if the party does not testify at trial. See §8.8.5.

The prior silence of the witness may in some circumstances give rise to an implication that his testimony is a recent contrivance. See, e.g., *Com. v. Heffernan*, 350 Mass 48, 51-52, 213 NE2d 399, 402-403 (1966) (defense counsel questioned prosecution witness's motive for not mentioning alleged bribe until he was arrested on unrelated charge). For a discussion of the method of rehabilitation of a witness impeached in this manner, see §6.16, infra.

In situations where the natural response of a person in possession of exculpatory evidence would be to come forward and disclose it to the police in order to avoid a mistaken prosecution of a relative or friend, the failure to do so might well cast doubt on the defense witness's subsequent exculpatory testimony at trial. The witness's silence in such circumstances may be used to impeach and suggest recent fabrication. See, e.g., *Com. v. Gregory*, 401 Mass 437, 444-445, 517 NE2d 454, 459-460 (1988) (cross-examination of alibi witness concerning failure to report information to police); *Com. v. Brown*, 11 Mass App 288, 295-297, 416 NE2d 218, 224 (1981) (same).[4]

A proper foundation must be laid for such impeachment by establishing that the witness knew of the pending charges in sufficient detail to realize that his information was exculpatory, that he had reason to make the information available, that he knew how to report it to the proper authorities, and that neither the defendant nor his lawyer asked him to refrain from reporting. *Com. v. Brown*, supra, 11 Mass App at 296, 416 NE2d at 224; *Com. v. Gregory*, supra, 401 Mass at 444-445, 517 NE2d at 459 (adopting the *Brown* guidelines). The goal is "to establish that the witness's pretrial silence is in fact inconsistent with his trial testimony." *Com. v. Brown*, supra, 11 Mass App at 296, 416 NE2d at 224. For more on the required foundation for this evidence, see *Com. v. Stewart*, 422 Mass 385, 387-388, 663 NE2d 255, 257-258 (1996); *Com. v. Egerton*, 396 Mass 499, 506-508, 487 NE2d 481, 486-487 (1986); *Com. v. Nickerson*, supra, 386 Mass at 57-58, 434 NE2d at 995 (pointing out that the examples in *Brown* of situations in which the witness would not be expected to come forward were not

---

[4] A prosecutor may also question a witness about the failure to come forward sooner to suggest an opportunity to collude. See, e.g., *Com. v. Passley*, 428 Mass 832, 840, 705 NE2d 269, 275 (1999).

exhaustive: "A witness may have a particular reason for not wanting to deal with the police." 386 Mass at 58 n.4, 434 NE2d at 995 n.4); *Com. v. Berth*, 385 Mass 784, 790-791, 434 NE2d 192, 196 (1982) (finding error in judge's failure to require prosecutor to lay the proper foundation); *Com. v. Cefalo*, 381 Mass 319, 338, 409 NE2d 719, 730-731 (1980); *Com. v. Hesketh*, 386 Mass 153, 162-164, 434 NE2d 1238, 1244-1246 (1982); *Com. v. Lopes*, 34 Mass App 179, 608 NE2d 749 (1993) (sufficient foundation laid where jury could draw inference that witness, who had been working toward degree in law enforcement, could reasonably be expected to provide police with information concerning shooting of one friend when another friend was charged). In the absence of an objection to the failure to lay a proper foundation, a defendant is entitled to relief on appeal only if the evidence and related argument created a substantial risk of a miscarriage of justice. See *Com. v. Epsom*, 399 Mass 254, 259, 503 NE2d 954, 958 (1987); *Com. v. Bassett*, 21 Mass App 713, 716-717, 490 NE2d 459, 462-463 (1986) (substantial risk of miscarriage of justice); *Com. v. Liberty*, 27 Mass App 1, 6, 533 NE2d 1383, 1386-1387 (1989) (error not prejudicial).

The use of silence to impeach a criminal defendant's own testimony presents a special situation raising constitutional questions. See §9.7.8, infra.

A statutory bar precludes reference to the fact that a criminal defendant failed to testify or offer evidence at the preliminary hearing on his case. See GL 278, §23.[5] See

---

[5] "At the trial of a criminal case in the superior court, upon indictment, or in a jury-of-six session in the district court, the fact that the defendant did not testify at any preliminary hearing in the first court, or that at such hearing he waived examination or did not offer any evidence in his own defense, shall not be used as evidence against him, nor be referred to or commented upon by the prosecuting officer." See *Com. v. Barber*, 14 Mass App 1008, 1010, 441 NE2d 763, 765 (1982). GL 278, §23 has been read in conjunction with the constitutional protections against self-incrimination. See generally §13.14.8, infra.

generally *Com. v. Sherick*, 23 Mass App 338, 341-346, 502 NE2d 156, 158-161 (1987); §13.14.8, infra. GL 278, §23 prevents the prosecution from asking a defense witness whether he had testified at any prior court hearing on the case, even when offered to suggest that his testimony was recently contrived. See *Com. v. Palmarin*, 378 Mass 474, 392 NE2d 534 (1979); *Com. v. Morrison*, 1 Mass App 632, 635-637, 305 NE2d 518, 521 (1973) (statute violated when prosecutor elicited from defense witnesses that they had been present at probable cause hearing but had not testified or told the judge the exculpatory information they testified to at trial). Compare *Com. v. Egerton*, supra, 396 Mass at 508, 487 NE2d at 486-487 (no violation where questions concerning alibi witnesses failure to come forward did not relate to earlier court proceedings) and *Com. v. Cefalo*, 381 Mass 319, 337-338, 409 NE2d 719, 730-731 (1980) (no violation where prosecutor elicited from defense witness that he had been present at probable cause hearing but had not told his story to any representative of the commonwealth at that time). A violation of GL 278, §23, may be harmless error. See *Com. v. Paradiso*, 368 Mass 205, 330 NE2d 825 (1975); *Com. v. Maguire*, 375 Mass 768, 774, 378 NE2d 445, 449 (1978) (violation of statute not reversible error where "there was no basis on which the jury could reasonably infer that the defendant's failure to call [non-pivotal] witness indicated a failure to offer any evidence in his defense in the lower court."). See also *Com. v. Gagliardi*, 29 Mass App 225, 238-239, 559 NE2d 1234, 1243-1244 (1990) (improper impeachment of defense witness by reference to his refusal to answer questions before grand jury not sufficiently prejudicial to require new trial).

Another statutory bar, together with constitutional protections, prohibits comment on the defendant's failure to testify at trial. See GL 233, §20, discussed at §13.14.8, infra.

f.   Mechanics of Impeachment/Extrinsic Proof

Massachusetts practice allows a witness to be examined concerning a prior statement without showing it to him or disclosing its contents at that time, but upon request it must be shown or disclosed to opposing counsel. *Hubley v. Lilley,* 28 Mass App 468, 471-472, 552 NE2d 573, 575-576 (1990); Proposed Mass R Evid 613(a).[6] "The purpose in not requiring disclosure during examination is to afford the advocate the tactical choice of not placing the witness on guard." Advisory Committee Note to Proposed Mass R Evid 613. Permitting opposing counsel to examine the statement protects against unwarranted suggestions that an inconsistent statement has been made and, further, prevents selective quotation by the questioner. *Hubley v. Lilley,* supra, 28 Mass App at 472, 552 NE2d at 575-576.

In many states and in the federal courts (see Fed R Evid 613(b)) W1's prior inconsistent statement cannot be put into evidence by extrinsic proof (for example, through W2) unless W1 has been asked on the stand whether he made the statement and been given an opportunity to explain it. Massachusetts departs from this practice, see Proposed Mass R Evid 613(b),[7] except in the case of impeachment of one's own witness. In this latter situation, GL 233, §23 provides that "before proof of such inconsistent statements is given, the circumstances thereof sufficient to designate the particular occasion shall be mentioned to the witness,

---

[6] "In examining a witness concerning a prior statement by him, whether written or not, the statement need not be shown nor its contents disclosed to him at that time, but on request the same shall be shown or disclosed to opposing counsel." PMRE 613(a).

[7] "Extrinsic evidence of a prior inconsistent statement by a witness is admissible whether or not the witness was afforded an opportunity to explain or deny the inconsistency." PMRE 613(b). See also *Sirk v. Emery,* 184 Mass 22, 25, 67 NE 668, 669 (1903) (extrinsic evidence of prior inconsistent statement may be offered against opponent's witness without laying foundation calling attention to statement).

and he shall be asked if he has made such statements, and, if so, shall be allowed to explain them." Thus, as a prerequisite to extrinsic proof, the party's own witness must be apprised of the time, place and content of the prior statement, and asked the prescribed preliminary questions. See *Com. v. Scott*, 408 Mass 811, 824 n.14, 564 NE2d 370, 379 n.14 (1990); *Com. v. Champagne*, 399 Mass 80, 88, 503 NE2d 7, 13 (1987); *Com. v. Festa*, 369 Mass 419, 425-426, 341 NE2d 276, 281 (1976); *Hubley v. Lilley*, supra, 28 Mass App at 473 n.7, 552 NE2d at 576 n.7. Compare *Fishman v. Brooks*, 396 Mass 643, 650-651, 487 NE2d 1377, 1382 (1986) (not necessary to lay foundation where adverse party witness testified extensively on cross-examination by his own attorney and explained his positions as if he had been called as a witness on his own behalf); *Com. v. Charles*, 397 Mass 1, 7, 489 NE2d 679, 683-684 (1986) (Commonwealth permitted to impeach its own witness with proof of prior inconsistent statement in apparent absence of foundation). See also §6.12, infra.

The designation of the circumstances of the prior statement is particularly important where a witness has made relevant statements on more than one occasion. See *Com. v. Ferrara*, 368 Mass 182, 192, 330 NE2d 837, 844 (1975).

It is not necessary to give the witness an opportunity to explain the statement where he testifies he has no recollection of having made it. *Com. v. Festa*, supra; *Com. v. Ferrara*, supra, 368 Mass at 193, 330 NE2d at 844 (denial must be unequivocal); *Com. v. Cappellano*, 17 Mass App 272, 278-279, 457 NE2d 1121, 1125 (1983).

A prosecutor may question his own witness about a prior inconsistent statement made during an interview of the witness by the prosecutor. *Com. v. Johnson*, 412 Mass 318, 325-327, 588 NE2d 684, 688-689 (1992). If extrinsic evidence is to be offered, the required foundation must be laid and, if no third person was present during the interview, the prosecutor would have to obtain leave to withdraw from the case in order to prove the statement. Id.

It has been held that it makes no difference whether prior inconsistent testimony is read by counsel or the witness. *Com. v. Fort*, 33 Mass App 181, 186, 597 NE2d 1056, 1059 (1992).

For discussion of the use of an audiotape to impeach a witness, see *Com. v. Gordon*, 389 Mass 351, 353-356, 450 NE2d 572, 574-576 (1983) (guidelines for use of recorded testimony); *Com. v. Supplee*, 45 Mass App 265, 266-268, 697 NE2d 547, 548-549 (1998) (error to refuse to permit defense counsel to impeach witness with audiotape of her police interview; but reversal not required).

On redirect examination, the witness who has been impeached by a prior inconsistent statement must be afforded the opportunity to explain or elaborate on the alleged inconsistencies. *Hubley v. Lilley*, supra, 28 Mass App at 473, 552 NE2d at 576 (& cases cited).

g. *Use of Statement Generally Limited to Impeachment/Exception for Substantive Use*

Massachusetts law has followed the "orthodox" view that the prior contradictory statement is admitted solely for its bearing on the credibility of the witness — to reveal to the fact finder that the account heard from the witness on the stand is but one of two or more inconsistent versions provided by him at different times. See generally *Com. v. Daye*, 393 Mass 55, 65-75, 469 NE2d 483, 496-499 (1984). The statement is deemed inadmissible hearsay for any other purpose (see Chapter 8) and thus cannot be used to prove the facts asserted. See *Com. v. Rosa*, 412 Mass 147, 587 NE2d 767 (1992) (reversing conviction where prosecutor argued in closing as though prior inconsistent statements were substantive evidence) (Text cited); *Com. v. Costello*, 411 Mass 371, 377-378, 582 NE2d 938, 941-942 (1991) (reversing conviction for rape of child because only evidence against defendant was prior inconsistent statement of alleged victim); *Wheeler v. Howes*, 337 Mass 425, 427, 150 NE2d 1, 2 (1958); *Com. v. Frisino*, 21 Mass App 551, 553, 488 NE2d 51,

53 (1986) (where only evidence of defendant's participation in crime consisted of two unsworn out-of-court statements of witnesses who repudiated statements at trial, a required finding of not guilty must follow). A party may not call a witness, who would provide no probative testimony, for the sole purpose of creating a basis for impeaching him with a prior inconsistent statement. See *Com. v. Benoit,* 32 Mass App 111, 586 NE2d 19 (1992) (prosecution witness); *Com. v. McGee,* 42 Mass App 740, 746, 679 NE2d 609, 612-613 (1997) (defense witness).

This approach differs somewhat from that taken by both Fed R Evid 801(d)(1) and Proposed Mass R Evid 801(d)(1),[8] which afford substantive effect for all probative purposes to prior inconsistent statements that were made under oath at an official proceeding and are offered against a declarant who is testifying at trial and subject to cross-examination concerning the statement.

In a significant move toward the federal approach, the Supreme Judicial Court has held that a prior inconsistent statement made under oath before a grand jury is admissible for all probative purposes (thus adopting Proposed Mass R Evid 801(d)(1)) provided that:

- the witness can be effectively cross-examined as to the accuracy of the statement;
- the statement was not coerced and was more than a mere confirmation or denial of the interrogator's assertion; and
- other evidence tending to prove the issue is presented.

---

[8] "Statements which are not hearsay. A statement is not hearsay if —
(1) Prior statement by witness. The declarant testifies at the trial or hearing and is subject to cross-examination concerning the statement, and the statement is (A) inconsistent with his testimony and was given under oath subject to the penalty of perjury at a trial, hearing, or other proceeding, or in a deposition. . . ." PMRE 801(d)(1).

Com. v. Daye, supra, 393 Mass at 75, 469 NE2d at 494 (Liacos, CJ, dissenting: "The court today abandons a time honored rule, honed in experience, developed to enhance the process of discovering the truth in favor of a rule of expediency that enhances the likelihood of convictions." 393 Mass at 79, 469 NE2d at 498). The court deferred consideration of the general admissibility of prior inconsistent statements. 393 Mass at 71, 469 NE2d at 483

For cases admitting prior grand jury testimony for substantive purposes, see *Com. v. Berrio,* 407 Mass 37, 43-46, 551 NE2d 496, 500-501 (1990); *Com. v. Rivera,* 37 Mass App 244, 249-250, 638 NE2d 1382, 1385-1386 (1994); *Com. v. Donnelly,* 33 Mass App 189, 198, 597 NE2d 1060, 1066 (1992) (state trooper's accident scene diagrams which he used to illustrate testimony before grand jury admissible by defendant as prior inconsistent statement for probative value); *Com v. Tiexeira,* 29 Mass App 200, 203-204, 559 NE2d 408, 410-411 (1990). But see *Com. v. Accetta,* 422 Mass 642, 645, 664 NE2d 830, 832 (1996) (speculative testimony before grand jury not admissible under *Daye*).

For a discussion of the requirement in *Daye* that other evidence tending to prove the issue be presented in order that the prior testimony achieve full probative status, see *Com. v. Noble,* 417 Mass 341, 343-347, 629 NE2d 1328, 1329-1331 (1994) (witness's grand jury testimony admissible for full probative value where it corroborates inferences already apparent from the circumstantial evidence of defendant's guilt). Compare *Idaho v. Wright,* 497 US 805, 823 (1990) (rejecting corroboration as acceptable evidence of reliability of a hearsay statement).

The *Daye* decision suggests that "[b]efore offering a prior inconsistent statement as probative evidence, counsel should ask for a voir dire, during which the witness should be reminded of the circumstances in which the statement was made and given an opportunity to explain the inconsistency." 393 Mass at 74 n.21, 469 NE2d at 495 n.21. This hearing has been construed as a mechanism for determining whether the conditions for admissibility have been met, and not an opportunity for the witness to explain the inconsistency in order to prevent the jury from hearing the prior statement. *Com. v. Fort*, 33 Mass App 181, 185-186, 597 NE2d 1056, 1059 (1992). Moreover, the witness's disavowal at trial of statements made to the grand jury does not render the statements inadmissible, but rather presents an issue of credibility for the jury. *Com. v. Noble*, supra, 417 Mass at 347, 629 NE2d at 1331.

The Supreme Judicial Court has refused to expand the *Daye* exception to statements made in circumstances lacking the formality of grand jury proceedings. See *Com. v. Weaver*, 395 Mass 307, 311, 479 NE2d 682, 685 (1985). See also *Com. v. Frisino*, supra, 21 Mass App at 554, 488 NE2d at 53-54 (refusing to extend *Daye* to signed, unsworn extrajudicial statements). The Appeals Court has extended *Daye* to inconsistent testimony given at a probable cause hearing. See *Com. v. Jenkins*, 34 Mass App 135, 144, 607 NE2d 756, 762 (1993) and *Com. v. Fort*, 33 Mass App 181, 184-185, 597 NE2d 1056, 1058-1059 (1992), departing from its previous decision in *Com. v. Gore*, 20 Mass App 960, 480 NE2d 1059 (1985).

Unless the prior statement was made before a grand jury or falls within another exception to the hearsay rule (see Chapter 8),[9] the judge on request will instruct the jury that the statement shall not be considered as evidence for its truth but only as it affects the weight to be accorded the witness's testimony. Failure to make the request for such instruction allows consideration of the statement for all probative purposes and precludes a claim of error on appeal. See *Com. v. Ashley*, 427 Mass 620, 627-628, 694 NE2d 862, 868 (1998); *Schwartz v. Goldstein*, 400 Mass 152, 154, 508 NE2d 97, 99 (1987); *Com. v. Luce*, 399 Mass 479, 482-483,

---

[9] If, for example, the witness who made the prior statement is a party to the action, the statement is admissible for all probative purposes under the admissions exception to the hearsay rule. See §8.8. Because a victim of crime is not a party in criminal proceedings, the victim's prior inconsistent statements are admissible only as to credibility. See *Com. v. Kennedy*, 389 Mass 308, 314, 450 NE2d 167, 172 (1983).

505 NE2d 178, 180 (1987); *Com. v. Gil*, 393 Mass 204, 220, 471 NE2d 30 (1984); *Com. v. Keaton*, 36 Mass App 81, 88, 628 NE2d 1286, 1290 (1994); *Genova v. Genova*, 28 Mass App 647, 652, 554 NE2d 1221, 1224 (1990). See also Proposed Mass R Evid 105 (discussed at §3.10, supra).

Although a limiting instruction may be of dubious value because it is "unrealistic to believe that a jury properly discriminates limited admissibility" (see Advisory Committee Note to Proposed Mass R Evid 801(d)(1)), a request that the evidence be limited to impeachment ensures a directed verdict if there is no other evidence of the fact asserted and the fact is essential to the claim. See, e.g., *Mroczek v. Craig*, 312 Mass 236, 239, 44 NE2d 644, 646 (1942); *Desmond v. Boston Elevated Railway Co.*, 319 Mass 13, 64 NE2d 357 (1946).

When a witness confronted with a prior inconsistent statement adopts the earlier statement as the truth, the statement acquires full probative value. See *Com. v. Fiore*, 364 Mass 819, 823, 308 NE2d 902, 905 (1974); *Com. v. Rivera*, supra, 37 Mass App at 250, 638 NE2d at 1385; *Com. v. Tiexeira*, supra, 29 Mass App at 202, 559 NE2d at 410.

§6.7.3   Self-Contradictory Statements Made at Trial

The testimony of a witness may be impeached by contradictory testimony of that witness given at the same proceeding. Where a witness gives conflicting testimony on direct and cross-examination, the general rule is that it is for the jury to determine which version to believe. Where, however, the witness on cross-examination is asked to make a choice between his contradictory statements and he affirmatively repudiates his testimony on direct, the witness is "bound by" that choice and the jury is not entitled to believe the repudiated version. See *Sullivan v. Boston Elevated Railway Co.*, 224 Mass 405, 406-407, 112 NE 1025 (1916); *Donovan v. Johnson*, 301 Mass 12, 16 NE2d 62

(1938). For cases applying the *Sullivan* rule, see *Harlow v. Chin*, 405 Mass 697, 706 n.11, 545 NE2d 602, 608 n.11 (1989); *Krasnow v. Fenway Realty Co.*, 352 Mass 781, 227 NE2d 501 (1967); *Osborne v. Boston Consolidated Gas Co.*, 296 Mass 441, 444, 6 NE2d 347, 348 (1937). Compare *Siira v. Shields*, 360 Mass 874, 277 NE2d 825 (1972) (no such final and conclusive election by witness among possibly conflicting accounts as to remove matter from the province of the jury); *Yanowitz v. Augenstern*, 343 Mass 513, 515, 179 NE2d 592, 593 (1962) (plaintiff witness refused to elect one of two dates on which fall occurred); *Ballou v. Boston & M.R.R.*, 341 Mass 696, 698, 171 NE2d 857, 858-859 (1961) (plaintiff witness did not definitively elect one version of accident over other); *Stinson v. Soble*, 301 Mass 483, 487, 17 NE2d 703, 705 (1938) (variance of five mph in testimony concerning speed of vehicle not a "material difference" for purposes of *Sullivan* rule); *Com. v. Geisler*, 14 Mass App 268, 273 n.6, 438 NE2d 375, 378 n.6 (1982) (& cases cited) (defendant not entitled to have testimony struck because the witness was not clearly asked to make a definite choice between his contradictory statements). The rule has been applied to nonparty witnesses. See *Pahigian v. Manufacturers' Life Insurance Co.*, 349 Mass 78, 83, 206 NE2d 660, 664 (1965); *Morris v. Logden*, 343 Mass 778, 179 NE2d 821 (1962).

For further discussion of the concept of "binding testimony," see §2.11, supra.

§6.8 By Challenging Testimonial Faculties

The credibility of W1's testimony is dependent upon his or her ability to accurately:

- perceive the event in question;
- remember what was perceived;
- articulate in court; and
- testify truthfully.

Each of these faculties, both in general and in the particular case, are open to challenge on cross-examination. See *Com. v. Carrion*, 407 Mass 263, 273-274, 552 NE2d 558, 564-565 (1990); *Com. v. Caine*, 366 Mass 366, 369, 318 NE2d 901, 905 (1974). Questions may be asked concerning the witness's use of alcohol, illegal drugs, or medication at the time of the events about which he or she is testifying. See *Morea v. Cosco, Inc.*, 422 Mass 601, 604, 664 NE2d 822, 825 (1996); *Com. v. Carrion*, supra, 407 Mass at 273-274, 552 NE2d at 564-565 (& cases cited); *Com. v. Bennett*, 13 Mass App 954, 431 NE2d 940 (1982); *Com. v. Ciminera*, 11 Mass App 101, 103, 414 NE2d 366, 368 (1981). Questions may similarly be addressed regarding a mental impairment if it is shown that it might affect perception, memory, or communication. See *Com. v. Gibbons*, 378 Mass 766, 771 n.9, 393 NE2d 400, 404 n.9 (1979) (& cases cited); *Com. v. Caine*, supra. The victim's prior misidentification of the former codefendant may raise questions about the accuracy of the witness's perceptions, and thus can be explored on cross-examination. See, e.g., *Com. v. Franklin*, 366 Mass 284-290, 318 NE2d 469, 472-474 (1974).

The parties are entitled to reasonable latitude on cross-examination concerning testimonial faculties, with discretion as to scope and extent left to the trial judge. See, e.g., *Com. v. Carrion*, supra, 407 Mass at 273, 552 NE2d at 565 (& cases cited) (judge did not abuse discretion in excluding question concerning prosecution witness's use of drugs in prison when defense counsel had already elicited that she was heroin addict); *Com. v. Russell*, 38 Mass App 199, 203-204, 646 NE2d 760, 763 (1995) (no error in excluding questions regarding prosecution witness's drug use at time of testimony where there was extensive evidence before jury about her use of drugs at time of incident). There must be some indication that the matter is relevant to credibility before it can be used to impeach, and the burden is on the cross-examiner to demonstrate this. *Com. v. Arce*, 426 Mass 601, 604, 690 NE2d 806, 808-809 (1998) (question regarding eyewitness's drug use properly excluded because such use, standing alone, did not relate to capacity to perceive or recall); *Com. v. Adrey*, 376 Mass 747, 752, 383 NE2d 1110, 1112-1113 (1978) (& cases cited) (no showing that question concerning witness's pattern of drug addiction or treatment was relevant to credibility, where counsel had already elicited that witness was under influence of drugs at time of incident); *Com. v. Caine*, supra, 366 Mass at 370, 318 NE2d at 905 (no showing that question concerning witness's commitment to state hospital was relevant to credibility); *Com. v. Beattie*, 29 Mass App 355, 366-367, 560 NE2d 714, 721 (1990) (no showing that questions relating to witness's hospitalization and psychiatric history were relevant to credibility); *Com. v. Williams*, 25 Mass App 210, 218, 517 NE2d 176, 181 (1987) (no showing that line of questions concerning witness's use of medication was relevant to credibility); *Com. v. Gonsalves*, 23 Mass App 184, 189-190, 499 NE2d 1229, 1232-1233 (1986) (no substantial basis for questions concerning witness's use of drugs on night of rape); *Com. v. Perreault*, 13 Mass App 1072, 435 NE2d 635 (1982) (no showing that witness's admission to mental hospital was relevant to her credibility); *Com. v. Maioli*, 11 Mass App 179, 180-181, 414 NE2d 1017, 1018 (1981) (no error in excluding question seeking to establish that witness was currently at Bridgewater State Hospital for observation where commitment was temporary and for purpose of determining competency to stand trial).

Expert testimony may be necessary to establish the relevance to credibility. See *Com. v. Lloyd*, 45 Mass App 931, 702 NE2d 395 (1998) (defendant needed to demonstrate that use of Prozac impairs ability to perceive or remember).

Extrinsic proof raising a substantial question about the witness's testimonial abilities may be admissible. See, e.g., *Com. v. Fayerweather*, 406 Mass 78, 82-84, 546 NE2d 345, 347-348 (1989) (hospital psychiatric report on complainant's mental status); *Com. v. Barber*, 261 Mass 281, 290, 158 NE 840, 843 (1927) (evidence that defense witness was drunk on morning of incident); *Joyce v. Parkhurst*, 150 Mass 243, 247, 22 NE 899, 900 (1889) (same); *Chadbourn v. Franklin*,

71 Mass (5 Gray) 312 (1855) (witnesses properly allowed to testify that W1 and W2 were not present at time of incident they testified to). Compare *Com. v. McLaughlin*, 352 Mass 218, 231, 224 NE2d 444, 452 (1967) (no error in excluding evidence that prosecution witness had been drunk prior to incident, because not relevant to testimonial capacities on day in question).

In appropriate circumstances, defense counsel may be permitted to search otherwise confidential and privileged records for evidence of how mental impairment might affect a victim witness's capacity to perceive, remember, and articulate the alleged events. See *Com. v. Figueroa*, 413 Mass 193, 203, 595 NE2d 779, 785-786 (1992); *Com. v. Gauthier*, 32 Mass App 130, 134-136, 586 NE2d 34, 37-38 (1992) (special education records). But compare *Com. v. Jones*, 34 Mass App 683, 615 NE2d 207 (1993) (defendant not automatically entitled to access records).

Various challenges to the honesty and truthfullness of the witness are discussed in the sections that follow.

§6.9   By Proving Bias, Prejudice, or Motive to Lie

A witness may be impeached by showing facts indicating bias, prejudice, or motive to lie on the part of the witness in favor of one side or the other. Such impeachment is commonly predicated on either the relationship between the witness and a party, or the interest (financial or otherwise) that the witness has in the outcome of the litigation. See, e.g., *Com. v. Frate*, 405 Mass 52, 54, 537 NE2d 1235, 1236 (1989) (cross-examination of witness concerning representation of other clients in similar circumstances relevant to bias and interest in outcome of lawsuit).

Because bias, prejudice, and motive to lie are not considered collateral matters, they may be demonstrated by extrinsic proof as well as on cross-examination. *United States v. Abel*, 469 US 45, 52 (1984) ("The 'common law of evidence' allowed the showing of bias by extrinsic evidence, while requiring the cross-examiner to 'take the answer of the witness' with respect to less favored forms of impeachment.”). See, e.g., *Com. v. Colon*, 408 Mass 419, 443-445, 558 NE2d 974, 989-990 (1990) (plea agreement admitted in evidence to illuminate witness's “incentives to please the prosecution”); *Com. v. Aguiar*, 400 Mass 508, 513-514, 510 NE2d 273, 276-277 (1987) (judge erred in precluding cross-examination and extrinsic testimony suggesting bias). There is no requirement that the opponent cross-examine on the matter as a foundation prior to offering extrinsic evidence. See *Com. v. Gabbidon*, 17 Mass App 525, 531, 459 NE2d 1263, 1268 (1983) (& citations); *Com. v. Brown*, 394 Mass 394, 397, 476 NE2d 184, 186-187 (1985) (defendant may introduce evidence of bias through cross-examination or extrinsic evidence).

Cross-examination to show bias, prejudice, or interest is a matter of right that in criminal cases assumes constitutional dimension under the confrontation clause of the Sixth Amendment to the United States Constitution and art. 12 of the Declaration of Rights.[1] *Com. v. Grenier*, 415 Mass 680, 686, 615 NE2d 922, 925 (1993) (& citations). The defendant has the right to bring to the jury's attention any “circumstance which may materially affect the testimony of an adverse witness which might lead the jury to find that the witness is under an 'influence to prevaricate.'” *Com. v. Haywood*, 377 Mass 755, 760, 388 NE2d 648, 652 (1979) (citation omitted). See, e.g., *Com. v. Stockhammer*, 409 Mass 867, 873-877, 570 NE2d 992, 996-999 (1991) (cross-examination of rape complainant designed to uncover evidence of bias and motive to lie); *Com. v. Koulouris*, 406 Mass 281, 285, 547 NE2d 916, 918 (1989) (witness's interest and involvement in pending federal forfeiture proceeding

---

§6.9   [1]Evidence tending to show that an important government witness is biased is exculpatory within the meaning of *Brady v. Maryland*, 373 US 83 (1963). See *Com. v. Jackson*, 388 Mass 98, 112, 445 NE2d 1033, 1041 (1983); *Com. v. Fuller*, 394 Mass 251, 262-264, 475 NE2d 381, 389 (1985).

involving defendant's house); *Com. v. Barnes*, 399 Mass 385, 393, 504 NE2d 624, 630 (1987); *Com. v. Ahearn*, 370 Mass 283, 346 NE2d 907 (1976) (& cases cited); *Com. v. Michel*, 367 Mass 454, 459-460, 327 NE2d 720, 723-724 (1975), *new trial granted*, 381 Mass 447 (1980) (& cases cited); *Com. v. Civello*, 39 Mass App 373, 375-377, 656 NE2d 1262, 1263-1264 (1995) (reversible error for trial court to preclude cross-examination on bias designed to show that complainant knew her accusations could result in defendant's removal from her home). See also *Com. v. Elliot*, 393 Mass 824, 828, 473 NE2d 1121, 1124 (1985) (right to demonstrate witness's motive to lie is particularly important in rape cases because the "right to cross-examine a complainant . . . to show a false accusation may be the last refuge of an innocent defendant") (citation omitted). For a general discussion of the right of cross-examination in criminal cases, see §3.3, supra.

Frequently the proffered evidence of bias takes the form of charges pending against the prosecution witness which, it is argued, provide an incentive to "please the prosecution." A defendant has a constitutional right to inquire on cross-examination whether the witness expects more favorable treatment from the government in return for his testimony. *Com. v. Schand*, 420 Mass 783, 792-793, 653 NE2d 566, 573 (1995) (but prosecutor's commitment to be "fair" to witness with regard to pending charges is not a promise of favorable treatment that must be disclosed). It has been held that the defendant is entitled to question the witness about a pending charge even if the Commonwealth has offered no inducements to the witness. See *Com. v. Hamilton*, 426 Mass 67, 72, 686 NE2d 975, 979 (1997) (& citations) (but noting that in certain circumstances the judge may limit examination; thus a voir dire showing consistency between witness's trial testimony and his statements made before any basis for bias existed may justify denying cross-examination regarding pending charges).

Although arrest, indictment, or the pendency of charges are generally not admissible to impeach a witness (see §6.10, infra), where relevant to particularized bias or motive to lie these matters may be developed on cross-examination. See cases collected in *Com. v. Smith*, 26 Mass App 673, 675-676, 532 NE2d 57, 59-60 (1988). For cases reversing convictions because the trial judge unduly restricted cross-examination concerning pending charges, see *Com. v. Colon*, 408 Mass 419, 443-445, 558 NE2d 974, 989-990 (1990); *Com. v. Henson*, 394 Mass 584, 586-590, 476 NE2d 947, 950-952 (1985); *Com. v. Connor*, 392 Mass 838, 840-842, 467 NE2d 1340, 1344 (1984); *Com. v. Martinez*, 384 Mass 377, 379-381, 425 NE2d 300, 302-303 (1981); *Com. v. Dean*, 17 Mass App 943, 457 NE2d 286 (1983); *Com. v. Lewis*, 12 Mass App 562, 569-573, 427 NE2d 934, 940 (1981). Compare *Com. v. DiMuro*, 28 Mass App 223, 228-229, 548 NE2d 896, 899-900 (1990) (judge did not abuse discretion in curtailing cross-examination on charges pending against chemist witness where he formed his opinion and wrote his report concluding that substance was cocaine before charges were brought against him); *Com. v. DiBlasio*, 17 Mass App 1008, 1010, 460 NE2d 200, 202 (1984) (no abuse of discretion in excluding evidence of charges pending against witness where defendant failed to establish that witness was the person against whom the charges were brought). Other related matters relevant to bias are a prosecution witness's past cooperation with the Commonwealth which led to favorable treatment, see *Com. v. Rodwell*, 394 Mass 694, 699-700, 477 NE2d 385, 389 (1985), and a witness's invocation of the privilege against self-incrimination and subsequent grant of immunity. See *Com. v. Voisine*, 414 Mass 772, 785-786, 610 NE2d 926, 934 (1993).

The testimony of a prosecution witness pursuant to a plea agreement founded on the witness's promise of truthful testimony poses special problems regarding motive to lie as well as the appearance that the prosecution is vouching for witness's truthfulness. For an extensive discussion of the trial judge's obligations in handling such witnesses, see *Com. v. Ciampa*, 406 Mass 257, 547 NE2d 314

(1989) (reversing convictions because judge failed to redact repeated references in written plea agreement to witness's obligation to tell the truth and failed to instruct jury adequately on incentives that could have influenced witness's testimony). When a prosecution witness testifies pursuant to a plea agreement containing such a promise, the judge should warn the jury that the government does not know whether the witness is telling the truth. See *Com. v. Meuse*, 423 Mass 831, 832, 673 NE2d 546, 547 (1996). Compare *Com. v. James*, 424 Mass 770, 785-786, 678 NE2d 1170, 1181-1182 (1997) (no special instruction required where no discussion before jury that agreement with Commonwealth was contingent on veracity of his testimony). For other cases dealing with the issues raised by these plea agreements, see *Com. v. Charles*, 428 Mass 672, 680-681, 704 NE2d 1137, 1145 (1999); *Com. v. Gordon*, 422 Mass 816, 833-835, 666 NE2d 122, 134-135 (1996); *Com. v. Brousseau*, 421 Mass 647, 653-655, 659 NE2d 724, 728-729 (1996); *Com. v. Fuller*, 421 Mass 400, 413, 657 NE2d 1251, 1258-1259 (1995); *Com. v. Grenier*, 415 Mass 680, 686-687, 615 NE2d 922, 925-926 (1993); *Com. v. Evans*, 415 Mass 422, 427-428, 614 NE2d 653, 657 (1993); *Com. v. Marangiello*, 410 Mass 452, 462-465, 573 NE2d 500 (1991); *Com. v. Sullivan*, 410 Mass 521, 524-525, 574 NE2d 966, 969 (1991) (*Ciampa* distinguished); *Com. v. Holmes*, 46 Mass App 550, 707 NE2d 1094 (1991) (language of *Ciampa* plea agreement distinguished); *Com. v. Barnes*, 40 Mass App 666, 672-675, 667 NE2d 269, 273-275 (1996).

While reference to the "truthful testimony" provisions of such plea agreements should be avoided, a prosecutor may use direct examination to bring out the fact that the witness has entered into a plea agreement and generally understands his obligations under it. See *Com. v. Martinez*, 425 Mass 382, 398, 681 NE2d 818, 829 (1997) (& citation).

For a discussion of the related problem of the "contingent fee witness" who testifies in the hope of an award of compensation from the proceeds of defendant's forfeited assets, see *Com. v. Luna*, 410 Mass 131, 139-140, 571 NE2d 603, 608 (1991).

The use of unrelated criminal charges pending against a defense witness for the purpose of establishing a generalized bias against the prosecution has been rejected as not sufficiently probative given the prejudicial nature of the evidence. See *Com. v. Smith*, 26 Mass App 673, 675-678, 532 NE2d 57, 59-61 (1988); *Com. v. Liberty*, 27 Mass App 1, 533 NE2d 1383 (1989).

For other grounds of bias or interest, see *Com. v. Dixon*, 425 Mass 223, 228-229, 680 NE2d 84, 88-89 (1997) (fact that it was necessary to arrest witnesses to ensure they would appear to testify could be basis for inference of bias in favor of defendant); *Com. v. Kirkpatrick*, 423 Mass 436, 446-447, 668 NE2d 790, 797 (1996) (witness married defendant after assertions of sexual abuse of daughter); *Com. v. Elliot*, supra, 393 Mass at 826-832, 473 NE2d at 1124-1126 (financial interest of complaining witness because of pending civil action); *Com. v. Ahearn*, supra, 370 Mass at 287, 346 NE2d at 909 (knowledge of complaining witness police officer that defendant had applied for civilian complaint against him); *Com. v. Graziano*, 368 Mass 325, 330, 331 NE2d 808, 811-812 (1976) (key prosecution witness knew he was himself a suspect); *Com. v. Kowalski*, 33 Mass App 49, 51-53, 595 NE2d 798, 800-801 (1992) (rape complainant's relationship to her boyfriend); *Com. v. McNickles*, 22 Mass App 114, 117-119, 491 NE2d 662, 665-666 (1986) (complainant's effort to regain custody of her children provided motive to fabricate rape story); *Com. v. Piedra*, 20 Mass App 155, 156-158, 478 NE2d 1284, 1286-1287 (1985) (sexual affair between defendant's son and the wife of key prosecution witness); *Com. v. Fetzer*, 19 Mass App 1024, 1025, 476 NE2d 981, 983 (1985) (favors that witness receives from party, here Commonwealth purchased new clothes for witness to wear to court). Compare *Israel v. Baker*, 170 Mass 12, 48 NE 621 (1897) (evidence of witness's pecuniary interest in result of litigation properly excluded because it revealed which party had prevailed in previous procceding).

The evidence proffered must be sufficiently probative of bias to justify its admission. See *Com. v. Bui*, 419 Mass 392,

401, 645 NE2d 689, 694-695 (1995) (defendant's bias theory too tenuous); *Com. v. Weichel,* 403 Mass 103, 105-106, 526 NE2d 760, 761-762 (1988) (proffered evidence had little relevance to bias and invited misuse by the jury); *Com. v. Brown,* 394 Mass 394, 397-398, 476 NE2d 184, 186-187 (1985); *Michnik-Zilberman v. Gordon's Liquor, Inc.,* 390 Mass 6, 15-16, 453 NE2d 430, 436 (1983) (evidence of witness's settlement with plaintiff three years earlier not sufficiently probative of bias); *Com. v. Haywood,* 377 Mass 755, 758-763, 388 NE2d 648, 652-654 (1979) (witness's arrest record offered to show motive to cooperate with prosecution properly excluded where arrests occurred after witness gave initial statements regarding defendant's criminal actions and trial testimony was consistent with initial statements); *Com. v. Souza,* 39 Mass App 103, 108-109, 653 NE2d 1127, 1131 (1995) (defendants failed to adequately connect victims' mothers' recovered memories of sexual abuse to possible bias against defendants); *Com. v. Stokes,* 38 Mass App 752, 761, 653 NE2d 180, 185 (1995) (release of witness despite warrant for her arrest insufficient to demonstrate police bias against defendant); *Com. v. Quegan,* 35 Mass App 129, 617 NE2d 651 (1993) (no indication that prior accusations of sexual abuse were false or had been used to secure custody of child); *Com. v. Huertas,* 34 Mass App 939, 941, 613 NE2d 113, 115 (1993) (no showing that chief prosecution witness's detention as material witness demonstrated bias); *Com. v. Allen,* 29 Mass App 373, 560 NE2d 704 (1990) (defendant failed to demonstrate that assault victim's prior arrest was relevant to bias or motive to lie); *Com. v. Johnson,* 16 Mass App 935, 936-937, 450 NE2d 1087, 1089 (1983) (where alleged bias of complaining witness arose more than a year after the complaint and identification had been made, and witness's trial testimony substantially tracked her earlier statements, no abuse of discretion in ecluding witness's arrest record).

Where it is not clear that the proffered question seeks evidence relevant to bias, the cross-examiner must be prepared to explain the relevance. See, e.g., *Com. v. Cheek,*

374 Mass 613, 614-615, 373 NE2d 1161, 1162-1163 (1978); *Com. v. Gonzalez*, 23 Mass App 913, 914, 500 NE2d 287, 289 (1986); *Com. v. Mazzola*, 22 Mass App 683, 685, 497 NE2d 280, 282 (1986); *Com. v. Bucknam*, 20 Mass App 121, 478 NE2d 747 (1985). "When a possibility of bias exists, however, even if remote, the evidence is for the jury to hear and evaluate." *Com. v. Henson*, 394 Mass 584, 587, 476 NE2d 947, 950-951 (1985). As in other contexts, the questioner must be prepared to state a good faith basis for questions concerning bias. See *Com. v. Dixon*, 425 Mass 223, 227-228, 680 NE2d 84, 88 (1997) (Commonwealth's information, although derived from questionable sources, nonetheless sufficed to permit questioning).

The right to cross-examine to show bias or prejudice is not infringed by reasonable limitations, for example where the matter sought to be elicited has been sufficiently aired. *Com. v. Smiledge*, 419 Mass 156, 159, 643 NE2d 41, 44 (1994). See, e.g., *Com. v. Doherty*, 394 Mass 341, 349-350, 476 NE2d 169, 174 (1985); *Com. v. Rodwell*, 394 Mass 694, 700, 477 NE2d 385, 389 (1985); *Com. v. Porter*, 384 Mass 647, 658, 429 NE2d 14, 21 (1981); *Com. v. Dougan*, 377 Mass 303, 309-310, 386 NE2d 1, 5-6 (1979); *Com. v. Traylor*, 43 Mass App 239, 242-243, 681 NE2d 1249, 1251-1252 (1997); *Com. v. Quegan*, 35 Mass App 129, 134-135, 617 NE2d 651, 654-655 (1993); *Com. v. Gonzalez*, supra, 23 Mass App at 914, 500 NE2d at 289; *Com. v. Morris*, 20 Mass App 114, 116-119, 478 NE2d 750, 751-754 (1985); *Com. v. Gauthier*, 21 Mass App 585, 588-590, 488 NE2d 806, 809 (1986); *Com. v. Maffei*, 19 Mass App 924, 471 NE2d 1364 (1984); *Olson v. Ela*, 8 Mass App 165, 169-171, 392 NE2d 1057, 1060-1061 (1979) (no error in restricting cross-examination of defendant's medical witness regarding the amount of compensation for testimony, given fact of compensation was established). See also *Com. v. Grenier*, 415 Mass 680, 686, 615 NE2d 922, 925 (1993) (testimony showing bias properly struck as not responsive to questions asked).

Because of its importance in weighing credibility, impeachment by showing bias is permissible even where it reveals confidential, privileged, or other inadmissible matters. *Davis v. Alaska*, 415 US 308, 94 S Ct 1105, 39 L Ed 2d 347 (1974). Thus, bias may be explored even though it involves:

(1)   prior sexual conduct of the victim. See *Com. v. Joyce*, 382 Mass 222, 415 NE2d 181 (1981) (rape shield statute, GL 233, §21B, does not preclude evidence of complaining witness's prior sexual conduct where relevant to bias or motive to lie). See generally §4.4.3.b, supra.

(2)   privileged matters contained in psychiatric or social worker records. See *Com. v. Figueroa*, 413 Mass 193, 203, 595 NE2d 779, 785-786 (1992), *Com. v. Stockhammer*, 409 Mass 867, 570 NE2d 992 (1991), and *Com. v. Bishop*, 416 Mass. 169, 617 NE2d 990 (1993), discussed in §13.5.4, infra; attorney-client privilege, see *Com. v. Michel*, 367 Mass 454, 459-460, 327 NE2d 720, 724-725 (1975); insurance coverage, see *Dempsey v. Goldstein Brothers Amusement Co.*, 231 Mass 461, 464-465, 121 NE 429, 430 (1919) (no error in allowing question on cross-examination eliciting that defendant's medical expert was retained by insurance company and thus suggesting bias, even though evidence of insurance coverage is usually inadmissible).

(3)   prior bad acts of the defendant. See *Com. v. Wright*, 411 Mass 678, 685, 584 NE2d 621, 626 (1992) (relationship of defendant and witness's mother could be shown to establish bias); *Com. v. Aguiar*, 400 Mass 508, 513-514, 510 NE2d 273, 276-277 (1987) (& citations) (evidence of motive to prevaricate admissible even though it reveals otherwise inadmissible fact, such as witness's criminal activity).

(4)   a prior arrest. See *Com. v. Allen*, 29 Mass App 373, 376-378, 560 NE2d 704, 706-707 (1990) (& cita-

tions) (extensive discussion of use of prior arrests to establish bias).

(5) the juvenile record of a witness. See *Com. v. Bembury*, 406 Mass 552, 556-561, 548 NE2d 1255, 1258-1261 (1990) (& citations) (if information contained in juvenile record indicates witness's testimony may be product of official pressure or inducement, record may be used to impeach despite GL 119, §60); *Com. v. Ferrara*, 368 Mass 182, 330 NE2d 837 (1975) (juvenile or criminal records). But see *Com. v. Santos*, 376 Mass 920, 384 NE2d 1202 (1978) (no absolute right to use sealed juvenile records; judge must balance defendant's need to cross-examine on bias against confidentiality interest).

Examination of a witness concerning possible bias toward a *non*-party is within the discretion of the judge and is not a matter of right. See *Com. v. D'Agostino*, 344 Mass 276, 280, 182 NE2d 133, 136 (1962) (no error in excluding question concerning prosecution witness's relationship to owner of restaurant where assault occurred); *Com. v. Harrison*, 342 Mass 279, 286, 173 NE2d 87, 92 (1961) (no error in excluding question concerning friendly relationship between prosecution witness and deputy police chief). It is permissible to show, however, that the witness is in the employ of the real party in interest. See *Stevens v. Stewart-Warner Speedometer Corp.*, 223 Mass 44, 47, 111 NE 771, 773 (1916).

The bias or interest of the witness may be shown by evidence of prior statements or conduct. See, e.g., *Omansky v. Shain*, 313 Mass 129, 131, 46 NE2d 524, 526 (1943) (plaintiff and defendant's wife took trip together); *Tasker v. Stanley*, 153 Mass 148, 26 NE 417 (1891) (statement); *Com. v. White*, 32 Mass App 949, 590 NE2d 716 (1992) (statement of child victim's mother that even if defendant did not commit the rape, she still hoped "all sorts of nasty things happen to him"); *Com. v. Gabbidon*, 17 Mass App 525, 530-532, 459 NE2d 1263, 1268-1269 (1983) (statements).

An expert witness is not immune from impeachment by evidence of bias or interest. See, e.g., *Com. v. Perkins*, 39 Mass App 577, 581, 658 NE2d 975, 978 (1995) (& citations) (prosecutor could show bias of defense expert by using statements from published article in which expert appeared to endorse pedophilia).

§6.10 By Proving Bad Character

The credibility of a witness may be impeached by attacking his or her character for truthfulness. Under long-established Massachusetts practice, this impeachment may take two forms: (1) evidence of the general reputation of the witness for truthfulness and veracity; and (2) evidence that the witness has been convicted of a crime. A third mode of character impeachment, cross-examination of the witness regarding prior bad acts, is not permitted by Massachusetts practice, but would be permitted by Proposed Mass R Evid 608(b).

§6.10.1 General Character for Truthfulness and Veracity

W1's credibility may be attacked by testimony of W2 that W1 has a poor reputation for truthfulness and veracity among those who know him. See *Eastman v. Boston Elevated Railway Co.*, 200 Mass 412, 86 NE 793 (1909). This mode of impeachment is limited to:

- reputation for truth and veracity, and not character in general. *Com. v. Cancel*, 394 Mass 567, 572-573, 476 NE2d 610, 615 (1985) (evidence that witness was a member of a street gang improperly admitted to attack his credibility).

- evidence of general reputation, and not specific acts of lying or misconduct. *Com. v. Arthur*, 31 Mass App 178, 180, 575 NE2d 1147, 1149 (1991). See §6.10.3.

Reputation in this context has been defined as follows: "Has the subject been so much discussed and considered that there is in the public mind a uniform and concurrent sentiment which can be stated as a fact?" *Com. v. Baxter*, 267 Mass 591, 593, 166 NE 742, 743 (1929). See also *Com. v. Dockham*, 405 Mass 618, 631, 542 NE2d 591, 599 (1989) (& citations).

Massachusetts practice does not permit opinion evidence from W2 regarding W1's truthfulness. See *Com. v. Dockham*, supra, 405 Mass at 631, 542 NE2d at 599 (& citations); *Eastman v. Boston Elevated Railway Co.*, supra (question as to whether W2 would believe W1 under oath properly excluded); *Com. v. Edgerly*, 13 Mass App 562, 576, 435 NE2d 641, 649-650 (1982) (& citations). Indeed, it is the longstanding rule that a witness, either lay or expert, may not offer an opinion regarding the credibility of another witness. See §6.6, supra.

Such opinion evidence is allowed by Fed R Evid 608(a) and Proposed Mass R Evid 608(a).[1] In support of the addition of opinion evidence, the Advisory Committee expressed its belief "that in practice the distinction between opinion and reputation testimony in this context is often difficult to preserve." Advisory Committee Note, PMRE 608. See also *Com. v. Belton*, 352 Mass 263, 269, 225 NE2d 53, 57 (1967).

The impeaching witness must have personal knowledge of W1's reputation for truth and veracity; and a sufficient

---

§6.10 [1] "The credibility of a witness may be attacked or supported by evidence in the form of opinion or reputation, but subject to these limitations: (1) the evidence may refer only to character for truthfulness or untruthfulness, and (2) evidence of truthful character is admissible only after the character of the witness for truthfulness has been attacked by opinion or reputation or otherwise." PMRE 608(a).

foundation must be demonstrated, so that a witness who has knowledge of the opinions of only a few members of W1's community is not qualified to testify to his general reputation. "It is what is said of the person under inquiry in the common speech of his neighbors and members of his community or territory of repute, from which his reputation for truth or falsehood arises, and not what the impeaching witness may have heard others say who numerically may be few and insignificant." *F. W. Stock & Sons v. Dellapenna*, 217 Mass 503, 506, 105 NE 378, 379 (1914). See also *Com. v. Belton*, supra, 352 Mass at 269, 225 NE2d at 57; *Com. v. Porter*, 237 Mass 1, 129 NE 298 (1921). Compare *Com. v. Baxter*, supra, 267 Mass at 593, 166 NE at 743 (stranger to community who was hired as investigator by a party and inquired of only five persons not qualified to testify that witness's reputation for truthfulness was bad), *Com. v. Phachansiri*, 38 Mass App 100, 109, 645 NE2d 60, 66 (1995) (testimony based on community of 10 to 12 adults properly excluded), *Com. v. Healey*, 27 Mass App 30, 39-40, 534 NE2d 301, 306-307 (1989) (judge properly excluded testimony of defense witness in sexual abuse case concerning victim's poor reputation in community for truth and veracity because the sources of knowledge were insufficient and foundation inadequate), and *Com. v. Gomes*, 11 Mass App 933, 416 NE2d 551 (1981) (judge properly excluded testimony concerning victim's poor reputation for truthfulness where based on views of only five people, and on remarks from a few other teachers in school community) with *Com. v. Arthur*, supra, 31 Mass App at 179-181, 575 NE2d at 1148-1149 (evidence of complainant witness's reputation for lying and exaggerating, presented by two eighth-grade classmates and drawn from her middle school class of 150, improperly excluded; the foundation established a discrete, identifiable community of middle school students, 50 or 60 of whom had expressed views about the victim's reputation for veracity, and an impeaching witness who knew complainant for six years and was in position to know of her reputation).

The information upon which the impeaching witness bases her testimony as to reputation must be current and not too attenuated. See *Com. v. Moore*, 379 Mass 106, 115, 393 NE2d 904, 910 (1979) (no error in excluding testimony that W1's reputation for veracity was poor where impeaching witness, W1's former wife, had moved out of the community seven years before trial); *Com. v. Phachansiri*, supra, 38 Mass App at 109, 645 NE2d at 66 (evidence of defendant's reputation for truthfulness five years earlier properly excluded).

At common law the reputation of the witness being impeached had to be drawn from the community where he resided, but GL 233, §21A, now makes reputation admissible where the witness works or has his business associations as well.[2] This has been held to include the school community to which a student belongs. See *Com. v. Arthur*, supra, 31 Mass App at 179, 575 NE2d at 1148.

Although not mandated by the caselaw (see *Wetherbee v. Norris*, 103 Mass 565 (1870) and *F. W. Stock & Sons v. Dellapenna*, supra, 217 Mass at 506-507, 105 NE at 379), the foundation for testimony from the impeaching witness may be established as follows:

(1)   Are you familiar with W1's general reputation for truth and veracity in the community in which he or she resides (or works)?

(2)   What is that reputation?

On cross-examination, a character witness's knowledge of W1's reputation may be tested by asking for specifics regarding the events that formed the basis for that reputation. See *Com. v. Arthur*, supra, 31 Mass App at 180, 575 NE2d at 1148-1149 (& citations); Proposed Mass R Evid

---

[2] Proposed Mass R Evid 608(a) "does not alter G.L. c. 233, §21A, as regards the source or basis of reputation evidence." Advisory Committee Note to PMRE 608.

405(a) and 608(b).[3] "The credibility of the witness is tested in the following manner—if the witness states that he has not heard of the report of prior misconduct, his professed knowledge of the defendant's reputation in the community may be doubted by the jury or, if he states that he has heard of the report but still testifies that the defendant's reputation is good in the community, the jury may consider whether the witness is fabricating or whether the community standards in regard to character are too low." *Com. v. Montanino*, 27 Mass App 130, 137, 535 NE2d 617, 621 (1989) (Commonwealth had right to cross-examine defendant's character witnesses about whether they had heard reports of prior misconduct concerning the character trait testified about). The thrust of such cross-examination goes to the weight of the evidence and not to its admissibility. *Com. v. Arthur*, supra. See also *Michelson v. United States*, 335 US 469 (1948); *Com. v. Brown*, 411 Mass 115, 117-118, 579 NE2d 153, 154-155 (1991) (Commonwealth had right to cross-examine defense witnesses testifying to defendant's reputation for truthfulness regarding allegedly false statements made by defendant regarding his military record); *Com. v. Deveau*, 34 Mass App 9, 14 n.2, 606 NE2d 921, 924 n.2 (1993) (prosecutor on cross-examination may inquire of witness who has testified to reputation if witness has heard rumors inconsistent with good reputation to which the witness has vouched on direct). The reputation witness may not be asked, however, if he would change his mind if he knew certain adverse facts because that suggests the existence of facts not in evidence. *Com. v. Deveau*, supra, 34 Mass App at 14 n.2, 606 NE2d at 924; *Com. v. Kamishlian*, 21 Mass App 931, 933-934, 486 NE2d 743, 746 (1986).

---

[3] "In all cases in which evidence of character or a trait of character is admissible, proof may be made by testimony as to reputation or by testimony in the form of an opinion. *On cross examination, inquiry is allowable into relevant specific instances of conduct.*" PMRE 405(a) (emphasis added). PMRE 608(b) permits cross-examination of a character witness regarding specific instances of conduct of the witness whose character is being testified about.

§6.10.2   Prior Convictions

W1 may be impeached by evidence that he or she has been convicted of a crime or crimes. In this mode of impeachment, the jury is implicitly asked to infer a readiness to lie from the witness's prior involvement in criminal activity.[4] See *Com. v. Fano*, 400 Mass 296, 302-303, 508 NE2d 859, 863-864 (1987) ("a defendant's earlier disregard for the law may suggest to the fact finder similar disregard for the courtroom oath") (citation omitted); *Com. v. Sheeran*, 370 Mass 82, 89, 345 NE2d 362, 367 (1976) ("it is not irrational to infer that a thief may also be a liar"); *Gertz v. Fitchburg Railroad Co.*, 137 Mass 77, 78 (1884). A conviction may be admissible for this purpose even though the underlying crime does not reflect directly on the defendant's truth-telling abilities. See *Com. v. Kowalski*, 33 Mass App 49, 50, 595 NE2d 798, 799-800 (1992) (& citations) (distribution of heroin and accessory after fact to armed robbery). The logic of impeachment by prior convictions has not escaped criticism over the years. See, e.g., *Com. v. DiMarzo*, 364 Mass 669, 682, 308 NE2d 538, 546 (1974) (Hennessey, J, concurring) ("Prior convictions, even as applied only to the credibility issue, have little or no probative value in most instances.").

Impeachment by prior convictions is available in both civil and criminal cases, and is controlled by GL 233, §21. If evidence of criminality or bad conduct is to be used to impeach a witness, it can be done only by production of records of criminal convictions pursuant to GL 233, §21. See *Com. v. Clifford*, 374 Mass 293, 305, 372 NE2d 1267, 1275 (1978); *Com. v. Dominico*, 1 Mass App 693, 713, 306 NE2d 835, 846 (1974). It has been held that the use of convictions

---

[4]A prior conviction may also be used to impeach where it specifically rebuts the testimony of a witness, as for example where the witness denies ever having carried or used a firearm in the past, that opens the door to the admission of his prior conviction for gun possession. See *Com. v. Roderick*, 429 Mass 271, 274-275, 707 NE2d 1065, 1068-1069 (1999) (& citations).

for impeachment does not infringe either the state or federal constitutional rights of criminal defendants. *Com. v. Drumgold*, 423 Mass 230, 249, 668 NE2d 300, 314 (1996); *Com. v. Diaz*, 383 Mass 73, 417 NE2d 950 (1981) (& cases cited); *Com. v. DiMarzo*, 364 Mass 669, 678, 308 NE2d 538, 544 (1974).

GL 233, §21, prescribes time limits after which convictions cannot be used to impeach a witness (unless intervening criminal convictions revive them)[5] as follows:

(1) misdemeanors cannot be used after five years from the date the sentence was imposed unless the witness has subsequently been convicted of a crime within five years of the time he testifies;

(2) felony convictions resulting in: (a) no sentence, (b) a suspended sentence, (c) a fine, or (d) a sentence to a correctional institution other than a state prison cannot be used after ten years from the date of conviction or sentence, whichever is applicable, unless the witness has subsequently been convicted of a crime within ten years of the time he testifies;

(3) felony convictions resulting in a sentence to state prison cannot be used after ten years from the expiration of the minimum term of imprisonment unless the witness has subsequently been convicted of a crime within ten years of the time he testifies;

(4) traffic violations for which a fine only was imposed shall not be used unless the witness was convicted of another crime or crimes within five years of the time he testifies. See, e.g., *Com. v. Burnett*, 417 Mass 740, 632 NE2d 1206 (1994) (judge properly excluded witness's prior convic-

---

[5] A plea of guilty tendered pursuant to a pretrial diversion program does not revitalize a stale conviction. See *Com. v. Jackson*, 45 Mass App 666, 669-670, 700 NE2d 848, 851-852 (1998)

tion for "operating to endanger" for which only a
fine had been imposed).

When the defendant is the witness being impeached,
the last clause of GL 233, §21 extends the time limitations
for any period of time during which the defendant was a
fugitive from justice.

Regarding the operation of the time limits, see generally *Com. v. Gladney*, 34 Mass App 151, 154-155, 607 NE2d
750, 752 (1993) and *Com. v. Childs*, 23 Mass App 33, 35, 499
NE2d 299 (1986).

Federal and out-of-state convictions are admissible
under GL 233, §21, provided that the convictions come
within the statute. See *Attorney General v. Pelletier*, 240 Mass
264, 310-312, 134 NE 407, 420 (1922) (federal crime); *Gertz
v. Fitchburg Railroad Co.*, supra (federal felony); *Com. v.
Gladney*, supra, 34 Mass App at 155, 607 NE2d at 753 (&
citations).

Subject to the limitations of GL 233, §21, the conviction may be for any type of crime regardless (as noted
above) of its logical relevance to the matter of credibility.
See *Quigley v. Turner*, 150 Mass 108, 22 NE 586 (1889)
(assault). See also *Com. v. Gallarelli*, 372 Mass 573, 579-580,
362 NE2d 923, 927 (1977) (criminal contempt).

An adjudication of juvenile delinquency based on a
criminal offense may be used for impeachment in the same
manner as a criminal conviction. GL 119, §60[6] otherwise
precludes the admission or use of delinquency records. See
Com. v. A Juvenile (No. 2), 384 Mass 390, 394-395, 425 NE2d
294, 297 (1981); *Com. v. Ferrara*, 368 Mass 182, 185-186, 330
NE2d 837, 841 (1975); *Com. v. Freeman*, 29 Mass App 635,
638-639, 564 NE2d 11, 13-14 (1990). See also Proposed
Mass R Evid 609(e); n.7, infra; *Com. v. Young*, 22 Mass App
237, 493 NE2d 213 (1986).

---

[6]The application of GL 119, §60, to the use of prior testimony for
impeachment is discussed at §6.7.2, supra.

Where the juvenile record is relevant to bias or prejudice, the court may be required to put aside any statutory protection of confidentiality and admit it to preserve the accused's constitutional right of confrontation. See *Com. v. A Juvenile (No. 2)*, supra, 384 Mass at 394, 425 NE2d at 297 (& citations); *Com. v. Ferrara*, supra, 368 Mass at 186-190, 330 NE2d at 840-843 (witness may have been motivated in his testimony by desire to please authorities). See also §6.9, supra. For a discussion of the factors to be weighed in deciding whether to permit the use of juvenile records to impeach a prosecution witness in such a situation, see *Com. v. Santos*, 376 Mass 920, 924-926, 384 NE2d 1202, 1204-1206 (1978).

A conviction based on a plea of nolo contendere is not admissible for impeachment. *Olszewski v. Goldberg*, 223 Mass 27, 111 NE 404 (1916). See also Mass R Crim P 12(f) and Proposed Mass R Evid 410.

Suggestions in earlier cases that a conviction followed by a pardon is not admissible for impeachment (see *Rittenberg v. Smith*, 214 Mass 343, 101 NE 989 (1913) and *Perkins v. Stevens*, 41 Mass (24 Pick) 277 (1883)) appear to have been undercut. See *Commissioner of the MDC v. Director of Civil Service*, 348 Mass 184, 193-196, 203 NE2d 95, 98-103 (1964). But see *Com. v. Childs*, supra, 23 Mass App at 36-37 (suggesting that GL 127, §152, providing for automatic sealing of criminal records of offenses for which a pardon has been granted, may preclude use of such convictions for impeachment). Proposed Mass R Evid 609(d) resolves the unsettled case law by providing that "[w]here a conviction has been followed by a pardon, both the conviction, if otherwise admissible, and the pardon shall be admissible." Compare Fed R Evid 609(c) (excluding impeachment use of convictions followed by pardons in certain circumstances).

Probation violations may not be used to impeach a witness's character for truthfulness, but may be used to show bias on the part of the witness who might want to curry favor with the prosecution. See *Com. v. Roberts*, 423 Mass 17, 20-21, 666 NE2d 475, 478 (1996).

Records that have been sealed or expunged under GL 94C, §§34, 35, 44 or GL 276, §§100A, 100B, 100C (discussed in §13.10, infra) may not be admitted in evidence or used in any way in court proceedings, and thus may not be used for impeachment. See also Proposed Mass R Evid 609(g); n.7, infra.

In order to be used to impeach, a conviction must be a final judgment. See *Wilson v. Honeywell, Inc.*, 409 Mass 803, 808-809, 569 NE2d 1011, 1014-1015 (1991); *Forcier v. Hopkins*, 329 Mass 668, 110 NE2d 126 (1953) (& cases cited). Thus, a conviction at a bench trial in the district court was not "final" for purposes of impeachment if the defendant filed an appeal under the former de novo system. *Wilson v. Honeywell, Inc.*, supra. A suspended sentence is a final judgment for purposes of the statute. *Com. v. Sheeran*, supra, 370 Mass at 88, 345 NE2d at 366; *Forcier v. Hopkins*, supra.

For felony crimes, a finding of guilty constitutes a conviction even if no sentence is imposed; for misdemeanors, the conviction alone in the absence of a sentence may not be used to impeach. See *Com. v. Devlin*, 365 Mass 149, 163, 310 NE2d 353, 362 (1974) (& cases cited). Probation on a conviction of a misdemeanor is not a sentence for purposes of the statute. *Com. v. Stewart*, 422 Mass 385, 387, 663 NE2d 255, 257 (1996); *Com. v. Rossi*, 19 Mass App 257, 259, 473 NE2d 708, 710 (1985). See also *Com. v. Edgerly*, 13 Mass App 562, 569-571, 435 NE2d 641, 646-647 (1982) (adjudication of paternity and support order is not "conviction").

A conviction resulting in a jail sentence cannot be used to impeach a defendant unless it is established that he was represented by counsel or waived counsel in the prior proceeding. *Com. v. Proctor*, 403 Mass 146, 147, 526 NE2d 765, 766-767 (1988) (& citations). The burden is on the Commonwealth to show representation or waiver. *Com. v. Stewart*, supra, 422 Mass at 386, 663 NE2d at 257. A docket sheet indicating counsel had been appointed satisfies the burden in absence of contrary evidence. Id. As to other methods available to the Commonwealth to establish either representation or waiver, see *Com. v. Napier*, 417 Mass 32, 627 NE2d 913 (1994) (& citations); *Com. v. Delorey*, 369 Mass 323, 328-331, 339 NE2d 746, 749-750 (1975).

The use of a conviction in the absence of a showing of representation or waiver is constitutional error, *Com. v. Stewart*, supra, 422 Mass at 386, 663 NE2d at 257; but it may be harmless beyond a reasonable doubt. *Com. v. Delorey*, supra, 369 Mass at 327, 339 NE2d at 748. Compare *Com. v. Brown*, 2 Mass App 76, 83, 308 NE2d 794, 798 (1974) (error harmless) with *Com. v. Proctor*, supra, 403 Mass at 149, 526 NE2d at 767-768 and *Com. v. Barrett*, 3 Mass App 8, 322 NE2d 89 (1975) (error not harmless).

The courts have left open the question whether a non-party witness may be impeached by uncounseled convictions, see *Com. v. Napier*, supra, 417 Mass at 33, 627 NE2d at 914 and *Com. v. Puleio*, 394 Mass 101, 104, 474 NE2d 1078, 1080-1081 (1985), as well as the use of uncounseled convictions to impeach a witness in a civil case. See *Carey v. Zayre of Beverly, Inc.*, 367 Mass 125, 324 NE2d 619 (1975); *Walter v. Bonito*, 367 Mass 117, 123 n.1, 324 NE2d 624, 627 n.1 (1975).

Where the defendant objects to the use of a conviction obtained in a foreign country to impeach him, the burden falls on the defendant to show that the conviction was obtained in proceedings so fundamentally unfair that the conviction should be excluded. *Com. v. Bourgeois*, 391 Mass 869, 882-883, 465 NE2d 1180, 1189 (1984).

It must be emphasized that the trial judge has the discretion to exclude evidence of a defendant's prior conviction even if it falls within the requirements of GL 233, §21, where the danger of unfair prejudice outweighs the probative value of the conviction for purposes of impeachment. *Com. v. Maguire*, 392 Mass 466, 470, 467 NE2d 112, 115 (1984). "The admission of evidence of a prior conviction, particularly a conviction of a crime not involving the defendant's truthfulness and one closely related to or identical to the crime with which the defendant is charged, may well divert the jury's attention from the question of the defendant's guilt to the question of the defendant's bad character. Moreover, the mere threat of the admission of evidence of a defendant's prior conviction of a crime may discourage him from testifying." *Com. v. Maguire,* supra, 392 Mass at 466, 467 NE2d at 114-115. "Impeachment of a defendant's credibility by means of prior convictions is always subject to possible misconstruction by a jury, who may improperly regard the impeachment as substantive evidence of guilt, despite careful limiting instructions." *Com. v. Childs,* supra, 23 Mass App at 38, 499 NE2d at 302.

The trial judge's ruling admitting evidence of a prior conviction may be reviewed on appeal under *Com. v. Maguire* on the question of whether there was an abuse of discretion because the probative value of the conviction for impeachment purposes was outweighed by the danger of unfair prejudice. See, e.g., *Com. v. Gallagher,* 408 Mass 510, 516-517, 562 NE2d 80, 84-85 (1990) (upholding decision to admit convictions for breaking and entering, larceny, and receiving stolen property in first degree murder trial); *Com. v. Feroli,* 407 Mass 405, 407-408, 553 NE2d 934, 935-936 (1990) (upholding decision to admit convictions for armed robbery in first-degree murder trial). Reversal is required where it appears that the judge was unaware of his discretion to exclude convictions. See *Com. v. Ruiz,* 400 Mass 214, 508 NE2d 607 (1987) (& cases cited).

As noted in *Com. v. Maguire,* the substantial similarity of the crime charged and the crime offered for impeachment is a factor weighing against admission because of the risk that the jury will engage in prejudicial propensity logic. 392 Mass at 471, 467 NE2d at 1180-1181. Where "the prior convictions relate to offenses similar to the [offense] at bar, there is an especially serious danger that a jury will disregard limiting instructions and allow the convictions to influence their deliberations as substantive evidence." *Walter v. Bonito,* supra, 367 Mass at 124, 324 NE2d at 628. It has been observed that "[g]enerally, a prior conviction must be substantially similar to the charged offense for the prejudicial effect to outweigh the probative value of prior conviction evidence." *Com. v. Drumgold,* 423 Mass 230, 250, 668 NE2d 300, 314 (1996). See also *Com. v. Preston,* 27 Mass App 16, 23, 534 NE2d 787, 791-792 (1989) ("It is at least difficult, if not impossible, to show an abuse of discretion [in the admission of prior convictions] in the absence of a 'substantial similarity' between the offenses being tried and the prior convictions.").

Nonetheless, the admission of a conviction substantially similar to the crime for which the defendant is on trial is not *per se* error, see *Com. v. Whitman,* 416 Mass 90, 94, 617 NE2d 625, 628 (1993) and *Com. v. Fano,* 400 Mass 296, 304, 508 NE2d 859, 864 (1987); and the admission of similar crimes has been upheld on several occasions. See, e.g., *Com. v. Whitman,* supra, 416 Mass at 94-95 (conviction for assault with intent to commit rape admitted in murder prosecution arising out of defendant's alleged sexual assault); *Com. v. Smith,* 403 Mass 489, 497-498, 531 NE2d 556, 561-562 (1988) (armed robbery convictions admitted in trial on armed assault); *Com. v. Walker,* 401 Mass 338, 345-346, 516 NE2d 1143, 1148-1149 (1987) (unarmed robbery, larceny, and assault convictions admitted in trial on murder and armed robbery); *Com. v. Boyer,* 400 Mass 52, 56-59, 507 NE2d 1024, 1026-1028 (1987) (conviction for prostitution in trial on prostitution charges); *Com. v. Chartier,* 43 Mass App 758, 762, 686 NE2d 1055, 1058 (1997) (conviction for violating domestic abuse order admitted in trial for same offense); *Com. v. Nutile,* 31 Mass App 614, 621, 582 NE2d 547, 551-552 (1991) (conviction for possession of cocaine admitted in trial on cocaine trafficking); *Com. v. Dwyer,* 22 Mass App 724, 726-728, 497 NE2d 1103, 1104-1106 (1986) (finding no abuse of discretion even though "[m]ost of the offenses could be viewed as similar in nature to that under consideration to the extent they reveal a propensity for assaultive behavior;" judge could properly consider defense counsel's declared intent to impeach credibility of victim with prior convictions for assault crime).

For other cases dealing with the admissibility of similar-crime convictions, see *Com. v. Sanchez*, 405 Mass 369, 378-379, 540 NE2d 1316, 1322-1323 (1989) (judge properly exercised discretion in rape and sexual assault trial when he "carefully excluded the defendant's prior convictions of crimes involving homosexual rapes of minors and admitted for impeachment purposes the conviction of a crime dissimilar to the ones being tried [arson]"); *Com. v. Mahoney*, 405 Mass 326, 330, 540 NE2d 179, 182 (1989) (in prosecution for breaking and entering, judge did not abuse discretion in denying defendant's motion in limine to bar use of prior convictions for armed robbery, kidnapping and assault by means of a deadly weapon, inasmuch as prior crimes were not so similar to crime charged as to require exclusion); *Com. v. Andrews*, 403 Mass 441, 456, 530 NE2d 1222, 1230-1231 (1988) (substantial difference between armed robbery and murder, even if that murder is committed in course of armed robbery); *Com. v. Cordeiro*, 401 Mass 843, 855, 519 NE2d 1328, 1335 (1988) (no abuse of discretion where judge admitted prior conviction for assault by means of dangerous weapon at trial for aggravated rape even though both incidents involved use of knife); *Com. v. Weaver*, 400 Mass 612, 618-619, 511 NE2d 545, 549 (1987) (convictions for assaultive crimes sufficiently dissimilar to firearm possessory offense); *Com. v. Reid*, 400 Mass 534, 537-540, 511 NE2d 331, 333-335 (1987) (defendant on trial for rape of a child without force and assault and battery on child properly impeached by evidence of 14 prior convictions, five of which involved assaults or threats). See also *Com. v. Guilfoyle*, 396 Mass 1003, 485 NE2d 679 (1985) (reversal required where trial judge stated that he was admitting the prior conviction *because of* the similarity between it and crime charged); *Com. v. Roucoulet*, 22 Mass App 603, 608, 496 NE2d 166, 169 (1986) (same).

Because a ruling on a defendant's motion to bar the use of convictions for impeachment may affect counsel's conduct of the entire trial, it is desirable for the trial judge to rule on it at "an early moment." *Com. v. Diaz*, supra, 383

Mass at 81, 417 NE2d at 955. But see *Com. v. Pina*, 406 Mass 540, 550, 549 NE2d 106, 112-113 (1990) (advance ruling not required); *Com. v. Andrews*, supra, 403 Mass at 456, 530 NE2d at 1230-1231 (same). The defendant may seek an order prohibiting use of his prior convictions by filing a motion in limine, see, e.g., *Com. v. Gallagher*, supra, 408 Mass at 516, 562 NE2d at 84-85; but the defendant is not required to make a motion in limine in order to object to the introduction of prior convictions at trial. See *Com. v. Ruiz*, supra, 400 Mass at 215-216, 508 NE2d at 608. For a discussion of the showing required for such a motion in limine, see *Com. v. Dwyer*, supra, 22 Mass App at 726-728, 497 NE2d at 1104-1106. Where defendants have testified in reliance upon representations or pretrial agreements by prosecutors that convictions would not be offered at trial, failure to comply has resulted in reversals on appeal. See, e.g., *Com. v. Felton*, 16 Mass App 63, 448 NE2d 1304 (1983) and *Com. v. Lavin*, 42 Mass App 711, 713-714, 679 NE2d 590, 592 (1997).

Unlike the federal courts, the Massachusetts courts have not required a defendant to testify in order to preserve for review the claim that a motion to exclude convictions was improperly denied. See *Com. v. Feroli*, supra, 407 Mass at 407-408, 553 NE2d at 935-936; *Com. v. Cordeiro*, supra, 401 Mass at 854, 519 NE2d at 1334-1335; *Com. v. Fano*, supra, 400 Mass at 301 n.9, 508 NE2d at 863 n.9; *Com. v. Gonzalez*, 22 Mass App 274, 277-280, 493 NE2d 516, 518-520 (1986) (comparing the federal rule, and discussing the record required for review in a case where defendant does not testify). But see *Com. v. Preston*, supra, 27 Mass App at 24, 534 NE2d at 792 ("It may not be necessary in our practice for a defendant to testify to preserve for appellate review the correctness of the denial of a [motion in limine to exclude prior convictions]. We think, however, that such an issue is not preserved for appellate review where a defendant neither presses for a ruling on the [motion in limine] nor testifies.").

Under Massachusetts practice a witness's conviction can be proved only by the court record or a certified copy of the record; it cannot be shown by cross-examination without production of record. See *Com. v. Puleio,* supra, 394 Mass at 104, 474 NE2d at 1080-1081; *Com. v. Atkins,* 386 Mass 593, 600, 436 NE2d 1203, 1207 (1982); *Com. v. Clifford,* supra, 374 Mass at 305, 372 NE2d at 1274; *Ford v. Kremer,* 360 Mass 870, 277 NE2d 679 (1972). But see *Com. v. Ferguson,* 365 Mass 1, 11 n.8, 309 NE2d 182, 188 n.8 (1974) (no error where prosecutor permitted to read prior convictions from the original records instead of introducing certified copies); *Com. v. Smith,* 342 Mass 180, 185-186, 172 NE2d 597, 601-602 (1961) (no error where prosecutor permitted to argue that fact that criminal record was not introduced did not mean that defendant did not have one, where defense counsel had argued that if defendant had a criminal record, prosecution would have introduced it). Proposed Mass R Evid 609(b) would relax this practice by also permitting proof "in such other manner as the court may approve."

The record of conviction must be properly authenticated to be admissible for impeachment, but this is easily accomplished under the provisions of Mass R Civ P 44, Mass R Crim P 39 & 40, and GL 233, §69. When admitted, the record of conviction may be taken by the jury into the jury room during deliberations. *Com. v. Rondoni,* 333 Mass 384, 386, 131 NE2d 187, 188 (1955).

It is proper to ask for purposes of identification whether the witness on the stand is the same person as the one whose name appears on the court record. See *Com. v. Millyan,* 399 Mass 171, 184 n.10, 503 NE2d 934, 941 n.10 (1987); *Com. v. Rondoni,* supra, 333 Mass at 386, 131 NE2d at 188. Indeed, it is necessary to establish in this manner or another that the witness is in fact the person referred to in the court record; mere identity of name is not sufficient. *Com. v. Rondoni,* supra; *Ayers v. Ratshesky,* 213 Mass 589, 593-595, 101 NE 78, 80 (1913) (proponent must present "confirmatory facts or circumstances"); *Com. v. Doe,* 8 Mass App

297, 299, 393 NE2d 426, 429 (1979) ("Slight confirmatory evidence is needed to establish identity of persons where there is identity of names."). Even where the fact of the defendant's convictions are already established through his testimony, certified copies of the convictions may be admitted into evidence. See *Com. v. White,* 27 Mass App 789, 795, 543 NE2d 703, 707 (1989).

Where certified copies of the prior convictions are admitted, care must be taken to avoid including extraneous material that could cause prejudice. See *Com. v. Ford,* 397 Mass 298, 300-301, 490 NE2d 1166, 1168 (1986) (docket entries showing defaults, warrants, arrests, and violations of probation erroneously admitted); *Com. v. Kowalski,* 33 Mass App 49, 51, 595 NE2d 798, 800 (1992) (error in admitting unexpurgated records of convictions, including docket entries showing defaults, warrants, and surrender for probation violation); *Com. v. White,* supra, 27 Mass at 795, 543 NE2d at 707 (error to include extraneous material consisting of victims' names, probation surrender and default; but no prejudice because materials were insignificant); *Com. v. Clark,* 23 Mass App 375, 380-383, 502 NE2d 564, 567-569 (1987). The "better practice" is to avoid mention of the crimes for which the defendant was indicted where he was only convicted of lesser offenses. *Com. v. Kowalski,* supra, 33 Mass App at 50, 595 NE2d at 799-800 (but no abuse of discretion where prosecutor was permitted to read to jury charges of armed robbery and robbery when defendant's conviction was for accessory after fact).

Once admitted, the record of conviction is conclusive and matters of explanation, extenuation, or aggravation are not admissible. See *Com. v. McGeoghean,* 412 Mass 839, 843, 593 NE2d 229, 231-232 (1992); *Com. v. Maguire,* supra, 392 Mass at 471 n.10, 467 NE2d at 155 n.10 ("the proponent of the witness may not undertake in rehabilitation of the witness to show the circumstances of the conviction"); *Lamoureux v. New York & N. H. & H. Railroad,* 169 Mass 338, 340, 47 NE 1009, 1010 (1897) (the guilt or innocence of the witness cannot be retried, and "it is impracticable to introduce what may be a long investigation of a wholly collateral matter into a case to which it is foreign"). If, however, one side is permitted to go into the matter, the other side must also be allowed to do so. *Com. v. McGeoghean*, supra, 412 Mass at 842-843, 593 NE2d at 231-232 (where cross-examination goes beyond simply establishing that witness is person named in record of conviction, proponent of witness may, in judge's discretion, inquire about those collateral matters in effort to rehabilitate witness); *Lamoureux v. New York & N. H. & H. Railroad*, supra; *Com. v. Callahan*, 358 Mass 808, 265 NE2d 382 (1970). Further, the witness should be allowed on redirect to explain an inconsistency between his testimony on direct and cross relating to the prior conviction. *Com. v. Donovan*, 17 Mass App 83, 86-88, 455 NE2d 1217, 1219-1221 (1983).

Where a prior conviction is admitted for impeachment, the judge should clearly instruct the jury that it is relevant solely in evaluating the credibility of the witness. See *Com. v. Gallagher*, supra, 408 Mass at 516, 562 NE2d at 84-85. See also *Com. v. Riccard*, 410 Mass 718, 723-724, 575 NE2d 57, 60-61 (1991) (reversing conviction because judge gave contradictory instructions on jury's use of prior convictions in determining credibility of witnesses); *Com. v. Kines*, 37 Mass App 540, 543, 640 NE2d 1117, 1119 (1994); *Com. v. Bassett*, 21 Mass App 713, 490 NE2d 459 (1986) (reversing conviction because judge's instructions allowed jury to use prior convictions to establish propensity of defendant for violence and threats); *Com. v. Felton*, 16 Mass App 63, 448 NE2d 1304 (1983) (reversing conviction because judge failed to give immediate limiting instruction). When admitting a defendant's conviction for impeachment, the trial judge (unless the defendant moves otherwise) should advise the jury of the nature of the conviction; revealing only the fact that the defendant had a prior conviction increases the risk of prejudice since it allows the jury to speculate as to what the conviction was for. See *Com. v. Ioannides*, 41 Mass App 904, 668 NE2d 845 (1996).

GL 233, §21, applies only where the past crime is being used to impeach the credibility of a witness at trial. Where evidence of a prior conviction is offered for another purpose, neither GL 233, §21, nor its restrictions — i.e., the time limitations or the requirement that proof be by certified copy of court record — apply. See *Care & Protection of Frank,* 409 Mass 492, 495, 567 NE2d 214, 217 (1991) (& cases cited). Thus, the statute is inapplicable where the prior crime is used circumstantially to motive, intent, plan, etc. (see §4.4.6, supra); or where a prior conviction is offered as an element of the crime charged, as in the case of a second offense of operating under the influence, *Com. v. Fortier,* 258 Mass 98, 155 NE 8 (1927) (prior conviction may be established by cross-examination of defendant without production of the record); or where the prior conviction is relevant to parental fitness. *Care & Protection of Frank,* supra; *Adoption of Irwin,* 28 Mass App 41, 545 NE2d 1193 (1989). In these situations, the fact of conviction may be established without the court record, and the evidence is admissible whether the defendant takes the stand as a witness or not. The fact that the witness has committed a crime may also be disclosed where it is referred to in a prior inconsistent statement otherwise admissible. *Com. v. West,* 312 Mass 438, 440-441, 45 NE2d 260, 262 (1942). For other evidentiary uses of a judgment of conviction, see §8.8.2, infra.

For a case discussing (but not permitting) the use of a third-party's conviction to impeach a witness, see *Com. v. Supplee,* 45 Mass App 265, 268, 697 NE2d 547, 549-550 (1998).

Where the prosecutor uses prior convictions not merely to impeach the defendant but to suggest propensity for violence, GL 233, §21, is violated. See *Com. v. Roberts,* 378 Mass 116, 126-127, 389 NE2d 989, 996 (1979) (but reversal not required because judge gave prompt limiting instructions).

The limitations on the introduction of prior crimes may be lifted if the defendant opens the subject of his prior record. See, e.g., *Com. v. Smith*, 342 Mass 180, 185-186, 172 NE2d 597, 601 (1961); *Com. v. Baldwin*, 385 Mass 165, 179, 435 NE2d 194, 202 (1982).

Proposed Mass R Evid 609[7] would modify present impeachment practice in several regards. See generally *Com. v. Diaz*, supra, 383 Mass at 80-82, 417 NE2d at 955-956. Most notably the rule imposes a fixed time limit of 15 years from the date of conviction (or five years from the date of expiration of the minimum sentence imposed), after which evidence of the conviction is not admissible. Proposed Mass R Evid 609(c). The discretion accorded the judge under Rule 609(a) to exclude a conviction offered to impeach a criminal defendant is consistent with present Massachusetts practice under *Com. v. Maguire*, supra. No discretion is permitted, however, to exclude a conviction offered to impeach the credibility of any witness other than the

---

[7] PMRE 609 provides:

(a) General rule. For the purpose of impeaching the credibility of a witness, evidence that he has been convicted of a crime is admissible. In a criminal case, the court shall have the discretion to exclude evidence of a prior conviction offered to impeach the credibility of the accused if it finds that its probative value is outweighed by the danger of unfair prejudice. There shall be no discretion to exclude a prior conviction offered to impeach the credibility of any other witness. A plea of guilty or a finding or verdict of guilty shall constitute a conviction.

(b) Type of evidence. The evidence of conviction shall be by the original or certified copy of the record of conviction, or in such other manner as the court may approve.

(c) Time limits. Evidence of a conviction is not admissible under this rule after fifteen years from the date of conviction, or five years from the date of expiration of the minimum term of confinement imposed by the court for that conviction, whichever is greater.

(d) Effect of pardon. Where a conviction has been followed by a pardon, both the conviction, if otherwise admissible, and the pardon shall be admissible.

(e) Juvenile adjudications. Evidence of a juvenile adjudication is not admissible, except by constitutional requirement or as otherwise provided by statute.

(f) Pendency of appeal. The pendency of an appeal therefrom does not render evidence of a conviction inadmissible. Evidence of the pendency of an appeal is admissible.

(g) Sealed records. Notwithstanding any other provisions of this rule, no evidence of a conviction shall be used or admissible, if the record of such has been sealed under the law of the jurisdiction where it occurred, except by constitutional requirement or as otherwise provided by statute.

accused. Rule 609(a). This is not consistent with current practice. See *Com. v. Burnett,* 417 Mass 740, 743 n.1, 632 NE2d 1206 n.1 (1994) and *Com. v. Bucknam,* 20 Mass App 121, 123-124, 478 NE2d 747, 749-750 (1985).

Fed R Evid 609 adopts an approach different from both GL 233, §21, and Proposed Mass R Evid 609. The federal rule limits the crimes that can be used for impeachment to those punishable by death or imprisonment for more than one year and those involving dishonesty or false statement. With regard to the former category (but not the latter), the judge is afforded discretion to exclude the conviction if the probative value is outweighed by the risk of prejudice. This discretion applies to both criminal defendants and other witnesses, although with a different balancing standard employed for the accused. The federal rule establishes a ten-year time limit on the use of a conviction but permits the judge to admit a conviction over ten years old if the probative value substantially outweighs its prejudicial effect. For a discussion of the federal approach, see *Walter v. Bonito,* 367 Mass 117, 123 n.2, 324 NE2d 624, 628 n.2 (1975).

The mere fact that the witness has been arrested or indicted is not admissible for impeachment. *Com. v. Baldwin,* 385 Mass 165, 178, 431 NE2d 194, 202-203 (1982); *Com. v. Haywood,* 377 Mass 755, 759-760, 388 NE2d 648, 651-652 (1979). See also §6.10.3, infra. Such evidence may be admissible if the fact of arrest or indictment shows bias or motive to lie. See §6.8. Special problems arise where mug shots, which reveal prior arrests, are used at trial for identification purposes. See §4.4.2, supra.

Prior convictions may be elicited during direct examination for tactical purposes. See §6.12.

§6.10.3   Prior Bad Acts

Massachusetts practice does not permit a witness to be impeached (either on cross-examination or by extrinsic proof) by use of specific acts of misconduct showing the witness to be untruthful (unless the act resulted in a criminal conviction, as discussed in the previous section). See *Com. v. Andrews*, 403 Mass 441, 459, 530 NE2d 1222, 1232 (1988); *Com. v. Hightower*, 400 Mass 267, 271, 508 NE2d 850, 853 (1987); *Com. v. Atkins*, 386 Mass 593, 600, 436 NE2d 1203, 1207-1208 (1982); *Com. v. Clifford*, 374 Mass 293, 305, 372 NE2d 1267, 1275 (1978); *Com. v. Johnson*, 41 Mass App 81, 669 NE2d 212 (1996) (defaults not admissible); *Com. v. McClendon*, 39 Mass App 122, 129-130, 653 NE2d 1138, 1143 (1995); *Com. v. Gonzalez*, 11 Mass App 932, 416 NE2d 539 (1981). But see *Com. v. LaVelle*, 33 Mass App 36, 39, 596 NE2d 364 (1992) (1993) (citing Text) (rule is not inflexible, as indicated by *Bohannon* exception for prior false allegations of rape, see below). However, such matters may be explored where the opposing party opens the subject on direct examination. See, e.g., *Com. v. Perez*, 390 Mass 308, 316-319, 455 NE2d 632, 637-638 (1983); *Com. v. Key*, 381 Mass 19, 28-29, 407 NE2d 327, 334 (1980); *Com. v. McClendon*, supra, 39 Mass App at 128, 653 NE2d at 1141.

"The reasons generally given [for the rule against impeachment by bad acts] are: That proof of separate instances of falsehood may have existed without impairing his general reputation for truthfulness. Or that the impeached witness is not required to be prepared to meet particular acts of which he has had no notice, although he is presumed to be capable of supporting his general reputation. Or that the attention of jurors will be distracted from the real issue to be tried by the introduction of collateral issues, which also would tend to prolong the trial unduly." *F. W. Stock & Sons v. Dellapenna*, 217 Mass 503, 506, 105 NE 378, 379 (1914).

An application of the principle that prior bad acts may not be used to impeach a witness's credibility forecloses impeachment by showing that the witness has testified falsely in a collateral proceeding. See *Com. v. Frey*, 390 Mass 245, 249, 454 NE2d 478, 480 (1983); *Com. v. Trenholm*, 14 Mass App 1038, 442 NE2d 745 (1982). The fact that a complainant has made prior false allegations of rape may, however, be admissible to challenge her credibility despite the general rule and the Rape-Shield Statute. See *Com. v. Bohannon*, 376 Mass 90, 378 NE2d 987 (1978) (discussed in §4.4.3).

Proposed Mass R Evid 608(b)[8] would bring Massachusetts into line with federal practice by permitting cross-examination (but not extrinsic proof) in the discretion of the court concerning specific instances of conduct of the witness that are deemed probative of untruthfulness. As always, such questions must be supported by a good faith basis.

§6.11   Impeachment by Religious Belief, Oaths, and Affirmations

A witness may not be impeached by evidence of his disbelief in God. GL 233, §19.[1] Proposed Mass R Evid 610[2] is in accord. As to the method of administering oaths and

---

[8] PMRE 608(b) provides:

> Specific instances of the conduct of a witness, for the purpose of attacking or supporting his credibility, other than conviction of crime as provided in Rule 609, may not be proved by extrinsic evidence. They may, however, in the discretion of the court, if probative of truthfulness or untruthfulness, be inquired into on cross-examination of the witness (1) concerning his character for truthfulness or untruthfulness, or (2) concerning the truthfulness or untruthfulness of another witness as to which character the witness being cross-examined has testified. The giving of testimony, whether by an accused or any other witness, does not operate as a waiver of his privilege against self-incrimination when examined with respect to matters which related only to credibility.

§6.11   [1]"A person believing in any other than the Christian religion may be sworn according to the appropriate ceremonies of his religion. A person not a believer in any religion shall be required to testify under the penalties of perjury, and evidence of his disbelief in the existence of God may not be received to affect his credibility as a witness."

[2]"Evidence of the beliefs or opinions of a witness on matters of religion is not admissible for the purpose of showing that by reason of their nature his credibility is impaired or enhanced." PMRE 610.

affirmations, see GL 233, §§15-19; Proposed Mass R Evid 603;[3] Mass R Civ P 43(d).

§6.12 Impeachment of One's Own Witness

Massachusetts practice permits impeachment of one's own witness, but in a restricted form. GL 233, §23, provides:

> The party who produces a witness shall not impeach his credit by evidence of bad character, but may contradict him by other evidence, and may also prove that he has made at other times statements inconsistent with his present testimony; but before proof of such inconsistent statements is given, the circumstances thereof sufficient to designate the particular occasion shall be mentioned to the witness, and he shall be asked if he has made such statements, and, if so, shall be allowed to explain them.

The prohibition against impeachment by evidence of bad character (specifically proof of prior convictions or reputation for untruthfulness) applies to any witness who is called by the proponent, even if the witness is the opposing party called under the provisions of GL 233, §22 (discussed at §3.2, supra). See *Walter v. Bonito*, 367 Mass 117, 120-123, 324 NE2d 624, 626-628 (1975)(& citations). See also Mass R Civ P 43(b) (forbidding impeachment of an adverse party "by evidence of bad character").

Regarding the restrictions of the statute, the Supreme Judicial Court has observed:

> We are aware that there is much sentiment and strong argument for allowing a party to impeach his own witness just as he can attack the opposition's, and particularly does the argument appear cogent when one's witness is the ad-

---

[3] "Before testifying, every witness shall be required to declare that he will testify truthfully, by oath or affirmation administered in a form calculated to awaken his conscience and impress his mind with his duty to do so." PMRE 603.

verse party, for here the fiction that by offering a witness one "vouches" for him is most vacuous. But regardless of what the degree of our own enthusiasm might be for such a rule, we do not consider ourselves free to adopt it by decision in defiance of the statute as previously interpreted.

Walter v. Bonito, supra, 367 Mass at 121, 324 NE2d at 627 (citations omitted).

GL 233, §23 expressly permits impeachment of one's own witness by contradiction (discussed in §6.7.1, supra) and by proof of prior inconsistent statements (discussed in §6.7.2, supra). The latter mode is generally subject to the same standards that apply to an opposing party's witness, except the statute inserts an additional requirement that a foundation be laid by bringing the statement to the attention of the witness with sufficient circumstances to designate the particular occasion on which it was made, asking the witness if he made the statement, and allowing him to explain it. See §6.7.2(f), supra.

As is generally the case, the prior inconsistent statement of one's own witness is admitted for the limited purpose of challenging the witness's credibility, and not for its truth. *Com. v. Rosa*, 412 Mass 147, 156, 587 NE2d 767, 772-773 (1992); *Com. v. Thompson*, 362 Mass 382, 386, 286 NE2d 333, 335 (1972); *Com. v. Anselmo*, 33 Mass App 602, 609, 603 NE2d 227, 232 (1992). It is generally presumed that the judge's limiting instructions are understood and followed by the jury. *Com. v. Rosa*, supra, 412 Mass at 159-160, 587 NE2d at 774-775 (but prosecutor's argument emphasizing the substantive use of the testimony overcomes the presumption).

Although the witness who claims a lack of memory regarding the subject generally cannot be impeached by prior statements because of the lack of inconsistency (see §6.7.2 and *Com. v. Reddick*, 372 Mass 460, 463, 362 NE2d 519, 521 (1977) (& citations)), the prior statements may in appropriate circumstances be used to "refresh recollection." *Com. v. Hartford*, 346 Mass 482, 487, 194 NE2d 401, 404

(1963); *Jensen v. McEldowney*, 341 Mass 485, 487, 170 NE2d 472, 473 (1960). And if the witness goes beyond asserting a lack of memory, impeachment may be allowed. See *Com. v. Cobb*, 379 Mass. 456, 463-464, 405 N.E.2d 97, 102 (1980); *Com. v. Reddick*, supra, 372 Mass at 463, 362 NE2d at 521; *Com. v. Greene*, 9 Mass App 688, 692-693, 404 NE2d 110, 113 (1980).

It should be noted that Massachusetts practice has not required that the party calling the witness be surprised by his testimony before being allowed to impeach him under GL 233, §23. See *Com. v. Bray*, 19 Mass App 751, 758, 477 NE2d 596, 601 (1985) (citing *Brooks v. Weeks*, 121 Mass 433 (1877)).

The tactical use of prior convictions on direct examination to minimize the impact of the record on the jury is not regarded as impeachment for purposes of the GL 233, §23 prohibition, and may be permitted within the judge's discretion. *Com. v. McTigue*, 384 Mass 814, 429 NE2d 707 (1981); *Com. v. Coviello*, 378 Mass 530, 392 NE2d 1042 (1979); *Com. v. Blodgett*, 377 Mass 494, 502-503, 386 NE2d 1042, 1046 (1979); *Com. v. Cadwell*, 374 Mass 308, 312, 372 NE2d 246, 249 (1978); *Com. v. Bandy*, 38 Mass App 329, 337, 648 NE2d 440, 445 (1995). It has similarly been held that the prosecutor may bring out on direct examination of its own witness the fact that he is testifying pursuant to an agreement for leniency. *Com. v. Griffith*, 404 Mass 256, 265-266, 534 NE2d 1153, 1158-1159 (1989).

Proposed Mass R Evid 607[1] would permit impeachment of a witness by any party, without regard to who called him and without limitations. The reasoning behind lifting the restrictions of GL 233, §23 is that it is unrealistic to assume that the party calling a witness thereby vouches for his credibility,[2] given the reality that a litigant rarely has a free

---

§6.12   [1]"The credibility of a witness may be attacked by any party, including the party calling him." PMRE 607.

[2]Illustrative of this traditional view is *Com. v. Hudson*, 77 Mass (11 Gray) 64, 66 (1858) (holding that witness called by Commonwealth and then recalled by defendant could not be impeached on cross-examina-

choice in selecting witnesses. See Advisory Committee Note to Proposed Mass R Evid 607. Conversely, it is improper for an attorney to vouch for or state in argument a personal belief in the witness's credibility. See §3.7, supra.

C. REHABILITATION

§6.13 Introduction

A witness who has been impeached may be rehabilitated in a variety of ways:

(1) where W1 has been impeached by the testimony of W2, by impeaching W2;

(2) where W1 has been impeached by challenging his character for veracity, by evidence of W1's good character for veracity;

(3) where W1 has been impeached on the ground that his testimony is a recent contrivance, by proof of W1's prior consistent statement;

(4) by evidence denying or explaining the impeaching evidence; and

(5) by proving facts bearing on the merits of the case that tend to make W1's testimony more credible.

For reasons of efficiency, logic and policy, evidence enhancing credibility is generally not admissible to bolster the testimony of a witness who has not been impeached. It should be noted that the attempt at impeachment need not be successful in order to open the door to rehabilitation; where "the opponent has insinuated the lack of truthfulness of the witness through attempted, though unsuccessful, impeachment, the party who put on the witness may adduce

---

tion by Commonwealth because "the party who first called him cannot be allowed to say or to show that he was unworthy of credit.")

evidence to establish his good character and truthfulness."
Com. v. Haraldstad, 16 Mass App 565, 571, 453 NE2d 472,
475 (1983).

In two situations discussed below — prior identification
and "fresh complaint" — prior consistent statements are
admissible in the absence of any attempt at impeachment.
See §6.19, infra.

§6.14   By Impeaching the Impeacher

In general, the same rules apply to impeachment of W2
(who impeached W1) as apply to the impeachment of W1.
It should be noted, however, that because impeachment of
an impeaching witness is remote from the merits of the
controversy, the trial judge can be expected to exclude
much of this evidence on the ground that it is too collateral.

§6.15   By Evidence of W1's Good Character for Veracity

Evidence of W1's good character for veracity is not admissible unless and until his character for veracity has been
attacked. *Com. v. Sheline,* 391 Mass 279, 288, 461 NE2d 1197,
1204 (1984); *Com. v. Clark,* 23 Mass App 375, 378-380, 502
NE2d 564, 567-568 (1987). Such an attack has occurred
when:

(1)   Records of W1's conviction for a crime have been
      introduced. See *Gertz v. Fitchburg Railroad Co.,* 137
      Mass 77 (1884).

(2)   Evidence of bad reputation for truthfulness and
      veracity has been introduced. *Quinsigamond Bank
      v. Hobbs,* 77 Mass (11 Gray) 250 (1858). It has
      been held that rehabilitation is permitted when-
      ever, in an effort to impeach, W2 is asked to tes-
      tify as to W1's character for veracity, even where
      the answer is that W1's character is good. *Com. v.*

Ingraham, 73 Mass (7 Gray) 46, 48 (1856) ("in the manner in which the answer is given, though in language apparently favorable to the witness, yet there might be conveyed the impression of doubt and uncertainty as to his reputation").

Impeachment by contradiction or by prior inconsistent statement does not constitute an attack on W1's character for veracity and thus does not permit rehabilitation by character evidence. *Com. v. Sheline*, supra, 391 Mass at 288-289, 461 NE2d at 1204 (& cases cited); *Gertz v. Fitchburg Railroad Co.*, supra; *Com. v. Clark*, supra, 23 Mass App at 380, 502 NE2d at 567-568.

The permissible form of the rehabilitation evidence is limited to reputation for truthfulness and veracity. W1's testimony may not be bolstered by evidence from W2 in the form of an opinion that W1 is truthful. *Com. v. Montanino*, 409 Mass 500, 502-505, 567 NE2d 1212, 1213-1215 (1991) (police officer improperly permitted to testify to typical manner in which sexual abuse victims report crime because that had same effect as stating opinion that victim testified truthfully).

Proposed Mass R Evid 608(a)[1] (which is identical to Fed R Evid 608(a)) would expand the avenues of rehabilitation to include opinion evidence of W1's good character for truthfulness, and 608(b)[2] would permit inquiry on cross-examination of W1 into specific instances of conduct showing him to be truthful. Proposed Mass R Evid 608 does not permit rehabilitation until W1's character for truthfulness has been "attacked by opinion or reputation or otherwise."

Both the case law and the Proposed Rules permit a witness who testifies to W1's reputation for truthfulness to be cross-examined as to specific acts of untruthfulness committed by W1. See *Com. v. Brown*, 411 Mass 115, 118,

---

§6.15   [1] See note 1, §6.10.
[2] See note 8, §6.10.

579 NE2d 153, 155 (1991); Proposed Mass R Evid 405(a) and 608(b).

§6.16   By Proof of Prior Consistent Statement

Prior statements of a witness consistent with his testimony at trial are generally not admissible to bolster his testimony. (But see §6.19.) "The reason for the rule is that the testimony of a witness in court should not need — and ought not — to be 'pumped up' by evidence that the witness said the same thing on some prior occasion." *Com. v. Kindell*, 44 Mass App 200, 202-203, 689 NE2d 845, 847 (1998).

When, however, W1 is impeached on the ground that his testimony is a recent contrivance,[1] or was the product of bias or undue influence, or that the facts described in the testimony have been concealed under conditions that warrant the belief that the witness would have disclosed them if true, then prior consistent statements made at a time before the motivation to falsify existed may be introduced to fortify his testimony. *Com. v. Retkovitz*, 222 Mass 245, 250, 110 NE 293, 294 (1915); *Com. v. Jiles*, 428 Mass 66,73-74, 698 NE2d 10, 14-15 (1998). See, e.g., *Com. v. Diaz*, 422 Mass 269, 274-275, 661 NE2d 1326, 1329-1330 (1996) (testimony from witness's lawyer on circumstances under which witness first told prosecutor about murders admissible to rebut implication of recent fabrication); *Com. v. Fryar*, 425 Mass 237, 252, 680 NE2d 901, 912 (1997) (witness properly rehabilitated with consistent testimony from first trial); *Com. v. Sullivan*, 410 Mass 521, 527, 574 NE2d 966, 970 (1991) (prosecution witness's 19-page handwritten statement made ten months before plea agreement admissible to counter allegation that witness's testimony was

---

§6.16   [1] A claim of recent contrivance, it must be emphasized, merely goes to the credibility of the witness and is not ground for exclusion of the testimony. See *Com. v. Gurney*, 13 Mass App 391, 406, 433 NE2d 471, 480 (1982) (citing Text).

product of inducement); *Com. v. Kater (Kater III)*, 409 Mass 433, 448, 567 NE2d 885, 894 (1991) (application to post-hypnotic testimony); *Com. v. Mayfield*, 398 Mass 615, 629-630, 500 NE2d 774, 783 (1986) (prior consistent statement of witness admissible where defendant raised inference that his trial testimony resulted from coercion by investigating officers); *Com. v. Haywood*, 377 Mass 755, 762-763, 388 NE2d 648, 653 (1979) (consistent statements made prior to witness's arrest would be admissible to rebut charge that prosecution witness's testimony was biased in favor of Commonwealth); *Com. v. Lacy*, 371 Mass 363, 370-371, 358 NE2d 419, 424-425 (1976) (prior consistent writing admissible to rebut charge that police officer witness recently fabricated testimony); *Com. v. Zukoski*, 370 Mass 23, 26-27, 345 NE2d 690, 693 (1976) (& cases cited); *Com. v. Heffernan*, 350 Mass 48, 51-52, 213 NE2d 399, 402-403 (1966) (after defense counsel questioned prosecution witness's motive for not reporting alleged bribe until he was arrested, Commonwealth properly permitted to introduce witness's earlier statement concerning it); *Com. v. Worcester*, 44 Mass App 258, 260-262, 690 NE2d 451, 453-454 (1998) (detective properly permitted to testify to witness's interview statement where defense counsel had raised on cross-examination inference that she received inducements from Commonwealth); *Com. v. Graves*, 35 Mass App 76, 87-88, 616 NE2d 817, 824 (1993) (rape victim properly allowed on redirect to read from her handwritten statement given to police shortly after incident where defense counsel had suggested on cross that her testimony about defendant's use of a knife was recent contrivance). Compare *Com. v. Henry*, 37 Mass App 429, 433, 640 NE2d 503, 507 (1994) (defendant's out-of-court statement denying guilt not admissible where no suggestion in prosecutor's cross of recent contrivance).

Prior consistent statements have been held admissible even where the assertion of recent contrivance is not explicit. See, e.g., *Com. v. Brookins*, 416 Mass 97, 617 NE2d 621 (1993) (judge erred in excluding defendant's prior consistent statement where, although prosecutor did not explicitly argue defendant's testimony was contrived, cross-examination focused on defendant's exposure to materials that informed him of Commonwealth's probable evidence and strongly implied he tailored his testimony to the evidence); *Com. v. Pickles*, 364 Mass 395, 400-401, 305 NE2d 107, 110-111 (1973) (jury might have "inferred" that witness's testimony was recent fabrication from cross-examination concerning her deal with prosecutor).

The trial judge has considerable discretion in determining whether a suggestion of recent fabrication has been made. See *Com. v. Andrews*, 403 Mass 441, 455, 530 NE2d 1222, 1230 (1988); *Com. v. Zukoski*, supra, 370 Mass at 27, 345 NE2d at 693; *Com. v. Tatro*, 4 Mass App 295, 304-305, 346 NE2d 724, 731 (1976). The judge may admit a prior consistent statement on direct examination, prior to any impeachment, when a claim of recent contrivance is inevitable on cross-examination. See *Com. v. Martinez*, 425 Mass 382, 397, 681 NE2d 818, 828-829 (1997) (& citation); *Com. v. Saarela*, 376 Mass 720, 383 NE2d 501 (1978).

Com. v. Retkovitz, supra, 222 Mass at 250, 110 NE at 294-295, indicates that if the claim of recent contrivance is abandoned, prior consistent statements admitted to refute such claim may be stricken if the change of position does not prejudice the adversary.

In order to be admitted, it must be demonstrated that the statement was made *prior to* the intervention of the pernicious impulses or the motivation to contrive; otherwise the statement is not probative in dispelling these suggestions. See *Com. v. DiLego*, 387 Mass 394, 399, 439 NE2d 807, 810 (1982); *Com. v. Pickles*, supra; *Com. v. Retkovitz*, supra. See also *Tome v. United States*, 115 S Ct 696 (1995) (Fed R Evid 801(d)(1)(B) permits admission of prior consistent statement only when statement was made prior to motive to fabricate arose). Compare *Com. v. Maioli*, 11 Mass App 179, 181-183, 414 NE2d 1017, 1019 (1981) (transcript of prosecution witness's grand jury testimony properly admitted to rebut inference that witness had falsified testimony to obtain favorable disposition of criminal charge brought against him shortly before trial, where it appeared that the witness was unaware of a default warrant on the charge outstanding against him at time he testified before grand jury) with *Com. v. Binienda*, 20 Mass App 756, 759, 482 NE2d 874, 876-877 (1985) (error to admit prior consistent statement made by complaining witness to effect he had been robbed because it was made after, and not before, alleged motive to fabricate came into existence) and *Com. v. Lareau*, 37 Mass App 679, 682-684, 642 NE2d 308, 310-311 (1994) (error to admit prior consistent statement that defendant threatened witness with gun where witness' antagonism toward defendant arose before statement). This "limitation serves to exclude, as inherently untrustworthy, self-serving statements made by a witness after the witness has a reason to build up his position, knowing that repetitions of his claims may be helpful later to blunt the force of an accusation that he is fabricating his testimony or is expressing a bias." *Com. v. Healey*, 27 Mass App 30, 35 n.5, 534 NE2d 301, 304 n.5 (1989) (letter written by child abuse victim to defendant referring to abuse admissible where defendant had tried to show on cross-examination that victim had earlier denied abuse and changed her story under pressure from social worker). For a discussion of the difficulty in some contexts of fixing a particular moment in time that a motive to fabricate may have emerged, see *Com. v. Healey*, supra, 27 Mass App at 37, 534 NE2d at 305-306 (& cases cited).

The ultimate "test [of admissibility] should remain one of probative value — whether the prior consistent statement has a logical tendency to meet and counter the suggestion that the witness has recently contrived his testimony for purposes of trial." *Com. v. Darden*, 5 Mass App 522, 530, 364 NE2d 1092, 1096 (1977). See also *Com. v. Kindell*, supra, 44 Mass App at 202-205, 689 NE2d at 848-849 (judge acted within discretion in admitting prior statements of witness that completed what he said to authorities, even though statements were made after motive to fabricate arose).

When admitted, the prior consistent statement is admissible only to show that the witness's testimony is not the product of the asserted bias or is not recently contrived; it is not admissible to prove the truth of the facts asserted. *Com. v. Diaz,* supra, 422 Mass at 275, 661 NE2d at 1330; *Com. v. Zukoski,* supra, 370 Mass at 27, 345 NE2d at 693; *Com. v. Darden,* supra, 5 Mass App at 527-528, 364 NE2d at 1097. Both Proposed Mass R Evid 801(d)(1)(B)[2] and its federal counterpart remove this limitation and give full substantive effect to a prior consistent statement offered to rebut the charge of recent fabrication as long as the witness is testifying at trial and subject to cross-examination concerning the statement.

Prior consistent statements are *not* admissible where W1 has been impeached only in the following manner:

- Testimony of W2 contradicting W1's testimony. See *Com. v. Reid,* 384 Mass 247, 259-260, 424 NE2d 495, 502-503 (1981).

- Prior statements of W1 inconsistent with his trial testimony. See *Com. v. Zukoski,* supra; *Wilson v. Jeffrey,* 328 Mass 192, 102 NE2d 426 (1951); *Com. v. Retkovitz,* supra, 222 Mass at 250, 110 NE at 294. But see *Com. v. Walker,* 370 Mass 548, 570-571, 350 NE2d 678, 694 (1976) (Commonwealth properly permitted to read into record portion of witness's prior testimony consistent with her trial testimony to put in context portions read by defendant that appeared to be inconsistent); *Com. v. Hoffer,* 375 Mass 369, 375-376, 377 NE2d 685, 690 (1978)

---

[2] "A statement is not hearsay if — The declarant testifies at the trial or hearing and is subject to cross-examination concerning the statement, and the statement is . . . (B) consistent with his testimony and is offered to rebut an express or implied charge against him of recent fabrication or improper influence or motive. . . ." PMRE 801(d)(1)(B).

(same); *Com. v. Manrique*, 31 Mass App 597, 599-602, 581 NE2d 1036, 1038-1039 (1992) (prosecutor properly permitted to elicit statement in trooper's police report where defense had shown trooper's grand jury testimony inconsistent with trial testimony); *Com. v. Horne*, 26 Mass App 996, 998, 530 NE2d 353, 356 (1988) ("If it can be made to appear that the inconsistent statement was the product of a peculiar and transient bias or pressure of some kind, the prior consistent statement may be admitted to shore up the consistent in-court statement.").

- Evidence of W1's bad reputation for veracity.

Since a person's prior consistent statements are relevant only to witness credibility and are admissible only to show that a witness's in-court testimony is not recently contrived, such statements may not be admitted unless the person actually testifies. *Com. v. Delaney*, 34 Mass App 732, 740, 616 NE2d 111, 117 (1993).

§6.17 By Evidence Denying or Explaining the Impeaching Evidence

When W1 has been impeached, the party who called W1 may introduce evidence that explains or contradicts the impeachment evidence. Thus, where W1 has been impeached with a self-contradictory statement or silence in circumstances calling for disclosure, his proponent may elicit from him an explanation of the contradiction or silence. *Com. v. Errington*, 390 Mass 875, 880, 460 NE2d 598, 602 (1984); *Com. v. DiLego*, 387 Mass 394, 399, 439 NE2d 807, 810 (1982). See, e.g., *Com. v. Watkins*, 377 Mass 385, 391 n.11, 385 NE2d 1387, 1391 n.11 (1979) (prosecution witness permitted to explain why she had made contradictory statement to police); *Com. v. Dougan*, 377 Mass 303, 309, 386 NE2d 1, 5 (1979) (prosecution witness permitted to explain delay in reporting incident to police); *Com. v. Hoffer*, 375 Mass 369, 375-376, 377 NE2d 685, 690 (1978) (prosecution witness permitted to explain apparent inconsistencies on redirect); *Com. v. Ferreira*, 373 Mass 116, 130-131, 364 NE2d 1264, 1274 (1977) (error to deny defendant oppportunity on redirect to explain failure to implicate third party when confronted by him at police station); *Com. v. Fatalo*, 345 Mass 85, 185 NE2d 754 (1962) (error to deny defendant opportunity on redirect to explain why he failed to assert alibi when arrested); *Com. v. Smith*, 329 Mass 477, 480, 109 NE2d 120, 122, (1952) (prejudicial error to deny alibi witness opportunity on redirect to explain inconsistency between testimony and prior statement); *Com. v. Donovan*, 17 Mass App 83, 87, 455 NE2d 1217, 1220 (1983) (error to exclude questions to defendant on redirect designed to explain inconsistency between his testimony on direct and cross-examination). Generally, however, testimony that reveals the defendant's bad acts is not admissible to explain why there was a delay in complaining or to show the victim's state of mind when he or she made the complaint. See *Com. v. Hynes*, 40 Mass App 927, 928, 664 NE2d 864, 866 (1996) (& citations). But compare *Com. v. Mitchell*, 38 Mass App 184, 195-196, 646 NE2d 1073, 1079 (1995) (witness could explain that he had lied to police out of fear of the defendant who had stabbed him just a few months earlier).

Similarly, it is well established that a witness may explain, modify, or correct damaging testimony that was elicited on cross-examination. *Com. v. Mandeville*, 386 Mass 393, 399-400, 436 NE2d 912, 917 (1982). See, e.g., *Com. v. Jackson*, 384 Mass 572, 584-585, 428 NE2d 289, 296-297 (1981) (prosecutor permitted to elicit facts underlying grants of immunity to witness "to correct any mistaken conclusions the jury may have drawn from defendant's questions as well as to rehabilitate the witness"). But compare *Com. v. Vanderpool*, 367 Mass 743, 748, 328 NE2d 833, 836 (1975) (no error in refusal of judge to allow defendant to explain his adverse reaction in court to testimony of prosecution witness); *Com. v. Barros,* 5 Mass App 887, 369 NE2d 464 (1977) (no error in excluding question calling on witness to comment on his own testimony).

Where the rehabilitation relates to an issue collateral to the merits of the lawsuit, the judge may impose reasonable limits on redirect examination. See *Footit v. Monsees,* 26 Mass App 173, 182, 525 NE2d 423, 429 (1988) (& cases cited).

§6.18 By Proof of Facts Tending to Make Witness's Testimony Credible

A witness's testimony may be corroborated by other admissible evidence of the material facts. See *Com. v. Grammo,* 8 Mass App 447, 455, 395 NE2d 476, 482-483 (1979) (& citation). Ordinarily, however, a witness may not be accredited before his credibility has been impeached. Thus, evidence whose purpose is not to prove material facts but merely to bolster credibility generally may not be admitted unless and until there has been an attack on credibility. See *Krupp v. Craig,* 247 Mass 273, 142 NE 69 (1924) (error to admit insurance policy to corroborate witness's testimony concerning address at particular point in time); *Com. v. Haraldstad,* 16 Mass App 565, 571, 453 NE2d 472, 475 (1983).

It has been held, nonetheless, that corroborating evidence (other than the witness's own prior consistent statements and acts, see §6.16, supra) may be admitted as a matter of discretion. See, e.g., *Com. v. DeBrosky,* 363 Mass 718, 725, 297 NE2d 496, 501 (1973) (hotel registration records admissible to corroborate testimony that defendants were at hotels on particular days); *Com. v. Galvin,* 310 Mass 733, 747, 39 NE2d 656, 663-664 (1942) (witness permitted to testify he had bankbook with him to corroborate testimony that he had consulted it to refresh his recollection as to date he made a particular payment to defendant). But compare *Com. v. Rego,* 360 Mass 385, 391, 274 NE2d 795, 799 (1971) (no abuse of discretion in exclusion of check to corroborate testimony of alibi witness as to presence of defendant at her home). It also has been held that where the "whiff of [the witness's] bias was inherent in his position as an alleged participant in the crime," rehabilitative evidence may be introduced even though no attack on credibility has occurred. *Com. v. Haraldstad,* supra, 16 Mass App at 571-572, 453 NE2d at 476. "If a witness in one case will be a defendant in another case based on the same facts, the presumption that the witness testifies truthfully falls away, and evidence enhancing credibility, if otherwise competent, may be admitted." *Com. v. Haraldstad,* supra, 16 Mass App at 571, 453 NE2d at 475.

§6.19 Prior Identification and Fresh Complaint

The general rule that prior statements of a witness are not admissible to bolster his credibility unless he is impeached has two important exceptions:

§6.19.1 *Prior Identification*

Where a witness identifies the defendant in a criminal case during his direct testimony, he or others may also testify as to a prior consistent identification on prior occasions to corroborate the courtroom identification. See §10.1, infra.

§6.19.2 *Fresh Complaint*

Where the defendant is charged with a sexual assault, evidence of a "fresh complaint" by the complaining witness has long been held admissible as part of the prosecution's case in chief to corroborate the witness's testimony. See *Com. v. Bailey,* 370 Mass 388, 391-397, 348 NE2d 746, 748-752 (1976) (victim's description of rape given in hospital the morning after it occurred; discussion of history and rationale of fresh complaint doctrine); *Com. v. Izzo,* 359 Mass 39, 42-43, 267 NE2d 631, 634-635 (1971) (victim's written statement given at police station several hours after crime); *Com. v. Gangi,* 243 Mass 341, 137 NE 643 (1923) (complaint made by victim to mother immediately after assault); *Com. v. Snow,* 30 Mass App 443, 445-446, 569 NE2d 838, 840 (1991) (citing Text). It is not a requirement for admissibility either that the complaining witness have been impeached, or that the complaint be a spontaneous utterance. See *Com. v. Sherry,* 386 Mass 682, 691 n.5, 437 NE2d 224, 229 n.5 (1982).

The fresh complaint doctrine is justified on the ground that a victim's failure to make a prompt complaint might be viewed by the jury as inconsistent with the charge of sexual assault, and in the absence of evidence of complaint the jury might assume that none was made. *Com. v. Bailey,* supra, 370 Mass at 392, 348 NE2d at 749. In *Com. v. Licata,* 412 Mass 654, 591 NE2d 672 (1992), the Supreme Judicial Court reconsidered and ultimately reaffirmed the rule, explaining:

> Troubled as we are by a doctrine which has its origins in outmoded, and invalid, sexual myths, we need not embrace those views to recognize the unfortunate skepticism that exists as to the truth of allegations of rape where the victim is perceived as having remained silent. Whatever may have been the historical origin of the fresh complaint doctrine, it should now be seen in relation to the common observation . . . that juries tend toward considerable and perhaps inordinate skepticism in rape cases, above all where there is a suggestion of willingness or acquiescence on the part of the victim. Thus, we continue to perceive a need for the fresh complaint doctrine. We cannot ignore the societal tendency to disbelieve sexual assault victims and to presume that a rape victim will make a prompt complaint. Accordingly, we conclude that fresh complaint evidence should remain admissible. . . .

412 Mass at 658, 591 NE2d at 674 (citations and internal quotes omitted). See also *Com. v. Scanlon*, 412 Mass 664, 592 NE2d 1279 (1992).

It has been held that the "defendant's right to show lack of fresh complaint is correlative with the Commonwealth's duty to show that such complaint was made." *Com. v. Pratt*, 42 Mass App 695, 701-702, 679 NE2d 579, 582-583 (1997) (citation omitted) (reversible error to exclude evidence of lack of fresh complaint by complainant in communication to DSS case worker).

Unlike evidence of a prior identification (see §6.19.1), evidence of a fresh complaint is admitted for the limited purpose of corroboration, with appropriate limiting instructions, and not for its full probative value. *Com. v. Scanlon*, supra, 412 Mass at 665 n.1, 592 NE2d at 1281 n.1; *Com. v. Dockham*, 405 Mass 618, 627, 542 NE2d 591, 596-597 (1989); *Com. v. Bailey*, supra, 370 Mass at 396, 348 NE2d at 751; *Com. v. McGrath*, 364 Mass 243, 247, 303 NE2d 108, 111 (1973). *Com. v. Snow*, supra, 30 Mass App at 446, 569 NE2d at 840. The courts have recognized, however, the considerable risk that the jury will use the evidence for substantive purposes, particularly where several fresh complaint witnesses testify. See *Com. v. Trowbridge*, 419 Mass 750, 761, 647 NE2d 413, 421 (1995); *Com. v. Lavalley*, 410 Mass 641, 646, 574 NE2d 1000, 1003-1004 (1991) (five fresh complaint witnesses and a videotape recording of victim's statement to police); *Com. v. Swain*, 36 Mass App 433, 442, 632 NE2d 1848 (1994).

Given the risk that the jury will improperly use fresh complaint testimony, trial judges are advised to instruct the jury at the time the evidence is admitted and again during the final charge that the testimony may not be used as substantive proof of the crime. *Com. v. Licata*, supra, 412 Mass at 660, 591 NE2d at 675; *Com. v. Trowbridge*, supra, 419 Mass at 761, 647 NE2d at 421. See also *Com. v. Goss*, 41 Mass App 929, 673 NE2d 80 (1996) (trial court's failure to instruct jury that testimony of rape victim's mother, although not called as fresh complaint witness, constituted fresh complaint evidence and was thus of limited admissibility required reversal).

On the adequacy of limiting instructions in particular cases, compare *Com. v. Trowbridge*, supra, 419 Mass at 760-762, 647 NE2d at 421-422 (instructions regarding four fresh complaint witnesses inadequate and created substantial risk of miscarriage of justice), *Com. v. Lorette*, 37 Mass App 736, 741, 643 NE2d 67, 70 (1994) (failure to give timely limiting instruction required reversal), and *Com. v. Almon*, 30 Mass App 721, 724-726, 573 NE2d 529, 531-532 (1991) (failure to instruct jury that fresh complaint testimony by several prosecution witnesses could be used only for corroborative purposes created substantial risk of miscarriage of justice, requiring new trial) with *Com. v. Scanlon*, supra, 412 Mass at 673-675, 592 NE2d at 1284-1285 (judge's final instructions, taken with previous explanations regarding limited use of fresh complaint evidence, sufficient to apprise jurors) and *Com. v. Lanning*, 32 Mass App 279, 287-288, 589 NE2d 318, 324 (1992) (failure to instruct jury in final charge did not constitute substantial risk of miscarriage of justice where jury had been previously advised as to limited use). As usual, it is presumed that jurors heed the judge's instructions. See *Com. v. Barbosa*, 399 Mass 841, 849, 507 NE2d 694, 699 (1987).

Unlike some other jurisdictions where only the fact of the complaint is admitted, under Massachusetts practice the entire statement including the details is admissible. *Com. v. Licata*, supra, 412 Mass at 657-659, 591 NE2d at 673-675. "When a witness is limited to testifying only that the victim made a complaint, the jury must rely on that witness's interpretation of the victim's statements. In our view, the better approach remains one which allows a jury to make their own interpretation based on the details of the statements." Id. See also *Com. v. Bailey*, supra, 370 Mass at 392, 348 NE2d at 751 (& citations). By way of limitation, fresh complaint witnesses may testify to "details" only where the testimony contains "no new information" and is "merely a short summary of the testimony the victim herself gave about the criminal events." *Com. v. Snow,* supra, 30 Mass App at 446, 569 NE2d at 840 (citation omitted).

Although only those details to which the victim has testified generally at trial are admissible as corroboration by way of evidence of a prior fresh complaint, *Com. v. Licata,* supra, 412 Mass at 659 n.8, 591 NE2d at 675 n.8, the Supreme Judicial Court "has never insisted that fresh complaint testimony be sanitized to match exactly the testimony of the complaining witness." *Com. v. Scanlon,* supra, 412 Mass at 670, 592 NE2d at 1283 (& cases cited). Witnesses may not testify to details which "add substantively to the complainant's account, and details which are so graphic, colorful, or gruesome as to have an important effect on the jury may be excluded." *Com. v. Snow,* supra, 30 Mass App at 446, 569 NE2d at 840 (& citations). Thus, a police officer should not have been permitted to testify to potentially prejudicial details of the complaint not included in the victim's own testimony. See *Com. v. Scanlon,* supra, 412 Mass at 670, 592 NE2d at 1283. But the fact that a fresh complaint witness gave detailed testimony regarding an incident about which the child complainant had testified more generally did not render the evidence inadmissible. See *Com. v. LeFave,* 407 Mass 927, 941, 556 NE2d 83, 92 (1990). Compare *Com. v. Flebotte,* 417 Mass 348, 351, 630 NE2d 265, 267 (1994) (error to allow fresh complaint testimony as to acts not testified to by child victim), *Com. v. Kirouac,* 405 Mass 557, 564-565, 542 NE2d 270, 274-275 (1989) (videotape of police interview with child victim that included serious criminal conduct not mentioned in her testimony could not be admitted), *Com. v. Demars,* 38 Mass App 596, 650 NE2d 368 (1995) (victim's father's testimony that victim put male doll's face on genitals of female doll exceeded scope of victim's testimony), *Com. v. McCaffrey,* 36 Mass App 583, 585, 633 NE2d 1062, 1064 (mother's testimony regarding additional incident exceeded proper scope), *Com. v. Kerr,* 36 Mass App 505, 632 NE2d 1244 (1994) (detective's testimony relating defendant's threatening statement to complainant and that complainant thought defendant was going to shoot her exceeded permissible scope), and *Com. v. Sugrue*, 34 Mass App 172, 607 NE2d 1045 (1993) (testimony of fresh complaint witnesses concerning incidents other than one testified to by victim was clearly outside permissible bounds of corroborative evidence) with *Com. v. Kirkpatrick*, 423 Mass 436, 444-445, 668 NE2d 790, 795-796 (1996) (police officer's testimony regarding incident of anal sex barely went beyond victim's testimony), *Com. v. Martins*, 38 Mass App 636, 638-639, 650 NE2d 821, 823 (1995) (portions of police officer's testimony that were at variance with victim's did not materially strengthen prosecution's case), *Com. v. Caracino*, 33 Mass App 787, 791-792, 605 NE2d 859, 862-863 (1993) (abuse specialist properly testified to child's complaint describing penile penetration, although victim testified only to digital and lingual penetration), *Com. v. Tingley*, 32 Mass App 706, 709-712, 594 NE2d 546, 548-550 (1992) (additional details and variances between fresh complaint testimony and child victim's did not render testimony inadmissible, but testimony as to incidents not testified to by child improperly admitted), and *Com. v. Coleman*, 30 Mass App 229, 236, 567 NE2d 956, 960 (1991) (discrepancies between fresh complaint testimony and victim's testimony consisted largely of peripheral details).

Fresh complaint evidence may not be used to fill gaps in the prosecution's case. See *Com. v. Scanlon*, supra, 412 Mass at 670, 592 NE2d at 1283 (& citations); *Com. v. Tingley*, supra, 32 Mass App at 710, 594 NE2d at 549; *Com. v. Lanning*, supra, 32 Mass App at 286-287, 589 NE2d at 324; *Com. v. Coleman*, supra, 30 Mass App at 236, 567 NE2d at 960; *Com. v. Gardner*, 30 Mass App 515, 527, 570 NE2d 1033, 1040 (1991) (judge erred in permitting jury to use fresh complaint testimony to supply explanation for failure of complainant to report assault at earlier time). The trial judge must closely watch the details of fresh complaint testimony "to ensure that the limited hearsay exception allowing fresh complaint testimony is not used to put inadmissible and prejudicial evidence into the case." *Com. v.*

Lagacy, 23 Mass App 622, 629, 504 NE2d 674, 679 (1987) (& cases cited). A fresh complaint witness may not testify regarding the credibility of the complainant. See *Com. v. Powers,* 36 Mass App 65, 627 NE2d 953 (1994) and §6.6, supra.

The preliminary question of whether a complaint is sufficiently "fresh" or "prompt" to be presented to the jury lies within the discretion of the trial judge. *Com. v. Montanino,* 409 Mass 500, 508, 567 NE2d 1212, 1216 (1991); *Com. v. McGrath,* supra, 364 Mass at 247, 303 NE2d at 111; *Com. v. Gardner,* supra, 30 Mass App at 524, 570 NE2d at 1038. The trial judge may, but is not required to, conduct voir dire on the complaint to determine promptness. See *Com. v. Lanning,* supra, 32 Mass App at 287, 589 NE2d at 324. If admitted, the jury should be instructed that they may disregard the evidence if they find the complaint was not made "reasonably promptly." *Com. v. Sherry,* supra, 386 Mass at 691, 437 NE2d at 229. See also *Com. v. Amirault,* 404 Mass 221, 230, 535 NE2d 193, 199-200 (1989) (judge should instruct jury that it should evaluate the weight of the fresh complaint testimony by assessing the spontaneity, promptness, and voluntariness of the statement); *Com. v. Densten,* 23 Mass App 981, 503 NE2d 1337 (1987). The ultimate responsibility for determining the freshness of the complaint lies with the jury, and it must be appraised by the trial judge of its proper role in this regard. *Com. v. Montanino,* supra, 409 Mass at 510-511, 567 NE2d at 1218.

It has often been observed that there is no absolute rule as to the time within which a sexual assault victim must make a complaint for that complaint to be a seasonable fresh complaint. *Com. v. Amirault,* supra, 404 Mass at 228, 535 NE2d at 198 (complaint made by child victim 18 months after alleged assault properly admitted as reasonably prompt in exceptional circumstances of case). The linchpin of "freshness" is not spontaneity, but reasonableness. *Com. v. Sherry,* supra. The test is whether the victim's actions were reasonable under the particular circumstances, and the courts "have not insisted on great promptness for fresh complaints in prosecutions involving child sexual abuse." *Com. v. Amirault,* supra, 404 Mass at 228-229, 535 NE2d at 198-199 (& cases cited); *Com. v. Dockham,* supra, 405 Mass at 625-627, 542 NE2d at 595-597; *Com. v. Tingley,* supra, 32 Mass App at 709, 594 NE2d at 548. As one court noted, the "cases involving children would appear to constitute a factually distinct branch of the doctrine that gives special consideration to the natural fear, ignorance and susceptibility to intimidation that is often part of a child's make-up." *Com. v. Lagacy,* supra, 23 Mass App at 626 n.6, 504 NE2d at 677 n.6.

The relationship of victim to assailant, the age of the victim, the defendant's control over the victim, and any threats against or intimidation of the victim are factors to be weighed in assessing the reasonableness of a delayed complaint. *Com. v. Fleury,* 417 Mass 810, 814, 632 NE2d 1230, 1233 (1994). "In cases where a young victim has been under the control of, and in reasonable fear of, a defendant who is a close relative, the promptness of a complaint is usually measured from the date when the victim leaves the defendant's control." *Com. v. Comtois,* 399 Mass 668, 672 n.9, 506 NE2d 503, 506 n.9 (1987). See, e.g., *Com. v. Dockham,* supra, 405 Mass at 626, 545 NE2d at 596 (complaint by four-year-old against his mother and purported father made 11 days after child left abusive setting properly admitted in light of exceptional circumstances).

For cases concluding that a delayed complaint was nonetheless "fresh," see *Com. v. Fleury,* supra, 417 Mass at 813-815, 632 NE2d at 1232-1233 (21-month delay); *Com. v. Thayer,* 418 Mass 130, 134, 634 NE2d 576, 579 (1994) (16-month delay); *Com. v. Scanlon,* supra, 412 Mass at 672, 592 NE2d at 1284 (seven months had elapsed from time of incident and victim had had numerous opportunities to report it); *Com. v. LeFave,* supra, 407 Mass at 930, 556 NE2d at 86 (child's statement 18 months after leaving day care center); *Com. v. McDonough,* 400 Mass 639, 651-653, 511 NE2d 551, 559-560 (1987) (complaint by child three months after father gained custody); *Com. v. Comtois,* supra,

399 Mass at 673-674, 506 NE2d at 506-507 (complaints by two teenage victims two months after they left defendant's home); *Com. v. King*, 387 Mass 464, 473-474, 441 NE2d 248, 253 (1982) (child's statement to police officer one month after she began living apart from defendant); *Com. v. Moreschi*, 38 Mass App 562, 566, 649 NE2d 1132, 1135 (1995) (friend of rape victim could testify that victim told her she was raped by defendant even though rape not mentioned during initial conversations regarding incident); *Com. v. Costello*, 36 Mass App 689, 692-695, 635 NE2d 255, 257-258 (1994) (12-month delay); *Com. v. McKinnon*, 35 Mass App 398, 620 NE2d 792 (1993) (34-month delay in minor rape victim's report); *Com. v. Tingley*, supra, 32 Mass App at 709, 594 NE2d at 548 (ten-month delay by a four-year-old child); *Com. v. Titus*, 32 Mass App 216, 222-223, 587 NE2d 800, 804 (1992) (complaints of child made two months after leaving defendant's home); *Com. v. Hyatt*, 31 Mass App 488, 490-492, 579 NE2d 1365, 1367-1368 (1991) (teenage victim's complaints made two years after event); *Com. v. Souther*, 31 Mass App 219, 222, 575 NE2d 1150, 1153 (1991) (child's complaint to mother nine months after last incident); *Com. v. Rockwood*, 27 Mass App 1137, 538 NE2d 40 (1989) (child's complaints four to six months after incident); *Com. v. Guy*, supra, 24 Mass App at 787-788, 513 NE2d at 704 (three days after incident, where victim was in fear of defendants); *Com. v. Densten*, supra, 23 Mass App at 981, 503 NE2d at 1338 (fresh complaint testimony of special needs child's mother concerning incident 17 days earlier); *Com. v. Gonsalves*, 23 Mass App 184, 186, 499 NE2d 1229, 1231 (1986) (testimony of friend concerning victim's statement several weeks after incident, and revealing more details than three prior statements, noting "[i]t is not at all implausible that feelings of humiliation, embarrassment, and violation of privacy might be particularly forceful in a teenage victim of a male homosexual rape and might account for a delay of several weeks in revealing all the details of the rape"); *Com. v. Lagacy*, supra, 23 Mass App at 624-627, 504 NE2d at 676-678 (complaints made three and

one-half weeks after incident, where victim was young, confused, and apparently in fear of defendant); *Com. v. Adams,* supra, 23 Mass App 534, 535-536, 503 NE2d 1315, 1317 (1987) (statement made by nine-year-old victim to police officer four months after victim first reported incident to mother, in view of victim's age, defendant's close relationship to family, and fact that victim was dependent upon mother to take her to police station); *Com. v. Crowe,* 21 Mass App 456, 479-480, 488 NE2d 780, 794-795 (1986) (statements made by victim hours after rape even though in period between incident and statement victim had seen and conversed with five men, including three police officers, and had not reported rape to any of them).

For cases concluding that a delayed complaint was not admissible, see *Com. v. Montanino,* supra, 409 Mass at 509-510, 567 NE2d at 1217-1218 (victim's complaint against scoutmaster delayed four years, where they did not live in same household, there was no evidence of threats against youth, and the two had no contact for several years); *Com. v. Shiek,* 42 Mass App 209, 675 NE2d 805 (1997) (interval of seven years between first incident and complaint, and 24 to 32 months from last incident); *Com. v. Traynor,* 40 Mass App 527, 666 NE2d 148 (1996) (minor's complaint to mother over two years after acts, where defendant was not authority figure, there were no threats, and no indicia of spontaneity); *Com. v. Perreira,* 38 Mass App 901, 644 NE2d 253 (1995) (complaints made seven years after alleged abuse); *Com. v. Spence,* 38 Mass App 88, 645 NE2d 58 (1995) (complaint made 15 months after alleged incident); *Com. v. Swain,* 36 Mass App 433, 632 NE2d 848 (1994) (six complaints made nine years after incidents began and ten months after last incident); *Com. v. Snow,* 35 Mass App 836, 626 NE2d 888 (1994) (child's reports of alleged abuse six years after acts ended and one year after defendant had left victim's home); *Com. v. Johnson,* 35 Mass App 211, 617 NE2d 1040 (1993) (child's reports of alleged sexual offenses 45 months after offenses); *Com. v. Davids,* 33 Mass App 421, 600 NE2d 1006 (1992) (17-year-old's disclosure to mother and police officer that defendant had abused him eight years before); *Com. v. Gardner*, supra, 30 Mass App at 526-527, 570 NE2d at 1040 (complaint made at least 38 months after alleged assault by victim who had not been threatened and who had moved out of defendant's home day after incident); *Com. v. Dion*, 30 Mass App 406, 413-414, 568 NE2d 1172, 1176-1177 (1991) (complaint made by teenager 18 months after alleged rape, where no evidence of threats or intimidation). See also cases collected in *Com. v. Dion*, supra, 30 Mass App at 416-417, 568 NE2d at 1177-1179, and *Com. v. Gardner*, supra, 30 Mass App at 524-526, 570 NE2d at 1038-1039.

The complaint must be "voluntary" to be admissible, but it may be deemed so even though elicited in part by questions provided they were not suggestive or leading. See, e.g., *Com. v. Amirault*, supra, 404 Mass at 228, 535 NE2d at 198-199 (fresh complaint properly admitted even though child made statements following investigatory interview); *Com. v. McGrath*, supra, 364 Mass at 246-250, 303 NE2d at 111-113 (police questioning); *Com. v. Hanger*, 357 Mass 464, 258 NE2d 555 (1970) (1,500-word account of conversation between police officer and complainant admissible despite fact it was elicited by questions from officer); *Com. v. Caracino*, 33 Mass App 787, 789-791, 605 NE2d 859, 861-862 (1993) (child's complaints properly admitted even though one made in response to pointed questions from abuse specialist in district attorney's office, and other in response to request that she repeat story to mother); *Com. v. Davids*, supra, 33 Mass App at 425-426, 600 NE2d at 1009 (child's complaint properly admitted even though result of persistent questioning by aunt); *Com. v. Lanning*, supra, 32 Mass App at 285, 589 NE2d at 323 (complaint made in course of interviews by social worker and investigator); *Com. v. Tingley*, supra, 32 Mass App at 709, 594 NE2d at 548 (mother's inquiry was sufficiently broad that the child's reply had a spontaneity that did not indicate mere acquiescence).

Fresh complaint evidence has been admitted where the complaint was written rather than oral. See *Com. v. Scanlon*, supra, 412 Mass at 668-669, 592 NE2d at 1282-1283 (note to friend); *Com. v. Graves*, 35 Mass App 76, 87-88, 616 NE2d 817, 824 (1993) (rape victim, who had been referred to portion of her written statement given to police in order to rebut defense counsel's assertion of recent fabrication, properly allowed to read entire statement under doctrine of fresh complaint); *Com. v. Lanning*, supra, 32 Mass App at 286, 589 NE2d at 323 (note given to investigator); *Com. v. Lagacy*, supra, 23 Mass at 625, 504 NE2d at 677 (police officer read victim's written statement to jury). In appropriate circumstances, a tape recording or videotape of the victim's complaint is admissible. See *Com. v. Lavalley*, supra, 410 Mass at 645, 574 NE2d at 1003; *Com. v. Jerome*, 36 Mass App 59, 627 NE2d 948 (1994).

Where a defendant is charged with other offenses that are tried together with the alleged sexual offense, the defendant is entitled to an instruction that the fresh complaint shall be considered only in relation to the sexual offense. *Com. v. Barbosa*, supra, 399 Mass at 849, 507 NE2d at 698-699; *Com. v. Blow*, 370 Mass 401, 404-406, 348 NE2d 794, 796 (1976); *Com. v. Moreschi*, supra, 38 Mass App at 566-569, 649 NE2d at 1135-1137 (because of nature of crimes, impossible to segregate facts only corroborating rape claim). But see *Com. v. Lanning*, supra, 32 Mass App at 286, 589 NE2d at 323 (fact that victim's complaint "might have pertained to acts outside the information provided by the bill of particulars did not require its exclusion, especially in view of the ongoing nature of the defendant's acts").

While a complainant may testify about the fact that she made a complaint to another, the person complained to must be produced as a witness to testify about the complaint and be subject to cross-examination. The complainant may not engage in self-corroboration. See *Com. v Peters*, 429 Mass 22, 28, 705 NE2d 1118, 1122 (1999). The governing principles provide that the complainant may testify only to the fact that a fresh complaint was made and to whom it was made. The complainant should not be allowed to testify about the details of the complaint, although defense counsel may cross-examine about the details. If defense counsel does so, the prosecutor may then go into the details in appropriate redirect examination. Otherwise, the details of the complaint can only be developed by testimony of the fresh complaint witness. *Com. v. Peters,* supra, 429 Mass at 30, 705 NE2d at 1123.

The reaction of third persons to an alleged sexual molestation may not be admitted as fresh complaint testimony. See *Com. v. Figueroa,* 413 Mass 193, 198, 595 NE2d 779, 783 (1992).

There is no per se rule as to how many fresh complaint witnesses may testify. *Com. v. Trowbridge,* supra, 419 Mass. at 761, 647 NE2d at 421; *Com. v. Kirkpatrick,* 423 Mass 436, 445 n.5, 668 NE2d 790, 796 n.5 (1996). The courts have, however, warned against the overuse of such evidence, see *Com. v. Trowbridge,* supra (& citations), and have admonished judges generally with regard to this evidence as follows:

> Trial judges should be cautious in admitting evidence of a fresh complaint. The trial judge should instruct the jury as the evidence is admitted and again during the jury instructions that fresh complaint testimony does not serve as substantive evidence that the crime in fact occurred. The judge should instruct the jury that the purpose of the fresh complaint evidence is to corroborate the victim's testimony, namely, as it relates to the credibility of the victim's testimony at trial. Fresh complaint evidence is corroborative only if it shows that the victim seasonably complained of the attack. Because the evidence is corroborative, the judge may exclude needless repetition of the details of the fresh complaints. When it appears that admission of details would operate unjustly — as by inciting a jury through a needless rehearsal of the particulars of a gruesome crime — the judge may well limit the testimony in his discretion. *Com. v. Licata,* supra, 412 Mass at 660, 591 NE2d at 675 (citations and quotation marks omitted).

> Trial judges should carefully scrutinize evidence of complaints that appear tardy. They should be mindful of the likelihood that the prejudice inherent in the admission of

borderline fresh complaint evidence might outweigh its probative value, particularly since the average jury might have difficulty in understanding and applying fairly the usual limiting instruction. *Com. v. Lagacy*, supra, 23 Mass App at 627, 504 NE2d at 678.

Regarding the admissibility of expert opinion concerning the typical behavior and symptoms of abused persons in conjunction with fresh complaint testimony, the Supreme Judicial Court has further warned: "Notwithstanding the theoretical right of a qualified fresh complaint witness also to testify to the general characteristics of sexually abused children, prosecutors would be well advised to avoid such juxtaposition and, if it occurs, trial judges should be alert to its considerable prejudicial potential." *Com. v. Swain*, supra, 36 Mass App at 444-445. See also *Com. v. Brouillard*, 40 Mass App 448, 665 NE2d 113 (1996) (reversing convictions because testimony of treating therapist, including fresh complaints, improperly bolstered complainants' credibility). For further discussion of the problem of bolstering with regard to expert testimony, see §§7.3, 7.7 and 7.8, infra.

D.   REVIVED AND ENHANCED TESTIMONY

§6.20   Present Recollection Revived

In the event that a witness has difficulty recalling the events about which he is asked to testify, there are three techniques that may be employed to elicit the information. First, leading questions may be used to aid the memory of the witness. See §3.5, supra. Second, the witness's memory may be stimulated by use of an item that revives his or her recollection, as discussed in this section. Third, when the memory of the witness is beyond revival, a document embodying his or her forgotten knowledge may be admissible under the doctrine of past recollection recorded, an exception to the hearsay prohibition. See §8.17, infra. The determination of whether the doctrine of present recollection revived or past recollection recorded is applicable is a question within the sound discretion of the trial judge. *Com. v. Pickles*, 364 Mass 395, 402, 305 NE2d 107 (1973); *Com. v. Dougherty*, 343 Mass 299, 306, 178 NE2d 584 (1961). For an excellent comparison of present recollection revived and past recollection recorded, see *United States v. Riccardi*, 174 F2d 883 (3d Cir 1949).

When a witness is unable to testify as to facts of which he apparently has knowledge, his recollection may be refreshed by showing him a writing or object which then permits him to recall the events from his own memory. The witness may use the writing to refresh his failing memory, but the testimony which the witness gives must be the product of the revived present recollection. *Com. v. Hoffer*, 375 Mass 369, 376, 377 NE2d 685, 690-691 (1978). Compare *Com. v. Walker*, 42 Mass App 14, 19, 674 NE2d 249, 252 (1997) (judge, in refusing to permit defense counsel to show nine-year-old witness social worker's report, could reasonably conclude that witness would not likely understand that document was only being used to refresh recollection).

Anything may be used to refresh a witness's memory, including (in the oft-cited words of Learned Hand) "a song, a scent, a photograph, an allusion, even a past statement known to be false." See *United States v. Rappy*, 157 F2d 964, 967 (2d Cir 1946). See also *Com. v. O'Brien*, 419 Mass 470, 478, 645 NE2d 1170, 1175 (1995); *Com. v. Cheek*, 374 Mass 613, 617-618, 373 NE2d 1161 (1978) (conversation overheard by witness); *Com. v. Hartford*, 346 Mass 482, 487, 194 NE2d 401 (1963) (witness's own prior statement); *Kuklinska v. Maplewood Homes, Inc.*, 336 Mass 489, 495, 146 NE2d 523, 527 (1957) (expert witness used United States Geological Survey map to refresh recollection). Most often it is a writing of some kind, and any writing that in fact refreshes the memory of the witness may be used by him for that purpose. An item typically employed in this manner is a transcript of the witness's grand jury testimony. See, e.g.,

Com. v. Silva, 401 Mass 318, 328, 516 NE2d 161, 168 (1987); *Com. v. Daye,* 393 Mass 55, 65 n.11, 469 NE2d 483, 490 n.11 (1984); *Com. v. Fiore,* 364 Mass 819, 823, 308 NE2d 902, 906 (1974).

It is not necessary that the writing be contemporaneous with the event it records or that it have been made by the witness. *Com. v. McDermott,* 255 Mass 575, 580-581, 152 NE 704, 705-706 (1926). See also *Gordon v. Medford,* 331 Mass 119, 124, 117 NE2d 284, 287 (1954) (plaintiff properly permitted to refresh his memory as to items of damage from paper prepared by another plaintiff); *Com. v. Levine,* 280 Mass 83, 91, 181 NE 851, 854 (1932) (immaterial that witness did not prepare ledger he used to refresh recollection). A witness may not, of course, be permitted to refer to a writing to refresh his recollection with reference to a matter about which he never had any knowledge. See *Kaplan v. Gross,* 223 Mass 152, 156, 111 NE 853, 855 (1916).

As noted above, the evidence admitted is the testimony of the witness, not the memorandum or object used to refresh recollection. *Com. v. Daye,* supra, 393 Mass at 65 n.11, 469 NE2d at 490 n.11; *Com. v. Bookman,* 386 Mass 657, 662 n.8, 436 NE2d 1228, 1232 n.8 (1982); *Com. v. A Juvenile,* 361 Mass 214, 217, 280 NE2d 144, 146 (1972). It is error, therefore, to show the writing to the jury, or to permit the witness to read the document into the record under the guise of refreshing his recollection. See *Com. v. Daye,* supra; *Davis v. Hotels Statler Co.,* 327 Mass 28, 30-31, 97 NE2d 187, 188-189 (1951); *Com. v. Parrotta,* 316 Mass 307, 312, 55 NE2d 456, 459 (1944); *Bendett v. Bendett,* 315 Mass 59, 63-65, 52 NE2d 2, 5 (1943); *Com. v. McDuffie,* 16 Mass App 1016, 455 NE2d 461 (1983) (error to admit medical report used by prosecution witnesses to refresh recollection of rape victim's statement). A frequently recurring question is whether a police officer is reading from his notes rather than testifying from recollection refreshed by those notes. See, e.g., *Com. v. Pike,* 324 Mass 335, 339-340, 86 NE2d 519, 521 (1949); *Com. v. Pickles,* 364 Mass 395, 401-402, 305 NE2d 107, 111 (1973) (no error in permitting police officer on direct examination to read from notes of conversation with defendant because, although judge did not distinguish between present recollection revived and past recollection recorded, it appears judge acted properly on basis of latter doctrine, discussed at §8.17, infra); *Com. v. Dougherty*, 343 Mass 299, 306, 178 NE2d 584, 588 (1961) (same). See also *Com. v. Reynolds*, 338 Mass 130, 138, 154 NE2d 130, 135-136 (1958) (no error where judge permitted, with limiting instructions, portion of testimony at first trial to be read to refresh defendant's recollection on cross-examination).

Because it is the refreshed memory of the witness that constitutes the evidence admitted, it is immaterial that the writing itself may be inadmissible, see *Allwright v. Skillings*, 188 Mass 538, 541, 74 NE 944, 945 (1905), or that the writing is a copy and not the original. *Com. v. Ford*, 130 Mass 64, 66 (1881).

Before attempting to refresh a witness's recollection, it must be established that his memory is clearly exhausted. *Com. v. O'Brien*, supra, 419 Mass at 478, 645 NE2d at 1175. See also *Com. v. Baldwin*, 385 Mass 165, 178-179, 431 NE2d 194, 202-203 (1982) (not sufficient if recollection is simply different from what examiner wishes it to be); *Com. v. Hennigan*, 11 Mass App 979, 417 NE2d 1232 (1981) (no error in refusing to allow tape recording to be used to refresh witness's recollection where witness had no failure of memory, indeed his testimony was unequivocal).

Under Massachusetts practice, opposing counsel is not entitled to inspect a writing used to refresh recollection on the witness stand *before* it is shown to the witness, but is entitled to do so afterwards and before cross-examination so that he may raise the question of whether it refreshes the witness's memory as claimed. *Com. v. O'Brien*, supra, 419 Mass at 478, 645 NE2d at 1175; *Begin's Case*, 354 Mass 594, 597, 238 NE2d 864, 866-867 (1968); *Jensen v. McEldowney*, 341 Mass 485, 486-487, 170 NE2d 472, 473 (1960); *Com. v. Greenberg*, 339 Mass 557, 581, 160 NE2d 181, 196 (1959). Opposing counsel may not, as of right, examine documents used by a witness to refresh his recollection *prior to* the witness's taking the stand, but the judge may permit such examination as a matter of discretion. See *Leonard v. Taylor*, 315 Mass 580, 583-584, 53 NE2d 705, 707 (1944) (discussed at §3.13.2, supra). Documents used by a witness to refresh recollection prior to taking the stand may also be sought through pretrial discovery. Mass R Civ P 26-37; Mass R Crim P 14.

A document used to refresh the memory of a witness *prior to* trial and examined upon demand by opposing counsel at trial may become admissible at the option of the party who produced the document under the doctrine of curative admissibility. See §3.13.2, supra. The doctrine does not, however, apply to the examination of documents used by the witness *while testifying* at trial. Neither inspection of such a document by opposing counsel in court nor use of it during cross-examination makes the document admissible in evidence at the option of the proponent. Id. See also *Com. v. Beaulieu*, 333 Mass 640, 648-650, 133 NE2d 226, 231-232 (1955).

A document used by a witness to refresh recollection and provided to opposing counsel may be introduced by the latter to show that it could not or did not aid the witness in any legitimate way. *Bendett v. Bendett*, supra, 315 Mass at 62, 52 NE2d at 5.

When materials otherwise protected by the work product doctrine are used by the examiner to refresh a witness's recollection on the stand, the protection afforded by the work product doctrine is waived and the opponent's attorney is entitled to inspect the writing. See *Com. v. O'Brien*, supra, 419 Mass at 478, 645 NE2d at 1175.

Proposed Mass R Evid 612 (which is in substance the same as Fed R Evid 612) is consistent with present practice in providing that the adverse party is entitled to examine any writing or object used by the witness while testifying to refresh his memory, but leaving the time of inspection to the court's discretion.[1] Items used by the witness before testifying may under the rule be ordered produced within the discretion of the court.[2] The party obtaining the writing or object may use it to cross-examine the witness and may introduce into evidence those portions that relate to the witness's testimony.[3]

In criminal cases, the right to inspect prior statements or notes used to refresh recollection is further provided by way of decisional law and court rules. Notes used by a witness to refresh recollection prior to taking the stand may be inspected in the discretion of the trial judge without a formal demand and, where the request occurs during voir dire (and thus not in a situation where counsel may be

---

§6.20   [1] "If, while testifying, a witness uses a writing or object to refresh his memory, an adverse party is entitled to have the writing or object produced at the trial, hearing, or deposition in which the witness is testifying." PMRE 612(a). "This rule leaves the time of inspection to the court's discretion." Advisory Committee Note to R 612.

[2] "If, before testifying, a witness uses a writing or object to refresh his memory for the purpose of testifying and the court in its discretion determines that the interests of justice so require, an adverse party is entitled to have the writing or object produced, if practicable, at the trial, hearing, or deposition in which the witness is testifying." PMRE 612(b).

[3] Rule 612(c) provides:

A party entitled to have a writing or object produced under this rule is entitled to inspect it, to cross-examine the witness thereon, and to introduce in evidence those portions which relate to the testimony of the witness. If production of the writing or object at the trial, hearing, or deposition is impracticable, the court may order it made available for inspection. If it is claimed that the writing or object contains matters not related to the subject matter of the testimony the court shall examine the writing or object in camera, excise any portions not so related, and order delivery of the remainder to the party entitled thereto. Any portion withheld over objections shall be preserved and made available to the appellate court in the event of an appeal. If a writing is not produced, made available for inspection, or delivered pursuant to order under this rule, the court shall make any order justice requires, except that in criminal cases when the state elects not to comply, the order shall be one striking the testimony or, if the court in its discretion determines that the interests of justice so require, declaring a mistrial.

"The provisions for inspection, cross-examination, and introduction are for the limited purpose of showing that the writing or object did not or could not have refreshed the witness's memory." Advisory Committee Note to R 612 (citation omitted).

grandstanding), "there are substantial reasons for exercising discretion in favor of the inspection." *Com. v. Marsh*, 354 Mass 713, 721-722, 242 NE2d 545, 550 (1968). Compare *Com. v. Walker*, 370 Mass 548, 562-563, 350 NE2d 678, 689 (1976) ("Where notes, memoranda, tapes or the like have not been used to refresh a witness's recollection, they, likewise, are not automatically to be made available to the defense."); *Com. v. Guerro*, 357 Mass 741, 756-757, 260 NE2d 190, 199 (1970) (judge not required to order production of entire file of notations and worksheet of police officer witnesses where there was no indication they were used to refresh recollection). See also Mass R Crim P 23.

§6.21 Hypnotically Enhanced Testimony

Testimony of a witness that has been enhanced or aided by use of hypnotism may not be admitted as probative evidence in the trial of a criminal case in the Massachusetts courts. See *Com. v. Kater*, 409 Mass 433, 567 NE2d 885 (1991) (*Kater III*) (& cases cited). As the court explained in *Kater I*, "testimony by a witness as to a fact that became available following hypnosis is generally inadmissible in the trial of criminal cases in the Commonwealth. . . . Hypnosis simply lacks general acceptability by experts in the field as a reliable method of enhancing the memory of a witness." *Com. v. Kater*, 388 Mass 519, 520-521, 447 NE2d 1190, 1193 (1983).

A witness may, however, testify based on what he knew before hypnosis. Id. The question of the admissibility of testimony from a witness who has been hypnotized must be resolved by the trial judge; "before admitting proffered testimony, the judge must be satisfied by a preponderance of the evidence presented at a hearing that the testimony is based on prehypnotic memory." *Com. v. Kater*, 394 Mass 531, 533, 476 NE2d 593, 594 (1985) (*Kater II*). For a description of the required procedures, see *Kater III*, supra, 409 Mass at

441-442, 567 NE2d at 890-891. See also *Com. v. Burke*, 20 Mass App 489, 481 NE2d 494 (1985).

The judge's findings on the issue of separating pre-hypnotic memory from post-hypnotic memory are accorded substantial deference and will be accepted absent clear error. *Com. v. Kater*, 412 Mass 800, 802, 592 NE2d 1328, 1329-1330 (1992) (*Kater IV*) (court properly suppressed testimony by witnesses identifying defendant's automobile where there was no evidentiary basis to conclude they could have identified automobile prior to hypnosis).

A criminal defendant has a constitutional right to testify to facts remembered after hypnosis. *Rock v. Arkansas*, 483 US 44, 107 S Ct 2704, 97 L Ed 2d 37 (1987); *Kater I*, supra, 388 Mass at 528-529 n.6, 447 NE2d 1197 n.6.

OPINION and EXPERT EVIDENCE

A.   OPINION RULE — GENERAL PRINCIPLES

§7.1   Traditional Rule

There are significant differences among legal jurisdictions in the scope of testimony that is admissible against an objection that it constitutes lay "opinion." Similarly, the rules vary substantially with respect to the subject matter on which experts may offer opinions, the permissible basis for such opinions, and the manner in which such testimony may be given.

For a general discussion of the history, theory, and nature of the opinion rule, see Wigmore §§1917-1929 (Chad rev 1978). The Proposed Massachusetts Rules of Evidence and the Federal Rules of Evidence incorporate several significant departures from prior Massachusetts practice. While the rules are not wholly discordant with Massachusetts law, their general impact is to permit a more flexible approach to the admissibility of opinion evidence by lay and expert witnesses. The focus of this chapter is on Massachusetts practice, but we shall note significant differences with the Federal Rules as various topics are discussed.

The so-called opinion rule traditionally requires that the witness testify as to facts known or observed by him and not give an opinion based on those facts. *DiMarzo v. American Mutual Insurance Co.*, 389 Mass 85, 103-104, 449 NE2d 1189, 1201 (1983) (witness properly testified to existence of custom and usage as a factual matter, but legal effect of custom or usage may not be proven by opinion); *Barrie v. Quinby*, 206 Mass 259, 265, 92 NE 451, 454 (1910).

The implication of the rule — that there is a clear distinction between fact and opinion — is not warranted by logic, experience, or the reported decisions. See *Gorham v. Moor*, 197 Mass 522, 84 NE 436 (1908). All testimony is to some extent an assertion of inference, or opinion, drawn by the witness from his or her perceptions. Courts tend to call testimony "fact" if it describes the witness's experience in terms of the most elemental logical ingredients that human nature and the English language permit — in terms of the words heard and the acts seen by the witness and of other sensory experiences of the witness. The further testimony goes in the direction of articulating inferences drawn from such elemental ingredients, the more likely it is to be ruled an "opinion."[1]

The purpose of the traditional opinion rule is to reserve for the jury the function of making inferences whenever that is feasible. The rule provides that where: (1) the witness can cast his or her knowledge in the form of facts; and (2) the jury is equipped to draw the inference from such facts, the witness may not usurp the province of the jury by drawing the inference. See *New England Glass Co. v. Lovell*, 61 Mass (7 Cush) 319 (1851).

For similar reasons, lay and expert witnesses are precluded from giving an opinion that involves a conclusion of law or in regard to a mixed question of fact and law. Thus, no witness may express an opinion or belief on the guilt or innocence of a party, the competency of a testator to make a will, or similar matters. *Perry v. Medeiros*, 369 Mass 836, 343 NE2d 859 (1976) (barring opinion interpreting building code and stating whether certain condition was in violation thereof); *Com. v. Brady*, 370 Mass 630, 351 NE2d 199 (1976)

---

§7.1 [1]The words in which the witness casts her testimony are not conclusive with respect to whether she has testified to facts or opinion. See, e.g., *Doherty v. Belmont*, 396 Mass 271, 485 NE2d 183 (1985) (plaintiff's testimony she "presumed" she tripped over spot where pipe had been removed held not unduly speculative, when in other testimony she stated she tripped over a bump, and any uncertainty goes to weight of evidence, not admissibility).

(insurance agent precluded from testifying as to the legal sufficiency of defendant's coverage); *S. D. Shaw & Sons v. Joseph Rugo, Inc.,* 343 Mass 635, 180 NE2d 446 (1962) (whether certain work is included in particular construction specification); *May v. Bradlee,* 127 Mass 414, 419 (1879) (competency of testator).

The opinion rule applies to most hearsay declarations. Evidence as to a hearsay declaration, although within a hearsay exception, is barred if the declaration is in the form of improper opinion. It should be remembered, however, that the opinion rule does not apply to evidentiary admissions (see §8.2.5) or to reputation evidence (see §8.19). Also, the courts are likely to be somewhat more lenient in cases where the declarant did not have the aid of an attorney in phrasing his declaration in non-opinion form. *Old Colony Trust Co. v. Shaw,* 348 Mass 212, 217-218, 202 NE2d 785, 790 (1964).

§7.2 Federal Rules

The Federal Rules allow substantially greater latitude than traditional Massachusetts practice in the reception of opinions by lay witnesses. Fed R Evid 701 provides:

> If the witness is not testifying as an expert, his testimony in the form of opinions or inferences is limited to those opinions or inferences which are (a) rationally based on the perception of the witness and (b) helpful to a clear understanding of his testimony or the determination of a fact in issue.

Proposed Mass R Evid 701 is the same as the federal rule. The intent of Rule 701 is to liberalize the admissibility of lay opinion testimony subject to the sound discretion of the trial judge. Rule 701 recognizes that need or convenience may justify the admission of lay opinion testimony yet it leaves room for the discretionary requirement of specific factual testimony that may advance the inquiry. The short-hand expression rule (collective fact doctrine), discussed infra, is a reflection of a similar pragmatic approach. To the extent that Rule 701 is more flexible, its adoption might cause relaxation in practice of the stricter aspects of the opinion rule in Massachusetts — e.g., the limitations on lay opinion testimony on matters such as sanity.

§7.3   Opinions on Ultimate Issues

§7.3.1   Opinion on Ultimate Issue Is Generally Permissible

In its strictest formulation, the traditional opinion rule precludes a witness from giving an opinion on the "ultimate issue" in a case, although the various decisions give no clear guideline as to the meaning of this proscription. Insofar as this rule has meaning, it seems to preclude a witness from giving an opinion as to the legal significance of facts in issue in such a manner as to interfere with the province of the jury. See *Com. v. Coleman*, 366 Mass 705, 322 NE2d 407 (1975) (medical examiner improperly allowed to testify that death was a homicide, but error not prejudicial); *DeCanio v. School Committee of Boston*, 358 Mass 116, 260 NE2d 676 (1970) (proper to exclude expert testimony that suspension and dismissal of probationary teachers "would have no legitimate educational purpose" as such was opinion on ultimate issue of whether statutes in issue were patently arbitrary); *Foley v. Hotel Touraine Co.*, 326 Mass 742, 96 NE2d 698 (1951) (treasurer of corporate defendant precluded from testifying whether assistant manager had "ostensible authority" to represent hotel); *Puopolo v. Honda Motor Co., Ltd.*, 41 Mass App 96, 668 NE2d 855 (1996) (suggesting that proffered opinion that an automobile without a starter interlock was "unreasonably dangerous" was properly excluded as a question framed in almost identical language to a special question submitted to the jury, holding that, in any event, exclusion of the testimony was not reversible error because expert's opinion on the ultimate issue was implicit in his answers to other questions); *Matteo v. Livingstone*, 40 Mass App 658, 666 NE2d 1309 (1996) (proper to exclude expert's opinion that a porch, as built and maintained, was "unsafe," as this issue was one the jury might decide without expert assistance) (Text cited).

Neither the rationales nor the holdings of the decided cases have been consistent. Exceptions to strict enforcement of the ultimate issue rule have always been made and in recent years the rule has been relaxed generally. In cases involving expert testimony, the Supreme Judicial Court has repeatedly held that an expert may testify on matters within the witness's field of expertise whenever it will aid the jury in reaching a decision, even if the expert's opinion touches on the ultimate issues that the jury must decide. See, e.g., *Com. v. Cruz*, 413 Mass 686, 689, 602 NE2d 1089, 1091 (1992) (in murder case where defense was inability to form intent, error to exclude expert testimony that defendant's blood alcohol level would have severely affected his judgment); *Sacco v. Roupenian*, 409 Mass 25, 564 NE2d 386 (1990) (whether defendant doctor should have diagnosed breast cancer); *Martel v. MBTA*, 403 Mass 1, 525 NE2d 662 (1988) (whether driver could have prevented accident).

For illustrative cases ruling that opinions reaching the ultimate issue are admissible, see *Com. v. Cyr*, 425 Mass 89, 96, 679 NE2d 550, 556 (1997) (medical examiner properly permitted to testify to presence of "defensive wounds"); *Com. v. Allen*, 395 Mass 448, 480 NE2d 630 (1985) (physician's opinion on cause of defendant's black eyes properly admitted); *Simon v. Solomon*, 385 Mass 91, 431 NE2d 556 (1982) (expert opinion that plaintiff tenant appeared sincere and honest admissible if it will aid jury in reaching a decision); *Everett v. Bucky Warren, Inc.*, 376 Mass 280, 380 NE2d 653 (1978) (neurosurgeon with extensive experience in sports medicine properly allowed to give opinion as to relative safety of two types of hockey helmets); *Com. v.*

Campbell, 375 Mass 308, 376 NE2d 872 (1978) (expert allowed to testify that wound was the result of a "purposeful" thrust with knife; if error, not prejudicial); *Com. v. La Corte*, 373 Mass 700, 369 NE2d 1006 (1978) (expert testimony that fingerprints on incriminating evidence were "identical" with those of defendant held to be proper and not to be usurping function of the jury); *Foreign Car Center, Inc. v. Salem Suede, Inc.*, 40 Mass App 15, 21, 660 NE2d 687, 693 (1996) (error to exclude expert testimony regarding whether company's manufacturing and emissions control equipment was "reasonable and appropriate"); *Com. v. Almeida*, 34 Mass App 901, 605 NE2d 1251 (1993) (FBI photo analyst properly permitted to testify that jacket on bank surveillance film was the same as one in evidence, seized from defendant); *Welch v. Keene Corp.*, 31 Mass App 157, 575 NE2d 766 (1991) (opinion about appropriate warnings on dangerous product); *Gleason v. Source Perrier, S.A.*, 28 Mass App 561, 553 NE2d 544 (1990) (opinions of doctor as to details of how glass fragment entered plaintiff's eye improperly excluded, however, error held harmless); *Burns v. 21 Combined Insurance Co. of America*, 6 Mass App 86, 373 NE2d 1189 (1978) (medical expert properly permitted to give opinion regarding date of plaintiff's total disability).

In some cases where the witness's evidence touches the ultimate issue, the testimony in dispute has been held admissible on the rationale that it did not constitute an opinion. See *Sherman v. MTA*, 345 Mass 777, 189 NE2d 536 (1963) (questioning of bus driver as to range of vision from operator's seat did not call for an opinion on the ultimate issue); *Com. v. Barrasso*, 342 Mass 680, 175 NE2d 251 (1961) (witness properly permitted to testify whether money paid to defendant was a "loan;" opinion rule not discussed); *Bachand v. Vidal*, 328 Mass 97, 101 NE2d 884 (1951) ("Was the insurance in effect?" deemed a proper question eliciting a fact and not opinion as to legal status of policy); *Robinson v. Springfield Street Railway*, 211 Mass 483, 98 NE 576 (1912) ("Was there anything you could have done that you didn't do to have avoided this collision?" a proper question eliciting facts and not opinion).

§7.3.2 Opinions about Credibility of Witnesses

A witness is not permitted to express an opinion on the credibility of other witnesses. *Com. v. Reed*, 417 Mass 558, 631 NE2d 552 (1994) (defendant not entitled to offer expert testimony on either witness's ability or willingness to tell the truth, hence defendant not entitled to discovery of witness's psychiatric files in order to obtain expert testimony on his veracity) (Text cited); *Com. v. Sires*, 413 Mass 292, 304, 596 NE2d 1018, 1026 (1992) (not error to exclude expert's testimony about defendant's state of mind on morning after killing, where it could have been viewed as opinion that defendant told the truth as to how much alcohol he drank); *Simon v. Solomon*, 385 Mass 91, 431 NE2d 556 (1982) (opinion on credibility of witnesses in eviction proceeding not admissible, but no error where judge so instructed jury and limited expert testimony to explanation of basis of his opinion); *Com. v. Syrafos*, 38 Mass App Ct 211, 646 NE2d 429) (1995) (expert could not give opinion as to whether sexual intercourse was consensual or forced, or render an opinion as to the victim's credibility); *Com. v. Powers*, 36 Mass App 65, 627 NE2d 953 (1994) (reversal required due to substantial risk of miscarriage of justice where fresh complaint witnesses testified without objection that they believed complaining witness). The special problems of "vouching" by expert witnesses in child abuse cases are discussed in §7.8.4.

§7.3.3 Opinions about Guilt of Criminal
Defendant

Opinions concerning the identity of a suspect or a perpetrator of a crime are normally irrelevant in a criminal trial. *Com. v. Lennon*, 399 Mass 443, 445, 504 NE2d 1051, 1053 (1987) (opinion by victim's wife that defendant was her husband's killer should have been excluded, but error harmless under circumstances of this trial) (& citations); *Com. v. Garcia*, 46 Mass App 466, 707 NE2d 328 (1999) (officer not qualified to give legal opinion on whether he had probable cause, court notes defendant's argument that question approached comment on his guilt). Such evidence may be admissible for an oblique purpose, however. See *Com. v. Miller*, 361 Mass 644, 282 NE2d 394 (1972) (evidence that police knew certain people suspected defendant, admissible, not to prove guilt, but for limited purpose of justifying undercover activity, and thus to rebut entrapment claim).

Because it amounts to a comment on the guilt of a defendant, it is impermissible for a police officer testifying as an expert to state that a given set of facts constituted a drug transaction, or that he observed a drug transaction taking place. *Com. v. Barbosa*, 421 Mass 547, 658 NE2d 966 (1995) (narcotics officer's testimony that drug transaction had taken place constituted comment on defendant's guilt and should not have been admitted; error harmless given strength of prosecution's case); *Com. v. Woods*, 419 Mass 366, 645 NE2d 1153 (1995) (same); *Com. v. Griffith*, 45 Mass App 784, 702 NE2d 17 (1998) (such testimony constituted part of a pattern of prosecutorial overreaching in the case); *Com. v. Lovejoy*, 39 Mass App 930, 656 NE2d 914 (1995) (officers' testimony that defendant's actions constituted a drug transaction and that defendant had swallowed cocaine constituted opinion on guilt of defendant and reversible error). A persuasive argument may be made that prosecutors should not be permitted to circumvent this rule by asking the officer whether the observations he made were "consistent with" a drug transaction. *Com. v. Tanner*, 45 Mass App 576, 581, 700 NE2d 282, 286 (1998) ("such semantical differences almost certainly make no difference to jurors"). As the court noted in *Tanner*, "The better practice in drug cases, especially when an expert is a percipient witness, is to confine opinion testimony to the explanation of specific unusual or cryptic conduct, without stating, in any form, whether such conduct amounts to a criminal offense." 45 Mass App at 581, 700 NE2d at 287.

It is not permissible to ask an expert for an opinion regarding the defendant's intent. *Com. v. Santiago*, 41 Mass App 916, 670 NE2d 199 (1996) (permissible to ask veteran detective whether a given amount of heroin was inconsistent with personal use, but error to permit him to testify that heroin "was intended for" distribution).

§7.3.4   *Rape and Sexual Abuse Cases*

In rape and sexual abuse cases, there are significant inconsistencies in the reported decisions concerning whether expert testimony improperly reached the ultimate issue. One line of cases appears to hold clearly that an expert witness may not express an opinion directly on the question of whether a rape, forcible assault, or sexual assault occurred. *Com. v. Federico*, 425 Mass 844, 849, 683 NE2d 1035, 1039 (1997); *Com. v. Colin C.*, 419 Mass 54, 643 NE2d 19 (1994) (error to permit expert testimony that children were sexually abused, noting distinction in cases between expert testimony relating generally to behavioral characteristics of sexual assault and sexual abuse victims, and testimony that an alleged victim was in fact sexually assaulted); *Com. v. Gardner*, 350 Mass 664, 216 NE2d 558 (1966) (reversible error where gynecologist allowed to give opinion that there had been "forcible entry" in rape prosecution); *Com. v. LaCaprucia*, 41 Mass App 496, 671 NE2d 984 (1996) (error to permit expert to give characteristic sexual profile testimony that presented defendant's family situation as prone to sexual abuse); *Com. v. Baldwin*, 24 Mass App Ct 200, 509 NE2d 4 (1987) (admission of portion of hospital record containing diagnosis of "sexual molestation" was reversible error); *Com. v. Mendrala*, 20 Mass App Ct 398,

480 NE2d 1039 (1985) (expert may not be asked directly whether a rape or sexual assault has occurred). Cf. *Com. v. McNickles*, 22 Mass App Ct 114, 491 NE2d 662 (1986) (doctor's "diagnosis" of "sexual assault" was improper, but reversal not required where curative instruction was given).[1]

Despite these cases, however, on occasion opinions touching in one way or another on the ultimate issue have been permitted. See *Com. v. Montmeny*, 360 Mass 526, 276 NE2d 688 (1971) (permissible for the prosecutor to ask a physician whether the observations he had made during his physical examination were "consistent with the history" [of rape] he had taken from the victim); *Com. v. Lanning*, 32 Mass App 279, 288, 589 NE2d 318, 324 (1992) (error, if any, was harmless where doctor testified hymenal ring was intact, leading to conclusion full penetration had not occurred, but observations were consistent with insertion of tip of penis into complainant's genitalia); *Com. v. Lewandowski*, 22 Mass App Ct 148, 491 NE2d 670 (1986) (prosecution's expert, a pediatrician, properly permitted to testify that results of his examination of the victim were consistent with sexual molestation); *Com. v. Howard*, 355 Mass 526, 246 NE2d 419 (1969) (doctor's testimony that the probable cause of a widening in the private area of a girl was male organ penetration, interpreted as equivalent to testimony that the physical condition observed was consistent with male penetration, held no error).

---

§7.3 [1] If the expert witness limits his testimony to observations made during his physical examination, and expresses no opinion on whether the alleged victim was "raped," the testimony is clearly admissible. *Com. v. Crichlow*, 30 Mass App Ct 901, 565 NE2d 816 (1991). See *Com. v. Wise*, 39 Mass App 922, 655 NE2d 643 (1995) (where medical records included notation "here for molestation rape evaluation" and contained heading "Record of Possible Sexual Assault," but contained no opinion by medical provider about whether sexual assault occurred, not error to admit them).

§7.3.5   Federal Rule 704 and Proposed
Massachusetts Rule 704

The Federal Rules of Evidence have explicitly abolished the ultimate issue rule, with the exception of testimony regarding sanity in a criminal case. Fed R Evid 704 provides:

Opinion on Ultimate Issue

(a) Except as provided in subdivision (b), testimony in the form of an opinion or inference otherwise admissible is not objectionable because it embraces an ultimate issue to be decided by the trier of fact.

(b) No expert witness testifying with respect to the mental state or condition of a defendant in a criminal case may state an opinion or inference as to whether the defendant did or did not have the mental state or condition constituting an element of the crime charged or of a defense thereto. Such ultimate issues are matters for the trier of fact alone.

Proposed Mass R Evid 704 is identical to paragraph (a) of the Federal Rule. There are two basic reasons for the relaxation of the ultimate issue rule: (1) the rule proved difficult to apply in that the distinction between ultimate and non-ultimate issues was often impossible to make; and (2) the rationale for the rule — that the rule usurped the province of the jury — is not justified in that the jury is free to disregard opinion testimony and draw its own conclusions. Rule 704 follows the basic approach of modern opinion rules, which is to admit opinions when admission is helpful to the trier of fact.

B.   LIMITATIONS ON THE OPINION RULE

§7.4   Rationale for Shorthand Expressions

Facts from which the jury is to draw an inference often cannot be described in testimony as precisely as they appeared to the witness. This may be because the witness's perception was a "composite" one — such as the perception of speed — that registered in the mind only in the form of a conclusion. Or it may be because the witness possessed certain knowledge — such as the mannerisms of a drunken person — that can reasonably be translated into language only in conclusory terms. In such cases, if the jury is to get the information at all, the witness must be permitted to articulate his or her knowledge in the form of conclusions. The general rule excluding opinion evidence is relaxed by a doctrine allowing shorthand expressions based upon the practical necessity that evidence as to such matters otherwise may be difficult or impossible to obtain. *Com. v. Sandler*, 368 Mass 729, 335 NE2d 903 (1975); *Com. v. Tracy*, 349 Mass 87, 95, 207 NE2d 16, 21 (1965).

When necessity dictates that shorthand expressions be allowed, the rule is that a conclusion is proper provided that:

(1)   the conclusion conveys a definite conception of facts;

(2)   the witness has personal knowledge of such foundation facts; and

(3)   the conclusion is one that people in general are capable of drawing.

Com. v. Sturtivant, 117 Mass 122 (1875). Such evidence may not be admissible if the subject matter to which it relates can be reproduced or described to the jury precisely as it appeared to the witness at the time. *Com. v. Austin*, 421 Mass 357, 366, 657 NE2d 458, 463 (1995) (error to allow non-expert to testify that defendant was the man in videotape when tape was available to jury); *Com. v. Smith*, 17 Mass App 918, 920-921, 456 NE2d 760, 763 (1983) (Text cited). Such opinions are often called conclusions of fact or shorthand expressions. The rule under which such opinions are admitted is sometimes called the collective facts doctrine. Such conclusions of fact are admissible even if they are not

reached at the time of the observation. *Copithorn v. Boston &
M.R.R. Co.*, 309 Mass 363, 366-367, 35 NE2d 254, 255-256
(1941).

§7.5 Examples of Shorthand Expressions

Testimony as to speed may be a shorthand expression.
Speed is an inference from distance, time, sound, dust trail,
and so on; yet the knowledge of a witness who perceived a
moving automobile cannot meaningfully be cast in a form
more elemental than speed. A conclusion as to speed
conveys a definite conception of facts and is one that jurors
in general are capable of drawing. A witness may give his
estimate in terms of miles per hour, *Snow v. Sulkoski*, 345
Mass 766, 186 NE2d 822 (1962) and *Com. v. Charland*, 338
Mass 742, 157 NE2d 538 (1959), or in terms of comparison
between two vehicles — e.g., that one vehicle was moving
"considerably faster" than another. *Sax v. Horn*, 274 Mass
428, 174 NE 673 (1931).

The observations of a witness as to the manner of
operation of a motor vehicle are also admissible. *Cushman v.
Boston, W. & N.Y. Street Railway Co.*, 319 Mass 177, 179, 65
NE2d 6, 8 (1946) (bus started with unusual jerk or jolt
worse than witness had ever experienced before); *McGrath
v. Fash*, 244 Mass 327, 139 NE 303 (1923) (truck appeared
to be "out of control of driver").

Matters relating to distance, size, color, weight, time,
and other similar phenomena are within the doctrine of
shorthand expressions described in *Com. v. Sturtivant*,
supra. See *Com. v. Olszewski*, 401 Mass 749, 519 NE2d 587
(1988) (police officer permitted to testify as lay witness that
chrome strip came from defendant's vehicle); *Com. v.
Robertson*, 357 Mass 559, 259 NE2d 553 (1970) (sound heard
was like that of people wrestling and falling to floor); *Com.
v. LePage*, 352 Mass 403, 418, 226 NE2d 200, 210 (1967)
(officer permitted to describe footprints in snow as "fresh");
Com. v. Cataldo, 326 Mass 373, 94 NE2d 761 (1950) (dust on

a criminal defendant was "similar to the dust one might get on oneself from the mortar on bricks"); *Com. v. Brusgulis*, 41 Mass App 386, 670 NE2d 207 (1996); *Com. v. Lopes*, 34 Mass App 179, 608 NE2d 749 (1993) (victim's mother permitted to testify that defendant had a gun because he held his hand in his pocket in a certain way).

The human features, likewise, are not capable of accurate description so as to enable the jury to determine whether the person the witness saw is the person the jury has before it. Thus, witnesses are permitted to testify as to the identity of persons whom they have seen. *Com. v. Kennedy*, 170 Mass 18, 24, 48 NE 770, 772 (1897). Cf. *Com. v. Gagnon*, 16 Mass App Ct 110, 127-128, 449 NE2d 686, 696 (1983) (where defendants had altered their appearance, there was no error in allowing police detective to testify that photographs taken by bank surveillance camera included photographs of the defendants); *Com. v. Bourgeois*, 391 Mass 869, 465 NE2d 1180 (1984) (Supreme Judicial Court explicitly agreed with Appeals Court on this issue). See Chapter 10.

Witnesses may also describe the emotional, mental, or physical condition of another in terms of summary description. See, e.g., *Proulx v. Basbanes*, 354 Mass 559, 238 NE2d 531 (1968) (nervous condition of plaintiff described); *Luz v. Stop & Shop, Inc. of Peabody*, 348 Mass 198, 208, 202 NE2d 771, 777 (1964) (driver of car characterized as "confused"); *Com. v. Harrison*, 342 Mass 279, 285, 173 NE2d 87, 93 (1961) (defendant described as "angry" and "upset"); *Kane v. Fields Corner Grille, Inc.*, 341 Mass 640, 647, 171 NE2d 287, 292 (1961) (person described as "boisterous" and having "an arrogant manner"); *Vieira v. East Taunton Street Railway Co.*, 320 Mass 547, 70 NE2d 841 (1947) (person had "failed" mentally or physically within a given period of time); *Com. v. Russell*, 38 Mass App 199, 646 NE2d 760 (1995) (victim described as angry and upset) (Text cited). Whether a person was drunk or intoxicated is also within the category of permissible summary description. *Com. v. Atencio*, 12 Mass App 747, 429 NE2d 37 (1981) (Text cited).

A lay witness, however, may not testify that he or she has a disease, the diagnosis of which requires expert knowledge. *Com. v. White*, 329 Mass 51, 106 NE2d 419 (1952) (syphilis). Similarly, he or she may not testify as to the cause of a physical or mental condition when that cause is a matter of expert medical knowledge. *Jones v. Spering*, 334 Mass 458, 136 NE2d 217 (1956) (cause of nervous breakdown). A criminal defendant may, however, testify to his feelings and recent history of psychiatric care to support an insanity defense. *Com. v. Guadalupe*, 401 Mass 372, 516 NE2d 1159 (1987) (error to exclude defendant's testimony that he used to hear noises, had visited a mental health clinic very shortly before alleged crime, and he felt better now because he was seeing a psychiatrist).[1]

In many states, a witness may state the meaning he drew from a conversation, even if he does not remember what was said or by whom. See Wigmore §1969 (Chad rev 1978). But in Massachusetts, the witness may not testify to his opinion of the effect of a conversation. *Ives v. Hamlin*, 59 Mass (5 Cush) 534 (1850). A witness should attempt to relate the words of the parties to a conversation as accurately as he can remember them. However, this does not mean that the witness is required to recite verbatim an oral conversation he has heard. He may give the substance of the conversation in the sense of what he heard the parties say, so long as he does not give his opinion as to the conversation's meaning or effect. *Com. v. Bonomi*, 335 Mass 327, 347, 140 NE2d 140, 156 (1957). See also *Collins v. Inhabitants of Greenfield*, 172 Mass 78, 81, 51 NE 454, 455 (1898).

---

§7.5 [1]Opinion evidence regarding insanity is discussed in more detail at §7.8.4.f.

C.   EXPERT TESTIMONY

§7.6   General Principles

§7.6.1   Admissible when Subject Matter Is Not within Ordinary Experience

Proposed Mass R Evid 702 provides:

> If scientific, technical, or other specialized knowledge will assist the trier of fact to understand the evidence or to determine a fact in issue, a witness qualified as an expert by knowledge, skill, experience, training, or education, may testify thereto in the form of an opinion or otherwise.

Fed R Evid 702 is identical with the proposed Massachusetts rule.

Proposed Mass R Evid 702 codifies existing Massachusetts case law, providing that prior to the admission of expert testimony the judge must determine whether the situation is a proper one for expert testimony and whether the proposed expert is properly qualified.[1] These determi-

---

§7.6 [1] Whether failure to give the opposing party notice of anticipated expert testimony prior to trial constitutes a significant enough abuse of discovery requirements for the testimony to be barred depends upon the individual circumstances of the case. Compare *Com. v. Chappee*, 397 Mass 508, 492 NE2d 719 (1986) (barring testimony), with *Resendes v. Boston Edison Co.*, 38 Mass App 344, 648 NE2d 757 (1995) (allowing testimony, noting that opposing party did not object to expert until lobby conference immediately before empanelment of jury and had not sought either a continuance or a deposition of the expert during the month before trial in which it had notice he would be called); *Com. v. Anderson*, 404 Mass 767, 537 NE2d 146 (1989) (allowing testimony, noting that information was disclosed in another form). Whether a continuance is required due to late notice of an expert also depends upon the circumstances. Compare *Com. v. Nester*, 32 Mass App 983, 594 NE2d 542 (1992) (error to deny defendant a continuance during trial to obtain expert to rebut unexpected evidence from Commonwealth's expert, whose testimony had gone significantly further than her report) with *Com. v. MeMaria*, 46 Mass App 114, 703 NE2d 1203 (1999) (not error to deny continuance where no bad faith or carelessness by prosecutor and no material prejudice resulted from denial), and *Com. v. Bandy*, 38 Mass App 329, 648 NE2d 440 (1995) (not error where continuance was denied when defendant was on notice on the prior trial day that expert would probably be required).

nations are governed by Proposed Mass R Evid 104(a). Past Massachusetts practice is in accord with Proposed Mass R Evid 702. See, e.g., *Simon v. Solomon*, 385 Mass 91, 105, 431 NE2d 556, 566 (1982) (court refers with approval to standard of admissibility of expert testimony as stated in Fed R Evid 702 and 704); *Terrio v. McDonough*, 16 Mass App 163, 175-176, 450 NE2d 190, 198 (1983) (expert testimony as to rape trauma syndrome, an area of specialized medical knowledge, properly admitted to assist jury in understanding evidence; court cited Proposed Mass R Evid 702).

The test used under the Rules in determining whether the situation is a proper one for expert testimony, as under case law, is whether the testimony will assist the trier of fact in determining a fact in issue or in understanding the evidence. *Com. v. Dockham*, 405 Mass 618, 628, 542 NE2d 591, 597 (1989); *Le Blanc v. Ford Motor Co.*, 346 Mass 225, 231-232, 191 NE2d 301, 305-306 (1963). This decision would be dependent on the facts of the case in question. Clearly, the testimony would be permitted where the inference to be drawn or opinion to be given is one for which more than the equipment of everyday experience is required. Additionally, when the testimony will be of assistance, it will be admissible, in the judge's discretion, even though the matter may be within the knowledge of the trier of fact.

Expert testimony may be appropriate in the discretion of the trial judge, even though not necessary.[2] *Bernier v.*

---

[2] The failure to consult with and employ expert witnesses may amount to ineffective assistance of counsel in criminal cases. *Com. v. Roberio*, 428 Mass 278, 700 NE2d 830 (1998) (failure to investigate insanity defense); *Com. v. Martin*, 427 Mass 816, 821, 696 NE2d 904, 907 (1998) (ineffective assistance not to insist upon confirmatory test, rather than relying upon screening test, to prove presence of LSD); *Com. v. Haggerty*, 400 Mass 437, 509 NE2d 1163 (1987) (murder conviction reversed where counsel failed to investigate whether victim's death was caused by heart problems, rather than beating by defendant, the sole defense available). However, where the decision not to call experts at trial is a reasonable tactical choice, failure to do so does not amount to ineffective assistance. *Com. v. Cormier*, 427 Mass 446, 451, 693 NE2d 1015, 1019 (1998) (fact that defense counsel consulted with experts does not

Boston Edison Co., 380 Mass 372, 403 NE2d 391 (1980). Cf. *Com. v. Fayerweather*, 406 Mass 78, 83, 546 NE2d 345, 347-348 (1989) (although some medical records may be unintelligible without expert explanation, they are generally admissible without expert testimony, although such testimony might be admissible if offered).

§7.6.2 *When Expert Testimony Is Required*

Findings of fact as to technical matters beyond the scope of ordinary experience are not warranted in the absence of expert testimony supporting such findings. *Com. v. Kirkpatrick*, 423 Mass 436, 447, 668 NE2d 790, 797 (1996) (expert testimony required to establish likelihood of transmission of sexually transmissible disease); *Enrich v. Windmere Corp.*, 416 Mass 83, 87, 616 NE2d 1081, 1084 (1993) (presence of defect in electric fan could not be inferred in absence of expert testimony); *Sullivan v. Boston Gas Co.*, 414 Mass 129, 138, 605 NE2d 805, 810 (1993) (expert medical testimony may be required to establish showing of objective corroboration of emotional distress in negligent infliction of emotional distress case); *Department of Revenue v. Sorrentino*, 408 Mass 340, 557 NE2d 1376 (1990) (error to admit human leukocyte antigen test results without expert testimony that proper testing procedures were employed); *Com. v. Lloyd*, 45 Mass App 931, 702 NE2d 395 (1998) (expert required to explain effects of Prozac on perception and memory); *Lally v. Volkswagen Aktiengesellschaft*, 45 Mass App 317, 322, 698 NE2d 28, 34 (1998) (expert required to prove

mean that it was ineffective assistance not to call them as witnesses); *Com. v. Anderson*, 398 Mass 838, 501 NE2d 515 (1986); *Com. v. Sowell*, 34 Mass App 229, 609 NE2d 492 (1993).

Where a new scientific test is developed after a conviction, a defendant may be entitled to a new trial. *Com. v. Meggs*, 30 Mass App 111, 565 NE2d 1249 (1991) (defendant sought new trial based on new tests that determine the blood grouping of semen donors; court held issue should not have been decided on affidavits alone, remanded for evidentiary hearing).

that paraplegic's injury was caused by striking open glove box door during crash); *Harris v. Magri*, 39 Mass App 349, 656 NE2d 585 (1995) (expert required on standard of care in legal malpractice action, whether viewed as negligence claim or contract claim); *Colucci v. Rosen, Goldberg, Slavet, Levenson & Wekstein*, 25 Mass App 107, 515 NE2d 891 (1987) (expert needed to establish standard of care in legal malpractice action and to prove plaintiff would have been successful in underlying claim, but for defendant attorney's negligence); *Triangle Dress, Inc. v. Bay State Service, Inc.*, 356 Mass 440, 252 NE2d 889 (1969) (expert required to prove cause of fire in air conditioner); *Stewart v. Worcester Gas Light Co.*, 341 Mass 425, 435, 170 NE2d 330, 337 (1960) (expert required to establish propriety of a "dresser coupling" in gas pipe close to house). See also *Edwards v. Boland*, 41 Mass App 375, 670 NE2d 404 (1996) (expert testimony may afford sufficient basis for application of res ipsa loquitur doctrine in medical malpractice cases); *Broderick v. Gibbs*, 1 Mass App 822, 296 NE2d 708 (1973) (possible disbelief of expert testimony as to good medical practice cannot fill void left by absence of expert testimony of bad medical practice).

For cases holding that expert testimony was not required, see *Com. v. Trowbridge*, 419 Mass 750, 647 NE2d 413 (1995) (trial judge not required to employ expert to determine whether eight-year-old victim was competent to testify); *Matter of Tobin*, 417 Mass 81, 628 NE2d 1268 (1994) (expert testimony not required to prove ethical violations by lawyers); *Com. v. Dockham*, 405 Mass 618, 542 NE2d 591 (1989) (no expert testimony required to sustain judge's conclusion that child witness would suffer emotional trauma if he testified in open court); *Collins v. Baron*, 392 Mass 565, 569, 467 NE2d 171, 173-174 (1984) (admission of defendant doctor may be sufficient to justify a finding of negligence); *Smith v. Ariens Co.*, 375 Mass 620, 625, 377 NE2d 954 (1978) (expert testimony is not always required to establish liability in design defect case, jury could find that protuberances on snowmobile were a defect based on their lay knowledge); *Com. v. Adames*, 41 Mass App 14, 668 NE2d 848 (1996) (expert testimony not required to lay foundation for police officer's testimony that bill dusted with fluorescent powder glowed under ultraviolet light); *Town of Shrewsbury v. Commissioner of Environmental Protection*, 38 Mass App 946, 648 NE2d 1287 (1995) (DEP not required to base its decision that a composting operation created a condition of air pollution upon scientific evidence); *Fall River Savings Bank v. Callahan*, 18 Mass App 76, 82-83, 463 NE2d 555, 560-561 (1984) (trial judge in legal malpractice case involving conveyancing may obviate the need for, or supplement, expert testimony by resort to opinions, standard texts, and articles in law reviews).

§7.6.3   Expert Testimony Is Not Binding on Trier of Fact

Experts' conclusions are not binding on the trier of fact, who may decline to adopt them in whole or in part. *In re Wyatt*, 428 Mass 347, 360, 701 NE2d 337, 346 (1998) (experts' opinions that petitioner was a sexually dangerous person were not entitled to conclusive weight, even though no contrary opinions were offered); *Com. v. Lyons*, 426 Mass 466, 688 NE2d 1350 (1998) (conflicting opinions regarding competence of defendant); *Guardianship of Brandon*, 424 Mass 482, 677 NE2d 114 (1997); *Com. v. DeMinico*, 408 Mass 230, 235, 557 NE2d 744, 747 (1990); *Com. v. Goulet*, 402 Mass 299, 522 NE2d 417 (1988); *Com. v. Sims*, 30 Mass App 25, 565 NE2d 463 (1991) (Text cited). As a corollary, where testimony from various experts is conflicting, it is for the trier of fact to determine which expert's testimony to accept, if any. *Ward v. Com.*, 407 Mass 434, 554 NE2d 25 (1990); *Dewan v. Dewan*, 30 Mass App Ct 133, 566 NE2d 1132 (1991). See *Com. v. Guiliana*, 390 Mass 464, 457 NE2d 275 (1983) (where the court acknowledged the power of the jury to disregard expert testimony, but nevertheless exercised its extraordinary power in a first degree murder case under GL 278, §33E, to set aside the conviction and order a new trial because of a substantial likelihood of miscarriage of justice). But cf. *New Boston Garden Corp. v. Board of Assessors of Boston*, 383 Mass 456, 471-472, 420 NE2d 298, 307-308 (1981) (while Appellate Tax Board is not bound by expert testimony, it must have basis in evidence for alternative finding).

The trial judge's disagreement with expert testimony does not constitute a sufficient ground for excluding it. *Com. v. Roberio*, 428 Mass 278, 700 NE2d 830 (1998) (error for court to deny new trial motion because he did not believe expert, credibility was for the jury); *Com. v. O'Brien*, 423 Mass 841, 854, 673 NE2d 552, 561, 562 (1996) (even when sitting without a jury, judge should recognize the difference between the admissibility and the weight of the evidence); *Com. v. Pallotta*, 36 Mass App 669, 634 NE2d 915 (1994) (error to exclude defendant's expert testimony on criminal responsibility; court notes, however, that there could be cases where an expert's opinion is transparently so wrong or misdirected that it could be excluded even in the absence of conflicting testimony).

The purpose of standard instructions on expert testimony is to remind the jury that they are the sole judges of credibility and to counteract the possibility that jurors may believe they cannot reject an expert witness's testimony. Nonetheless, in the absence of a request for such an instruction, or an objection to the court's failure to give one, it has been held that there was no substantial risk of a miscarriage of justice where the court failed to instruct the jury on its role in evaluating expert testimony. *Com. v. Richardson*, 423 Mass 180, 185, 667 NE2d 257, 262 (1996).

§7.6.4   *Degree of Certitude Required of Expert*

Where an expert's opinion is based on facts in evidence, that it relies on extrapolations made from those facts will not render the testimony inadmissible. *Sacco v. Rou-*

penian, 409 Mass 25, 564 NE2d 386 (1990) (expert deduced that cancer could have been diagnosed at time of defendant doctor's exam, by working back from size of tumor he observed, using the rate of "doubling time" of breast cancer, trial court erred in rejecting evidence as "far-fetched"). In addition, the fact that a witness expresses his opinion by stating that given causes of a condition are "consistent with" his observations does not render the testimony inadmissible. Where other evidence is introduced tending to prove the cause, such expert testimony is relevant to show that the expert or scientific evidence is not inconsistent with the claimed cause. *Com. v. Nadworny*, 396 Mass 342, 359, 486 NE2d 675, 686 (1985) (no error to admit testimony of pathologist despite lack of certainty as to time and cause of death; noting cases going both ways on whether evidence of presence of blood is admissible when it cannot be said whether it is animal or human, admission no error here where no prejudice shown); *Resendes v. Boston Edison Co.*, 38 Mass App 344, 352, 648 NE2d 757, 763 (1995) (expert's characterization of his opinion as a "reasonable explanation" of how accident occurred did not render it inadmissible); *Com. v. Azar*, 32 Mass App 290, 302, 588 NE2d 1352, 1361 (1992) (doctor's testimony that injuries were consistent with victim's chest having been compressed and her body shaken was not "speculative"). Cf. *Com. v. Wright*, 411 Mass 678, 584 NE2d 621 (1992) (fact that chemist could not determine if blood found on murder victim's kitchen floor was human affected weight of evidence, but not admissibility).

Where an expert's opinion is sufficiently grounded in the evidence, that certain facts were unknown to the expert or that mistakes were made in some of the expert's assumptions does not render the testimony inadmissible, but rather goes to the weight of the evidence. *Simmons v. Monarch Mach. Tool Co., Inc.*, 413 Mass 205, 212, 596 NE2d 318, 323 (1992) (some facts unknown); *Sullivan v. First Massachusetts Financial*, 409 Mass 783, 791, 569 NE2d 814, 820 (1991) (some assumptions incorrect). Cf. *Board of Assessors of Boston v. Ogden Suffolk Downs*, 398 Mass 604, 499 NE2d 1200 (1986) (witness examined property in 1982, opinion as to value in 1979 was properly struck due to blatant error of overlooking in excess of $2,000,000 in improvements between 1979 and 1982).

However, an expert's opinion that is a "mere guess or conjecture . . . in the form of a conclusion from basic facts that do not tend toward that conclusion any more than toward a contrary one has no evidential value." *Toubiana v. Priestly*, 402 Mass 84, 91, 520 NE2d 1307, 1312 (1988), citing *Kennedy v. U-Haul Co.*, 360 Mass 71, 73-74, 271 NE2d 346 (1971); *Goffredo v. Mercedes-Benz Truck Co.*, 402 Mass 97, 103, 520 NE2d 1315, 1318 (1988); *Van Brode Group v. Bowditch & Dewey*, 36 Mass App 509, 520, 633 NE2d 424, 430 (1994) (expert prediction of dramatic new profits to be realized in a business turnaround from a historic record of losses, based on only one month of profitability, was properly excluded in the discretion of the trial judge). An opinion expressed as a mere assertion of a possibility of a causal connection is insufficient alone to sustain a finding. *Goffredo v. Mercedes-Benz Truck Co.*, supra (directed verdict was proper where witness expressed opinion in terms of possibilities, rather than probabilities); *Imbimbo v. Ahrens*, 360 Mass 847, 274 NE2d 349 (1971) (testimony insufficient). Cf. *Blood v. Lea*, 403 Mass 430, 530 NE2d 344 (1988) (medical expert's assessment of a "probable" causal link between alleged negligent act and injury was sufficient to submit case to trier of fact).

§7.7   Foundation for Expert Testimony

Expert opinion is the product of special knowledge applied to the particular facts of the case in dispute. Thus, as foundation for expert opinion evidence, it must be established that: (1) the scientific principles and methodology on which the expert's opinion is based are reliable; (2) the witness is qualified with special knowledge; and (3) the witness has sufficient knowledge of the particular facts to bring his expertise meaningfully to bear.[1]

§7.7.1   Determination of Reliability by Trial Court

One determination that must be made with respect to the propriety of scientific testimony is whether the body of scientific or expert knowledge on which the witness's testimony is based is sufficiently reliable. The classic definition of the standard was articulated in *Frye v. United States*, 293 F 1013, 1014 (DC Cir 1923), where it was held that, "while courts will go a long way in admitting expert testimony deduced from a well-recognized scientific principle or discovery, the thing from which the deduction is made must be sufficiently established to have gained general acceptance in the particular field in which it belongs."[2]

In *Daubert v. Merrell Dow Pharmaceuticals, Inc.*, 509 US 579, 113 S Ct 2786 (1993), the United States Supreme Court held that by adoption of Fed R Evid 702, the *Frye* test had been abandoned in the federal courts. The Court held that the "general acceptance" standard of the *Frye* test had not been silently incorporated into Rule 702. The Court

---

§7.7   [1]A party may not obtain expert testimony by summonsing an involuntary witness solely for the expertise he may bring to the trial, in the absence of any personal knowledge on his part related to the issues before the court. *Bagley v. Illyrian Gardens, Inc.*, 401 Mass 822, 519 NE2d 1308 (1988); *Com. v. Vitello*, 367 Mass 224, 327 NE2d 819 (1975). A court does have discretionary power to require, without payment of expert fees, that an expert witness testify as to an opinion already formed; however, such power is exercised sparingly, and only when necessary for the purposes of justice. *Bagley v. Illyrian Gardens, Inc., supra*, 401 Mass at 827, 519 NE2d at 1311 (& citations).

[2]The requirement of general acceptance in the scientific community was intended to ensure "that those most qualified to assess the general validity of a scientific method will have the determinative voice" as to whether such evidence may be accepted in trials. *Com. v. Lykus*, 367 Mass 191, 202, 327 NE2d 671, 678 (1975) (permitting expert testimony as to voice identification based on voice print spectrogram or on aural comparison and analysis). The premise of the requirement is that those most qualified are not judges, but scientists with specialized knowledge.

reasoned that the doctrine would be at odds with the "liberal thrust" of the Federal Rules of Evidence and their "general approach of relaxing the traditional barriers to 'opinion' testimony," 509 US at 588, citing *Beech Aircraft Corp. v. Rainey*, 488 US 153, 169 (1988).

In *Daubert*, the Court emphasized that Fed R Evid 702 continues to impose on trial judges the obligation to make an initial determination of whether scientific testimony and evidence is relevant and reliable. The Court noted that the subject of such testimony must be "scientific . . . knowledge," which requires that inferences or assertions must be derived by the scientific method. The Court suggested several guidelines that might be used in assessing such testimony, although it indicated that none of the individual guidelines were strict requirements. The Court indicated that it would be relevant to determine:

(1)   whether or not a given theory or technique had been subjected to peer review and publication;
(2)   whether a particular scientific technique had a known or potential rate of error;
(3)   whether there were standards controlling the operation of the technique; and
(4)   whether the theory or technique did have general acceptance in the relevant scientific community. The Court emphasized that the inquiry envisioned by Rule 702 is a flexible one.

The decision for the trial judge is the threshold one of whether testimony is sufficiently reliable to be admissible. The Court concluded that risks of inappropriate scientific evidence are further minimized through the adversary system by vigorous cross-examination and the presentation of contrary evidence, and by careful instruction to jurors by trial judges on the burden of proof.

In *Com. v. Lanigan*, 419 Mass 15, 641 NE2d 1342 (1994) (*Lanigan II*), the Supreme Judicial Court held that the general acceptance standard of the Frye test is not the exclusive means by which the admissibility of scientific evidence is to be determined in Massachusetts courts.[3] The court held that the "ultimate test . . . is the reliability of the theory or process underlying the expert's testimony." 419 Mass at 24. Although it did not specifically adopt Proposed Mass R Evid 702, which is identical to the Federal Rule, the court indicated that the "general proposition set forth in the *Daubert* opinion seems sound, although that opinion gives little guidance for the application of that proposition to the facts of a given case." 419 Mass at 25.

The Supreme Judicial Court stated that the trial judge has a "gatekeeper role" in determining whether the process or theory underlying a scientific expert's opinion lacks reliability. The court concluded:

> We accept the basic reasoning of the *Daubert* opinion because it is consistent with our test of demonstrated reliability. We suspect that general acceptance in the relevant scientific community will continue to be the significant, and often the only, issue. We accept the idea, however, that a proponent of scientific opinion evidence may demonstrate the reliability or validity of the underlying scientific theory or process by some other means, that is, without establishing general acceptance.

Lanigan II, supra, 419 Mass at 26, 641 NE2d at 1349.

Lanigan II did not establish a specific checklist or test for determining the reliability of the principles or methodology upon which expert testimony is based. 419 Mass at 26, 641 NE2d 1342. In *Adoption of Hugo,* 428 Mass 219, 234, 700 NE2d 516, 526 (1998), the court reviewed a child's challenge to the methodology of the parents' expert witness, a clinical social worker. The court rejected the child's argu-

---

[3] The *Frye* test had been subjected to substantial criticism. See *Com. v. Mendes,* supra, 406 Mass 201, 212, 547 NE2d 35, 41 (1989) (Liacos, CJ, dissenting) and authorities cited therein. The rule was inherently conservative and was questioned on the ground that it may bar otherwise reliable probative evidence simply because the scientific community had not yet adequately digested and approved of its foundation.

ment that the reliability of the testimony could only be established by one of the five factors discussed in *Lanigan II*.[4] See also *Higgins v. Delta Elevator Service Corp.*, 45 Mass App 643, 700 NE2d 833 (1998) (criticizing a jury instruction regarding the reliability of expert testimony which supplied four specific criteria similar to the *Daubert* factors; court rejected plaintiff's argument that it was error to limit the jury's reliability determination to consideration of those factors, because the trial judge had described them to the jury as factors they "may consider").

In *Kumho Tire Co., Ltd. v. Carmichael*, 526 US 137, 119 S Ct 1167 (1999) (admissibility of testimony of tire failure analyst), the United States Supreme Court held that Rule 702 imposes a "gatekeeping" obligation on the trial court to determine that all expert testimony, not just that from scientific experts, is reliable. In so doing, trial courts may apply the factors suggested in *Daubert*, or employ other criteria, depending upon the circumstances. The Court again emphasized that the test of reliability is "flexible." 119 S Ct at 1171.

Whether the Supreme Judicial Court will follow *Kumho* and establish a "gatekeeper" role for trial courts with respect to the reliability of non-scientific expert testimony remains to be seen. In Massachusetts, the requirement of a showing of "general acceptance" in the scientific community before expert testimony would be allowed seemed to concern only the problem of unproven or disputed scientific instruments or scientific theories. Experts who developed their own particular techniques based on accepted instruments or theories generally were allowed to give their opinions. See, e.g., *Com. v. Cifizzari*, 397 Mass 560, 492 NE2d 357 (1986) (affirming admission of expert testimony making an identification from bite marks); *Com. v. Devlin*, 365

---

[4]The court approved the methodology employed, which consisted of using knowledge gained from the expert's training and experience, reviewing the case file, interviewing the parties, and gathering information from service providers, the same methods used by the child's and DSS's experts.

Mass 149, 310 NE2d 353 (1974) (identification of dismembered torso by x-ray comparisons); *Com. v. Gilbert,* 366 Mass 18, 314 NE2d 111 (1974) (same).

In addition, where an expert's testimony did not involve the use of a scientific technique or test, the validity of which might be subject to dispute, the *Frye* test was not employed. See *Com. v. Avellar,* 416 Mass 409, 418, 622 NE2d 625, 630 (1993) (testimony by pediatrician that father's response upon seeing deceased son's body constituted an inappropriate grief reaction did not involve scientific testing methods, *Frye* test inapplicable); *Com. v. Ghee,* 414 Mass 313, 320, 607 NE2d 1005, 1010 (1993) (expert testimony on the basis of photographic techniques that witness could identify a latent fingerprint, and testimony that by comparing stripes running lengthwise in plastic bags, expert could conclude that one bag was made on the same day as others, constituted physical comparisons that experts made using their knowledge of particular techniques; *Frye* test did not apply).

The Supreme Judicial Court also held that opinions "based on personal observations rather than dependent on scientific theories or principles," were not governed by *Frye. Com. v. Gordon,* 422 Mass 816, 841, 666 NE2d 122, 138 (1996) (chemist's testimony that ortho-tolidine procedure was a presumptive test for the presence of blood, among other iron-containing substances, but that based on her observations she could rule out false positive test results when she observed a brilliant blue color on the filter paper used in the test, was admissible and not subject to the *Frye* test).

Following *Lanigan II,* in *Com. v. Sands,* 424 Mass 184, 185-186, 675 NE2d 370, 371 (1997), the court reaffirmed that "a party seeking to introduce scientific evidence may lay a foundation either by showing that the underlying scientific theory is generally accepted within the relevant scientific community, or by showing that the theory is reliable or valid through other means." The court suggested, however, that if the subject matter of expert testimony is understandable to jurors, separate expert testimony on the reliability of the theory behind it may not be required:

> Expert testimony on the scientific theory is needed if the subject of expert testimony is beyond the common knowledge or understanding of the lay juror. If jurors can evaluate an expert's testimony with common sense and experience and can understand the underlying methods or theories of the testimony, then the expert's qualifications and the logical basis of the testimony can be effectively tested through cross-examination and rebuttal evidence.

424 Mass at 186, 675 NE2d at 371. In *Sands*, the court concluded that evidence of a Horizontal Gaze Nystagmus (HGN) field sobriety test would not be admissible in the absence of expert testimony, because its underlying assumption — that there is a correlation between intoxication and nystagmus — is not within the common experience of jurors.

In other recent cases, however, the appellate courts have suggested that a reliability determination by the trial court is necessary with regard to non-scientific expert testimony. In *Com. v. Roberio*, 428 Mass 278, 700 NE2d 830 (1998), in reference to a psychologist testifying with respect to criminal responsibility, the court stated that "assuming the expert's testimony met the standard of [*Lanigan II*]," issues of the witness's credibility were for the jury, not the judge. The court evidently assumed that testimony from a clinical psychologist on criminal responsibility was susceptible to a *Lanigan II* reliability analysis, although no challenge to the expert's discipline or methodology was made in the case.

In *Ducharme v. Hyundai Motor America*, 45 Mass App 401, 698 NE2d 412 (1998), the court held that the trial court had properly excluded the testimony of the plaintiff's expert with regard to whether a vehicle would have satisfied the requirements of a particular Federal Motor Vehicle

Safety Standard. The expert had conceded that he had not employed any of the objective criteria specified in the test protocol. The court found that his opinion, based on a post-collision examination of the vehicle and crash test reports involving other Hyundai automobiles, was speculative and properly excluded "pursuant to the judge's 'gatekeeper' function against unreliable expert testimony." 45 Mass App at 407, 698 NE2d at 416. In *Hicks v. Brox Industries, Inc.*, 47 Mass App 103, 711 NE2d 179 (1999), the court noted in dictum that the argument that a *Lanigan/Daubert* analysis did not apply to engineering opinions had been discredited in *Kumho.*

In the event that the Supreme Judicial Court does determine that a formal reliability determination must be made by a trial judge with respect to all expert testimony, the continuing vitality of some previous decisions discussed above may be called into question. See, e.g., *Com. v. Ghee,* 414 Mass 313, 607 NE23d 1005 (1993) (identification of plastic bags); *Com. v. Gordon,* 422 Mass 816, 666 NE2d 122 (1996) (individual observations of expert deemed sufficient to rule out false positive results from chemical test).

Where the reliability of scientific or other principles or methodology is disputed, and the court entertains the challenge, it should hold a voir dire examination of the experts for the purpose of determining reliability. Jurors should not be permitted to hear the testimony of any expert in support of the validity of a given scientific procedure until after the court has made its determination that the expert's testimony will be admitted. *Com. v. Curnin,* 409 Mass 218, 565 NE2d 440 (1991).

The existence of a stipulation between the parties as to the admissibility of a scientific test is not always sufficient to justify its admission. *Com. v. Mendes,* 406 Mass 201, 547 NE2d 35 (1989); *Com. v. Walker,* 392 Mass 152, 466 NE2d 71 (1984) (polygraph evidence as to witnesses inadmissible, even if all parties stipulate to admissibility). However, where evidence has been received pursuant to a stipulation, a challenge to the admissibility of the evidence on appeal must demonstrate a substantial likelihood of a miscarriage of justice to obtain a reversal. *Com. v. Phoenix,* 409 Mass 408, 420, 567 NE2d 193, 200 (1991) (conviction affirmed where genetic allotype blood testing admitted following stipulation that such testing has general acceptance in scientific community).

In Massachusetts, the standard of review on the appeal of reliability determinations is broader than in federal court.[5] The appellate court will make its "own determination without regard to the conclusions of the trial or motion judge." *Com. v. Lanigan,* 413 Mass 154, 160, 596 NE2d 311, 314 (1992) (*Lanigan I*). A record where objections are properly preserved is ordinarily required for appellate de novo review of the trial court's rulings admitting expert testimony; and where a party preserves only a limited basis for objecting to the evidence, the court will ordinarily review only that basis. *Vassallo v. Baxter Healthcare Corp.,* 428 Mass 1, 11, 696 NE2d 909, 917 (1998) (declining to reach the defendants' objections to experts under *Lanigan II* asserted on appeal in silicone breast implant case). However, where a criminal defendant fails to object to scientific evidence at trial on the ground that tests performed were not generally accepted, and does not request a voir dire hearing to make that determination, an appellate court will review the issue only to determine if admission of the evidence created a substantial risk of a miscarriage of justice. *Com. v. Daye,* 411 Mass 719, 741, 587 NE2d 194, 207 (1992).

Examples of scientific evidence that have passed the reliability hurdle, or have been held admissible without an explicit finding with respect to reliability, are discussed in §7.8 infra.

---

[5] Federal appellate courts apply an "abuse of discretion" standard when reviewing the admission of expert testimony pursuant to the reliability determination. *General Electric Co. v. Joiner,* 522 US 136, 118 S Ct 512 (1997). Kumho declared that the same standard applies to review of the method by which trial courts determine reliability.

Proposed scientific evidence was excluded under both *Frye* and *Lanigan II* in *Rotman v. National Railroad Passenger Corp.*, 41 Mass App 317, 669 NE2d 1090 (1996) (expert testimony that trauma exacerbated preexisting optic neuritis was not supported by evidence indicating that the opinion was either generally accepted or otherwise had scientific validity). Based upon a lack of sufficient acceptance in the scientific community, a number of types of evidence have been held properly excluded. *Com. v. Mendes*, 406 Mass 201, 204, 547 NE2d 35, 37 (1989) (holding that polygraph evidence had failed to gain sufficient general acceptance among scientific authorities to be admissible);[6] *Croall v. MBTA*, 26 Mass App 957, 526 NE2d 1320 (1988) (rejecting expert testimony concerning "microbursts" of wind); *Com. v. Kater*, 388 Mass 519, 447 NE2d 1190 (1983) (*Kater I*) (rejecting hypnotically aided testimony).[7]

§7.7.2 Expert's Special Knowledge (Qualifications)

An expert witness must show to the trial court's satisfaction that he or she possesses sufficient special knowledge

---

[6] *Mendes* reversed a line of authority that had permitted polygraph evidence under certain limited conditions. See *Com. v. Vitello,* 376 Mass 426, 381 NE2d 582 (1978); *Com. v. A Juvenile,* 365 Mass 421, 313 NE2d 120 (1974). *Mendes* was followed in *Com. v. Tanso,* 411 Mass 640, 583 NE2d 1247 (1992). The issue of whether polygraph test results might be admissible after *Lanigan II* was noted in *Com. v. Stewart,* 422 Mass 385, 663 NE2d 255 (1996) (issue not reached because defendant made no showing regarding the reliability of polygraph evidence) and *Com. v. Kent K.,* 427 Mass 754, 763, 696 NE2d 511, 518 (1998) (juvenile made no attempt to meet "demanding Stewart standard").

[7] Where a witness has been hypnotized, testimony to be admissible must be based on pre-hypnotic memory. The trial court must determine the substance of a witness's pre-hypnotic memory and compare it to the proposed trial testimony, then exclude from evidence details "remembered" for the first time after hypnosis. For a detailed discussion of the problems of such evidence, see *Com. v. Kater,* 412 Mass 800, 592 NE2d 1328 (1992) (*Kater IV*); *Com. v. Kater,* 409 Mass 433, 567 NE2d 885 (1991) (*Kater III*); *Com. v. Kater,* 394 Mass 531, 476 NE2d 593 (1985) (*Kater II*); and cases cited therein. See also §6.20.

and experience to be able to give competent aid to the jury in construing the particular facts of the case in dispute. "The crucial issue is whether the witness has sufficient education, training, experience and familiarity with the subject matter of the testimony." *Letch v. Daniels*, 401 Mass 65, 68, 514 NE2d 675-677 (1987) (testimony of orthodontist permissible in dental malpractice action against defendant pedodontist). The witness need not have encountered precisely the same facts before. *McLaughlin v. Board of Selectmen of Amherst*, 422 Mass 359, 662 NE2d 687 (1996) (error to exclude testimony of real estate expert because she had not bought, sold, or owned land in the locality about which she intended to testify); *Boston Gas Co. v. Assessors of Boston*, 334 Mass 549, 573-574, 137 NE2d 462, 479-481 (1956); *Marchand v. Murray*, 27 Mass App 611, 616, 541 NE2d 371, 374 (1989) (questions of whether economist had previously evaluated fast food franchises, as opposed to other types of restaurants or businesses, did not preclude testimony); *Com. v. Siano*, 4 Mass App 245, 344 NE2d 920 (1976); *Edinberg v. Merry*, 11 Mass App 775, 420 NE2d 1 (1981).

It is not essential that an expert be a specialist within his profession. The Supreme Judicial Court has held: "There is no requirement that testimony on a question of discrete knowledge come from an expert qualified in that subspecialty rather than from an expert more generally qualified." *Com. v. Fryar*, 425 Mass 237, 251, 680 NE2d 901, 911 (1997) (supervising chemist in state police lab, who had taken courses on blood spatter patterns, was competent to testify on physics of blood spattering and knife's ability to inflict wounds). See *Adoption of Hugo*, 428 Mass 219, 700 NE2d 516 (1998) (licensed social worker experienced in working with children and families qualified to testify in adoption case, despite lack of specific clinical experience with foster care and adoption problems); *Com. v. Avellar*, 416 Mass 409, 415, 622 NE2d 625, 629 (1993) (court had discretion to allow board-certified physician in emergency medicine and pediatrics to testify that father's response to viewing the child after death demonstrated an inappropriate grief response); *Com. v. Mahoney*, 406 Mass 843, 852, 550 NE2d 1380, 1385-1386 (1990) (testimony of chemist was admissible that substance on victim's shirt and defendant's footwear was consistent with "residual stomach contents," although expert had no particular training in chemical analysis of same); *Keville v. McKeever*, 42 Mass App 140, 151, 675 NE2d 417, 426 (1997) (psychiatrist who had treated 10 to 20 patients who suffered from dementia, but did not hold himself out as an expert in dementia, was properly qualified to render opinion that person was suffering from severe dementia); *Com. v. Estep*, 38 Mass App 502, 649 NE2d 775 (1995) (permissible to allow chemist, who had testified that paint on wood chip matched paint on ax handle, to also testify that the wood on both items matched); *Cronin v. McCarthy*, 22 Mass App 448, 494 NE2d 411 (1986) (police officers permitted to give opinions that, at point of impact, decedent's vehicle was in defendant's lane, although officers lacked training and experience in accident reconstruction). But see *Com. v. Barresi*, 46 Mass App 907, 705 NE2d 639 (1999) (physician who generally treated the elderly and had limited experience with sexually transmitted diseases was properly excluded from testifying about the likelihood of the transmission of chlamydia).

The court has also held repeatedly that a medical expert need not be a specialist in the area concerned or be practicing in the same field as a medical malpractice defendant in order to give an opinion.[8] *Letch v. Daniels*, supra, and cases cited therein.

Whether a person who might qualify as an expert in one subject is qualified to give an expert opinion in another

---

[8] The standard used to judge the qualifications of an expert before a medical malpractice tribunal is "extremely lenient." *Heyman v. Knirk*, 35 Mass App 946, 626 NE2d 5 (1994) (tribunal should have accepted opinion by podiatrist, not a physician, in case involving foot surgery by orthopedic surgeon); *Blake v. Avedikian*, 412 Mass 481, 482, 590 NE2d 183, 184 (1992). The tribunal should consider a proffered opinion if a trial judge might properly rule the expert to be qualified, even though if that exercise of discretion were in the tribunal's province, it would find the expert not qualified. *Blake v. Avedikian*, supra (& citations).

somewhat related subject will depend upon the circumstances of the case. Compare *Com. v. Griffith*, 404 Mass 256, 534 NE2d 1153 (1989) (no error for prosecution's ballistics expert to testify that blow to defendant's arm would not have caused gun to discharge accidentally) and *Com. v. Sullivan*, 17 Mass App 981, 459 NE2d 117 (1984) (medical examiner, although not a ballistics specialist, properly allowed to extrapolate from nature of wound the approximate distance from which shotgun was fired) with *Com. v. Seit*, 373 Mass 83, 91-92, 364 NE2d 1243, 1249 (1977) (ballistician not allowed to testify whether bullet wound to forehead would cause victim to spin around where witness had no expertise in area of physiology or pathology). See *Com. v. Thayer*, 418 Mass 130, 634 NE2d 576 (1994) (licensed and experienced psychiatric social worker was qualified to testify regarding behavior characteristics of sexually abused children; medical doctor was not required); *Com. v. Simmons*, 419 Mass 426, 646 NE2d 97 (1995) (chemist with experience in blood pattern analysis was properly qualified as an expert on that subject); *Timmons v. MBTA*, 412 Mass 646, 591 NE2d 667 (1992) (vocational rehabilitation counselor qualified to give opinion about plaintiff's impairment of earning capacity between accident and trial based on adequate medical records, but not qualified to testify about permanence of injury absent medical evidence on the issue) (Text cited); *Howe v. Marshall Contractors, Inc.*, 38 Mass App 981, 651 NE2d 1245 (1995) (not error to allow vocational expert to testify that plaintiff was permanently disabled and, in practical effect, unemployable where opinion was predicated on ample testimony from physicians); *Com. v. Olszewski*, 401 Mass 749, 519 NE2d 587 (1988) (police officer not permitted to testify "within a reasonable degree of police certainty" that a chrome strip originally came from victim's automobile, because court does not recognize such a standard; error held not prejudicial because same testimony could be given by witness as a lay person); *Com. v. Garabedian*, 399 Mass 304, 503 NE2d 1290 (1987) (not error to permit psychiatrists to testify about organophosphate intoxication, on issue of whether defendant suffered from mental disease or defect); *Com. v. Weichell*, 390 Mass 62, 78, 453 NE2d 1038, 1048 (1983) (expertise in the area of photography does not qualify a witness to testify on the subject of human perception; also, ability of person to perceive is within the common experience of a jury); *Drake v. Goodman*, 386 Mass 88, 434 NE2d 1211 (1982) (attending orthopedic surgeon properly allowed to testify that plaintiff's clenched fist caused by psychological, not physical, problem); *Com. v. Neverson*, 35 Mass App 913, 619 NE2d 344 (1993) (no error in court's refusal to allow professor of physics and biomechanics, lacking medical qualifications, to testify regarding effect on child of fall from a given height); *Com. v. Azar*, 32 Mass App 290, 301, 588 NE2d 1352, 1360 (1992) (forensic pathologist qualified to give opinions regarding deceased infant, although not a "pediatric pathologist"); *Moore v. Fleet Refrigeration*, 28 Mass App 971, 552 NE2d 127 (1990) (error to assume that social worker was not qualified to give opinion on psychological matters, particularly where judge did not even permit testimony on her credentials); *McNeill v. American Cyanamid Co.*, 3 Mass App 738, 326 NE2d 366 (1975) (metallurgist not allowed to give opinion as to manufacture or processing of molded compound). Cf. *Com. v. Cantres*, 405 Mass 238, 540 NE2d 149 (1989) (identification of drug does not require chemist; police officer or user may testify to identity of substance if court makes determination he has sufficient experience to do so).

Where the court has determined that an expert has sufficient qualifications to render an opinion, further questions and criticisms by the opponent as to the witness's education, training, knowledge, and professional experience are said to go to the weight of the testimony and not its admissibility. See *Letch v. Daniels*, 401 Mass 65, 69, 514 NE2d 675 (1987); *Com. v. Schulze*, 389 Mass 735, 740, 452 NE2d 216, 220 (1983); *Marchand v. Murray*, 27 Mass App 611, 616, 541 NE2d 371, 374 (1989).

Knowledge of details — e.g., points of medicine, law, real estate values — gained through reading the works of others may contribute to the opinion of an expert witness, though the sources from which the knowledge was obtained are inadmissible as hearsay. *Kuklinska v. Maplewood Homes, Inc.*, 336 Mass 489, 496, 146 NE2d 523, 528 (1957) (geological survey); *Johnson v. Lowell*, 240 Mass 546, 550, 134 NE 627, 629 (1922) (real estate); *Barker v. United States Fidelity & Guaranty Co.*, 228 Mass 421, 117 NE 894 (1917) (foreign law); *Finnegan v. Fall River Gas Works Co.*, 159 Mass 311, 34 NE 523 (1893) (medicine); *Donahue v. Draper*, 22 Mass App 30, 491 NE2d 260 (1986) (business executives' compensation). See also *National Bank of Commerce v. New Bedford*, 175 Mass 257, 261, 56 NE 288, 290 (1900), where Holmes, CJ, said, "An expert may testify to value, although his knowledge of details is chiefly derived from inadmissible sources, because he gives the sanction of his general experience. But the fact that an expert may use hearsay as a ground of opinion does not make the hearsay admissible." See *Shaw v. Keown & McEvoy, Inc.*, 243 Mass 221, 137 NE 258 (1922) (opinion as to value of potatoes allowed although based on expert's inquiries as to market conditions). Cf. *Framingham v. Department of Public Utilities*, 355 Mass 138, 145, 244 NE2d 281, 285-286 (1969) (not error to exclude witness's evaluation of studies in which he had not been personally engaged).

Where the expert draws upon hearsay sources for his generalized knowledge and evaluation of specific facts and states such to be the basis, in part, of his opinion, this will not necessarily make the hearsay admissible. *National Bank of Commerce v. New Bedford*, supra; *Com. v. Howard*, 355 Mass 526, 246 NE2d 419 (1969); *Newton Girl Scout Council, Inc. v. Massachusetts Turnpike Authority*, 355 Mass 189, 199, 138 NE2d 769, 776 (1956); *Com. v. Kendall*, 9 Mass App 152, 399 NE2d 1115 (1980).

The qualifications of an expert must be passed on by the trial judge as a preliminary question of fact. *Leibovich v. Antonellis*, 410 Mass 568, 574 NE2d 978 (1991). It is thus important to be clear about whether a given witness is called as an expert or as a lay witness. Otherwise, the proponent of the witness may be relieved of satisfying the requirements of offering him as an expert; the court may fail to make necessary findings; the jury may not be properly instructed on the considerations that apply in evaluating expert testimony; and appellate review of the admissibility of the evidence will be more difficult in the absence of an appropriate record. See *Com. v. Wolcott*, 28 Mass App 200, 207-208, 548 NE2d 1271, 1275 (1990) (police officer was improperly permitted to testify concerning tactics and organization of Jamaican gangs, where he was not identified and qualified as an expert).

The better practice is for the trial judge to make an explicit finding on whether the witness has been qualified as an expert at the time any objection is made to the solicitation of his opinion. However, the fact that the court heard the witness's qualifications and then permitted the testimony has been held to imply a finding that the witness qualified as an expert. *Leibovich v. Antonellis*, supra; *Com. v. Boyd*, 367 Mass 169, 326 NE2d 320 (1975); *Com. v. Allen*, 40 Mass App 458, 468, 665 NE2d 105, 112 (1996). The judge need not entertain the proffer of a witness as an expert or make the preliminary finding that the witness is qualified as an expert before the jury. *Com. v. Richardson*, 423 Mass 180, 184, 667 NE2d 257, 261 (1996) (Text cited). It is error for the judge to refuse to make a preliminary finding on qualifications and expressly leave the question of whether a witness has qualified as an expert to the jury. *Com. v. Boyd*, supra; *Winthrop Products Corp. v. Elroth Co.*, 331 Mass 83, 117 NE2d 157 (1954). However, once the judge does make a preliminary finding that a witness is qualified to render expert opinion, the jury is entitled to continue to evaluate the witness's qualifications and to take them into account in determining how much or whether to credit the expert's testimony. *Leibovich v. Antonellis*, supra.

The trial courts have discretion in determining whether or not experts are qualified, and the decision, being one of fact, will not be reversed unless there is no evidence to warrant the conclusion. *Com. v. Benoit*, 410 Mass 506, 520, 574 NE2d 347, 355 (1991); *Com. v. Garabedian*, supra; *Prudential Insurance Co. v. Board of Appeals of Westwood*, 23 Mass App 278, 502 NE2d 137 (1986) (trial court had discretion to refuse to qualify town police sergeant as expert on traffic conditions in a zoning case); *Com. v. Ranahan*, 23 Mass App 201, 500 NE2d 1349 (1986) (no error in failure to qualify chemist as expert on reliability of breathalyzer). Cf. *McLaughlin v. Board of Selectmen*, supra, 422 Mass 359, 662 NE2d 687 (appropriate to reverse trial judge where exclusion of expert was based on improper factor that real estate expert was required to have practical knowledge and sales experience in the area in which she proposed to evaluate property) (Text cited); *Com. v. Banuchi*, 335 Mass 649, 655, 141 NE2d 835, 839 (1957) (judge was reversed where expert's testimony was excluded because of misunderstanding of relevance of testimony on issues of fact).

Opposing counsel cannot preclude the sponsor of an expert from producing evidence to establish his expertise by stipulating or conceding the expert's qualifications.

A provision for nonpartisan experts is made for testimony before the Industrial Accident Board. GL 152, §9. Proposed Mass R Evid 706 and Fed R Evid 706 provide that the court may appoint experts on its own motion or on the motion of any party.

§7.7.3   Expert's Knowledge of Particular Facts

An expert witness may base her opinion about the particular facts of the case upon: (1) facts observed by herself; (2) evidence already in the record or which the parties represent will be presented during the course of the proceedings, which facts may be assumed to be true in questions put to the witness; and (3) facts or data not in evidence, including hearsay, if the facts or data are independently admissible and constitute a permissible basis for an expert to consider in formulating an opinion. *Sacco v. Roupenian*, 409 Mass 25, 564 NE2d 386 (1990); *Department of Youth Services v. A Juvenile*, 398 Mass 516, 499 NE2d 812 (1986) (modifying Massachusetts law, which had previously foreclosed an expert from gaining knowledge about the particular facts of the case from facts or data that were themselves not in evidence). The expert's opinion may be based on a combination of facts derived from those various sources.

Whether an expert has sufficient knowledge of the particular facts of the dispute to be qualified to render an opinion is in the discretion of the trial court, which will seldom be reversed with respect to such determinations. *Com. v. McDonough*, 400 Mass 639, 648, 511 NE2d 551, 557 (1987) (court did not err in excluding proposed defense experts on question of whether victim could distinguish real episodes of sexual abuse from imagined ones, based on witnesses' lack of knowledge of victim's mental and emotional condition).

a. Personal Observation

Where an expert witness has personally observed the facts on which his opinion is based, he may bring his general knowledge to bear upon those facts and render expert opinions. *Com. v. Benoit*, 410 Mass 506, 574 NE2d 347 (1991) (pathologist who was present at an autopsy, although he did not perform it, was competent to testify as to the autopsy results); *Com. v. Freiberg*, 405 Mass 282, 540 NE2d 1289 (1989) (medical examiner competent to testify that injuries could have been caused by a stove, based upon photographs of stove and personal observations of victim during autopsy); *Adoption of Frederick*, 405 Mass 1, 537 NE2d 1208 (1989) (psychiatrist's interview with mother provided sufficient basis for opinion regarding her "intellectual shortcomings"); *Com. v. Pikul*, 400 Mass 550, 511 NE2d 336 (1987) (expert who performed autopsy may testify that injuries observed could have been caused in a particular way or by a specified instrumentality); *Fourth Street Pub, Inc. v. National Union Fire Insurance Co.*, 28 Mass App 157, 161, 547 NE2d 935, 937-938 (1989) (error to exclude fire expert's testimony based on examination of scene, although there were inadequacies in investigation). Questions put to such an expert need not be in hypothetical form, nor must the inquiry of the expert on direct examination call for the reasons upon which his opinion is based. *City Welding & Manufacturing Co. v. Gidley-Eschenheimer Corp.*, 16 Mass App 372, 451 NE2d 734 (1983) (Text cited). The trial court has broad discretion in determining the admissibility of testimony based on personal observations made at some time in the past. *Com. v. Rosenberg*, 410 Mass 347, 355, 573 NE2d 949, 954 (1991) (no error to admit testimony of doctor who examined defendant on one occasion over three years before trial, where doctor had reviewed defendant's records since that time). See *Stark v. Patalano Ford Sales, Inc.*, 30 Mass App 194, 200, 567 NE2d 1237, 1241 (1991) (expert's examination of truck six years after delivery, in breach of warranty case, was sufficient—weaknesses in testimony went to its weight, not admissibility).

Where an expert has examined an item of real evidence and either intentionally or negligently destroyed or lost it, upon request of the opposing party the court should preclude the expert's testimony based on the examination. The rule is necessary to avoid the unfair advantage that might result were the testimony received. *Nally v. Volkswagen of America, Inc.*, 405 Mass 191, 197-198, 539 NE2d 1017, 1021 (1989); *Bolton v. MBTA*, 32 Mass App 654, 593 NE2d 248 (1992). See §11.7.

b.   Facts in Evidence, Hypothetical Questions

An expert may testify in response to a hypothetical question whether she has personally observed the subject in dispute or not.[9] See, e.g., *Davis v. Seller*, 329 Mass 385, 108

---

[9] For a more general discussion of hypothetical questions, see Wigmore §§672-686 (Chad rev 1979).

NE2d 656 (1952). However, even where an expert's opinion is not based on her personal observations, counsel is under no obligation to use hypothetical questions in eliciting opinions. In *Department of Youth Services v. A Juvenile*, 398 Mass 516, 499 NE2d 812 (1986), the court approved Proposed Mass R Evid 705, which provides that an expert may give his opinions and the reasons therefore without prior disclosure of the underlying facts or data, unless the court requires otherwise. The thrust of the rule is to eliminate the requirement for using hypothetical questions. Cf. *Hanover Insurance Co. v. Talhouni*, 413 Mass 781, 789, 604 NE2d 689, 694 (1992) (doctor properly permitted to testify on the basis of deposition testimony and medical records, where facts on which the doctor relied were later testified to at trial).

Counsel may still find it advisable, for tactical reasons or for clarity of presentation, to employ hypothetical questions. In a properly constructed hypothetical question, alleged facts, evidence of which has previously been introduced or may fairly be expected to be introduced, are summed up by counsel and the expert is asked to state his opinion on the assumption that the alleged facts are true. *Wing v. Com.*, 359 Mass 286, 268 NE2d 658 (1971). Where the question is based on evidence expected to be introduced, failure to introduce such evidence will, of course, vitiate the opinion based upon such question.

The scope of hypothetical questions is within the sound discretion of the trial judge. *Com. v. Merola*, 405 Mass 529, 542 NE2d 249 (1989); *Cohen v. Maritime Transportation Co.*, 353 Mass 760, 233 NE2d 215 (1968). The judge may allow separate hypothetical questions designed to elicit the opinion of the expert rather than requiring one question to sum up the whole issue. *Com. v. Noxon*, 319 Mass 495, 538, 66 NE2d 814, 841 (1946). It is not necessary that the question include all relevant facts; the effect of omission of relevant facts upon the expert's opinion may be tested on cross-examination. *Com. v. Burke*, 376 Mass 539, 382 NE2d 192 (1978); *MacKay v. Ratner*, 353 Mass 563, 233 NE2d 745

(1968); *Foreign Car Center, Inc. v. Salem Suede, Inc.*, 40 Mass App 15, 21, 660 NE2d 687, 693 (1996) (Text cited); *Drivas v. Barnett*, 24 Mass App 750, 753, 513 NE2d 696, 698 (1987) (Text cited).

The trial judge may require that certain facts be included in a hypothetical question, however. *O'Brien v. Wellesley College*, 346 Mass 162, 173, 190 NE2d 879, 886 (1963). Failure to include sufficient facts in the hypothetical question may also destroy the value of the expert's opinion based thereon. *Bearse v. Fowler*, 347 Mass 179, 196 NE2d 910 (1964); *Milch v. Boston Consolidated Gas Co.*, 341 Mass 230, 167 NE2d 845 (1960). A question based on assumptions not in evidence is improper. *Roddy v. Fleischman Distilling Sales Corp.*, 360 Mass 623, 277 NE2d 284 (1971); *Hopping v. Whirlaway, Inc.*, 37 Mass App 121, 637 NE2d 866 (1994).

So, too, a question is improper where it contains a material misstatement of facts, *Buck's Case*, 342 Mass 766, 770-771, 175 NE2d 369, 372-373 (1961), or is confusingly double and creates a prejudicial ambiguity in the answer. *Molloy v. Kizelewicz*, 343 Mass 402, 179 NE2d 247 (1961). The jury should, on request, be instructed that it may give weight to the expert's opinion only if it finds all of the assumed facts to be true. *Com. v. Bjorkman*, 364 Mass 297, 306, 303 NE2d 715, 721-722 (1973); *Com. v. Taylor*, 327 Mass 641, 649, 100 NE2d 22, 27 (1951).

Where testimony has been in conflict, it is improper to ask an expert: "Basing your opinion on all the testimony you have heard given in this case, what is the cause of X's condition?" This requires the witness to perform the jury's function of believing or disbelieving testimony and gives the jury no opportunity to discard the opinion if the wrong facts have been assumed as its basis. *Connor v. O'Donnell*, 230 Mass 39, 119 NE 446 (1918). It is probably permissible, but not good practice, to base a hypothetical question on all the testimony of a single witness. See *Nolan v. Newton Street Railway*, 206 Mass 384, 92 NE 505 (1910). Cf. *Com. v. Harrison*, 342 Mass 279, 286, 173 NE2d 87, 93 (1961) (question excluded).

   c.　Facts and Data Not in Evidence but which
     Would Be Admissible

In *Department of Youth Services v. A Juvenile,* 398 Mass 516, 499 NE2d 812 (1986), the Supreme Judicial Court held that an expert may gain his knowledge of the particular facts in dispute from facts that are not in evidence, but which would be admissible in evidence. In reaching this decision, the court considered whether to adopt proposed Mass R Evid 703, which provides:

Bases of Opinion Testimony By Experts

   The facts or data in the particular case upon which an expert bases an opinion or inference may be those perceived by or made known to him at or before the hearing. If of a type reasonably relied upon by experts in the particular field in forming opinions or inferences upon the subject, the facts or data need not be admissible in evidence.

The proposed rule is identical with Fed R Evid 703.

   The court concluded that allowing an expert to rely on facts not admissible in evidence would constitute a radical departure from prior practice, and that the rule raised a serious potential for abuse. The court was concerned that experts may be permitted in recounting the bases for their opinions to put before the jury material inadmissible in evidence that it would otherwise not hear. As a result, the court declined to adopt the full reach of the proposed rule. It did, however, conclude that allowing an expert to base an opinion on facts that would be admissible in evidence if offered was a reasonable modification that would eliminate the necessity of producing exhibits and witnesses whose sole function would be to construct a proper foundation for an expert's opinion.

   The new rule has been followed in subsequent cases. See *Com. v. O'Brien,* 423 Mass 841, 851, 673 NE2d 552, 560 (1996) (proper for expert to rely on admissible evidence not offered but furnished to him by prosecutor); *Com. v.*

Daye, 411 Mass 719, 742, 587 NE2d 194, 207 (1992) (expert's testimony concerning analysis of bullet lead was admissible, although radiation testing was performed by a technician); *Anthony's Pier Four, Inc. v. HBC Associates,* 411 Mass 451, 480, 583 NE2d 806, 824-825 (1991) (expert's opinion on value of real estate based on "comparables" was admissible where he spoke to a party involved in each transaction and their testimony would have been independently admissible); *Adoption of Kirk,* 35 Mass App 533, 623 NE2d 492 (1993) (social worker's diagnosis of father as paranoid schizophrenic was properly based on witness's knowledge of his psychiatric history as contained in hospital records); *Adoption of Seth,* 29 Mass App 343, 560 NE2d 708 (1990) (psychiatrist's testimony may be based on reports of treatment by others only where that information is independently admissible).

Although medical records regarding treatment and history that would be admissible in evidence may form the basis of expert opinion, when they involve a diagnosis that is controversial or involves difficulties in interpretation, the judge may preclude the use of such material as a foundation for an expert opinion. *Com. v. Waite,* 422 Mass 792, 803-804, 665 NE2d 982, 990 (1996) (not error to exclude opinion offered on the basis of a written preliminary diagnosis by another physician, which was considered to be only an "initial impression").

Although the Supreme Judicial Court has rejected inadmissible hearsay as a permissible basis for an expert's knowledge of the facts in dispute, the fact that an expert has relied in part on such hearsay in forming his opinion does not automatically render his testimony inadmissible. See, e.g., *Com. v. Roman,* 414 Mass 235, 606 NE2d 1333 (1993) (psychiatrist was permitted to testify regarding defendant's multiple personalities, having stated that he could reach his opinion without relying on letter he reviewed from second physician who made multiple personality diagnosis, although second physician's letter itself was inadmissible hearsay); *Com. v. Pikul,* 400 Mass 550, 555, 511

NE2d 336, 340 (1987) (& citations). In addition, the fact that a witness has been exposed to hearsay does not imply that he has relied on it in the formation of his opinion. *Hanover Insurance Co. v. Talhouni*, 413 Mass 781, 789, 604 NE2d 689, 694 (1992).

§7.7.4   Disclosure of Bases of Opinion

a.   Under Rule 705

In *Department of Youth Services v. A Juvenile*, 398 Mass 516, 499 NE2d 812 (1986), the Supreme Judicial Court approved the rule articulated in Proposed Mass R Evid 705:

Disclosure of Facts or Data
Underlying Expert Opinion

The expert may testify in terms of opinion or inference and give his reasons therefore, without prior disclosure of the underlying facts or data, unless the court requires otherwise. The expert may in any event be required to disclose the underlying facts or data on cross-examination.

The rule is virtually identical with Fed R Evid 705.

The rule allows a witness to state his opinion or inferences he has drawn from the evidence, without first setting out during direct examination the underlying facts or data on which the testimony is based. The thrust of the rule is to eliminate the necessity for posing a hypothetical question to expert witnesses.

In *Department of Youth Services v. A Juvenile*, supra, the court specifically noted that the use of the word "may" in the second sentence of the rule does not permit a judge to exclude questions designed to elicit the underpinnings of the expert's opinion. It would appear, therefore, that opposing counsel has a clear right to examine the expert on the bases of his opinion.

It remains permissible to draw out on direct examination the facts or circumstances on which the expert has relied, prior to eliciting an opinion. How far one may go in having the expert provide details, where such details would themselves be inadmissible, has not been entirely clarified in the reported cases. The Supreme Judicial Court has noted that a statement by the expert of the facts on which he relied, as part of the foundation of his testimony, may be of great use to the jury in determining what weight to accord the testimony. *Simon v. Solomon*, 385 Mass 91, 105, 431 NE2d 556, 566 (1982); *Newton Girl Scout Council, Inc. v. Mass Turnpike Authority*, 335 Mass 189, 199, 138 NE2d 769, 776 (1956). The court has stated that where "an expert's statements concerning matters on which he has relied are admitted for the limited purpose of laying the foundation for his opinion and are presented to the jury or judge, in a manner that avoids prejudice to the opposing party, the trial judge's discretion should not be disturbed." *Anthony's Pier Four v. HBC Associates*, 411 Mass 451, 480-481, 583 NE2d 806, 825 (1991) (witness testified to prices and square footage of comparable properties) (citing *Simon v. Solomon, supra*, 385 Mass at 106, 431 NE2d at 567).

The court has also stated that an expert witness may not, under the guise of stating the reasons for an opinion, testify to matters of hearsay during the direct examination, unless such matters are admissible under an exception to the hearsay rule. *Grant v. Lewis/Boyle, Inc.*, 408 Mass 269, 272-273, 557 NE2d 1136, 1138-1139 (1990) (although proper for doctor to testify that he relied on the reports of other physicians in reaching his opinion, not proper for him to introduce their out-of-court diagnoses unless they came within an exception to hearsay rule) (citing Text); *Care and Protection of Martha*, 407 Mass 319, 324, 553 NE2d 902, 905 (1990) (inappropriate to admit hearsay statements by minors regarding alleged sexual abuse made to psychotherapist, where therapist had developed plan for the children and court's role was to evaluate the plan); *Com. v. Martin*, 17 Mass App 717, 461 NE2d 1244 (1984) (expert's testimony as to inculpatory statements by defendant, otherwise inadmissible, constitutes reversible error, even absent objection). Where an expert has stated the information on which he relied, such facts are not admitted to prove their truth, and the trier of fact may not rely on them in making findings. *Care and Protection of Rebecca*, 419 Mass 67, 83, 643 NE2d 26, 35 (1994) (statements by alleged sexual abuse victims to expert witness were not admissible for their truth) (citing Text).

b. Statutory Admissibility of Hearsay in Child Abuse and Neglect Reports

Hearsay that forms the basis for opinions may be rendered admissible by statute in particular instances. See, e.g., GL 119, §§21 and 24 (reports regarding child abuse and neglect); *Custody of a Minor (No. 2)*, 378 Mass 712, 723, 393 NE2d 379, 386 (1979); *Adoption of Kenneth*, 31 Mass App 946, 580 NE2d 392 (1991); *Custody of Tracy*, 31 Mass App 481, 579 NE2d 1362 (1991). See *Adoption of Paula*, 420 Mass 716, 724-725, 651 NE2d 1222, 1229 (1995) (GL 119, §24 reports, as well as testimony of investigator, are admissible in proceeding dispensing with parents' consent to adoption); *Adoption of Mary*, 414 Mass 705, 610 NE2d 898 (1993); *Adoption of Sean*, 36 Mass App 261, 630 NE2d 604 (1994) (guardian ad litem reports containing hearsay are admissible in proceedings to dispense with consent for adoption under GL 215, §56A).

The Supreme Judicial Court has recognized that it is error to admit hearsay from GL 119, §24 reports unless there is "an opportunity to refute the investigator *and the investigator's sources* through cross-examination and other means." *Adoption of Carla*, 416 Mass 510, 514, 623 NE2d 1118, 1120 (1993) (emphasis added) (citing *Custody of Michel*, 28 Mass App 260, 266, 549 NE2d 440 (1990)). See *Care and Protection of Rebecca*, 419 Mass 67, 82, 643 NE2d 26, 35 (1994) (hearsay in §24 report which is inadmissible under *Adoption of Carla* may not be used to bolster reliability determination in order to admit hearsay under GL 233, §83); *Adoption of Iris,* 43 Mass App Ct 95, 680 NE2d 1188 (1997) (requiring parents to call court investigator on direct examination, denial of right to conduct cross-examination, was error); *In re Leo,* 38 Mass App 237, 646 NE2d 1086 (1995) (where party was given opportunity to call as witnesses the sources in investigator's report, but refused to do so, he waived right to complain of hearsay in §24 report); *Care and Protection of Inga,* 36 Mass App 660, 634 NE2d 591 (1994) (hearsay accusations of child from GL 119, §51A report inadmissible where child does not testify and judge has no other means to assess accuracy of statements).

§7.8   Subject Matter of Expert Testimony

§7.8.1   Introduction

The circumstances under which expert testimony might be employed are bounded only by the limits of imagination. Expert testimony is admissible when it relates to matters within the witness's field of expertise and the evidence will aid the jury in reaching a decision. The court should consider whether the inference to be drawn or the material to be understood is something for which more than the equipment of everyday experience is required. See, e.g., *Com. v. Crawford,* 429 Mass 60, 65, 706 NE2d 289, 293 (1999) (error to decline to receive expert testimony regarding voluntariness of confession, despite judge's claim to be familiar with PTSD and battered woman's syndrome); *Com. v. Cruz,* 413 Mass 686, 691, 602 NE2d 1089, 1092 (1992) (in absence of expert testimony, jury would not have known what effect a given blood alcohol level would have on defendant's mental processes in case where defense was diminished capacity); *Harlow v. Chin,* 405 Mass 697, 714, 545 NE2d 602, 612 (1989) (expert on medical economics permitted to give opinion on future medical expenses); *Com. v. Boudreau*, 362 Mass 378, 380, 285 NE2d 915, 917 (1972) (doctor may give an opinion, where layman could not, that brain injury was caused by blows around the head); *Coyle v. Cliff Compton, Inc.*, 31 Mass App 744, 749, 583 NE2d 875, 878 (1992) (exclusion of expert testimony about standards of installation of overhead doors was proper — jurors could comprehend the matter without it); *Adams v. U.S. Steel Corp.*, 24 Mass App 102, 506 NE2d 893 (1987) (judge properly excluded testimony of safety engineer on whether hole in parking lot was dangerous). Further examples of the subjects of expert testimony are provided below.

Some of the cases cited in the following sections are illustrative of varying results that may occur on superficially similar subjects. As stated above, expert testimony may be essential in certain areas; in others it may not be necessary although appropriate. In these latter situations the discretion of the trial judge seems to be given great weight on the question of the propriety of such evidence. See, e.g., *Goldhor v. Hampshire College*, 25 Mass App 716, 521 NE2d 1381 (1988) (within court's discretion to exclude expert testimony that termination from an academic position makes it difficult to be hired elsewhere in the academic community). See also Wigmore §§555-561 (Chad rev 1979).

§7.8.2   Physical Sciences

a.   Speed Detection

In *Com. v. Whynaught*, 377 Mass 14, 384 NE2d 1212 (1979), the court, based on reported decisions from other jurisdictions that had taken judicial notice of the underlying scientific principles at issue, took judicial notice that the radar speedmeter was an accurate and reliable means of measuring velocity. Radar evidence is admissible when the prosecution can demonstrate the accuracy of the particular device on which the defendant's speed was measured.

b.   Ballistics

Com. v. Daye, 411 Mass 719, 587 NE2d 194 (1992) (bullet fragments from victim's body identified as manufactured by the same party on approximately the same date as bullet found in defendant's basement; although there was conflicting evidence at trial from experts as to whether methods of conducting elemental analysis of bullet lead were accepted in the relevant scientific community, the defendant had not challenged at trial the admissibility of the prosecution expert's testimony and the Supreme Judicial Court found no substantial risk of a miscarriage of justice); *Com. v. Ellis*, 373 Mass 1, 364 NE2d 808 (1977) (spent projectile in victim's car identified as coming from same gun which had been used to fire shots into tree, by person who sold weapon to defendant; although murder weapon itself was never found, deviation from traditional methods of obtaining comparison bullets went to weight, not admissibility of evidence); *Com. v. Giacomazza*, 311 Mass 456, 42 NE2d 506 (1942) (evidence admissible that a particular projectile was fired from a particular barrel, based on rifling marks).

c.   Trace Evidence

Com. v. Sullivan, 410 Mass 521, 574 NE2d 966 (1991) (photos of microscopic comparison of hairs were admissible); *Com. v. Tarver*, 369 Mass 302, 345 NE2d 671 (1975) (microscopic comparison of hair samples in order to exclude classes of suspects; record demonstrated that microscopic examination was accepted by the relevant scientific community); *Com. v. Ghee*, 414 Mass 313, 607 NE2d 1005 (1993) (photographic techniques employed to identify latent fingerprint of defendant on a shotgun; court specifically held that *Frye* test was not relevant, expert had made a physical comparison using his knowledge of a particular technique).

d.   Voice Recognition

Voice identification based on visual analysis of specto-grams (voice prints) was held to be generally accepted in the relevant scientific community in *Com. v. Lykus,* 367 Mass 191, 327 NE2d 671 (1975).[1]

e.   Handwriting[2]

The problem of proving the authorship of a piece of handwriting is merely that of securing a witness with suffi-cient knowledge of the alleged author's hand to enable the witness to give an opinion as to the authorship of the specimen in dispute. Whether the witness has such knowl-edge as to enable him to give an opinion is a preliminary question of fact for the trial judge. *Com. v. Ryan,* 355 Mass 768, 247 NE2d 564 (1969); *Nunes v. Perry,* 113 Mass 274 (1873).

The most usual method of identifying handwriting is to have some person testify on the basis of having seen writings of the alleged author in the past and being familiar with his handwriting. *Foye v. Patch,* 132 Mass 105, 108 (1882). See also *Pataskas v. Judeikas,* 327 Mass 258, 98 NE2d 265 (1951); *Sheinkopf v. Eskin,* 4 Mass App 826, 350 NE2d 469 (1976).

Where a genuine specimen of the alleged author's handwriting has been obtained, an expert may give his opinion as to whether the genuine specimen and the specimen in dispute are by the same hand. *Moody v. Rowell,* 34 Mass (17 Pick) 490 (1836). See *Priorelli v. Guidi,* 251 Mass 449, 146 NE 770 (1925) (handwriting specimen obtained from defendant while she was on the witness stand). If such specimen is admitted in evidence, the court or jury may compare it with the disputed document to determine the authenticity of the latter. *Buker v. Melanson,* 8 Mass App 325, 330, 393 NE2d 436, 439 (1979). But a lay witness may not

---

§7.8   [1]Justice Kaplan dissented on this point, emphasizing that scientific opinion was divided on the reliability of the technique.
   [2]See also §12.3.2.

do so; nor may he offer an opinion in such event as to the authenticity of the disputed document based on his familiarity with the writing of the purported author. *Noyes v. Noyes*, 224 Mass 125, 112 NE 850 (1916).

The genuineness of the specimen itself is to be determined by the trial judge before it can be used in evidence as a basis of comparison by the expert witness or by the trier of fact. *Davis v. Meenan*, 270 Mass 313, 169 NE 145 (1930). In criminal cases, such a preliminary determination of fact by the trial judge must be made, but the same issue will be submitted to the jury if the genuineness of the specimen is disputed. *Com. v. Tucker*, 189 Mass 457, 473-474, 76 NE 127, 132-133 (1905).

The genuineness of the standard may be established by direct or circumstantial evidence but not by the opinion of witnesses, lay or expert. *Com. v. Di Stasio*, 297 Mass 347, 362, 8 NE2d 923, 931 (1937); *Newton Centre Trust Co. v. Stuart*, 201 Mass 288, 292, 87 NE 630, 631 (1909). See also *Taylor-Wharton Iron & Steel Co. v. Earnshaw*, 259 Mass 554, 156 NE 855 (1927).

Fed R Evid 901 and Proposed Mass R Evid 901 would allow nonexpert opinion as to the genuineness of handwriting where familiarity was not acquired for purposes of litigation. The Rules would also permit comparisons by the trier of fact or by experts with specimens that have been authenticated.

f.   Accident Reconstruction

Testimony by experts is frequently offered, but not always admitted, in the litigation of automobile accidents. Compare *Hallett v. Town of Wrentham*, 398 Mass 550, 499 NE2d 1189 (1986) (police officer's testimony about cause of skid marks properly excluded because jury had as much knowledge as officer to draw conclusion); *Bernier v. Boston Edison Co.*, 380 Mass 372, 403 NE2d 391 (1980) (expert permitted to give opinion on speed and on how a light pole was caused to fall when it was struck by a motor vehicle);

Turcotte v. DeWitt, 332 Mass 160, 124 NE2d 241 (1955) (no expert testimony permitted as to whether certain wheel marks, which had been described to jury, were caused by automobiles involved in collision); *Reardon v. Marston*, 310 Mass 461, 38 NE2d 644 (1941) (Registry of Motor Vehicles inspector can testify that skid marks on road showed that defendant's brakes were not in good working order); *Jackson v. Anthony*, 282 Mass 540, 185 NE 389 (1933) (where two automobiles collided, causing very extensive damage not only to the bodies of the cars but to their structural parts, the manner of the happening of the accident was a matter upon which expert repairmen could give an opinion). See *Lally v. Volkswagen Aktiengesellschaft*, 45 Mass App 317, 698 NE2d 28 (1998) (testimony of accident reconstruction expert admitted without objection; objection to video shown to illustrate his opinion properly overruled on ground there was no prejudice because video was cumulative).

For boating cases, compare *New England Glass Co. v. Lovell*, 61 Mass (7 Cush) 319 (1851) (whether bales of goods could be washed out of a hole in the hull of a wreck was not the subject of expert knowledge) and *Sargent v. Massachusetts Accident Co.*, 307 Mass 246, 29 NE2d 825 (1940) (probability of survival in a canoe descent of rapids in a Canadian river was a subject for expert testimony).

g. Construction Cases

Compare these efforts to use expert testimony in cases dealing with construction and related problems: *Roberts v. Southwick*, 415 Mass 465, 614 NE2d 659 (1993) (majority and dissenting justices disagree about whether exclusion of expert testimony regarding the force required to pull down stacked sheet rock was harmless error); *Wilson v. Boston Redevelopment Authority*, 371 Mass 841, 359 NE2d 1306 (1977) (expert allowed to opine on whether a grate over an elevator shaft had ever been secured thereto); *Stimpson v. Wellington Service Corp.*, 355 Mass 685, 246 NE2d 801 (1969) (expert testimony was not required, although admissible, to support the inference that if an overloaded truck drives over a buried pipe, one end of the pipe would be depressed and the other end would rise); *Thomas v. Tom's Food World, Inc.*, 352 Mass 449, 226 NE2d 188 (1967) (expert testimony not required to show hazard of individual walking down greasy wooden ramp at 45-degree grade while carrying a quarter of beef); *Merwin v. DeRaptellis*, 338 Mass 118, 153 NE2d 893 (1958) (expert testimony was not necessary for a jury to find that a clicking sound of a marble stair tread, when stepped upon, indicated that the tread was loose and could slip out of place); *Scully v. Joseph Connolly Ice Cream Sales Corp.*, 336 Mass 392, 145 NE2d 826 (1957) (expert testimony that construction and maintenance of booth in ice cream parlor were improper was properly excluded because such question was easily comprehended by the jury); *Johnson v. Orange*, 320 Mass 336, 69 NE2d 587 (1946) (where jury had viewed place where plaintiff fell, court excluded expert testimony as to whether construction of driveway was unusual and improper); *Harrington v. Boston Elevated Railway Co.*, 229 Mass 421, 118 NE 880 (1918) (whether a given temporary subway structure was properly constructed was matter for expert testimony).

h.   Computer Simulations

Computer-generated models or simulations have been treated like other scientific tests. In *Commercial Union Insurance Co. v. Boston Edison Co.*, 412 Mass 545, 549, 591 NE2d 165, 168 (1992), admissibility was held to be conditioned on a sufficient showing that: "(1) the computer is functioning properly; (2) the input and underlying equations are sufficiently complete and accurate (and disclosed to the opposing party, so that they may challenge them); and (3) the program is generally accepted by the appropriate community of scientists." A variety of different computer simulation cases from other jurisdictions are noted in

Commercial Union. See also *Schaeffer v. General Motors Corp.,* 372 Mass 171, 177, 360 NE2d 1062, 1066-1067 (1977).

§7.8.3   Biological Sciences

a.   Anatomy and Anthropology

In *Com. v. Gilbert,* 366 Mass 18, 314 NE2d 111 (1974) and *Com. v. Devlin,* 365 Mass 149, 310 NE2d 353 (1974), the court upheld the admissibility of identification by means of x-ray comparison of bones and joints. The court specifically held that the testimony was not subject to a *Frye* analysis because it did not involve a "scientific instrument" or "scientific theory," and the experts relied on experienced-based knowledge.

Com. v. Festo, 251 Mass 275, 146 NE 700 (1925) held that a medical examiner is permitted to testify regarding the course of a projectile through a victim's body and the position of body at the time of the shooting.

b.   Time of Death

Several methods of estimating the time of death have been held admissible. See *Com. v. Bennett,* 424 Mass 64, 674 NE2d 237 (1997) ("12-12-12 rule" — during the first 12 hours after death, rigor begins to form, then it is generally complete and stays on full rigor for the next 12 hours, over the last 12 hours rigor starts to wane and eventually disappears; court finds that there is substantial authority demonstrating the reliability of time of death evidence, citing *Com. v. Haas,* 373 Mass 545, 563, 369 NE2d 692 (1977)); *Com. v. Campbell,* 378 Mass 680, 393 NE2d 820 (1979) (estimate based upon observations of corpse by medical examiner and a prison medic; court held that a medical opinion regarding time of death is not objectionable merely because it was not based on objective scientific evidence, suggested in dictum that a rectal thermometer could have provided objective evidence); *Com. v. Haas,* 373 Mass 545, 563, 369

NE2d 692 (1977) (estimate of time of death formulated at the scene without benefit of scientific testing was admissible; court found, without citations, that there is substantial authority demonstrating the reliability of time of death evidence).

c.   Blood Spatter

Experts have been permitted to testify concerning the analysis of blood patterns in order to deduce how the blood was deposited on surfaces and the movement of persons during an incident. See *Com. v. Fryar*, 425 Mass 237, 680 NE2d 901 (1997); *Com. v. Simmons*, 419 Mass 426, 646 NE2d 97 (1995). In neither of the cited cases did the defendant challenge the reliability of blood pattern analysis; in both cases the challenge to the evidence was limited to the qualifications of the witness.

d.   Odontology

Identification by comparing bite marks with dental impressions has been held admissible. In *Com. v. Cifizzari*, 397 Mass 560, 492 NE2d 357 (1986), the court indicated that the witnesses' testimony merely aided the jury in comparing photographs of the bite marks with the dental impressions. The court held that in order to admit such testimony, including the opinion that no two people have the same bite mark, there was no need to establish that such evidence has gained general acceptance in the scientific community. The court concluded it would be sufficient to establish the reliability of the procedures involved, such as x-rays, models, and photographs.

e.   DNA

In the landmark case, *Com. v. Lanigan*, 413 Mass 154, 596 NE2d 311 (1992) (*Lanigan II*), the court held that DNA evidence was properly admitted where the probability of a random DNA match was based on the "ceiling principle"

recommended in a 1992 report by a committee of the National Research Council of the National Academy of Sciences (NRC Report). The ceiling principle was found to be a conservative approach to determining the likelihood of a match, which the court found was sufficiently reliable to be admissible.

For further development of DNA-related issues, see *Com. v. Rosier*, 425 Mass 807, 685 NE2d 739 (1997) (Polymerasechain reaction (PCR)-based DNA tests at short tandem repeat (STR) loci are scientifically reliable); *Com. v. Sok*, 425 Mass 787, 683 NE2d 671 (1997) (PCR-based DNA tests at DQA1, PM, and D1S80 loci generally meet test of reliability, case remanded to determine if technique used followed appropriate protocols); *Com. v. Fowler*, 425 Mass 819, 685 NE2d 746 (1997) (based upon 1996 NRC Report, product rule is permissible in calculating DNA profile frequencies, ceiling principle is not required; RFLP method of analysis found to be scientifically reliable); *Com. v. Daggett*, 416 Mass 347, 622 NE2d 272 (1993) (court divided on question of whether DNA evidence was admissible where the likelihood of a match was expressed in non-numerical terms, but any error in admission of evidence held harmless); *Com. v. Teixeira*, 40 Mass App 236, 662 NE2d 726 (1996) (contention on appeal that prosecution had not established proficiency of DNA laboratory, a significant variable noted in the NRC Report, would not justify reversal either on the ground that there was a substantial risk of a miscarriage of justice or on the "clairvoyance exception" that constitutional error had not yet been fully developed where the point was not raised in the trial court).

§7.8.4 Behavioral Sciences

a. Battered Woman's Syndrome (BWS)

Evidence of a history of abuse and expert testimony regarding such abuse are admissible by statute, GL 233,

§23F in criminal cases where the defendant claims to have been a victim of abuse. *Com. v. Crawford,* 429 Mass 60, 706 NE2d 289 (1999) (defendant entitled to present evidence as BWS and PTSD with respect to voluntariness of confession). The statute allows expert testimony on: the common patterns in abusive relationships; the nature and effects of abuse and typical responses thereto; how those effects relate to the perception of the imminent nature of the threat of death or serious bodily harm; the relevant facts and circumstances that form the basis for the opinion; and evidence of whether the defendant displayed characteristics common to victims of abuse. The statute is gender neutral.

Given the passage of this statute in 1994, the Massachusetts appellate courts have not found an occasion to determine explicitly whether the theory on which battered woman's syndrome is based is scientifically reliable. The Appeals Court has noted that such evidence has been admitted in numerous jurisdictions. *Com. v. Goetzendanner,* 42 Mass App Ct 637, 679 NE2d 240 (1997).

In *Com. v. Rodriquez,* 418 Mass 1, 10, 633 NE2d 1039, 1042 (1994), the court reversed a manslaughter conviction where evidence of the history of abuse had been excluded, employing a traditional self-defense analysis. The court did not decide the issue of the admissibility of evidence of battered woman's syndrome as such. It did note that when self-defense is at issue with respect to a crime involving the use of force against another, "where there is evidence of a pattern of abuse of the defendant by the victim, expert testimony on common patterns in abusive relationships and the typical emotional and behavioral responses of persons who are battered may be admissible."

In *Com. v. Goetzendanner,* supra, 42 Mass App at 646, 679 NE2d at 246, the court addressed the question of whether expert testimony regarding BWS is admissible when the alleged vicitim of a crime claims to have been abused. It held that such evidence of battered woman's syndrome may be admitted "to enlighten jurors about behavioral or emotional characteristics common to most victims of battering and to show that an individual victim or victim witness has exhibited similar characteristics." The purpose of the evidence is to explain what might otherwise seem to be counter-intuitive behavior by a victim, which could diminish her credibility. The court ruled that evidence of the syndrome is not limited to those situations expressly authorized by statute. See *R.H. v. B.F.*, 39 Mass App 29, 37-38, 653 NE2d 195, 200 (1995) (in custody dispute, expert testimony that mother suffered from battered woman's syndrome was admissible when father put in issue mother's use of force against him).

b.   Rape Trauma Syndrome

Expert testimony concerning rape trauma syndrome has been held sufficiently reliable to be admissible. *Com. v. Mamay*, 407 Mass 412, 553 NE2d 945 (1990) (medical community has generally recognized existence of rape trauma syndrome; questions of whether sexual assault and battery victims are affected by the syndrome and whether it applies in the context of a trust relationship were within professional knowledge and experience of witness);[3] *Terrio v. McDonough*, 16 Mass App Ct 163, 450 NE2d 190 (1983) (RTS evidence admissible in civil suit for sexual assault and battery).

c.   Sexually Abused Children

Expert testimony concerning the characteristics of sexually abused children has been held admissible as "beyond the common knowledge of jurors and of assistance in assessing a victim witness's testimony and credibility." *Com. v. Dockham*, 405 Mass 618, 629, 542 NE2d 591, 598 (1989); *Com. v. Hudson*, 417 Mass 536, 540, 631 NE2d 50, 52 (1994)

---

[3] See concurring opinion by Liacos, CJ, questioning whether evidence was sufficient to conclude there was a scientific basis for the testimony regarding the behavior of sexual assault victims in a trust relationship. 407 Mass at 427, 553 NE2d at 954.

(citing *Dockham;* further noting that expert testimony is not admissible to prove that victim was in fact sexually abused, court held that testimony regarding symptoms of post-traumatic stress disorder (PTSD) was admissible and relevant to jury's assessment of victim's testimony and credibility; testimony established that victim's stomachaches and nightmares were typical symptoms of PTSD, and that PTSD could result from a traumatic event such as sexual abuse).[4] In *Dockham,* the court relied upon decisions from other jurisdictions to demonstrate admissibility on the ground that the testimony addressed issues beyond the common knowledge of jurors, but did not discuss the scientific basis for the testimony or its general acceptance in the scientific community.

The appellate courts have recognized the substantial danger that such testimony may amount to impermissible vouching for the credibility of the complainant. An expert may not directly opine on whether an alleged victim was in fact subjected to sexual abuse. The Supreme Judicial Court has concluded that an expert may not directly refer to or compare the behavior of specific child complainants to the general characteristics of sexual abuse victims. The court has warned that opinion testimony may constitute impermissible vouching even when it does not explicitly link an opinion to a child witness, and the danger of implicit vouching is greater when the witness testifies both as a direct witness who examined the complainant and as an expert, particularly when the witness offers fresh complaint testimony. See *Com. v. Pare,* 427 Mass 427, 693 NE2d 1002 (1998) (error to admit social worker's reference to child's "truthful" disclosures); *Com. v. Federico,* 425 Mass 844, 849, 683 NE2d 1035, 1039 (1997) (testimony of one expert improperly admitted, could be understood as indicating

---

[4] See dissent by O'Connor, J and Liacos, CJ, arguing that stomachaches and nightmares are not "behavior" which might reflect negatively on the victim's credibility and thus need to be explained; PTSD evidence was wrongly used to prove that the victim was in fact sexually assaulted. 417 Mass at 543, 631 NE2d at 54.

that sexual abuse occurred in the case; testimony of second expert who stated lack of physical trauma was not "inconsistent" with abuse was permissible); *Com. v. Richardson*, 423 Mass 180, 185, 667 NE2d 257, 262 (1996); *Com. v. Trowbridge*, 419 Mass 750, 647 NE2d 413 (1995) (testimony that symptoms and physical condition of child at issue were consistent with the type of non-violent sexual abuse that was alleged came impermissibly close to an endorsement of child's credibility; expert testimony that mother's animosity could have influenced child to make false accusations of sexual abuse was properly excluded as an impermissible comment on the credibility of the child witness); *Care and Protection of Rebecca*, 419 Mass 67, 643 NE2d 26 (1994) (expert's testimony that children had been sexually abused, identifying the persons who had abused them, and opining that their mother was present amounted to testimony that he believed children and was inadmissible); *Com. v. Colin C.*, 419 Mass 54, 643 NE2d 19 (1994) (expert testimony that victims were sexually abused was essentially a statement vouching for their credibility); *Com. v. Montanino*, 409 Mass 500, 504, 567 NE2d 1212, 1214 (1991) (error to admit police officer's testimony that most sexual assault victims provide more complete details of the incident in later as compared to initial interviews — would be taken by jury as endorsement of victim's credibility) (Text cited); *Com. v. Ianello*, 401 Mass 197, 515 NE2d 1181 (1987) (no error in exclusion of testimony by defendant's expert, a psychologist, which amounted to opinion on veracity of minor rape victim); *Com. v. Spear*, 43 Mass App Ct 583, 593, 686 NE2d 1037, 1044 (1997) (direct comparison between general characteristics of child victims and complainants was improper); *Com. v. LaCaprucia*, 41 Mass App 496, 671 NE2d 984 (1996) (school counselor's description of her observations of complainant, coupled with her observations of her experience with other traumatized children amounted to impermissible vouching); *Com. v. Allen*, 40 Mass App 458, 665 NE2d 105 (1996) (not error to allow therapist to testify about general symptoms associated with sexual abuse where prosecution brought out the fact that witness was the child's treating therapist only briefly at the end of testimony; not error to allow doctor to testify that complainant's hymen was a normal shape and that the majority of girls examined with regard to a finding of sexual abuse have a normal exam); *Com. v. Brouillard*, 40 Mass App 448, 665 NE2d 113 (1996) (error to admit testimony from expert who explicitly connected complainants to general syndrome associated with sexual abuse and otherwise conveyed to the jury his belief in the complainants' credibility); *Com. v. Perkins*, 39 Mass App 577, 583, 658 NE2d 975, 979 (1995) (where expert testified as to general characteristics of sexually abused children and then answered a series of hypothetical questions regarding particularized behavior of children that matched children in the case, testimony was tantamount to endorsement of credibility of complaining witnesses, and admission was error); *Com. v. McCaffrey*, 36 Mass App 583, 591, 633 NE2d 1062, 1067 (1994) (allowing psychologist to testify as both behavioral expert and treating therapist may have amounted to vouching for victim's credibility by suggesting that therapist had accepted child as a patient to be treated because she accepted her allegations as true); *Com. v. O'Brien*, 35 Mass App 827, 626 NE2d 892 (1994) (trial court properly limited expert's testimony to general characteristics of sexually abused children without addressing truthfulness of victim).

In *Com. v. Rather*, 37 Mass App 140, 150, 638 NE2d 915, 920 (1994), the court suggested guidelines for cases in which either side intends to offer expert evidence as to patterns of disclosure of child abuse victims. The guidelines include: (1) early notification to trial judge; (2) voir dire of the expert witness; (3) specific advice to the witness not to render an opinion as to the credibility of the alleged victim or the general veracity of sexually abused children; (4) jury instructions on the role of experts, including, on request, that expert testimony is not affirmative evidence of sexual abuse and that the expert did not assess the credibility of the alleged victim; (5) proponent of the testimony should not imply in closing argument that expert vouched for credibility of victim.

d.   Battered Child Syndrome

Expert testimony concerning the battered child syndrome has been held sufficiently reliable to be admissible. *Com. v. Day*, 409 Mass 719, 724, 569 NE2d 397, 399-400 (1991) (battered child syndrome is "a well recognized medical diagnosis, dependent on inferences, not a matter of common knowledge, but within the area of expertise of physicians whose familiarity with numerous instances of injuries accidentally caused qualifies them to express with reasonable probability that a particular injury or group of injuries is not accidental or is not consistent with the explanation offered therefor but is instead the result of physical abuse by a person of mature strength"); *Adoption of Iris*, 43 Mass App 95, 101 n. 8, 680 NE2d 1188 (1997); *Com. v. Azar*, 32 Mass App 290, 301, 588 NE2d 1352, 1360 (1992); *Com. v. Collins*, 26 Mass App 1021, 533 NE2d 214 (1989) (finding "shaken infant syndrome" to be a recognized medical diagnosis); *Com. v. Labbe*, 6 Mass App Ct 73, 373 NE2d 227 (1978).

In *Estelle v. McGuire*, 498 US 1119, 111 S Ct 1071 (1991), the Court reviewed the admission under California law of evidence that an alleged child murder victim suffered from "battered child syndrome." The Court ruled that the evidence of prior abuse was relevant to prove that someone had intentionally, as opposed to accidentally, harmed the child, although there was no direct evidence linking the prior incidents to defendant. The Court held there was no constitutional due process violation in the admission of such evidence.

e.   Eyewitness Identification

Expert testimony on the capacity of eyewitnesses to make identifications is not admissible as of right. It is, however, admissible in the proper exercise of discretion by the trial judge.[5] *Com. v. Ashley,* 427 Mass 620, 624 n.3, 694 NE2d 862, 866 (1998) (court refused to adopt Commonwealth's argument that expert testimony on eyewitness identification is never admissible); *Com. v. DiBenedetto,* 427 Mass 414, 693 NE2d 1007 (1998); *Com. v. Santoli,* 424 Mass 837, 680 NE2d 1116 (1997); *Com. v. Hyatt,* 419 Mass 815, 818, 647 NE2d 1168, 1171 (1995); *Com. v. Francis,* 390 Mass 89, 453 NE2d 1204 (1983) (extensive review of authorities on expert testimony on eyewitness identification); *Com. v. Jones,* 362 Mass 497, 287 NE2d 599 (1972). In *Com. v. Sowers,* 388 Mass 207, 446 NE2d 51 (1983), the court found no error in the admission of an ophthalmologist's testimony that a victim, who was legally blind, could identify a person from a certain distance, stating that the testimony dealt with only the clarity and distinctness of the victim's vision, not the reliability of the identification in issue.

f. Insanity

In Massachusetts it is held that testimony as to sanity is within the opinion rule — i.e., that persons not expert in mental disease may testify only as to facts observed and may not draw the conclusion of sanity or insanity. *Com. v. Monico,* 396 Mass 793, 488 NE2d 1168 (1986) (citing Text); *Com. v. Schulze,* 389 Mass 735, 452 NE2d 216 (1983).

Under our state law, a witness qualified in the treatment of mental diseases may give an opinion on the criminal responsibility of the defendant. *Com. v. Monico,* supra; *Com. v. Schulze,* supra; *Com. v. Boyd,* 367 Mass 169, 181-183, 326 NE2d 320, 328-329 (1975). Although an expert is allowed to give an opinion on the ultimate issue of criminal responsibility, she is not required to do so. An expert may testify as to her observations of the defendant and supply psychiatric explanations for a defendant's actions, without

---

[5] See also §10.4.

providing an opinion on criminal responsibility. *Com. v. Kappler*, 416 Mass 574, 585, 625 NE2d 513, 519 (1993).

Under the Federal Rules, an expert may not express an opinion on the ultimate issue of whether the defendant had a mental state or condition constituting an element of the crime charged or of a defense thereto. Fed R Evid 704(b).[6]

In Massachusetts, a doctor without a specialty in psychiatry who has examined a criminal defendant may testify as to his observations, diagnosis, and treatment of the defendant's condition.[7] However, he may not render an opinion on criminal responsibility if he is not specially qualified in the treatment of mental diseases. *Com. v. Monico*, supra; *Com. v. Schulze*, supra. A witness may be so qualified without possessing a medical degree — the issue is the witness's experience and the probative value of the testimony. *Com. v. Monico*, supra (psychologist may give opinion on criminal responsibility).

Expert testimony is not required to raise an insanity defense. The issue may be presented on the facts of the case, through prosecution witnesses, by lay testimony of observations of the defendant, or a combination of such evidence. *Com. v. Guadalupe*, 401 Mass 372, 516 NE2d 1159 (1987); *Blaisdell v. Com.*, 372 Mass 753, 765, 364 NE2d 191, 201-202 (1977). A criminal defendant may testify himself as to the symptoms he suffered from and to the fact that he felt better after psychiatric care. *Com. v. Guadalupe*, supra.[8] Cf. *Com. v. Seabrooks*, 425 Mass 507, 681 NE2d 1198 (1997) (nature of crime itself, suicide attempt, and defendant's testimony that "he freaked out" and "lost control" were not

---

[6] See §7.3 for text of the rule.

[7] In *Com. v. Stockwell*, 426 Mass 17, 686 NE2d 426 (1997), it was held that the trial judge had not abused his discretion by denying the defendant's request to videotape the examination by the Commonwealth's psychiatrist.

[8] In *Guadalupe*, the court held that failure to give notice of an insanity defense pursuant to Mass R Crim P 14(b)(2) will not bar evidence on the issue unless the defendant has refused to submit to a court-ordered psychiatric examination. In accord, see *Com. v. Dotson*, 402 Mass 185, 521 NE2d 395 (1988).

enough to raise insanity defense); *Com. v. Johnson,* 422 Mass 420, 663 NE2d 559 (1996) (suicidal ideation, absent more, provides insufficient basis for finding of lack of criminal responsibility; bizarre or inexplicable nature of crime alone does not provide foundation for insanity defense).

Once the defendant has raised the issue of insanity, the prosecution must prove that a defendant is sane beyond a reasonable doubt. *Com. v. Keita,* 429 Mass 843, 712 NE2d 65 (1999) (rejecting suggestion that burden of proving insanity should be placed upon the defendant). The prosecution need not present expert testimony to meet its burden of proving sanity. *Com. v. Keita,* supra (evidence of the defendant's conduct after his arrest, although "thin," was sufficient along with presumption of sanity to carry Commonwealth's burden); *Com. v. Kappler,* supra (although defendant introduced testimony from experts who concluded he was not criminally responsible, and prosecution's experts failed to reach that ultimate issue, evidence was sufficient for jury to find defendant was sane). In each case in which the defendant's criminal responsibility is raised, the court should give a jury instruction permitting the jury to consider the "presumption of sanity," the fact that a great majority of people are sane, and the probability that any particular person is sane. *Com. v. Keita,* supra.

If an expert does testify, he may be asked questions regarding the defendant's demeanor during the trial, if relevant to the sanity issues involved. *Com. v. Hunter,* 427 Mass 651, 655, 695 NE2d 653, 657 (1998) (not error to permit government expert to comment on defendant's demeanor during showing of Vietnam film in case where insanity claim was based on PTSD); *Com. v. Smiledge,* 419 Mass 156, 643 NE2d 41 (1994).

In a homicide case, where a defendant presents expert testimony that his mental condition impaired his ability to form specific intent, the defendant is entitled to a jury instruction on the question of whether his mental condition impaired his ability to engage in deliberate premeditation. *Com. v. Ward,* 426 Mass 290, 688 NE2d 227 (1997).

In a civil case, a judge has discretion to admit testimony from physicians who are not psychiatrists concerning a party's mental capacity. *Barshak v. Buccheri*, 406 Mass 187, 547 NE2d 23 (1989).

In a will case, an attesting witness can give his opinion as to sanity formed at the time of execution of the will, but not his opinion as to sanity formed either before or after that time. *Williams v. Spencer*, 150 Mass 346, 23 NE 105 (1890). The testator's attending physician can give his opinion, even if he is not a qualified expert in mental disease. *Duchesneau v. Jaskoviak*, 360 Mass 730, 277 NE2d 507 (1972); *Greene v. Cronin*, 314 Mass 336, 50 NE2d 36 (1943).

§7.8.5　Law Enforcement

a.　General Issues

Law enforcement officers may be permitted to render opinions about instrumentalities and evidence of crime. See *Com. v. Luna*, 418 Mass 749, 754, 641 NE2d 1050, 1053 (1994) (assistant district attorney permitted to testify regarding materiality of defendant officer's statements in prosecution for perjury and filing false police reports); *Com. v. Johnson*, 413 Mass 598, 603, 602 NE2d 555, 558 (1992) (narcotics officer permitted to testify that manner in which cocaine was packaged was consistent with intent to distribute); *Com. v. Johnson*, 410 Mass 199, 571 NE2d 623 (1991) (narcotics officer permitted to testify that given amount of cocaine was not consistent with personal use but was consistent with intent to distribute); *Com. v. Munera*, 31 Mass App 380, 578 NE2d 418 (1991) (opinion admissible that method of carrying cocaine was consistent with dealer's sample; explanation of "stash pads" permissible to rebut defendant's claim of simple lifestyle inconsistent with dealing drugs, but court notes that expert evidence about drug profiles is suspect if offered to prove that because defendant fit profile he must be guilty of particular offense); *Com. v. Pope*, 19

Mass App 627, 476 NE2d 969 (1985) (police officer permitted to testify that paper with notations was a bookmaker's gambling memorandum); *Com. v. LaBella,* 17 Mass App 973, 458 NE2d 763 (1984) (no error in the admission of a state trooper's opinion describing habits of bookmakers and significance of evidence seized); *Com. v. Kimball,* 16 Mass App 974, 453 NE2d 465 (1983) (judge had discretion to admit police officer's opinion on footprints and tracks) (Text cited). Cf. *Com. v. Goguen,* 361 Mass 846, 279 NE2d 666 (1972) (testimony of vexillologist as to contemporary use and treatment of American flag properly excluded; flag on seat of pants could be found not to articulate any idea of redeeming social importance).

b.   *Syndrome Evidence about Perpetrator of Crime*

Expert testimony offered by the government regarding the expected characteristics of perpetrators of crime is not admissible. *Com. v. Federico,* 425 Mass 844, 683 NE2d 1035 (1997); *Com. v. Day,* 409 Mass 719, 569 NE2d 397 (1991) (error to admit expert opinion describing child battering profile); *Com. v. Roche,* 44 Mass App Ct 372, 691 NE2d 946 (1998) (error to admit expert's profile of "abusive male"); *Com. v. LaCaprucia,* 41 Mass App 496, 499, 671 NE2d 984, 987 (1996) (error to permit expert to give characteristic sexual profile testimony that presented defendant's family situation as prone to sexual abuse). Compare *Com. v. Jackson,* 45 Mass App 666, 700 NE2d 848 (1998) (officer's statement that it was very common for drug buyers to refuse to identify sellers because of fear of retribution was an inadmissible description of characteristic of drug buyers, rather than permissible explanation of modus operandi of drug sales) with *Com. v. Robinson,* 43 Mass App Ct 257, 682 NE2d 903 (1997) (testimony about characteristics of two-person street drug transactions was admissible so long as it was more akin to description of modus operandi rather than profile of a drug dealer) and *Com. v. Dennis,* 33 Mass App 666, 604 NE2d 48 (1992) (defendant's conviction of trafficking reversed on other grounds, but court indicated that experienced narcotics officer's testimony as to how street level dealers conduct their business was admissible, court concluding it was more akin to a description of the dealers' modus operandi, than a "profile" of a drug dealer).

§7.8.6   Foreign Law

Expert testimony is admissible in certain situations to prove what the law is in other jurisdictions. See *Sullivan v. First Massachusetts Financial Corp.*, 409 Mass 783, 793, 569 NE2d 814, 821 (1991) (affirming trial court's discretion to admit expert testimony on question of whether a bank qualified for subchapter S status under federal tax law). Where the point in dispute between experts is a question of settled law, the judge should instruct the jury about the applicable law on the subject, and not permit it to return a verdict premised on an erroneous view of the law. In such a case, the judge's instruction on the point of law, or his or her ruling in a trial to the court, will be subject to appellate review in the same manner as any other instruction or ruling. *Romano v. Weiss*, 26 Mass App Ct 162, 524 NE2d 1381 (1988) (leaving open the question of whether the same approach is required if the legal point is the subject of uncertainty).

§7.8.7   Value

Testimony as to the value of property, business interests, investments, and the like may be given by properly qualified experts.[9] See, e.g., *Anthony's Pier Four, Inc. v. HBC Associates*, 411 Mass 451, 479, 583 NE2d 806, 824 (1991) (real estate development); *Barshak v. Buccheri*, 406 Mass 187,

---

[9] For a discussion of proof of value based on the sale price of similar land, see §4.4.9.b.

191, 547 NE2d 23, 26 (1989) (value of apartment complex); *Board of Assessors of Brookline v. Buehler*, 396 Mass 520, 487 NE2d 493 (1986) (real property); *Dewan v. Dewan*, 30 Mass App 133, 566 NE2d 1132 (1991) (value of pension); *Foley v. Foley*, 27 Mass App 221, 537 NE2d 158 (1989) (expert on value of real estate brokerage business improperly excluded); *Cataldo v. Zuckerman*, 20 Mass App 731, 744, 482 NE2d 849, 858 (1985) (testimony by CPA properly admitted on value of party's share of developer's equity in several projects).

An expert may base his opinions on value in part upon "trustworthy sources of information." *Olympia & York State v. Board of Assessors*, 428 Mass 236, 700 NE2d 533 (1998) (appraiser could rely upon his staff for market data); *McLaughlin v. Board of Selectmen of Amherst*, 422 Mass 359, 662 NE2d 687 (1996) (error to exclude opinion of real estate appraiser on real estate value, although witness had no brokering experience in the particular locality involved); *Analogic Corp. v. Peabody Board of Assessors*, 45 Mass App 605, 700 NE2d 548 (1998) (appraiser may rely on admissible data from interested parties).

In assessing the value of real property, whether it is appropriate to use the capitalization of income method of valuation rather than sale prices depends on the circumstances. See *Olympia & York State v. Board of Assessors*, supra (capitalization of income); *Pepsi-Cola Bottling Co. v. Board of Assessors of Boston*, 397 Mass 447, 491 NE2d 1071 (1986) (sale price had been adversely affected by uneconomic lease, "comparable" sales differed materially from subject property); *Board of Assessors of Boston v. Diab*, 396 Mass 560, 487 NE2d 491 (1986) (error to reject sale price in favor of capitalization of income method where decision was based on error of law regarding tax factors). In *Clifford v. Algonquin Gas Transmission Co.*, 413 Mass 809, 816, 604 NE2d 697, 702 (1992), it was held that the trial court had properly admitted expert testimony on the value of a large tract of land based on the "lot" method of appraising a potential subdivision. The court reasoned that the admissibility of such testimony turns on the particular facts and the extent to which a development has progressed toward completion, and that a trial judge is afforded discretion to determine whether a proposed subdivision plan is too speculative or remote as to preclude its submission to the jury. Under appropriate circumstances, a trial judge also has the discretion to permit expert testimony valuing land pursuant to the depreciated reproduction cost (DRC) method, for special purpose properties, although the method is disfavored. See *Correia v. New Bedford Redevelopment Authority*, 375 Mass 360, 366-367, 377 NE2d 909 (1978); *Lodge No. 65 v. Lawrence Redevelopment Authority*, 33 Mass App 701, 604 NE2d 715 (1992).

Testimony as to value is usually given by experts, but it may also be given by non-experts who are particularly familiar with the property in question. Admission of such opinion testimony by non-experts is a matter of sound judicial discretion upon establishment of a proper foundation of competency. *Menici v. Orton Crane & Shovel Co.*, 285 Mass 499, 504, 189 NE 839, 841 (1934); *Com. v. Shagoury*, 6 Mass App 584, 594, 380 NE2d 708, 714 (1978) (Text cited).

At one time, it was thought that an owner was presumed to have sufficient familiarity with his property to testify to its value. It is clear, however, that an owner, like any other witness, must be particularly familiar with property to testify as to its value. *Von Henneberg v. Generazio*, 403 Mass 519, 524, 531 NE2d 563, 566 (1988); *Blais-Porter, Inc. v. Simboli*, 402 Mass 269, 272, 521 NE2d 1013, 1016 (1988); *Fechtor v. Fechtor*, 26 Mass App 859, 865 (1989) (Text cited); *McCormick v. Travelers Indemnity Co.*, 22 Mass App 636, 496 NE2d 174 (1986) (Text cited); *Turner v. Leonard*, 17 Mass App 909, 455 NE2d 1215 (1983) (error to admit owner's testimony as to value of automobile absent evidence of familiarity with vehicle) (Text cited). A fortiori, an officer of a corporation, must show particular familiarity with the land or property owned by the corporation to testify as to its value. *Newton Girl Scout Council, Inc. v. Massachusetts Turnpike*

Authority, 335 Mass 189, 198, 138 NE2d 769, 773 (1956); *Winthrop Products Corp. v. Elroth Co.,* 331 Mass 83, 117 NE2d 157 (1954).

The recent assessed valuations of real estate are, by statute, admissible in eminent domain proceedings as evidence of fair market value of the property. GL 79, §35; *Bennett v. Brookline Redevelopment Authority,* 342 Mass 418, 173 NE2d 815 (1961); *Stewart v. Burlington,* 2 Mass App 712, 319 NE2d 921 (1974) (construing the 1969 amendment to §35). For discussion of the permissible methods of valuation by experts as to so-called specialized use properties, see *Correia v. New Bedford Redevelopment Authority,* 375 Mass 360, 377 NE2d 909 (1978) and *Saxon Theatre Corp. of Boston v. Hayden,* 7 Mass App 695, 389 NE2d 1020 (1979). See also *Alstores Realty Corp. v. Board of Assessors of Peabody,* 391 Mass 60, 460 NE2d 1276 (1984); *Montaup Electric Co. v. Board of Assessors of Whitman,* 390 Mass 847, 460 NE2d 583 (1984); *Boston Edison Co. v. Board of Assessors of Watertown,* 387 Mass 298, 439 NE2d 763 (1982); *Young Men's Christian Association of Quincy v. Sandwich Water District,* 16 Mass App 666, 454 NE2d 514 (1983).

A person can testify as to the value of his own services even though he has never been paid for them. *Cushman v. Boston, W. & N.Y. Street Railway Co.,* 319 Mass 177, 180, 65 NE2d 6, 8 (1946). However, if it appears that the opinion of the value of the witness's services is based primarily on the opinions of others as to such value, the evidence is inadmissible. *Downey v. Union Trust Co. of Springfield,* 312 Mass 405, 416, 45 NE2d 373, 380 (1942). In any event, testimony as to value of services is admissible only if such services are shown to have some market value. *Williamson v. Feinstein,* 311 Mass 322, 41 NE2d 185 (1942); *Matloff v. Chelsea,* 308 Mass 134, 31 NE2d 518 (1941). See also *Elbaum v. Sullivan,* 344 Mass 662, 183 NE2d 712 (1962). A finding as to the fair value of such services may be made without expert testimony. *Mason v. Black,* 341 Mass 347, 169 NE2d 899 (1960); *Levey v. Curry,* 12 Mass App 925, 424 NE2d 1147 (1981).

§7.9 Statutory Provisions for Expert Testimony

Massachusetts statutes provide for the discretionary admissibility of expert opinion evidence in certain cases. Some of these statutes are discussed in the following sections.

§7.9.1 Obscenity Cases

GL 272, §28F, provides that in actions to suppress an allegedly obscene book, "the court may receive the testimony of experts and may receive evidence as to the literary, artistic, political or scientific character of said book and as to the manner and form of its dissemination." This statute makes permissible expert testimony that would not have been admissible under the common-law criteria set forth above. Cf. *Com. v. United Books, Inc.*, 389 Mass 888, 894-896, 453 NE2d 406, 411-413 (1983) (reversible error to exclude qualified expert's testimony on contemporary community standards and question of serious artistic, social, political, and scientific value of film); *Com. v. Dane Entertainment Services, Inc. (No. 2)*, 389 Mass 917, 452 NE2d 1135 (1983) (same). Compare *Com. v. Dane Entertainment Services, Inc. (No. 1)*, 389 Mass 902, 910-915, 452 NE2d 1126, 1131-1134 (1983) (no error to exclude investigator's testimony as to community standards; although court may have ruled otherwise, it affirmed judge's discretion); *Attorney General v. Book Named "John Cleland's Memoirs of a Woman of Pleasure,"* 349 Mass 69, 206 NE2d 403 (1965) (expert literary testimony admitted and utilized by appellate court in two latter cases to determine whether books were hard-core pornography); *Attorney General v. Book Named "Tropic of Cancer,"* 345 Mass 11, 184 NE2d 328 (1962); *Com. v. Isenstadt*, 318 Mass 543, 62 NE2d 840 (1945) (testimony of literary and other experts properly excluded).

Section 28F, however, has been construed strictly as to the type of expert testimony it makes permissible. *Attorney General v. Book Named "Forever Amber,"* 323 Mass 302, 81

NE2d 663 (1948) (§28F does not permit testimony of psychiatrist that book had no tendency to incite lascivious thoughts or did not violate current sex mores). Cf. *District Attorney v. Three Way Theatres Corp.*, 371 Mass 391, 357 NE2d 747 (1976) (injunctive proceedings under GL 272, §30; error for judge to require expert testimony on the subject of community standards for proof of obscenity). The concept of the statute may not be extended into other types of proceedings. *Supreme Malt Products Co. v. Alcoholic Beverages Control Commission*, 334 Mass 59, 63-64, 133 NE2d 775, 779 (1956) (psychiatric testimony to effect that retail price of liquor has nothing to do with alcoholism was properly excluded in proceeding challenging minimum price law).

§7.9.2   *Malpractice Actions — Treatises*

GL 233, §79C, provides that in actions of contract or tort for malpractice or error in treatment by specified medical practitioners, facts and opinions from authoritative treatises are admissible.[1] The party intending to use a text must give 30 days' notice prior to trial. See *Ramsland v. Shaw*, 341 Mass 56, 63-64, 166 NE2d 894, 900 (1960) (even where defendant admitted authoritativeness of treatise, trial judge has discretion to exclude same as irrelevant); *Redding-*

---

§7.9   [1] The statute provides:

Statements of facts or opinions on a subject of science or art contained in a published treatise, periodical, book or pamphlet shall, insofar as the court shall find that the said statements are relevant and that the writer of such statements is recognized in his profession or calling as an expert on the subject, be admissible in actions of contract or tort for malpractice, error or mistake against physicians, surgeons, dentists, optometrists, hospitals and sanitaria, as evidence tending to prove said facts or as opinion evidence; provided, however, that the party intending to offer as evidence any such statements shall, not less than thirty days before the trial of the action, give the adverse party or his attorney notice of such intention, stating the name of the writer of the statements, the title of the treatise, periodical, book or pamphlet in which they are contained, the date of publication of the same, the name of the publisher of the same, and wherever possible or practicable the page or pages of the same on which said statements appear.

ton v. Clayman, 334 Mass 244, 134 NE2d 920 (1956) (bio-
graphical data in front of treatise cannot be used to
establish authoritativeness of author; nor can court take
judicial notice of same).

In *Mazzaro v. Paull*, 372 Mass 645, 363 NE2d 509
(1977), the court suggested that a *Who's Who* might be used
to establish the expertise of authors of medical treatises, if
the requirements of the Commercial Lists Statute, GL 233,
§79B, were met. See §8.12 for discussion.

In *Simmons v. Yurchak*, 28 Mass App 371, 551 NE2d 539
(1990), the court held that §79C did not authorize the
admission of a videotape produced by the American Medical Association. The court acknowledged that videotapes
are now frequently used for informational and instructional
purposes and that exclusion was not compelled by the fact
that they were not mentioned in the statute, because they
did not exist when it was drafted in 1949. However, the
court reasoned that published written works have "an
imprimatur of reliability" as a result of the careful, professional criticism attendant to the editorial and publishing
process. Lacking information about whether similar care is
taken in the production of videotapes, the court concluded
that it should be left to the legislature to indicate whether
videotapes are admissible under §79C.

Evidence of treatises is not limited to the use permitted
by the statute. In *Com. v. Sneed*, 413 Mass 387, 394-397, 597
NE2d 1346, 1350-1351 (1992), the court adopted Proposed
Mass R Evid 803(18), which allows authoritative treatises to
be used during the cross-examination of expert witnesses.
For a fuller discussion, see §8.18.

§7.9.3 Physicians' Reports

GL 233, §79G, permits medical opinions regarding
diagnosis, treatment, prognosis, and causation to be introduced in the form of written reports that would otherwise
constitute hearsay. The statute requires that notice of the

intention to offer a report into evidence be provided no less than ten days before its introduction at trial. The opposing party is then free to summon into court at his own expense the author of the report, for the purposes of cross-examination. For the text of the statute and additional discussion, see §8.11.3.

§7.9.4   Blood and Genetic Marker Tests

GL 209C, §17, provides for the administration of tests to establish paternity.[2] The statute provides, inter alia, that

---

[2]The statute provides:

In an action under this chapter to establish paternity of a child born out of wedlock, the court shall, on a motion of a party and upon a proper showing except as provided in this section, order the mother, the child and the putative father to submit to one or more genetic marker tests of a type generally acknowledged as reliable and performed by a laboratory approved by an accreditation body designated by the federal Secretary of Health and Human Services pursuant to Title IV, Part D of the Social Security Act: An affidavit by the mother or the putative father alleging that sexual intercourse between the mother and the putative father occurred during the probable period of conception shall be sufficient to establish a proper showing. If during the probable period of conception, the mother was married to someone other than the putative father, the court may order genetic marker tests only after notice pursuant to subsection (c) of section 6 to the spouse or former spouse. The court or the IV-D agency as provided in section 3A of chapter 119A may order any person properly made a party under this chapter to submit to such testing. Unless a party objects in writing to the test results upon notice of the hearing date or within thirty days prior to the hearing, whichever is shorter, the report of the results of genetic marker tests, including a statistical probability of the putative father's paternity based upon such tests, shall be admissible in evidence without the need for laying a foundation or other proof of authenticity or accuracy; provided, further, that such report shall not be considered as evidence of the occurrence of intercourse between the mother and the putative father; and provided, however, that such report shall not be admissible absent sufficient evidence of intercourse between the mother and the putative father during the period of probable conception. If such report indicates a statistical probability of paternity of ninety-seven percent or greater, there shall be a rebuttable presumption that the putative father is the father of such child and, upon motion of any party or on its own motion, the court shall issue a temporary order of support. If the report of the results of genetic marker tests or an expert's analysis of inherited characteristics is disputed, the court may then order that an additional test be made at the same laboratory or different laboratory at the expense of the party requesting additional testing. Verified documentation of the chain of custody of genetic marker or agencies accredited pursuant to Title IV, Part D of the Social Security Act, as well as a court, have authority to order testing. The statute by its terms applies only to establishing the paternity of children born out of wedlock. It further provides that if the mother was married to someone other than the putative father during the probable period of conception, notice to that spouse is required before testing may be ordered. Upon a showing that there is a statistical probability of paternity of 97 percent or greater, the statute establishes a rebuttable presumption that the putative father is the father.

Section 17 applies to all blood or genetic marker tests that may be used to attempt to establish paternity. The statute allows a court to order tests of all parties to a paternity action, based on a "proper showing" that such tests would be appropriate. The statute specifically provides that an affidavit by either the mother or the putative father that sexual intercourse occurred during the probable period of conception is sufficient to establish a proper showing. In *G.E.B. v. S.R.W.*, 422 Mass 158, 661 NE2d 646 (1996), the court held that proof of intercourse to trigger the statute is judged by a preponderance of the evidence standard and it refused to read a clear and convincing evidence standard into the statute.

---

other specimens is competent evidence to establish such chain of custody. The fact that any party refuses to submit to genetic marker test shall be admissible and the court may draw an adverse inference from such refusal. The cost of making any tests ordered pursuant to this section shall, in the first instance, be chargeable against the party making the motion. The court in its discretion may order the costs of such testing to be apportioned among the parties provided, however, the court may not direct the IV-D agency as set forth in chapter 119A to pay for such tests, unless said IV-D agency is the moving party and provided further, that if the putative father is found to be the father, the court shall order the putative father to reimburse the IV-D agency or the other party. Payment for the costs of such tests shall be considered a necessary expense and if any party chargeable with the costs of the genetic marker tests is indigent as provided in section twenty-seven A of chapter two hundred and sixty-one, the court may direct payment of such costs by the commonwealth regardless of the type of tests requested by the moving party. (Pursuant to Secs. 234-246 of St. 1998, c. 64.)

Under §17, such tests may be introduced not only to exclude the possibility of a putative father's paternity, but also to establish the statistical probability of a putative father's paternity.[3] Significantly, such a positive result establishes no presumption of paternity, but is simply a factor to be weighed along with other evidence of paternity.

Under §17, blood and genetic marker tests may not be used as evidence of the occurrence of intercourse between the mother and the putative father. Reports of such tests are not admissible unless there is sufficient other evidence of intercourse between the mother and putative father during the period of probable conception. *Department of Revenue v. Sorrentino*, 408 Mass 340, 345 n.1, 557 NE2d 1376, 1379 n.1 (1990).

Section 17 provides that the refusal by a party to submit to a blood test is admissible in evidence. In *Department of Revenue v. B. P.*, 412 Mass 1015, 593 NE2d 1305 (1992), the court held that there was no constitutional impediment to the admission in evidence in a civil action of a party's refusal to take such tests and stated that there was no constitutional bar to the imposition of other sanctions for failure to comply with discovery orders under Dist/Mun Cts R Civ P 37(b)(2).[4]

The statute provides for the payment and apportionment of costs of the test and for the payment by the Commonwealth for costs for indigent parties.

---

[3]The use of blood tests to exclude the possibility of paternity has long been held reliable, even in the absence of a statute. *Com. v. Sasville*, 35 Mass App 15, 22, 616 NE2d 476, 481 (1993) (citing *Com. v. Stappen*, 336 Mass 174, 143 NE2d 221 (1957)).

[4]At present, there is no statute permitting a court to require a criminal defendant in a paternity action to submit to blood tests. It would appear that a refusal to submit to blood testing in a criminal proceeding would not be admissible in evidence, based on the defendant's constitutional right not to furnish evidence against himself. *Opinion of the Justices*, 412 Mass 1201, 591 NE2d 1073 (1992) (declaring unconstitutional proposed legislation that would have rendered admissible the refusal to submit to blood tests in connection with the charge of driving under the influence).

A report of the results of blood or genetic marker tests on the issue of paternity is not admissible in evidence unless offered through the testimony of an expert who describes and establishes the adequacy of the testing procedures used. *Department of Revenue v. Sorrentino*, supra; *Com. Beausoleil*, 397 Mass 206, 490 NE2d 788 (1986).

Where parties voluntarily consent to submit to such tests, the results are admissible if the other requirements of the statute are met, even though the tests were not taken pursuant to a court order. *Department of Revenue v. Sorrentino*, supra.

Under Mass R Civ P 35(a) and Mass R Dom Rel P 35(a), a court may order a physical or mental examination, including blood or genetic marker tests. *Symonds v. Symonds*, 385 Mass 540, 432 NE2d 700 (1982) (results of such tests are admissible in annulment and divorce proceedings, even in absence of statutory authority). *Symonds* further stated that despite the rule barring spouses from testifying as to non-access where the legitimacy of a child born during wedlock is issue (see *Taylor v. Whittier*, 240 Mass 514, 138 NE 6 (1922) (Lord Mansfield rule)), scientific evidence is not only admissible but may conclusively establish non-paternity. The Supreme Judicial Court has held that probable cause to believe either that a man is or is not the father of a child is sufficient to meet the constitutional standard for ordering parties to submit to blood tests. *A. R. v. C. R.*, 411 Mass 570, 576, 583 NE2d 840, 844 (1992) (leaving open question of whether something less than probable cause might also suffice to justify court-ordered blood testing in civil proceedings). See *R. R. K. v. S. G. P.*, 400 Mass 12, 18, 507 NE2d 736, 740 (1987) (concurring op, Liacos, CJ) ("improper in the extreme" for a judge to order parties to submit to psychological evaluations and to blood tests based solely on the unsworn, unverified complaint of plaintiff).

The court does not have the power to require a blood test in a proceeding for non-support of a minor child under

GL 273, §1, but expert testimony of blood grouping tests showing the exclusion of the defendant as the father of the child whose support is sought is admissible. The presumption of legitimacy of a child born during wedlock may be rebutted by such an exclusionary blood grouping. *Symonds v. Symonds,* supra; *Com. v. Stappen,* 336 Mass 174, 143 NE2d 221 (1957). Where there is evidence of a blood grouping test properly administered that definitely excludes the paternity of the alleged father, he must be adjudged not to be the father as a matter of law. *Symonds v. Symonds,* supra; *Com. v. D'Avella,* 339 Mass 642, 162 NE2d 19 (1959).

§7.9.5   *Blood Alcohol Tests*

GL 90, §24(1)(e), provides for blood and breath testing of drivers for the presence of alcohol. It permits an inference that a defendant is intoxicated if the percentage of alcohol in the blood is .08% or greater. The test gives rise to a "permissive inference" of intoxication at that level, rather than a "presumption," as the former version of the statute had provided. The case law had already indicated that a jury should not be charged in terms of presumptions with respect to such evidence. See *Com. v. Moreira,* 385 Mass 792, 434 NE2d 196 (1982). A driver's license may be suspended when an arrestee refuses to submit to a test.

The Commonwealth may offer as prima facie evidence of blood alcohol percentage a signed, sworn statement of a chemist of the Department of State Police or the Department of Public Health.

In *Com. v. Brooks,* 366 Mass 423, 319 NE2d 901 (1974) and in *Com. v. Bernier,* 366 Mass 717, 322 NE2d 414 (1975), the court engaged in an extensive discussion of the legal and chemical meaning of the terms of §24 with particular reference to the so-called breathalyzer. Further discussion of the scientific principles underlying the use of a breathalyzer is found in *Com. v. Neal*, 392 Mass 1, 464 NE2d 1356 (1984). In *Neal* and in *Com. v. Doyle*, 392 Mass 23, 465 NE2d 1192 (1984), the court rejected a number of constitutional arguments against the use of breathalyzer evidence where breath samples or test ampules had not been preserved for the defendant's experts to test.

The reliability of the instrumentation employed and the specific procedures followed present legitimate issues that may be contested in individual cases involving breathalyzer evidence. The court must make a preliminary finding in a given case that the breathalyzer test result is sufficiently reliable to go to the jury. *Com. v. Durning*, 406 Mass 485, 548 NE2d 1242 (1990). See *Com. v Marley*, 396 Mass 433, 486 NE2d 715 (1985) (delay in time from when police were dispatched to accident at 4:30 A.M. until administration of breathalyzer test at 7:05 A.M. was not unreasonable and did not require exclusion of test results, nor was defendant entitled to a jury instruction on the effect of the time delay, in the absence of scientific evidence to support claim that delay was harmful to him); *Com. v. Neal*, supra (potential effect of radio frequency interference on S & W model 900A breathalyzer units is sufficient to require that admission of results be conditioned on demonstration to trial judge of the accuracy of the particular unit at the time test was performed). Performance of simulator tests is a common method for establishing the reliability of the machines. See *Com. v. Durning*, supra (no requirement that a simulator test be performed immediately after the breathalyzer examination of defendant, simulations performed 19 days before and 13 days after the defendant's, together with certification of the device 11 days before and a beam attenuator test 5 days after, were sufficient); *Com. v. Cochran*, 25 Mass App 260, 517 NE2d 498 (1988) (where simulator deviation exceeds the permissible tolerance according to the testimony, test results are inadmissible).

Problems of reliability are specifically addressed by GL 90, §24K,[5] and the regulations promulgated thereunder, 501 Code Mass. Regs., §2.41. The regulations stipulate that testing shall be performed by the police using the breathalyzer equipment and that the mandatory calibration of a breathalyzer prior to each use shall be deemed to be a test of the device. The regulations were found to be in compliance with the statutory mandate in *Morris v. Com.*, 412 Mass 861, 593 NE2d 241 (1992), where the court rejected a challenge based on the assertion that delegation of the testing to the police was improper and that the regulations

---

[5]The statute provides:

§24K. Chemical breath analysis; validity; testing procedures; report forms

Chemical analysis of the breath of a person charged with a violation of this chapter shall not be considered valid under the provisions of this chapter, unless such analysis has been performed by a certified operator, using infrared breath-testing devices according to methods approved by the secretary of public safety. The secretary of public safety shall promulgate rules and regulations regarding satisfactory methods, techniques and criteria for the conduct of such tests, and shall establish a statewide training and certification program for all operators of such devices and a periodic certification program for such breath testing devices; provided, however, that the secretary may terminate or revoke such certification at his discretion.

Said regulations shall include, but shall not be limited to the following:

(a) that the chemical analysis of the breath of a person charged be performed by a certified operator using a certified infrared breath-testing device in the following sequence:
(1) one adequate breath sample analysis;
(2) one calibration standard analysis;
(3) a second adequate breath sample analysis;
(b) that no person shall perform such a test unless certified by the secretary of public safety;
(c) that no breath testing device, mouthpiece or tube shall be cleaned with any substance containing alcohol.

The secretary of public safety shall prescribe a uniform form for reports of such chemical analysis to be used by law enforcement officers and others acting in accordance with the provisions of this chapter. Such forms shall be sequentially numbered. Each chief of police or other officer or official having charge or control of a law enforcement agency shall be responsible for the furnishing and proper disposition of such uniform forms. Each party so responsible shall prepare or cause to be prepared such records and reports relating to such uniform forms and their disposition in such manner and at such times as the secretary of public safety shall prescribe.

should have provided a fixed period or regular interval for "periodic" testing. In *Com. v. Barbeau*, 411 Mass 782, 585 NE2d 1392 (1992), the court had held that breathalyzer test results were inadmissible where the Commonwealth had not offered any evidence that a periodic testing program existed.

The regulations require that the breathalyzer must not only be tested each time it is used, but that the operator must change the simulator solution in the device, run calibration analyses, and record test results in a prescribed manner. See *Com. v. Smith*, 35 Mass App 655, 661, 624 NE2d 604, 608 (1993); *Com. v. Livers,* 420 Mass 556, 650 NE2d 791 (1995) (Commonwealth was required to have a periodic testing program of devices, but statute did not require adoption of regulations for periodic testing of devices); *Com. v. Kelley*, 39 Mass App 448, 657 NE2d 1274 (1995) (neither statutes nor regulations require certification by Office of Alcohol Testing of known value of simulator solution every time a device is used).

For the results of a breathalyzer examination to be admissible, the analysis must be performed by a certified operator. GL 90, §24K. The Secretary of Public Safety may delegate the process of certification to the Criminal Justice Training council. *Com. v. Smigliano*, 427 Mass 490, 694 NE2d 341 (1998). The qualifications of a police officer as an expert to testify as to breathalyzer test results is discussed in *Com. v. Shea*, 356 Mass 358, 252 NE2d 336 (1969) (officer's infirmities in knowledge and skill in administering test go to weight and not admissibility of testimony).

A defendant is entitled to call a properly qualified expert to testify about various particulars of breathalyzer examination and the effect of alcohol upon the body. *Com. v. Smythe*, 23 Mass App 348, 502 NE2d 162 (1987) (error to exclude proposed testimony regarding installation, maintenance, testing, calibration and operation of machine, whether or not defendant on videotape displayed the clinically observable signs expected of an individual with a 0.17 percent blood alcohol content, the amount of alcohol a person of defendant's size would need to consume during relevant time period to obtain a 0.17 reading, what defendant's blood alcohol content would have been if he had consumed only the amount of alcohol he claimed). But see *Com. v. Connolly*, 394 Mass 169, 474 NE2d 1106 (1985) (where defendant refused to take breathalyzer, it was proper for trial court to exclude evidence from expert regarding what blood alcohol level a person of defendant's size would have had after consuming a given amount of alcohol, and of the effect of that amount of alcohol on his person).

In *Com. v. Smith*, supra, the trial court had excluded evidence offered by the prosecution of "retrograde extrapolation," a calculation that attempts to determine from a given reading at the time of the test what the operator's blood alcohol level would have been earlier at the time of the alleged offense. The defendant complained on appeal of prejudice resulting from the prosecutor's mention of such evidence in the opening. The court rejected the argument, noting that there was no authority in this state requiring exclusion of such evidence, that it had been ruled admissible in a number of jurisdictions, and suggesting it might be admissible under an analysis pursuant to *Daubert v. Merrell Dow Pharmaceuticals, Inc.*, 509 US 579, 113 S Ct 2786 (1993), 125 L Ed 2d 469. (See §7.7.1.)

The constitutionality of GL 90, §24(1)(f), which requires an immediate suspension of the right to operate a motor vehicle where the terms of §24(1)(f) have been complied with, was upheld against a claim of denial of due process of law absent a hearing prior to suspension. *Mackey v. Montrym*, 443 US 1, 99 S Ct 2612 (1979) (upholding 90-day suspension in former version of statute).

In *Com. v. Brennan*, 386 Mass 772, 438 NE2d 60 (1982), the court held that the use of a breathalyzer and field sobriety tests to determine intoxication does not involve testimonial communication; hence, introduction of such tests is not barred by the Fifth Amendment to the United States Constitution or by art. 12 of the Massachusetts Declaration of Rights. In *Com. v. Brazelton*, 404 Mass 783, 537 NE2d 142 (1989), the court held that there is no constitutional right to consult with counsel before deciding whether or not to submit to a breathalyzer examination. However, in *Opinion of the Justices*, 412 Mass 1201, 591 NE2d 1073 (1992), the Justices expressed the view that under art. 12 of the Declaration of Rights, a proposed amendment to the statute would be unconstitutional that would have made the refusal to consent to such an examination admissible in evidence. The Justices noted that although the use of test results does not involve testimonial evidence, a refusal to take a test is testimonial and an arrestee is constitutionally entitled to refuse to furnish such evidence against himself, under the Declaration of Rights.[6]

An earlier version of GL 90, §24(1)(e), had provided that when no evidence of the blood alcohol level is presented at trial, the trial judge must instruct the jury that a person has a legal right not to take the test, that there might be a number of reasons why a person would not take the test and why a test would not be administered, and that the jury is not allowed to speculate as to the reason for the absence of the test. Jury instructions pursuant to this statute were held unconstitutional in *Com. v. Zevitas*, 418 Mass 677, 639 NE2d 1076 (1994). The court reasoned that the trial judge was, in effect, informing the jury that the defendant had refused the test and that a jury would be likely to draw inferences adverse to the defendant. The court held that the question was the same, for all practical purposes, as the issue the Justices had considered in *Opinion of the Justices*, supra, and that this portion of the statute would compel an

---

[6] It should be noted that the United States Supreme Court had earlier held that the admission in evidence of a refusal to submit to a breathalyzer test does not violate the Fifth Amendment to the United States Constitution. *South Dakota v. Neville*, 459 US 553, 103 S Ct 916 (1983). For a further discussion of the difference between testimonial and non-testimonial material and the protection afforded by the privilege against self-incrimination, see §13.14.2.b.

accused to furnish evidence against himself, in violation of art. 12 of the Declaration of Rights.

Collateral comments made by a defendant during a discussion with the police about the breathalyzer may be admissible in evidence where no evidence is offered that the defendant refused the test. *Com. v. Sands,* 424 Mass 184, 189, 675 NE2d 370, 373 (1997) (not error to admit statement, "I'm not drunk, but I'm over."). See *Com. v. Conroy,* 396 Mass 266, 485 NE2d 180 (1985) (error for trooper to testify that defendant was offered a breathalyzer examination, when no such test results were offered at trial, because it implied that defendant had refused the examination; error was ruled harmless in the circumstances of the case). Determining whether or not one has "consented" to a breathalyzer examination is a question of whether the person gave actual consent, as opposed to having been forced to submit to the testing. It is not essential that the Commonwealth demonstrate that the decision to submit to the test was "knowing, voluntary, and intelligent," as is required when demonstrating a waiver of constitutional rights. *Com. v. Davidson,* 27 Mass App 846, 545 NE2d 55 (1989).

In addition to the provision in GL 90, §24(1)(e), that the defendant shall be afforded "a reasonable opportunity, at his request and at his expense, to have another such test or analysis made by a person or a physician selected by him," a correlative right for private examination is provided in GL 263, §5A.[7]

---

[7] The statute provides:

A person held in custody at a police station or other place of detention, charged with operating a motor vehicle while under the influence of intoxicating liquor, shall have the right, at his request and at his expense, to be examined immediately by a physician selected by him. The police official in charge of such station or place of detention, or his designee, shall inform him of such right immediately upon being booked, and shall afford him a reasonable opportunity to exercise it. Such person shall, immediately upon being booked, be given a copy of this section unless such a copy is posted in the police station or other place of detention in a conspicuous place to which such person has access.

The statutes require that the police afford a person in custody a reasonable opportunity to obtain an independent examination, and inform him of his right to do so. See *Com. v. King,* 429 Mass 169, 706 NE2d 685 (1999); *Com. v. Rosewarne,* 410 Mass 53, 571 NE2d 354 (1991) (police not required to assist defendant in obtaining independent test, not required to drive him to hospital); *Com. v. Durning,* 406 Mass 485, 548 NE2d 1242 (1990) (requirement was met where defendant was given a reasonable opportunity to obtain an independent blood test, although he was unsuccessful in locating a physician to perform one); *Com. v. Marley,* 396 Mass 433, 486 NE2d 715 (1985) (police waited until after taking defendant from two-hour stay at hospital to police station before advising him of rights under GL 263, §5A, no violation because statute requires advice of rights only "upon being booked"; but see concurring opinion by Liacos, CJ, which would have found a violation and applied a standard of reasonableness to the giving of notice of rights); *Com. v. Lindner,* 395 Mass 144, 478 NE2d 1267 (1985) (police not responsible for loss or destruction of defendant's blood sample left at hospital). An indigent defendant has no constitutional right to have a private test or examination at public expense under either GL 90, §24(1)(e), or GL 263, §5A. *Com. v. Tessier,* 371 Mass 828, 360 NE2d 304 (1977).

The police may not, however, prevent or hinder an arrested person's reasonable and timely attempt to obtain an independent examination. GL 263, §5A, together with the statutory right to prompt release on bail, GL 276, §§42, 57, 58, require that the police promptly telephone a bail commissioner and inform him that an arrestee has requested an independent medical examination or allow the detainee to do so directly. The bail commissioner is obliged to respond promptly. *Com. v. King,* supra (six-hour guideline for providing a bail hearing does not apply once an independent medical exam is requested, because the evidence will be destroyed during that length of time; violation of rights occurred when bail commissioner refused to come to station because arrestee had refused breatha-lyzer); *Com. v. Hampe,* 419 Mass 514, 646 NE2d 387 (1995). Compare *Com. v. Priestley,* 419 Mass 678, 646 NE2d 754 (1995) (although there was no evidence that defendant was advised by police that he could make contact with bail commissioner, evidence showed he made numerous tele-phone calls, obtained advice from his lawyer, and talked with friends; hence, defendant was not prevented from seeking bail on his own); *Com. v. Maylott,* 43 Mass App Ct 516, 684 NE2d 10 (1997) (permissible to require arrestee to complete booking procedure before allowing him to exer-cise statutory rights). It is required that an arrested party inform the police that he wishes to exercise his right under §5A to an independent examination or blood tests to support a finding of an obstruction of his rights under the statute. *Com. v. Finelli,* 422 Mass 860, 666 NE2d 144 (1996); *Com. v. Chistolini,* 38 Mass App 966, 650 NE2d 1278 (1995); *Com. v. Falco,* 43 Mass App Ct 253, 682 NE2d 900 (1997) (holding arrestee for six and one-half hours without bail hearing, because he refused breathalyzer, where he was advised of right to telephone call and independent medical exam and requested neither, did not violate his rights).

In *Com. v. King,* supra, the court held that dismissal is the presumptive remedy for a violation of the statute. The court concluded:

> the violation itself is prima facie evidence that the defendant has been prejudiced in that his opportunity to obtain and present potentially exculpatory evidence has been restricted or destroyed. This presumption of prejudice, however, may be overcome by overwhelming evidence of intoxica-tion . . . or by other evidence indicating that the omission was not prejudicial in the circumstances.

429 Mass at 180-181, 706 NE2d at 693-694.[8] See *Com. v. Ames,* 410 Mass 603, 574 NE2d 986 (1991) (police offered

---

[8] In *Com. v. King,* the court did not explicitly state whether a remedy other than dismissal is appropriate when the Commonwealth overcomes

defendant a blood test when he was at hospital, although they did not specifically mention §5A right, court found defendant would not have exercised right, hence no prejudice); *Com. v. McIntyre*, 36 Mass App 193, 629 NE2d 355 (1994) (not error to refuse to dismiss for failure to notify defendant of rights where he was an attorney who knew of right to have an independent examination and requested one). In *Com. v. Neal*, 392 Mass 1, 464 NE2d 1356 (1984), the court held that this statutory right of a second test discharges the due process obligation of the Commonwealth to preserve breath samples and breathalyzer ampules for retesting by the defendant.

In *Irwin v. Ware*, 392 Mass 745, 748-752, 467 NE2d 1292, 1296-1298 (1984), the court held that a doctor's letter as to blood alcohol analysis was not admissible under GL 233, §78, as a business record, and that there was insufficient evidence to authenticate the blood samples analyzed — i.e., to show the blood to be that of the motor vehicle operator.

§7.10 Court-Appointed Experts

Proposed Mass R Evid 706(a), which is identical with the federal rule, provides that the court on its own motion or on the motion of any party may enter an order to show cause why an expert witness should not be appointed and may require the parties to submit nominations. The purpose of the rule is to make available nonpartisan expert testimony. The rule makes explicit a power that has been

---

the presumption of prejudice. In *Com. v. Hampe*, supra, the court had suggested that where dismissal is inappropriate, ordinarily the results of the breathalyzer should be suppressed as well as any police testimony about events occurring after the violation of the right. Because the *King* presumption in favor of dismissal is not based on an exclusionary rule analysis, but rather on the prejudice to the defendant's right to establish his innocence, it is not clear that suppression would still be appropriate where no prejudice exists.

implicit in Massachusetts for years (see *Abodeely v. County of Worcester*, 352 Mass 719, 227 NE2d 486 (1967)) and does not disturb statutory schemes for appointment of experts. See GL 123, §15. See also Mass R Crim P 41.

Proposed Mass R Evid 706(b) provides for reasonable compensation of the appointed expert. This section diverges from the federal rule to accommodate state practice. Rule 706(c), which also diverges from the federal rule, prohibits disclosure to the jury through any source of the fact that the court has appointed the witness. Federal Rule 706(c) leaves this matter to the discretion of the court. Rule 706(d), which is the same as the federal rule, makes it clear that the appointment of an expert by the court does not preclude the parties from calling their own expert witnesses.

8

HEARSAY

A.   GENERAL NATURE OF HEARSAY

§8.1   Definition

The hearsay rule forbids the admission in evidence of extra-judicial statements offered to prove the truth of the matters asserted in the statements.[1] Proposed Mass R Evid 802; Fed R Evid 802. Proposed Mass R Evid 801(c) and Fed R Evid 801(c) define hearsay as "a statement, other than one made by the declarant while testifying at the trial or hearing, offered in evidence to prove the truth of the matter asserted." A "statement" is defined by both rules as: "(1) an oral or written assertion; or (2) nonverbal conduct of a person, if it is intended by him as an assertion." Rule 801(a).[2] A "declarant" is a person "who makes a statement." Rule 801(b). The definitions in the rules are consistent with the Massachusetts articulation of the hearsay rule. *Com. v. Keizer*, 377 Mass 264, 269 n.4, 385 NE2d 1001, 1004 n.4 (1979) (definition of hearsay) (citing Text); *Opinion of the Justices*, 412 Mass 1201, 1209, 591 NE2d 1073, 1077 (1992) (conduct as an assertion) (citing Text); *Com. v. Diaz*, 426 Mass 548, 689 NE2d 804 (1998) (statement offered to prove the truth of an assertion is not admissible "to show the general atmosphere of what was occurring").

An extrajudicial statement may contain within it one or more other statements that also constitute assertions offered for their truth. In such multiple hearsay problems, each layer of hearsay must be independently admissible. *Com. v. McDonough*, 400 Mass 639, 643, 511 NE2d 551, 554 (1987). Current Massachusetts law is in accord with Proposed Mass R Evid 805: "Hearsay included within hearsay is not excluded under the hearsay rule if each part of the

---

§8.1   [1] In certain proceedings, the proscription against hearsay may be relaxed. See §1.2.

[2] Nonverbal conduct that is not intended as an assertion is not hearsay, although it may constitute circumstantial evidence of the actor's state of mind. See, e.g., §4.2.1 (consciousness of guilt and consciousness of liability).

combined statements conforms with an exception to the hearsay rule provided by law or in these rules." Fed R Evid 805 is similar.[3]

The principal reason for the hearsay rule is that extra-judicial statements, unlike statements in court, are not immediately tested by cross-examination. Thus, there may be no way to determine whether extrajudicial statements accurately and fully depict the matters asserted. Hearsay statements are not admissible merely because they may have been made under oath. *Moran v. School Committee of Littleton,* 317 Mass 591, 595, 59 NE2d 279, 281 (1945) (affidavits are hearsay). Hearsay evidence is nevertheless admissible in many instances, either because the extrajudicial statements were made under circumstances that insure accuracy or because no better evidence is available.

Determining the admissibility of extrajudicial statements requires a two-step analysis. First, is the statement hearsay — i.e., is it offered for a hearsay purpose, to prove the truth of the matter asserted in the statement? Second, if it is hearsay, does it fall within an exception to the rule?

§8.2   Extrajudicial Statements that Are Not Hearsay

The word "hearsay" does not embrace an extrajudicial statement offered to prove something other than the truth of the statement. The variety of other purposes for which extrajudicial statements may be offered is endless, and many do not fall neatly within any particular category. For example, in *Com. v. Koney,* 421 Mass 295, 303, 657 NE2d 210, 215 (1995), the Commonwealth sought to prove that the defendant had received notice that his driver's license had been revoked. A police officer had testified that he received a Massachusetts identification card from the de-

---

[3] The requirement that each level of hearsay be independently admissible may be modified by statute. See GL 119, §§21, 24, and cases cited in §7.7.4.b.

fendant, and the court concluded that although the card could not be offered for the hearsay purpose of proving that the defendant actually was the person named on the card and lived at the address on the card, it could be offered for the more limited purpose of establishing that the defendant held himself out to be a person of that name, residing at that address, and hence was connected with the address to which the notices of revocation had been mailed. In *Com. v. Sullivan*, 410 Mass 521, 526, 574 NE2d 966, 970 (1991), a police officer testified that *D*'s sister told him that *V* left her apartment in a cab. The statement was not offered to prove that *V* left in a cab, for she had not. It was offered to prove that *D* told his sister to claim that *V* left in that way, evidence of his consciousness of guilt, and an effort to cover up his crime. In *Com. v. Gabbidon*, 398 Mass 1, 494 NE2d 1317 (1986), there was testimony that after a shooting, *D* became known by nicknames, such as "Top Ranking," "Rankin" and "General," whereas before he was "just another person." The court held that the nicknames were not hearsay, and were admissible as relevant to *D*'s motives for the shooting.[1] In *Com. v. Sullivan*, 123 Mass 221 (1877), the court held that if the existence of an event described in an extrajudicial statement is proved otherwise, the statement is admissible to prove that the event occurred before the statement.

Previous statements by a witness may be either consistent or inconsistent with her present testimony. Where such statements are offered for the truth of their assertions, they would constitute hearsay. Where offered simply to impeach or to bolster credibility, they are not offered for a

---

§8.2   [1] This case demonstrates the subtlety of analysis that some hearsay problems require. Note that the evidence that *D* became known by the nicknames in question is not relevant unless one implicitly assumes that those originating the use of the nicknames believed that *D* had earned them, which in terms of the prejudicial effect of the testimony is close to the hearsay assertion that he was a killer. Limiting instructions may not always be sufficient to limit the use to which jurors put such evidence.

hearsay purpose. The use and admissibility of such evidence is discussed in §6.7.2 (prior inconsistent statements) and §6.16 (prior consistent statements).

In the following sections we discuss several types of extrajudicial statements offered for something other than their truth, but the various categories should be viewed as illustrative, rather than exhaustive.

§8.2.1   Speech Evidencing Condition of Speaker

An extrajudicial declaration is not hearsay if it is offered to prove that the declarant was conscious at the time of the declaration. *Hayes v. Pitts-Kimball Co.*, 183 Mass 262, 67 NE 249 (1903). Nor is it hearsay if it is offered as proof of a cry of distress or emotion. *Com. v. Tracy*, 349 Mass 87, 96, 207 NE2d 16, 21 (1965).

§8.2.2   Statement Offered as Proof of Notice, Knowledge, Motive

An extrajudicial statement is not hearsay when offered to prove that the person to whom it was addressed had notice or knowledge of the contents of the statement. *Com. v. Bush*, 691 NE2d 218 (1998) (witness's statements to defendant about victim were admissible to prove reasons for defendant to be angry, to anticipate a confrontation, and to arm himself); *McNamara v. Honeyman*, 406 Mass 43, 546 NE2d 139 (1989) (in medical malpractice action, the statement of decedent's boyfriend to ward attendant that she told him she had attempted to choke herself admissible to show notice to the hospital staff of the danger of suicide, but not to prove that she actually had tried to harm herself); *Com. v. Therenin*, 33 Mass App 588, 603 NE2d 223 (1992) (statement to *D* by friend prior to alleged rape that *V* had "crabs" admissible to show *D*'s disinclination to have contact with her).

A party's knowledge of the contents of statements must be material for them to be admissible on this basis. *Com. v. Pleasant*, 366 Mass 100, 315 NE2d 874 (1974); *Com. v. Stokes*, 38 Mass App 752, 653 NE2d 180 (1995) (defendant's evidence of out-of-court statement by witness to police officers, otherwise hearsay, was not admissible to show that police had ignored the information, as evidence of their bias, where interview with witness did not contain exculpatory evidence and defendant's account of her other statements lacked reasonable guarantee of trustworthiness).

On occasion it has been felt necessary to permit testimony relating to the investigative background which led to the taking of specific action by police officers. *Com. v. La-Velle*, 414 Mass 146, 155, 605 NE2d 852, 858 (1993) (extrajudicial statements regarding informant's past relationship with police were admissible as relevant to state of police knowledge that led them to use that person as an informant and to seek out defendant as a possible drug trafficker); *Com. v. Cohen*, 412 Mass 375, 393, 589 NE2d 289, 300 (1992) (testimony that defendant's father told police that defendant was not home while he pointed to another room in the apartment and allowed the police to enter was admissible to show state of police knowledge that impelled approach to defendant). The rationale for allowing such testimony is that it makes the discovery of the identity of the suspect, or the presence of an officer at a scene, "seem more natural and less mysterious." *Com. v. Perez*, 27 Mass App 550, 554, 540 NE2d 697, 699 (1989). The cost of eliminating the mystery, however, may be the introduction of inculpatory hearsay accusations that cannot be cross-examined. The specific details of the police investigation, when based upon hearsay statements by third parties, "are seldom needed and present the likelihood of serious prejudice." *Com. v. Soto*, 45 Mass App 109, 113, 695 NE2d 683, 687 (1998). "For this reason a statement that an officer acted 'upon information received,' or 'as a consequence of a conversation,' or words to that effect — without further detail — satisfy the purpose of explaining police conduct." Id. (citations omitted).[2] The admission of unnecessary and prejudicial hearsay details has been held to amount to reversible error. *Com. v. Soto,* supra.

Where a defendant raises the defense of entrapment, a detailed explanation of what led the police to him may be more relevant. See *Com. v. Miller,* 361 Mass 644, 658, 282 NE2d 394, 403-404 (1972) (evidence that drug pushers had mentioned defendant's name was relevant to government's good faith where defendant alleged shocking and offensive entrapment). But see *Com. v. Urena,* 42 Mass App 20, 674 NE2d 253 (1997) (officer's testimony that informant stated following his arrest that defendant was his drug source was hearsay and not admissible to explain the state of police knowledge that impelled the approach to defendant, who made entrapment defense).

Statements of a victim of a crime made prior to the event may be admissible in order to prove a motive or relevant state of mind of the defendant, if there is evidence they were communicated to the defendant. *Com. v. Seabrooks,* 425 Mass 507, 511 n.5, 681 NE2d 1198, 1202 (1997) (victim's intention to require child support for defendant to see his child); *Com. v. Qualls,* 425 Mass 163, 680 NE2d 61 (1997) (victim's attitude of contempt or hostility toward defendant); *Com. v. Cyr,* 425 Mass 89, 679 NE2d 550 (1997) (statements of victim relative to her desire to seek custody of children); *Com. v. Cruz,* 424 Mass 207, 675 NE2d 764 (1997) (police testimony that domestic violence victim indicated defendant had broken her door lock and that she would apply for a restraining order and move away from him was admissible where evidence showed that defendant knew victim, victim had tried to separate herself from him, and victim had communicated to him her desire to be rid of him); *Com. v. Fiore,* 364 Mass 819, 308 NE2d 902 (1974) (*V*'s challenging remark to group of which *D* was a member

---

[2] See McCormick, Evidence §249, at 104 (4th ed. 1992); Mueller & Kirkpatrick, Modern Evidence §8.18, at 1101-1102 (1995).

admissible to demonstrate state of mind of the group prior to assault on *V*).

Where there is no evidence that the defendant learned of a statement, the statement constitutes hearsay and demonstrates only the victim's state of mind. Unless the defendant has placed it in issue, the state of mind of the victim has no independent relevance. Statements that merely go to prove the victim's state of mind, rather than the defendant's, will not be admissible in evidence. *Com. v. Vinnie*, 428 Mass 161, 172, 698 NE2d 896, 906 (1998) (victim's state of mind irrelevant if unknown to defendant, error harmless); *Com. v. Taylor*, 426 Mass 189, 687 NE2d 631 (1997) (victim's stated impression that defendant was mad at her and "hated" her went only to her state of mind, not relevant or admissible); *Com. v. Olszewski*, 401 Mass 749, 519 NE2d 587 (1988) (*V*'s statement to *W* that she would tell police of *D*'s involvement in robberies inadmissible in absence of evidence it was communicated to *D*). See *Com. v. Demars*, 38 Mass App 596, 650 NE2d 368 (1995) (evidence that victim's father had concerns about sexual abuse of his daughter after speaking with someone about the defendant was evidence of father's state of mind, but that was not relevant to determination of defendant's guilt).[3]

Direct evidence that the victim's statements were known to the defendant is not required; circumstantial evidence is sufficient. *Com. v. Purcell*, 423 Mass 880, 673 NE2d 53 (1996) (defendant's niece properly permitted to testify that she had told defendant to get his things and leave, jury was warranted in inferring that defendant knew of victim's

---

[3] But see *Com. v. Hunter*, 416 Mass 831, 626 NE2d 873 (1994) (not error to allow testimony from friend of homicide victim that several months before death she advised victim to move out of her house and not allow defendant to know where she was going, and that victim stated she planned to do something about her situation; comments were not hearsay, but evidence of victim's state of mind, and therefore defendant's motive for killing her; court indicated that evidence of a "hostile relationship" between defendant and victim may be admitted as relevant to defendant's motive, without discussion of fact that there was no evidence victim's comments had been communicated to defendant).

state of mind); *Com. v. Todd,* 394 Mass 791, 477 NE2d 999 (1985) (not error to allow *V*'s mother to testify that prior to shooting, *V* tore up marriage license for *V* and *D*— inference is permissible that if *V* was willing to tell third parties of deteriorating relationship, she told *D*); *Com. v. Borodine,* 371 Mass 1, 8-9, 353 NE2d 649, 654 (1976) (*V*'s statements she intended to leave *D* were admissible, jury could infer *V* communicated feelings to *D*); *Com. v. Williams,* 30 Mass App 543, 503 NE2d 1 (1991) (same).

Statements of a victim indicating prior assaults or threats by the defendant, or expressing fear of the defendant, are not relevant or admissible to prove a motive, even if known to the defendant. They are inadmissible as hearsay. *Com. v. Wilson,* 427 Mass 336, 348, 693 NE2d 158, 170 (1998); *Com. v. Arce,* 426 Mass 601, 690 NE2d 806 (1998); *Com. v. Magraw,* 426 Mass 589, 690 NE2d 400 (1998); *Com. v. Jenner,* 426 Mass 163, 686 NE2d 1313 (1997); *Com. v. Sea-brooks,* supra; *Com. v. Qualls,* supra; *Com. v. Cyr,* supra; *Com. v. Andrade,* 422 Mass 236, 239, 661 NE2d 1308, 1311 (1996).

Although it is an error to admit evidence of the victim's fear of the defendant, such error may be deemed harmless on appeal where there was substantial other admissible evidence of a violent or abusive relationship between the victim and the defendant. *Com. v. Squailia,* 429 Mass 101, 706 NE2d 636 (1999); *Com. v. Vinnie,* supra; *Com. v. Wilson,* supra.

A defendant may open the door to the victim's extrajudicial statements, if he raises an issue to which the evidence would constitute logical rebuttal — e.g., by making a claim the victim committed suicide, that the victim would have willingly gone with him, or that the victim and the defendant were on friendly terms. Under such circumstances, the extrajudicial statements of the victim may be proof of her state of mind, the relevance of which has been put in issue by the defendant. *Com. v. Magraw,* supra.

Where a statement is offered to prove the effect it had on the listener's state of mind, that state of mind must be relevant to an issue properly in the case. *Com. v. Weichel*, 403 Mass 103, 526 NE2d 760 (1988) (evidence that other prisoners told *D* that guards had assaulted inmates could be relevant to *D*'s state of mind on a self-defense theory, but admissible only if there was sufficient evidence of self-defense to raise the issue).

Statements offered to prove notice or knowledge frequently do contain assertions that the proponent would like the jury to accept, although the evidence would be hearsay if offered for that purpose. If a limiting instruction would not cure the potential harm, a court may in appropriate cases decline to accept such evidence as more prejudicial than probative. *Com. v. Harris*, 409 Mass 461, 567 NE2d 899 (1991) (statement that members of *D*'s group were carrying knives was relevant to *V*'s state of mind where *D* claimed *V* was the aggressor, but unfairly suggested that *D* had a knife).[4]

---

[4] The Supreme Judicial Court employed the notice and knowledge analysis of statements that are not hearsay in an unusual context in *Com. v. Fourteen Thousand Two Hundred Dollars*, 421 Mass 1, 653 NE2d 153 (1995). In this forfeiture action, the Commonwealth offered out-of-court statements by declarant to a police officer regarding the location and packaging of the funds that it sought to have forfeited. The court treated them not as hearsay, but as evidence of the police officer's state of mind and, in turn, the reasonableness of the Commonwealth's decision to institute the forfeiture action, which it equated with probable cause to institute the action. The court noted that out-of-court statements that are inadmissible at trial are also inadmissible at probable cause hearings, but found the forfeiture action to be more closely analogous to grand jury proceedings, where hearsay statements may be used. But see the dissent by Liacos, CJ, noting that probable cause determinations "deal with articulable facts and circumstances, not just reasonable states of mind," and concluding that it is unfair to allow the Commonwealth to establish probable cause by using hearsay evidence and then shift the burden of proof to the claimant of the property involved when he has no opportunity to cross-examine and impeach the absent declarant. 421 Mass at 14-15, 653 NE2d at 160-161.

§8.2.3   Conversations Evidencing the Nature of a Place or a Thing

A difficult group of cases is that in which extrajudicial conversations are admitted in evidence to prove the nature of a place or thing associated with the conversations. *Com. v. Niemic*, 427 Mass 718, 725, 696 NE2d 117, 122 (1998) (statement of merchant to defendant to put away knife and leave store so there would be no trouble admissible to show by merchant's reaction that object was a weapon, not merely a fishing knife) (Text cited); *Com. v. Massod*, 350 Mass 745, 217 NE2d 191 (1966) (proved telephone was "apparatus" for registering bets by testimony of policeman as to words heard on that telephone); *Com. v. Kimball*, 73 Mass (7 Gray) 328, 330 (1856) (proved house to be house of ill fame by testimony of eavesdropper as to conversations of inmates); *Com. v. Washington*, 39 Mass App 195, 654 NE2d 334 (1995) (evidence was held not hearsay and admissible where police officer seized defendant's beeper after a search, returned telephone calls following beeps, and spoke with persons who sought to purchase drugs) (Text cited). But cf. *Com. v. Lopera*, 42 Mass App 133, 136, 674 NE2d 1340 (1997) (statements by alleged prostitute that defendant kept apartment where she worked a shift were not admissible to show nature of the place, because declarant knew she was talking to a police officer and it could not be said that there was a patent absence of motive to falsify) (Text cited). Such extrajudicial declarations are treated as nonhearsay in spite of the fact that the implications of the declarations must be believed for the declarations to have probative value. It should be noted that in such cases there is a patent absence of motive to falsify on the part of the declarant and that there is a large volume of independent items of evidence that can be consistent with one another only if the hypothesis is true.

§8.2.4   Verbal Acts

Some physical acts have legal significance only when accompanied by a particular intention or declaration of intention — that is, without an accompanying intention or declaration of intention, a physical act may be legally ambiguous. Such declarations are in any event admissible to resolve such ambiguities. They are admitted under what is known as the verbal act doctrine. Thus, where *A* moves from one town to another, his declaration at that time of his intention to make the second town his home would be admissible to prove change of residence. See *Salem v. Lynn,* 54 Mass (13 Metc) 544 (1847); *Com. v. McCray,* 40 Mass App 936, 665 NE2d 127 (1996) (error to exclude defendant's testimony that complainant, in response to his request for sex, answered affirmatively, statement constituted verbal act of consent) (Text cited). The doctrine applies only in the case where a physical act needs explaining and a concurrent declaration helps to explain it. *Com. v. Wallace,* 346 Mass 9, 13-14, 190 NE2d 224, 227-228 (1963). Many declarations admissible under the verbal act doctrine would also be admissible as a declaration of mental condition, a hearsay exception. See §8.15. For a more detailed discussion and a more expansive definition of verbal acts, see Mueller and Kirkpatrick, *Evidence,* §8.16 (1999).

§8.2.5   Operative Words

Where extrajudicial statements are offered as the basis, in whole or in part, of the cause of action or the defense, they are admissible under the so-called operative words doctrine. For example, defamatory statements, words constituting a contract, or words constituting a criminal offense are admissible. See *Fahey v. Rockwell Graphic Systems, Inc.,* 20

Mass App 642, 482 NE2d 519 (1985) (*D*'s employee's statements to *P* that guard on a machine should be removed not hearsay, admissible as the operative fact of *P*'s negligent instruction case); *Telecon, Inc. v. Emerson-Swan, Inc.*, 17 Mass App 671, 672-673, 461 NE2d 1227, 1228 (1984) (words of modification of contract admissible) (Text cited); *Com. v. Walter*, 388 Mass 460, 466, 446 NE2d 707, 711 (1983) (advertisement admitted not for truth, but to prove its publication in violation of statute).

§8.2.6   State of Mind

Many types of statements reflect circumstantially on the state of mind of the speaker. Such statements may be offered as evidence of state of mind without implicating the hearsay rule if the statements either do not contain assertions or are offered without regard to whether the assertions are true. See *Com. v. Trowbridge*, 419 Mass 750, 760, 647 NE2d 413, 421 (1995) (error to admit multiple hearsay in statement by grandmother to doctor following gynecological exam that child had told grandmother "that's what it felt like when her father touched her," despite limiting instruction that statement was offered not for its truth but for what led the child to talk to the doctor); *Keville v. McKeever*, 42 Mass App 140, 152, 675 NE2d 417, 427 (1997) (proper to admit transcript of unrelated proceeding in which incapacitated transferor was unable to give his correct age, as evidence of his state of mind) (Text cited); *Com. v. White*, 32 Mass App 949, 590 NE2d 716 (1992) (statement demonstrating declarant's bias improperly excluded, although error ruled harmless). See generally Wigmore §1790 (Chad rev 1976). In the well-known example, the statement, "I am Napoleon," is not offered to prove that the speaker is Napoleon, but as evidence of his insanity.

Where a statement is offered to prove the contents of the assertion it contains respecting the declarant's state of mind, it must qualify under the hearsay exception for declarations as to mental condition to be admissible. See §8.15.

§8.2.7   Silence

Under some circumstances, a person's silence may be as probative as a statement. Of course, silence may also be ambiguous in the absence of cross-examination. Silence is admissible against a hearsay objection if used as circumstantial evidence to support an inference, but inadmissible if offered as an implicit assertion. Where a witness is shown a photo spread and asked if he can identify a suspect, his silence in response is equivalent to an assertion that he cannot, and is therefore hearsay. *Com. v. Baker*, 20 Mass App 926, 928, 479 NE2d 193, 195 (1985). On the other hand, in *Silver v. New York Central Railroad Co.*, 329 Mass 14, 19, 105 NE2d 923, 926 (1952), to prove that a Pullman car was not cold, a porter was permitted to testify that no passenger other than the plaintiff had complained of cold. Cf. *Jacquot v. William Filene's Sons Co.*, 337 Mass 312, 317, 149 NE2d 635, 639 (1958) (evidence of no complaint on sale of 500 fingernail kits apparently received without objection); *Foreign Car Center, Inc. v. Salem Suede, Inc.*, 40 Mass App 15, 19, 660 NE2d 687, 692 (1996) (evidence that neither employees nor owners of other nearby businesses had complained of symptoms caused by odors or emissions from company was not admissible where it was not shown that they were similarly situated to plaintiffs in case or that mechanism for receiving complaints existed).

§8.3   Hearsay Admitted Without Objection

Hearsay admitted without objection may be considered by the jury and may be given any probative value it possesses. *Adoption of Kimberly,* 414 Mass 526, 609 NE2d 73 (1993); *Com. v. Keevan,* 400 Mass 557, 562, 511 NE2d 534, 538 (1987) (citing Text); *Com. v. Stewart,* 398 Mass 535, 499 NE2d 822 (1986); *Freyermuth v. Lufty,* 376 Mass 612, 616-617, 382 NE2d 1059, 1063 (1978). Cf. *Com. v. Stovall,* 22 Mass App 737, 498 NE2d 126 (1986) (court expressed concern about prospect of affirming conviction if only evidence were inadmissible hearsay). See also §3.8.4.

A general objection to a question may not be sufficient to preserve a hearsay objection. See *Com. v. Cancel,* 394 Mass 567, 476 NE2d 610 (1985) (general objection to hearsay accusation against *D* insufficient because until *D*'s response was related it was unclear whether he had unequivocally denied it, or whether it would be admissible as an adoptive admission; after *W* testified to *D*'s denial, *D* was obliged to renew objection or move to strike). An objection on an incorrect ground may not preserve a hearsay objection. *Com. v. Raymond,* 424 Mass 382, 388 n.5, 676 NE2d 824, 829 n.5 (1997) (objection based on authenticity is insufficient to preserve a hearsay objection); *Blake v. Hendrickson,* 40 Mass App 579, 666 NE2d 164 (1996) (on appeal, court considers only the grounds asserted at trial in opposition to hearsay evidence); *Genova v. Genova,* 28 Mass App 647, 649, 554 NE2d 1221 (1990) (objection that testimony was "self-serving" did not preserve hearsay objection).

When it becomes apparent through subsequent examination that a witness's earlier testimony was not based on personal knowledge, but on hearsay, a motion to strike should be allowed. *Giannasca v. Everett Aluminum, Inc.,* 13 Mass App 208, 212, 431 NE2d 596, 598-599 (1982).

Where an extrajudicial statement is admitted for any nonhearsay purpose, counsel should ask for, and receive, an instruction to the jury as to the limited purpose for which such evidence is admitted. See *Com. v. Costa*, 354 Mass 757, 236 NE2d 94 (1968); *Regan v. John J. Amara & Sons Co.*, 348 Mass 734, 737, 205 NE2d 705, 707 (1965). The failure to do so may result in the admission of the evidence for all purposes. *Genova v. Genova*, supra, 28 Mass App at 652, 554 NE2d at 1224; *Com. v. Fitzpatrick*, 14 Mass App 1001, 441 NE2d 559 (1982) (no duty on judge to give limiting instruction on his own motion).[1] Cf. *G.E.B. v. S.R.W.*, 422 Mass 158, 167, 661 NE2d 646, 654 (1996) (record did not make clear in nonjury trial whether letter was offered for a hearsay purpose or for a proper nonhearsay purpose; decision admitting the evidence over a general objection affirmed, court assumed that ruling was based on the proper ground).

B.   EXCEPTIONS TO THE HEARSAY RULE

§8.4   General Principles

§8.4.1   *Rationale for Hearsay Exceptions*

The common-law exceptions to the hearsay rule in almost every case are based on two elements: (1) a strong necessity for the evidence the rule would otherwise exclude; and (2) a guarantee of trustworthiness in the circumstances surrounding the making of the particular declaration for which an exception is created. Despite the many exceptions, some commentators believe that the application of the hearsay rule to exclude certain extrajudicial statements brings about results that appear to be onerous and, in some instances, unjustifiable. The result may be particularly onerous where the extrajudicial declarant is unavailable to testify at the trial, especially if the word "unavailable" is as narrowly defined as it was at common law. Recent cases and

---

§8.3   [1] See also Proposed Mass R Evid 105 and Fed R Evid 105; §3.8.4.

rules of evidence have broadened the definition of unavailability, with the result that the "necessity" to admit statements as an exception to the hearsay rule is more easily
shown. See §8.4.2.

Some hearsay evidence may be deemed more reliable
than others. The Federal Rules of Evidence, through the
catchall exceptions, permit the admissibility of some hearsay evidence where there exist special indicia of reliability.
See Fed R Evid 803(24) and 804(b)(5). Neither provision is
included in the Proposed Massachusetts Rules of Evidence.
The Supreme Judicial Court has specifically declined to
adopt these general exceptions. See §8.21.

Efforts to dilute or enforce the exclusionary aspects of
the hearsay rule raise special problems with regard to criminal proceedings. The right of confrontation provided by the
Sixth Amendment to the United States Constitution, art. 12
of the Massachusetts Declaration of Rights, and the hearsay
rule safeguard similar values. We discuss confrontation
clause problems as they arise in connection with individual
topics.[1] While the confrontation right and the hearsay rule
are not identical,[2] the essential right both principles protect
is the right of effective cross-examination. See *White v.
Illinois*, 502 US 346, 356, 112 S Ct 736, 743 (1992); *Com. v.
Canon*, 373 Mass 494, 507-513, 368 NE2d 1181, 1188-1192
(1977) (Liacos, J, dissenting); Liacos, *The Right of Confrontation and the Hearsay Rule: Another Look*, 34 Am Trial LJ 153
(1972); Liacos, *The Right of Confrontation*, 33 Am Trial LJ 243
(1970).

Statutes may create additional exceptions to the hearsay rule. These statutes supersede the common-law exceptions to the hearsay rule only to the extent to which the
statutes would admit evidence not within a common-law
exception. By way of illustration, consider: GL 79, §35

---

§8.4 [1] See §3.3 (scope of cross-examination); §10.2 (evidence of
prior identification); §8.7.2 (use of prior testimony).
[2] See the concurring opinion of Justice Breyer in *Lilly v. Virginia*, ___
US ___, 119 S Ct 1887 (1999), for his view of the need to re-examine the
differences between the two doctrines.

(assessed value of real estate); GL 152, §20B (medical reports of deceased physician); GL 175, §4 (commissioner of insurance report of examination of insurance company); GL 185C, §21 (housing inspection report); GL 233, §65 (declarations of deceased persons); GL 233, §65A (answers of deceased party to interrogatories); GL 233, §66 (declarations of testator); GL 233, §70 (judicial notice of law); GL 233, §79 (hospital records); GL 233, §79B (commercial lists); GL 233, §79C (medical treatises in malpractice actions); GL 233, §79F (public way); GL 233, §79G (medical and hospital bills and reports); GL 233, §79H (medical reports of deceased physicians); Mass R Civ P 32(a)(3) (depositions); Mass R Crim P 35(g) (depositions). Such exceptions are incorporated into the Proposed Massachusetts Rules of Evidence by Rule 802, which provides: "Hearsay is not admissible except as provided by law or by these rules or by other rules prescribed by the Supreme Judicial Court." Fed R Evid 802 takes a similar approach. The more significant statutory exceptions are discussed below.

§8.4.2   Unavailability of Declarant

The "unavailability" of a witness may be established by a showing of death, *Com. v. Mustone*, 353 Mass 490, 233 NE2d 1 (1968), or an inability to locate the witness after due and diligent search. *Com. v. Charles*, 428 Mass 672, 678, 704 NE2d 1137, 1143 (1999) (declarant was a fugitive from prosecution as a co-defendant in the same case); *Com. v. Clark*, 363 Mass 467, 295 NE2d 163 (1973); *Com. v. Gallo*, 275 Mass 320, 175 NE2d 718 (1931). However, the mere absence of the witness from the jurisdiction without a showing that he cannot be found or that a deposition cannot be taken is an insufficient showing of unavailability. *Ibanez v. Winston*, 222 Mass 129, 109 NE 814 (1915).[3]

---

[3] See §8.7.2 for a discussion of criminal cases on unavailability and the confrontation clause.

The issue is not the physical presence of a witness, but the availability of her testimony. Therefore, a valid claim of privilege by a witness makes her "unavailable." *Com. v. DiPietro*, 373 Mass 369, 367 NE2d 811 (1977) (wife's claim of statutory privilege under GL 233, §20); *Com. v. Galloway*, 404 Mass 204, 208, 534 NE2d 778 (1989) (claim of privilege against self-incrimination). Cf. *Com. v. Charles*, supra (assumed that fugitive witness would exercise Fifth Amendment privilege if located where he would be a co-defendant in case on trial).

Proposed Mass R Evid 804(a) and Fed R Evid 804(a) take a broad view of what constitutes unavailability and go beyond the case law. Proposed Mass R Evid 804(a) provides a witness is "unavailable" if there is:

(1)   a valid claim of privilege;
(2)   the witness persists in refusing to testify despite a court order to do so;
(3)   the witness testifies to a lack of memory;
(4)   the witness is unable to be present or to testify because of death or a then-existing physical or mental illness or infirmity; or
(5)   the witness is absent and the proponent has been unable to procure his attendance by process or "other reasonable means."

Rule 804(a) also provides that a declarant is not unavailable if "his exemption, refusal, claim of lack of memory, inability, or absence is due to the procurement or wrongdoing of the proponent . . . for the purpose of preventing the witness from attending or testifying." Fed R Evid 804(a) contains the same provisions, except for 804(a)(5), which reads: "is absent from the hearing and the proponent of his statement has been unable to procure the declarant's attendance (or in the case of a hearsay exception under subdivision (b)(2), (3), or (4), the declarant's attendance or testimony) by process or other reasonable means." The effect of this difference is that as to statements offered as declarations against interest under Proposed Mass R Evid

804(b)(3), statements of belief of impending death under 804(b)(2), and statements of personal or family history under 804(b)(4), no attempt to procure testimony by deposition or interrogatories is required by the proposed Massachusetts rule before the declarant is deemed "unavailable."

§8.4.3 Impeachment of Declarant

Proposed Mass R Evid 806 and Fed R Evid 806 provide for the impeachment of hearsay statements admitted as exceptions to the hearsay rule or as vicarious admissions admitted under Rule 801(d)(2)(C), (D), or (E). The rule, which seems essentially consistent with common practice, provides:

Attacking and Supporting Credibility of Declarant

When a hearsay statement, or a statement defined in Rule 801(d)(2), (C), (D) or (E), has been admitted in evidence, the credibility of the declarant may be attacked, and if attacked may be supported, by any evidence which would be admissible for those purposes if declarant had testified as a witness. Evidence of a statement or conduct by the declarant at any time, inconsistent with his hearsay statement, is not subject to any requirement that he may have been afforded an opportunity to deny or explain. If the party against whom a hearsay statement has been admitted calls the declarant as a witness, the party is entitled to examine him on the statement as if under cross-examination.[4]

§8.5   Declarations of Deceased Persons

§8.5.1   GL 233, §65

In any action or other civil judicial proceeding, a declaration of a deceased person shall not be inadmissible in evidence as

---

[4]See §6.6.

hearsay or as private conversation between husband and wife, as the case may be, if the court finds that it was made in good faith and upon the personal knowledge of the declarant.[1]

This statute does not apply to criminal cases. *Com. v. Cormier,* 427 Mass 446, 449 n.1, 693 NE2d 1015, 1018 n.1 (1998). The federal rules have no specific comparable provision. Proposed Mass R Evid 804(b)(5) specifically incorporates this hearsay exception.[2]

To render evidence admissible under §65, the trial judge must find that the statement in question was made in good faith and on personal knowledge. It is error to leave this preliminary finding to the jury. *Horan v. Boston Elevated Railway Co.,* 237 Mass 245, 129 NE 355 (1921). These factual findings by the trial court generally will be affirmed if there is any evidence to support them. *Kelley v. Jordan Marsh Co.,* 278 Mass 101, 106, 179 NE 299, 302 (1932). For illustrative cases, see *Barbosa v. Hopper Feeds, Inc.,* 404 Mass 610, 537 NE2d 99 (1989) (statement after accident of deceased co-worker to *W* that he advised *P* on proper operation of machine not made in good faith because of incentive for declarant to avoid blame himself); *Old Colony Trust Co. v. Shaw,* 348 Mass 212, 217-219, 202 NE2d 785, 789-790 (1964) (declarant's general duties as bookkeeper permitted conclusion that a specific memo was written in good faith, on personal knowledge). Compare *Anselmo v. Reback,* 400 Mass 865, 513 NE2d 1270 (1987) (failure to diagnose cancer case, videotape of deceased, answering questions from her

---

§8.5 [1] Section 65 applies to proceedings before the Industrial Accident Board. *Stanton's Case,* 331 Mass 378, 119 NE2d 388 (1954). It also applies to disbarment proceedings. *In re Keenan,* 287 Mass 577, 192 NE 65 (1934). Cf. *In re Troy,* 364 Mass 15, 23, 306 NE2d 203, 164 (1973) (assumed to apply in judicial misconduct proceeding).

[2] As to the effect of §65 on what would otherwise be a privilege for private conversations between spouses, see §13.2.

attorney, made without notice to known potential defendants, held inadmissible for failure to afford defendants cross-examination as provided in GL 233, §§46, 47, and Mass R Civ P 27 (a)), with *Cusher v. Turner*, 22 Mass App 491, 495 NE2d 311 (1986) (failure to diagnose cancer case, tape recording, and diary of decedent regarding her mental and physical health properly admitted).

Where the trial judge has admitted the statement, it will be assumed the preliminary facts were found, unless the record demonstrates otherwise. *Warren v. Ball*, 341 Mass 350, 356, 170 NE2d 341, 345 (1960); *Horan v. Boston Elevated Railway Co.*, supra; *Mitchell v. Hastings & Koch Enterprises, Inc.*, 38 Mass App 271, 274, 647 NE2d 78, 81 (1995). Where the statement was excluded at trial, the court will be affirmed unless the record demonstrates proof of the material facts. *Virta v. Mackey*, 343 Mass 286, 178 NE2d 571 (1961). Where a statement of a deceased person has been introduced for another purpose, its use will be limited to that purpose, where the preliminary findings required by GL 233, §65, have not been made. *Flanagan v. John Hancock Mutual Life Insurance Co.*, 349 Mass 405, 208 NE2d 497 (1965) (declarations of deceased insured in application for insurance policy admitted on behalf of insurer as part of contract were not received under GL 233, §65, and therefore could not be used by plaintiff for truth of matter).

The requirement of a finding that the statement was made in good faith was held to include a requirement that the court find that the statement was in fact made by the declarant. *Slotofski v. Boston Elevated Railway Co.*, 215 Mass 318, 102 NE 417 (1913). The requirement of personal knowledge is held to exclude most declarations of opinion. The requirement has been held to exclude opinion evidence that depends upon the expert qualifications of the declarant, even if the opinion is based on personal observation. *Middlesex Supply, Inc. v. Martin & Sons*, 354 Mass 373, 237 NE2d 692 (1968); *Buck's Case*, 342 Mass 766, 772, 175 NE2d 369, 373 (1961).

The "personal knowledge" requirement does not exclude a class of "shorthand expression" opinion statements [3] that would not be improper if uttered on the witness stand. *Samuel Cohen Shoe Co. v. Cohen*, 329 Mass 281, 107 NE2d 817 (1952); *Eldredge v. Barton*, 232 Mass 183, 122 NE 272 (1919). When the form of the statement leaves doubt as to whether the statement is one of fact or opinion, the judge must decide in which sense the declaration was made. *Shamgochian v. Drigotas*, 343 Mass 139, 177 NE2d 580 (1961). See also *Old Colony Trust Co. v. Shaw*, supra. In *Knapp v. Bronson Building* Co., 226 Mass 416, 115 NE 671 (1917), the court held that a claim by a deceased person to have heard an admission of fault by the opposing party raises a different risk of error and falsification from a decedent's account of facts observed, and excluded the statement. This is an exception to the normal rule that multiple hearsay is admissible provided that each link in the testimonial chain falls within a hearsay exception.

The declarations of a deceased person that otherwise qualify are admissible whether made orally or in writing and need not be reproduced in the exact words used by the declarant. *Bellamy v. Bellamy*, 342 Mass 534, 174 NE2d 358 (1961); *Desrosiers v. Germain*, 12 Mass App 852, 858, 429 NE2d 385, 388-389 (1981) (oral statements).

GL 233, §65A, permits answers to interrogatories to be admitted in favor of the personal representative of the answering party where such party dies during the pendency of the litigation. This same result would probably be reached under §65. *Thornton v. First National Stores, Inc.*, 340 Mass 222, 163 NE2d 264 (1960) (interrogatories admissible under either section). Note that since the answers to the interrogatories have been obtained by the adverse party, §65A dispenses with the necessity of showing "good faith."

It should be noted that GL 233, §65, does not supersede the common-law rules as to admissibility of statements by a party opponent. Thus, where an administrator is suing

---

[3] See §§7.4 and 7.5.

upon a contract claim of his intestate, statements of the intestate are admissible when offered by the defendant even if the requirements of §65 are not complied with. *Bendett v. Bendett*, 315 Mass 59, 52 NE2d 2 (1943). The statute does not make admissible a declaration of a deceased person that is inadmissible for other reasons. Thus, the court in *Taylor v. Whittier*, 240 Mass 514, 138 NE 6 (1922) (will contest), held, under the law of the time, that testimony as to a declaration by a husband (deceased at the time of the trial) was inadmissible because it tended to prove the illegitimacy of a child born to his wife while she was married to him. [4]

§8.5.2   GL 233, §66

If a cause of action brought against an executor or administrator is supported by oral testimony of a promise or statement made by the testator or intestate of the defendant, evidence of statements, written or oral, made by the decedent, memoranda and entries written by him, and evidence of his acts and habits of dealing tending to disprove or to show the improbability of the making of such promise or statement, shall be admissible.

The two preliminary requirements regarding the admission of evidence under §65 do not apply to evidence admissible under §66. Thus, no finding of good faith is required. *Rothwell v. First National Bank of Boston*, 286 Mass 417, 190 NE 812 (1934). The single preliminary requirement to the admission of evidence under §66 is that oral testimony of a statement of the deceased be presented by the party suing the executor or administrator. For an application of these words of the statute, see *Huebener v. Childs*, 180 Mass 483, 62 NE 729 (1902). The kinds of evidence this section admits are very broadly described. *Quaere:* Is the statute broad enough to admit evidence of the character of

---

[4] The legal rule regarding the disqualification of the testimony of spouses as to illegitimacy has been changed. See §13.2.4.

the deceased? *Loweth v. Bradford,* 227 Mass 584, 116 NE 892 (1917).

§8.5.3 Other

Medical reports of deceased physicians are admissible under separate statutes. GL 233, §79H (actions of tort); GL 152, §20B (workmen's compensation proceedings). Both statutes allow medical opinion evidence to be admitted in the discretion of the judge or hearing member, but §79H bars any statement that "has reference to the question of liability." GL 152, §20B, is broader than GL 233, §79H, in two respects. First, it provides for discretionary admission of medical reports of deceased physicians and also reports of physicians who are "incapacitated" or "disabled." Second, §20B was amended by St 1977, c 777, to delete the limitation on admissibility relating to the question of liability.

§8.6   Dying Declarations

The common-law hearsay exception for dying declarations is narrower than the statutory exceptions just described. The rule provides that: (1) in a prosecution for homicide (2) committed upon declarant, (3) declarant's statement in regard to the manner in which he met his death is admissible (4) provided he believes at the time of the statement that he is to die immediately and (5) provided he does die within a very short time.[1] *Com. v. Vona,* 250 Mass 509, 146 NE 20 (1925); *Com. v. Cooper,* 87 Mass (5 All) 495 (1862). Each of these five elements is necessary. The trial judge

---

§8.6 [1] The common-law exception was expanded by GL 233, §64, which provides:

> In prosecutions under [GL 272, §19, illegal procurement of abortion], in which the death of a woman is alleged to have resulted from the means therein described, her dying declarations shall be admissible in evidence.

must make the finding that the necessary elements are present in order to admit the evidence. *Com. v. Green*, 420 Mass 771, 781, 652 NE2d 572, 579 (1995). For discussion of the exception, see *Com. v. Nolin*, 373 Mass 45, 364 NE2d 1224 (1977); *Com. v. Lacy*, 371 Mass 363, 358 NE2d 419 (1976); *Com. v. Dunker*, 363 Mass 792, 298 NE2d 813 (1973). In *Com. v. Key*, 381 Mass 19, 407 NE2d 327 (1980), the court modified the common-law rule that precluded the admissibility of a dying declaration relating to the death of one other than the declarant. The court held that where multiple homicides result from one felonious act, the dying declaration of one victim should be admitted to prove the homicides of the other victims.

The declarant's apprehension of death may be inferred from circumstances, even if he has made no explicit statement on the matter. *Com. v. Key*, supra, 381 Mass at 24, 407 NE2d at 332. The declarant must have no expectation of recovery, although he need not expressly state that he has "abandoned every last flicker of hope." *Com. v. Viera*, 329 Mass 470, 473, 109 NE2d 171, 173 (1952). See *Com. v. Gaskins*, 419 Mass 809, 647 NE2d 429 (1995) (victim's statements did not constitute dying declarations where there was no evidence that he believed he was facing imminent death).

Whether the elements of a dying declaration are established is initially a preliminary question of fact for the trial judge. *Com. v. Cantor*, 253 Mass 509, 149 NE 205 (1925). If the judge finds that the declaration is admissible, he must instruct the jury that it can reconsider the question of admissibility and may consider the declaration as probative evidence only if it finds the existence of the preliminary facts by a preponderance of the evidence. *Com. v. Green*, supra, 420 Mass at 781, 652 NE2d at 579 (Text cited); *Com. v. Key*, supra, 381 Mass at 22, 407 NE2d at 330-331; *Com. v. Polian*, 288 Mass 494, 193 NE 68 (1934).[2] Cf. *Com. v. Mayne*, 38 Mass App 282, 287, 647 NE2d 89, 93 (1995) (where trial

---

[2] See §3.9.1.

judge failed to instruct jury it must find that victim believed his death was imminent, but defendant failed to object, there was no substantial risk of a miscarriage of justice — statement was introduced by prosecution as a prior inconsistent statement of its own witness and defense counsel did not request a limiting instruction, and victim made statement after having been shot seven times and lay bleeding on the floor having stated he was dying).

Proposed Mass R Evid 804(b)(2) provides for the admission of the following dying declarations:

> In a prosecution for homicide or for unlawful procurement of an abortion or in a civil action or proceeding, a statement made by a declarant while believing that the declarant's death was imminent, concerning the cause or circumstances of what he believed to be his impending death.

Fed R Evid 804(b)(2) is the same as the proposed Massachusetts rule except that it does not include the phrase "or for unlawful procurement of an abortion," which was included in the Massachusetts version to conform to GL 233, §64. Both versions of the rule apply to civil matters as well as criminal matters.

Since the admissibility of a statement under Fed R Evid 804(b)(2) depends not on a showing of the death of the declarant but simply on a showing of the declarant's "unavailability" — as more broadly defined in Fed R Evid 804(a)[3] — this exception is broader than the common-law dying declaration exception or even the statutory exception for declarations of deceased persons created for civil proceedings by GL 231, §65. [4] Fed R Evid 804(b)(2) may be more restrictive than *Com. v. Key*, supra, in that it appears to preclude statements relating to the death of one other than the declarant.

---

[3] See §8.4.2.

[4] Compare Proposed Mass R Evid 804(b)(5) (incorporating the statutory exception of GL 231, §65, and also limiting "unavailability" to situations where the declarant is dead).

§8.7   Reported Testimony

§8.7.1   *General Principles*

Prior testimony of a presently unavailable witness is admissible if it was given under oath in a proceeding where the issues were substantially the same as in the current proceeding and the party against whom it is offered had an opportunity and a similar motive to cross-examine the witness. *Com v. Trigones*, 397 Mass 633, 638, 492 NE2d 1146, 1149-1150 (1986). This hearsay exception is embodied in Proposed Mass R Evid 804(b)(1) and Fed R Evid 804(b)(1).[1] What constitutes the "unavailability" of a witness under the hearsay rules is discussed in §8.4.2; "unavailability" under the confrontation clause, in §8.7.2.

The prior testimony rule has been applied to testimony given in a previous trial between the same parties, *Com. v. Clark*, 363 Mass 467, 470, 295 NE2d 163, 165-166 (1973); *Com. v. Gallo*, 275 Mass 320, 175 NE2d 718 (1931); testimony from a probable cause hearing, *Com. v. Salim*, 399 Mass 227, 503 NE2d 1267 (1987); *Com. v. Bohannon*, 385 Mass 733, 434 NE2d 163 (1982); *Com. v. Caine*, 366 Mass 366, 318 NE2d 901 (1974); *Com. v. Mustone*, 353 Mass 490, 233 NE2d 1 (1968); testimony from the probable cause portion of a juvenile transfer proceeding, *Com. v. Ortiz*, 393 Mass 523, 471 NE2d 1321 (1984); testimony from a motion to suppress, *Com. v. Trigones*, 397 Mass 633, 492 NE2d 1146 (1986); and testimony from a former civil trial where the defendant in a later criminal proceeding had been an adverse party to the witness, *Com. v. Canon*, 373 Mass 494, 368 NE2d 1181 (1977). Provided the requirements of the rule are met, there is no principled reason why testimony

---

§8.7   [1] The Rules would go further than the common law and allow prior inconsistent statements given under oath in a trial, hearing, proceeding, or deposition to be admitted for substantive purposes where the declarant testifies at trial and is subject to cross-examination concerning his former statements. Proposed Mass R Evid 801(d)(1); Fed R Evid 801(d)(1). See §6.7.2 (prior inconsistent statements).

from other types of proceedings would not be similarly admissible.

Deposition testimony is admissible under the rule, pursuant to Mass R Civ P 32(a)(3) and Mass R Crim P 35(g). See *Shear v. Gabovitch*, 43 Mass App Ct 650, 666 n.17, 685 NE2d 1168, 1180 (1997) (error to refuse to admit deposition where witness was living in Florida, not amenable to Massachusetts process); *Caron v. General Motors Corp.*, 37 Mass App 744, 643 NE2d 471 (1994) (trial court properly excluded deposition testimony from out-of-state expert where proponent had not demonstrated he made a reasonable effort to secure expert's presence at trial, and opinions expressed during deposition were in response to objectionable questions and possibly speculative). Where a videotaped deposition has been taken pursuant to Mass R Civ P 30(a), it is not necessary to establish the witness's unavailability to use the deposition at trial. *Roche v. MBTA*, 400 Mass 217, 508 NE2d 614 (1987). The court further held in *Roche* that the admissibility of the deposition does not automatically quash a subpoena by the opposing party for the live testimony of the witness, because that would improperly restrict the opponent's right of cross-examination.

The Supreme Judicial Court has not determined whether a criminal defendant may offer against the Commonwealth the grand jury testimony of a witness unavailable at trial, although the court has noted that admissibility may be supported by Proposed Mass R Evid 804(b)(1) and Fed R Evid 804(b)(1). *Com. v. Martinez*, 384 Mass 377, 381-385, 425 NE2d 300, 303-305 (1981); *Com. v. Meech*, 380 Mass 490, 403 NE2d 1174 (1980). Although the government does not typically cross-examine its witnesses at the grand jury, direct examination may be held to be the equivalent, as provided by the Rules. However, at a minimum, the defendant would have to establish that the government had a "similar motive" to develop the issues germane to the trial at the time of the grand jury testimony. *Com. v. Martinez*, supra; *Com. v. Meech*, supra. See *US v. Salerno*, 505 US 317, 112 S Ct 2503

(1992) (admissibility of grand jury testimony against the government under Fed R Evid 804(b)(1) requires proof of similar motive, requirement may not be avoided to ensure "adversarial fairness").[2] Grand jury testimony of unavailable witnesses may not be offered by the government against a criminal defendant, because he has had no opportunity to cross-examine or question the witness. *Com. v. Meech*, supra, 380 Mass at 494, 403 NE2d at 1178.

Admissibility of prior testimony depends upon a reliable record or report of the former testimony. A stenographic transcript is the preferable way of establishing its content; the use of such a transcript is authorized under GL 233, §80. See *Com. v. Mustone*, supra. See also Mass R Civ P 80; Fed R Civ P 80. In the absence of such a transcript, a witness who can state the testimony with substantial accuracy may testify as to the testimony of the unavailable witness. *Com. v. Bohannon*, supra, 385 Mass at 746-747, 434 NE2d at 171-172 (citing Text); *Com. v. Di Pietro*, 373 Mass 369, 392-393, 367 NE2d 811, 825 (1977) (citing Text).

§8.7.2 *As Affected by Confrontation Clause in Criminal Cases*

Although the rule pertaining to the admissibility of reported testimony applies to both civil and criminal cases, a criminal defendant has a constitutional right to confront the witnesses against him, under art. 12 of the Massachusetts Declaration of Rights and the Sixth Amendment to the United States Constitution. *Pointer v. Texas*, 380 US 400, 85 S Ct 1065, 13 L Ed 2d 923 (1965) (Sixth Amendment applicable to the states). The rights provided by the state and federal constitutional provisions are equivalent. *Com. v.*

---

[2] Grand jury testimony is not admissible as prior recollection recorded where there is no evidence that the witness adopted the transcript as accurate at or about the time of the events described. *Com. v. Bookman*, 386 Mass 657, 436 NE2d 1228 (1982). See §8.17 (prior recollection recorded).

Childs, 413 Mass 252, 260, 596 NE2d 351 (1992); *Com. v. Siegfriedt,* 402 Mass 424, 430, 522 NE2d 970, 974-975 (1988) (holding that state law does not impose a stricter standard). GL 263, §5, provides the same protection. For a general discussion of the history and meaning of the confrontation clause, see *Opinion of the Justices to Senate,* 406 Mass 1201, 1205-1210, 547 NE2d 8, 10-12 (1989); *Com. v. Bergstrom,* 402 Mass 534, 541-548, 524 NE2d 366, 371-375 (1988).

The confrontation clause imposes two requirements on the state's use of prior reported testimony against a criminal defendant. First, the witness must be shown to be unavailable.[3] Second, the prior testimony must be reliable.[4] *Ohio v. Roberts,* 448 US 56, 65, 100 S Ct 2531 (1980); *Com. v. Siegfriedt,* 402 Mass 424, 427, 522 NE2d 970, 973 (1988); *Com. v. Bohannon,* 385 Mass 733, 741, 434 NE2d 163, 168 (1982). We discuss these requirements in turn.

The unavailability requirement derives from a constitutional preference for face-to-face accusation and recognizes that the Sixth Amendment establishes a rule of necessity to justify the hearsay use of prior reported testimony. In order to use the testimony of a witness from a former proceeding, the Commonwealth must establish that the witness is unavailable and that it has made a good faith and diligent

---

[3] Despite the broad language of *Ohio v. Roberts,* supra, which appeared to suggest that the confrontation clause may impose the unavailability requirement on the use of all hearsay in criminal cases, the Supreme Court has subsequently held that these requirements apply with respect to prior reported testimony, but not to other classes of hearsay. *White v. Illinois,* 502 US 346, 112 S Ct 736 (1992) (spontaneous utterances and statements made in the course of receiving medical care); *United States v. Inadi,* 475 US 387, 106 S Ct 1121 (1986) (co-conspirator hearsay). The Supreme Judicial Court held that unavailability was not required in *Com. v. Jones,* 400 Mass 544, 511 NE2d 17 (1987) (adoptive admission). See *Com. v. Napolitano,* 42 Mass App Ct 549, 678 NE2d 447 (1997) (excited utterance exception is deemed so specially reliable that confrontation rights do not require proof of declarant's unavailability).

[4] The reliability requirement is generally applicable to the use of hearsay against a criminal accused. It is satisfied, however, by any hearsay exception which is "firmly rooted." We discuss the application of this standard to specific exceptions as we reach them in the text.

effort to locate the witness and produce him at trial. *Com. v. Childs*, supra, 413 Mass at 260, 596 NE2d at 356. Whether a court will rule that the Commonwealth has made a sufficient showing involves a fact-based determination and will depend upon what reasonableness requires under the circumstances. Compare *Barber v. Page*, 390 US 719, 88 S Ct 1318 (1968) (insufficient showing of unavailability where witness was incarcerated in federal prison and state made no effort to produce him at trial); *Mancusi v. Stubbs*, 408 US 204, 92 S Ct 2308 (1972) (absent witness living in Sweden and beyond reach of court's process was sufficiently "unavailable"); *Ohio v. Roberts*, supra (witness within United States who could not be located after good faith effort was "unavailable," although not every potential lead had been exhausted); *Com. v. Childs*, supra (although Commonwealth had computer information suggesting witness was in Florida and did not exhaust all available means of locating him, efforts taken were sufficient to demonstrate unavailability); *Com. v. Lopera*, 42 Mass App 133, 674 NE2d 1340, 1343 (1997) (declarant's supposed declarations against penal interest not admissible because witness not shown to be unavailable where she was subpoenaed for prior trial date, but not actual trial date, and prosecutor did not describe specific steps taken by police or DA's Office to attempt to locate witness); *Com. v. Hunt*, 38 Mass App 291, 647 NE2d 433 (1995) (witness was unavailable where he lived in England, had been contacted by prosecutor, and had refused to come to United States to testify); *Com. v. Cook*, 12 Mass App 920, 423 NE2d 1056 (1981) (mere out-of-court refusal by witness to testify is insufficient).

The evidence must demonstrate that the witness is unavailable at the time of trial. In *Com. v. Bohannon*, supra, the court held that rulings 8 and 13 months before trial that it would be an undue hardship to require an out-of-state witness to return to Massachusetts did not establish unavailability at trial. Compare *Com. v. Siegfriedt*, supra (where the second trial began within a week of a mistrial, not error to rely on finding made in first trial that witness could not be located, together with testimony that police made additional fruitless efforts to locate witness, and to use testimony from probable cause hearing). It has been held that it is not unreasonable for the Commonwealth to commence its efforts to locate a witness shortly before trial. *Com. v. Childs*, supra, 413 Mass at 261, 596 NE2d at 356.

Where a witness has been located out of state, in determining unavailability the court should consider whether the Commonwealth has made recourse to the Uniform Act to Secure the Attendance of Witnesses from without a State in Criminal Proceedings, GL 233, §13A. *Barber v. Page*, supra; *Com. v. Bohannon*, supra. Earlier recourse to the Uniform Act to produce the witness in the past, however, will not establish his unavailability at the time of trial. Id.

The test for reliability requires first, that the testimony be shown to be reliable when given, and second, that the testimony was accurately preserved. *Com. v. Siegfriedt*, supra, 402 Mass at 428, 522 NE2d at 974. Most of the challenges to the use of former testimony have focused on the first requirement.

The essential right protected by the confrontation clause, and on which the reliability of testimony depends, is the right of cross-examination. See *California v. Green*, 399 US 149, 90 S Ct 1930 (1970); *Com. v. Canon*, 373 Mass 494, 507-513, 368 NE2d 1181, 1189 (1977) (dissenting op, Liacos, J); Liacos, *The Right of Confrontation and the Hearsay Rule: Another Look*, 34 Am Trial LJ 153 (1972); Liacos, *The Right of Confrontation*, 33 Am Trial LJ 243 (1970). For prior testimony to be admissible, it must have been given "in a proceeding addressed to substantially the same issues as in the current proceeding, with reasonable opportunity and similar motivation on the prior occasion for cross-examination of the declarant by the party against whom the testimony is now being offered." *Com. v. Trigones*, 397 Mass 633, 638, 492 NE2d 1146, 1149-1150 (1986). Where cross-examination has been denied and the prior testimony admitted, a reversal of a conviction is required unless the error was harmless beyond a reasonable doubt. The prosecution bears the burden of proving that admission of the uncross-examined testimony was not a substantial factor in the jury's decision to convict. *Com. v. DiBenedetto*, 413 Mass 37, 605 NE2d 811 (1992).

The Supreme Judicial Court noted both in *Trigones*, supra, and in *Com. v. Bohannon*, supra, 385 Mass at 747 n.12, 434 NE2d at 172 n.12, that the United States Supreme Court has left open the issue of whether the opportunity to cross-examine is sufficient to establish reliability where no cross-examination was conducted, citing *Ohio v. Roberts*, supra, 448 US at 61-62, 70. However, the Supreme Court had suggested in *California v. Green*, 399 US at 165 that the opportunity was sufficient, and the Supreme Judicial Court has indicated that it is. *Com. v. Tanso*, 411 Mass 640, 647, 583 NE2d 1247, 1252 (1992).

A defendant may not be adequately prepared to cross-examine a witness against him when the matter is first reached at a preliminary hearing. However, the court may set a reasonable deadline by which cross-examination must be conducted or waived. *Com. v. Tanso*, supra (where defendant claimed inability to cross-examine at hearing, failure of court to set deadline or to rule that defendant had enjoyed a reasonable opportunity to cross-examine precluded later use of the testimony).

Where a defendant has cross-examined the unavailable witness at the time the previous testimony was given, the issue is whether the examination permitted or conducted was constitutionally adequate. See, e.g., *Com. v. DiBenedetto*, 413 Mass 37, 605 NE2d 811 (1992) (restricting cross-examination of witness to the area in which he had been promised immunity by the prosecution was a denial of right to cross-examine requiring reversal); *Com. v. Siegfriedt*, supra (cross-examination sufficient despite defendant's claim he only learned later of witness's real name and that he had overstated his employment status while testifying); *Com. v. Trigones*, supra (prior testimony sufficiently reliable, even though defendant did not adequately pursue opportunity to cross-examine on bias); *Com. v. Taylor*, 32 Mass App 570, 591 NE2d 1108 (1992) (cross-examination adequate, although improperly restricted by judge on one issue).[5]

Where the prior reported testimony was involuntarily given, its use at trial would offend fundamental fairness, and it is not admissible. *Com. v. Rosa*, 412 Mass 147, 161, 587 NE2d 767, 775 (1992) (remanding for determination of voluntariness of *W*'s waiver of spousal privilege).

§8.8   Statements by a Party-Opponent

§8.8.1   General Principles[1]

Any extrajudicial statement by a party may be admitted in evidence against that party by an opponent, and will not be excluded on the ground it constitutes hearsay.[2] Statements of others for which a party is vicariously responsible are similarly admissible.[3] Conduct of a party intended as an assertion is treated as a statement and when offered by an opponent is not barred by the hearsay rule. Conduct of a party that was not intended as an assertion may be relevant because it suggests a state of mind of the party inconsistent with the position he has taken in the litigation. Proof of such conduct is admissible as circumstantial evidence, but because no assertion or statement was made, the evidence is simply not governed by the hearsay rule. The admissibility of such evidence is properly analyzed as a question of relevance.[4]

---

[5] See §3.3 for a more detailed discussion of the scope of cross-examination constitutionally required.

§8.8   [1] See also §§2.2-2.5 (judicial admissions); §6.7.2 (prior inconsistent statements).

[2] Statements of the opponent obtained through formal discovery proceedings are admissible against a hearsay objection. See Mass R Civ P 32(a)(2), 33(b), and 36(b).

[3] See §8.8.6 (vicarious admissions).

[4] See, e.g., §4.2.1 (consciousness of guilt and consciousness of liability).

Traditionally, the extrajudicial statements of a party have been labeled "admissions." The term, however, is misleading. There is no requirement that an extrajudicial statement of a party be incriminating, inculpatory, or inconsistent with his perceived interests at the time it was made to be admissible. Any statement of a party is admissible against him when offered by an opponent, if not objectionable on grounds other than hearsay.[5] Such statements are admissible without regard to whether the party against whom they are offered testifies in his own behalf. Both oral and written statements are admissible. See, e.g., *Com. v. Morgan*, 422 Mass 373, 379, 663 NE2d 247, 252 (1996) (defendant's oral statements to fellow prisoner are admissible) (Text cited); *Com. v. Pero*, 402 Mass 476, 524 NE2d 63 (1988) (written notes from *D* to co-conspirator regarding the cutting of cocaine and directions for its distribution). Statements of a party-opponent are admissible under both Proposed Mass R Evid 801(d)(2) and Fed R Evid 801(d)(2).

Authorities differ as to whether statements by a party-opponent are hearsay. The contention that they are not hearsay is based on the view that their admissibility is the result of the adversary system, rather than satisfaction of the conditions of the hearsay rule, and that no guarantee of trustworthiness is required in the case of an admission. Adv. Com. Note to Fed R Evid 801(d)(2).[6] It may be noted that a

---

[5] Certain statements of a party would be admissible as against a hearsay objection, but are excluded for policy reasons. See, e.g., §4.6 (offers of compromise and withdrawn guilty pleas).

[6] Parties who are not opponents in a pleadings sense may have adverse positions on a given issue. In some circumstances, evidence offered by one such party of a statement by the other may be admissible as a statement by a "party opponent." *Flood v. Southland Corp.*, 416 Mass 62, 71, 616 NE2d 1068 (1993). An unusual case led to an interesting ruling based on who the real adversaries in interest were in *Genova v. Genova*, 28 Mass App 647, 554 NE2d 1221 (1990). The plaintiff sued her own husband as a result of injuries suffered in an auto accident. At trial, the court allowed the defendant husband's counsel to introduce his prior statement, which was more favorable to the defense position than his trial testimony. The Appeals Court reasoned that it could be received as an admission, because the insurance company was the real party in interest

party cannot logically assert a lack of opportunity to cross-examine himself as the basis of excluding evidence of his own extrajudicial statements. The contention that such statements are hearsay is based on the fact that the statement or assertive conduct, the truth of which is important, occurred while the party was not a sworn witness in the case at bar. This theoretical difference is of no practical importance. Both the Proposed Massachusetts Rules of Evidence and the Federal Rules of Evidence treat admissions as nonhearsay.

The Opinion Rule Does Not Apply to Admissions. Statements of a party-opponent need not be made on personal knowledge to be admissible; they are not subject to the opinion rule. *Hallett v. Rimer*, 329 Mass 61, 106 NE2d 427 (1952) (to prove defendant's gross negligence witness testified that defendant had said he had had "one too many"); *LaPlante v. Maguire*, 325 Mass 96, 89 NE2d 1 (1949) (to disprove defendant's negligence, witness testified that plaintiff had said "he didn't believe any of them were going too fast"); *Ellis v. Pierce*, 172 Mass 220, 51 NE 974 (1898) (defendant advised plaintiff to sue defendant to recover from defendant's insurer).

Statements of a Party-Opponent Distinguished from Declarations against Interest. Statements of a party-opponent differ from the exception to the hearsay rule for declarations against interest (§8.10) in that: (1) the latter must be against the declarant's interest when made, whereas the former need not be;[7] (2) the latter can be offered by the declarant's estate, the opponent, or a third person, whereas admissions can be offered only by the party-opponent; (3) the latter are admissible only when the declarant is unavailable, whereas the former are admissible without regard to

---

on the defense side, and the husband stood to benefit if his wife won the case. It should perhaps be noted that there were alternative grounds relied upon to support the court's ruling that the statement was admissible.

[7] This is true in spite of the loose language ("admission against interest") used in cases such as *Stern v. Stern*, 330 Mass 312, 316-317, 113 NE2d 55, 58 (1953).

any unavailability of the party-declarant; and (4) admissions need not be based on the firsthand knowledge of the declarant, but declarations against interest are not admissible unless the declarant was speaking on the basis of firsthand knowledge.

Statements of a Party-Opponent Distinguished from Prior Inconsistent Statements. Admissions differ from prior inconsistent statements used to impeach (see §6.7.2) in that: (1) the latter are admissible when made by any witness, whereas the former are admissible only when chargeable to a party; (2) the probative effect of the latter is usually limited to impeachment, whereas statements by a party-opponent are admissible for all purposes; and (3) in some instances a foundation must be laid before proof of a prior inconsistent statement, whereas no foundation is required before proof of an admission.

Evidentiary Admissions Are Not Conclusive. Where the trier of fact believes that a statement by a party was made, the statement is not binding on the party, but is only some evidence of the facts asserted. *Brown v. MTA*, 345 Mass 636, 189 NE2d 214 (1963). Unlike a judicial admission (see §2.2), it is error for the court to charge the jury that an evidentiary admission is conclusive on the party making the statement. *Tully v. Mandell*, 269 Mass 307, 168 NE 923 (1929). The same rule applies to one's answers to the interrogatories of the party opponent. *Chaplain v. Dugas*, 323 Mass 91, 80 NE2d 9 (1948).

§8.8.2   Guilty Pleas

A guilty plea to a criminal charge and statements made by the criminal defendant during the taking of the plea are admissible against him in a later civil trial in which the former defendant is a party. *Aetna Casualty v. Niziolek*, 395 Mass 737, 481 NE2d 1356 (1985). Neither the plea nor the statements constitute conclusive proof of the facts admitted, however. *Department of Revenue v. W. Z. Jr.*, 412 Mass 718, 592 NE2d 1297 (1992); *Aetna Casualty v. Niziolek*, supra.[8]

The Supreme Judicial Court has accepted the principles of Proposed Mass R Evid 803(22), substantively identical to Fed R Evid 803(22), which provides that the hearsay rule does not bar evidence of a final judgment of a criminal conviction, following either a trial or guilty plea, to prove any fact essential to sustain the judgment. *Flood v. Southland Corp.*, 416 Mass 62, 70, 616 NE2d 1068 (1993). See §8.21. Such a conviction, however, is not conclusive proof of such facts. The admissibility of such evidence under Rule 803(22) does not depend on whether the person convicted is a party to the case in which the evidence is offered. Cf. *Com. v. Santiago*, 425 Mass 491, 681 NE2d 1205, 1215 (1997) (admissibility of guilty pleas of a shooter, other than defendant, in a gun battle described as within the trial court's discretion, evidently with respect to relevance, no reference made to *Flood v. Southland Corp.*).

For a discussion of the effect to be given an admission to sufficient facts in the state district courts, see *Com. v. Duquette*, 386 Mass 834, 438 NE2d 334 (1982); *Davis v. Allard*, 37 Mass App 508, 641 NE2d 121 (1994) (admission to sufficient facts on crimes of operating under the influence and operating an automobile to endanger life and safety are admissible in evidence as testimonial admissions in later civil action).

Where a motorist has been issued a citation and the clerk has found him "responsible," the fact that he pays a fine and foregoes an appeal to the judge will not be admissible against him in later civil proceedings. In *LePage v. Bumila*, 407 Mass 163, 552 NE2d 80 (1990), the court reasoned that because many people choose to pay traffic fines simply to avoid the inconvenience of contesting them, such

---

[8]A conviction following a guilty plea does not bar the defendant from contesting the underlying facts in later civil litigation under principles of collateral estoppel, although a conviction after a trial on the merits will preclude the defendant from relitigating the issues. *Aetna Casualty v. Niziolek*, supra.

conduct could not fairly be taken as an assertion that the person had actually committed the violation.

A withdrawn guilty plea is not admissible in later proceedings. Mass R Crim P 12(f); Proposed Mass R Evid 410; Fed R Crim P 11(e)(6); Fed R Evid 410. See §4.6.

It is merely a straightforward application of the rule admitting statements of a party-opponent that the testimony of a defendant in a criminal trial will be admissible against him in later trials where a conviction is followed by a reversal and a new trial. *Com. v. Marley*, 396 Mass 433, 486 NE2d 715 (1985); *Com. v. Cassidy*, 29 Mass App 651, 564 NE2d 400 (1990). In the absence of a transcript, any competent witness to the testimony from the first trial may recount the defendant's statements. *Com. v. Marley*, supra (assistant district attorney present at first trial could testify at second) (citing Text).

§8.8.3   Civil Pleadings

GL 231, §87, provides: "In any civil action pleadings shall not be evidence on the trial." Cf. Mass R Civ P 15; Fed R Civ P 15. But, except as to mere formal allegations, pleadings in one case are admissible as statements by a party in other cases, even if there is no evidence that they were dictated or approved by the party against whom they are offered. *DiMare v. Capaldi*, 336 Mass 497, 504, 146 NE2d 517, 520 (1957); *Clarke v. Taylor*, 269 Mass 335, 168 NE 806 (1929); *Hibernia Savings Bank v. Bomba*, 35 Mass App 378, 620 NE2d 787 (1993) (pleadings from another case are admissible, but are not "judicial admissions" and are not binding against a party) (see §2.4.2); *Pinshaw v. Metropolitan District Commission*, 33 Mass App 733, 737, 604 NE2d 1321, 1324 (1992) (Text cited). Cf. *Maney v. Maney*, 340 Mass 350, 164 NE2d 146 (1960) (allegations of unliquidated damage in prior proceeding in writ, declaration, or probate notice of claim not an admission as to true value of party's claim). If a pleading is amended, the superseded pleading cannot be introduced in evidence as an admission at the trial of the case, nor can the differences between the original and the amended pleading be commented upon in argument. *Harrington v. MTA*, 345 Mass 371, 187 NE2d 818 (1963); *Stoney v. Soar*, 322 Mass 408, 76 NE2d 645 (1948); *Taft v. Fiske*, 140 Mass 250, 5 NE 621 (1885).

In an action for personal injury, a party's written statements or his or her statements taken on a recording instrument that are given to the other party or his representative are inadmissible in evidence and may not be referred to at the trial unless a copy of the recorded statement or a verbatim written transcript of such statement is furnished to the party making it within ten days of written request therefor. GL 233, §23A. *Spellman v. MTA*, 328 Mass 446, 104 NE2d 493 (1952). But see *Mazzoleni v. Cotton*, 33 Mass App 147, 597 NE2d 59 (1992) (statement not furnished upon demand for same admissible in discretion of trial court where statement was ultimately furnished in discovery long before trial and plaintiff could demonstrate no prejudice from delay). GL 152, §7B, has similar provisions as to workmen's compensation proceedings. GL 271, §44 prohibits the admission in evidence of, or reference to, written and signed settlements, general releases, and statements made by hospitalized patients within 15 days of their injuries. The statute does not apply, however, to tape-recorded statements. *Fahey v. Rockwell Graphic Systems, Inc.*, 20 Mass App 642, 656, 482 NE2d 519, 528 (1985).

GL 233, §23B, provides that no statement made by a defendant during the course of a psychiatric examination under GL 123, §§15 and 16, shall be admissible on any issue other than that of his mental condition; nor shall any statement be admissible on that issue if the statement constitutes a confession of guilt for the crime charged. For discussion of the relationship of GL 233, §23B, to the privilege against self-incrimination, see *Blaisdell v. Com.*, 372 Mass 753, 364 NE2d 191 (1977). See also §13.14.6.

§8.8.4 Safety Standards

The fact that a company has provided a written rule of care for the conduct of its employees is admissible as an admission of the standard of care required if that rule was designed for the protection of persons in the position of the plaintiff. *Stevens v. Boston Elevated Railway Co.*, 184 Mass 476, 69 NE 338 (1904). Evidence of violation of safety standards or regulations promulgated by governmental organizations, trade associations, industry groups, or governmental and nongovernmental testing organizations may be admitted as evidence of negligence. In products liability cases, such evidence may be admitted under theories of admissibility other than that of an admission of a party. See, e.g., *Afienko v. Harvard Club of Boston*, 365 Mass 320, 312 NE2d 196 (1974) (violation of Department of Labor and Industries regulations admissible); *Campbell v. Leach*, 352 Mass 367, 225 NE2d 594 (1967) (violation of Department of Public Safety regulations admissible); *Woodcock v. Trailways of New England, Inc.*, 340 Mass 36, 40-41, 162 NE2d 658, 662-663 (1959) (violation of Interstate Commerce Commission (ICC) regulations admissible); *Torre v. Harris-Seybold Co.*, 9 Mass App 660, 404 NE2d 96 (1980) (extensive discussion of principles and authorities).

Evidence of violation of safety standards entered into by contract is admissible against a party to the contract. *Corsetti v. Stone Co.*, 396 Mass 1, 11 n.8, 483 NE2d 793 (1985) (contract provides evidence of the standards the parties considered material to due care); *Banaghan v. Dewey*, 340 Mass 73, 162 NE2d 807 (1959) (contract between owner of building and defendant elevator company); *Kushner v. Dravo Corp.*, 339 Mass 273, 158 NE2d 858 (1959) (defendant's contract with Metropolitan District Commission). Compare *Ted's Master Service, Inc. v. Farina Brothers Co.*, 343 Mass 307, 178 NE2d 268 (1961) (contract not admissible; contained no relevant safety standards); *Clough v. New England Tel. & Tel. Co.*, 342 Mass 31, 172 NE2d 113 (1961) (violation of safety rule not proximate cause of injury). It was held that this does not apply to a rule that is only given to employees orally, for the dangers of abuse in admitting evidence of such rules is too great. *Gerry v. Worcester Consolidated Street Railway Co.*, 248 Mass 559, 564-565, 143 NE 694, 696 (1924). If the rule or regulation is printed, oral testimony as to its contents will not be allowed. *Passanessi v. C. J. Maney Co.*, 340 Mass 599, 604, 165 NE2d 590, 593 (1960). See §12.6 (Best Evidence Rule).

§8.8.5   *Adoptive Admissions*

Silence in the presence of a statement is admissible against the silent party as an admission of the truth of the statement only when: (1) the person to whom the statement is made hears and understands it and has sufficient knowledge to reply to it; and (2) the statement is made under circumstances in which the ordinary person would contradict it if it were false. *Brown v. Com.*, 407 Mass 84, 90, 551 NE2d 531, 534 (1990) (silence in response to accusation of crime by coworker); *Com. v. Brown*, 394 Mass 510, 515, 476 NE2d 580, 583 (1985) (admission by silence inferred where witness could not recall which of two defendants made individual statements in incriminating conversation at which both were present). Such statements are sometimes called "adoptive admissions." They are included among statements that are admissible under Proposed Mass R Evid 801(d)(2)(B) and Fed R Evid 801(d)(2)(B) as a "statement of which the party has manifested an adoption or belief in its truth."

Where a statement is properly admitted as an adoptive admission, the Supreme Judicial Court has held there is no violation of the confrontation clause, although the maker of the statement is not produced for cross-examination and his unavailability is not established. *Com. v. Jones*, 400 Mass 544, 547, 511 NE2d 17, 19 (1987).[9]

---

[9] See §8.7.2 for further discussion of the confrontation clause.

The Supreme Judicial Court has indicated that evidence of an adoptive admission is "to be received with caution." *Com. v. Mackenzie*, 413 Mass 498, 506, 597 NE2d 1037, 1043 (1992) (noting that the meaning of a response, or lack thereof, to an accusatory statement is often ambiguous) (Text cited); *Com. v. Boris*, 317 Mass 309, 58 NE2d 8 (1944) (evidence of defendant's silence should have been excluded because he could not be expected to deny allegation that ran against third person). The court has described its attitude as "general wariness of adoptive admissions." *Com. v. Rembiszewski*, 363 Mass 311, 293 NE2d 919 (1973) (defendant could not be expected to reply to doctor's comment about x-ray results, while feigning incoherence and when he had been advised of *Miranda* rights). Ordinarily, a statement made face-to-face calls for contradiction if it is not true; therefore failure to contradict may be an implied admission. *Attorney General v. Pelletier*, 240 Mass 264, 134 NE 407 (1922). In *Leone v. Doran*, 363 Mass 1, 292 NE2d 19 (1973), the court indicated it is "not inclined to extend the scope of the doctrine of admission by silence," and it refused to allow evidence of silence in response to an accusation made in a telephone conversation.

A statement made in the presence of a party, but not directed to him, may not require a reply. His silence in such circumstances may not amount to an adoptive admission. *Com. v. Rembiszewski*, supra; *Com. v. Valcourt*, 333 Mass 706, 713, 133 NE2d 217, 222-223 (1956); *Com. v. Stevenson*, 46 Mass App 506, 511, 707 NE2d 385, 389 (1999) (defendants' mere presence in vicinity of conversation in which they were not participants did not establish that they could hear, let alone understand and respond to the allegations made). Nor does a statement that does not constitute in any way an accusation of guilt or liability require a reply. *Com. v. Wallace*, 346 Mass 9, 14-15, 190 NE2d 224, 227 (1963) (statement by wife of deceased that "I could kill you!" was an emotional outburst; failure to reply did not constitute an adoptive admission). If one is in a situation in which one believes oneself not entitled to speak, one's silence is not an adoptive admission. *Com. v. Kenney,* 53 Mass (12 Metc) 235 (1847). Similarly, silence is inadmissible as evidence if the person reasonably believes that the assertion has already been denied. *Refrigeration Discount Corp. v. Catino,* 330 Mass 230, 112 NE2d 790 (1953).

If instead of remaining silent when a statement requiring contradiction is made the party makes an equivocal reply or a reply that partially admits the statement, the statement and the reply are admissible in evidence. *Brown v. Com.,* supra (coworker asked *D* if he "did it," and he sarcastically replied "yeah, right"); *Com. v. Jones,* 400 Mass 544, 547, 511 NE2d 17, 19 (1987) (*D* and alleged accomplice conversed with *W,* whether *D*'s comments and tears constituted adoption of accomplice's statements was properly question for jury); *Com. v. Earltop,* 372 Mass 199, 361 NE2d 220 (1977) (statement made to *D,* "you have a gun," to which he replied, "so what if I do"); *Com. v. Sazama,* 339 Mass 154, 158 NE2d 313 (1959) (evasive or equivocal reply admissible, but not if intended to assert right to counsel). See §9.7.8.

Where police confronted the defendant with a lengthy statement by his co-defendant, his apparent acceptance of portions of the statement did not justify admitting the statement in its entirety. *Com. v. MacKenzie,* supra. In *MacKenzie,* the defendant waived his objections to the inadmissible portions, however, by virtually conceding admissibility of testimony and failing to distinguish between admissible and inadmissible portions of the statement.

Ordinarily, statements in letters are not to be taken as admitted if they are not contradicted. *Wagman v. Ziskind,* 234 Mass 509, 125 NE 633 (1920). But see *Elwell v. Athol,* 325 Mass 41, 88 NE2d 635 (1949).

If a defendant, while under arrest, is charged with a crime by a statement made in his presence and he makes an equivocal reply, a reply susceptible of being interpreted as an admission, or a reply not likely to be made by an innocent man, the statement and the reply may be admissible.

However, admissibility of such evidence depends upon whether a violation of defendant's right to counsel or privilege against self-incrimination is involved. These problems are discussed in §9.7.8 (confessions).

§8.8.6 Vicarious Admissions

There are a variety of situations in which a statement of a third person may be admitted against a party who is held to have responsibility for the statement, although he did not make it. These situations are covered by Fed R Evid 801(d)(2) and Proposed Mass R Evid 801(d)(2). We discuss with respect to specific issues the extent to which Massachusetts case law has adopted or differs from the rules and federal cases.

a. Statements of an Agent Offered Against Principal

Proposed Mass R Evid 801(d)(2)(D) provides that: "A statement is not hearsay if . . . the statement is offered against a party and is . . . a statement by his agent or servant concerning a matter within the scope of his agency or employment, made during the existence of the relationship." Fed R Evid 801(d)(2)(D) is identical. In *Ruszcyk v. Secretary of Public Safety*, 401 Mass 418, 517 NE2d 152 (1988), the Supreme Judicial Court adopted the rule and abrogated the prior common-law rule under which an agent's extrajudicial statement might be admitted against the principal only where the agent had actual authority to make the statement offered. See *Herson v. New Boston Garden Corp.*, 40 Mass App 779, 667 NE2d 907 (1996) (affirming finding under *Ruszcyk* that hearsay was properly excluded where subject matter of statements was not within declarant's scope of employment); *Blake v. Hendrickson*, 40 Mass App 579, 666 NE2d 164 (1996) (letters by plaintiff's counsel were properly admitted as vicarious statements of agent).

Ruszcyk represents a substantial departure from prior law and changes the analysis from an inquiry into the agent's specific authorization to speak about the subject matter in question to an inquiry into his general authority to act in the area. The universe of statements that are potentially admissible is much broader under the new rule than the old. However, the change does not mean that every statement by an agent concerning matters within the general scope of her duties will be admissible against the principal. In *Ruszcyk*, the court directed trial judges to make an additional determination whether the probative value of the statement is substantially outweighed by the danger of unfair prejudice before admitting it, as suggested by Proposed Mass R Evid 403 and Fed R Evid 403:

> This determination, which should take place outside the hearing of the jury, see Proposed Mass R Evid 104(c), takes into account the particular circumstances of each case, including the credibility of the witness; the proponent's need for the evidence, e.g., whether the declarant is available to testify; and the reliability of the evidence offered, including consideration of whether the statement was made on first-hand knowledge and of any other circumstances bearing on the credibility of the declarant. In short, this approach rejects a rigid per se rule in favor of a flexible, fact-sensitive standard applied on a case-by-case basis.

401 Mass at 422-423.

In *Ruszcyk*, the party opposing admission of the statement had argued that there should be a requirement of firsthand knowledge, although in general statements of a party-opponent are admissible without such a showing. The court rejected the argument, holding that firsthand knowledge is not required, although it may be taken into account in determining whether the probative value of the evidence is outweighed by danger of prejudice, and considered as well by the trier of fact in determining the weight to be given to the statement.

Out-of-court statements of an alleged agent are inadmissible to prove his agency. See *Poulin v. H. A. Tobey*

Lumber Corp., 337 Mass 146, 148 NE2d 277 (1958); *DuBois v. Powdrell*, 271 Mass 394, 397, 171 NE 474, 475-476 (1930). The alleged agent can be called as a witness and the agency established by his testimony. *Eastern Paper & Box Co. v. Herz Manufacturing Corp.*, 323 Mass 138, 80 NE2d 484 (1948); *Campbell v. Olender*, 27 Mass App 1197, 543 NE2d 708 (1989); *Republic Floors of New England, Inc. v. Weston Racquet Club, Inc.*, 25 Mass App 479, 486, 520 NE2d 160, 165 (1988). Under the Federal Rules, the out-of-court statement of an agent is admissible on the existence of the agency relationship and the scope thereof, but is not alone sufficient to prove it. Fed R Evid 801(d)(2). The Proposed Massachusetts Rules of Evidence do not address this specific issue.

b. Statements of Co-conspirators and Participants in Joint Ventures

The extrajudicial statements of a co-conspirator or a fellow participant in a joint venture are admissible against the other conspirators or participants if the statements are made during the pendency of the cooperative effort and in furtherance of its goal. *Com. v. Colon-Cruz*, 408 Mass 533, 543, 562 NE2d 797, 806 (1990); *Com. v. Borans*, 379 Mass 117, 145-148, 393 NE2d 911, 928-930 (1979) (extensive discussion of authorities; rule applies to joint ventures as well as to co-conspirators); *Com. v. Beckett*, 373 Mass 329, 366 NE2d 1252 (1977) (statement must be made in furtherance of conspiracy; this exception does not violate *Bruton* rule); *Com. v. White*, 370 Mass 703, 352 NE2d 904 (1976) (review of pertinent authorities); *Com. v. Pleasant*, 366 Mass 100, 315 NE2d 874 (1974); *Com. v. Cartagena*, 32 Mass App 141, 586 NE2d 43 (1992); Proposed Mass R Evid 801(d)(2)(E); Fed R Evid 801(d)(2)(E). The Proposed Massachusetts Rules of Evidence and the Federal Rules of Evidence treat this type of statement as nonhearsay rather than as an exception to the hearsay rule, but no difference in result obtains from the difference in nomenclature.

The existence of the conspiracy or joint venture must be proved by means other than the extrajudicial statement in question, as a condition of the statement's admissibility. *Com. v. Colon-Cruz,* supra; *Com. v. Bongarzone,* 390 Mass 326, 340, 455 NE2d 1183, 1192 (1983); *Com. v. Ali,* 43 Mass App Ct 549, 684 NE2d 1200 (1997); *Com. v. Treadwell,* 37 Mass App 968, 643 NE2d 60 (1994). The Massachusetts rule differs from the federal rule, where the statement itself may be taken into account in determining whether a conspiracy existed and whether the defendant was a member of it. Even under the federal rule, the statement alone is not sufficient to prove the existence of the conspiracy. Fed R Evid 801(d)(2). See *Bourjaily v. United States,* 483 US 171, 107 S Ct 2775 (1987).

The court need not make a preliminary finding that the joint criminal enterprise existed before admitting the evidence; it may be admitted subject to a later motion to strike if the prosecution fails to prove the defendant was part of a conspiracy or joint enterprise. *Com. v. Collado,* 426 Mass 675, 690 NE2d 424 (1998); *Com. v. Colon-Cruz,* supra. The existence of the conspiracy may be proved by circumstantial evidence. *Com. v. Soares,* 384 Mass 149, 159, 424 NE2d 221, 227 (1981); *Com. v. Stasiun,* 349 Mass 38, 50, 206 NE2d 672, 680 (1965); *Com. v. Cartagena,* 32 Mass App 141, 144, 586 NE2d 43, 45 (1992). The prior acquittal in a separate trial of the alleged co-conspirator who made the statement does not render it inadmissible. *Com. v. Anselmo,* 33 Mass App 602, 603 NE2d 227 (1992).

When statements of a co-conspirator have been admitted, the court should instruct the jury that they may consider the statement against the defendant only if they determine on the basis of other evidence that a conspiracy or joint venture existed and the defendant was a member of it. *Com. v. Soares,* 384 Mass 149, 159-160, 424 NE2d 221, 227 (1981); *Com. v. Beckett,* 373 Mass, 329, 340, 366 NE2d 1252, 1259 (1977). Cf. *Com. v. Fernandes,* 427 Mass 90, 692 NE2d 3 (1998) (error in failing to give charge did not create substantial risk of miscarriage of justice where defendant did not request it); *Com. v. Cartagena*, supra (error in failing to give charge did not create substantial risk of miscarriage of justice, where *D* did not request it).

A statement or confession by a co-conspirator or joint venturer made after the termination of the common enterprise does not come within this exception and may be admitted as against the declarant only. Admission of such a statement against the declarant may require a severance where the declarant does not testify and the remaining defendants have no opportunity to cross-examine him on the statement. See *Com. v. Bongarzone*, supra, and §8.8.7. However, statements made during a period in which the conspirators were still acting to conceal evidence of their crime and to avoid detection and detention may be held to be during the pendency of the conspiracy and therefore admissible. *Com. v. Clarke*, 418 Mass 207, 218, 635 NE2d 1197, 1204 (1994); *Com. v. Angiulo*, 415 Mass 502, 518, 615 NE2d 155, 166 (1993); *Com. v. Colon-Cruz*, supra. Statements made after the declarant has been apprehended and incarcerated are held to be after the termination of the conspiracy and not admissible. *Com. v. Drew*, 397 Mass 65, 71, 489 NE2d 1233, 1238 (1986); *Com. v. White*, supra.

c.   Other Vicarious Admissions

An admission of default by a principal is admissible against a surety, at least in an action against both. *Singer Manufacturing Co. v. Reynolds*, 168 Mass 588, 47 NE 438 (1897). Compare *Atlas Shoe Co. v. Bloom*, 209 Mass 563, 568-569, 95 NE 952, 954 (1911).

Admissions of lack of title made by a predecessor in title while in possession, according to the theory of the case of the party against whom the admission is offered, are admissible. *Abbott v. Walker*, 204 Mass 71, 90 NE 405 (1910).

§8.8.7   Statements by Co-defendant in Criminal Cases (**Bruton** Problems)

In *Bruton v. United States*, 391 US 123, 88 S Ct 1620 (1968), the Court held that where a co-defendant does not testify, the admission of his confession denies the non-confessing defendant's Sixth Amendment right of confrontation. The Court held that limiting instructions are not sufficient to cure the problem and that the appropriate remedy is to sever the trials where the government is not willing to forego use of the statement. The Supreme Judicial Court has held that:

> According to *Bruton*, severance is constitutionally required where: a co-defendant's extrajudicial statements are offered in evidence at a joint trial; the statements are "clearly inadmissible" as against the defendant; the co-defendant is not subject to cross-examination because he does not testify; and, finally, there is a substantial possibility that, in determining the defendant's guilt, the jury relied on the co-defendant's "powerfully incriminating extrajudicial statements" notwithstanding any limiting instructions from the judge.

Com. v. Pontes, 402 Mass 311, 314, 522 NE2d 931, 933 (1988) (citing *Bruton v. United States*, supra, 391 US at 128 and n.3, 135-136).

If the co-defendant's statement incriminates the defendant, severance is required even though the Commonwealth argues to the jury that the statement should not be believed. *Com. v. Hawkesworth*, 405 Mass 664, 674, 543 NE2d 691, 697 (1989) (rejecting argument that admission was harmless because full weight of Commonwealth's case was contrary to statement).

For *Bruton* to be implicated, the co-defendant's extrajudicial statement must inculpate the defendant. Where the statement does not name the defendant, or explicitly identify him, the inculpatory connection may be established by the content of the statement taken together with other evidence in the case. *Com. v. Johnson,* 412 Mass 318, 588 NE2d 684 (1992) (despite lack of objection, substantial likelihood of miscarriage of justice found where jury could have concluded defendant was the person referred to in co-defendant's statement). However, where the challenged statement does not directly inculpate the defendant, an appropriate limiting instruction may be sufficient to protect the defendant's rights. *Com. v. Charles,* 428 Mass 672, 676, 704 NE2d 1137, 1142 (1999); *Com. v. Wilson,* 46 Mass App 292, 296, 705 NE2d 313, 316 (1999) (declarant's statement, "we stabbed him," did not explicitly identify the defendant). Other evidence should be considered to determine "if the risk of contextual implication is pressing enough to invalidate the effect of limiting instructions." *Com. v. James,* 424 Mass 770, 780, 678 NE2d 1170, 1178 (1997) (noting that statement that does nothing more than raise an association between defendants is not sufficient by itself to give rise to *Bruton* challenge); *Com. v. Keevan,* 400 Mass 557, 570, 511 NE2d 534, 542 (1987); *Com. v. Cifizzari,* 397 Mass 560, 573, 492 NE2d 357, 365 (1986); *Com. v. LeBlanc,* 364 Mass 1, 8, 299 NE2d 719, 723 (1973); *Com. v. Crowe,* 21 Mass App 456, 478, 488 NE2d 780, 794 (1986). See *Richardson v. Marsh,* 481 US 200 (1987).

Where the co-defendant's statement is equivocal, *Bruton* may not apply. *Com. v. Santiago,* 30 Mass App 207, 215, 567 NE2d 943 (1991) (co-defendants' jailhouse remark, "We are all f - d," was equivocal, not necessarily incriminating).

The Supreme Court has suggested that a confession so heavily edited that it eliminates any reference to the non-testifying defendant may be admissible. *Richardson v. Marsh,* 481 US 200 (1987). The Court has held, however, that simply replacing inculpating references to the defendant with a blank space, or the word "deleted" is insufficient to protect the defendant's rights. *Gray v. Maryland,* 523 US 185, 118 S Ct 1151 (1998).

Decisions subsequent to *Bruton* have made it clear that if the declarant takes the stand and is available for cross-examination at trial, there is no violation of the confrontation right even if he denies making the statement or confession. *Nelson v. O'Neill*, 402 US 622, 91 S Ct 1723, 29 L Ed 2d 222 (1971). Cf. *California v. Green*, 399 US 149, 90 S Ct 1930, 26 L Ed 2d 489 (1970); *Dutton v. Evans*, 400 US 74, 91 S Ct 210, 27 L Ed 2d 213 (1970). The significance of these three cases is discussed in Liacos, *The Right of Confrontation and The Hearsay Rule: Another Look*, 34 Am Trial LJ 153 (1972).

The opportunity to cross-examine a testifying co-defendant who by his silence may have "adopted" the statements of a non-testifying declarant is not, for *Bruton* purposes, the equivalent of cross-examining the declarant. *Com. v. Bongarzone*, 390 Mass 326, 344, 455 NE2d 1183, 1194 (1983).

The confrontation clause does not permit the use of the non-testifying co-defendant's confession incriminating the defendant, even where the defendant himself has confessed and his own statement is introduced in evidence. *Cruz v. New York*, 481 US 186, 193 (1987). Introduction of such a statement may, however, constitute harmless error in some circumstances. The Supreme Judicial Court applies a "stringent test" to determine if the error was harmless beyond a reasonable doubt. *Com. v. Dias*, 405 Mass 131, 136, 539 NE2d 59, 63 (1989); *Com. v. Sinnott*, 399 Mass, 863, 872, 507 NE2d 699, 705 (1987); *Com. v. Twing*, 39 Mass App 75, 653 NE2d 1123 (1995) (*Bruton* violation found harmless). The test is whether any "spillover" created by those portions of statements that do not perfectly interlock, "was without effect on the jury and did not contribute to the verdict." *Com. v. Cunningham*, 405 Mass 646, 649, 543 NE2d 12, 14 (1989); *Com. v. Libran*, 405 Mass 634, 642, 543 NE2d 5, 10 (1989). In *Com. v. Adams*, 416 Mass 55, 617 NE2d 594 (1993), the court rejected the prosecution's argument that because the confession of each co-defendant contained sufficient evidence from which the jury could infer that he intended to commit the crime, the *Bruton* error was harmless. Reversal was required where each defendant's confession had portrayed the other as the mastermind and himself as a reluctant follower.

In *Com. v. Gordon,* 422 Mass 816, 826, 666 NE2d 122, 131 (1996), the co-defendant's attorney said in his opening that there would be evidence that the defendant had stabbed the victims and admitted it to the co-defendant. Subsequently, the co-defendant's case was mistried and severed, before the co-defendant had testified, giving the defendant no opportunity to cross examine the co-defendant or to challenge counsel's opening. It was held that the defendant's motion for a mistrial was properly denied because the opening was not evidence and the jury would be presumed to follow the trial court's instructions to that effect.

There is no violation of the confrontation clause where the co-defendant's statement is independently admissible against the defendant as an admission by a fellow partici-pant in a joint enterprise or conspiracy, or as an admission by silence by the defendant who was present at the time the statement was made. *Com. v. Collado,* 426 Mass 675, 690 NE2d 424 (1998); *Com. v. Brown,* 394 Mass 510, 515, 476 NE2d 580, 583 (1985); *Com. v. Rogers,* 38 Mass App 395, 647 NE2d 1228 (1995).

The fact that a co-defendant's statement inculpating the defendant may have been against the co-defendant's penal interest will not render it admissible in violation of the defendant's confrontation clause rights protected by *Bruton. Lilly v. Virginia,* ___ US ___, 119 S Ct 1887 (1999).

§8.9   Prior Inconsistent Statements by Witnesses

The general rule is that prior inconsistent statements are not admissible as substantive evidence of the matters as-serted, but only for the impeachment purpose of demon-strating the inconsistency of the witness's accounts. The Supreme Judicial Court has recognized an exception for grand jury testimony under oath, provided the witness can be effectively cross-examined as to the accuracy of the statement, the statement was not coerced and was more than a mere confirmation or denial of the interrogator's assertion, and other evidence tending to prove the issue is presented. Under these circumstances, the prior inconsistent statement may be admissible as substantive evidence. *Com. v. Daye*, 393 Mass 55, 469 NE2d 483 (1984). For a fuller discussion of these issues, see §6.7.2.

§8.10   Declarations Against Interest

Statements of a declarant against his own pecuniary or proprietary interest at the time the statements are made have long been admissible for the truth of the matters asserted under the circumstances herein described. *Cunningham v. Davis*, 175 Mass 213, 56 NE 2 (1900). Statements against penal interest were recognized as admissible under this exception to the hearsay rule much later in *Com. v. Carr*, 373 Mass 617, 369 NE2d 970 (1977).

Declarations against interest are statements made by witnesses, not parties to the litigation or their privies or representatives.[1] The declarant must be unavailable for the statement to be admissible,[2] and the statement must have been made on the basis of firsthand knowledge. The statement may be admitted upon offer of either party. See Wigmore, §§1455-1477 (Chad rev 1974).

The common law did not recognize a statement that rendered the declarant subject to prosecution for a crime, a "declaration against penal interest," as being within the scope of this exception to the hearsay rule.[3] The decision in *Com. v. Carr*, supra, adopts the position taken by Fed R Evid

---

§8.10 [1] Such latter statements may be admissible as statements by a party-opponent. See §8.8.

[2] For a discussion of what constitutes "unavailability," see §8.4.2.

[3] For a discussion of the common law and recent statutory history of the admissibility of declarations against penal interest, see *Lilly v. Virginia*, ___ US ___, 119 S Ct 1887 (1999).

804(b)(3), which provides in pertinent part that a statement that "so far tended to subject" the declarant to criminal liability "that a reasonable man in his position would not
have made the statement unless he believed it to be true"
may be admissible.[4]

Whether a statement is sufficiently adverse to the declarant's penal interest to be admissible is judged by whether
the declarant would have been inclined to make a truthful
statement under the circumstances because of his concern
for the penal consequences of the statement. See *Com. v.
Charles,* 428 Mass 672, 679, 704 NE2d 1137, 1144 (1999)
(admission that accident for which an insurance claim had
been made was fictional was against penal interest); *Com. v.
Pope,* 397 Mass 275, 280, 491 NE2d 240, 243 (1986) (suicide
note confessing to a murder was inadmissible because
declarant had already decided to kill himself and would not
be motivated by penal consequences of statement). In *Com.
v. Drew,* 397 Mass 65, 74, 489 NE2d 1233, 1239-1240 (1986),
the court questioned whether the statement, which admitted little other than presence at a murder, was sufficiently
inculpatory. However, the court noted that the exception
was "not so narrow as to preclude all declarations but direct
admissions of guilt." The court reasoned that "it is not the
fact that the declaration is against interest but the awareness
of that fact by the declarant which gives the statement
significance," citing Jefferson, *Declarations Against Interest:
An Exception to the Hearsay Rule,* 58 Harv L Rev 1, 17 (1944).
Because a layman might have believed he would be incriminated by an admission of presence at a murder scene,

---

[4] In *Lilly v. Virginia,* ___ US ___, 119 S Ct 1887 (1999), the Court
considered whether the admission of a confession by a co-defendant that
inculpated the defendant violated the constitutional rights of the
defendant under the confrontation clause. Four of the Justices found
that a declaration against penal interest offered for these purposes was
not within a "firmly rooted" hearsay exception, and insufficiently
trustworthy to satisfy the reliability requirement of *Ohio v. Roberts,* 448 US
56, 100 S Ct 2531 (1980). See §8.8.7. The remainder of the Court did not
reach this issue, finding the statement in question inadmissible for other
reasons.

the court indicated the statement was probably a declaration against penal interest.

The courts have found statements insufficiently incriminating in a variety of circumstances. *Com. v. Slonka*, 42 Mass App Ct 760, 770, 680 NE2d 103, 110 (1997) (witness's interview statement to defense counsel that he smoked "a couple of bowl fulls" with victim was not made under circumstances suggesting declarant's awareness that statement was against penal interest); *Com. v. Hearn*, 31 Mass App 707, 583 NE2d 279 (1991) (statement that essentially exculpated declarant/defendant and admitted only uncontested facts was not against penal interest); *Com. v. Fernandes*, 30 Mass App 335, 338, 568 NE2d 604, 607 (1991) (affirming exclusion of statement in part because the incriminating declaration was "clearly affected by the exigencies of the plea bargaining"); *Com. v. Marple*, 26 Mass App 150, 524 NE2d 863 (1988) (court questioned whether a statement qualified as against penal interest where declarant spoke after he believed his case was already lost).

The United States Supreme Court has held that only those statements within a longer narrative that are individually self-incriminating are admissible under Fed R Evid 804(b)(3). In *Williamson v. United States*, 512 US 594, 114 S Ct 2431, 129 L Ed 2d 476 (1994), the Court held that non-self-inculpatory statements are not admissible as declarations against interest, even if made within a broader narrative that is generally self-inculpatory. See *Com. v. Lilly*, supra, 119 S Ct at 1887 (concurring op by Rehnquist, CJ) (statements in confession by co-defendant that were against his penal interest were separate from those which exculpated him and inculpated the defendant); *Com. v. Lopera*, 42 Mass App 133, 674 NE2d 1340 (1997) (statements by alleged prostitute that she gave defendant a portion of her fee and that defendant kept the apartment in question were not sufficiently against declarant's penal interest to be admissible).

Fed R Evid 804(b)(3) and Proposed Mass R Evid 804(b)(3), as adopted in *Com. v. Carr*, supra, provide: "A statement tending to expose the declarant to criminal liability and offered to exculpate the accused is not admissible unless corroborating circumstances clearly indicate the trustworthiness of the statement." The Supreme Judicial Court has held that corroboration of trustworthiness is also required when the government seeks to introduce a statement against penal interest by an unavailable declarant that would inculpate the defendant.[5] *Com. v. Charles,* 428 Mass 672, 679, 704 NE2d 1137, 1144 (1999). See *Com. v. Pope,* 397 Mass 275, 280, 491 NE2d 240, 243 (1986).

The Supreme Judicial Court has declared that in assessing whether a statement is sufficiently corroborated, a court should "not be stringent," and where the issue is close, a court should favor admission, relying on the good sense of the jury to correct any prejudicial impact. *Com. v. Charles,* supra, 428 Mass at 679-680, 704 NE2d at 1144 (Text cited); *Com. v. Drew,* 397 Mass 65, 75 and n.10, 489 NE2d 1233, 1241 and n.10 (1986); *Com. v. Gagnon,* 408 Mass 185, 194, 557 NE2d 728, 734 (1990); *Com. v. Galloway,* 404 Mass 204, 208, 534 NE2d 778, 781 (1989) (reversing trial court's exclusion of statement). The question is not whether the trial judge is satisfied that the statement is actually true, but whether there is some reasonable likelihood that the statement could be true. *Com. v. Drew,* supra, 397 Mass at 75-76, 489 NE2d at 1241.

In making the determination, the court should take into account the degree of disinterestedness of the witnesses giving corroborating testimony, the plausibility of that testimony in the light of the rest of the proof, the credibility of the declarant and the credibility and probative quality of his statement, the timing of the declaration, the relationship between the declarant and the witness, the

---

[5] Such a statement may not be admissible under the confrontation clause if the declarant does not testify and the statement explicitly identifies the defendant. See §8.8.7.

reliability and character of the declarant, whether the statement was made spontaneously, whether other people heard the out-of-court statement, whether there is any apparent motive for declarant to misrepresent the matter, and whether and in what circumstances the statement was repeated. *Com. v. Drew*, supra, 397 Mass at 75-76, 489 NE2d at 1241. The judge should not base her determination, however, on the credibility of the witness who testifies as to the making of the statement by the declarant, because the jury should assess that witness's credibility. *Com. v. Drew*, supra, 397 Mass at 76, 489 NE2d at 1241. Where the proponent of the evidence has failed to make a record of corroborating evidence, an appellate court will affirm a trial court's exclusion of the evidence. *Com. v. Piper*, 426 Mass 8, 686 NE2d 191 (1997); *Com. v. Stewart*, 422 Mass 385, 663 NE2d 255 (1996); *Com. v. Zuluaga*, 43 Mass App Ct, 629, 686 NE2d 463 (1997); *Com. v. Burgos*, 36 Mass App 903, 627 NE2d 471 (1994) (where declarant was identified only by first name, no efforts were made to locate him, and nothing was offered to bolster his statement, it was not error to exclude it); *Com. v. Cintron*, 29 Mass App 983, 562 NE2d 108 (1990).

In a criminal trial, due process requirements may dictate that when the defendant seeks to introduce reliable declarations against penal interest that exculpate him, he be allowed to adduce such evidence even if it would not qualify as an exception to the hearsay rule under state law. *Green v. Georgia*, 442 US 95, 99 S Ct 2150 (1979); *Chambers v. Mississippi*, 410 US 284, 93 S Ct 1038, 35 L Ed 2d 297 (1973). Where there is insufficient evidence of trustworthiness or reliability, and insufficient corroboration demonstrating trustworthiness, constitutional due process principles do not require the admission of a hearsay statement that would exculpate the accused. *Com. v. Drew*, supra.

The common-law exception did not recognize a statement exposing the declarant to future civil liability as being a statement sufficiently against interest to qualify. Both

Proposed Mass R Evid 804(b)(3) and Fed R Evid 804(b)(3) provide that a statement that "so far tended to subject the declarant to civil . . . liability, or to render invalid a claim by him against another" may qualify as an exception. The rules thus provide for a broader range of extrajudicial statements against interest that may be admissible than that which is allowed by common law.

Declarations of a landowner, now deceased, made during his ownership in disparagement of his title are admissible. *Rowell v. Doggett*, 143 Mass 483, 10 NE 182 (1887). Such declarations may come into evidence as declarations against interest or as admissions if they were made by a predecessor in title of the party against whom they are offered.[6] A local doctrine analogous to the doctrine of declarations against interest makes such declarations of a deceased owner admissible in any event if offered to prove boundaries and if the owner was on the land pointing out such boundaries when the statement was made. *Long v. Colton*, 116 Mass 414 (1875).

Declarations of deceased persons are more liberally admitted under GL 233, §65, than as declarations against interest. See §8.5.1. However, unlike the statutory exception, this common-law exception applies to both civil and criminal cases.

---

[6] Other hearsay exceptions created by the rules of evidence may be a basis for admission of evidence pertaining to ownership or boundaries of land. See, e.g., Proposed Mass R Evid 803(14) and Fed R Evid 803(14) (records of documents recorded in a public office that affect an interest in property); Fed R Evid 803(15) (statements in documents affecting an interest in property; this exception is not adopted by the Proposed Massachusetts Rules of Evidence); Proposed Mass R Evid 803(16) and Fed R Evid 803(16) (statements in ancient documents); Proposed Mass R Evid 803(20) and Fed R Evid 803(20) (reputation concerning boundaries or customs affecting lands); Proposed Mass R Evid 803(23) and Fed R Evid 803(23) (inter alia judgments pertaining to boundaries; no common-law equivalent in Masschusetts).

§8.11   Regular Business Entries

The admission in evidence of business entries is principally controlled by two Massachusetts statutes and two common-law rules. Proposed Mass R Evid 803(6), discussed infra, would combine the two statutory exceptions into one and modify them. The statutory rules were designed to liberalize the rather strict common-law rules pertaining to the admissibility of business entries. The common-law rules are still extant but are of only occasional utility. These exceptions to the hearsay rule overlap one another. If evidence can be brought within any one of them, it is admissible. Business records may be used like any other memorandum to refresh the recollection of a witness (see §6.19) or as past recollection recorded (see §8.17).

§8.11.1   Statutory Exceptions: MGL 233, §78

Section 78 of GL 233 provides for the admissibility of ordinary business records.[1] Four preliminary findings by the

---

§8.11   [1] The statute provides:

An entry in an account kept in a book or by a card system or by any other system of keeping accounts, or a writing or record, whether in the form of an entry in a book or otherwise, made as a memorandum or record of any act, transaction, occurrence or event, shall not be inadmissible in any civil or criminal proceeding as evidence of the facts therein stated because it is transcribed or because it is hearsay or self-serving, if the court finds that the entry, writing or record was made in good faith in the regular course of business and before the beginning of the civil or criminal proceeding aforesaid and that it was the regular course of such business to make such memorandum or record at the time of such act, transaction, occurrence or event or within a reasonable time thereafter. For the purposes hereof, the word "business," in addition to its ordinary meaning, shall include profession, occupation and calling of every kind. The court, in its discretion, before admitting such entry, writing or record in evidence, may, to such extent as it deems practicable or desirable, but to no greater extent than the law required before April 11, 1913, require the party offering the same to produce and offer in evidence the original entry, writing, document or account or any other form which the entry, writing or record offered and the facts therein stated were transcribed or taken, and to call as his witness any person who made the entry, writing or record offered or the original or any other entry, writing, document or account from which the entry, writing or

judge have to be made to admit such records: (1) the entry
was made in good faith; (2) in the regular course of business; (3) before the action was begun; and (4) it was the
usual course of business to make the entry at the time of the
event recorded or within a reasonable time thereafter. The
admission of the records in civil cases imports the necessary
preliminary findings by the judge. *Sawyer & Co. v. Southern
Pacific Co.*, 354 Mass 481, 238 NE2d 357 (1968). But cf.
Fisher v. Swartz, 333 Mass 265, 266, 130 NE2d 575, 577
(1955) (no such finding can be implied where record revealed no attempt to bring record within the statute).[2]

In 1982, the legislature adopted GL 233, §79J, which
provides a method for the use of certified copies of business
records. While the statute does not vary the prerequisites of
admissibility of a business record set forth in GL 233 §78
(from the point of view of the hearsay rule), it does provide
for a method of authentication and use of copies of such
records comparable to that provided for hospital records in
the second paragraph of GL 233, §79 (see §8.11.2).[3]

---

record offered or the facts therein stated were transcribed or taken, or who
has personal knowledge of the facts stated in the entry, writing or record
offered. When any such entry, writing or record is admitted, all other
circumstances of the making thereof, including lack of personal knowledge
by the entrant or maker, may be shown to affect its weight and when such
entry, writing or record is admitted in a criminal proceeding all questions of
fact which must be determined by the court as the basis for the admissibility
of the evidence involved shall be submitted to the jury, if a jury trial is had
for its final determination.

[2] See *Friedman v. Kurker*, 14 Mass App 152, 157-158, 438 NE2d 76, 79
(1982) (where parties stipulated to admissibility of business records, fact
there was evidence of some inaccuracies in same did not bar their use for
all purposes) (Text cited).

[3] The statute provides:

A record kept by any business which is required to be produced in court by
any party shall be certified by the affidavit of the person in custody thereof
to be a true and complete record and shall be delivered by such business to
the clerk of such court who shall keep the same in his custody until its
production is called for at the trial or hearing by the party requiring the said
record. Such record, so certified and delivered, shall be deemed to be
sufficiently identified to be admissible in evidence if admissible in all other
respects. The party requiring the production of said record and, in the
discretion of the court, any other party may examine said record in the
custody of the clerk at any time before it is produced in court. The clerk

Under §78 the unavailability of the declarant is not required for the record to be admissible. The section applies to criminal as well as civil cases. The section removes the objection not only to the hearsay rule but also to the best evidence rule to some extent.

The prerequisites of admissibility, and the nature of material in a purported business record that may qualify within the statutory exception, are discussed in both the main and the concurring opinion (joined in by the court) in *Wingate v. Emery Air Freight Corp.*, 385 Mass 402, 408, 432 NE2d 474, 479 (1982). The proponent of the evidence must establish that it was the business duty of the preparer of the record to make the memorandum or entry in the regular course of business. See *Tosti v. Ayik*, 394 Mass 482, 476 NE2d 928 (1985) (proper to exclude personnel memo regarding investigation into plaintiff's conduct where no showing it was made in the regular course of business); *Irwin v. Ware*, 392 Mass 745, 748-751, 467 NE2d 1292, 1296 (1984) (letter reporting blood test results not shown to be a business record made in the regular course of business); *Burke v. Memorial Hospital*, 29 Mass App 948, 558 NE2d 1146 (1990) (memorandum in personnel file not a business record because not placed in file as part of the regular practice of employer); *Alcan Aluminum v. Carlton Aluminum*, 35 Mass App 161, 617 NE2d 1005 (1993) (exhibit listing expenses of plaintiff, based on plaintiff's records, was inadmissible where records themselves were not introduced and it was undisputed that exhibit did not constitute a business record). Compare *Com. v. LaPlante*, 416 Mass 433, 441, 622 NE2d 1357, 1362 (1993) (foundation for invoice must be laid by witness from company issuing invoice, rather than

---

upon completion of such trial or hearing shall notify such business that said record is no longer required and will be returned by mail unless an authorized representative of the business calls for the same at the office of said clerk within seven days of said notice.

A copy of such record made by the photographic process may be delivered to the clerk of such court in place of the original and, if certified as hereinbefore provided, shall be admitted in evidence equally with the original.

keeper of records at company where order was picked up, but error harmless under circumstances) with *Quinn Brothers, Inc. v. Wecker*, 414 Mass 815, 611 NE2d 234 (1993) (invoices from vendors offered as evidence of costs constituted business records of the customer where they were maintained as part of the customer's business records with checks written against them).

The fact that a business record itself is admissible does not mean that every statement in a record is admissible. Where records contain multiple hearsay, each level of hearsay must satisfy an exception to the hearsay rule to be admissible. See *Wingate v. Emery Air Freight Corp.*, supra; *Kelly v. O'Neil*, 1 Mass App 313, 296 NE2d 223 (1973); §8.1.

In *Com. v. Trapp*, 396 Mass 202, 208 n.5, 485 NE2d 162, 166 n.5 (1985), the court explicitly held that "the extra assurance of unbiased assertions guaranteed by the requirement that a record must have been made before a proceeding began is a necessary component of the Massachusetts business records exception." The court refused to adopt Proposed Mass R Evid 803(6) to the extent that it eliminates this requirement. See *DiMarzo v. American Mutual Insurance Co.*, 389 Mass 85, 105-106, 449 NE2d 1189, 1202 (1983) (records made during pendency of action lacked sufficient indicia of reliability to fall within ambit of statute); *Simon v. Solomon*, 385 Mass 91, 106-107 n.10, 431 NE2d 556, 567 n.10 (1982) (telephone records made after suit commenced not admissible under §78 but could be used for impeachment purposes); *Com. v. Reyes*, 19 Mass App 1017, 476 NE2d 978 (1985) (telephone records — not objectionable that the actual document introduced in evidence was produced after commencement of litigation where the record itself was stored in the regular course of business before litigation began). Cf. *American Velodur Metal, Inc. v. Schinabeck*, 20 Mass App 460, 481 NE2d 209 (1985) (where party was entitled to attorneys' fees from opponent, not error to admit under this exception billing records of law firm, although prepared after litigation commenced).

In criminal cases, the judge, after finding the four preliminary facts and admitting the evidence, must instruct the jury that it should disregard the evidence if it fails to find any one of the preliminary facts. (See §3.9.1.) Failure to resubmit the question to the jury will not be reversible error, however, in the absence of an objection or request by the defendant. *Com. v. Stubbs*, 4 Mass App 777, 341 NE2d 695 (1976); *Com. v. Devlin*, 335 Mass 555, 563, 141 NE2d 269, 273 (1957). In the absence of evidence to the contrary, the admission of such records by the judge in a criminal case also imports a finding by him that the conditions of admissibility contained in the statute have been satisfied. *Com. v. Monahan*, 349 Mass 139, 170, 207 NE2d 29, 44 (1965); *Com. v. Greenberg*, 339 Mass 557, 579, 160 NE2d 181, 187 (1959).

Among other documents, bills of lading, way bills, delivery sheets, and invoices are admissible. *Wiley & Foss, Inc. v. Saxony Theatres*, 332 Mass 172, 124 NE2d 903 (1955); *Chadwick & Carr Co. v. Smith*, 293 Mass 293, 295, 199 NE 903, 904 (1936). Computer printouts are admissible under §78. *Com. v. Reed*, 23 Mass App 294, 502 NE2d 147 (1986) (that the witness does not understand how the system works is irrelevant to admissibility, but may go to the weight of the evidence); *Com. v. Hogan*, 7 Mass App 236, 250-251, 387 NE2d 158, 167 (1979). Specifications from an engineering department also have qualified as business records. *Ricciutti v. Sylvania Electric Products, Inc.*, 343 Mass 347, 349, 178 NE2d 857, 860 (1961).

Police records may constitute business records under §78. *Adoption of Paula*, 420 Mass 716, 727, 651 NE2d 1222, 1230 (1995) (report of police officers' firsthand observations of conditions in home) (Text cited); *Com. v. Sellon*, 380 Mass 220, 402 NE2d 1329 (1980) (police log showing time telephone call was received); *Com. v. Walker*, 379 Mass 297, 397 NE2d 1105 (1979) (police record of report of stolen car). But compare *Kelly v. O'Neil*, 1 Mass App 313, 296 NE2d 223 (1973), holding that §78 does not authorize admission of statements of second-level hearsay—i.e., statements made by third persons that are incorporated into a police officer's report—and that accident reports filed by a motor vehicle operator are not business records. Records of the probation office of the probate court qualify under §78. *Furtado v. Furtado*, 380 Mass 137, 402 NE2d 1024 (1980). See also *Sawyer & Co. v. Southern Pacific Co.*, supra (government records may be considered business records). Official records are discussed in §8.13.

Employer's reports of injury received by a worker's compensation insurer are not business records of the insurer. *Wingate v. Emery Air Freight Corp.*, 385 Mass 402, 432 NE2d 474 (1982). Nor are wage reports received by the Department of Public Welfare from the employer of an employee business records of the Department. *Com. v. Hussey*, 14 Mass App 1015, 441 NE2d 783 (1982). A school file consisting of reports received as to the victim of a crime is not a business record of the school. *Com. v. Wilson*, 12 Mass App 942, 426 NE2d 162 (1981).

Some hospital medical records not admissible under §79 (see §8.11.2) have been held admissible under §78. *Com. v. Hogg*, 365 Mass 290, 311 NE2d 63 (1974) (hospital receipt for bullets taken from victim's body). Business records of hospitals are, of course, within the scope of §78. *Brockton Hospital v. Cooper*, 345 Mass 616, 188 NE2d 922 (1963).

Opinions contained in business records offered under §78 are not admissible. *Julian v. Randazzo*, 380 Mass 391, 403 NE2d 931 (1980) (following the same rule as applied to official records offered as an exception to the hearsay rule); *Burke v. Memorial Hospital*, 29 Mass App 948, 558 NE2d 1146 (1990) (performance evaluations in personnel records constituted inadmissible opinions); *Wiik v. Rathore*, 21 Mass App 399, 487 NE2d 235 (1986) (doctor's opinion in medical record regarding cause of injury was inadmissible opinion). But see *Vassallo v. Baxter Healthcare Corp.*, 428 Mass 1, 18, 696 NE2d 909, 921 (1998) (scientific studies containing primarily factual data, although including some interpretations of data, were properly admitted as against a general objection to the studies as a whole where opponent made no request to strike those portions containing opinions). Compare Proposed Mass R Evid 803(6) and Fed R Evid 803(6), which allow statements of opinion.

Opinions in hospital and medical records regarding the diagnosis, prognosis, or causation of a medical condition may be admissible under MGL 233, §79G. See §8.11.3.

§8.11.2   Statutory Exceptions: MGL 233, §79

Section 79, GL 233 provides for the admissibility of hospital records.[4] The admissibility of hospital records in

---

[4] The statute provides:

Records kept by hospitals, dispensaries or clinics, and sanatoria under GL 111, §70: shall be admissible, and records which the court finds are required to be kept by the laws of any other state or territory, or the District of Columbia, or by the laws and regulations of the United States of America pertaining to the department of national defense and the veterans administration, by hospitals, dispensaries or clinics, and sanatoria similarly conducted or operated or which, being incorporated, offer treatment free of charge, may be admitted by the court, in its discretion, as evidence in the courts of the Commonwealth so far as such records relate to the treatment and medical history of such cases and the court may, in its discretion, admit copies of such records, if certified by the persons in custody thereof to be true and complete; but nothing therein contained shall be admissible as evidence which has reference to the question of liability. Copies of photographic or microphotographic records so kept by hospitals, dispensaries or clinics, or sanatoria, when duly certified by the person in charge of the hospital, dispensary or clinic, or sanatorium, shall be admitted in evidence equally with the original photographs or microphotographs.

A record kept by any hospital, dispensary or clinic, or sanatorium under section seventy of chapter one hundred and eleven which is required to be produced in court by any party shall be certified by the affidavit of the person in custody thereof to be a true and complete record, and shall be delivered by such hospital, dispensary or clinic, or sanatorium to the clerk of such court, who shall keep the same in his custody until its production is called for at the trial or hearing by the party requiring the said record. Such record, so certified and delivered shall be deemed to be sufficiently identified to be admissible in evidence if admissible in all other respects. The party requiring the production of said record and, in the discretion of the court, any other party may examine said record in the custody of the clerk at any time before it is produced in court. The clerk upon the completion of such trial or hearing shall notify such hospital that said worker's compensation proceedings is governed by GL 152, §20. The word "records" in §79 has been construed to include technical reports. See *Com. v. Franks*, 359 Mass 577, 270 NE2d 837 (1971) (laboratory reports); *Kramer v. John Hancock Mutual Life Insurance Co.*, 336 Mass 465, 146 NE2d 357 (1957) (electrocardiograms); *Whipple v. Grandchamp*, 261 Mass 40, 158 NE 270 (1927) (x-rays taken in the course of diagnosis and treatment together with the evaluative reports of the doctors).

The oft-stated purpose of §79 is primarily to relieve physicians and nurses working at hospitals from the inconvenience of attending court as witnesses to facts ordinarily recorded in hospital records. *Com. v. Gogan*, 389 Mass 255, 263, 449 NE2d 365, 370 (1983); *Com. v. Bohannon*, 385 Mass 733, 749, 434 NE2d 163, 173 (1982). Thus, hospital records containing facts relevant to medical history or treatment are admissible without need for and despite the absence of testimonial corroboration. *Com. v. Gogan*, supra, 389 Mass at 264, 449 NE2d at 270; *Com. v. Copeland*, 375 Mass 438, 377 NE2d 930 (1978). But compare *Diaz v. Eli Lilly & Co.*, 14 Mass App 448, 440 NE2d 518 (1982) (diagnostic statements in record that involve difficulties of interpretation, or are unusual or controversial, may lack sufficient indicia of reliability to be admitted as part of record); *Com. v. Ennis*, 2 Mass App 864, 314 NE2d 922 (1974) (no error to exclude diagnostic statements that could not be understood without expert testimony and that posed problems of multiple-level hearsay). Although the presence of the maker of the record is not required, the statute does not limit the admissibility of hospital records to those cases where the preparers of the reports are absent. The report is admissible, even if it would be cumulative. *Com. v. McNickles*, 22 Mass App 114, 123, 491 NE2d 662, 669 (1986).

---

record is no longer required and will be returned to the hospital by certified mail unless an authorized representative of the hospital calls for the same at the office of said clerk within seven days of said notice.

In *Bouchie v. Murray*, 376 Mass 524, 531, 381 NE2d 1295, 1300 (1978), the court set out a four-part test to determine whether material contained in a hospital record is admissible under §79:

> First, the document must be the type of record contemplated by G.L. c. 233, §79. Second, the information must be germane to the patient's treatment or medical history... Third, the information must be recorded from the personal knowledge of the entrant or from a compilation of the personal knowledge of those who are under a medical obligation to transmit such information. Fourth, voluntary statements of third persons appearing in the record are not admissible unless they are offered for reasons other than to prove the truth of the matter contained therein or, if offered for their truth, come within another exception to the hearsay rule or the general principles discussed supra.

The reference to "general principles" apparently refers to information from a person with reason to know of the patient's medical history by reason of his or her relationship to the patient, which the court indicated should be admissible if the circumstances guaranteed its trustworthiness. For application of the statute, see *Doyle v. Dong*, 412 Mass 682, 591 NE2d 1084 (1992) (reference in hospital record to throat culture results from a second hospital was admissible, although source of note was never explained); *Com. v. Hartman*, 404 Mass 306, 316, 534 NE2d 1170, 1177 (1989) (proper to redact defendant's "self-diagnosis" from hospital record where he failed to establish it was within any exception to hearsay rule); *Com. v. Dunne*, 394 Mass 10, 17, 474 NE2d 538, 543 (1985) (record excluded where defendant made no attempt to demonstrate that psychological evaluation of alleged rape victim taken to hospital for physical exam fit within meaning of "treatment and medical history;" record also included potential hearsay statements of victim's mother); *Com. v. Sargent*, 24 Mass App 657, 512 NE2d 285 (1987) (not error to admit results of blood alcohol test not ordered by physician nor used in treating defendant where test was conducted as part of normal procedure on every trauma patient); *Terrio v. McDonough*, 16 Mass App 163, 175, 450 NE2d 190, 197 (1983). Cf. *Com. v. Perry*, 385 Mass 639, 641-644, 433 NE2d 446, 448-450 (1982) (judge may require the entire relevant portion of a record to be placed in evidence, or none of it; where defendant had successfully caused exclusion of part of records, no error to exclude related portions, even if otherwise admissible under hearsay exception) (citing Text).

Most of the litigation involving §79 deals with the clause "but nothing therein contained shall be admissible as evidence which has reference to the question of liability."[5] The rule is that those parts of the hospital record that relate mainly to the treatment and medical history of the patient are admitted in evidence even if incidentally the facts recorded may bear on the question of liability. References to alcohol are generally admissible. *Com. v. Gogan*, 389 Mass 255, 263, 449 NE2d 365, 370 (1983) (references in record to defendant's intoxication and belligerence related to treatment and hence properly admitted); *Leonard v. Boston Elevated Railway Co.*, 234 Mass 480, 125 NE 593 (1920) (patient had the odor of alcohol on his breath and vomited a fluid smelling like whiskey). Hospital records containing medical tests of blood alcohol content are admissible to show that a defendant had consumed intoxicating liquor shortly before his arrest for driving under the influence. *Com. v. Dube*, 413 Mass 570, 574, 601 NE2d 467, 469 (1992) (& citations); *Com. v. St. Hilaire*, 43 Mass App Ct 743, 686 NE2d 1045 (1997) (preliminary findings of reliability of testing apparatus not required where testing administered at hospital and results recorded in hospital record); *Com v. Riley*, 22 Mass App 698, 497 NE2d 651 (1986) (also rejecting defendant's argument that admission of the evidence violated the confrontation clause, relying on the presumption

---

[5] Compare a similar clause in GL 46, §19; see §8.13.

of reliability that attaches to hospital records by their very nature).[6] Cf. *Com. v. Sheldon*, 423 Mass 373, 667 NE2d 1153 (1996) (where information concerning alcohol in defendant's blood was not obtained pursuant to a hospital protocol or any medical goal, but rather to prove whether or not defendant was intoxicated, it would not be admissible under §79).

In *Com. v. DiMonte*, 427 Mass 233, 242, 692 NE2d 45, 52 (1998), the court concluded that "unqualified statements in the wife's hospital record that report the ultimate conclusion of the crime charged—an assault and battery—should be redacted," but "more fact-specific references to the reported cause of the wife's injuries are part of her medical history and are relevant to treatment." The court concluded it was not error to admit the latter statements, although incidental to liability. An entry of diagnosis of "Cerebral hemorrhage (traumatic in origin)" is admissible as a specification of the type of injury. *Caccamo's Case*, 316 Mass 358, 362, 55 NE2d 614, 616 (1944). But an entry that "While patient was running along the road she was run over by an automobile" is not. *Inangelo v. Pettersen*, 236 Mass 439, 128 NE 713 (1920). Compare *Com. v. Baldwin*, 24 Mass App 200, 509 NE2d 4 (1987) (error to admit that portion of record stating "Diagnosis: Sexual molestation") with *Com. v. McNickles*, 22 Mass App 114, 123, 491 NE2d 662, 669 (1986) (not error to admit record containing notation "alleged rape").

The broad language of §79: allows copies of original records to be admitted, as well as original records; gives the court discretion to admit certified copies without requiring the attendance of a witness; and applies to records of state and federal hospitals outside the Commonwealth of Massachusetts but within the United States or its territories. A party may obtain hospital records pertaining to another person by procuring a judicial order under the authority of

---

[6] See §8.7.2 for a more detailed discussion of the confrontation clause.

GL 111, §70. Where records are obtained upon such order, the second paragraph of GL 233, §79, governs. For alternative methods of discovery of hospital and medical records, see Mass R Civ P 26, 30, and 34. See also Mass R Civ P 35 (providing for physical and mental examination of persons). Discovery as to such matters in criminal cases may be sought under Mass R Crim P 14.

§8.11.3   Statutory Exceptions: MGL 233, §79G

Section 79G of GL 233 provides a broad hearsay exception for medical and dental records prepared and offered according to its terms. The statute provides for the admissibility of records reflecting diagnosis and prognosis and opinions with respect to the causation of conditions and disability or incapacity caused by conditions. Such records are also admissible as evidence of the fair and reasonable charge for services and the necessity of services or treatments. The statute requires pretrial notice to the opponent of an intention to offer such records.[7]

---

[7] The statute provides:

In any proceeding commenced in any court, commission or agency, an itemized bill and reports, including hospital medical records, relating to medical, dental, hospital services, prescriptions, or orthopedic appliances rendered to or prescribed for a person injured, or any report of any examination of said injured person, including, but not limited to hospital medical records subscribed and sworn to under the penalties of perjury, by the physician, dentist, authorized agent of a hospital or health maintenance organization rendering such services or by the pharmacist or retailer of orthopedic appliances, shall be admissible as evidence of the fair and reasonable charge for such services or the necessity of such services or treatments, the diagnosis of said physician or dentist, the prognosis of such physician or dentist, the opinion of such physician or dentist as to proximate cause of the condition so diagnosed, the opinion of such physician or dentist as to disability or incapacity, if any, proximately resulting from the condition so diagnosed; provided, however, that written notice of the intention to offer such bill or report as such evidence, together with a copy thereof, has been given to the opposing party or parties, or to his or their attorneys, by mailing the same by certified mail, return receipt requested, not less than ten days before the introduction of same into evidence, and that an affidavit of such notice and the return receipt is filed with the clerk of the court forthwith after said receipt has been returned.

In *Gompers v. Finnell*, 35 Mass App 91, 616 NE2d 490 (1993), the plaintiff offered hospital records accompanied by a form drafted for use under §79G, on which the authorized agent of the hospital certified under the penalties of perjury that particular services had been rendered to the injured person and that charges were necessary, fair, and reasonable. In addition, the authorized agent of the hospital, not a physician, had typed in that the personal injuries for which the services were rendered were sustained as a result of the accident at issue in the litigation. The court held that this constituted an extraneous opinion by the hospital's agent, not admissible under §79G, and that it was error not to redact it. In *Ortiz v. Stein*, 31 Mass App 643, 582 NE2d 560 (1991), the court held that an affidavit setting out opinions on the liability of the defendant in a medical malpractice case, by a physician who had neither treated nor examined the plaintiff, would not be admissible under the statute. The court reasoned that it could not find an intent to make such a radical change in the trial of such claims in the absence of a clear statutory expression.

The authority of a trial court to afford the same treatment to similar records is not limited by the statute. In *Phelps v. MacIntyre*, 397 Mass 459, 462, 491 NE2d 1067, 1069 (1986), the court affirmed the admission of a bill of an ambulance service under the procedures of the statute, although ambulance services are not included in its terms. The court held that the trial judge had discretion to admit the bill under its authority to adopt appropriate common-law rules of evidence.

Nothing contained in this section shall be construed to limit the right of any party to the action to summon, at his own expense, such physician, dentist . . . for the purpose of cross-examination with respect to such bill, record and report or to rebut the contents thereof, or for any other purpose, nor to limit the right of any party to summon any other person to testify in respect to such bill, record or report or for any other purpose.

There is no hearsay exception comparable to §79G in either the Proposed Massachusetts Rules of Evidence or the Federal Rules of Evidence; the closest analogy found in the rules is Rule 803(6) (business records). In *Grant v. Lewis/Boyle, Inc.*, 408 Mass 269, 557 NE2d 1136 (1990), the court decided it was unnecessary to adopt Rule 803(6) with respect to physician's reports, given the existence of §79G.

§8.11.4   Rules 803(6) and 803(7)

The exceptions to the hearsay rule created by GL 233, §78 (business records) and §79 (hospital records), would be merged if Proposed Mass R Evid 803(6) is adopted. The drafters of this rule follow the federal approach where one exception rather than two provides the means of admissibility of business and hospital records. The federal exception was statutory (28 USC §1732 (1975)) but now is found in Fed R Evid 803(6). Proposed Mass R Evid 803(6) is identical with the federal rule, providing:

(6) Records of Regularly Conducted Activity

A memorandum, report, record, or data compilation, in any form, of acts, events, conditions, opinions, or diagnoses, made at or near the time by, or from information transmitted by, a person with knowledge, if kept in the course of a regularly conducted business activity, and if it was the regular practice of that business activity to make the memorandum, report, record, or data compilation, all as shown by the testimony of the custodian or other qualified witness, unless the source of information or the method of circumstances of preparation indicate lack of trustworthiness. The term "business" as used in this paragraph includes business, institution, association, profession, occupation, and calling of every kind, whether or not conducted for profit.

Rule 803(6) differs from Massachusetts practice in several respects. First, it would allow the admission of opinions contained in business records rather than only medical opinions (diagnoses), as is provided by GL 233, §§78 and 79. Second, hospital records other than those described under GL 111, §70, would come within the rule. Third, questions of admissibility as to both business and medical records would be governed by Proposed Mass R Evid 104 (Fed R Evid 104 is the same for these purposes). Proposed Mass R Evid 104 does not provide for the continuation of the practice whereby the jury may reconsider the admissibility of business records, as is now provided by §78 (a similar requirement is not found in §79 as to hospital records). Fourth, the rule does not explicitly require, as does §78, that the record be "made in good faith;" nor does it require that the record be made "before the beginning of the civil or criminal proceeding." (§79 does not have these limitations of §78.) Fifth, the provisions of §§78 and 79 as to the admissibility of certified copies is lacking; but see Proposed Mass R Evid 1003 and Fed R Evid 1003 (duplicates admissible to same extent as original). Sixth, the explicit language of §79 (not found in §78) precluding the admissibility of any evidence "which has reference to the question of liability" is not found in the rule. The drafters of the rule indicate that the same exclusionary results will be reached under the phrasing of the rule, but this would appear doubtful. Seventh, the absence of an entry would not be admissible under either statute to establish the non-occurrence of an event. This problem is covered by Proposed Mass R Evid 803(7) and Fed R Evid 803(7), which allow evidence of lack of entry to be admitted:

(7) Absence of Entry in Records Kept in Accordance with the Provisions of Paragraph (6)

Evidence that a matter is not included in the memoranda, reports, records, or data compilations, in any form, kept in accordance with the provisions of paragraph (6), to prove the nonoccurrence or nonexistence of the matter, if the

matter was of a kind of which a memorandum, report, record, or data compilation was regularly made and preserved,
unless the sources of information or other circumstances indicate lack of trustworthiness.

§8.11.5   *Common-Law Exceptions*

Entries made in the regular course of business are
admissible in evidence. *Welsh v. Barrett,* 15 Mass (15 Tyng)
379 (1819). Admissibility is subject to the following limitations:

(1)   The witness must be dead or otherwise unavailable. This limitation does not apply to dispatch
sheets kept by railroads or steamship companies.[8]
The Supreme Judicial Court has refused to extend this principle beyond dispatch sheets. Thus,
records kept in a hospital are inadmissible under
this exception and the person keeping the record
cannot testify as to information therein contained
received from another hospital employee unless
the other employee is unavailable. *Delaney v.
Framingham Gas Co.,* 202 Mass 359, 88 NE 773
(1909). However, such records are likely to be admissible under GL 233, §§78 or 79, discussed
above.

(2)   The entry must be regular (i.e., not isolated) and
in the course of business (i.e., not a personal diary). But there need not be any duty to a third
person to keep the entry. *Kennedy v. Doyle,* 92
Mass (10 All) 161 (1865) (baptismal record).

---

[8] *Hines v. Eastern Steamship Lines,* 245 Mass 385, 139 NE 823 (1923);
Donovan v. Boston & M.R.R., 158 Mass 450, 33 NE 583 (1893). The
dispatcher keeping the sheet is allowed to testify as to the information
received from station agents along the line without producing station
agents or accounting for their absence, and the sheets themselves are
admissible in evidence.

(3)   The entry must be made ante litem motam, and there must be no motive to misrepresent.

(4)   The evidence contained in the entry must be within the personal knowledge of the person making the entry. *Household Fuel Corp. v. Hamacher*, 331 Mass 653, 655, 121 NE2d 846, 848 (1954).

§8.12   Commercial Lists

GL 233, §79B, provides:

> Statements of facts of general interest to persons engaged in an occupation contained in a list, register, periodical, book or other compilation, issued to the public, shall, in the discretion of the court, if the court finds that the compilation is published for the use of persons engaged in that occupation and commonly is used and relied upon by them, be admissible in civil cases as evidence of the truth of any fact so stated.

An excellent discussion of this statute is found in *Torre v. Harris-Seybold Co.*, 9 Mass App 660, 404 NE2d 96 (1980) and *Mazzaro v. Paull*, 372 Mass 645, 363 NE2d 509 (1977). For application of the statute, see *Jordan Marsh Co. v. Board of Assessors of Malden*, 359 Mass 106, 267 NE2d 912 (1971) (publication entitled "Operating Results of Department and Specialty Stores" held properly admitted by Appellate Tax Board in abatement proceeding);[1] *Petition of Boat Demand, Inc.*, 160 F Supp 833, 834 (D Mass 1958) (pamphlet entitled "Fire Protection Standards for Motor Craft" issued by the National Fire Protection Association); *Boston Consolidated Gas Co. v. Department of Public Utilities*, 327 Mass 103, 97

---

§8.12   [1] Market quotations are also admissible under GL 106, §2-724.

NE2d 521 (1951) (*Handy's Indices,* a book useful in the determination of reproduction cost in rate-making). Title standards adopted and published by the Massachusetts Conveyancers' Association, however, were viewed as expressions of professional opinion, not statements of fact, and hence were improperly admitted under §79B. *Fall River Savings Bank v. Callahan,* 18 Mass App 76, 83, 463 NE2d 555, 561 (1984).

In *Reddington v. Clayman,* 334 Mass 244, 134 NE2d 920 (1956), the plaintiff unsuccessfully offered medical treatises in evidence under GL 233, §79C (see §8.18). To prove their authoritativeness, he offered a directory of medical specialists and an English edition of *Who's Who* but did not offer these latter texts under §79B. The court implied, but did not decide, that these latter texts might be admissible under this section. See also *Ramsland v. Shaw,* 341 Mass 56, 64, 166 NE2d 894, 900 (1960).

Subsequently, the Supreme Judicial Court has emphasized that in order to use a *Who's Who* under §79B to qualify a treatise under §79C, the offering party must offer evidence to persuade the trial judge that the *Who's Who* is, as required by the statute: (1) issued to the public; (2) published for persons engaged in the applicable occupation; and (3) commonly used and relied on by such persons. *Mazzaro v. Paull,* 372 Mass 645, 363 NE2d 509 (1977) (also exhorting trial judges to consider the remedial purpose of §79C and not to frustrate legitimate attempts to qualify authoritative treatises by use of §79B). On the requisite preliminary findings for admission under §79B, see also *Ricciutti v. Sylvania Electric Products, Inc.,* 343 Mass 347, 350-351, 178 NE2d 857, 860 (1961) and *Torre v. Harris-Seybold Co.,* supra. Proposed Mass R Evid 803(17) and Fed R Evid 803(17) provide an exception to the hearsay rule similar to that created by §79B except that, unlike the statute, the exception applies to criminal cases as well as to civil cases.

§8.13   Official Records

§8.13.1   Common-Law Rules

Official records may be admitted in evidence in certain instances as evidence of the truth of the facts recorded therein, under a common-law exception to the hearsay rule. Not every official record will qualify under this exception, which provides that an official record of a primary fact made by a public officer in the performance of official duty may be introduced in evidence as proof of the facts recorded. *Com. v. Slavski*, 245 Mass 405, 140 NE 465 (1923) (extensive listing of types of records admissible). See, e.g., *Lodge v. Congress Taxi Association*, 340 Mass 570, 165 NE2d 94 (1960) (plaintiff established identity of owner of taxi as being defendant through Boston police records pertaining to licensing of hackneys); *Adoption of George*, 27 Mass App 265, 537 NE2d 1251 (1989) (DSS case records admissible, not restricted by requirement applicable to business records that records be generated prior to commencement of proceedings). Cf. *Jacobs v. Hertz Corp.*, 358 Mass 541, 265 NE2d 588 (1970) (allegation in complaint in court record about registration of vehicle was not official record of primary fact).

The official records exception as stated by Proposed Mass R Evid 803(8) and Fed R Evid 803(8) incorporates this common-law exception but with some modification. Rule 803(8) provides for the admission of:

Public Records and Reports

Records, reports, statements, or data compilations, in any form, of public offices or agencies, setting forth (A) the activities of the office or agency, or (B) matters observed pursuant to duty imposed by law as to which matter there was a duty to report, excluding, however, in criminal cases matters observed by police officers and other law enforcement personnel, or (C) in civil actions and proceedings and against the Commonwealth in criminal cases, factual findings resulting from an investigation made pursuant to authority granted by law, unless the sources of information or other circumstances indicate lack of trustworthiness.

The language of Rule 803(8) would both widen and narrow the common-law exception. Under the federal rule, factually based conclusions and opinions are admissible. *Beech Aircraft Corp. v. Rainey*, 488 US 153, 109 S Ct 439 (1988) (conclusions concerning cause of airplane crash admissible). However, law enforcement reports are not admissible against the defendant in criminal cases.

Evaluative reports and other official records may be admissible by virtue of a specific statutory exception, apart from the common-law exception or Rule 803(8). The possibility of such statutory exceptions is recognized by Proposed Mass R Evid 802, which states: "Hearsay is not admissible except as provided by law or by these rules or by other rules prescribed by the Supreme Judicial Court." Cf. Fed R Evid 802. A sampling of such statutes is given below.

The fact that a document has been filed with a government agency by a private party may make it a "public record" in the sense that it is available for public inspection, or with regard to whether it is privileged. See *Lord v. Registrar of Motor Vehicles*, 347 Mass 608, 199 NE2d 316 (1964) (accident reports filed with the Registry of Motor Vehicles are public records). This will not make a document an official record, however, for the purpose of coming within this common-law exception to the hearsay rule. *Kelly v. O'Neil*, 1 Mass App 313, 319, 296 NE2d 223, 226 (1973) (accident report filed with police department not an official record within hearsay exception); *Genova v. Genova*, 28 Mass App 647, 654, 554 NE2d 1221, 1225 (1990) (dissenting op. by Brown, J). This is because a record must have been prepared by a public official acting within the scope of his duty before it falls within this exception. See *Com. v. Kirk*, 39 Mass App 225, 654 NE2d 938 (1995) (identification of defendant in GL 209A order was merely a replication of complainant's assertion in her affidavit that defendant was her abuser and could not be regarded as a record of a "primary fact made by a public officer in the performance of official duty") (Text cited). One should note that whether or not a report is admissible under a statute or the common law, a public record may be available for use for nonhearsay purposes — e.g., to show constructive notice, recording, or as the source of admissions or prior inconsistent statements.

Where the official record is offered as an exception to the hearsay rule, both the common-law and the statutory exceptions require that the recorded statement of fact be made by one who has a duty to do so. The duty may be imposed by a foreign law, and the official may be a foreign official. The duty need not be imposed directly by statute.

Statements of opinion, judgmental observations, and the results of investigations do not come within the common-law exception. *Julian v. Randazzo*, 380 Mass 391, 403 NE2d 931 (1980) (recognizing also that police investigative reports may be treated as official records or as business records under GL 233, §78, and applying the same limitation under either theory of admissibility); *Herson v. New Boston Garden Corp.*, 40 Mass App 779, 792, 667 NE2d 907, 917 (1996) (evaluative reports are not admissible); *Adoption of George*, supra (appropriate to screen expressions of opinion, evaluation, or judgment from DSS records before admission).

The fact that the official has a duty generally to keep records is not sufficient. It must be shown that he has a public duty to record that particular type of fact. *Building Inspector of Chatham v. Kendrick*, 17 Mass App 928, 456 NE2d 1151 (1983) (minutes of meetings of zoning board of appeals admissible only to show specific matters that statute requires to be recorded; error to admit as evidence of truth of statements made to board) (Text cited). A duty to record facts is ordinarily not construed to include expressions of opinion, conclusions, or statements as to causes and effects. *Passanessi v. C. J. Maney Co.*, 340 Mass 599, 603, 165 NE2d 590, 593 (1960). Thus, where a statute requires a medical examiner's report to contain "every fact tending to show the condition of the body and the cause and manner of death," the portion of a report that gives, in addition to such facts, the conclusion of the medical examiner as to the cause of death is inadmissible. *Jewett v. Boston Elevated Railway Co.*, 219 Mass 528, 107 NE 433 (1914); *Amory v. Com.*, 321 Mass 240, 72 NE2d 549 (1947) (details in annual report of Metropolitan District Water Commission held inadmissible). See *Rice v. James Hanrahan & Sons*, 20 Mass App 701, 706, 482 NE2d 833, 837 (1985) (environmental regulations barring insulation were not records of primary facts.)

Reports of conclusions may be made admissible by statute, allowing them to be introduced in evidence. *Shamlian v. Equitable Accident Co.*, 226 Mass 67, 115 NE 46 (1917). Such conclusions or opinions may not only become admissible under a statute but may also be given the qualitative force of prima facie evidence. *Miles v. Edward O. Tabor, M.D., Inc.*, 387 Mass 783, 787, 443 NE2d 1302, 1304 (1982) (death certificate admitted under GL 46, §19, is not conclusive but only prima facie evidence); *Pahigian v. Manufacturers' Life Insurance Co.*, 349 Mass 78, 85, 206 NE2d 660, 665 (1965). See also *General Motors, Petitioner*, 344 Mass 481, 182 NE2d 815 (1962). Cf. *Resendes v. Boston Edison Co.*, 38 Mass App 344, 354, 648 NE2d 757, 764 (1995) (GL 82, §40, which provides that failure to give a "dig safe" notice is prima facie evidence of negligence, did not authorize the admission in evidence of a written DPU decision that a contractor had failed to give such notice where the statute did not explicitly provide that the DPU document or record was admissible in evidence, hence no error where trial judge redacted conclusions from report).

§8.13.2   Statutory Rules

GL 46, §19, provides for the admissibility of birth, marriage, and death records.[1] See *Com. v. Lykus*, 406 Mass 135, 144, 546 NE2d 159, 165 (1989) (death certificate is prima facie evidence of time of death); *Com. v. Garabedian*, 399 Mass 304, 308, 503 NE2d 1290, 1293 (1987) (death certificate is prima facie evidence of identity of deceased).

The troublesome clause in §19 — as in §79, dealing with hospital records (§8.11.2) — is that forbidding the use in evidence of anything in a record of death "which has reference to the question of liability for causing the death." See *Com. v. Lannon*, 364 Mass 480, 306 NE2d 248 (1974), for a discussion of the history of this insertion in the statute. Fed R Evid 803(9) provides a similar exception but without the limitation as to statements relating to cause of death. Proposed Mass R Evid 803(9), however, incorporates the statutory language. See also Proposed Mass R Evid 803(12) and Fed R Evid 803(12). In an action against a taxi driver for the death of a passenger, the clause was held not to bar that part of the death certificate that said, inter alia, "Cause of death . . . Accident, 9/1/44; Taxi Cab; Injuries to Side of Head, Ear and Arm." *Trump v. Burdick*, 322 Mass 253, 76 NE2d 768 (1948). Cf. *Krantz v. John Hancock Mutual Life Insurance Co.*, 335 Mass 703, 141 NE2d 719 (1957).

In *Wadsworth v. Boston Gas Co.*, 352 Mass 86, 223 NE2d 807 (1967), the court stated that where the hospital records (GL 233, §79) and the death certificate (GL 49, §19) recited that the injury or death came about from the inhala-

---

§8.13   [1] The statute provides:

> The record of the town clerk relative to a birth, marriage or death shall be prima facie evidence of the facts recorded, but nothing contained in the record of a death which has reference to the question of liability for causing the death shall be admissible in evidence. A certificate of such a record, signed by the town clerk or assistant clerk, or a certificate of the copy of the record relative to a birth, marriage or death required to be kept in the department of public health signed by the commissioner of public health, or the registrar of vital records and statistics, shall be admissible as evidence of such record.

tion of illuminating gas, this alone did not impute fault. Also, in finding no error, the court relied on the rule stated in *Trump*, supra, that where the words have reference to the injuries of the deceased they are admissible even though incidentally they may have some bearing on liability. However, it has been stated that the better and safer course is to delete from the death certificate admitted in a criminal trial such words as "homicide," "suicide," or "accident." *Com. v. Griffin*, 8 Mass App 276, 279-280, 392 NE2d 1220, 1223 (1979) (judge properly excluded word "accident" from autopsy report offered by defendant); *Com. v. Ellis*, 373 Mass 1, 364 NE2d 808 (1977); *Com. v. Lannon*, supra.

Other statutes may allow official statements in evidence. For example, GL 79, §35, allows evidence of assessed valuation of the real estate taken by eminent domain to be admitted. Admission of these official statements of value as evidence of value was not permissible at common law. *Bennett v. Brookline Redevelopment Authority*, 342 Mass 418, 173 NE2d 815 (1961). The use of such evidence is wholly dependent on the statute. *Wenton v. Com.*, 335 Mass 78, 138 NE2d 609 (1956). Similarly, GL 90, §30, provides that certified copies of records of the Registry of Motor Vehicles pertaining to applications, certificates, and licenses issued may be admissible to prove the facts contained therein. Again, this hearsay exception is wholly statutory and will not be extended beyond the terms of the statute. *Carney v. Carrier*, 333 Mass 382, 130 NE2d 879 (1955) (notations with Registry stamp on letter of inquiry as to ownership of automobile did not come within exception).

§8.13.3   *Authentication*

Generally, proof of official records is made by a certified copy of the original records, as provided in GL 233, §76. The method of authenticating official written statements is almost always a matter of some precision. Statutes are specific in their requirements, and these requirements

— involving attestations, certificates, affidavits, and seals —
are rigidly insisted upon. For the requirements in Massachusetts courts, see GL 233, §§69, 75-77, 79, 79A. Cf. Mass R
Civ P 44; Mass R Crim P 39, 40. See *Com. v. Key*, 381 Mass
19, 31, 407 NE2d 327, 335-336 (1980) (interpreting the
requirements of GL 233, §69). It should be noted that the
proper authentication of a public record does not compel
the conclusion that its contents are admissible to prove the
truth of assertions made therein, if it does not otherwise
come within this exception to the hearsay rule. *Rice v. James
Hanrahan & Sons*, 20 Mass App 701, 482 NE2d 833 (1985).
Except where provided to the contrary by statute, there is
no authority in a public officer to provide anything other
than the entire official statement. *Wayland v. Ware*, 109 Mass
248, 250 (1872).

Apart from the statutory modes of documentary proof,
the authenticity of an official written statement may be
proved by the testimony of a person with personal knowledge of the recorded statement. *Kaufman v. Kaitz*, 325 Mass
149, 89 NE2d 505 (1949). For further discussion see Chapter 12. (The use of testimony to *authenticate* a document
should not be confused with the use of testimony or other
secondary evidence *in lieu of* a document. The latter process
is dealt with in Chapter 12, Best Evidence Rule.)

A public officer usually has no authority to give a
certificate that a record does not exist. But such authority is
expressly given in Mass R Civ P 44(b) and Mass R Crim P
40(b). Cf. Proposed Mass R Evid 803(10). Comparable
provisions are found in Fed R Evid 803(10), Fed R Civ P
44(b), and Fed R Crim P 27. Any person who has searched
the records can testify that he has so searched and has
found no record. *Blair's Foodland, Inc. v. Shuman's Foodland*,
311 Mass 172, 175, 40 NE2d 303, 306 (1942).

The official written statements exception to the hearsay
rule obviously conflicts with the best evidence rule where
the statement is a copy of a document whose contents are in
issue. The registry copy of a deed is a case in point. Proof of

contents of Massachusetts deeds by means of the registry is treated as a best evidence problem; proof of contents of foreign deeds is usually treated as a hearsay problem under this exception to the hearsay rule. Both problems are discussed in §12.7.5.

§8.14   Declarations as to Physical Condition

Expressions of present pain, whether articulate or inarticulate and whether or not made to a physician, are admissible in Massachusetts. *Murray v. Foster*, 343 Mass 655, 180 NE2d 311 (1962); *Bacon v. Charlton*, 61 Mass (7 Cush) 581 (1851). Cf. *Simmons v. Yurchak*, 28 Mass App 371, 374, 551 NE2d 539, 542 (1990) (trial court may exclude such evidence where the evidence is untrustworthy and the danger of prejudice outweighs its probative value). A comparable hearsay exception is found in Proposed Mass R Evid 803(3) and Fed R Evid 803(3). Some states refuse to admit articulate expressions unless made to a physician, but admit inarticulate expressions regardless of the person to whom they are made.

A physician may testify as to statements of past pain, symptoms, and condition made to him when he was consulted by declarant for purposes of diagnosis and treatment. *Com. v. Comtois*, 399 Mass 668, 675, 506 NE2d 503, 508 (1987) (citing Text). Such statements are admissible as an exception to the hearsay rule. If the primary purpose of such statements was to obtain medical treatment, they are admissible even if made after the commencement of the litigation. *Barber v. Mirriam*, 93 Mass (11 All) 322 (1865). See also the dictum in *Meaney v. United States*, 112 F2d 538 (2d Cir 1940) and *Roosa v. Boston Loan Co.*, 132 Mass 439 (1882). Testimony as to such statements is also admissible to show the basis of the doctor's expert testimony. *Uberto v. Kaufman*, 348 Mass 171, 202 NE2d 822 (1964); *Kramer v. John Hancock Mutual Life Insurance Co.*, 336 Mass 465, 146 NE2d 357 (1957).

Narration of circumstances — e.g. a patient's story of how injuries were suffered — is not admissible, even if made to a physician. *Com. v. Howard*, 355 Mass 526, 246 NE2d 419 (1969); *Com. v. Spare*, 353 Mass 263, 230 NE2d 798 (1967); *Roosa v. Boston Loan Co.*, supra.

Proposed Mass R Evid 803(4) is the same as Fed R Evid 803(4) and provides a similar exception to the hearsay rule. Rule 803(4) allows in evidence:

Statements for Purposes of Medical Diagnosis or Treatment

Statements made for purposes of medical diagnosis or treatment and describing medical history, or past or present symptoms, pain, or sensations, or the inception or general character of the cause or external source thereof insofar as reasonably pertinent to diagnosis or treatment.

Rule 803(4) differs from Massachusetts law in that the declaration need not have been made to a physician nor need have been made primarily for the purpose of obtaining treatment. Therefore, it would appear to allow admission of statements made for the purpose of enabling a physician to testify. The rule implies also the possible admission of statements as to how the injuries were suffered. Last, the rule suggests that statements made by one other than the patient may also qualify as an exception to the hearsay rule.

The Supreme Judicial Court has suggested in dictum in *Bouchie v. Murray*, 376 Mass 524, 381 NE2d 1295 (1978), that statements as to medical history based on personal knowledge of the declarant may be admissible as an exception to the hearsay rule even if the declarant is not the patient. In *Bouchie*, however, it was made clear that such statements would qualify only if made to a physician consulted for treatment and only if the statements were pertinent to diagnosis and treatment. Additionally, the court suggested that in such instances it must be shown that the circumstances in which the statements were made would "guarantee" the trustworthiness of the statements. It would appear that Rule 803(4) would go beyond the expanded limits of the common-law exception suggested by the *Bouchie* dictum.

In *White v. Illinois*, 502 US 346, 112 S Ct 736 (1992), the Court held that the admission of declarations made during medical examinations under the hearsay exception did not violate the confrontation clause, despite the failure of the prosecution to produce the declarant at trial or to demonstrate unavailability of the witness.[1]

§8.15   Declarations as to Mental Condition

Statements of a person as to his present friendliness, hostility, intent, knowledge, or other mental condition are admissible to prove such mental condition. *Com. v. Lowe*, 391 Mass 97, 104-106, 461 NE2d 192, 197-198 (1984) (discussion of distinction between statements of memory and belief, which are inadmissible, and statements of present state of mind, which are admissible); *Com. v. Borodine*, 371 Mass 1, 353 NE2d 649 (1976); *Com. v. Tracy*, 349 Mass 87, 207 NE2d 16 (1965).

Fed R Evid 803(3) and Proposed Mass R Evid 803(3) provide for the admissibility of such "state of mind" statements by declaring that the following is not excluded by the hearsay rule:

> A statement of the declarant's then existing state of mind, emotion, sensation, or physical condition (such as intent, plan, motive, design, mental feeling, pain, and bodily health), but not including a statement of memory or belief to prove the fact remembered or believed unless it relates to the execution, revocation, identification, or terms of declarant's will.

---

§8.14   [1]See §8.7.2 for a fuller discussion of the confrontation clause.

This rule comports with Massachusetts practice except as to statements of a testator to prove execution of a will (other statements by a testator showing state of mind have been admissible where material). See *Mahan v. Perkins*, 274 Mass 176, 174 NE 275 (1931). The rule would allow the admission of such statements.

State of mind evidence is frequently offered to prove that the declarant did a certain act. To prove that the declarant did the act it is circumstantially relevant to show that at a time before or after the alleged act, not unreasonably remote from the act, the declarant declared a state of mind from which the act can be inferred. *White v. White*, 346 Mass 76, 190 NE2d 102 (1963).

A declaration of intention to commit an act may be offered to prove that the declarant later performed the act in question. *Com. v. Fernandes*, 427 Mass 90, 692 NE2d 3 (1998) (threat to kill another); *Com. v. Caldron*, 383 Mass 86, 417 NE2d 958 (1981) (error to exclude defendant's statements in argument with co-defendant immediately after robbery, to the extent they revealed defendant's lack of intention to rob another); *Com. v. Trefethen*, 157 Mass 180, 31 NE 961 (1892) (intention to commit suicide); *Com. v. Vermette*, 43 Mass App Ct 789, 801, 686 NE2d 1071, 1079 (1997) (intention to lie and falsely confess to a shooting). See *Mutual Life Insurance Co. v. Hillmon*, 145 US 285 (1892) (letters stating that declarant intended to travel to a certain destination with another). Compare *Com. v. Stewart*, 411 Mass 345, 355, 582 NE2d 514, 520-521 (1991) (*D*'s statements making arrangements to have lunch with his mother not offered to prove he did so, but that he intended to do so, rather than having intent to kill anybody, hence inadmissible).

The one state of mind excluded from this exception is memory or belief as to past facts. See, e.g., *Shepard v. United States*, 290 US 96, 54 S Ct 22 (1933) (to prove that deceased wife did not have suicidal intent when she drank whiskey allegedly poisoned by her husband, it was not permissible to prove that she subsequently told nurse at hospital, "Dr. Shepard has poisoned me."). See *Com. v. Pope*, 397 Mass 275, 281, 491 NE2d 240, 244 (1986) (suicide note, "I killed Jimmy," inadmissible because went to past conduct, not intent to act); *Custody of Jennifer*, 25 Mass App 241, 517 NE2d 187 (1988) (hearsay statements of alleged child abuse victims not admissible on "state of mind" theory—constituted statements of memory or belief to prove fact remembered).[1]

§8.16 Spontaneous Exclamations

A statement made under the impulse of excitement or shock is admissible if its utterance was spontaneous to a degree that reasonably negated premeditation or possible fabrication and if it tended to qualify, characterize, or explain the underlying event. *Com. v. Snell*, 428 Mass 766, 777, 705 NE2d 236, 244 (1999) (domestic abuse victim's complaint to neighbor immediately after assault, while highly distraught); *Com. v. Whelton*, 428 Mass 24, 26, 696 NE2d 540, 544 (1998) (victim's daughter's statement to police shortly after assault); *Com. v. Giguere*, 420 Mass 226, 648 NE2d 1279 (1995) (admitting telephone call from murder victim's wife to police immediately after the shooting); *Com. v. Cohen*, 412 Mass 375, 589 NE2d 289 (1992) (admitting several exclamations of shooting victims shortly after the event); *Com v. Young*, 401 Mass 390, 517 NE2d 130 (1987) (statement shortly after a shooting by one who saw it, "That security guard killed that boy.") (citing Text); *Com. v. Fuller*, 399 Mass 678, 506 NE2d 852 (1987) (statement by child abuse victim to mother in car en route to doctor, a few moments after incident); *Com. v. Williams*, 399 Mass 60, 503 NE2d 1 (1987) (statement by stabbing victim within three

---

§8.15 [1] Hearsay declarations may be admissible to prove the state of mind of a victim of a crime where that state of mind was known to the defendant and may have been relevant to motive. See §8.2.2.

minutes of event, while still in shock, admissible, although he had been able to telephone police, calm down, and stop mumbling); *Com. v. Rivera*, 397 Mass 244, 248, 490 NE2d 1160, 1163 (1986) (victim's statement to mother within minutes after rape, "Oh yes, my God, I will never forget that face."); *Com. v. Brown*, 46 Mass App 279, 705 NE2d 631 (1999) (911 calls describing home invasion and assault) (Text cited); *Com. v. Napolitano*, 42 Mass App Ct 549, 678 NE2d 447 (1997) (admitting victim's statements to witness and EMTs who came to her aid respecting details of her boyfriend's attempt to drown her, although she later recanted them); *Com. v. Rockett*, 41 Mass App 5, 667 NE2d 1168 (1996) (unknown voice calls defendant's first name as burglar flees from stabbing occupant of premises) (Text cited); *Com. v. Kirk*, 39 Mass App 225, 654 NE2d 938 (1995) (crying, very upset, very dishevelled victim blurted out, "My boyfriend just beat me up."); *Com. v. Alvarado*, 36 Mass App 604, 634 NE2d 132 (1994) (alleged victim's statements to police, while very emotional, that defendant had hit and bit her just before police arrived at her apartment were admissible, despite victim's later testimony denying that defendant had bitten her and claiming that she had arranged for a friend to bite her); *Com. v. Tiexeira*, 29 Mass App 200, 205, 559 NE2d 408, 411 (1990) (statement by *W* to *D* shortly after his encounter with *V*, "Why did you have to hit him with the club? Why couldn't you just — if you wanted — to him, why couldn't you use your own hands?"). See *Com. v. Capone*, 39 Mass App 606, 659 NE2d 1196 (1996) (declarant's intoxication went to the weight of the evidence, but did not render it insufficiently reliable for admission).

Earlier cases sometimes justified the admissibility of such statements by labeling them part of the "res gestae" of the event. The Supreme Judicial Court has disapproved the use of this term, which is ambiguous, confusing and unnecessary, and prefers that such declarations be referred to as spontaneous exclamations or utterances. *Com. v. Sellon*, 380 Mass at 229 n.14, 402 NE2d at 1337 n.14; *Com. v. McLaugh-*

lin, 364 Mass 221, n.3, 303 NE2d 338, 346 n.3 (1973); *Com. v. Tiexeira*, supra, 29 Mass App at 205, 559 NE2d at 412.

Statements need not be strictly contemporaneous with the exciting cause to be admissible, provided that the underlying event has not lost its sway and been dissipated. *Com. v. Grant*, 418 Mass 76, 634 NE2d 565 (1994) (statements of shooting victim were admissible where due to circumstances of shooting and provision of medical treatment she had been close to hysterical from the time of the shooting to her interview by police 60 minutes later); *Com. v. Crawford*, 417 Mass 358, 629 NE2d 1332 (1994) (child's statement within hours of murder that "Daddy shot Mummy" was admissible, court takes into account fact that child had remained in the presence of alleged perpetrator until shortly before she made the statement); *Com. v. Brown*, 413 Mass 693, 602 NE2d 575 (1992) (statements made five hours after scalding episode by child victim were admissible); *Com. v. Fuller*, supra, 399 Mass at 682, 506 NE2d at 855; *Com v. Puleio*, 394 Mass 101, 104-105, 474 NE2d 1078, 1081 (1985) (following a shot and a scream, someone ran into bar, asked bartender to telephone police, she did so and then went outside and asked who shot — at first there was no answer, then someone named the defendant — admissible); *Com. v. Hampton*, 351 Mass 447, 221 NE2d 766 (1966) (statement made five to six minutes after stabbing was properly admitted); *Rocco v. Boston-Leader, Inc.*, 340 Mass 195, 197, 163 NE2d 157, 158 (1960); *Com v. Tiexeira*, supra, 29 Mass App at 206, 559 NE2d at 412. See Wigmore §1750 (Chad rev 1976).[1]

A statement may be considered spontaneous and admissible, although made in response to questions. *Com. v. Fuller*, supra, 399 Mass at 682-683, 506 NE2d at 855; *Com. v.*

---

§8.16 [1] The older cases required that the statement be contemporaneous with the event, but they have been eclipsed by modern practice. See *Eastman v. Boston & M.R.R.*, 165 Mass 342, 43 NE 115 (1896) (statement by injured plaintiff no more than five minutes after incident; excluded); *Lane v. Bryant*, 75 Mass (9 Gray) 245 (1857).

Williams, supra; *Com. v. Hampton*, supra, 351 Mass at 449-450, 221 NE2d at 786.

Where the circumstances do not demonstrate that a statement was spontaneous and made without an opportunity for reflection that would undermine its reliability, it may be excluded. See *Com. v. DiMonte*, 427 Mass 233, 692 NE2d 45 (1998) (error to admit facsimile describing alleged assault sent several hours later, some contents of which suggested a premeditated message); *Com. v. Gilbert*, 423 Mass 863, 673 NE2d 46 (1996) (defendant's statement the day after his wife's death that she had killed herself was lacking the spontaneity that would have negated possible fabrication); *Com. v. Trowbridge*, 419 Mass 750, 647 NE2d 413 (1995) (child's statements to teacher on Friday afternoons that she did not want to visit her father were inadmissible where there was no evidence that the child was under the influence of any startling or exciting event); *Com. v. Burnett*, 417 Mass 740, 632 NE2d 1206 (1994) (statements by second driver in motor vehicle homicide made 90 minutes after accident were inadmissible where there was no testimony that declarant was excited or upset); *Com. v. Reid*, 384 Mass 247, 258-259, 424 NE2d 495, 502 (1981) (statement made after declarant made two telephone calls and after considerable time lag properly excluded); *Com. v. Joubert*, 38 Mass App 943, 647 NE2d 1238 (1995) (child's statements to aunt that father had touched her sexually were inadmissible where there was nothing in record to show circumstances of the touching or when it occurred); *Com. v. Bandy*, 38 Mass App 329, 648 NE2d 440 (1995) (defendant's exculpatory statements to nurses a month after accident and shortly after he was served with a citation were properly excluded). Compare *Com. v. Santos*, 402 Mass 775, 785, 525 NE2d 388, 394 (1988) (suggestive police station identification was not a spontaneous utterance) with *Com. v. Mendrala*, 20 Mass App 398, 480 NE2d 1039 (1985) (*V*'s identification of attacker shortly after event, at end of police chase, admissible as spontaneous exclamation, although not under exception for identifications, because did not meet requirements of *Com. v. Daye*, 393 Mass 55, 469 NE2d 483 (1984)).[2]

To be admissible, a statement must tend to qualify, characterize, or explain the underlying event. This requirement is seldom litigated. In *Com. v. Zagranski*, 408 Mass 278, 558 NE2d 933 (1990), a wife encountered her husband handcuffed by the police in their kitchen, and upon being told he was arrested for murder, exclaimed, "Where's the body?" The court held the statement was relevant as tending to show that the husband had told his wife he killed *V* and then hid the body. The husband objected to the statement, arguing that the underlying event was the murder and the wife's statement did not relate to it. The court, however, held the startling event was the wife's discovery her husband was under arrest, and her statement was admissible because it explained her perception of the arrest.

Proposed Mass R Evid 803(2) is consistent with recent Massachusetts case law, as is Fed R Evid 803(2). Rule 803(2) provides that "a statement relating to a startling event or condition made while the declarant was under the stress of excitement caused by the event or condition" is an exception to the hearsay rule. Proposed Mass R Evid 803(1) would provide a new (and related) exception not known to Massachusetts practice, the so-called present sense impression. See *Houston Oxygen Co. v. Davis*, 139 Tex 1, 161 SW2d 474 (1942). This exception provides that "a statement describing or explaining an event or condition made while the declarant was perceiving the event or condition, or immediately thereafter, except when such statement is made under circumstances that indicate its lack of trustworthiness" need not be excluded as hearsay. The availability or unavailability of the declarant is not relevant to the issue of admissibility. Note that under this exception there need not be shown an exciting or startling event; nor need it be demonstrated that the declarant was excited. The theory of reliability under this exception is that spontaneous and

---

[2] See §11.1.

routine remarks contemporaneously describing an event to another in a position to verify the description are sufficiently trustworthy to be admitted. *Houston Oxygen Co. v. Davis,* supra. Fed R Evid 803(1) is in accord except that it does not contain the redundant last clause ("except . . .").

In *White v. Illinois,* 502 US 346, 112 S Ct 736 (1992), the Court held that the admission of spontaneous declarations under the hearsay exception did not violate the confrontation clause, despite the failure of the prosecution to produce the declarant at trial or to demonstrate unavailability of the witness.[3] In *Com. v. Whelton,* 428 Mass 24, 27, 696 NE2d 540, 545 (1998), the court held that the confrontation protections of art. 12 of the Massachusetts Declaration of Rights do not require proof of the unavailability of a declarant before evidence under the spontaneous exclamation exception may be received, because such an utterance is highly reliable and falls within a "firmly rooted" hearsay exception.

The case of *Com. v. Harris,* 376 Mass 201, 380 NE2d 642 (1978), illustrates a problem analytically distinct from, but easily confused with, this hearsay exception. The statement of an unidentified bystander ("Shoot that m . . . f . . .!), made immediately before a shooting, was admitted. The statement is not hearsay, because no assertion was made. It is not necessary to consider whether it would otherwise constitute a spontaneous declaration. Nor is it necessary or helpful to ask whether it was part of the so-called res gestae. The statement is admissible because statements and other circumstances made or existing prior to, during, and shortly after a crime was committed are admissible to give the jury the benefit of the complete occurrence. See *Com. v. Murphy,* 356 Mass 604, 254 NE2d 895 (1970); *Com. v. Ward,* 45 Mass App 901, 694 NE2d 395 (1998) (statement by participant in drug transaction that he was selling drugs; also admissible as statement by joint venturer) (Text cited).

---

[3] See §8.7.2 for a more extensive discussion of the confrontation clause.

§8.17 Past Recollection Recorded

A witness often has difficulty in recalling the events about which he is asked to testify. In such instances, either of two doctrines may be utilized to procure his knowledge for the jury's consideration. These doctrines are designated "present recollection revived" and "past recollection recorded." See generally Wigmore §§758-765 (Chad rev 1970) (recollection revived); §§734-755 (recollection recorded). See Proposed Mass R Evid 612, 803(5); Fed R Evid 612, 803(5). While there has been some tendency toward confusion of the two doctrines, the courts in Massachusetts and in other jurisdictions have come to recognize that they are distinct doctrines to which differing principles and consequences apply. See, e.g., *United States v. Riccardi*, 174 F2d 883 (3rd Cir 1949).

Under the doctrine of present recollection revived the witness has some memory of the events he observed but is unable to testify without the assistance of some stimulus to that memory. The stimulating factor may be a writing or any object that revives his memory. See §6.20 for a detailed discussion of this doctrine. Reviving the present memory of a witness does not implicate the hearsay rule. However, when the memory of the witness is beyond revival, a document embodying his forgotten knowledge may be admissible under the more stringent rules of the doctrine of past recollection recorded. Such a document offered for the truth of the assertions it contains is hearsay, but an exception has been recognized for its admission.

Where a witness who once had personal knowledge of facts has insufficient recollection to testify fully and accurately and no memorandum can refresh his recollection, if he can testify that a memorandum presented to him was made or seen by him when the events were fresh in his mind, that the memorandum at the time it was made or seen accurately described the events, and that the paper presented is the memorandum, he may, in the discretion of the trial judge, incorporate the memorandum in his testimony by reading it. It is also within the judge's discretion to permit the proposing party to introduce the writing in evidence. *Cricenti v. Weiland*, 427 Mass 541, 694 NE2d 350 (1998) (witness remembered some details of her statement, but not others); *Com. v. Dougherty*, 343 Mass 299, 306, 178 NE2d 584, 588 (1961) (witness read document to jury); *Fisher v. Swartz*, 333 Mass 265, 130 NE2d 575 (1955) (overruling *Bendett v. Bendett*, 315 Mass 59, 52 NE2d 2 (1943) on the matter of admitting the writing in evidence); *Com. v. Galvin*, 27 Mass App 150, 152, 535 NE2d 623, 625 (1989) (citing Text). Contrast *Com. v. McDuffie*, 16 Mass App 1016, 455 NE2d 461 (1983) (error to allow report in evidence as past recollection recorded where transcript showed witnesses used report to refresh recollection); *Com. v. Murphy*, 6 Mass App 335, 343, 375 NE2d 366, 372 (1978) (where memo refreshed witness's recollection, no error in refusal of judge to allow it to be read in evidence).

It is not necessary that the memorandum be made in the regular course of business or that the witness's memory be exhausted before recourse is had to the memorandum. *Guiffre v. Carapezza*, 298 Mass 458, 11 NE2d 433 (1937).

The traditional requirement that the memorandum be made at or about the time of the event recorded has been somewhat relaxed by *Catania v. Emerson Cleaners, Inc.*, 362 Mass 388, 286 NE2d 341 (1972) (where trial took place four years after accident in question, signed statement of witness given eight months after accident and remembered as better and true recollection was admissible not only to impeach but as past recollection recorded). In *Catania*, the trial judge first excluded the memorandum and allowed it to be marked as an exhibit but after the close of evidence retracted it as an exhibit; thus, it was neither read nor shown to the jury. This change of rulings was held to be error. Although the time lapse is not specified in the opinion, a similar relaxation of contemporaneity occurred in *Ralston v. Anthony*, 5 Mass App 859, 364 NE2d 1289 (1977) (memorandum drafted by an attorney for a party some time after negotiations completed admissible as past recollection recorded).

It is not necessary that the witness be the author of the memorandum as long as he saw and approved it when his memory of events was fresh. However, a document that the witness has never seen or approved is not admissible. *Com. v. Bookman*, 386 Mass 657, 662-665, 436 NE2d 1228, 1231-1233 (1982) (transcript of grand jury testimony of witness improperly admitted as past recollection recorded absent evidence or a finding that witness adopted transcript as accurate at or about the time of the event). In accord, *Com. v. Daye*, 393 Mass 55, 76, 469 NE2d 483 (1984).[1] See *Com. v. Fryar*, 414 Mass 732, 745, 610 NE2d 903, 911 (1993) (where witness was not shown her grand jury testimony for one year, she did not adopt it as accurate at or about the time of events and it was inadmissible). See also *Parsons v. Manufacturers' Insurance Co.*, 82 Mass (16 Gray) 463 (1860) (memorandum signed by witness who could not remember it to be a true statement of facts does not qualify). Although the witness must assert that the record was accurate when made, it is not required that the witness adopt the statement as true or accurate at the time of trial — indeed, for the rule to come into play he would not be able to do so because of a failure of recollection. *Com. v. Greene*, 9 Mass App 688, 690, 404 NE2d 110, 112 (1980).

The original memorandum must be produced or its absence accounted for. *Whitney v. Sawyer*, 77 Mass (11 Gray) 242 (1858). A witness must, at the time he wrote or saw and approved the memorandum, have had personal knowledge of the events recorded; if he did not, he may not testify. *Kent v. Garvin*, 67 Mass (1 Gray) 148 (1854). However, if *A* has reported events to *B*, who has recorded them, the re-

---

§8.17 [1]In *Daye*, the court also indicated that, under certain safeguards, prior inconsistent statements made before a grand jury will be admissible as probative evidence where the witness is available for cross-examination at trial, incorporating a modified version of Rule 801(d)(1)(A)). See §6.6.2. See also §8.7 with respect to whether grand jury testimony is admissible as prior recorded testimony.

cord made by *B* may be used if *A* will testify that he reported correctly and if *B* will testify that he recorded correctly. Allowing admission of such memoranda merely represents a double application of the principle of past recollection recorded. *Com. v. Galvin,* supra (citing Text); *Whitney v. Sawyer,* 77 Mass (11 Gray) 242 (1858).

Proposed Mass R Evid 803(5) and Fed R Evid 803(5) deal with the doctrine of past recollection recorded in identical language. The document that constitutes past recollection recorded is declared an exception to the hearsay rule by both. Both rules are in accordance with prior Massachusetts practice, except that under the rules only the opposing party may offer the document itself in evidence. Proposed Mass R Evid 803(5) defines an admissible document as follows:

> A memorandum or record concerning a matter about which a witness once had knowledge but now has insufficient recollection to enable him to testify fully and accurately, shown to have been made or adopted by the witness when the matter was fresh in his memory and to reflect that knowledge correctly. If admitted, the memorandum or record may be read into evidence but may not itself be received as an exhibit unless offered by an adverse party.

§8.18   Learned Treatises

In *Com. v. Sneed,* 413 Mass 387, 394-397, 597 NE2d 1346, 1350-1351 (1992), the Supreme Judicial Court adopted Proposed Mass R Evid 803(18), establishing a new exception for learned treatises, rendering admissible:[1]

> To the extent called to the attention of an expert witness upon cross-examination, statements contained in published treatises, periodicals, or pamphlets on a subject of history,

---

§8.18 [1] Prior to *Sneed,* the only permitted use of treatises was pursuant to GL 233, §79C.

medicine, or other science or art, established as a reliable authority by the testimony or admission of the witness or by other expert testimony or by judicial notice. If admitted, the statements may be read into evidence but may not be received as exhibits.

Fed R Evid 803(18) is the same as the proposed Massachusetts rule except that it also provides that such a treatise is admissible to the extent relied on by the expert in direct examination. Proposed Mass R Evid 803(18) as adopted by the court in *Sneed* does not allow the admission of a learned treatise in evidence as part of a party's case in chief since its applicability is related to cross-examination only. See *Brusard v. O'Toole*, 45 Mass App 288, 697 NE2d 1000 (1998) (error to forbid use of chart in treatise on cross-examination, although insufficient foundation to admit it in evidence under §79C).

In *Com. v. Sneed*, supra, 413 Mass at 396, 597 NE2d at 1351, the court offered the following guidance for the use of treatises:

> Proposed Rule 803(18) requires that an opponent of the expert witness bring to the witness's attention a specific statement in a treatise that has been established, to the judge's satisfaction, as reliable authority. The witness should be given a fair opportunity to assess the statement in context and to comment on it, either during cross-examination or on redirect examination. The judge, of course, will have to determine the relevance and materiality of the statement and should consider carefully any claimed unfairness or confusion that admission of the statement may create.

The court further noted: "We can imagine a situation in which, in fairness, portions of a learned treatise not called to the attention of a witness during cross-examination should be admitted on request of the expert's proponent in order to explain, limit, or contradict a statement ruled admissible under rule 803(18)." *Com. v. Sneed*, supra, 413 Mass at 396 n.8, 597 NE2d at 1351 n.8.

The only other circumstances in which the contents of learned treatises are admissible in evidence to prove the truth of their assertions is as provided in GL 233, §79C. That statute is discussed in §7.9.2 and §8.12.

§8.19   Reputation

Reputation evidence may or may not be hearsay. It is hearsay if offered for a purpose that requires a belief that the reputation truthfully reflects the reputed facts; otherwise, it is not. Evidence of the plaintiff's bad reputation, for example, is not hearsay when offered by the defendant to mitigate damages in a defamation case. See, e.g., *Clark v. Brown*, 116 Mass 504 (1875). Similarly, in a homicide case, evidence of the decedent's reputation for quarrelsomeness is not hearsay when offered to prove that the defendant acted in self-defense in reasonable fear of great bodily harm. See, e.g., *Com. v. Dilone*, 385 Mass 281, 285-286, 431 NE2d 576, 579 (1982); *Com. v. Gibson*, 368 Mass 518, 333 NE2d 400 (1975); *Com. v. Edmonds*, 365 Mass 496, 313 NE2d 429 (1974). In such cases, it is the reputation itself, not the truth of the reputation, that is in issue. See §4.4.4.

An infrequent instance of hearsay use of reputation evidence involves the establishment of a public or general right — e.g., the ownership or location of boundaries of public lands. See *Inhabitants of Enfield v. Woods*, 212 Mass 547, 99 NE 331 (1912). Cf. Proposed Mass R Evid 803(20) and Fed R Evid 803(20) (reflecting this exception but extending it to include reputation evidence of boundaries of private lands).

Hearsay use of reputation evidence is most commonly encountered in cases involving a person's character or pedigree.

Character. The use of reputation evidence to prove character is discussed at §4.4.4 (character as evidence of an act) and §6.9 (character to impeach). See also Proposed

Mass R Evid 404(a), 405(a), 608(a), and 803(21) and the parallel federal rules.

Pedigree (see also §8.20). Family reputation, such as appears in the family Bible and in inscriptions on tombstones, may be admissible to prove the truth of the matters reputed. *North Brookfield v. Warren*, 82 Mass (16 Gray) 171 (1860). The matters that can be proved in this way are limited to birth, death, marriage, and the relationships between persons. And, contrary to the rule in some jurisdictions, the evidence can be used in cases other than "pedigree cases;" it can be used in any action in which reputed family fact is relevant. *North Brookfield v. Warren*, supra. To be admissible under this exception, the writing must have been created ante litem motam and be of such nature that any errors would have been corrected by members of the family. There is some question as to the admissibility of family reputation evidence if persons with personal knowledge of the disputed fact are available as witnesses. Closely related to this exception to the hearsay rule is the rule that reputation within a family as to births, marriages, and deaths of members of the family may be testified to by any member of the family. *Butrick v. Tilton*, 155 Mass 461, 29 NE 1088 (1892).

Proposed Mass R Evid 803(19) and Fed R Evid 803(19) state the family reputation exception more broadly than the common-law rule. Rule 803(19) allows evidence of:

> [r]eputation among members of a person's: family by blood, adoption, or marriage, or among his associates, or in the community, concerning a person's birth, adoption, marriage, divorce, death, legitimacy, relationship by blood, adoption, or marriage, ancestry, or other similar fact of his personal or family history.

There is no requirement in the rule concerning "unavailability" and no requirement that a writing offered to establish reputation be ante litem motam. Other provisions of the Proposed Massachusetts Rules of Evidence and the

Federal Rules of Evidence relating to the admissibility of evidence of family history and relationships are Rule 803(11) (records of religious organizations), Rule 803(12) (marriage, baptismal, and similar certificates), Rule 803(13) (family records), Rule 803(16) (statements in ancient documents), and Rule 803(23) (judgments as to matters of personal, family, or general history or as to boundaries). See also Rule 803(19) (public records of vital statistics).

§8.20   Declarations of Pedigree

Declarations of pedigree are distinguishable from reputation of pedigree in that the declarant is known and meets certain qualifications. Thus, an entry in a family Bible, mentioned as an example under reputation of pedigree, may also be a declaration of pedigree if the person making the entry can be identified and meets the qualifications. This exception to the hearsay rule applies to the same facts and in the same kinds of actions as the exception for reputation of pedigree. Also, the declaration must have been made ante litem motam. Special rules applicable to declarations of pedigree relate to the declarant:

(1)   The persons who can be declarants are limited to blood members of the family whose pedigree is in question or spouses of blood members.

(2)   The declarant must be unavailable to testify.

See generally *North Brookfield v. Warren*, 82 Mass (16 Gray) 171 (1860). Cf. Proposed Mass R Evid 804(b)(4) and Fed R Evid 804(b)(4). The rule requires a showing of unavailability (more broadly defined than at common law by virtue of Rule 804(a)). Under the rule, statements of nonfamily members are admissible if the declarant was "so intimately associated with the other's family as to be likely to have accurate information concerning the matter declared."

§8.21   The Catchall and Other Exceptions

The Proposed Massachusetts Rules of Evidence and the Federal Rules of Evidence set forth exceptions to the hearsay rule not described thus far in this topic. In addition to the exceptions set forth in this section, see ancient documents, discussed in §12.3.1.

§8.21.1   Catchall Exception

Fed R Evid 803(24) and 804(b)(5) provide the so-called innominate exception — a catchall exception not urged for adoption as part of the Proposed Massachusetts Rules of Evidence. Fed R Evid 803(24) provides for situations where the declarant is available that are not covered by any other exception:

Other Exceptions

A statement not specifically covered by any of the foregoing exceptions but having equivalent circumstantial guarantees of trustworthiness, if the court determines that

(A) the statement is offered as evidence of a material fact;

(B) the statement is more probative on the point for which it is offered than any other evidence which the proponent can procure through reasonable efforts; and

(C) the general purposes of these rules and the interests of justice will best be served by the admission of the statement into evidence.

However, a statement may not be admitted under this exception unless the proponent of it makes known to the adverse party sufficiently in advance of the trial or hearing to provide the adverse party with a fair opportunity to prepare to meet it, his intention to offer the statement and the particulars of it, including the name and address of the declarant.

Where the declarant is unavailable, Fed R Evid 804(b)(5) provides the same exception in identical language. Proposed Mass R Evid 804(b)(5) rejects this exception and instead provides an exception for statements of deceased persons comparable to that found in GL 233, §65. See §8.5.1.

The Supreme Judicial Court has stated, "we do not regard the common-law hearsay exceptions as frozen in their established contours, and have been prepared on suitable occasions to venture forth." *Com. v. Meech*, 380 Mass 490, 497, 403 NE2d 1174, 1179 (1980). The court consistently, however, has refused to adopt the general exception to the hearsay rule embodied in Fed R Evid 803(24) or 804(b)(5). *Com. v. Semedo*, 422 Mass 716, 665 NE2d 638 (1996) (recorded statements of eyewitnesses to assault, although reliable and trustworthy, were hearsay and not admissible); *Com. v. Costello*, 411 Mass 371, 377, 582 NE2d 938, 942 (1991); *Com. v. Pope*, 397 Mass 275, 281, 491 NE2d 240, 244 (1986); *Com. v. Meech*, supra; *Com. v. White*, 370 Mass 703, 352 NE2d 904 (1976).

§8.21.2 *Judgments in Criminal Cases*

Judgments in criminal cases become an exception to the hearsay rule under Proposed Mass R Evid 803(22), which would allow:

> Evidence of a final judgment, entered after a trial or upon a plea of guilty (but not upon a plea of nolo contendere), adjudging a person guilty of a crime punishable by death or confinement in excess of one year, to prove any fact essential to sustain the judgment, but not including, when offered by the Commonwealth in a criminal prosecution for

purposes other than impeachment, judgments against persons other than the accused. The pendency of an appeal may be shown but does not affect admissibility.

This hearsay exception was adopted by the Supreme Judicial Court in *Flood v. Southland Corp.,* 416 Mass 62, 70, 616 NE2d 1068 (1993). Fed R Evid 803(22) is essentially the same as the proposed Massachusetts rule. As the rule itself makes clear, a conviction based on a plea by one party cannot be used in evidence by the Commonwealth against another, other than to impeach the convicted person if he or she appears as a witness. *Com. v. Powell,* 40 Mass App 430, 665 NE2d 99 (1996). See also Proposed Mass R Evid 803(23), Fed R Evid 803(23) (judgments as to personal, family, or general history or as to boundaries may be admitted), and Fed R Evid 803(15) (statements in documents affecting an interest in property; 803(15) has not been proposed for adoption in Massachusetts).

§8.21.3   Alleged Victims of Child Abuse

The Supreme Judicial Court has considered whether an exception to the hearsay rule should be created for extrajudicial declarations by children alleged to be victims of child abuse. In *Opinion of the Justices,* 406 Mass 1201, 547 NE2d 8 (1989), the court held that proposed legislation, which would have created such an exception for child sexual abuse, was unconstitutional, in violation of the confrontation clause in art. 12 of the Declaration of Rights. The legislation would have permitted out-of-court statements to be admitted for their truth under a variety of circumstances, including where the child was unavailable as a witness for any of several reasons, including a refusal to testify, and there was corroborative evidence of sexual contact. The court found significant that under the bill such statements did not have to be made under oath, there was no explicit requirement of good faith and due diligence in establishing unavailability, and concluded that a refusal to testify could not be equated with that measure of necessity which justifies other hearsay exceptions. The court held that the criteria for determining the reliability of admissible statements under the legislation were inadequate and that the exception as drafted did not have the same guarantees of reliability as other hearsay exceptions.

In 1990, the Legislature passed three statutes creating hearsay exceptions for statements by child abuse victims, GL §§81, 82 and 83. These statutes were evidently drafted with an eye toward responding to the concerns of the Supreme Judicial Court in *Opinion of the Justices,* supra.

Section 81 governs the admissibility of such statements in criminal proceedings.[1] Section 81 was discussed at length

---

§8.21   [1] The statute provides:

§81. Admissibility in Criminal Proceeding of Out-of-Court Statement of Child Abuse Victim: Unavailability of Victim; Reliability of Statement.

(a) An out-of-court statement of a child under the age of ten describing an act of sexual contact performed on or with the child, the circumstances under which it occurred, or which identifies the perpetrator shall be admissible as substantive evidence in any criminal proceeding; provided, however, that the statement is offered as evidence of a material fact and is more probative on the point for which it is offered than any other evidence which the proponent can procure through reasonable efforts; the person to whom the statement was made or who heard the child make the statement testifies; the judge finds pursuant to subsection (b) that the child is unavailable as a witness: and the judge finds pursuant to subsection (c) that the statement is reliable.

(b) The proponent of such statement shall demonstrate a diligent and good faith effort to produce the child and shall bear the burden of showing unavailability. A finding of unavailability shall be supported by specific findings on the record, describing facts with particularity, demonstrating that:

(1) the child is unable to be present or to testify because of death or physical or mental illness or infirmity; or

(2) by a ruling of the court, the child is exempt on the ground of privilege from testifying concerning the subject matter of such statement; or

(3) the child testifies to a lack of memory of the subject matter of such statement; or

(4) the child is absent from the hearing and the proponent of such statement has been unable to procure the attendance of the child by process or by other reasonable means; or

in *Com. v. Colin C.*, 419 Mass 54, 643 NE2d 19 (1994). The defendant made a challenge to the facial constitutionality of the statute. However, the Supreme Judicial Court did not reach that issue because it reversed the defendant's conviction on other grounds. The court did state that in addition to the procedures and protections set forth in the statute, it would impose certain other requirements before such hearsay could be admitted in criminal cases.

The court requires that before the statute can be invoked, the Commonwealth must give prior notice to a criminal defendant that it will seek to use such hearsay statements, in order to provide a meaningful opportunity to respond to hearsay allegations. Second, the Commonwealth must show by proof beyond a reasonable doubt that there is a compelling need for the use of the hearsay. Third, the court required that any separate hearing regarding the

---

(5) the court finds, based upon expert testimony from a treating psychiatrist, psychologist, or clinician, that testifying would be likely to cause severe psychological or emotional trauma to the child; or

(6) the child is not competent to testify.

(c) If a finding of unavailability is made, the out-of-court statement shall be admitted if the judge further finds:

(1) after holding a separate hearing, that such statement was made under oath, that it was accurately recorded and preserved, and there was sufficient opportunity to cross-examine; or

(2) after holding a separate hearing and, where practicable and where not inconsistent with the best interests of the child, meeting with the child, that such statement was made under circumstances inherently demonstrating a special guarantee of reliability.

For the purposes of finding circumstances demonstrating reliability pursuant to clause (2) of subsection (c), a judge may consider whether the relator documented the child witness's statement, and shall consider the following factors:

(i) the clarity of the statement, meaning, the child's capacity to observe, remember, and give expression to that which such child has seen, heard, or experienced; provided, however, that a finding under this clause shall be supported by expert testimony from a treating psychiatrist, psychologist, or clinician;

(ii) the time, content and circumstances of the statement;

(iii) the child's sincerity and ability to appreciate the consequences of such statement.

(d) An out-of-court statement which is admissible by common law or by statute shall remain admissible notwithstanding the provisions of this section.

reliability of the out-of-court statement be on the record, and that the judge's determination of reliability be supported by specific findings on the record. The court noted that where possible, without causing severe emotional trauma to the child witness, the defendant and counsel should be given the opportunity to be present at the hearing. Fourth, the court noted that where the judge determines that a child witness was unavailable because she was incompetent to testify, the judge's reasons for finding the witness incompetent should not be those that call into question the reliability of the out-of-court statements. Finally, the court required that in order to admit such hearsay statements for substantive purposes, there must be other independently admitted evidence that corroborated the out-of-court statements. See *Com. v. Jaubert*, 38 Mass App 943, 647 NE2d 1238 (1995) (hearsay by alleged child sexual abuse victim was not admissible where the trial judge made none of the requisite findings required by §81).

Section 82, which governs all civil cases except for care and protection cases, is substantially identical to §81, with the exception that §82 specifically directs the judge to consider the existence of corroborating evidence in determining whether the out-of-court statement is reliable under subsection (c). The Supreme Judicial Court upheld the constitutionality of §82 in *Adoption of Quentin*, 424 Mass 882, 678 NE2d 1325 (1997), suggesting that although they may not be required in every civil case, the better part of caution would be for judges to employ the procedures discussed in *Com. v. Colin C.*, supra, in §82 proceedings. See *Adoption of Tina*, 45 Mass App 727, 701 NE2d 671 (1998) (trial court's findings were inadequate to demonstrate reliability of child's hearsay statements); *Edward E. v. Department of Social Services*, 42 Mass App 478, 678 NE2d 163 (1997) (holding that circumstances of the case did not demonstrate the reliability of the child's statements).

Section 83 governs care and protection proceedings.[2] Section 83 was discussed at length in *Care and Protection of Rebecca*, 419 Mass 67, 643 NE2d 26 (1994). The court rejected the claim that the statute violated due process and equal protection provisions of the Fourteenth Amendment to the U.S. Constitution and art. 12 of the Massachusetts Declaration of Rights. The court also rejected the claim that §83 contained an implicit requirement that a judge find that the child witness is unavailable before admitting such evidence. The court noted that such a requirement was explicitly set forth in §§81 and 82, and that its absence from §83 would be deemed to be intentional by the Legislature. The court did conclude, however, that there is an implicit requirement in the statute that a judge assess the reliability of such out-of-court statements in connection with deciding how much weight to afford to them. The court noted that the judge is required "to treat this evidence with caution." 419 Mass at 79. It noted that the person through whom the statement is introduced is subject to cross-examination concerning the circumstances in which the statement was made and related matters, and also noted that the legislation does not foreclose a judge from holding a voir dire to assess the child's capacity to remember and relate and the child's ability to perceive the necessity of telling the truth. The court stated that in determining the weight to give to

---

[2] The statute provides:

§83. Admissibility in Proceeding to Place Child in Foster Care of Out-of-Court Statement of Child Abuse Victim.

(a) Any out-of-court statements of a child under the age of ten describing any act of sexual contact performed on or with the child, the circumstances under which it occurred, or which identifies the perpetrator offered in an action brought under subparagraph C of section twenty-three or section twenty-four of chapter one hundred and nineteen shall be admissible; provided, however, that the person to whom the statement was made, or who heard the child make the statement testifies, and the judge finds that the statement is offered as evidence of a material fact and is more probative on the point for which it is offered than any other evidence with the proponent can procure through reasonable effort.

(b) An out-of-court statement admissible by common law or by statute shall remain admissible notwithstanding the provisions of this section.

such statements, a judge should consider whether other admissible evidence corroborated the existence of child abuse. Finally, the court required that a judge's reason for relying on §83 evidence must appear clearly in the specific and detailed findings required in a care and protection case.

In *Com. v. Costello*, 411 Mass 371, 582 NE2d 938 (1991), the court declined to recognize prior inconsistent statements by alleged child sexual abuse victims as substantive evidence. The Commonwealth had not argued for such an exception to the ordinary rule limiting the use of such statements to impeachment purposes; however, the court recognized that some other states allow such evidence. The court noted that Massachusetts has no general exception to the hearsay rule for statements by child sexual abuse victims.

It should be noted that statements by alleged child sexual abuse victims might be admissible as spontaneous exclamations (see §8.16), or as fresh complaint evidence (see §6.19). Solicitude for the sensitivity of such victims as witnesses may also be shown by making special arrangements for the receipt of their testimony, consistent with protecting the rights of the defendant. See §3.3.

§8.21.4   Reports Regarding Child Abuse and Neglect

Hearsay statements in reports regarding child abuse and neglect have been made admissible by statute. GL 119, §§21 and 24. See *Adoption of Paula*, 420 Mass 716, 724-725, 651 NE2d 1222, 1229 (1995) (GL 119, §24 reports, as well as testimony of investigator, are admissible in proceeding dispensing with parents' consent to adoption); *Adoption of Mary*, 414 Mass 705, 610 NE2d 898 (1993); *Adoption of Sean*, 36 Mass App 261, 630 NE2d 604 (1994) (guardian ad litem reports containing hearsay are admissible in proceedings to dispense with consent for adoption under GL 215, §56A); *Adoption of Arthur*, 34 Mass App 914, 609 NE2d 486 (1993) (same); *Adoption of Kenneth*, 31 Mass App 946, 580 NE2d 392 (1991); *Custody of Tracy*, 31 Mass App 481, 579 NE2d 1362 (1991).

The Supreme Judicial Court has recognized, however, that it is error to admit hearsay from GL 119, §24 reports unless there is "an opportunity to refute the investigator *and the investigator's sources* through cross-examination and other means." *Adoption of Carla*, 416 Mass 510, 514, 623 NE2d 1118, 1120 (1993) (citing *Custody of Michel*, 28 Mass App 260, 266, 549 NE2d 440 (1990), emphasis added in *Carla*). See *Care and Protection of Rebecca*, 419 Mass 67, 82, 643 NE2d 26, 35 (1994) (hearsay in §24 report which is inadmissible under *Adoption of Carla* may not be used to bolster reliability determination in order to admit hearsay under GL 233, §83); *Adoption of Iris*, 43 Mass App Ct 95, 680 NE2d 1188 (1997) (requiring parents to call court investigator on direct examination, denial of right to conduct cross-examination, was error); *In re Leo*, 38 Mass App 237, 646 NE2d 1086 (1995) (where party was given opportunity to call as witnesses the sources in investigator's report, but refused to do so, he waived right to complain of hearsay in §24 report); *Care and Protection of Inga*, 36 Mass App 660, 634 NE2d 591 (1994) (hearsay accusations of child from GL 119, §51A report inadmissible where child does not testify and judge has no other means to assess accuracy of statements).

The standards for the admissibility of confessions derive from both common law and constitutional sources. While much of the common law has been altered by the evolving constitutional jurisprudence, some remains relevant to the question of the admission of an accused's statements, most notably the "humane practice." See §9.1.

Several doctrines control the admissibility of confessions and incriminating statements: (1) the voluntariness standard under the Due Process Clause; (2) the *Miranda* doctrine under the Fifth Amendment; (3) the right to counsel approach under the Sixth Amendment; (4) the "fruit of the poisonous tree" doctrine under the Fourth Amendment; and (5) miscellaneous nonconstitutional exclusionary rules.

§9.1   The "Humane Practice" Doctrine

Under the so-called humane practice followed in the Commonwealth for many years (and cited with approval in *Jackson v. Denno*, 378 US 368, 378-385, 84 S Ct 1774, 1781-1785, 12 L Ed 2d 908, 916-917 (1964)), a confession may be admitted in evidence only after a preliminary hearing in the absence of the jury and a judicial determination of its voluntariness. See *Com. v. Crawford*, 429 Mass 60, 65, 706 NE2d 289, 293 (1999); *Com. v. Tavares*, 385 Mass 140, 149-150, 430 NE2d 1198, 1204-1205 (1982). See also Proposed Mass R Evid 104(c) ("Hearings on the admissibility of confessions shall in all cases be conducted out of the hearing of the jury."). If the judge concludes that the confession was involuntary, it is excluded. If the judge determines that the confession was voluntary and admits it, the jury is instructed that they are not to consider the confession unless satisfied that it was the voluntary act of the defendant. *Com. v. Tavares*, supra, 385 Mass at 149-150, 430 NE2d at 1205. See also Proposed Mass R Evid 104(f) ("In a criminal case tried to a jury, if the court admits evidence of a confession . . . it shall submit for determination by the jury the respective questions of the voluntariness of the confession. . . .").

Thus, the defendant is given two opportunities to challenge a confession: first before the judge who may decide to exclude it; and then before the jury who may decide to disregard it.[1] But see *Com. v. Griffin*, 345 Mass 283, 286, 186 NE2d 909, 910-911 (1963) (in a jury-waived trial, such duplication is unnecessary); *Com. v. Parker*, 412 Mass 353, 589 NE2d 306 (1992) (*Parker II*) (defendant's motion to suppress confession, which was denied at first trial, could be denied on retrial without conducting hearing where defendant raised no new issues and applicable law had not

---

§9.1   [1]While the hearing and determination before the judge is constitutionally mandated, see *Jackson v. Denno*, supra, the "second prong" of the humane practice, jury reconsideration, is not. See *Lego v. Twomey*, 404 US 477, 489-490, 92 S Ct 619, 30 L Ed 2d 618 (1972); *Com. v. Cole*, 380 Mass 30, 40, 402 NE2d 55, 62 (1980) (& citations).

changed); *Com. v. Griffin*, 19 Mass App 174, 184-185, 472 NE2d 1354, 1361 (1985) (where motion judge already conducted hearing, no requirement that trial judge hold new hearing in absence of new facts or change in applicable law).

For an extensive discussion of the treatment of confessions and admissions under the "humane practice," see *Com. v. Paszko*, 391 Mass 164, 179-183, 461 NE2d 222, 232-234 (1984) and *Com. v. Tavares*, supra, 385 Mass at 149-153, 430 NE2d at 1204-1206.

The defendant bears the burden of going forward at the suppression hearing with evidence that his statement was involuntary. It is then the Commonwealth's burden to prove voluntariness beyond a reasonable doubt.[2] If the judge concludes that the defendant's statement was voluntary beyond a reasonable doubt, that conclusion must appear with "unmistakable clarity" from the record.[3] If voluntariness is a live issue at trial, the judge must instruct the jury to disregard the statement unless the Commonwealth has met its burden of proving beyond a reasonable doubt that the statement was voluntary. The Commonwealth is thus required to prove the voluntariness of a confession or admission beyond a reasonable doubt to both

---

[2] Under federal due process standards, the burden on the prosecution at this proceeding is to establish voluntariness merely by a preponderance of the evidence. See *Lego v. Twomey*, supra, 404 US at 489.

[3] Evidence of voluntariness must affirmatively appear in the record. See *Com. v. Fernette*, 398 Mass 658, 662-663, 500 NE2d 1290, 1293 (1986). But see *Com. v. Mello*, 420 Mass 375, 381-383, 649 NE2d 1106, 1112-1113 (1995) (failure of judge to make specific findings of fact to support denial of defendant's motion to suppress confession did not warrant new trial; judge's denial implied resolution of factual and credibility issues in favor of Commonwealth); *Com. v. Brady*, 380 Mass 44, 52, 410 NE2d 695, 700 (1980) ("Although we have stated that 'it is both prudent and desirable for a judge to make a record of facts found in a voir dire hearing on the admissibility of evidence,' we have not held that 'unmistakable clarity' mandates 'an absolute requirement that such a record be made.'") (citation omitted).

the judge and the jury. *Com. v. Tavares*, supra, 385 Mass at 151-152, 430 NE2d at 1206 (& citations).[4]

The judge is required to conduct a preliminary hearing sua sponte and make a determination of voluntariness whenever there is credible evidence placing the voluntariness of the confession in issue. See *Com. v. Harris*, 371 Mass 462, 467-472, 358 NE2d 982, 989 (1976) (evidence that defendant confessed only after having been beaten by police); *Com. v. Collins*, 11 Mass App 126, 133-134, 414 NE2d 1008, 1012 (1981) (defendant forced to lie naked with hands handcuffed during time he gave statements). Compare *Com. v. Burke*, 414 Mass 252, 258-259, 607 NE2d 991, 996 (1993) (defense strategy did not make voluntariness an issue); *Com. v. Benoit*, 410 Mass 506, 512-513, 574 NE2d 347, 351-352 (1991) (no evidence of involuntariness presented at suppression hearing); *Com. v. Hall*, 45 Mass App 146, 157, 696 NE2d 151, 160-161 (1998) (statement in question was important to self-defense strategy); *Com. v. Pavao*, 46 Mass App 271, 274-275, 705 NE2d 307, 310-311 (1999) (lack of affirmative credible evidence of involuntariness). A mere assertion by counsel does not amount to the "credible evidence" required to trigger a voir dire. See *Com. v. Watkins*, 33 Mass App 7, 15 n.8, 595 NE2d 786, 791 n.8 (1992).

Where credible psychiatric evidence of mental impairment or insanity is presented, the judge has an obligation to hold a voir dire to determine voluntariness and to instruct the jury to consider the voluntariness of the confession,

---

[4]Regarding the instructions to be given the jury on its determination of voluntariness, see *Com. v. Grenier*, 415 Mass 680, 687-688, 615 NE2d 922, 926 (1993); *Com. v. Williams*, 388 Mass 846, 856-857, 448 NE2d 1114, 1121-1122 (1983); *Com. v. Nadworny*, 396 Mass 342, 370, 486 NE2d 675, 691-692 (1985). The judge should not inform the jury of his determination of voluntariness, as this would "diminish the benefit of independent jury determination required by our long-established humane rule." *Com. v. Tavares*, supra, 385 Mass at 152 n.18, 430 NE2d at 1206 n.18 (citation and internal quotations omitted). See also *Com. v. Chung*, 378 Mass 451, 460 n.12, 392 NE2d 1015, 1021 n.12 (1979) (& citations). The Supreme Judicial Court has refused to impose a unanimity requirement on the jury's determination of voluntariness. See *Com. v. Watkins*, 425 Mass 830, 836, 683 NE2d 653, 657 (1997).

even in the absence of a request from defendant. *Com. v. Sheriff,* 425 Mass 186, 192-196, 680 NE2d 75, 79-81 (1997); *Com. v. Vazquez,* 387 Mass 96, 102-103, 438 NE2d 856, 860 (1982); *Com. v. Vick,* 381 Mass 43, 45-46, 406 NE2d 1295, 1296-1297 (1980). See also *Com. v. Callahan,* 401 Mass 627, 631 n.5, 519 NE2d 245, 248 n.5 (1988) (judge properly submitted to jury question of effect of defendant's mental state as described in psychiatric testimony); *Com. v. Louraine,* 390 Mass 28, 39, 453 NE2d 437, 445 (1983) (in light of evidence of insanity, court must determine whether confession was product of rational intellect, even where the confession was spontaneously made while defendant was not in custody). Compare *Com. v. Benoit,* 410 Mass 506, 513-516, 574 NE2d 347, 352-353 (1991) (insufficient evidence of psychosis, intoxication, or injury to raise issue of voluntariness); *Com. v. Brady,* 380 Mass 44, 49, 410 NE2d 695, 699-700 (1980) (mere evidence of drinking alcohol or using drugs does not trigger judge's obligation to inquire into voluntariness of confession absent defendant's objection).

A defendant is entitled to present expert testimony (at both the suppression hearing and trial) on the issue of voluntariness in appropriate cases. See *Com. v. Crawford,* 429 Mass 60, 706 NE2d 289 (1999) (expert testimony on battered woman syndrome and post-traumatic stress disorder).

The judge has no duty to ask the jury to pass on voluntariness unless it is made a live issue at trial. *Com. v. Nichypor,* 419 Mass 209, 218-219, 643 NE2d 452, 458 (1994); *Com. v. Ferreira,* 417 Mass 592, 600, 632 NE2d 392 (1994); *Com. v. Burke,* supra, 414 Mass at 259-260; *Com. v. Benoit,* supra, 410 Mass at 511-513, 574 NE2d at 351-352 (& citations) (defendant's theory at trial was that he did not make the incriminating statement, not that it was involuntary). Where voluntariness is an issue, the judge must submit all relevant evidence to the jury. See *Com. v. Adams,* 416 Mass 55, 60-61, 617 NE2d 594, 597-598 (1993) (error to exclude testimony of defendant's mother and forensic psychiatrist tending to show that defendant was psychologically coerced into confessing).

Although the common law at one time distinguished between confessions, to which the humane practice safeguards applied, and incriminating statements falling short of a confession, which were not subject to the practice, the distinction has been abandoned and all "incriminating statements made by the accused" are within the protection. *Com. v. Tavares*, supra, 385 Mass at 150, 430 NE2d at 1204-1205 (citing Text).

§9.2   Involuntariness under the Common Law and Due Process: The Totality of the Circumstances Analysis[1]

The common law excluded involuntary confessions on the rationale that they are of doubtful reliability and thus "have no just and legitimate tendency to prove the facts admitted." *Com. v. Morey*, 67 Mass (1 Gray) 461 (1854). See also *Com. v. Myers*, 160 Mass 530, 532, 36 NE 481 (1894); *Com. v. Knapp*, 26 Mass (9 Pick) 495, 502 (1830). Since 1936, the due process clause of the Fourteenth Amendment to the United States Constitution has also been held to require exclusion of coerced confessions. *Brown v. Mississippi*, 297 US 278 (1936). The constitutional focus shifted to the fundamental unfairness of extracting and using such statements at trial. Justice Frankfurter explained:

> Our decisions under [the Fourteenth] Amendment have made clear that convictions following admission into evidence of confessions which are involuntary, i.e., the product of coercion, either physical or psychological, cannot stand. This is so not because such confessions are unlikely to be true but because the methods used to extract them offend an underlying principle in the enforcement of our criminal

---

§9.2   [1] The Massachusetts cases do not generally distinguish between the voluntariness issue under the common law and under the Constitution, so both will be treated together.

law: that ours is an accusatorial and not an inquisitorial system — a system in which the State must establish guilt by evidence independently and freely secured and may not by coercion prove its charge against an accused out of his own mouth.

Rogers v. Richmond, 365 US 534, 540, 81 S Ct 735, 5 L Ed 2d 760 (1961).

The question of voluntariness turns on whether the suspect's free will had been overborne by law enforcement officials. See *Rogers v. Richmond,* supra, 365 US at 544. This requires an examination of the circumstances of the interrogation to determine "whether the processes were so unfair or unreasonable as to render a subsequent confession involuntary." *Michigan v. Tucker,* 417 US 433, 441, 94 S Ct 2357, 41 L Ed 2d 182 (1974). A conviction founded in whole or in part on statements that are the product of physical or psychological coercion deprives the defendant of his right to due process of law under the Fourteenth Amendment. *Com. v. Mahnke,* 368 Mass 662, 679, 335 NE2d 660, 671 (1975).

The coercion may take many forms, mental as well as physical. It may involve threats, inducements or promises of immunity or favor. Frequently the coercion involves prolonged questioning under adverse circumstances. See *Com. v. Makarewicz,* 333 Mass 575, 585-586, 132 NE2d 294, 299-300 (1956) (& citations).

There is no "acid test" of voluntariness. *Com. v. Mahnke,* supra, 368 Mass at 680, 335 NE2d at 671. Rather, the question is determined on a case-by-case basis in light of the "totality of the circumstances." *Procunier v. Atchley,* 400 US 446, 453, 91 S Ct 485, 27 L Ed 2d 524 (1971); *Com. v. Cruz,* 373 Mass 676, 688, 369 NE2d 996, 1000-1001 (1977). The relevant factors in assessing voluntariness include the time and conditions under which the questioning took place, the content and form of the questions put to the suspect, and the physical and mental condition of the suspect during the period of interrogation. *Com. v. Makarewicz,* supra, 333 Mass at 587, 132 NE2d at 301. Regarding the suspect, courts look to the defendant's age, education, intelligence, emotional stability, and experience with and in the criminal justice system. Regarding the interrogation, courts look to who initiated any discussion of a deal or leniency, and whether *Miranda* warnings were given. *Com. v. Mandile*, 397 Mass 410, 413, 492 NE2d 74, 76 (1986); *Com. v. Azar*, 32 Mass App 290, 297-298, 588 NE2d 1352, 1357-1358 (1992).

The focus is on the manner and duration of the interrogation as well as the vulnerabilities of the defendant at the time. *Procunier v. Atchley*, supra, 400 US at 453-454. The process weighs the circumstances of pressure against the suspect's power of resistance. *Fikes v. Alabama*, 352 US 191, 197-198, 77 S Ct 281, 1 L Ed 2d 246 (1957). The task is to ascertain whether this *particular* defendant's will was overcome by the *particular* pressures exerted upon him. *Com. v. Harris*, 364 Mass 236, 242, 358 NE2d 982, 986 (1973); *Com. v. Selby*, 420 Mass 656, 662-663, 651 NE2d 843, 848 (1995).

As with any balancing test, no one factor is generally determinative. Thus, while prolonged detention and interrogation alone might constitute sufficient coercion to render a confession involuntary, findings to the contrary have been upheld on appeal. See, e.g., *Com. v. Makarewicz*, supra, 333 Mass at 584-589, 132 NE2d at 299-302 (interrogation of 15-year-old boy over course of nine hours); *Com. v. Banuchi*, 335 Mass 649, 656-657, 141 NE2d 835, 839-840 (1957) (interrogation over course of two and one-half days).

In determining voluntariness, the Supreme Judicial Court has become "increasingly sensitive to consideration of the defendant's mental condition."[2] *Com. v. Chung*, 378 Mass 451, 456, 392 NE2d 1015 (1979) (insanity of defendant). See also *Com. v. Cole*, 380 Mass 30, 40-41, 402 NE2d

---

[2]Earlier decisions had affirmed findings of voluntariness in the face of evidence of mental disability. See, e.g., *Com. v. Tracy*, 349 Mass 87, 99, 207 NE2d 16, 22, (1965) (defendant seriously wounded by gunfire and in pain); *Com. v. Harrison*, 342 Mass 279, 284-285, 173 NE2d 87, 91 (1961) (defendant had bullet wound in head and severe brain injury).

55, 62 (1980) (evidence of psychosis); *Com. v. Banuchi,* supra, 335 Mass at 654-656, 141 NE2d at 839 (evidence of effect upon defendant of withdrawal from alcohol at time of confession). Statements attributable to a defendant's debilitated condition, such as insanity, drug abuse or withdrawal symptoms, intoxication, or head injury have been suppressed. See *Com. v. Allen,* 395 Mass 448, 455, 480 NE2d 630, 635-636 (1985) (& citations). A statement is inadmissible if it would not have been obtained but for the effects of the confessor's mental disease or defect. See *Com. v. Libran,* 405 Mass 634, 639, 543 NE2d 5, 8-9 (1989) (citation omitted); *Com. v. Cifizzari,* 19 Mass App 981, 474 NE2d 1174, 1175-1176 (1985). But compare *Com. v. Perrot,* 407 Mass 539, 543, 554 NE2d 1205, 1208 (1990) (fact that defendant was depressed and on suicide watch at time of confession does not mandate conclusion that it was involuntary); *Com. v. Libran,* supra, 405 Mass at 638-639, 543 NE2d at 8 (fact that defendant was retarded and suffering from schizophrenic reaction and manic-depressive condition did not render statements involuntary); *Com. v. Davis,* 403 Mass 575, 578-581, 531 NE2d 577, 579-581 (1988) (confession made in third person by defendant with psychiatric history was voluntary where the interrogation bore no evidence that defendant's will had been broken); *Com. v. Allen,* supra, 395 Mass at 457-458, 480 NE2d at 636 (defendant's statements to nurse were voluntary even though he was recovering from self-inflicted gunshot wound to head); *Com. v. Bandy,* 38 Mass App 329, 331, 648 NE2d 440, 442 (1995) (claim of hallucination resulting from physical injury); *Com. v. Cifizzari,* supra, 19 Mass App at 982, 474 NE2d at 1177 (confession was voluntary despite uncontested evidence that defendant suffered from chronic paranoid schizophrenia).

Although intoxication alone is insufficient to render a statement involuntary, "special care" must be taken to review the issue of voluntariness where the defendant claims to have been under the influence of drugs or alcohol. *Com. v. Mello,* 420 Mass 375, 383, 649 NE2d 1106, 1113

(1995). Thus, the defendant's statement was found involuntary where he was under the influence of alcohol, nervous and upset, and was questioned by three officers at a late hour. *Com. v. Scherben*, 28 Mass App 952, 550 NE2d 899 (1990). But compare *Com. v. Ward*, 426 Mass 290, 294-295, 688 NE2d 227, 231 (1997) ("defendant was a tolerant alcoholic who was often intoxicated but nevertheless able to make apparently rational decisions"); *Com. v. Smith*, 426 Mass 76, 81-82, 686 NE2d 983, 988 (1997); *Com. v. Koney*, 421 Mass 295, 304-305, 657 NE2d 210, 215-216 (1995) (rational denials made by motor vehicle homicide defendant demonstrated voluntariness of statements despite his intoxication and emotional state); *Com. v. Mello*, supra, 420 Mass at 383, 649 NE2d at 1113 (despite evidence that defendant ingested beer and inhaled heroin night before arrest, suppression not required where defendant spoke coherently, appeared sober, explained preparation and crime in detail, did not complain of illness, signed waiver form, stated he understood his rights, and agreed to talk to police); *Com. v. Simmons*, 417 Mass 60, 65-66, 627 NE2d 917, 921 (1994) (although defendant was intoxicated, statement was voluntary); *Com. v. Parker*, 402 Mass 333, 341, 522 NE2d 924, 928 (1988) (*Parker I*); *Com. v. Pavao*, 46 Mass App 271, 274, 705 NE2d 307, 310-311 (1999) (cases collected).

The fact that a confession was obtained without a warning to the accused of his constitutional rights[3] is a factor to be weighed in determining voluntariness, but does not automatically bar its admission under Massachusetts law. See *Com. v. Tavares*, 385 Mass 140, 153 n.19, 430 NE2d 1198, 1206 n.19 (1982); *Com. v. Chung*, supra, 378 Mass at 458-459 n.9, 392 NE2d at 1020 n.9; *Com. v. Valcourt*, 333 Mass 706, 711, 133 NE2d 217, 221 (1956). Where the statement is made in a noncustodial setting, and thus warnings are not required, it is within the judge's discretion to exclude testimony concerning failure to give warnings. *Com. v. Nadworny*, 396 Mass 342, 369-370, 486 NE2d 675, 691-692

---

[3] See §9.7.1, infra.

(1985). The Supreme Judicial Court has declined to impose a requirement that before a statement may be considered voluntary, a suspect must be advised of his status as such or that he is charged with a particular crime. *Com. v. Wills*, 398 Mass 768, 776-777, 500 NE2d 1341, 1346-1347 (1986).

While the police may not use threats or inducements to secure a confession, not every promise or inducement renders a statement involuntary. *Com. v. Berg*, 37 Mass App 200, 203-204, 638 NE2d 1367, 1370 (1994) (citation omitted) (confession not inadmissible because police truthfully explained to defendant that his mother would be charged unless ownership of drugs was established). As always, voluntariness is determined on the totality of the circumstances. Id. See also *Com. v. Cunningham*, 405 Mass 646, 657-658, 543 NE2d 12, 19 (1989) (neither advice of detective and priest that it would be better if defendant told truth nor detective's comment that defendant had nothing to worry about if he told truth invalidated waiver); *Com. v. Doe*, 37 Mass App 30, 32-33, 636 NE2d 308, 309-310 (1994) (no showing that officers misled informant into making incriminatory statement).

Regarding inducements, an officer may suggest that it would be better for a suspect to tell the truth, may indicate that the suspect's cooperation will be brought to the attention of the prosecutor or judge, and may state that cooperation has been considered favorably by the courts in the past. What is prohibited is an assurance, express or implied, that it will aid the defense or result in a lesser sentence. *Com. v. Souza*, 418 Mass 478, 481-482, 702 NE2d 1167, 1170 (1998); *Com. v. Raymond*, 424 Mass 382, 395-396, 676 NE2d 824, 833-834 (1997); *Com. v. Mandile*, supra, 397 Mass at 414-415, 492 NE2d at 77; *Com. v. Meehan*, 377 Mass 552, 564, 387 NE2d 527, 534 (1979) (& cases cited).

An officer's promise of psychiatric help to a suspect is an interviewing technique which may result in a coerced confession, especially if the help is offered as a quid pro quo for the statement. The promise alone, however, will not invalidate a confession. The issue is whether the promise was so manipulative as to overcome the free will of a person with the defendant's characteristics. See *Com. v. Felice*, 44 Mass App 709, 712-713, 693 NE2d 713, 716 (1998) (& citations).

The use of false information or trickery by the police to elicit a statement is relevant in determining its voluntariness, but does not of itself render the statement involuntary. See *Com. v. Colby*, 422 Mass 414, 416-417, 663 NE2d 808, 810 (1996) (Virginia police officer's misrepresentations that polygraph test was infallible and results admissible did not render defendant's statement involuntary); *Com. v. Edwards*, 420 Mass 666, 673-674, 651 NE2d 398, 402-403 (1995) (detectives' false statement that defendant's handprint had been recovered at murder scene insufficient to render statement involuntary); *Com. v. Selby*, supra, 420 Mass at 663-664, 651 NE2d at 848-849 (false representation that defendant's handprint placed him in victim's house did not invalidate statement); *Com. v. Dustin*, 373 Mass 612, 614, 368 NE2d 1388, 1390-1391 (1977) (deceptive statement by police officer implying that defendant's statement could not be used against him did not render suspect's incriminating statements involuntary).

Where the defendant during interrogation makes self-serving statements to the police that are helpful to his case, a finding that his will was overborne is less likely. See *Com. v. Pavao*, 46 Mass App 271, 276, 705 NE2d 307, 311 (1999); *Com. v. Fuentes*, 45 Mass App 934, 936, 702 NE2d 814, 817 (1998).

Although the range of variables is almost infinite, the following is a sampling of cases emphasizing the two major points of reference in the voluntariness analysis:

The mental or physical state of the defendant: *Mincey v. Arizona*, 437 US 385, 98 S Ct 2408, 57 L Ed 2d 290 (1978) (seriously wounded suspect questioned in hospital while in considerable pain and barely conscious; statement involuntary); *Townsend v. Sain*, 372 US 293, 83 S Ct 745, 9 L Ed 2d 770 (1963) (confession obtained while defendant was under the influence of drug having the effect of a "truth serum" was involuntary); *Gallegos v. Colorado*, 370 US 49, 82 S Ct 1209, 8 L Ed 2d 325 (1962) (youth and immaturity of 14-year-old suspect rendered statement involuntary); *Culombe v. Connecticut*, 367 US 568, 81 S Ct 1860, 6 L Ed 2d 1037 (1961) (mentally retarded person's statement involuntary); *Blackburn v. Alabama*, 361 US 199, 80 S Ct 274, 4 L Ed 2d 242 (1960) (insane person); *Fikes v. Alabama*, supra (uneducated defendant of low mentality); *Com. v. Magee*, 423 Mass 381, 387-389, 668 NE2d 339, 344-345 (1996) (defendant's debilitated physical and emotional state, and officer's withholding of medical treatment until she gave statement). Compare *Colorado v. Connelly*, 479 US 157 (1987) (mental disorder of defendant not determinative on voluntariness issue in absence of coercive police conduct); *Com. v. Colon-Cruz*, 408 Mass 533, 539-540, 562 NE2d 797, 803-804 (1990) (no evidence that defendant's physical condition was so disabling as to render his statement involuntary, or that the interview involved excessive or unfair pressure, or that defendant was unusually susceptible to police pressure); *Com. v. Wills*, 398 Mass 768, 776, 500 NE2d 1341 (1986) (defendant's statements voluntary despite fact they were made while he was receiving treatment in hospital for knife wounds); *Com. v. Paszko*, 391 Mass 164, 175, 461 NE2d 222, 232-234 (1984) (no per se rule excluding as involuntary statements made during drug withdrawal); *Com. v. Vazquez*, 387 Mass 96, 100, 438 NE2d 856, 859 (1982) (no per se rule that statements given by individual suffering severe psychotic conditions is inadmissible; statement inadmissible only if it would not have been obtained but for the effects of the defendant's psychosis).

The means used to obtain the confession: *Arizona v. Fulminante*, 499 US 279, 111 S Ct 1246 (1991) (defendant was motivated to confess by fear of physical violence from other inmates and promise of protection from police informant); *Brooks v. Florida*, 389 US 413, 88 S Ct 541, 19 L Ed 2d 643 (1967) (defendant confined in punishment cell on restricted diet for 14 days, completely under control and domination of jailers); *Haynes v. Washington*, 373 US 503, 83 S Ct 1336, 10 L Ed 2d 513 (1963) (defendant held incommunicado for 16 hours and denied permission to call wife unless he confessed); *Rogers v. Richmond*, supra, 365 US at 540-542 (police officer pretended during interrogation to place call ordering defendant's wife to be taken into custody); *Spano v. New York*, 360 US 315, 79 S Ct 1202, 3 L Ed 2d 1265 (1959) (prolonged interrogation and trickery by the police); *Watts v. Indiana*, 338 US 49, 52-55, 69 S Ct 1347, 93 L Ed 2d 1801 (1949) (prolonged detention in solitary confinement in cell with no place to sit or sleep, and interrogation by relays of police officers); *Com. v. Lahti*, 398 Mass 829, 831, 501 NE2d 511, 512 (1986) (defendant's statements were induced by detective's promises and threats); *Com. v. Meehan*, 377 Mass 552, 563-564, 387 NE2d 527, 534-535 (1979) (defendant confessed after being told that case against him was established and after being assured the confession would help his defense). Compare *Com. v. Souza*, 418 Mass 478, 702 NE2d 1167 (1998) (confession voluntary even though defendant interrogated in his underwear, handcuffed to wall, and questioned by series of officers over three and one-half hours); *Com. v. Fryar*, 414 Mass 732, 741-743, 610 NE2d 903, 909-910 (1993) (confession voluntary even though defendant, 17-years-old, had been drinking, had been isolated for over four hours without food or sleep, and was falsely told by police that he had been charged with stabbing victim; and when he gave second statement, he had been handcuffed in room for additional four hours, alone and with no food or sleep); *Com. v. Bousquet*, 407 Mass 854, 862, 556 NE2d 37, 42 (1990) (no evidence of physical coercion or that defendant's ingestion of drugs impaired his mind); *Com. v. Medeiros*, 395 Mass 336, 348, 479 NE2d 1371, 1379-1380 (1985) (practice of voluntarily subjecting suspect to lie detector test and accurately informing him that results reveal he is lying not coercive per se); *Com. v. Makarewicz*, supra, 333 Mass at 584-589, 132 NE2d at 299-302 (15-year-old boy's confession not involuntary even though police officer during interrogation remarked about taking defendant into the "back room to beat your ears").

For additional cases illustrating the weighing of factors under the totality standard, compare *Com. v. Meehan*, supra, 377 Mass at 562-568, 387 NE2d at 535-536 (confession was involuntary where defendant was 18-years-old, with poor educational background, uninformed of his right to reach his family or friends, his judgment impaired through intoxication, and he confessed after being misinformed by police officer that case against him was established and after receiving assurance that confession would assist his defense) with *Com. v. Larkin*, 429 Mass 426, 438, 708 NE2d 674, 682-683 (1999) (no evidence of any disability and defendant was veteran of criminal process) and *Com. v. Mandile*, supra, 397 Mass at 413-414, 492 NE2d at 76 (judge erred in holding confession involuntary where defendant was not intoxicated, or emotional, or detached from reality; was of sufficient age, educational background, and intelligence to comprehend the meaning of his actions and was familiar with the criminal justice system; was given *Miranda* warnings three times; was aware of his right to talk to counsel and in fact exercised that right; and it was defendant who initiated the discussion of leniency and sought deal). See also *Com. v. Signorine*, 404 Mass 400, 408-409, 535 NE2d 601, 606-607 (1989) (judge did not err in admitting as voluntarily made a statement by defendant during a telephone conversation with his brother-in-law, which was overheard by a police officer where defendant, without any request for privacy, chose a telephone located six feet from the officer).

It must be emphasized that the voluntariness of a suspect's statement on due process grounds and the voluntariness of the waiver of *Miranda* rights are separate and distinct issues, but they are both determined in light of the totality of the circumstances and they share many of the same relevant factors. *Com. v. Edwards*, supra, 420 Mass at 673, 651 NE2d at 403. See §9.7.4, infra.

The United States Supreme Court has held that "coercive police activity is a necessary predicate to the finding that a confession is not 'voluntary' within the meaning of the Due Process Clause of the Fourteenth Amendment." *Colorado v. Connelly*, 479 US 157, 164, 107 S Ct 515, 522, 93 L Ed 2d 473 (1986). No Massachusetts case has yet adopted this specific requirement for a determination of involuntariness.

The imprecise nature of the due process "totality of the circumstances" analysis led the Supreme Court to develop correlative doctrines applying more specific rules derived from the Fourth, Fifth, and Sixth Amendments to the United States Constitution, as outlined in the sections below. These doctrines, it must be emphasized, supplement but do not supplant the due process standard.

§9.3   Statements to Private Parties

Under Massachusetts law, statements extracted by private citizens, even absent governmental involvement, are subject to suppression under the involuntariness standard. See *Com. v. Mahnke*, 368 Mass 662, 679-681, 335 NE2d 660, 672 (1975). As the Supreme Judicial Court has observed: "[A] statement obtained through coercion and introduced at trial is every bit as offensive to civilized standards of adjudication when the coercion flows from private hands as when official depredations elicit a confession. Statements extracted by a howling lynch mob or a lawless private pack of vigilantes from a terrorized, pliable suspect are repugnant to due process mandates of fundamental fairness and protection against compulsory self-incrimination." 368 Mass at 681.

With regard to admissions by a defendant to private citizens, involuntariness has been found primarily where there has been actual physical or psychological coercion. See *Com. v. Watkins*, 33 Mass App 7, 14, 595 NE2d 786, 791 (1992) (& citations) (no involuntariness in student's statements to university investigator); *Com. v. Taylor*, 426 Mass 189, 196, 687 NE2d 631, 636 (1997) (defendant's statement to sister not involuntary even though made while handcuffed at police station). See also *Com. v. Blanchette*, 409 Mass 99, 106-108, 564 NE2d 992, 996 (1991) (defendant's written and oral statements to uncle and visitor at state hospital were product of a rational mind and voluntary); *Com. v. Libran*, 405 Mass 634, 639-640, 543 NE2d 5, 8-9 (1989) (defendant's statements overheard by another prisoner not involuntary because not result of coercion or mental impairment).

When the voluntariness of defendant's statements to private citizens is in issue, Massachusetts law requires the same "humane practice" applied to statements elicited by law enforcement personnel: The judge should conduct a voir dire to determine the voluntariness of the statements. If the judge determines that the statements are voluntary, the issue of voluntariness should be submitted to the jury for consideration. The Commonwealth has the burden of proving to the judge and the jury the voluntariness of the statements beyond a reasonable doubt. *Com. v. Hunter*, 416 Mass 831, 626 NE2d 873 (1994); *Com. v. Blanchette*, supra, 409 Mass at 106, 564 NE2d at 996. It has been suggested that the "better practice" is to treat statements to private citizens as if they were statements to the police. *Com. v. Paszko*, 391 Mass 164, 182-183, 461 NE2d 222, 234 (1984). The question of the voluntariness of statements made to private citizens must be raised by the defendant, and he must offer some proof to support his claim. See *Com. v. Smith*, 426 Mass 76, 82, 686 NE2d 983, 988 (1997).

Conduct by private citizens does not implicate the federal constitutional prohibition against coerced statements. See *Colorado v. Connelly*, 479 US 157, 166 (1987) ("The most outrageous behavior by a private party seeking to secure evidence against a defendant does not make that evidence inadmissible under the due process clause.").

§9.4   Subsequent Statements and Derivative Evidence

A finding that an earlier statement was involuntary does not necessarily require suppression of a later statement by the accused. The issue becomes whether the taint from the initial illegal interrogation has been eliminated, in which case the later statement may be admitted. The courts follow two lines of analysis in making this determination. In the first, the question is whether there had been a "break in the stream of events" so that the subsequent statement is sufficiently insulated from the coercive circumstances. The second analysis looks at the defendant's state of mind to determine whether the subsequent statement resulted from the erroneous impression that the "cat was already out of the bag." See generally *Com. v. Smith*, 412 Mass 823, 830-831, 593 NE2d 1288, 1292 (1992) (citations omitted). For further discussion of the two analyses, see *Com. v. Mahnke*, 368 Mass 662, 682-683, 686, 335 NE2d 660, 674-675, 676 (1975); *Com. v. Gallant*, 381 Mass 465, 469, 410 NE2d 704, 707 (1980); *Com. v. Watkins*, 375 Mass 472, 480-483, 379 NE2d 1040, 1046-1047 (1978) (extensive discussion of "cat out of the bag" theory and authorities); *Com. v. Meehan*, 377 Mass 552, 569-571, 387 NE2d 527, 537 (1979) (there is strong basis for drawing inference that second confession was product of first, and for permitting inference to be overcome only by such insulation as the advice of counsel or lapse of a long period of time). For a discussion of the same issue in the *Miranda* context, see §9.7.5.

Where a defendant takes the stand at trial in response to a confession admitted into evidence but subsequently determined to have been coerced, the defendant's testimony may not be introduced at a subsequent trial. See *Com. v. Brusgulis*, 41 Mass App 386, 389-390, 670 NE2d 207, 209-210 (1996) (& citations). Compare *Com. v. Luna*, 418 Mass 749, 751-752, 641 NE2d 1050, 1052 (1994) (even if defendant's affidavit was involuntary, it did not compel him to testify at trial).

Under early common law, the exclusion of a confession did not require the exclusion of evidence obtained as a result of that confession. See *Com. v. Knapp*, 26 Mass (9 Pick) 495, 510-511 (1830). More recent case law suggests the opposite conclusion. See *Com. v. Meehan*, supra, 377 Mass at 568-569, 387 NE2d at 536 (& citations) (evidence seized pursuant to search warrant based on involuntary confession was inadmissible). See also *Com. v. Lahti*, 398 Mass 829, 501 NE2d 511 (1986) (suppressing on Fifth Amendment grounds two victims' anticipated testimony as the tainted fruit of defendant's involuntary statements to police).

§9.5   Appellate Review of the Voluntariness Determination

Where voluntariness is in issue the appellate court must examine the entire record and make an independent determination of the ultimate issue. *Miller v. Fenton*, 474 US 104 (1985) (voluntariness not factual, but legal, issue); *Beckwith v. United States*, 425 US 341 (1976); *Com. v. Tavares*, 385 Mass 140, 144-145, 430 NE2d 1198, 1206 (1982). The judge's subsidiary fact findings will not be disturbed, however, if they are warranted by the evidence, and a finding of voluntariness is entitled to substantial deference. *Com. v. Fryar*, 414 Mass 732, 742, 610 NE2d 903, 909 (1993); *Com. v. Cunningham*, 405 Mass 646, 655, 543 NE2d 12, 17 (1989); *Com. v. Tavares*, supra, 385 Mass at 144-145, 430 NE2d at 1206.

The Supreme Court has held that harmless error analysis applies to coerced confessions. *Arizona v. Fulminante*, 499 US 279, 111 S Ct 1246, 113 L Ed 2d 302 (1991). Where a confession has been erroneously admitted, the prosecution has the burden of demonstrating beyond a reasonable doubt that the admission of the confession did not contribute to the defendant's conviction. Id.

§9.6   Electronic Recording of Interrogations

Noting that defendants, prosecutors, and courts "spend an enormous amount of time and effort trying to determine precisely what transpires during custodial interrogations" and that the electronic recording of interrogations would therefore be a "helpful tool in evaluating the voluntariness of confessions," the Supreme Judicial Court has nonetheless refused to mandate such a rule under either the common law or the Massachusetts Declaration of Rights. See *Com. v. Ardon*, 428 Mass 496, 498, 702 NE2d 808, 810 (1998); *Com. v. Fryar*, 414 Mass 732, 742 n.8, 610 NE2d 903, 909 n.8 (1993). See also *Com. v. Fernandes*, 427 Mass 90, 98, 692 NE2d 3, 8-9 (1998).

In *Com. v. Diaz*, 422 Mass 269, 661 NE2d 1326 (1996) the Court, while declining to adopt a rule suppressing custodial statements unless they had been electronically recorded, observed:

> There is force to a recording requirement particularly if a defendant is being questioned at a police station. The cost of the equipment and its operation is minimal. The machinery is not difficult to use. A recording speaks for itself literally on questions concerning what was said and in what manner. Recording would tend to eliminate certain challenges to the admissibility of defendants' statements and to make easier the resolution of many challenges that are made. Police officials should be alert to the merits of recording custodial interrogations and be warned that the time may come when recording in places of detention, at least, will be mandatory if a statement obtained during custodial interrogation is to be admissible.

422 Mass at 272-273, 661 NE2d at 1328-1329 (citations omitted). See also *Com. v. Baldwin*, 426 Mass 105, 110-113, 686 NE2d 1001, 1005-1007 (1997) (declining to require electronic recording of court-ordered psychiatric evaluation); *Com. v. Stockwell*, 426 Mass 17, 19-20, 686 NE2d 426,

429 (1997) (no abuse of discretion in denying motion to videotape psychiatric interview).

Moreover, defense counsel are:

> entitled to pursue the failure of the police to record a defendant's statements. Counsel may, for example, inquire of a testifying police officer . . . whether he or she was aware of the availability of recorders to use during the questioning of suspects. Counsel may argue to a jury and to a judge as factfinder that the failure of the police to record electronically statements made in a place of custody should be considered in deciding the voluntariness of any statement, whether the defendant was properly advised of his rights, and whether any statement attributed to the defendant was made.

Com. v. Diaz, supra, 422 Mass at 273, 661 NE2d at 1329. See, e.g., *Com. v. Larkin,* 429 Mass 426, 438 n.10, 708 NE2d 674, 683 n.10 (1999) (defense counsel cross-examined troopers about access to recorders).

Where a confession is taped, the "better practice" is to leave the recorder on during the entire interview, including silences, emotional displays, and casual conversation among the participants, so that the judge and jury are better able to assess the totality of the circumstances. *Com. v. Fernette,* 398 Mass 658, 665, 500 NE2d 1290, 1295 (1986).

§9.7   Confessions under the Fifth Amendment *Miranda* Doctrine

§9.7.1   *The Safeguards*

Premised upon the Fifth Amendment privilege against self-incrimination (applied to the states in *Malloy v. Hogan,* 378 US 1 (1964)), the landmark decision of *Miranda v. Arizona,* 384 US 436 (1966) adopted a prophylactic scheme designed to limit the coercion inherent in custodial interrogation. See generally *Com. v. Garcia,* 379 Mass 422, 430, 399 NE2d 460, 466-467 (1980). In the absence of the warnings and a valid waiver, a statement obtained as a result of custodial interrogation (whether incriminating or exculpatory)[1] is inadmissible at trial. Massachusetts has not adopted the *Miranda* scheme as a means of protecting state constitutional rights, but has established certain state law adjuncts to the *Miranda* rules, as discussed below. *Com. v. Ghee*, 414 Mass 313, 318 n.5, 607 NE2d 1005, 1009 n.5 (1993); *Com. v. Snyder*, 413 Mass 521, 531, 597 NE2d 1363 (1992).

Prior to any questioning, the accused must be advised in clear and unequivocal terms of his right to remain silent and his right to consult with an attorney. He must also be advised that anything he says can be used against him in court and that if he cannot afford an attorney one will be appointed at state expense. The required warnings need not be given in the precise language contained in *Miranda*. See *California v. Prysock*, 453 US 355, 101 S Ct 2806, 69 L Ed 2d 696 (1981) (warnings not defective even though suspect not explicitly advised that he was entitled to the services of a free lawyer prior to questioning); *Duckworth v. Eagan*, 492 US 195 (1989) (warnings not defective even though suspect

---

§9.7   [1] The Court ruled:

> The warnings required and the waiver necessary in accordance with [Miranda] are . . . prerequisites to the admissibility of any statement made by a defendant. No distinction can be drawn between statements which are direct confessions and statements which amount to "admissions" of part or all of an offense. The privilege against self-incrimination protects the individual from being compelled to incriminate himself in any manner; it does not distinguish degrees of incrimination. Similarly, for precisely the same reason, no distinction may be drawn between inculpatory statements and statements alleged to be merely "exculpatory." If a statement made was in fact truly exculpatory it would, of course, never be used by the prosecution. In fact, statements merely intended to be exculpatory by the defendant are often used to impeach his testimony at trial or to demonstrate untruths in the statement given under interrogation and thus to prove guilt by implication. These statements are incriminating in any meaningful sense of the word and may not be used without the full warnings and effective waiver required for any other statement.

Miranda v. Arizona, supra, 384 US at 476-477.

Thus, even if the defendant's motivation for making an admission is to clear himself or another, *Miranda* is designed to ensure that he has the requisite information about his rights before he speaks. *Com. v. Rubio*, 27 Mass App 506, 514, 540 NE2d 189, 194 (1989).

advised that free lawyer would be appointed "if and when you go to court"); *Com. v. Colon-Cruz*, 408 Mass 533, 539, 562 NE2d 797, 803 (1990) (warnings not defective even though Spanish translator used two words not on *Miranda* card); *Com. v. Colby*, 422 Mass 414, 418-419, 663 NE2d 808, 811 (1996) (officer's departure from standard warning, telling defendant "if he could not afford an attorney, the Commonwealth would attempt to provide one for him," was harmless). But compare *Com. v. Ghee*, supra, 414 Mass at 317-318 (warning that implied that, although suspect did not have to talk about offenses with which he was charged, he did have to talk about other offenses, not adequate; but error harmless); *Com. v. Adams*, 389 Mass 265, 268-269, 450 NE2d 149, 151-152 (1983) (where officer failed to inform defendant that any statements made by him could be used against him in court, warnings inadequate); *Com. v. Dustin*, 373 Mass 612, 615-616, 368 NE2d 1388, 1390-1391 (1977) (police officer's response to defendant's question, which carried implication that defendant's statement could not be used against him, directly contradicted required warning); *Com. v. Miranda*, 37 Mass App 939, 641 NE2d 139 (1994) (failure to inform defendant of right to presence of attorney during interrogation rendered warnings inadequate); *Com. v. Coplin*, 34 Mass App 478, 612 NE2d 1188 (1993) (complete set of warnings at time of arrest could not be deemed to carry over to remedy omission at station house of warning about possible consequences of forgoing privilege to remain silent).[2]

---

[2] The Supreme Judicial Court has left open the issue of whether the judge is required to submit to the jury the preliminary factual questions regarding compliance with *Miranda*, including questions as to whether the warnings were given. See *Com. v. Garcia*, supra, 379 Mass at 431-432, 391 NE2d at 474; *Com. v. Chung*, 378 Mass 451, 458 n.9, 392 NE2d 1015, 1020 n.9 (1979). For cases upholding the trial judge's refusal to credit defendant's testimony that he did not receive proper warnings, see *Com. v. Corriveau*, 396 Mass 319, 329-330, 486 NE2d 29, 36-37 (1985); *Com. v. Day*, 387 Mass 915, 919, 444 NE2d 384, 386 (1983); *Com. v. Williams*, 378 Mass 217, 226, 391 NE2d 1202, 1207-1208 (1979). See also *Com. v. Johnson*, 41 Mass App 81, 88-89, 669 NE2d 212, 217 (1996) (Common-

The Supreme Judicial Court has approved the practice of police reading the *Miranda* warnings to the suspect from a card: "We believe that much of the trial time now spent in trying to establish exactly what warning was given to a suspect or defendant could be saved if he were also given a copy of the card to be kept by him. We also approve the practice of admitting a police copy of the card in evidence. No useful purpose is served by testing on the witness stand the officer's ability to recite acurately from memory the *Miranda* warnings he read." *Com. v. Lewis*, 374 Mass 203, 204-205, 371 NE2d 775, 776 (1978). See also *Com. v. Perez*, 411 Mass 249, 255, 581 NE2d 1010, 1014-1015 (1991) (rejecting defendant's contention that he was misinformed of his rights because Spanish translations on *Miranda* cards were incomplete and inaccurate). There is no requirement that a suspect be given written *Miranda* warnings. See *Com. v. Smith*, 426 Mass 76, 81, 686 NE2d 983, 988 (1997).

Although *Miranda* warnings, once given, are not to be accorded "unlimited efficacy or perpetuity," they are generally viewed as sufficient to keep the suspect apprised of his rights even if there is a significant lapse of time between the warnings and an inculpatory statement. See *Com. v. Cruz*, 373 Mass 676, 687, 369 NE2d 996, 1003 (1977). Thus, a lapse of six hours between the warnings and a second confession did not negate the defendant's waiver. See *Com. v. Mello*, 420 Mass 375, 385-386, 649 NE2d 1106, 1114 (1995). See also *Com. v. Colby*, 422 Mass 414, 417-418, 663 NE2d 808, 810 (1996) (new warnings not required after defendant failed polygraph); *Com. v. Ghee*, 414 Mass 313, 317, 607 NE2d 1005, 1009 (1993) (rejecting claim that warnings given by trooper at 7:23 A.M. were not sufficient to advise defendant of his rights when other officers began questioning him at 9:00 A.M.); *Com. v. Penta*, 32 Mass App 36, 44, 586 NE2d 996, 1001 (1992) (police not required to re-advise defendant of his rights during ride in the cruiser after

---

wealth entitled to introduce transcript of tape recording of interview to rebut defendant's testimony that he had not received warnings).

arrest). Compare *Com. v. Harvey*, 390 Mass 203, 454 NE2d 105, 106 (1983) (statement suppressed where defendant was advised of his rights, declined to be questioned, and approximately eight hours later police elicited statement without re-advising him of his rights); *Com. v. Doe*, 37 Mass App 30, 35-36, 636 NE2d 308, 311 (1994) (lapse of weekend rendered warnings ineffective). As a general rule, if a valid waiver is obtained from a suspect, the police are not required to re-advise the suspect of his rights or obtain a second waiver absent a break in the interrogation, such as an exercise of the right to remain silent or to counsel, or a significant lapse of time between the waiver and the statement. *Com. v. Edwards*, 420 Mass 666, 671, 651 NE2d 398, 401 (1995).

If the suspect at any time prior to or during interrogation indicates that he does not wish to respond to questions or wishes to consult with counsel, interrogation must cease. *Miranda v. Arizona*, supra, 384 US at 473-474. The suspect has, in other words, the continuing right to cut off questioning and to consult with counsel. *Com. v. Hussey (No. 1)*, 410 Mass 664, 671, 574 NE2d 995, 999 (1991); *Com. v. Bradshaw*, 385 Mass 244, 265, 431 NE2d 880, 893 (1982). There is, however, no requirement that a suspect be specifically advised in a "fifth warning" that he could stop the questioning at any time. See *Com. v. Smith*, 426 Mass 76, 81 686 NE2d 983, 988 (1997); *Com. v. Day*, 387 Mass 915, 918 n.7, 444 NE2d 384, 385 n.7 (1983); *Com. v. Lewis*, 374 Mass 203, 371 NE2d 775 (1978) (but the better practice is to give the "fifth warning").

If the suspect wishes to cut off questioning, he must indicate this in some affirmative manner. *Miranda v. Arizona*, supra, 384 US at 473. "For the rule of *Miranda* regarding the termination of questioning to apply, there must be either an expressed unwillingness to continue or an affirmative request for an attorney." *Com. v. Pennellatore*, 392 Mass 382, 387, 467 NE2d 820, 823 (1984) (defendant's statements "I guess I'll have to have a lawyer for this" and

"Can we stop please?", when viewed in context, were not meant as assertion of right to remain silent). Compare *Com. v. Boncore*, 412 Mass 1013, 593 NE2d 227 (1992) (defendant's "No comment" and telephone call seeking his brother, an attorney, constituted invocation of right to remain silent) and *Com. v Cobb*, 374 Mass 514, 516-520, 373 NE2d 1145, 143 (1978) (defendant's responses "What can I say?" and "I have nothing to say" construed as invocation of right to remain silent) with *Com. v. James*, 427 Mass 312, 315, 693 NE2d 148, 151 (1997) (by declining to make formal statement, defendant neither terminated questioning nor invoked right to silence), *Com. v. Raymond*, 424 Mass 382, 393-394, 676 NE2d 824, 832-833 (1997) (defendant silently shaking head in response to questioning did not constitute invocation of right to silence), *Com. v. Selby*, 420 Mass 656, 660-662, 651 NE2d 843, 847 (1995) (defendant did not invoke right to silence by responding "no" to detective's question whether he had completed taped statement), *Com. v. Hussey (No. 1)*, supra, 410 Mass at 671, 574 NE2d at 999 (defendant's statement that he "had nothing else to say" after denying involvement in the robbery did not constitute expression of unwillingness to be interviewed and did not qualify as invocation of right to cut off questioning), *Com. v. Roberts*, 407 Mass 731, 733-734, 555 NE2d 588, 590 (1990) (defendant's refusal to reply to certain questions not assertion of right to remain silent), *Com. v. Mandeville*, 386 Mass 393, 402-403, 436 NE2d 912, 919 (1982) (defendant's momentary silence after receiving warnings and being asked "Do you wish to talk to us now" did not indicate desire to remain silent), *Com. v. Bradshaw*, supra, 385 Mass at 265-266, 431 NE2d at 893-894 (in context of the interrogation, suspect's "I don't want to talk" not intended to stop questioning), and *Com. v. Ewing*, 30 Mass App 285, 287, 567 NE2d 1262, 1263 (1991) (defendant's refusal to answer particular question did not constitute invocation of right to terminate questioning).

Invocation of the right to remain silent does not, however, create an impenetrable wall against further questioning. Rather, the police are permitted to resume interrogation as long as the suspect's right to silence has been "scrupulously honored." *Michigan v. Mosley*, 423 US 96 (1975). The police may not wear down the resistance of a suspect who had previously cut off questioning. See *Com. v. Atkins*, 386 Mass 593, 598, 436 NE2d 1203, 1206-1207 (1982); *Com. v. Brant*, 380 Mass 876, 406 NE2d 1021 (1980) (where law enforcement officials acted to overcome defendant's resistance to interrogation immediately after he invoked his right to silence, statement inadmissible); *Com. v. Jackson*, 377 Mass 319, 325-327, 386 NE2d 15, 19 (1979) (police persistence in questioning and use of trickery in obtaining statement despite fact that defendant twice invoked right to silence rendered statement inadmissible). Police may not deliberately elicit a statement from a suspect who has invoked his *Miranda* rights. See *Com. v. Harvey*, supra, 390 Mass at 206, 454 NE2d at 107 (statement suppressed where obtained by confronting defendant with confessed accomplice, a meeting designed to elicit an incriminating response); *Com. v. Gallant*, 381 Mass 465, 410 NE2d 704 (1980) (statement obtained by confronting defendant with his brother's inculpatory statement immediately after defendant asserted right to remain silent inadmissible). But compare *Michigan v. Mosley*, 423 US 96 (1975) (where different police officer gave renewed warnings after two-hour lapse and questioned defendant about different crime, earlier refusal to answer questions did not bar admission of the statements obtained in second interrogation); *Com. v. Williams*, 388 Mass 846, 854-855, 448 NE2d 1114, 1120-1121 (1983) (detective's questioning of other suspect in defendant's presence could not be characterized as an impermissible attempt to vitiate defendant's exercise of his *Miranda* rights).

It has been held permissible for the police, subsequent to a suspect's invocation of the right to silence, to accurately advise him of a change in circumstances (such as an accomplice's confession) "so that the suspect may make a realistic evaluation of his position." *Com. v. Jackson,* supra, 377 Mass at 327 n.7, 386 NE2d at 20 n.7. See also *Com. v. Hunt,* 12 Mass App 841, 844 n.4, 429 NE2d 379, 380-381 n.4 (1981) (citing cases permitting truthful advice regarding release of relative if confession is made).

If the suspect invokes his right to counsel, an additional safeguard applies — interrogation must cease until an attorney is present (or, as discussed below, the suspect himself initiates further communication). *Edwards v. Arizona,* 451 US 477, 101 S Ct 1880, 68 L Ed 2d 378 (1981); *Miranda v. Arizona,* supra, 384 US at 474; *Com. v. Brant,* supra, 380 Mass at 882, 406 NE2d at 1025-1026; *Com. v. Watkins,* 375 Mass 472, 483-484, 379 NE2d 1040, 1047-1048 (1978) (but rejecting argument that *Miranda* prohibits *any* interrogation after suspect requests an attorney); *Com. v. D'Entremont,* 36 Mass App 474, 478, 632 NE2d 1239 (1994). Merely providing the suspect with an opportunity to consult with counsel outside the interrogation room is not sufficient; the accused is entitled to have counsel present during questioning. See *Minnick v. Mississippi,* 498 US 146 (1990).

As with the right to remain silent, the suspect must make some affirmative statement that can reasonably be construed as a request for counsel; an ambiguous or equivocal reference to an attorney does not require cessation of questioning. *Davis v. United States,* 512 US 452, 114 S Ct 2350, 129 L Ed 2d 362 (1994) (suspect's remark "maybe I should talk to a lawyer" not request for counsel). Compare *Com. v. Hussey (No. 1),* supra, 410 Mass at 672, 574 NE2d at 999 (defendant did not invoke right to counsel when he unsuccessfully sought to reach his attorney by telephone and then said "I'm not going to wait. All right. I'll tell you what happened."), *Com. v. Todd,* 408 Mass 724, 726-727, 563 NE2d 211, 213 (1990) (defendant "wondered aloud about the advisability of having a lawyer" but made no affirmative request), and *Com. v. Corriveau,* 396 Mass 319, 331, 486 NE2d 29, 38 (1985) (defendant's statement, "It's beginning to sound like I need a lawyer" did not constitute request for counsel) with *Com. v. Judge,* 420 Mass 433, 450, 650 NE2d

1242, 1252-1253 (1995) (defendant's initial request that his uncle, an attorney, be called sufficient to invoke right to counsel despite fact that defendant continued to talk to police).

Once the right to counsel is invoked and questioning is thus terminated, interrogation may be resumed in the absence of counsel only if the suspect himself initiates further communication with the police. *Edwards v. Arizona,* 451 US 477 (1981); *Solem v. Stumes,* 465 US 638 (1984); *Com. v. Perez,* supra, 411 Mass at 256-259, 581 NE2d at 1015-1017 (general discussion of *Edwards* rule). This constraint upon further interrogation applies even if the resumed questioning concerns an unrelated offense. See *Arizona v. Roberson,* 486 US 675 (1988). Fresh warnings and evidence of voluntariness are not sufficient to overcome the presumption that any subsequent waiver in the absence of counsel is invalid. *Edwards v. Arizona,* supra, 451 US at 484-487; *Com. v. Perez,* supra, 411 Mass at 257, 581 NE2d at 1015-1016. The purpose of the *Edwards* rule is to protect the suspect from being worn down in his effort to obtain the assistance of counsel. *Minnick v. Mississippi,* supra, 498 US at 150-151; *Com. v. Perez,* supra, 411 Mass at 257-258, 581 NE2d at 1015-1016. It has been recognized that enforcement of this purpose requires a bright line rule: when the suspect asks for a lawyer, discussion of the charge should cease unless the suspect later clearly indicates a change of mind (explicitly or by conduct). See *Com. v. Perez,* supra, 411 Mass at 258, 581 NE2d at 1016; *Com. v. Chadwick,* 40 Mass App 425, 429, 664 NE2d 874, 876 (1996).

The *Edwards* rule indefinitely terminating questioning applies only where there is continuous custody of the suspect. When there is a break in custody, *Edwards* does not require the exclusion of a subsequent statement even in the absence of counsel. *Com. v. Galford,* 413 Mass 364, 370, 597 NE2d 410, 414 (1992) (defendant released after first interview). Where custody is continuous, however, even a lapse of six months between termination of the initial interrogation and the subsequent questioning cannot justify a violation of *Edwards*. See *Com. v. Perez*, supra, 411 Mass at 258, 581 NE2d at 1016.

As noted above, interrogation may resume after invocation of the right to counsel where the suspect himself initiates communication. For cases defining "initiation" in this context, see *Oregon v. Bradshaw*, 462 US 1039, 103 S Ct 2830, 77 L Ed 2d 405 (1983) (although questions relating to routine incidents of custody do not constitute "initiation," suspect's question "What is going to happen to me now?" evidenced desire for further discussion about investigation, thus permitting interrogation to resume); *Com. v. Phinney*, 416 Mass 364, 371, 622 NE2d 617, 622 (1993) (suspect initiated further conversation by asking "What's going to happen to me next?"); *Com. v. Richmond*, 379 Mass 557, 560, 399 NE2d 1069, 1072 (1980) (police could resume interrogation after defendant questioned police as to details of crime); *Com. v. Watkins*, supra, 375 Mass at 484-485, 379 NE2d at 1048-1049 (police could resume questioning after defendant's spontaneous declaration of his desire to make further statement); *Com. v. D'Entremont*, supra, 36 Mass App at 480 (defendant's statement that he wanted to tell his side of story constituted "initiation"). See also *Com. v. Nom*, 426 Mass 152, 156-158, 686 NE2d 1017, 1022 (1997) (officer's asking defendant why he wanted attorney was not re-interrogation, but only request for clarification regarding defendant's initiation of conversation).

The Commonwealth has the burden of proving beyond a reasonable doubt that a defendant who has earlier invoked his right to counsel has nonetheless decided independently to confess without an attorney. *Com. v. Judge*, supra, 420 Mass at 450-451, 650 NE2d at 1253.

Neither a request to consult with a probation officer, see *Fare v. Michael C.*, 442 US 707, 99 S Ct 2560, 61 L Ed 2d 197 (1979), nor a family member, see *Com. v. Bradshaw*, 385 Mass 244, 263-264, 431 NE2d 880, 893 (1982) and *Com. v. Carey*, 26 Mass App 339, 343, 526 NE2d 1329, 1332 (1988), constitutes a request for counsel for purposes of cutting off questioning. See also *Com. v. Jackson*, supra, 377 Mass at 322 n.4, 386 NE2d at 17 n.4 (leaving open question whether request to see parole officer constitutes invocation of rights). There is no constitutional right to have a family member present during custodial interrogation. *Com. v. Bradshaw*, supra, 385 Mass at 264, 431 NE2d at 893.

A person subjected to custodial interrogation is entitled to the benefit of the *Miranda* safeguards regardless of the nature or severity of the offense of which he is suspected or for which he was arrested. *Berkemer v. McCarty*, 468 US 420, 434 (1984) (misdemeanor traffic offense); *Com. v. Brennan*, 386 Mass 772, 438 NE2d 60 (1982) (driving under the influence charge).

The silence of the defendant following *Miranda* warnings may not be used against him at trial. See §9.7.8.

§9.7.2   *Custody*

Custodial interrogation, the event that triggers the *Miranda* protections, is defined as "questioning initiated by law enforcement officers after a person has been taken into custody or otherwise deprived of his freedom of action in any significant way." *Miranda v. Arizona*, 384 US 436, 443 (1966). A person is in "custody" if he is under formal arrest or subject to a "restraint on freedom of movement of the degree associated with a formal arrest." *Thompson v. Keohane*, 516 US 99, 112, 116 S Ct 457 (1995); *New York v. Quarles*, 467 US 649 (1984); *Minnesota v. Murphy*, 465 US 420, 430 (1984). Any formal distinction between "arrest" and "detention" becomes immaterial in light of this definition. See, e.g., *Com. v. Garcia*, 379 Mass 422, 427, 399 NE2d 460, 464 (1980) (defendant was in custody from time police placed him in cruiser because from that moment he was not free to leave).

There is no specific formulation on which courts can rely in determining whether a person's freedom of action is sufficiently curtailed so as to require the *Miranda* warnings. *Com. v. Haas*, 373 Mass 545, 552, 369 NE2d 692, 698 (1977). Rather, the test is how a reasonable person in the defendant's position would have understood his situation. *Com. v. A Juvenile*, 402 Mass 275, 277, 521 NE2d 1368, 1370 (1988) (& citations). The court in *Com. v. Bryant*, 390 Mass 729, 737, 459 NE2d 792, 798 (1984) set forth four indicia of custody:

1.   The place of the interrogation.
2.   Whether the investigation has begun to focus on the suspect, including whether there is probable cause to arrest the suspect.
3.   The nature of the interrogation, including whether the interview was aggressive or, instead, informal and influenced in its contours by the suspect.
4.   Whether, at the time the incriminating statement was made, the suspect was free to end the interview by leaving the locus of the interrogation or by asking the interrogator to leave, as evidenced by whether the interview terminated with the defendant's arrest.

See also *Com. v. Vinnie*, 428 Mass 161, 170-171, 698 NE2d 896, 905 (1998); *Com. v. Morse*, 427 Mass 117, 121-122, 691 NE2d 566, 569-570 (1998); *Com. v. Jung*, 420 Mass 675, 688, 651 NE2d 1211, 1220 (1995); *Com. v. Haas*, supra, 373 Mass at 552, 369 NE2d at 698; *Com. v. Gallati*, 40 Mass App 111, 661 NE2d 948 (1996); *Com. v. King*, 33 Mass App 905, 906, 595 NE2d 795, 796-797 (1992).

The fact that the investigation has begun to focus on the defendant is not, in itself, sufficient to trigger the *Miranda* protections. *Beckwith v. United States*, 425 US 341, 345-347, 96 S Ct 1612, 48 L Ed 2d 1 (1976); *United States v. Ventura*, 85 F3d 708, 712 (1st Cir 1996); *Com. v. Vinnie*, supra, 428 Mass at 171, 698 NE2d at 905; *Com. v. Jung*, supra, 420 Mass at 689, 651 NE2d at 1220; *Com. v. Phinney*,

416 Mass 364, 370, 622 NE2d 617, 621 (1993); *Com. v. Tart,* 408 Mass 249, 259, 557 NE2d 1123, 1131 (1990) (& citation); *Com. v. Azar,* 32 Mass App 290, 297, 588 NE2d 1352, 1357-1358 (1992). The duration of the questioning is not determinative. *Com. v. Comolli,* 14 Mass App 607, 610-611, 441 NE2d 536, 539 (1982) (interrogation of defendant at scene of accident not necessarily custodial even though defendant was questioned in police cruiser for over an hour); *Com. v. Doyle,* 12 Mass App 786, 794 n.2, 429 NE2d 346, 351 n.2 (1981). Nor does an interrogation become custodial simply because a suspect's voluntary statements give the police probable cause to arrest, unless the police do in fact arrest the suspect or the suspect reasonably believes himself to be restrained. *Com. v. Bryant,* supra, 390 Mass at 738-739, 549 NE2d at 799 (interrogation did not become custodial where, after suspect stated, "I did it, I shot him," officer made non-accusatorial inquiry as to whether the suspect had anything more to say). The non-arrest of the suspect at the close of the interrogation is indicative of the lack of custodial atmosphere during interrogation. *Com. v. Bryant,* supra, 390 Mass at 742 n.15, 459 NE2d at 800 (& citations).

The issue of whether an interrogation has occurred in custodial circumstances "is a vexing one, susceptible to resolution in most instances only by close scrutiny of the particular questioning session." *Com. v. Bryant,* supra, 390 Mass at 736, 459 NE2d at 797. "The difficulties inherent in determining whether a given confrontation between suspect and police is appropriately characterized as custodial derive from the necessity of answering what is essentially a subjective inquiry—whether, from the point of view of the person being questioned, the interrogation took place in a coercive environment—by reference to objective indicia." Id.

The courts apply an objective standard of "custody," *Com. v. Bryant,* supra, 390 Mass at 739 n.11, 459 NE2d at 799 n.11, in which the ultimate issue is whether a reasonable person in the position of the person being questioned would not feel free to leave the place of questioning. *Com. v. Larkin,* 429 Mass 426, 432, 708 NE2d 674, 679 (1999) (& citations); *Com. v. Morse,* supra, 427 Mass at 124-125, 691 NE2d at 571-572 (& citations) (officer's pointing out inconsistency between defendant's and witness's statements would not suggest to reasonable person that he was not free to leave). Thus, although the police officer may have had an intent to restrain the suspect, this does not enter into the "custody" determination unless it is communicated to the suspect. *Stansbury v. California,* 511 U.S. 318, 323, 114 S Ct 1526 (1994); *Com. v. Bryant,* supra; *Com. v. Morse,* supra, 427 Mass at 123-124, 691 NE2d at 570-571; *Com. v. Cameron,* 44 Mass App 912, 689 NE2d 1365 (1998) (officer formed opinion that motorist was intoxicated, but did not communicate it to him). Similarly, the issue is not how the defendant actually felt, but whether there were "objective features of the interrogation that would reasonably lead the defendant to believe that his freedom of action had been curtailed. To emphasize a defendant's purely subjective feelings about 'custody,' without considering the reasonableness of those feelings, would allow issues to turn not on the objective circumstances of the questioning, but on the personal idiosyncracies that are neither within the control of, nor necessarily observable by, investigating personnel. The law imposes no burden on the police to divine a suspect's subjective impressions." *Com. v. Comolli,* supra, 14 Mass App at 611-612, 441 NE2d at 539-540 (citations omitted).

Custodial interrogation may occur anywhere — one need not be in a police station to be deemed in custody. See, e.g., *Orozco v. Texas,* 394 US 324 (1969) (suspect in custody when interrogated by four officers in his bedroom). But compare *Beckwith v. United States,* supra, 425 US 341 (defendant not in custody when questioned at home by special agents of IRS conducting criminal investigation); *Com. v. Eagles,* 419 Mass 825, 832-833, 648 NE2d 410, 416 (1995) (defendant not in custody at residence); *Breese v. Com.,* 415 Mass 249, 255-256, 612 NE2d 1170, 1173-1174

(1993) (no custody where defendant was questioned in familiar surroundings of home and workplace); *Com. v. Tart*, supra, 408 Mass at 258, 557 NE2d at 1131 (no custody where defendant was questioned on board his own fishing vessel surrounded by his employees); *Com. v. Bryant*, supra, 390 Mass at 737-738, 459 NE2d at 797-798 (no custodial interrogation where confession occurred during friendly chat in defendant's home with defendant's acquiescence); *Com. v. McNelley*, 28 Mass App 985, 554 NE2d 37 (1990) (no custody where defendant was interviewed outside his van on the road).

Conversely, the fact that the interrogation occurs in a police station does not in itself establish it as "custodial." See, e.g., *California v. Beheler*, 463 US 1121 (1983) (suspect, informed he was not under arrest, agreed to accompany police to station for questioning); *Oregon v. Mathiason*, 429 US 492 (1977) (suspect reported to station voluntarily at officer's request, was informed he was not under arrest, and was not restricted in his freedom to depart); *Com. v. Osachuk*, 418 Mass 229, 234-235, 635 NE2d 1192, 1195 (1995) (although in police interview room, defendant was free to leave); *Com. v. Mayfield*, 398 Mass 615, 626-627, 500 NE2d 774, 781-782 (1986) (defendant, one of several suspects, went to the police station voluntarily by prearrangement, was told he was free to leave an any time, and did leave at the end of the interrogation session); *Com. v. Gil*, 393 Mass 204, 212, 471 NE2d 30 (1984) (questioning of defendant at police station concerning homicide of defendant's estranged wife and boyfriend noncustodial until officer observed that pattern on soles of defendant's shoes matched footprints at murder scene); *Com. v. Sim*, 39 Mass App 212, 220-221, 654 NE2d 340, 345 (1995) (defendant came willingly to police station, was allowed to roam about, and was not told he was required to stay); *Com. v. Wallen*, 35 Mass App 915, 619 NE2d 365 (1993) (no indication defendant's presence at police station to give his version of events was not voluntary); *Com. v. Greenberg*, 34 Mass App 197, 200-201,

609 NE2d 90, 92-93 (1993) (juvenile defendant not in custody when, at police request, he and his father drove to police station and he was questioned, with father present, for one hour, but not arrested until four days later); *Com. v. Azar*, supra, 32 Mass App at 297, 588 NE2d at 1357 (defendant agreed to go to police station for further questioning); *Com. v. Comolli*, supra, 14 Mass at 610, 441 NE2d at 539 (use of police premises such as a cruiser for questioning does not necessarily imply custodial interrogation). See also *Minnesota v. Murphy*, supra, 465 US at 430-434 (probationer appearing for required appearance before probation officer not "in custody" for purposes of *Miranda* protections).

A suspect incarcerated on an unrelated charge has been held not to be in custody where he would not reasonably feel himself confined beyond the usual constraints of prison life. See *Com. v. Larkin*, supra, 429 Mass at 434-436, 708 NE2d 680-681 (& citations) (defendant told he did not have to meet with troopers, they met in lawyer's interview room, and defendant was free to end interview at any time).

Because of its noncustodial nature, "on the scene questioning" does not generally require warnings. *Miranda v. Arizona*, supra, 384 US at 477; *Com. v. Callahan*, 401 Mass 627, 630, 519 NE2d 245, 247 (1988) (police officer's "What happened?" question at homicide scene); *Com. v. Podlaski*, 377 Mass 339, 342-343, 385 NE2d 1379, 1382-1383 (1979) (preliminary inquiry to defendant aimed at discovering what he knew about the circumstances of the assault); *Com. v. Merritt*, supra, 14 Mass App at 604, 441 NE2d at 534 (investigating officer went to defendant's home after accident and asked defendant outside building whether he had been operator of vehicle involved).

Roadside questioning of a motorist during a routine traffic stop has similarly been viewed as noncustodial (although subsequent events may render the motorist "in custody"). See *Berkemer v. McCarthy*, 468 US 420, 435-442, 104 S Ct 3138, 82 L Ed 2d 317 (1984). *Com. v. Smith*, 35 Mass App 655, 657, 624 NE2d 604, 606 (1993) ("when a police officer makes a motor vehicle pull over, the driver is not free to move away, but it would surely be untoward to require that a police officer approach a stopped vehicle declaiming the Miranda warnings"); *Com. v. Cameron,* supra, 44 Mass App at 913-914, 689 NE2d at 1367-1368 (*Miranda* warnings not required during temporary detention, questioning, and field sobriety tests). But see *Com. v. Torres,* 424 Mass 153, 158, 674 NE2d 638, 642 (1997) and *Com. v. Bartlett,* 41 Mass App 468, 671 NE2d 515 (1996) (police inquiry in routine traffic stop must end on production of valid license and registration unless police have reasonable suspicion of crime).

Roadside sobriety tests have been held to be noncustodial and thus not subject to *Miranda. Pennsylvania v. Bruder,* 488 US 9, 109 S Ct 205 (1988); *Vanhouten v. Com.,* 424 Mass 327, 331-332, 676 NE2d 460, 463-464 (1997) (recitation of alphabet); *Com. v. Cameron,* supra, 44 Mass App at 913-914, 689 NE2d at 1367-1368; *Com. v. D'Agostino,* 38 Mass App 206, 646 NE2d 767 (1995). Moreover, since such tests seek physical and not testimonial evidence, they do not trigger the Fifth Amendment privilege against self-incrimination. *Com. v. Cameron,* supra, 44 Mass App at 913, 689 NE2d at 1367 (& citations). When a suspect is asked for a response requiring him to communicate a fact or belief, such as being asked when his sixth birthday is, there is a testimonial dimension to the response which may implicate the privilege. See *Com. v. Ayre,* 31 Mass App 17, 21 & n.8, 574 NE2d 415, 418 & n.8 (1991) (citing *Pennsylvania v. Muniz,* 496 US 582, 592-600 (1990)).

For cases applying the *Miranda* principles to motor vehicle accident scenes, see *Com. v. Seymour,* 39 Mass App 672, 679-680, 660 NE2d 679, 683 (1996) (fact that police officer observed defendant smelled of alcohol made her focal point of investigation, but did not transform encounter into custodial interrogation); *Com. v. Smith,* supra, 35 Mass App at 657-658 (in case of motor vehicle accidents, some preliminary questions are permissible without warnings to enable police to orient themselves); *Com. v. Merritt,* supra, 14 Mass App at 604-605, 441 NE2d at 535 (because immediate investigative goal is usually to determine whether crime was committed, limited preliminary questioning is not subject to *Miranda*); *Com. v. Comolli*, supra, 14 Mass App at 610-613, 441 NE2d at 539; *Com. v. Doyle*, supra, 12 Mass App at 793-794, 429 NE2d at 351 (questions posed to defendant at hospital and on way to police station designed to obtain preliminary investigative information about fatal accident and did not constitute custodial interrogation).

"Drawing the line between custodial interrogation and general investigative questioning has not been an easy task for the courts." *Com. v. Doyle*, supra, 12 Mass App 792, 429 NE2d at 350. The Supreme Court has provided the following guidance:

> Any interview of one suspected of a crime by a police officer will have coercive aspects to it, simply by virtue of the fact that the police officer is part of a law enforcement system which may ultimately cause the suspect to be charged with a crime. But police officers are not required to administer *Miranda* warnings to everyone whom they question. Nor is the requirement of warnings to be imposed simply because the questioning takes place in the station house, or because the questioned person is one whom the police suspect. *Miranda* warnings are required only where there has been such a restriction on a person's freedom as to render him "in custody." It was *that* sort of coercive environment to which *Miranda* by its terms was made applicable, and to which it is limited.

Oregon v. Mathiason, supra, 429 US at 495.

The imparting of *Miranda* warnings does not itself transform a noncustodial situation into a custodial one. See *Com. v. Lawrence*, 404 Mass 378, 386, 536 NE2d 571, 577 (1989); *Com. v. Parker*, 402 Mass 333, 339 n.2, 522 NE2d 924, 928 n.2 (1988) *(Parker I)*. While not constitutionally required, it is the suggested practice to inform a suspect explicitly of the change of his condition from noncustodial to custodial. *Com. v. Alicea*, 376 Mass 506, 514, 381 NE2d 144, 150 (1978). See also *Com. v. Cruz*, 373 Mass 676, 686-687, 369 NE2d 996, 1003 (1977) (rejecting defendant's assertion that he was not aware of the change in his status from noncustodial to custodial).

For a sampling of cases dealing with the issue of custodial status, compare *Com. v. Jung*, supra, 420 Mass at 688-689, 651 NE2d at 1219-1220 (although investigation focused solely on defendants, interrogation was noncustodial because not conducted in aggressive manner, suspects went to police station voluntarily, were free to leave at any time, and were not arrested at end of interview), *Com. v. Nadworny*, 396 Mass 342, 367-369, 486 NE2d 675, 690-691 (1985) (neither statements made to police officer over telephone, nor conversation at defendant's family home, were custodial), *Com. v. Martinez*, 393 Mass 612, 615, 473 NE2d 167, 168-169 (1985) (defendant's statement, overheard by police officer while she was not in custody and not the product of police questioning, was admissible without proof of warnings), *Com. v. Accaputo*, 380 Mass 435, 451-452, 404 NE2d 1204, 1214 (1980) (questioning at defendant's place of business in presence of his employees and occasional customers not custodial), *Com. v. Alicea*, supra, 376 Mass at 513-514, 381 NE2d at 149-150 (defendant not in custody while taken in cruiser to police station as possible witness; custody began when defendant was identified at station as culprit and placed in handcuffs), and *Com. v. Borodine*, 371 Mass 1, 4-5, 353 NE2d 649, 653 (1976) (defendant not in custody while questioned in basement where homicide had just occurred) with *Estelle v. Smith*, 451 US 454, 466-469, 101 S Ct 1866, 68 L Ed 2d 359 (1981) (pretrial court-ordered psychiatric examination constituted custodial interrogation and thus required warnings), *Com. v. Damiano*, 422 Mass 10, 660 NE2d 660 (1996) (defendant in custody while handcuffed in back seat of cruiser; fact that police asserted defendant was not under arrest but in protective custody is not controlling where reasonable person would have believed he was not free to leave), *Com. v. A Juvenile*, 402 Mass 275, 277-278, 521 NE2d 1368, 1370 (1988) (confession made by juvenile in detention facility to assistant director custodial), *Com. v. Cruz*, supra, 373 Mass at 682-684; 369 NE2d at 1001 (defendant voluntarily accompanied police to station for questioning, but after one hour of questioning he was no longer free to leave and thus in custody), and *Com. v. Gallati*, 40 Mass App 111, 661 NE2d 948 (1996) (defendant correctional officer in custody even though not under arrest when questioned by superior in his office, investigation had focused on him, and questioning was domineering and relentless).

§9.7.3   Interrogation

In addition to "custody" there must also be "interrogation" before the *Miranda* doctrine is applicable. Spontaneous, unsolicited statements or confessions do not come within *Miranda* even if the defendant is in custody at the time such statements are made. See *Com. v. Woods*, 427 Mass 169, 173, 693 NE2d 123, 125 (1998); *Com. v. Smallwood*, 379 Mass 878, 885-887, 401 NE2d 802, 807-808 (1980); *Com. v. O'Brien*, 377 Mass 772, 776, 388 NE2d 658, 661 (1979); *Com. v. Goulet*, 374 Mass 404, 417, 372 NE2d 1288, 1297 (1978) (defendant blurted out incriminating words in midst of *Miranda* warnings); *Com. v. Frongillo*, 359 Mass 132, 135-136, 268 NE2d 341, 343 (1971) (statement volunteered as arresting officer was passing defendant's jail cell); *Com. v. Mitchell*, 35 Mass App 909, 619 NE2d 619 (1993); *Com. v. King*, 17 Mass App 602, 607-608, 460 NE2d 1299, 1302, 1303 (1984) (defendant exclaimed, "I did it. I did it. I raped that girl and I need help." upon completion of booking procedure). See also *Com. v. Delrio*, 22 Mass App 712, 717-718, 497 NE2d 1097, 1100 (1986) (where there is a factual dispute as to whether defendant's statement was spontaneous or in response to question by police, judge is required to hold voir dire).

"Interrogation" occurs when law enforcement officers subject a person to either express questioning or its functional equivalent — i.e., words or actions (other than those normally attendant to arrest and custody) that the police should have known were reasonably likely to elicit an incriminating response from the suspect, given their knowledge of his susceptibility to particular forms of persuasion. *Rhode Island v. Innis*, 446 US 291, 100 S Ct 1682, 64 L Ed 2d 297 (1980) (no "interrogation" where police could not reasonably have expected conversation concerning possibility of handicapped children finding hidden shotgun to elicit incriminating statement). Compare *Com. v. Rubio*, 27 Mass App 506, 511-512, 540 NE2d 189, 192-193 (1989) (defendant subjected to "interrogation" when officer showed him cocaine found during the search of apartment: "Showing the cocaine in the pocketbook to the defendant in this setting was clearly confrontational and had the force of an implicit question: 'Is this yours?'") and *Com. v. Chadwick*, 40 Mass App 425, 427-429, 664 NE2d 874, 876 (1996) (police officer's unsolicited explanation of rape constituted impermissible interrogation) with *Com. v. Harkess*, 35 Mass App 626, 632, 624 NE2d 581, 585 (1993) (defendant's statement not product of questioning where police officer handled gun merely as piece of evidence collected at scene, and not as accusatory police question: "How do you explain this?") and *Com. v. Rogers*, 38 Mass App 395, 406-407, 647 NE2d 1228, 1234 (1995) (second fingerprinting of defendant not functional equivalent of questioning). The police are not expected to be clairvoyant in predicting a defendant's response to their words or conduct. See *Com. v. King*, supra, 17 Mass App at 608-609, 460 NE2d at 1304 (no interrogation where officer, at defendant's request, showed him arrest warrant).

Courts evaluate both the perceptions of the suspect as to whether he is being subjected to coercive pressures, and the conduct of the police as to the use of compelling influences or psychological ploys. See *Arizona v. Mauro*, 481 US

520, 528, 107 S Ct 1931, 95 L Ed 2d 458 (1987) (no "interrogation" where police permitted defendant and his wife, both suspects in murder of their child, to speak together in presence of officer and tape recorder); *Illinois v. Perkins*, 496 US 292, 110 S Ct 2394 (1990) (no "interrogation" where suspect made incriminating statements in conversation with undercover agent placed in jail cell).

The test for determining the functional equivalent of interrogation can be stated as follows: if an objective observer (with the same knowledge of the suspect as the police officer) would conclude that the officer's speech or conduct was designed to elicit an incriminating response, interrogation occurred. *Com. v. Rubio*, supra, 27 Mass App at 512, 540 NE2d at 193 (citation omitted). As an objective test, the intent of the officers to elicit an incriminating statement is not conclusive, but certainly bears on whether the officers should have known that their words and actions were likely to evoke an incriminating response. See *Com. v. Brant*, 380 Mass 876, 883, 406 NE2d 1021, 1026-1027 (1980) (defendant "interrogated" where officer informed him confederate had already made statement and allowed defendant to confer with confederate); *Com. v. Harvey*, 390 Mass 203, 206, 454 NE2d 105, 106-107 (1983) (statement suppressed where obtained by confronting defendant with confessed accomplice, designed to elicit incriminating response). Compare *Com. v. Williams*, 388 Mass 846, 854-855, 448 NE2d 114, 1120-1121 (1983) (no evidence that interrogation of another suspect in presence of defendant was designed to, or had the effect of, eliciting incriminating response); *Com. v. Chipman*, 418 Mass 262, 273, 635 NE2d 1204, 1211 (1994) (no indication that police responses to defendant's questions designed to elicit inculpatory comments); *Com. v. D'Entremont*, 36 Mass App 474, 478-480, 632 NE2d 1239 (1994) (detective's statement to defendant that if he changed his mind she would be willing to speak with him did not constitute interrogation); *Com. v. Mitchell*, supra, 35 Mass App at 910-911 (no evidence suggesting that conversation among officers in booking room was an ingenious contrivance to make defendant utter incriminating statement).

In sum, the intent of the police is not entirely irrelevant, because it bears on whether they should have known their words or actions were likely to elicit an incriminating response; but awareness of the possibility of eliciting an incriminating statement is itself insufficient to establish the functional equivalent of interrogation. *Com. v. Torres*, 424 Mass 792, 796-797, 678 NE2d 847, 850-851 (1997). Conversely, testimony from the officers that they had *not* expected their conversations to elicit incriminating responses is entitled to some weight. *Com. v. Messere*, 14 Mass App 1, 8 n.5, 436 NE2d 414, 418 n.5 (1982).

Where the suspect waives his *Miranda* rights (see §9.7.4, infra) and indicates a willingness to talk to the police, there is no bar to interrogation and it is not improper for the police "to attempt, within proper bounds, to elicit a confession from the defendant." See *Com. v. MacKenzie*, 413 Mass 498, 512-513, 597 NE2d 1037, 1046 (1992).

Miranda warnings are not required prior to routine booking questions regarding the arrestee's name, address, and related matters. *Pennsylvania v. Muniz*, 496 US 582, 110 S Ct 2638 (1990); *Com. v. Mahoney*, 400 Mass 524, 528-529, 510 NE2d 759, 762-763 (1987) (videotape recording of defendant made during booking procedure properly admitted despite lack of *Miranda* warnings because questions were normally attendant to arrest and custody); *Com. v. Kacavich*, 28 Mass App 941, 550 NE2d 397 (1990) (& cases collected). See also *Com. v. White*, 422 Mass 487, 501-503, 663 NE2d 834, 844-845 (1996) (defendant's statement of telephone number he wished to call not result of custodial interrogation).

Where, however, an arrestee's employment status may prove incriminatory, the police must give *Miranda* warnings before asking booking questions about employment. See

Com. v. Woods, 419 Mass 366, 372-374, 645 NE2d 1153, 1157 (1995); *Com. v. Guerrero,* 32 Mass App 263, 266-269, 588 NE2d 716, 718-719 (1992). See also *Com. v. Acosta,* 416 Mass 279, 283-284, 620 NE2d 780 (1993) (suggesting a broader prohibition might be derived from art. 12 of state constitution for incriminatory evidence obtained by compulsion in response to booking questions); *Com. v. Sheriff,* 425 Mass 186, 198-199, 680 NE2d 75, 82-83 (1997) (suggesting that questions to ascertain whether defendant is aware of his surroundings may be in same category as booking questions).

Interrogation by a private person acting as an instrument or agent of the police has been held to trigger the *Miranda* protections. See *Com. v. A Juvenile,* 402 Mass 275, 278, 521 NE2d 1368, 1370 (1988) (& citations) (assistant director at youth detention facility). Compare *Com. v. Snyder,* 413 Mass 521, 530-532, 597 NE2d 1363, 1368-1369 (1992) (*Miranda* inapplicable where school principal, not acting on behalf of law enforcement officials, questioned student in her office); *Com. v. Sanchez,* 405 Mass 369, 378 n.6, 540 NE2d 1316, 1322 (1989) (no *Miranda* waiver required where information obtained by county nurse acting as private citizen conducting routine medical inquiry); *Com. v. Tynes,* 400 Mass 369, 372-374, 510 NE2d 244, 246-247 (1987) (*Miranda* did not apply where un-uniformed, off-duty police officers directed questions to stopped motorist); *Com. v. Rancourt,* 399 Mass 269, 271-275, 503 NE2d 960, 962-965 (1987) (fellow inmate acted as private party and not government agent when he induced defendant to write letter describing the details of crime); *Com. v. Allen,* 395 Mass 448, 453-454, 480 NE2d 630, 635 (1985) (hospital nurse not acting as agent of police when questioning patient even though officer was present and did nothing to stop the questioning). The fact that the private party had every intention of providing the police with evidence does not make her an agent or instrument of the police. *Com. v. Snyder,* supra, 413 Mass at 532, 597 NE2d at 1369.

§9.7.4   Waiver

a.   Standards and Burden of Proof

If a statement is obtained from a suspect during custodial interrogation, the statement may be admitted at trial only if the prosecution demonstrates that the warnings and procedures required by *Miranda* were "scrupulously observed," and that the suspect "knowingly, intelligently and voluntarily" waived his or her privilege against self-incrimination and right to counsel. *Com. v. Corriveau*, 396 Mass 319, 330, 486 NE2d 29, 37-38 (1985). There can be no valid waiver in the absence of adequate warnings. *Com. v. Adams*, 389 Mass 265, 270, 450 NE2d 149, 152 (1983).

Because courts indulge every reasonable presumption against waiver of fundamental constitutional rights (see *Johnson v. Zerbst*, 304 US 458, 464, 58 S Ct 1019, 1023, 82 L Ed 2d 1461, 1466 (1938)), the Commonwealth has a "heavy burden" in demonstrating such waiver. *Miranda v. Arizona*, 384 US 436, 475, 86 S Ct 1602, 16 L Ed 2d 694 (1966); *Com. v. Taylor*, 398 Mass 725, 728, 500 NE2d 799, 801 (1986); *Com. v. Forde*, 392 Mass 453, 454, 466 NE2d 510, 512 (1984); *Com. v. Coplin*, 34 Mass App 478, 482, 612 NE2d 1188, 1190 (1993).

As a matter of Massachusetts practice, the Commonwealth must prove a knowing, intelligent, and voluntary waiver beyond a reasonable doubt. See *Com. v. Judge*, 420 Mass 433, 447, 650 NE2d 1242, 1251 (1995); *Com. v. Day*, 387 Mass 915, 920-921, 444 NE2d 384, 387 (1983). Compare *Colorado v. Connelly*, 479 US 157, 107 S Ct 515, 93 L Ed 2d 473 (1986) (under federal standard, waiver need be proven only by a preponderance of the evidence). While a written waiver of *Miranda* rights is some evidence of voluntariness, it is not dispositive; the court must still analyze the totality of the circumstances. See *Com. v. Magee*, 423 Mass 381, 387 n.8, 668 NE2d 339, 344 n.8 (1996).

There is no rule requiring that a waiver be made expressly in writing or orally. Rather a waiver may be found even in the absence of an explicit statement to that effect; it may be inferred from the suspect's words and actions. See *North Carolina v. Butler*, 441 US 369, 99 S Ct 1755, 60 L Ed 2d 286 (1979); *Com. v. Corriveau*, supra, 396 Mass at 330, 486 NE2d at 38 (waiver established where officer, after informing defendant of rights, asked him whether he understood them and defendant, an experienced and well-educated businessman, responded affirmatively). While mere silence in response to the warnings is not sufficient to establish a waiver, "the defendant's silence, coupled with an understanding of his rights and a course of conduct indicating waiver" may suffice. *North Carolina v. Butler*, supra, 441 US at 374 (defendant refused to sign waiver form but agreed to talk about the robbery being investigated). Compare *Com. v. Watkins*, 375 Mass 472, 484-485, 379 NE2d 1040, 1048-1049 (1978) (defendant's spontaneous declaration of desire to make statement constituted implied waiver of previously claimed desire to speak with counsel) with *Com. v. Cain*, 361 Mass 224, 228-229, 279 NE2d 706, 709 (1972) (mere fact that minor defendant made statement after acknowledging rights does not establish waiver).

Whether express or implied, a waiver must be shown to have been "knowing, intelligent and voluntary." The judge is not required to submit to the jury the question of the validity of a waiver of *Miranda* rights apart from the over-all determination of voluntariness discussed in §9.2. *Com. v. Tavares*, 385 Mass 140, 153 n.19, 430 NE2d 1198, 1206 n.19 (1982); *Com. v. Day*, supra, 387 Mass at 923, 444 NE2d at 388. Compliance with *Miranda* is a prerequisite for admissibility and is a question of law for the judge. *Com. v. Tavares*, supra; *Com. v. Todd*, 408 Mass 724, 727, 563 NE2d 211, 213 (1990). But see *Com. v. Chung*, 378 Mass 451, 458-460, 392 NE2d 1015, 1019-1029 (1979) (where there was credible evidence that defendant was insane at time he made confession, judge erred in failing to adequately instruct jury that knowing, intelligent, and voluntary waiver is prerequisite to questioning). See also *Com. v. Cole*, 380 Mass 30, 41-42 & n.14, 402 NE2d 55, 63 & n.14 (1980) (leaving open question whether jury should be given limiting instructions when defendant's responses to *Miranda* warnings are admitted in evidence).

b. Knowing, Intelligent, and Voluntary

Waiver requires both comprehension of the rights involved and voluntary relinquishment of them. *Com. v. Dustin*, 373 Mass 612, 615, 368 NE2d 1388, 1391 (1977). As the Supreme Court has explained:

> First, the relinquishment of the right must have been voluntary in the sense that it was the product of a free and deliberate choice rather than intimidation, coercion, or deception. Second, the waiver must have been made with a full awareness of both the nature of the right being abandoned and the consequences of the decision to abandon it. Only if the "totality of the circumstances surrounding the interrogation" reveal both an uncoerced choice and the requisite level of comprehension may a court properly conclude that the Miranda rights have been waived.

Moran v. Burbine, 475 US 412, 421, 106 S Ct 1135, 89 L Ed 2d 410 (1986). The ultimate question is: "Did the defendant, with a full knowledge of his legal rights, knowingly and intentionally relinquish them?" *Com. v. Cruz*, 373 Mass 676, 687, 369 NE2d 996, 1003 (1977) (citation omitted).

Knowing and Intelligent. The first two requirements focus on whether the defendant understood his or her rights and the consequences of relinquishing them. See *Moran v. Burbine*, supra, 475 US at 421. "A confession can be voluntary in the legal sense only if the suspect actually understands the import of each *Miranda* warning." *Com. v. Garcia*, 379 Mass 422, 429, 399 NE2d 460, 466 (1980). But see *Connecticut v. Barrett*, 479 US 523 (1987) (defendant's ambiguous conduct in refusing to make written statement and then giving oral confession did not invalidate waiver on grounds it was not knowing and intelligent).

A misrepresentation of the *Miranda* rights, even if innocent, renders suspect a claim that the defendant knowingly waived those rights. *Com. v. Dustin*, supra, 373 Mass at 616, 368 NE2d at 1390-1391 (officer implied that defendant's statement could not be used against him). See also *Com. v. Magee*, 423 Mass 381, 386-387, 668 NE2d 339, 344 (1996) (officer's response to defendant's inquiry about getting attorney was inadequate and weighed against valid waiver). Compare *Com. v. Grenier*, 415 Mass 680, 682-684, 615 NE2d 922, 923-924 (1993) (police officer's answer to defendant's question about meaning of *Miranda* warning not misleading or false).

The prosecution may not rely on any presumption that the suspect understood the warnings, but must affirmatively demonstrate such understanding — for example, by showing that the suspect answered affirmatively when asked whether he understood the warnings. *Tague v. Louisiana*, 444 US 469 (1980). Understanding of the warnings may, however, be inferred from "the suspect's outward behavior, most notably his indication that he understands his rights, waives them, and wishes to talk." *Com. v. Garcia*, supra, 379 Mass at 430, 399 NE2d at 465. Compare *Com. v. Cain*, 361 Mass 224, 228, 279 NE2d 706, 709 (1972) (minor defendant's response, "Yes, I didn't do anything" to question whether he waived rights did not indicate with sufficient clarity an understanding of rights and an intelligent waiver) and *Com. v. Coplin*, 34 Mass App 478, 482, 612 NE2d 1188, 1190 (1993) (insufficient proof that defendant, handcuffed and lying on floor, understood warnings) with *Com. v. Cook*, 419 Mass 192, 201, 644 NE2d 203, 209 (1994) (evidence supported finding that defendant either signed waiver card or indicated he understood rights) and *Com. v. Williams*, 378 Mass 217, 225-226, 391 NE2d 1202, 1207-1209 (1979) (police attempted to ascertain whether defendant wanted to waive his rights, and he responded affirmatively).

For cases involving non-English speaking defendants, see *Com. v. Iglesias*, 426 Mass 574, 577, 689 NE2d 1315, 1318 (1998) (fact that warnings given in English without interpreter to native Spanish speaker does not invalidate otherwise valid waiver); *Com. v. Bui,* 419 Mass 392, 396-397, 645 NE2d 689, 692 (1995) (evidence supported finding that defendant understood his rights when they were given to him in both English and Vietnamese); *Com. v. Perez,* 411 Mass 249, 255-256, 581 NE2d 1010, 1014-1015 (1991) (evidence was sufficient to establish that defendant read and understood Spanish translations warnings on *Miranda* card); *Com. v. Colon-Cruz,* 408 Mass 533, 539, 562 NE2d 797, 803 (1990) (judge's determination that Spanish translator succeeded in communicating the warnings to defendant was supported by the record); *Com. v. Garcia,* supra, 379 Mass at 430, 399 NE2d at 465 (rejecting defendant's contention that he had been unable to understand Spanish interpreter's explanation of rights); *Com. v. Alves,* 35 Mass App 935, 625 NE2d 559 (1993) (rejecting Portuguese-speaking defendant's claims that language differences and errors in written Portuguese *Miranda* card precluded his understanding of rights).

"In certain limited circumstances [such as intoxication and mental retardation], the police are charged with observing greater caution in relying on signs by the accused that he understands and waives his *Miranda* rights." *Com. v. Garcia,* supra, 379 Mass at 430 n.4, 399 NE2d at 466 n.4 (& cases cited). "[P]articularly when a suspect is brought in on a charge of drunkenness the police should not assume they can immediately receive a knowing and intelligent waiver of *Miranda* rights and commence interrogation." *Com. v. Hosey,* 368 Mass 571, 579, 334 NE2d 44, 49 (1975). But see *Com. v. Lanoue,* 392 Mass 583, 588-589, 467 NE2d 159, 163 (1984) (rejecting the contention that the police have obligation to ensure valid waiver through administration of sobriety tests; police are ordinarily entitled to rely on a suspect's outward behavior when deciding whether to proceed with an interrogation); *Com. v. Dunn,* 407 Mass 798, 805, 556 NE2d 30, 34-35 (1990) (defendant did not indicate to officers that he was intoxicated or give any outward appearance of intoxication).

Although factors such as the youthful age, intoxication, or diminished mental capacity of the defendant do not automatically invalidate a waiver, see *Com. v. Wanderlick*, 12 Mass App 970, 428 NE2d 328 (1981) (& cases cited), the mental condition of the defendant is a significant factor to be weighed in determining whether the waiver was knowing and intelligent. Compare *Com. v. Hosey*, 368 Mass 571, 574-579, 334 NE2d 44, 49 (1975) (defendant was "extremely high," "extremely emotional," and "detached from reality;" waiver not intelligent), *Com. v. Magee*, 423 Mass 381, 386-387, 668 NE2d 339, 344 (1996) (defendant suffering from lack of sleep and emotionally distraught), and *Com. v. White*, 374 Mass 132, 137-138, 371 NE2d 777, 780 (1977) (waiver invalid because defendant intoxicated by drugs or alcohol) with *Com. v. Mello*, 420 Mass 375, 383, 649 NE2d 1106, 1113 (1995) (despite evidence that defendant ingested beer and inhaled heroin night before arrest, waiver valid where defendant spoke coherently, appeared sober, explained preparation and crime in detail, did not complain of illness, signed waiver form, stated he understood his rights, and agreed to talk to police), *Com. v. Prater*, 420 Mass 569, 578-579, 651 NE2d 833, 839-840 (1995) (waiver valid, even though defendant intoxicated and had low IQ where he had been subject to custodial interrogation before and stated on videotape that the effects of alcohol had worn off), *Com. v. Bousquet*, 407 Mass 854, 861-862, 556 NE2d 37, 42 (1990) (defendant's ability to explain details of murder indicative that his mind was not overtaken by drugs), *Com. v. Libran*, 405 Mass 634, 638-639, 543 NE2d 5, 8 (1989) (any mental impairment that retarded and schizophrenic defendant suffered did not impede his ability to effectively waive *Miranda* rights), *Com. v. Parker*, 402 Mass 333, 340, 522 NE2d 924, 928 (1988) (*Parker I*) (evidence presented contradicted defendants' assertions that they were too tired and intoxicated to make valid waiver), *Com. v. Shipps*, 399 Mass 820, 826-827, 507 NE2d 671, 676-677 (1987) (defendant minor not precluded from making valid waiver by reason of youth, low intelligence, or intoxication), *Com. v. Taylor*, supra, 398 Mass at 728-729, 500 NE2d at 800-801 (although defendant had consumed some alcohol, he was not intoxicated and made valid waiver), *Com. v. Medeiros*, 395 Mass 336, 347, 479 NE2d 1371, 1379 (1985) (defendant's diminished mental capacity did not prevent him from effectively waiving rights), *Com. v. Duffy*, 36 Mass App 937, 629 NE2d 1347 (1994) (judge could properly conclude that neither defendant's mental impairments nor consumption of alcohol impeded his ability to waive rights), *Com. v. Matos*, 36 Mass App 958, 963, 634 NE2d 138, 143 (1994) (even if defendant suffered from diminished mental capacity, evidence of totality of circumstances established valid waiver), *Com. v. Wallen*, 35 Mass App 915, 619 NE2d 365 (1993) (judge could properly conclude that defendant with IQ between 60 and 70 and third or fourth grade reading level validly waived rights), and *Com. v. Griffin*, 19 Mass App 174, 181-184, 472 NE2d 1354, 1360 (1985) (neither defendant's intoxication nor alleged concussion rendered his waiver invalid).

It has been suggested that expert testimony be presented to aid in the evaluation of the effect of custodial interrogation on a mentally deficient defendant. *Com. v. Cameron*, 385 Mass 660, 666 n.5, 433 NE2d 878, 883 n.5 (& citation). See also *Com. v. Crawford*, 429 Mass 60, 706 NE2d 289 (1999) (defendant entitled to present expert testimony on battered woman syndrome and post-traumatic stress disorder on issue of voluntariness of her confession to police).

The fact that a suspect selectively asserted rights to certain questions has been held to exhibit a knowing and intelligent waiver as to questions that were answered. See *Com. v. Mandeville*, 386 Mass 393, 404, 436 NE2d 912, 920 (1982).

Despite the requirement that a waiver be knowing and intelligent, a suspect need not be made aware of all the possible subjects or crimes to be covered in the interrogation in order to make his waiver valid. See *Colorado v. Spring*, 479 US 564 (1987) (interrogation switched from firearms charge, for which defendant was arrested, to a homicide); *Com. v. Medeiros*, supra, 395 Mass at 345, 479 NE2d at 1377-1378 (police not required to re-advise suspect of rights when questioning changed from theft to murder; but suspect's ignorance of subject of interrogation is factor to be weighed in totality of circumstances analysis); *Com. v. Hooks*, 38 Mass App 301, 304-305, 647 NE2d 440, 442-443 (1995). The police are not required to explain all the possible legal ramifications of the defendant's conduct, such as the theory of joint venture. See *Com. v. Cunningham*, 405 Mass 646, 656-657, 543 NE2d 12, 18-19 (1989). Nor is it necessary that the person being questioned be told that he is a suspect. *Com. v. Raymond*, 424 Mass 382, 392-393, 676 NE2d 824, 832 (1997); *Com. v. Borodine*, 371 Mass 1, 6, 353 NE2d 647, 653 (1976).

Although Massachusetts precedent suggested that the failure to inform the suspect that his attorney had requested to be present during questioning or to consult with him invalidated any waiver as unknowing (see *Com. v. Sherman*, 389 Mass 287, 291-296, 450 NE2d 566 (1983), *Com. v. Mahnke*, 368 Mass 691-692, 335 NE2d 660 (1975) (& cases cited), *Com. v. McKenna*, 355 Mass 313, 323-326, 244 NE2d 560 (1969), and *Com. v. DiMuro*, 28 Mass App 223, 226-228, 548 NE2d 896 (1990)), these decisions have been "undermined" by *Moran v. Burbine*, 475 US 412 (1986), holding that the fact that police failed to inform defendant that an attorney retained by a relative to represent him was attempting to see him at the police station did not invalidate the waiver. See *Com. v. Cryer*, 426 Mass 562, 567, 689 NE2d 808, 812 (1998); *Com. v. Phinney*, 416 Mass 364, 371-373, 622 NE2d 617, 622-623 (1993) (police officer not obligated to tell attorney who had previously represented defendant that defendant was at police station being interrogated).

The Supreme Judicial Court has reserved the issue of whether *Moran v. Burbine* extends to claims under art. 12 of the Declaration of Rights. See *Com. v. Cryer*, supra, 426 Mass at 568, 689 NE2d at 812-813 (but holding that art. 12 would not apply in any event where it was the New Hampshire police who failed to inform defendant and the Massachusetts officers who interrogated him that defendant's attorney on an unrelated matter had left instructions that he not be questioned).

The Court has cautioned: "That a waiver of rights must be knowing and intelligent does not mean that with the hindsight of conviction the defendant would not have chosen to talk to the police. Rather, it means that police procedures must scrupulously respect the suspect's free choices, made with actual knowledge of his rights at the time of interrogation." *Com. v. Garcia*, supra, 379 Mass at 431, 399 NE2d at 466.

Voluntary. The voluntariness of a waiver is tested by examining "the totality of all the surrounding circumstances." *Com. v. Borodine*, supra, 371 Mass at 6, 353 NE2d at 653. The determination involves essentially the same inquiry as the due process standard discussed in §9.2, supra, focusing on the characteristics of the defendant as well as the circumstances of the interrogation.[3] See, e.g., *Colorado v. Connelly*, 479 US 157, 107 S Ct 515, 93 L Ed 2d 473 (1986) (emphasis on police coercion); *Com. v. Forde*, 392 Mass 453, 455-456, 466 NE2d 510, 512 (1984); *Com. v. Williams*, supra, 378 Mass at 226-227, 391 NE2d at 1209; *Com. v. Watkins*, supra, 375 Mass at 485, 379 NE2d at 1049; *Com. v. Cruz*, 373 Mass 676, 688, 369 NE2d 996, 1004 (1977); *Com. v. Coplin*, 34 Mass App 478, 482, 612 NE2d 1188, 1190 (1993).

An important factor to be weighed in determining the voluntariness of a waiver is the length of the interrogation, which if excessive may "raise a suspicion that the police were trying to wear down the defendant's inner resources." *Com. v. Bradshaw*, 385 Mass 244, 268, 431 NE2d 880, 895

---

[3] *Com. v. Edwards*, 420 Mass 666, 670, 651 NE2d 398, 401 (1995). It must be emphasized, however, that the issues of the voluntariness of the waiver and the confession are separate and distinct. See *Com. v. Williams*, 388 Mass 846, 851 n.2, 448 NE2d 1114, 1118 n.2 (1983) (& citations); *Com. v. Wallen*, 35 Mass App 915, 917, 619 NE2d 365, 367 (1993).

(1982) (& citation). "Off-hour questioning," such as during the early morning hours, is looked upon with disfavor but does not, in itself, constitute coercion. See *Com. v. Hunter*, 426 Mass 715, 722 n.3, 690 NE2d 815, 822 n.3 (1998) (& citations).

A waiver that is the result of police threats, trickery, promises, or deliberate misrepresentations is not voluntary. *Miranda v. Arizona*, supra, 384 US at 476; *Com. v. Medeiros*, supra, 395 Mass at 345, 479 NE2d at 1378. See *Com. v. Jackson*, 377 Mass 319, 327-329, 386 NE2d 15, 20-21 (1979) (officer falsely told defendant that his girlfriend had given police incriminatory statement); *Com. v. Meehan*, 377 Mass 552, 563-564, 387 NE2d 527, 537 (1979) (misrepresentations concerning strength of Commonwealth's case and that confession would benefit defendant); *Com. v. Magee*, 423 Mass 381, 387, 668 NE2d 339, 344 (1996) (promise by officers that defendant would receive psychological help she was seeking if she provided information created quid pro quo undermining validity of waiver); *Com. v. Hunt*, 12 Mass App 841, 844, 429 NE2d 379, 381 (1981) (& citations) (implicit threat or promise that defendant's wife would be released if he confessed and did not implicate her). Trickery alone, however, may not invalidate a waiver if there is evidence, in light of other surrounding circumstances, that it was made voluntarily. *Com. v. Edwards*, 420 Mass 666, 671, 651 NE2d 398, 402 (1995) (waiver not rendered involuntary by detectives' false statement that defendant's handprint had been recovered at murder scene); *Com. v. Selby*, 420 Mass 656, 663-664, 651 NE2d 843, 848-849 (1995) (false representation that defendant's handprint placed him in victim's house did not invalidate waiver); *Com. v. Forde*, supra, 392 Mass at 455-456, 466 NE2d at 511-512 (defendant made valid waiver even though police officer falsely suggested that his fingerprints had been found on victim's body; the fact that the statement was evoked by trickery is "relevant but not conclusive"). See also *Com. v. Corriveau*, 396 Mass 319, 331-332, 486 NE2d 29, 38-39 (1985) (officer's statement to defendant that others had already spoken to police did not make defendant's waiver the product of coercion where defendant had already observed friend talking to police at the stationhouse).

An officer may suggest that it would be better for a suspect to tell the truth, as long as there is no assurance that a statement will aid the defense. See *Com. v. Souza*, 418 Mass 478, 481-482, 702 NE2d 1167, 1170 (1998) (& citations). See also *Com. v. Williams*, 388 Mass 846, 852, 448 NE2d 1114, 1121 (1983) (officer's promise to make known to district attorney's office and to the judge the defendant's cooperation in making a statement did not invalidate the waiver).

When an accused has invoked his right to silence or to counsel, a valid waiver cannot be established merely by showing that he responded to further police-initiated custodial interrogation, even if further interrogation is preceded by *Miranda* warnings. See *Michigan v. Mosley*, 423 US 96, 96 S Ct 321, 46 L Ed 2d 313 (1975) and *Edwards v. Arizona*, 451 US 477, 101 S Ct 1880, 68 L Ed 2d 378 (1981), discussed in §9.7.1, supra. "Where a desire to remain silent was made known to the police, it is infrequent that a valid waiver of constitutional rights will be found when only a short interval existed between the time when a defendant asserted his right to terminate questioning and the time when interrogation was subsequently resumed." *Com. v. Mandeville*, 386 Mass 393, 403, 436 NE2d 912, 919 (1982). But compare *Com. v. Richmond*, 379 Mass 557, 560, 399 NE2d 1069, 1072 (1980) (defendant waived right to counsel shortly after invoking it by questioning police about the details of crime).

c.   Waiver by Juvenile: "Interested Adult" Rule

The Supreme Judicial Court has observed that "circumstances and techniques of custodial interrogation which pass constitutional muster when applied to a normal adult may not be constitutionally tolerable as applied to one who is immature or mentally deficient." *Com. v. Daniels*, 366 Mass 601, 606, 321 NE2d 822, 826 (1975) (moderately retarded young man). See also *Com. v. Williams*, 388 Mass 846, 852, 448 NE2d 1114, 1119 (1983) (& citations). Thus, while both juveniles and mentally deficient adults may make effective waivers, "special caution" must be taken in scrutinizing the totality of the circumstances. *Com. v. Philip S., a Juvenile*, 414 Mass 804, 808, 611 NE2d 226, 230 (1993); *Com. v. Tavares*, 385 Mass 140, 146, 430 NE2d 1198, 1202 (1982).

Recognizing the unique problems that arise with respect to waiver when the accused is a juvenile, Massachusetts has adopted a modified "interested adult" rule regarding confessions. See *Com. v. A Juvenile*, 389 Mass 128, 449 NE2d 654 (1983). In order to demonstrate a knowing and intelligent waiver by a juvenile, the Commonwealth must generally show that a parent or interested adult was present, understood the warnings, and had the opportunity to explain his rights to the juvenile so that he would understand the significance of waiver. 389 Mass at 134, 449 NE2d at 657, 658. Where the juvenile is under the age of 14, no waiver can be effective without this protection. Where the juvenile has reached the age of 14, a waiver in the absence of such protection is valid only if the circumstances demonstrate a high degree of intelligence, experience, knowledge, or sophistication on the part of the juvenile. Id.; *Com. v. Berry*, 410 Mass 31, 34-35, 570 NE2d 1004, 1006-1007 (1991).

The standards for determining whether a juvenile has been given sufficient opportunity for consultation have a common-law basis and are not constitutionally mandated. *Com. v. A Juvenile*, 402 Mass 275, 279, 521 NE2d 1368, 1371 (1988).

In deciding whether an adult advising a juvenile during interrogation is an "interested adult" for purposes of the rule, the facts must be viewed from the perspective of the officials conducting the interview. *Com. v. Philip S., a Juvenile*, supra, 414 Mass at 809, 611 NE2d at 230-231. "If, at the time of the interrogation (as assessed by objective standards), it should have been reasonably apparent to the officials questioning a juvenile that the adult who was present on his or her behalf lacked capacity to appreciate the juvenile's situation and to give advice, or was actually antagonistic toward the juvenile, a finding would be warranted that the juvenile has not been assisted by an interested adult and did not have the opportunity for consultation contemplated by our rule." Id. The interested adult rule is not violated, however, merely because a parent fails to provide "what, in hindsight and from a legal perspective, might have been optimum advice." Id. Nor does the fact that the adult has a relationship with the victims preclude her from acting as an interested adult. See *Com. v. McCra*, 427 Mass 564, 568-569, 694 NE2d 849, 852-853 (1998) (defendant's aunt was sister of one of victims).

The "interested adult" rule requires a showing that the juvenile and the adult were provided *the opportunity* to consult; it does not require that an *actual* consultation occur. *Com. v. McCra*, supra, 427 Mass at 567-568, 694 NE2d at 852; *Com. v. Philip S., a Juvenile*, supra, 414 Mass at 811-813, 611 NE2d at 232; *Com. v. Berry*, supra, 410 Mass at 35 & n.2, 570 NE2d at 1007 & n.2.

"[T]he ultimate question is whether the juvenile has understood his rights and the potential consequences of waiving them before talking to the police." *Com. v. MacNeill*, 399 Mass 71, 79, 502 NE2d 938, 943 (1987). Compare *Com. v. Philip S., a Juvenile*, supra, 414 Mass at 813-814, 611 NE2d at 233 (nothing to show that juvenile was impaired or that investigating officials used threats, promises, or subterfuge to induce him to talk), *Com. v. Tevenal*, 401 Mass 225, 227-228, 515 NE2d 1191, 1192-1193 (1987) (judge was warranted in finding that defendant and his mother understood his *Miranda* rights, that he had an opportunity to consult with his mother, and that he voluntarily waived his rights), and *Com. v. King*, 17 Mass App 602, 609-611, 460 NE2d 1299, 1305-1306 (1984) (although 16-year-old defendant did not have opportunity to consult with his mother before being questioned by police, evidence warranted finding that waiver was valid) with *Com. v. Guyton*, 405 Mass 497, 502-504, 541 NE2d 1006, 1009-1010 (1989) (Commonwealth failed to sustain burden of establishing that 16-year-old defendant, who did not have the opportunity to consult with "interested adult," had capacity of waiving his rights without consultation), *Com. v. A Juvenile*, supra, 402 Mass at 280, 521 NE2d at 1371-1372 (juvenile did not have high degree of intelligence, experience, knowledge, or sophistication to make valid waiver), and *Com. v. Cain*, 361 Mass 224, 228, 279 NE2d 706, 709 (1972) (waiver not knowing and intelligent where minor denied access to father).

The Supreme Judicial Court has refused to adopt a fixed rule that a minor's opportunity to consult with an interested adult requires that the police expressly inform the minor and the adult that they may confer *in private*. While the police may not properly deny them that right, it is sufficient if the minor and adult are generally advised of their right to confer. See *Com. v. Ward*, 412 Mass 395, 397, 590 NE2d 173, 174 (1992). Nor are the officials required to expressly inform a juvenile and his parent that they should use their opportunity to confer for a discussion of the juvenile's rights. The better practice, however, is for the investigating officers to explicitly inform the juvenile's parent, or other interested adult, that "an opportunity is being furnished for the two to confer about the juvenile's rights." *Com. v. Philip S., a Juvenile*, supra, 414 Mass at 811 n.5, 611 NE2d at 232 n.5.

d. Appellate Review

A trial judge's finding of waiver of *Miranda* rights is entitled to substantial deference by the appellate court. Subsidiary findings of fact and credibility will not be disturbed where they are warranted by the evidence, but ultimate findings of constitutional dimension are open for review and independent determination. *Com. v. Boncore*, 412 Mass 1013, 593 NE2d 227 (1992); *Com. v. Berry*, 410 Mass 31, 34, 570 NE2d 1004, 1006-1007 (1991); *Com. v. Tavares*, 385

Mass 140, 144-145, 430 NE2d 1198, 1202-1203 (1982); *Com. v. Jackson*, 377 Mass 319, 325, 386 NE2d 15, 19 (1979) (& citations); *Com. v. Hunt*, 12 Mass App 841, 843, 429 NE2d 379, 380 (1981). See, e.g., *Com. v. Herbert*, 421 Mass 307, 313, 656 NE2d 899, 902 (1995) (judge's findings that defendant did not request attorney, was not told by any officer that he should tell truth, and was not told that no attorney was available properly based on rejection of defendant's testimony and on reasonable inferences from police witnesses); *Com. v. Colon*, 408 Mass 419, 426, 558 NE2d 974, 980 (1990) (judge entitled to discredit defendant's testimony concerning circumstances of waiver); *Com. v. Benjamin*, 399 Mass 220, 222-223, 503 NE2d 660, 663 (1987) (judge's rejection of defendant's assertion that he was confused about rights supported by record).

The use at trial of statements elicited from a defendant in violation of *Miranda* is subject to harmless-error analysis. See *Com. v. Ghee*, 414 Mass 313, 318-319, 607 NE2d 1005, 1009 (1993); *Com. v. Perez*, 411 Mass 249, 259, 581 NE2d 1010, 1017 (1991); *Com. v. Coplin*, 34 Mass App 478, 483-484, 612 NE2d 1188, 1191 (1993) (in view of government's heavy emphasis on defendant's statement in closing argument, error could not be found harmless); *Com. v. Marquetty*, 28 Mass App 690, 695-696, 554 NE2d 1230, 1233-1234 (1990).

§9.7.5   Subsequent Statements and Derivative Evidence

Under federal constitutional law, a statement obtained from a suspect subsequent to the elicitation of an earlier statement in violation of *Miranda* is not presumptively inadmissible. "[A]bsent deliberately coercive or improper tactics in obtaining the initial statement, the mere fact that a suspect has made an unwarned admission does not warrant a presumption of compulsion. A subsequent administration of *Miranda* warnings to a suspect who has given a voluntary but unwarned statement ordinarily should suffice to remove the conditions that precluded admission of the earlier statement." *Oregon v. Elstad,* 470 US 298, 314, 105 S Ct 1285, 84 L Ed 2d 222 (1985). See also *Michigan v. Tucker,* 417 US 433, 94 S Ct 2357, 41 L Ed 2d 182 (1974); *Com. v. Rubio,* 27 Mass App 506, 515 & n.9, 540 NE2d 189, 194 & n.9 (1989). Thus, where the accused's initial statement obtained in violation of *Miranda* is followed by a subsequent statement, the latter is not tainted by the prior illegality.

Massachusetts law, however, departs from *Oregon v. Elstad* and provides "additional protections." *Com. v. Snyder,* 413 Mass 521, 530, 597 NE2d 1363, 1368 (1992). See generally Katherine E. McMahon, "Cat-Out-of-the-Bag" & "Break-in-the-Stream-of-Events": Massachusetts' Rejection of Oregon v. Elstad for Suppression of Warned Statements Made after a Miranda Violation, 20 W.N.Eng.L.Rev. 173 (1998). As a common-law rule of evidence, where a statement follows an earlier statement obtained in violation of *Miranda* requirements, the second statement is presumed to be tainted by the first and the prosecution is required to show more than the belated administration of *Miranda* warnings in order to dispel that taint. *Com. v. Smith,* 412 Mass 823, 836-837, 593 NE2d 1288, 1295-1296 (1992) (& citations). The presumption may be overcome by showing either: (1) there was a break in the stream of events after the illegally obtained statement that sufficiently insulated the second statement from the taint of the first; or (2) the illegally obtained statement did not incriminate the defendant, so that "the cat was not out of the bag." *Com. v. Larkin,* 429 Mass 426, 436-438, 708 NE2d 674, 682 (1999); *Com. v. Nom,* 426 Mass 152, 155-156, 686 NE2d 1017, 1021 (1997); *Com. v. Torres,* 424 Mass 792, 799-800, 678 NE2d 847, 852 (1997); *Com. v. Prater,* 420 Mass 569, 579-581, 651 NE2d 833, 840-841 (1995); *Com. v. Osachuk,* 418 Mass 229, 235, 635 NE2d 1192, 1196 (1994).

"The focus and ultimate goal of undertaking either or both lines of analysis is a determination of the voluntariness of the later confession. If the defendant's subsequent statements were not a product of coercion, either by coercive external forces or primarily by a sense of futility that he has already incriminated himself with the first statement, then the Fifth Amendment to the United States Constitution does not require suppression of the subsequent statement." *Com. v. Prater*, supra, 420 Mass at 581, 651 NE2d at 841 (defendant's videotaped statement 90 minutes after first statement sufficiently removed and thus admissible). See also *Com. v. Damiano*, 422 Mass 10, 13, 660 NE2d 660, 662 (1996) (defendant's later statements not free from taint of earlier *Miranda* violation where questioning was continuous and earlier statement was incriminating); *Com. v. Osachuk*, supra, 418 Mass at 235-237, 635 NE2d at 1196-1197; *Com. v. Smallwood*, 379 Mass 878, 886 n.2, 401 NE2d 802, 807 n.2 (1980) (& citations); *Com. v. Watkins*, 375 Mass 472, 480-483, 379 NE2d 1040, 1045-1047 (1978). See also §9.4, supra.

Under Massachusetts law, statements obtained in violation of *Miranda* cannot be considered in determining probable cause to secure a search warrant or to arrest. See *Com. v. Haas*, 398 Mass 806, 808 n.2, 501 NE2d 1154, 1156 (1986); *Com. v. White*, 374 Mass 132, 138-139, 371 NE2d 777, 781 (1977).

§9.7.6   *Inapplicability of* **Miranda** *to Statements Obtained by Private Citizens, to Grand Jury Witnesses, and at Parole Revocation Hearings*

Miranda is inapplicable where a statement is obtained by a private citizen not acting in concert with police. The sole inquiry in such cases is whether the statement was voluntarily made, as discussed in §9.2, supra. *Com. v. Snyder*, 413 Mass 521, 531-532, 597 NE2d 1363, 1369 (1992) (school principal); *Com. v. Mahnke*, 368 Mass 662, 676-678, 335

NE2d 660, 669-670 (1975) (private citizens abducted and questioned defendant about missing girl). Compare *Com. v. A Juvenile*, 402 Mass 275, 278, 521 NE2d 1368, 1370 (1988) (assistant director of youth detention facility acted as instrument of the police in questioning juvenile).

The *Miranda* protections are not applicable to a grand jury witness. *United States v. Mandujano*, 425 US 564, 96 S Ct 1768, 48 L Ed 2d 212 (1976). Although a grand jury witness has no constitutional right to assistance of counsel, the witness has a statutory right under GL 277, §14A "to consult with counsel and to have counsel present at . . . examination before the grand jury. . . ." *Com. v. Griffin*, 404 Mass 372, 374, 535 NE2d 594, 595-596 (1989); *Com. v. Gilliard*, 36 Mass App 183, 629 NE2d 349 (1994) (& citations) (suggesting that grand jury witness may have right under art. 12 of Massachusetts Declaration of Rights to be warned if he is a potential defendant).

Inculpatory statements obtained in violation of *Miranda* are nonetheless admissible at probation revocation hearings. *Com. v. Vincente*, 405 Mass 278, 540 NE2d 669 (1989) (& citations).

§9.7.7 Exceptions to the Miranda Doctrine— Public Safety and Impeachment

Miranda does not apply to custodial interrogations concerning matters that pose an immediate danger to public safety. See *New York v. Quarles*, 467 US 649, 104 S Ct 2626, 81 L Ed 2d 550 (1984) ("The gun is over there" in response to police question admissible despite absence of warnings). The Supreme Judicial Court has left open the question of whether *Quarles* applies to a situation in which the safety of police and not the public generally is threatened. See *Com. v. Bourgeois*, 404 Mass 61, 66, 533 NE2d 638, 642 (1989). But see *Com. v. Kitchings*, 40 Mass App 591, 598, 666 NE2d 511, 516-517 (1996) (trooper not required to give warnings before demanding to know where gun was located in car, because his safety was in jeopardy).

Statements obtained in violation of the *Miranda* safeguards but otherwise uncoerced, voluntary and trustworthy, may be used to impeach the defendant if he takes the witness stand. See *Oregon v. Hass*, 420 US 714 (1975); *Harris v. New York*, 401 US 222, 91 S Ct 643, 28 L Ed 2d 1 (1971); *Com. v. Harris*, 364 Mass 236, 358 NE2d 982 (1973); *Com. v. Mahnke*, 368 Mass 662, 692-697, 335 NE2d 660, 678-681 (1975). Involuntary statements cannot be used even for the limited purpose of impeachment. *Mincey v. Arizona*, 437 US 385, 398, 98 S Ct 2408, 57 L Ed 2d 290 (1978).

§9.7.8   Pre- and Post-Arrest Silence

In accordance with federal constitutional protections and state law, the post-arrest silence of a defendant (such as a failure to deny an accusation) may not be used as substantive evidence of guilt. *Com. v. Nickerson*, 386 Mass 54, 59 n.5, 434 NE2d 992, 995 n.5 (1982) (& citations). Nor can the prosecutor make reference to the defendant's silence after *Miranda* warnings. *Com. v. Egardo*, 426 Mass 48, 50-52, 686 NE2d 432, 434-435 (1997); *Com. v. Crichlow*, 30 Mass App 901, 565 NE2d 816 (1991) (prosecutor's reference during opening statement to defendant's exercise of right to remain silent after *Miranda* warnings was error, but harmless). See also *Com. v. Somers*, 44 Mass App 920, 691 NE2d 225 (1998) (error to admit *Miranda* form indicating defendant asserted right to remain silent). Neither the prosecution nor the defense can admit a defendant's denial of an accusation after warnings. See *Com. v. Nawn*, 394 Mass 1, 4-5, 474 NE2d 545, 549 (1985) (defense) (& citations; citing Text); *Com. v. Waite*, 422 Mass 792, 800-801, 665 NE2d 982, 989

(1996); *Com. v. Henry*, 37 Mass App 429, 432-433, 640 NE2d 503, 506 (1994) (defense).[4]

Under federal constitutional standards, the defendant's post-arrest silence may be used for impeachment purposes if the silence preceded *Miranda* warnings and the circumstances meet the usual requirements for an adoptive admission — i.e., an ordinary person would be expected to contradict the accusation if false (see §8.8.5, supra). See *Fletcher v. Weir*, 455 US 603, 102 S Ct 1309, 71 L Ed 2d 490 (1982). A defendant who takes the stand is subject to cross-examination about prior inconsistent statements voluntarily made, and such inconsistencies may include omissions from a statement where it would have been natural to include the omitted fact. See *Com. v. Rivera*, 425 Mass 633, 639-640, 682 NE2d 636, 641-642 (& citations). A prosecutor may comment on such omissions. Id.

Silence of the defendant *following* the warnings cannot be used to impeach under either federal or state law. *Doyle v. Ohio*, 426 US 610, 96 S Ct 2240, 49 L Ed 2d 91 (1976); *Com. v. Rivera*, supra, 425 Mass at 639, 682 NE2d at 641; *Com. v. MacKenzie*, 413 Mass 498, 507 n.8, 597 NE2d 1037, 1043 n.8 (1992); *Com. v. Haas*, 373 Mass 545, 559, 369 NE2d 692, 702 (1977).

The use of silence to impeach a criminal defendant's testimony raises what the Supreme Judicial Court has re-

---

[4]Where a defendant while under arrest makes an equivocal response to an accusation, both the accusation and reply may be admissible as an admission (providing there is no violation of defendant's right to counsel or privilege against self-incrimination). *Com. v. Grenier*, 415 Mass 680, 688-689, 615 NE2d 922, 926-927 (1993) (& citations); *Com. v. Valliere*, 366 Mass 479, 488, 321 NE2d 625, 632 (1974); *Com. v. Estep*, 38 Mass App 502, 507 n.1, 649 NE2d 775, 778 n.1 (1995). An assertion of a constitutional right (such as the right to counsel) is not deemed an equivocal response within this rule. See *Com. v. Burke*, 339 Mass 521, 532-533, 159 NE2d 856, 863 (1963); *Com. v. Sazama*, 339 Mass 154, 158 NE2d 313 (1959). But see *Com. v. Cole*, 380 Mass 30, 42, 402 NE2d 55, 63 (1980) (defendant's responses to *Miranda* warnings admitted on issue of sanity). False statements made by a defendant may be admissible to show consciousness of guilt. *Com. v. Mayne*, 38 Mass App 282, 284, 647 NE2d 89, 91 (1995). See §4.2.1.

ferred to as "troublesome questions." *Com. v. Nickerson*, 386 Mass 54, 58, 59 n.5, 434 NE2d 992, 994, 995 n.5 (1982) (noting that use of defendant's post-arrest silence raises separate question under art. 12 of the Declaration of Rights of the Commonwealth). The Court has advised that "[e]vidence of this nature is to be received with caution, especially in criminal cases, due to the fact that the meaning of a defendant's response, or lack thereof, to an accusatory statement is often ambiguous." *Com. v. MacKenzie*, supra, 413 Mass at 506, 597 NE2d at 1043 (1992) (defendant's response, "We never meant to hurt the woman," did not adopt all details of accusatory statements and should not have been admitted as adoptive admission).

Thus, there is substantial doubt whether Massachusetts law would permit the use of post-arrest silence to impeach a defendant under *any* circumstances. See *Com. v. Amirault*, 404 Mass 221, 236-238, 535 NE2d 193, 203-204 (1989) (prosecutor's comments on defendant's post-arrest silence improper); *Com. v. Cobb*, 374 Mass 514, 380 NE2d 142 (1978) (evidence of defendant's post-arrest refusal to respond to questions improperly admitted); *Com. v. Freeman*, 352 Mass 556, 562-563, 227 NE2d 3, 8 (1967) (judge erred in instructing jury on admission by silence where defendant, although not under arrest, was represented by counsel and entitled to leave all talking to attorney); *Com. v. King*, 34 Mass App 466, 612 NE2d 690 (1993) (error to permit police officer to testify that defendant refused to answer questions during interrogation after receiving *Miranda* warnings); *Com. v. Ferrara*, 31 Mass App 648, 652, 582 NE2d 961, 964 (1991) (& citations) (no admission by silence may be offered after defendant has been read his *Miranda* rights, placed under arrest, or so significantly deprived of freedom as to be effectively in police custody); *Com. v. Corridori*, 11 Mass App 469, 417 NE2d 969 (1981) (defendant's silence after threshold stop inadmissible); *Com. v. Morrison*, 1 Mass App 632, 305 NE2d 518 (1973) (improper for prosecutor to ask defendant on cross-examination if he remembered third person making incriminating statement to police in his presence after arrest; defendant under no obligation to say anything, let alone contradict a statement allegedly made in his presence). See also *Com. v. Waite*, supra, 422 Mass at 800-802, 665 NE2d at 989 (improper for prosecutor in closing to refer to failure to give honest answers when arrested); *Com. v. Grenier*, 415 Mass 680, 690-691, 615 NE2d 922, 927 (1993) (jury should not have been permitted to hear that defendant terminated questioning after being asked whether he wanted to give police truthful statement as to involvement in murder); *Com. v. Egardo*, 42 Mass App 41, 674 NE2d 1088 (1997) (defense counsel's failure to object to prosecutor's comments regarding defendant's post-arrest silence required new trial).

Evidence relating to post-arrest silence has been admitted only on rare occasions. See *Com. v. Thurber*, 383 Mass 328, 333-335, 418 NE2d 1253, 1258 (1981) (escape defendant's post-arrest silence properly allowed to impeach assertion that he had told police he had escaped where issue opened on cross-examination); *Com. v. Waite*, supra, 422 Mass at 798-799, 665 NE2d at 987-988 (& citations) (when defendant has cut off questioning, testimony regarding cessation may be appropriate to prevent jury confusion even though evidence of post-*Miranda* silence); *Com. v. Halsey*, 41 Mass App 200, 204-205, 669 NE2d 774, 778 (1996) (testimony regarding defendant's demeanor after receiving warnings relevant on issue of voluntariness and not offered for sole purpose of having jurors infer guilt from silence).

Evidence of a defendant's exercise of his *Miranda* rights is inadmissible to establish his sanity, see *Com. v. Mahdi*, 388 Mass 679, 694-696, 448 NE2d 704, 713-714 (1983), or to rebut a defense of necessity. See *Com. v. Thurber*, 383 Mass 328, 333-335, 418 NE2d 1253, 1258 (1981) (but prosecution properly sought to impeach defendant's testimony by showing that after he was captured, he made no statement that he had escaped from Concord institution, because defense counsel failed to make timely objection).

There is no federal constitutional bar to the use of a defendant's *pre*-arrest silence to impeach his testimony. *Jenkins v. Anderson*, 447 US 231, 239, 100 S Ct 2124, 65 L Ed 2d 86 (1980). *Com. v. Nickerson* holds, however, that pre-arrest silence of the defendant should not be admitted where it would not have been natural for the defendant to disclose the information because it would have incriminated him — "his failure to come forward in these circumstances says little about the truth of his trial testimony." 386 Mass at 60-61, 434 NE2d at 996. The Court observed:

> In general, impeachment of a defendant with the fact of his pre-arrest silence should be approached with caution, and, whenever it is undertaken, it should be prefaced by a proper demonstration that it was "natural" to expect the defendant to speak in the circumstances. A trial judge should feel free to conduct a voir dire on the question of impeachment of a witness (particularly a defendant) by his silence; and, if admitted, the judge should, on request, instruct the jury to consider that silence for the purpose of impeachment only if they find that the witness naturally should have spoken up in the circumstances.

386 Mass at 62, 434 NE2d at 997. A defendant's failure to report information to someone other than the police would, the Court added, be "an appropriate subject for cross-examination where it would have been natural for the defendant to report those facts." Id. at n.8. Compare *Com. v. Barnoski*, 418 Mass 523, 535, 638 NE2d 9, 16 (1994) (questions concerning defendant's failure to call ambulance for shooting victim were proper) and *Com. v. Lopes*, 34 Mass App 179, 184, 608 NE2d 749, 752 (1993) (because it would have been natural for defendant to discuss incident with brother, cross-examination regarding what defendant told brother was proper) with *Com. v. Martinez*, 34 Mass App 131, 608 NE2d 740 (1993) (improper for prosecutor to suggest inference of guilt from rape defendant's failure to offer to furnish district attorney with physical evidence).

For a discussion of the bounds of permissible comment upon, and inference from, a defendant's pretrial silence, see §13.14.8, infra.

The wrongful use of post-arrest silence to impeach the defendant at trial does not automatically constitute reversible error; if the judge immediately instructs the jury to disregard the questions, reprimands the proscecutor, and explains why the questions are improper, the error may be found harmless. See *Com. v. Morgan*, 369 Mass 332, 338-344, 339 NE2d 723, 727-730 (1975); *Com. v. Rembiszewski*, 363 Mass 311, 316-317, 293 NE2d 919, 923 (1973). It has been noted, however, that the "nature of [such an] error is so egregious that reversal is the norm, not the exception." *Com. v. Mahdi*, supra, 388 Mass at 698 (discussing factors to be considered); *Com. v. King*, supra, 34 Mass App at 469.

Where the defendant chooses not to remain silent but speaks to police about matters concerning the crime for which he has been arrested, the prosecutor may cross-examine the defendant about, and comment to the jury upon, any omission from his statement that is at variance with his trial testimony, as with any prior inconsistent statement (see §6.7.2, supra). See *Com. v. Rivera*, supra, 425 Mass at 639-640, 682 NE2d at 641-642; *Com. v. Martino*, 412 Mass 267, 282-284, 588 NE2d 651 (1992); *Com. v. Seymour*, 39 Mass App 672, 679-680, 660 NE2d 679, 683 (1996); *Com. v. McClary*, 33 Mass App 678, 685-686, 604 NE2d 706, 710 (1993) (& citations).

§9.7.9   *Relationship of* Miranda *and Voluntariness Standard*

If a statement has been obtained in violation of *Miranda* requirements, it is inadmissible even if found to be voluntary under due process and common-law standards (see §9.2, supra). *Michigan v. Mosley*, 423 US 96, 99-100, 96 S Ct 321, 46 L Ed 2d 313 (1975). Conversely, a statement obtained in compliance with *Miranda* is nonetheless inadmissible if found to be involuntary. "The question of the voluntariness of a waiver of *Miranda* rights is separate and differs from the determination of the voluntariness of a confession. Once it is clear that a defendant has made a knowing and voluntary waiver of his or her *Miranda* rights, the issue becomes whether the confession itself was voluntary." *Smith v. Duckworth*, 856 F2d 909, 911 (7th Cir 1988); *Com. v. Garcia*, 379 Mass 422, 428, 399 NE2d 460, 464-465 (1980) ("The question of the voluntariness of the waiver of [*Miranda*] rights and that of the voluntariness of the statements which Garcia made to the police may be interrelated, but they are separate and distinct questions. The former is whether the *Miranda* requirement of warnings was scrupulously observed and whether Garcia knowingly, intelligently and voluntarily waived the rights covered by the warnings. The latter is whether Garcia's statements were made freely and voluntarily when considering the 'totality of the circumstances' in which they were made."); *Com. v. Cruz*, 373 Mass 676, 688, 369 NE2d 996, 1003 (1977).

§9.8   Confessions under the Sixth Amendment *Massiah* Doctrine

The Sixth Amendment (made applicable to the states in *Gideon v. Wainwright*, 372 US 335, 83 S Ct 792, 9 L Ed 2d 799 (1963)) has been held to require the exclusion of incriminatory statements "deliberately elicited" from a defendant by law enforcement officials[1] in the absence of counsel. See *Massiah v. United States*, 377 US 201, 84 S Ct 1199, 12 L Ed 2d 246 (1964) (co-defendant Colson, at request of federal agents, initiated conversation with Massiah resulting in admissions surreptitiously recorded by agents

---

§9.8   [1] The Sixth Amendment is not violated when a private citizen, unconnected with law enforcement authorities, elicits an incriminating statement. *Com. v. Allen*, 395 Mass 448, 454, 480 NE2d 630, 635 (1985) (hospital nurse).

and offered into evidence); *Brewer v. Williams*, 430 US 387, 97 S Ct 1232, 51 L Ed 2d 424 (1977) (detective used "Christian burial speech" to elicit incriminating statements about missing girl). For Massachusetts cases recognizing and discussing the *Massiah* doctrine, see *Com. v. Reynolds*, 429 Mass 388, 392-395, 708 NE2d 658, 663-664 (1999) (& citations); *Com. v. Cote*, 386 Mass 354, 359-361, 435 NE2d 1047, 1050-1051 (1982); *Com. v. Brant*, 380 Mass 876, 882, 406 NE2d 1021, 1026 (1980); *Com. v. Williams*, 378 Mass 217, 227 n.10, 391 NE2d 1202, 1209 n.10 (1979) (citations omitted); *Com. v. Frongillo*, 359 Mass 132, 136-137, 268 NE2d 341, 344 (1971) (*Massiah* did not require suppression of incriminating statement voluntarily made in conversation initiated by defendant in hope of help on disposition).

The *Massiah* doctrine "in general terms stated a rule against interrogation after indictment in the absence of counsel." *Com. v. McCarthy*, 348 Mass 7, 11-12, 200 NE2d 264, 266 (1964). In order to make out a violation, the defendant must demonstrate that the police either interrogated him or took some action designed to elicit the incriminating statements. See *Com. v. Bandy*, 38 Mass App 329, 334-335, 648 NE2d 440, 443 (1995) (no showing that probation officer's comment was other than inadvertent). *Massiah* represents a basis for suppression of statements distinct from, and in addition to, the *Miranda* framework. See generally *Com. v. Rainwater*, 425 Mass 540, 542-546, 681 NE2d 1218, 1221-1223 (1997) (extensive discussion of relationship between doctrines).

The doctrine applies only after the initiation of adversary judicial criminal proceedings—i.e., after indictment, information, arraignment, or preliminary hearing—because that is the point at which the right to counsel attaches. See *Kirby v. Illinois*, 406 US 682, 92 S Ct 1877, 32 L Ed 2d 411 (1972). The issuance of a complaint and arrest warrant does not constitute the commencement of adversary proceedings in Massachusetts. *Com. v. Ortiz*, 422 Mass 64, 67 n.1, 661 NE2d 925, 927 n.1 (1996); *Com. v. Smallwood*, 379 Mass 878, 884-885, 401 NE2d 802, 806 (1980). See also

Com. v. Phinney, 416 Mass 364, 371 n.4, 622 NE2d 617, 622 n.4 (1993) (no right to counsel during interrogation where defendant had not been charged); *Com. v. Mahoney*, 400 Mass 524, 528-529, 510 NE2d 759, 762 (1987) (right to counsel does not apply during booking procedure); *Com. v. Mandeville*, 386 Mass 393, 436 NE2d 912 (1982) (where neither defendant nor attorney asked that attorney's presence be secured at time of arrest, statements obtained on route to police station following arrest did not violate Sixth Amendment even though police knew that defendant was represented by counsel and had been informed by counsel six days prior to arrest that defendant did not wish to speak to police). In this context, it should be noted that there is no federal or state constitutional right to consult with an attorney before deciding whether to submit to a breathalyzer test. See *Com. v. Brazelton*, 404 Mass 783, 537 NE2d 142 (1989).

Prior to the commencement of formal proceedings, incriminatory statements deliberately elicited from the defendant in the absence of counsel are not rendered inadmissible by the doctrine. See *Moulton v. Maine*, 474 US 159, 180 n.16, 106 S Ct 477, 88 L Ed 2d 481 (1985).

The Sixth Amendment is offense specific, so that even if the right to counsel has attached with regard to one offense, this does not preclude interrogation regarding a different, unrelated offense. *Moulton v. Maine*, supra (incriminating remarks relating to crimes not then charged not subject to exclusion); *McNeil v. Wisconsin*, 501 US 171, 111 S Ct 2204 (1991); *Com. v. Rainwater*, supra, 425 Mass at 546-550, 681 NE2d at 1223-1225 (discussion of "inextricably related" crime exception); *Com. v. Shipps*, 399 Mass 820, 827-828, 507 NE2d 671, 677-678 (1987) (even if police aware defendant had been represented on an unrelated charge the year before, no violation by interrogating him on the current charge); *Com. v. Chase*, 42 Mass App 749, 757, 679 NE2d 1012, 1027 (1997).

The standard for waiver of the right to counsel would appear to be the same as the standard for waiver of *Miranda* rights — knowing, intelligent, and voluntary. See *Patterson v. Illinois,* 487 US 285, 292, 108 S Ct 2389, 101 L Ed 2d 261 (1988). Some waivers, however, will pass muster for *Miranda* purposes but not *Massiah,* as for example where the suspect is not informed his attorney is seeking to reach him during questioning. *Patterson v. Illinois,* supra, 487 US at 297 n.9, distinguishing *Moran v. Burbine,* 475 US 412, 421, 106 S Ct 1135, 1141, 89 L Ed 2d 410 (1986), discussed at §9.7.4, supra. A defendant may waive the Sixth Amendment right to counsel without consulting with or notifying counsel. See *Com. v. Cote,* supra, 386 Mass at 360 n.9, 435 NE2d at 1051 n.9.

Once the right to counsel has been invoked, a valid waiver can be made out only if the suspect initiated further communication with the police. See *Michigan v. Jackson,* 475 US 625 (1986) (applying the *Edwards v. Arizona* rule, discussed in §9.7.1, supra). But see *Michigan v. Harvey,* 494 US 344 (1990) (statement obtained in violation of *Michigan v. Jackson* may be used to impeach defendant at trial).

The right to counsel applies to post-indictment, court-ordered psychiatric evaluations. See *Estelle v. Smith,* 451 US 454, 101 S Ct 1866, 68 L Ed 2d 359 (1981) (where defense counsel was not notified psychiatric examination would encompass issue of client's future dangerousness — an issue material to capital sentencing proceeding — examination violated defendant's Sixth Amendment rights). But see *Com. v. Baldwin,* 426 Mass 105, 110, 686 NE2d 1001, 1005 (1997) (decision to undergo psychiatric evaluation is "critical stage," but interview itself is not; thus no right to attendance of counsel at interview); *Com. v. Trapp,* 423 Mass 356, 359, 668 NE2d 327 (1996).

The right to counsel does not include the right to have family members present at custodial interrogations. *Com. v. Bradshaw,* 385 Mass 244, 431 NE2d 880 (1982). But see *Com. v. A Juvenile (No. 1),* 389 Mass 128, 134, 449 NE2d 654, 657 (1983) (in order to demonstrate knowing and intelligent waiver by juvenile, Commonwealth must demonstrate in most cases that parent or interested adult was present at time of waiver).

For application of the *Massiah* doctrine to "jail plant" cases, compare *United States v. Henry*, 447 US 264, 100 S Ct 2183, 65 L Ed 2d 115 (1980) (post-indictment statements obtained from incarcerated defendant by undercover government informant placed in cell constituted "surreptitious interrogation" which violated Sixth Amendment right to counsel) and *Com. v. Reynolds*, supra, 429 Mass at 392-395, 708 NE2d at 663-664 (jailhouse informant was agent of government at time he elicited statements from defendant if he was promised recognition of cooperation) with *Kuhlmann v. Wilson*, 477 US 436, 106 S Ct 2616, 91 L Ed 2d 364 (1986) (because informant was merely passive listener, police had not "deliberately elicited" statements and Sixth Amendment not violated). See also *Com. v. Gajka*, 425 Mass 751, 752-753, 682 NE2d 1345, 1347 (1997) (cellmate not agent of government when he initiated questioning of defendant).

The Supreme Judicial Court has declined to provide more protection under art. 12 of the Declaration of Rights than is provided by the Sixth Amendment. See *Com. v. Rainwater*, supra, 425 Mass at 553-555, 681 NE2d at 1227-1228.

The Supreme Court has refused to adopt a "public safety" exception (analagous to *New York v. Quarles*, discussed in §9.7.7, supra) to the *Massiah* doctrine. See *Moulton v. Maine*, supra, 474 US at 180.

§9.9   Confessions under the Fourth Amendment "Fruit of the Poisonous Tree" Doctrine

The rule excluding evidence seized in violation of the Fourth Amendment (imposed upon the states in *Mapp v.*

Ohio, 367 US 643 (1961)) applies to admissions or confessions obtained as a result of an illegal search, arrest, or detention. See *Dunaway v. New York*, 442 US 200 (1979); *Brown v. Illinois*, 422 US 590 (1975); *Wong Sun v. United States*, 371 US 471 (1963); *Com. v. Reyes*, 38 Mass App 483, 649 NE2d 166 (1995). But compare *Com. v. Corriveau*, 396 Mass 319, 326-329, 486 NE2d 29, 36-37 (1985) (defendant's statement at police station not product of unlawful arrest because defendant voluntarily accompanied police to the station); *Com. v. Bookman*, 386 Mass 657, 659-660, 436 NE2d 1228, 1230 (1982) (although officers lacked probable cause to arrest, defendant voluntarily accompanied them to police station for questioning); *Com. v. Cruz*, 373 Mass 676, 681-685, 369 NE2d 996, 1004 (1977) (defendant's incriminating statements not result of illegal detention).

A statement that is the product of police conduct violative of the Fourth Amendment is thereby subject to suppression even if the statement is "voluntary" under the due process standard (see §9.2, supra) and complies with the requirements of *Miranda* (see §9.7, supra). *Taylor v. Alabama*, 457 US 687 (1982); *Dunaway v. New York*, supra, 442 US at 216-217; *Com. v. Cote*, 386 Mass 354, 361-362, 435 NE2d 1047, 1051 (1982).

The critical question under this derivative evidence analysis is whether the statement was obtained by exploitation of the initial illegality (in which case it must be suppressed), or whether the causal connection had become sufficiently attenuated by the intervention of time or circumstances. *Taylor v. Alabama*, supra, 457 US at 689-690; *Dunaway v. New York*, supra, 442 US at 217-219 (provision of *Miranda* warnings not suffcient to purge taint of illegal arrest); *Brown v. Illinois*, supra, 422 US at 600-604 (same; discussing factors to be weighed in attenuation analysis). For Massachusetts cases applying this analysis, see *Com. v. Shipps*, 399 Mass 820, 829-830, 507 NE2d 671, 678 (1987); *Com. v. Cote*, supra, 386 Mass at 362, 435 NE2d at 1051-1052; *Com. v. Bradshaw*, 385 Mass 244, 258-259, 431 NE2d 880, 895 (1982) (confession properly admitted because taint of illegal arrest had been purged); *Com. v. Haas,* 373 Mass 545, 551, 554, 369 NE2d 692, 700, 703 (1977) (statement following illegal arrest); *Com. v. Fielding,* 371 Mass 97, 113-115, 353 NE2d 719, 729-730 (1976) (confession properly admitted because taint of illegal arrest had been purged; discussion of *Brown* factors); *Com. v. Reyes,* supra, 38 Mass App at 487-488, 649 NE2d at 169 (given temporal circumstances of illegal search and arrest and defendant's confession, and lack of an intervening event, confession must be suppressed). For a general discussion of the "fruit of the poisonous tree" doctrine and the two exceptions for evidence obtained through an independent source and evidence that would have been inevitably discovered by lawful means, see *Com. v. Fedette,* 396 Mass 455, 458-461, 486 NE2d 1112, 1115-1116 (1985); *Com. v. Benoit,* 382 Mass 210, 415 NE2d 818 (1980).

The discovery of a witness through unconstitutional police conduct does not automatically preclude that witness's testimony. Admissibility turns on whether the witness's decision to testify was voluntary. See *United States v. Ceccolini,* 435 US 268, 98 S Ct 1054, 55 L Ed 2d 268 (1978) (Fourth Amendment violation); *Michigan v. Tucker,* 417 US 433, 94 S Ct 2357, 41 L Ed 2d 182 (1974) (Fifth Amendment violation); *Com. v. Caso,* 377 Mass 236, 385 NE2d 979 (1979). See also *Com. v. Lahti,* 398 Mass 829, 501 NE2d 511 (1986) (suppressing on Fifth Amendment grounds two victims' anticipated testimony as tainted fruit of defendant's involuntary statements to police).

§9.10 Other Exclusionary Rules

§9.10.1   Delayed Arraignment

Prior to its decision in *Miranda v. Arizona* (discussed above in §9.7), the Supreme Court adopted an automatic rule of exclusion applicable in federal proceedings for statements (even if voluntary) obtained from a defendant during a period of unreasonable delay between arrest and arraignment. See *Mallory v. United States*, 354 US 449, 77 S Ct 1356, 1 L Ed 2d 1479 (1957); *McNabb v. United States*, 318 US 332, 63 S Ct 608, 87 L Ed 819 (1943). The so-called *McNabb-Mallory* rule was purportedly overturned by legislation in 1968, see 18 USC §3501(c), and its current status remains somewhat in doubt. See generally *Com. v. Rosario*, 422 Mass 48, 55-56, 661 NE2d 71, 76-77 (1996) (& citations). Cf. *United States v. Dickerson*, 166 F3d 667 (4th Cir 1999) (holding that *Miranda v. Arizona* was superceded by 18 USC §3501(b)).

Although unreasonable delay in arraignment is a factor to be weighed in determining the voluntariness of a confession under due process concepts (see §9.2, supra), the automatic rule of exclusion has not been applied to the state courts. See *Fikes v. Alabama*, 352 US 191, 199 n.1, 77 S Ct 281, 1 L Ed 2d 246 (1957) (Frankfurter, J, concurring); *Com. v. Cote*, 386 Mass 354, 360, 435 NE2d 1047, 1051 (1982). See also *Cleary v. Bolger*, 371 US 392, 83 S Ct 385, 9 L Ed 2d 390 (1963). Compare *County of Riverside v. McLaughlin*, 500 US 44, 111 S Ct 1661, 114 L Ed 2d 49 (1991) (setting 48-hour period for holding of probable cause hearing for persons arrested without warrant).

In the Massachusetts courts, exclusion of a confession has been deemed an appropriate sanction for violation of Mass R Crim P 7(a), requiring prompt presentment of an arrestee before a court, if it is determined that the delay was arranged by the police with the purpose of procuring a statement from the defendant. *Com. v. Cote*, supra, 386 Mass at 361, 435 NE2d at 1051. See, e.g., *Com. v. Fryar*, 414 Mass 732, 743, 610 NE2d 903, 910 (1993) (police had not intentionally delayed defendant's arraignment for purpose of interrogating him further without assistance of counsel); *Com. v. Hodgkins*, 401 Mass 871, 876-878, 520 NE2d 145, 149 (1988) (evidence did not support defendant's assertion that delay in arraignment was contrived to procure his participation in videotape reenactment of crime). For discussion of the interaction of Rule 7(a) and the bail statute, GL 276,

§58, in the context of suppression of evidence, see *Com. v. Perito*, 417 Mass 674, 679-680, 632 NE2d 1190, 1193-1194 (1994) and *Com. v. Chistolini*, 422 Mass 854, 855-858, 665 NE2d 994, 996-997 (1996). See also *Com. v. Falco*, 43 Mass App 253, 682 NE2d 900 (1997) (no violation of statutory right to prompt bail hearing where motorist who refused blood alcohol test was held for six and one-half hours).

In 1996, the Supreme Judicial Court adopted a "safe harbor" rule: An otherwise admissible statement is not to be excluded on the ground of unreasonable delay in arraignment if the statement is made within six hours of the arrest or if at any time the defendant made an informed and voluntary written or recorded waiver of his right to be arraigned without unreasonable delay. See *Com. v. Rosario*, supra, 422 Mass at 56, 661 NE2d at 76-77. See also *Com. v. Ortiz*, 422 Mass 64, 661 NE2d 925 (1996) (informed and voluntary waiver of prompt arraignment would excuse delay, but no waiver necessary if questioning occurs within six-hour period). The rule is designed to eliminate (or at least reduce) debate over the reasonableness of any delay and to bar admission of a statement made after the six-hour period unless there is a waiver of prompt arraignment. The rule applies without regard to whether or not court is in session during the time period. See generally *Com. v. Butler*, 423 Mass 517, 668 NE2d 832 (1996) (extensive discussion; rule not to be applied retroactively); *Com. v. Hunter*, 426 Mass 715, 720-721, 690 NE2d 815, 820-821 (1998) (applying pre-*Rosario* analysis).

A statement obtained during the six-hour period is still, of course, subject to suppression if the requirements of *Miranda* are not met (see §9.7, supra), or if the statement is shown to be involuntary (see §§9.2, supra), or if the arrestee's right to use the telephone pursuant to GL 276, §33A, is violated (see §9.10.2, infra). Moreover, the six-hour safe harbor period is tolled if the arrestee is incapacitated because of a self-induced disability, such as the consumption of drugs, or if for other reasons not attributable to the police interrogation is not possible or must be suspended. *Com. v. Rosario,* supra, 422 Mass at 56-57, 661 NE2d at 77.

§9.10.2   Right to Use Telephone

An inculpatory statement obtained as a result of a violation of GL 276, §33A, providing that a person in custody must be permitted to use the telephone within one hour and to be so informed, is subject to suppression under a judge-made exlusionary rule. See *Com. v. Alicea,* 428 Mass 711, 716, 705 NE2d 233, 236 (1999); *Com. v. Caze,* 426 Mass 309, 310, 687 NE2d 1251, 1252 (1997); *Com. v. Jones,* 362 Mass 497, 502-503, 287 NE2d 599, 603-604 (1972). Moreover, a violation of the statute factors into the equation of deciding the voluntariness of a confession. See *Com. v. Meehan,* 377 Mass 552, 387 NE2d 527 (1979).

Exclusion has not been required, however, where the violation is found to have been unintentional. See *Com. v. Johnson,* 422 Mass 420, 429, 663 NE2d 559, 565 (1996) (delay designed to allow other officers to be present, and defendant not questioned during delay); *Com. v. Parker,* 402 Mass 333, 341, 522 NE2d 924, 929 (1988) (*Parker I*); *Com. v. Bradshaw,* 385 Mass 244, 266, 431 NE2d 880, 895 (1982); *Com. v. Alicea,* 376 Mass 506, 511 n.11, 381 NE2d 144, 148 (1978); *Com. v. Santiago,* 30 Mass App 207, 219-220, 567 NE2d 943, 950-951 (1991). See also *Com. v. Borodine,* 371 Mass 1, 5, 353 NE2d 649, 652-653 (1976) (basement of victim's home was not a "place of detention" within meaning of statute); *Com. v. Carey,* 26 Mass App 339, 343, 526 NE2d 1329, 1332-1333 (1988) (no violation of statute where defendant required to wait until completion of booking procedure to use phone, but within one hour statutory period, even though inculpatory videotape made during booking).

Evidence obtained by police from a defendant's telephone call has been held admissible at trial. See, e.g., *Com. v. White,* 422 Mass 487, 499-500, 663 NE2d 834, 843-844

(1996) (telephone number defendant called during booking).

§9.10.3   Right to Interpreter for Hearing-Impaired Person/No Right to Interpreter for Non-English Speaking Defendant

A deaf or hearing-impaired person under arrest is entitled to the assistance of a qualified interpreter regarding interrogation, warnings, notification of rights, or the taking of a statement. GL 221, §92A. The statute renders inadmissible in evidence any answer, statement, or admission elicited other than through a qualified interpreter, unless there was a knowing, voluntary, and intelligent waiver of the right to an interpreter. See generally *Com. v. Kelley*, 404 Mass 459, 461-462, 535 NE2d 1251, 1253-1254 (1989).

There is no requirement that police provide an independent interpreter when questioning a non-English speaking defendant. A police officer may act as interpreter. *Com. v. Ardon*, 428 Mass 496, 499-500, 702 NE2d 808, 810-811 (1998); *Com. v. Alves*, 35 Mass App 935, 937, 625 NE2d 559, 561 (1993).

§9.10.4   Statement Made by a Defendant during a Court-Ordered Psychiatric Examination

A statement made by a defendant during a court-ordered psychiatric examination is rendered inadmissible by GL 233, §23B, discussed in §13.5.5, infra.

§9.10.5   Statements Made during Plea Negotiations, in Connection with Assignment of Counsel, and during Pretrial Diversion Assessment

Massachusetts practice bars the use in evidence of statements made by a defendant during plea negotiations.

See §4.6, supra. Information provided in connection with assignment of counsel based on indigency may not be used in any criminal or civil proceeding except a prosecution for perjury committed in providing the information. SJC Rule 3:10, Sec 9. No statement made by a defendant during the course of assessment for a pretrial diversion program may be disclosed to a prosecutor or other law enforcement officer in connection with the charge or charges pending against defendant. GL c 276A, §5.

§9.11   Procedure for Challenging Confessions

The proper method for challenging the admissibility of a confession or other statement is a pretrial motion to suppress or for a voir dire. Mass R Crim P 13(c)(2); Superior Court Rule 61; *Com. v. Rubio*, 27 Mass App 506, 511, 540 NE2d 189, 192 (1989). Defendants have, however, been permitted to rely upon an objection at trial. Id; *Com. v. Adams*, 389 Mass 265, 269-270 & n.1, 450 NE2d 149, 152 & n.1 (1983) ("Even if the defendant has not moved to suppress his statements the burden is still on the Commonwealth, upon seasonable objection, to prove affirmatively, prior to the admission of these statements, that the statements were properly obtained and that the defendant waived his rights."). "When an objection is made at trial to the admission of a defendant's incriminating statement on the ground that it was obtained in violation of the *Miranda* case or was involuntary, or both, and no pretrial hearing has been held, the prudent thing for the judge to do is to stop the trial and conduct an appropriate inquiry." *Com. v. Rubio*, supra, 27 Mass App at 511, 540 NE2d at 192.

§9.12   Corroboration Requirement

Under Massachusetts law, a criminal defendant may not be convicted solely on the basis of his uncorroborated confession. *Com. v. Forde,* 392 Mass 453, 457-458, 466 NE2d 510, 513 (1984). The corroboration rule has been extended to admissions as well as confessions. See *Com. v. Leonard,* 401 Mass 470, 517 NE2d 157 (1988). The corroboration required, however, may be quite minimal. There need only be some evidence besides the confession that the criminal act actually occurred. The corroborating evidence need not point to the accused as the perpetrator. *Com. v. Leonard, supra,* 401 Mass at 458, 517 NE2d at 159; *Com. v. Manning,* 41 Mass App 18, 668 NE2d 850 (1996) (rejecting federal rule that corroborative evidence must implicate the accused; automobile's position sufficiently corroborated defendant's admission to operating under influence). See also *Com. v. Jackson,* 428 Mass 455, 467, 702 NE2d 1158, 1166 (1998); *Com. v. Phinney,* 416 Mass 364, 373, 622 NE2d 617, 623 (1993) (Commonwealth not required to offer physical evidence to support confession where it was undisputed that murder had occurred and confession was supplemented by other evidence pointing to defendant). Compare *Com. v. Landenburg,* 41 Mass App 23, 668 NE2d 1306 (1996) (lack of corroborating evidence required reversal of larceny conviction).

Testimony admitted as a prior inconsistent statement (and not as substantive evidence) cannot constitute corroboration. *Com. v. Costello,* 411 Mass 371, 374-375, 582 NE2d 938, 940-941 (1991). Nor can one extrajudicial confession be used to corroborate another extrajudicial confession. Id. (& citations).

CHAPTER
10

EYEWITNESS IDENTIFICATION EVIDENCE

§10.1   Use and Admissibility of Identification Evidence

A person suspected or accused of a crime may be the subject of police-initiated identification procedures, either formal or informal in nature. Through the process of observation of such a person (or his photograph) by the victim or a witness, the person so viewed may either be exculpated or inculpated.

Requiring a person to participate in a lineup or show-up does not violate the privilege against self-incrimination guaranteed by the Fifth Amendment. *United States v. Wade,* 388 US 218, 222 (1967) ("compelling the accused merely to exhibit his person for observation by a prosecution witness prior to trial involves no compulsion of the accused to give evidence having testimonial significance"); *Com. v. Holland,* 410 Mass 248, 259 n.10, 571 NE2d 625, 632 n.10 (1991); *Com. v. Simmonds,* 386 Mass 234, 239, 434 NE2d 1270, 1274 (1982). Nor does compelled participation violate the Fourth Amendment so long as there is probable cause to detain the suspect. See *United States v. Crews,* 445 US 463 (1980); *Dunaway v. New York,* 442 US 200 (1979); *Brown v. Illinois,* 422 US 590 (1975); *Davis v. Mississippi,* 394 US 721 (1969); *Com. v. Napolitano,* 378 Mass 599, 607, 393 NE2d 338, 344 (1979) (absent probable cause, suspect cannot be detained for investigatory purposes).

§10.1.1   Use at Trial of Pretrial Identifications

If the subject of an identification procedure is brought to trial, *Com. v. Swenson,* 368 Mass 268, 272, 331 NE2d 893, 896 (1975) sets out the three primary purposes for which proof of a pretrial identification of the subject may be offered in evidence:

   (1)   for corroborative purposes (i.e., to corroborate an in-court identification). See, e.g., *Com. v. Gunter,* 427 Mass 259, 692 NE2d 515 (1998); *Com.*

v. Weaver, 395 Mass 307, 310, 479 NE2d 682, 685 (1985).[1]

(2)   for impeachment purposes, when the prior identification has been disclaimed by the witness. See, e.g., *Com. v. Swenson*, supra, 368 Mass at 273-274, 331 NE2d at 897 (testimony of officer who had presented array of photographs was admissible to impeach witness who testified at trial that he had not identified defendant's photograph in pretrial procedure).

(3)   as substantive evidence, which may serve as the basis for denial of a motion for directed verdict and the probative value of which is left for the jury. See *Com. v. Daye*, 393 Mass 55, 60, 469 NE2d 483, 487 (1984) (& citations),[2] and *Com. v. Swenson*, supra, 368 Mass at 272, 331 NE2d at 896.

A prior identification by the witness of someone *other than* the defendant may be brought out to impeach an in-court identification. See *Com. v. Roselli*, 335 Mass 38, 40, 138 NE2d 607, 608 (1956). Similarly, the failure of the witness to identify the defendant in a photographic array or lineup has impeachment value if the witness makes a subsequent identification of the defendant. See, e.g., *Com. v. Paszko*, 391 Mass 164, 171-172, 461 NE2d 222, 228 (1984); *Com. v. Correia*, 381 Mass 65, 79-80, 407 NE2d 1216, 1226 (1980)

Assigning full probative value to a pretrial identification has been held particularly appropriate "where the witness, because of the time lapse before trial, is unable to

---

§10.1   [1] "Since juries may have trouble making the distinction between corroboration evidence and substantive evidence, the elimination of this distinction is salutary." *Com. v. Weichell*, 390 Mass 62, 71, 453 NE2d 1038, 1044 (1983), and "identification evidence formerly admissible as corroborative is now admissible for its probative value." *Com. v. Daye*, 393 Mass 55, 60 n.8, 72, 469 NE2d 483, 487, n.8, 494 (1984).

For a discussion of the use of a prior identification to bolster trial testimony even before the identifying witness has been impeached, see §6.19.

[2] For further discussion of *Com. v. Daye*, see §6.7.2.c.

make an in-court identification but clearly recollects having positively identified the defendant earlier." *Com. v. Swenson,* supra, 368 Mass at 272 n.3, 331 NE2d at 896-897 n.3. "A pretrial identification is regarded as having equal or greater testimonial value than one made in court because the circumstances of the earlier identification often were less suggestive and because that identification occurred closer to the time of the offense." *Com. v. Torres,* 367 Mass 737, 739, 327 NE2d 871, 873 (1975). "Furthermore, it is appropriate to recognize the possibility that fear will motivate a person who has made a pretrial identification to disclaim the ability to do so at trial." *Com. v. Warren,* 403 Mass 137, 141, 526 NE2d 250, 252 (1988).

It is thus established that a "defendant's due process rights are not violated so long as the identifying witness is present in court, is available to be cross-examined, and acknowledges the extra-judicial identification." Id.; *Com. v. Schand,* 420 Mass 783, 795-796, 653 NE2d 566, 574-575 (1995). See also *Com. v. Paszko,* supra, 391 Mass 164 at 171 n.8, 461 NE2d at 228 n.8 ("An out-of-court identification is admissible as substantive evidence if the witness does not identify the defendant in court, provided the defendant's due process and confrontation rights are observed."); *Com. v. Vitello,* 376 Mass 426, 458-461, 381 NE2d 582, 600-601 (1978) (police officer was properly allowed to testify that witness, who made a positive in-court identification of defendant's photograph and testified that he remembered making a pretrial identification of the photograph but was unable to identify defendant in court, had made a positive pretrial identification of the same photograph; the testimony was admissible as independent substantive evidence of defendant's guilt);[3] *Com. v. Fitzgerald,* 376 Mass 402, 407-

---

[3]Moreover, the police officer could testify that in his opinion, the photograph selected by a witness prior to trial depicted the defendant, who had lost 25 pounds since the date of the crime. *Com. v. Vitello,* supra, 376 Mass at 459-460, 381 NE2d at 601. But compare *Com. v. Nassar,* 351 Mass 37, 41-42, 218 NE2d 72, 76 (1966) (police officer should not have been permitted to testify that photograph of defendant looked like

409, 381 NE2d 123, 129 (1978) (prior identification of defendants by witness admissible not merely to impeach but as substantive evidence where witness testified at trial that defendants were not the perpetrators, but affirmed that she had made the earlier identifications and thus could be cross-examined concerning them); *Com. v. Torres,* supra, 367 Mass at 738-740, 327 NE2d 873-874 (pretrial voice identification of defendant by blind victim, who did not identify defendant at trial, was admissible for probative purposes where defendant's constitutional right of confrontation was satisfied); *Com. v. Crowley,* 29 Mass App 1, 7, 556 NE2d 1043, 1047 (1990) ("a nonidentifying witness may testify to corroborate an extrajudicial identification if the testimony does not differ in material respects from that of the identifying witness"); *Com. v. Pacheco,* 12 Mass App 109, 120-121, 421 NE2d 1239, 1247 (1981) (pretrial voice identification of defendant by blind victim, who did not attempt to identify defendant at trial, was admissible for probative purposes).

If a witness at trial makes no in-court identification and disclaims any pretrial identification, third-party evidence of a pretrial identification is not admissible for substantive purposes. *Com. v. Daye,* supra, 393 Mass at 60-63, 469 NE2d 487-489 ("Where there is a dispute not only as to the accuracy of a pretrial identification, but also as to whether the identification was in fact made, 'the evidential value of the prior identification is almost completely dissipated.'") (citation omitted). "Thus, a police officer's attribution to a witness of a positive identification denied by the witness at trial is not admissible to prove the identification. Its effect is limited to impeachment." 393 Mass at 61, 469 NE2d at 488 (& citations). See also *Com. v. Martin,* 417 Mass 187, 198, 629 NE2d 297, 304 (1994) (witness did not establish her extrajudicial identification at trial, nor did she sufficiently

composite of perpetrator); *Com. v. Anderson,* 19 Mass App 968, 473 NE2d 1165, 1166 (1985) (non-eyewitness testimony that videotape and photographs depicted defendant was improperly admitted).

adopt it during her testimony); *Com. v. Kater*, 409 Mass 433, 447, 567 NE2d 885, 893 (1991) (*Kater III*) (composite likeness prepared by prosecution witness but that she refused to acknowledge at trial was admissible for impeachment purposes only); *Com. v. Scott*, 408 Mass 811, 824, 564 NE2d 370, 379 (1990); *Com. v. Jones*, 407 Mass 168, 552 NE2d 90 (1990); *Com. v. Kirk*, 39 Mass App 225, 230-231, 654 NE2d 938, 942-943 (1995) (conviction based on extrajudicial identification by nontestifying victim in affidavit and on complaint for abuse protection order violated defendant's right of confrontation); *Com. v. Muse*, 35 Mass App 466, 622 NE2d 640 (1993) (Commonwealth's failure to ask witness at trial whether he recognized photograph that detective testified he had selected during pretrial identification violated defendant's right of confrontation; but error harmless). Compare *Com. v. Dinkins*, 415 Mass 715, 722-723, 615 NE2d 570, 574 (1993) (no substantial risk of miscarriage of justice where judge admitted police officer's testimony concerning photographic identification denied by witness at trial); *Com. v. Meadows*, 33 Mass App 534, 540-541, 602 NE2d 583, 587 (1992) (variation in testimony of police officer and robbery victim witness was not a material one where officer testified victim rated his certainty as a ten on scale of one-to-ten when he identified two mug shots, and victim's own testimony was that he rated it seven; officer's testimony admissible); *Com. v. Mendrala*, 20 Mass App 398, 400-401, 480 NE2d 1039, 1041 (1985) (although witness's failure to acknowledge a pretrial identification of defendants precluded its admission under *Com. v. Daye*, the identification was nevertheless admissible under the spontaneous utterance exception to the hearsay rule). Cf. *Com. v. Perez*, 27 Mass App 550, 553-556, 540 NE2d 697, 699-700 (1989) (case remanded to determine whether judge improperly considered as substantive evidence testimony from police officer as to informant's description of perpetrator).

An identification made under oath before the grand jury and inconsistent with trial testimony may, however, be used substantively. *Com. v. Daye*, supra, 393 Mass at 73-74, 469 NE2d at 493 (adopting in part Proposed Mass R Evid 801(d)(1)(A)). See also *Com. v. Jenkins*, 34 Mass App 135, 145, 607 NE2d 756, 762 (1993), *superseded*, 416 Mass 736, 625 NE2d 1344 (1993) (witness's prior identifications of defendant at probable cause hearing and grand jury proceedings, acknowledged by witness at trial, admissible for full probative value). Moreover, where a witness who proves to be "vague and forgetful" has sufficiently adopted on voir dire extrajudicial statements of identification, third-party evidence of the pretrial identification is also admissible for substantive purposes. *Com. v. Cappellano*, 17 Mass App 272, 276-278, 457 NE2d 1121, 1124 (1983). Evidence that a witness, under oath and subject to cross-examination, identified the defendant at a probable cause hearing is admissible at trial if the witness is then "unavailable." *Com. v. Furtick*, 386 Mass 477, 480, 436 NE2d 396, 398 (1982) (but record did not establish "unavailability").

When offered substantively, evidence of a pretrial identification is admissible even though it might otherwise be considered hearsay. See Proposed Mass R Evid 801(d)(1)(C);[4] *Com. v. Vitello*, supra, 376 Mass at 458-459, 381 NE2d at 600 (citing with approval Fed R Evid 801(d)(1)(C)); *Com. v. Robinson*, 19 Mass App 1010, 476 NE2d 268 (1985).

---

[4] "A statement is not hearsay if — (1) Prior statement by a witness. The declarant testifies at the trial or hearing and is subject to cross-examination concerning the statement, and the statement is . . . (C) one of identification of a person after perceiving him." The Advisory Committee's Note explains: "The rationale for affording substantive effect to these statements is two-fold. It is unrealistic to believe that a jury properly discriminates limited admissibility in these matters though so instructed, and the declarant is available and subject to cross-examination." See also Fed R Evid 801(d)(1)(C).

§10.1.2   Composite Drawings and Sketches

Composite drawings and sketches are admissible for substantive purposes unless prepared under suggestive circumstances. See *Com. v. Weichell*, 390 Mass 62, 68-73, 453 NE2d 1038, 1044-1045 (1983) (but noting that the court "would not, at this time, sustain a conviction where such composite constituted the only evidence of identification, absent a more general acceptance of such evidence or a greater demonstration of its reliability." 390 Mass at 72 n.8, 453 NE2d at 1044-1045 n.8.); *Com. v. Thornley*, 400 Mass 355, 359-361, 509 NE2d 908, 911-912 (1987) (*Thornley I*); *Com. v. Kater*, 409 Mass 433, 443, 567 NE2d 885, 891 (1991) (*Kater III*). An Identikit composite sketch does not fall within the hearsay rule. *Com. v. Thornley I*, supra, 400 Mass at 361-362, 509 NE2d at 912 (& citations) (holding admissible a composite even though it was prepared by two witnesses, one of whom was unavailable to testify at trial).[5] Compare *Com. v. Susi*, 394 Mass 784, 789-790, 477 NE2d 995, 999 (1985) (a written description of the robber accompanying a composite drawing was not admissible where there was no evidence as to the source of the statement).

§10.1.3   Identifications Following Hypnosis

Identification evidence concerning matters not remembered before hypnosis is inadmissible. See *Com. v. Kater III*, supra, 409 Mass at 437-439, 567 NE2d 888-889 (statement of the procedures to be used by the trial judge to determine whether proffered identification testimony of a witness who had been subjected to hypnosis was based on the witnesses'

---

[5]But see (Liacos, J, dissenting),"[A] composite created by two witnesses interacting with the police officer should be inadmissible — at least, where one of the witnesses later misidentifies a person in a fair lineup and then is unavailable for trial examination." 400 Mass at 366, 509 NE2d at 915.

prehypnotic memory; declining to adopt an absolute prohibition of all posthypnotic identifications); *Com. v. Dodge*, 391 Mass 636, 462 NE2d 1363 (1984); *Com. v. Brouillet*, 389 Mass 605, 451 NE2d 128 (1983); *Com. v. Watson*, 388 Mass 536, 447 NE2d 1182 (1983); *Com. v. Kater*, 388 Mass 519, 447 NE2d 1190 (1983) (*Kater II*). See also §6.21.

§10.1.4   Mug Shots

Because of the risk of prejudice to the defendant inherent in the admission of photographs of the "mug shot" variety (see §4.4.2.), judges and prosecutors are required to "use reasonable means to avoid calling the jury's attention to the source of [such] photographs used to identify the defendant." *Com. v. Blaney*, 387 Mass 628, 638, 442 NE2d 389, 395 (1982). See *Com. v. Richardson*, 425 Mass 765, 682 NE2d 1354 (1997) (not error to admit over objection front and side views of defendant without separating them where all information on photos was sanitized and trial judge determined photos should go to jury in same condition as viewed by witness; judge did not err in not giving curative instruction where none was requested); *Com. v. Cohen*, 412 Mass 375, 382, 589 NE2d 289, 294-295 (1992) (use of phrase "mug shot" should not have been used by prosecutor in his opening; but it did not create a substantial likelihood of miscarriage of justice); *Com. v. Perez*, 405 Mass 339, 344, 540 NE2d 681, 684 (1989); *Com. v. Tuitt*, 393 Mass 801, 808-809, 473 NE2d 1103, 1109 (1985)(even if jury inferred from detective's testimony that photographs of defendant were mug shots, judge gave prompt limiting instructions and thus no prejudicial error); *Com. v. Gee*, 36 Mass App 154, 628 NE2d 1296 (1994) (admission of unsevered and unsanitized mug shots was reversible error where identity was main issue in case, jury could have reasonably inferred from photograph that defendant had been involved in prior misconduct, and jury instruction was not adequate to cure error); *Com. v. Payton*, 35 Mass App 586, 623 NE2d 1127 (1993) (no abuse of discretion in allowing unsevered mug shots in evidence where profile shot was of some assistance in identifying perpetrator and trial counsel did not object for tactical reasons); *Com. v. Bassett*, 21 Mass App 713, 720, 490 NE2d 459, 463 (1986) (references to identification of defendant from "mug book" improperly suggested that he had a prior criminal record).

While there is no per se rule excluding mug shots, their introduction into evidence is limited by the following criteria: (1) the prosecution must show some need to introduce the mug shots; (2) the mug shots, to the extent possible, should not indicate a prior record; and (3) the mug shots should not call attention to their origins and implications. *Com. v. Gee*, supra, 36 Mass App at 157-158 (citations omitted). Compare *Com. v. Weaver*, 400 Mass 612, 620, 511 NE2d 545, 550 (1987) (evidence of a photographic identification should not have been admitted where identification was not a live issue at trial and the evidence tended to show that defendant had had prior trouble with the criminal law) and *Com. v. Smith*, 21 Mass App 619, 622-623, 489 NE2d 203, 205 (1986) (reversible error to admit police photograph of defendant where his presence at scene of crime was not disputed) with *Com. v. Holmes*, 32 Mass App 906, 909-910, 584 NE2d 1150, 1154 (1992) (no error in admission of mug shots where *Com. v. Blaney* procedures were strictly followed and identification was live issue at trial). Cf. *Com. v. McNickles*, 22 Mass App 114, 122, 491 NE2d 662, 668 (1986) (rape defendant charged on joint enterprise theory was not entitled to instruction that the jury should draw no negative inferences concerning defendant from the victim's photographic identification of defendant's alleged companion). See also *Com. v. Austin*, 421 Mass 357, 365, 657 NE2d 458, 463 (1995) (videotape depicting another bank robbery admissible even though not amenable to sanitation procedures).

§10.2   Constitutional Issues

"[E]yewitness identification often plays a major, if not a determinative, role in the trial of criminal offenses, and the dangers of mistaken identification are great and the result possibly tragic. . . ." *Com. v. Dickerson*, 372 Mass 783, 789, 364 NE2d 1052, 1056 (1977). Pretrial confrontations arranged by the police between the accused and the victim or witnesses to a crime to obtain identification evidence are "peculiarly riddled with innumerable dangers and variable factors which might seriously, even crucially, derogate from a fair trial." *United States v. Wade*, 388 US 218, 228 (1967). The overriding danger inherent in such confrontations is that they might cause unreliable or mistaken identifications. Id.; *Manson v. Brathwaite*, 432 US 98, 111-114 (1977).

Decisions of the United States Supreme Court and of the Massachusetts courts have therefore developed legal principles based largely on the Fifth, Sixth, and Fourteenth Amendments to the United States Constitution that are designed to lessen the dangers of misidentification. These principles sometimes require that identification evidence be excluded from evidence at trial, as discussed below.

An eyewitness identification may also be suppressed on the grounds that it was the product of conduct violative of the Fourth Amendment, such as an illegal arrest. See *United States v. Crews*, 445 US 463 (1980); *Com. v. Cao*, 419 Mass 383, 644 NE2d 1294 (1995) (field interrogation was not "seizure" for purposes of determining whether resulting photograph was admissible in subsequent identification procedure); *Com. v. Howell*, 394 Mass 654, 657-659, 477 NE2d 126, 130 (1985); *Com. v. Manning*, 44 Mass App Ct 695, 693 NE2d 704 (1998) (although photo used in identification of defendant by witness was taken following illegal arrest, suppression was not required because purpose of arrest was not to gather evidence for unrelated crime, illegal arrest was not flagrant police misconduct, and photo was taken pursuant to standard police procedure); *Com. v.*

Pandolfino, 33 Mass App 96, 98-99, 596 NE2d 390, 391-392 (1992).

§10.2.1   Right to Counsel

The right to counsel, guaranteed by the Sixth Amendment, extends to each critical stage of a criminal proceeding, which has been held to include a lineup (or other physical confrontation) occurring *after* the defendant has been indicted or adversary criminal proceedings have been otherwise initiated. Conducting such a lineup in the absence of defense counsel or a valid waiver thereof thus constitutes a denial of the right to counsel, and the evidence of identification that results from the lineup is inadmissible at trial. *United States v. Wade,* 388 US 218 (1967); *Gilbert v. California,* 388 US 263 (1967); *Moore v. Illinois,* 434 US 220 (1977) (extending rule of per se inadmissibility to a one on one confrontation at a preliminary hearing held to determine whether accused should be bound over to the grand jury and to set bail); *Com. v. Donovan,* 392 Mass 647, 467 NE2d 198 (1984) (applying rule of per se inadmissibility to an identification initiated by a police officer without notice to counsel while defendant was seated in courtroom awaiting his probable cause hearing); *Com. v. Cooper,* 356 Mass 74, 80-84, 248 NE2d 253, 258-259 (1969) (discussion of *Wade-Gilbert* doctrine); *Com. v. Guillory,* 356 Mass 591, 254 NE2d 427 (1970). Compare 18 USC §3502 (1968), which purports to override *Wade* but is of doubtful constitutional validity.

The right to have counsel present does not apply to a lineup or other corporeal identification conducted *prior to* the initiation of adversary judicial criminal proceedings by way of indictment, information, arraignment, or preliminary hearing. See *Kirby v. Illinois,* 406 US 682 (1972) (plurality refused to apply *Wade-Gilbert* rule to robbery victim's one on one station house identification of an uncounseled suspect after his arrest but before judicial proceedings have been initiated); *Com. v. Simmonds*, 386 Mass 234, 237-238, 434 NE2d 1270, 1273-1274 (1982) (neither Sixth Amendment nor art. 12 of Massachusetts Declaration of Rights entitles defendant to assistance of counsel at lineup occurring prior to indictment or formal charge); *Com. v. Smallwood*, 379 Mass 878, 884-885, 401 NE2d 802, 806 (1980) (complaint and arrest warrant procedures do not constitute initiation of adversary proceedings); *Com. v. Clifford*, 374 Mass 293, 302, 372 NE2d 1267, 1274 (1978) (per se rule of exclusion is inapplicable where defendant has been arrested but no criminal complaint, indictment, or other formal charge has been issued against him); *Com. v. Key*, 19 Mass App 234, 237-239, 472 NE2d 1381, 1384 (1985) (right to counsel did not extend to courtroom identification of defendant following his arrest but just before his arraignment).

The right to have counsel present does not apply to a photographic identification, even if the prosecution has already initiated adversary criminal proceedings. See *United States v. Ash*, 413 US 300 (1973). The Court reasoned that a photographic identification procedure was not a critical stage of the criminal proceeding and that, inasmuch as the accused himself would not be present at the procedure, counsel was not needed to protect the accused from being misled or to counterbalance possible prosecutorial overreaching. See also *Com. v. Jackson*, 419 Mass 716, 729 n.13, 647 NE2d 401, 409 n.13 (1995). Compare *Com. v. Torres*, 367 Mass 737, 740, 327 NE2d 871, 874 (1975) (suggesting that right to counsel would apply to live voice identification procedure).

There is no right to have counsel present at a post-lineup interview with the witness. See *Com. v. Tanso*, 411 Mass 640, 653-654, 583 NE2d 1247, 1255-1256 (1992); *Com. v. Charles*, 397 Mass 1, 6, 489 NE2d 679, 683 (1986) (although it was unnecessary to decide the issue, "the cases holding that defense counsel does not have a right to be present at a post-lineup interview would appear to represent the better reasoned view").

The right to counsel may be waived. See *Com. v. Davis,* 380 Mass 1, 8, 401 NE2d 811, 816 (1980) (defendant who, after arrest, was warned of his right to counsel before participating in lineup and signed a consent form validly waived his right to counsel). But "[o]nce the right to counsel arises in connection with an identification procedure the person in custody must specifically and seasonably be informed of that right before the procedure commences," and waiver must be knowing and intelligent. *Com. v. Cooper,* supra, 356 Mass at 83, 248 NE2d at 259. Merely advising a suspect of his *Miranda* rights does not suffice. Id.; *Com. v. Mendes,* 361 Mass 507, 509-510, 281 NE2d 243, 245 (1972) ("The police, contrary to well-established law which we are required to apply, did not inform the defendant of his right to counsel *at the lineup,* and in these circumstances the defendant could not make a knowing and intelligent waiver of his *Wade* rights."); *Com. v. Guillory,* 356 Mass 591, 593, 254 NE2d 427, 429 (1970). Cf. *Com. v. Santos,* 402 Mass 775, 782-783, 525 NE2d 388, 393 (1988) (no waiver of constitutional rights occurred when defendant assented to one on one confrontation).

The primary purpose of ensuring defense counsel's presence at pretrial identification procedures is to avoid suggestive influences (either intentional or unintentional) that may result in a mistaken identification. *United States v. Wade,* supra, 388 US at 228-239; *Com. v. Napolitano,* 378 Mass 599, 604, 393 NE2d 338, 342 (1979) (counsel is present to "ferret out" any suggestive influences he perceives in the identification procedures). Moreover, "because of the potential for prejudice at a pretrial lineup, there is a critical need for counsel at that stage to 'assure a meaningful confrontation at trial.'" *Com. v. Cooper,* supra, 356 Mass at 82, 248 NE2d at 259 (citation omitted). When counsel is present, counsel's role depends on the setting in which the prosecution conducts the identification procedure. At trial or at a probable cause hearing, of course, "counsel has the responsibility, by way of cross-examination, to bring to the attention of the trier of facts any circumstances which tend to cast doubt upon a witness's identification testimony." *Com. v. Jones*, 362 Mass 497, 500-501, 287 NE2d 599, 602 (1972). Counsel, moreover, may suggest steps to eliminate the risk of mistaken identification, such as seating the defendant in the courtroom audience rather than at the counsel table or in the dock. *Com. v. Jones*, supra, 362 Mass at 501, 287 NE2d at 602 (but absent a showing of abuse of discretion that prejudices defendant's opportunity for a fair trial, the trial judge's ruling denying request will not be disturbed; no abuse of discretion where witness was not unusually impressionable or otherwise unreliable); *Com. v. Libby*, 21 Mass App 650, 656-657, 489 NE2d 702, 707 (1986) (judge did not abuse his discretion in requiring defendant to choose between absenting himself from the courtroom and refraining from asking the victim whether he saw the perpetrator, and remaining in the courtroom and asking the victim to identify the defendant). See also *Com. v. Moore*, 379 Mass 106, 107-111, 393 NE2d 904, 906-908 (1979) (extensive discussion of history and use of prisoner's dock, together with authorities; holding that a judge confronted with a request that the defendant be permitted to sit at counsel table rather than the dock should grant the request unless unusual security measures are necessary); *Walker v. Butterworth*, 599 F2d 1074 (1st Cir 1979) (suggesting in dictum that the Massachusetts prisoner's dock may be unconstitutional because it dilutes the presumption of innocence).

Opportunities contrived to allow witnesses improperly to observe the defendant in the courtroom may lead to suppression of an identification. See *Martin v. Donnelly*, 391 F Supp 1241 (D Mass 1974) (contrived confrontation in courtroom prior to arraignment of defendant, apparently calculated to bolster identifications by witnesses and made without knowledge of defendant or his counsel, violated *Wade-Gilbert*); *Com. v. Donovan*, supra, 392 Mass at 649-651, 467 at NE2d at 199-200 (identification initiated by a police officer without notice to counsel while defendant was seated in courtroom awaiting his probable cause hearing violated

Wade-Gilbert); *Com. v. Wheeler*, 3 Mass App 387, 389 n.1, 331 NE2d 815, 816 n.1 (1975) (trial judge suppressed identification of defendant seated in dock because he was not satisfied that victim's presence in courtroom on that occasion was "accidental").

Counsel can also request postponement of an identification until a lineup can be arranged in a less suggestive setting or request that others be seated in the dock with the defendant. *Com. v. Napolitano*, supra, 378 Mass at 604 n.8 393 NE2d at 342 n.8; *Com. v. Cincotta*, 379 Mass 391, 395, 398 NE2d 478, 480-481 (1979). See also *Com. v. Core*, 370 Mass 369, 372, 348 NE2d 777, 780 (1976) (no abuse of discretion in denial of motion for pretrial lineup); *Com. v. Pearsall*, 370 Mass 413, 415, 348 NE2d 428, 430 (1976) (same).

Counsel has an affirmative duty to raise the issue of the danger of suggestiveness and request corrective action. See *Com. v. Cincotta*, supra, 379 Mass at 395, 398 NE2d at 480-481 ("[C]ounsel has a responsibility to be alert and, as far as he thinks necessary or useful, to try to eliminate any suggestive influence. . . . If precautionary measures are not sought, complaint cannot be later made of suggestiveness."); *Com. v. Napolitano*, supra, 378 Mass at 604, 393 NE2d at 342 (failure of counsel to make request at probable cause hearing to have in-court lineup or to seat defendant in audience); *Com. v. Jones*, 375 Mass 349, 359, 377 NE2d 903, 909 (1978) (counsel at probable cause hearing failed to seek alteration in identification procedures). If counsel wishes to employ a particular in-court identification procedure, a request should be made by written motion filed in advance of the court date. See *Com. v. Ceria*, 13 Mass App 230, 237, 431 NE2d 608, 612-613 (1982) (no abuse of discretion in denying oral request for lineup made on date of probable cause hearing). Cf. *Com. v. Florentino*, 396 Mass 689, 691, 488 NE2d 403, 405 (1986) (defendant was not denied effective assistance of counsel even though his attorney failed to move to suppress pretrial identifications).

At a lineup or show-up, counsel's role is primarily that of an observer who may deter abuse and provide the basis (as well as the ability to reconstruct the event) for a later challenge to the identification by a motion to suppress or by cross-examination. See *United States v. Wade,* supra, 388 US at 229-237; *United States v. Ash,* supra, 413 US at 312-313; *Com. v. Crowe,* 21 Mass App 456, 466 n.10, 488 NE2d 780, 787 n.10 (1986) (observing in response to defendant's argument that although his counsel was present, he had no say in the makeup of the lineup: "[T]he defendant has no *right* to anything beyond the presence of counsel at a lineup."). Cf. *Com. v. Clifford,* supra, 374 Mass at 302, 372 NE2d at 1274 (the "better practice" is to give the attorney a meaningful opportunity to become acquainted with the case and the prospective witnesses prior to the lineup).

It must be emphasized that the *Wade-Gilbert* rule of per se inadmissibility, founded on the Sixth Amendment right to counsel, is separate from and independent of any issue concerning the fairness of an identification premised on due process standards (discussed in §10.2.2). *Com. v. Donovan,* supra, 392 Mass at 648-650, 467 NE2d at 199 (& citations).

§10.2.2   Due Process

Of wider application than the *Wade-Gilbert* rule of per se inadmissibility is the requirement that *any* identification procedure conducted at *any* time in investigative process (whether before or after the initiation of formal proceedings) conform to standards of fundamental fairness. See *Com. v. Simmonds,* 386 Mass 234, 239, 434 NE2d 1270, 1274 (1982) (due process considerations are applicable to lineup conducted prior to arrest); *Com. v. Chase,* 372 Mass 736, 743, 363 NE2d 1105, 1110 (1977) (due process considerations are applicable to informal identification procedures conducted prior to arrest). Under due process standards evolved from the Fifth and Fourteenth Amendments, evidence of a pretrial identification is inadmissible if obtained in a manner so impermissibly suggestive as to give rise to a substantial likelihood of mistaken identification. See *Kirby v. Illinois*, 406 US 682, 690-691 (1972) (pre-indictment stationhouse show-up); *Simmons v. United States*, 390 US 377 (1968) (pre-indictment photographic identification); *Stovall v. Denno*, 388 US 293 (1967) (hospital room show-up); *Com. v. Odware*, 429 Mass 231, 707 NE2d 347 (1999); *Com. v. Dinkins*, 415 Mass 715, 720-721, 615 NE2d 570, 573 (1993); *Com. v. Botelho*, 369 Mass 860, 343 NE2d 876 (1976) (suppressing identifications; extensive discussion of due process analysis). As the Supreme Judicial Court has observed:

> The law has not taken the position that a jury can always be relied on to discount the value of an identification by a proper appraisal of the unsatisfactory circumstances in which it may have been made. On the contrary, this court, like others, has read the Constitution to require that where the conditions are shown to have been highly and unnecessarily suggestive, the identification should not be brought to the attention of the jury.

Com. v. Marini, 375 Mass 510, 519, 378 NE2d 51, 57 (1978) (citations omitted).

a.   *Unnecessarily Suggestive*

Utilizing a totality of the circumstances approach, the court under the due process test must determine whether the identification procedure was: (1) suggestive; (2) unnecessary (i.e., because there was no exigent circumstance or other justification); and (3) unreliable. Only if all three elements are found will the identification be suppressed. See *Manson v. Brathwaite*, 432 US 98 (1977); *Com. v. Melvin*, 399 Mass 201, 205, 503 NE2d 649, 652 (1987). The Supreme Judicial Court has emphasized that the constitutional issue in identification cases is not whether "the witness was or might be mistaken but whether any possible mistake was or would be the product of improper suggestions made by the police." *Com. v. Andrews,* 427 Mass 434, 438, 694 NE2d 329, 333 (1998); *Com. v. Rancourt,* 399 Mass 269, 276 n.10, 503 NE2d 960, 965 n.10 (1987) (& citations). See also *Com. v. Warren,* 403 Mass 137, 140, 526 NE2d 250, 252 (1988).

The first two elements require an analysis of both the prejudicial nature of the challenged procedure and the circumstances that necessitated resort to it. Thus, in *Stovall v. Denno,* supra, where the handcuffed black suspect was brought into the victim's hospital room by white police officers who asked if he was "the man," the court concluded that the concededly suggestive procedure was nonetheless "imperative" because it was unclear how long the victim would live. See also *Simmons v. United States,* 390 US at 384-385 (arguably suggestive display of photographs was not "unnecessary" because a serious felony had been committed, the perpetrators were still at large, and it was essential for FBI to determine whether they were on the right track); *Com. v. Dickerson,* 372 Mass 783, 790, 364 NE2d 1052, 1058 (1977) (hospital room confrontation was not "unnecessarily" suggestive because it took place in the immediate aftermath of the crime as part of reasonable police investigation); *Com. v. Barnett,* 371 Mass 87, 91-94, 354 NE2d 879, 882-883 (1976) (hospital confrontation arranged by police between victim and defendant while both were being treated for gunshot wounds was not violative of due process). "The evil to be avoided is *needless* suggestiveness." *Com. v. O'Loughlin,* 17 Mass App 972, 458 NE2d 767 (1984). Compare *Com. v. Kazonis,* 356 Mass 649, 255 NE2d 333 (1970) (confrontation at police headquarters two months after robbery was conducted in a manner so impermissibly suggestive and conducive to misidentification as to amount to a denial of due process; the procedure could not be justified by urgency, efficient police work, or some other relevant factor).

b.   Reliability Factors

If the court concludes that the identification was unnecessarily suggestive, under Supreme Court doctrine it must then determine whether the evidence was nonetheless reliable. Reliability is "the linchpin" in determining the admissibility of identification testimony under federal standards. *Manson v. Brathwaite,* supra, 432 US at 114. See also *Neil v. Biggers,* 409 US 188 (1972). Even if the result of unnecessarily suggestive procedures, identification evidence is admissible if it possesses sufficient indicia of reliability to reduce the possibility of irreparable mistaken identification. See, e.g., *Com. v. Dickerson,* supra, 372 Mass at 790-791, 364 NE2d at 1057-1058 (the suggestiveness of the hospital confrontation was overriden by the facts that the witness had had ample opportunity to observe the assailant and promptly gave the police a description that fit the defendant).

The factors to be considered regarding reliability include:

(1)   the opportunity the witness had to view the criminal at the time of the crime;

(2)   the witness's degree of attention;

(3)   the accuracy of the witness's prior description of the criminal;

(4)   the level of certainty demonstrated by the witness at the confrontation; and

(5)   the length of time between the crime and the confrontation.

(These factors are also relevant in determining whether there is an independent basis for an in-court identification when the pretrial identification has been ruled inadmissible. See §10.2.3). "[O]f most importance are the victim's attentiveness and opportunity to observe the assailant during the commission of the crime." *Com. v. Riley,* 26 Mass App 550, 554, 530 NE2d 181, 184 (1988). "Against these factors is to be weighed the corrupting effect of the suggestive identification itself." *Manson v. Brathwaite,* supra, 432 US at 114.

The Supreme Judicial Court has, however, rejected the "reliability test" set forth in *Manson v. Brathwaite* and has held that identification procedures that are unnecessarily suggestive require per se exclusion under the due process requirements of the Massachusetts Declaration of Rights. *Com. v. Johnson,* 420 Mass 458, 461, 650 NE2d 1257, 1259 (1995); *Com. v. Day,* 42 Mass App 242, 676 NE2d 467 (1997). Persuaded that "the dangers present whenever eyewitness evidence is introduced against an accused require the utmost protection against mistaken identifications," *Com. v. Johnson,* supra, 420 Mass at 465, 650 NE2d at 1261. The court has ruled that once a defendant meets the burden of demonstrating (by a preponderance of the evidence) that the identification was unnecessarily suggestive, the prosecution is barred from using the evidence at trial. Regarding other identifications the witness may have made of the defendant, only those which the prosecution can show by clear and convincing evidence are not the product of the suggestive confrontation — i.e., that have an independent source are admissible at trial. See §10.2.3.

c. Types of Identification Procedures

Significant to the issue of suggestiveness is the type of identification procedure used, as well as what the police did when using the particular procedure. There are essentially four identification procedures: (1) lineup, (2) photographic array, (3) informal pre-arrest procedures, and (4) one on one confrontation either in person or by photograph.

The lineup is the preferred procedure, especially when defense counsel is present. *Com. v. Storey,* 378 Mass 312, 318-319, 391 NE2d 898, 903 (1979); *Com. v. Marini,* supra, 375 Mass at 519, 378 NE2d at 57. The police are not required, however, to use a lineup over other identification procedures, even where the accused is already in custody. *Com. v. Jackson*, 419 Mass 716, 729 n.13, 647 NE2d 401, 409 n.13 (1995). Where there is evidence that a defendant has altered his appearance to avoid identification, the state may require him to undo the alteration. *Com. v. Cinelli*, 389 Mass 197, 205-207, 449 NE2d 1207, 1213 (1983) (where there was evidence that defendant had been relatively clean shaven on the day of the crime, compelling him to shave his full beard prior to a lineup did not violate his right of due process).

Although (as noted in §10.1) absent probable cause the police may not detain an individual for investigatory purposes or require him to participate in a lineup,[1] *Com. v. Napolitano*, 378 Mass 599, 607, 393 NE2d 338, 344 (1979), the police may seek to arrange a noncustodial and informal pre-arrest identification procedure. "Informal identification procedures during the initial investigatory stages of the criminal process may free innocent suspects and allow the police to follow other more productive leads." *Com. v. Napolitano*, supra, 378 Mass at 606, 393 NE2d at 343. Such a procedure is permissible where the witness views the suspect in a non-suggestive setting that does not isolate the suspect from others. See, e.g., *Com. v. Napolitano*, supra, 378 Mass at 605-608, 393 NE2d 343-344 (1979) (defendant identified while being arraigned on unrelated charge; evidence was admissible even though defendant was in prisoner's dock because he sat with two other males in the busy courtroom and the police did not direct the witness's attention to the dock); *Com. v. Chase*, 372 Mass 736, 741-745, 363 NE2d 1105, 1111-1112 (1977) (defendant identified in a public lounge; evidence was admissible even though defendant, a bartender, had a prominent role at lounge, because there were approximately 25 patrons and two bartenders and the

---

§10.2 [1]A subject may agree voluntarily to participate in a lineup. See, e.g., *Com. v. Simmonds*, 386 Mass 234, 238, 434 NE2d 1270, 1274 (1982). Evidence that a defendant was requested to voluntarily submit to a lineup but refused should not be admitted. See *Com. v. Holland*, 410 Mass 248, 256-261, 571 NE2d 625, 630-633 (1991) (but error harmless).

police made no suggestion to witness concerning identification of the defendant); *Com. v. Marks,* 12 Mass App 511, 514-515, 426 NE2d 1172, 1176 (1981) (defendant identified while being arraigned on an unrelated charge). A suspect need not be advised that an informal identification procedure is taking place. See *Com. v. Chase,* supra, 372 Mass at 743, 363 NE2d at 1111; *Com. v. Napolitano,* supra, 378 Mass at 605, 393 NE2d at 343.

One on one confrontations, whether in person or by photograph, pose particularly serious dangers of suggestiveness and are thus generally disfavored. *Stovall v. Denno,* 388 US 293, 302 (1967); *Com. v. Johnson,* 420 Mass 458, 461, 650 NE2d 1257, 1259 (1995); *Com. v. Santos,* 402 Mass 775, 781, 525 NE2d 388, 392 (1988). Nonetheless, evidence produced by a one on one confrontation is not subject to a rule of per se exclusion. *Com. v. Johnson,* supra, 420 Mass at 461, 650 NE2d at 1259; *Com. v. Otsuki,* 411 Mass 218, 234, 581 NE2d 999, 1008 (1991); *Com. v. Freiberg,* 405 Mass 282, 295, 540 NE2d 1289, 1298 (1989); *Com. v. Pacheco,* 12 Mass App 109, 118, 421 NE2d 1239, 1245 (1981) (voice identification; the "use of a single taped voice raises suspicion of a constitutional violation, but that factor alone will not constitute sufficient ground for exclusion of the out of court identification"). Rather, whether the evidence is admissible under the controlling due process standard will depend on when, where, and why the confrontation occurred. *Stovall v. Denno,* supra, 388 US at 302.

One on one confrontations have been held permissible where there are exigent circumstances or where they represent an effort to provide the witness with an opportunity to view the suspect in the immediate aftermath of the crime. See *Stovall v. Denno,* supra, 388 US at 302 (hospital room confrontation with victim in critical condition); *Com. v. Thompson,* 427 Mass 729, 735, 696 NE2d 105, 109 (1998) (identifications were justified because they constituted efficient police investigation in the immediate aftermath of a crime); *Com. v. Austin,* 421 Mass 357, 657 NE2d 458 (1995) (witnesses were shown videotape depicting another bank robbery); *Com. v. Eagles,* 419 Mass 825, 833-834, 648 NE2d 410, 416 (1995) (field identification outside of defendant's residence); *Com. v. Freiberg,* supra, 405 Mass at 295, 540 NE2d at 1298 (field identification by witness who had observed defendant burying victim in backyard of house); *Com. v. Santos,* supra, 402 Mass at 783-784, 525 NE2d at 393-394 (field confrontation immediately after defendant's apprehension); *Com. v. Melvin,* 399 Mass 201, 206 n.7, 503 NE2d 649, 653 n.7 (1987) (& citations); *Com. v. Leaster,* 395 Mass 96, 102-103, 479 NE2d 124, 128-129 (1985) (& citations) (parking lot confrontation in immediate aftermath of crime); *Com. v. Howell,* 394 Mass 654, 660, 477 NE2d 126, 131 (1985) (show-up at hospital within one or two hours of incident); *Com. v. Barnett,* 371 Mass 87, 91-94, 354 NE2d 879, 883-884 (1976) (confrontation occurred while both witness and suspect were in same hospital for wounds received during the crime; it makes no difference that witness's life was not in such jeopardy as to make confrontation imperative); *Com. v. Rogers,* 38 Mass App 395, 402-405, 647 NE2d 1228, 1232-1233 (1995) (defendants brought to window of victim's ambulance). But compare *Com. v. Johnson,* supra, 420 Mass at 461, 650 NE2d at 1259 (show-up conducted 18 hours after crime was unnecessarily suggestive).

Even where there has been a substantial time lapse between the crime and the confrontation, the identification may nonetheless be admissible if it is determined that, in the totality of circumstances, it was not unnecessarily suggestive. *Com. v. Walker,* 421 Mass 90, 95, 653 NE2d 1080, 1083 (1995) (quick identification of a recently spotted at-large suspect proper even though 16 days lapsed between crime and show-up); *Com. v. Levasseur,* 32 Mass App 629, 635-637, 592 NE2d 1350, 1354-1355 (1992) (victim requested show-up, which occurred nearly six months after crime, after she had described assailant and selected defendant's photograph).

Whether an identification procedure is unnecessarily or impermissibly suggestive involves an inquiry into whether "good reason exists for the police to use a one on one identification procedure." *Com. v. Austin*, supra, 421 Mass at 361-362, 657 NE2d at 461. (But see dissenting opinion of O'Connor, J, joined by Liacos, CJ: "The question . . . is not 'whether good reason exists for the police to use a one on one identification procedure' [but whether the procedure was] 'so impermissibly or unnecessarily suggestive and conducive to irreparable misidentification as to deprive the defendant of his due process rights.'" 421 Mass at 368, 657 NE2d at 465). "Relevant to the good reason examination are the nature of the crime involved and corresponding concerns for public safety; the need for efficient police investigation in the immediate aftermath of a crime; and the usefulness of prompt confirmation of the accuracy of investigatory information, which, if in error, will release the police quickly to follow another track." 421 Mass at 362, 657 NE2d at 461.

Single-photograph identifications have been upheld in circumstances similar to one on one confrontations. See *Simmons v. United States*, supra, 390 US at 383-384; *Com. v. Venios*, 378 Mass 24, 29, 389 NE2d 395, 398 (1979); *Com. v. Nolin*, 373 Mass 45, 51, 364 NE2d 1224, 1228 (1977) (single photograph shown to victim who was seriously wounded and near death); *Com. v. Laaman*, 25 Mass App 354, 361, 518 NE2d 861, 865 (1988) (display of driver's license photo three hours after armed attack on two State troopers; "[s]ome suggestiveness is permitted in such cases in order to speed detection of the offender or to exonerate the suspect"). But see *Com. v. Moon*, 380 Mass 751, 758, 405 NE2d 947, 952 (1980) (photographs of only one person should not be shown to witnesses in the absence of exigent circumstances).

Neither the absence of exigent circumstances nor the fact that the police had ample time to conduct a lineup itself renders a one on one confrontation unconstitutional. The procedure may be justified by the need for efficient investigation in the immediate aftermath of the crime. See *Com. v. Austin*, supra, 421 Mass at 361-362, 657 NE2d at 461;

Com. v. Leonardi, 413 Mass 757, 761, 604 NE2d 23, 26 (1992); *Com. v. Leaster,* supra, 395 Mass at 103, 479 NE2d at 129 (& citations); *Com. v. Libby,* 21 Mass App 650, 656, 489 NE2d 702, 706 (1986) (the fact that a lineup could have been conducted does not itself render the one on one confrontation unlawful). "Such [confrontations] are particularly valuable and permitted where the police are working from a description of the criminal provided by the victim immediately after the crime." *Com. v. Coy,* 10 Mass App 367, 372, 407 NE2d 1310, 1314 (1980) (extensive discussion of authorities); *Com. v. Libby,* supra, 21 Mass App at 656, 489 NE2d at 706. "Of course, if there are special elements of unfairness, indicating a desire on the part of the police to 'stack the deck' against the defendant, an identification resulting from a one on one confrontation would be inadmissible." *Com. v. Leaster,* supra, 395 Mass at 103, 479 NE2d at 129 (& citations). See, e.g., *Com. v. Moon,* supra, 380 Mass at 758, 405 NE2d at 952. Compare *Com. v. Leonardi,* supra, 413 Mass at 761-762 (& cases cited) (although it would have been better if detective had not told victim that he was bringing in someone who fit description given by victim, statement did not create special element of unfairness).

Because it has been recognized that one on one identifications may be less reliable than identifications based on a lineup where evidence of the former has been admitted the defendant is entitled to that portion of the pattern jury instruction (see §10.3, infra) stating that "an identification made by picking the defendant out of a group of similar individuals is generally more reliable than one which results from the presentation of a defendant alone to the witness." *Com. v. Cuffie,* 414 Mass 632, 639-640, 609 NE2d 437, 440-441 (1993).

While the Supreme Judicial Court has recognized that an identification obtained in the course of a confrontation at a probable cause hearing or other pretrial proceeding has an undeniable element of suggestion because of the isolation of the defendant at defense table or in the dock, evidence of such identification may be admitted so long as counsel is present to "ferret out [any] suggestive influences" by cross-examination or otherwise. *Com. v. Jones*, 362 Mass 497, 500-501, 287 NE2d 599, 602 (1972). See also *Com. v. Colon-Cruz*, 408 Mass 533, 541-542, 562 NE2d 797, 805 (1990) (no impermissible suggestion where witness identified defendant from among seven suspects at probable cause hearing); *Com. v. Freiberg*, 405 Mass 282, 295, 540 NE2d 1289, 1298 (1989) (isolation in courtroom not sufficient to render identification impermissibly suggestive); *Com. v. Napolitano*, supra, 378 Mass at 603-605, 393 NE2d at 342 (identification of defendant by witnesses at probable cause hearing was not impermissibly suggestive merely because defendant was seated in the prisoner's dock); *Com. v. Cincotta*, 379 Mass 391, 394-395, 398 NE2d 478, 480-481 (1979) (spontaneous and uncontrived identification of defendant while seated in courtroom awaiting probable cause hearing was not unduly suggestive); *Com. v. Riley*, 26 Mass App 550, 555, 530 NE2d 181, 185 (1988) (defendant failed to produce evidence that the particular circumstances of the courtroom identification, where defendant was one of six men seated in the prisoner's dock, were suggestive). But compare *Moore v. Illinois*, 434 US 220 (1977) (evidence excluded where defendant, not represented by counsel, was identified by victim at preliminary hearing after she was told she was going to view a suspect, observed him called up to the bench, and heard the prosecutor recite the evidence against him).

d.   Voice Identification

Voice identifications have been treated as suspect, and "police and prosecutors are warned to take particular pains to avoid suggestive conditions in making arrangements for out-of-court tests where a witness tries to match live voices with his recollections of a voice heard in the usually stressful original setting." *Com. v. Marini*, 375 Mass 510, 516-519, 378 NE2d 51, 55-56 (1978) (one on one voice identification of defendant by victim at trial was unnecessarily suggestive). See also *Com. v. Torres*, 367 Mass 737, 740-741, 327 NE2d 871, 874 (1975); *Com. v. Enos*, 26 Mass App 1006, 530 NE2d 805 (1988) ("Although voice identification evidence has been accepted under circumstances thought appropriate or sufficiently hedged with safeguards (e.g., the presence of counsel), the cases manifest apprehension about its too free use to identify a defendant."); *Com. v. Gauthier*, 21 Mass App 585, 587-588, 488 NE2d 806, 808 (1986). The preferred precautionary procedures for conducting voice identifications include avoiding one-on-one auditions, not having the witness view the speaker as he listens to the voice, and not choosing for repetition the words used by the perpetrator at the scene of the crime. *Com. v. Marini*, supra, 375 Mass at 517, 375 NE2d at 56. But compare *Com. v. DeMaria*, 46 Mass App 114, 118, 703 NE2d 1203, 1206 (1999) (it would have been better not to refer to defendant by same number in voice identification procedure as in preceding visual line-up, but where witness testified she was not influenced by number, it was not unduly suggestive); *Com. v. Burgos*, 36 Mass App 903, 904, 627 NE2d 471, 473 (1994) (*Marini* precautions do not apply in a "show-up"). For a case following the *Marini* procedures, see *Com. v. Miles*, 420 Mass 67, 78-81, 648 NE2d 719, 727-729 (1995). See also *Com. v. Carpinto*, 37 Mass App 51, 636 NE2d 1349 (1994) (identification of voice on taped telephone call); §12.4.

e.   *Police Conduct and Suggestiveness*

Any identification procedure may become unnecessarily suggestive due to the way in which the police conduct it. See, e.g., *Com. v. Weichell*, 390 Mass 62, 72-73, 453 NE2d 1038, 1045 (1983) (identification by composite will be set aside if the process was so impermissibly suggestive as to give rise to a substantial likelihood of irreparable misidentification). For cases finding undue suggestiveness, see *Foster v. California*, 394 US 440 (1969) (identification improperly admitted where witness identified defendant only after police first displayed defendant to witness in a three-man lineup in which defendant stood out from the others due to his height and jacket similar to that worn by robber, and then police permitted a one-on-one confrontation); *Com. v. Riccard*, 410 Mass 718, 722-723, 575 NE2d 57, 60 (1991) (display of defendant's photograph to witness during meeting with prosecutor days before trial unnecessarily suggestive); *Com. v. Santos*, 402 Mass 775, 780-785, 525 NE2d 388, 391-394 (1988) (one-on-one stationhouse identification unconstitutionally suggestive in light of suggestibility of moderately retarded identifying witness; testimony corroborating the unconstitutional identification must also be suppressed); *Com. v. Moon*, 380 Mass 751, 756-759, 405 NE2d 947, 951-952 (1980) (identification evidence suppressed where victim identified defendant after police named defendant in victim's presence and then showed victim a single photograph of defendant); *Com. v. Day*, 42 Mass App 242, 676 NE2d 467 (1997) (giving witnesses opportunity to view for 20 to 30 minutes a police flyer containing the same photograph of defendant which was used in the array from which they made an identification, where flyer advised that defendant had shot someone, was impermissibly suggestive); *Com. v. Marks*, 12 Mass App 511, 514-516, 426 NE2d 1172, 1176 (1981) (where two witnesses were permitted to view defendant jointly with result that mother identified him in the presence of her daughter, who then also identified him, there was risk of suggestiveness and judge was required to make findings as to whether daughter's identification had an independent source or was otherwise reliable).

For cases finding no impermissible suggestion, see *Com. v. Andrews*, 427 Mass 434, 438, 694 NE2d 329, 333 (1998) (detective's question whether perpetrator might have been light-skinned black man, rather than Hispanic as initially described by witness, was not impermissibly suggestive where police had no suspect in mind); *Com. v. Tanso*, 411 Mass 640, 651-653, 583 NE2d 1247, 1254-1255 (1992) (identification procedures used in three separate police lineups not unnecessarily suggestive; the "fact that each person in the lineup may not have closely resembled the defendant does not render the lineup impermissibly suggestive"); *Com. v. Thornley*, 400 Mass 355, 359-361, 509 NE2d 908, 911-912 (1987) (*Thornley I*) (police procedure used to create Identi-kit composite sketch not so impermissibly suggestive as to give rise to substantial likelihood of misidentification even though the two witnesses participated in a single session to produce the composite) (Liacos, J, dissenting); *Com. v. Simmonds*, 386 Mass 234, 239-240, 434 NE2d 1270, 1275 (1982) (lineup not unduly suggestive even though only three of seven participants were clean-shaven, defendant among them, and witnesses had described the assailant as clean-shaven; and even though several participants wore regulation police pants); *Com. v. Toney*, 385 Mass 575, 586-587, 433 NE2d 425, 432-433 (1982) (mentioning of defendant's name by police not, by itself, unduly suggestive and thus did not taint the in-court identification); *Com. v. Cincotta*, supra, 379 Mass at 393-394, 398 NE2d at 480 (witness not unduly influenced by choice of defendant's photograph made by other witness); *Com. v. Clifford*, 374 Mass 293, 303-304, 372 NE2d 1267, 1275 (1978) (lineup not impermissibly suggestive even though defendant wore a jacket similar to one used during the crime); *Com. v. O'Loughlin*, 17 Mass App 972, 458 NE2d 767 (1984) (one on one confrontation that allowed the victim to listen to defendant's voice as part of the identification process not unduly suggestive where confrontation occurred within three hours of crime and defendant spoke in a normal conversation rather than uttering the words spoken by victim's assailant during crime). See also *Com. v. Lopes*, supra, 362 Mass at 453-454, 287 NE2d at 121-122 (& citations) (nothing inherently suggestive about use of "two-way mirror" to view suspect).

For cases finding photographic arrays unnecessarily suggestive, see *Com. v. Thornley*, 406 Mass 96, 98-101, 546 NE2d 350, 351-353 (1989) (*Thornley II*) (photographic identification impermissively suggestive where defendant's picture was only one in array showing him wearing eyeglasses); *Com. v. LaFaille*, 46 Mass App 144, 150, 704 NE2d 206, 210 (1999) (two photos of defendant in single array shown to witness 29 days following crime); *Com. v. Gordon*, 6 Mass App 230, 239, 374 NE2d 1228, 1231 (1978) (showing victim an array of photographs that included only one depiction of a person with braided hair such as victim had described to police was unnecessarily suggestive; but identification evidence was nonetheless admissible as reliable).

Compare *Com. v. Miles*, 420 Mass 67, 77-78, 648 NE2d 719, 727 (1995) (nine photograph array did not distinguish defendant on basis of age, not otherwise unduly suggestive); *Com. v. Jackson*, 419 Mass 716, 728-730, 647 NE2d 401, 408-409 (1995) (post-identification statements by police did not render photographic identification suggestive); *Com. v. Wallace*, 417 Mass 126, 129, 627 NE2d 935, 938 (1994) (duplication of defendant's photograph in successive arrays not sufficient to compel suppression of resulting identification); *Com. v. Dinkins*, 415 Mass 715, 720-721, 615 NE2d 570, 573 (1993) (same; no substantial risk of miscarriage of justice where witness asked to see defendant's photograph after another eyewitness selected it in his presence); *Com. v. Downey*, 407 Mass 472, 478-479, 553 NE2d 1303, 1307 (1990) (photographic arrays not unnecessarily suggestive even though a "look-alike" photograph was removed); *Com. v. Melvin*, 399 Mass 201, 503 NE2d 649 (1987) (photographic array not impermissibly suggestive even though defendant's photograph was the only one depicting a person wearing a sling, and the witness had observed the intruder injure his shoulder while escaping from the scene of the crime); *Com. v. Shipps*, 399 Mass 820, 831, 507 NE2d 671, 679 (1987) (identification of defendant from photographs of two persons shown to witness not so suggestive as to give rise to a substantial likelihood of misidentification); *Com. v. Paszko*, 391 Mass 164, 167-171, 461 NE2d 222, 227-228 (1984) (photographic arrays not unduly suggestive even though defendant's photograph was only one shown in both arrays); *Com. v. Porter*, 384 Mass 647, 656-658, 429 NE2d 14, 21 (1981) (showing of one more photograph, taken from officer's pocket, after witness had been unable to identify defendant's photograph from among a group shown to him, was merely a continuation of an ongoing process and was not unduly suggestive); *Com. v. Clark,* 378 Mass 392, 399-401, 393 NE2d 296, 301 (1979) (photographic array not impermissibly suggestive even though defendant's photograph was one of two snapshots in a group including 11 "mug shots"); *Com. v. Mobley,* 369 Mass 892, 344 NE2d 181 (1976) (photographic array not impermissibly suggestive even though defendant was only person depicted wearing a ski cap and and such a cap was worn by the robber); *Com. v. Manning,* 44 Mass App Ct 695, 693 NE2d 704 (1998) (although defendant's photo was the only one in array of nine photos which witness had not previously seen, array was not unduly suggestive where judge credited witness's testimony that he did not realize the other eight photos were from prior array); *Com. v. Caldwell,* 36 Mass App 570, 579-580, 634 NE2d 124, 130 (1994) (although police had to reconstruct array after 10 to 12 photographs were lost, no showing of impermissible suggestiveness); *Com. v. Ayles,* 31 Mass App 514, 517-518, 580 NE2d 394, 397 (1991) (photograph identification not unduly suggestive even though police officer told rape victim that he "had a good idea of who did it" before displaying the photographs to her); *Com. v. Laaman,* 25 Mass App 354, 361, 518 NE2d 861, 865 (1988) (photographic identification not unduly suggestive even though police mentioned suspect's name inadvertently); *Com. v. Riley,* 17 Mass App 950, 457 NE2d 660 (1983) (fact that array contained two markedly different photographs of defendant did not render it impermissibly suggestive).

There is a line of authority supporting the proposition that where the pretrial identification of the suspect "is the product of something other than improper action by the state, due process does not require the suppression of it or its repetitions." *Com. v. Wheeler,* 3 Mass App 387, 392, 331 NE2d 815, 818 (1975) (original identification was utterly independent of the police). See also *Com. v. Holland,* 410 Mass 248, 253, 571 NE2d 625, 629 (1991) (what is forbidden by the due process clause is that a witness be "subjected *by the State* to an identification so unnecessarily suggestive") (emphasis added). Thus, identification evidence from an accidental confrontation is unobjectionable. See *Com. v. Otsuki*, supra, 411 Mass at 233-234, 581 NE2d at 1008 (witness's observation of wanted poster portraying defendant was accidental and not the result of improper police conduct); *Com. v. Leaster*, 362 Mass 407, 410-411, 287 NE2d 122, 125 (1972) (& citations); *Com. v. McMaster*, 21 Mass App 722, 725 n.2, 490 NE2d 464, 468 n.2 (1986). Similarly, the fact that a witness has observed the defendant's likeness in the media does not, absent police involvement and misconduct, taint an identification. See *Com. v. Otsuki*, supra, 411 Mass at 234-235, 581 NE2d at 1009 (witness identified defendant from a newspaper photograph); *Com. v. Colon-Cruz*, 408 Mass 533, 542, 562 NE2d 797, 805 (1990) ("If police have not in any way manipulated press reports, then simple exposure to the media is not sufficient ground to suppress an identification."). See also *Com. v. Currier*, 15 Mass App 929, 445 NE2d 158 (1983) (original identification of the defendant by the victim was made as a result of an encounter arranged by a friend of the victim); *Com. v. Mattias*, 8 Mass App 786, 788-789, 397 NE2d 1134, 1136 (1979) (first witness recognized defendant on a public street; second witness had accidental encounter with defendant).

The Supreme Judicial Court has held, however, that an in-court identification of a defendant is not admissible where there is no independent basis for it and it is the product of an earlier suggestive confrontation with the defendant, whether or not government agents had a hand in causing the confrontation. *Com. v. Jones*, 423 Mass 99, 666 NE2d 994 (1996). The court's decision was not based on constitutional grounds but on common-law principles of fairness which dictate that an unreliable identification arising from especially suggestive circumstances should not be admitted. See §10.2.3.

f. Application to Other Identification Evidence

The due process principles discussed in this section apply principally to the direct identification of the defendant as the person who committed a crime. Defendants have unsuccessfully argued that these same principles should govern other identification evidence. See *Com. v. Spann,* 383 Mass 142, 146-148, 418 NE2d 328, 331-332 (1981) (pretrial photographic identification of deceased victim); *Com. v. Simmons,* 383 Mass 46, 48-52, 417 NE2d 1193, 1195-1196 (1981) (pretrial one on one identification of automobile allegedly driven by victim's assailant). See also *Com. v. Shipps,* 399 Mass 820, 833, 507 NE2d 671, 680 (1987) (photographic identification of defendant's gun was not unnecessarily suggestive). While rejecting this argument, the Supreme Judicial Court has nonetheless recognized that in an extreme case, the degree of suggestiveness in the identification procedures involving inanimate objects or persons other than the perpetrator might be so great as to violate due process. *Com. v. Spann,* supra, 383 Mass at 148, 418 NE2d at 332; *Com. v. Simmons,* supra, 383 Mass at 51-52, 417 NE2d at 1196. See also *Com. v. Jones,* 25 Mass App 55, 62, 514 NE2d 1337, 1341 (1987). Accordingly, law enforcement officers should exercise care to avoid unduly suggestive procedures. The court has also recognized that "it would be desirable to conduct a voir dire on a challenge based on a claimed suggestive 'confrontation' in the identification of an inanimate object." *Com. v. Simmons,* supra, 383 Mass at 53 n.3, 417 NE2d at 1197 n.3.

§10.2.3   *Fruits of Illegal Identification Procedures — In-Court Identification*

If evidence of a pretrial identification is suppressed because the accused's right to counsel was abridged (see §10.2.1, supra) or because the procedure is found to have been impermissibly suggestive (see §10.2.2, supra), the question arises as to whether the witness will nonetheless be permitted to make an in-court identification. Generally, evidence derived even indirectly from a constitutional violation is subject to suppression as the "the fruit of the poisonous tree." See *Wong Sun v. United States*, 371 US 471 (1963). The test for determining the admissibility of such derivative evidence is whether it "has been come at by exploitation of [the initial] illegality or instead by means sufficiently distinguishable to be purged of the primary taint." 371 US at 488. See also *United States v. Crews*, 445 US 463, 472-473 (1980) (in-court identification rested on witness's independent recollection of her initial encounter with the assailant and was not the product of defendant's illegal arrest or pretrial identifications); *Com. v. Crowe*, 21 Mass App 456, 462-465, 488 NE2d 780, 785-787 (1986) (extensive discussion of derivative evidence doctrine and authorities). Compare *Com. v. Lyons*, 397 Mass 644, 646-649, 492 NE2d 1142, 1145-1146 (1986) (the fact that defendant's identification was obtained as a result of an arrest on a warrant issued in violation of GL 218, §35A, but otherwise lawful, does not require suppression of the resulting identification).

An in-court identification must therefore be excluded if it is the product of the illegal pretrial procedure. If, however, it can be established that the in-court identification has an independent origin, such as the opportunity the witness had to observe the perpetrator at the time of the crime, it may be admitted. *United States v. Wade*, 388 US 218, 239-241 (1967); *Com. v. Johnson*, 420 Mass 458, 467, 650 NE2d 1257, 1260-1261 (1995) (per se approach excluding impermissibly suggestive identifications notwithstanding their reliability does not render inadmissible a subsequent identification shown to come from an independent source); *Com. v. Hill*, 38 Mass App 982, 652 NE2d 621 (1995) (same). The issue is whether the witness's observations made during the course of the crime fixed in his mind the features of the offender and thus provided an independent source for the identification at trial. *Com. v. Ross*, 361 Mass 665, 676, 282

NE2d 70, 77 (1972), *vacated on other grounds*, 410 US 901 (1973). The prosecution bears the burden of demonstrating by "clear and convincing evidence" that the in-court identification is based upon observations of the suspect other than the tainted pretrial identification. *United States v. Wade*, supra, 388 US at 240; *Com. v. Johnson*, supra, 420 Mass at 463-464, 650 NE2d at 1260-1261; *Com. v. Bodden*, 391 Mass 356, 359, 461 NE2d 803, 806 (1984); *Com. v. Venios*, 378 Mass 24, 30, 389 NE2d 395 (1979).

Several factors have been set forth as germane to the determination of whether a subsequent identification has an independent origin:

(1) the prior opportunity to observe the alleged criminal act;

(2) the existence of any discrepancy between the witness's description of the perpetrator and the defendant's actual personal characteristics;

(3) any prior identification of another person as the perpetrator;

(4) the identification of the defendant by picture prior to the impermissible procedure;

(5) the failure to identify the defendant on a prior occasion; and

(6) the length of time between the alleged act and the identification procedure.

United States v. Wade, supra, 388 US at 241. It will be observed that these factors are similar to those used to measure the reliability of a pretrial identification under the *Biggers-Brathwaite* test discussed above. See *Com. v. Thornley*, 406 Mass 96, 98 n.2, 546 NE2d 350, 352 n.2 (1989) (*Thornley II*); *Com. v. Crowe*, 21 Mass App 456, 468 n.13, 488 NE2d 780, 788 n.13 (1986) ("The independent source and the reliability tests are essentially the same."). "The crucial determination in both instances is whether the identification sought to be admitted in evidence is the product of the witness's observations at the time of the crime or is instead the product of improper suggestions by the police." *Com. v. Wheeler*, 3 Mass App. 387, 392, 331 NE2d 815, 818 (1975).

Application of these factors depends upon the context of the particular case, and each factor is not necessarily entitled to equal weight. *Com. v. Ross*, supra, 361 Mass at 671, 282 NE2d at 74. The extent of the witness's opportunity to observe the perpetrator at the time of the crime is probably the most important single factor, as the firmer the contemporaneous impression, the less the witness is subject to be influenced by subsequent events. 361 Mass at 671-672, 282 NE2d at 74; *Com. v. Bodden*, supra, 391 Mass at 361, 461 NE2d at 807; *Com. v. Mendes*, supra, 361 Mass at 511, 281 NE2d at 246. A witness's knowledge of and opportunity to observe the subject prior to the incident is also relevant to the determination of whether a subsequent identification has an independent source. *Com. v. Crowe*, supra, 21 Mass App at 466, 488 NE2d at 787.

These principles regarding derivative identification evidence apply whether the primary illegality involves the denial of the defendant's right to counsel or right to due process. Compare *United States v. Wade*, supra, 388 US at 242 and *Gilbert v. California*, 388 US 263, 272 (1967) (remanding to determine whether in-court identification had a source independent of a lineup identification conducted in the absence of counsel) with *Com. v. Moon*, 380 Mass 751, 756-759, 405 NE2d 947, 951-952 (1980) (judge properly determined that naming defendant in presence of victim and then showing victim a single photograph of defendant was so violative of due process as to taint any subsequent in-court identification) and *Com. v. Jackson*, 377 Mass 319, 329-332, 386 NE2d 15, 21-22 (1979) (concluding that there was sufficient evidence to warrant a finding that witness's in-court identification had a source independent of an impermissibly suggestive pretrial photographic procedure). When, however, the primary illegality involves denial of the defendant's right to counsel, the prosecution is not entitled to show that the witness's *pretrial* identification had an independent source. See *Moore v. Illinois*, 434 US 220, 226,

231-232 (1977); *Gilbert v. California,* supra, 388 US at 272-274 ("Only a per se exclusionary rule as to such testimony can be an effective sanction to assure that law enforcement authorities will respect the accused's constitutional right to the presence of his counsel at the critical lineup.").

For cases finding that the in-court identification had an independent source, see *Com. v. Holland,* 410 Mass 248, 256, 571 NE2d 625, 630 (1991) (witness had opportunity to observe assailant close up and face-to-face while he stood over her for some time in well lit parking lot); *Com. v. Freiberg,* 405 Mass 282, 295, 540 NE2d 1289, 1298 (1989) (witness, with excellent vision, observed defendant for more than three minutes on sunny day from unobstructed view); *Com. v. Bodden,* supra, 391 Mass at 359-363, 461 NE2d at 806-807 (witness had opportunity to "quite easily" observe defendant at time of crime for a period of several minutes, and thus, trial judge properly concluded that in-court identification rested on independent recollection even though witness failed to identify defendant positively when he first saw him after crime); *Com. v. Cooper,* 356 Mass 74, 84-85, 248 NE2d 253, 260 (1969) (witnesses had ample opportunity to observe offenders and ample capacity to remember what they observed, and one witness selected defendant's photograph before the suggestive lineup); *Com. v. Hill,* 38 Mass App 982, 652 NE2d 621 (1995) (officer's initial encounter with defendant provided basis for in-court identification independent of later suggestive identification); *Com. v. Ayles,* 31 Mass App 514, 518-520, 580 NE2d 394, 397-398 (1991) (police officer's post-identification statement to victim that person whose photograph she selected was a suspect in other assaults on women did not taint in-court identification where her prior identification was made with certitude and without undue hesitation).

For cases finding no independent source, see *Com. v. Thornley,* 406 Mass 96, 101, 546 NE2d 350, 353 (1989) (*Thornley II*) (Commonwealth failed to demonstrate that lineup and courtroom identification were based on source independent of suggestive photographic identification);

Com. v. A Juvenile, 402 Mass 275, 280, 521 NE2d 1368, 1372 (1988) (Commonwealth did not meet heavy burden of proving that proffered in-court identification would be free of taint of suggestive pretrial procedure); *Com. v. Botelho*, 369 Mass 860, 868-870, 343 NE2d 876, 882 (1976) (where witness's observation of assailant was over a substantial distance in dim lighting when she was influenced by alcohol, her description of the gunman immediately after incident was very general, she failed to identify picture of defendant, and on a prior occasion she stated that defendant was positively not the assailant, court was warranted in finding that subsequent in-court identifications of defendant were tainted by suggestive confrontation at courthouse); *Com. v. Kazonis*, 356 Mass 649, 653, 255 NE2d 333, 336 (1970) (highly unlikely that in-court identification more than two years after crime could have occurred independently of suggestive police station confrontation); *Com. v. White*, 11 Mass App 953, 417 NE2d 44 (1981) (in-court identification should have been suppressed as lacking source independent of suggestive out-of-court identification where witness's description was at variance with defendant's height and weight and she failed to identify defendant's photograph prior to suggestive show-up).

§10.3   Challenging Identification Evidence

§10.3.1   *Motion to Suppress*

When an allegedly impermissible pretrial identification has occurred, the defendant must seasonably raise the issue by filing a motion to suppress the evidence before trial. Mass R Crim P 13; Mass Superior Court R 61; Fed R Crim P 12(b)(3). A defendant who fails to make a pretrial motion is not entitled to object to an in-court identification at trial. See *Com. v. Cooper*, 356 Mass 74, 78-79, 248 NE2d 253, 257 (1969) (decided under Superior Court Rule 101, the predecessor of Rule 61). See also *Com. v. Stanley*, 363 Mass 102, 104, 292 NE2d 694, 697 (1973).

A defendant has a right to be informed of the details of any out-of-court identification, and may request a voir dire of the relevant witnesses to obtain such details. The Supreme Judicial Court has emphasized that "full exploration of the circumstances surrounding eyewitness identification is necessary to ensure a fair trial." *Com. v. Dougan*, 377 Mass 303, 316-317, 386 NE2d 1, 9-10 (1979) (conviction reversed because defendant had been denied any opportunity to explore the identification process). See also *Com. v. Dickerson*, 372 Mass 783, 789, 364 NE2d 1052, 1056-1057 (1977) ("In a case suggestive of unfairness in the confrontation process, failure to allow full development [on cross-examination] of the circumstances surrounding the identification might well warrant setting aside the verdict of guilt."). Compare *Com. v. Leaster*, 395 Mass 96, 104-105, 479 NE2d 124, 129-130 (1985) (newly discovered evidence suggesting a different version of the pretrial identification than was testified to at trial did not entitle defendant to new trial); *Com. v. Wilson*, 46 Mass App 292, 705 NE2d 313 (1999) (voir dire unnecessary where prosecutor had accurately informed defense counsel of the information).

When a timely motion is filed, the practice in Massachusetts is to hold a pretrial hearing or voir dire examination in the absence of the jury to determine the admissibility of pretrial and in-court identifications. See, e.g., *Com. v. Dickerson*, supra. But see *Com. v. Hicks*, 377 Mass 1, 6-7, 384 NE2d 1206, 1210 (1979) (voir dire unnecessary at second trial where court had before it the transcript from the voir dire held during first trial). While a judicial determination outside the jury's presence of the admissibility of identification evidence is the preferred proceeding, the due process clause of the Fourteenth Amendment of the United States Constitution does not require such a proceeding whenever a defendant contends that an improper identification occurred. See *Watkins v. Sowders*, 449 US 341, 345-349 (1981); *Com. v. Walker*, 421 Mass 90, 94, 653 NE2d 1080,

1083 (1995). See also *Com. v. Simmons*, 383 Mass 46, 47, 417 NE2d 1193, 1194 (1981) (although not constitutionally required, better practice is to conduct a voir dire to determine whether witness's pretrial identification of motor vehicle was unduly suggestive).

On a motion to suppress identification evidence, it is the defendant's burden to prove by a preponderance of the evidence that the pretrial procedure was so unnecessarily suggestive and conducive to mistaken identity as to deny the defendant due process of law. *Com. v. Odware*, 429 Mass 231, 235, 707 NE2d 347, 351 (1999). Upon such a showing, the prosecution may not offer the identification in evidence. If the court excludes evidence of the pretrial identification and the prosecution desires to offer an in-court identification, it must (as discussed in §10.2.3, supra) show by clear and convincing evidence that the proffered identification has a source independent of the suggestive procedure. See *United States v. Wade*, 388 US 218, 240 (1967); *Com. v. Smith*, 414 Mass 437, 442-443, 608 NE2d 1018, 1022 (1993); *Com. v. Otsuki*, 411 Mass 218, 232, 581 NE2d 999, 1007-1008 (1991); *Com. v. Thornley*, 406 Mass 96, 98-99, 546 NE2d 350, 351-352 (1989) (*Thornley II*); *Com. v. Thornley*, 400 Mass 355, 363, 509 NE2d 908, 913 (1987) (*Thornley I*).

§10.3.2   Cross-Examination and Closing Argument

It should be added that a ruling admitting evidence of a pretrial identification does not end the matter. The testimony presented to the jury is subject to cross-examination on the question of the fairness and reliability of the procedure, and the matter will almost certainly be addressed in closing argument. *Com. v. Barnett*, 371 Mass 87, 94, 354 NE2d 879, 884 (1976). "Where identification evidence has not been suppressed, its infirmities are a matter for consideration by the jury. The defendant [is] entitled not only to inform the jury of procedures used which might have been somewhat suggestive, but also to establish the existence of fairer procedures which the police chose to ignore." *Com. v. Rodriguez*, 378 Mass 296, 308, 391 NE2d 889, 896 (1979) (citations omitted) (judge improperly excluded evidence regarding pretrial identification procedures employed by the police). See also *Com. v. Colon-Cruz*, 408 Mass 533, 542 n.3, 562 NE2d 797, 805 n.3 (1990) ("Defense counsel took ample advantage of his remedy [for the admission of identification evidence]: on cross-examination he thoroughly explored [the witness's] exposure to the press and the consequent reliability of his identification."); *Com. v. Enos*, 26 Mass App 1006, 530 NE2d 805 (1988) ("When the voice identification is of a person other than the defendant, we may rely on cross-examination and argument to illuminate weaknesses in the identification, whether by reason of suggestion or conditions for observation."); *Com. v. Allen*, 22 Mass App 413, 417-423, 494 NE2d 55, 58-61 (1986) (judge erred in excluding a partial transcript of a telephone conversation between the victim and a police emergency operator that the defense offered to impeach the victim's testimony concerning his initial identification). Compare *Com. v. Montez*, 45 Mass App 802, 810, 702 NE2d 40, 46 (1998) (no violation of defendant's rights where court refused to allow defense counsel to present photo array to witness with only eyes and noses exposed).

§10.3.3   Jury Instructions

A defendant who fairly raises the issue of mistaken identification at trial is ordinarily entitled to jury instructions on the factors relevant to reliability. Model instructions were set out in *Com. v. Rodriguez*, 378 Mass 296, 302, 310-311, 391 NE2d 889, 892-893, 897-898 (1979).

The *Rodriguez* instructions have been added to and revised subsequently. In *Com. v. Hallet*, 427 Mass 552, 558, 694 NE2d 845, 849 (1998), the court criticized the *Rodriguez* language which invited the jury to consider "the length of time that passed between the occurrence of the crime and the next opportunity any identification witness had to see the defendant." Such language "implies inappropriately that the witness saw the defendant at the crime scene." Id. See *Com. v. Cuffie*, 414 Mass 632, 640-641, 609 NE2d 437, 441-442 (1993); *Com. v. Fitzpatrick*, 18 Mass App 106, 111 & n.8, 463 NE2d 571 (1984).

In *Com. v. Santoli*, 424 Mass 837, 680 NE2d 1116 (1997), the court revised a portion of the standard *Rodriguez* identification charge, which had suggested that jurors take into account the strength of an identification in assessing its reliability. The court noted significant doubt about a supposed correlation between a witness's confidence in an identification and the accuracy of her recollection. The court concluded that in the future this matter should be left to cross-examination and arguments of counsel and, in the ordinary course, not be a subject of jury instruction. See *Com. v. Ashley*, 427 Mass 620, 628, 694 NE2d 862, 869 (1998) (*Santoli* is not retroactive).

In *Com. v. Pressley*, 390 Mass 617, 457 NE2d 1119 (1983), the court held that the judge's refusal to instruct the jury on the possibility of a good faith mistake in the identification of defendant by the victim constituted reversible error. See *Com. v. Odware*, 429 Mass 231, 707 NE2d 347 (1999) (error not to give *Pressley* instruction, but harmless under particular facts of the case); *Com. v. Rosado*, 428 Mass 76, 696 NE2d 943 (1998) (same); *Com. v. Spencer*, 45 Mass App 33, 39, 695 NE2d 677, 681 (1998) ("constancy in the testimony of identification witnesses by itself is insufficient reason to deny a requested *Pressley* charge where, in the circumstances of the case, the accuracy of the identification might reasonably be questioned by the jury and independent evidence linking the defendant to the alleged crime is not overwhelming"); *Com. v. Adderley*, 36 Mass App 918, 921, 629 NE2d 308, 311 (1994) (reversible error not to give *Pressley* instruction); *Com. v. Caparrotta*, 34 Mass App 473, 612 NE2d 696 (1993) (same). Cf. *Com. v. Montez*, 45 Mass App 802, 811, 702 NE2d 40, 47 (1998) (not ineffective assistance of counsel not to request *Pressley* instruction where jury was apprised by other means of possibility of good faith mistake in identification); *Com. v. Carter*, 423 Mass 506, 515, 669 NE2d 203, 209 (1996) (not ineffective assistance of counsel for defense lawyer to request a *Rodriguez/Pressley* jury instruction, rather than making different tactical choices for handling eyewitness testimony).

A judge is not required to give all the suggested instructions set out in *Rodriguez*; they may be modified as the evidence at trial requires. *Com. v. Payton*, 35 Mass 586, 596, 623 NE2d 1127, 1134 (1993). See also *Com. v. Jackson*, 419 Mass 716, 732-733, 647 NE2d 401, 410-411 (1995) (although instructions varied from recommended model, they made clear to jury that identification was subject to error and suggestion). Compare *Com. v. Hallet*, 427 Mass 552, 694 NE2d 845 (1998) (reversible error not to charge on presenting defendant to witness for identification, one on one confrontation, and failure to make identification, when these issues were relevant to case) with *Com. v. Walker*, supra, 421 Mass at 99-103, 653 NE2d at 1085-1087 (omission of portion of charge addressing suggestive one on one confrontation and error in instruction regarding length of time between crime and identification did not create substantial risk of miscarriage of justice); *Com. v. Elam*, 412 Mass 583, 587, 591 NE2d 186, 189 (1992) (no error in refusal to charge jury on possibility of good faith mistake in identification); *Com. v. Grace*, 43 Mass App Ct 905, 681 NE2d 1265 (1997) (same); *Com. v. McMaster*, 21 Mass App 722, 726-728, 490 NE2d 464, 469-470 (1986) (omission of certain portions of *Rodriguez* charge did not create substantial risk of miscarriage of justice). See also *Com. v. Walker*, 33 Mass App 915, 916-917, 597 NE2d 72, 72-73 (1992) (error for judge to instruct jury on identification, including factors relating to misidentification, where defense is that crime never occurred; but no prejudice).

There is no right to an instruction regarding the asserted difficulty of interracial identification, but a judge in the exercise of discretion may instruct the jury that in determining the weight to be given eyewitness identification testimony, it may consider the fact of any cross-racial identification and whether the identification by a person of different race from the defendant may be less reliable than identification by a person of the same race. *Com. v. Hyatt,* 419 Mass 815, 818-819, 647 NE2d 1168, 1171 (1995). See also *Com. v. Charles,* 397 Mass 1, 8, 489 NE2d 679 (1986); *Com. v. Engram,* 43 Mass App Ct 804, 686 NE2d 1080 (1997) (cross-racial identification instruction not required given circumstances under which identification was made); *Com. v. Burgos,* 36 Mass App 903, 904, 627 NE2d 471, 473 (1994); *Com. v. Horne,* 26 Mass App 996, 999, 530 NE2d 353 (1988). Similarly, the decision as to whether to allow expert testimony on the subject of cross-racial identifications is within the judge's discretion. See *Com. v. Walker,* supra, 421 Mass at 96, 653 NE2d at 1084 (& citations). See also §10.4.

§10.3.4   Harmless Error

When identification evidence has been wrongly admitted into evidence, either in violation of the defendant's right to counsel or in violation of due process, reversal is not mandatory; the error may be harmless beyond a reasonable doubt. See *Moore v. Illinois,* 434 US 220, 232, 98 S Ct 458, 54 L Ed 2d 424 (1977); *United States v. Wade,* 388 US 218, 242 (1967); *Gilbert v. California,* 388 US 263, 274 (1967); *Com. v. Thornley,* 406 Mass 96, 101, 546 NE2d 350, 353-354 (1989) (*Thornley II*); *Com. v. Morgan,* 30 Mass App 685, 691-693, 573 NE2d 989, 993 (1991). Whether an error is harmless depends on a variety of factors, including whether the erroneously admitted evidence was merely cumulative of other evidence properly before the jury; the "essential question is whether the error had or might have had an effect on the jury and whether the error contributed to or might have contributed to the verdict." *Com. v. Thornley II,* supra, 406 Mass at 101-102, 546 NE2d at 354. For more on the standards for harmless error, see *Chapman v. California,* 386 US 18 (1967).

§10.4   Expert Testimony

Expert testimony concerning eyewitness identification is not admissible as of right, but is admissible in the proper exercise of discretion by the trial judge. See *Com. v. Kent K.*, 427 Mass 754, 762, 696 NE2d 511, 518 (1998); §7.7, note 1 and accompanying text.

REAL and
DEMONSTRATIVE
EVIDENCE

A.   GENERAL PRINCIPLES

§11.1   Definition

All evidence is "real" evidence in the sense that it must be perceived by the trier of fact in order to have probative value. The courts, however, apply the term "real" only to nontestimonial evidence. Real evidence is such evidence as is addressed directly to the physical senses of the court or jury without the direct intervention of the testimony of witnesses. Real evidence thus includes things and events introduced in evidence in the courtroom; it also includes things and events viewed by the jury outside the courtroom. Real evidence is often designated demonstrative evidence. Wigmore describes it by use of the term "autoptic proference." See generally Wigmore §§1150-1169 (Chad rev 1972).

Real evidence is subject to no general rules not applicable to testimonial evidence.[1] However, because of its peculiar nature, certain conditions of admissibility of evidence are particularly important in the case of real evidence.

§11.2   Accessibility of Material Characteristics

Real evidence must be such that the jurors are able to perceive the characteristic for which the evidence is offered. For example, jurors are able through their sense of taste to determine if water from a well is salty; they are not able to determine by taste whether a fruit juice is "adulterated" within the meaning of a statute. See, e.g., *Bruce's Juices v. United States*, 194 F2d 935, 937 (5th Cir 1952). The water is

---

§11.1   [1]There is no "best evidence rule" with respect to physical objects not produced in court. The existence or condition of a tangible object may be described by witnesses without producing the article itself. *Com. v. Pope*, 103 Mass 440 (1869). The best evidence rule with respect to the contents of documents is discussed at §12.6.

thus proper real evidence to prove its salty taste; the juice is not proper real evidence to prove its adulteration.

§11.3   Authenticity, Chain of Custody

An item of real evidence must be authenticated, or "identified," as the thing or event its proponent represents it to be.[1] *Com. v. LaCorte*, 373 Mass 700, 704, 369 NE2d 1006, 1009 (1977); *Nesci v. Angelo*, 249 Mass 508, 144 NE 287 (1924). Authentication is usually accomplished by the testimony of a witness who testifies that the object is what it purports to be. *Com. v. Drayton*, 386 Mass 39, 48, 434 NE2d 997, 1005 (1982) (Text cited). If the object is one the witness can identify by observation, his testimony that he recognizes it will be sufficient. If not, it may be necessary for him to have placed an identifying mark or label thereon, or to otherwise create a "chain of custody" that will help him authenticate the object. *Com. v. Hogg*, 365 Mass 290, 311 NE2d 63 (1974). Cf. *Com. v. Rodriquez*, 364 Mass 87, 300 NE2d 192 (1973).

The fact that there may be weaknesses in the identification or chain of custody of evidence usually goes to the weight rather than the admissibility of the evidence. *Com. v. Viriyahiranpaiboon*, 412 Mass 224, 230, 588 NE2d 643, 648 (1992); *Com. v. Andrews*, 403 Mass 441, 530 NE2d 1222 (1988); *Com. v. Paszko*, 391 Mass 164, 196, 461 NE2d 222, 241 (1984); *Com. v. Berth*, 385 Mass 784, 791, 434 NE2d 192, 196 (1982); *Com. v. Colon*, 33 Mass App 304, 309, 598 NE2d 1143, 1146 (1992). Compare *Irwin v. Ware*, 392 Mass 745, 750-751, 467 NE2d 1292, 1296-1298 (1984) (failure to produce specific evidence to establish chain of custody; evidence of blood test results improperly admitted).

---

§11.3   [1] See §12.1.

§11.4   Circumstantial Use of Real Evidence

Real evidence of the direct kind is always relevant — e.g., the exhibition of a scar when offered to show the extent of injury. Where real evidence is used circumstantially, the item of evidence must be not only authenticated, but also shown to tend to prove a material fact. (See Chapter 4 for a general discussion of principles of relevance.) See *Com. v. Merola*, 405 Mass 529, 542 NE2d 249 (1989) (photos of bruises on child's body not linked to defendant or to child's death held admissible to show, inter alia, consciousness of guilt, as defendant denied seeing any bruises); *Com. v. Drayton*, 386 Mass 39, 48, 434 NE2d 997, 1005 (1982) (defendant's fingerprints on box found at scene of incident involving a murder were circumstantial evidence of his identity as killer); *Com. v. Stroud*, 375 Mass 265, 272, 376 NE2d 849, 853 (1978) (bloodstained shirt relevant to manner in which victim died); *Com. v. Lamoureux*, 348 Mass 390, 392-393, 204 NE2d 115, 117 (1965) (photos of open scalp wounds demonstrated probability that blood would flow onto clothing of one assaulting victim in a particular physical position); *Com. v. Bartolini*, 299 Mass 503, 511-512, 13 NE2d 382, 387-388 (1938) (twine found in residence of defendant admissible as similar to that with which deceased was tied).

§11.5   Similar and Altered Objects

The relevancy of certain real evidence may be brought into particular question if the object is similar to but not identical with the object in question. Evidence that a commonplace article similar to one involved in a crime, but not the article itself, was found in a place connected to a criminal defendant may well be more prejudicial than probative. Where the item is less common, evidence that the defendant keeps that type of item about may be more probative. It has frequently been held, however, that similar items are admissible. See, e.g., *Com. v. Paszko*, 391 Mass at 195, 461 NE2d at 241 (1984) (drugs found in defendant's car corresponded to those missing from pharmacy where druggist was killed); *Com v. Johnson*, 46 Mass App 398, 706 NE2d 716 (1999) (knife recovered from defendant's residence admissible as one similar to knife used by robber); *Com. v. McDonald*, 11 Mass App 944, 416 NE2d 992 (1981) (safety pin found at scene, similar to one used by defendant; jackknife on defendant's person when arrested consistent with wounds of victim); *Com. v. Kinney*, 12 Mass App 915, 423 NE2d 1017 (1981) (hats found in apartment similar to those defendant had been seen wearing were relevant to show his control of apartment); *Com. v. McJunkin*, 11 Mass App 609, 620-621, 418 NE2d 1259, 1266-1267 (1981) (knife surrendered by defendant on arrest properly allowed to be described by victim as "similar" to one used in assault). Contrast *Com. v. Chasson*, 383 Mass 183, 423 NE2d 306 (1981) (knives offered by defendant allegedly discovered at crime scene after fruitless intensive search for same by police were properly excluded in discretion of judge). See §4.1.2.

An object similar to the article in issue, but unconnected with any party to the case, may be offered as merely illustrative of the object. *Com. v. Luna*, 46 Mass App 90, 703 NE2d 740 (1998) (gun). Any differences between the item offered and the one in issue must be such that the jury can perceive and take account of them. *Flynn v. First National Stores*, 296 Mass 521, 6 NE2d 814 (1937).

If an article is identified as the identical article in issue but has changed in its condition, similar requirements would seem appropriate. The fact that the article has changed does not bar its admissibility but only affects the weight to be given the evidence. *Poirier v. Plymouth*, 374 Mass 206, 210, 372 NE2d 212, 213 (1978) (construction plans). However, the nature of the change must be shown to be such as either not to affect its evidentiary value or as to allow the jury to perceive and take account of it. *Cutter v. Hamlen*, 147 Mass 471, 18 NE 397 (1888) (house drains). Cf.

Com. v. Sheeran, 370 Mass 82, 345 NE2d 362 (1976) (witness's verification of photograph as representing earlier condition sufficient to indicate no change had taken place); *Droney v. Doherty,* 186 Mass 205, 71 NE 547 (1904) (in absence of evidence of change there is a presumption that article is in same condition).

Whether an item of real evidence is relevant is essentially a discretionary matter for the trial court. *Alholm v. Wareham,* 371 Mass 621, 358 NE2d 788 (1976). See generally Chapter 4.

§11.6   Evidence Arguably Inflammatory or Prejudicial

Real evidence tends to be powerful, even sensational. It may excite the passions of jurors and raise a possibility that decisions may not be based on reason and logic, but on emotions. Such evidence should not be admitted if unduly prejudicial or confusing. It is within the sound discretion of the trial judge to exclude such evidence, although relevant, if its prejudicial effect outweighs its probative value.[1]

The issue that has been most frequently litigated is the admissibility of photographs of a crime victim or crime scene. Where such photographs have probative value, they are not rendered inadmissible merely because they are gruesome or may be considered inflammatory. *Com. v. DeSouza,* 428 Mass 667, 704 NE2d 190 (1999); *Com. v. Jackson,* 428 Mass 455, 702 NE2d 1158 (1998); *Com. v. Repoza,* 382 Mass 119, 129, 414 NE2d 591, 596-597 (1980) (*Repoza I*) ("where the allegedly inflammatory element of a photograph offered as evidence is a natural and inevitable incident of the crime, and the photograph is otherwise probative, there is little basis to disturb the ruling of a trial judge as to its admissibility"). The admissibility of photographic evidence is a matter left to the sound discretion of the judge, and a defendant bears a heavy burden of demon-

---

§11.6   [1] See §4.3, Fed R Evid 403, Proposed Mass R Evid 403.

strating an abuse of that discretion. *Com. v. Stockwell,* 426 Mass 17, 686 NE2d 426 (1997) (not error to admit gruesome photo of victim discovered nine days after death, although picture was of debatable relevance); *Com. v. Glowacki,* 398 Mass 507, 512, 499 NE2d 290, 293 (1986). Indeed, the courts "have rarely reversed a conviction because of the production of photographs of a victim." *Com. v. Nadworny,* 396 Mass 342, 366, 486 NE2d 675, 689-690 (1985). Cf. *Com. v. Hrycenko,* 31 Mass App 425, 578 NE2d 809 (1991) (error to send inflammatory photos to deliberating jury in response to question, after photos had originally been excluded, because counsel had no opportunity to mount defense to their effect, although it would not have been error to admit them originally).

Photographs generally will not be excluded merely because an expert or other witness has already provided a detailed description of the crime scene or victim's wounds. *Com. v. DeSouza,* supra; *Com. v. Paradise,* 405 Mass 141, 539 NE2d 1006 (1989); *Com. v. Benoit,* 389 Mass 411, 429, 451 NE2d 101, 112 (1983). Nor will a party's offer to stipulate as to the matters demonstrated by the photographs preclude their admissibility. *Com. v. Nadworny,* supra, 396 Mass at 367, 486 NE2d at 690 ("a judge may generally admit relevant evidence even if a party has agreed to stipulate to the fact that the offered evidence tends to prove"); *Com. v. Torres,* 367 Mass 737, 327 NE2d 871 (1975). However, in determining the probative value of such evidence, it may be useful for the trial court to voir dire an appropriate witness outside the presence of the jury to learn if photographs will be of assistance in understanding the testimony. See *Com. v. Medeiros,* 395 Mass 336, 479 NE2d 1371 (1985).

The judge should caution the jurors to curb their emotional reactions to such photographs, in order to alleviate any prejudicial impact they may have. An admonition to the jury is one factor to be weighed in determining whether the risk of prejudice has been avoided. See *Com. v. Jackson,* supra; *Com. v. Rosado,* 408 Mass 561, 562 NE2d 790 (1990); *Com. v. Richenburg,* 401 Mass 663, 673, 518 NE2d 1143, 1148

(1988) (judge instructed the jurors to be "cold, calculating and professional in dealing with this type of evidence" and not to "get fired up").

Numerous cases have held photographs of the victim admissible on the issue of extreme atrocity and cruelty, or deliberate premeditation, in murder prosecutions. See *Com. v. Jackson*, supra (crime scene and autopsy photos); *Com. v. Meinholz*, 420 Mass 633, 651 NE2d 385 (1995) (photos depicted differences between discoloration caused by blunt object and discolorations resulting from decomposition); *Com. v. Berry*, 420 Mass 95, 648 NE2d 732 (1995) (photograph of victim's naked body); *Com. v. Simmons*, 419 Mass 426, 431, 646 NE2d 97, 100 (1995) (autopsy photo of victim showing 11 stab wounds); *Com. v. Phinney*, 416 Mass 364, 375, 622 NE2d 617, 624 (1993) (autopsy photographs); *Com. v. Blake*, 409 Mass 146, 564 NE2d 1006 (1991) (11 photos from the scene and autopsy, each depicting a different aspect of injuries); *Com. v. Gallagher*, 408 Mass 510, 562 NE2d 80 (1990) (included autopsy photo showing interior of the skull); *Com. v. Lawrence*, 404 Mass 378, 536 NE2d 571 (1989) (also affirming admission of an autopsy photo of fetus to show that victim's pregnancy would have been obvious to third parties); *Com. v. Clifford*, 374 Mass 293, 305-306, 372 NE2d 1267, 1276 (1978) (badly burned victim); *Com. v. Cadwell*, 374 Mass 308, 372 NE2d 246 (1978) (four-year-old child); *Com. v. Estep*, 38 Mass App 502, 649 NE2d 775 (1995) (autopsy photos depicting bruises on brain); *Com. v. Talbot*, 35 Mass App 766, 778, 625 NE2d 1374, 1381-1382 (1994) (fact that photographs displayed post-mortem decomposition did not render them inadmissible on issue of extreme cruelty); *Com. v. King*, 33 Mass App 905, 595 NE2d 795 (1992).

For cases holding photographs of the victim admissible for other purposes, see *Com. v. Andrade*, 422 Mass 236, 661 NE2d 1308 (1996) (two videotapes of crime scene, depicting blood, multiple photos of victim, and autopsy photos were admissible); *Com. v. Benson*, 419 Mass 114, 642 NE2d 1035 (1994) (color photos of victim's facial injuries were relevant to dispute self-defense claim and to support witness's testimony on manner in which defendant used metal pipe to beat victim); *Com. v. Robertson*, 408 Mass 747, 563 NE2d 223 (1990) (photo of homicide victim taken after earlier beating by defendant relevant to show hostility); *Com. v. Merola*, 405 Mass 529, 544-545, 542 NE2d 249, 258-259 (1989) (photos of child victim's bruises helped jury understand medical testimony and assess defendant's credibility inasmuch as he had denied seeing any bruises); *Com. v. Nadworny*, 396 Mass 342, 366-367, 486 NE2d 675, 689-690 (1985) (photo of body showing advanced state of decomposition relevant to pathologist's testimony that he was unable to determine precise cause and time of death; photo of victim while she was alive showing "youthful and smiling face" was relevant as tending to show that death due to ill health or suicide was unlikely); *Com. v. Todd*, 394 Mass 791, 796, 477 NE2d 999, 1003-1004 (1985) (photos probative of degree of guilt, tended to refute defendant's claim of intoxication, and showed direction from which shot came); *Com. v. Perry*, 385 Mass 639, 644, 433 NE2d 446, 450 (1982) (photos of room where fire occurred and of victim's body relevant to refute claim of accidental smoking death) (Text cited); *Com. v. Tarver*, 369 Mass 302, 317, 345 NE2d 671, 680 (1975) (photos of body of six-year-old girl who had been raped and murdered admissible to show sexual abuse); *Com. v. Holmes*, 32 Mass App 906, 584 NE2d 1150 (1992) (autopsy photo showing depth of wound admissible to prove wound was consistent with defendant's knife). Cf. *Com. v. Darby*, 37 Mass App 650, 642 NE2d 303 (1994) (error to admit photo of child sexual abuse victim sitting in bathtub alone naked, fondling himself, where there was already a plethora of evidence on the issue of child's sexual knowledge).

Photographs have been held admissible, although arguably inflammatory, when they identify or describe the defendant in a material way. See *Com. v. Lamoureux*, 348 Mass 390, 392-393, 204 NE2d 115, 117 (1965) (photos of open scalp wounds demonstrated probability that blood would flow onto clothing of one assaulting victim); *Com. v. Appleby*, 389 Mass 359, 374-375, 377, 450 NE2d 1070, 1080-1081 (1983) (photographs of defendant's residence); *Com. v. Izzo*, 359 Mass 39, 267 NE2d 631 (1971) (photos of rape defendant wearing swastikas and German helmet admissible as a fair representation of his appearance at time of alleged crime). Cf. *Com. v. Darby*, supra (error to admit grossly offensive and inflammatory photo of defendant alone, sitting fully dressed, with penis exposed in turgid state, where defendant did not claim impotence or sexual dysfunction).

Photographs showing the victim's body in an altered state (as in the course of an autopsy) present special problems and, on rare occasions, their admission has been held reversible error. See *Com. v. Bastarache*, 382 Mass 86, 105-106, 414 NE2d 984, 997 (1980); *Com. v. Richmond*, 371 Mass 563, 358 NE2d 999 (1976) (conviction reversed because of the admission of photos showing victim with severe post-mortem facial injuries). The Supreme Judicial Court has provided the following guidance:

> [T]he judge should carefully assess the photographs. If they are apt to be inflammatory or otherwise prejudicial, he should admit them, in his discretion, only if they are important to the resolution of any contested fact in the case. In some instances, an expert may testify and be cross-examined concerning autopsy photographs without any need to show them to the jury. Unless the viewing of an autopsy photograph would aid the jury, as lay people, in making a finding of fact on a contested point, the actual viewing of a photograph showing the body as altered in the course of an autopsy would serve no proper purpose. It may often be difficult to determine the admissibility of such photographs before any expert testifies, and a decision to exclude such photographs might properly be changed during or after the testimony of one or more experts. The exercise of discretion to admit such photographs should be based in part on an assessment of the contested issues of fact.

Bastarche, supra, 382 Mass at 106, 414 NE2d at 997. However, while reversing the defendant's conviction in *Richmond,* supra, the court cautioned: "[W]e have never, so far as we know, upset a verdict on this type of error, and this opinion is not to be taken to indicate that we are likely to do so again, but there are limits to the employment of judicial discretion and those limits were exceeded in this instance." 371 Mass at 566, 358 NE2d at 1001. Indeed, there are a substantial number of cases where the admission of autopsy photographs or pictures showing a body in a state of decomposition has been affirmed. See *Com. v. Vazquez,* 419 Mass 350, 644 NE2d 978 (1995) (photo of murder victim's broken hyoid bone after removal from body was admissible on issue of whether victim had been strangled); *Com. v. Medeiros,* 395 Mass 336, 479 NE2d 1371 (1985); *Com. v. Paszko,* 391 Mass 164, 196, 461 NE2d 222, 241 (1984); *Com. v. Allen,* 377 Mass 674, 387 NE2d 553 (1979) (photographs and slides of victim's body in state of "moderately advanced decomposition" questionably admitted, but conviction reversed on other grounds); *Com. v. Holmes,* 32 Mass App 906, 584 NE2d 1150 (1991).

The fact that photographs are in color is not a sufficient reason to exclude them. See *Com. v. Paszko,* 391 Mass 164, 196, 461 NE2d 222, 241 (1984); *Com. v. Horton,* 376 Mass 380, 398-399, 380 NE2d 687, 698-699 (1978); *Com. v. Makarewicz,* 333 Mass 575, 583-584, 132 NE2d 294, 299 (1956) (enlarged color slides properly admitted).

Disturbing photographs of other subject matters have also been held admissible. See *Com. v. Simmons,* 419 Mass 426, 646 NE2d 97 (1995) (photographs and videotape of blood-stained apartment were admissible to prove prosecution's contentions about defendant's movements); *Com. v. Perry,* 385 Mass 639, 644, 433 NE2d 446, 450 (1982) (photo of room where fire occurred).

With respect to the use of provocative photographs in civil litigation, compare *Horowitz v. Bokron,* 337 Mass 739, 742, 151 NE2d 480, 483 (1958) (color slides showing unpleasant injuries to face and neck of plaintiff properly admitted within discretion of judge) with *Herwitz v. MBTA*, 353 Mass 594, 233 NE2d 726 (1968) (in wrongful death case, error to admit slides to show mutilated and disfigured body of deceased solely on basis of degree of culpability of defendants).

The proffer of items of real evidence other than photographs may also provoke claims of prejudice. Here, also, the appellate courts rarely reverse a trial court's determination that probative value outweighed prejudice. See *Com. v. Berry*, 420 Mass 95, 109, 648 NE2d 732, 741 (1995) (display of victim's bedclothing and introduction in evidence of her nightgown was proper to demonstrate that each item had a single knife cut in a blood-stained area; court noted that, "In the future, however, trial judges must take care to avoid exposing the jury unnecessarily to inflammatory material that might inflame the jurors' emotions and possibly deprive the defendant of an impartial jury."); *Com. v. Zagranski*, 408 Mass 278, 558 NE2d 933 (1990) (affirming admissibility of bloodstained clothing, even though only "marginally relevant" because obvious that person shot as victim was would bleed on clothes); *Com. v. Appleby*, 389 Mass 359, 374-375, 377, 450 NE2d 1070, 1080-1081 (1983) (voodoo doll found in defendant's home corroborated victim's testimony). Compare *Tuttle v. McGeeney*, 344 Mass 200, 181 NE2d 655 (1962) (judge may bar exhibition of scars on plaintiff's body in his discretion).[2]

§11.7   Destruction of Real Evidence

When significant physical items are lost or destroyed, intentionally or accidentally, before trial, fairness may require the taking of remedial measures to avoid the possibility that the party who had access to the evidence may obtain an improper advantage.

---

[2] See §11.10 for additional cases on the exhibition of wounds and scars before the jury.

§11.7.1   Criminal Cases

In a criminal case when potentially exculpatory real evidence is discarded, lost or destroyed (including during destructive testing by experts), a defendant may seek to have the charges dismissed, or to preclude the prosecution from relying on the evidence in question. In deciding what, if any, sanctions are appropriate, the court must weigh the culpability of the government, the materiality of the evidence, and the potential for prejudice. *Com. v. DiBenedetto,* 427 Mass 414, 419, 693 NE2d 1007, 1011 (1998) (no prejudice shown where Commonwealth failed to make available evidence per pretrial conference report, prosecution expert wiped away blood on sneaker during test, but defense expert found blood on other sneaker); *Com. v. Martinez,* 420 Mass 622, 629, 651 NE2d 380, 384 (1995) (conviction affirmed); *Com. v. Willie,* 400 Mass 427, 432, 510 NE2d 258, 261-262 (1987) (remanded for hearing by trial judge on prejudice). The defendant has an initial burden of establishing "a reasonable possibility, based on concrete evidence and not on mere speculation, that the Commonwealth's actions deprived him of evidence that would have been favorable to his case." *Com. v. Olszewski,* 416 Mass 707, 714, 625 NE2d 529, 535 (1993) (conviction affirmed).

For cases affirming convictions despite the destruction or loss of evidence, see, e.g., *Com. v. Woodward,* 427 Mass 659, 679, 694 NE2d 1277, 1292 (1998) (prosecution was responsible for medical examiner's failure to preserve tissue samples, the lost evidence was material, but there was not sufficient prejudice to warrant dismissal of the indictment); *Com. v. Eakin,* 427 Mass 590, 696 NE2d 499 (1998) (no prejudice when city destroyed house containing alleged building code violations, because defendants had opportunity to photograph it and have it examined by expert prior to demolition); *Com. v. Hunter,* 426 Mass 715, 690 NE2d 815 (1998) (dismissal not required by destruction of fingerprint during testing where defendant had been furnished enlarged photos of same, or by loss of police notes of witness interview, no bad faith shown); *Com. v. Taylor,* 426 Mass 189, 687 NE2d 631 (1997) (no reversible error based on failure of prosecution's expert to cut sneakers into sections before testing for presence of gasoline, in order to determine where on sneaker it was found); *Com. v. Nom,* 426 Mass 152, 686 NE2d 1017 (1997) (dismissal not required by standard procedure of recording over tape of police telephone calls where defendant could not establish reasonable possibility it contained favorable evidence); *Com. v. Waters,* 420 Mass 276, 649 NE2d 724 (1995) (conviction affirmed; court considered, among other factors, that defendant had been permitted to depose a number of witnesses as mitigation of police error in losing tapes of radio and telephone calls); *Com. v. Otsuki,* 411 Mass 218, 230, 581 NE2d 999, 1007 (1991) (conviction affirmed, despite missing bullet fragments); *Com. v. Troy,* 405 Mass 253, 540 NE2d 162 (1989) (conviction affirmed against argument that potentially exculpatory blood samples were not retained); *Com. v. Richenburg,* 401 Mass 663, 668, 518 NE2d 1143 (1988) (*D*'s claim of error rejected, in part, because *D* made no request for smear slides he later argued were improperly discarded); *Com. v. Shipps,* 399 Mass 820, 836, 507 NE2d 671, 682 (1987) (better practice is to photograph stages of destructive testing, but error, if any, was harmless here); *Com. v. Burns,* 43 Mass App Ct 263, 683 NE2d 284 (1997) (dismissal not required by destruction of fingerprints, where defendant could point to no evidence showing they were exculpatory, or by destruction of original police notes where summary was provided); *Com. v. Chase,* 42 Mass App Ct 749, 679 NE2d 1021 (1997) (no error where prosecution negligently released truck involved in homicide before defense inspection, with result it was repaired before seen by defense); *Com. v. Mitchell,* 38 Mass App 184, 646 NE2d 1073 (1995) (conviction affirmed although Commonwealth did not do blood tests on murder weapon, a knife, and fingerprint tests on knife handle destroyed ability to do blood testing later, court noted that absence of defendant's blood on knife was of marginal materiality); *Com. v. Green-*

berg, 34 Mass App 197, 609 NE2d 90 (1993) (conviction affirmed where defendant's jacket was lost by Commonwealth, but jury was shown photo of jacket and told that chemists found no blood or accelerants on it). Cf. *Com. v. DeCicco*, 44 Mass App Ct 111, 688 NE2d 1010 (1998) (under circumstances, no ineffective assistance of counsel based on lawyer's failure to inspect evidence apparently lost by prosecution).

For cases allowing a defendant some measure of relief as the result of the destruction or loss of evidence, see, e.g., *Com. v. Gliniewicz*, 398 Mass 744, 500 NE2d 1324 (1986) (defendants entitled to new trial where evidence altered by Commonwealth's experts, comparable testing no longer possible, destruction of items was either intended or condoned by Commonwealth, evidence was material and its destruction prejudicial); *Com. v. Sasville*, 35 Mass App 15, 616 NE2d 476 (1993) (dismissal required where Commonwealth failed to notify defendant that fetus was being preserved following abortion performed on alleged rape victim, then allowed fetus to be destroyed without opportunity for defendant to conduct blood tests). Cf. *Com. v. Fitzgerald*, 402 Mass 517, 524 NE2d 72 (1988) (defendant entitled to new trial in rape case based on newly discovered medical bill proving vasectomy—due diligence demonstrated in part by proof insurance company had destroyed its records).

Compare *Com. v. Holman*, 27 Mass App 830, 544 NE2d 598 (1989) (defendant not entitled to dismissal of charge of operating under influence of liquor, despite erasure of arguably exculpatory videotape of booking) with *Com. v. Cameron*, 25 Mass App 538, 520 NE2d 1326 (1988) (conviction of operating under influence of liquor reversed, defendant not entitled to dismissal, but error to refuse to allow defendant to question about and comment upon Commonwealth's failure to produce videotape of booking).

There are special circumstances attendant to defense requests for access to, and the Commonwealth's responsibility for preserving evidence from a homicide victim's body.

In *Com. v. Woodward*, 427 Mass 659, 676, 694 NE2d 1277, 1290 (1998), the court noted that, "Autopsy procedures are inherently destructive . . . ". Under the circumstances of the case, the court held that the defendant was not entitled to relief based on the claims of lost body parts, delay in supplying defense attorneys with medical information, and the denial of a motion for an independent autopsy. The court noted that whatever due process rights a defendant might have to an independent autopsy must be balanced against the statutory right of the victim's family to return of the body following the medical examiner's autopsy. It concluded that a defendant would have to show cause and a specific need in a motion for access to a victim's body. The court suggested that "the optimal balancing and reconciliation of each party's interests could have been by allowing [defendant's] expert to be present at the [medical examiner's] autopsy." 427 Mass at 676 n.29.

§11.7.2　Civil Cases

In civil cases, the Supreme Judicial Court has held that where an item of physical evidence has been lost, destroyed or materially altered by an expert, where he knew or should have known that the item in its original form might be material to litigation, an opposing party is entitled to an order precluding the expert from testifying about the appearance of the item before its disappearance or alteration and from expressing any opinion based thereon. *Nally v. Volkswagen of America, Inc.*, 405 Mass 191, 197-198, 539 NE2d 1017, 1021 (1989). In *Bolton v. MBTA*, 32 Mass App 654, 593 NE2d 248 (1992), the Appeals Court extended the rule to cover the destruction of evidence by the party after inspection by its expert.

Sanctions for spoliation of evidence cannot be justified where the threat of a lawsuit is not sufficiently apparent that a reasonable person would realize the possible importance of the evidence to the resolution of the potential dispute.

Kippenhan v. Chaulk Services, Inc., 420 Mass 124, 127, 697 NE2d 527, 530 (1998). Sanctions for spoliation are also not appropriate against those parties in a case who played no role in the spoliation. *Kippenhan v. Chaulk Services, Inc.,* supra (plaintiff in action against ambulance attendants and manufacturer of stretcher were not foreclosed from offering evidence about condition of stretcher prior to its loss by ambulance company).[1]

B.   SPECIAL INSTANCES OF REAL EVIDENCE

§11.8   Documents

Documents are real evidence. When the truth of their contents is in issue, documents also have many of the attributes of testimonial evidence. The special problems of documentary evidence are treated in Chapter 12.

§11.9   Views

GL 234, §35, provides:

> The court may, upon motion, allow the jury in a civil case to view the premises or place in question or any property, matter or thing relative to the case. . . . The court may order a view by a jury impaneled to try a criminal case.

---

§11.7   [1] In *Nally v. Volkswagen of America, Inc.,* supra, the court had suggested that the rule barring testimony from an expert would apply without regard for whether the expert's conduct occurred before or after she was retained by a party to the case. In *Kippenhan v. Chaulk Services, Inc.,* supra, the court indicated that circumstances might make inappropriate such a hard and fast rule.

Section 35 essentially confirms the inherent common-law power of the court, sitting with or without jury, to take a view either upon request of a party or upon its own motion. *Madden v. Boston Elevated Railway Co.*, 284 Mass 490, 188 NE 234 (1933). Whether a view will be taken rests in the sound discretion of the court; a view should be allowed whenever the judge determines it would be of assistance to understand better the testimony that has been or may be presented. *Com. v. Cataldo*, 423 Mass 318, 327 n.8, 668 NE2d 762, 767 n.8 (1996) (within court's discretion to refuse view where it would not likely have helped jurors because events at issue took place in early morning hours on street crowded with noise of patrons leaving bars and restaurants, a situation not amenable to replication before jury); *Com. v. King*, 391 Mass 691, 694, 463 NE2d 1168, 1070-1071 (1984); *Terrio v. McDonough*, 16 Mass App 163, 173, 450 NE2d 190, 196 (1983). See also *Frade v. Costa*, 342 Mass 5, 171 NE2d 863 (1961) (master took a view). In certain cases, by statute, a view may be a matter of right upon the request of a party. GL 79, §22 (eminent domain cases); GL 80, §9 (betterment assessments); GL 253, §7 (mill flowage cases). Cf. *Jarvinen v. Com.*, 353 Mass 339, 231 NE2d 366 (1967) (trial judge is not required to attend a view taken under GL 79, §22).

The information acquired at a view is not evidence in a strict and narrow sense, but the jury may use it in reaching a verdict. *Com. v. Curry*, 368 Mass 195, 330 NE2d 819 (1975). Cf. *Rivers v. Town of Warwick*, 37 Mass App 593, 641 NE2d 1062 (1994) (view of dirt roads running through woods could not assist jury in determining whether roads were public or private, thus fact that jury took a view could not be given dispositive effect on appeal); *Com. v. Jefferson*, 36 Mass App 684, 635 NE2d 2 (1994) (trial court's instruction to jury that it could use the view as evidence was technically incorrect, but not error that created a substantial risk of a miscarriage of justice requiring reversal in the absence of objection). The proper procedure for taking a view is described in *Com. v. Dascalakis*, 246 Mass 12, 29-30, 140 NE

470, 477 (1923). No evidence should be taken or testimonial comments made during the taking of a view.

In a trial without a jury, a view ought not be taken without notice to the parties or counsel, in order that they can be present. *Sargeant v. Traverse Building Trust*, 267 Mass 490, 167 NE 233 (1929). Cf. *Berlandi v. Com.*, 314 Mass 424, 449-453, 50 NE2d 210, 225-226 (1943) (taking of view without parties held nonprejudicial error in light of judge's statement that view did not affect his decision). In a jury trial, an unauthorized view by one or more jurors may constitute sufficient grounds for a new trial.[1] See *Com. v. Cuffie*, 414 Mass 632, 609 NE2d 437 (1993) (new trial required where juror made independent visit to scene of crime); *Markee v. Biasetti*, 410 Mass 785, 789, 575 NE2d 1083, 1085 (1991) (new trial required where several jurors visited scene, made measurements); *Com. v. Coles*, 44 Mass App Ct 463, 691 NE2d 969 (1998) (new trial affirmed where jurors visited scene and came back with "totally different information than the lawyers presented"). Compare *Com. v. Jones*, 15 Mass App 692, 448 NE2d 400 (1983) (unauthorized view of much used public facility was improper, but not prejudicial under circumstances of case). Since no evidence is taken, it is not error to refuse a criminal defendant the right to be present, so long as he is represented by counsel. *Com. v. Mack*, 423 Mass 288, 667 NE2d 867 (1996); *Com. v. Gordon*, 422 Mass 816, 849, 666 NE2d 122, 142 (1996) (holding that conducting a view in absence of defendant violates neither the Fourteenth Amendment nor art. 12 of Declaration of Rights); *Com. v. Snyder*, 282 Mass 401, 413, 185 NE 376, 379-380 (1933), *aff'd*, 291 US 97 (1934), *overruled on other grounds*, *Malloy v. Hogan*, 378 US 1 (1964). Cf. *Com. v.*

---

§11.9 [1]The court may receive testimony from jurors to show that an unauthorized view occurred, but not with respect to the role the improper influence played in the jury's decisions. The judge "must focus on the probable effect of the extraneous facts on a hypothetical average jury." *Com. v. Cuffie*, 414 Mass at 637; *Com. v. Fidler*, 377 Mass 192, 196-197, 385 NE2d 513, 515 (1979); *Com. v. Cuffie*, 597 NE2d 1069, 1072 (1992). See §13.7.

Curry, supra (not error to refuse to allow defendant to consult with counsel during view).

A judge is not required to allow a view to be taken at the same time of day the crime occurred or under the same weather conditions that prevailed when the crime occurred. *Com. v. Curry*, supra; *Com. v. Gabbidon*, 17 Mass App 525, 535, 459 NE2d 1263, 1270 (1984) (judge may set the limits of any view he authorizes); *Com. v. Washburn*, 5 Mass App 195, 360 NE2d 908 (1977). During the taking of a view, counsel may point out objects or features to be noted by the jury but may not otherwise comment; but an impropriety occurring on a view generally can be cured by cautionary instruction and will not require a mistrial. *Com. v. Cresta*, 3 Mass App 560, 336 NE2d 910 (1975).

§11.10   Demonstrations

Sworn witnesses may, within the discretion of the judge, demonstrate the manner in which events occurred. Such demonstrations, although inconsistent with the witness's oral description of the event, are evidence sufficient to support a finding of fact. *Whalen v. Shivek*, 326 Mass 142, 93 NE2d 393 (1950).

Demonstration of the manner in which an event occurred is to be distinguished from demonstration of a condition or fact within the peculiar control of a witness — e.g., if a witness offers to show that certain handwriting is not his by demonstrating his handwriting in court, there is a danger that he may alter his writing. Such a demonstration properly may be barred. *King v. Donahue*, 110 Mass 155 (1872). So, too, a voice demonstration on the question of voice identification may be barred, especially if the witness is not under oath. *Com. v. Scott*, 123 Mass 222, 234 (1877). A trial judge may refuse to allow a party to come into court on a stretcher and testify therefrom. *Blanchard v. Holyoke Street Railway Co.*, 186 Mass 582, 72 NE 94 (1904). A plaintiff was allowed to demonstrate the working of the machine upon which he was injured to show how the accident in question happened; he was not allowed to use the demonstration as evidence that he lacked the strength to operate the machine properly. *Probert v. Phipps*, 149 Mass 258, 21 NE 370 (1889). Compare *Com. v. Shea*, 401 Mass 731, 737, 519 NE2d 1283, 1287 (1988) (tapping of defendant's shoes against rail by prosecutor in closing argument to illustrate sound they made was permissible where shoes were in evidence and witness had testified to "clicking sound" of shoes of perpetrator).

The danger of undiscoverable fraud inherent in subjective demonstrations leads to a reluctance upon the part of the court to sanction them. Distinguishable from such demonstrations is an exhibition of the body or a part thereof on such questions as identification, the extent of wounds or scars, or other relevant facts. In such instances, the danger of fraud is removed but there remains problems of indecent exposure, inflammatory tendencies, and probative worth. The extent of such an exhibition or "demonstration" is thus left within the sound discretion of the trial judge.

With respect to identification of a defendant, compare *Com. v. Kater*, 388 Mass 519, 533, 447 NE2d 1190, 1199 (1983) (would be proper to ask defendant to display his bare arms to jury); *Com. v. Burke*, 344 Mass 243, 247, 182 NE2d 127, 135 (1962) (retrial; no error to refuse to allow defendant's son to walk and look back to illustrate possible misidentification); *Com. v. Burke*, 339 Mass 521, 535, 159 NE2d 856, 864 (1959) (no error in requiring defendant to walk and look back in connection with testimony of an identifying witness); *Com. v. Happnie*, 3 Mass App 193, 326 NE2d 25 (1975) (witness to crime had not testified to anything unusual about perpetrator's hands, defendant properly refused exhibition of tattoo on hand because he did not testify and offered no other proof tattoo existed at time of crime).

The traditional rule in Massachusetts was that in a paternity suit a child could be exhibited to the jury for comparison with the features of the alleged father. *Scott v. Donovan*, 153 Mass 378, 26 NE 871 (1891). However, in *Com. v. Kennedy*, 389 Mass 308, 313-314, 450 NE2d 167, 171-172 (1983), the court held that in the future such exhibitions should not be allowed absent expert testimony concerning the probability that specific physical characteristics were inherited from the defendant.

Whether scars or wounds may be exhibited is within the discretion of the court. Compare *Com. v. MacDonald*, 368 Mass 395, 400, 333 NE2d 189, 192-193 (1975) (exhibition of scar allowed); *Tuttle v. McGeeney*, 344 Mass 200, 205, 181 NE2d 655, 658 (1962) (exhibition of scars refused); *Com. v. Bertuzzi*, 6 Mass App 937, 381 NE2d 1312 (1978) (victim allowed to display wound caused by surgical intervention, not by defendant's attack); *Com. v. Beaulieu*, 3 Mass App 786, 337 NE2d 710 (1975) (gruesome and hideous scars inflicted by defendant exhibited); *Com. v. Perry*, 3 Mass App 308, 329 NE2d 150 (1975) (victim allowed to display scar caused by stab wound inflicted by defendant even though other scars were caused by subsequent surgery).

§11.11 Demeanor

The trier of fact may consider the demeanor of a witness on the stand as evidence. See, e.g., *Breton v. Breton*, 332 Mass 317, 125 NE2d 121 (1955). Demeanor may be considered not only on questions of credibility but also on the fitness of a parent contesting custody of a child. *O'Brien v. O'Brien*, 347 Mass 765, 197 NE2d 192 (1964). The appearance or demeanor of a witness may be considered in determining his age. *Com. v. Hollis*, 170 Mass 433, 49 NE 632 (1898); *Com. v. Emmons*, 98 Mass 6 (1867). The trier of fact is entitled to consider a criminal defendant's demeanor in court on the issue of his mental condition or sanity. *Com. v. Smiledge*, 419 Mass 156, 643 NE2d 41 (1994) (expert may be asked questions regarding defendant's demeanor during trial, if relevant to sanity issues); *Com. v. Gurney*, 413 Mass

97, 595 NE2d 320 (1992) (where defense was diminished capacity to form specific intent to commit crime, error to exclude evidence that defendant was taking antipsychotic medication during trial that affected his outward appearance); *Com. v. Louraine*, 390 Mass 28, 34-38, 453 NE2d 437, 442-444 (1983) (under the facts of the case, to compel defendant asserting insanity defense to appear before jury in a medicated state was reversible error). Intelligence or competence to perform particular work may be so determined. *Leistritz v. American Zylonite Co.*, 154 Mass 382, 28 NE 294 (1891); *Keith v. New Haven & Northampton Co.*, 140 Mass 175, 3 NE 28 (1885).

The demeanor of a victim may also constitute demonstrative evidence that may be considered by a jury. *Com. v. Roderick*, 411 Mass 817, 819, 586 NE2d 967, 969 (1992) (not error to permit non-testifying victim to sit in spectator section where jury could observe her conduct, including noises she made).

Within appropriate limits, closing argument is permitted with respect to the demeanor of testifying witnesses, including parties. *Com. v. Houghton*, 39 Mass App 94, 654 NE2d 932 (1995) (prosecutor's comment on victim's crying after testifying did not raise a substantial risk of miscarriage of justice; court suggested comment may not have been improper) (Text cited); *Com. v. White*, 2 Mass App 258, 311 NE2d 81 (1974). Closing argument by a prosecutor on the demeanor of a criminal defendant who has not testified is dangerous and may be inappropriate in several respects.[1] Remarks reasonably susceptible of being interpreted as comment on the defendant's failure to take the stand are impermissible. *Com. v. Domanski*, 332 Mass 66, 69, 123 NE2d 368, 371 (1954). See *Borodine v. Douzanis*, 592 F2d 1202, 1210-1211 (1st Cir 1979). Evidence of guilt may not be implied from a defendant sitting calmly in the courtroom. *Com. v. Young*, 399 Mass 527, 505 NE2d 186 (1987); *Com. v. Borodine*, 371 Mass 1, 11, 353 NE2d 649, 650 (1976). A

---

§11.11   [1] For a more extensive discussion, see §13.4.8.

prosecutor may not suggest that normal courtroom behavior demonstrates a consciousness of guilt. *Com. v. Valliere*, 366 Mass 479, 494, 321 NE2d 625, 635 (1974); *Com. v. Pullum*, 22 Mass App 485, 488, 494 NE2d 1355, 1358 (1986) (error to permit prosecutor to argue that defendant's failure to bare his teeth during trial demonstrated consciousness of guilt, when he was not asked to do so). It is improper for a prosecutor's comment to suggest that he has particular knowledge of a fact about the defendant unknown to the jury. *Com. v. Kater*, 388 Mass 519, 533, 447 NE2d 1190, 1199 (1983) (not proper to argue defendant wore long-sleeved shirts to trial to hide hairy arms in absence of evidence he had hairy arms). It has been held proper to comment on affirmative behavior of a defendant plainly visible in the courtroom. *Com. v. Smith*, 387 Mass 900, 907, 444 NE2d 374, 380 (1983) (squirming, smirking, laughing).

§11.12   Experiments

Experiments conducted in court are considered real evidence.[1] The admissibility of such experiments is within the sound discretion of the court. *LeBlanc v. Ford Motor Co.*, 346 Mass 225, 232, 191 NE2d 301, 306 (1963). The judge may allow an experiment to be conducted if he finds that it will be fair and informative and that the circumstances in court are sufficiently similar to those at the time in issue or surrounding the event in issue to make the demonstration relevant. *Griffin v. General Motors Corp.*, 380 Mass 362, 403 NE2d 402 (1980); *Com. v. Medina*, 372 Mass 772, 782, 364 NE2d 203, 209 (1977) (no error to refuse request to fire gunshot in courtroom); *Com. v. Flynn*, 362 Mass 455, 472-473, 287 NE2d 420, 433-434 (1972) (no error to refuse to

---

§11.12 [1]Testimony as to experiments performed out of the presence of the jury is not real evidence. Evidence of such experiments is discussed in §4.4.9.c.

allow lady's stocking to be placed over face to demonstrate effect on features). The use of the factfinder as a participant in an experiment or demonstration is problematic and has been discouraged. *Com. v. DeDomenicis*, 42 Mass App 76, 674 NE2d 1099 (1997) (error for motion judge to "frisk" defendant to determine whether wad of bills would have felt like a weapon to officer during a pat-down, court noting that courtroom circumstances were different than those facing officer on the street).

Allowing the jury to take exhibits to the jury room during deliberations provides a potential opportunity for the jurors to conduct their own experiments with the exhibits. Nonetheless, whether to send exhibits to the jury room is within the judge's discretion. *Com. v. Pixley*, 42 Mass App 927, 677 NE2d 273 (1997).

Given the low cost and easy availability of videotaping equipment, proffers of videotapes of experiments conducted outside of trial may become more common. Whether such videotapes or films of experiments are admissible is within the discretion of the trial judge and should be determined by the same criteria that govern experiments performed in court. Compare *Szeliga v. General Motors Corp.*, 728 F2d 566 (1st Cir 1984) (films of experimental auto crashes admissible to illustrate expert's theory of cause of accident); *Com. v. Chipman*, 418 Mass 262, 635 NE2d 1204 (1994) (videotaped simulation of the view from the fatal shooting site through the defendant's telescopic site was admissible); *Welch v. Keene Corp.*, 31 Mass App 157, 166, 575 NE2d 766, 772 (1991) (videotaped experiment showing visibility of dust concentrations was admissible); *Com. v. Nadworny*, 30 Mass App 912, 566 NE2d 625 (1991) (excluding videotaped re-creation of accident); *Terrio v. McDonough*, 16 Mass App 163, 173, 450 NE2d 190, 196 (1983) (excluding videotape of re-enacted fall down stairs).

§11.13 Photographs, Maps, Tapes, and Chalks[1]

§11.13.1 Admissible Evidence

Photographs, maps, plans, and so on may be used as independent evidence or as substitutes for the narrative of a witness on the stand. Maps, photographs, and similar objects professing scientific accuracy are admitted in evidence as exhibits. It is a preliminary question of fact to be found by the trial judge whether the exhibit is sufficiently verified by proof that it is a true representation of the subject. If the offered exhibit is so verified, its admission or exclusion is not a matter of discretion but is governed by the usual rules of law as to admissibility of relevant evidence. *Horowitz v. Bokron*, 337 Mass 739, 742, 151 NE2d 480, 483 (1958); *Howe v. Boston*, 311 Mass 278, 281, 41 NE2d 1, 3 (1942).

The surveyor or photographer who drew a plan or made a photograph may testify as to the circumstances under which it was drawn or made. Such testimony is ordinarily required before a plan is admitted, but it is not error for the court to admit a photograph without such testimony if some witness testifies that it accurately represents the object in issue at the relevant time. *Eldredge v. Mitchell*, 214 Mass 480, 102 NE 69 (1913). Indeed, on occasion the foundation has been held to be implicit in a witness's testimony describing the scene pictured in a photo, even when the witness was not directly asked if the photo accurately depicted the scene. *Com. v. Sheeran*, 370 Mass 82, 345 NE2d 362 (1976).

If a photograph admittedly shows an object as being different from its condition at the relevant time, it may be admitted if witnesses can supplement the photograph by oral testimony explaining the differences. *Com. v. Sullivan*, 410 Mass 521, 533, 574 NE2d 966, 973 (1991) (photos of comparison hair samples properly admitted; witness ade-

---

§11.13 [1]See also Chapter 12.

quately explained differences resulting from focusing error); *Com. v. Rodriguez*, 364 Mass 87, 300 NE2d 192 (1973).

Films and videotapes are admissible in evidence "if they are relevant, they provide a fair representation of that which they purport to depict, and they are not otherwise barred by an exclusionary rule." *Com. v. Mahoney*, 400 Mass 524, 527, 510 NE2d 759, 761-762 (1987). In *Mahoney*, the court held that a videotape of a booking was properly authenticated by the arresting officer who viewed the tape prior to trial and testified as to the procedure used in the videotaping process and the contents of the tape. See *Com. v. Lawson*, 425 Mass 528, 682 NE2d 845 (1997) (videotape made one and one-half years after crime, which was never represented to be a fair and accurate representation of the scene at the relevant time, was properly excluded); *Com. v. Carey*, 26 Mass App 339, 526 NE2d 1329 (1988) (videotape of field sobriety test was admissible, but testimonial statements by defendant on tape would not be if violated *Miranda* rights).

Use of videotape or film at trials may be expected to increase. See *Com. v. Simmons*, 419 Mass 426, 646 NE2d 97 (1995) (videotape that provided panoramic views of apartment where murder was committed was admissible; videotape demonstrated that apartment was not quite as blood-drenched as photographs in evidence might have suggested); *Com. v. Lavalley*, 410 Mass 641, 574 NE2d 100 (1991) (not error to admit videotape of fresh complaint by victim); *Com. v. Mulica*, 401 Mass 812, 820-821, 520 NE2d 134, 138-139 (1988) (not error to exclude in first trial documentary film of Vietnam War, but on remand trial court should exercise broad discretion to consider admitting film either as evidence illustrating Vietnam experience similar to defendant's, relevant to diagnosis of post-traumatic stress syndrome (PTSD), or as chalk to illustrate expert's explanation of PTSD). Compare *Kord v. Baystate Medical Center, Inc.*, 13 Mass App 909, 429 NE2d 1045 (1982) (not error to exclude nurse's training film, although trial court's view of evidence characterized as "narrow"). Videotapes or films may, of course, be inadmissible for substantive reasons. See, e.g., *Com. v. Bergstrom*, 402 Mass 534, 547, 524 NE2d 366, 374 (1988) (statute that allows victim of sexual abuse to testify outside of courtroom through videotape or simultaneous transmission violates confrontation rights).[2]

Audio tapes are admissible to prove the content of prior speech, if not objectionable for substantive reasons. In *Com. v. Gordon*, 389 Mass 351, 355-356, 450 NE2d 572, 575-576 (1983), the court established guidelines for the use of audio tapes.[3] The tape must be authenticated. A judge may require it to be edited to include only relevant material. The proponent of the evidence must bring to court a recording that provides an adequate, audible, and coherent rendition of the material, and ensure that proper equipment is provided for playing it. The judge may allow a properly authenticated transcript to be provided to the jury as an aid to understanding the recording, but the court explicitly held that the lack of a transcript is not a sufficient reason to refuse to admit audio tapes. For other cases, see *Com. v. Freiberg*, 405 Mass 282, 540 NE2d 1289 (1989) (not error to play 911 tape twice, over objection it was inflammatory); *Com. v. Silva*, 401 Mass 318, 516 NE2d 161 (1987) (security system tape recording of sounds during a larceny properly admitted); *Com. v. Fernette*, 398 Mass 658, 664, 500 NE2d 1290, 1294 (1986) (not error to admit taped confession, although recorder was turned off several times during interview; in future better practice is to stop recorder only for purpose of changing tapes); *Com. v. Wheeler*, 42 Mass App 933, 678 NE2d 168 (1997) (not error to exclude 911 tape where it was not authenticated by the evidence) (Text cited); *Com. v. Jerome*, 36 Mass App 59, 627 NE2d 948 (1994) (incomplete recording of fresh complaint interviews may render tapes inadmissible, but no error here in absence of

---

[2] See §3.3.

[3] The best evidence rule with respect to documents does not apply to oral communications. Therefore, a tape recording is not required to prove what was said; any competent witness may testify to what she heard. *Com. v. Gordon*, supra.

prejudice to defendant); *Com. v. Carpenter,* 22 Mass App 911, 491 NE2d 1077 (1986) (proper to admit cassette copy, rather than original reel-to-reel tape of electronic surveillance).

A device may record on paper an impression that the human senses have not perceived or cannot perceive — e.g., an x-ray picture. The testimony of a witness who identifies an x-ray as that of the person and bone in issue and shows that the picture was taken by a qualified technician in the standard manner upon a machine in good operating condition will serve to verify and admit the x-ray. *Doyle v. Singer Sewing Machine Co.,* 220 Mass 327, 107 NE 949 (1915). The same type of testimony is required to verify other scientific recording devices — e.g., electrocardiograms. *Kramer v. John Hancock Mutual Life Insurance Co.,* 336 Mass 465, 146 NE2d 357 (1957). X-rays or recordings taken of normal persons may be admitted as a basis of comparison to aid the jury in understanding the nature of the injury or disease in issue. *McGrath v. Fash,* 244 Mass 327, 139 NE 303 (1923). X-rays, coupled with expert testimony, may also be used to identify a body. *Com. v. Devlin,* 365 Mass 149, 310 NE2d 353 (1974).

§11.13.2   *Chalks*

Models, sketches, and so on not rising to the dignity of a scientifically accurate representation are frequently admitted as "chalks." Chalks are used to illustrate testimony and do not become a part of the record; they are not evidence in the ordinary sense of the word. *Aselbekian v. Massachusetts Turnpike Authority,* 341 Mass 398, 402, 169 NE2d 863, 865 (1960).

The trial judge has considerable, but not unrestrained, discretion as to the degree to which chalks can be used. *Alholm v. Wareham,* 371 Mass 621, 631, 358 NE2d 788, 794 (1974); *Everson v. Casualty Co.,* 208 Mass 214, 220, 94 NE 459, 461-462 (1911). See *Com. v. Trowbridge,* 419 Mass 750, 757, 647 NE2d 413, 419 (1995) (within judge's discretion to allow child sexual abuse victim to use anatomically correct doll during her testimony) (citing Text); *Goldstein v. Gontarz*, 364 Mass 800, 309 NE2d 196 (1974) (plaintiff's counsel used blackboard to tabulate elements of damages); *LeBlanc v. Ford Motor Co.*, 346 Mass 225, 191 NE2d 301 (1963) (expert witness used models to illustrate testimony); *Com. v. Shea*, 38 Mass App 7, 644 NE2d 244 (1995) (not error to allow Commonwealth to use videotapes as chalks to illustrate victims' testimony concerning condition of ocean when defendant threw them into water and abandoned them); *Teller v. Schepens*, 25 Mass App 346, 518 NE2d 868 (1988) (not error to allow expert to use slides as chalks); *Com. v. Walter*, 10 Mass App 255, 406 NE2d 1304 (1980) (not error to permit jury to use chalk during deliberations).

Charts summarizing voluminous records or other documents may be used as chalks. See *Welch v. Keene Corp.*, 31 Mass App 157, 165, 575 NE2d 766, 771 (1991) (expert's use of chart containing redacted versions of articles on asbestos); *Com. v. Greenberg*, 339 Mass 557, 581-582, 160 NE2d 181, 197 (1959) (chart collating evidence of checks and deposit slips of defendant used in conjunction with accountant's testimony and later admitted in evidence). Where a chart contains summaries, "care must be taken to insure that summaries accurately reflect the contents of the underlying documents and do not function as pedagogical devices that unfairly emphasize part of the proponent's proof. . . ." *Welch v. Keene Corp.*, 31 Mass App at 165-166, 575 NE2d at 771. Cf. Fed R Evid 1006; Proposed Mass R Evid 1006.

DOCUMENTARY
EVIDENCE
and
RELATED MATTERS

A.   AUTHENTICATION

§12.1   In General

The materiality of any evidence depends upon its authenticity. This is so whether the evidence is a witness, a viewed parcel of land, or a gun, photograph, or document. The evidence must be the person or the thing its proponent represents it to be. Witnesses identify themselves. A thing, however, rarely authenticates itself. If it does not authenticate itself, its authenticity must be stipulated or proved as a preliminary fact. Such proof of authenticity usually takes the form of testimony from a qualified witness that either: (1) the thing is what its proponent represents it to be; or (2) circumstances exist that imply that the thing is what its proponent represents it to be. *Com. v. Wheeler,* 42 Mass 933, 678 NE2d 168 (1997) (Text cited). Proving the authenticity of tangible objects other than documents, along with chain of custody problems, are discussed in the chapter on real evidence. See §11.3.

The process of authenticating objects, documents, and analogous items of evidence — e.g., computer printouts, voice identification, and telephone conversations — is often affected not only by common-law rules or statutes but also by a number of rules of court.[1] The primary rules in

---

§12.1 [1] See §11.13 for verification of photographs; Opinion Evidence, Handwriting, §7.8.2.e. For a general discussion of documents, see Wigmore §§2128-2169 (Chad rev 1978).

this regard are Proposed Mass R Evid 901-903, Fed R Evid 901-903, Mass R Civ P 44, Fed R Civ P 44, Mass R Crim P 39-40, and Fed R Crim P 27. Rules pertaining to discovery procedures also offer a method of establishing the authenticity of evidence that is likely to be offered at trial. See, e.g., Mass R Civ P 26, 30, 34, 36, and 37. Mass R Civ P 36 may be particularly helpful in that it provides a pretrial procedure to establish the genuineness of documents served on the adversary in accordance with its provisions.

The modern trend in resolving authentication problems is reflected in Proposed Mass R Evid 901(a), identical to Fed R Evid 901(a):

> **General provision.**   The requirement of authentication or identification as a condition precedent to admissibility is satisfied by evidence sufficient to support a finding that the matter in question is what its proponent claims.

§12.2   General Modes of Proof

Most authenticity problems relate to documents. A document may be authenticated by the following evidence other than the document itself:

(1) By a judicial admission on behalf of opponent (see §2.2).

(2) By testimony (a) of the writer of the genuine document; (b) of a witness who saw the genuine document written (see Proposed Mass R Evid 901(b)(1); Fed R Evid 901(b)(1)) or who is familiar with the handwriting on the document (see Proposed Mass R Evid 901(b)(2); Fed R Evid 901(b)(2)); (c) of document experts (see §7.8.2.e.); Proposed Mass R Evid 901(b)(3); Fed R Evid 901(b)(3)); or (d) of a witness who offers information as to circumstantial facts. For example, see *Frick Co. v. New England Insulation Co.*,

347 Mass 461, 468-469, 198 NE2d 433, 438 (1964) (bill authenticated by variety of facts as well as by direct testimony); cf. Proposed Mass R Evid 901(b)(4) and Fed R Evid 901(b)(4).

(3)　By documentary standards and other real evidence. This last class of proof includes the authenticating certificates provided for in numerous Massachusetts statutes and rules (see §12.3.4).

§12.3　Selected Authenticating Circumstances

There are a number of circumstances that occur frequently and have been recognized by the courts as tending to authenticate a document. Authentication by circumstantial evidence is not limited to the configurations set forth here. Rather, proof of any circumstances that would support a finding of genuineness will serve to authenticate a document or other item of evidence. See Proposed Mass R Evid 901(a), 902; Fed R Evid 901(a), 902, which provide additional illustrations of methods of authentication.

§12.3.1　Age

The rule regarding the age of the document, which relates to the genuineness of the document, should be distinguished from the ancient document hearsay exception, which relates to the truth of the recitals in documents.

Age alone authenticates a document when the following requirements are met:

(1)　The document must be at least 30 years old. *Drury v. Midland Railroad,* 127 Mass 571 (1879);

Tolman v. Emerson, 21 Mass (4 Pick) 160 (1826). The age of the document is determined from the date of execution to the date of the offer in evidence. This is an arbitrary requirement. The 30 years of existence must be proved by extrinsic evidence; the date on the face of the document and even the appearance of age of the document as a rule are not sufficient. Proposed Mass R Evid 901(b)(8) would liberalize authentication under the ancient document rule by reducing the required age to 20 years. The other requirements (honest and ancient appearance and appropriate custody) would remain intact. See also Fed R Evid 901(b)(8), which is the same as the proposed Massachusetts rule.

(2) The document must present an honest and ancient appearance. *Green v. Chelsea*, 41 Mass (24 Pick) 71 (1883). See Proposed Mass R Evid 901(b)(8); Fed R Evid 901(b)(8).

(3) The document must come from a place of custody where a genuine document of its kind would be likely to be found. *Whitman v. Shaw*, 166 Mass 451, 44 NE 333 (1896). See Proposed Mass R Evid 901(b)(8); Fed R Evid 901(b)(8).

(4) In some states, it is held that where the document is a deed to land the person relying upon authentication by age must be in possession. While there is language in some cases indicating a similar requirement in Massachusetts — e.g., *Phillips v. Watuppa Reservoir Co.*, 184 Mass 404, 68 NE 848 (1903) — it would appear that possession is not a requirement and that Massachusetts will follow the modern trend toward admissibility upon proof of any proper confirmatory circumstances. See *Cunningham v. Davis*, 175 Mass 213, 56 NE 2 (1900); *Boston v. Richardson*, 105 Mass 351, 371-372 (1870).

§12.3.2   Contents and Handwriting

Where a letter is sent by *A* to *B* containing information that *B* presumably does not know and, in course of post, *A* receives a letter purporting to be sent by *B* and containing an answer to *A*'s inquiries or an indication that *B* now knows the information conveyed by *A*'s letter, this is usually sufficient authentication of the return letter as a letter of *B*'s. *Connecticut v. Bradish*, 14 Mass (14 Tyng) 296, 300 (1817).

Where the nature of the contents of the document or other circumstantial facts indicate its authenticity, the document may be admitted. *Irving v. Goodimate Co.*, 320 Mass 454, 70 NE2d 414 (1946). See also *Eveland v. Lawson*, 240 Mass 99, 104, 132 NE 719, 721 (1921). This principle is embodied in Proposed Mass R Evid 901(b)(4) and Fed R Evid 901(b)(4).

Authenticity of a document may be inferred from the authenticity of the signature on the document. *Simpson v. Davis*, 119 Mass 269 (1876). Cf. *W. A. Robinson, Inc. v. Burke*, 327 Mass 670, 100 NE2d 366 (1951). But the authenticity of the signature does not import the authority of the author to bind his principal. *In re Sargent's Case*, 347 Mass 250, 253, 197 NE2d 592, 594 (1964). Furthermore, if the only evidence of authenticity of the document relied upon is that it was received in the mail from a person signing himself as the alleged author, the document is inadmissible. Cf. *Pataskas v. Judeikas*, 327 Mass 258, 260, 98 NE2d 265, 266 (1951); *Nunes v. Perry*, 113 Mass 274 (1873). If there has been an intelligent correspondence between the witness and the alleged author and the witness has acted upon that correspondence, the witness is a competent witness to identify the author's handwriting. *Chaffee v. Taylor*, 85 Mass (3 All) 598 (1862).

An expert may examine a document and its contents and give an opinion as to its authenticity (see §7.8.2.e); Proposed Mass R Evid 901(b)(3); Fed R Evid 901(b)(3)). In such cases, the chief problem is often that of securing a genuine handwriting specimen with which the disputed specimen may be compared. But see *Priorelli v. Guidi*, 251 Mass 449, 146 NE 770 (1925), where a specimen was procured from the defendant while she was on the witness stand.

Where the genuineness of the specimen is not admitted, genuineness is a preliminary question of fact for the judge. *Costelo v. Crowell*, 139 Mass 588, 590, 2 NE 698, 699 (1885). See Proposed Mass R Evid 104; Fed R Evid 104. The jury may also determine authorship by comparison of genuine and disputed specimens in the same manner as the expert. *Moody v. Rowell*, 34 Mass (17 Pick) 490 (1835).

§12.3.3   Custody

Where a document that is a public record is produced from the custody of a person upon whom the law places a duty to keep custody of the document, the document is sufficiently authenticated. See Proposed Mass R Evid 901(b)(7); Fed R Evid 901(b)(7) (the rules apply to "public records or reports," including writings authorized by law to be filed or recorded and in fact so filed or recorded in a public office). Cf. *Kaufman v. Kaitz*, 325 Mass 149, 89 NE2d 505 (1949). Even private documents, such as business records, may be authenticated by testimony as to their proper custody. *Com. v. Duddie Ford, Inc.*, 28 Mass App 426, 435, 551 NE2d 1211, 1212 (1990) (loan documents provided by customer not admissible to prove truth of contents, but admissible to show what was on record at and relied upon by bank in making loan, when properly authenticated by bank officer,); *W. A. Robinson, Inc. v. Burke*, 327 Mass 670, 100 NE2d 366 (1951).

§12.3.4   Official Certificates and Seals; Miscellaneous Statutes and Rules

The matter of official certificates and seals is considered together with the official written statement exception to the hearsay rule. See §8.13.3. See also §§12.7.4 and 12.7.6. With regard to official certificates and seals, the pertinent rules are Mass R Civ P 44 and Fed R Civ P 44 (domestic and foreign records); Mass R Crim P 40 and Fed R Crim P 27 (same); Proposed Mass R Evid 901(b)(7) and Fed R Evid 901(b)(7) (public records or reports); and Proposed Mass R Evid 901(b)(10) and Fed R Evid 901(b)(10) (recognizing any method of authentication provided by statute or by other rules of court).

Proposed Mass R Evid 902 and Fed R Evid 902 deal with so-called self-authentication — i.e., instances where extrinsic evidence of authenticity is not required as a condition precedent to admissibility. Many of the provisions of Rule 902 cover matters affected by statutory enactments but may not be identical with statutory provisions, as previously set forth in the discussion of the best evidence rule. The portions of Rule 902 that may come into play in areas covered by statute are 902(1) (domestic public documents under seal), 902(2) (domestic public documents not under seal), 902(3) (foreign public documents), 902(4) (certified copies of public records), 902(5) (official publications), 902(6) (newspapers and periodicals), 902(8) (acknowledged documents), and 902(9) (commercial paper and related documents).

Each of the statutes or rules referred to in these sections has its own requirements, which, if met, serve to authenticate the document in question. For example:

- GL 233, §69, requires both an attestation and a seal with regard to records of foreign (out-of-state) courts. *Rossi v. Rossi*, 348 Mass 796, 206 NE2d 53 (1965). See also *Com. v. Key*, 381 Mass 19, 31, 407 NE2d 327, 335-336 (1980).
- Under Mass R Crim P 40(a)(2), a trial judge has discretion to admit foreign documents without final certification where there is "good cause shown" and "reasonable opportunity . . . to investigate the authenticity and accuracy of the documents,"

which may require an evidentiary hearing. *Com. v. Martinez*, 425 Mass 382, 395, 681 NE2d 818, 828 (1997).

- GL 233, §75, allows printed copies of acts of legislative or administrative bodies, including municipal ordinances and bylaws, to be admitted without attestation unless their genuineness is questioned. Cf. *Bowes v. Inspector of Buildings of Brockton*, 347 Mass 295, 197 NE2d 676 (1964) (municipal ordinances and maps may be authenticated by testimony of city clerk).

- GL 233, §76, requires that state and municipal records other than records of the department of telecommunications and energy relating to common carriers and records of the registry of motor vehicles, be attested under seal.

- GL 233, §76A (records of Securities and Exchange Commission must be attested under a certificate of a member).

- GL 233, §76B (printed copies of rate schedules of Interstate Commerce Commission that show an ICC number and date admissible without certification).

- GL 233, §77 (copies of records of banks and trust companies doing business in the Commonwealth must have an affidavit acknowledged before notary public or clerk of court under seal of same).

- §79 (hospital records may be authenticated by certificate or affidavit only). Cf. *Custody of Two Minors*, 19 Mass App 552, 560, 476 NE2d 235, 240-241 (1985) (admission of hospital record certified before notary, but without affidavit or statement under penalties of perjury, not error).

See also GL 233, §78 (business records); §79J (business records and photocopies thereof may be certified by affidavit); §79A (certain public and private records); §79D (newspapers and photographic prints); §79E (reproductions of public or business records); *Com. v. Monahan*, 349 Mass 139, 167, 207 NE2d 29, 46 (1965) (interpreting §§77, 78, and 79E); *Ricciutti v. Sylvania Electric Products, Inc.*, 343 Mass 347, 349, 178 NE2d 857, 859-860 (1961) (records admitted under §78). See also *Com. v. Reynolds*, 36 Mass App 963, 635 NE2d 254 (1994) (certificate of narcotics analysis under GL 111, §13, was admissible although notary before whom analyst signed certificate did not affix a seal; noting that seal was generally an anachronism and holding that there was no express provision in the statute requiring that certificate of analysis bear a seal in the jurat).

Other statutes may be of assistance in authenticating a document — e.g., GL 233, §68, provides that "[a] signature to an attested instrument or writing, except a will, may be proved in the same manner as if it were not attested." See *Brigham v. Palmer*, 85 Mass (3 All) 450 (1862), for a statement of the common-law rule as to authentication of an attested document. Proposed Mass R Evid 903 would not vary prior Massachusetts practice; Fed R Evid 903 provides that the local practice is to be followed — i.e., "the laws of the jurisdiction whose laws govern the validity of the writing."

GL 233, §73, provides that an acknowledgement taken by a notary public of another state under his official seal is to be recognized in Massachusetts. It would seem that such an acknowledgment would serve to authenticate the document. See Wigmore §2165 (Chad rev 1978). Cf. *Kirby v. Kirby*, 338 Mass 263, 155 NE2d 165 (1959); Proposed Mass R Evid 902(8); Fed R Evid 902(8).

Other pertinent rules and statutes involving authentication by judicial admission are discussed in §§2.3, 2.4. Note also that a statute in a specialized area may make a document prima facie genuine — e.g., GL 106, §1-202 (certain third-party documents prima facie genuine). Cf. Proposed Mass R Evid 902 and Fed R Evid 902, providing, "Extrinsic evidence of authenticity as a condition precedent to admissibility is not required with respect to (9) commercial paper, signatures thereon, and documents relating thereto to the extent provided by general commercial law."

§12.4   Telephone Conversations

There are a variety of circumstances that will suffice to authenticate the identity of a person with whom a witness has had a telephone conversation. It is sufficient if the witness testifies that she recognizes the voice on the other end of the telephone, regardless of who initiated the conversation. *Com. v. Leonardi*, 413 Mass 757, 604 NE2d 23 (1992) (victim could identify telephone caller as defendant from hearing voice during earlier assault); *Com. v. Perez*, 411 Mass 249, 262, 581 NE2d 1010, 1018 (1991); *Chartrand v. Registrar of Motor Vehicles*, 345 Mass 321, 187 NE2d 135 (1963). The witness need not have met the individual to be identified in person, if she has had previous telephone conversations and there is evidence of circumstances attending those calls tending to establish the individual's identity. *Com. v. Anderson*, 404 Mass 767, 770, 537 NE2d 146, 148 (1989); *Com. v. Hartford*, 346 Mass 482, 487-488, 194 NE2d 401, 404-405 (1963) (other circumstances were sufficient evidence of identity of speaker). In *Com. v. Anderson*, 404 Mass at 770, 537 NE2d at 148, the court cited with approval Proposed Mass R Evid 901(b)(5), which is identical to Fed R Evid 901(b)(5), which provides that the following establishes an adequate identification:

> **Voice identification.** Identification of a voice, whether heard firsthand or through mechanical or electronic transmission or recording, by opinion based upon hearing the voice at any time under circumstances connecting it with the alleged speaker.

In accord, *Com. v. Mezzanotti*, 26 Mass App 522, 527, 529 NE2d 1351, 1355 (1988) (citing Proposed Mass R Evid 901(b)(5) to support identification of voice heard through a wall where baseboard had been removed). In *Com. v. Carpinto*, 37 Mass App 51, 636 NE2d 1349 (1994), the victim of obscene and threatening telephone calls was unable to identify the speaker at the time she received the calls. However, she recorded them on her answering machine and was later able to identify the voice as that of the defendant, after she heard him speaking in court. This was the first time she had heard him speak in her presence in several years. The court held that where a recording of a telephone conversation exists and is deemed an accurate representation, a witness may offer identification testimony upon a showing that she is familiar with the speaker's voice.

When the witness has telephoned a number listed in the directory as belonging to a certain business or entity and the person answering takes the call on behalf of the entity, there is sufficient proof to admit the evidence of the call as one to that entity. *Bond Pharmacy, Inc. v. Cambridge*, 338 Mass 488, 490-491, 156 NE2d 34, 36-37 (1959); *Pietroforte v. Yellow Cab of Somerville, Inc.*, 19 Mass App 961, 473 NE2d 1148 (1985). When the witness has called the listed number of a specific individual, the person answering says he is that individual, and there is evidence that no other person is at that number, the conversation is admissible as a call with that individual. *Massachusetts N.E. Street Railway v. Plum Island Beach Co.*, 255 Mass 104, 114, 151 NE 84, 86-87 (1926). However, testimony that a witness made a call to an address not stated, and the person answering claimed to be a certain individual, is not sufficient to authenticate that the call was with that person. *Virta v. Mackey*, 343 Mass 286, 291, 178 NE2d 571, 574 (1961).

Although the rules are phrased somewhat differently from the language used in the decided cases, most cases involving telephone calls to listed numbers would probably be decided the same way under the case law and the rules. Proposed Mass R Evid 901(b)(6) and Fed R Evid 901(b)(6) provide that the following is adequate for authentication:

Telephone conversations, by evidence that a call was made to the number assigned at the time by the telephone company to a particular person or business, if (A) in the case of a person, circumstances, including self identification, show the person answering to be the one called, or (B) in the case of a business and the conversation related to business reasonably transacted over the telephone.

Other circumstantial evidence may suffice to authenticate the identity of a person on the telephone, even where the witness does not recognize the voice. See *Com. v. Anderson*, supra; *Com. v. Hartford*, supra; *Com. v. Loach*, 46 Mass App 313, 705 NE2d 642 (1999); *Com. v. Wojcik*, 43 Mass App 595, 606, 686 NE2d 452, 460 (1997).

However, when a witness has received an incoming call from a person claiming to be *A*, without more, this is insufficient evidence to admit the call as a conversation with *A*. *Com. v. Gettigan*, 252 Mass 450, 148 NE 113 (1925); *Com. v. Howard*, 42 Mass App 322, 677 NE2d 233 (1997).

When a court has admitted evidence that a telephone conversation was had with a given party, it ultimately remains an issue for the jury to determine whether the call was with that party. *Com. v. Hartford*, 346 Mass 482, 488, 194 NE2d 401, 405 (1963).

§12.5   Trademarks; Process or System (Computers and X-Rays)

The rules of evidence add two significant aspects to the rules of authentication. As to trademarks, Proposed Mass R Evid 902(7) and Fed R Evid 902(7) provide: "Extrinsic evidence of authenticity as a condition precedent to admissibility is not required with respect to . . . [I]nscriptions, signs, tags, or labels purporting to be affixed in the course of business and indicating ownership, control, or origin." See *Smith v. Ariens Co.*, 375 Mass 620, 377 NE2d 954 (1978).

Proposed Mass R Evid 901(b)(9) and Fed R Evid 901(b)(9) provide that "evidence describing a process or system used to produce a result and showing that the process or system produces an accurate result" is sufficient authentication to support the admission of such evidence. This rule would apply to a variety of technological or scientific processes — e.g., computers and x-rays.

B.   THE BEST EVIDENCE RULE

§12.6   The Rule Itself

The best evidence rule requires that where the contents of a document are to be proved, the party must either produce the original document or show a sufficient excuse for its nonproduction. See, e.g., *Com. v. Koney*, 421 Mass 295, 303, 657 NE2d 210, 215 (1995) (police officer testified that defendant gave him original identification card and officer made photocopy and returned original to defendant; photocopy was admissible, evidence accounted for nonproduction of original and no contention was made that photocopy was inaccurate or fraudulent); *Bank of Boston v. Haufler*, 20 Mass App 668, 671, n.7, 482 NE2d 542, 545 n.7 (1985); *Jacobs v. Hertz Corp.*, 358 Mass 541, 265 NE2d 588 (1970). Compare *Com. v. Lawrence Ready-Mix Concrete Corp.*, 4 Mass App 804, 345 NE2d 919 (1976).

Under the Proposed Mass Rules and the Federal Rules, the application of this rule extends to recordings and photographs. Proposed Mass R Evid 1002, Fed R Evid 1002. See Proposed Mass R Evid 1001 and Fed R Evid 1001 for definition of the matters and objects covered by the rules. Massachusetts case law, however, has rejected extension of the best evidence rule to photographs. *Com. v. Weichell*, 390

Mass 62, 77, 453 NE2d 1038, 1047 (1983) (noting contrary Proposed Mass R Evid 1002).

The best evidence rule is designed to: (1) protect against the possibility of error, which is proverbially very large in the repetition by memory of the contents of documents, particularly documents with legal significance; and (2) secure for the court the peculiarities of handwriting, paper, ink, and so on that may have great bearing on the genuineness of the document. See Wigmore, §§1177, 1179-1180 (Chad rev 1972). The requirement that the original document must be produced does not apply to writings so simple in their nature that the possibility of error is negligible — e.g., the label on a whiskey bottle. *Com. v. Blood,* 77 Mass (11 Gray) 74 (1859). See also *Snow v. Massachusetts Turnpike Authority,* 339 Mass 620, 161 NE2d 759 (1959) (best evidence rule not applicable to photographic copy of plan).

Expert testimony as to the contents of complicated accounts is admissible (*Boston & W.R.R. v. Dana,* 67 Mass (1 Gray) 83, 104 (1854); *Com. v. Greenberg,* 339 Mass 557, 581-582, 160 NE2d 181, 197 (1959); *Com. v. Baker,* 368 Mass 58, 84, 330 NE2d 794, 808 (1975)), but only if the books and documents upon which the testimony is based are produced in court and made available for purposes of cross-examination (*Cabel v. United States,* 113 F2d 998, 1001 (1st Cir 1940). See Proposed Mass R Evid 1006; Fed R Evid 1006).

The significance of the best evidence rule has declined appreciably in recent decades. The rule predates the invention of photocopy machines and computers, and also the modern discovery rules. Most potential best evidence problems are probably resolved today by stipulations between counsel who have satisfied themselves during discovery that there is no necessity to insist upon the production at trial of original documents.

§12.7   Cases in Which Production of Original Is Excused

§12.7.1   Where Document Is Lost or Destroyed

Where the original document is alleged to be lost or destroyed or otherwise unavailable, production may be excused if the trial judge finds that the original has become unavailable otherwise than through the serious fault of the proponent, provided that, where appropriate, reasonable search has been made for it. *Old Colony Trust Co. v. Shaw*, 348 Mass 212, 219, 202 NE2d 785, 790 (1964); *Com. v. Fay*, 14 Mass App 371, 439 NE2d 855 (1982) (photocopy of confession properly admitted where prosecution could not find original and testimony indicated copy did not differ from the original). See Proposed Mass R Evid 1004(1); Fed R Evid 1004(1). It is a preliminary question of fact whether these requirements have been sufficiently established; it is for the trial judge to decide this matter, and his decision ordinarily will be sustained. *Smith v. Brown*, 151 Mass 338, 24 NE 31 (1890). Thus, where evidence warranting a finding that the original once existed is introduced, the judge must assume its existence and allow secondary evidence if he decides the previously enumerated preliminary questions of fact in favor of proponent. *Fauci v. Mulready*, 337 Mass 532, 540-543, 150 NE2d 286, 291-293 (1958). But the questions of whether an original document ever existed or whether secondary evidence correctly reflects the content of the original are not preliminary questions of fact but questions for the jury. See Proposed Mass R Evid 1008; Fed R Evid 1008.

If the document was destroyed by the proponent, secondary evidence of the contents ordinarily will not be admitted, there being a presumption that if the proponent destroyed the document it contained matter unfavorable to him. *Capitol Bank & Trust Co. v. Richman*, 19 Mass App 515, 521-522 & n.7, 475 NE2d 1236, 1240-1241 n.7 (1985) (citing Text); *Joannes v. Bennett*, 87 Mass (5 All) 169 (1862). Proponent can overcome this presumption by showing a satisfactory reason for destruction such as will refute the imputation of culpable negligence or of fraudulent or improper intent — e.g., that proponent had no reason to anticipate the need for the document, *Smith v. Holyoke,* 112 Mass 517 (1873), or that the destruction was inadvertent.

GL 233, §§79D and 79E, provide for the use in evidence of photographic reproductions of certain lost or destroyed documents. These statutes recognize the practical necessity of destruction of certain business or public records as part of the regular course of business.

§12.7.2   *Where Document Is in Control of Adversary*

Where the document is in control of the opponent (*O*), the proponent (*P*) can introduce secondary evidence of the contents of the document only if he gives *O* sufficient notice to produce the document at the trial and *O* fails to produce it. The only notice required is notice enough to give *O* time to get the document to the courtroom. Thus, if *O* has the document in court, oral notice at the trial is enough. (See §3.13.2 for the effect of such notice on admissibility of the document for *O*). In certain cases that involve the contents of documents, the pleadings themselves are notice to produce and no other notice is necessary. *Com. v. Slocomb,* 260 Mass 288, 157 NE 350 (1927). The principles stated in this paragraph are incorporated in Proposed Mass R Evid 1004(3) and Fed R Evid 1004(3).

If proper notice to produce is given and *O* does not produce the original, *P* can produce secondary evidence. *Fisher v. Swartz,* 333 Mass 265, 271, 130 NE2d 575, 579 (1955); *Cregg v. Puritan Trust Co.,* 237 Mass 146, 129 NE 428 (1921). Case law also provides that *O* cannot thereafter bring forth the original or otherwise offer evidence of the contents of the document, *Gage v. Campbell,* 131 Mass 566 (1881), but this limitation is not contained in either Fed R

Evid 1004(3) or Proposed Mass R Evid 1004(3). If the document is in court or readily available, it is within the power of the court to order *O* to produce it on pain of contempt proceedings. *Kincaide v. Cavanagh*, 198 Mass 34, 84 NE 307 (1908). Cf. Mass R Civ P 34. Failure of *O* to produce a material document within his control is the proper basis for comment by P and for an inference by the jury that the document, if produced, would be unfavorable to *O*.

The fact that *O*'s privilege against self-incrimination covers production by *O* of the document does not excuse *P* from giving *O* notice as foundation for use of secondary evidence. Nor does the privilege prevent P from putting in secondary evidence of the contents of the document if proper notice has been given. *Com. v. Perry*, 254 Mass 520, 528, 150 NE 854, 858 (1926). Despite some of the language in the *Perry* case, it would seem appropriate in light of United States Supreme Court decisions to give the defendant notice to produce in writing or, if notice is given orally, to give notice out of the presence of the jury in order to avoid the possibility of appearing to infringe upon his right to remain silent. See *Griffin v. California*, 380 US 609 (1965).

A notice to produce under the best evidence rule must be distinguished from a subpoena duces tecum. The notice to produce is nothing but a basis for the introduction of secondary evidence in the event of nonproduction. It can be given orally or by letter. The subpoena duces tecum is an order of the court under pain of contempt proceedings to bring the document to court. Insofar as the use of secondary evidence is concerned, a subpoena duces tecum has the effect of a notice to produce. *Cregg v. Puritan Trust Co.*, supra. Nevertheless, the usual practice is to give notice in addition to having the subpoena served.

§12.7.3   Where Document Is in Control of Third Person

Where the document is in the control of some third person and the person is within the jurisdiction, a subpoena duces tecum must be issued ordering him to bring the document into court. If the person is outside of the jurisdiction, his absence is sufficient excuse for nonproduction and permits the introduction of secondary evidence. Cf. Proposed Mass R Evid 1004(2); Fed R Evid 1004(2). The language of the rules ("The original is not required ... [if] ... [n]o original can be obtained by any available judicial process or procedure. ...") requires that even if the original is in the possession of a person outside the jurisdiction an effort must be made to obtain the original by such judicial process as may be available before a claim of unavailability sufficient to permit the introduction of secondary evidence will be allowed. An example of such judicial process authorizing depositions to be taken outside the Commonwealth to obtain testimony of documents is found in GL 223A, §10.

§12.7.4   Where Document Is a Public Record

Where the document is a Massachusetts public record, a certified copy is by statute competent evidence if the record itself was competent. GL 233, §76 (set out in §8.13). See also GL 233, §§69, 75-76B, 79A, 79D, and 79E, all of which contain provisions making copies of one kind or another equally competent with specific classes of original public documents. Compare *Com. v. Rondoni*, 333 Mass 384, 131 NE2d 187 (1955) (copy of document properly admitted under GL 233, §69) with *Rossi v. Rossi*, 348 Mass 796, 206 NE2d 53 (1965) (same statute; copies improperly admitted).

GL 223A, §12, which governed the admissibility of domestic records in long-arm statute actions, and GL 223A, §13, which governed foreign records in such actions, were repealed by St 1979, c 344, §6. The statutory procedures simplifying the use of copies of such public records have been duplicated and, to some extent, amplified by the enactment of various rules of court. For example, Fed R Evid 1005 provides:

> The contents of an official record, or, of a document authorized to be recorded and filed and actually recorded and filed, including data compilations in any form, if otherwise admissible may be proved by copy certified as correct in accordance with Rule 902 or testified to be correct by a witness who has compared it with the original. If a copy which complies with the foregoing cannot be obtained by the exercise of reasonable diligence, then other evidence of the contents may be given.

Proposed Mass R Evid 1005 is in accord with the federal rule. Additionally, see Mass R Civ P 44 and Fed R Civ P 44, which deal with the proof of official records, both domestic and foreign. Both rules specifically provide in subdivision (b) for proof of "lack of record." The language of Mass R Civ P 44(b) is as follows:

> A written statement that after diligent search no record or entry of a specified tenor is found to exist in the records designated by the statement, authenticated as provided in subdivision (a)(1) of this rule in the case of a domestic record, or complying with the requirements of subdivision (a)(2) of this rule for a summary in the case of a foreign record, is admissible as evidence that the records contain no such record or entry.

Subdivision (c) of Rule 44 also provides: "This rule does not prevent the proof, by any other method authorized by law, of the existence of, or the lack of, an official record, or of entry, or of lack of entry therein." (For further discussion, see §8.13).

Mass R Civ P 44 follows prior Massachusetts practice except that as to records kept within the Commonwealth no double certification is required. Compare, e.g., GL 233, §76 (requiring, except as to certain records of the Department of Public Utilities, certification of the genuineness of the signature of the attesting officer). In this regard, Mass R Civ P 44 also differs from Fed R Civ P 44, which retains the double certification requirement for domestic records. As to criminal matters, Mass R Crim P 40 is the same as Mass R Civ P 44. Cf. Fed R Crim P 27 (incorporating by reference the provisions of Fed R Civ P 44). Proposed Mass R Evid 1005 applies to criminal matters as well as to civil proceedings.

§12.7.5   *Proof of Contents of Deeds by Means of the Registry*[1]

a.   *Massachusetts Deeds*

GL 233, §76 (see §8.13) has no practical application to the proof of deeds by means of copies in the registry. There are two reasons for this:

(1)   The registry copy of a deed is itself secondary evidence and may be inadmissible as such. In Massachusetts, the best evidence rule applies in full force to any deed of which either party is a grantee. *Com. v. Emery*, 68 Mass (2 Gray) 80 (1854). Cf. *Gleason v. Galvin*, 374 Mass 574, 373 NE2d 357 (1978) (harmless error to admit certified registry copy in absence of dispute as to its accuracy). The rule does not apply, however, where the grantee is not a party to the action,

---

§12.7   [1] See also official written statements exception to the hearsay rule, §8.13.

and it is immaterial that the grantee and the original deed are available. *Scanlan v. Wright*, 30 Mass (13 Pick) 523 (1833).

(2)   If the registry copy would itself be admissible, there is a common-law procedure simpler than that provided by GL 233, §76, for getting a copy of the registry copy of a Massachusetts deed into evidence. The copy of the registry copy, verified only by the registrar's attestation, is admissible in evidence to prove the contents of the original deed. *Scanlan v. Wright*, supra. Proposed Mass R Evid 1005 would apply to recorded instruments as well as to official records. Cf. Mass R Civ P 44 (applies to official records only).

Rule 1005 carries forward the certification aspects of *Scanlan* and adds two alternative methods of verifying the accuracy of a copy of such a recorded instrument. See discussion of Rule 1005 and other related rules in §12.7.4.

Where a party seeks to prove the contents of a deed not made directly to him or the other party as grantee, the original evidence of a deed acknowledged and recorded in accordance with the statutes is the certified copy from the registry instead of the deed itself. *Samuels v. Borrowscale*, 104 Mass 207 (1870).

b.   Foreign Deeds

Proof of the contents of a deed recorded in a sister state or in a foreign country is within the official written statements exception to the hearsay rule (see §8.13.1; Proposed Mass R Evid 803(14); Fed R Evid 803(14)). Proof is required that the foreign law imposed the duty of keeping a deed registry upon the person who copied the deed and that it imposes the duty of giving certified copies upon the person who made the copy. The duty to make the certified copy is usually presumed from the duty to keep the documents. The great seal, together with the attestation of the secretary of state of the foreign state or country, would have to be affixed to the document to show that the person certifying the copy was the present incumbent of the office of registrar and that the signature and seal appearing on the document were genuine.

The above cumbersome manner of proof is not, in practice, used to prove the contents of deeds registered in sister states. The method for proving the nonjudicial records of sister states is set out in 28 USC §1739. To make a recorded deed admissible under this statute, affirmative evidence must be introduced that the person signing the paper produced in court is its custodian under the laws of the sister state. Evidence must also be introduced regarding what effect is given in the sister state to the paper produced in court. Observe that this statute requires the paper to be sealed by "the keeper" of the records and attested by "the presiding justice" of a court. See *Willock v. Wilson*, 178 Mass 68, 59 NE 757 (1901), for an indication of how strictly this requirement is enforced. But cf. *Portland Maine Publishing Co. v. Eastern Tractors Co.*, 289 Mass 13, 193 NE 888 (1935).

The admissibility of copies of foreign deeds is affected also by Proposed Mass R Evid 1005 and Fed R Evid 1005, in interplay with both Proposed Mass R Evid 803(14) and 902 and Fed R Evid 803(14) and 902. Rule 1005 applies to copies of deeds. *Amoco Production Co. v. United States*, 455 F Supp 46 (D Utah 1977); 5 Weinstein, Evidence §1005(04) (1978). Unlike Mass R Civ P 44 and Fed R Civ P 44 (applying only to official records), Rule 1005 applies not only to official records but also to a "document authorized to be recorded or filed and actually recorded or filed." A deed, mortgage, or other instrument so recorded or filed that affects "an interest in property" is admissible as an exception to the hearsay rule. Proposed Mass R Evid 803(14); Fed R Evid 803(14). A certified copy of such an instrument may be authenticated under Proposed Mass R Evid 902(4) or Fed R Evid 902(4), which provide that extrinsic evidence of authenticity is not required for:

A copy of an official record or report or entry therein, or of a document authorized by law to be recorded or filed and actually recorded or filed in a public office, including data compilations in any form, certified as correct by the custodian or other person authorized to make the certification, by certificate complying with paragraph (1), (2) or (3) of this rule or complying with any Act of Congress or rule prescribed by the Supreme Court pursuant to statutory authority.

Proposed Mass R Evid 1005 and Fed R Evid 1005 recognize the certification procedures of Rule 902(4) but provide alternatively that a copy may be admitted if "testified to be correct by a witness who has compared it with the original." Rule 1005 provides further: "If a copy which complies with the foregoing cannot be obtained by the exercise of reasonable diligence, then other evidence of the contents may be given."

The evidentiary rules, while creating a clear preference for certified or compared copies, would provide for a more flexible approach to the proof of such records than has hitherto been allowed under local or federal statutes or case law.

§12.7.6   Miscellaneous Statutes

GL 233, §§77-79A, 79D, and 79E, provide for the admissibility of certified copies and identified photographic reproductions of records of hospitals, banks, trust companies, insurance companies, and other businesses and of photographic reproductions of newspapers. GL 233, §79J (added by St 1982, c 101), now provides for certification by affidavit and the use of certified photocopies of business records, which are required "to be produced in court by any party." Certified business records, or certified copies thereof, may now be deposited with the clerk of court for use in evidence, if the record is otherwise admissible. (See §8.11). See *Com. v. Monahan*, 349 Mass 139, 167, 207 NE2d 29, 46 (1965) (photostatic reproductions of checks properly admitted under GL 233, §79E); *Com. v. Gogan*, 389 Mass 255, 264, 449 NE2d 365, 370 (1983) (certified copy of hospital record admissible under GL 233, §79, "without need for and despite the absence of, testimonial corroboration"); *Com. v. Hubbard*, 371 Mass 160, 175-176, 355 NE2d 469, 479 (1976) (while records of hospital at Massachusetts Correctional Institution at Norfolk may be hospital records within meaning of GL 233, §79, uncertified photocopies unauthenticated by any other means — e.g., by testimony of a witness — were properly excluded); *Com. v. Johnson*, 371 Mass 862, 870-871, 359 NE2d 1286, 1291-1292 (1977) (Rhode Island Hospital records kept in accordance with Rhode Island law, properly certified, admissible under GL 233, §79).

§12.8   What Is the Original?

§12.8.1   Multiple Originals

Where a lease or other instrument is executed in multiple copies, each of which is intended by the parties to have legal effect, each of the copies so executed is considered an original. Cf. Proposed Mass R Evid 1001(3); Fed R Evid 1001(3). Production of any such "original" is sufficient without accounting for the other. *Quinn v. Standard Oil Co. of New York*, 249 Mass 194, 144 NE 53 (1924). The fact that a copy is mechanically reproduced by letterpress or otherwise does not give it the legal significance of an original unless circumstances showing such intent are established — e.g., a carbon copy of a letter is not an original. See *Augur Steel Axle & Bearing Co. v. Whittier*, 117 Mass 451 (1875) (letterpress copy treated as secondary evidence). But any such copy of a libelous handbill or newspaper that had publication might be so treated. The statutes cited above in §§12.7.4 and 12.7.6 may make mechanically reproduced copies equally admissible with the original documents where the prerequisites of the statute are satisfied.

Where there are multiple originals, production of all of them must be properly excused before secondary evidence is admissible. *Peaks v. Cobb*, 192 Mass 196, 77 NE 881 (1906).

§12.8.2   Duplicates

Proposed Mass R Evid 1001(4) and Fed R Evid 1001(4) define certain documents as "duplicates." Rather than focusing on the intent of the parties, these rules emphasize the accuracy of the reproductive process. Fed R Evid 1001(4) provides:

> A "duplicate" is a counterpart produced by the same impression as the original, or from the same matrix, or by means of photography, including enlargements and miniatures, or by mechanical or electronic re-recording, or by chemical reproduction, or by other equivalent techniques which accurately reproduce the original.

Proposed Mass R Evid 1001(4) is substantially the same.

Proposed Mass R Evid 1003 and Fed R Evid 1003 provide:

> A duplicate is admissible to the same extent as an original unless (1) a genuine question is raised as to the authenticity of the original or (2) in the circumstances it would be unfair to admit the duplicate in lieu of the original.

While copies subsequently produced manually, whether typed or handwritten, are not within the definition of a duplicate given by the rules, copies that meet the requirements of Rules 1001(4) and 1003 are for all practical purposes given the status of originals. Thus, the common-law approach is considerably modified so as to make such copies freely admissible.

§12.8.3   Telegrams

Where contents of a telegram are the subject of proof, the original is: (1) the telegram *sent*, if the receiver was the one to initiate the use of the telegraph; or (2) the telegram *received*, if the sender was the one to initiate use of the telegraph. *Nickerson v. Spindell*, 164 Mass 25, 41 NE 105 (1895).

§12.9   Limitations and Exceptions to the Rule

(1)   The best evidence rule applies only to the proof of the *contents* of *documents*. There is no general rule requiring proof of the nature of tangible items by the "best evidence." See *Com. v. Balukonis*, 357 Mass 721, 260 NE2d 167 (1970) (best evidence rule does not apply to composite picture of defendants); *Com. v. Valleca*, 358 Mass 242, 263 NE2d 468 (1970) (best evidence rule does not preclude picture of purloined item). The rule does not apply to proof of a document's existence, its execution, or transactions with it. Thus, the fact that a note was sold and delivered can be proved without production of the document.

(2)   The rule does not apply to the proof of an oral utterance even if the oral utterance was previously or subsequently written down.

(3)   An admission on the witness stand by opponent (*O*) as to the contents of a document is admissible to prove the contents of the document even if other secondary evidence would be inadmissible under the best evidence rule. See Proposed

Mass R Evid 1007; Fed R Evid 1007. In Massachusetts, an admission by *O* outside court and reported by a witness on the stand is also admissible, even if other secondary evidence would be excluded. *Smith v. Palmer*, 60 Mass (6 Cush) 513 (1850). Fed R Evid 1007 does not go this far. Proposed Mass R Evid 1007 adopts the federal approach and therefore would be more restrictive than prior Massachusetts practice in this regard. However, where conviction of prior crime is used to impeach *O* or any other witness, the record of conviction may not be proved by *O*'s admission. See §6.10.2.

(4)   If the requirements of the best evidence rule as to excuse for nonproduction of the original and any multiple original documents have been met, any secondary evidence is admissible. There is no preference for an immediate copy over a copy of a copy or for a copy over oral testimony based on recollection. There are no degrees of secondary evidence so far as admissibility is concerned. *Goodrich v. Weston*, 102 Mass 362 (1869); *Bellamy v. Bellamy*, 342 Mass 534, 174 NE2d 358 (1961). Both Proposed Mass R Evid 1004 and Fed R Evid 1004 are in accordance with prior Massachusetts practice.

PRIVILEGES and
DISQUALIFICATIONS

§13.1   Introduction

As noted in §6.3, supra, any person of "sufficient understanding" may testify in any proceeding, civil or criminal. GL 233, §20.[1] The fact that a witness is a party to or has an interest in the litigation is no longer a disqualification in Massachusetts. "[T]he bias of a witness goes only to his credibility, and is not a reason for exclusion of his testimony." *Assessors of Pittsfield v. W. T. Grant Co.*, 329 Mass 359, 361,108 NE2d 536, 537 (1952).[2]

---

§13.1   [1] GL 233, §20 provides:

> Any person of sufficient understanding, although a party, may testify in any proceeding, civil or criminal, in court or before a person who has authority to receive evidence, except as follows:
>
> First, Except in a proceeding arising out of or involving a contract made by a married woman with her husband, a proceeding under chapter two hundred and nine D and in a prosecution begun under sections one to ten, inclusive, of chapter two hundred and seventy-three, any criminal proceeding in which one spouse is a defendant alleged to have committed a crime against the other spouse or to have violated a temporary or permanent vacate, restraining, or no-contact order or judgment issued pursuant to section eighteen, thirty-four B or thirty-four C of chapter two hundred and eight, section thirty-two of chapter two hundred and nine, section three, three B, three C, four, or five of chapter two hundred and nine A, or sections fifteen or twenty of chapter two hundred and nine C, or a similar protection order issued by another jurisdiction, obtained by the other spouse, and except in a proceeding involving abuse of a person under the age of eighteen, including incest, neither husband nor wife shall testify as to private conversations with the other.
>
> Second, Except as otherwise provided in section seven of chapter two hundred and seventy-three and except in any proceeding relating to child abuse, including incest, neither husband nor wife shall be compelled to testify in the trial of an indictment, complaint or other criminal proceeding against the other;
>
> Third, The defendant in the trial of an indictment, complaint or other criminal proceeding shall, at his own request, but not otherwise, be allowed to testify; but his neglect or refusal to testify shall not create any presumption against him.
>
> Fourth, An unemancipated, minor child, living with a parent, shall not testify before a grand jury, trial of an indictment, complaint or other criminal proceeding, against said parent, where the victim in such proceeding is not a member of said parent's family and who does not reside in the said parent's household. For the purposes of this clause the term "parent" shall mean the natural or adoptive mother or father of said child.

[2] Nor is a witness disqualified from testifying merely because he has a long association with the court and has testified frequently before the

GL 233, §20 sets out two exceptions to the general rule of competency in the form of disqualifications for testimony regarding private conversations between spouses (see §13.2.1, infra), and for the testimony of a minor child against a parent in certain circumstances (see §13.3, infra). The statute also creates a privilege of a spouse not to testify against the other spouse in a criminal case (see §13.2.2), and of a criminal defendant not to testify in the proceedings against him (see §13.13, infra).

These disqualifications and privileges, as well as others discussed below, deprive courts of probative evidence but are justified by important policy concerns such as marital harmony and the protection of confidential relationships. The Supreme Judicial Court has observed in this regard:

> Testimonial privileges are exceptions to the general duty imposed on all people to testify. Such privileges diminish the evidence before the court, and contravene the fundamental principle that the public has a right to every man's evidence. As such, they must be strictly construed, and accepted only to the very limited extent that permitting a refusal to testify or excluding relevant evidence has a public good transcending the normally predominant principle of utilizing all rational means for ascertaining truth.

Three Juveniles v. Com., 390 Mass 357, 359-360, 455 NE2d 1203, 1205 (1983) (internal quotes and citations omitted).

Matters of privilege and disqualification in the federal courts are not specifically enumerated in the evidentiary rules but are governed by constitutional, statutory, or common law. See Fed R Evid 501. In diversity cases, the federal courts apply the state evidentiary rules of privilege and competence pursuant to *Erie Railroad Co. v. Tompkins*, 304 US 64 (1938); Fed R Evid 501, 601. See, e.g., *Kowalski v. Gagne*, 914 F2d 299, 306-308 (1st Cir 1990) (Massachusetts spousal disqualification would apply in wrongful death

---

judge trying the case. See *Salvato v. DiSilva Transportation Co., Inc.*, 329 Mass 305, 313, 108 NE2d 51, 56 (1952).

action). The Proposed Massachusetts Evidence Rules, modeled on a draft of proposed federal rules rejected by Congress, do enumerate privileges and disqualifications. See Proposed Mass R Evid 501-512 (discussed throughout this chapter).

A party in a civil action may resist discovery on the basis of privilege. Mass R Civ P 26(b)(1). Having done so, the party may not rely on the privileged information as evidence at trial. *G.S. Enterprises, Inc. v. Falmouth Marine, Inc.*, 410 Mass 262, 270-271, 571 NE2d 1363, 1368 (1991). Conversely, a party may waive the privilege and then offer the information as evidence. A party following the latter course should waive the privilege before raising it as a bar to discovery, to allow his adversary sufficient time for discovery and preparation. "A waiver on the virtual eve of trial is insufficient and, depending on the circumstances, may justify an order barring the use of the privileged evidence." 410 Mass at 271.

For a case discussing the evolving right of privacy as it manifests itself in a privilege against disclosure of personal information in the course of litigation, see *Planned Parenthood of Massachusetts v. Blake*, 417 Mass 467, 476-479, 631 NE2d 985, 991-993 (1994).

§13.2   Husband-Wife

GL 233, §20 disqualifies spouses from testifying as to private conversations with each other (see §13.2.1), and privileges a spouse from testifying against the other in any criminal proceeding (see §13.2.2).[1] A common-law disqualification that prevented a spouse from testifying as to impotency or non-access when the legitimacy of a child born in wedlock is in issue has been abandoned (see §13.2.4).

---

§13.2 [1] The Supreme Judicial Court has not determined whether testimony produced in violation of the statutory spousal privilege or disqualification should be admissible for impeachment purposes. See *Com. v. Paszko*, 391 Mass 164, 191 n.31, 461 NE2d 222, 238 n.31 (1984).

§13.2.1   Disqualification of Spouses to Disclose Private Conversations

GL 233, §20, cl First (see note 1, §13.1 supra) provides that "neither husband nor wife shall testify as to private conversations with the other." The disqualification does not apply:

- in proceedings arising out of a contract between husband and wife.
- in proceedings to enforce support or a prosecution for nonsupport.[2]
- in any criminal proceeding in which one spouse is alleged to have committed a crime against the other or to have violated a court order protecting the other.
- in a proceeding involving abuse of a person under age 18.

The disqualification applies in divorce cases, but would not apply to mere abusive language addressed by one spouse to the other outside the context of a conversation. See *French v. French*, 80 Mass (14 Gray) 186, 188 (1859). See also *Freeman v. Freeman*, 238 Mass 150, 161, 130 NE 220, 222 (1921).

The rule is one of disqualification, not privilege. The spouses are forbidden (upon objection of the party against whom it is offered) to testify about the conversation, even if both wish the evidence to be received. See *Gallagher v. Goldstein*, 402 Mass 457, 459-460, 524 NE2d 53, 54-55 (1988) (testimony of husband regarding conversation with wife concerning her symptoms properly excluded in medical malpractice case) (citing text); *Kaye v. Newhall*, 356 Mass

---

[2] In a prosecution for nonsupport, "both husband and wife shall be competent witnesses to testify against each other to any relevant matters;" and "any existing statute or rule of law prohibiting the disclosure of confidential communications between husband and wife" shall be inapplicable. GL 273, §7.

300, 304, 249 NE2d 583, 585 (1969); *Com. v. Cronin*, 185 Mass 96, 69 NE 1065, 1066 (1904) (defendant unsuccessfully offered, to support insanity defense, testimony of wife concerning private conversation in which he contemplated suicide); *Com. v. Azar*, 32 Mass App 290, 303-304, 588 NE2d 1352, 1361, 412 Mass 1105 (1992).

If no objection is made when the evidence of the private conversation is offered, testimony as to the conversation may be admitted for its full probative value. *Com. v. Stokes*, 374 Mass 583, 595 n.8, 374 NE2d 87, 95 n.8 (1978); *MacDonald's Case*, 277 Mass 418, 422, 178 NE 647, 649 (1931); *Com. v. Sylvia*, 35 Mass App 310, 315-316, 619 NE2d 360, 364 (1993); *Com. v. Azar*, 32 Mass App 290, 304, 588 NE2d 1352, 1361 (1992); *Bak v. Bak*, 24 Mass App 608, 611 n.3, 511 NE2d 625, 628 n.3 (1987).

The disqualification applies only to conversations between persons validly married at the time of the conversation. Conversations occurring before marriage are not included. *Com. v. Barronian*, 235 Mass 364, 366, 126 NE 833, 834 (1920). The disqualification does not terminate with the death of one of the spouses (see *Dexter v. Booth*, 84 Mass (2 All) 559, 561 (1861)), unless the conversation may be admitted as a declaration of a deceased person within the terms of GL 233, §65, discussed in §8.5.1, supra.

If a third person is present and hears the conversation, it is not "private" and the disqualification is inapplicable. *Com. v. Paszko*, 391 Mass 164, 190 n.30, 461 NE2d 222, 238 n.30 (1984); *Com. v. O'Brien*, 377 Mass 772, 774, 388 NE2d 658, 661 (1979); *Fay v. Guynon*, 131 Mass 31, 33 (1881).

Whether a conversation between husband and wife that occurs in the proximity of other persons was "private" depends upon the distance of the other persons, whether they were within earshot, and whether they were paying attention to the conversation. Compare *Freeman v. Freeman*, 238 Mass 150, 161-162, 130 NE 220, 222 (1921) (testimony properly excluded because it did not appear that any passers-by on public street paid any attention to conversation or could even hear it) with *Linnell v. Linnell*, 249

Mass 51, 54, 143 NE 813, 814 (1924) (testimony regarding two conversations properly admitted because first conversation took place while daughter was in next room just across hall, door was open, wife's voice was angry and excited, and afterwards daughter came into room where husband and wife were and was crying; and second conversation took place in train station waiting room where from 30 to 40 persons were coming and going and anyone who had been listening could have heard it within four or five feet). Whether a conversation in the presence of a child was "private" depends upon the child's intellectual ability to pay attention and understand what was being said. *Freeman v. Freeman*, supra, 238 Mass at 161, 130 NE at 222 (conversation in front of nine-year-old daughter and younger siblings properly admitted). See also *Com. v. Stokes*, supra, 374 Mass at 595, 374 NE2d at 95.

The subject matter of the conversation need not be of a confidential nature in order to fit within the disqualification. Business conversations between husband and wife are included. *Com. v. Hayes*, 145 Mass 289, 293, 14 NE 151, 153 (1887) (testimony of defendant concerning directions she gave husband, as her agent, relating to their business properly excluded). By its terms, however, GL 233, §20, does not disqualify a spouse from testifying to private conversations concerning the disputed transactions in an action arising out of or involving a contract between the spouses. See, e.g., *Hutchinson v. Hutchinson*, 6 Mass App 705, 710-711, 383 NE2d 82, 85-86 (1978) (action by husband for equitable relief seeking reconveyance of stock transferred to wife).

Threats and verbal assaults are not considered "private conversations" and thus do not come within the disqualification. See *Com. v. Gillis*, 358 Mass 215, 217, 263 NE2d 437, 439 (1970) (& cases cited) (at trial of charge that defendant assaulted wife, she was properly permitted to testify to his threats to kill her). "Whether the policy is to protect the marital relationship or to encourage confidence between spouses, or merely reflects legislative reticence concerning marital confidences, the purpose does not logically extend to words constituting or accompanying abuse, threats, or assaults of which the other spouse is the victim." 358 Mass at 217-218, 263 NE2d at 439-440. See also *Com. v. O'Brien*, supra, 377 Mass at 774, 388 NE2d at 661; *French v. French*, supra, 80 Mass at 186. But see *Sherry v. Moore*, 265 Mass 189, 194, 163 NE 906, 907 (1928) (statement by husband to wife that he wished she were dead not "abusive language" and thus properly excluded). Spontaneous exclamations of pain are similarly not subject to the disqualification. *Com. v. Jardine*, 143 Mass 567, 10 NE 250 (1887).

Written communications are not deemed "conversations" within the meaning of the statute. See *Com. v. Szczuka*, 391 Mass 666, 678 n.14, 464 NE2d 38, 46 n.14 (1984) (letters from defendant to wife); *Com. v. Caponi*, 155 Mass 534, 30 NE 82 (1892) (letter from husband to wife properly admitted). Compare Proposed Mass R Evid 504(b)(1) (see note 3 infra), which substitutes the broader phrase "communications" and thus includes acts other than conversations "by which ideas may be transmitted from one person to another." See Advisory Committee Note to R 504(b)(1) (citation omitted).

The statutory disqualification covers the contents of the private conversation, but not the fact that a conversation occurred. "There is a plain line of demarcation between the occurrence of the fact of a private conversation between husband and wife, which [where relevant] may be competent, and a narration of the substance of that conversation by either of them, which is not competent." *Sampson v. Sampson*, 223 Mass 451, 458-459, 112 NE 84, 87 (1916) (wife properly permitted to testify that conversation occurred and, as result, she took certain action). See also *Freeman v. Freeman*, supra, 238 Mass at 161, 130 NE at 222 (wife properly permitted to testify she refrained from engaging in certain social affairs in consequence of conversation with husband).

While spouses are forbidden to testify concerning the conversation, a third person who overheard may testify about it. "The circumstance that the conversation was between a husband and wife while they were physically alone is no ground for objection. There is no rule of law that third persons who hear a private conversation between a husband and wife shall be restrained from testifying what it was." *Com. v. Wakelin*, 230 Mass 567, 574, 120 NE 209, 212 (1918). See also *Com. v. O'Brien*, 377 Mass 772, 774-775, 388 NE2d 658, 661 (1979).

Proposed Mass R Evid 504(b)[3] is for the most part consistent with present practice concerning the disqualification of testimony from a spouse regarding conversations with the other spouse.

Characterizing GL 233, §20, cl 1, as a "statutory preservation of a remnant of an outdated common-law concept," the Supreme Judicial Court has nonetheless left any reform of the disqualification to the Legislature:

> It seems imprudent to prohibit testimony as to a marital conversation when both parties to the conversation want disclosure and the interests of the marital unit would be furthered by disclosure. However, the Legislature has enacted a statute stating a clear and unambiguous preference for the marital disqualification. We have consistently ruled that the

---

[3] The rule provides:

Disqualified Communication

(1) *General Rule.* Neither husband nor wife shall testify as to confidental communications with the other.

(2) *Definition.* A communication is confidential if it is made by any person to his or her spouse and is not intended for disclosure to any other person.

(3) *Exceptions.* The foregoing disqualification of confidential communications does not apply:

(i) In a civil proceeding to a declaration of a deceased spouse if the court finds that it was made in good faith and upon the personal knowledge of the declarant.

(ii) In a proceeding arising out of or involving a contract made between a husband and wife.

(iii) In a proceeding under G.L. c. 273A, Uniform Reciprocal Enforcement of Support Act.

(iv) In any prosecution for nonsupport, desertion, or neglect of parental duty.

PMRE 504(b). "In most respects this rule is proposed from current Massachusetts law." See Advisory Committee's Note to Rule 504.

statute renders spouses incompetent to testify as to the contents of their private conversations with their marital partners. . . . While we agree with the plaintiff that many of the stated policy reasons for this statute are anachronistc and that those that are not outmoded, such as the preservation of marital confidentiality and harmony, are not furthered by the inadmissibility of this testimony, we must construe the statute as written. Were this strictly a common law rule, we would not hesitate to transform it from a rule of disqualification to one of privilege. However, given the existence of the statute, that decision is for the Legislature.

Gallagher v. Goldstein, supra, 402 Mass at 460-461, 524 NE2d at 55 (citations omitted). It has been held that the policies behind the disqualification may be outweighed by a criminal defendant's constitutional rights to confrontation and a fair trial. See *Com. v. Sugrue,* 34 Mass App 172, 177-178, 607 NE2d 1045, 1048-1049 (1993) (private conversation in which defendant threatened to obtain custody of children in event of divorce admissible in prosecution for indecent assault on defendant's son, as it provided evidence of motive for wife to lie about incident).

§13.2.2   Privilege of Spouse Not to Testify Against Other Spouse in Criminal Case

Except in a prosecution for nonsuppport or a proceeding relating to child abuse (including incest), "neither husband nor wife shall be compelled to testify in the trial of an indictment, complaint or other criminal proceeding against the other." GL 233, §20, cl Second. The statutory privilege replaced the common-law prohibition preventing a spouse from being a witness in any case (civil or criminal) in which the other spouse was a party. *Com. v. Maillet,* 400 Mass 572, 575-576, 511 NE2d 529, 531-532 (1987); *Kelly v. Drew,* 94 Mass (12 All) 107, 109 (1866).

While application of the spousal disqualification discussed above is contingent upon marriage at the time of the conversation, availablity of the privilege depends upon marriage at time of testifying. The Supreme Judicial Court has refused to establish an analogous common-law privilege for unmarried persons who live together. See *Com. v. Diaz,* 422 Mass 269, 273-274, 661 NE2d 1326, 1329 (1996).

The privilege is personal; it can be claimed by the witness-spouse only, and may be waived over the objection of the other spouse. *Com. v. Stokes,* 374 Mass 583, 595, 374 NE2d 87, 96 (1978). The "spouse facing criminal prosecution [has] no voice in controlling the witness stand appearance of the other." *Com. v. Maillet,* supra, 400 Mass at 576, 511 NE2d at 532 (citation omitted). Consequently, the defendant-spouse has no standing to assert error in the admission of privileged testimony from the other spouse, or assert the waiver was invalid. Id.; *Com. v. Rosa,* 412 Mass 147, 160-162, 587 NE2d 767, 775-776 (1992) (but spouse's testimony cannot be used where her decision to testify is found to have been involuntary) (citing Text); *Com. v. Paszko,* 391 Mass 164, 190, 461 NE2d 222, 238 (1984); *Com. v. Sylvia,* 35 Mass App 310, 316-317, 619 NE2d 360, 364 (1993).

Because one spouse may testify against the other in a criminal case only if willing to do so, the Supreme Judicial Court has advised that "good trial practice" requires that the judge "satisfy himself, outside the presence of the jury, that the spouse who is about to testify against the other in a criminal proceeding knowingly waives his or her statutory privilege." *Com. v. Stokes,* supra, 374 Mass at 595 n.9, 374 NE2d at 96 n.9.

Where it is clear that a witness, if called to testify, will invoke the privilege, the witness should not be called or, alternatively, should be questioned in the absence of the jury. "[The witness] should not be put in the position of having to exercise the privilege before the jury, lest they draw inferences adverse to the party against whom the witness is called to testify." *Com. v. Labbe,* 6 Mass App 73, 79, 373 NE2d 227, 232 (1978). But see *Com. v. DiPietro,* 373 Mass 369, 388-391, 367 NE2d 811, 823 (1977) (no error in permitting Commonwealth to call defendant's spouse in front of jury to assert privilege because Commonwealth was entitled to lay foundation for admission of spouse's prior testimony, especially in light of fact that defendant's own act in marrying the principal witness against him four days before trial compelled Commonwealth to resort to witness's prior testimony).

The privilege has been held to apply where the spouse is called as a witness *by* the defendant to testify *for him*, as well as where the spouse is called to testify against the defendant. See *Com. v. Maillet*, supra, 400 Mass at 575-578, 511 NE2d at 531-533 (& cases cited) (phrase "against the other" in GL 233, §20, cl 2, refers to nature of proceeding and not content of spousal testimony).

By explicit words of the statute, the privilege does not apply "in any proceeding relating to child abuse." GL 233, §20, cl 2. This has been held to render the privilege inapplicable even where the child victim is not related to either husband or wife and does not live with them. See *Villalta v. Com.*, 428 Mass 429, 702 NE2d 1148 (1998).

Recognizing that the constitutional right to present a defense might be implicated in a case where the spousal privilege deprives the defendant of material evidence favorable to his defense, the Supreme Judicial Court has nonetheless not yet resolved the potential conflict. See *Com. v. Maillet*, supra, 400 Mass at 578 n.8, 511 NE2d at 533 n.8. See also *Com. v. Sugrue*, supra, 34 Mass App at 177-178, 607 NE2d at 1048-1049.

There is no privilege for a spouse not to testify against the other spouse in a civil action, "even if that testimony may be highly destructive of the marital relationship." *Three Juveniles v. Com.*, 390 Mass 357, 361, 455 NE2d 1203, 1206 (1983). The issue of applicability of the privilege in grand jury proceedings has not been resolved. See *Com. v. Paszko*, supra, 391 Mass at 189 n. 29, 461 NE2d at 238 n. 29 (but implicitly suggesting that the statutory language may exclude grand jury proceedings); *Com. v. Szczuka*, 391 Mass 666, 677-78, 464 NE2d 38, 46 (1984).

Proposed Mass R Evid 504(a)[4] is consistent with present practice in recognizing a privilege not to testify against one's spouse in a criminal proceeding, but extends the privilege to nontrial settings such as the grand jury. See Advisory Committee Note to R 504(a)(1).

Federal practice is in accord with that of Massachusetts in recognizing a privilege in the witness-spouse that may be asserted (or waived) only by that spouse and not the defendant. See *Trammel v. United States*, 445 US 40, 100 S Ct 906, 63 L Ed 2d 186 (1980).

§13.2.3   Comparison Between the Statutory Disqualification and Privilege

The following are the distinctions between the disqualification for private spousal conversations, GL 233, §20, cl 1, and the privilege not to testify against a spouse in a criminal case, GL 233, §20, cl 2:

(1)   The disqualification applies in all actions, civil and criminal, and regardless of whether one of the spouses is a party or not; the privilege applies only in criminal cases where the spouse is the defendant.

(2)   The disqualification affects only testimony concerning private conversations between the spouses; the privilege affects all testimony.

(3)   The disqualification operates whether or not one or both spouses want to disclose the conversa-

---

[4]Rule 504(a) provides:

(a) *Testimonial Privilege*

(1) *General Rule.* In any criminal proceeding, neither husband nor wife shall be compelled to testify against the other.

(2) *Exceptions.* The foregoing shall not apply in any prosecution for nonsupport, desertion, neglect of parental duty, or abuse of family or household member.

tion; the privilege operates only if invoked (and not waived) by the witness-spouse.

(4)   The disqualification prevents both spouses from testifying; the privilege excuses only the non-defendant spouse from testifying.

(5)   The disqualification depends upon the existence of the marriage relationship at the time of the conversation; the privilege depends upon the existence of the relation at the time of trial.

For further discussion of these differences, see *Com. v. Spencer*, 212 Mass 438, 450-451, 99 NE 266, 271 (1912); *Com. v. McCreary*, 12 Mass App 690, 695-697, 428 NE2d 361, 366 (1981) (testimony of wife concerning private conversations with husband-defendant properly excluded, although judge apparently confused statutory disqualification and privilege, because defense counsel failed to specify grounds supporting admission).

§13.2.4   Abandonment of Lord Mansfield's Rule Disqualifying Spouses from Testifying as to Illegitimacy of Child

Where the legitimacy of a child born in lawful wedlock is in issue, a judge-made disqualification commonly known as Lord Mansfield's Rule prevented either husband or wife from testifying as to impotency or as to nonaccess between them. See *Taylor v. Whittier*, 240 Mass 514, 515-516, 138 NE 6, 7 (1922) (will contest). The rule was based on reasons of "decency and policy; especially because of the effect it may have upon the child, who is in no fault." 240 Mass at 516, 138 NE at 7 (citation omitted). The disqualification did not apply to evidence other than the spouse's testimony. See *Sayles v. Sayles*, 323 Mass 66, 69, 80 NE2d 21, 23 (1948) (testimony of third party to wife's admission of adultery); *Symonds v. Symonds*, 385 Mass 540, 544, 432 NE2d 700, 702-703 (1982) (blood grouping tests).

Lord Mansfield's Rule was subject to considerable criticism (see *Symonds v. Symonds*, supra, 385 Mass at 543-545, 432 NE2d at 702-703), and would be abrogated by Proposed Mass R Evid 601, establishing a general rule of competence. See Advisory Committee Note to R 601.

In *C. C. v. A. B.*, 406 Mass 679, 550 NE2d 365 (1990), the Supreme Judicial Court abandoned the disqualification. Explaining that "[m]odern trends in the law, combined with changes in social attitudes, have brought into question the continuing validity of archaic rules which obfuscate the truth-seeking principles our system of jurisprudence strives to achieve," the Court held: "As a matter of the common law, a wife and a husband are no longer incompetent, by operation of Lord Mansfield's Rule, to testify as to nonaccess or impotence during the time relevant to conception." 406 Mass at 688, 550 NE2d at 371.

§13.3   Parent-Child

GL 233, §20, was amended in 1986 to add the Fourth Clause providing that "[a]n unemancipated, minor child, living with a parent, shall not testify before a grand jury, trial of an indictment, complaint or other criminal proceeding, against said parent, where the victim in such proceeding is not a member of said parent's family and who does not reside in the said parent's household." St 1986, c 145.

Adoption of the statutory disqualification followed the Supreme Judicial Court's refusal to recognize a common-law privilege permitting a child to refuse to testify against a parent in criminal proceedings. See *Three Juveniles v. Com.*, 390 Mass 357, 455 NE2d 1203 (1983). Three dissenters argued (with apparent persuasion in the Legislature):

> The State should not make unrealistic demands on its citizens, especially its children. A requirement that an unemancipated minor child, living with his or her parents, must

incriminate one or both of them is an unrealistic demand, at least when a family member is not a victim of the crime under investigation. The demand is unrealistic because it is insensitive to the needs of children, and to the nature of the normal relationship between children and their parents, involving, as it does, love, trust, loyalty, and dependency. This court should recognize a public policy against imposing on the conscience of a child responsibility for incriminating his or her parent. Society's interest in its children should be recognized as sufficiently important to outweigh the need for probative evidence in the administration of criminal justice in the circumstances presented by this case.

390 Mass at 366, 455 NE2d at 1209 (O'Connor, J, Hennessey, CJ, and Lynch, J, dissenting).

§13.4   Attorney-Client

§13.4.1   Introduction

Where a person, as a client or prospective client, consults a member of the bar in his or her capacity as such, the communication in confidence of matters that are (or that the client reasonably supposes to be) necessary to the proper conduct of legal business is privileged at the option of the client. See *In the Matter of a John Doe Grand Jury Investigation*, 408 Mass 480, 482, 562 NE2d 69 (1990); *Panell v. Rosa*, 228 Mass 594, 596, 118 NE 225, 226 (1918); *Foster v. Hall*, 29 Mass (12 Pick) 89 (1831); Proposed Mass R Evid 502(b).[1] The purpose of the privilege is "to encourage full and frank communication between attorneys and their clients and thereby promote broader public interests in the observance of law and administration of justice. The privi-

---

§13.4 [1]"A client has a privilege to refuse to disclose and to prevent any other person from disclosing confidential communications made for the purpose of facilitating the rendition of professional legal services to the client. . . ." PMRE 502(b).

lege recognizes that sound legal advice or advocacy serves public ends and that such advice or advocacy depends upon the lawyer being fully informed by the client." *Upjohn Co. v. United States,* 449 US 383, 389 (1981).

The Supreme Judicial Court has assigned "extraordinarily high value" on "the right of every citizen to obtain the thoughtful advice of a fully informed attorney concerning legal matters." *In the Matter of a John Doe Grand Jury Investigation,* supra, 408 Mass at 485, 562 NE2d at 69 (attorney-client privilege of deceased husband not overridden by society's interest in ascertaining truth concerning murder of wife); *Com. v. Goldman,* 395 Mass 495, 501-502, 480 NE2d 1023, 1028 (1985) (privilege of prosecution witness not overriden in the interest of justice by defendant's need for testimony). The court has recognized, however, that the attorney-client privilege may have to yield to a constitutionally based claim of denial of the right of confrontation or to a fair trial. *Com. v. Goldman,* supra, 395 Mass at 502 n.8, 480 NE2d at 1028 n.8; *Com. v. Michel,* 367 Mass 454, 460, 327 NE2d 720, 724 (1975), *new trial granted,* 381 Mass 447, 409 NE2d 1293 ("in certain circumstances assertion of an attorney-client privilege in such a way as to prevent the defense from exposing the bias of an important witness may deprive the defendant of his constitutional rights.").

As with any doctrine that deprives the court of probative evidence, the attorney-client privilege is ordinarily strictly construed. *In re Reorganization of Electric Mutual Liability Insurance Co.,* 425 Mass 419, 421, 681 NE2d 838, 840 (1997) (& citations). The burden of establishing that the privilege applies to a communication rests on the party asserting it. This burden extends to showing the existence of the privilege, and that it has not been waived. Id.

The privilege is reinforced by an attorney's ethical duty to preserve the confidences and secrets of the client. See SJC Rule 3:07, Rules of Prof Conduct, Rule 1.6 (formerly DR 4-101, Canons of Ethics and Disciplinary Rules Regulating the Practice of Law, SJC Rule 3:07, 382 Mass 768, 778-779 (1981)).

§13.4.2   "Client" or "Prospective Client" Defined

It is not necessary that a fee be paid by the client or that the attorney be actually retained for the privilege to attach. *Foster v. Hall*, 29 Mass (12 Pick) 89, 93 (1831). The privilege may extend to "preliminary communications looking toward representation even if representation is never undertaken." *Com. v. O'Brien*, 377 Mass 772, 775-776, 388 NE2d 658, 661 (1979) (but defendant's request "Will you be my lawyer?" moments after shooting not within privilege because not viewed as intended to be confidential). An attorney-client relationship need not rest on an express contract, but may be implied when: "(1) a person seeks advice or assistance from an attorney, (2) the advice or assistance sought pertains to matters within the attorney's professional competence, and (3) the attorney expressly or impliedly agrees to give or actually gives the desired advice or assistance." *Bays v. Theran*, 418 Mass 685, 690, 639 NE2d 720, 723 (1994) (citations omitted) (preliminary consultations between condominium unit owner and attorney gave rise to attorney-client relationship). See also *Neitlich v. Peterson*, 15 Mass App 622, 624, 447 NE2d 671, 672 (1983) (initiating letter to obtain legal services falls within privilege). But see *Mailer v. Mailer*, 390 Mass 371, 372-375, 455 NE2d 1211, 1213 (1983) (fact that wife had on one occasion five years earlier consulted husband's attorney concerning divorce did not establish attorney-client relationship requiring disqualification of attorney in subsequent divorce proceedings).

The privlege of course applies even after the relation of attorney and client has ceased. *Hatton v. Robinson*, 31 Mass (14 Pick) 416, 421-422 (1833) ("the mouth of the attorney shall be for ever sealed."); *Foster v. Hall*, supra, 29

Mass at 93 (communications subject to privilege "cannot be disclosed at any future time").

The attorney-client privilege may extend to communications from the client's agent or employee to the attorney. See *Ellingsgard v. Silver*, 352 Mass 34, 40, 223 NE2d 813, 817 (1967).

Proposed Mass R Evid 502(a)(1) defines "client" as "a person, public officer, or corporation, association, or other organization or entity, either public or private, who is rendered professional legal services by a lawyer, or who consults a lawyer with a view to obtaining professional legal services." The rule adopts a "control group" test that limits the category of "representative of the client" to those "having authority to obtain professional legal services, or to act on advice rendered pursuant thereto, on behalf of the client." Proposed Mass R Evid 502(a)(2). For a discussion of the attorney-client privilege as it applies to corporate clients, see *Upjohn Co. v. United States*, 449 US 383 (1981) (rejecting "control group" test and extending privilege to communications from employees concerning matters within the scope of their duties and made at direction of corporate superiors). Compare *United States v. Sawyer*, 878 F Supp 295 (D Mass 1995) (defendant had obligation to assist employer's in-house counsel with internal investigation of his activities, and thus was not "client" so that he could not assert privilege with respect to communications).

§13.4.3   "Member of the Bar" Defined

Under Massachusetts case law, the would-be client takes the risk that the person whom he consults and discloses information to is not an attorney; and if he is mistaken, there is no privilege. *Barnes v. Harris*, 61 Mass (7 Cush) 576 (1851) (disclosure to student in attorney's office not privileged even though client supposed him to be an attorney); *Foster v. Hall*, supra, 29 Mass at 98.

Proposed Mass R Evid 502(a)(3) would extend the privilege to communications to persons "reasonably believed by the client to be authorized" to practice law. The privilege would also apply to communications made to a "representative of the lawyer" — i.e., a person "used by the lawyer to assist the lawyer in the rendition of professional legal services." Proposed Mass R Evid 502(a)(4). See also former DR 4-101(D), supra, 382 Mass at 779 ("A lawyer shall exercise reasonable care to prevent his employees, associates, and others whose services are utilized by him from disclosing or using confidences or secrets of a client. . . .").

§13.4.4   "Communications"/"Facts" Distinguished

The privilege protects only those communications from the client made for the purpose of obtaining legal advice. See *Purcell v. District Attorney for the Suffolk District*, 424 Mass 109, 115, 676 NE2d 436, 440 (1997) (& citations) (question on remand as to whether tenant informed attorney of his intention to commit arson for purpose of receiving legal advice); *Judge Rotenberg Educational Center, Inc., v. Commissioner of Department of Mental Retardation*, 424 Mass 430, 457 n.26, 677 NE2d 127, 145 n.26 (1997) (general policy meeting not privileged because participants neither supplied counsel with information necessary to provide legal advice, nor sought legal advice); *Hatton v. Robinson*, supra, 31 Mass at 423-424 (privilege did not apply to disclosures debtor made to attorney drawing up mortgage deed regarding debtor's motives for transaction; no legal advice was asked and none given). See also *Grant v. Lewis/Boyle, Inc.*, 408 Mass 269, 271-272, 557 NE2d 1136, 1138 (1990) (engineering expert previously retained by party in that capacity not precluded by attorney-client privilege from testifying in subsequent action against that party where although expert was also an attorney, he had provided no legal representation and possessed no confidential information). Proposed Mass R Evid 502(d)(4) would not apply the privilege to a communication to a lawyer in his capacity as attesting witness to a document.

The communication need not be made in regard to a lawsuit that has been or is to be brought; communications seeking legal advice are privileged regardless of whether litigation is involved. See *Foster v. Hall*, supra, 29 Mass at 97 ("the rule is not strictly confined to communications made for the purpose of enabling an attorney to conduct a cause in court, but does extend so as to include communications made by one to his legal advisor, whilst engaged and employed in that character, and when the object is to get his legal advice and opinion as to legal rights and obligations").

"The protection of the privilege extends only to *communications* and not to facts. A fact is one thing and a communication concerning that fact is an entirely different thing. The client cannot be compelled to answer the question, 'What did you say or write to the attorney?' but may not refuse to disclose any relevant fact within his knowledge merely because he incorporated a statement of such fact into his communication to his attorney." *Upjohn Co. v. United States*, supra, 449 US at 395-396 (citation omitted). See also *Foster v. Hall*, supra, 29 Mass at 98-99 (& cases cited).

For examples of protected "communications," see *Ellingsgard v. Silver*, supra, 352 Mass at 40, 223 NE2d at 817, (written statement relative to accident given by client to attorney); *Vigoda v. Barton*, 348 Mass 478, 485, 204 NE2d 441, 446 (1965) (letters written by defendant to attorneys seeking legal assistance in lawsuit). Compare *Ramacorti v. Boston Redevelopment Authority*, 341 Mass 377, 380-381, 170 NE2d 323, 326 (1960) (no breach of privilege where witness disclosed selling price of property because not confidential communication). An attorney's impressions about the truthfulness of his or her client are as much a part of the privileged information as the communication itself. See

Com. v. Martinez, 425 Mass 382, 391-392, 681 NE2d 818, 825 (1997).

§13.4.5   "In Confidence" Defined/Disclosure to Third Persons

The essence of the privilege is that it is recognized only to protect the confidential relation between attorney and client. Communications that are intended to be conveyed to others are not privileged. Thus, "[w]hile an attorney's advice to his client on whether to accept the offer of the prosecution [of a plea arrangement] may be confidential, it is evident that the attorney's recitation of that offer is not confidential, for necessarily the offer is known to the prosecutor and it is likely to become the basis of a statement for the record in court." *Com. v. Michel,* 367 Mass 454, 460-461, 327 NE2d 720, 724 (1975), *new trial granted,* 381 Mass 447, 409 NE2d 1293 (1980). See also *Com. v. O'Brien,* 377 Mass 772, 775-776, 388 NE2d 658, 661 (1979); *Com. v. Goulet,* 374 Mass 404, 418-419, 372 NE2d 1288, 1298 (1978) (error to allow claim of attorney-client privilege to prosecution witness asked on cross-examination if he caused his lawyer to send letter to victim threatening an injunction, because not intended to stop with lawyer but to be communicated to victim); *Peters v. Wallach,* 366 Mass 622, 627-628, 321 NE2d 806, 809 (1975) (client's grant of authority to attorney to settle case must be communicated to other party, and thus not confidential); *Rent Control Board of Cambridge v. Praught,* 35 Mass App 290, 296, 619 NE2d 346, 350 (1993) (completed documents such as offer form, purchase and sale agreement, or declaration of trust, while the ultimate product of lawyer-client communications, do not fall within privilege); *Com. v. Anolik,* 27 Mass App 701, 709-710, 542 NE2d 327, 332 (1989) (attorney's testimony concerning real estate documents and insurance claim did not violate privilege because documents not intended to stop with attorney, but were meant to be passed along to third parties); Proposed Mass R Evid 502(a)(5).[2]

Disclosure of the communication to a third person (other than a necessary agent of the attorney or client) destroys the privilege. *Drew v. Drew*, 250 Mass 41, 44-45, 144 NE 763, 764 (1924) (letter given to attorney was shown to husband). But see *Blount v. Kimpton*, 155 Mass 378, 29 NE 590 (1892) ("[A]s between the client and attorney [communications] are still confidential, though made in the presence or hearing of a third party. The only effect of that is they are less confidential in fact, and that such third party may testify to them. It does not qualify the attorney as a witness.").

Communications between an attorney and a third party are, of course, not within the attorney-client privilege. *Com. v. Noxon*, 319 Mass 495, 543-544, 66 NE2d 814, 844 (1946) (conversation between defense counsel and expert witness).

§13.4.6   *"Privileged at the Option of the Client"*

The privilege belongs to the client, not to the attorney, and thus the latter cannot disclose the communication unless released from the obligation by the former. *In the Matter of a John Doe Grand Jury Investigation*, 408 Mass 480, 483, 562 NE2d 68, 70 (1990) (& cases cited) (privilege can be waived only by client, or in some instances by executor or administrator of client's estate); *Foster v. Hall*, 29 Mass (12 Pick) 89, 92-93 (1831). See also *Bermingham v. Thomas*, 3 Mass App 742, 326 NE2d 733 (1975) (third parties had no right to assert attorney-client privilege); Proposed Mass

---

[2] "A communication is 'confidential' if not intended to be disclosed to third persons other than those to whom disclosure is made in furtherance of the rendition of professional legal services to the client or those reasonably necessary for the transmission of the communication." PMRE 502(a)(5).

R Evid 502(c).[3] The attorney may not testify concerning the communication even if called as a witness in a lawsuit in which the client is not a party and has no interest in. *Bermingham v. Thomas, supra.*

The attorney-client privilege survives the client's death. *In the Matter of a John Doe Grand Jury Investigation,* supra, 408 Mass at 483, 562 NE2d at 70 (& citations). See also *Swidler & Berlin v. United States,* 524 US 399, 118 S Ct 2081, 141 L Ed 2d 379 (1998). "A rule that would permit or require an attorney to disclose information given to him or her by a client in confidence, even though such disclosure might be limited to the period after the client's death, would in many instances . . . so deter the client from 'telling all' as to seriously impair the attorney's ability to function effectively." *In the Matter of a John Doe Grand Jury Investigation,* supra, 408 Mass at 485, 562 NE2d at 71. The privilege may be exercised or waived after the client's death by his executor or other personal representative. *Phillips v. Chase,* 201 Mass 444, 449, 87 NE 755, 758 (1909); *District Attorney for Norfolk District v. Magraw,* 417 Mass 169, 172-173, 628 NE2d 24, 26 (1994) (probate judge had duty to remove husband as executor of wife's estate where, as suspect in her murder, husband had conflict of interest regarding waiver of privileges).

Individual directors are not entitled to waive the corporation's attorney-client privilege. *Symmons v. O'Keeffe,* 419 Mass 288, 299 n.10, 644 NE2d 631, 638 n.10 (1995). A trustee who seeks legal advice about a potential conflict of interest with the beneficiaries may claim the privilege to

---

[3] "The privilege may be claimed by the client, his guardian or conservator, the personal representative of a deceased client, or the successor, trustee, or similar representative of a corporation, association, or other organization, whether or not in existence. The lawyer or the lawyer's representative or the person who was the lawyer or the lawyer's representative at the time of the communication is presumed to have authority to claim the privilege but only on behalf of the client." PMRE 502(c).

preclude the beneficiaries from discovering memoranda prepared by counsel. 419 Mass at 301, 644 NE2d at 639-640.

§13.4.7   Exceptions

Several exceptions to the attorney-client privilege have been carved out. The privilege does not apply to:

(1)   Information concerning the commission of a future crime or fraud. *In the Matter of a John Doe Grand Jury Investigation,* supra, 408 Mass at 486, 562 NE2d at 72 (& citations). See generally *Purcell v. District Attorney for the Suffolk District,* 424 Mass 109, 676 NE2d 436 (1997) (extensive discussion of crime-fraud exception). The crime-fraud exception focuses not on the attorney's conduct, but on whether the client sought services to enable or aid someone to commit a crime. *In re Ellis,* 425 Mass 332, 335-336, 680 NE2d 1154, 1158 (1997). See also SJC Rule 3:07, Rules of Prof Conduct, Rule 1.6(b)(1) ("A lawyer may reveal [and in certain defined circumstances] must reveal, such information to prevent the commission of a criminal or fraudulent act that the lawyer reasonably believes is likely to result in death or substantial bodily harm, or in substantial injury to the financial interests or property of another, or to prevent the wrongful execution or incarceration of another."); former DR4-101(C)(3), supra, 382 Mass at 778 ("A lawyer may reveal the intention of his client to commit a crime and the information necessary to prevent the crime.").

(2)   Disputes between parties claiming through the same deceased client. See *Philips v. Chase,* supra, 201 Mass at 449, 87 NE at 758; *Panell v. Rosa,* 228 Mass 594, 596-597, 118 NE 225, 226-227 (1917).

(3)   Disputes between joint clients who share the same attorney. See *Beacon Oil Co. v. Perelis*, 263 Mass 288, 293, 160 NE 892, 894 (1928); *Thompson v. Cashman*, 181 Mass 36, 62 NE 976 (1902).

(4)   Directions given an attorney by a deceased client concerning the drafting of a will, to determine whether the instrument presented for probate is the actual will. See *Doherty v. O'Callaghan*, 157 Mass 90, 93, 31 NE 726, 727 (1892).

(5)   Disputes between client and attorney regarding collection of the fee or allegations of wrongful conduct against the attorney. See *Com. v. Brito*, 390 Mass 112, 119, 453 NE2d 1217, 1221 (1983); *Com. v. Woodberry*, 26 Mass App 636, 637, 530 NE2d 1260, 1261 (1988) ("if a client assails his attorney's conduct the privilege as to confidential communications is waived because the lawyer has a right to defend himself"). See also SJC Rule 3:07, Rules of Prof Conduct, Rule 1.6(b)(2); former DR 4-101(C)(4), supra, 382 Mass at 778.

Although the attorney-client privilege is treated as waived when the client charges the attorney with misconduct, "counsel's obligation may continue to preserve confidences whose disclosure is not relevant to the defense of the charge of his ineffectiveness as counsel." *Com. v. Brito*, supra, 390 Mass at 119, 453 NE2d at 1221. See also *Com. v. Woodberry*, supra, 26 Mass App at 637-640, 530 NE2d at 1261-1262 (attorney's testimony at hearing on defendant's motion to withdraw guilty pleas, covering entire range of discussions between attorney and client regarding pleas, was properly admitted because relevant to counsel's defense of charge of misconduct).

The circumstances in which in-house counsel may pursue a claim for wrongful discharge are limited by the obligation to protect client confidences. See *GTE Products Corp. v. Stewart*, 421 Mass 22, 32, 653 NE2d 161, 167-168

(1995) (it must be established that claim can be proved without violation of confidentiality obligation).

Proposed Mass R Evid 502(d)[4] essentially incorporates the existing exceptions, and additionally removes communications between a public officer or agency and its lawyers from the protection of the privilege except in certain situations. See Proposed Mass R Evid 502(d)(6).

§13.4.8   Waiver

A client does not waive the attorney-client privilege by testifying at trial as to events that have been a topic of a privileged communication. See *Com. v. Goldman*, 395 Mass 495, 498-502, 480 NE2d 1025, 1027-1029 (1985) (resolving long-standing conflict in the case law). See also *Neitlich v.*

---

[4]Rule 502(d) provides:

Exceptions. There is no privilege under this rule:

(1) *Furtherance of crime or fraud.* If the services of the lawyer were sought or obtained to enable or aid anyone to commit or plan to commit what the client knew or reasonably should have known to be a crime or fraud;

(2) *Claimants through same deceased client.* As to a communication relevant to an issue between parties who claim through the same deceased client, regardless of whether the claims are by testate or intestate succession or by *inter vivos* transaction;

(3) *Breach of duty by a lawyer or client.* As to a communication relevant to an issue of breach of duty by the lawyer to his client or by the client to his lawyer;

(4) *Document attested by a lawyer.* As to a communication relevant to an issue concerning an attested document to which the lawyer is an attesting witness;

(5) *Joint clients.* As to a communication relevant to a matter of common interest between or among two or more clients if the communication was made by any of them to a lawyer retained or consulted in common, when offered in an action between or among any of the clients; or

(6) *Public officer or agency.* As to a communication between a public officer or agency and its lawyers unless the communication concerns a pending investigation, claim, or action and the court determines that disclosure will seriously impair the ability of the public officer or agency to process the claim or conduct a pending investigation, litigation, or proceeding in the public interest.

PMRE 502(d).

Peterson, 15 Mass App 622, 626-627, 447 NE2d 671, 673 (1983). A waiver may be found, however, where the client testifies as to the contents of a privileged communication. *Com. v. Goldman*, supra, 395 Mass at 500, 480 NE2d at 1027; *Com. v. Woodberry*, 26 Mass App 636, 639, 530 NE2d 1260, 1262 (1988) ("By giving testimony concerning privileged communication about his plea decision the defendant waived his privilege and permitted counsel to introduce testimony 'as to all consultations relating to the same subject.'") (citation omitted). See also Proposed Mass R Evid 510.[5]

The fact that a document may have been stolen or disclosed in bad faith does not result in a waiver where it can be shown that reasonable precautionary steps were taken. See *In re Reorganization of Electric Mutual Liability Insurance Co.*, 425 Mass 419, 681 NE2d 838 (1997) (rejecting traditional view that once contents of document became public by any means, confidentiality is destroyed).

§13.4.9   Comment upon Claim of Privilege

Case law permits opposing counsel to comment upon a party's claim of the attorney-client privilege and to argue to the jury that the claim is an implied admission that the privileged matter would be harmful to the party's case. *Phillips v. Chase*, 201 Mass 444, 450, 87 NE 755, 758 (1909). Counsel may similarly comment on the claim of privilege

---

[5] "A person upon whom these rules confer a privilege against disclosure waives the privilege, if he or his predecessor while holder of the privilege voluntarily discloses or consents to disclosure of any significant part of the privileged matter. This rule does not apply if the disclosure itself is privileged." PMRE 510. The Advisory Committee Note explains that under this rule, "there is no waiver [where a party witness voluntarily takes the stand] unless the direct testimony discloses a 'significant part of the privileged matter.'" See also Proposed Mass R Evid 511: "A claim of privilege is not defeated by a disclosure which was (a) compelled erroneously or (b) made without opportunity to claim the privilege."

by a witness who is closely aligned with a party and has an interest in the outcome of the proceeding. *Neitlich v. Peterson*, supra, 15 Mass App at 628, 447 NE2d at 674 (& cases cited) (but trial judge properly refused to permit comment because witness was not so aligned with defendant as to make defendant responsible for witness's claim of privilege). Proposed Mass R Evid 512(a) would preclude an adverse comment or inference based upon a claim of privilege in a criminal case.[6]

It has been held that a party may be called before the jury even though it is known that the party will claim the attorney-client privilege. *Kendall v. Atkins*, 374 Mass 320, 325-326, 372 NE2d 764, 767-768 (1978). But compare Proposed Mass R Evid 512(b) ("In criminal cases tried to a jury, proceedings shall be conducted to the extent practicable, so as to facilitate the making of claims of privilege without the knowledge of the jury.").

§13.4.10   Work Product

Mass R Civ P 26(b)(3) codifies the privilege first recognized in *Hickman v. Taylor*, 329 US 495 (1947), to refuse discovery of documents prepared in anticipation of litigation by or for a party, his attorney, insurer, or agent. See, e.g., *Lindsey v. Ogden*, 10 Mass App Ct 142, 153-155, 406 NE2d 701, 710 (1980) (bank documents containing notations of party's accountants and tax attorney and their respective worksheets within privilege).

The privilege may be overcome upon a showing of "substantial need" for the materials. Mass R Civ P 26(b)(3).

---

[6]"The claim of a privilege, whether in the present proceeding or upon a prior occasion, is not a proper subject of comment by judge or counsel in a criminal case. No inference may be drawn therefrom." PMRE 512(a).

However, in ordering discovery of such materials when the required showing has been made, "the court shall protect against disclosure of the mental impressions, conclusions, opinions, or legal theories of an attorney or other representative of a party concerning the litigation."

The privilege applies in a more limited fashion in criminal cases. See Mass R Crim P 14(5) and *Com. v. Paszko,* 391 Mass 164, 187-188, 461 NE2d 222, 236-237 (1984) (Mass R Crim P 14(a)(5) protects only materials that reveal mental processes of attorney, but unlike federal doctrine, excludes statements of witnesses other than defendant and nonlegal reports from the definition of work product).

The work product doctrine is "intended to enhance vitality of the adversary system of litigation by insulating counsel's work from intrusions, interferences, or borrowings by other parties as he prepares for the contest." *Ward v. Peabody,* 380 Mass 805, 817, 405 NE2d 973, 980 (1980). In order to fit within the privilege, the materials must have been prepared in relation to litigation, pending or prospective. Id. See also *Com. v. Fall River Motor Sales, Inc.,* 409 Mass 302, 308-309, 565 NE2d 1205, 1210 (1991) (internal documents and other information requested by defendant appear to have been prepared for litigation by Attorney General and to contain litigation strategies and policies of that office).

§13.4.11   *Attorney as Witness*

Except in limited circumstances, an attorney cannot take part in a trial in which he is to be a witness. See *Kendall v. Atkins,* 374 Mass 320, 323-325, 372 NE2d 764, 766-767 (1978) (discussion of propriety of calling opposing counsel as witness); SJC Rule 3:07, Rules of Prof Conduct, Rule 3.7 (formerly SJC Rule 3:07, DR 5-101 and 102); Superior

Court Rule 12. See also *Com. v. Rondeau*, 378 Mass 408, 392 NE2d 1001 (1979) (defendant deprived of effective assistance of counsel by failure of attorney to withdraw when it became apparent his testimony as alibi witness was necessary to defense); *Borman v. Borman*, 378 Mass 775, 785-792, 393 NE2d 847, 854-858 (1979) (judge erred in disqualifying law firm from representing husband merely because he was member of firm and, as litigant, would testify in proceeding; extensive discussion of applicable ethical rules and policy); *Byington v. City of Boston*, 37 Mass App 907, 640 NE2d 115 (1994) (representation of wife by husband's law partner not precluded where, although husband had knowledge of wife's pain and suffering, the issue could be addressed by other testimony and partner had no intention of calling husband as witness); *Serody v. Serody*, 19 Mass App 411, 474 NE2d 1171 (1985) (judge did not abuse discretion in requiring wife's attorney to withdraw from case after husband's attorney gave notice he intended to call attorney as witness).

§13.5   Physician-Patient; Psychotherapist-Patient; Social Worker-Client; Counselor-Victim; Court-Ordered Psychiatric Examination

No physician-patient, psychotherapist-patient, or social worker-client privileges existed at common law. *Com. v. Mandeville*, 386 Mass 393, 409, 436 NE2d 912, 922 (1982) (psychotherapist-patient); *Kramer v. John Hancock Mutual Life Insurance Co.*, 336 Mass 465, 467, 146 NE2d 357, 359 (1957) (physician-patient). Privileges have been established by statute for communications between pyschotherapist and patient, between social worker and client, and between sexual-assault or domestic-violence counselor and victim. A statutory disqualification renders inadmissible for certain purposes in a criminal case statements made by the defendant during a court-ordered psychiatric examination. In addition, a nonstatutory civil remedy has been recognized for breach of a physician's duty of confidentiality.

§13.5.1   Physician-Patient Confidentiality

Other than the psychotherapist-patient privilege discussed in §13.5.2, infra, no statutory testimonial privilege applies to physicians and their patients. *Com. v. Dube*, 413 Mass 570, 572 n.3, 601 NE2d 467, 468 n.3 (1992) (& citations); *Alberts v. Devine*, 395 Mass 59, 67, 479 NE2d 113, 118 (1985), *cert denied sub nom, Carroll v. Alberts*, 474 US 1013 (1985).

A duty of confidentiality arising from the physician-patient relationship has been recognized by the Supreme Judicial Court, violation of which gives rise to a tort claim against the physician. *Alberts v. Devine*, supra. The duty covers medical facts communicated to or discovered by the physician, 395 Mass at 65, 479 NE2d at 118, and proscribes *out-of-court* disclosure of such information without the patient's consent, except to meet a serious danger to the patient or to others. 395 Mass at 66-68, 479 NE2d at 119.

The court has, however, refused to create an exclusionary rule for disclosures in violation of the duty of confidentiality, relying instead on the damages remedy. See *Schwartz v. Goldstein*, 400 Mass 152, 154, 508 NE2d 97, 99 (1987). See also *Tower v. Hirshhorn*, 397 Mass 581, 585, 492 NE2d 728, 731-732 (1986).

A physician's duty of confidentiality to a patient has been read into administrative regulations concerning the profession. See *Hellman v. Board of Registration in Medicine*, 404 Mass 800, 537 NE2d 150 (1989); *Sugarman v. Board of Registration in Medicine*, 422 Mass 338, 662 NE2d 1020 (1996) (Board had authority to sanction psychiatrist who, as expert witness in custody case, released confidential report to press).

§13.5.2   Psychotherapist-Patient Privilege

GL 233, §20B provides:

> Except as hereinafter provided, in any court proceeding and in any proceeding preliminary thereto and in legislative and administrative proceedings, a patient shall have the privilege of refusing to disclose, and of preventing a witness from disclosing, any communication, wherever made, between said patient and a psychotherapist relative to the diagnosis or treatment of the patient's mental or emotional condition. This privilege shall apply to patients engaged with a psychotherapist in marital therapy, family therapy, or consultation in contemplation of such therapy.
>
> If a patient is incompetent to exercise or waive such privilege, a guardian shall be appointed to act in his behalf under this section. A previously appointed guardian shall be authorized to so act.
>
> Upon the exercise of the privilege granted by this section, the judge or presiding officer shall instruct the jury that no adverse inference may be drawn therefrom.

The purpose of the statute is to "protect justifiable expectations of confidentiality that people who seek psychotherapeutic help have a right to expect." *Com. v. Clancy,* 402 Mass 664, 667, 524 NE2d 395, 397 (1988).

Section 20B defines "psychotherapist" as "a person licensed to practice medicine, who devotes a substantial portion of his time to the practice of psychiatry," and also includes licensed psychologists and psychiatric nurses.[1] "Communications" are defined as "conversations, correspondence, actions and occurrences relating to diagnosis or treatment before, during or after institutionalization, regardless of the patient's awareness of such conversations, correspondence, actions and occurrences, and any records,

---

§13.5   [1]St 1989, c 373 removed the former requirement that a psychologist have a doctoral degree in psychology in order to be considered a "psychotherapist." See, e.g., *Com. v. McDonough,* 400 Mass 639, 644-645, 511 NE2d 551, 555-556 (1987).

memoranda or notes of the foregoing." "Patient" is defined as "a person who, during the course of diagnosis or treatment, communicates with a psychotherapist."

The courts have required that "some confidential relationship" exist between patient and psychotherapist before the privilege may be invoked. *Com. v. Mandeville*, 386 Mass 393, 409, 436 NE2d 912 (1982); *Com. v. Clemons*, 12 Mass App 580, 586-587, 427 NE2d 761, 765 (1981). Thus, where the facts suggested that the defendant did not consult the psychotherapist for treatment or diagnosis, but rather to minimize the legal and family impact of the charges, the relationship was not that of patient and psychotherapist and the privilege would not apply. See *Com. v. Berrio*, 407 Mass 37, 42-43, 551 NE2d 496, 500 (1990). But see *Robinson v. Com.*, 399 Mass 131, 503 NE2d 31 (1987) (judge erred in ruling that privilege did not apply because defendant had not been a "patient" undergoing "diagnosis or treatment" while conversing privately with staff psychiatrist at latter's initiation in hospital where critically ill infant victim was being treated).

The Supreme Judicial Court has indicated that it is not inclined "to extend the patient-psychotherapist privilege beyond the bounds established by the Legislature." *Com. v. Rosenberg*, 410 Mass 347, 353, 573 NE2d 949, 953 (1991); *Com. v. Mandeville*, supra, 386 Mass at 409, 436 NE2d at 992-923. Thus, communications to therapists who do not meet the specifications of the statute do not fall within the privilege, even though the therapist is working under the supervision of a qualifying psychotherapist. *Com. v. Rosenberg*, supra, 410 Mass at 353, 573 NE2d at 953; *Adoption of Diane*, 400 Mass 196, 200-201, 508 NE2d 837, 840 (1987); *Com. v. Mandeville*, supra, 386 Mass at 408-409, 436 NE2d at 922 (unlicensed community health center staff psychologist); *Com. v. Clemons*, supra, 12 Mass App at 584-587, 427 NE2d at 764 (unlicensed family therapist). Still open is the question whether the privilege might apply to an agent or assistant of the psychotherapist in order to protect an existing confidential relationship. *Com. v. Rosenberg*, supra,

410 Mass at 354, 573 NE2d at 954; *Com. v. Mandeville*, supra, 386 Mass at 409, 436 NE2d at 923; *Com. v. Clemons*, supra, 12 Mass App at 586-587, 427 NE2d at 765.[2]

Proposed Mass R Evid 503 would broaden the definition of "psychotherapist" to include persons "reasonably believed by the patient to be [a licensed psychotherapist, psychologist, or social worker]," Rule 503(a)(2), and would extend the applicability of the privilege to "persons who are participating in the diagnosis or treatment under the direction of the psychotherapist, including members of the patient's family." Rule 503(b). The rule also excepts from the "third persons" to whom disclosure (or intended disclosure) destroys confidentiality those "persons present to further the interest of the patient in the consultation, examination, or interview, persons reasonably necessary for the transmission of the communication, or persons who are participating in the diagnosis and treatment under the direction of the psychotherapist, including members of the patient's family." Proposed Mass R Evid 503(a)(3).

GL 233, §20B, establishes a privilege, not a disqualification. The patient must therefore affirmatively exercise the privilege in order to prevent the psychotherapist from disclosing confidential communications at trial, and failure to do so precludes assertion of the privilege on appeal. *Com. v. Benoit*, 410 Mass 506, 518-519, 574 NE2d 347, 354-355 (1991) (& citations). See also *Adoption of Carla*, 416 Mass 510, 515, 623 NE2d 1118, 1121 (1993) (mother's failure to object at trial to testimony of psychotherapist on grounds of privilege precluded appellate review; mother's assertion of privilege in motion in limine insufficient to preserve appellate rights); *Com. v. Hawkesworth*, 405 Mass 664, 672 n.6, 543 NE2d 691, 696 n.6 (1989) (failure to claim §20B privilege at trial limits consideration on appeal to whether there was substantial likelihood of miscarriage

---

[2] GL 112, §129A requires licensed psychologists as well as their colleagues, agents, or employees (professional, clerical, academic, or therapeutic) to maintain the confidentiality of patient communications.

of justice); *Petitions of the Department of Social Services to Dispense with Consent to Adoption*, 399 Mass 279, 290 n.21, 503 NE2d 1275, 1282 n.21 (1987) (burden on patient to assert privilege); *Adoption of Christine*, 405 Mass 602, 605-606, 542 NE2d 582, 584 (1989) (failure to assert privilege not prejudicial); *Adoption of Abigail*, 23 Mass App 191, 198, 499 NE2d 1234, 1239 (1986) (privilege issue cannot be raised as second thought of appellate counsel). Where the patient's counsel questions the psychotherapist about privileged communications and records, the privilege is waived. See *Care and Protection of Bruce*, 44 Mass App 758, 764-765, 694 NE2d 27, 31-32 (1998) (& citations).

It has been held that a psychotherapist has standing to raise the privilege on behalf of a patient. See *Com. v. Kobrin*, 395 Mass 284, 287 n.8, 479 NE2d 674, 677 n.8 (1985) (psychiatrist had standing to raise patient's claims of privilege when grand jury investigating Medicaid fraud demanded patient's records). See also Proposed Mass R Evid 503(c) ("The person who was the psychotherapist at the time of the communication is presumed to have authority to claim the privilege but only on behalf of the patient."). The parent of a patient, however, has no right to assert the privilege on behalf of the child; pursuant to §20B only the child or a guardian appointed by the court may do so. *Adoption of Diane*, supra, 400 Mass at 201-202, 508 NE2d at 840 (mother in adoption consent case could not challenge testimony of psychotherapists regarding communications with child); *Adoption of George*, 27 Mass App 265, 275, 537 NE2d 1251, 1258 (1989) (mother, whose interests in litigation conflict with those of the child, may not invoke privilege on child's behalf). See generally *Com. v. Pellegrini*, 414 Mass 402, 407-409, 608 NE2d 717, 721-722 (1993) (parents have no privacy right to exclude child's medical record).

Like the attorney-client privilege (see §13.4.6, supra), the psychotherapist-patient privilege survives the death of the patient and may be invoked or waived by the administrator or executor of the estate. *District Attorney for Norfolk*

District v. Magraw, 417 Mass 169, 172-174, 628 NE2d 24, 26-27 (1994).

The privilege protects only communications, not facts. Those parts of a psychiatric record that contain "conclusions based on objective indicia rather than on communications from [the patient]" may be admitted in evidence. *Adoption of Seth*, 29 Mass App 343, 353, 560 NE2d 708, 713-714 (1990) ("To the extent that the psychiatrist's opinions may have been grounded on such a mixed foundation, the recommended approach would be for the [patient's] counsel to request a voir dire to determine the basis of the expert opinion."). Similarly a psychotherapist must disclose portions of records documenting times and lengths of patient appointments, fees, diagnoses, and treatment plans; but those portions of the records which reflect the patients' "thoughts, feelings, and impressions, or contain the substance of the psychotherapeutic dialogue" are protected. See *Com. v. Kobrin*, supra, 395 Mass at 294-295, 479 NE2d at 681. See also *Com. v. Clancy*, 402 Mass 664, 667, 524 NE2d 395, 397 (1988); *Adoption of Abigail*, supra, 23 Mass App at 198-199, 499 NE2d at 1239

The privileged status of a communication is not lost by reason of being recorded in a hospital record otherwise admissible. See *Usen v. Usen*, 359 Mass 453, 455-456, 269 NE2d 442, 443-444 (1971). See also *Com. v. Rexach*, 20 Mass App 919, 478 NE2d 744 (1985) (patient's statements to psychiatrists contained in hospital records are protected). On the other hand, the fact that hospital records contain some references to psychiatric matters does not compel the conclusion that the entire record is privileged. *Petitions of the Department of Social Services to Dispense with Consent to Adoption*, supra, 399 Mass at 287-288, 503 NE2d at 1280-1281.

The fact that the patient later repeated some of the information communicated to other persons does not necessarily defeat the privilege. *See Robinson v. Com.*, supra, 399 Mass at 135, 503 NE2d at 34.

A prosecution witness retains the privilege as to protected communications not testified to on direct examination. See *Com. v. Clancy*, supra, 402 Mass at 666-669, 524 NE2d at 397-398 ("a witness does not relinquish all protection by merely testifying to events falling within the subject matter of a privilege.").

Section 20B sets out six exceptions to the privilege:

(a)   where the psychotherapist determines that the patient is in need of treatment in a hospital for mental or emotional illness, or is a threat to himself or others, and discloses the communication for the purpose of placing or retaining the patient in a hospital or under arrest;[3]

(b)   where the patient was informed that his communications would not be privileged in the context of a court-ordered examination, but such communications are admissible only on issues involving the patient's mental or emotional condition, and not as a confession or admission of guilt;[4]

---

[3] This exception is inapplicable to communications made by a defendant already in custody and undergoing examination for possible commitment as a sexually dangerous person. *Com. v. Lamb*, 365 Mass 265, 268-269, 311 NE2d 47, 50 (1974). Such communications are governed by exception (b).

[4] See *Com. v. Benoit*, supra, 410 Mass at 518-519, 574 NE2d at 334-335. This exception and its notice requirement have been held applicable to court-ordered examinations in the context of:

- a sexually-dangerous person determination. See *Com. v. Barboza*, 387 Mass 105, 109, 438 NE2d 1064, 1070-1071 (1982); *Com. v. Lamb*, supra note 3; *Petition of Sheridan*, 412 Mass 599, 604, 591 NE2d 193, 196 (1992).
- a request to extend a juvenile's commitment beyond his 18th birthday. See *Department of Youth Services v. A Juvenile*, 398 Mass 516, 524-527, 499 NE2d 812, 817-818 (1986); *Com. v. Traylor*, 29 Mass App 584, 590 n.2, 563 NE2d 243, 247 n.2 (1990).
- a petition to dispense with need of mother's consent to adoption of her child. See *Petition of the Department of Social Services to Dispense with Consent to Adoption*, 396 Mass 485, 487, 487 NE2d 184, 185-186 (1986).

See also §13.5.5, infra.

(c) where the patient places his mental or emotional condition in issue in any proceeding except one involving child custody, adoption, or adoption consent, but only if the judge determines that "it is more important to the interests of justice that the communication be disclosed than that the relationship between patient and psychotherapist be protected;"[5]

(d) where the patient is dead and his mental or emotional condition is placed in issue by a party claiming or defending through or as a beneficiary of the patient, but only if the judge determines that "it is more important to the interests of justice that the communication be disclosed than that the relationship between patient and psychotherapist be protected;"

(e) in child custody, adoption, and adoption consent cases, where the judge determines that the evidence bears significantly on the patient's ability to provide suitable care or custody and that "it is more important to the welfare of the child that the communication be disclosed than that the relationship between patient and psychotherapist be protected;"[6] and

---

[5] See, e.g., *McMillan v. Massachusetts Society for the Prevention of Cruelty to Animals*, 24 MLW 509 (D Mass 1995) (plaintiff seeking emotional distress damages in GL 151B employment discrimination action must disclose her therapist's session notes during discovery, and therapist may be deposed).

[6] See, e.g., *Adoption of Adam*, 23 Mass App 922, 500 NE2d 816 (1986); *Custody of a Minor (No. 3)*, 16 Mass App 998, 1002, 454 NE2d 924, 927 (1983). See also *Usen v. Usen*, supra, 359 Mass at 456-457, 269 NE2d at 444. Section 20B(e) was amended by St 1986, c 594, to include adoption and adoption-consent cases together with child-custody cases. Compare *Petition of Catholic Charitable Bureau to Dispense with Consent to Adoption*, 392 Mass 738, 467 NE2d 866 (1984) (petition to dispense with parent's consent to adoption not within original language).

(f)   in any proceeding against the psychotherapist where disclosure is necessary to the defense.[7]

The trial judge is required to treat the determinations in these exceptions with "meticulous observance," and the findings should be shown on the record or transcript. *Usen v. Usen*, supra, 359 Mass at 456-457, 269 NE2d at 444.

In addition to the statutory exceptions, the privilege is not infringed when a psychotherapist reports a suspected instance of child abuse as required by GL 119, §51A. See *Com. v. Souther*, 31 Mass App 219, 222-224, 575 NE2d 1150, 1153-1154 (1991) (patient not entitled to dismissal of indictments founded on report by psychotherapist filed on §51A). The privilege §20B confers is not absolute but "hedged," and by requiring reports pursuant to §51A the Legislature "gave higher priority to the protection of children than the protection of psychotherapist-patient confidences." 31 Mass App at 224, 575 NE2d at 1154.

Finally, the psychotherapist-patient (as well as the social worker-client privilege discussed in the next section) may be overridden by the defendant's constitutional rights. See §13.5.4.

§13.5.3   Social Worker-Client Confidentiality and Privilege

Massachusetts law provides for both the confidentiality of communications between social worker and client, as well as a privilege that attaches to certain of those communications.

GL 112, §135A (as amended as of 1989) mandates the confidentiality of "all communications"[8] between a licensed

---

[7]Proposed Mass R Evid 503(d)(1) through (6) adopts these exceptions.

[8]"Communications" is defined to include "conversations, correspondence, actions and occurrences regardless of the client's aware-

social worker or a social worker employed in a state, county or municipal government agency,[9] and a client.[10] "No such social worker, colleague, agent, or employee of any social worker, whether professional, clerical, academic or therapeutic, shall disclose any information acquired or revealed in the course of or in connection with the performance of the social worker's professional services, including the fact, circumstances, findings or records of such services." Disclosure is permitted in the following circumstances:

(a)   where the communication falls within an exception to the privilege created by GL 135B, discussed below;

(b)   upon express, written consent of the client or a guardian appointed to act in the client's behalf, and in the case of marital or family therapy, with the consent of each adult participant;

(c)   upon the need to disclose information that is necessary to protect the safety of the client or others if the client presents a clear and present danger to himself, or has communicated to the social worker an explicit threat to kill or inflict serious bodily injury upon a reasonably identified victim or victims;[11]

---

ness of such conversations, correspondence, actions and occurrences and any records, memoranda or notes of the foregoing." GL 112, §135.

[9] The confidentiality provisions of §135A and the privilege provided for in §135B apply to unlicensed persons employed by governmental agencies to perform social work. See *Bernard v. Com.*, 424 Mass 32, 673 NE2d 1220 (1996) (state trooper employed as peer counselor).

[10] A "client" is defined in GL 122, §135 as "a person with whom a social worker has established a social worker-client relationship."

[11] The predecessor to §135A more broadly excepted communications that reveal "the contemplation or commission of a crime or a harmful act." See *Com. v. Collett*, 387 Mass 424, 431-435, 439 NE2d 1223, 1228-1230 (1982); *Com. v. Berrio*, 407 Mass 37, 40-41, 551 NE2d 496, 498-499 (1990); *Com. v. Merola*, 405 Mass 529, 535-536, 542 NE2d 249, 253-254 (1989); *Allen v. Holyoke Hospital*, 398 Mass 372, 389-390, 496 NE2d 1368, 1377-1379 (1986) (Abrams, J, dissenting); *Com. v. LeCain*, 19 Mass App 1034, 477 NE2d 205 (1985). The Advisory Committee for

(d)   in order to collect amounts owed by the client for professional services rendered by the social worker or his employees;

(e)   in order to initiate or give testimony in a care and protection proceeding or petition to dispense with consent to adoption;[12]

(f)   where the social worker has acquired the information while acting as an elder protective services worker; and

(g)   where the social worker has acquired the information while conducting an investigation into abuse of a disabled person.

GL 112, §135B creates a privilege that permits the client to refuse to disclose and to prevent a witness from disclosing in any court, legislative, or administrative proceeding any communication "relative to the diagnosis or treatment of the client's mental or emotional condition" between the client and a licensed social worker, or a social worker employed in a state, county, or municipal governmental agency. The judge is required to instruct the jury that no adverse inference may be drawn from assertion of the privilege.

The privilege is "a legislative recognition that the confidentiality of a person's communications to a social worker is a necessity for successful social work intervention. . . . The purpose of enacting a social worker-client privilege is to prevent the chilling effect which routine disclosures may have in preventing those in need of help from seeking that help." *Com. v. Collett*, 387 Mass 424, 428,

---

the Proposed Massachusetts Rules of Evidence concluded, in rejecting this formulation, that this exception was "so ambiguous and broad as to drastically impair the value and meaning of the privilege." Advisory Committee Note to Proposed R 503.

[12] See, e.g., *Adoption of Diane*, 400 Mass 196, 198-200, 508 NE2d 837, 838-839 (1987); *Petition of the Department of Social Services to Dispense with Consent to Adoption*, 397 Mass 659, 662-664, 467 NE2d 866, 869-870 (1986) (exception applies to permit social worker to disclose information even if she was not party bringing the petition).

439 NE2d 1223, 1226 (1982) (decided under predecessor statute).

By its terms, the privilege encompasses only those statements made for the purpose of diagnosis and treatment of the client's mental or emotional condition, as compared to the broader reference to "all communications" in §135A. See *Com. v. Wojcik*, 43 Mass App 595, 608-609, 686 NE2d 452, 461-462 (1997).

Both §135A and 135B apply to the disclosure of "communications." Information contained in DSS records that was acquired through the personal observations of the social worker in the subject's home is not therefore within the prohibition. See *Allen v. Holyoke Hospital*, 398 Mass 372, 378, 496 NE2d 1368, 1372 (1986); *Custody of a Minor (No. 3)*, 16 Mass App 998, 454 NE2d 924 (1983).

The privilege established by §135B does not apply to the following communications:[13]

(a)   where the social worker determines that the patient is in need of treatment in a hospital for mental or emotional illness, or is a threat to himself or others, and discloses the communication for the purpose of placing or retaining the patient in a hospital;

(b)   where the patient was informed that his communications would not be privileged in the context of a court-ordered examination, but such communications are admissible only on issues involving the patient's mental or emotional condition, and not as a confession or admission of guilt;

(c)   where the patient places his mental or emotional condition in issue in any proceeding except one involving child custody, adoption or adoption consent, but only if the judge determines that "it

---

[13] The exceptions essentially track those applying to the psychotherapist-patient privilege discussed in §13.5.2, supra.

is more important to the interests of justice that the communication be disclosed than that the relationship between client and social worker be protected;"

(d)   where the client is dead and his mental or emotional condition is placed in issue by a party claiming or defending through or as a beneficiary of the client, but only if the judge determines that "it is more important to the interests of justice that the communication be disclosed than that the relationship between client and social worker be protected;"

(e)   in the initiation or giving of testimony in certain child protection proceedings;

(f)   in any proceeding whereby the social worker has acquired the information while conducting an investigation of child abuse pursuant to GL 119, §51B;[14]

(g)   in child custody, adoption, and adoption consent cases, where the judge determines that the evidence bears significantly on the client's ability to provide suitable care or custody and that "it is more important to the welfare of the child that the communication be disclosed than that the relationship between client and social worker be protected;" and

---

[14] In the context of criminal prosecutions, see also *Com. v. Jones*, 404 Mass 339, 535 NE2d 221 (1989) (defendant entitled to have judge make in camera inspection of entire Department of Social Services (DSS) file for exculpatory evidence concerning alleged abuse); *Com. v. O'Brien*, 27 Mass App 184, 536 NE2d 361 (1989) (defendant entitled to DSS investigatory report on incident without any showing of particularized need); *Com. v. Pratt*, 42 Mass App 695, 679 NE2d 579 (1997) (reversible error to exclude defendant's evidence of lack of fresh complaint by complainant in her communications with DSS case worker). But see *Com. v. Hyatt*, 31 Mass App 488, 492-493, 579 NE2d 1365, 1368-1369 (1991) (underlying raw file of DSS remains confidential).

     (h)   in any proceeding brought by the client against the social worker and in any malpractice, criminal or license revocation proceeding in which disclosure is necessary or relevant to the claim or defense of the social worker.

The Legislature has thus determined that "while the preservation of the confidential relationship is an important objective, under certain circumstances, this goal must give way in favor of other societal interests," such as the protection of children. *Com. v. Collett*, supra, 387 Mass at 428, 434, 439 NE2d at 1226.

Proposed Mass R Evid 503 (discussed in §13.5.2) combines the psychotherapist-patient and social worker-client privilege.

An earlier version of GL 112, §135, prohibited disclosure of any information "acquired from persons consulting [the social worker] in his professional capacity," and was interpreted as extending the privilege to communications regardless of whether such persons were "clients" of the social worker or whether the social worker initiated the contact. See *Com. v. Collett*, supra, 387 Mass at 427-430, 439 NE2d at 1226-1228 (information obtained from interviews with victim's family members); *Allen v. Holyoke Hospital*, 398 Mass 372, 376-378, 496 NE2d 1368, 1371-1372 (1986) (communications to DSS social workers from child decedent's grandparents and foster parents fell within privilege and were not subject to discovery in wrongful death action) (Liacos, CJ, dissenting, concluded that the statutory obligation of confidentiality applies only to communications from persons "consulting" the social worker—i.e., seeking advice and assistance); *In re Production of Records to Grand Jury*, 618 F Supp 440 (D Mass 1985) (recognizing, as matter of federal evidentiary law, a qualified privilege for DSS records containing communications made to social worker from either patient or third parties). The current version of §135A and 135B, as noted above, applies only to communications between client and social worker.

In addition to the statutory exceptions, the social worker-client privilege may in a criminal case have to yield to a defendant's constitutional right to use privileged communications in his defense. See §13.5.4, infra.

The federal courts now recognize a privilege protecting confidential communications between psychotherapist and patient. See *Jaffee v. Redmond,* 518 US 1, 116 S Ct 1923, 135 L Ed 2d 337 (1996) (statements that defendant police officer made to licensed social worker in course of psychotherapy, and notes taken during counseling sessions, were protected from compelled disclosure in civil rights action).

§13.5.4   *Privilege Overridden by Constitutional Rights*

Both the psychotherapist-patient and social worker-client privilege may be overriden by the defendant's constitutional rights to confront his accusers and to present relevant evidence in his favor. The Supreme Judicial Court has, in a series of decisions in rape and sexual abuse cases, confronted the difficult task of balancing the competing interests of disclosure and confidentiality. See *Com. v. Bishop,* 416 Mass 169 (1993); *Com. v. Figueroa,* 413 Mass 193, 595 NE2d 779 (1992); *Com. v. Stockhammer,* 409 Mass 867, 570 NE2d 992 (1991).

Beginning with its decision in *Com. v. Stockhammer,* supra, 409 Mass at 880-884, 570 NE2d at 1001-1003, the court held that defense counsel was entitled under art. 12 of the Massachusetts Declaration of Rights to review a rape complainant's privileged psychiatric records to seek evidence of bias, prejudice, or motive to lie. See also §§4.4.3(b) and 6.9, supra. *Stockhammer* rejected the federal standard requiring only in camera review by trial judge. *Com. v. Figueroa,* supra, 413 Mass at 202-203, applied *Stockhammer* retroactively, and extended the disclosure rule to privileged records concerning the condition of mental retardation or impairment of a complaining witness:

"[D]efense counsel must also be allowed to search the records for evidence of how that impairment might affect her capacity to perceive, remember and articulate the alleged events. This type of evidence, like evidence of bias, prejudice, or motive to lie, can be used to impeach the credibility of the complaining witness." See also *Com. v. Hrycenko*, 31 Mass App 425, 433-434, 578 NE2d 809, 814-815 (1991) (defense counsel must be permitted to examine DMH records concerning victim); *Com. v. Arthur*, 31 Mass App 178, 182, 575 NE2d 1147, 1149-1150 (1991) (DSS investigation records); *Com. v. Simcock*, 31 Mass App 184, 199-200, 575 NE2d 1137, 1145-1146 (1991) (notes concerning victim's therapy).

In *Com. v. Bishop*, 416 Mass 169, 617 NE2d 990 (1993), however, the Court drew back significantly on the right of defense counsel to review privileged records regarding the complainant. Starting from the proposition that the privileges for mental health records should be pierced only in those cases in which "there is a reasonable risk that nondisclosure may result in an erroneous conviction," 416 Mass at 177, the court devised a procedural scheme for determining whether disclosure was required:

- **Stage 1 — Privilege determination.** Defendant in a case of rape or sexual abuse moves to compel production of the various records pertaining to the complainant. If the keeper of the records refuses to produce them because of a statutory privilege, the judge must decide whether the records are indeed privileged and prepare a written determination of that issue.

- **Stage 2 — Relevancy determination.** If the judge determines the documents are privileged, defense counsel must submit to the judge, in writing, the theory or theories under which the particular records sought are likely to be relevant to an issue in the case.[15] If the judge decides that the records are likely to be relevant,[16] the judge then reviews the records in camera to determine whether the records, or any portion thereof, are relevant.

- **Stage 3 — Access to relevant material.** The judge then allows defense counsel and the prosecutor access to the relevant portions of the privileged records for the sole purpose of determining whether disclosure of the relevant communications to the trier of fact is required to provide the defendant a fair trial.

- **Stage 4 — Disclosure of relevant communications.** The burden is on the defendant to demonstrate by written motion that disclosure of the relevant portions of the records to the trier of fact is required to provide the defendant a fair trial. If the defendant meets this burden, the judge must permit disclosure, and may condition it on appropriate terms and conditions. See Model Order, 416 Mass at 189. In arriving at this determination the judge shall resolve any doubt he or she may have in the defendant's favor. The reasons for the decision must be set forth in a written memorandum.

----

[15] A defendant seeking privileged records is not entitled to an ex parte hearing on his submission as to relevance. See *Pare v. Com.*, 420 Mass 216, 648 NE2d 1277 (1995). "The defendant need not make a showing that the records actually contain information that carries, for example, the potential for establishing the unreliability of either the criminal charge or a witness on whose testimony the charge depends. The defendant must, however, advance, in good faith, at least some factual basis which indicates how the privileged records are likely to be relevant to an issue in the case and 'that the quest for its contents is not merely a desperate grasping at a straw.'" *Com. v. Bishop*, supra, 416 Mass at 180, 617 NE2d at 996-997.

[16] "In considering the defendant's request the judge may consider, among other things, the nature of the privilege claimed, the date the target records were produced relative to the date or dates of the alleged incident, and the nature of the crimes charged." *Com. v. Bishop*, supra, 416 Mass at 180, 617 NE2d at 997.

- **Stage 5 — Trial.** At trial, the judge determines in a voir dire examination the admissibility of the particular records that counsel wishes to introduce.

Com. v. Bishop, supra, 416 Mass 169, 181-183, 617 NE2d 990, 997-998. For cases utilizing this approach, compare *Com. v. Reed*, 417 Mass 558, 561-562, 631 NE2d 552, 554 (1994) (in camera review of prosecution witness's psychological records revealed no evidence of promises, inducements, or rewards), *Com. v. Syrafos*, 38 Mass App 211, 213-216, 646 NE2d 429, 431-433 (1995) (defendant failed to demonstrate relevance of victim's clinic records and failed to justify disclosure of records to mental health expert), and *Com. v. Souza*, 39 Mass App 103, 107-109, 653 NE2d 1127, 1130-1131 (1995) (defendants charged with molesting their grandchildren not entitled to notes of victims' mothers' psychotherapists; suggests that "a judge might reasonably hold access on a somewhat tighter leash" when dealing with records of noncomplaining witnesses) with *Com. v. Pare*, 427 Mass App 427, 693 NE2d 1002 (1998) (extensive discussion of *Bishop/Fuller* protocol) (reversible error to deny counsel access to child's "sexual information and trauma team" (SITT) records) and *Com. v. Pratt*, 42 Mass App 579, 679 NE2d 579 (1997) (reversible error to deny defendant evidence of lack of fresh complaint by complainant in her communications with DSS case worker).

In *Com. v. Fuller*, 423 Mass 216, 667 NE2d 847 (1996), the court addressed the procedure to be followed and the standards to be applied when a defendant seeks access to the complainant's rape counseling records, which are privileged under GL 233, §20J (see §13.5.6, infra). Expressing general adherence to the procedures set forth in *Bishop*, the court subjected rape counseling records to somewhat more stringent controls. The defendant must file a written motion seeking production and explaining in detail his reasons for doing so. Such a motion should be "the last step" in the defendant's pretrial discovery, exhausting all other potential sources for the information, and must contain a showing that the material sought is not available elsewhere. A judge should undertake an in camera review of records privileged under §20J only when the defendant's motion has demonstrated "a good faith, specific, and reasonable basis for believing that the records will contain exculpatory evidence which is relevant and material to the issue of the defendant's guilt." "Material evidence" means evidence that not only is admissible, but that "also tends to create a reasonable doubt that might not otherwise exist." 423 Mass at 226, 667 NE2d at 855. A credible showing that the complainant had previously fabricated allegations of sexual assault or a showing of bias against the defendant or credible evidence that the complainant has difficulty distinguishing fantasy from reality might, the court suggested, suffice to warrant in camera inspection of the records. Emphatically repeating its admonition in *Bishop*, however, there is to be no "unrestrained foray into confidential records in the hope that the unearthing of some unspecified information would enable [the defendant] to impeach the witness." Id. The *Bishop-Fuller* procedures are to be followed with regard to requests for information protected by the domestic counselor privilege, GL 233, §20K, as well. *Com. v. Tripolone*, 425 Mass 487, 681 NE2d 1216 (1997). See §13.5.6, infra.

The Commonwealth has no obligation to seek information (for use by the defense) from the complainant concerning any mental health treatment she has received or any records which may exist; nor is the prosecutor under a duty to affirmatively facilitate the questioning of the complainant by defendant. See *Com. v. Beal*, 429 Mass 530, 709 NE2d 413 (1999).

The principle allowing a criminal defendant access to privileged records in certain cases has been held inapplicable to noncriminal proceedings. See *Herridge v. Board of Registration in Medicine*, 420 Mass 154, 157, 648 NE2d 745, 747 (1995).

§13.5.5   Inadmissibility of Statements Made during Court-Ordered Psychiatric Examination

GL 233, §23B, provides:

> In the trial of an indictment or complaint for any crime, no statement made by a defendant therein subjected to psychiatric examination pursuant to [GL 123, §15 or 16] for the purposes of such examination or treatment shall be admissible in evidence against him on any issue other than that of his mental condition, nor shall it be admissible in evidence against him on that issue if such statement constitutes a confession of guilt of the crime charged.[17]

The relationship between GL 233, §23B, and the constitutional privilege against self-incrimination (see §13.14, infra) is discussed in *Blaisdell v. Com.*, 372 Mass 753, 761-764, 364 NE2d 191, 198-199 (1977), holding that the protections afforded by §23B to a defendant subjected to a compelled psychiatric examination are not coextensive with the greater protection afforded by the constitutional privilege. The court established certain requirements in order to meet the constitutional mandate, such as construction of "confession" to include inculpatory statements falling short of a full acknowledgment of guilt. 372 Mass at 763, 364 NE2d at 198-199. The procedures mandated by the court (372 Mass at 767-769) are now found in Mass R Crim P 14(b)(2).

For cases applying §23B, see *Com. v. Harvey*, 397 Mass 803, 807-809, 494 NE2d 382, 385-386 (1986) (prosecutor's introduction of evidence obtained as result of court-ordered psychiatric examination was improper before defendant had introduced any evidence of mental impairment;

---

[17] See also discussion of exception (b) to GL 233, §20B, in §13.5.2, infra.

but error harmless because defendant subsequently offered psychiatric testimony); *Com. v. Martin*, 393 Mass 781, 786-787, 473 NE2d 1099, 1103 (1985) (defendant's admissions during court-ordered psychiatric examination regarding his state of mind at time of shooting were improperly admitted, requiring reversal even in absence of objection); *Com. v. Callahan*, 386 Mass 784, 787-789, 438 NE2d 45, 48 (1982) (reversal required because inculpatory statements, tending to show premeditation, made in course of court-ordered psychiatric examination were admitted in violation of GL 233, §23B, even though statements fell short of full confession); *Com. v. O'Connor*, 7 Mass App 314, 387 NE2d 190 (1979) (inculpatory statements made by defendant during court-ordered psychiatric examination should have been excluded, but error harmless). But see *Com. v. Williams*, 30 Mass App 543, 551, 571 NE2d 29, 33 (1991) (defendant may waive privilege by testifying about the matters).

Nontestimonial evidence such as scientific and objective psychological test results obtained during a court-ordered examination are not privileged either under GL 233, §23B, or the privilege against self-incrimination. *Blaisdell v. Com.*, supra, 372 Mass at 759, 765, 767-769, 364 NE2d at 196, 199, 201-202; *Com. v. Marshall*, 373 Mass 65, 68, 364 NE2d 1237, 1241 (1977). See also Mass R Crim P 14(b)(2)(B)(ii).

Psychiatric evaluations may not be introduced against a juvenile in the course of proceedings to retain custody beyond age 18 (see GL 120, §17) unless the juvenile is warned, when interviewed, that the results of the interview may be used against him. *Department of Youth Services v. A Juvenile*, 398 Mass 516, 524-527, 499 NE2d 812, 817-818 (1986); *Com. v. Traylor*, 29 Mass App 584, 590 n.2, 563 NE2d 243, 247 n.2 (1990). On the applicability of the constitutional privilege against self-incrimination to court-ordered psychiatric evaluations held in connection with juvenile transfer hearings, GL 119, §61, see *Com. v. Wayne*, 414 Mass 218, 226-232, 606 NE2d 1323, 1328-1332 (1993).

§13.5.6   *Confidential Communications to Sexual Assault and Domestic Violence Counselors*

GL 233, §20J, provides:

> A sexual assault counsellor shall not disclose [a] confidential communication [defined as information transmitted in confidence by and between a victim of sexual assault and a sexual assault counsellor by a means which does not disclose the information to a person other than a person present for the benefit of the victim, or to those to whom disclosure of such information is reasonably necessary to the counselling and assisting of such victim], without the prior written consent of the victim; provided, however, that nothing in this chapter shall be construed to limit the defendant's right of cross-examination of such counsellor in a civil or criminal proceeding if such counsellor testifies with such written consent.
>
> Such confidential communications shall not be subject to discovery and shall be inadmissible in any criminal or civil proceeding without the prior written consent of the victim to whom the report, record, working paper or memorandum relates.

Unlike the privileges pertaining to psychotherapists and social workers discussed above (see §13.5.2 and 13.5.3, supra), the privilege created by GL 233, §20J, has no statutory exceptions (other than the consent of the victim), and has thus been characterized as "absolute." See *Com. v. Two Juveniles*, 397 Mass 261, 265, 491 NE2d 234, 237 (1986). See also *Com. v. Stockhammer*, 409 Mass 867, 883, 570 NE2d 992, 1002 (1991); *Com. v. Jones*, 404 Mass 339, 342, 535 NE2d 221, 223 (1989); *Com. v. Gauthier*, 32 Mass App 130, 135, 586 NE2d 34, 37-38 (1992).

Nonetheless, "in certain circumstances the absolute privilege expressed in §20J . . . must yield to the constitutional right of a criminal defendant to have access to privileged communications." *Com. v. Two Juveniles*, supra, 397 Mass at 266, 491 NE2d at 238. But see *Com. v. Giacalone*, 24

Mass App 166, 170, 507 NE2d 769, 772 (1987) (no sufficient showing made to justify resort to privileged records).
In *Com. v. Fuller,* 423 Mass 216, 667 NE2d 847 (1996),
discussed fully in §13.5.4, supra, the court established the
procedure to be followed and the standards to be applied
when a defendant seeks access to the complainant's rape
counseling records. These procedures are also to be followed with regard to requests for information protected by
the domestic counselor privilege, GL 233, §20K, discussed
immediately below. See *Com. v. Tripolone,* 425 Mass 487, 681
NE2d 1216 (1997).

A privilege for rape counseling records has also been
recognized under federal law. See *United States v. Lowe,* 948
F Supp 97 (D Mass 1996).

GL 233, §20K, provides:

> A domestic violence victims' counselor shall not dis-
> close . . . confidential communications without the prior
> written consent of the victim, except as herinafter provided.
> Such confidential communication shall not be subject to
> discovery in any civil, legislative or adminstrative proceeding
> without the prior written consent of the victim to whom
> such confidential communication relates. In criminal ac-
> tions such confidential communications shall be subject to
> discovery and shall be admissible as evidence but only to the
> extent of information contained therein which is exculpa-
> tory in relation to the defendant; provided, however, that
> the court shall first examine such confidential communica-
> tion and shall determine whether or not such exculpatory
> information is therein contained before allowing such dis-
> covery or the introduction of such evidence.

§13.6   Priest-Penitent

There is no priest-penitent privilege at common law. *Com.
v. Drake,* 15 Mass 161 (1818). A privilege is established by
GL 233, §20A, which provides:

> A priest, rabbi or ordained or licensed minister of any church or an accredited Christian Science practitioner shall not, without the consent of the person making the confession, be allowed to disclose a confession made to him in his professional character, in the course of discipline enjoined by the rules or practice of the religious body to which he belongs; nor shall a priest, rabbi or ordained or licensed minister of any church or an accredited Christian Science practitioner testify as to any communication made to him by any person in seeking religious or spiritual advice or comfort, or as to his given advice thereon in the course of his professional duties or in his professional character, without the consent of such person.

The word "communication" in the statute is not limited to conversation and includes other acts by which ideas may be transmitted from one person to another. *Com. v. Zezima*, 365 Mass 238, 241, 310 NE2d 590, 592 (1974) (defendant's display of gun to clergyman may have constituted "communication").

A penitent may waive the privilege, and as a result the priest may be required to disclose confidential communications. See, e.g., *Com. v. Kane*, 388 Mass 128, 135-138, 445 NE2d 598, 602-603 (1983).

Unlike the psychotherapist-patient privilege (see §13.5.2), the priest-penitent privilege is absolute, indicating that the "legislative concern for the inviolability of the communications [protected] is more substantial." Consequently, courts should be cautious in accepting arguments of waiver by an executor or administrator of the deceased. See *Ryan v. Ryan*, 419 Mass 86, 95-96, 642 NE2d 1028, 1034-1035 (1994).

Proposed Mass R Evid 505 would expand the "religious privilege" by including "other similar functionary of a religious organization" in its definition of "clergyman," as well as "an individual reasonably believed so to be by the person consulting him." Proposed Mass R Evid 505(a)(1). The Rule provides that a person holding the privilege may bar disclosure by third parties, 505(b), and that the privilege survives the death of the claimant, 505(c), matters upon which GL 233, §20A, is silent.

§13.7   Deliberations of Jurors and Judicial Officers/Extraneous Influences upon Jury Deliberations/Post-Verdict Interviews/Attorney as Witness

The deliberations of judicial or quasi-judicial bodies may not be testified to by members of the bodies. *Philips v. Town of Marblehead*, 148 Mass 326, 330, 19 NE 547, 549 (1889) (deliberations of selectmen acting in a quasi judicial capacity assessing value of land taken by the town); *Day v. Crowley*, 341 Mass 666, 669-670, 172 NE2d 251, 253 (1961) (judge cannot properly state the secret and unexpressed reasons which actuated his decision) (citation omitted).

Grand and petit jurors are not permitted to testify as to opinions expressed or discussions occurring during deliberations. *Markee v. Biasetti*, 410 Mass 785, 789, 575 NE2d 1083, 1085 (1991) ("To uphold the integrity of the verdict and to keep the jury free from unwarranted intrusions, juror testimony is generally not admissible to impeach the jury's verdict."); *Philips v. Marblehead*, supra, 148 Mass at 330, 19 NE at 549. See also *Com. v. Geagan*, 339 Mass 487, 499, 159 NE2d 870, 879 (1959) (no inquiry permitted into grand jury deliberations); GL 277, §5, and Mass R Crim P 5(d) (secrecy of grand jury); *Globe Newspaper Co. v. Police Commissioner of Boston*, 419 Mass 852, 865-866, 648 NE2d 419, 428-429 (1995).

It has been held that jurors are competent witnesses to prove an error in the recording of their verdict. *Cassamasse v. J. G. Lamotte & Sons, Inc.*, 391 Mass 315, 318, 461 NE2d 785, 788 (1984); *Capen v. Stoughton*, 82 Mass (16 Gray) 364 (1860). See also *Latino v. Crane Rental Co.*, 417 Mass 426, 429-430, 630 NE2d 591 (1994) (judge entitled to conduct inquiry of jury to determine whether they had agreed on the special verdicts they announced). But see *Com. v.*

Brown, 367 Mass 24, 27-29, 323 NE2d 902, 905 (1975) (proof other than testimony of jurors may be received to correct formal or clerical error in recording of verdict); *Lapham v. Eastern Massachusetts Street Railway Co.*, 343 Mass 489, 492-493, 179 NE2d 589, 591 (1962) (same). Compare *Carzis v. Hassey*, 6 Mass App 13, 15-16, 371 NE2d 1375, 1377 (1978) (verdicts regular on face cannot be disturbed on basis of foreman's representations of jury's intentions).

Jurors may not testify as to the internal decision-making process of jury deliberations. They may, however, give testimony about extraneous influences or matters (such as unauthorized views[1] or facts communicated by a third party) that may have improperly tainted the deliberations.[2] See *Com. v. Fidler*, 377 Mass 192, 385 NE2d 513 (1979) (extensive discussion of authorities; judge properly refused to consider portions of juror affidavit concerning matters discussed during deliberations, but allegation that another juror referred to fact not in evidence indicated possibility of extraneous influence and entitled defendant to hearing); *Com. v. Cuffie*, 414 Mass 632, 634-638, 609 NE2d 437, 438-440 (1993) (judge erred in inquiring into deliberative processes of jury to determine potential influence of juror who allegedly made unauthorized view of crime scene). Compare *Com. v. Dixon*, 395 Mass 149, 479 NE2d 159 (1985) (assertion that juror's husband had conversations with some witnesses during course of trial and made them known to juror required trial judge to investigate possibility of extraneous influence) and *Com. v. Hunt*, 392 Mass 28, 37-43, 465 NE2d 1195, 1201-1205 (1984) (& citations) (juror's independent knowledge of defendant's criminal record, when established through testimony of other jurors, is an extraneous factor that may be used to impeach verdict) with *Com. v. Drumgold*, 423 Mass 230, 260-261, 668 NE2d 300, 320-321 (1996) (discussion among jurors about

---

§13.7 [1] For further discussion of views, see §11.9, supra.

[2] For a discussion of the issue of juror impartiality prior to empanelment, see §3.14, supra.

option of mistrial not "extraneous influence;" court officer's remark that he hoped alternate juror favoring mistrial "is not on the deliberating jury or else this trial will be dragged on and it is already costing the state too much money" did not qualify as extraneous influence so to warrant mistrial), *Com. v. Kamara*, 422 Mass 614, 664 NE2d 825 (1996) (court employed proper procedures upon being told by juror during deliberations that another juror had said she knew defendant, he was member of gang, and she thought he was guilty), *Com. v. Hanlon*, 44 Mass App 810, 816, 694 NE2d 358, 364 (1998) (videotape of post-trial television news interview with jurors could not be used to attack verdict), *Com. v. Hynes*, 40 Mass App 927, 664 NE2d 864 (1996) (court properly denied defendant's request for post-verdict inquiry of juror where juror merely wrote letter to judge claiming to have struggled with illness similar to defendant's and stating that jury was in deliberation for quite awhile because of juror's concern about rehabilitation available to defendant upon conviction), *Com. v. Royster*, 15 Mass App 970, 446 NE2d 1078 (1983) (trial judge committed error when he granted new trial based on juror assertion that she was intimidated by fellow jurors into voting to convict, because that did not constitute external influence), and *Com. v. Scanlan*, 9 Mass App 173, 182-184, 400 NE2d 1265, 1271-1272 (1980) (& cases cited) (judge properly refused to interrogate jurors where allegations were that they failed to follow judge's instructions not to discuss case with one another until deliberations). See also *Com. v. Maltais*, 387 Mass 79, 91, 438 NE2d 847, 854 (1982) (judge properly concluded after inquiry that conversation between jury foreman and another juror regarding weight to be given expert's answer did not taint jury); *Com. v. Schoen*, 24 Mass App 731, 512 NE2d 1157 (1987) (judge properly denied motion for mistrial where he thoroughly interrogated jurors concerning allegation of extraneous influence and found none); *Com. v. Jones*, 15 Mass App 692, 694-696, 448 NE2d 400, 402 (1983) (defendant did not suffer prejudice from unauthorized views of scene by some jurors). See generally Greaney, *Juror Impeachment and Post-Verdict Interrogation of Jurors,* 64 Mass L Rev 85 (1979).

Evidence of a juror's racially or ethnically prejudiced comments during deliberations presents a "difficult case" of distinguishing extraneous factors from internal deliberative processes. See *Com. v. Tavares,* 385 Mass 140, 153-157, 430 NE2d 1198, 1208 (1982) (trial judge properly concluded that jury was impartial notwithstanding comments). While juror bias is generally not an "extraneous matter" within the *Fidler* rule, see *Com. v. Grant,* 391 Mass 645, 651-653, 464 NE2d 33, 38 (1984) (daughter of juror in rape trial had been rape victim ten years earlier), a juror affidavit asserting that three other jurors made racist verbal attacks on defendant throughout deliberations raised a question about defendant's fundamental right to a fair trial by an impartial jury and thus required a hearing to determine truth of assertions. See also *Com. v. Laguer,* 410 Mass 89, 94-99, 571 NE2d 371, 375-377 (1991) (affirming denial of motion for new trial on judge's findings that juror's allegations of ethnically oriented statements were not true); *Com. v. Delp,* 41 Mass App 435, 672 NE2d 114 (1996) (trial judge, viewing juror's post-verdict testimony concerning his own bias against defendant because of his homosexuality, properly denied motion for new trial).

"[J]uror testimony is admissible to establish the existence of an improper influence on the jury, but is not admissible to show the role which the improper influence played in the jury's decisions." *Com. v. Fidler,* supra, 377 Mass at 196, 385 NE2d at 516. "[A]ny inquiry into whether any juror was actually influenced would violate the principle . . . that inquiry into the subjective mental process of jurors is impermissible." *Com. v. Smith,* 403 Mass 489, 497, 531 NE2d 556, 561 (1988). See also *Cassamasse v. J. G. Lamotte & Sons, Inc.,* supra, 391 Mass at 317-318, 461 NE2d at 787 (& citations). Proposed Mass R Evid 606[3] is in accord. The judge reviewing the matter is to determine, therefore, not the *actual* effect the extraneous material had on the jury's deliberations, but whether the extraneous matter might have affected the verdict of a hypothetical average jury. *Com. v. Cuffie*, supra, 414 Mass at 637, 609 NE2d at 439; *Com. v. Fidler*, supra, 377 Mass at 201, 385 NE2d at 519; *Markee v. Biasetti*, supra, 410 Mass at 789, 575 NE2d at 1085; *Fitzpatrick v. Allen*, 410 Mass 791, 796, 575 NE2d 750, 753 (1991); *Com. v. Kamara*, 37 Mass App 769, 643 NE2d 1056 (1994) (upon determining that highly prejudicial extraneous information concerning defendant's gang membership had entered jury room, judge erred in questioning individual jurors about its impact and refusing to order new trial based on their responses).

Post-verdict interviews of jurors by counsel, litigants, or their agents must be conducted under the supervision and direction of the judge; the jurors may not be independently contacted. Counsel may, however, investigate unsolicited information to determine whether it should be brought to the judge's attention. *Com. v. Fidler*, supra, 377 Mass at 202-204, 385 NE2d at 520; *Com. v. Dixon*, supra, 395 Mass at 153, 479 NE2d at 162-163. See also SJC Rule 3:07, Rules of Prof Conduct Rule 3.5(d) (formerly Supreme Judicial Court Rule 307, DR 7-108). For the view that Rule 3.5(d) may violate a criminal defendant's constitutional rights, see Wilkins, The New Massachusetts Rules of Pro-

---

[3] PMRE 606(b) provides:

> Upon an inquiry into the validity of a verdict or indictment, a juror may not testify as to any matter or statement occurring during the course of the jury's deliberations or to the effect of anything upon his or any other juror's mind or emotions as influencing him to assent to or dissent from the verdict or indictment or concerning his mental processes in connection therewith, except that a juror may testify on the question whether extraneous prejudicial information was improperly brought to the jury's attention or whether any outside influence was improperly brought to bear upon any juror. Nor may his affidavit or evidence of any statement by him concerning a matter about which he would be precluded from testifying be received for these purposes.

See also Fed R Evid 606.

fessional Conduct: An Overview, 82 Mass L Rev 261, 264 (1997).

The judge must be provided with sufficiently clear, detailed, and reliable information to recognize the need for supervised post-verdict inquiry. *Cassamasse v. J.G. Lamotte & Sons, Inc.*, supra, 391 Mass 318-319, 461 NE2d at 788 (affidavit of plaintiff's counsel containing hearsay conclusory statements from unidentified source insufficient); *Com. v. Taylor*, 32 Mass App 570, 579-580, 591 NE2d 1108, 1114-1115 (1992) (party requesting investigation must make colorable showing that extrinsic influence may have had impact on jury's impartiality). See also *Com. v. Luna*, 418 Mass 749, 754, 641 NE2d 1050, 1053 (1994) (trial judge properly refused to allow post-verdict interviews of jurors based on claim that during deliberations juror indicated he was prejudiced against police officers, as that was not extraneous influence).

Once it is determined that the jury has been exposed to extraneous matter, the burden shifts to the non-moving party to show that there was no prejudice. The burden on the Commonwealth in a criminal case is to show beyond a reasonable doubt that no prejudice resulted to the defendant. *Com. v. Cuffie*, supra, 414 Mass at 637, 609 NE2d at 439. In a civil case, a lesser standard of "no reasonable likelihood of prejudice" is imposed. *Fitzpatrick v. Allen*, supra, 410 Mass at 794-795, 575 NE2d at 752. Where, however, there was "active juror participation in an effort to resolve key issues by resort to material not in evidence," prejudice is presumed and a new trial must be granted. *Fitzpatrick v. Allen*, supra, 410 Mass at 796, 575 NE2d at 753 (jurors at medical malpractice trial consulted home reference medical book not in evidence); *Markee v. Biasetti*, supra, 410 Mass 789, 575 NE2d at 1085 (at least two jurors conducted unauthorized on-site investigation of accident scene).

The disqualification of jurors and judicial officers to disclose deliberations should be distinguished from the disqualification of such persons from testifying in a proceeding in which they are acting. See Proposed Mass R Evid 605 ("The judge presiding at the trial may not testify in that trial as a witness.") and 606(a) ("A member of the jury may not testify as a witness before that jury in the trial of the case in which he is sitting as a juror.")

§13.8   Informers/Surveillance Location

Communications made to a district attorney or other prosecuting officer in order to secure the enforcement of law are privileged, as is the identity of the informer. *Com. v. Bakoian*, 412 Mass 295, 306-307, 588 NE2d 667, 673-674 (1992); *District Attorney for Norfolk District v. Flatley*, 419 Mass 507, 510, 646 NE2d 127, 129 (1995); *Worthington v. Scribner*, 109 Mass 487 (1872) (defendants in malicious prosecution case could not be compelled to answer interrogatories concerning information given treasury officials regarding alleged illegal importation by plaintiff).

As stated in *Worthington*:

> It is the duty of every citizen to communicate to his government any information which he has of the commission of an offence against its laws. To encourage him in performing this duty without fear of consequences, the law holds such information to be among the secrets of state, and leaves the question how far and under what circumstances the names of the informers and the channel of communication shall be suffered to be known, to the absolute discretion of the government, to be exercised according to its views of what the interests of the public require. Courts of justice therefore will not compel or allow the discovery of such information, either by the subordinate officer to whom it is given, by the informer himself, or by any other person, without the permission of the government. The evidence is excluded, not for the protection of the witness or of the party in the particular case, but upon general grounds of public policy because of the confidential nature of such communications.

109 Mass at 488-489. See also *Hutchinson v. New England Tel. & Tel. Co.*, 350 Mass 188, 191, 214 NE2d 57, 59 (1966).

The privilege not only protects the release of the name of the informant, but also the disclosure of details that would in effect identify the informant. See *Com. v. John*, 36 Mass App 702, 706, 635 NE2d 261, 264 (1994) (& citations). The privilege does not apply where the informer's identity or the substance of the communication has already been disclosed. *Pihl v. Morris*, 319 Mass 577, 579-580, 66 NE2d 804, 806 (1946); *Com. v. McMiller*, 29 Mass App 392, 406, 560 NE2d 732, 739-740 (1990) (newspaper article disclosed informer's identity). See also *Com. v. Johnson*, 365 Mass 534, 544-545, 313 NE2d 571, 577-578 (1974) (discussion of informer privilege in context of trial court's refusal to elicit identity of other participants in crime from prosecution witness).

Where the disclosure of an informer's identity or of the contents of his communication is necessary to the defense of the criminal case, as where the informer was a participant in or witness to the crime, the privilege must give way. See *Roviaro v. United States*, 353 US 53, 60-61, 77 S Ct 623, 1 L Ed 2d 639 (1957) (disclosure required where "relevant and helpful" to defense or "essential to a fair determination of a cause"); *Com. v. Healis*, 31 Mass App 527, 529-532, 580 NE2d 1047, 1048-1050 (1991) (judge erred in denying defendant's motion for disclosure of informer where he was active participant in crime, the only non-government witness to events, and he had arranged meeting at which arrest occurred); *Com. v. Ennis*, 1 Mass App 499, 301 NE2d 589 (1973) (extensive discussion of issue; privilege inapplicable where informer had arranged sale of marijuana from defendant to police officer and was only other person present).

Where the informant did not participate in the crime and acted only as a tipster, the privilege will not be overriden. See *Com. v. Brzezinski*, 405 Mass 401, 408, 540 NE2d 1325, 1330 (1989). See also *Com. v. Signorine*, 404 Mass 400, 407-408, 535 NE2d 601, 606 (1989) (judge did not abuse discretion in limiting cross-examination of two prosecution witnesses regarding identity of confidential informant where evidence sought had no tendency to exculpate defendant); *Com. v. Mott*, 2 Mass App 47, 53, 308 NE2d 557, 561 (1974) (judge properly denied motion for disclosure where informant did not participate in crime charged and continued to assist police in narcotics investigations); *Com. v. Swenson*, 368 Mass 268, 331 NE2d 893 (1975) (although fact that informer was eyewitness to crime weighs heavily in favor of disclosure, defendant failed to meet burden of demonstrating disclosure was necessary to defense).

For an extensive discussion of the problem of police perjury regarding informants, see *Com. v. Lewin*, 405 Mass 566, 542 NE2d 275, 277 (1989) (vacating order dismissing indictments because Commonwealth failed to produce informant allegedly relied upon in obtaining search warrant) (Liacos, CJ, & Abrams, J, dissenting). See also *Com. v. Nelson*, 26 Mass App 794, 536 NE2d 1094 (1989) (vacating order dismissing indictments for Commonwealth's refusal to disclose identity of informer).

For a discussion of the government's duty to produce an informer, as distinguished from its duty to merely disclose, see *Com. v. Curcio*, 26 Mass App 738, 746-749, 532 NE2d 699, 704-705 (1989); *Com. v. Manrique*, 31 Mass App 597, 599-602, 581 NE2d 1036, 1038-1039 (1991) (rejecting claim that defendant was denied access to informer).

The privilege generally applies to prevent a criminal defendant from obtaining the identification of an informer where the issue is not guilt or innocence but rather the supression of illegally obtained evidence. See *McCray v. Illinois*, 386 US 300 (1967); *Com. v. Snyder*, 413 Mass 521, 532-533, 597 NE2d 1363, 1369-1370 (1992); *Com. v. Ennis*, supra, 1 Mass App at 501, 301 NE2d at 590 (& citations). Upon a sufficient preliminary showing to demonstrate that the affidavit in support of a warrant contained a deliberate or reckless misstatement of facts (under the principles discussed in *Franks v. Deleware*, 438 US 154 (1978)), however, the court may order disclosure of the informant, preferably during an in camera procedure. "The conflict between the government's interest in protection of the informant and a defendant's interest in proving that the affiant lied concerning either the existence of an informant or what the informant said may be resolved by the judge conducting a preliminary hearing at which the affiant testifies but without revealing the informant's identity. Further, if it appears necessary, the judge may hold an in camera hearing in which he questions the affiant further, and, if he deems it appropriate, the informant himself." *Com. v. Douzanis*, 384 Mass 434, 441, 425 NE2d 326, 331 (1981). See also *Com. v. Amral*, 407 Mass 511, 554 NE2d 1189 (1990) (where defendant by affidavit asserts facts that cast reasonable doubt on veracity of material representations made by affiant concerning informer, judge must order in camera hearing to interrogate affiant and, if necessary, informer, to determine whether *Franks* hearing is required); *Com. v. Salvati*, 420 Mass 499, 505-506, 650 NE2d 782, 786 (1995) (same); *Com. v. Ramirez*, 416 Mass 41, 53-54, 617 NE2d 983, 990 (1993) (same); *Com. v. Signorine*, 404 Mass 400, 405-407, 535 NE2d 601, 605-606 (1989) (defendant's affidavits failed to demonstrate that either affiant or informer made any misstatement of fact, and thus judge properly denied motion for disclosure of informer); *Com. v. Abdelnour*, 11 Mass App 531, 535-537, 417 NE2d 463, 466-467 (1981) (request for disclosure in warrant affidavit cases should be denied unless defendant makes "adequate threshold demonstration" of fabrication).

Where the judge concludes that the defendant challenging the seizure of evidence should have the opportunity to question the informant, the Commonwealth presumably has the option of making disclosure or accepting dismissal of the charges. *Com. v. Douzanis*, supra, 384 Mass at 442 n.13, 425 NE2d at 332 n.13.

The informant of course retains the Fifth Amendment right against self-incrimination if called as a witness. See *Com. v. Zuluaga*, 43 Mass App 629, 641 n.14, 686 NE2d 463, 472 n.14 (1997).

In the absence of a specific request by the defendant, the Commonwealth is not bound to disclose that it had used an informer or to disclose the identity of the informer. *Com. v. Monteiro*, 396 Mass 123, 129, 484 NE2d 999, 1004 (1985); *Com. v. Ramos*, 30 Mass App 915, 917, 566 NE2d 1141, 1143 (1991).

Disclosure of the informant may be required in a prison disciplinary hearing where relevant to the defense. See *Nelson v. Commissioner of Correction*, 390 Mass 379, 394 n.19, 456 NE2d 1100, 1109 n.19 (1983).

Proposed Mass R Evid 509 is generally consistent with present practice regarding the informer privilege.[1]

A "surveillance location privilege" has been recognized which permits the prosecution in appropriate cases to withhold the exact location from which observations of

---

§13.8   [1]"The United States or a state or subdivision thereof has a privilege to refuse to disclose the identity of a person who has furnished information relating to or assisting in an investigation of a possible violation of a law to a law enforcement officer or member of a legislative committee or its staff conducting an investigation." PMRE 509(a).

"If it appears from the evidence in the case or from other showing by a party that an informer may be able to give testimony necessary to a fair determination of the issue of guilt or innocence in a criminal case or of a material issue on the merits in a civil case to which the public entity is a party, and the informed public entity invokes the privilege, the judge shall give the public entity an opportunity to show in camera facts relevant to determining whether the informer can, in fact, supply that testimony. The showing will ordinarily be in the form of affidavits, but the judge may direct that testimony be taken if he finds that the matter cannot be resolved satisfactorily upon affidavit. If the judge finds that there is a reasonable probability that the informer can give the testimony, and the public entity elects not to disclose his identity, the judge on motion of the defendant in a criminal case shall dismiss the charges to which the testimony would relate, and the judge may do so on his own motion. In civil cases, he may make any order that justice requires. . . ." PMRE 509(c)(2).

"If information from an informer is relied upon to establish the legality of the means by which evidence was obtained and the judge is not satisfied that the information was received from an informer reasonably believed to be reliable or credible, he may require the identity of the informer disclosed. The judge shall, on request of the public entity, direct that the disclosure be made in camera. . . ." PMRE 509(c)(3).

criminal activity were made. See *Com. v. Lugo,* 406 Mass 565, 570-574, 548 NE2d 1263, 1265-1267 (1990). The privilege must give way when disclosure would provide "material evidence needed by the defendant for a fair presentation of his case to the jury." 406 Mass at 574 (disclosure required where prosecution's entire case rested on the officer's credibility and ability to observe from hidden location, his testimony was not corroborated in any respect, and inconsistencies existed as to location and whether it provided clear view). See also *Com. v. Hernandez,* 421 Mass 272, 275, 656 NE2d 1237, 1239 (1995) (disclosure of surveillance location required where testimony of observing officers was crucial to Commonwealth's case). Moreover, the Commonwealth's interest in preserving the confidentiality of a surveillance point cannot justify exclusion of the defendants from a portion of their trial during which a police officer testified concerning the location from which he observed the unlawful sales of drugs. *Com. v. Rios,* 412 Mass 208, 588 NE2d 6 (1992).

A defendant seeking to overcome the surveillance location privilege must make an affirmative showing that disclosure of the information would provide evidence needed to defend the case. It is not enough simply to assert such a need. See *Com. v. Grace,* 43 Mass App 905, 906, 681 NE2d 1265, 1267 (1997).

§13.9　Journalists

Massachusetts does not recognize a privilege of a news reporter to refuse to disclose the identity of or communications with a confidential news source. No such privilege exists at common law or under the federal or state constitutions. See *In re John Doe Grand Jury Investigation,* 410 Mass 596, 598, 574 NE2d 373, 375 (1991); *Com. v. Corsetti,* 387 Mass 1, 438 NE2d 805 (1982) (newsman has no constitutional right to refuse to testify at criminal proceeding concerning information acquired in confidence, and no common-law privilege to refuse to testify as to information already disclosed in newspaper article); *In re Roche*, 381 Mass 624, 411 NE2d 466 (1980) (newsman not privileged by First Amendment to refuse to divulge at deposition in civil matter his confidential sources used in preparing investigative report); *In re Pappas*, 358 Mass 604, 266 NE2d 297 (1971) (no newsman's privilege under First Amendment to refuse to appear and testify before court or grand jury).

The Supreme Judicial Court has refused to establish an evidentiary privilege by rule, see *Petition for the Promulgation of Rules Regarding the Protection of Confidential News Sources and Other Unpublished Information*, 395 Mass 164, 479 NE2d 154 (1985), and the Legislature has failed on several ocasions to enact a statutory press shield law. See *In re Roche*, supra, 381 Mass at 635 n.13, 411 NE2d at 474 n.13; *Petition for the Promulgation of Rules*, supra, 395 Mass at 164, 479 NE2d at 157. Accordingly, a reporter must appear and testify when summonsed.

The Supreme Judicial Court has indicated, however, that "some protection" is provided by the First Amendment to the United States Constitution for "any person" who gathers information and prepares it for expression. *In re Roche*, supra, 381 Mass at 632, 411 NE2d at 472. Three justices noted their "willingness to consider, in future cases, whether the central role a free discussion of public issues plays in a self-governing society requires, as a matter of Massachusetts practice, that persons addressing such issues be afforded more clearly defined protection against intrusive discovery than that provided by the discretionary supervision contemplated by Mass R Civ P 26(c)." 381 Mass at 638-639, 411 NE2d at 476.

While the Supreme Judicial Court has not adopted a shield against all sanctions for failure to provide confidential information, it has nonetheless recognized that "the availability of alternative remedies to compelled disclosure should be considered. Likewise, a judge is obliged to consider the effect of compelled disclosure on values underlying the First Amendment and art. 16. Thus, a judge has the authority to prevent 'harassing' or the 'needless disclosure of confidential relationships.'" *Petition for the Promulgation of Rules*, supra, 395 Mass at 171-172, 479 NE2d at 158 (citations omitted). Moreover, the First Amendment protects reporters against grand jury investigations initiated or conducted in bad faith. *Branzburg v. Hayes*, supra, 408 US at 707.

In ruling on a motion to quash a subpoena issued to a news reporter to discover the identity of a confidential news source, a judge must balance the public interest in having every person's evidence against the public interest in the free flow of information. *In re John Doe Grand Jury Investigation*, supra, 410 Mass at 599, 574 NE2d at 375 (judge properly allowed motions to quash grand jury subpoenas). The threshold inquiry is whether the unwilling witness has made "some showing that the asserted damage to the free flow of information is more than speculative or theoretical." Id. (citation omitted). Such a showing is made where the witness demonstrates that he would not have received the information without the promise of anonymity to the source and that his future news-gathering ability would be impaired if he violated the promise. 410 Mass at 600. In assessing the public interest in obtaining the evidence, the judge should consider the particular circumstances of the grand jury inquiry and the importance of the evidence sought.

On several occasions the Supreme Judicial Court has affirmed the Superior Court's refusal to compel investigative news reporters to disclose confidential sources. See *Com. v. Bui*, 419 Mass 392, 402, 645 NE2d 689, 695 (1995); *In re John Doe Grand Jury Investigation*, supra, 410 Mass at 596-597, 574 NE2d at 373; *Sinnott v. Boston Retirement Board*, 402 Mass 581, 524 NE2d 100 (1988). See also *Ayash v. Dana-Farber Cancer Institute*, 46 Mass 384, 706 NE2d 316 (1999) (finding that reporter had made threshold showing against disclosure of sources, and remanding for performance of balancing test).

§13.10 Public Records and Reports; "Governmental Privilege"

Public records (as defined by GL 4, §7(26)) are subject to inspection and copying and thus are not privileged from disclosure. See GL 66, §10 (Public Records Act). See generally *Globe Newspaper Co. v. Police Commissioner of Boston*, 419 Mass 852, 648 NE2d 419 (1995) (extensive discussion of exemptions); *District Attorney for Norfolk District v. Flatley*, 419 Mass 507, 646 NE2d 127 (1995); *Lambert v. Executive Director of Judicial Nominating Council*, 425 Mass 406, 681 NE2d 285 (1997) (questionnaire completed by applicants for judicial appointment not public record); *Attorney General v. Collector of Lynn*, 377 Mass 151, 385 NE2d 505 (1979); *Hastings & Sons Publishing Co. v. City Treasurer of Lynn*, 374 Mass 812, 375 NE2d 299 (1978).

GL 4, §7(26) has, however, the following exemptions:

- records "related solely to internal personnel rules and practices of the government unit, provided however, that such records shall be withheld only to the extent that proper performance of necessary governmental functions requires such withholding;" §7(26)(b)
- "personnel and medical files or information; also any other materials or data relating to a specifically named individual, the disclosure of which may constitute an unwarranted invasion of personal privacy;" §7(26)(c)[1]

---

§13.10 [1]Application of the privacy exemption requires a balancing between a claimed invasion of privacy and the interest of the public in disclosure. See generally *Globe Newspaper Co. v. Police Comm'r of Boston*, supra, 419 Mass at 857-868, 648 NE2d at 425-430 (transcripts and audio tapes of citizen witness statements and police officer statements compiled by police internal affairs division not protected by privacy exemption). Compare *Globe Newspaper Co. v. Chief Medical Examiner*, 404 Mass 132, 533 NE2d 1356 (1989) (reports of autopsies conducted by medical examiner exempt from disclosure), *Globe Newspaper Co. v. Boston Retirement Board*, 388 Mass 427, 446 NE2d 1051 (1983) (medical and

- "inter-agency or intra-agency memoranda or letters relating to policy positions being developed by the agency; but this subclause shall not apply to reasonably completed factual studies or reports on which the development of such policy positions has been or may be based;" §7(26)(d)
- "notebooks and other materials prepared by an employee of the Commonwealth which are personal to him and not maintained as part of the files of the governmental unit;" §7(26)(e)
- "investigatory materials necessarily compiled out of the public view by law enforcement or other investigatory officials the disclosure of which materials would probably so prejudice the possibility of effective law enforcement that such disclosure would not be in the public interest;" §7(26)(f)[2]

---

personnel files pertaining to disability pensions exempt where they are of personal nature and relate to particular individual), and *Connolly v. Bromery*, 15 Mass App 661, 447 NE2d 1265 (1983) (written evaluations of faculty and courses by students at public university constitute "personnel files or information" and thus exempt from disclosure) with *Attorney General v. Collector of Lynn*, supra (lists of tax delinquents not "intimate details of a highly personal nature," and not within privacy exemption), *Hastings & Sons Publishing Co. v. City Treasurer of Lynn*, supra (payroll records of municipal employees not within privacy exemption), *Brogan v. School Committee of Westport*, 401 Mass 306, 516 NE2d 159 (1987) (individual absentee records of school employees not records of "personal nature" and not exempt from disclosure), and *Pottle v. School Committee of Braintree*, 395 Mass 861, 482 NE2d 813 (1985) (names and addresses of employees of municipal school department not within privacy exemption). See also *Com. v. Beauchemin*, 410 Mass 181, 185, 571 NE2d 395, 398 (1991) (judge erred in excluding complainant's school records during cross-examination because, although exempt from public disclosure under §7(26)(c), they were lawfully subpoenaed); *Reinstein v. Police Comm'r of Boston*, 378 Mass 281, 292-293, 391 NE2d 881, 885-887 (1979) (privacy exemption not blanket exemption for all records of police department relating to discharge of firearms by officers).

[2] See generally *Globe Newspaper Co. v. Police Comm'r of Boston*, supra, 419 Mass at 857-868, 648 NE2d at 425-430 (transcripts and audio tapes of citizen witness' statements and police officer statements compiled by police internal affairs division not protected by investigatory exemption; certain homicide hotline records within exemption); *District Attorney for*

- "trade secrets or commercial or financial information voluntarily provided to an agency for use in developing governmental policy and upon a promise of confidentiality; but this subclause shall not apply to information submitted as required by law or as a condition of receiving a governmental contract or other benefit;" §7(26)(g)
- proposals and bids to enter into any contract or agreement until the time for the opening of bids; §7(26)(h)
- appraisals of real property until a final agreement is entered into, or litigation arising therefrom is terminated; §7(26)(i)
- the names and addresses of persons applying for firearm permits or firearm identification cards; §7(26)(j)
- materials related to tests and examinations; §7(26)(l)
- certain contracts for hospital or related health care services; §7(26)(m)
- records that are "specifically or by necessary implication exempted from disclosure by statute;" §7(26)(a).

Norfolk District v. Flatley, supra, 419 Mass at 512, 646 NE2d at 130; *WBZ-TV4 v. District Attorney for the Suffolk District,* 408 Mass 595, 603, 562 NE2d 817, 822 (1990) (exemption does not operate to exclude from disclosure all information contained in law enforcement files, but requires case by case consideration of whether access would prejudice law enforcement); *Reinstein v. Police Comm'r of Boston,* supra, 378 Mass at 289-292, 391 NE2d at 882-885 (same); *Bougas v. Chief of Police of Lexington,* 371 Mass 59, 354 NE2d 872 (1976) (police reports and letters to police from private citizens regarding incident resulting in misdemeanor charges exempt from disclosure).

A criminal defendant's right of access to relevant records is not constrained by the exemptions to the public records law. See *Com. v. Wanis,* 426 Mass 639, 690 NE2d 407 (1998) and *Com. v. Rodriguez,* 426 Mass 647, 692 NE2d 1 (1998), holding that a defendant is entitled to statements obtained from percipient witnesses that are contained in police department internal affairs records.

A sampling of the exempting statutes referred to in this provision follows.

GL 66A (Fair Information Practices Act) restricts access to "personal data" maintained by a state agency and not contained in a public record. See, e.g., *Allen v. Holyoke Hospital*, 398 Mass 372, 378-382, 496 NE2d 1368, 1372-1374 (1986) (DSS records containing social worker's personal observations of family of deceased child); *Torres v. Attorney General*, 391 Mass 1, 460 NE2d 1032 (1984) (information derived from DSS client's case file relating to his whereabouts on particular dates). GL 46, §2A, restricts access to "records and returns of children born out of wedlock or abnormal sex births, or fetal deaths."

GL 71B, §3, limits access to special education records to parents, guardians, or persons with custody of the child. But see *Com. v. Figueroa*, 413 Mass 193, 203, 595 NE2d 779, 785-786 (1992) and *Com. v. Gauthier*, 32 Mass App 130, 134-135, 586 NE2d 34, 37 (1992) (where information is relevant to witness's credibility, statutory privilege must yield to defendant's constitutional right to defend himself).

GL 66, §10, exempts from disclosure the home address and home telephone number of law enforcement, judicial, prosecutorial, department of youth services, correctional, and any other public safety and criminal justice personnel; the names of family members of such personnel; and the home address, telephone number, and place of employment or education of crime victims or persons involved in family planning services.

Several statutes limit access to criminal, probation, and juvenile records. See GL 6, §§167-178 (Criminal Offender Record Information System ["CORI"]); GL 94C, §34 (providing for sealing of certain drug offense records); GL 119, §60 (restricting admissibility of juvenile records and proceedings);[3] GL 276, §§100, 100A-C (restricting access to

---

[3]GL 119, §60, does not preclude use of a juvenile record in subsequent sentencing proceedings. *Department of Youth Services v. A Juvenile*, 384 Mass 784, 786-787, 429 NE2d 709, 711 (1981); *Com. v.*

probation records; providing for sealing, expungement, and inadmissibility of certain criminal records).[4] For discussion of the statutory framework pertaining to the maintenance of criminal history records and the statutes authorizing sealing and expungement, see *Com. v. Doe*, 420 Mass 142, 648 NE2d 1255 (1995) (setting out procedures for GL 276, §100C, 2d para., authorizing sealing of records in cases of nolle prosequi or dismissal); *Com. v. Balboni*, 419 Mass 42, 642 NE2d 576 (1994) (sealing statute supersedes expungement remedy for adult defendants); *Com. v. Roe*, 420 Mass 1002, 648 NE2d 744 (1995) (same); *Com. v. Rob-*

Rodriguez, 376 Mass 632, 634-641, 382 NE2d 725, 729-731 (1978) (juvenile records admissible in action, in lieu of sentence, for commitment as sexually dangerous person).

See also GL 119, §60A, which opens to public inspection the records of certain youthful offender proceedings, and GL 6, §78C et seq., the Sexual Offender Registration Act, which sets forth procedures for the dissemination of otherwise confidential information. In *Doe v. Attorney General*, 425 Mass 210, 680 NE2d 92 (1997), the Supreme Judicial Court held that the disclosure provisions of the Sexual Offender Registration Act prevailed over the confidentiality provisions of GL 119. For a discussion of the constitutional limits on GL 119, §60, when the information is relevant to a prosecution witness's bias, see §6.9, supra.

[4]Sealing does not operate to erase the fact of the prior conviction, and such conviction may thus be considered by the police when issuing or revoking firearms licenses. See *Rzeznik v. Chief of Police of Southampton*, 374 Mass 475, 480, 373 NE2d 1128, 1132 (1978). See also *Dickerson v. New Banner Inst., Inc.*, 460 US 103, 103 S Ct 986, 74 L Ed 2d 845 (1983) (provisions of federal gun control law that make it unlawful for person convicted of felony to ship firearm apply even though record is expunged under state law); *Com. v. Doe*, 420 Mass 142, 151 n.9, 648 NE2d 1255, 1260 n.9 (1995) (records sealed pursuant to Section 100C, 2, remain accessible to law enforcement personnel and courts); *Com. v. Roberts*, supra, 39 Mass App at 356, 656 NE2d at 1260-1261. A district court has no authority to direct expungement of a record from the statewide domestic abuse violence record keeping system maintained pursuant to GL 209, §7. See *Vaccaro v. Vacarro*, 425 Mass 153, 680 NE2d 55 (1997).

The provisions of §100C which automatically seal records of cases ending with acquittal or finding of no probable cause have been declared unconstitutional. See *Globe Newspaper Co. v. Pokaski*, 868 F2d 497 (1st Cir 1989) (extensive discussion of sealing statutes).

Sealed records may be admissible to establish bias of the witness. See §6.9, supra.

erts, 39 Mass App 355, 656 NE2d 1260 (1995) (same); *Com. v. Vickey*, 381 Mass 762, 412 NE2d 877 (1980); *Police Commissioner of Boston v. Municipal Court of the Dorchester District*, 374 Mass 640, 374 NE2d 272 (1978); *Com. v. S.M.F.*, 40 Mass App 42, 660 NE2d 701 (1996) (where sealing statutes are not applicable, trial courts retain inherent power to expunge criminal records). See also *Reinstein v. Police Commissioner of Boston*, 378 Mass 281, 293-296, 391 NE2d 881, 888 (1979) (relationship between CORI and GL 66, §10); *New Bedford Standard-Times Publishing Co. v. Clerk of Third District Court*, 377 Mass 404, 387 NE2d 110 (1979) (CORI's applicability to court records).

Reports required to be filed with governmental agencies pursuant to certain statutes are privileged. For example, an employer's report of an accident to the Division of Industrial Accidents required by GL 152, §19, has been held privileged and inadmissible in a tort action arising out of the accident, and on grounds that indicate that many reports required by executive departments or administrative bodies may be similarly privileged. *Gerry v. Worcester Consolidated Street Railway Co.*, 248 Mass 559, 566-568, 143 NE 694, 696 (1924). Agreements for the payment of compensation filed under GL 152, §6, are not admissible in evidence. *Ricciutti v. Sylvania Electric Products, Inc.*, 343 Mass 347, 349, 178 NE2d 857, 859 (1961). A statement by a workers' compensation claimant (either in writing or taken on a recording instrument) and given to the insurer is inadmissible unless a copy of the statement has been furnished to the claimant or his attorney upon request. GL 152, §7B. Medical records from an employer's or insurer's hospital or clinic are similarly inadmissible against the claimant unless provided upon request. GL 152, §20A. Information secured by the Department of Employment and Training is inadmissible except in limited circumstances. GL 151A, §46.

GL 111, §204, protects the confidentiality of proceedings, reports, and records of a hospital's medical peer review committee. See *Com. v. Choate-Symmes Health Services,*

Inc., 406 Mass 27, 545 NE2d 1167 (1989) (hospital not required to produce peer review committee materials in response to subpoena issued by Board of Registration).

The following are open for inspection and not protected from disclosure:

- A corporation's certificate of condition and annual report, filed with the secretary of state of the Commonwealth. *Union Glass Co. v. Somerville*, 228 Mass 202, 203-204, 117 NE 184, 185 (1917); *Brackett v. Com.*, 223 Mass 119, 127, 111 NE 1036, 1040 (1916).
- Communications to a board of assessors stating the value of corporate property. *Union Glass Co. v. Somerville*, supra.
- An accident report filed by a motor vehicle operator as required by GL 90, §26. *Lord v. Registrar of Motor Vehicles*, 347 Mass 608, 199 NE2d 316 (1964). Such reports are generally admissible in personal injury actions. *Genova v. Genova*, 28 Mass App 647, 653, 554 NE2d 1221, 1225 (1990). But see *Kelly v. O'Neil*, 1 Mass App 313, 317-319, 296 NE2d 223, 227 (1973) (hearsay rule limitations). A motorist may properly assert his privilege against self-incrimination in refusing to file an accident report where criminal charges are pending against him. See *Com. v. Sasu*, 404 Mass 596, 536 NE2d 603 (1989).

Whether a particular report will be considered privileged depends upon the court's conclusion as to whether the legislature intended the document to be open to the public, whether it would be fair to permit it to be used, and whether permitting it to be put in evidence would tend to defeat the purpose of the statute by discouraging complete disclosure of information. *Carr v. Howard*, 426 Mass 514, 689 NE2d 1304 (1998) (incident reports protected by peer review committee privilege); *Gerry v. Worcester Consolidated*

Street Railway Co., supra, 248 Mass at 568, 143 NE at 697; *Swatch v. Treat*, 41 Mass App 559, 671 NE2d 1004 (1996) (proceeding before hearing panel of national association of social workers protected by statute).

The Supreme Judicial Court has refused to create a common-law evidentiary "governmental" privilege for documents relating to the development of policy in the executive branch. See *Babets v. Secretary of Human Services*, 403 Mass 230, 526 NE2d 1261 (1988); *District Attorney for Norfolk District v. Flatley*, supra, 419 Mass at 510, 646 NE2d at 129. Among the documents exempted from mandatory disclosure under the Public Records Act discussed above, however, are "inter-agency or intra-agency memoranda or letters relating to policy positions being developed by the agency." GL 4, §7(26)(d). This exemption protects such documents from disclosure only while policy is "being developed" — i.e., while the deliberative process is "ongoing and incomplete." *Babets v. Secretary of Human Services*, supra, 403 Mass at 237 n.8, 526 NE2d at 1266 n.8. Once the process is completed, the documents generated become publicly available. Id.

For a discussion of "executive privilege" in the federal context, see *United States v. Nixon*, 418 US 683, 94 S Ct 3090, 41 L Ed 2d 1039 (1974) (Watergate tapes case); *Clinton v. Jones*, 520 US 681, 703-704, 117 S Ct 1636, 137 L Ed 2d 945 (1997). See also Proposed Mass R Evid 508 (recognizing privileges created by the federal Constitution, 508(a), but providing that "[n]o other governmental privilege is recognized except as created by the Constitution or statutes of the Commonwealth." 508(b)).

§13.11   Tax Returns/Accountant Privilege

GL 62C, §21 (as amended in 1998) generally prohibits public employees from disclosing (to anyone other than the taxpayer or his representative) information set forth in a tax return or document filed with the Commonwealth.

The statute and its predecessor "embody the policy of the Commonwealth to preserve the confidentiality of State tax returns." *Finance Commissioner of Boston v. Commissioner of Revenue*, 383 Mass 63, 71, 417 NE2d 945, 950 (1981) (extensive discussion of GL 62C, §21). Exemptions permit disclosure in the context of tax and certain other enumerated investigations and proceedings. See also GL 62C, §74 (tax preparer nondisclosure provisions).

The courts have recognized a privilege against the disclosure and use in evidence of state tax documents. See *Leave v. Boston Elevated Railway Co.*, 306 Mass 391, 398-403, 28 NE2d 483, 487-489 (1940) (plaintiff privileged to refuse to make individual state income tax returns available to defendant, and such returns would be inadmissible); *James Millar Co. v. Com.*, 251 Mass 457, 464, 146 NE 677, 678 (1925) (corporation excise tax returns properly excluded). See also *In re Hampers*, 651 F2d 19 (1st Cir 1981) (recognizing qualified privilege against disclosure of state tax records in federal grand jury proceeding). The privilege cannot be circumvented by inquiring of the individual who filed the return as to its contents. *James Millar Co. v. Com.*, supra, 251 Mass at 464, 146 NE at 679. But see *Com. v. Ventola*, 351 Mass 703, 221 NE2d 395 (1966) (defendant's admission that he failed to report alleged income admissible to impeach testimony that he had been employed). The fact that municipal payroll records reveal information that could also be found in tax returns does not prevent disclosure of the payroll information as a public record. *Hastings & Sons Publishing Co. v. City Treasurer of Lynn*, 373 Mass 812, 820 n.10, 375 NE2d 299, 304-305 n.10 (1978).

Although federal officials and certain other persons receiving tax information must preserve the confidentiality of tax returns (see 26 USC §6103), copies of federal tax returns in the hands of the taxpayer are not absolutely privileged. *Town Taxi, Inc. v. Police Commissioner of Boston*, 377 Mass 576, 586-588, 387 NE2d 129, 135-136 (1979) (& cases cited). Such returns may be discovered from the taxpayer on a sufficient showing of need. Id.; *Finance Com-*

missioner of Boston v. McGrath, 343 Mass 754, 766-768, 180 NE2d 808, 816-817 (1962). See also *Com. v. Garabedian*, 8 Mass App 442, 446, 395 NE2d 467, 470 (1979) (federal income tax returns admissible in prosecution for failure to file state returns); *Com. v. Ianelli*, 17 Mass App 1011, 1013, 460 NE2d 203, 206 (1984) (no error in admitting defendant's tax returns through his accountant).

Neither the Proposed Massachusetts Rules of Evidence nor the Federal Rules of Evidence deal with the matter of the admissibility of tax returns.

Accountants are required to maintain the confidentiality of information communicated by clients relating to and in connection with services rendered. GL 112, §78E (but exempting disclosures required in court proceedings and investigations). The Internal Revenue Service Restructuring and Reform Act of 1998 creates a privilege for accountants to refuse to disclose client communications in noncriminal matters before the IRS or in federal court. Internal Revenue Code §7525.

§13.12   Political Vote

In order to encourage participation in the election process, the Supreme Judicial Court has concluded that good faith voters may not be asked to reveal the candidate for whom they cast their ballots. *McCavitt v. Registrars of Voters of Brockton*, 385 Mass 833, 846-850, 434 NE2d 620, 629-631 (1982). So fundamental is society's interest in the secret ballot that the right at stake does not belong to the individual voter. Accordingly, the good faith voter may not waive the "privilege" and disclose his vote. 385 Mass at 849, 434 NE2d at 630. The question whether courts may require illegal voters to reveal the candidate for whom they voted has not been resolved. See *McCavitt*, supra, 385 Mass at 848 n.18, 434 NE2d at 630 n.18.

Proposed Mass R Evid 506 provides a privilege to refuse to disclose the tenor of one's vote in a political election, except where the court finds that the vote was cast illegally or where "disclosure should be compelled pursuant to the election laws of the Commonwealth."

§13.13   Trade Secrets

Massachusetts case law does not recognize a testimonial privilege as to trade secrets. *Gossman v. Rosenberg*, 237 Mass 122, 124, 129 NE 424, 426 (1921). Mass R Civ P 26(c)(7), however, authorizes the issuance of a protective order during the discovery process providing that "a trade secret or other confidential research, development, or commercial information not be disclosed or be disclosed only in a designated way." And as noted in §13.10, supra, the Public Records Act, GL 4, §7(26)(g), exempts from disclosure "trade secrets or commercial or financial information voluntarily provided to an agency for use in developing governmental policy and upon a promise of confidentiality."

Proposed Mass R Evid 507 creates an evidentiary privilege "to refuse to disclose and to prevent other persons from disclosing a trade secret" provided "the allowance of the privilege will not tend to conceal fraud or otherwise work injustice."

§13.14   Privilege Against Self-Incrimination

§13.14.1 Introduction

The privilege against self-incrimination derives from constitutional, statutory, and common-law sources. It is established by the Fifth Amendment to the United States

Constitution,[1] which was held applicable to the states by way of the Fourteenth Amendment in *Malloy v. Hogan*, 378 US 1, 84 S Ct 1489, 12 L Ed 2d 653 (1964). It is also recognized by the Massachusetts Constitution in Part 1, Article 12,[2] and is provided for in GL 233, §20(3)[3] and GL 231, §63.[4] The privilege was also recognized at common law. See *Com. v. Brennan*, 386 Mass 772, 780, 438 NE2d 60, 65-66 (1982) (& cases cited).

The effect of *Malloy v. Hogan* is to apply federal standards to the determination of whether a claim of Fifth Amendment privilege is justified in state proceedings. See *Com. v. Borans*, 388 Mass 453, 456, 446 NE2d 703, 705 (1983) (& citations). A state may of course interpret its own constitutional provisions to provide more protection than the federal decisions, but may not fall short of the federal standard in applying Fifth Amendment protections. *Attorney General v. Colleton*, 387 Mass 790, 795-796, 444 NE2d 915, 918-919 (1982); *Com. v. Brennan*, supra, 386 Mass at 779-780, 438 NE2d at 65. The Supreme Judicial Court has in fact "consistently held that art. 12 requires a broader interpretation than that of the Fifth Amendment." *Opinion of the Justices to the Senate*, 412 Mass 1201, 1210, 591 NE2d 1073, 1078 (1992). "Our Constitution adds an additional element not found in most other jurisdictions. Art. 12 of the Declaration of Rights of the Massachusetts Constitution provides in part that no person shall 'be compelled to accuse, or furnish evidence against himself.'" 412 Mass at 1206, 591 NE2d at 1076. See also *Com. v. Burgess*, 426 Mass

---

§13.14   [1] "No person . . . shall be compelled in any criminal case to be a witness against himself." US Const., amend v.

[2] "No subject shall . . . be compelled to accuse, or furnish evidence against himself." Mass Const., pt 1, art. xii.

[3] "The defendant in the trial of an indictment, complaint, or other criminal proceeding shall, at his own request, but not otherwise, be allowed to testify; but his neglect or refusal to testify shall not create any presumption against him."

[4] "[N]o party interrogated [by way of interrogatory] shall be obliged to answer a question or produce a document tending to criminate him. . . ."

206, 217-219, 688 NE2d 439, 447-448 (1997); *Com. v. Harvey*, 397 Mass 351, 356 n.4, 491 NE2d 607, 610 n.4 (1986).

For a full discussion of the topic of confessions and admissions, see Chapter 9.

§13.14.2 Availability of the Privilege

The privilege against self-incrimination is available when three conditions exist:

- the person claiming the privilege must be under *governmental compulsion* to furnish evidence.
- the evidence required must be *testimonial* in nature.
- the evidence must have a *reasonable possibility of incriminating the witness in criminal proceedings*.

a. Governmental Compulsion

First, the person claiming the privilege must be under *governmental compulsion*[5] to furnish evidence. *Com. v. Harvey*, 397 Mass 351, 355-357, 491 NE2d 607, 610-611 (1986) (statements made by police officer during internal affairs investigation not result of overt threat or pressure, and thus not "compelled"). Absent such compulsion, the privilege does not apply. See *Selective Service System v. Minnesota Public Interest Research Group*, 468 US 841, 104 S Ct 3348, 82 L Ed 2d 632 (1984) (no coercion where legislative scheme requires persons who have failed to register with Selective Service to acknowledge their non-registration and thereby confess to crime in order to obtain financial aid, because non-registrants under no compulsion to seek financial aid); *Minnesota v. Murphy*, 465 US 420, 427-429, 104 S Ct 1136, 79 L Ed 2d 409 (1984) (no coercion where probationer makes

---

[5] Statements extracted by private coercion are subject to suppression under Massachusetts due process standards. See §9.3.

incriminating statements to probation officer even though probationer has general obligation to appear and answer questions truthfully); *United States v. Doe*, 465 US 605, 610-612, 104 S Ct 1237, 79 L Ed 2d 552 (1984) (contents of business records subpoenaed from respondent by grand jury not privileged because records voluntarily prepared by him and thus no compulsion); *South Dakota v. Neville*, 459 US 553, 562, 103 S Ct 916, 74 L Ed 2d 748 (1983) (no coercion when motorist refuses to submit to blood-alcohol test);[6] *Andresen v. Maryland*, 427 US 463, 470-477, 96 S Ct 2737, 49 L Ed 2d 627 (1976) (no compulsion where law enforcement personnel seized suspect's business records during search); *Fisher v. United States*, 425 US 391, 396-401, 96 S Ct 1569, 48 L Ed 2d 39 (1976) (no compulsion where taxpayer's documents were obtained by IRS summons from attorney); *Garner v. United States*, 424 US 648, 653-656, 96 S Ct 1178, 47 L Ed 2d 370 (1976) (privilege not violated by introduction of incriminating statements that petitioner chose to make on tax returns); *Couch v. United States*, 409 US 322, 328-329, 93 S Ct 611, 34 L Ed 2d 548 (1973) (no compulsion where taxpayer's documents were obtained by IRS summons from taxpayer's accountant).

The threat of the loss of one's livelihood may constitute compulsion. See *Walden v. Board of Registration*, 395 Mass 263, 266, NE2d 665, 668 (1985) (& citations) (certification that applicant for renewal of license as registered nurse has complied with state tax laws treated as compelled, but no substantial threat of prosecution).

A court-ordered psychiatric examination is considered compelled production. See *Estelle v. Smith*, 451 US 454, 468-

---

[6] But see *Opinion of the Justices to the Senate*, 412 Mass 1201, 591 NE2d 1073 (1992) (proposed statute making defendant's refusal to submit to chemical test or analysis of breath admissible as evidence in criminal proceeding would violate art. 12 of Massachusetts Declaration of Rights because there is compulsion on subject to chose between two alternatives, both of which are capable of producing adverse evidence). See also *Com. v. McGrail*, 419 Mass 774, 779, 647 NE2d 712, 715 (1995) (same/field sobriety test).

469, 101 S Ct 1866, 68 L Ed 2d 359 (1981) (admission at penalty phase of capital trial of psychiatrist's damaging testimony on crucial issue of future dangerousness violated Fifth Amendment privilege against compelled self-incrimination because based on defendant's statements during examination to determine competency to stand trial); *Com. v. Baldwin*, 426 Mass 105, 109-110, 686 NE2d 1001, 1004 (1997) (but defendant who testifies at trial or proffers expert witness opinion based on his out-of-court statements as to criminal responsibility waives privilege and opens to the Commonwealth opportunity to rebut); *Com. v. Wayne*, 414 Mass 218, 228 n.11, 606 NE2d 1323, 1330 n.11 (1993); *Blaisdell v. Com.*, 372 Mass 753, 757-758, 364 NE2d 191, 195-196 (1977).[7]

b.   Testimonial Evidence

Second, the evidence required must be *testimonial* in nature. *Com. v. Hughes*, 380 Mass 583, 588, 404 NE2d 1239, 1242 (1980). "Testimonial evidence" is evidence "which reveals the subject's knowledge or thoughts concerning some fact." *Com. v. Brennan*, 386 Mass 772, 778, 438 NE2d 60, 64 (1982).

Where, however, the subject is merely the source of real, physical, or identification evidence, the privilege does not apply, as in the following:

- Field sobriety tests. *Pennsylvania v. Muniz*, 496 US 582, 110 S Ct 2638, 110 L Ed 2d 528 (1990); *Vanhouten v. Com.*, 424 Mass 327, 333-337, 676 NE2d 460, 464-466 (1997) (field sobriety tests and alphabet recitation); *Com. v. Brennan*, supra, 386 Mass at 776-779, 438 NE2d at 63-64 (breathalyzer and field sobriety tests). See also *Com. v. Carey*, 26 Mass App

---

[7]There is no constitutional right to have the *Blaisdell* interview electronically recorded. *Com. v. Baldwin*, supra, 426 Mass at 111 n. 4, 686 NE2d at 1005 n.4; *Com. v. Lo*, 428 Mass 45, 47-48, 696 NE2d 935, 938 (1998).

339, 340-341, 526 NE2d 1329, 1331 (1988) (video-tape of defendant performing sobriety tests).

- Fingernail scrapings. *Cupp v. Murphy*, 412 US 291, 93 S Ct 2000, 36 L Ed 2d 900 (1973).
- Handwriting exemplars. *United States v. Mara*, 410 US 19, 93 S Ct 774, 35 L Ed 2d 99 (1973); *Com. v. Buckley*, 410 Mass 209, 214-216, 571 NE2d 609, 612-613 (1991); *Com. v. Nadworny*, 396 Mass 342, 362-365, 486 NE2d 675, 687-688 (1985) (handwriting exemplar including defendant's declaration of right-handedness).
- Voice exemplars. *United States v. Dionisio*, 410 US 1, 93 S Ct 764, 35 L Ed 2d 67 (1973).
- Extraction of blood sample from motorist. *Schmerber v. California*, 384 US 757, 86 S Ct 1826, 16 L Ed 2d 908 (1966); *Com. v. Beausoleil*, 397 Mass 206, 222-223, 490 NE2d 788, 795 (1986) (blood test).
- Requirement that driver stop at scene after "hit and run." *California v. Byers*, 402 US 424, 91 S Ct 1535, 29 L Ed 2d 9 (1971).
- Line-ups. *United States v. Wade*, 388 US 218, 87 S Ct 1926, 18 L Ed 2d 1149 (1967). See also *Com. v. Burke*, 339 Mass 521, 159 NE2d 856 (1959) (forcing defendant to assume posture in court to aid identification not testimonial).
- Booking photographs. *Com. v. Fryar*, 425 Mass 237, 250, 680 NE2d 901, 911 (1997). See also *United States v. Bullard*, 37 F3d 765, 768-769 (1st Cir 1995) (requiring defendant to wear hat for identification photograph).
- Videotape of booking procedure for OUI suspect. *Com. v. Mahoney*, 400 Mass 524, 527-528, 510 NE2d 759, 762 (1987).
- Compelled execution of forms authorizing disclosure of federal tax return information. *Com. v. Burgess*, 426 Mass 206, 688 NE2d 439 (1997).
- Body examination. *Com. v. Miles*, 420 Mass 67, 82 n.16, 648 NE2d 719, 729 n.16 (1995).

- Scientific tests such as CAT-scan and psychological tests. *Com. v. Trapp*, 396 Mass 202, 212, 485 NE2d 162, 169 (1985).

See also *Com. v. Barnoski*, 418 Mass 523, 538 n.10, 638 NE2d 9, 18 n.10 (1994) (act of defendant rubbing hand through hair allegedly to remove gunshot residue); *Com. v. Billings*, 42 Mass App 261, 264 n.7, 676 NE2d 62, 64 n.7 (1997) (suspect's lifting of foot to show sole of sneaker); *Com. v. Fallon*, 38 Mass App 366, 375, 648 NE2d 767, 772 (1995), *rev'd on other grounds*, 423 Mass 92 (financial records obtained from the defendant under court order in the civil case); *Com. v. Billups*, 13 Mass App 963, 432 NE2d 105 (1982) (exposure of defendant's underwear and genital area).

In some instances, however, the manner in which these procedures are conducted may convert a non-testimonial exercise into a testimonial message. An order requiring defendant to supply a handwriting exemplar that would have shown his choice of spelling and thus link him in an incriminating way to a particular document was, for example, held to violate the Fifth Amendment. *United States v. Campbell*, 732 F2d 1017, 1020-1021 (1st Cir 1984). See also *Pennsylvania v. Muniz*, supra, 110 S Ct at 2645-2649 (motorist's answer to "sixth birthday" question of field sobriety test incriminating because of its content and thus "testimonial"); *Com. v. Hughes*, supra, 380 Mass at 592, 404 NE2d at 1244 (order to produce gun violated defendant's Fifth Amendment privilege because compelled implicit statements as to existence, location, and control of weapon); *Com. v. Ayre*, 31 Mass App 17, 21 & n.8, 574 NE2d 415, 418 n.8 (1991) (potential testimonial dimension to roadside sobriety tests); *Com. v. Carey*, supra, 26 Mass App at 341-342, 526 NE2d at 1331-1332 (testimonial component of OUI booking procedure).

Moreover, where a refusal to submit to a test or procedure may be viewed as an implicit admission of guilt, the refusal will be deemed testimonial and the privilege applicable in Massachusetts. The refusal to take a field sobriety test or to submit to breathalyzer constitutes testimonial evidence under art. 12, and the admission of evidence of the refusal violates the state constitutional privilege. *Com. v. McGrail*, 419 Mass 774, 647 NE2d 712 (1995) (field sobriety test); *Opinion of the Justices to the Senate*, supra, 412 Mass at 1208-1211, 591 NE2d at 1077-1078 (breathalyzer); *Com. v. Seymour*, 39 Mass App 672, 660 NE2d 679 (1996) (evidence that defendant refused breathalyzer inadmissible even though she had testified on direct that officer had asked her to submit to test; prosecutor's closing argument commenting on refusal also violated privilege). Compare *South Dakota v. Neville*, supra, 459 US at 562 (evidence of motorist's refusal to submit to blood-alcohol test does not violate Fifth Amendment of federal constitution). A driver's "negotiation" with an officer about taking the test may be deemed the equivalent of a refusal and thus inadmissible. See *Com. v. Grenier*, 45 Mass App 58, 695 NE2d 1075 (1998).

For other forms of refusal evidence, see *Com. v. Hinckley*, 422 Mass 261, 661 NE2d 1317 (1996) (evidence of defendant's refusal to turn over sneakers during criminal investigation violated privilege); *Com. v. Lydon*, 413 Mass 309, 313-315, 597 NE2d 36, 39-40 (1992) (admission of defendant's refusal to allow police to swab hands for evidence that he had fired gun amounted to self-accusation and violated art. 12 privilege against self-incrimination); *Com. v. Vermette*, 43 Mass App 789, 797-798, 686 NE2d 1071, 1076-1077 (1997) (testimony about defendant's refusal to consent to search of car violated state constitutional privilege); *Com. v. Martinez*, 34 Mass App 131, 608 NE2d 740 (1993) (right against self-incrimination violated where prosecutor suggested inference of guilt could be drawn from rape defendant's failure to voluntarily offer to furnish district attorney with physical evidence). Compare *Mello v. Hingham Mutual Fire Insurance Co.*, 421 Mass 333, 656 NE2d 1247 (1995) (plaintiff insured's refusal to submit to examination under oath not justified by privilege against self-incrimination). Refusal evidence may be admitted to correct a misimpression created by defendant's direct testimony. See, e.g., *Com. v. Johnson*, 46 Mass App 398, 404-406, 706 NE2d 716, 722-723 (1999).

In *Com. v. Zevitas*, 418 Mass 677, 639 NE2d 1076 (1994), the court found that the statutorily-mandated instruction concerning a defendant's failure to take a blood alcohol test had the same effect as the admission of refusal evidence and thus violated the privilege against self-incrimination. *Zevitas* has been held retroactively applicable. See *Com. v. D'Agostino*, 421 Mass 281, 657 NE2d 217 (1995); *Com. v. Koney*, 421 Mass 295, 657 NE2d 210 (1995). But compare *Com. v. Adams*, 421 Mass 289, 657 NE2d 455 (1995) and *Com. v. Madigan*, 38 Mass App 965, 650 NE2d 363 (1995) (no retroactive application where case was tried after *Opinion of the Justices*, supra, which foreshadowed *Zevitas*).

Finally, even where *the contents* of the records sought are not protected, there are certain situations where the *act of producing them* is deemed "testimonial incrimination," and thus the Fifth Amendment is applicable. See *United States v. Doe*, 465 US 605, 104 S Ct 1237, 79 L Ed 2d 552 (1984) (because by producing business records, which were not themselves compelled testimony, owner would tacitly admit their existence and authenticity as well as his possession, act of producing documents was privileged and could not be compelled without a statutory grant of use immunity); *Com. v. Doe*, 405 Mass 676, 679, 544 NE2d 860, 862 (1989); *In re Kenney*, 399 Mass 431, 440-441, 504 NE2d 652, 658 (1987) (& cases cited) ("Production of the documents is an admission that the records exist, that they are in the possession of the person and that they are authentic; such an admission could be incriminating.").

c. Reasonable Possibility of Incriminating the Witness in Criminal Proceedings

Third, the evidence must have a *reasonable possibility of incriminating the witness in criminal proceedings. Lefkowitz v.*

Turley, 414 US 70, 77, 84, 94 S Ct 316, 38 L Ed 2d 274 (1973). It is not sufficient that the evidence may subject the witness to civil liability or otherwise adversely affect his pecuniary interest. *United States v. Ward*, 448 US 242, 248-256, 100 S Ct 2636, 65 L Ed 2d 742 (1980) (statutory reporting requirement regarding oil spills did not violate Fifth Amendment because monetary fine was "civil" in nature); *Bull v. Loveland*, 27 Mass (10 Pick) 9, 14 (1830). See also *Com. v. Johnson*, 365 Mass 534, 543-544, 313 NE2d 571, 577 (1974) (witness may not refuse to respond on grounds that answer might embarrass him or place him in danger). Nor may the witness refuse to testify about matters on which the statute of limitations has run. *In re DeSaulnier (No. 2)*, 360 Mass 761, 763-764, 276 NE2d 278, 280 (1971).

The privilege does not prevent disclosures from being used in noncriminal commitment proceedings. See *Com. v. Barboza*, 387 Mass 105, 114, 438 NE2d 1064, 1067 (1982) (GL 123A proceeding for commitment as sexually dangerous person). Compare *Estelle v. Smith*, 451 US 454, 101 S Ct 1866, 68 L Ed 2d 359 (1981) (admission of statements to psychiatrist at sentencing stage of capital trial violated defendant's right against self-incrimination). Nor does the privilege apply in child custody cases. *Custody of Two Minors*, 396 Mass 610, 616-618, 487 NE2d 1358, 1363 (1986) (privilege, which prevents drawing of negative inference from defendant's failure to testify in criminal proceeding, did not prevent judge in custody case from drawing such inference).

The privilege is not violated where the information sought may result not in a criminal prosecution, but rather in loss of the witness's employment.[8] *Lefkowitz v. Turley*, supra, 414 US at 84-85. Thus, a state may properly insist that public employees either answer questions (under an

---

[8] As to the applicability of the Fifth Amendment to disciplinary proceedings in which a license might be revoked, the Supreme Court has held that lawyer could not be disbarred on the ground that he claimed the privilege during an investigation into his professional conduct. See *Spevack v. Klein*, 385 US 511 (1967).

adequate grant of immunity from criminal prosecution, see §13.14.7.b., infra) concerning the performance of their jobs or suffer loss of employment. *Lefkowitz v. Turley*, supra, 414 US at 84; *Uniformed Sanitation Men Association, Inc. v. Commissioner of Sanitation*, 392 US 280, 284-285, 88 S Ct 1917, 20 L Ed 2d 1089 (1968); *Gardner v. Broderick*, 392 US 273, 276-279, 88 S Ct 1913, 20 L Ed 2d 1082 (1968); *Com. v. Dormady*, 423 Mass 190, 193-194, 667 NE2d 832, 834 (1996). Police officers may be required to answer questions or submit to a polygraph examination in connection with the performance of their duties provided they are granted immunity from the use of their responses in a criminal prosecution. See *Patch v. Mayor of Revere*, 397 Mass 454, 492 NE2d 77 (1986); *Baker v. Lawrence*, 379 Mass 322, 409 NE2d 710 (1979); *Reinstein v. Police Commissioner of Boston*, 378 Mass 281, 391 NE2d 881 (1979); *Broderick v. Police Commissioner of Boston*, 368 Mass 33, 330 NE2d 199 (1975); *Silverio v. Municipal Court of the City of Boston*, 355 Mass 623, 628-630, 247 NE2d 379, 382 (1969) (privilege did not bar dismissal of officer who refused to answer superior's questions concerning his testimony before grand jury where answers could not be used to prosecute him).

The threat of dismissal renders involuntary any incriminating statements made by the employee in response thereof, thus rendering the statements inadmissible under the Fifth Amendment in any subsequent criminal proceeding. See *Garrity v. New Jersey*, 385 US 493, 500, 87 S Ct 616, 17 L Ed 2d 562 (1967); *Carney v. City of Springfield*, 403 Mass 604, 607-608 n.5, 532 NE2d 631, 634 n.5 (1988) (this is form of "informal immunity," because although not under the umbrella of statutory immunity, statements compelled by the threat of job sanction are inadmissible in criminal proceedings). See also *Patch v. Mayor of Revere*, supra, 397 Mass at 456, 492 NE2d at 78. Where the employee invokes art. 12 of the Massachusetts Declaration of Rights, a grant of transactional immunity (see §13.14.7.b., infra) with respect to the answers sought is required to supplant the privilege and compel the testimony. See

Baglioni v. Chief of Police of Salem, 421 Mass 229, 656 NE2d 1223 (1995); *Com. v. Kerr,* 409 Mass 11, 14, 563 NE2d 1364, 1366-1367 (1990); *Carney v. City of Springfield,* supra, 403 Mass at 610-611, 532 NE2d at 635.

A witness may not claim the privilege out of fear that he will be prosecuted for perjury for what he is about to say, but he may claim the privilege if his new testimony might suggest that he had previously perjured himself at a prior proceeding. *Com. v. Martin,* 423 Mass 496, 503-504, 668 NE2d 825, 830 (1996) (& citations). The privilege "does not condone perjury. It grants a privilege to remain silent without risking contempt, but 'it does not endow the person who testifies a license to perjury.'" *United States v. Wong,* 431 US 174, 178, 97 S Ct 1823, 52 L Ed 2d 231 (1977) (citation omitted). See also *Com. v. Steinberg,* 404 Mass 602, 607, 536 NE2d 606, 610 (1989).

At its most basic, the privilege permits a criminal defendant to refuse to testify at trial. More generally, it permits any person to refuse to furnish information that could be used against him in a criminal prosecution. A witness protected by the privilege "may rightfully refuse to answer unless and until he is protected at least against the use of his compelled answers and evidence derived therefrom in any subsequent criminal case in which he is a defendant. . . . Absent such protection, if he is nevertheless compelled to answer, his answers are inadmissible against him in a later criminal prosecution." *Minnesota v. Murphy,* 465 US 420, 426, 104 S Ct 1136, 79 L Ed 2d 409 (1984) (citations omitted).

The privilege extends not only to evidence that would support a conviction but to any information "which would furnish a link in the chain of evidence needed to prosecute" the claimant of the privilege. *Hoffman v. United States,* 341 US 479, 486, 71 S Ct 814, 95 L Ed 1118 (1951); *Malloy v. Hogan,* 378 US 1, 11-12 (1964); *Com. v. Borans,* 388 Mass 453, 456, 446 NE2d 703, 705 (1983); *Taylor v. Com.,* 369 Mass 183, 187-188, 338 NE2d 823, 826 (1975). It also protects a person from having to disclose the names of persons who could testify against him. *Com. v. Prince*, 313 Mass 223, 229-231, 46 NE2d 755, 758-759 (1943), *aff'd*, 321 US 158 (1944).

The protection, however, must be confined to instances where the witness has "reasonable cause to apprehend danger from a direct answer. The witness is not exonerated from answering merely because he declares that in so doing he would incriminate himself—his say-so does not of itself establish the hazard of incrimination. It is for the court to say whether his silence is justified, and to require him to answer if 'it clearly appears to the court that he is mistaken.'" *Hoffman v. United States*, supra, 341 US at 486 (citations omitted). See also *Republic of Greece v. Koukouras*, 264 Mass 318, 323, 162 NE 345, 347 (1928).

A person's right to be free from self-incrimination is a fundamental principle of our system of justice and, accordingly, it is to be "construed liberally in favor of the claimant." *Com. v. Borans*, supra, 388 Mass at 455, 446 NE2d at 704 (& citations). It will be sustained where it is "evident from the implications of the question, in the setting in which it is asked, that a responsive answer to the question or an explanation of why it cannot be answered might be dangerous because injurious disclosure could result." *Malloy v. Hogan*, supra, 378 US at 11-12; *Emspak v. United States*, 349 US 190, 198-199, 75 S Ct 687, 99 L Ed 997 (1955); *Hoffman v. United States*, supra, 341 US at 486-487.

To deny the privilege, it must be "*perfectly clear*, from a careful consideration of all the circumstances in the case, that the witness is mistaken, and that the answer[s] *cannot possibly* have such tendency to incriminate." *Hoffman v. United States*, supra, 341 at 488 (citation and internal quotes omitted). See also *Com. v. Tracey*, 416 Mass 528, 538, 624 NE2d 84, 90 (1993) (since exact nature of relationship between witness and police was unclear, it was not perfectly clear that witness's testimony could not incriminate him); *Com. v. Pennellatore*, 392 Mass 382, 389, 467 NE2d 820, 824 (1984); *Com. v. Borans*, supra, 388 Mass at 456, 446 NE2d at 705; *Powers v. Com.*, 387 Mass 563, 564-565, 441 NE2d 1025,

1026 (1982); *Com. v. Baker*, 348 Mass 60, 62-63, 201 NE2d 829, 832 (1964); *Com. v. LaBonte*, 25 Mass App 190, 196, 516 NE2d 1193, 1197 (1987) (claim of privilege should be allowed "if there was even slender ground for apprehending that testimony on the part of [the witness] might tend to incriminate him.").

Put another way, the privilege may be denied only where there is no "real or substantial danger that the evidence supplied will lead to a charge of crime or to the securing of evidence to support such a charge." *Com. v. Joyce*, 326 Mass 751, 756, 97 NE2d 192, 196 (1951). See also *Leary v. United States*, 395 US 6, 16, 89 S Ct 1532, 23 L Ed 2d 57 (1969).

Any circumstance that eliminates a witness's exposure to prosecution — the running of the statute of limitations on the alleged crime, a conviction or acquittal for the alleged crime, the granting of a pardon — bars the privilege. *Com. v. Borans*, supra, 388 Mass at 459, 446 NE2d at 707 (conviction; but witness does not lose privilege concerning other matters not included in conviction); *In re DeSaulnier (No. 2)*, supra, 360 Mass at 763, 276 NE2d at 280 (statute of limitations); *Com. v. Crawford*, 12 Mass App 776, 784, 429 NE2d 54, 59 (1981) (guilty plea). But see *Com. v. Colantonio*, 31 Mass App 299, 305-306, 577 NE2d 314, 318 (1991) ("Although [the witness's] testimony could not expose him to prosecution for the crime to which he had pleaded guilty, testimony concerning the episode could expose him to prosecution for a related crime, such as conspiracy;" thus judge did not err in permitting witness to assert privilege).

It is now well-settled that a witness may claim the privilege even though the sovereign that is seeking the testimony is not the same sovereign that may institute criminal proceedings. One jurisdiction within the federal structure may not, absent an immunity provision, compel a witness to give testimony that might incriminate him under the laws of another jurisdiction. The Fifth Amendment thus provides protection for a witness in a state proceeding against incrimination under federal (or another state's) law, and for a witness in a federal proceeding against incrimination under state law. *Murphy v. Waterfront Commission of New York*, 378 US 52, 84 S Ct 1594, 12 L Ed 2d 678 (1964).

The federal government is not required, however, when it seeks to compel testimony, to grant immunity co-extensive with the immunity the state would grant if it were seeking the testimony. Thus, a witness is not entitled to transactional immunity from the federal government on grounds that Massachusetts would grant the broader immunity. See *In Re Bianchi*, 542 F2d 98, 101 (1st Cir 1976); §13.14.7.b., infra.

Fear of prosecution in a foreign country is beyond the scope of the Fifth Amendment. *United States v. Balsys*, 118 S Ct 2218 (1998) (resident alien subpoenaed to testify about wartime activities in Europe could not claim privilege based on fear of prosecution in Lithuania). See also *Com. v. Steinberg*, supra, 404 Mass at 607-608, 536 NE2d at 610.

The privilege does not generally extend to self-reporting schemes that primarily further noncriminal regulatory objectives. See, e.g., *California v. Byers*, 402 US 424, 433-444 (1971) (statute requiring motorist involved in accident to stop and furnish name and address does not violate privilege even though information could lead to prosecution) and *Com. v. Joyce*, 326 Mass 751, 97 NE2d 192 (1950) (same). But where there is a "real and appreciable" threat of incrimination, the privilege will apply. See *Com. v. Sasu*, 404 Mass 596, 600-601, 536 NE2d 603, 605-606 (1989) (while criminal charges stemming from accident were pending against defendant, and information requested on accident report included identity of operator, which was essential element of Commonwealth's case against him, furnishing of any information on report would have constituted "a link in the chain of evidence needed to prosecute"). See also *Leary v. United States*, 395 US 6, 16 (1969) (requirement to complete a tax form on the transfer of marijuana violates the privilege); *Grosso v. United States*, 390 US 62 (1968) (requirement to file form and pay excise tax on gambling proceeds violates privilege); *Marchetti v. United States*, 390 US 39 (1968) (required registration of persons liable for occupational tax relating to gambling violates privilege); *Albertson v. Subversive Activities Control Board*, 382 US 70 (1965) (required registration of members of Communist Party violates privilege).

Where there is a question about the propriety of the claim of privilege and insufficient information upon which the judge can rule, an *in camera* hearing may be conducted. See *Com. v. Martin*, 423 Mass 496, 504-505, 668 NE2d 825, 831-832 (1996).

§13.14.3   Assertion in Civil or Criminal Proceeding

Although the privilege protects only against disclosures that might be used in a criminal proceeding, it can be asserted in any proceeding, civil or criminal, administrative or judicial, investigatory or adjudicatory. *Kastigar v. United States*, 406 US 441, 444, 92 S Ct 1653, 32 L Ed 2d 212 (1972). See also *United States v. Washington*, 431 US 181, 186, 97 S Ct 1814, 52 L Ed 2d 238 (1977); *In the Matter of a John Doe Grand Jury Investigation*, 418 Mass 549, 551, 637 NE2d 858, 860 (1994) (grand jury); *Malloy v. Hogan*, 378 US 1, 11 (1964) (state investigation); *Watkins v. United States*, 354 US 178, 188, 77 S Ct 1173, 1 L Ed 2d 1273 (1957) (congressional committee investigation); *Wansong v. Wansong*, 395 Mass 154, 157, 478 NE2d 1270 (1985) (civil action); *Attorney General v. Colleton*, 387 Mass 790, 794, 444 NE2d 915, 917 (1982) (civil investigative demand by Attorney General); *Emery's Case*, 107 Mass 172 (1871) (state legislative investigation). The privilege also extends to a person subjected to custodial interrogation by law enforcement officials. See *Miranda v. Arizona*, discussed in §9.7, supra.

Unlike a criminal case, invocation of the privilege in a civil case may result in sanctions against the litigant. See

Department of Revenue v. B. P., 412 Mass 1015, 1016, 593 NE2d 1305, 1306 (1992) (because paternity action under GL 209C is civil action, compelling putative father to submit to testing or be subject to sanctions would not violate privilege against self-incrimination); *Wansong v. Wansong,* supra, 395 Mass at 157-158 (judge did not abuse discretion by dismissing plaintiff's complaint for divorce and imposing other discovery sanctions for plaintiff's refusal at deposition to answer questions about relationship with another woman). In determining the effect the claim of privilege should have on the case, "[t]he judge's task is to balance any prejudice to the other civil litigants which might result . . . against the potential harm to the party claiming the privilege if he is compelled to choose between defending the civil action and protecting himself from criminal prosecution." *Wansong v. Wansong,* supra, 395 Mass at 157-158 (citations omitted)

§13.14.4   *Required Records Exception*

A "required records" exception has been read into both the Fifth Amendment and art. 12 privileges and applies where:

(1)   the purpose of the official inquiry is essentially regulatory;
(2)   the records sought are of a kind that the regulated party must customarily keep; and
(3)   the records themselves have assumed "public aspects" such that they are analogous to public documents.

See *In re Kenney,* 399 Mass 431, 437-442, 504 NE2d 652, 656-658 (1987) (enforcement of subpoena requiring attorney to produce certain records would not infringe on right against compulsory self-incrimination because documents met test for "required records"); *Stornanti v. Com.,* 389 Mass

518, 521-522, 451 NE2d 707, 710 (1983) (records required to be maintained by pharmacy under Medicaid program not privileged). In such situations, there is said to be no compelled self-incrimination. *In re Kenney*, supra, 399 at Mass 442, 504 NE2d at 658.

§13.14.5   Who May Claim Privilege

The privilege against self-incrimination is personal and may not be asserted by another party. *Com. v. Simpson*, 370 Mass 119, 121, 345 NE2d 899, 902 (1976) (defendant had no standing to argue that testimony from two witnesses was product of improper grants of immunity); *Com. v. Rivera*, 37 Mass App 244, 251, 638 NE2d 1382, 1386 (1994); *Com. v. Tiexeira*, 29 Mass App 200, 207, 559 NE2d 408, 412-413 (1990) (defendant had no standing to challenge judge's denial of witnesses' right to claim privilege). Similarly, where the defendant's papers are produced by a third party, the privilege does not apply because a "party is privileged from producing the evidence but not from its production." *Johnson v. United States*, 228 US 457, 458, 33 S Ct 572, 57 L Ed 919 (1913). See also *Couch v. United States*, 409 US 322, 327-329 (1973) (no violation of privilege where petitioner's records were summonsed from his accountant).

Moreover, the Fifth Amendment privilege protects only natural persons, not organizations or corporations. Thus, the privilege cannot be claimed by an individual to avoid production of the records of an organization that he holds in a representative capacity as agent or custodian, even if the production may incriminate him. *Braswell v. United States*, 487 US 99, 108 S Ct 2284, 101 L Ed 2d 98 (1988) (custodian of corporate records; extensive discussion); *Fisher v. United States*, 425 US 391, 96 S Ct 1569, 48 L Ed 2d 39 (1976) (attorney could not claim privilege for tax records entrusted him by client); *Bellis v. United States*, 417 US 85, 94 S Ct 2179, 40 L Ed 2d 678 (1974) (records of law firm partnership); *Campbell Painting Corp. v. Reid,* 392 US 286, 88 S Ct 1978, 20 L Ed 2d 1094 (1968) (corporation cannot invoke privilege); *Rogers v. United States,* 340 US 367, 71 S Ct 438, 95 L Ed 2d 344 (1951) (petitioner could not claim privilege with respect to books and records of Communist Party that she held in representative capacity, even though production might incriminate her personally); *United States v. White,* 322 US 694, 64 S Ct 1248, 88 L Ed 2d 1542 (1944) (officer of labor union could not claim privilege to avoid production of union's records); *In re Hampers,* 651 F2d 19 (1st Cir 1981) (state commissioner of revenue had no privilege to refuse production of state sales tax records); *In the Matter of a John Doe Grand Jury Investigation,* 418 Mass 549, 552, 637 NE2d 858, 860 (1994).

In *Com. v. Doe,* 405 Mass 676, 679, 544 NE2d 860, 862 (1989), however, the Supreme Judicial Court rejected the "fiction" that the custodian acts only as a representative of the entity and thus cannot claim the privilege regarding the entity's papers. "The act of production is demanded *of the witness* and the possibility of self-incrimination is inherent in that act. The witness's status as a representative does not alter the fact that in so far as he is a natural person he is entitled to the protection of art. 12. It would be factually unsound to hold that requiring *the witness* to furnish corporate records, the act of which would incriminate him, is not *his act.* . . . [The witness's] status as custodian of the corporation's records does not require that he lose his individual privilege under art. 12." 405 Mass at 679-680, 544 NE2d at 862. Thus, the sole stockholder and custodian of corporate records in *Doe* could not be held in contempt for invoking his privilege under art. 12 in refusing to produce corporate documents that were asserted to be incriminatory. 405 Mass at 681, 544 NE2d at 863.

The personal privilege against self-incrimination possessed by individual representatives of a corporation does not extend to the corporation's papers and records. That privilege protects only those papers that are the private property of the person claiming the privilege, or in the possession of such person in a purely private capacity. The custodian retains the privilege against self-incrimination by compelled oral testimony and by an act of production, but the corporate records themselves are outside the protection. *In the Matter of a John Doe Grand Jury Investigation,* supra, 418 Mass at 552-553, 637 NE2d at 861. If the custodian of the corporate records cannot produce the records without implicating his or her personal art. 12 rights, an alternate keeper of the records can be appointed to do so. Id.

Even when the books and records of an organization cannot themselves be protected by the Fifth Amendment privilege on the part of their custodian, the latter may nonetheless claim the privilege to avoid giving oral testimony that might incriminate him, including answering questions concerning the whereabouts of the records. *Braswell v. United States,* supra, 487 US at 113-114; *Curcio v. United States,* 354 US 118, 122, 77 S Ct 1145, 1 L Ed 2d 1225 (1957).

§13.14.6   Claim of the Privilege

The Fifth Amendment privilege against compelled self-incrimination is not self-executing; it may not be relied upon unless it is invoked in a timely fashion.[9] *Roberts v. United States,* 445 US 552, 559, 100 S Ct 1358, 63 L Ed 2d 622 (1980); *Minnesota v. Murphy,* 465 US 420, 427-428, 104 S Ct 1136, 79 L Ed 2d 409 (1984). A "witness must claim his privilege in the outset, when the testimony he is about to give, will, if he answers fully all that appertains to it, expose

---

[9] It has been suggested that one of the consequences of the broader protection of art. 12 of Massachusetts Declaration of Rights may include "the extent to which and the manner in which an applicant would have to assert the protection of art. 12, in contrast to the Fifth Amendment, in order to receive the benefit of her art. 12 rights." *Walden v. Board of Registration,* 395 Mass 263, 270, NE2d 665, 671 (1985). Nonetheless, art. 12 has not been held to be self-executing. See *Com. v. Harvey,* 397 Mass 351, 357 n.6, 491 NE2d 607, 611 n.6 (1986).

him to a criminal charge, and if he does not, he waives it altogether." *Com. v. Funches*, 379 Mass 283, 289, 397 NE2d 1097, 1100 (1979) (citation omitted); *Com. v. Fallon*, 38 Mass App 366, 375, 648 NE2d 767, 773 (1995) (testimony from deposition and contempt hearing admissible in criminal case where defendant failed to assert privilege in previous proceedings).

Although a judge is not generally required by Massachusetts law to warn a witness at trial that he need not answer questions tending to incriminate him, in circumstances where the witness is ignorant, misinformed or confused about his rights, and there is danger to him in the testimony sought to be elicited, it is a "commendable practice" for the judge to intervene and advise the witness. *Taylor v. Com.*, 369 Mass 183, 192, 338 NE2d 823, 828 (1975) (citation omitted) (special caution is indicated where witness is juvenile). See also *Com. v. Slaney*, 345 Mass 135, 141-142, 185 NE2d 919, 924 (1962); *Com. v. LaFontaine*, 32 Mass App 529, 532, 591 NE2d 1103, 1105 (1992) (better practice is to dispense advice outside hearing of jury); *Com. v. Crawford*, 12 Mass App 776, 779, 429 NE2d 54, 56 (1981); *Com. v. Carballo*, 9 Mass App 57, 59, 399 NE2d 34, 36 (1980). But see *Webb v. Texas*, 409 US 95, 93 S Ct 351, 34 L Ed 2d 330 (1972) (trial court's extended warning to defendant's only witness discouraged witness from testifying and deprived defendant of due process of law).

Where the witness is unrepresented and appears to need assistance, the better practice is to provide counsel to assist him. See *Com. v. Funches*, supra, 379 Mass at 287, 397 NE2d at 1099; *Com. v. Crawford*, supra, 12 Mass App at 779, 429 NE2d at 56; *Com. v. Holmes*, 34 Mass App 916, 609 NE2d 489 (1993) (no prejudicial error when judge interrupted testimony of defense witness at suppression hearing to appoint counsel to advise her of right against self-incrimination, with result that witness declined to testify any further and previous testimony was stricken).

The witness must himself claim the privilege, although in practice the witness's counsel (assuming the witness is represented) may usually claim the privilege for him. See *Jones v. Com.*, 327 Mass 491, 495 n.4, 99 NE2d 456, 458 n.4 (1951).

A claim of the privilege does not require any ritualistic formula or special combination of words. "Plainly a witness need not have the skill of a lawyer to invoke the protection of the Self-Incrimination Clause. If an objection to a question is made in any language that a [questioner] may reasonably be expected to understand as an attempt to invoke the privilege, it must be respected. . . ." *Quinn v. United States*, 349 US 155, 162-163, 75 S Ct 668, 99 L Ed 964 (1955). See also *Com. v. Dormady*, 423 Mass 190, 195, 667 NE2d 832, 835 (1996).

Where it is known that a prosecution witness will claim the privilege in front of the jury, the witness should not be called to testify. Questioning of a material witness in order to provoke a claim of privilege and thus raise improper inferences in the minds of the jurors constitutes prosecutorial misconduct necessitating reversal of the conviction. See *Com. v. Martin*, 372 Mass 412, 414, 362 NE2d 507, 508 (1977). Even in the absence of such misconduct, there is reversible error "when the impression made on the jurors by the witness's demurral is thought to add the 'critical weight' that brings about the verdict of guilty." Id.; *Com. v. LaFontaine*, supra, 32 Mass App at 533, 591 NE2d at 1105-1106. This is not true in a civil case. See *Kaye v. Newhall*, 356 Mass 300, 305, 249 NE2d 583, 586 (1969) (plaintiff in civil case had right to call defendant as witness even though he knew defendant would claim privilege, and counsel had right to comment on claim during closing argument).

Where there is doubt about what the prosecution witness will do, he may be called. "A prosecutor need not go on an assumption that a witness, if called, will balk at testifying, but may make the test by actually calling him." *Com. v. Martin*, supra, 372 Mass at 420, 362 NE2d at 511. See also *Com. v. Fazio*, 375 Mass 451, 456, 378 NE2d 648, 652 (1978) ("The prosecutor was not obliged to guess at the time of his opening as to whether this previously cooperative individual would claim his Fifth Amendment privilege at trial, whether the claim ultimately would be upheld, and whether [the witness] would choose to suffer contempt rather than testify if the claim were not upheld."). Cf. *Com. v. Phoenix*, 409 Mass 408, 428-429, 567 NE2d 193, 204-205 (1991) (although it may have been improper for judge to permit witness to claim privilege in front of jury, defendant suffered no prejudice since his theory was that witness had committed crime). In the context of other privileges, see *Com. v. Kane*, 388 Mass 128, 135-140, 445 NE2d 598, 602-604 (1983) (no abuse of discretion where judge permitted prosecutor to question witness regarding conversation with defendant even though witness, a priest, had stated during voir dire that he would assert religious privilege; prosecutor could "reasonably have assumed that the priest might change his mind and testify, in light of the judge's admonishment"); *Com. v. DiPietro*, 373 Mass 369, 389, 367 NE2d 811, 823 (1977) ("The judge was not required to accept the defendant's statement that [the witness] would exercise the [spousal] privilege, [and] the prosecutor was not precluded from calling her to the stand in the presence of the jury to inquire of her to the point where she claimed the privilege. . . .;" moreover, prosecutor entitled to proceed before jury to establish unavailability of witness for purpose of introducing prior testimony).

The "sound practice," however, is to put the questions to the witness under oath in the absence of the jury in order to determine whether he or she should be called. *Com. v. Martin*, supra, 372 Mass at 421 n.17, 362 NE2d at 512 n.17; *Com. v. Fazio*, supra, 375 Mass at 460, 378 NE2d at 654; *Com. v. LaFontaine*, supra, 32 Mass App at 532-533, 591 NE2d at 1105-1106. See also Proposed Mass R Evid 512(b) ("In criminal cases tried to a jury, proceedings shall be conducted to the extent practicable, so as to facilitate the making of claims of privilege without the knowledge of the jury.").

A criminal defendant has no right (either under the federal or state constitutions) to call a witness to the stand solely in order for the witness to invoke his privilege against self-incrimination, as the witness's invocation of the privilege would not furnish any probative evidence and would be likely to have an illegitimate impact on the jury's deliberations. *Com. v. Gagnon*, 408 Mass 185, 194-198, 557 NE2d 728, 734-737 (1990); *Com. v. Hesketh*, 386 Mass 153, 155-160, 434 NE2d 1238, 1241-1243 (1982).

A defendant in a criminal trial effectively claims the privilege when he chooses not to testify, and no comment may be made upon or presumption drawn from this choice. See GL 233, §20, Third, and §13.14.8.

A person subjected to custodial interrogation must be advised of his right to remain silent and warned of the implications of failing to assert that right; in the absence of warnings, incriminating statements obtained are inadmissible. See §9.7.

§13.14.7   Overcoming the Privilege

When the privilege against self-incrimination applies, it may be overcome only by either: (1) a valid waiver of the privilege by the person who possesses it; or (2) a constitutionally adequate grant of immunity. *Blaisdell v. Com.*, 372 Mass 753, 761, 364 NE2d 191, 198 (1977).

a.   Waiver

An individual may waive the privilege expressly by affirmatively relinquishing the right against self-incrimination, as in the case of a *Miranda* waiver. See §9.7.4, supra. The term "waiver" as used in the context of self-incrimination oftentimes refers however to an implied waiver, or "waiver by testimony." This occurs when a witness who may claim the privilege does not do so and instead testifies or otherwise discloses the information. See generally *Garner v. United States*, 424 US 648, 653-654, 96 S Ct 1178, 47 L Ed 2d 370 (1976) (but noting that "waiver" is not appropriate term: if witness makes disclosures instead of claiming privilege, the government has not "compelled" him to incriminate himself); *Com. v. Martin*, 423 Mass 496, 500, 668 NE2d 825, 829 (1996); *Taylor v. Com.*, 369 Mass 183, 189, 338 NE2d 823, 827-828 (1975).

When a defendant in a criminal case voluntarily takes the stand, under Massachusetts law he waives his privilege against self-incrimination as to all facts relevant to the crime charged and thus renders himself open to cross-examination on such facts. *Com. v. Judge*, 420 Mass 433, 445, 650 NE2d 1242, 1250 (1995) (privilege waived by testimony at suppression hearing as well as at trial); *Com. v. West*, 357 Mass 245, 249, 258 NE2d 22, 24 (1970); *Jones v. Com.*, 327 Mass 491, 493-495, 99 NE2d 456, 457 (1951); *Com. v. Mandile*, 17 Mass App 657, 661-662, 461 NE2d 838, 841 (1984). The defendant does not waive the privilege with respect to matters not pertinent to the issue or improper for impeachment. See *Com. v. Seymour*, 39 Mass App 672, 675-677, 660 NE2d 679, 681-682 (1996). In the federal courts, the privilege is waived only as to matters reasonably related to the subject matter of direct examination. See *Jenkins v. Anderson*, 447 US 231, 237 n.3, 100 S Ct 2124, 65 L Ed 2d 86 (1980) (& citations). The different approaches appear to reflect the distinction between the respective rules on the permissible scope of cross-examination. Compare Fed R Evid 611(b) with Proposed Mass R Evid 611(b), discussed in §3.2.

A defendant may also be deemed to have waived the privilege when his own statements are offered into evidence by an expert on his behalf. See *Blaisdell v. Com.*, 372 Mass 753, 761, 764-766, 364 NE2d 191, 197-200 (1977) (when defendant in criminal case voluntarily submits to psychiatric interrogation on mental responsibility for alleged crime and submits evidence of statements as basis for psychiatric expert opinion, he waives privilege against self-incrimination with respect to court-ordered interrogation); *Com. v. Wayne*, 414 Mass 218, 226-232, 606 NE2d 1323, 1328-1332 (1993) (juvenile defendant who voluntarily chooses at transfer hearing to present expert psychiatric testimony that includes juvenile's own statements is not denied his constitutional privilege against self-incrimination if he is ordered to submit to examination by psychiatrist retained by Commonwealth).

A non-party witness who voluntarily testifies to a fact of an incriminating nature is held to have thereby waived his privilege as to subsequent questions seeking related facts. *Com. v. Martin*, supra; *Taylor v. Com.*, supra; *Com. v. Funches*, 379 Mass 283, 289-291, 397 NE2d 1097, 1100-1101 (1979) (& citations).

The doctrine of waiver by testimony is based on twin rationales: (1) that once a witness has testified to incriminating facts, there is little risk that further testimony about the same transaction will incriminate him further; and (2) that a witness should not be permitted unilaterally to select and choose which facts to reveal regarding the transaction. *Taylor v. Com.*, supra, 369 Mass at 190, 338 NE2d at 828. See also *Loud v. Loud*, 386 Mass 473, 475-476, 436 NE2d 164, 166 (1982) (where husband chose to answer questions asked by wife's counsel about cohabitation with another woman, husband waived privilege for subsequent questions on same topic).

In order for a waiver by testimony to occur, the witness must admit to at least one element of a crime. *Com. v. Funches*, supra, 379 Mass at 291, 397 NE2d at 1101 (witness who testified that defendants had come to his house and told him they wanted to buy heroin had not admitted to element of crime and thus had not waived privilege). See also *McCarthy v. Arndstein*, 262 US 355, 359, 43 S Ct 562, 67 L Ed 1023 (1923) (if previous disclosure by witness is not incriminatory, he does not relinquish privilege of "stopping short in his testimony whenever it may fairly tend to incriminate him").

Even when incriminating information is disclosed, however, there is no waiver as to further disclosures that pose a "real danger of legal detriment" — i.e., disclosures that would supply an additional link in the chain of evidence. *Com. v. Funches*, supra, 379 Mass at 290, 397 NE2d at 1101. Moreover, by testifying with respect to one unlawful act, the witness does not thereby waive his privilege of refusing to reveal other unlawful acts. *Com. v. Francis*, 375 Mass 211, 217, 375 NE2d 1221, 1225 (1978) (citation omitted) (witness's testimony concerning breaking and entering did not constitute waiver of privilege for questions that would have incriminated him with respect to separate offenses of larceny and conspiracy); *Com. v. Voisine*, 414 Mass 772, 784-785, 610 NE2d 926, 933 (1993) (witness who had pled guilty as accessory after fact to murder did not, by so pleading, waive privilege with respect to testifying in murder prosecution as to his own involvement in the murder, because testimony might furnish a link in chain of evidence needed to prosecute witness on additional charge as principal).

To constitute a valid waiver, the witness's testimony must have been given freely and voluntarily. See *Garrity v. New Jersey*, 385 US 493, 87 S Ct 616, 17 L Ed 2d 562 (1967) (where police officer testifies under threat of dismissal, testimony is not voluntary and thus inadmissible in subsequent criminal proceedings); *Com. v. Koonce*, 418 Mass 367, 378-379, 636 NE2d 1305, 1311 (1994) (witness's testimony at prior trial not voluntary because of his level of education and ignorance of the privilege); *Com. v. Ortiz*, 393 Mass 523, 530, 471 NE2d 1321, 1327 (1984) (juvenile did not waive privilege by testifying at prior hearing because testimony, against advice of counsel, not given freely and voluntarily); *Com. v. Turner*, 371 Mass 803, 810, 359 NE2d 626, 630-631 (1977) (witnesses who testified before grand jury about prior crimes in mistaken belief that crimes were within grant of immunity did not thereby waive privilege); *Taylor v. Com.*, supra, 369 Mass at 190-193, 338 NE2d at 827-829 (testimony of confused juvenile, unrepresented by counsel and not advised of rights by judge, "not so freely and voluntarily given as to effect a waiver of his privilege on later questioning"); *Com. v. Holmes*, 34 Mass 916, 919, 609 NE2d 489, 491 (1993) (initial willingness of witness to testify for defendant at suppression hearing did not constitute waiver where she was not represented by counsel and was ignorant of rights). Compare *Com. v. Slonka*, 42 Mass App 760, 769, 680 NE2d 103, 109 (1997) (if witness's sworn statement to defense counsel about drug use with victim was given freely and voluntarily, then witness waived privilege); *Com. v. Weed*, 17 Mass App 463, 459 NE2d 144 (1984) (witness who testified at the grand jury after prosecutor had given her detailed recitation of rights had done so freely and voluntarily and thus could not invoke privilege at trial; but witness who had been misinformed by prosecuting attorney as to consequences of testimony before grand jury and at hearing on motion to suppress could not be deemed to have waived privilege).

As a general rule, waiver by testimony is limited to the proceeding in which it is given and does not extend to subsequent proceedings. *Com. v. Borans*, 388 Mass 453, 457, 446 NE2d 703, 705 (1983) (witness's testimony at grand jury proceedings and at his own trial did not constitute waiver extending to his testimony at trial of another defendant). The Supreme Judicial Court has recently reaffirmed that testimony before a grand jury should not be considered a waiver of the witness's privilege against self-incrimination for the purpose of testifying at a subsequent trial on an indictment returned by that grand jury. See *Com. v. Martin*, supra, 423 Mass at 500-501, 668 NE2d at 829-830. See also *Palaza v. Superior Court*, 393 Mass 1001, 464 NE2d 60 (1984).

In certain circumstances, however, where the witness testifies in a proceeding that was the "probable, logical, or natural continuation or outgrowth of the proceeding or inquiry" in which he previously waived the privilege, waiver by testimony may act as a continuing waiver as to matters previously addressed. See *Luna v. Superior Court*, 407 Mass 747, 751, 555 NE2d 881, 883 (1990) (prospective witness in criminal case who voluntarily submitted affidavit in conjunction with Commonwealth motion waived privilege against self-incrimination as to further proceedings in same case); *In re DeSaulnier (No. 2)*, 360 Mass 761, 765-766, 276 NE2d 278, 281 (1971) (indicating in dicta that witness who answered questions during preliminary inquiry on judicial misconduct could not assert privilege in later proceedings relating to same misconduct); *Com. v. Penta*, 32 Mass App 36, 44-46, 586 NE2d 996, 1001-1002 (1992) (prospective witness at criminal trial who voluntarily testified at two pretrial hearings involving same charges and same defendant waived privilege as to questions at trial seeking related facts). See also *Com. v. Judge*, supra, 420 Mass at 445 n.8, 650 NE2d at 1250 n.8 (defendant who testified at suppression hearing waived privilege as if he had testified at trial).

Unsworn statements made during police interrogation do not constitute "testimony" for purposes of the waiver doctrine so as to deprive the witness of the privilege during subsequent in-court testimony. *Com. v. Dormady*, 423 Mass 190, 195 n.3, 667 NE2d 832, 835 n.3 (1996); *Taylor v. Com.*, supra, 369 Mass at 190-191, 338 NE2d at 828. Nor do guilty pleas previously entered by the witness constitute "testimony." See *Com. v. Voisine*, supra, 414 Mass at 784-785, 610 NE2d at 933.

An individual undergoing police interrogation in custody does not waive the privilege by answering questions. He may claim the privilege at any stage of the interrogation; and if he indicates at any time prior to or during questioning that he wishes to remain silent or to consult with counsel, the interrogation must cease. See §9.7.1, supra.

Neither the Federal Rules of Evidence nor the Proposed Massachusetts Rules of Evidence purport to deal with the privilege against self-incrimination. See Advisory Committee's Note to Proposed Mass R Evid 501 (constitutional privileges are "preserved without further reference"). But see Advisory Committee's Note to Proposed Mass R Evid 512, suggesting that the rule regarding comment upon or inference from the claim of privilege does purport to apply to self-incrimination contexts.

b. *Removal by Grant of Immunity*

Neither a "practical unlikelihood of prosecution nor the prosecutor's denial of an intention to prosecute negates an otherwise proper invocation of the Fifth Amendment." *Com. v. Borans*, 388 Mass 453, 459, 446 NE2d 703, 707 (1983) (citation omitted). A constitutionally adequate grant of immunity does however bar the privilege and compel the testimony. *United States v. Mandujano*, 425 US 564, 575, 96 S Ct 1768, 48 L Ed 2d 212 (1976).

The United States may compel testimony from an unwilling witness who invokes the Fifth Amendment privilege by conferring immunity pursuant to statute. *Kastigar v. United States*, 406 US 441, 92 S Ct 1653, 32 L Ed 2d 212 (1972). The immunity must be coextensive with the scope of the privilege, which has been held to require that the grant of immunity bar both the use and derivative use of the witness's testimony in any subsequent proceeding. *Kastigar v. United States*, supra, 406 US at 453 (transactional immunity, which completely bars prosecution for offense to which compelled testimony relates, not constitutionally required).

The Commonwealth may compel testimony from an unwilling witness who invokes the privilege by conferring immunity in the manner prescribed by GL 233, §§20C-20I (as amended by St 1998, c 188).[10] Article 12 of the Declaration of Rights of the Massachusetts Constitution has been read to require a broader grant of immunity than the Fifth Amendment. Thus, a witness's privilege can be displaced only by a grant of transactional immunity, which bars prosecution for offenses to which the compelled testimony relates. *Com. v. Dormady*, 423 Mass 190, 194, 667 NE2d 832,

---

[10] The Supreme Judicial Court has held that the statute "covers the entire subject of immunity" at least for witnesses in the specified proceedings, and has refused to recognize an inherent common-law authority of the Attorney General or a district attorney to grant immunity. See *Com. v. Dalrymple*, 428 Mass 1014, 1015-1016, 699 NE2d 344, 345-346 (1998) (& citations).

835 (1996) (transactional immunity required to compel police officer to answer questions during internal affairs investigation); *Attorney General v. Colleton*, 387 Mass 790, 444 NE2d 915 (1982) (immunity granted by GL 93A, §6(7), inadequate under art. 12 because it provides only use immunity); *Com. v. Upton*, 390 Mass 562, 577, 458 NE2d 717, 726 (1983), *rev'd on other grounds*, 466 US 727 (1984). The statutory scheme provides for such transactional immunity. See GL 233, §20G;[11] *In re Pressman*, 421 Mass 514, 516, 658 NE2d 156, 158 (1995); *In re a John Doe Grand Jury Investigation*, 405 Mass 125, 129, 539 NE2d 56, 58 (1989).

Where immunity has been granted, a refusal to testify may result in a citation for contempt. GL 233, §20H. See, e.g., *Com. v. Santaniello*, 369 Mass 606, 341 NE2d 259 (1976).

A justice of the Supreme Judicial Court, Appeals Court or Superior Court may, upon request of the attorney general or a district attorney,[12] and after a hearing, grant immunity for enumerated crimes[13] to a witness called before a grand jury or criminal proceeding. GL 233, §20D, 20E. The

---

[11] "A witness who has been granted immunity as provided [by this statute] shall not be prosecuted or subjected to any penalty or forfeiture for or on account of any transaction matter, or thing concerning which he is so compelled, after having claimed his privilege against self-incrimination, to testify or produce evidence, nor shall testimony so compelled be used as evidence in any criminal or civil proceeding against him in any court of the commonwealth, except in a prosecution for perjury or contempt committed while giving testimony or producing evidence under compulsion. . . ."

[12] An application for immunity may be signed by an assistant district attorney or assistant attorney general as well. See *Lindegren v. Com.*, 427 Mass 696, 695 NE2d 207 (1998).

[13] The crimes as to which the witness is immunized are not only those crimes listed in §20D, but also any crime related to a transaction about which the witness is compelled to testify. See *In re a John Doe Grand Jury Investigation*, supra, 405 Mass at 129, 539 NE2d at 58-59 (defining the scope of "transactional immunity").

Immunity may only be granted to a grand jury witness when the grand jury is investigating one or more of the enumerated crimes. See *Petition of the District Attorney for the Plymouth District*, 391 Mass 723, 726-727, 464 NE2d 62, 65 (1984).

district attorney has no power to grant immunity; therefore his assurance of immunity does not remove the privilege. *Grand Jurors for Middlesex County for the Year 1974 v. Wallace*, 369 Mass 876, 343 NE2d 844 (1976) (grand jury witnesses not required to testify on being given written offer of immunity signed by assistant district attorney). The district attorney does, however, have authority to withdraw charges and to thereby in effect confer immunity within his district. *Baglioni v. Chief of Police of Salem*, 421 Mass 229, 233, 656 NE2d 1223, 1225 (1995). Moreover, where a witness reasonably relies on a prosecutor's promise of immunity, the courts will enforce the promise to the same extent as a formal grant of immunity. See *Com. v. Dormady*, 423 Mass 190, 196-198, 667 NE2d 832, 836-837 (1996); *In re DeSaulnier (No. 2)*, 360 Mass 761, 764, 276 NE2d 278, 280 (1971) (& citation). See also *Grand Jurors for Middlesex County for the Year 1974 v. Wallace*, supra, 369 Mass at 880, 343 NE2d at 845-846.

Before a judge may grant immunity under the statutory scheme, it must be found that the witness validly refused to answer questions or produce evidence on the ground that such testimony might tend to incriminate him. GL 233, §20E. The Supreme Judicial Court has rejected the contention that the Commonwealth must make an additional showing that the testimony sought is necessary to its investigation, although it has suggested that "certain rare circumstances may arise where the relevancy of a particular line of questioning may be slight or nonexistent, and where the need for the testimony may be outweighed by legitimate privacy interests." *Petition of the District Attorney for the Plymouth District*, 395 Mass 1005, 1006, 479 NE2d 1370, 1371 (1985) (& citations).

Under GL 233, §20E, only the prosecutor may request an order of immunity. Accordingly, the defendant has no right under the statute to an order granting immunity to one of his witnesses. *Com. v. Curtis*, 388 Mass 637, 643, 448 NE2d 345, 348-349 (1983). Although the assertion by a witness of his Fifth Amendment right may impair a defendant's ability to present an effective defense, the Supreme Judicial Court has held that the question whether to seek a grant of immunity "primarily involves public interest considerations best evaluated by the prosecutor." 388 Mass at 645-646, 448 NE2d at 350. See also *Com. v. Pennellatore*, 392 Mass 382, 389, 467 NE2d 820, 824-825 (1984).

Although the court has acknowledged that in some unique circumstances "due process may require the granting by a judge of a limited form of immunity" to a defense witness, *Com. v. Curtis*, supra, 388 Mass at 646, 448 NE2d at 350 (but Commonwealth established that it had a strong interest in opposing grant of immunity to witness who was potential suspect in continuing investigation), it has declined to recognize a defendant's constitutional right to such a judicial grant of immunity. *Com. v. Doherty*, 394 Mass 341, 343-346, 476 NE2d 169, 173 (1985) (barring unique circumstances, "any inquiry into the question of immunity is foreclosed if the prospective witness is an actual or potential target of prosecution"). See also *Com. v. Reynolds*, 429 Mass 388, 400, 708 NE2d 658, 667-668 (1999) (proffered testimony was not clearly exculpatory); *Com. v. Grimshaw*, 412 Mass 505, 512, 590 NE2d 681, 685-686 (1992) (fact that case involved battered-woman-syndrome defense did not create unique circumstance); *Com. v. Upton*, supra, 390 Mass at 575-577, 458 NE2d at 725-726 (no showing that judicial grant of immunity was constitutionally required); *Com. v. Toney*, 385 Mass 575, 587-588, 433 NE2d 425, 433 (1982) (no showing that witness if called would invoke privilege or would testify to exculpatory facts). Cf. *Com. v. Turner*, 393 Mass 685, 473 NE2d 679 (1985) (no substantial risk of miscarriage of justice in permitting two prosecution witnesses, defendant's alleged accomplices whose direct testimony was under grant of immunity, to invoke privilege against self-incrimination during cross-examination by defense counsel).

A defendant in federal court similarly has no right to obtain immunity for a defense witness, nor has the federal district court the general power to grant such immunity or order the government to request it. *United States v. Davis,* 623 F2d 188, 192-193 (1st Cir 1980). In certain narrow circumstances, however, it has been held that the federal defendant's constitutional right to a fair trial may require that his witness be granted immunity. See *United States v. Davis,* supra, 623 F2d at 193 (& cases cited) (but no such showing where witness's testimony went merely to credibility of prosecution witness and was cumulative); *United States v. Drape,* 668 F2d 22, 26-27 (1st Cir 1982) (but no showing that witness's evidence would have been exculpatory and essential to defense).

A state witness may not be compelled to give testimony that may be incriminating under federal law unless the compelled testimony and its fruits cannot be used in any manner by federal officials in connection with a criminal prosecution against him. *Murphy v. Waterfront Commission of New York,* 378 US 52, 79 (1964). See also *Com. v. Stone,* 369 Mass 965, 341 NE2d 284 (1976) (nothing that immunized witness may say before Hampden County grand jury could be used against him in federal proceeding). The federal government is not required to grant transactional immunity to a Massachusetts witness on grounds that the Commonwealth would grant the broader immunity. *In Re Bianchi,* 542 F2d 99, 101 (1st Cir 1976); *Baglioni v. Chief of Police of Salem,* supra, 421 Mass at 234, 656 NE2d at 1226 (fact that state grant of transactional immunity only translates into use immunity for federal purposes does not preclude compelling person to answer questions).

Testimony given by a witness immunized pursuant to GL 233, §§20C-20I, may not be used against him in any criminal or civil proceeding in the Commonwealth, except in a prosecution for perjury or contempt committed while giving testimony or producing evidence under compulsion. GL 233, §20G. Nor may the immunized testimony be used against him in a prosecution in any other jurisdiction in the United States. *Com. v. Steinberg,* 404 Mass 602, 607, 536 NE2d 606, 610 (1989).

Testimony given pursuant to an immunity agreement in another jurisdiction may be used in non-criminal proceedings in the Commonwealth. See *In re Pressman*, supra, 421 Mass 514, 658 NE2d 156 (federal grant of immunity to attorney does not foreclose use of immunized testimony in Massachusetts bar disciplinary proceeding); *Adoption of Astrid*, 45 Mass App 538, 543-544, 700 NE2d 275, 279 (1998) (statement given by mother in her home state under immunity agreement could be admitted in child custody proceeding in Commonwealth).

Testimony given by a witness in response to a grant of immunity may not be used for either substantive or impeachment purposes. *New Jersey v. Portash*, 440 US 450, 99 S Ct 1292, 59 L Ed 2d 501 (1979). The immunity does not, however, preclude the use of the testimony in a perjury prosecution against the witness arising out of the immunized testimony. *United States v. Apfelbaum*, 445 US 115, 100 S Ct 948, 63 L Ed 2d 250 (1980) (if any part of immunized testimony is false, witness's entire testimony may be used against him at perjury trial). See also *Pillsbury Co. v. Conboy*, 459 US 248, 103 S Ct 608, 74 L Ed 2d 430 (1983) (grant of use immunity to grand jury witness did not preclude him from asserting Fifth Amendment privilege in deposition in subsequent civil case, even though deposition testimony sought closely tracked prior immunized testimony).

Under Massachusetts law, a conviction cannot be based solely on the testimony of an immunized witness. See GL 233, §20I. See also *Com. v. Shaheen*, 15 Mass App 302, 305-306, 445 NE2d 619, 622 (1983) (& cases cited). The corroboration required need not be proof of defendant's actual participation in the crime; it need only provide support for the credibility of the immunized witness. *Com. v. Fernandes*, 425 Mass 357, 681 NE2d 270 (1997) (reaffirming *Com. v. DeBrosky*, 363 Mass 718, 297 NE2d 496 (1973)). To provide the requisite credibility, "there must be some evidence in support of the testimony of an immunized witness on at least one element of proof essential to convict the defendant." *Com. v. Fernandes*, 425 Mass at 360, 681 NE2d at 272 (citation omitted).

For a discussion of the special jury instructions to be given regarding an immunized witness, see *Com. v. Gagliardi*, 29 Mass App 225, 240-242, 559 NE2d 1234 (1990); *Com. v. Kindell*, 44 Mass App 200, 207, 689 NE2d 845, 850 (1998).

§13.14.8   Comment upon and Adverse Inference from Claim of Privilege

In a civil case, a party's claim of the privilege against self-incrimination can be commented upon by opposing counsel, and an inference adverse to the party may properly be drawn. *Frizado v. Frizado*, 420 Mass 592, 596, 651 NE2d 1206, 1210 (1995) (inference adverse to defendant may properly be drawn in domestic abuse prevention case, even if criminal proceedings are pending or might be brought); *Quintal v. Commissioner of Department of Employment and Training*, 418 Mass 855, 861, 641 NE2d 1338, 1342 (1994); *Department of Revenue v. B. P.*, 412 Mass 1015, 593 NE2d 1305 (1992) (& citations). It has been held that such an inference may be drawn against an employer where its employee has invoked the privilege. See *Shafnacker v. Raymond James & Associates*, 425 Mass 724, 735-736, 683 NE2d 662, 670 (1997) (& citations).

In a criminal case, however, the rule in Massachusetts has long been that the failure of the defendant to take the stand is not a proper subject for comment and "shall not create any presumption against him." GL 233, §20, Third. See generally *Com. v. Paradiso*, 368 Mass 205, 211, 330 NE2d 825, 828-829 (1975) (GL 233, §20 must be read in conjunction with art. 12 of Declaration of Rights). The Supreme Court elevated this rule to constitutional status and made it applicable to the states as well as the federal government in *Griffin v. California*, 380 US 609, 85 S Ct 1229, 14 L Ed 2d 106 (1965). See also *Roberts v. United States*, 445 US 552, 100

S Ct 1358, 63 L Ed 2d 622 (1980) (suggesting that judge, when sentencing, may not draw adverse inference from the defendant's refusal to assist in criminal investigation if failure is justified by timely claim of privilege against self-incrimination).

A comment is improper if it is reasonably susceptible of being interpreted as a comment on the defendant's failure to take the stand. See *Com. v. Phoenix*, 409 Mass 408, 427, 567 NE2d 193, 203 (1991) (citations omitted) (prosecutor's suggestion that defendant offered no proof of alibi); *Com. v. Sherick*, 401 Mass 302, 304-305, 516 NE2d 157, 158 (1987) (extensive discussion). Compare *Com. v. Young*, 399 Mass 527, 505 NE2d 186 (1987) (prosecutor's closing argument, which urged jury to draw inferences adverse to defendant because he sat impassively at trial, prejudicial and required reversal), *Com. v. Cancel*, 394 Mass 567, 573-576, 476 NE2d 610, 616 (1985) (impermissible comment on defendant's failure to call alibi witnesses), *Com. v. Smith*, 387 Mass 900, 908-909, 444 NE2d 374, 381 (1983) (impermissible reference to defendant's silence at trial), *Com. v. Hawley*, 380 Mass 70, 83-84, 401 NE2d 827, 835 (1980) (references to certain facts as "uncontested" improper when defendant himself is only one who can contradict evidence), *Com. v. Borodine*, 371 Mass 1, 10-11, 353 NE2d 649, 655-656 (1976) (same), *Com. v. Domanski*, 332 Mass 66, 69-71, 123 NE2d 368, 371 (1954) (improper comment on defendant's failure to take stand and to call witnesses), and *Com. v. Pullum*, 22 Mass App 485, 487-489, 494 NE2d 1355, 1357-1358 (1986) (prosecutor's closing argument, which called the jury's attention to defendant's failure to testify, required reversal) with *Com. v. Grant*, 418 Mass 76, 82-83, 634 NE2d 565, 569-570 (1994) (prosecutor's rhetorical questions inviting jurors to examine defendant's intent at time of shooting did not improperly focus attention on defendant's silence at trial), *Com. v. Walker*, 413 Mass 552, 560, 600 NE2d 583, 588 (1992) (comment by prosecutor as to who might be able to tell jury about what happened at murder scene was at worst oblique reference to defendant and was remedied by judge's instruction), *Com. v. Martino*, 412 Mass 267, 283-284, 588 NE2d 651, 661 (1992) (no infringement of right to remain silent where prosecutor commented on defendant's failure in lengthy statement to police to disclose certain facts), *Com. v. McGeoghean*, 412 Mass 839, 842, 593 NE2d 229, 231 (1992) (prosecutor entitled to refer to defendant's failure to provide explanation for scars on daughter's body), *Com. v. Feroli*, 407 Mass 405, 408-409, 553 NE2d 934, 936-937 (1990) (prosecutor is entitled to emphasize strong points of Commonwealth's case and weaknesses of defendant's even though he may, in so doing, prompt passing reflection on defendant's failure to testify), *Com. v. Smallwood*, 379 Mass 878, 891-893, 401 NE2d 802 (1980) (prosecutor's oblique reference to defendant's failure to testify remedied by corrective instructions), *Com. v. Cepulonis*, 374 Mass 487, 500-501, 373 NE2d 1136, 1145 (1978) (prosecutor's remarks could not be reasonably construed as referring to defendant's failure to testify), *Com. v. DiCicco*, 44 Mass App 111, 120, 688 NE2d 1010, 1016-1017 (1998) (prosecutor's statement that defendant "has a right to just sit there and make us prove our case" not improper comment on failure to testify), *Com. v. Coyne*, 44 Mass App 1, 7-8, 686 NE2d 1321, 1325 (1997) (prosecutor's comment that defendants were "trying to run and hide" should have been avoided, but could not have been understood as comment on failure to testify), *Com. v. Lashway*, 36 Mass App 677, 682, 634 NE2d 930, 933 (1994) (prosecutor's remark that "there is no other evidence before you" not improper comment on defendant's failure to testify where defense counsel challenged victim's credibility and prosecutor argued victim's testimony was corroborated by witness and there was no contradictory evidence from any source), *Com. v. King*, 33 Mass App 905, 907, 595 NE2d 795, 797 (1992) (prosecutor's labeling of certain facts in closing argument as "not in dispute" not directed at defendant's failure to testify), and *Com. v. Johnson*, 32 Mass App 989, 594 NE2d 899 (1992) (one-sentence reference in closing argument to defendant's silence did not create substantial risk of miscarriage of justice).

Where the defendant's sanity is in issue, the prosecutor may alert the jury to inconsistencies between his conduct at trial and his alleged mental illness. See *Com. v. Hunter*, 427 Mass 651,657, 695 NE2d 653, 655 (1998); *Com. v. Smiledge*, 419 Mass 156, 160, 643 NE2d 41, 44 (1994) (prosecutor's question to defense expert on mental disease as to whether he found it surprising defendant was able to sit quietly through trial not improper comment on failure to testify).

Improper comment may issue from the judge as well as the prosecutor. See, e.g., *Griffin v. California*, supra, 380 US at 610 (judge improperly instructed jury they could draw adverse inference from defendant's failure to testify); *Com. v. Sneed*, 376 Mass 867, 872, 383 NE2d 843, 845-846 (1978) (charge gave jurors erroneous impression about defendant's election not to testify); *Com. v. Goulet*, 374 Mass 404, 410-414, 372 NE2d 1288, 1294-1296 (1978) (reversible error where judge's charge implied that testimony of defense witness should be devalued because defendant himself had not taken stand). See also *Com. v. Carrion*, 407 Mass 263, 269-272, 552 NE2d 558, 562-564 (1990) (although judge's embellishment on instruction regarding defendant's right not to testify "teeters on the brink of reversible error," viewed in context reversal not required).

For a case involving comment on the privilege in the form of an outburst by the victim on the witness stand, see *Com. v. Farnkoff*, 16 Mass App 433, 441-442, 452 NE2d 249, 255 (1983). See also *Com. v. Ries*, 337 Mass 565, 585, 150 NE2d 527, 541 (1958) (judge properly refused to permit defendant to comment in closing argument upon prosecution witness's invocation of privilege on cross-examination).

Proposed Mass R Evid 512 would preclude both comment upon and an adverse inference from a claim of privilege.[14] Further, it directs that in criminal cases tried to a jury, "proceedings shall be conducted to the extent practicable, so as to facilitate the making of claims of privilege without the knowledge of the jury." Proposed Mass R Evid 512(b).

GL 278, §23, precludes comment at trial upon the fact that the defendant failed to testify or offer evidence at the preliminary hearing.[15] See §6.7.2.e. The statute is not violated by pointing out inconsistencies between a defendant's testimony on the stand and a prior voluntary statement, including omissions from the prior statement where it would have been natural to include the omitted fact. *Com. v. Rivera*, 425 Mass 633, 640, 682 NE2d 636, 642 (1997).

As the Supreme Court has recognized, "[e]ven without adverse comment, the members of a jury, unless instructed otherwise, may well draw adverse inferences from a defendant's silence." *Carter v. Kentucky*, 450 US 288, 301, 101 S Ct 1112, 67 L Ed 2d 241 (1981). Accordingly, a defendant who chooses not to testify is constitutionally entitled upon request to an instruction that he is not compelled to testify and that no adverse inference may be drawn from his failure to do so. 450 US at 305. See also Proposed Mass R

---

[14] "The claim of a privilege, whether in the present proceeding or upon a prior occasion, is not a proper subject of comment by judge or counsel in a criminal case. No inference may be drawn therefrom." PMRE 512(a).

[15] When a criminal defendant takes the stand, early decisions held that his *prior* claim of privilege could be the subject of comment as affecting the credibility of his present testimony. *Raffel v. United States*, 271 US 494, 497, 46 S Ct 566, 70 L Ed 1054 (1926) (prior claim of privilege at first trial); *Com. v. Smith*, 163 Mass 411, 430-433, 40 NE 189, 196 (1895) (prior claim before grand jury). The vitality of these decisions seems quite questionable. See *Grunewald v. United States*, 353 US 391, 415-424, 77 S Ct 963, 1 L Ed 2d 931 (1957) (prejudicial error for trial judge to permit defendant to be cross-examined regarding assertion of privilege before grand jury); *Com. v. Bennett*, 2 Mass App 575, 582 n.3, 317 NE2d 834 n.3 (1974) (citing Text).

Evid 512(c).[16] But see *Com. v. Gilchrist*, 413 Mass 216, 218, 597 NE2d 32 (1992) (defendant does not have right to specify precise language of judge's instruction, which is reviewed in context of entire charge).

"No aspect of the charge to the jury requires more care and precise expression than that used with reference to the right of a defendant in a criminal case to remain silent and not be compelled to incriminate himself. . . . Even an unintended suggestion that might induce the jury to draw an unfavorable inference is error." *Com. v. Thomas*, 400 Mass 676, 679, 511 NE2d 1095, 1097-1098 (1987) (citations omitted). To avoid prejudice to the defendant, the judge in instructing the jury should avoid use of the phrase "the right not to incriminate oneself" and instead substitute "the right to remain silent." *Com. v. Charles*, 397 Mass 1, 9, 489 NE2d 679, 684-685 (1986) (& cases cited). See also *Com. v. Jenkins*, 416 Mass 736, 741, 625 NE2d 1344, 1347 (1993) (although reference to "no adverse inference" is preferable form of instruction, judge's instruction that jury "absolutely" not consider defendant's failure to testify not reversible error); *Com. v. Powers*, 9 Mass App 771, 774, 404 NE2d 1260, 1263 (1980).

As a matter of federal constitutional law, the no-adverse-inference instruction may be given over the defendant's objection without violating his privilege. See *Lakeside v. Oregon*, 435 US 333 (1978) (instruction does not constitute improper comment on failure to testify). Under Massachusetts law, however, the judge must accede to a defendant's request that the jury not be so instructed, and the giving of the no-adverse-inference charge over his objection is reversible error. *Com. v. Buiel*, 391 Mass 744, 746, 463 NE2d 1172, 1173 (1984). Compare *Com. v. Jackson*, 419 Mass 716, 731-732, 647 NE2d 401, 410 (1994) (no error

---

[16] "Upon request, any accused in a criminal case against whom the jury might draw an adverse inference from a claim of privilege is entitled to an instruction that no inference may be drawn therefrom." PMRE 512(c).

in instructing jury in absence of defendant's request that judge not give instruction).

When the judge or prosecutor has made an improper comment, it is not per se reversible error; it may be harmless beyond a reasonable doubt. See, e.g., *United States v. Hasting*, 461 US 499 (1983); *Com. v. Paradiso*, 368 Mass 205, 213, 330 NE2d 825, 828-829 (1975); *Com. v. Ayre*, 31 Mass App 17, 23-24, 574 NE2d 415, 419 (1991). See also *Com. v. Walker*, 421 Mass 90, 97-99, 653 NE2d 1080, 1084-1085 (1995); *Com. v. Pope*, 406 Mass 581, 588-591, 549 NE2d 1120, 1125-1126 (1990) (no substantial likelihood of miscarriage of justice where judge, at defendant's request, instructed jury as to defendant's right to remain silent).

For discussion of the use of a defendant's prior silence to impeach his credibility, see §9.7.8, supra.

§13.15   Privileges and Disqualifications in Proceedings Arising out of Abuse of Disabled Persons

In the case of an investigation of possible abuse against a disabled person, GL 19C, §5 provides as follows:

> Any privilege created by statute or common law relating to confidential communications or any statute prohibiting the disclosure of information shall neither preclude the disclosure of such documents to the [Disabled Persons Protection] commission or its designated agency nor prevent the admission of such documents in any civil or disciplinary proceeding arising out of the alleged abuse or neglect of the disabled person; provided, however, that absent the written consent of an individual to whom the requested documents relate, any information which is protected by the attorney-client privilege, the psychotherapist-client privilege, or the clergy-penitent privilege shall not be subject to such disclosure.

EVIDENCE in ADMINISTRATIVE PROCEEDINGS

§14.1   Evidentiary Matters: GL 30A, §11

The State Administrative Procedure Act, GL 30A, which applies to almost all state administrative agencies, departments, boards, and commissions (see GL 30A, §1(2) for exceptions including the parole board, the division of dispute resolution of the department of industrial accidents, the personnel administrator, the civil service commission, and the appellate tax board), provides in §11 the following with regard to evidentiary and related matters:

(2) Unless otherwise provided by any law, agencies need not observe the rules of evidence observed by courts, but shall observe the rules of privilege recognized by law. Evidence may be admitted and given probative effect only if it is the kind of evidence on which reasonable persons are accustomed to rely in the conduct of serious affairs. Agencies may exclude unduly repetitious evidence, whether offered on direct examination or cross-examination of witnesses.

(3) Every party shall have the right to call and examine witnesses, to introduce exhibits, to cross-examine witnesses who testify, and to submit rebuttal evidence.

(4) All evidence, including any records, investigation reports, and documents in the possession of the agency of which it desires to avail itself as evidence in making a decision, shall be offered and made a part of the record in the proceeding, and no other factual information or evidence shall be considered, except as provided in paragraph (5) of this section. Documentary evidence may be received in evidence in the form of copies or excerpts, or by incorporation by reference.

(5) Agencies may take notice of any fact which may be judicially noticed by the courts, and in addition, may take notice of general, technical or scientific facts within their specialized knowledge. Parties shall be notified of the material so noticed, and they shall be afforded an opportunity to contest the facts so noticed. Agencies may utilize their experience, technical competence, and specialized knowledge in the evaluation of the evidence presented to them.

(6) Agencies shall make available an official record, which shall include testimony and exhibits, and which may be in narrative form, but the agency need not arrange to transcribe shorthand notes or sound recordings unless otherwise requested by a party. If so requested, the agency may, unless otherwise provided by any law, require the party to pay the reasonable costs of the transcript before the agency makes the transcript available to the party.

(7) If a majority of the officials of the agency who are to render the final decision have neither heard nor read the evidence, such decision, if adverse to any party other than the agency, shall be made only after (a) a tentative or proposed decision is delivered or mailed to the parties contain-

ing a statement of reasons and including determination of each issue of fact or law necessary to the tentative or proposed decision; and (b) an opportunity is afforded each party adversely affected to file objections and to present argument, either orally or in writing as the agency may order, to a majority of the officials who are to render the final decision. The agency may by regulation provide that, unless parties make written request in advance for the tentative or proposed decision, the agency shall not be bound to comply with the procedures of this paragraph.

(8) Every agency decision shall be in writing or stated in the record. The decision shall be accompanied by a statement of reasons for the decision, including determination of each issue of fact or law necessary to the decision, unless the General Laws provide that the agency need not prepare such statement in the absence of a timely request to do so. Parties to the proceeding shall be notified in person or by mail of the decision; of their rights to review or appeal the decision within the agency or before the courts, as the case may be; and of the time limits on their rights to review or appeal. A copy of the decision and of the statement of reasons, if prepared, shall be delivered or mailed upon request to each party and to his attorney of record.

It should be noted that §11 makes no evidence inadmissible except that which is privileged. See also *Morris v. Board of Registration in Medicine*, 405 Mass 103, 107-108 & n.2, 539 NE2d 50, 52-53 & n.2 (1989). An agency has wide discretion in ruling on evidence. *Massachusetts Automobile Rating & Accident Prevention Bureau v. Commissioner of Insurance*, 401 Mass 282, 285-286, 516 NE2d 1132, 1134-1135 (1987) (& citations) (error for commissioner to exclude, without explanation, proffered documentary evidence where same kind of evidence had been admitted and relied upon in previous rate proceedings); *Planning Board of Braintree v. Department of Public Utility*, 420 Mass 22, 30-31, 647 NE2d 1186, 1192 (1984); *Northeast Metropolitan Regional Vocational School District School Committee v. Massachusetts Commission Against Discrimination*, 31 Mass App 84, 88, 575

NE2d 77 (1991) (hearing commissioner has discretion to admit evidence, even if it would be inadmissible under rules of evidence, if it bears indicia of reliability). Hearsay may be admitted. See *Town of Brookline v. Commissioner of Department of Environmental Quality Engineering*, 387 Mass 372, 389, 439 NE2d 792, 805 (1982) (& citations).

Notwithstanding GL 30A, some agencies bind themselves to abide by some or all of the usual rules of evidence. See, e.g., GL 211C, §7(3) (at hearing before Commission on Judicial Conduct, "the rules of evidence applicable to civil proceedings shall apply"), construed in *Matter of King*, 409 Mass 590, 600, 568 NE2d 588, 593 (1991). Furthermore, apart from any statutory or agency rules, the courts impose minimum requirements to ensure that the hearing is fair. Compare *Boott Mills v. Board of Conciliation & Arbitration*, 311 Mass 223, 40 NE2d 870 (1942) with *Mayor of Everett v. Superior Court*, 324 Mass 144, 85 NE2d 214 (1949).

§14.2   Burden of Proof

In the absence of a statutory provision to the contrary, proof by a preponderance of the evidence is the standard generally applicable to administrative and quasi-judicial proceedings. *Medical Malpractice Joint Underwriting Association of Massachusetts v. Commissioner of Insurance*, 395 Mass 43, 46-47, 478 NE2d 936, 939 (1985); *Craven v. State Ethics Commission*, 390 Mass 191, 200, 454 NE2d 471, 477 (1983) (& citations); *City of Gloucester v. Civil Service Commission*, 408 Mass 292, 297, 557 NE2d 1141, 1144 (1990); *Sevigny's Case*, 337 Mass 747, 151 NE2d 258 (1958) (probable cause of disease); *Mayor of Revere v. Civil Service Commission*, 31 Mass App 315, 321, 577 NE2d 325, 329-330 (1991); *Fire Commissioner of Boston v. Joseph*, 23 Mass App 76, 82, 498 NE2d 1368, 1372 (1986).

§14.3   Subpoenas: GL 30A, §12

GL 30A, §12, provides:

> In conducting adjudicatory proceedings, agencies shall issue, vacate, modify and enforce subpoenas in accordance with the following provisions: —
>
> (1) Agencies shall have the power to issue subpoenas requiring the attendance and testimony of witnesses and the production of any evidence, including books, records, correspondence or documents, relating to any matter in question in the proceeding. Agencies may administer oaths and affirmations, examine witnesses, and receive evidence. The power to issue subpoenas may be exercised by any member of the agency or by any person or persons designated by the agency for such purpose.
>
> (2) The agency may prescribe the form of subpoena, but it shall adhere, in so far as practicable, to the form used in civil cases before the courts, unless another manner is provided by any law. Witnesses summoned shall be paid the same fees for attendance and travel as in civil cases before the courts, unless otherwise provided by any law.

See also *Matter of Tobin*, 417 Mass 92, 102-103, 628 NE2d 1273, 1279 (1994) (hearing committee's refusal to issue subpoenas requested by attorney was appropriate because information sought not relevant to proceeding).

§14.4   Findings

The provisions of GL 30A, §11(8) (quoted above in §14.1) require that the agency make subsidiary findings of fact on all issues relevant and material to the ultimate issue to be decided and specify the manner in which it reasoned from the subsidiary facts so found to the ultimate decision reached. *Maryland Casualty Co. v. Commissioner of Insurance,*

372 Mass 554, 363 NE2d 1087 (1977). See also *Malone-Capagna v. Director of Division of Employment Security*, 391 Mass 399, 402, 461 NE2d 818, 820 (1984) (absent a finding on a critical factual issue, the agency's decision cannot stand even if supported by substantial evidence).

The agency has a duty to make such findings, including subsidiary findings as to each issue of fact or law, so that the appellate court may exercise its function of appellate review. *Massachusetts Automobile Rating & Accident Prevention Bureau v. Commissioner of Insurance*, 401 Mass 282, 287-288, 516 NE2d 1132, 1135-1136 (1987) (agency should not leave counsel and the courts without the "guidance of proper findings . . . to determine from a voluminous record . . . whether [its] conclusions can be sustained on the evidence") (citation omitted); *Smith v. Director of Division of Employment Security*, 376 Mass 563, 382 NE2d 199 (1978); *Westborough v. Department of Public Utilities*, 358 Mass 716, 267 NE2d 110 (1971).

The agency need not make findings on every controverted issue of fact or law so long as findings indicate the "over-all basis" of the decision and permit effective appellate review. *Aetna Casualty & Surety Co. v. Commissioner of Insurance*, 408 Mass 363, 374, 558 NE2d 941, 948 (1990); *Costello v. Department of Public Utilities*, 391 Mass 527, 538, 462 NE2d 301, 309 (1984); *Massachusetts Automobile Rating & Accident Prevention Bureau v. Commissioner of Insurance*, supra, 401 Mass 289 n.3, 292, 516 NE2d at 1137 n.2, 1138.

§14.5   Judicial Review: "Substantial Evidence"

GL 30A, §14(7)(e), provides that the finding of an agency must be supported by "substantial evidence" in order to withstand the judicial review. "Substantial evidence" is defined as "such evidence as a reasonable mind might accept as adequate to support a conclusion." GL 30A, §1(6). For further discussion and application of the substantial evidence test, see *Tennessee Gas Pipeline Co. v. Board of Assessors of Agawam,* 428 Mass 261, 262, 700 NE2d 818, 819 (1998); *New Boston Garden Corp. v. Board of Assessors of Boston,* 383 Mass 456, 420 NE2d 298 (1981); *Benmosche v. Board of Registration in Medicine,* 412 Mass 82, 86, 588 NE2d 621, 623 (1992); *Zachs v. Department of Public Utilities,* 406 Mass 217, 221-222, 547 NE2d 28, 30-31 (1989) (substantial evidence standard in context of nonadjudicative, policy-making judgments rather than party-specific fact finding); *Wardell v. Director of Division of Employment Security,* 397 Mass 433, 436-437 & n.5, 491 NE2d 1057, 1059-1060 (1986) (employee's admission in district court to sufficient facts, absent subsequent finding of guilt, does not constitute substantial evidence that alleged misconduct occurred); *Medical Malpractice Joint Underwriting Association of Massachusetts v. Commissioner of Insurance,* 395 Mass 43, 54, 478 NE2d 936, 943 (1985) (substantial evidence standard indistinguishable from reasonable evidence standard); *Workers' Compensation Rating & Inspection Bureau v. Commissioner of Insurance,* 391 Mass 238, 244-245, 461 NE2d 1178, 1183-1184 (1984) (test of whether findings are supported by substantial evidence same as whether findings have "reasonable support in the evidence"); *Utility Workers of America, Local 466 v. Labor Relations Commission,* 389 Mass 500, 506, 451 NE2d 124, 127-128 (1983) (court may not treat proceeding as trial de novo or substitute its judgment for that of agency); *Hotchkiss v. State Racing Commission,* 45 Mass App 684, 688-689, 701 NE2d 642, 647 (1998). For a comparison of federal judicial review under 20 USC §1415(e)(2) (Education of the Handicapped Act) and GL 30A, §14, see *School Committee of Brookline v. Bureau of Special Education Appeals,* 389 Mass 705, 715-716, 452 NE2d 476, 483 (1983) (concluding that under either standard agency decision was properly affirmed).

The substantial evidence standard is also generally applied to agencies not subject to the Administrative Procedure Act. See *Boston Gas Co. v. Board of Assessors of Boston,* 402 Mass 346, 348-349 n.1, 522 NE2d 921, 922 n.1 (1988)

(& citations); *Blue Cross of Massachusetts, Inc. v. Commissioner of Insurance*, 397 Mass 117, 120 n.2, 489 NE2d 1249, 1251 n.2 (1986) (proceedings under GL 176B, §4); *Towle v. Commissioner of Revenue*, 397 Mass 599, 601-602, 492 NE2d 739, 741 (1986) (& citations); *Murphy v. Superintendent, Massachusetts Correctional Institution*, 396 Mass 830, 833, 489 NE2d 661, 663 (1986) (prison disciplinary proceedings).

Substantial evidence has been held to be the appropriate standard in administrative proceedings notwithstanding the fact that the alleged violation underlying the proceeding involves a criminal statute. See *Goldstein v. Board of Registration of Chiropractors*, 426 Mass 606, 612 n.5, 689 NE2d 1320, 1325 n.5 (1998) (& citations).

The evidence necessary to support the agency's decision must be found in the record. *D'Amour v. Board of Registration in Dentistry*, 409 Mass 572, 585, 567 NE2d 1226, 1233-1234 (1991). Nonacceptance of testimony or evidence by the agency does not create substantial evidence to the contrary. *Salisbury Water Supply Co. v. Department of Public Utilities*, 344 Mass 716, 721, 184 NE2d 44, 47-48 (1962). The administrative agency cannot use the computations and opinions of its staff unless they are introduced in evidence. *New England Tel. & Tel. Co. v. Department of Public Utilities*, 372 Mass 678, 363 NE2d 519 (1977).

A finding based on incomplete evidence will not stand. *Holyoke Street Railway Co. v. Department of Public Utilities*, 347 Mass 440, 198 NE2d 413 (1964). See also *Retirement Board of Somerville v. Contributory Retirement Appeal Board*, 38 Mass App 673, 651 NE2d 1241 (1995) (appeal board's decision was arbitrary and would be reversed, even though substantial evidence supported decision, where final adjudication contradicted earlier interim determination made on same record and no reason was given explaining or supporting change).

The agency may not use its own expertise and rely on undisclosed evidence unless it takes official notice thereof as a matter of record, in compliance with GL 30A, §11(5). *D'Amour v. Board of Registration in Dentistry,* supra, 409 Mass at 583, 585, 567 NE2d at 1233. While the agency may put its expertise to use in evaluating the complexities of technical evidence, it may not use its expertise as a substitute for evidence in the record. *Id., Salisbury Water Supply Co. v. Department of Public Utilities,* supra, 344 Mass at 721, 184 NE2d at 47-48. An agency or board may not sit as a "silent witness" where expert testimony is required to establish an evidentiary basis for its conclusions, but it is free to evaluate evidence in light of its own technical expertise. *Langlitz v. Board of Registration of Chiropractors,* 396 Mass 374, 381, 486 NE2d 48, 53 (1985) (citations omitted).

Hearsay evidence may constitute substantial evidence if it contains sufficient indicia of reliability and probative value. *School Committee of Brockton v. Massachusetts Against Discrimination,* 423 Mass 7, 15, 666 NE2d 468, 474 (1996) (physicians' letters); *Embers of Salisbury v. Alcoholic Beverages Control Commission,* 401 Mass 526, 530, 517 NE2d 830, 832 (1988) (transcript of testimony by defendant at her criminal trial, corroborated in certain particulars by stipulated testimony of other persons); *Murphy v. Superintendent, Massachusetts Correctional Institution,* supra, 396 Mass at 834, 489 NE2d at 663 (informants' statements); *Moran v. School Committee of Littleton,* 317 Mass 591, 59 NE2d 279 (1945) (dismissal of teacher affirmed although affidavits were considered by school committee). See also *Martorano v. Department of Public Utilities,* 401 Mass 257, 261-263, 516 NE2d 131, 133-134 (1987) (sufficient evidence in record, other than unsworn letter, to justify decision); *LaPointe v. License Board of Worcester,* 389 Mass 454, 459, 451 NE2d 112, 116 (1983) (substantial evidence even apart from the hearsay statements to support the board's decision). For discussion of the older rule requiring a "residuum" of legal evidence to support a decision, see *Embers of Salisbury v. Alcoholic Beverages Control Commission,* supra, 401 Mass at 532-536, 517 NE2d at 833-835 (Lynch, J, dissenting).

§14.6   Deference to Agency's Findings

In reviewing an agency decision, the court is required by GL 30A, §14(7), to give "due weight to the experience, technical competence, and specialized knowledge of the agency, as well as to the discretionary authority conferred upon it." This standard of review is highly deferential to the agency on questions of fact and reasonable inferences drawn therefrom. *Flint v. Commissioner of Public Welfare*, 412 Mass 416, 420, 589 NE2d 1224, 1227 (1992) (& citations). See also *Koch v. Commissioner of Revenue*, 416 Mass 540, 555, 624 NE2d 91, 99 (1993) (in reviewing mixed questions of fact and law, Appellate Tax Board's expertise must be recognized); *Alsabti v. Board of Registration in Medicine*, 404 Mass 547, 549, 536 NE2d 357, 358 (1989); *Cherubino v. Board of Registration of Chiropractors*, 403 Mass 350, 354-355, 530 NE2d 151, 154-158 (1988) (board is free to evaluate evidence in light of its own technical expertise); *Attorney General v. Commissioner of Insurance*, 403 Mass 370, 376, 530 NE2d 142, 146-147 (1988); *Bournewood Hospital v. Massachusetts Commission Against Discrimination*, 371 Mass 303, 317, 358 NE2d 235, 243 (1976). The agency's conclusion will stand if it "*could* have been made by reference to the logic of experience." *Benmosche v. Board of Registration in Medicine*, 412 Mass 82, 86, 588 NE2d 621, 623 (1992) (emphasis in original) (citations omitted).

A court cannot disturb an agency's decision unless it is based upon an error of law, unsupported by substantial evidence, arbitrary or capricious, an abuse of discretion, or otherwise not in accordance with law. GL 30A, §14(7); *Blue Cross of Massachusetts, Inc. v. Commissioner of Insurance*, 397 Mass 117, 120, 489 NE2d 1249, 1251 (1986); *Sugrue v. Contributory Retirement Appeal Board*, 45 Mass App 1, 5 n.5, 694 NE2d 391, 394 n.5 (1998). See also *Care and Protection of Isaac*, 419 Mass 602, 611, 646 NE2d 1034, 1039 (1995) (not de novo review).

If there is substantial evidence to support the findings of the agency, the court will not substitute its own view of the facts. *Doherty v. Retirement Board of Medford*, 425 Mass 130, 141, 680 NE2d 45, 52 (1997); *D'Amour v. Board of Registration in Dentistry*, supra, 409 Mass at 581, 567 NE2d at 1232; *Zachs v. Department of Public Utilities*, 406 Mass 217, 224, 547 NE2d 28, 32 (1989); *M & T Charters, Inc. v. Commissioner of Revenue*, 404 Mass 137, 140, 533 NE2d 1359, 1361 (1989) (court will set aside board's findings only if evidence points to "no appreciable probability of the conclusion or points to an overwhelming probability of the contrary") (citation omitted); *Utility Workers of America, Local 466 v. Labor Relations Commission*, 389 Mass 500, 451 NE2d 124 (1983) (court may not engage in de novo review); *Craven v. State Ethics Commission*, 390 Mass 191, 201, 454 NE2d 471, 477 (1983) (same; court may not substitute its judgment for that of agency); *Southern Worcester Regional Vocational School District v. Labor Relations Commissioner*, 377 Mass 897, 389 NE2d 389 (1979); *School Committee of Boston v. Board of Education*, 363 Mass 125, 128, 292 NE2d 870, 872 (1973). But the administrative agency's decision is subject to judical review of the entire record to determine if it is upheld by substantial evidence, and the substantiality of evidence must take into account whatever in the record detracts from its weight. *D'Amour v. Board of Registration in Dentistry*, supra, 409 Mass at 584, 567 NE2d at 1233; *Entis v. Rent Control Board of Brookline*, 399 Mass 158, 161, 503 NE2d 640, 642 (1987); *Cohen v. Board of Registration in Pharmacy*, 350 Mass 246, 214 NE2d 63 (1966); *St. Elizabeth's Hospital v. Labor Relations Commission*, 2 Mass App 782, 321 NE2d 837 (1975).

§14.7 Assessing Witness Credibility

The task of assessing the credibility of witnesses is one uniquely within an agency's discretion. *Matter of Tobin*, 417 Mass 92, 99, 628 NE2d 1273, 1277 (1994) (attorney disciplinary proceeding); *Cherubino v. Board of Registration of Chiropractors*, 403 Mass 350, 356, 530 NE2d 151, 155 (1988);

Embers of Salisbury v. Alcoholic Beverages Control Commission, 401 Mass 526, 529, 517 NE2d 830, 832 (1988); *Martorano v. Department of Public Utilities,* 401 Mass 257, 261, 264-265, 516 NE2d 131 (1987). *Boston Police Superior Officers Federation v. Civil Service Commission,* 35 Mass App 688, 695, 624 NE2d 617, 621 (1993).

The reviewing court may, however, modify or set aside findings and conclusions on credibility that are arbitrary or unsupported by substantial evidence. *Bettencourt v. Board of Registration in Medicine,* 408 Mass 221, 227, 558 NE2d 928, 930 (1990) (in deciding whether to believe patient or doctor, board improperly disregarded relevant evidence tending to show that doctor would not have engaged in alleged misconduct; proceeding remanded to board for further consideration of credibility issue); *Herridge v. Board of Registration in Medicine,* 420 Mass 154, 163-166, 648 NE2d 745, 750-751 (1995) (*Herridge I*) (board required to make credibility determination regarding patient's testimony; board could not choose to rely on portions of testimony, reject other portions, and fail to explain its reasons for doing so); *Herridge v. Board of Registration in Medicine,* 424 Mass 201, 675 NE2d 386 (1997) (*Herridge II*). Compare *Friedman v. Board of Registration in Medicine,* 408 Mass 474, 476-477, 561 NE2d 859, 860-861 (1990) (board's decision "thoroughly and logically analyzed the evidence and explained why the board believed the patient's testimony . . . and why the board disbelieved the doctor's explanation. . . . We should not, and do not, consider Friedman's various arguments on matters of credibility. They were for the board to resolve, and it did so."). See also *Zachs v. Department of Public Utilities,* 406 Mass 217, 224-225, 547 NE2d 28, 32 (1989) (deference to agency's credibility determinations); *Morris v. Board of Registration in Medicine,* 405 Mass 103, 106-114, 539 NE2d 50, 51-56 (1989) (& citations) (board owed substantial deference to credibility findings made by administrative magistrate who heard witnesses). Cf. *City of Salem v. Massachusetts Commission Against Discrimination,* 404 Mass 170, 534 NE2d 283 (1989) (remand for new hearing required where credibility of witnesses could not be evaluated on basis of record of hearing held before commissioner who died before rendering decision).

§14.8   Additional Evidence: GL 30A, §14

Under GL 30A, §14(6), a reviewing court may order that additional evidence be taken before the agency but only upon a showing that it is "material" and that there was "good reason" for the failure to present it in the original agency proceeding. See *Benmosche v. Board of Registration in Medicine*, 412 Mass 82, 88, 588 NE2d 621, 624 (1992) (& citations). See also *Northeast Metropolitan Regional Vocational School District School Committee v. Massachusetts Commission Against Discrimination*, 35 Mass App 813, 626 NE2d 884 (1994); *Medical Malpractice Joint Underwriting Association of Massachusetts v. Commissioner of Insurance*, 395 Mass 43, 57, 478 NE2d 936, 945 (1985) (remanding case for reconsideration).

§14.9   Occupational and Business Licenses

In regard to certain adjudicatory proceedings involving the issuance or revocation of occupational or business licenses, the right to a hearing and procedural due process has been held to be constitutionally required. See *Langlitz v. Board of Registration of Chiropractors*, 396 Mass 374, 376, 486 NE2d 48, 50-51 (1985); *LaPointe v. License Board of Worcester*, 389 Mass 454, 457-459, 451 NE2d 112, 115-116 (1983); *Konstantopoulos v. Whately*, 384 Mass 123, 132-136, 424 NE2d 210, 217-219 (1981) (extensive review of cases of minimum requirements of due process); *Milligan v. Board of Registration in Pharmacy*, 348 Mass 491, 204 NE2d 504 (1965) (& citations). Compare *Kearney v. Board of Registration in Pharmacy*, 4 Mass App 25, 340 NE2d 515 (1975) and *Palmer v. Rent*

Control Board of Brookline, 7 Mass App 110, 386 NE2d 1047 (1979) (hearing required) with *Lotto v. Com.,* 369 Mass 775, 343 NE2d 855 (1976) (no hearing required). See also *Matter of Tobin,* 417 Mass 92, 101-102, 628 NE2d 1273, 1278-1279 (1994) (bar counsel's resting on documentary evidence without introducing any live testimony in disciplinary proceeding did not violate due process on ground attorney was unable to confront witnesses); *Friedman v. Board of Registration in Medicine,* 408 Mass 474, 478-479, 561 NE2d 859, 861-862 (1990) (due process does not require a post-decision evidentiary hearing); *Aetna Casualty & Surety Co. v. Commissioner of Insurance,* 408 Mass 363, 373, 558 NE2d 941, 947-948 (1990) (commissioner's adoption of findings made in prior decision not impermissible where parties were afforded adequate opportunity to present evidence and arguments); *Embers of Salisbury v. Alcoholic Beverages Control Commission,* 401 Mass 526, 531, 517 NE2d 830, 833 (1988) (admission in evidence before commission of transcript of testimony at trial on criminal charges did not deprive licensees of constitutional rights to confront witnesses where licensees did not invoke their right to call the witness); *Massachusetts Outdoor Advertising Council v. Outdoor Advertising Board,* 9 Mass App 775, 405 NE2d 151 (1980) (review of authorities as to when administrative summary judgment procedures may be utilized).

For a discussion of the right to an impartial hearing officer, see *D'Amour v. Board of Registration in Dentistry,* 409 Mass 572, 579-581, 567 NE2d 1226, 1231 (1991); *Civil Service Commission v. Boston Municipal Court Department,* 27 Mass App 343, 347-349, 538 NE2d 49, 52 (1989).

Table of Cases

897

Table of Cases

Table of Cases

Table of Cases

Table of Cases

Table of Cases

Table of Cases

Table of Cases

Table of Cases

915

Table of Cases

Table of Cases

Table of Cases

Table of Cases

Table of Cases

Table of Cases

Table of Cases

Table of Cases

Table of Cases

Table of Cases

Table of Cases

Table of Cases

Table of Statutes

Table of Statutes

**Massachusetts Constitution
Part 1, Declaration of Rights**

Table of Statutes

Table of Rules
of Court

Table of Rules of Court

Index

Index

Index

Index

Suppression. *See* Admissibility;
Confessions, suppression;
Exclusion of evidence;
Identification evidence,
suppression
Surveillance location privilege,
13.8

Tax returns
confidentiality, 13.11
self-incrimination, privilege
inapplicable, 13.14.2.b
Testimony. *See also* Cross-
examination; Self-
incrimination, privilege
against; Witnesses
authentication of evidence,
11.3, 12.1, 12.2
binding. *See* Binding testimony
children, 3.3, 6.4, 13.3
competency. *See* Privileges and
disqualifications
disbelief, 4.2.3, 5.2.1
exclusion. *See* Exclusion of
evidence
hypnotically enhanced, 6.21
motion to strike, 3.8.1, 3.8.2,
6.5, 8.3
negative, 4.2.3
official records, authentication
of, 8.13.3
opinion. *See* Opinion
time limits, 3.1
unsworn statement in lieu of,
3.1
Time limits
closing argument, 3.7
prior convictions,
impeachment of witness,
6.10.2
self-incrimination, claim of,
13.14.6
testimony, 3.1
Trade secrets, 13.10, 13.13
Treatises
cross-examination of experts,
use during, 7.9.2

hearsay exceptions, 8.4.1, 8.12,
8.18

Uniform Commercial Code
burden of persuasion, 5.3.1.b
presumptions, 5.5.3.b

Verbal act doctrine, 8.2.4
Verbal completeness, rule of, 3.12
Verdict, setting aside, 5.2.1
Victim
autopsy, 11.7.1
character evidence, 4.4.1, 4.4.3
demeanor, 11.11
dying declaration, 8.6
effect of crime on, 4.3
hearsay statements, 8.2.2,
8.21.3
photographs of, admissibility,
11.6
rape shield law, 4.4.3.b, 6.9
sympathy, closing argument,
3.7
Videotaped evidence
admissibility, 7.9.2, 11.2,
11.13.1
depositions, 8.7.1
experiments, 11.12
malpractice actions, 7.9.2
Voice identification, 10.2.2.d,
12.4, 13.14.2.b
Voir dire
confessions, admissibility, 3.9.1,
9.1, 9.11
jury, 3.14
witnesses, 6.3, 6.7.2.g, 7.7.1,
10.3.1

Wade-Gilbert rule, 10.2.1
Warrants, 1.2, 9.7.5
Weight of evidence
chain of custody, 11.3
character of criminal
defendant, 4.4.2
experiments, 4.4.9.c